Durhan
of Ca

- Fourteen volumes cover the state of California by region

- The most complete California place-name series

- *Durham's Place-Names of California's Gold Country Including Yosemite National Park:* **Includes Mariposa, Tuolumne, Calaveras, Amador, El Dorado, Placer, Sierra & Nevada Counties** ISBN 1-884995-25-X

- *Durham's Place-Names of the California North Coast:* **Includes Del Norte, Humbolt, Lake, Mendocino & Trinity Counties** ISBN 1-884995-26-8

- *Durham's Place-Names of California's Old Wine Country:* **Includes Napa & Sonoma Counties** ISBN 1-884995-27-6

- *Durham's Place-Names of Greater Los Angeles:* **Includes Los Angeles, Orange & Ventura Counties** ISBN 1-884995-28-4

- *Durham's Place-Names of California's Central Coast:* **Includes Santa Barbara, San Luis Obispo, San Benito, Monterey & Santa Cruz Counties** ISBN 1-884995-29-2

- *Durham's Place-Names of California's Eastern Sierra:* **Includes Alpine, Inyo & Mono Counties** ISBN 1-884995-30-6

- *Durham's Place-Names of California's Desert Counties:* **Includes Imperial, Riverside & San Bernardino Counties** ISBN 1-884995-31-4

- *Durham's Place-Names of* **San Diego County** ISBN 1-884995-32-2

- *Durham's Place-Names of Central California:* **Includes Madera, Fresno, Tulare, Kings & Kern Counties** ISBN 1-884995-33-0

- *Durham's Place-Names of California's North Sacramento Valley:* **Includes Butte, Glenn, Shasta, Siskiyou & Tehama Counties** ISBN 1-884995-34-9

- *Durham's Place-Names of The San Francisco Bay Area:* **Includes Marin, San Francisco, San Mateo, Contra Costa, Alameda , Solano & Santa Clara Counties** ISBN 1-884995-35-7

- *Durham's Place-Names of California's South Sacramento Valley:* **Includes Colusa, Sacramento, Sutter, Yuba & Yolo Counties** ISBN 1-884995-36-5

- *Durham's Place-Names of California's North San Joaquin Valley:* **Includes San Joaquin, Stanislaus & Merced Counties** ISBN 1-884995-37-3

- *Durham's Place-Names of Northeastern California:* **Includes Lassen, Modoc & Plumas Counties** ISBN 1-884995-38-1

The above titles are available at better bookstores, online bookstores or by calling 1-800-497-4909

Durham's

Place-Names
of
Central
California

Includes Madera, Fresno, Tulare,
Kings & Kern Counties

David L. Durham

Clovis, California

Printed in the United States of America
Published by
Quill Driver Books/Word Dancer Press, Inc.
8386 N. Madsen
Clovis, CA 93611
559-322-5917
800-497-4909

Word Dancer Press books may be purchased at special prices for educational, fund-raising, business or promotional use. Please contact Special Markets, Quill Driver Books/Word Dancer Press, Inc. at the above address or phone number.

To order another copy of this book or another book in the Durham's Place-Names of California series, please call 1-800-497-4909.

Quill Driver Books/Word Dancer Press, Inc. project cadre:
Doris Hall, Dave Marion, Stephen Blake Mettee

ISBN 1-884995-33-0

Library of Congress Cataloging-in Publication Data

Durham, David L., 1925-
   Durham's place names of central California : includes Madera, Fresno, Tulare, Kings & Kern counties / David L. Durham.
   p. cm.
   Includes bibliographical references (p.).
   ISBN 1-884995-33-0
   1. Names, Geographical--California. 2. California--History, Local. 3. Madera County (Calif.)--History, Local. 4. Fresno County (Calif.)--History, Local. 5. Tulare County (Calif.)--History, Local. 6. Kings County (Calif.)--History, Local. 7. Kern County (Calif.)--History, Local. I Title: Place names of central California. II. Title.

F859 .D88 2001
917.94'8'003--dc21

                                        00-054629

Cover photographs:
"Devils Postpile National Monument, CA," by Dennis Flaherty, courtesy of Dennis Flaherty Photography, Bishop, California (760-872-3805; www.dennis.flaherty.com; dennis@flaherty.com.)
"Valley Foothills," by Stephen Blake Mettee

Contents

California Map
Central California Counties Shaded VI

Introduction VII

Regional Setting IX

Geographic Terms XIII

Gazetteer

Madera, Fresno, Tulare, Kings and
Kern Counties 1

References Cited 311

About the Author 322

CALIFORNIA
CENTRAL CALIFORNIA
COUNTIES SHADED

INTRODUCTION

Purpose, organization and scope

This gazetteer, which lists geographic features of Madera, Fresno, Tulare, Kings, and Kern counties, California, is one of a series of fourteen books that cover the whole state. This series is derived from *California's Geographic Names: A Gazetteer of Historic and Modern Names of the State,* David L. Durham's definitive gazetteer of California. Each book contains all the entries for the counties covered that are included in the larger volume.United States government quadrangle maps, which are detailed, somewhat authoritative, and generally available, are the primary source of information. Included are features that are named on quadrangle maps, or that can be related to features named on the maps. The books list relief features, water features, and most kinds of cultural features, but omit names of streets, parks, schools, churches, cemeteries, dams and the like. Some names simply identify a person or family living at a site because such places are landmarks in sparsely settled parts of the state.

The listing of names is alphabetical, and multiword names are alphabetized as one word. Terms abbreviated on maps are given in full in the alphabetical list, and numerals in names are listed in alphabetical order rather than in numerical order. In addition to the principal entries, the list includes cross references to variant names, obsolete names and key words in multiword English-language names. For each principal entry, the name is followed by the name of the county or counties in which the feature lies, a classifying term, general and specific locations, identification of one or more quadrangle maps that show the name and other information. All features named in an entry generally belong to the same county. The classifying terms are defined under the heading "Geographic Terms" beginning on page *xiii*.

Locations and measurements are from quadrangle maps, distances and directions are approximate, and latitude and longitude generally are to the nearest five seconds. Distances between post offices are measured by road, as the mail would be carried. Other distances are measured in a straight line unless the measurement is given with a qualifying expression such as "downstream" or "by road." For streams, the location given generally is the place that the stream joins another stream, enters the sea or a lake, or debouches into a canyon or valley. For features of considerable areal extent, the location given ordinarily is near the center, except for cities and towns, for which the location given is near the center of the downtown part, or at the city hall or civic center. Measurements to or from areal features usually are to or from the center. Specific locations are omitted for some very large or poorly defined places. Books, articles, and miscellaneous maps are listed under "References Cited." The references identify sources of data and provide leads to additional information. If a name applies to more than one feature in a county, the features are numbered and identified elsewhere in the list by that number in parentheses following the name.

REGIONAL SETTING

General.—This book concerns geographic features in five counties—Fresno, Kern, Kings, Madera and Tulare—that lie in and around the south part of San Joaquin Valley. Townships (T) North and Ranges (R) West refer to San Bernardino Base and Meridian; Townships South and Ranges East refer to Mount Diablo Base and Meridian. San Joaquin Valley is the south part of the Central Valley, or Great Valley, of California, and takes its name from San Joaquin River, which drains most of it. Early Spanish explorers in the valley found a lake that they called Laguna de los Tulares because of the tules or cattails around it, and later the Spaniards called the valley itself Los Tulares (Mitchell, A.R., p. 5). The *Californian* newspaper used the name "Toolary valley" on August 22, 1846, and Carson (p. 93, 95) used the names "Tulare Valley" and "Tulare Plains" in 1852. The valley is called Tulares Valley on Derby's (1850) map. The whole Central Valley is called Buena Ventura Valley on Wilkes' (1841) map. Map makers apparently devised many names for features in and near Kettleman Hills, names that may have little or no local use.

The map on page *iv* shows the location of the counties included in this book. The Sierra Nevada lies east of San Joaquin Valley. United States Board on Geographic Names (1933a, p. 692) ruled against the form "Sierra Nevadas" for the name of the range. The term "High Sierra" commonly is accepted for the part of the range that includes the high peaks (Gudde, 1949, p. 148). Garces gave the name "Sierra de San Marcos" to the present Sierra Nevada in 1776 (Boyd, p. 3), Wilkes (p. 44) called it the California Range in 1841, Lyman (p. 307) called it "Sierra Nevada, or Snowy Mountains" in 1849, and Kip (p. 46) called it Snowy Range in 1850. Whitney (1865, p. 2) pointed out that the range was long known to the Spaniards as Sierra Nevada, or Snowy Range, because "the most distant and loftiest elevations are never entirely bare of snow, and for a large portion of the year are extensively covered with it." Diablo Range is along the west side of San Joaquin Valley from Contra Costa County to the northwest corner of Kern County. The range is called Sierra del Monte Diablo on Parke's (1854-1855) map. Whitney (1865, p. 2) called the feature Monte Diablo Range and stated that it "is so called from the conspicuous point [Mount Diablo] of that name." United States Board on Geographic Names (1933a, p. 246) rejected the names "Monte Diablo Range," "Mount Diablo Range," and "Sierra del Monte Diablo" for the feature. The southeasternmost part of the region lies in Mojave Desert. The name "Mojave" is from the designation of Indians that lived near Colorado River at the east side of the desert (Gudde, 1949, p. 219); United States Board on Geographic Names (1934, p. 11) rejected the form "Mohave Desert" for the name, and cited local usage for the decision.

Madera County.—Madera County extends from the crest of the Sierra Nevada southwestward into San Joaquin Valley. It was organized in 1893 from the part of Fresno County that lay north and west of San Joaquin River; the county boundaries have not changed (Coy, p. 157). The county name is from the principal town, Madera, which always has been the county seat (Hoover, Rensch, and Rensch, p. 170).

Fresno County.—Fresno County extends from the crest of the Sierra Nevada westward across San Joaquin Valley into Diablo Range. The state legislature created the county in 1856 from what previously had been the south part of Merced County and the south and east parts of Mariposa County. The original territory of Fresno County had three major reductions: the part east of the crest of Sierra Nevada went to Mono County when that county was organized in 1861; the northwest part went to San Benito County in 1887; and the north part went to form Madera County in 1893 (Coy, p. 101, 104-105). Millerton was the first county seat, but in 1874 the county government moved to Fresno, where it remains; *fresno* means "ash tree" in Spanish—early Spanish explorers used the name in the region because of the abundance of ash trees along watercourses there (Hoover, Rensch, and Rensch, p. 89).

Tulare County.—Tulare County extends from the crest of the Sierra Nevada westward into San Joaquin Valley. The state legislature created the county in 1852 from the south part of Mariposa County and the north part of Los Angeles County; Wood's Cabin, or Woodsville, was the first county seat, but the county government moved to Visalia in 1853, and remains there (Hoover, Rensch, and Rensch, p. 558, 561). The original Tulare County lost considerable territory with the formation of Fresno County in 1856, with the formation of Inyo and Kern Counties in 1866, and with the formation of Kings County in 1893 (Coy, p. 282-287). The name "Tulare" is from the Spanish term for the cattails, or tules, that grow in profusion at Tulare Lake, which was in the original territory of the county.

Kings County.—Kings County lies mainly in San Joaquin Valley, where it includes most of the bed of Tulare Lake, but also extends southwest from the valley across Kettleman Hills into Diablo Range. The state legislature formed Kings County in 1893 from territory of Tulare County; Kings County gained some land from Fresno County in 1909 (Coy, p. 120-121). The county name is from Kings River; Hanford is and always has been the county seat (Hoover, Rensch, and Rensch, p. 135).

Kern County.—Kern County extends eastward from Temblor Range across San Joaquin Valley and the Sierra Nevada into Mojave Desert. The state legislature created the county in 1866 from parts of previously organized Tulare County and Los Angeles County; the original boundaries of Kern County have had only minor changes (Coy, p. 116-119). The name is from Kern River; Havilah was the county seat until 1874, when the county government moved to Bakersfield (Hoover, Rensch, and Rensch, p. 121).

Geographic Terms

Area —A tract of land, either precisely or indefinitely defined.

Bend —A pronounced curve in the course of a stream, and the land partly enclosed therein.

Canyon —A narrow elongate depression in the land surface, generally confined between steep sides and usually drained by a stream.

Cave —A naturally formed subterranean chamber.

City —An inhabited place that has a population greater than about 25,000 in an urban setting.

District —Part of an inhabited place, either precisely or indefinitely defined.

Dry lake —A lake bed that normally lacks water.

Dry wash —A normally dry watercourse that on a map is shown without a stream.

Embayment —An indentation in the shoreline of a body of water.

Escarpment —A cliff or a nearly continuous line of steep slopes.

Glacier —A slowly moving mass of ice.

Gully —A small canyon-like depression in the land surface.

Hill —A prominent elevation on the land surface that has a well-defined outline on a map, and that rises less than 1000 feet above its surroundings.

Intermittent lake —A lake that ordinarily contains water only part of the time.

Island —A tract of normally dry land, or of marsh, that is surrounded by water.

Lake —A body of standing water, either natural or artificial.

Land grant —A gift of land made by Spanish or Mexican authority and eventually confirmed by the United States government.

Locality —A place that has past or present cultural associations.

Marsh —A poorly drained wet area.

Military installation —Land or facility used for military purposes.

Mountain —A prominent elevation on the land surface that has a well-defined outline on a map, and that rises more than 1000 feet above its surroundings.

Narrows —The constricted part of a channel, river, canyon, valley, or pass.

Pass —A saddle or natural depression that affords passage across a range or between peaks.

Peak —A prominent high point on a larger elevated land surface.

Promontory —A conspicuous, but not

necessarily high, elevation of the land surface that protrudes into a body of water or into a lowland.

Range —An elevated land surface of ridges and peaks.

Relief feature —A general term for a recognizable form of the land surface produced by natural causes.

Ridge —A prominent elongate elevation on the land surface; occurs either independently or as part of a larger elevation.

Settlement —An informal inhabited place.

Spring —A natural flow of water from the ground.

Stream —A body of water that moves under gravity in a depression on the land surface; includes watercourses that have intermittent flow and watercourses that are modified by man.

Town —An inhabited place that has a population of about 500 to 25,000 in an urban setting.

Valley —A broad depression in the land surface, or a wide place in an otherwise narrow depression.

Village —An inhabited place that has a compact cluster of buildings and a population less than about 500.

Waterfall —A perpendicular or very steep descent of the water in a stream.

Water feature —A general term for something or some place involving water.

Well —A hole sunk into the ground to obtain water.

– A –

Abbot: see **Mount Abbot** [FRESNO].

Abbott: see **Abbott Mill** [FRESNO].

Abbott Creek [FRESNO]: *stream,* flows 4.5 miles to Mill Flat Creek 11 miles south-south-east of Balch Camp (lat. 36°46'20" N, long. 119°01' W; sec. 23, T 13 S, R 27 E). Named on Patterson Mountain (1952) and Tehipite Dome (1952) 15' quadrangles.

Abbott Mill [FRESNO]: *locality,* 3.5 miles west-southwest of Hume (lat. 36°46'15" N, long. 118°58' W; sec. 19, T 13 S, R 28 E); the place is north of Abbott Creek. Named on Tehipite (1903) 30' quadrangle. California Mining Bureau's (1917a) map has the name "Abbott" at the site. The mill was built in 1902 to handle timber cut on the Millwood side of Hoist Ridge; the place also was called Camp Three (Johnston, p. 76).

Abel Mountain: see **Cerro Noroeste** [KERN].

Abilene [TULARE]: *locality,* 4.5 miles southsoutheast of Lindsay along Visalia Electric Railroad (lat. 36°08'45" N, long. 119°03'10" W; sec. 33, T 20 S, R 27 E). Named on Lindsay (1928) 7.5' quadrangle.

Academy [FRESNO]: *settlement,* 10 miles east-northeast of Clovis (lat. 36°33'15" N, long. 119°32'15" W; sec. 14, T 12 S, R 22 E). Named on Academy (1964) 7.5' quadrangle. Postal authorities established Academy post office in 1876, discontinued it in 1877, reestablished it in 1892, discontinued it in 1903, reestablished it in 1905, and discontinued it in 1951 (Salley, p. 1). The name "Academy" is from a private secondary school that was started in the neighborhood in 1872 (Hoover, Rensch, and Rensch, p. 94). Postal authorities established Big Dry Creek post office 2 miles north of Academy in 1870, moved it 2.5 miles south in 1888, and discontinued it in 1893 (Salley, p. 21).

Acrodectes Peak: see **Mount Baxter** [FRESNO].

Actis [KERN]: *locality,* 6.5 miles north of Rosamond (lat. 34°57'30" N, long. 118°08'55" W; at W line sec. 15, T 10 N, R 12 W). Named on Soledad Mountain (1973) 7.5' quadrangle. Called Gloster on Soledad Mountain (1947) 7.5' quadrangle. Thompson's (1921) map shows Runnington P.O. at present Actis. Postal authorities established Highberg post office in 1917, changed the name to Runnington in 1918, and discontinued it in 1927 (Frickstad, p. 56, 59).

Adair Lake [MADERA]: *lake,* 850 feet long, 3.5 miles north-northwest of Merced Peak (lat. 37°41' N, long. 119°24'25" W). Named on Merced Peak (1953) 15' quadrangle. Browning (1988, p. 1) associated the name with Charles F. Adair, a ranger at Yosemite National Park from 1914 until 1935, who planted golden trout in the lake—Browning pointed out that the feature also was known as Obelisk Lake and as Cirque Lake.

Adams Flat [TULARE]: *area,* 4 miles southeast of Auckland (lat. 36°33'10" N, long. 119°02'45" W; in and near sec. 9, T 16 S, R 27 E). Named on Auckland (1966) 7.5' quadrangle.

Adams Gap [TULARE]: *pass,* 4 miles southeast of Auckland (lat. 36°32'30" N, long. 119°03'35" W; near N line sec. 17, T 16 S, R 27 E); the pass is 1 mile southwest of Adams Flat. Named on Auckland (1966) 7.5' quadrangle.

Adelaide: see **Mount Adelaide** [KERN].

Administration Point: see **Admiration Point** [TULARE].

Admiration Point [TULARE]: *relief feature,* nearly 4 miles east-southeast of Yucca Mountain (lat. 36°33'10" N, long. 118°48'15" W). Named on Giant Forest (1956) 15' quadrangle. United States Board on Geographic Names (1933a, p. 80) rejected the name "Administration Point" for the feature.

Adobe Canyon [KERN]: *canyon,* drained by a stream that flows 8.5 miles to Poso Creek 3.5 miles south-southeast of Knob Hill (lat. 35°31' N, long. 118°35'15" W; near SW cor. sec. 1, T 28 S, R 28 E). Named on Knob Hill (1965) and Pine Mountain (1965) 7.5' quadrangles.

Adobe Flat [FRESNO]: *area,* 13 miles west of Coalinga (lat. 36°15'25" N, long. 120°35'20" W; near SE cor. sec. 20, T 19 S, R 13 E). Named on Santa Rita Peak (1969) 7.5' quadrangle.

Adobe Hill [MADERA]: *hill,* 13 miles south of Raymond (lat. 37°02' N, long. 119°51'40" W; sec. 26, T 10 S, R 19 E). Altitude 669 feet. Named on Little Table Mountain (1962) 7.5' quadrangle.

Adobe Station [KERN]: *locality,* 12 miles south of Bakersfield (lat. 35°11'45" N, long. 118°58' W; near SW cor. sec. 27, T 31 S, R 28 E). Named on Caliente (1914) 30' quadrangle. Telegraph Stage Company had a station at the place in the 1870's (Boyd, p. 42).

Advance [TULARE]: *locality,* 4.25 miles south-southwest of Yucca Mountain along North Fork Kaweah River (lat. 36°31' N, long.

118°54'10" W). Named on Giant Forest (1956) 15' quadrangle. The place was the site of the administrative center, general store, post office, and school for Kaweah Cooperative Colony, a socialistic experiment begun in 1885 and ended in 1891 (Kaiser, p. 63, 67). Postal authorities established Advance post office in 1890, changed the name to Kaweah the same year, and moved it to Kaweah in 1910 (Mitchell, A.R., p. 64).

Aerial Acres [KERN]: *locality,* 5.5 miles east-southeast of Castle Butte in Peerless Valley (lat. 35°05'20" N, long. 117°47'20" W; sec. 36, T 12 N, R 9 W). Named on North Edwards (1973) 7.5' quadrangle.

Agassiz: see **Mount Agassiz** [FRESNO].

Agassiz Col [FRESNO]: *pass,* 10.5 miles east of Mount Goddard on Fresno-Inyo county line (lat. 36°06'25" N, long. 119°31'45" W); the pass is 1600 feet south of Mount Agassiz. Named on Mount Goddard (1948) 15' quadrangle.

Agassiz Needle: see **Mount Agassiz** [FRESNO].

Agnew Meadows [MADERA]: *area,* 4.25 miles north-northwest of Devils Postpile (lat. 37°41'05" N, long. 119°05'45" W). Named on Devils Postpile (1953) 15' quadrangle. The name is for Theodore (Tom) Agnew, a miner who settled at the place in 1877 (Smith, Genny, p. 13).

Agnew Pass [MADERA]: *pass,* 8 miles north-northwest of Devils Postpile on Madera-Mono county line (lat. 37°44'05" N, long. 119°08'35" W; sec. 31, T 2 S, R 26 E). Named on Devils Postpile (1953) 7.5' quadrangle. The name commemorates Theodore Agnew of Agnew Meadows (Hanna, p. 2).

Agua Caliente: see **Caliente** [KERN]; **Scovern Hot Springs** [KERN].

Agua Caliente Creek: see **Caliente Creek** [KERN].

Agua de los Alamos: see **Sinks of the Tejon**, under **Tejon Creek** [KERN].

Agua Fria Spring [KERN]: *spring,* 9 miles east of Mount Adelaide (lat. 35°25' N, long. 118°35'25" W; sec. 7, T 29 S, R 32 E). Named on Breckenridge Mountain (1972) 7.5' quadrangle.

Ahart Meadow [FRESNO]: *area,* 8 miles southeast of Dinkey Dome along East Fork Deer Creek (3) (lat. 37°01'15" N, long. 119°02'30" W; near W line sec. 33, T 10 S, R 27 E). Named on Huntington Lake (1953) 15' quadrangle. The name commemorates John Ahart, who patented land at the place about 1890 (Hanna, p. 4). According to Browning (1986, p. 2), the landowner had the name "John Earthart."

Ahwahnee [MADERA]: *settlement,* 5.25 miles west of Yosemite Forks (lat. 37°22' N, long. 119°43'30" W; on W line sec. 31, T 6 S, R 21 E). Named on Bass Lake (1953) 15' quadrangle. The word "Ahwahnee" is from the Indian name for the largest Indian village in Yosemite Valley, and for the valley itself

(Kroeber, p. 34). Postal authorities established Ahwahnee post office in 1893, discontinued it in 1896, reestablished it in 1900 when they moved Gertrude post office 2 miles north and changed the name to Ahwahnee, discontinued it in 1907, and reestablished it in 1917 (Salley, p. 2). They established Gertrude post office in 1881, discontinued it in 1893, reestablished it in 1896, moved it 2 miles south in 1899, and discontinued it in 1900; the name was for Gertrude Haley, first postmaster (Salley, p. 84). Gertrude post office was at a place called String Town before the post office was established (Clough, p. 79-80).

Ahwahnee: see **Wassamma** [MADERA].

Aido Spring [KERN]: *spring,* 2 miles southeast of Orchard Peak (lat. 35°42'55" N, long. 120°06'40" W; on S line sec. 26, T 25 S, R 17 E). Named on Sawtooth Ridge (1961) 7.5' quadrangle. Two oil prospectors named the spring one hot summer day from initial letters of the phrase "all in, down and out" (Waring, p. 368).

Air Compressor Springs: see **Miracle Hot Springs** [KERN].

Airplane Flat [KERN]: *area,* 12.5 miles north of Mojave (lat. 35°13'45" N, long. 118°11'40" W; near S line sec. 14, T 31 S, R 35 E). Named on Cache Peak (1973) 7.5' quadrangle.

Alabama Settlement: see **Borden** [MADERA].

Alameda [KERN]: *locality,* 9 miles south of Bakersfield (lat. 35°14'15" N, long. 119°00'10" W; at SW cor. sec. 8, T 31 S, R 28 E). Named on Conner (1954) 7.5' quadrangle. A farming colony called Winter Garden was situated south of present Alameda in 1888 and 1889 (Bailey, 1962, p. 59).

Alamo Solo Spring [KERN]: *spring,* 14 miles north-northwest of present Blackwells Corner (lat. 35°46'50" N, long. 119°59'55" W; sec. 2, T 25 S, R 18 E). Named on Lost Hills (1914) 30' quadrangle. The name is for a single cottonwood tree at the spring—*alamo solo* means "lone cottonwood" in Spanish (Arnold and Johnson, p. 19). After the spring dried up, a well at the place was called Light Well for the Light family, who lived there (Latta, 1949, p. 299).

Alaska Flat [KERN]: *area,* 4.25 miles north-northwest of Claraville (lat. 35°30' N, long. 118°21'25" W; sec. 18, T 28 S, R 34 E). Named on Claraville (1972) and Woolstalf Creek (1972) 7.5' quadrangles.

Albanita Meadows [TULARE]: *area,* 5.5 miles south of Monache Mountain (lat. 36°07'40" N, long. 118°11'45" W; sec. 3, 4, T 21 S, R 35 E). Named on Monache Mountain (1956) 15' quadrangle.

Alcalde [FRESNO]: *locality,* 4.5 miles southwest of Coalinga along Warthan Creek (lat. 35°05'45" N, long. 120°25' W; near SW cor. sec. 13, T 21 S, R 14 E). Named on Coalinga (1912) 30' quadrangle, which shows the place in Alcalde Canyon. Postal authorities established Alcalde post office in 1888 and discontinued it in 1904; they established Warthan post office 10 miles west of Alcalde in 1880 and discontinued it in 1902, when they moved the service to Alcalde (Salley, p. 4, 234).

Alcalde Canyon [FRESNO]: *canyon,* drained by a stream that flows 2.5 miles to Warthan Creek 4.5 miles southwest of Coalinga (lat. 36°05'50" N, long. 120°25' W; near SW cor. sec. 13, T 21 S, R 14 E). Named on Curry Mountain (1969) 7.5' quadrangle. On Coalinga (1912) 30' quadrangle, the canyon of Warthan Creek (present Warthan Creek) has the name "Alcalde Canyon." Arnold and Anderson (1908, p. 15) applied the name "Alcalde Canyon" to only the lower part of the canyon of Warthan Creek "extending from the edge of Waltham Valley, where the stream cuts between Juniper Ridge and Curry Mountain, to Pleasant Valley."

Alcalde Creek: see **Warthan Creek** [FRESNO].

Alcalde Hills [FRESNO]: *range,* 5 miles west-northwest of Coalinga (lat. 36°10' N, long. 120°26'30" W). Named on Alcalde Hills (1969) and Curry Mountain (1969) 7.5' quadrangles. Arnold and Anderson (1908, p. 14) gave the name "Alcalde Hills" to "the foothills between Los Gatos and Waltham Creeks, east of Juniper Ridge, northwest of Alcalde and west of Coalinga."

Alder Creek [KERN]: *stream,* flows 3.25 miles to Cedar Creek 3.5 miles west of Alta Sierra (lat. 35°43'05" N, long. 118°36'50" W; sec. 26, T 25 S, R 31 E). Named on Alta Sierra (1972) 7.5' quadrangle.

Alder Creek [TULARE]:
(1) *stream,* flows 3.5 miles to Dry Meadow Creek 9 miles southeast of Camp Nelson (lat. 36°02'15" N, long. 118°30'55" W; near NW cor. sec. 10, T 22 S, R 32 E). Named on Camp Nelson (1956) 15' quadrangle.
(2) *stream,* flows 2 miles to Tyler Creek nearly 2 miles north-northeast of California Hot Springs (lat. 35°54'10" N, long. 118°39'10" W; sec. 29, T 23 S, R 31 E). Named on California Hot Springs (1958) 15' quadrangle.

Alder Creek: see **North Alder Creek** [TULARE]; **South Alder Creek** [TULARE]; **Whiskey Creek** [MADERA] (2).

Alder Creek Campground [KERN]: *locality,* 3.5 miles west of Alta Sierra (lat. 35°43'10" N, long. 118°36'40" W; near SE cor. sec. 26, T 25 S, R 31 E); the place is near the mouth of Alder Creek. Named on Alta Sierra (1972) 7.5' quadrangle.

Alder Springs [FRESNO]: *village,* 5.5 miles west-southwest of Shaver Lake Heights (present town of Shaver Lake) (lat. 37°04' N, long. 119°24' W; sec. 18, T 10 S, R 24 E). Named on Shaver Lake (1953) 15' quadrangle.

Alexander's Corner: see **Weed Patch** [KERN].

Alex Cook Spring [KERN]: *spring,* 10 miles southwest of Blackwells Corner (lat.

35°30'35" N, long. 119°59' W; sec. 12, T 28 S, R 18 E). Named on Shale Point (1953) 7.5' quadrangle.

Alfac [TULARE]: *locality,* 2 miles south of Tipton along Southern Pacific Railroad (lat. 36°01'55" N, long. 119°18'25" W; sec. 7, T 22 S, R 25 E). Named on Tipton (1928) 7.5' quadrangle.

Alfonce Well [KERN]: *well,* 11 miles southeast of Orchard Peak along Packwood Creek (lat. 35°36'25" N, long. 120°01'10" W; sec. 3, T 27 S, R 18 E). Named on Packwood Creek (1961) 7.5' quadrangle.

Alfonsos [KERN]: *locality,* 13 miles south-southeast of Orchard Peak (lat. 35°34'15" N, long. 120°00'50" W; near SW cor. sec. 14, T 27 S, R 18 E). Named on Cholame (1917) 30' quadrangle.

Algoso [KERN]: *locality,* 4.5 miles east-south-east of downtown Bakersfield along the railroad (lat. 35°21'35" N, long. 118°55'30" W; sec. 36, T 29 S, R 28 E). Named on Lamont (1954) 7.5' quadrangle. The place was called Weed Patch before the railroad reached the site; railroad officials chose the name "Algoso" for the station to avoid confusion with another place called Weed Patch—*algoso* means "weedy" in Spanish (Gudde, 1949, p. 7).

Alila: see **Earlimart** [TULARE].

Alkali City: see **Bakersfield** [KERN].

Alkali Flat [TULARE]: *area,* 8 miles south-southwest of Springville (lat. 36°01' N, long. 118°51'05" W; sec. 16, T 22 S, R 29 E). Named on Globe (1956) 7.5 quadrangle.

Allard: see **Bealville** [KERN].

Allen: see **Royal Allen Lake**, under **Little Kern Lake** [TULARE].

Allen Gap [TULARE]: *pass,* 7.5 miles northeast of Exeter (lat. 36°21'45" N, long. 119°02'10" W; sec. 15, T 18 S, R 27 E); the pass is 1 mile northwest of Allen Hill. Named on Rocky Hill (1951) 7.5' quadrangle.

Allen Hill [TULARE]: *ridge,* southwest-trending, nearly 1 mile long, 7.5 miles east-northeast of Exeter (lat. 36°21' N, long. 119°01'35" W; on E line sec. 22, T 18 S, R 27 E). Named on Rocky Hill (1951) 7.5' quadrangle.

Allen's Camp: see **Caliente** [KERN].

Allensworth [TULARE]: *village,* 6.5 miles west-southwest of Earlimart (lat. 35°51'50" N, long. 119°23'20" W; near SW cor. sec. 4, T 24 S, R 24 E). Named on Allensworth (1954) 7.5' quadrangle. The name commemorates Lieutenant Colonel Allen Allensworth, an army chaplain who was born a slave in 1842 and who started the village as a Negro colony after 1902 (Hanna, p. 7). Postal authorities established Allensworth post office in 1909 and discontinued it in 1933 (Frickstad, p. 209).

Alpaugh [TULARE]: *town,* 12 miles west of Earlimart (lat. 35°53'15" N, long. 119°29'10" W; mainly in sec. 33, T 23 S, R 23 E). Named on Alpaugh (1953) 7.5' quadrangle. Called

Alspaugh on California Mining Bureau's (1917b) map. Postal authorities established Alpaugh post office in 1906 (Frickstad, p. 209). The name commemorates John Alpaugh, a founder of the community (Mitchell, A.R., p. 67). The town is on a slight elevation of the valley floor that escaped winter floods; Judge J.J. Atwell of Visalia used the land as pasture for hogs in the 1850's, and the place then became known as Atwell's Island (Hoover, Rensch, and Rensch, p. 560). It also was called Root Island and Hog Island (Mitchell, A.R., p. 67). During highest water the west end of Atwell's Island became a separate island that was called Skull Island for Indian remains found there by early settlers (Hoover, Rensch, and Rensch, p. 560).

Alpaugh: see **West Alpaugh** [TULARE].

Alphie Canyon [KERN]: *canyon,* drained by a stream that flows 9.5 miles to Jawbone Canyon 4.5 miles north-northwest of Cinco (lat. 35°19'10" N, long. 118°04'30" W; near SE cor. sec. 14, T 30 S, R 36 E). Named on Cinco (1972) and Dove Spring (1972) 7.5' quadrangles. Called Gold Canyon on Cross Mountain (1943) 15' quadrangle, and United States Board on Geographic Names (1975b, p. 8) gave this name as a variant.

Alphie Spring [KERN]: *spring,* 7.5 miles north-northwest of Cinco (lat. 35°22'05" N, long. 118°04'40" W; sec. 35, T 29 S, R 36 E); the spring is in Alphie Canyon. Named on Cinco (1972) 7.5' quadrangle.

Alpine Col [FRESNO]: *pass,* 8 miles north of Mount Goddard on Glacier Divide (lat. 37°12'55" N, long. 118°41'35" W). Named on Mount Goddard (1948) 15' quadrangle.

Alpine Creek [FRESNO]: *stream,* flows 4.5 miles to Middle Fork Kings River 10 miles west of Marion Peak (lat. 36°56'45" N, long. 118°41'35" W). Named on Marion Peak (1953) and Mount Goddard (1948) 15' quadrangles.

Alpine Creek [TULARE]: *stream,* flows 6.5 miles to Little Kern River 8 miles northeast of Camp Nelson (lat. 36°13'50" N, long. 118°30'45" W; sec. 33, T 19 S, R 32 E). Named on Camp Nelson (1956) and Mineral King (1956) 15' quadrangles.

Alpine Lake [MADERA]: *lake,* 450 feet long, 2.5 miles south-southeast of Merced Peak (lat. 37°36' N, long. 119°22'35" W). Named on Merced Peak (1953) 15' quadrangle. Ansel F. Hall and Al Solinski named the feature in 1922 (Browning, 1988, p. 3).

Alpine Meadow [TULARE]: *area,* 7.5 miles north of Camp Nelson (lat. 36°14'55" N, long. 118°35'55" W; sec. 27, T 19 S, R 31 E). Named on Camp Nelson (1956) 15' quadrangle.

Alspaugh: see **Alpaugh** [TULARE].

Alta: see **Sultana** [TULARE].

Alta Meadow [TULARE]: *area,* 7 miles west of Triple Divide Peak (lat. 36°34'50" N, long.

118°39'15" W; near E line sec. 36, T 15 S, R 30 E). Named on Triple Divide Peak (1956) 15' quadrangle. Tom Witt, N.B. Witt, and W.B. Wallace named the place in 1876 for its high elevation (Hanna, p. 9).

Alta Peak [TULARE]: *peak,* 7.5 miles west of Triple Divide Peak (lat. 36°35'25" N, long. 118°39'45" W; sec. 25, T 15 S, R 30 E); the peak is 1 mile northwest of Alta Meadow. Altitude 11,204 feet. Named on Triple Divide Peak (1956) 15' quadrangle. The feature first was known as Tharps Peak for Hale Tharp, a mountaineer—Tharps Rock is at the place (Hanna, p. 9).

Alta Sierra [KERN]: *town,* 8.5 miles east of Glennville (lat. 35°43'45" N, long, 118°33' W; in and near sec. 28, T 25 S, R 32 E). Named on Alta Sierra (1972) 7.5' quadrangle.

Altha Lake [MADERA]: *lake,* 1100 feet long, 7 miles north-northwest of Devils Postpile (lat. 37°42'45" N, long. 119°08'40" W). Named on Devils Postpile (1953) 15' quadrangle.

Alum Creek [FRESNO]: *stream,* flows 1.5 miles to Deep Well Canyon 3 miles east of Smith Mountain (2) (lat. 36°04'35" N, long. 120°32'35" W; sec. 26, T 21 S, R 13 E). Named on Smith Mountain (1969) 7.5' quadrangle.

Amalie: see **Loraine** [KERN].

Amargo: see **Boron** [KERN].

Amargo Springs [KERN]: *springs,* 5 miles south of Arvin (lat. 35°08'15" N, long. 118°49'25" W). Named on Arvin (1955) 7.5' quadrangle.

Ambition Lake [FRESNO]: *lake,* 2100 feet long, 2.25 miles east of Blackcap Mountain (lat. 37°04'40" N, long. 118°45'05" W). Named on Blackcap Mountain (1953) and Mount Goddard (1948) 15' quadrangles.

Ambler [TULARE]: *settlement,* 1.5 miles south-southeast of Visalia (lat. 36°18'30" N, long. 119°16'45" W; sec. 5, T 19 S, R 25 E). Named on Visalia (1949) 7.5' quadrangle.

Ambrose Well [KERN]: *well,* 9 miles south-southeast of Orchard Peak (lat. 35°37'05" N, long. 120°03'30" W; sec. 32, T 26 S, R 18 E). Named on Packwood Creek (1961) 7.5' quadrangle.

Ames Hole [TULARE]: *relief feature,* 2.5 miles south of California Hot Springs along White River (1) (lat. 35°50'30" N, long. 118°40'10" W; sec. 18, T 24 S, R 31 E). Named on California Hot Springs (1958) 15' quadrangle.

Amphitheater Lake [FRESNO]: *lake,* 2800 feet long, 13 miles east-southeast of Mount Goddard (lat. 37°01'30" N, long. 118°30'35" W). Named on Mount Goddard (1948) 15' quadrangle. J.N. LeConte named the lake in 1902 (Farquhar, 1923, p. 382).

Amphitheater Lake [TULARE]: *lake,* 1600 feet long, 2.5 miles east of Mineral King (lat. 36°26'45" N, long. 118°33'05" W). Named on Mineral King (1956) 15' quadrangle. W.F. Dean named the feature in 1889 (Browning, 1986, p. 5).

Amphitheater Point [TULARE]: *relief feature,* 5.5 miles east-southeast of Yucca Mountain (lat. 36°32'15" N, long. 118°46'50" W). Named on Giant Forest (1956) 15' quadrangle.

Anderson Point [TULARE]: *peak,* 3 miles east of Monache Mountain (lat. 36°12'20" N, long. 118°08'40" W; near NW cor. sec. 12, T 20 S, R 35 E). Named on Monache Mountain (1956) 15' quadrangle.

Andress Spring [KERN]: *spring,* 4.5 miles north-northwest of Weldon (lat. 35°43'30" N, long. 118°19'45" W). Named on Weldon (1972) 7.5' quadrangle.

Andrews: see **Figarden** [FRESNO].

Andy Berry's Landing: see **Millwood** [FRESNO].

Angel Creek [KERN]: *stream,* flows 5.25 miles to Poso Creek 1.25 miles southwest of Glennville (lat. 35°43' N, long. 118°43'15" W; at S line sec. 26, T 25 S, R 30 E). Named on California Hot Springs (1958) 15' quadrangle, and on Glennville (1972) 7.5' quadrangle. United States Board on Geographic Names (1960a, p. 5) rejected the name "Angle Creek" for it.

Angiola [TULARE]: *village,* 13 miles west-northwest of Earlimart (lat. 35°59'25" N, long. 119°28'25" W; sec. 27, T 22 S, R 23 E). Named on Alpaugh (1953) 7.5' quadrangle. Postal authorities established Angiola post office in 1898 and discontinued it in 1927 (Frickstad, p. 209). Mr. Bacigalupi, who owned property at the place, named the village for his wife, Angela (Mitchell, A.R., p. 67).

Angle Creek: see **Angel Creek** [KERN].

Angora Creek [TULARE]: *stream,* flows 2 miles to Kern River 7.25 miles west-southwest of Kern Peak (lat. 36°16'10" N, long. 118°24'15" W); the stream heads near Angora Mountain. Named on Kern Peak (1956) 15' quadrangle.

Angora Mountain [TULARE]: *peak,* 9.5 miles west-southwest of Kern Peak on Great Western Divide (lat. 36°15'50" N, long. 118° 26'45" W). Altitude 10,202 feet. Named on Kern Peak (1956) 15' quadrangle. Called Sheep Mtn. on Olancha (1907) 30' quadrangle, but United States Board on Geographic Names (1938, p. 4) rejected this name for the feature. A sheepman named the peak for an Angora goat that led his flock (Browning, 1986, p. 5).

Anna Mills: see **Mount Anna Mills**, under **Mount Guyot** [TULARE].

Anne Lake [FRESNO]: *lake,* 2400 feet long, 12.5 miles west-northwest of Mount Abbot on the north side of Silver Divide (lat. 37°27'40" N, long. 118°59'25" W). Named on Mount Abbot (1953) 15' quadrangle.

Anne Lake [MADERA]: *lake,* 700 feet long, nearly 3 miles south-southeast of Merced Peak (lat. 37°36' N, long. 119°21'55" W). Named on Merced Peak (1953) 15' quadrangle.

Annette [KERN]: *locality,* 6.5 miles south-southwest of Orchard Peak (lat. 35°39'05" N, long. 120°10'40" W; sec. 19, T 26 S, R 17 E); the place is 1.5 miles northeast of Palo Prieto Pass. Named on Orchard Peak (1961) 7.5' quadrangle. The locality first was called Palo Prieto (Dillon, p. 5). Postal authorities established Annette post office in 1889, moved it 2.5 miles southwest in 1894, and discontinued it in 1930; the name was for Annette L. Jenness, first postmaster (Salley, p. 8).

Anona Lake [MADERA]: *lake,* 900 feet long, nearly 4 miles west-southwest of Devils Postpile (lat. 37°36'30" N, long. 119°08'55" W). Named on Devils Postpile (1953) 15' quadrangle.

Ansel [KERN]: *locality,* 3 miles north-northeast of Rosamond along Southern Pacific Railroad (lat. 34°54'20" N, long. 118°09'10" W; near N line sec. 4, T 9 N, R 12 W). Named on Soledad Mountain (1973) 7.5' quadrangle.

Ansel Adams: see **Mount Ansel Adams**, under **Foerster Peak** [MADERA].

Ansel Lake: [TULARE]: *lake,* 600 feet long, 4 miles south of Mineral King (lat. 36°23'30" N, long. 118°35'50" W). Named on Mineral King (1956) 15' quadrangle. The name is for Ansel Franklin Hall, a ranger and later information officer at Sequoia National Park (Browning 1986, p. 6).

Ant Canyon [TULARE]: *canyon,* drained by a stream that flows 4 miles to Kern River 3.5 miles southeast of Fairview (lat. 35°53'05" N, long. 118°27'30" W; sec. 31, T 23 S, R 33 E). Named on California Hot Springs (1958) and Kernville (1956) 15' quadrangles.

Antelope Canyon [KERN]:
(1) *canyon,* drained by a stream that flows 5 miles to Tehachapi Valley 2.25 miles south of Tehachapi (lat. 35°05'55" N, long. 118° 26'35" W; sec. 33, T 32 S, R 33 E). Named on Tehachapi South (1966) 7.5' quadrangle.
(2) *canyon,* drained by a stream that flows 3 miles to lowlands 7.5 miles south-southwest of Liebre Twins (lat. 34°51'45" N, long. 118°38'30" W; near SW cor. sec. 13, T 9 N, R 17 W). Named on La Liebre Ranch (1965) and Winters Ridge (1966) 7.5' quadrangles.

Antelope Creek [TULARE]: *stream,* flows 6.5 miles to lowlands 1.5 miles north of Woodlake (lat. 36°26'15" N, long. 119°05'45" W; sec. 19, T 17 S, R 27 E). Named on Auckland (1966) and Woodlake (1952) 7.5' quadrangles.

Antelope Hills [KERN]: *range,* 6.5 miles southeast of Blackwells Corner (lat. 35°32'30" N, long. 119°48'30" W). Named on Blackwells Corner (1953) 7.5' quadrangle. Arnold and Johnson (p. 19) proposed the name for "the group of low hills" that "are a range for the few wild antelope left in this region."

Antelope Mountain [TULARE]: *ridge,* generally west-trending, 1.25 miles long, 2 miles northeast of Woodlake (lat. 36°25'50" N, long. 119°04'15" W); the ridge is south of Antelope Valley. Named on Woodlake (1952) 7.5' quadrangle. Called Woodlake Mtn. on Lemon Cove (1928) 7.5' quadrangle.

Antelope Plain [KERN]: *valley,* southwest of the village of Lost Hills (lat. 35°38' N, long. 119°50' W). Named on Antelope Plain (1954), Avenal Gap (1954), Blackwells Corner (1953), Emigrant Hill (1953), and Shale Point (1953) 7.5' quadrangles.

Antelope Spring [KERN]: *spring,* 7.25 miles west-northwest of Carneros Rocks (lat. 35°28'45" N, long. 119°58'05" W; sec. 19, T 28 S, R 19 E). Named on Las Yeguas Ranch (1959) 7.5' quadrangle, which has a windmill symbol at the place.

Antelope Valley [KERN]:
(1) *valley,* 8 miles southeast of Orchard Peak (lat. 35°39'30" N, long. 120°01'30" W). Named on Emigrant Hill (1953), Orchard Peak (1961), Packwood Creek (1961), Sawtooth Ridge (1961), and Shale Point (1953) 7.5' quadrangles.
(2) *area,* part of Mojave Desert southeast of Tehachapi Mountains on Kern-Los Angeles county line. Named on Los Angeles (1975) and San Bernardino (1957) 1°x 2° quadrangles. Called Palma Plain on Williamson's (1853) map.

Antelope Valley [TULARE]: *valley,* 2.5 miles north-northeast of Woodlake (lat. 36°26'50" N, long. 119°04'15" W); the valley is north of Antelope Mountain. Named on Woodlake (1952) 7.5' quadrangle.

Antes [TULARE]: *locality,* 1.25 miles north-northeast of Exeter along Atchison, Topeka and Santa Fe Railroad (lat. 36°18'35" N, long. 119°07'45" W; sec. 2, T 19 S, R 26 E). Named on Exeter (1952) 15' quadrangle.

Ant Hill [KERN]: *peak,* 7.25 miles east-northeast of downtown Bakersfield (lat. 35°25'35" N, long. 118°53'10" W; at N line sec. 8, T 29 S, R 29 E). Altitude 960 feet. Named on Oil Center (1954) 7.5' quadrangle.

Anticline Canyon: see **Cooper Canyon** [FRESNO].

Anticline Ridge [FRESNO]: *ridge,* southeast-trending, 11 miles long, 6.5 miles north-northeast of Coalinga (lat. 36°14' N, long. 120°19'30" W). Named on Coalinga (1956), Guijarral Hills (1956), and Joaquin Rocks (1969) 7.5' quadrangles. The ridge "is formed by a perfect anticlinal nose" that gives the feature its name (Arnold and Anderson, 1908, p. 13)

Antimony Flat [KERN]: *valley,* 1.25 miles south of Cross Mountain (lat. 35°15'30" N, long. 118°08'15" W). Named on Cross Mountain (1972) 7.5' quadrangle.

Antimony Peak [KERN]:
(1) *peak,* 2.5 miles south-southeast of Eagle Rest Peak (lat. 34°52'35" N, long. 119°06'40" W; sec. 10, T 9 N, R 21 W). Altitude 6848 feet. Named on Pleito Hills (1958) 7.5' quadrangle. Antimony has been mined on the slopes of the peak (Troxel and Morton, p. 56).

(2) *peak,* 3 miles southwest of Loraine (lat. 35°16'50" N, long. 118° 28'35" W; sec. 31, T 30 S, R 33 E); the peak is at the north end of Antimony Ridge (1). Named on Loraine (1972) 7.5' quadrangle.

Antimony Ridge [KERN]:
(1) *ridge,* north-trending, less than 1 mile long, 3 miles southwest of Loraine (lat. 35°16'30" N, long. 118°28'30" W; sec. 31, T 30 S, R 33 E). Named on Loraine (1972) 7.5' quadrangle
(2) *ridge,* northwest-trending, 0.25 mile long, nearly 6 miles northwest of Emerald Mountain (lat. 35°19'10" N, long. 118°20'55" W; at S line sec. 17, T 30 S, R 34 E). Named on Emerald Mountain (1972) 7.5' quadrangle.

Apollo Lake [FRESNO]: *lake,* 1400 feet long, 7 miles west-southwest of Mount Abbot (lat. 37°20' N, long 118°53'25" W). Named on Mount Abbot (1953) 15' quadrangle.

Aqueduct: see **Monolith** [KERN].

Aramburu Canyon [KERN]: *canyon,* 1 mile long, 8.5 miles west of McKittrick (lat. 35°18'45" N, long. 119°46'30" W; on E line sec. 13, T 30 S, R 20 E). Named on McKittrick Summit (1959) 7.5' quadrangle. The name commemorates John L. Aramburu, a Portuguese settler who lived at the mouth of the canyon (Arnold and Johnson, p. 19).

Araujo Spring: see **Lower Araujo Spring** [KERN]; **Upper Araujo Spring** [KERN].

Arbios [FRESNO]: *locality,* 6.5 miles southeast of Firebaugh along Southern Pacific Railroad (lat. 36°46'35" N, long. 120°23'50" W; sec. 25, T 13 S, R 14 E). Named on Firebaugh (1956) 7.5' quadrangle.

Archer Camp [FRESNO]: *locality,* 15 miles northwest of Coalinga (lat. 36°17'55" N, long. 120°33'55" W; sec. 3, T 19 S, R 13 E); the place is nearly 1 mile southwest of Archer mine. Named on Santa Rita Peak (1969) 7.5' quadrangle.

Arch Rock [FRESNO]: *relief feature,* 12.5 miles north-northeast of Kaiser Peak (lat. 37°26'50" N, long. 119°04'20" W). Named on Kaiser Peak (1953) 15' quadrangle.

Arc Pass [TULARE]: *pass,* 2.25 miles southeast of Mount Whitney on Tulare-Inyo county line (lat. 36°33'05" N, long. 118°16'05" W). Named on Mount Whitney (1956) 15' quadrangle. Chester Versteeg proposed the descriptive name in 1936 (Browning 1986, p. 6).

Arcola: see **Borden** [MADERA].

Arctic Lake [FRESNO]: *lake,* 800 feet long, 4 miles north of Blackcap Mountain (lat. 37°07'50" N, long. 118°47'45" W). Named on Blackcap Mountain (1953) 15' quadrangle.

Arctic Lake [TULARE]: *lake,* 1100 feet long, 1 mile west-northwest of Mount Whitney (lat. 36°35' N, long. 118°18'25" W). Named on Mount Whitney (1956) 15' quadrangle. Chester Versteeg proposed the name in 1953 (Browning 1986, p. 6).

Arkansas Creek [FRESNO]: *stream,* flows nearly 2 miles to Dinkey Creek (1) 0.25 mile northeast of Dinkey Dome (lat. 37°07' N, long. 119°07'35" W; sec. 27, T 9 S, R 26 E). Named on Huntington Lake (1953) 15' quadrangle.

Arkansas Meadow [FRESNO]: *area,* 1 mile southeast of Dinkey Dome (lat. 37°06'20" N, long. 119°07'05" W; sec. 34, T 9 S, R 26 E); the place is along Arkansas Creek. Named on Huntington Lake (1953) 15' quadrangle.

Armistead [KERN]: *locality,* 9 miles southwest of Inyokern (lat. 35° 32'50" N, long. 117°55'40" W; sec. 31, T 27 S, R 38 E). Named on Freeman Junction (1972) 7.5' quadrangle.

Armitage Field [KERN]: *military installation,* 5 miles north of Ridgecrest (lat. 35°41'30" N, long. 117°41' W). Named on Ridgecrest (1953) 15' quadrangle. The place now is called Inyokern Airport (Darling, p. 62).

Armona [KINGS]: *town,* 3.5 miles west-southwest of Hanford (lat. 36°18'55" N, long. 119°42'30" W; in and near sec. 32, 33, T 18 S, R 21 E). Named on Hanford (1954) 7.5' quadrangle. The name applied to a railroad station in the 1880's, and was transferred to the present location on Southern Pacific Railroad in 1891 (Gudde, 1949, p. 15). Postal authorities established Armona post office in 1887—the name was coined by switching the first two letters of the name "Ramona" (Salley, p. 10).

Armstrong [FRESNO]: *village,* 0.5 mile southwest of Shaver Lake before the lake was enlarged; near present Rock Haven (lat. 37°07'25" N, long. 119°18'45" W; near NW cor. sec. 25, T 9 S, R 24 E). Named on Kaiser (1904) 30' quadrangle.

Army Pass [TULARE]: *pass,* 17 miles northnorthwest of Olancha Peak on Tulare-Inyo county line (lat. 36°29'50" N, long. 118°14'20" W). Named on Olancha (1956) 15' quadrangle.

Army Pass: see **New Army Pass** [TULARE].

Arnett Spring [TULARE]: *spring,* 4.25 miles north of Cliff Peak (lat. 36°37'05" N, long. 119°09'35" W; near W line sec. 16, T 15 S, R 26 E). Named on Stokes Mountain (1966) 7.5' quadrangle.

Arnold Creek [MADERA]: *stream,* flows 5.5 miles to Fine Gold Creek 5.5 miles westsouthwest of the town of North Fork (lat. 37° 11'50" N, long. 119°36'10" W; near N line sec. 31, T 8 S, R 22 E). Named on North Fork (1965) 7.5' quadrangle.

Arnold Meadow [MADERA]: *area,* 5.5 miles northeast of Shuteye Peak (lat. 37°25' N, long. 119°22' W; sec. 8, T 6 S, R 24 E). Named on Shuteye Peak (1953) 15' quadrangle. James H. Arnold patented land in section 8 in 1892 (Browning, 1986, p. 7).

Arnold Spring [MADERA]: *spring,* nearly 4 miles west-southwest of the town of North Fork (lat. 37°12'25" N, long. 119°34'20" W; sec. 28, T 8 S, R 22 E); the spring is along

Arnold Creek. Named on North Fork (1965) 7.5' quadrangle.

Arosi: see **East Orosi** [TULARE].

Arp's Addition: see **Riverview**, under **Bakersfield** [KERN].

Arrastra Canyon [TULARE]: *canyon,* drained by a stream that flows 1.25 miles to Dry Creek (1) 4.25 miles east-northeast of Woodlake (lat. 36°25'40" N, long. 119°01'30" W; near NW cor. sec. 26, T 17 S, R 27 E). Named on Woodlake (1952) 7.5' quadrangle.

Arrastre Creek [KERN-TULARE]: *stream,* heads in Kern County and flows 8.5 miles to White River (1) 7 miles southeast of Fountain Springs at White River (2) in Tulare County (lat. 35°48'50" N, long. 118°50'40" W; sec. 28, T 24 S, R 29 E). Named on White River (1952) 15' quadrangle.

Arrojo los Gates: see **Los Gatos Creek** [FRESNO].

Arrow Creek [FRESNO]: *stream,* flows 4.5 miles to South Fork Kings River 6 miles south of Marion Peak (lat. 36°52'15" N, long. 118°30'50" W); the stream is southeast of Arrow Ridge. Named on Marion Peak (1953) and Mount Pinchot (1953) 15' quadrangles.

Arrowhead Lake [FRESNO]: *lake,* 700 feet long, 9.5 miles west-northwest of Mount Abbot (lat. 37°25'30" N, long. 118°56'50" W). Named on Mount Abbot (1953) 15' quadrangle. The outline of the lake on a map has the shape of an arrowhead.

Arrow Peak [FRESNO]: *peak,* 5 miles westsouthwest of Mount Pinchot (lat. 36°55'40" N, long. 118°29'20" W). Altitude 12,958 feet. Named on Mount Pinchot (1953) 15' quadrangle. Bolton C. Brown made the first ascent of the peak and named it in 1895 (Browning 1986, p. 7).

Arrow Ridge [FRESNO]: *ridge,* northeasttrending, 3 miles long, 3 miles south-southeast of Marion Peak (lat. 36°54'30" N, long. 118° 30'30" W); the ridge extends southwest from Arrow Peak. Named on Marion Peak (1953) and Mount Pinchot (1953) 15' quadrangles.

Arroyo Ancho [KERN]: *stream,* 2 miles long, ends 11 miles north-northwest of Blackwells Corner (lat. 35°46' N, long. 119°55'05" W; near W line sec. 10, T 25 S, R 19 E). Named on Avenal Gap (1954) 7.5' quadrangle. United States Board on Geographic Names (1933b, p. 2) noted that *ancho* means "broad" in Spanish.

Arroyo Bifido [KINGS]: *stream,* flows 2 miles to lowlands 5 miles north-northeast of Avenal (lat. 36°03'55" N, long. 120°05'10" W; near S line sec. 25, T 21 S, R 17 E). Named on La Cima (1963) 7.5' quadrangle. United States Board on Geographic Names (1933b, p. 2) noted that the name is from the two branches near the head of the stream—*bifido* means "two-forked" in Spanish.

Arroyo Chico [KINGS]: *stream,* flows less than

2 miles to Kettleman Plain 1.5 miles east-southeast of Avenal (lat. 36°00' N, long. 120°06'15" W; sec. 23, T 22 S, R 17 E). Named on La Cima (1963) 7.5' quadrangle. United States Board on Geographic Names (1933b, p. 2) noted that the name is descriptive—*chico* means "small" in Spanish.

Arroyo Ciervo [FRESNO]: *stream, flows 8 miles to lowlands 15 miles southwest of Tranquility (lat. 36°31' N, long. 120°27'50" W; near SE cor. sec. 20, T 16 S, R 14 E); the stream is in Ciervo Hills. Named on Ciervo Mountain (1969) 7.5' quadrangle.

Arroyo Conchoso [KINGS]: *stream, flows nearly 3 miles to Kettleman Plain 3.5 miles east-southeast of Avenal (lat. 35°58'40" N, long. 120°04'25" W; near SW cor. sec. 30, T 22 S, R 18 E). Named on Kettleman Plain (1953) and La Cima (1963) 7.5' quadrangles. The name refers to the abundance of fossil shells at the place—*conchoso* means "shelly" in Spanish (United States Board on Geographic Names, 1933b, p. 2).

Arroyo Corto [FRESNO]: *stream, flows 1.5 miles to Kettleman Plain 12 miles east-southeast of Coalinga (lat. 36°03'05" N, long. 120°10'35" W; near S line sec. 31, T 21 S, R 17 E). Named on Avenal (1954) 7.5' quadrangle. United States Board on Geographic Names (1933b, p. 2) noted that the name is descriptive—*corto* means "short" in Spanish

Arroyo Culebrino [KINGS]: *stream, flows 3.25 miles to lowlands 5.5 miles south-southeast of Kettleman City (lat. 35°56' N, long. 119°55'50" W; near NW cor. sec. 16, T 23 S, R 19 E). Named on Los Viejos (1954) 7.5' quadrangle. United States Board on Geographic Names (1933b, p. 2) noted that *culebrino* means "snaky" in Spanish.

Arroyo Curvo [KINGS]: *stream, flows nearly 2 miles to Kettleman Plain 1 mile north-northwest of Avenal (lat. 36°01'05" N, long. 120°08'10" W; sec. 16, T 22 S, R 17 E). Named on Avenal (1954) 7.5' quadrangle. United States Board on Geographic Names (1933b, p. 2) pointed out that *curvo* means "bent" in Spanish.

Arroyo Degollado [KINGS]: *stream, flows 2.5 miles to lowlands nearly 1.5 miles west-northwest of Kettleman City (lat. 36°01' N, long. 119°59' W; near E line sec. 14, T 22 S, R 18 E). Named on Kettleman City (1963) and La Cima (1963) 7.5' quadrangles. The name refers to the apparent capture of the headwaters of the stream by Arroyo Robador—*degollado* means "beheaded" in Spanish (United States Board on Geographic Names, 1933b, p. 2).

Arroyo de las Encinas: see **Liveoak Canyon** [KERN].

Arroyo de las Uvas: see **Grapevine Creek** [KERN].

Arroyo del Camino [KINGS]: *stream, flows 1.5 miles to Kettleman Plain at Avenal (lat. 36°00'30" N, long. 120°07'15" W; sec. 15, T 22 S, R 17 E). Named on La Cima (1963) 7.5' quadrangle. United States Board on Geographic Names (1933b, p. 4) related the name to a road that follows the stream, and pointed out that *camino* means "road" in Spanish. On Discovery Well (1930) 7.5' quadrangle, the canyon of the stream has the name "Tar Canyon."

Arroyo del Conejo [KINGS]: *stream, flows 3 miles before ending 5.25 miles south of Kettleman City (lat. 35°55'50" N, long. 119°57'30" W; sec. 18, T 23 S, R 19 E). Named on Los Viejos (1954) 7.5' quadrangle. United States Board on Geographic Names (1933b, p. 4) pointed out that *conejo* means "rabbit" in Spanish.

Arroyo Delgado [KINGS]: *stream, flows 2.25 miles to Kettleman Plain 5.5 miles east-southeast of Avenal (lat. 35°57'40" N, long. 120°02'50" W; sec. 5, T 23 S, R 18 E). Named on Kettleman Plain (1953) 7.5' quadrangle. United States Board on Geographic Names (1933b, p. 2-3) related the name to the narrow course of the stream—*delgado* means "slender" in Spanish.

Arroyo de los Alamos: see **Tejon Creek** [KERN].

Arroyo de los Alizos: see **Sycamore Canyon** [KERN] (1).

Arroyo de los Osos: see **Williams Canyon** [KERN].

Arroyo del Paso [KINGS]: *stream, flows 4.25 miles to end 5 miles south of Kettleman City (lat. 35°56'45" N, long. 119°57'45" W; sec. 7, T 23 S, R 19 E). Named on Kettleman Plain (1953) and Los Viejos (1954) 7.5' quadrangles. United States Board on Geographic Names (1933b, p. 4) connected the name with the nearby pass called El Paso.

Arroyo del Tejon: see **Tejon Creek** [KERN].

Arroyo de Tecuya: see **Tecuya Creek** [KERN].

Arroyo Doblegado [KINGS]: *stream, flows 4 miles to lowlands 6.5 miles east-northeast of Avenal (lat. 36°01'40" N, long. 120°00'45" W; sec. 10, T 22 S, R 18 E). Named on La Cima (1963) 7.5' quadrangle. United States Board on Geographic Names (1933b, p. 3) noted that the name is descriptive—*doblegado* means "twisted" in Spanish.

Arroyo Escaso [KINGS]: *dry wash*, extends for 1 mile to Kettleman Plain 8 miles southeast of Avenal (lat. 35°56'10" N, long. 120° 01' W; near S line sec. 10, T 23 S, R 18 E). Named on Kettleman Plain (1953) 7.5' quadrangle. United States Board on Geographic Names (1933b, p. 3) pointed out that *escaso* means "short" (in the sense of "scarce") in Spanish.

Arroyo Esquinado [KINGS]: *stream, flows 2 miles to Kettleman Plain at Avenal (lat. 36°00'45" N, long. 120°07'35" W; sec. 15, T 22 S, R 17 E). Named on La Cima (1963) 7.5' quadrangle. United States Board on Geographic Names (1933b, p. 3) related the descriptive name to a sharp bend in the watercourse—*esquinado* means "angled" in Spanish.

Arroyo Estrecho [KINGS]: *stream,* flows 4.5 miles to lowlands 3.5 miles south-southeast of Kettleman City (lat. 35°57'45" N, long. 119°56'20" W; near N line sec. 5, T 23 S, R 19 E). Named on Los Viejos (1954) 7.5' quadrangle. The name is descriptive—*estrecho* means "narrow" in Spanish (United States Board on Geographic Names, 1933b, p. 3).

Arroyo Finito [KINGS]: *stream,* flows 1.5 miles to lowlands 6.25 miles east-northeast of Avenal (lat. 36°02'05" N, long. 120°01'30" W; near N line sec. 9, T 22 S, R 18 E). Named on La Cima (1963) 7.5' quadrangle. The name refers to the restricted drainage area of the stream—*finito* means "limited" in Spanish (United States Board on Geographic Names, 1933b, p. 3).

Arroyo Hondo [FRESNO]: *stream,* heads in San Benito County and flows 14 miles to lowlands 24 miles north of Coalinga (lat. 36° 28'45" N, long. 120°26' W; sec. 3, T 17 S, R 14 E). Named on Ciervo Mountain (1969) and Lillis Ranch (1956) 7.5' quadrangles. United States Board on Geographic Names (1933a, p. 104) rejected the name "Dry Creek" for the stream.

Arroyo Hondo [KINGS]: *stream,* flows 2.5 miles to lowlands 5.5 miles east-northeast of Avenal (lat. 36°02'40" N, long. 120°02'20" W; near E line sec. 5, T 22 S, R 18 E). Named on La Cima (1963) 7.5' quadrangle. United States Board on Geographic Names (1933b, p. 3) pointed out that *hondo* means "deep" or "low" in Spanish.

Arroyo Largo [FRESNO-KINGS]: *stream,* heads in Kings County and flows 5 miles to lowlands 14 miles east-southeast of Coalinga in Fresno County (lat. 36°04'45" N, long. 120°06'45" W; near N line sec. 27, T 21 S, R 17 E). Named on La Cima (1963) 7.5' quadrangle. The name is descriptive—*largo* means "long" in Spanish (United States Board on Geographic Names, 1933b, p. 3).

Arroyo Larguito [KINGS]: *stream,* heads just inside Fresno County and flows 1.25 miles to Kettleman Plain 2 miles north-northwest of Avenal (lat. 36°01'45" N, long. 120°09'45" W; sec. 8, T 22 S, R 17 E). Named on Avenal (1954) 7.5' quadrangle. United States Board on Geographic Names (1933b, p. 3) pointed out that *larguito* means "a little long" in Spanish.

Arroyo las Gatos: see **Los Gatos Creek** [FRESNO].

Arroyo Leona [FRESNO]: *stream,* flows 6.5 miles to Cantua Creek 5.5 miles south-southeast of Ciervo Mountain (lat. 36°23'40" N, long. 120°32'10" W; near E line sec. 3, T 18 S, R 13 E). Named on Ciervo Mountain (1969) and Santa Rita Peak (1969) 7.5' quadrangles.

Arroyo Mellado [KINGS]: *stream,* flows 2 miles to Kettleman Plain 2 miles east-southeast of Avenal (lat. 35°59'30" N, long. 120°05'40" W; near NE cor. sec. 26, T 22 S, R 17 E). Named on Kettleman Plain (1953) and La Cima (1963) 7.5' quadrangles. United States Board on Geographic Names (1933b, p. 3) noted that the name is descriptive—*mellado* means "jagged" in Spanish.

Arroyo Menudo [KINGS]: *stream,* flows 1.5 miles to Kettleman Plain 9 miles south of Kettleman City (lat. 35°52'30" N, long. 119°59'45" W; near N line sec. 2, T 24 S, R 18 E). Named on Avenal Gap (1954) and Los Viejos (1954) 7.5' quadrangles. The name is descriptive—*menudo* means "small" in Spanish (United States Board on Geographic Names, 1933b, p. 3).

Arroyo Murado [KINGS]: *stream,* flows 2.5 miles to Arroyo Torcido 4.25 miles northeast of Avenal (lat. 36°02'50" N, long. 120°04'20" W; sec. 6, T 22 S, R 18 E). Named on La Cima (1963) 7.5' quadrangle. The name is descriptive—*murado* means "walled" in Spanish (United States Board on Geographic Names, 1933b, p. 3).

Arroyo Passajero: see **Los Gatos Creek** [FRESNO].

Arroyo Pastoria: see **Pastoria Creek** [KERN].

Arroyo Pequeño [KINGS]: *stream,* flows 2 miles to lowlands 5.5 miles east-northeast of Avenal (lat. 36°02'25" N, long. 120°02' W; sec. 4, T 22 S, R 18 E). Named on La Cima (1963) 7.5' quadrangle. The name is descriptive—*pequeño* means "small" in Spanish (United States Board on Geographic Names, 1933b, p. 3).

Arroyo Petreo [KINGS]: *stream,* flows 1.25 miles to Kettleman Plain 10.5 miles south of Kettleman City (lat. 35°51'10" N, long. 119°58'25" W; sec. 12, T 24 S, R 18 E). Named on Avenal Gap (1954) 7.5' quadrangle. The name refers to gravel in the stream bed—*petreo* means "stony" in Spanish (United States Board on Geographic Names, 1933b, p. 3).

Arroyo Pino [KINGS]: *stream,* flows 3 miles to lowlands 2 miles south-southeast of Kettleman City (lat. 35°58'45" N, long. 119°57' W; near SE cor. sec. 30, T 22 S, R 19 E). Named on Los Viejos (1954) 7.5' quadrangle. United States Board on Geographic Names (1933b, p. 4) pointed out that *pino* means "steep" in Spanish.

Arroyo Pinoso [FRESNO]: *canyon,* drained by a stream that flows 5 miles to Zapato Chino Creek 4.5 miles north-northeast of Castle Mountain (lat. 36°00'05" N, long. 120°19' W; near E line sec. 23, T 22 S, R 15 E). Named on The Dark Hole (1961) 7.5' quadrangle, where the name applies to the stream in the canyon. On Cholame (1917) 30' quadrangle, and on The Dark Hole (1937) 7.5' quadrangle, the name applies to the canyon. Arnold and Anderson (1908, p. 16) called the feature Sulphur Spring Canyon "from the abundance of sulphur water that issues in it." The Dark Hole (1937) 7.5' quadrangle shows ruins of Pinoso house in the canyon (sec. 2, T 23 S, R 15 E). United States Board on Geographic Names (1964c, p. 15) rejected the names "Arroyo Piñoso," "Sulphur Spring Canyon," and "West Fork Zapato Creek" for the feature, and classified Arroyo Pinoso as a valley.

Arroyo Poso de Chane: see **Los Gatos Creek** [FRESNO].

Arroyo Ramoso [KINGS]: *stream,* flows 2.5 miles to Kettleman Plain nearly 5 miles east-southeast of Avenal (lat. 35°58' N, long. 120°03'20" W; near W line sec. 32, T 22 S, R 18 E). Named on Kettleman Plain (1953) 7.5' quadrangle.

Arroyo Raso [KINGS]: *stream,* flows 2 miles to Kettleman Plain 6.5 miles southeast of Avenal (lat. 37°57' N, long. 120°01'50" W; near S line sec. 4, T 23 S, R 18 E). Named on Kettleman Plain (1953) 7.5' quadrangle. United States Board on Geographic Names (1933b, p. 4) noted that *raso* means "open" or "unobstructed" in Spanish.

Arroyo Recodo [KINGS]: *stream,* flows 2.25 miles before ending at La Porteria 8 miles south-southeast of Kettleman City (lat. 35°53'55" N, long. 119°55'05" W; sec. 28, T 23 S, R 19 E). Named on Los Viejos (1954) 7.5' quadrangle. United States Board on Geographic Names (1933b, p. 4) noted that the name is descriptive—*recodo* means "winding" in Spanish.

Arroyo Recto [FRESNO]: *stream,* flows 1.5 miles to Kettleman Plain 10.5 miles east-southeast of Coalinga (lat. 36°04'10" N, long. 120° 11'45" W; sec. 25, T 21 S, R 16 E). Named on Avenal (1954) 7.5' quadrangle. The name is descriptive—*recto* means "straight" in Spanish (United States Board on Geographic Names, 1933b, p. 4).

Arroyo Robador [KINGS]: *stream,* flows 5 miles to lowlands 1 mile south of Kettleman City (lat. 35°59'35" N, long. 119°57'45" W; near SW cor. sec. 19, T 22 S, R 19 E). Named on Kettleman City (1963), Kettleman Plain (1953), La Cima (1963), and Los Viejos (1954) 7.5' quadrangles. The name refers to the apparent capture of the headwaters of Arroyo Degollado by Arroyo Robador—*robador* means "robber" in Spanish (United States Board on Geographic Names, 1933b, p. 4).

Arroyo San Arminio: see **San Emigdio Creek** [KERN].

Arroyo Seco [FRESNO]: *stream,* flows 2.5 miles to lowlands 11 miles east-southeast of Coalinga (lat. 36°06' N, long. 120°10' W; sec. 18, T 21 S, R 17 E). Named on Avenal (1954) 7.5' quadrangle. The name is descriptive—*seco* means "dry" in Spanish (United States Board on Geographic Names, 1933b, p. 4).

Arroyo Somero [KINGS]: *stream,* flows nearly 2 miles to Kettleman Plain 1 mile east of Avenal (lat. 36°00'05" N, long. 120°06'30" W;

sec. 23, T 22 S, R 17 E). Named on La Cima (1963) 7.5' quadrangle. United States Board on Geographic Names (1933b, p. 4) pointed out that *somero* means "shallow" in Spanish.

Arroyo Torcido [KINGS]: *stream,* flows 4 miles to lowlands 5.25 miles northeast of Avenal (lat. 36°03'25" N, long. 120°03'40" W; sec. 31, T 21 S, R 18 E). Named on La Cima (1963) 7.5' quadrangle. The name is descriptive—*torcido* means "twisted" in Spanish (United States Board on Geographic Names, 1933b, p. 4).

Arroyo Tozo [KINGS]: *stream,* flows 1 mile to lowlands 13 miles south-southeast of Kettleman City (lat. 35°49'20" N, long. 119°53'30" W; sec. 23, T 24 S, R 19 E). Named on Avenal Gap (1954) 7.5' quadrangle. United States Board on Geographic Names (1933b, p. 4) pointed out that *tozo* means "small" or "dwarf" in Spanish.

Arroyo Vadoso [FRESNO]: *stream,* flows 3.5 miles to lowlands 13 miles east-southeast of Coalinga (lat. 36°05'25" N, long. 120°08'15" W; sec. 21, T 21 S, R 17 E). Named on Avenal (1954) and La Cima (1963) 7.5' quadrangles. The name is descriptive—*vadoso* means "shallow" in Spanish (United States Board on Geographic Names, 1933b, p. 4).

Arroyo Venado [FRESNO]: *stream,* flows 2.5 miles to Arroyo Leona 6 miles south-southeast of Ciervo Mountain (lat. 36°23'05" N, long. 120°32'35" W; near N line sec. 10, T 18 S, R 13 E). Named on Ciervo Mountain (1969) and Santa Rita Peak (1969) 7.5' quadrangles.

Artwell: see **Bannister** [KERN].

Arvin [KERN]: *town,* 15 miles southeast of Bakersfield (lat. 35°12'30" N, long. 118°49'45" W; in and near sec. 23, 26, T 31 S, R 29 E). Named on Arvin (1955) 7.5' quadrangle. Postal authorities established Arvin post office in 1914 (Frickstad, p. 54), and the town incorporated in 1960. The first postmaster, Mrs. Birdie Heard, named the place for Arvin Richardson, a pioneer in construction and installation of concrete irrigation pipe in the region (Hanna, p. 18).

Ashely Hot Spring [KERN]: *spring,* 5 miles north-northwest of Weldon (lat. 35°44'05" N, long. 118°18'55" W). Named on Weldon (1972) 7.5' quadrangle.

Ash: see **Tillman** [MADERA].

Ashbrook Creek [MADERA]: *stream,* flows 2.5 miles to Coarse Gold Creek 4 miles southsoutheast of Knowles (lat. 37°10'05" N, long. 119°50'15" W; sec. 7, T 9 S, R 20 E). Named on Knowles (1962) 7.5' quadrangle.

Ash Creek: see **Ash Slough** [MADERA]; **Little Ash Creek** [MADERA].

Ashley Lake [MADERA]: *lake,* 1200 feet long, 4 miles west of Devils Postpile (lat. 37°37' N, long. 119°09'20" W). Named on Devils Postpile (1953) 15' quadrangle.

Ash Peaks [TULARE]: *peaks,* 3.25 miles south-

southeast of Yucca Mountain (lat. 36°31'30"
N, long. 118°51'15" W). Named on Giant
Forest (1956) 15' quadrangle.

Ash Peaks Ridge [TULARE]: *ridge,* southwest-
trending, 4.5 miles long, 3 miles southeast of
Yucca Mountain (lat. 36°32' N, long.
118°50'10" W); Ash Peaks are at the southwest end of the ridge. Named on Giant Forest
(1956) 15' quadrangle. United States Board
on Geographic Names (1933a. p. 105) rejected the name "Park Road Ridge" for the
feature.

Ash Slough [MADERA]: *stream,* diverges from
Chowchilla River 8 miles northeast of Fairmead and flows 29 miles to Fresno River 16
miles west-southwest of Chowchilla (lat.
37°01'45" N, long. 120° 31'50" W; sec. 27, T
10 S, R 13 E). Named on Chowchilla (1960),
Le Grand (1961), and Santa Rita Park (1962)
15' quadrangles. Called Ash Creek on Le
Grand (1918) and Plainsburg (1919) 7.5'
quadrangles.

Ash Spring Mountain [TULARE]: *peak,* 2
miles east of Auckland (lat. 36°35'30" N, long.
119°04'05" W; near W line sec. 29, T 15 S, R
27 E). Named on Auckland (1966) 7.5' quadrangle.

Ashton Slough [MADERA]: *stream,* flows 2.25
miles to Merced County 15 miles west-southwest of Chowchilla (lat. 37°03'50" N, long.
120°31' W; sec. 14, T 10 S, R 13 E). Named
on Santa Rita Bridge (1922) 7.5' quadrangle.

Aspen Meadow [FRESNO]: *area,* 5.5 miles west
of Kaiser Peak (lat. 37°16'45" N, long.
119°17'25" W; near NW cor. sec. 31, T 7 S, R
25 E). Named on Shuteye Peak (1953) 15'
quadrangle.

Asphalto: see **McKittrick** [KERN].

Aster Lake [TULARE]: *lake,* 600 feet long, 8
miles west of Triple Divide Peak (lat.
36°36'10" N, long. 118°40'40" W; sec. 24, T
15 S, R 30 E). Named on Triple Divide Peak
(1956) 15' quadrangle. Colonel John R. White
named the feature in the early 1920's for flowers that grow along the lake shore (Browning
1986, p. 8).

Atwell Creek [TULARE]: *stream,* flows 1.5
miles to East Fork Kaweah River 4.25 miles
west of Mineral King (lat. 36°27'20" N, long.
118°40'20" W). Named on Mineral King
(1956) 15' quadrangle, which shows Atwell
Mill ranger station by the stream. Atwell Mill
was a sawmill built in 1879 and later owned
by A.J. Atwell of Visalia (Hanna, p. 19).

Atwell Mill: see **Atwell Creek** [TULARE].

Atwell's Island: see **Alpaugh** [TULARE].

Auberry [FRESNO]: *town,* 9.5 miles east-southeast of Shaver Lake Heights (present town of
Shaver Lake) along Little Sandy Creek (lat.
37°04'45" N, long. 119°29'05" W; sec. 8, T
10 S, R 23 E). Named on Shaver Lake (1953)
15' quadrangle. On Kaiser (1904) 30' quadrangle. the name "Auberry" applies to a place
located 1.25 miles farther north-northwest at

present New Auberry. The name "Auberry"
is for Al Yarborough, but the spelling follows
the common pronunciation of Yarborough's
name (Gudde, 1949, p. 18). Postal authorities established Auberry post office in 1884,
moved it 1.5 miles southwest in 1887, moved
it 1.5 miles south in 1888, and moved it 8
miles northeast in 1906 (Salley, p. 12). They
established Thermal post office 5 miles southwest of Auberry in 1889 and discontinued it
in 1900—the post office was at a resort built
around hot springs (Salley, p. 221).

Auberry: see **New Auberry** [FRESNO].

Auberry Valley [FRESNO]: *valley,* 2.5 miles
west of Prather (lat. 37°02' N, long.
119°33'45" W). Named on Millerton Lake
East (1965) 7.5' quadrangle.

Auckland [TULARE]: *locality,* 16 miles east-
northeast of Dinuba along Cottonwood Creek
(lat. 36°35'20" N, long. 119°06'20" W; at W
line sec. 25, T 15 S, R 26 E). Named on
Auckland (1966) 7.5' quadrangle. Dunlap
(1944) 15' quadrangle shows Auckland ranch
at the site. Settlers from Auckland, New Zea-
land, named the place about 1860 (Mitchell,
A.R., p. 67).

Aux-um-ne: see **Merced River** [MADERA].

Avalanche Creek [FRESNO]: *stream,* flows 3
miles to South Fork Kings River 12 miles
south of Marion Peak in Kings Canyon (lat.
36°47'15" N, long. 118°33'45" W); the stream
is east of Avalanche Peak. Named on Marion
Peak (1953) 15' quadrangle.

Avalanche Lake [FRESNO]: *lake,* 500 feet long,
1.5 miles northeast of Kaiser Peak (lat.
37°18'35" N, long. 119°10' W). Named on
Kaiser Peak (1953) 15' quadrangle.

Avalanche Pass [FRESNO]: *pass,* 20 miles east
of Hume (lat. 36°44'50" N, long. 118°33'25"
W); the pass is 0.5 mile east of Palmer Mountain, which originally was called Avalanche
Peak. Named on Triple Divide Peak (1956)
15' quadrangle.

Avalanche Peak [FRESNO]: *peak,* 14 miles
south-southwest of Marion Peak (lat. 36°46'
N, long. 118°34'55" W). Altitude 10,077 feet.
Named on Marion Peak (1953) 15' quadrangle. John Muir named the feature in 1891;
on some maps the name applies to present
Palmer Mountain, situated 1.5 miles farther
southeast (United States Board on Geographic
Names, 1933a, p. 108).

Avalon: see **Kaweah** [TULARE].

Avenal [KINGS]: *town,* 35 miles southwest of
Hanford (lat. 36°00'20" N, long. 120°07'50"
W; sec. 15, 16, 21, 22, T 22 S, R 17 E). Named
on Avenal (1954), Garza Peak (1953), and La
Cima (1963) 7.5' quadrangles. Postal authorities established Avenal post office in 1929
(Frickstad, p. 60), and the town incorporated
in 1979. The name is from *avena*, which
means "oats," usually "wild oats," in Spanish
(Stewart, p. 29). United States Board on Geographic Names (1988b, p. 2) approved the

name "Zwang Peak" for a feature, altitude 3078 feet, located 8 miles southwest of Avenal (lat. 35°56'48" N, long. 120°14'48" W; sec. 9, T 23 S, R 16 E); the name commemorates Jake Zwang, who came to the neighborhood in 1906 and started a cattle ranch southwest of Avenal.

Avenal Canyon [FRESNO-KINGS]: *canyon,* drained by Little Avenal Creek, which heads in Fresno County and flows 18 miles to Avenal Creek 10 miles south of Avenal in Kings County (lat. 35°51'35" N, long. 120°08'45" W; near NW cor. sec. 9, T 24 S, R 17 E). Named on Garza Peak (1953), Tent Hills (1942), and The Dark Hole (1961) 7.5' quadrangles.

Avenal Creek [KINGS]: *stream,* flows 7.5 miles to Sunflower Valley 10.5 miles south of Avenal (lat. 35°51' N, long. 120°07' W; sec. 10, T 24 S, R 17 E). Named on Pyramid Hills (1953) and Tent Hills (1942) 7.5' quadrangles. United States Board on Geographic Names (1991, p. 3) rejected the names "Avendale Creek," "Dicks Creek," and "Little Avenal Creek" for the feature.

Avenal Creek: see **Little Avenal Creek** [FRESNO-KINGS]; **Little Avenal Creek**, under **Lovel Canyon** [KINGS].

Avenal Gap [KINGS]: *pass,* 11.5 miles south of Kettleman City between Middle Dome and South Dome of Kettleman Hills (lat. 35°50'15" N, long. 119°57' W). Named on Avenal Gap (1954) 7.5' quadrangle.

Avenal Ridge [KINGS]: *ridge,* northwest-trending, 11 miles long, southeast of Lovel Canyon (lat. 35°49'30" N, long. 120°09'45" W). Named on Pyramid Hills (1953) and Tent Hills (1942) 7.5' quadrangles. Arnold and Anderson (1908, p. 14) applied the name to "the southernmost of the spurs of Diablo Range" between Avenal Creek and McLure (present Sunflower) Valley; they noted that "the name, which means a field of oats, is appropriate because the hills forming the ridge are rounded and grass grown."

Avenal Ridge: see **Bluestone Ridge** [KERN].

Avendale Creek: see **Avenal Creek** [KINGS].

Avocado [FRESNO]: *locality,* nearly 2 miles southwest of Piedra on the southeast side of Kings River (lat. 36°47'20" N, long. 119°24'10" W; sec. 19, T 13 S, R 24 E). Named on Piedra (1965) 7.5' quadrangle. Orangedale School (1923) 7.5' quadrangle shows the place along the Atchison, Topeka and Santa Fe Railroad branch line to Piedra.

Avocado Lake [FRESNO]: *lake,* 0.5 mile long, 2.25 miles southwest of Piedra on lowlands near Kings River (lat. 36°47'15" N, long. 119°24'40" W); on E line sec. 24, T 13 S, R 23 E); the lake is 0.25 mile west of Avocado. Named on Piedra (1965) 7.5' quadrangle.

Aweetasal Lake [FRESNO]: *lake,* 1100 feet long, 6.5 miles south of Mount Abbot (lat. 37°17'35" N, long. 118°48'25" W). Named on Mount Abbot (1953) 15' quadrangle. Elden

H. Vestal of California Department of Fish and Game named the lake in 1951; Vestal believed that the word "aweetasal" refers to a kind of Indian back carrier for babies (Browning 1986, p. 9).

Azalea Campground [FRESNO-TULARE]: *locality,* less than 1 mile west-northwest of Wilsonia on Tulare-Fresno county line (lat. 36° 44'30" N, long. 118°57'55" W; at S line sec. 31, T 13 S, R 28 E). Named on Giant Forest (1956) 15' quadrangle.

– B –

Babbitt: see **Camp Babbitt**, under **Visalia** [TULARE].

Baby King Canyon [KINGS]: *canyon,* 1 mile long, 6 miles southwest of Avenal (lat. 35°56'30" N, long. 120°12'25" W); the canyon is at the head of Baby King Creek. Named on Garza Peak (1953) 7.5' quadrangle.

Baby King Creek [KINGS]: *stream,* flows 5 miles to Kettleman Plain 2.5 miles southsouthwest of Avenal (lat. 35°58'10" N, long. 120°08'55" W; sec. 32, T 22 S, R 17 E). Named on Garza Peak (1953) 7.5' quadrangle.

Baby Lake [FRESNO]: *lake,* 550 feet long, 15 miles northeast of Kaiser Peak (lat. 37°28'20" N, long. 119°02'15" W). Named on Kaiser Peak (1953) 15' quadrangle. The lake is one of the group called Margaret Lakes

Backbone Creek [FRESNO]: *stream,* flows 2.25 miles to San Joaquin River 8.5 miles west of Shaver Lake Heights (present town of Shaver Lake) (lat. 37°06'35" N, long. 119°28'15" W; near N line sec. 33, T 9 S, R 23 E); the stream heads east of Backbone Mountain. Named on Shaver Lake (1953) 15' quadrangle.

Backbone Creek [TULARE]: *stream,* flows 4.5 miles to North Fork Tule River 17 miles southeast of Kaweah (lat. 36°15'05" N, long. 118°47'40" W; at SW cor. sec. 24, T 19 S, R 29 E). Named on Kaweah (1957) and Mineral King (1956) 15' quadrangles.

Backbone Mountain [FRESNO]: *ridge,* northnorthwest-trending, nearly 0.5 mile long, 8.5 miles west-southwest of Shaver Lake Heights (present town of Shaver Lake) (lat. 37°04'30" N, long. 119°28' W). Named on Shaver Lake (1953) 15' quadrangle. Members of United States Geological Survey applied the name in 1904 for the shape of the ridge (Gudde, 1949, p. 19).

Back Canyon [KERN]: *canyon,* 8 miles long, along Caliente Creek above a point 2.5 miles east of Loraine (lat. 35°18'40" N, long. 118°23'25" W; at N line sec. 24, T 30 S, R 33 E). Named on Emerald Mountain (1972) and Loraine (1972) 7.5' quadrangles.

Bacon Hill [TULARE]: *hill,* 5.25 miles westnorthwest of Woodlake (lat. 26°27'05" N, long. 119°10'50" W; sec. 17, T 17 S, R 26 E). Named on Exeter (1952) 15' quadrangle.

Bacon Hills [KERN]: *ridge,* northwest-trending, 2.5 miles long, 3 miles northeast of Carneros Rocks (lat. 35°28'05" N, long. 119°48'30" W). Named on Carneros Rocks (1959) 7.5' quadrangle.

Bacon Meadow [TULARE]: *area,* 2.25 miles east-southeast of Wilsonia (lat. 36°43'45" N, long. 118°55' W; at S line sec. 3, T 14 S, R 28 E). Named on Giant Forest (1956) 15' quadrangle. The name commemorates Fielding Bacon, a pioneer stockman (Hanna, p. 21).

Badger [TULARE]: *locality,* 11 miles east of Tucker Mountain (lat. 36°37'55" N, long. 119°00'45" W; sec. 11, T 15 S, R 27 E); the place is along Badger Creek. Named on Miramonte (1966) 7.5' quadrangle. Postal authorities established Camp Badger post office in 1879 and changed the name to Badger in 1894 (Frickstad, p. 210). Myron Woodard, who came from the Badger State of Wisconsin, named the place in 1870 (Mitchell, A.R., p. 67).

Badger Canyon [KERN]: *canyon,* drained by Badger Creek, which flows 4.25 miles to Poso Creek 1.5 miles south-southeast of Pine Mountain (lat. 35°32'55" N, long. 118°45'35" W; at N line sec. 33, T 27 S, R 30 E). Named on Democrat Hot Springs (1972) 7.5' quadrangle.

Badger Creek [FRESNO-TULARE]: *stream,* heads in Fresno County and flows 7 miles to Dry Creek (1) 6.25 miles east-northeast of Auckland in Tulare County (lat. 36°37'10" N, long. 119°00' W; sec. 13, T 15 S, R 27 E); the stream goes past Badger. Named on Auckland (1966) and Miramonte (1966) 7.5' quadrangles.

Badger Creek [KERN]: *stream,* flows 4.25 miles to Poso Creek 1.5 miles south-south-east of Pine Mountain (lat. 35°32'35" N, long. 118°45'35" W; at N line sec. 33, T 27 S, R 30 E); the stream drains Badger Canyon. Named on Pine Mountain (1965) 7.5' quadrangle.

Badger Flat [FRESNO]: *area,* 4.5 miles east-southeast of Kaiser Peak (lat. 37°16'05" N, long. 119°06'45" W; sec. 3, T 8 S, R 26 E). Named on Kaiser Peak (1953) 15' quadrangle. Called Badger Flats on Kaiser (1904) 30' quadrangle.

Badger Gap [KERN]: *pass,* 2 miles northwest of Democrat Hot Springs (lat. 35°32'45" N, long. 118°41'25" W; near SW cor. sec. 30, T 27 S, R 31 E). Named on Democrat Hot Springs (1972) 7.5' quadrangle.

Badger Hill [KINGS]: *peak,* 12.5 miles south of Kettleman City (lat. 35°49'40" N, long. 119°55'50" W; near W line sec. 21, T 24 S, R 19 E). Named on Avenal Gap (1954) 7.5' quadrangle.

Badger Hill [TULARE]: *peak,* 2.5 miles east-northeast of Exeter (lat. 36°18'20" N, long. 119°05'25" W; sec. 6, T 19 S, R 27 E). Altitude 1152 feet. Named on Rocky Hill (1951) 7.5' quadrangle.

Badger Lake: see **Garnet Lake** [MADERA].

Badger Lakes [MADERA]: *lakes,* largest 700 feet long, 8 miles north-northwest of Devils Postpile (lat. 37°43'40" N, long. 119°08'55" W; sec. 31, T 2 S, R 26 E). Named on Devils Postpile (1953) 15' quadrangle.

Bad Name Spring [KERN]: *spring,* 9.5 miles west of Liebre Twins (lat. 34°57'55" N, long. 118°44' W; sec. 7, T 10 N, R 17 W). Named on Winters Ridge (1966) 7.5' quadrangle.

Bagby Hill [TULARE]: *peak,* 8 miles south of Springville (lat. 36°00'55" N, long. 118°50'25" W; near E line sec. 16, T 22 S, R 29 E). Named on Globe (1956) 7.5' quadrangle.

Bago: see **Mount Bago** [FRESNO].

Bailey Flats [MADERA]: *area,* 10 miles north-northeast of Raymond (lat. 37°20'30" N, long. 119°49'20" W; in and near sec. 7, T 7 S, R 20 E). Named on Horsecamp Mountain (1947) 7.5' quadrangle. Mist post office was in a general store at Bailey Flats near Mariposa county line (Clough, p. 94). Postal authorities established Mist post office in 1913 and discontinued it in 1935; the name was from the mist of nearby waterfalls (Salley, p. 143).

Bakeoven Meadows [TULARE]: *area,* 2 miles north of Monache Mountain (lat. 36°14' N, long, 118°12' W; near NW cor. sec. 33, T 19 S, R 35 E). Named on Monache Mountain (1956) 15' quadrangle.

Bakeoven Pass [TULARE]: *pass,* 13 miles south of Monache Mountain (lat. 36°00'40" N, long. 118°12'50" W; sec. 17, T 22 S, R 35 E). Named on Monache Mountain (1956) 15' quadrangle. The name is from a rock oven at the place (Browning 1986, p. 10).

Baker [KERN]: *locality,* 3 miles north-north-west of Boron (lat. 35° 02'30" N, long. 117°40' W; at NW cor. sec. 19, T 11 N, R 7 W). Named on Boron (1954) 15' quadrangle, which shows Boron P.O. at the place.

Baker: see **West Baker** [KERN].

Baker Meadow [TULARE]: *area,* 8.5 miles east-southeast of California Hot Springs (lat. 35°51'15" N, long. 118°31'20" W; sec. 9, T 24 S, R 32 E); the place is 0.5 mile southsouthwest of Baker Peak on Baker Ridge. Named on California Hot Springs (1958) 15' quadrangle.

Baker Peak [TULARE]: *peak,* 8.5 miles east of California Hot Springs (lat. 35°51'35" N, long. 118°31'15" W; on E line sec. 9, T 24 S, R 32 E); the peak is near the north end of Baker Ridge. Altitude 7926 feet. Named on California Hot Springs (1958) 15' quadrangle.

Baker Point [TULARE]: *peak,* 10 miles east of California Hot Springs (lat. 35°51'10" N, long. 118°30'05" W; on E line sec. 10, T 24 S, R 32 E); the feature is on the east side of Baker Ridge. Altitude 7753 feet. Named on California Hot Springs (1958) 15' quadrangle.

Baker Ridge [TULARE]: *ridge,* south- to south-southeast-trending, 5.5 miles long, 9 miles east-southeast of California Hot Springs (lat. 35°50' N, long. 118°31'20" W); Baker Peak is near the north end of the ridge. Named on California Hot Springs (1958) 15' quadrangle.

Bakersfield [KERN]: *city,* just west of the center of Kern County on the east side of San Joaquin Valley near the entrance of Kern River to the valley (lat. 35°22'30" N, long. 119°00' W). Named on Gosford (1954), Lamont (1954), Oil Center (1954), and Oildale (1954) 7.5' quadrangles. Postal authorities established Bakersfield post office in 1868 (Frickstad, p. 54). The city incorporated in 1873, disincorporated in 1876, and incorporated again in 1898 (Bailey, 1967, p. 1). The name "Bakersfield" originated with a fenced field of about 20 acres that Colonel Thomas Baker had at the place (Latta, 1976, p. 35). Early names for the site were Kern Island, given for its location between watercourses of Kern River (Hoover, Rensch, and Rensch, p. 132), and Alkali City (Bailey, 1967, p. 1). United States Geological Survey's (1906) map shows a community called Kern located 1.5 miles east of Bakersfield (lat. 35°22'40" N, long. 118°59'25" W). Officials of Southern Pacific Railroad had Kern laid out in 1874 after the railroad bypassed Bakersfield because of a dispute with the city; the railroad community first was called Sumner and later was called Kern, Kern City, and East Bakersfield (Bailey, 1967, p. 7). Postal authorities established Sumner post office in 1876, changed the name to Kern in 1893, and discontinued it in 1924; the name "Sumner" was for Joseph W. Sumner, mine owner, rancher, and judge (Salley, p. 111, 215). The community became part of Bakersfield in 1909 (Hoover, Rensch, and Rensch, p. 133). California Mining Bureau's (1917c) map shows a place called Nome located about 2 miles northwest of downtown Bakersfield along Southern Pacific Railroad. California Mining Bureau's (1909a) map shows a place called Pylema situated 10 miles south-southwest of Bakersfield by stage line. Postal authorities established Pylema post office in 1895 and discontinued it in 1905; the name was for Mary R. Pyle, a pioneer settler and later postmaster (Salley, p. 179). In 1881 Isaac Rumford started a small Utopian colony called Joyfull, officially known as Association of Brotherly Cooperation, located about 2 miles southwest of present Bakersfield; the colony disbanded in 1884 (Bailey, 1967, p. 12). Postal authorities established Joyful post office in 1883 and discontinued it in 1884 (Frickstad, p. 56). A community called Riverview is situated just north of Bakersfield across Kern River; it first was called Arp's Addition for James H. Arp, a real estate developer (Bailey, 1967, p. 23). Postal authorities established Clarkson post office 16 miles northeast of Bakersfield in 1890 and discontinued it in 1891; they established

Glenburn post office 7 miles northwest of Bakersfield in 1890 and discontinued it in 1891; they established Unadilla post office 24 miles southeast of Bakersfield in 1892 and discontinued it in 1899; they established Toolwass post office 25 miles southeast of Bakersfield in 1892 and discontinued it in 1899; they established Langdon post office 16 miles southeast of Bakersfield in 1898 and discontinued it in 1900 (Salley, p. 45, 85, 117, 223, 227).

Balance Rock [TULARE]:
(1) *relief feature,* 5.25 miles south of California Hot Springs (lat. 35°48'15" N, long. 118°39'20" W; near S line sec. 29, T 24 S, R 31 E). Named on California Hot Springs (1958) 15' quadrangle.
(2) *settlement,* 5.25 miles south of California Hot Springs (lat. 35°48'20" N, long. 118°39'10" W; near S line sec. 29, T 24 S, R 31 E); the place is east of Balance Rock (1). Named on California Hot Springs (1958) 15' quadrangle. Postal authorities established Balance Rock post office in 1935 and discontinued it in 1950 (Frickstad, p. 209). Mrs. Shively named the place in 1900 for its proximity to Balance Rock (1) (Gudde, 1949, p. 20).

Balch Camp [FRESNO]: *village,* 38 miles east-northeast of Fresno near the confluence of Dinkey Creek (1) and North Fork Kings River (lat. 36°54'20" N, long. 119°07'20" W; sec. 10, T 12 S, R 26 E). Named on Patterson Mountain (1952) 15' quadrangle.

Balch Park: see **Milo** [TULARE].

Bald Eagle Peak [KERN]: *peak,* 3 miles south of Bodfish (lat. 35°32'40" N, long. 118°28'40" W; near S line sec. 30, T 27 S, R 33 E). Altitude 6181 feet. Named on Lake Isabella South (1972) 7.5' quadrangle.

Bald Hills [KERN]: *ridge,* southwest-trending, 1 mile long, 4 miles north-northeast of Glennville (lat. 35°47'10" N, long. 118°41'10" W; mainly in sec. 6, T 25 S, R 31 E). Named on California Hot Springs (1958) 15' quadrangle.

Bald Knob [TULARE]: *peak,* 5 miles west-southwest of California Hot Springs (lat. 35°50'50" N, long. 118°45' W; near NW cor. sec. 16, T 24 S, R 30 E). Altitude 2720 feet. Named on California Hot Springs (1958) 15' quadrangle.

Bald Mill Creek [FRESNO]: *stream,* flows 3.5 miles to San Joaquin River 8.5 miles west of Shaver Lake Heights (present town of Shaver Lake) (lat. 37°06'50" N, long. 119°28'05" W; sec. 28, T 9 S, R 23 E); the stream heads at Bald Mountain (1). Named on Shaver Lake (1953) 15' quadrangle. Corlew Mill was along the creek; the stream was named for the mill and for Bald Mountain (Gudde, 1949, p. 21). United States Board on Geographic Names (1978b, p. 3) rejected the name "Ball Mill Creek" for the stream.

Bald Mountain [FRESNO]:
(1) *ridge,* northwest-trending, 2 miles long, 6

miles west-southwest of Shaver Lake Heights (present town of Shaver Lake) (lat. 37° 04' N, long. 119°24'45" W). Named on Shaver Lake (1953) 15' quadrangle. United States Board on Geographic Names (1980, p. 4) rejected the name "Ball Mountain" for the ridge.

(2) *peak,* 4 miles west-southwest of Dinkey Dome (lat. 37°06'15" N, long. 119°12'15" W; near E line sec. 35, T 9 S, R 25 E). Altitude 7832 feet. Named on Huntington Lake (1953) 15' quadrangle.

(3) *peak,* 11 miles south-southwest of Balch Camp (lat. 36°46' N, long. 119°12'05" W; sec. 25, T 13 S, R 25 E). Altitude 3605 feet. Named on Patterson Mountain (1952) 15' quadrangle.

(4) *ridge,* north-northwest-trending, nearly 1 mile long, 5 miles north-northeast of Charley Mountain on Fresno-Monterey county line (lat. 36°12'25" N, long. 120°37'40" W; sec. 12, T 20 S, R 12 E). Named on Priest Valley (1969) 7.5' quadrangle.

(5) *ridge,* northwest-trending, 4 miles long, 4 miles north-northwest of Coalinga Mineral Springs (lat. 36°11'30" N, long. 120°35'30" W). Named on Sherman Peak (1969) 7.5' quadrangle.

Bald Mountain [TULARE]:

(1) *peak,* 7.5 miles southeast of Fountain Springs (lat. 35°48'40" N, long. 118°49'40" W; sec. 27, T 24 S, R 29 E). Altitude 2397 feet. Named on White River (1965) 7.5' quadrangle.

(2) *peak,* 15 miles south-southeast of Hockett Peak (lat. 36°01'15" N, long. 118°15'10" W). Altitude 9382 feet. Named on Hockett Peak (1956) and Monache Mountain (1956) 15' quadrangles.

Baldy: see **Big Baldy** [TULARE]; **Little Baldy** [TULARE].

Baldy Saddle: see **Little Baldy Saddle** [TULARE].

Balfour: see **Oilfields** [FRESNO]; **Strathmore** [TULARE].

Ball Dome [TULARE]: *peak,* 11.5 miles northwest of Triple Divide Peak (lat. 36°41'05" N, long. 118°42' W). Altitude 9357 feet. Named on Triple Divide Peak (1956) 15' quadrangle.

Ballinger Canyon [KERN]: *canyon,* drained by a stream that flows 2.25 miles to Ventura County 14 miles west of Eagle Rest Peak (lat. 34°52'50" N, long. 119°22'45" W; near W line sec. 7, T 9 N, R 23 W). Named on Ballinger Canyon (1943) and Santiago Creek (1943) 7.5' quadrangles.

Ball Meadow [TULARE]: *area,* 11.5 miles south-southeast of Monache Mountain (lat. 36°03'55" N, long. 118°04'55" W); the place is 0.5 mile east of Ball Mountain. Named on Monache Mountain (1956) 15' quadrangle.

Ball Mill Creek: see **Bald Mill Creek** [FRESNO].

Ball Mountain [KERN]:

(1) *peak,* 3 miles northwest of Democrat Hot Springs (lat. 35°33'30" N, long. 118°42'25"

W; on S line sec. 24, T 27 S, R 30 E). Named on Democrat Hot Springs (1972) 7.5' quadrangle.

(2) *peak,* 2 miles east-southeast of Miracle Hot Springs (lat. 35°34'10" N, long. 118°30'10" W; sec. 23, T 27 S, R 32 E). Named on Miracle Hot Springs (1972) 7.5' quadrangle.

Ball Mountain [TULARE]: *peak,* 11.5 miles south-southeast of Monache Mountain (lat. 36°03'50" N, long. 118°05'35" W). Altitude 9256 feet. Named on Monache Mountain (1956) 15' quadrangle.

Ball Mountain: see **Bald Mountain** [FRESNO] (1).

Balloon Dome [MADERA]: *peak,* 13 miles northeast of Shuteye Peak (lat. 37°27'50" N, long. 119°13'30" W; sec. 27, T 5 S, R 25 E). Altitude 6881 feet. Named on Kaiser Peak (1953) 15' quadrangle. The feature reminded Brewer "of the top of a gigantic balloon struggling to get up through the rock" (Whitney, 1865, p. 401). The peak also was called Dome or Great Dome (Gudde, 1949, p. 22).

Balls [MADERA]: *relief feature,* 9 miles south-southeast of Merced Peak (lat. 37°30'25" N, long. 119°21'05" W). Named on Merced Peak (1953) 15' quadrangle.

Balsam Creek [FRESNO]: *stream,* flows 3 miles to Big Creek (1) 7 miles north-northeast of Shaver Lake Heights (present town of Shaver Lake) (lat. 37°11'45" N, long. 119°15'35" W; sec. 32, T 8 S, R 25 E). Named on Huntington Lake (1953) and Shaver Lake (1953) 15' quadrangles. Bradley (p. 456) noted a resort called Balsam Grove Springs that was located 0.25 mile from Carlson Station on San Joaquin and Eastern Railroad. From Bradley's description, the resort probably was near the mouth of Balsam Creek. Kaiser (1904) 30' quadrangle shows San Joaquin and Eastern Railroad near the mouth of the stream.

Balsam Grove Springs: see **Balsam Creek** [FRESNO].

Banada Ridge [KERN]: *ridge,* south-trending, 2 miles long, 8.5 miles north-northeast of Caliente (lat. 35°24'35" N, long. 118°34'50" W). Named on Breckenridge Mountain (1972) 7.5' quadrangle.

Bandit Rocks: see **Robbers Roost** [KERN].

Banner [KINGS]: *locality,* 3 miles north-northwest of Hanford along Atchison, Topeka and Santa Fe Railroad (lat. 36°22'30" N, long. 119°39'50" W; on N line sec. 14, T 18 S, R 21 E). Named on Hanford (1926) 7.5' quadrangle.

Bannister [KERN]: *locality,* 9.5 miles southwest of Bakersfield along Sunset Railroad (lat. 35°15'55" N, long. 119°06' W; near N line sec. 5, T 31 S, R 27 E). Named on Gosford (1954) 7.5' quadrangle. California Mining Bureau's (1917c) map shows a place called Artwell located 2.5 miles south of Bannister along the railroad.

Barbarossa Ridge [KERN]: *ridge,* east-southeast- to south-trending, 2.5 miles long, center 2.25 miles north of Loraine (lat. 35°20'05" N, long. 118°26'40" W). Named on Loraine (1972) 7.5' quadrangle, which shows Barbarossa mine on the ridge.

Barberry Spring [FRESNO]: *spring,* 5 miles northwest of Coalinga Mineral Springs (lat. 36°11'40" N, long. 120°37'15" W; sec. 13, T 20 S, R 12 E). Named on Sherman Peak (1969) 7.5' quadrangle.

Barbour: see **Camp Barbour**, under **Old Fort Miller** [FRESNO].

Bare Island Lake [MADERA]: *lake,* 1000 feet long, 10.5 miles north-northwest of Shuteye Peak (lat. 37°29'45" N, long. 119°29'25" W; sec. 18, T 5 S, R 23 E). Named on Shuteye Peak (1953) 15' quadrangle.

Barigan Stringer [TULARE]: *stream,* flows 3.5 miles to Golden Trout Creek 7.25 miles north of Kern Peak (lat. 36°24'45" N, long. 118°16'35" W; sec. 27, T 17 S, R 34 E). Named on Kern Peak (1956) 15' quadrangle.

Barillo Valley: see **Barrel Valley** [KERN].

Barker Creek [KERN]: *stream,* flows 3.5 miles to Cottonwood Creek (2) 2.25 miles south-southeast of Mount Adelaide (lat. 35° 24' N, long. 118°43'50" W; at S line sec. 14, T 29 S, R 30 E). Named on Mount Adelaide (1972) 7.5' quadrangle. Called Parker Creek on Breckenridge Mountain (1943) 15' quadrangle, and United States Board on Geographic Names (1975b, p. 8) gave this name as a variant.

Barnard: see **Mount Barnard** [TULARE].

Barn Canyon [KERN]: *canyon,* 1.5 miles long, 3.25 miles south of Alta Sierra along Stable Creek (lat. 35°40'50" N, long. 118°32'25" W; sec. 9, T 26 S, R 32 E). Named on Alta Sierra (1972) 7.5' quadrangle.

Barnes Mountain [FRESNO]: *ridge,* northwest-to north-trending, 3 miles long, 9.5 miles southwest of Dinkey Dome (lat. 37°00'30" N, long. 119°14'30" W). Named on Huntington Lake (1953), Patterson Mountain (1952), and Shaver Lake (1953) 15' quadrangles.

Barnes Settlement: see **Old River** [KERN].

Barn Spring [FRESNO]: *spring,* 9 miles northwest of Coalinga (lat. 36°13'35" N, long. 120°28'35" W; sec. 32, T 19 S, R 14 E). Named on Alcalde Hills (1969) 7.5' quadrangle.

Barrel Spring [KERN]: *spring,* 3.25 miles west-northwest of Emerald Mountain (lat. 35°16'40" N, long. 118°20' W). Named on Emerald Mountain (1972) 7.5' quadrangle.

Barrel Valley [KERN]: *valley,* 5.5 miles south of Orchard Peak (lat. 35°39'40" N, long. 120°07'30" W). Named on Orchard Peak (1961) and Sawtooth Ridge (1961) 7.5' quadrangles. Called Barril Valley on Arnold and Johnson's (1910) map, but United States Board on Geographic Names (1933a, p. 124) rejected the names "Barril Valley" and "Barillo Valley" for the feature.

Barren Ridge [KERN]: *ridge,* northeast-trend-

ing, 7 miles long, 11 miles north-northeast of Mojave (lat. 35°12'15" N, long. 118°07'45" W). Named on Cache Peak (1973) and Mojave NE (1973) 7.5' quadrangles.

Barrett Lakes [FRESNO]: *lakes,* largest 1800 feet long, 11 miles east of Mount Goddard in Palisade Basin (lat. 37°05' N, long. 118°31'30" W). Named on Mount Goddard (1948) 15' quadrangle.

Barril Valley: see **Barrel Valley** [KERN].

Barrington Spring [KERN]: *spring,* 3.5 miles southeast of Caliente (lat. 35°15'50" N, long. 118°34'35" W; sec. 6, T 31 S, R 32 E). Named on Oiler Peak (1972) 7.5' quadrangle.

Barris Hill [TULARE]: *peak,* 2.5 miles east-northeast of Dinuba at the south end of Smith Mountain (1) (lat. 36°33'30" N, long. 119°21' W; sec. 10, T 16 S, R 24 E). Named on Orange Cove South (1966) 7.5' quadrangle. On Sultana (1923) 7.5' quadrangle, the name applies to a feature situated less than 0.5 mile farther south.

Barr Spring [FRESNO]: *spring,* 4 miles north-northeast of Coalinga Mineral Springs (lat. 36°11'50" N, long. 120°31'45" W; near N line sec. 13, T 20 S, R 13 E). Named on Sherman Peak (1969) 7.5' quadrangle.

Barstow [FRESNO]: *locality,* 3.25 miles west-southwest of Herndon (lat. 36°48'55" N, long. 119°58'10" W; near W line sec. 12, T 13 S, R 18 E). Named on Herndon (1964) 7.5' quadrangle.

Bartolas Country [KERN]: *area,* 7 miles north of Weldon (lat. 35° 46' N, long. 118°16' W); the place is on upper reaches of Bartolas Creek. Named on Kernville (1956) and Lamont Peak (1956) 15' quadrangles, and on Onyx (1972) and Weldon (1972) 7.5' quadrangles. The name commemorates a Frenchman who ran sheep in the area in the early days (Gudde, 1969, p. 22).

Bartolas Creek [KERN]: *stream,* flows 7.5 miles to South Fork Kern River 4.5 miles north-northeast of Onyx (lat. 35°44'45" N, long. 118°11'05" W). Named on Kernville (1956) and Lamont Peak (1956) 15' quadrangles, and on Onyx (1972) 7.5' quadrangle.

Barton: see **Steve Barton Point** [TULARE]; **Sunnyside** [FRESNO].

Barton Creek [TULARE]: *stream,* flows 3 miles to Roaring River 7.25 miles north-northwest of Triple Divide Peak and 2.5 miles east of Barton Peak (lat. 36°41'40" N, long. 118°33'25" W). Named on Triple Divide Peak (1956) 15' quadrangle.

Barton Hills: see **Devils Den** [KERN] (1).

Barton Peak [TULARE]: *peak,* 8 miles north-northwest of Triple Divide Peak (lat. 36°41'30" N, long. 118°35'55" W). Altitude 10,370 feet. Named on Triple Divide Peak (1956) 15' quadrangle. United States Board on Geographic Names (1933a, p. 125) rejected the name "Mount Moraine" for the peak, and noted that the Sierra Club proposed the name "Barton" to commemorate James Barton, a local stockman.

Barton Ranch: see **Kaweah** [TULARE].

Barton's: see **Mineral King** [TULARE].

Bartons: see **Devils Den** [KERN] (1).

Bartons Resort [FRESNO]: *locality,* 3 miles northeast of Hume (lat. 36°49'05" N, long. 118°53'10" W). Named on Tehipite Dome (1952) 15' quadrangle. Clyde Barton and Virginia Barton started a resort at what originally was called Burro Flat (Forest M. Clingan, personal communication, 1990).

Basin [FRESNO]: *locality,* 15 miles southwest of Kaiser Peak along San Joaquin and Eastern Railroad (lat. 37°07'30" N, long. 119°22'15" W; near NE cor. sec. 29, T 9 S, R 24 E); the place is in Jose Basin. Named on Kaiser (1904) 30' quadrangle. California Mining Bureau's (1917a) map shows a place called Webstone located along the railroad between Lodge and Duncan Mill, at or near the site of Basin.

Basin: see **Huntington Lake** [FRESNO] (2); **The Basin**, under **Huntington Lake** [FRESNO] (1)

Basin Creek [FRESNO]: *stream,* flows 2 miles to North Fork Kings River 1 mile east of Balch Camp (lat. 36°54'20" N, long. 119°06'20" W; sec. 11, T 12 S, R 26 E). Named on Patterson Mountain (1952) 15' quadrangle.

Basin Creek: see **Walker Basin Creek** [KERN].

Basket Flat [KERN]: *area,* nearly 5 miles south-southeast of Glennville (lat. 35°39'55" N, long. 118°39'55" W; sec. 17, T 26 S, R 31 E); the place is less than 2 miles west-northwest of Basket Peak. Named on Glennville (1972) 7.5' quadrangle.

Basket Pass [KERN]: *pass,* 6.5 miles southeast of Glennville (lat. 35° 39'25" N, long. 118°37'40" W; sec. 22, T 26 S, R 31 E); the pass is 0.5 mile east-northeast of Basket Peak on Basket Ridge. Named on Glennville (1972) 7.5' quadrangle.

Basket Peak [KERN]: *peak,* 6.25 miles south-southeast of Glennville (lat. 35°39'10" N, long. 118°38'20" W; sec. 22, T 26 S, R 31 E). Altitude 6122 feet. Named on Glennville (1972) 7.5' quadrangle.

Basket Ridge [KERN]: *ridge,* generally west-trending, 4 miles long, center is 6 miles south-southeast of Glennville (lat. 35°39'15" N, long. 118°39' W); Basket Peak is on the ridge. Named on Alta Sierra (1972) and Glennville (1972) 7.5' quadrangles.

Basque Encino [KERN]: *locality,* 2.5 miles southwest of Liebre Twins (lat. 34°56' N, long. 118°36'15" W; at N line sec. 19, T 10 N, R 16 W). Named on Neenach (1943) 15' quadrangle.

Bass Lake [MADERA]:
(1) *lake,* about 4.5 miles long, behind a dam on North Fork Willow Creek (2) 7.5 miles southeast of Yosemite Forks (lat. 37°17'30" N, long. 119°31'45" W; sec. 26, T 7 S, R 22

E). Named on Bass Lake (1953) 15' quadrangle. Water of the lake covers most of Crane Valley, but United States Board on Geographic Names (1964b, p. 11) rejected the name "Crane Valley Lake" for the feature. A dam formed the lake in 1895, and a second dam enlarged the lake in 1910; the name "Bass Lake" was given after the lake was stocked with bass (Clough, p. 82-83).
(2) *settlement,* 4.5 miles southeast of Yosemite Forks (lat. 37°19'30" N, long. 119°34' W; sec. 15, 16, T 7 S, R 22 E); the place is on the northeast side of Bass Lake (1). Named on Bass Lake (1953) 15' quadrangle. Postal authorities established Bass Lake post office in 1912 (Frickstad, p. 84).

Bateman Ridge [TULARE]: *ridge,* north-trending, 1.5 miles long, 3 miles southwest of Camp Nelson (lat. 36°07'10" N, long. 118° 39' W). Named on Camp Nelson (1956) 15' quadrangle.

Bates: see **Bates Station** [MADERA].

Bates Slough [TULARE]: *water feature,* discontinuous watercourse that extends for 9 miles in lowlands to a point 10 miles southwest of Tulare (lat. 36°06'50" N, long. 119°29'25" W; sec. 9, T 21 S, R 23 E). Named on Paige (1950), Taylor Wier (1950), and Tulare (1950) 7.5' quadrangles. Called Packwood Cr. on Lake View School (1927) 7.5' quadrangle, and called North Fork Deep Creek on Paige (1927) 7.5' quadrangle. On Taylor Weir (1950, photo-revised 1969) 7.5' quadrangle, the feature extends to Deep Creek (2).

Bates Station [MADERA]: *locality,* 10.5 miles south-southeast of Raymond (lat. 37°05'25" N, long. 119°48'05" W; near E line sec. 5, T 10 S, R 20 E). Named on Little Table Mountain (1962) 7.5' quadrangle. Called Bates on Mariposa (1912) 30' quadrangle. Postal authorities established Bates post office in 1883, moved it 5 miles south in 1891, and discontinued it in 1903 (Salley, p. 15). The post office name was for George Bates, who operated Bates Station and was the first postmaster; Henry J. Prewett became postmaster in 1889, and the place sometimes was called Prewett Station, but the post office retained the old name—the final site of Bates post office was about 3 miles down Cottonwood Creek from the original site (Clough, p. 83). Postal authorities established Media post office 5 miles southwest of Bates post office in 1894 and discontinued it in 1898; the name was from the belief that the place was at the geographical center of California (Salley, p. 137).

Bathtub Lake [FRESNO]: *lake,* 1100 feet long, 14 miles northeast of Kaiser Peak (lat. 37°27'50" N, long. 119°02'20" W). Named on Kaiser Peak (1953) 15' quadrangle. The feature is one of the group called Margaret Lakes.

Battalion Lake [FRESNO]: *lake,* 1200 feet long, 3.25 miles south-southwest of Mount

Goddard (lat. 37°03'25" N, long. 118°44'25" W); the lake is 0.5 mile east-southeast of Division Lake. Named on Mount Goddard (1948) 15' quadrangle.

Battle Creek [TULARE]: *stream,* flows less than 1 mile to South Fork Kaweah River 9.5 miles southeast of Kaweah (lat. 36°21'35" N, long. 118°49' W; sec. 15, T 18 S, R 29 E). Named on Kaweah (1957) 15' quadrangle. The name stems from a battle between a mountain lion and a burro, won by the burro (United States Board on Geographic Names, 1970a, p. 2). Salley (p. 16) listed Battle Mound post office, established 25 miles northeast of Porterville in 1871, and discontinued the same year; the named was from the same incident.

Battle Creek: see **Bennett Creek** [TULARE].

Battle Mound: see **Battle Creek** [TULARE].

Battle Mountain [TULARE]: *hill,* 17 miles south-southeast of Kaweah near North Fork Tule River (lat. 36°15'10" N, long. 118° 47'15" W). Altitude 2936 feet. Named on Kaweah (1957) 15' quadrangle, and on Springville (1957) 7.5' quadrangle. The place was the site of a battle with Indians in 1856 (Gist, p. 22).

Baxter: see **Mount Baxter** [FRESNO]; **Wade Baxter Spring** [KINGS].

Baxter Creek [FRESNO]: *stream,* flows nearly 4 miles to South Fork Woods Creek 5.5 miles south of Mount Pinchot (lat. 36°51'05" N, long. 118°24'35" W); the stream heads near Baxter Pass and goes through Baxter Lakes. Named on Mount Pinchot (1953) 15' quadrangle.

Baxter Lakes [FRESNO]: *lakes,* largest 1900 feet long, 7 miles south of Mount Pinchot (lat. 36°50'50" N, long. 118°22'45" W); the lakes are southwest of Mount Baxter along Baxter Creek. Named on Mount Pinchot (1953) 15 quadrangle.

Baxter Pass [FRESNO]: *pass,* 8 miles south of Mount Pinchot on Fresno-Inyo county line (lat. 36°50'10" N, long. 118°22'30" W); the pass is 2 miles south-southwest of Mount Baxter. Named on Mount Pinchot (1953) 15' quadrangle.

Beach Creek [TULARE]: *stream,* flows 6.5 miles to Rattlesnake Creek (3) 9 miles south-southeast of Hockett Peak (lat. 36°05'40" N, long. 118°20'25" W; sec. 18, T 21 S, R 34 E); the stream goes through Beach Meadows. Named on Hockett Peak (1956) 15' quadrangle. Called Smith Cr. on Olancha (1907) 30' quadrangle.

Beach Meadows [TULARE]: *area,* 9 miles southeast of Hockett Peak (lat. 36°07'10" N, long. 118°17'40" W); the place is along Beach Creek. Named on Hockett Peak (1956) 15' quadrangle.

Beale: see **Bealville** [KERN].

Bealville [KERN]: *locality,* 1.25 miles south of Caliente along Southern Pacific Railroad (lat. 35°16'20" N, long. 118°37'30" W). Named on Bena (1972) and Oiler Peak (1972) 7.5'

quadrangles. Postal authorities established Beale post office at the place in 1879 and discontinued it in 1881 (Salley, p. 17). The name commemorates Edward Fitzgerald Beale, owner of El Tejon grant (Hanna, p. 27). California Division of Highways' (1934) map shows a place called Allard located about 2 miles west-northwest of Bealville along the railroad.

Bean [KINGS]: *locality,* 3.25 miles north-northwest of Corcoran along Atchison, Topeka and Santa Fe Railroad (lat. 36°08'20" N, long. 119°35'05" W). Named on Waukena (1928) 7.5' quadrangle.

Bean Canyon [KERN]: *canyon,* drained by a stream that flows 6.25 miles to lowlands 6.5 miles northwest of the village of Willow Springs (lat. 34°57'30" N, long. 118°21'45" W; at W line sec. 15, T 10 N, R 14 W). Named on Tehachapi South (1966), Tylerhorse Canyon (1965), and Willow Springs (1965) 7.5' quadrangles.

Bean Gulch [MADERA]: *canyon,* 1 mile long, 5.5 miles east-northeast of Knowles along Spangle Gold Creek (lat. 37°14'35" N, long. 119°46'45" W). Named on Knowles (1962) 7.5' quadrangle.

Bean Spring [KERN]: *spring,* 1 mile west of the village of Willow Springs (lat. 34°52'55" N, long. 118°18'50" W; sec. 12, T 9 N, R 14 W). Named on Willow Springs (1965) 7.5' quadrangle. Darling (p. 10) associated the name with Charles M. Bean, who owned land in the neighborhood in the 1880's.

Bear Butte [FRESNO]: *peak,* 6.5 miles east-northeast of the town of Big Creek (lat. 37°14'30" N, long. 119°08'05" W; near S line sec. 9, T 8 S, R 26 E). Altitude 8598 feet. Named on Huntington Lake (1953) 15' quadrangle.

Bear Canyon [FRESNO]: *canyon,* drained by a stream that flows 5.5 miles to Los Gatos Creek 8 miles north-northwest of Coalinga Mineral Springs (lat. 36°14'45" N, long. 120°36'45" W; sec. 30, T 19 S, R 13 E). Named on Priest Valley (1969) and Sherman Peak (1969) 7.5' quadrangles.

Bear Canyon [KERN]:
(1) *canyon,* 2.25 miles long, along Delonegha Creek above a point 4.5 miles west of Miracle Hot Springs (lat. 35°34'25" N, long. 118°36'50" W). Named on Democrat Hot Springs (1972) and Miracle Hot Springs (1972) 7.5' quadrangles.
(2) *canyon,* drained by a stream that flows 1.25 miles to El Paso Creek 6 miles west of Liebre Twins (lat. 34°58'20" N, long. 118° 40'35" W; sec. 3, T 10 N, R 17 W). Named on Winters Ridge (1966) 7.5' quadrangle.
(3) *canyon,* drained by a stream that heads in Los Angeles County and flows 1.5 miles to Castac Valley 1 mile southeast of Lebec (lat. 34°49'30" N, long. 118°51'15" W; near E line sec. 35, T 9 N, R 19 W). Named on Lebec (1958) 7.5' quadrangle.

Bear Canyon: see **Little Bear Canyon** [FRESNO].

Bear Creek [FRESNO]:

(1) *stream,* flows 2.25 miles to Huntington Lake (1) 3 miles south of Kaiser Peak (lat. 37°15'05" N, long. 119°10'45" W; sec. 7, T 8 S, R 26 E). Named on Kaiser Peak (1953) 15' quadrangle.

(2) *stream,* formed by the confluence of East Fork, South Fork, and West Fork, flows 10.5 miles to South Fork San Joaquin River 12.5 miles west-southwest of Mount Abbot (lat. 37°19'15" N, long. 118° 59'30" W). Named on Mount Abbot (1953) 15' quadrangle. East Fork and South Fork each are 5 miles long, and West Fork is 3.5 miles long. All three forks are named on Mount Abbot (1953) 15' quadrangle. Hilgard Branch enters 9 miles upstream from the mouth of the main stream; it heads near Bear Creek Spire, is 6.5 miles long, and is named on Mount Abbot (1953) 15' quadrangle. United States Board on Geographic Names (1983a, p. 3) rejected the name "Bear Meadow Creek" for Bear Creek (2).

(3) *stream,* flows 7.5 miles to Dinkey Creek (1) 5.5 miles south of Dinkey Dome (lat. 37°02'15" N, long. 119°08'30" W; near N line sec. 28, T 10 S, R 26 E); the stream goes past Bear Meadow (2). Named on Huntington Lake (1953) 15' quadrangle.

(4) *stream,* flows 3.5 miles to White Deer Creek 8 miles south-southwest of Balch Camp (lat 36°47'50" N, long. 119°10'30" W; sec. 17, T 13 S, R 26 E). Named on Patterson Mountain (1952) 15' quadrangle.

Bear Creek [KERN]: *stream,* flows 5 miles to Cedar Creek 4 miles east-southeast of Glennville (lat. 35°42'30" N, long. 118°38'20" W; sec. 34, T 25 S, R 31 E). Named on Alta Sierra (1972) and Glennville (1972) 7.5' quadrangles.

Bear Creek [TULARE]:

(1) *stream,* flows 7.25 miles to Dry Creek (1) 7 miles southeast of Auckland (lat. 36°31' N, long. 119°01'05" W; near E line sec. 22, T 16 S, R 27 E); the stream heads at Bear Mountain. Named on Auckland (1966) 7.5' quadrangle. United States Board on Geographic Names (1967d, p. 4) rejected the name "Murry Creek" for the feature.

(2) *stream,* flows 8.5 miles to North Fork Tule River 3.5 miles north-northeast of Springville (lat. 36°10'40" N, long. 118°47'45" W; near NW cor. sec. 24, T 20 S, R 29 E). Named on Camp Nelson (1956) and Springville (1957) 15' quadrangles.

(3) *stream,* flows 2.5 miles to South Fork of Middle Fork Tule River less than 1 mile southwest of Camp Nelson (lat. 36°07'55" N, long. 118°37'15" W; sec. 3, T 21 S, R 31 E). Named on Camp Nelson (1956) 15' quadrangle.

(4) *stream,* flows nearly 3 miles to join Double Bunk Creek and form South Creek 8 miles northeast of California Hot Springs (lat. 35°57'35" N, long. 118°34'20" W; near E line sec. 1, T 23 S, R 31 E); the stream goes through Bear Meadow (3). Named on California Hot Springs (1958) 15' quadrangle.

(5) *stream,* flows 2.5 miles to North Fork Kaweah River 5 miles south-southwest of Yucca Mountain (lat. 36°30'15" N, long. 118°54'20" W). Named on Giant Forest (1956) and Kaweah (1957) 15' quadrangles.

(6) *stream,* flows 4.25 miles to South Fork Tule River 9.5 miles south-southwest of Camp Nelson (lat. 36°01'40" N, long. 118°42'15" W). Named on California Hot Springs (1958) and Camp Nelson (1956) 15' quadrangles.

Bear Creek: see **South Bear Creek** [TULARE].

Bear Creek Spine: see **Bear Creek Spire** [FRESNO].

Bear Creek Spire [FRESNO]: *peak,* 1.5 miles southeast of Mount Abbot on Fresno-Inyo county line (lat. 37°22'05" N, long. 118° 46' W); the peak is near the head of Hilgard Branch Bear Creek (2). Altitude 13,713 feet. Named on Mount Abbot (1953) 15' quadrangle. United States Board on Geographic Names (1933a, p. 131) rejected the name "Bear Creek Spine" for the feature.

Bear Dens [KERN]: *relief feature,* 4.5 miles northeast of Glennville (lat. 35°45'45" N, long. 118°38'15" W; near SW cor. sec. 10, T 25 S, R 31 E). Named on California Hot Springs (1958) 15' quadrangle.

Bear Dome [FRESNO]: *peak,* 10 miles west-southwest of Mount Abbot (lat. 37°19'45" N, long. 118°57' W). Altitude 9947 feet. Named on Mount Abbot (1953) 15' quadrangle.

Bear Flat [KERN]: *area,* 4.5 miles north of Caliente (lat. 35°21'20" N, long. 118°37'30" W; on S line sec. 35, T 29 S, R 31 E). Named on Bena (1972) and Oiler Peak (1972) 7.5' quadrangles.

Bear Flat [TULARE]: *area,* 3 miles east of Auckland (lat. 36°34'50" N, long. 119°03'05" W; at W line sec. 33, T 15 S, R 27 E); the place is along Bear Creek (1). Named on Auckland (1966) 7.5' quadrangle.

Bear Gulch [FRESNO]: *canyon,* drained by a stream that flows 1.25 miles to Bear Canyon 7 miles north-northwest of Coalinga Mineral Springs (lat. 36°13'45" N, long. 120°37'20" W; sec. 36, T 19 S, R 12 E). Named on Priest Valley (1969) and Sherman Peak (1969) 7.5' quadrangles.

Bear Hallow Creek: see **Bear Hollow Creek** [KERN].

Bear Hill [TULARE]: *peak,* 5.5 miles east of Yucca Mountain (lat. 36°33'40" N, long. 118°46'05" W; sec. 6, T 16 S, R 30 E). Named on Giant Forest (1956) 15' quadrangle.

Bear Hollow [KERN]: *valley,* 2.2 miles west-southwest of Glennville (lat. 35°43'05" N, long. 118°44'40" W). Named on Glennville (1972) 7.5' quadrangle.

Bear Hollow Creek [KERN]: *stream,* flows 5.25 miles to Poso Creek 3 miles south-southwest of Glennville (lat. 35°41'35" N, long. 118°43'55" W; sec. 3, T 26 S, R 30 E); the stream goes through Bear Hollow. Named on White River (1965) and Woody (1965) 7.5' quadrangles. Called Bearwallow Creek on White River (1936) and Woody (1935) 15' quadrangles, but United States Board on Geographic Names (1966b, p. 4) rejected the names "Bearwallow Creek" and "Bear Hallow Creek" for the stream.

Bear Lake: see **Big Bear Lake** [FRESNO]; **Little Bear Lake** [FRESNO].

Bear Meadow [FRESNO]:
(1) *area*, 11 miles north-northeast of Kaiser Peak (lat. 37°26'55" N, long. 119°07'40" W). Named on Kaiser Peak (1953) 15' quadrangle.
(2) *area*, 4 miles southeast of Dinkey Dome (lat. 37°04'15" N, long. 119°04'50" W; sec. 12, T 10 S, R 26 E); the place is along Bear Creek (3). Named on Huntington Lake (1953) 15' quadrangle.
(3) *area*, 7 miles south-southwest of Dinkey Dome (lat. 37°01'05" N, long. 119°10'25" W; sec. 31, T 10 S, R 26 E). Named on Huntington Lake (1953) 15' quadrangle.

Bear Meadow [TULARE]:
(1) *area*, 10 miles north-northwest of Olancha Peak (lat. 36°24'05" N, long. 118°10' W; sec. 34, T 17 S, R 35 E). Named on Olancha (1956) 15' quadrangle.
(2) *area*, 1.5 miles north of Kern Peak (lat. 36°19'55" N, long. 118° 17'30" W; sec. 28, T 18 S, R 34 E). Named on Kern Peak (1956) 15' quadrangle.
(3) *area*, 6.5 miles northeast of California Hot Springs (lat. 35°56'45" N, long. 118°35' W; sec. 12, T 23 S, R 31 E); the place is along Bear Creek (4). Named on California Hot Springs (1958) 15' quadrangle.

Bear Meadow Creek [FRESNO]: *stream*, flows 6 miles to Dinkey Creek (1) 4 miles north-northwest of Balch Camp (lat. 36°57'20" N, long. 119°08'25" W); the stream goes through Bear Meadow (3). Named on Huntington Lake (1953) and Patterson Mountain (1952) 15' quadrangles.

Bear Meadow Creek: see **Bear Creek** [FRESNO] (2).

Bear Mountain [FRESNO]:
(1) *peak*, 2.5 miles east-southeast of Dinkey Dome (lat. 37°05'45" N, long. 119°05'35" W; near SW cor. sec. 36, T 9 S, R 26 E). Altitude 9512 feet. Named on Huntington Lake (1953) 15' quadrangle.
(2) *ridge*, northeast-trending, about 1.5 miles long, 9 miles north-northeast of Orange Cove (lat. 36°45' N, long. 119°16'35" W). Named on Orange Cove North (1966) and Pine Flat Dam (1965) 7.5' quadrangles.

Bear Mountain [KERN]: *peak*, 6 miles south of Caliente (lat. 35°12'15" N, long. 118°38'15" W; sec. 27, T 31 S, R 31 E). Altitude 6913 feet. Named on Bear Mountain (1966) 7.5' quadrangle. Called Bear Peak on

Wheeler's (1875-1878) map, which shows White Wolf Spr. located 4.5 miles northwest of the peak. The name "White Wolf" is from packs of white wolves formerly found in the neighborhood (Wilke and Lawton *in* Davidson, p. 38). The name "Bear Mountain" is from the numerous bears that lived on the slopes of the peak (Bailey, 1962, p. 65). The peak also was called Livermore Mountain (Wines, p. 86).

Bear Mountain [TULARE]: *peak*, 3.25 miles east of Auckland (lat. 36°35'45" N, long. 119°02'45" W; sec. 28, T 15 S, R 27 E). Altitude 4116 feet. Named on Auckland (1966) 7.5' quadrangle.

Bearpaw Lake [FRESNO]: *lake*, 1200 feet long, nearly 4 miles south of Mount Abbot (lat. 37°19'50" N, long. 118°47'40" W). Named on Mount Abbot (1953) 15' quadrangle. Elden H. Vestal of California Department of Fish and Game named the lake in 1952; the name also has the form "Bear Paw Lake" (Browning 1986, p. 13).

Bearpaw Meadow [TULARE]: *area*, 5.5 miles west-southwest of Triple Divide Peak (lat. 36°33'55" N, long. 118°37'20" W). Named on Triple Divide Peak (1956) 15' quadrangle. The name was given after a bear caught its foot in a trap at the place (Browning 1986, p. 13-14).

Bearpaw Meadow: see **Little Bearpaw Meadow** [TULARE].

Bear Peak: see **Bear Mountain** [KERN].

Bear Ridge [FRESNO]: *ridge*, southwest-trending, 5 miles long, 10.5 miles west-southwest of Mount Abbot (lat. 37°21'45" N, long. 118°57'45" W). Named on Mount Abbot (1953) 15' quadrangle.

Bearskin Creek [FRESNO-TULARE]: *stream*, heads just inside Tulare County and flows nearly 3 miles to Tenmile Creek 2 miles south-southeast of Hume in Fresno County (lat. 36°45'40" N, long. 118°53'55" W; sec. 26, T 13 S, R 28 E); the mouth of the stream is at Bearskin Meadow. Named on Giant Forest (1956) and Tehipite Dome (1952) 15' quadrangles.

Bearskin Meadow [FRESNO]: *area*, 2 miles south-southeast of Hume (lat. 36°45'35" N, long. 118°54' W; sec. 26, T 13 S, R 28 E); the place is along Bearskin Creek. Named on Tehipite Dome (1952) 15' quadrangle. The name reportedly is from the resemblance of a snow patch at the place to a bearskin (Browning 1986, p. 14).

Bear Spring [KERN]:
(1) *spring*, 4.5 miles north of Caliente (lat. 35°21'25" N, long. 118° 36'55" W; near SE cor. sec. 35, T 29 S, R 31 E); the spring is 0.5 mile east-northeast of Bear Flat. Named on Oiler Peak (1972) 7.5' quadrangle.
(2) *spring*, 6 miles east-southeast of Mount Adelaide (lat. 35°23'10" N, long. 118°39' W; near SE cor. sec. 21, T 29 S, R 31 E). Named

on Mount Adelaide (1972) 7.5' quadrangle.

Bear Trap Canyon [KERN]:

(1) *canyon,* drained by a stream that flows 2.5 miles to East Fork Erskine Creek 9.5 miles south-southwest of Weldon (lat. 35°32'35" N, long. 118°22'15" W). Named on Woolstalf Creek (1972) 7.5' quadrangle.

(2) *canyon,* 9.5 miles long, along Pastoria Creek above a point 6 miles northeast of Lebec (lat. 34°54'10" N, long. 118°47'50" W). Named on Pastoria Creek (1958) and Winters Ridge (1966) 7.5' quadrangles.

Bear Trap Canyon [TULARE]: *canyon,* drained by a stream that flows 1.5 miles to White River (1) 3.5 miles southwest of California Hot Springs (lat. 35°50'10" N, long. 118°42'25" W; sec. 14, T 24 S, R 30 E). Named on California Hot Springs (1958) 15' quadrangle.

Beartrap Creek [KERN]: *stream,* flows 2.5 miles to Walker Basin Creek 3.25 miles west of Piute Peak (lat. 35°26'30" N, long. 118°26'55" W; near N line sec. 4, T 29 S, R 33 E). Named on Piute Peak (1972) 7.5' quadrangle. United States Board on Geographic Names (1975b, p. 8) gave the form "Bear Trap Creek" as a variant.

Beartrap Creek: see **Woodward Creek** [TULARE].

Beartrap Lake [FRESNO]: *lake,* 600 feet long, 3.5 miles south-southwest of Mount Abbot (lat. 37°20'30" N, long. 118°49'15" W). Named on Mount Abbot (1953) 15' quadrangle.

Bear Trap Meadow [TULARE]: *area,* 5.25 miles east-northeast of Monache Mountain (lat. 36°13'50" N, long. 118°06'25" W). Named on Monache Mountain (1956) 15' quadrangle

Beartrap Meadow [TULARE]: *area,* 3.5 miles west-southwest of Shell Mountain along Woodward Creek (lat. 36°40'30" N, long. 118°51'30" W; sec. 29, T 14 S, R 29 E). Named on Giant Forest (1956) 15' quadrangle.

Bear Trap Ridge [TULARE]: *ridge,* west- to west-northwest-trending, 1.5 miles long, 3.5 miles south-southeast of California Hot Springs (lat. 35°49'50" N, long. 118°38'45" W). Named on California Hot Springs (1958) 15' quadrangle.

Bear Trap Spring [KERN]: *spring,* 8.5 miles north of Caliente (lat. 35°24'45" N, long. 118°36'10" W; on N line sec. 13, T 29 S, R 31 E). Named on Breckenridge Mountain (1972) 7.5' quadrangle.

Bear Trap Spring [TULARE]: *spring,* 4 miles south-southeast of California Hot Springs (lat. 35°49'30" N, long. 118°38'50" W; sec. 20, T 24 S, R 31 E); the spring is south of Bear Trap Ridge. Named on California Hot Springs (1958) 15' quadrangle.

Beartrap Spring [KERN]: *spring,* 4 miles southwest of Loraine (lat. 35°16'05" N, long. 118°29'15" W; on N line sec. 1, T 31 S, R 32 E). Named on Loraine (1972) 7.5' quadrangle.

Bear Twin Lakes [FRESNO]: *lakes,* two, each 500 feet long, 6.25 miles west-southwest of Mount Abbot (lat. 37°21'10" N, long. 118°53'10" W); the lakes are along a branch of Bear Creek (2). Named on Mount Abbot (1953) 15' quadrangle.

Bear Valley [KERN]: *valley,* 9 miles south of Caliente (lat. 35°09'45" N, long. 118°38'15" W). Named on Bear Mountain (1966) and Keene (1966) 7.5' quadrangles. The first settlers in the valley named the place for the large number of bears found there (Latta, 1976, p. 199).

Bear Wallow [FRESNO]: *area,* 3.5 miles east-southeast of Balch Camp (lat. 36°52'40" N, long. 119°0420" W; near N line sec. 19, T 12 S, R 27 E). Named on Patterson Mountain (1952) 15' quadrangle.

Bear Wallow Creek [FRESNO]: *stream,* flows nearly 3 miles to Dinkey Creek (1) 4 miles north of Balch Camp (lat. 36°57'50" N, long. 119°07'30" W). Named on Patterson Mountain (1952) 7.5' quadrangle.

Bearwallow Creek: see **Bear Hollow Creek** [KERN].

Beasore Creek [MADERA]: *stream,* flows 9 miles to Chiquito Creek 5.25 miles north-northeast of Shuteye Peak (lat. 37°25' N, long. 119°23'05" W; sec. 7, T 6 S, R 24 E). Named on Shuteye Peak (1953) 15' quadrangle.

Beasore Meadow Campground [MADERA]: *locality,* 7 miles north of Shuteye Peak (lat. 37°26'55" N, long. 119°27'10" W; near SE cor. sec. 33, T 5 S, R 23 E); the place is along Beasore Creek 1.5 miles downstream from Beasore Meadows. Named on Shuteye Peak (1953) 15' quadrangle.

Beasore Meadows [MADERA]: *area,* 7 miles north-northwest of Shuteye Peak (lat. 37°26'15" N, long. 119°28'45" W; mainly in sec. 5, T 6 S, R 23 E); the place is near the head of Beasore Creek. Named on Shuteye Peak (1953) 15' quadrangle. The name commemorates Tom Beasore, the first settler at the site (Crampton *in* Eccleston, p. 76). The place also was called Chiquito Meadows (Gudde, 1949, p. 66).

Beaver Canyon [KERN]: *canyon,* extends for 1 mile above the mouth of Delonegha Creek, which is 4.5 miles west-southwest of Miracle Hot Springs (lat. 35°33'15" N, long. 118°36'25" W). Named on Miracle Hot Springs (1972) 7.5' quadrangle.

Beck Canyon [KERN]: *canyon,* drained by a stream that flows 2.25 miles to Harper Canyon 4.25 miles northeast of Caliente (lat. 35°19'30" N, long. 118°33'50" W; near S line sec. 8, T 30 S, R 32 E). Named on Oiler Peak (1972) 7.5' quadrangle.

Becketts Backbone [TULARE]: *ridge,* southwest-trending, 4 miles long, 8 miles west-southwest of Yucca Mountain (lat. 36°31'15" N, long. 118°59'30" W). Named on Auckland (1966) 7.5' and Giant Forest (1956) 15' quadrangles.

Beck Lakes [MADERA]: *lakes,* two, largest 1900 feet long, 4.25 miles west-northwest of Devils Postpile (lat. 37°38'15" N, long. 119°09'30" W). Named on Devils Postpile (1953) 15' quadrangle. John Beck, a miner, named the lakes for himself about 1882 (Browning, 1986, p. 14).

Beck Meadows [TULARE]: *area,* 4 miles southeast of Monache Mountain (lat. 36°09'45" N, long. 119°09'45" W). Named on Monache Mountain (1956) 15' quadrangle.

Beck Spring: see **Lower Beck Spring** [KERN]; **Upper Beck Spring** [KERN].

Bee Canyon [FRESNO]: *canyon,* drained by a stream that flows nearly 2 miles to Warthan Creek 3.25 miles west of Coalinga Mineral Springs (lat. 36°08'15" N, long. 120°36'45" W; sec. 6, T 21 S, R 13 E). Named on Priest Valley (1969) and Sherman Peak (1969) 7.5' quadrangles.

Beer Keg Meadow [TULARE]: *area,* 7.5 miles east of Hockett Peak (lat. 36°14'20" N, long. 118°15'20" W). Named on Hockett Peak (1956) 15' quadrangle.

Beetlebug Lake [FRESNO]: *lake,* 1650 feet long, 16 miles northeast of Kaiser Peak at the head of Long Canyon (lat. 37°28'20" N, long. 119°00'15" W). Named on Kaiser Peak (1953) 15' quadrangle.

Bela Vista [KERN]: *locality,* 2 miles west-south-west of Weldon (lat. 35°39'10" N, long. 118°19'15" W; sec. 22, T 26 S, R 34 E). Named on Weldon (1972) 7.5' quadrangle.

Belknap Creek [TULARE]: *stream,* flows 2.5 miles to South Fork of Middle Fork Tule River 0.5 mile east of Camp Nelson (lat. 36°08'25" N, long. 118°35'50" W; sec. 34, T 20 S, R 31 E). Named on Camp Nelson (1956) 15' quadrangle. Corrington G. Belknap patented land near the stream in 1891 (Browning, 1986 p. 15).

Bell: see **Iva Bell Hot Springs**, under **Fish Creek Hot Springs** [FRESNO].

Bell Camp Meadow [TULARE]: *area,* nearly 3 miles north-northwest of Olancha Peak (lat. 36°18' N, long. 118°08'30" W; near W line sec. 1, T 19 S, R 35 E). Named on Olancha (1956) 15' quadrangle.

Belleville: see **Poplar** [TULARE].

Bellevue [KERN]: *locality,* 7.5 miles west-south-west of Bakersfield (lat. 35°20' N, long. 119°07'30" W; sec. 7, T 30 S, R 27 E). Named on Buena Vista Lake (1912) 30' quadrangle.

Beltran Creek [FRESNO]: *stream,* flows 5 miles to Zapato Chino Creek 10 miles south-south-east of Coalinga (lat. 36°00'30" N, long. 120°17'10" W; sec. 18, T 22 S, R 16 E). Named on Kreyenhagen Hills (1956) and The Dark Hole (1961) 7.5' quadrangles.

Bellview [MADERA]: *locality,* 5.5 miles south-southwest of O'Neals (lat. 37°03'25" N, long. 119°42'50" W; sec. 18, T 10 S, R 21 E). Site named on Millerton Lake West (1965) 7.5' quadrangle. Called Sesame on Mariposa (1912) 30' quadrangle. Postal authorities es-

tablished Bellview post office in 1894 and discontinued it in 1896; they established Sesame post office in 1902 and discontinued it in 1913 (Frickstad, p. 85, 86).

Bena [KERN]: *locality,* 7 miles west-northwest of Caliente along Southern Pacific Railroad (lat. 35°19'35" N, long. 118°44'20" W). Named on Bena (1972) 7.5' quadrangle. Called Pampa on Mendenhall's (1908) map. Postal authorities established Pampa post office in 1889, discontinued it in 1890, reestablished it in 1901, and discontinued it the same year (Frickstad, p. 58). The name "Pampa" was from Pampa Peak (Wines, p. 34). California (1891) map shows a place called Sand Cut located along the railroad about halfway between Pampa and Wade (present Edison).

Bench Canyon [MADERA]: *canyon,* drained by a stream that flows 3 miles to North Fork San Joaquin River 9 miles west-northwest of Devils Postpile (lat. 37°40'05" N, long. 119°14'30" W). Named on Devils Postpile (1953) and Merced Peak (1953) 15' quadrangles.

Bench Lake [FRESNO]: *lake,* 3400 feet long, 3.25 miles west of Mount Pinchot (lat. 36°56'50" N, long. 118°27'40" W). Named on Mount Pinchot (1953) 15' quadrangle. J. N. LeConte named the lake in 1902 (Browning, 1986, p. 15). The name describes the topographic setting of the lake (Versteeg, p. 422).

Bench Lakes: see **Double Peak** [FRESNO].

Bench Valley [FRESNO]: *canyon,* 3 miles long, 1.5 miles northwest of Blackcap Mountain along Fall Creek (lat. 37°05'15" N, long. 118°48'45" W). Named on Blackcap Mountain (1953) 15' quadrangle.

Bender [FRESNO]: *locality,* 2 miles north of Lanare along Southern Pacific Railroad (lat. 36°27'45" N, long. 119°57'15" W; sec. 8, T 17 S, R 19 E). Named on Burrel (1927) 7.5' quadrangle.

Benedict Meadow [MADERA]: *area,* 7.25 miles south of Shuteye Peak (lat. 37°14'50" N, long. 119°25'50" W; sec. 11, T 8 S, R 23 E). Named on Shaver Lake (1953) 15' quadrangle. Called Ellis Meadow on Kaiser (1904) 30' quadrangle, but United States Board on Geographic Names (1960b, p. 15) rejected this name for the place, and approved the name "Benedict Meadow" to honor Maurice Abbott Benedict, supervisor of Sierra National Forest from 1909 until 1914.

Benight Pond [FRESNO]: *intermittent lakes,* two, largest 1300 feet long, 3.25 miles southwest of Selma (lat. 36°31'45" N, long. 119°39'10" W; sec. 23, T 16 S, R 21 E). Named on Conejo (1963) 7.5' quadrangle. On Selma (1946) 15' quadrangle, the name applies to a permanent lake and two intermittent lakes.

Benita: see **Delano** [KERN].

Benito [FRESNO]: *locality,* 2.5 miles south-southeast of Firebaugh along Southern Pacific

Railroad (lat. 36°49'15" N, long. 120°26'10" W; at N line sec. 10, T 13 S, R 14 E). Named on Firebaugh (1956) 7.5' quadrangle.

Bennett Creek [TULARE]: *stream,* flows 4 miles to South Fork Kaweah River 10 miles southeast of Kaweah (lat. 36°21'25" N, long. 118°48'15" W; sec. 14, T 18 S, R 29 E). Named on Kaweah (1957) 15' quadrangle. Kaweah (1909) 30' quadrangle has the name "Battle Creek" for the lower part of present Bennett Creek, and for a west branch of present Bennett Creek. The name "Bennett" commemorates William F. Bennett, a stockman in the neighborhood in the 1870's (United States Board on Geographic Names, 1933a, p. 137).

Bennett Mill [FRESNO]: *locality,* 20 miles southwest of Kaiser Peak (lat. 37°05'30" N, long. 119°25'45" W; sec. 2, T 10 S, R 23 E). Named on Kaiser (1904) 30' quadrangle.

Benninger Canyon [KERN]: *canyon,* drained by a stream that flows 3 miles to Walker Basin Creek 6 miles north of Caliente (lat. 35°22'25" N, long. 118°36'10" W; sec. 25, T 29 S, R 31 E). Named on Breckenridge Mountain (1972) 7.5' quadrangle.

Benson Gulch [KERN]: *canyon,* drained by a stream that flows less than 1 mile to Fremont Valley 2.5 miles northeast of Garlock (lat. 35°25'30" N, long. 117°45'10" W; near W line sec. 12, T 29 S, R 39 E). Named on Garlock (1967) 7.5' quadrangle.

Benson Well [KERN]: *well,* 6.5 miles northwest of Randsburg (lat. 35°25'30" N, long. 117°44'50" W; sec. 12, T 29 S, R 39 E). Named on El Paso Peaks (1967) 7.5' quadrangle.

Bequette Canyon [TULARE]: *canyon,* drained by a stream that flows 1 mile to Dry Creek (1) nearly 5 miles northeast of Woodlake (lat. 36°27'10" N, long. 119°27'10" W; sec. 15, T 17 S, R 27 E). Named on Woodlake (1952) 7.5' quadrangle.

Berenda Creek [MADERA]: *stream,* enters lowlands 11 miles east-northeast of Fairmead (lat. 37°08'30" N, long. 120°01' W) and flows 16 miles to a ditch 5.5 miles south-southwest of Fairmead. Named on Firebaugh (1962) and Le Grand (1961) 15' quadrangles.

Berenda Reservoir [MADERA]: *lake,* behind a dam on Berenda Slough 3.5 miles north of Fairmead (lat. 37°07'40" N, long. 120° 11'10" W; near S line sec. 23, T 9 S, R 16 E). Named on Le Grand (1961, photorevised 1981) 7.5' quadrangle.

Berenda Slough [MADERA]: *stream,* diverges from Ash Slough 7 miles north-northeast of Fairmead, and flows 25 miles to Fresno River 22 miles west of Madera (lat. 36°59'45" N, long. 120°28'15" W; sec. 8, T 11 S, R 14 E). Named on Chowchilla (1960) and Le Grand (1961) 15' quadrangles, and on Firebaugh NE (1961) and Poso Farm (1962) 7.5' quadrangles. United States Board on Geographic

Names (1933a, p. 137) rejected the forms "Berendo Slough" and "Berrendo Slough" for the name.

Berendo: see **Berenda** [MADERA].

Berendo Slough: see **Berenda Slough** [MADERA].

Berrendo: see **Berenda** [MADERA].

Berrendo Slough: see **Berenda Slough** [MADERA].

Berry: see **Andy Berry's Landing,** under **Millwood** [FRESNO].

Berry Hill [MADERA]: *peak,* 5.5 miles south-southwest of O'Neals (lat. 37°03'05" N, long. 119°43'15" W; sec. 19, T 10 S, R 21 E). Named on Millerton Lake West (1965) 7.5' quadrangle.

Berts Canyon [KERN]: *canyon,* drained by a stream that flows 4 miles to Canebrake Creek 5 miles north-northwest of Walker Pass (lat. 34°43'25" N, long. 118°04'25" W; near W line sec. 25, T 25 S, R 36 E). Named on Walker Pass (1972) 7.5' quadrangle. Called Indian Wells Canyon on Kernville (1908) 30' quadrangle.

Beryl Lake [FRESNO]: *lake,* 800 feet long, 4.5 miles north-northeast of Dinkey Dome (lat. 37°10'40" N, long. 119°06'20" W; sec. 2, T 9 S, R 26 E). Named on Huntington Lake (1953) 15' quadrangle.

Bethel: see **North Fork** [MADERA].

Betty Lake [FRESNO]: *lake,* 350 feet long, 3 miles east-southeast of Dinkey Dome (lat. 37°06'15" N, long. 119°04'45" W; on E line sec. 36, T 9 S, R 26 E). Named on Huntington Lake (1953) 15' quadrangle.

Betty Spring [TULARE]: *spring,* 1 mile southeast of California Hot Springs (lat. 35°52'05" N, long. 118°39'40" W; sec. 5, T 24 S, R 31 E). Named on California Hot Springs (1958) 15' quadrangle.

Betty Waller Meadow [TULARE]: *area,* 3 miles southeast of California Hot Springs (lat. 35°51' N, long. 118°38' W; sec. 9, T 24 S, R 31 E). Named on California Hot Springs (1958) 15' quadrangle.

Beulah: see **Mineral King** [TULARE].

Beulah Camp: see **Mineral King** [TULARE].

Beverly: see **Lou Beverly Lake** [FRESNO].

Beville Lake [TULARE]: *lake,* 650 feet long, 10 miles west-northwest of Triple Divide Peak (lat. 36°39'40" N, long. 118°41'25" W). Named on Triple Divide Peak (1956) 15' quadrangle. The name commemorates a family from Visalia (Browning 1986, p. 16).

Bickel Camp [KERN]: *locality,* 5.25 miles north of Saltdale (lat. 35° 26'10" N, long. 117°53'10" W). Named on Saltdale NW (1967) 7.5' quadrangle.

Big Arroyo [TULARE]: *stream,* flows 14 miles to Kern River 11.5 miles northwest of Kern Peak (lat. 36°26'15" N, long. 118°24'45" W). Named on Kern Peak (1956), Mineral King (1956), and Triple Divide Peak (1956) 15' quadrangles. Called The Big Arroyo on

Olmsted's (1900) map. On Olancha (1907) and Tehipite (1903) 30' quadrangles, the name applies to the canyon of the stream. The canyon was called Jenny Lind Cañon in the early days when the stream itself was called Crabtree Creek—the name "Jenny Lind" was from Jenny Lind mine (Browning 1986, p. 16).

Big Baldy [TULARE]: *peak,* 7 miles north of Yucca Mountain (lat. 36°40'20" N, long. 118°52'50" W; near SE cor. sec. 25, T 14 S, R 28 E). Altitude 8209 feet. Named on Giant Forest (1956) 15' quadrangle. The name is from the bare summit of the feature (Browning 1986, p. 16).

Big Baldy Ridge [TULARE]: *ridge,* south-trending, 4 miles long, 7.5 miles north of Yucca Mountain (lat. 36°40'30" N, long. 118°52'45" W); the peak called Big Baldy is on the ridge. Named on Giant Forest (1956) 15' quadrangle.

Big Bear Lake [FRESNO]: *lake,* 1200 feet long, 4 miles south-southwest of Mount Abbot (lat. 37°19'55" N, long. 118°48'05" W); the feature is 600 feet upstream from Little Bear Lake. Named on Mount Abbot (1953) 15' quadrangle. Elden H. Vestal of California Department of Fish and Game named the lake in 1952 (Browning 1986, p. 16).

Big Bend [FRESNO]: *bend,* 6.5 miles west of Prather along San Joaquin River on Fresno-Madera county line (lat. 37°01'15" N, long. 119°38' W). Named on Millerton Lake West (1965) 7.5' quadrangle. Water of Millerton Lake now covers the place.

Big Bend [MADERA]: *bend,* 8 miles south-southeast of O'Neals along San Joaquin River on Madera-Fresno county line (lat. 37° 01'15" N, long. 119°38' W). The feature now is in Millerton Lake. Named on Millerton Lake West (1965) 7.5' quadrangle.

Big Bird Lake [TULARE]: *lake,* 4000 feet long, 4 miles west-northwest of Triple Divide Peak (lat. 36°37'15" N, long. 118°35'30" W). Named on Triple Divide Peak (1956) 15' quadrangle. United States Board on Geographic Names (1962a, p. 5) rejected the name "Dollar Lake" for the feature, and noted that the name "Big Bird" was given about 1902 for the tracks of a large bird found on the lake shore.

Big Blue Hills [FRESNO]: *range,* 16 miles north-northwest of Coalinga between Cantua Creek and Domengine Creek (lat. 36°22' N, long. 120°25' W). Named on Domengine Ranch (1956), Joaquin Rocks (1969), Lillis Ranch (1956), and Tres Picos Farms (1956) 7.5' quadrangles. Anderson and Pack (p. 17) named the feature because "the central and most prominent summits in the group are high, domelike hills of light-blue color formed of serpentine fragments derived from the beds locally known as the Big Blue."

Big Blue Mill [KERN]: *locality,* nearly 2 miles south of present Kernville and 1 mile north of the original site of Kernville (lat. 35° 43'45"

N, long. 118°25'40" W). Named on Isabella (1943) 15' quadrangle, which shows Big Blue mine situated 0.5 mile west-southwest of the place. Lovely Rogers discovered gold about 1 mile north of the original site of Kernville in 1861, and a town to be called Rogersville was laid out there, but failed to materialize; resumption of mining at the place in 1873 resulted in a new community called Quartzburg, and a camp located 0.5 mile farther north called Burkeville for Edwin Burke, co-owner of Big Blue mine—Burkeville also was called Millville and Milltown (Hensher and Peskin, p. 11).

Big Brewer Lake [TULARE]: *lake,* 1700 feet long, 8 miles north of Triple Divide Peak (lat. 36°42'10" N, long. 118°30'30" W); the lake is along Brewer Creek. Named on Triple Divide Peak (1956) 15' quadrangle.

Big Campbell [TULARE]: *peak,* 8.5 miles east of Porterville (lat. 36° 05'35" N, long. 118°52'05" W; near N line sec. 20, T 21 S, R 29 E); the peak is southeast across Tule River from Little Campbell. Altitude 1328 feet. Named on Globe (1956) 7.5' quadrangle.

Big Chief Lake [FRESNO]: *lake,* 2200 feet long, 8.5 miles south-southwest of Mount Abbot (lat. 37°16' N, long. 118°49'20" W). Named on Mount Abbot (1953) 15' quadrangle. Elden H. Vestal of California Department of Fish and Game named the lake in 1951 (Browning 1986, p. 16).

Big Creek [FRESNO]:

(1) *stream,* formed by the confluence of East Fork and South Fork, flows 17 miles to San Joaquin River 7.25 miles north of Shaver Lake Heights (present town of Shaver Lake) (lat. 37°12'40" N, long. 119°19'45" W; near W line sec. 26, T 8 S, R 24 E). Named on Huntington Lake (1953) and Shaver Lake (1953) 15' quadrangles. East Fork is 4 miles long, and South Fork is 6.5 miles long; both forks are named on Huntington Lake (1953) 15' quadrangle.

(2) *stream,* flows 15 miles to Pine Flat Reservoir nearly 7 miles west of Balch Camp (lat. 36°54'30" N, long. 119°14'30" W; near NW cor. sec. 10, T 12 S, R 25 E). Named on Huntington Lake (1953), Patterson Mountain (1952), and Shaver Lake (1953) 15' quadrangles.

(3) *town,* 7 miles south-southwest of Kaiser Peak (lat. 37°12'15" N, long. 119°14'35" W; sec. 28, T 8 S, R 25 E); the town is along Big Creek (1). Named on Huntington Lake (1953) and Shaver Lake (1953) 15' quadrangles. The name is from the Big Creek project of Southern California Edison Company, started in 1911 (Hanna, p. 32). The railroad station at the place was called Cascada until 1926; the area near the present town was known as Big Creek Flats in the 1870's, and as Manzanita Park in 1902 (Redinger, p. 13, 20). Postal authorities established Big Creek post office

in 1912 (Frickstad, p. 31). California Mining Bureau's (1917a) map shows a place called Portal along the railroad between Shaver and the town of Big Creek.

Big Creek [MADERA]: *stream,* heads in Madera County and flows 15 miles to South Fork Merced River 0.5 mile west of Wawona in Mariposa County (lat. 37°32'20" N, long. 119°40' W; near E line sec. 33, T 4 S, R 21 E). Named on Bass Lake (1953) and Yosemite (1956) 15' quadrangles.

Big Creek, North Fork: see **Rancheria Creek** [FRESNO] (1).

Big Creek Canyon [FRESNO]: *canyon,* 7.5 miles long, along Big Creek (1) between Huntington Lake (1) and the confluence of Big Creek (1) and San Joaquin River, 7.5 miles north of Shaver Lake Heights (present town of Shaver Lake) (lat. 37°12'40" N, long. 119°19'45" W; near W line sec. 26, T 8 S, R 24 E). Named on Huntington Lake (1953) and Shaver Lake (1953) 15' quadrangles.

Big Creek Flats: see **Big Creek** [FRESNO] (3).

Big Dry Creek: see **Academy** [FRESNO]; **Dry Creek** [FRESNO].

Big Dry Meadow [TULARE]: *area,* 3.5 miles north-northwest of Olancha Peak along Dry Creek (3) (lat. 36°18'45" N, long. 118° 08' W; sec. 36, T 18 S, R 35 E). Named on Olancha (1956) 15' quadrangle.

Big Dry Meadows [TULARE]: *area,* nearly 3 miles west of Monache Mountain (lat. 36°12'35" N, long. 118°14'40" W; sec. 1, 12, T 20 S, R 34 E). Named on Monache Mountain (1956) 15' quadrangle. Called Dry Meadows on Olancha (1907) 30' quadrangle.

Big E Spring [KERN]: *spring,* 3.25 miles east-southeast of Caliente in Deer Canyon (lat. 35°16'15" N, long. 118°34'35" W; near SE cor. sec. 31, T 30 S, R 32 E). Named on Oiler Peak (1972) 7.5' quadrangle.

Big Five Lakes [TULARE]: *lakes,* five, largest 0.5 mile long, 4.5 miles east-northeast of Mineral King (lat. 36°28'50" N, long. 118° 31'15" W). Named on Mineral King (1956) 15' quadrangle. United States Board on Geographic Names (1933a, p. 142) rejected the name "The Five Lakes" for the group.

Big Hart Canyon [KERN]: *canyon,* drained by a stream that flows 2 miles to Hart Canyon 8 miles north of Emerald Mountain (lat. 35° 22'10" N, long. 118°18'50" W). Named on Claraville (1972) and Emerald Mountain (1972) 7.5' quadrangles.

Bighorn Lake [FRESNO]:
(1) *lake,* 2000 feet long, 8 miles northwest of Mount Abbot (lat. 37° 28'05" N, long. 118°52'45" W). Named on Mount Abbot (1953) 15' quadrangle.
(2) *lake,* 1100 feet long, 2 miles east of Blackcap Mountain (lat. 37° 04'05" N, long 118°45'25" W). Named on Blackcap Mountain (1953) 15' quadrangle.

Bighorn Plateau [TULARE]: *area,* 5.5 miles west-northwest of Mount Whitney (lat. 36°37' N, long. 118°22'30" W). Named on Mount Whitney (1956) 15' quadrangle. Called Sandy Plateau on Mount Whitney (1907) 30' quadrangle, but United States Board on Geographic Names (1933a, p. 142) rejected this name for the feature.

Big Last Chance Canyon [KERN]: *canyon,* drained by a stream that flows 1.5 miles to Caliente Creek 2 miles west of Loraine (lat. 35°18'05" N, long. 118°28'15" W; sec. 19, T 30 S, R 33 E); the canyon is less than 1 mile east of Little Last Chance Canyon. Named on Loraine (1972) 7.5' quadrangle.

Big Margaret Lake [FRESNO]: *lake,* 3500 feet long, 14 miles northeast of Kaiser Peak (lat. 37°27'30" N, long. 119°02' W); the feature is the largest of the group called Margaret Lakes. Named on Kaiser Peak (1953) 15' quadrangle.

Big Maxson Meadow [FRESNO]: *area,* 2.5 miles west-southwest of Blackcap Mountain along North Fork Kings River (lat. 37°03'05" N, long. 118°50' W); the place is 7.5 miles east-southeast of Maxson Meadows. Named on Blackcap Mountain (1953) 15' quadrangle.

Big Meadow [TULARE]: *area,* 9.5 miles east-southeast of Fairview (lat. 35°52'45" N, long. 118°20'15" W). Named on Kernville (1956) 15' quadrangle.

Big Meadows [TULARE]: *area,* 2.5 miles west-northwest of Shell Mountain (lat. 36°42'40" N, long. 118°50'30" W). Named on Giant Forest (1956) 15' quadrangle. Called Big Meadow on Tehipite (1903) 30' quadrangle. The name is in use by the 1860's (Browning 1986, p. 17).

Big Meadows Creek [TULARE]: *stream,* flows 6 miles to Boulder Creek (1) 3 miles northeast of Shell Mountain at Tulare-Fresno county line (lat. 36°44'25" N, long. 118°47' W; at N line sec. 1, T 14 S, R 29 E); the stream goes through Big Meadows. Named on Giant Forest (1956) 15' quadrangle. Called Big Meadow Creek on Tehipite (1903) 30' quadrangle.

Big Moccasin Lake [FRESNO]: *lake,* 1000 feet long, 8 miles south of Mount Abbot (lat. 37°46'30" N, long. 118°48' W); the lake is 400 feet northeast of Little Moccasin Lake. Named on Mount Abbot (1953) 15' quadrangle.

Big Panoche Creek: see **Panoche Creek** [FRESNO].

Big Pete Meadow [FRESNO]: *area,* 6.5 miles east of Mount Goddard along Middle Fork Kings River (lat. 37°06'40" N, long. 118°36'15" W); the place is 0.5 mile upstream from Little Pete Meadow. Named on Mount Goddard (1948) 15' quadrangle.

Big Pine Meadow [TULARE]: *valley,* 10 miles north of Lamont Peak (lat. 35°56'15" N, long. 118°03'30" W). Named on Lamont Peak (1956) 15' quadrangle.

Big Sandy Bluffs [FRESNO]: *escarpment,* northwest-trending, 3.5 miles long, 7.5 miles west-southwest of Shaver Lake Heights (present town of Shaver Lake) (lat. 37°03'15" N, long. 119° 26'15" W); the feature is northeast of Big Sandy Valley. Named on Shaver Lake (1953) 15' quadrangle. United States Board on Geographic Names (1980, p. 4) approved the form "Big Sandy Bluff" for the name.

Big Sandy Campground [MADERA]: *locality,* 7.25 miles north-northeast of Yosemite Forks (lat. 37°28' N, long. 119°34'55" W; sec. 29, T 5 S, R 22 E); the place is along Big Creek 1 mile downstream from Little Sandy Campground. Named on Bass Lake (1953) 15' quadrangle.

Big Sandy Creek [FRESNO]: *stream,* flows 10.5 miles to San Joaquin River 3.5 miles west-northwest of Prather (lat. 37°03'45" N, long. 119°34' W; sec. 16, T 10 S, R 22 E); the stream goes through Big Sandy Valley. Named on Shaver Lake (1953) 15' quadrangle, and on Millerton Lake East (1965) 7.5' quadrangle.

Big Sandy Valley [FRESNO]: *valley,* 9 miles west-southwest of Shaver Lake Heights (present town of Shaver Lake) (lat. 37°02'30" N, long. 119°27'30" W); the valley is along Big Sandy Creek. Named on Shaver Lake (1953) 15' quadrangle.

Big Spring [KERN]: *spring,* 8 miles west of Inyokern (lat. 35°37'30" N, long. 117°57'30" W; sec. 36, T 26 S, R 37 E). Named on Freeman Junction (1972) and Owens Peak (1972) 7.5' quadrangles.

Big Spring [TULARE]: *spring,* 11 miles southwest of Mineral King in Putnam Canyon (lat. 36°20'35" N, long. 118°44'40" W). Named on Mineral King (1956) 15' quadrangle.

Big Springs [TULARE]: *spring,* 6 miles northnorthwest of Yucca Mountain in Redwood Canyon (lat. 36°39'15" N, long 118°54'15" W; sec. 2, T 15 S, R 28 E). Named on Giant Forest (1956) 15' quadrangle.

Big Sycamore Canyon [KERN]: *canyon,* drained by a stream that flows 4 miles to lowlands 10 miles southwest of Liebre Twins (lat. 34°50'35" N, long. 118°41' W; sec. 28, T 9 N, R 17 W); the mouth of this canyon is 1 mile northeast of the mouth of Little Sycamore Canyon (2). Named on La Liebre Ranch (1965) and Winters Ridge (1966) 7.5' quadrangles.

Big Tar Canyon [KINGS]: *canyon,* 3 miles long, 6 miles south-southwest of Avenal (lat. 35°55'30" N, long. 120°10' W); the canyon is on upper reaches of Big Tar Creek. Named on Garza Peak (1953) 7.5' quadrangle, which shows a tar seep in the canyon.

Big Tar Creek [KINGS]: *stream,* flows 6 miles to Kettleman Plain 4.25 miles south-southeast of Avenal (lat. 35°56'50" N, long. 120° 06'30" W; sec. 11, T 23 S, R 17 E); the stream drains Big Tar Canyon. Named on Garza Peak (1953) and Kettleman Plain (1953) 7.5' quadrangles.

Big Tenant Spring [KERN]: *spring,* 2.25 miles north of Democrat Hot Springs (lat. 35°33'35" N, long. 118°39'40" W; near SE cor. sec. 20, T 27 S, R 31 E); the spring is 0.5 mile northeast of Little Tenant Spring near the head of Tenant Creek. Named on Democrat Hot Springs (1972) 7.5' quadrangle.

Big West Meadow: see **Big Wet Meadow** [TULARE].

Big Wet Meadow [TULARE]: *area,* 5 miles north of Triple Divide Peak along Roaring River in Cloud Canyon (lat. 36°39'45" N, long. 118°31'50" W). Named on Triple Divide Peak (1956) 15' quadrangle. United States Board on Geographic Names (1968b, p. 5) rejected the name "Big West Meadow" for the feature.

Big Whitney Meadow [TULARE]: *area,* 9 miles north of Kern Peak on upper reaches of Golden Trout Creek (lat. 36°26' N, long. 118° 16' W; in and near sec. 23, T 17 S, R 34 E); the place is 6 miles northeast of Little Whitney Meadow. Named on Kern Peak (1956) 15' quadrangle. Called Whitney Meadows on Olancha (1907) 30' quadrangle. United States Board on Geographic Names (1933a, p. 816) rejected the name "Golden Trout Meadows" for the feature.

Biledo Meadow [MADERA]: *area,* 6.5 miles south-southwest of Buena Vista Peak (lat. 37°30'10" N, long. 119°34' W; on S line sec. 9, T 5 S, R 22 E). Named on Yosemite (1956) 15' quadrangle. United States Board on Geographic Names (1990, p. 5) rejected the form "Billiedo Meadow" for the feature. The name commemorates Thomas Biledo, or Biledeaux, a French-Canadian miner who built a log cabin at the place in 1890 (Uhte, p. 51).

Billiedo Meadow: see **Biledo Meadow** [MADERA].

Bill Lake [FRESNO]: *lake,* 450 feet long, 1 mile west-northwest of Kaiser Peak (lat. 37°18' N, long. 119°12' W; near E line sec. 23, T 7 S, R 25 E). Named on Kaiser Peak (1953) 15' quadrangle.

Bill Moore Canyon [TULARE]: *canyon,* drained by a stream that flows about 1.5 miles to Dry Creek (1) 5 miles east-southeast of Auckland (lat. 36°34'15" N, long. 119°01'15" W; near N line sec. 3, T 16 S, R 27 E); the canyon is northeast of Bill Moore Ridge. Named on Auckland (1966) 7.5' quadrangle.

Bill Moore Ridge [TULARE]: *ridge,* east-southeast- to southeast-trending, 1.5 miles long, 4 miles east-southeast of Auckland (lat. 36°34'30" N, long. 119°02'15" W). Named on Auckland (1966) 7.5' quadrangle.

Billy Creek [FRESNO]:
(1) *stream,* flows 1 mile to Huntington Lake (1) 2.5 miles north-northeast of the town of Big Creek (lat. 37°14'15" N, long. 119°13'45" W; sec. 15, T 8 S, R 25 E). Named on Huntington Lake (1953) 15' quadrangle.
(2) *stream,* flows 2.5 miles to Pine Flat Reser-

voir 1 mile south of Trimmer (lat. 36°53'25" N, long. 119°17'40" W; near W line sec. 18, T 12 S, R 25 E). Named on Trimmer (1965) 7.5' quadrangle.

Billy Spring [KERN]: *spring,* 3.5 miles northwest of Caliente (lat. 35°19'35" N, long. 118°40'25" W). Named on Bena (1972) 7.5' quadrangle.

Bino Springs [KERN]: *springs,* 13 miles southsoutheast of Arvin (lat. 35°00'55" N, long. 118°45'20" W; near NW cor. sec. 25, T 11 N, R 18 W). Named on Tejon Hills (1955) 7.5' quadrangle.

Biola [FRESNO]: *town,* 6 miles north-northeast of Kerman (lat. 36° 48'10" N, long. 120°01' W; sec. 16, T 13 S, R 18 E). Named on Biola (1963) 7.5' quadrangle. William Kerchoff started the town in 1912 and coined the name from initial letters of the term "Bible Institute of Los Angeles" (Gudde, 1949, p. 31). Postal authorities established Biola post office in 1915, discontinued in it 1918, and reestablished it in 1920 (Frickstad, p. 31).

Biola Junction [FRESNO]: *locality,* 5.5 miles west-northwest of downtown Fresno along Southern Pacific Railroad (lat. 36°48'05" N, long. 119°52'05" W; sec. 14, T 13 S, R 19 E). Named on Fresno North (1965) 7.5' quadrangle.

Birch: see **Hildreth** [MADERA].

Bird Spring [KERN]: *spring,* 5.5 miles northeast of Pinyon Mountain (lat. 35°29'55" N, long. 118°04'35" W). Named on Dove Spring (1972) 7.5' quadrangle.

Bird Spring Canyon [KERN]: *canyon,* drained by a stream that flows 7.25 miles to Indian Wells Valley 7 miles east-northeast of Pinyon Mountain (lat. 35°29'40" N, long. 118°02'45" W; at E line sec. 13, T 28 S, R 36 E); Bird Spring is in the canyon. Named on Cane Canyon (1972), Dove Spring (1972), and Horse Canyon (1972) 7.5' quadrangles.

Bird Spring Pass [KERN]: *pass,* 1 mile southsouthwest of Skinner Peak (lat. 35°33'10" N, long. 118°07'55" W); the pass is at the head of Bird Spring Canyon. Named on Cane Canyon (1972) 7.5' quadrangle.

Bishop Pass [FRESNO]: *pass,* 10 miles east of Mount Goddard on Fresno-Inyo county line (lat. 37°06'55" N, long. 118°32'40" W). Named on Mount Goddard (1948) 15' quadrangle.

Bissell [KERN]: *locality,* 13 miles northeast of Rosamond along Atchison, Topeka and Santa Fe Railroad (lat. 34°59'40" N, long. 118°00' W; sec. 1, T 10 N, R 11 W). Named on Bissell (1973) and Edwards (1973) 7.5' quadrangles. On Bissell (1947) 7.5' quadrangle, the name is at a site situated 2 miles farther southwest along an abandoned railroad grade (lat. 34°58'15" N, long. 118°01'20" W; near SW cor. sec. 11, T 10 N, R 11 W).

Bissell Hills [KERN]: *range,* 10 miles eastnortheast of Rosamond (lat. 34°56' N, long.

118°00' W); the range is south of Bissell. Named on Bissell (1973) and Edwards (1973) 7.5' quadrangles.

Bitter Creek [KERN]: *stream,* flows 10 miles to lowlands 5 miles southeast of Maricopa (lat. 35°01'15" N, long. 119°20'25" W; near S line sec. 21, T 11 N, R 23 W). Named on Ballinger Canyon (1943), Pentland (1953), and Santiago Creek (1943) 7.5' quadrangles. The name is from the quality of water in the stream (Arnold and Johnson, p. 19).

Bitter Creek [TULARE]: *stream,* flows 3.5 miles to South Fork Kern River 12.5 miles south-southeast of Monache Mountain (lat. 36°02'05" N, long. 118°08' W; sec. 6, T 22 S, R 36 E). Named on Monache Mountain (1956) 15' quadrangle.

Bitter Creek: see **Bitterwater Creek** [KERN] (1).

Bitterwater Canyon [KERN]: *canyon,* 5 miles long, on Kern-San Luis Obispo county line along Bitterwater Creek (2) above a point 14 miles south of Orchard Peak (lat. 35°32' N, long. 120°04'45" W; sec. 31, T 27 S, R 18 E). Named on La Panza NE (1966) and Packwood Creek (1961) 7.5' quadrangles.

Bitterwater Creek [KERN]:

(1) *stream,* heads just inside San Luis Obispo County and flows 12.5 miles to end 4.5 miles northeast of Maricopa (lat. 35°06'50" N, long. 119°21' W; sec. 25, T 32 S, R 24 E). Named on Ballinger Canyon (1943), Maricopa (1951), and Pentland (1953) 7.5' quadrangles. United States Board on Geographic Names (1990, p. 6) rejected the name "Bitter Creek" for the stream.

(2) *stream,* flows 15 miles, partly in San Luis Obispo County, to Antelope Plain 6 miles west-southwest of Blackwells Corner (lat. 35°35'10" N, long. 119°58' W; at N line sec. 18, T 27 S, R 19 E); the stream drains Bitterwater Canyon and Bitterwater Valley. Named on Emigrant Hill (1953), La Panza NE (1966), Packwood Creek (1961), and Shale Point (1953) 7.5' quadrangles. Called East Palo Prieto Cr. on Mendenhall's (1908) map. The name "Bitterwater" is from the quality of water in the stream (Arnold and Johnson, p. 19).

Bitterwater Spring [KERN]:

(1) *spring,* 16 miles south-southeast of Orchard Peak (lat. 35°31'05" N, long. 120°04' W; near W line sec. 5, T 28 S, R 18 E); the spring is in Bitterwater Canyon. Named on Packwood Creek (1961) 7.5' quadrangle.

(2) *spring,* 5 miles south-southwest of Maricopa (lat. 35°00'05" N, long. 119°27'15" W; near NW cor. sec. 33, T 11 N, R 24 W); the spring is along Bitterwater Creek (1). Named on Maricopa (1951) 7.5' quadrangle.

Bitterwater Valley [KERN]: *valley,* along Bitterwater Creek (2) above the entrance of the stream into Antelope Plain 6 miles westsouthwest of Blackwells Corner (lat.

35°35'10" N, long. 119° 58' W; at N line sec. 18, T 27 S, R 19 E). Named on Packwood Creek (1961) and Shale Point (1953) 7.5' quadrangles. United States Board on Geographic Names (1933a, p. 147) rejected the name "Palo Prieto Valley" for the feature.

Bitterwater Wells [KERN]: *well,* 13 miles south-southeast of Orchard Peak (lat. 35°34'20" N, long. 120°00'55" W; near SE cor. sec. 15, T 27 S, R 18 E); the feature is in Bitterwater Valley along Bitterwater Creek (2). Named on Packwood Creek (1961) 7.5' quadrangle.

Black Bear Lake [FRESNO]: *lake,* 1500 feet long, 3.25 miles south of Mount Abbot (lat. 37°20'15" N, long. 118°47'35" W). Named on Mount Abbot (1953) 15' quadrangle. Elden H. Vestal of California Department of Fish and Game named the lake in 1952 (Browning 1986, p. 20).

Black Bill Peak [KERN]: *peak,* nearly 4 miles north-northwest of Loraine (lat. 35°21' N, long. 118°28'15" W; sec. 6, T 30 S, R 33 E); the peak is on Black Bill Ridge. Altitude 5067 feet. Named on Loraine (1972) 7.5' quadrangle.

Black Bill Ridge [KERN]: *ridge,* generally north-northeast-trending, 1 mile long, 4 miles north-northwest of Loraine (lat. 35°21'10" N, long. 118°28' W). Named on Loraine (1972) 7.5' quadrangle.

Black Bob Canyon [KERN]: *canyon,* drained by a stream that flows 5.25 miles to Salt Creek (2) 6.25 miles east of Eagle Rest Peak (lat. 34°54'35" N, long. 119°01'20" W; near NW cor. sec. 33, T 10 N, R 20 W). Named on Frazier Mountain (1958), Grapevine (1958), and Pleito Hills (1958) 7.5' quadrangles. Frazier Mountain (1958) 7.5' quadrangle shows Black Bob mine in the canyon.

Blackburn Canyon [KERN]: *canyon,* drained by a stream that flows 5.25 miles to Tehachapi Valley 3 miles southeast of Tehachapi (lat. 35°05'45" N, long. 118°24'45" W; at N line sec. 31, T 12 N, R 14 W). Named on Tehachapi South (1966) 7.5' quadrangle.

Blackcap Basin [FRESNO]: *area,* 2 miles east of Blackcap Mountain at the head of North Fork Kings River (lat. 37°04' N, long. 118° 46' W). Named on Blackcap Mountain (1953) and Mount Goddard (1948) 15' quadrangles.

Blackcap Mountain [FRESNO]: *peak,* 4.5 miles west-southwest of Mount Goddard (lat. 37°04'20" N, long. 118°47'35" W). Altitude 11,559 feet. Named on Blackcap Mountain (1953) 15' quadrangle.

Black Divide [FRESNO]: *ridge,* north-north-west- to north-trending, 7 miles long, between LeConte Canyon and Enchanted Gorge (lat. 37°04' N, long, 118°38' W); Black Giant is at the north end of the ridge. Named on Mount Goddard (1948) 15' quadrangle. George R. Davis of United States Geological Survey named the feature about 1907 (Farquhar, 1923, p. 384).

Black Giant [FRESNO]: *peak,* 4 miles east of Mount Goddard (lat. 37°06'10" N, long. 118°38'50" W); the peak is at the north end of Black Divide. Altitude 13,330 feet. Named on Mount Goddard (1948) 15' quadrangle. J.N. LeConte gave the name "Black Giant" to the peak, but members of United States Geological Survey later called it Mount Goode (Farquhar, 1923, p. 399). United States Board on Geographic Names (1933a, p. 149) rejected the name "Mount Goode" for the peak, and then (1978b, p. 3) rejected the form "Black Giant Peak" for the name.

Black Giant Peak: see **Black Giant** [FRESNO].

Black Gulch [KERN]: *canyon,* drained by a stream that flows 4.25 miles to Kern River 1.25 miles north-northeast of Miracle Hot Springs (lat. 35°35'35" N, long. 118°31'40" W). Named on Alta Sierra (1972) and Miracle Hot Springs (1972) 7.5' quadrangles.

Blackhawk Mountain [MADERA]: *ridge,* northeast-trending, 1.5 miles long, 2 miles north-northwest of O'Neals (lat. 37°09'15" N, long. 119°42'35" W). Named on O'Neals (1965) 7.5' quadrangle.

Black Hills [KERN]: *range,* 8.5 miles north of Saltdale on the northwest side of El Paso Range (lat. 35°28'30" N, long. 117°51'30" W). Named on Garlock (1967), Inyokern SE (1972), and Saltdale NW (1967) 7.5' quadrangles.

Black Hills Well [KERN]: *well,* 9.5 miles north of Saltdale (lat. 35° 29'35" N, long. 117°55'15" W); the well is west of Black Hills. Named on Saltdale NW (1967) 7.5' quadrangle.

Blackie Lake [MADERA]: *lake,* 400 feet long, 4 miles south-southeast of Merced Peak (lat. 37°34'45" N, long. 119°22'40" W). Named on Merced Peak (1953) 15' quadrangle. Warden Herb Black told employees of California Department of Fish and Game in 1946 that the lake sometimes was called Blackie Lake after himself (Browning, 1986, p. 21).

Black Kaweah [TULARE]: *peak,* 3.25 miles south-southeast of Triple Divide Peak (lat. 36°32'45" N, long. 118°30'55" W); the peak is on Kaweah Peaks Ridge. Altitude 13,765 feet. Named on Triple Divide Peak (1956) 15' quadrangle. United States Board on Geographic Names (1969d, p. 8) approved the name "Kaweah Queen" for a peak located less than 1 mile north-northeast of Black Kaweah on Kaweah Peaks Ridge.

Blackmans Bar [MADERA]: *locality,* 3 miles northeast of Shuteye Peak along West Fork Chiquito Creek (lat. 37°22'30" N, long. 119° 23' W; sec. 30, T 6 S, R 24 E). Named on Shuteye Peak (1953) 15' quadrangle.

Black Mountain [FRESNO]:
(1) *ridge,* west-northwest-trending, 2 miles long, 10 miles southwest of Shaver Lake Heights (present town of Shaver Lake) (lat. 37°00'30" N, long. 119°26'45" W). Named

on Shaver Lake (1953) 15' quadrangle.

(2) *peak,* 9.5 miles south of Mount Pinchot on Fresno-Inyo county line (lat. 36°48'30" N, long. 118°22'40" W). Altitude 13,289 feet. Named on Mount Pinchot (1953) 15' quadrangle. Members of the Wheeler survey named the peak in the late 1870's (Browning 1986, p. 20).

(3) *peak,* 3 miles east-southeast of Joaquin Rocks (lat. 36°18'15" N, long. 120°24'05" W; sec. 1, T 19 S, R 14 E). Altitude 3640 feet. Named on Joaquin Rocks (1969) 7.5' quadrangle.

(4) *peak,* 9.5 miles southwest of Coalinga (lat. 36°01'40" N, long. 120°27'30" W; on W line sec. 10, T 22 S, R 14 E). Altitude 2447 feet. Named on Curry Mountain (1969) 7.5' quadrangle.

(5) *ridge,* east-trending, 4 miles long, east of Castle Mountain (lat. 35°56'30" N, long. 120°18'30" W). Named on The Dark Hole (1961) 7.5' quadrangle.

Black Mountain [KERN]:

(1) *peak,* 1.5 miles northeast of Alta Sierra (lat. 35°44'30" N, long. 118°31'25" W; sec. 22, T 25 S, R 32 E). Altitude 7438 feet. Named on Alta Sierra (1972) 7.5' quadrangle.

(2) *peak,* 4.5 miles south-southeast of Keene (lat. 35°09'50" N, long. 118°31'40" W; sec. 10, T 32 S, R 32 E). Altitude 5686 feet. Named on Keene (1966) 7.5' quadrangle.

(3) *ridge,* east- to northeast-trending, 1 mile long, 5.5 miles northwest of Garlock (lat 35°28'15" N, long. 117°50'45" W). Named on Garlock (1967) 7.5' quadrangle. The name is from the mantle of dark volcanic rock that covers the feature (Fairbanks, 1897, p. 36).

Black Mountain: see **Madera Peak** [MADERA].

Black Mountain [TULARE]:

(1) *peak,* 7.5 miles west-southwest of Camp Nelson (lat. 36°05'50" N, long. 118°44' W; near W line sec. 15, T 21 S, R 30 E). Named on Camp Nelson (1956) 15' quadrangle.

(2) *peak,* 12.5 miles west-northwest of Lamont Peak (lat. 35°51'10" N, long. 118°14'15" W). Named on Lamont Peak (1956) 15' quadrangle.

Black Mountain Saddle [KERN]: *pass,* 1.25 miles north-northeast of Alta Sierra (lat. 35°44'35" N, long. 118°32'15" W; sec. 21, T 25 S, R 32 E); the pass is nearly 1 mile west of Black Mountain (1). Named on Alta Sierra (1972) 7.5' quadrangle.

Black Oak Flat [FRESNO]: *area,* 3.5 miles east of Dunlap (lat. 36° 44'40" N, long. 119°03'15" W; around SE cor. sec. 32, T 13 S, R 27 E). Named on Miramonte (1966) 7.5' quadrangle.

Black Pass: see **Black Rock Pass** [TULARE].

Black Peak [FRESNO]: *peak,* 6.5 miles northeast of Dinkey Dome (lat. 37°10'55" N, long. 119°03' W; sec. 5, T 9 S, R 27 E). Altitude 9771 feet. Named on Huntington Lake (1953) 15' quadrangle. United States Board on Geographic Names (1983b, p. 4) rejected the names "Potato Butte" and "Potato Mountain" for the feature.

Black Peak: see **Madera Peak** [MADERA].

Black Peak Fork: see **Madera Creek** [MADERA].

Black Point [FRESNO]: *peak,* 10 miles north-northeast of Shaver Lake Heights (present town of Shaver Lake) (lat. 37°14'20" N, long. 119°15'30" W; sec. 17, T 8 S, R 25 E). Altitude 8111 feet. Named on Shaver Lake (1953) 15' quadrangle.

Black Rock [FRESNO]: *relief feature,* 4.25 miles east-northeast of Balch Camp (lat. 36°55'55" N, long. 119°03'10" W; sec. 32, T 11 S, R 27 E). Named on Patterson Mountain (1952) 15' quadrangle.

Black Rock Creek [FRESNO]: *stream,* flows 1 mile to North Fork Kings River 5.25 miles east of Balch Camp (lat. 36°55' N, long. 119°01'40" W; sec. 4, T 12 S, R 27 E); the stream heads near Black Rock. Named on Patterson Mountain (1952) 15' quadrangle.

Blackrock Lake [FRESNO]: *lake,* 1200 feet long, 4 miles north-northwest of Blackcap Mountain (lat. 37°07'45" N, long. 118°48'45" W). Named on Blackcap Mountain (1953) 15' quadrangle.

Blackrock Mountain [TULARE]: *peak,* 7 miles east-southeast of Hockett Peak (lat. 36°10'45" N, long. 118°16'35" W). Named on Hockett Peak (1956) 15' quadrangle. Hunters named the feature for a large black boulder at the summit (Browning 1986, p. 21).

Black Rock Pass [TULARE]: *pass,* 3.5 miles northeast of Mineral King on Great Western Divide (lat. 36°29'05" N, long. 118°23'05" W). Named on Mineral King (1956) 15' quadrangle. The name is from a band of black rock that contrasts with red and white rocks that prevail nearby (United States Board on Geographic Names, 1933a, p. 149). The feature also was called Black Pass and Cliff Pass (Browning, p. 20).

Black Rock Reservoir [FRESNO]: *lake,* behind a dam on North Fork Kings River 5.5 miles east of Balch Camp (lat. 36°55'10" N, long. 119°01'20" W; sec. 3, T 12 S, R 27 E); the lake is 2 miles east-southeast of Black Rock. Named on Patterson Mountain (1952) 15' quadrangle.

Blackwells Corner [KERN]: *locality,* 50 miles west-northwest of Bakersfield (lat. 35°36'55" N, long. 119°52' W; at NE cor. sec. 1, T 27 S, R 19 E). Named on Blackwells Corner (1953) 7.5' quadrangle. The name commemorates George Blackwell, who started a travelers stop at the place in 1921 (Bailey, 1967, p. 2).

Blanco [TULARE]: *locality,* 7 miles south of Waukena along Atchison, Topeka and Santa Fe Railroad (lat. 36°02'10" N, long. 119°30'40" W; at N line sec. 8, T 22 S, R 23 E). Named on Corcoran (1954) 7.5' quadrangle.

Blaney Meadows [FRESNO]: *area,* 13 miles north-northwest of Blackcap Mountain along South Fork San Joaquin River (lat. 37° 14'30" N, long. 118°53'45" W; sec. 15, T 8 S, R 28 E). Named on Blackcap Mountain (1953) 15' quadrangle. United States Board on Geographic Names (1971a, p. 2) approved the name "Blayney Meadows" for the feature, and gave the names "Blaney Meadows," "Hidden Valley," "Hidden Valley Meadows," and "Lost Valley" as variants. At the same time the Board noted that the name "Blayney" commemorates William Farris Blayney, who grazed sheep in the neighborhood in the 1870's. Waring (p. 54) described Blaney Meadows Hot Springs, located "about a mile above the upper end of Blaney Meadows," where bathing pools were dug out at three or four springs.

Blaney Meadows Hot Springs: see **Blaney Meadows** [FRESNO].

Blayney Meadows: see **Blaney Meadows** [FRESNO].

Block Hill [KINGS]: *peak,* 7.5 miles east-southeast of Avenal (lat. 35°58'25" N, long. 120°00'05" W; near W line sec. 35, T 22 S, R 18 E). Named on Kettleman Plain (1953) 7.5' quadrangle. United States Board on Geographic Names (1933b, p. 5) noted that the name is descriptive

Blossom Lakes [TULARE]: *lakes,* largest 700 feet long, 5.5 miles south of Mineral King (lat. 36°22'15" N, long. 118°35'45" W). Named on Mineral King (1956) 15' quadrangle. R.B. Marshall of United States Geological Survey named the lake in 1909 for Charles W. Blossom, a ranger at Sequoia National Park (Hanna, p. 35).

Blossom Peak [TULARE]: *peak,* 3.5 miles south-southeast of Kaweah (lat. 36°25'25" N, long. 118°53'15" W; on E line sec. 25, T 17 S, R 28 E). Altitude 2539 feet. Named on Kaweah (1957) 15' quadrangle.

Blue Canyon [FRESNO]:
(1) *canyon,* 9.5 miles long, along Big Creek (2) 7.5 miles northwest of Balch Camp (lat. 35°58'30" N, long. 119°13'30" W; sec. 15, T 11 S, R 25 E). Named on Huntington Lake (1953), Patterson Mountain (1952), and Shaver Lake (1953) 15' quadrangles.
(2) *canyon,* 5 miles long, drained by Blue Canyon Creek, which joins Middle Fork Kings River 12.5 miles west of Marion Peak (lat. 36°55'50" N, long. 118°44'35" W). Named on Marion Peak (1953) and Tehipite Dome (1952) 15' quadrangles. Frank Dusy and Gustav Eisen named the canyon in the late 1870's (Browning 1986, p. 22).

Blue Canyon [TULARE]:
(1) *canyon,* drained by a stream that flows 1.5 miles to Collier Creek nearly 4 miles south of Auckland (lat. 36°32' N, long. 119° 06' W; sec. 13, T 16 S, R 26 E). Named on Auckland (1966) 7.5' quadrangle.
(2) *canyon,* 1 mile long, opens into the canyon

of Blue Creek 6 miles southeast of Springville (lat. 36°03'25" N, long. 118°45'20" W). Named on Globe (1956) 7.5' quadrangle.

Blue Canyon Creek [FRESNO]: *stream,* flows 8.5 miles to Middle Fork Kings River 12.5 miles west of Marion Peak (lat. 36°55'50" N, long. 118°44'35" W); the stream heads near Blue Canyon Peak and goes through Blue Canyon (2). Named on Mount Goddard (1948) 15' quadrangle.

Blue Canyon Falls [FRESNO]: *waterfall,* 13 miles west of Marion Peak near Middle Fork Kings River (lat. 36°55'50" N, long. 118° 44'50" W); the feature is in Blue Canyon (2). Named on Marion Peak (1953) 15' quadrangle. Frank Dusy and Gustav Eisen named the falls in the late 1870's (Browning 1986, p. 22).

Blue Canyon Peak [FRESNO]: *peak,* 5.25 miles south of Mount Goddard (lat. 37°01'45" N, long. 118°42'30" W); the peak is near the head of Blue Canyon Creek. Altitude 11,849 feet. Named on Mount Goddard (1948) 15' quadrangle.

Blue Creek [TULARE]: *stream,* flows 4.5 miles to South Fork Tule River 7 miles south-east of Springville (lat. 36°02'25" N, long. 118°45'35" W). Named on Camp Nelson (1956) and Springville (1957) 15' quadrangles.

Blue Dome: see **Little Blue Dome** [TULARE].

Blue Flower Pass: see **Glen Pass** [FRESNO].

Blue Jay Lakes [FRESNO]: *lakes,* largest 600 feet long, 6.5 miles northwest of Mount Abbot (lat. 37°26'45" N, long. 118°52'30" W). Named on Mount Abbot (1953) 15' quadrangle.

Blue Lake [MADERA]: *lake,* 1200 feet long, 7 miles east-northeast of Merced Peak (lat. 37°40'50" N, long. 119°16'55" W). Named on Merced Peak (1953) 15' quadrangle.

Blue Mountain [KERN]: *ridge,* generally east-southeast- to south-trending, 5.5 miles long, 5.5 miles northeast of Woody (lat. 35°45'35" N, long. 118°46'10" W). Named on California Hot Springs (1958) 15' quadrangle, and on Glennville (1972), White River (1965), and Woody (1965) 7.5' quadrangles.

Blue Mountain [TULARE]: *ridge,* east- to east-southeast-trending, 2.5 miles long, 3 miles south-southeast of Auckland (lat. 36°33'10" N, long. 119°04'40" W). Named on Auckland (1966) 7.5' quadrangle.

Blue Point [KERN]: *relief feature,* nearly 5 miles north-northwest of Cinco (lat. 35°19'15" N, long. 118°04'55" W; near S line sec. 14, T 30 S, R 36 E). Named on Cinco (1972) 7.5' quadrangle.

Blue Ridge [KERN]: *ridge,* generally west-trending, 2.5 miles long, 7 miles west of Eagle Rest Peak (lat. 34°53'40" N, long. 119°15'20" W). Named on Eagle Rest Peak (1942) and Santiago Creek (1943) 7.5' quadrangles.

Blue Ridge [TULARE]: *ridge,* south-southwest- to south-trending, 4 miles long, 15 miles south-southeast of Kaweah (lat. 36°16' N, long. 118°51' W). Named on Kaweah (1957) and Springville (1957) 15' quadrangles.

Bluestone Ridge [KERN]: *ridge,* southeast- to east-trending, 8 miles long, center near Orchard Peak (lat. 35°44'15" N, long. 120° 08' W). Named on Orchard Peak (1961), Sawtooth Ridge (1961), and Tent Hills (1942) 7.5' quadrangles. Called Avenal Ridge on Sawtooth Ridge (1943) 7.5' quadrangle. Marsh (p. 41) noted that the feature has the local name "Orchard Ridge."

Board Camp Creek: see **Garfield Creek** [TULARE].

Bobby Lake [FRESNO]: *lake,* 250 feet long, 2000 feet west-northwest of Kaiser Peak (lat. 37°17'45" N, long. 119°11'25" W; near S line sec. 24, T 7 S, R 25 E). Named on Kaiser Peak (1953) 15' quadrangle.

Bobcat Point [TULARE]: *relief feature,* 6.25 miles east-southeast of Yucca Mountain (lat. 36°32'45" N, long. 118°45'30" W). Named on Giant Forest (1956) 15' quadrangle.

Bobcat Spring [KERN]: *spring,* nearly 6.5 miles east of Caliente (lat. 35°16'20" N, long. 118°31' W; sec. 35, T 30 S, R 32 E). Named on Oiler Peak (1972) 7.5' quadrangle.

Bob Rabbit Canyon [KERN]: *canyon,* 3.25 miles long, drained by Dry Meadow Creek above a point 7 miles south of Weldon (lat. 35°34'05" N, long. 118°16'20" W). Named on Woolstalf Creek (1972) 7.5' quadrangle, which shows the site of Bob Rabbit place near the mouth of the canyon. United States Board on Geographic Names (1974b, p. 2) approved the name "Bob Rabbit Place" and gave the name "Roberts" as a variant; the Board noted that Robert Roberts, known as Bob Rabbit, was an Indian who hunted cottontail rabbits in the neighborhood.

Bobs Flat [FRESNO]: *area,* 4 miles north of Trimmer (lat. 36°57'55" N, long. 119°17'40" W; near NE cor. sec. 24, T 11 S, R 24 E). Named on Trimmer (1965) 7.5' quadrangle.

Bobs Lake [FRESNO]: *lake,* 1500 feet long, 9.5 miles northwest of Mount Abbot (lat. 37°28'30" N, long. 118°55' W). Named on Mount Abbot (1953) 15' quadrangle. United States Board on Geographic Names (1969a, p. 5) approved the name "Warrior Lake" for the feature.

Bob Spring [KERN]: *spring,* 5.5 miles east-southeast of Caliente (lat. 35°15'25" N, long. 118°32'05" W; sec. 3, T 31 S, R 32 E). Named on Oiler Peak (1972) 7.5' quadrangle.

Bodfish [KERN]: *town,* 32 miles east-northeast of Bakersfield (lat. 35°35'20" N, long. 118°29'15" W; around SE cor. sec. 12, T 27 S, R 32 E). Named on Lake Isabella South (1972) 7.5' quadrangle. Called Vaughn on Kernville (1908) 30' quadrangle, which shows Bodfish P.O. at the place. Postal authorities established Bodfish post office in 1892, discontinued it in 1895, and reestablished it in 1906 (Salley, p. 24). The name Bodfish is for George Homer Bodfish, who came to California about 1867 (Hanna, p. 36). Postal authorities established Vaughn post office 5 miles south of Isabella post office in 1897 and discontinued it in 1906, when they moved it to Bodfish; they established Borel post office 2.5 miles southwest of Vaughn post office in 1904 and discontinued it in 1908—the name "Vaughn" was for Edward Vaughn, first postmaster, and the name "Borel" was from Borel Canal Construction Company (Salley, p. 25, 230).

Bodfish Canyon [KERN]: *canyon,* 6.25 miles long, drained by Bodfish Creek above a point 2 miles east-southeast of Bodfish (lat. 35° 34'50" N, long. 118°27'20" W; sec. 17, T 27 S, R 33 E). Named on Lake Isabella South (1972) 7.5' quadrangle.

Bodfish Creek [KERN]: *stream,* flows 9 miles to Kern River less than 1 mile north-north-west of Bodfish (lat. 35°36' N, long. 118° 29'45" W; near N line sec. 12, T 27 S, R 32 E); the stream drains Bodfish Canyon. Named on Lake Isabella South (1972) 7.5' quadrangle.

Bodfish Peak [KERN]: *peak,* 3.25 miles southeast of Bodfish (lat. 35°33' N, long. 118°27'10" W; sec. 29, T 27 S, R 33 E). Altitude 6038 feet. Named on Lake Isabella South (1972) 7.5' quadrangle.

Bog Creek: see **Ferguson Creek** [TULARE].

Boggs Slough [KINGS]: *water feature,* extends for 4 miles from near North Fork Kings River to Fresno Slough 10 miles northwest of Lemoore (lat. 36°23'40" N, long. 119°55'15" W; near W line sec. 4, T 18 S, R 19 E). Named on Burrel (1954) and Vanguard (1956) 7.5' quadrangles.

Boggy Meadow [FRESNO]: *area,* 11 miles east-northeast of Kaiser Peak (lat. 37°22'30" N, long. 119°00'30" W). Named on Kaiser (1904) 30' quadrangle. Water of Lake Thomas A. Edison now covers the place.

Boggy Meadow [MADERA]:

(1) *area,* 7.5 miles north-northeast of Yosemite Forks along Big Creek (lat. 37°27'30" N, long. 119°33' W; sec. 34, T 5 S, R 22 E). Named on Bass Lake (1953) 15' quadrangle. Called Boggy Meadows on Mariposa (1912) 30' quadrangle.

(2) *area,* 5.25 miles northeast of Shuteye Peak (lat. 37°24'10" N, long. 119°21'30" W; on W line sec. 16, T 6 S, R 24 E). Named on Shuteye Peak (1953) 15' quadrangle.

Bog Hole Spring [KERN]: *spring,* 3.25 miles north-northeast of Democrat Hot Springs (lat. 35°34' N, long. 118°38' W). Named on Democrat Hot Springs (1972) 7.5' quadrangle.

Bohna Creek [KERN]: *stream,* flows 2.5 miles to Cedar Creek 4.25 miles east-southeast of Glennville (lat. 35°42'50" N, long. 118°37'35" W; near NE cor. sec. 34, T 25 S, R 31 E). Named on Alta Sierra (1972) and Glennville (1972) 7.5' quadrangles.

Bohna Peak [KERN]: *peak,* 6.5 miles east-northeast of Glennville (lat. 35°45'35" N, long. 118°35'35" W; at N line sec. 13, T 25 S, R 31 E). Named on California Hot Springs (1958) 15' quadrangle.

Boiler Spring [KERN]: *spring,* nearly 7 miles east of Caliente (lat. 35°16'15" N, long. 118°30'30" W; sec. 35, T 30 S, R 32 E). Named on Oiler Peak (1972) 7.5' quadrangle. The name is for a small boiler that was abandoned at the place (Bailey, 1962, p. 17).

Boiler Spring: see **Lower Boiler Spring** [KERN].

Bolsillo Campground [FRESNO]: *locality,* 8 miles east of Kaiser Peak (lat. 37°18'50" N, long. 119°02'30" W); the place is along Bolsillo Creek. Named on Kaiser Peak (1953) 15' quadrangle.

Bolsillo Creek [FRESNO]: *stream,* flows 3 miles to South Fork San Joaquin River 9 miles east-northeast of Kaiser Peak (lat. 37°19'45" N, long. 119°01'55" W). Named on Kaiser Peak (1953) 15' quadrangle.

Bolton Brown: see **Mount Bolton Brown** [FRESNO].

Bonanza Gulch [KERN]: *canyon,* drained by a stream that flows 3.5 miles to Last Chance Canyon 5.25 miles north of Saltdale (lat. 35° 26' N, long. 117°53'30" W). Named on Garlock (1967) and Saltdale NW (1967) 7.5' quadrangles. The canyon had rich gold placers in 1893 (Wynn, 1963, p. 64).

Bond Creek [TULARE]: *stream,* flows 7.5 miles to South Fork Tule River 7.25 miles south-southeast of Springville (lat. 36°02'15" N, long. 118°45'25" W). Named on California Hot Springs (1958), Camp Nelson (1956), and Springville (1957) 15' quadrangles.

Bone Canyon [TULARE]: *canyon,* drained by a stream that flows 1 mile to lowlands 4.5 miles north of Woodlake (lat. 36°28'45" N, long. 119°05'30" W; sec. 6, T 17 S, R 27 E). Named on Woodlake (1952) 7.5' quadrangle.

Bone Creek [TULARE]: *stream,* flows 5 miles to Nobe Young Creek 11 miles northeast of California Hot Springs (lat. 35°59'55" N, long. 118°02'10" W; sec. 20, T 22 S, R 32 E). Named on California Hot Springs (1958) and Camp Nelson (1956) 15' quadrangles.

Bone Meadow [TULARE]: *area,* 9 miles north-northeast of California Hot Springs (lat. 35°59'45" N, long. 118°36'30" W; near NE cor. sec. 27, T 22 S, R 31 E); the place is at the head of Bone Creek. Named on California Hot Springs (1958) 15' quadrangle.

Boneyard Meadow [FRESNO]: *area,* 3 miles east of the town of Big Creek (lat. 37°12' N, long. 119°11'10" W; on S line sec. 25, T 8 S, R 25 E). Named on Huntington Lake (1953) 15' quadrangle. The name is from the bones of sheep that died at the place during a heavy spring snowstorm in the 1870's (Browning 1986, p. 23).

Bonita [MADERA]: *locality,* 8 miles west of Madera (lat. 36°57'10" N, long. 120°12'05" W; near NE cor. sec. 27, T 11 S, R 16 E). Named on Bonita Ranch (1963) 7.5' quadrangle.

Bonita Creek [TULARE]: *stream,* flows 1.5 miles to Rattlesnake Creek (3) 13 miles south-southeast of Hockett Peak (lat. 36°02'30" N, long. 118°18'10" W). Named on Hockett Peak (1956) 15' quadrangle.

Bonita Flat [TULARE]: *area,* 9 miles south-southeast of Hockett Peak (lat. 36°06' N, long. 118°20'30" W; sec. 18, T 21 S, R 34 E). Named on Hockett Peak (1956) 15' quadrangle.

Bonita Meadows [TULARE]: *area,* 13 miles south-southeast of Hockett Peak (lat. 36°02'20" N, long. 118°19'50" W); the place is at the head of Bonita Creek. Named on Hockett Peak (1956) 15' quadrangle.

Bonnie Lake [FRESNO]: *lake,* 600 feet long, 0.5 mile west-northwest of Kaiser Peak (lat. 37°17'50" N, long. 119°11'40" W; near S line sec. 24, T 7 S, R 25 E). Named on Kaiser Peak (1953) 15' quadrangle.

Bonsall Hill [TULARE]: *ridge,* west-trending, 1 mile long, 7.5 miles south-southwest of Springville (lat. 36°01'35" N, long. 118°52'05" W). Named on Globe (1956) 7.5' quadrangle.

Boone Lake: see **Pine Flat Reservoir** [FRESNO].

Boone Meadow [TULARE]: *area,* 10.5 miles east-northeast of Fairview along Trout Creek (lat. 35°59'50" N, long. 118°19'45" W; sec. 20, T 22 S, R 34 E). Named on Kernville (1956) 15' quadrangle.

Bootleg Canyon [KERN]: *canyon,* drained by a stream that flows 2 miles to Oak Creek Canyon 7.5 miles south of Tehachapi (lat. 35° 01'10" N, long. 118°25'40" W; sec. 25, T 11 N, R 15 W). Named on Tehachapi South (1966) 7.5' quadrangle.

Boreal Plateau [TULARE]: *area,* 10 miles north-northwest of Kern Peak (lat. 36°26'30" N, long. 118°21' W). Named on Kern Peak (1956) 15' quadrangle. Oliver Kehrlein suggested the name to reflect the frigid, windswept nature of the place (Browning 1986, p. 23).

Borel: see **Bodfish** [KERN].

Borel Canyon [KERN]: *canyon,* drained by a stream that flows 5.25 miles to Adobe Canyon 2.5 miles east of Knob Hill (lat. 35°33'20" N, long. 118°54'05" W; sec. 30, T 27 S, R 29 E). Named on Knob Hill (1965) 7.5' quadrangle.

Boron [KERN]: *town,* 15 miles east-southeast of Castle Butte (lat. 35°00'05" N, long. 117°38'55" W; sec. 31, 32, T 11 N, R 7 W). Named on Boron (1973) and Leuhman Ridge (1973) 7.5' quadrangles. Postal authorities established Boron post office in 1938; the name is from the borate mines nearby (Salley, p. 25). Kramer (1942) 15' quadrangle has the name "Amargo" at the site.

Boron: see **Baker** [KERN].

Borreguero Spring [FRESNO]: *spring,* 2.5 miles south of Ciervo Mountain along Arroyo Hondo (lat. 36°25'40" N, long. 120°34'35" W; sec. 29, T 17 S, R 13 E). Named on Ciervo Mountain (1969) 7.5' quadrangle.

Borrough: see **Burrough Valley** [FRESNO].

Boulder Canyon [KERN]:

(1) *canyon,* drained by a stream that flows 6.25 miles to Sage Canyon 6 miles east of Skinner Peak (lat. 35°33'30" N, long. 118° 01'05" W). Named on Horse Canyon (1972) and Walker Pass (1972) 7.5' quadrangles.

(2) *canyon,* drained by a stream that flows 1.5 miles to Indian Wells Valley 10.5 miles north-northwest of Inyokern (lat. 35°47'10" N, long. 118°53'50" W; near SW cor. sec. 4, T 25 S, R 38 E). Named on Little Lake (1954) 15' quadrangle.

Boulder Creek [FRESNO]: *stream,* flows 4.5 miles to Florence Lake 14 miles northwest of Blackcap Mountain (lat. 37°14'35" N, long. 118°56'45" W; sec, 18, T 8 S, R 28 E). Named on Blackcap Mountain (1953) 15' quadrangle.

Boulder Creek [FRESNO-TULARE]: *stream,* heads in Tulare County and flows 11.5 miles to South Fork Kings River 6 miles east-north-east of Hume in Fresno County (lat. 36°48'35" N, long. 118° 48'35" W). Named on Giant Forest (1956) and Tehipite Dome (1952) 15' quadrangles. The stream was called Glacier Creek in the 1860's and 1870's (Forest M. Clingan, personal communication, 1990).

Boulder Creek [TULARE]: *stream,* flows 3 miles to South Fork of Middle Fork Tule River 2 miles east of Camp Nelson (lat. 36°08'15" N, long. 118°34'25" W; near W line sec. 36, T 20 S, R 31 E). Named on Camp Nelson (1956) 15' quadrangle.

Boulder Creek: see **Little Boulder Creek** [FRESNO].

Boulder Gulch [KERN]: *canyon,* drained by a stream that flows 1.5 miles to Last Chance Canyon 5.25 miles north of Saltdale (lat. 35° 26'10" N, long. 117°53'05" W). Named on Saltdale NW (1967) 7.5' quadrangle.

Boulder Gulch Campground [KERN]: *locality,* 2.5 miles south-southwest of Wofford Heights (lat. 35°40'20" N, long. 118°28'10" W; near NE cor. sec. 18, T 26 S, R 33 E). Named on Lake Isabella North (1972) 7.5' quadrangle.

Boulder Hill [KINGS]: *peak,* 10 miles south-southeast of Kettleman City (lat. 35°51'55" N, long. 119°54'40" W; sec. 3, T 24 S, R 19 E). Named on Avenal Gap (1954) 7.5' quadrangle. The name refers to conglomerate that covers the peak (United States Board on Geographic Names, 1933b, p. 5).

Boulder Spring [KERN]: *spring,* 5.5 miles east of Skinner Peak (lat. 35°34'45" N, long. 118°01'40" W); the spring is in Boulder Canyon (1). Named on Horse Canyon (1972) 7.5' quadrangle. Called Boulder Springs on

Kernville (1908) 30' quadrangle.

Boundary Creek [MADERA]: *stream,* flows 2 miles to Middle Fork San Joaquin River 1.25 miles south of Devils Postpile (lat. 37°36'15" N, long. 119°04'35" W); the mouth of the stream is near the east boundary of Devils Postpile National Monument. Named on Devils Postpile (1953) 15' quadrangle.

Boust City: see **Taft Heights** [KERN].

Bowen: see **Joe Bowen Canyon** [TULARE].

Bowerbank [KERN]: *locality,* 3.5 miles east of Buttonwillow along Southern Pacific Railroad (lat. 35°23'55" N, long. 119°24'30" W; at N line sec. 21, T 29 S, R 24 E). Named on Buttonwillow (1954) 7.5' quadrangle.

Bowles [FRESNO]: *village,* 11 miles south of downtown Fresno (lat. 36°36'10" N, long. 119°45'05" W; near NW cor. sec. 25, T 15 S, R 20 E). Named on Caruthers (1963) and Conejo (1963) 7.5' quadrangles. Postal authorities established Bowles post office in 1904 and discontinued it in 1943 (Frickstad, p. 31). The name is from a pioneer family in the region (Hanna, p. 39).

Boyden Cave [FRESNO]: *cave,* 6 miles east-northeast of Hume along South Fork Kings River (lat. 36°48'55" N, long. 118°49' W). Named on Tehipite Dome (1952) 15' quadrangle. Pete Boyden discovered the cave (Gudde, 1969, p. 36).

Bracchi Spring [KERN]: *spring,* nearly 3 miles south-southwest of Piute Peak (lat. 35°24'50" N, long. 118°24'45" W; sec. 11, T 29 S, R 33 E). Named on Piute Peak (1972) 7.5' quadrangle.

Bradford Mountain [FRESNO]: *ridge,* northwest-trending, 1 mile long, 3 miles north-northeast of Trimmer (lat. 36°56'45" N, long. 119°17'10" W; mainly in sec. 30, T 11 S, R 25 E). Named on Trimmer (1965) 7.5' quadrangle.

Bradley: see **Mount Bradley** [TULARE].

Bradley Canyon [KERN]: *canyon,* drained by a stream that flows 2.5 miles to Black Bob Canyon 7.5 miles west-northwest of Lebec (lat. 34°52'25" N, long. 118°59'30" W; near W line sec. 10, T 9 N, R 20 W). Named on Cuddy Valley (1943) and Frazier Mountain (1958) 7.5' quadrangles.

Bradshaw Creek [KERN]: *stream,* flows 5 miles to Lilly Canyon 1.5 miles west of Miracle Hot Springs (lat. 35°34'45" N, long. 118° 33'30" W). Named on Alta Sierra (1972) and Miracle Hot Springs (1972) 7.5' quadrangles.

Bradys [KERN]: *locality,* 5 miles northwest of Inyokern (lat. 35°42'05" N, long. 117°52'05" W; near E line sec. 3, T 26 S, R 38 E). Named on Inyokern (1943) 15' quadrangle.

Braitman Spring [KERN]: *spring,* 8.5 miles northwest of Cross Mountain (lat. 35°22'25" N, long. 118°14'15" W; sec. 32, T 29 S, R 35 E). Named on Cross Mountain (1972) 7.5' quadrangle.

Brave Lake [FRESNO]: *lake,* 950 feet long, 11.5

miles northwest of Mount Abbot (lat. 37°29'15" N, long. 118°56'45" W). Named on Mount Abbot (1953) 15' quadrangle.

Bravo Lake [TULARE]: *lake*, 1 mile long, at southeast edge of Woodlake (lat. 36°24'30" N, long. 119°05'30" W; sec. 31, T 17 S, R 27 E). Named on Woodlake (1952, photorevised 1969) 7.5' quadrangle. Called Wood Lake on Lemon Cove (1928) 7.5' quadrangle. According to local tradition, the name "Bravo Lake" was given by Indians who saw a fight between two Irishmen by the lake—*bravo* means "brave" in Spanish (Hanna, p. 358).

Breckenridge Campground [KERN]: *locality*, 10 miles east-northeast of Mount Adelaide (lat. 35°28' N, long. 118°34'50" W; sec. 30, T 28 S, R 32 E); the place is near the northeast end of Breckenridge Mountain. Named on Breckenridge Mountain (1972) 7.5' quadrangle.

Breckenridge Lodge: see **Breckenridge Meadows** [KERN].

Breckenridge Meadows [KERN]: *area*, about 8 miles east-northeast of Mount Adelaide (lat. 35°28' N, long. 118°36'25" W; sec. 26, T 28 S, R 31 E); the place is 1.25 miles west of Breckenridge Mountain. Named on Breckenridge Mountain (1972) 7.5' quadrangle. Breckenridge Mountain (1943) 15' quadrangle shows the abandoned Breckenridge Lodge at the place.

Breckenridge Mountain [KERN]: *ridge*, generally southwest-trending, 2.25 miles long, 9 miles east of Mount Adelaide (lat. 35°27'30" N, long. 118°35'05" W). Named on Breckenridge Mountain (1972) 7.5' quadrangle. Called Mt. Breckenridge on Olmsted's (1900) map, and called Canon Mt. on Williamson's (1853) map. The peak also was known as Cross Mountain (Wines, p. 86). The name "Breckenridge" was applied at the time of the Civil War, presumably by Southern sympathizers to honor John C. Breckenridge of Kentucky, who was a presidential candidate in the election of 1860 (Bailey, 1962, p. 74).

Breeze Lake [MADERA]: *lake*, 1600 feet long, 4 miles south of Merced Peak (lat. 37°34'35" N, long. 11??'3'30" W). Named on Merced Peak (1953 quadrangle. Lieutenant H.C. Benson named the lake for William H. Breeze of Breeze Creek (United States Board on Geographic Names, 1934a, p. 3).

Bretz Mill [FRESNO]: *settlement*, 8 miles southwest of Dinkey Dome in Blue Canyon (1) (lat. 37°02'20" N, long. 119°14'30" W; near NW cor. sec. 27, T 10 S, R 25 E). Named on Huntington Lake (1953) 15' quadrangle.

Bretz Mill: see **Old Bretz Mill** [FRESNO].

Brewer: see **Mount Brewer** [TULARE].

Brewer Creek [TULARE]: *stream*, flows 4.5 miles to Roaring River 7.5 miles north-north-west of Triple Divide Peak (lat. 36°42' N, long. 118°33'35" W); the stream heads near Mount Brewer. Named on Mount Whitney (1956)

and Triple Divide Peak (1956) 15' quadrangles.

Brewer Lake [FRESNO]: *lake*, 600 feet long, 3.5 miles north of Dinkey Dome (lat. 37°10' N, long. 119°07'20" W; sec. 10, T 9 S, R 26 E). Named on Huntington Lake (1953) 7.5' quadrangle.

Brewer Lake: see **Big Brewer Lake** [TULARE]; **East Lake** [TULARE].

Bridge: see **El Prado** [FRESNO] (1).

Bridge Camps [TULARE]: *locality*, 4.5 miles east of Yucca Mountain along Marble Fork Kaweah River (lat. 36°34'40" N, long. 118° 47'20" W). Named on Tehipite (1903) 30' quadrangle.

Bright Star Canyon [KERN]: *canyon*, 9 miles long, along Kelso Creek, and a branch of that creek, above a point 3.5 miles west-northwest of Pinyon Mountain (lat. 35°29' N, long. 118°12'45" W). Named on Claraville (1972), Pinyon Mountain (1972), and Woolstalf Creek (1972) 7.5' quadrangles.

Brights Valley: see **Brite Valley** [KERN].

Brin Canyon [TULARE]: *canyon*, drained by a stream that flows 2.5 miles to Kern River 1.5 miles northeast of Fairview (lat. 35°56'45" N, long. 118°28'35" W). Named on Kernville (1956) 15' quadrangle.

Brinn Canyon: see **Gold Ledge Creek** [TULARE].

Brite Creek [KERN]: *stream*, flows 10 miles to Tehachapi Creek 2.5 miles northwest of Tehachapi (lat. 35°09'25" N, long. 118°28'30" W; sec. 7, T 32 S, R 33 E). Named on Cummings Mountain (1966), Keene (1966), Tehachapi North (1966), and Tehachapi South (1966) 7.5' quadrangles.

Brite Valley [KERN]: *valley*, 5.5 miles northnortheast of Cummings Mountain (lat. 35°07' N, long. 118°32'30" W). Named on Cummings Mountain (1966) and Keene (1966) 7.5' quadrangles. Goodyear (1888a, p. 310) called the feature Brights Valley. The name "Brite" is for John M. Brite, who settled in the valley in 1857 (Boyd, p. 172).

Broad Creek [KERN]: *stream*, heads in Midway Valley and flows 9 miles to end in Buena Vista Valley 5 miles northeast of Taft (lat. 35°11'55" N, long. 119°23'50" W; sec. 28, T 31 S, R 24 E). Named on Fellows (1951) and Taft (1950) 7.5' quadrangles.

Broder Meadows [TULARE]: *area*, 3.5 miles south of Monache Mountain (lat. 36°09'15" N, long. 118°11'15" W; in and near sec. 28, T 20 S, R 35 E). Named on Monache Mountain (1956) 15' quadrangle.

Broken Hill [KINGS]: *peak*, 2.5 miles southsouthwest of Kettleman City (lat. 35°58'20" N, long. 119°58'45" W; sec. 36, T 22 S, R 18 E). Altitude 715 feet. Named on Los Viejos (1954) 7.5' quadrangle. The name refers to strata that are broken by faults (United States Board on Geographic Names, 1933b, p. 6).

Bronco Canyon [KERN]:

(1) *canyon*, drained by a stream that flows 3.25 miles to lowlands 9 miles southwest of Liebre Twins (lat. 34°51'30" N, long. 118°40'20" W; sec. 22, T 9 N, R 17 W). Named on La Liebre Ranch (1965) and Winters Ridge (1966) 7.5' quadrangles.

(2) *canyon*, drained by a stream that flows 5.5 miles to El Paso Creek 7 miles west-north-west of Liebre Twins (lat. 34°59'25" N, long. 118°40'50" W; sec. 34, T 11 N, R 17 W). Named on Liebre Twins (1965) and Winters Ridge (1966) 7.5' quadrangles.

Bronge [FRESNO]: *locality*, 4.25 miles southsoutheast of Clovis along Fresno Interurban Railroad (lat. 36°45'55" N, long. 119°40'55" W; near NE cor. sec. 33, T 13 S, R 21 E). Named on Clovis (1922) 7.5' quadrangle.

Brown [KERN]: *locality*, 9 miles north-north-west of Inyokern along Southern Pacific Railroad (lat. 35°46'30" N, long. 117°51'W; near E line sec. 11, T 25 S, R 38 E); the place is 8.5 miles east-northeast of Owens Peak. Named on Little Lake (1954) 15' quadrangle. Postal authorities established Brown post office in 1909, changed the name to Mount Owen in 1948, and discontinued it in 1950 (Frickstad, p. 54, 57). The place first was called Siding 18 and was along the rail line built to carry supplies for construction of the aqueduct that takes Owens Valley water from Inyo County to Los Angeles; the name "Brown" was for George Brown, who built a hotel at the site (Hensher and Peskin, p. 32). The place also was known as Front (Wines, p. 86).

Brown: see **Mount Bolton Brown** [FRESNO].

Brown Bear Lake [FRESNO]: *lake*, 1650 feet long, 3 miles south-southwest of Mount Abbot (lat. 37°20'45" N, long. 118°48'35" W). Named on Mount Abbot (1953) 15' quadrangle. Employees of California Department of Fish and Game named the lake in the 1950's (Browning 1986, p. 27).

Brown Butte [KERN]: *hill*, 11.5 miles northeast of Rosamond (lat. 34°59'05" N, long. 118°01'55" W; at S line sec. 3, T 10 N, R 11 W). Altitude 2906 feet. Named on Bissell (1973) 7.5' quadrangle.

Brown Canyon: see **Browns Canyon** [KERN].

Brown Cone [FRESNO]: *peak*, 8 miles northnorthwest of Kaiser Peak (lat. 37°24'15" N, long. 119°13'55" W; sec. 15, T 6 S, R 25 E). Altitude 7130 feet. Named on Kaiser Peak (1953) 15' quadrangle.

Brown Cow Camp [TULARE]: *locality*, 3 miles west-northwest of Olancha Peak (lat. 36°16'30" N, long. 118°10' W; sec. 15, T 19 S, R 35 E); the place is in Brown Meadow. Named on Olancha (1956) 15' quadrangle.

Brown Flat [TULARE]: *area*, 3 miles east-southeast of Auckland (lat. 36°34'25" N, long. 119°03'20" W; sec. 32, T 15 S, R 27 E). Named on Auckland (1966) 7.5' quadrangle.

Brown Meadow [KERN]: *area*, 2.25 miles

north-northwest of Piute Peak along Clear Creek (1) (lat. 35°29' N, long. 118°24'15" W; sec. 23, T 28 S, R 35 E); the place is 1 mile east of Brown Peak. Named on Piute Peak (1972) 7.5' quadrangle.

Brown Meadow [TULARE]: *area*, 3 miles westnorthwest of Olancha Peak (lat. 36°17'15" N, long. 118°09'55" W); Brown Cow Camp is at the place. Named on Olancha (1956) 15' quadrangle.

Brown Mountain [TULARE]: *peak*, 3.5 miles west of Olancha Peak (lat. 36°15'35" N, long. 118°10'45" W; sec. 22, T 19 S, R 35 E). Altitude 9958 feet. Named on Olancha (1956) 15' quadrangle.

Brown Peak [FRESNO]: *peak*, 4.25 miles east of Dinkey Dome (lat. 37°07'30" N, long. 119°03'20" W; on N line sec. 29, T 9 S, R 27 E). Altitude 10,349 feet. Named on Huntington Lake (1953) 15' quadrangle.

Brown Peak [KERN]: *peak*, 3 miles northwest of Piute Peak (lat. 35° 29'05" N, long. 118°25'25" W; near N line sec. 22, T 28 S, R 33 E). Altitude 8095 feet. Named on Piute Peak (1972) 7.5' quadrangle. The name commemorates Charlie Brown, a miner who lived in the neighborhood in the early 1900's (United States Board on Geographic Names, 1975b, p. 8).

Brown's: see **North Fork** [MADERA].

Browns Canyon [KERN]: *canyon*, 1.5 miles long, 6 miles west-southwest of McKittrick on Kern-San Luis Obispo county line (lat 35°16' N, long. 119°43' W; in and near sec. 33, T 30 S, R 21 E). Named on Reward (1951) 7.5' quadrangle. Called Brown Canyon on Arnold and Johnson's (1910) map.

Browns Creek [MADERA]: *stream*, flows 5.5 miles to join Sand Creek and form Willow Creek (2) 5 miles southwest of Shuteye Peak (lat. 37°17'55" N, long. 119°29'40" W; near NE cor. sec. 30, T 7 S, R 23 E); the stream heads at Browns Meadow. Named on Shuteye Peak (1953) 15' quadrangle.

Browns Meadow [MADERA]: *area*, 1 mile southwest of Shuteye Peak (lat. 37°20'20" N, long. 119°26'25" W; sec. 10, T 7 S, R 23 E); the place is at the head of Browns Creek. Named on Shuteye Peak (1953) 15' quadrangle.

Browns Mill [KERN]: *locality*, 5 miles southsouthwest of Alta Sierra (lat. 35°39'25" N, long. 118°34'15" W; near NE cor. sec. 19, T 26 S, R 32 E). Site named on Alta Sierra (1972) 7.5' quadrangle.

Brown Spring [KERN]: *spring*, 4.25 miles eastsoutheast of Weldon (lat. 35°36'50" N, long. 118°15'10" W; near NW cor. sec. 5, T 27 S, R 35 E). Named on Woolstalf Creek (1972) 7.5' quadrangle.

Brown Valley: see **Indian Wells Valley** [KERN].

Broza Ridge [KERN]: *ridge*, generally north-northwest-trending, 1 mile long, 6.5 miles east of Caliente (lat. 35°17'30" N, long. 118°

30'55" W). Named on Oiler Peak (1972) 7.5' quadrangle.

Bruce: see **Mount Bruce**, under **Merced Peak** [MADERA].

Brush Canyon [FRESNO]: *canyon,* drained by a stream that flows 2.5 miles to Middle Fork Kings River nearly 6 miles northeast of Hume (lat. 36°51' N, long. 118°51'10" W). Named on Tehipite Dome (1952) 15' quadrangle.

Brush Creek [TULARE]: *stream,* flows 8.5 miles to Kern River 3 miles north-northeast of Fairview (lat. 35°57'55" N, long. 118°28'45" W; sec. 36, T 22 S, R 32 E). Named on Kernville (1956) 15' quadrangle.

Brush Creek: see **Little Brush Creek**, under **Cannell Creek** [KERN-TULARE].

Brush Meadow [FRESNO]: *area,* 7.5 miles south-southeast of Dinkey Dome (lat. 37°00'45" N, long. 119°04'50" W; near SE cor. sec. 36, T 10 S, R 26 E). Named on Huntington Lake (1953) 15' quadrangle.

Brush Meadow [TULARE]: *area,* 4.5 miles northeast of Monache Mountain (lat. 36°15' N, long. 118°08' W). Named on Monache Mountain (1956) and Olancha (1956) 15' quadrangles.

Brush Mountain [KERN]: *peak,* 5.5 miles west-southwest of Eagle Rest Peak (lat. 34°53'10" N, long. 119°13'35" W; at NW cor. sec. 10, T 9 N, R 22 W). Named on Eagle Rest Peak (1942) 7.5' quadrangle.

Brushy Hill [KERN]: *peak,* 5 miles south-southwest of Knob Hill (lat. 35°30'20" N, long. 118°59'55" W; sec. 7, T 28 S, R 28 E). Named on Knob Hill (1965) 7.5' quadrangle.

Bryanthus Lake: see **Bullfrog Lake** [FRESNO] (2).

Bubbs Creek [FRESNO-TULARE]: *stream,* heads in Tulare County and flows 18 miles to South Fork Kings River 12 miles south of Marion Peak in Fresno County (lat. 36°47'20" N, long. 118°33' W). Named on Mount Whitney (1907) 30' quadrangle, and on Marion Peak (1953) and Mount Pinchot (1953) 15' quadrangles. The name commemorates John Bubbs, who crossed Kearsarge Pass with a party of prospectors in 1864 (Hanna, p. 42).

Buchanan: see **Eastman Lake** [MADERA].

Buchanan Hollow: see **Eastman Lake** [MADERA].

Buchanan Reservoir: see **Eastman Lake** [MADERA].

Buck Camp [MADERA]: *locality,* 7.25 miles southwest of Merced Peak (lat. 37°33'50" N, long. 119°29'20" W; near N line sec. 30, T 4 S, R 23 E); the place is along Buck Creek. Named on Mount Lyell (1901) 30' quadrangle. The name supposedly is from the so-called buck privates who were on army duty at the place (Browning, 1988, p. 17).

Buck Canyon [TULARE]:

(1) *canyon,* 2.5 miles long, along Buck Creek above a point 6 miles west-southwest of Triple

Divide Peak (lat. 36°34' N, long. 118° 38' W). Named on Triple Divide Peak (1956) 15' quadrangle.

(2) *canyon,* drained by a stream that flows 1 mile to Dry Creek (1) nearly 6 miles east-southeast of Auckland (lat. 36°33' N, long. 119°00'45" W; sec. 11, T 16 S, R 27 E). Named on Auckland (1966) 7.5' quadrangle.

Buck Creek [MADERA]: *stream,* flows 2.25 miles to South Fork Merced River 8 miles southwest of Merced Peak (lat. 37°32'30" N, long. 119°29'10" W); Buck Camp is along the stream.. Named on Merced Peak (1953) 15' quadrangle.

Buck Creek [TULARE]: *stream,* flows 6.5 miles to Middle Fork Kaweah River 8.5 miles west-southwest of Triple Divide Peak (lat. 36°32'20" N, long. 118°40'10" W). Named on Triple Divide Peak (1956) 15' quadrangle.

Buckeye Creek [TULARE]: *stream,* flows less than 1 mile to Cottonwood Creek 0.5 mile north of Auckland (lat. 36°35'50" N, long. 119°06'15" W; near W line sec. 25, T 15 S, R 26 E). Named on Auckland (1966) 7.5' quadrangle.

Buckeye Flat [TULARE]:

(1) *area,* 7 miles east-southeast of Yucca Mountain along Middle Fork Kaweah River (lat. 36°31'15" N, long. 118°45'45" W). Named on Giant Forest (1956) 15' quadrangle.

(2) *area,* 5 miles north of Woodlake (lat. 36°29'20" N, long. 119° 05'25" W; on E line sec. 36, T 16 S, R 26 E). Named on Woodlake (1952) 7.5' quadrangle.

Buckeye Gulch [TULARE]: *canyon,* drained by a stream that flows 1.5 miles to North Fork Tule River 2.25 miles north-northeast of Springville (lat. 36°09'35" N, long. 118°48' W; sec. 26, T 20 S, R 29 E). Named on Springville (1957) 7.5' quadrangle.

Buckeye Mountain [MADERA]: *ridge,* north-west- to west-trending, 3 miles long, 7 miles southwest of Yosemite Forks (lat. 37°18'10" N, long. 119°43'40" W). Named on Bass Lake (1953) and Mariposa (1947) 15' quadrangles.

Buckeye Spring [FRESNO]: *spring,* 11 miles south-southwest of Coalinga (lat. 36°00'05" N, long. 120°26'20" W; near W line sec. 23, T 22 S, R 14 E). Named on Curry Mountain (1969) 7.5' quadrangle.

Buckey Spring [KERN]: *spring,* 2 miles north-east of Caliente (lat. 35°18'50" N, long. 118°36'20" W). Named on Oiler Peak (1972) 7.5' quadrangle.

Buckhorn Lake [KERN]: *dry lake,* 4 miles south-southwest of Edwards at Kern-Los Angeles county line (lat. 34°49'45" N, long. 117°58'30" W). Named on Redman (1973) 7.5' quadrangle. Johnson's (1911) map shows Buckhorn Springs located about 2 miles east-northeast of the center of Buckhorn Lake (sec. 27, T 9 N, R 10 W).

Buckhorn Springs: see **Buckhorn Lake** [KERN].

Buck Meadow [FRESNO]: *area,* about 8.5 miles

south-southeast of Dinkey Dome along Deer Creek (3) (lat. 37°00'20" N, long. 119° 03'45" W; near E line sec. 6, T 11 S, R 27 E). Named on Huntington Lake (1953) 15' quadrangle.

Buck Meadow [TULARE]: *area*, 1.5 miles west of Olancha Peak (lat. 36°16'10" N, long. 118°08'45" W). Named on Olancha (1956) 15' quadrangle.

Buck Peak [FRESNO]: *peak*, 11 miles south of Marion Peak (lat. 36° 48'15" N, long. 118°33'25" W). Altitude 8776 feet. Named on Marion Peak (1953) 15' quadrangle.

Buck Peak [TULARE]:

(1) *peak*, 5.25 miles east-northeast of Fountain Springs (lat. 35° 55'05" N, long. 118°49'35" W; near N line sec. 22, T 23 S, R 29 E). Altitude 2318 feet. Named on Gibbon Peak (1965) 7.5' quadrangle.

(2) *peak*, nearly 5 miles south-southwest of California Hot Springs (lat. 35°49'20" N, long. 118°43'10" W; near E line sec. 22, T 24 S, R 30 E). Named on California Hot Springs (1958) 15' quadrangle.

Buck Rock [TULARE]: *peak*, 4.5 miles northwest of Shell Mountain (lat. 36°44'10" N, long. 118°51'30" W; near E line sec. 6, T 14 S, R 29 E). Altitude 8500 feet. Named on Giant Forest (1956) 15' quadrangle. The feature originally was called Finger Rock or Finger Peak (Forest M. Clingan, personal communication, 1989).

Buck Rock Campground [TULARE]: *locality*, 3.25 miles west-northwest of Shell Mountain (lat. 36°43'10" N, long. 118°50'50" W; sec. 8, T 14 S, R 29 E); the place is 1.5 miles southsoutheast of Buck Rock. Named on Giant Forest (1956) 15' quadrangle.

Buck Rock Creek [FRESNO]: *stream*, flows 1.5 miles to Little Boulder Creek 5.5 miles eastsoutheast of Hume (lat. 36°45'10" N, long. 118°49'20" W). Named on Giant Forest (1956) 15' quadrangle.

Buck Slide [TULARE]: *relief feature*, 6 miles north of California Hot Springs (lat. 35°58' N, long. 118°41' W; near E line sec. 36, T 22 S, R 30 E). Named on California Hot Springs (1958) 15' quadrangle.

Buena Ventura Valley: see "Regional setting."

Buena Vista: see **Buttonwillow** [KERN]; **Visalia** [TULARE].

Buenavista [TULARE]: *locality*, 2.5 miles southeast of Wilsonia near the head of Redwood Creek (1) (lat. 36°42'45" N, long. 118°55' W; sec. 15, T 14 S, R 28 E). Named on Tehipite (1903) 30' quadrangle.

Buena Vista Canal Slough: see **Kern River** [KERN-TULARE].

Buena Vista Canyon [KERN]: *canyon*, 2 miles long, 9 miles west-northwest of Inyokern (lat. 35°41'20" N, long. 117°57'45" W). Named on Owens Peak (1972) 7.5' quadrangle.

Buena Vista Creek [KERN]: *stream*, flows 17 miles, mainly through Buena Vista Valley, to end 6 miles northeast of Taft at Buena Vista

Lake Bed (lat. 35°12'15" N, long. 119°23' W; sec. 27, T 31 S, R 24 E). Named on Fellows (1951), Panorama Hills (1954), Taft (1950), and West Elk Hills (1954) 7.5' quadrangles.

Buena Vista Creek [MADERA]: *stream*, heads in Madera County and flows 6 miles to Illilouette Creek 7.25 miles southeast of Yosemite Village in Mariposa County (lat. 37° 40' N, long. 119°30'05" W; near NE cor. sec. 24, T 3 S, R 22 E). Named on Merced Peak (1953) and Yosemite (1956) 15' quadrangles.

Buena Vista Creek [TULARE]: *stream*, flows 1 mile to Redwood Creek (1) 3.5 miles southeast of Wilsonia (lat. 36°42' N, long. 118° 54'40" W; near SW cor. sec. 14, T 14 S, R 28 E); the stream heads near Buena Vista Peak. Named on Giant Forest (1956) 15' quadrangle.

Buena Vista Crest [MADERA]: *ridge*, east- to northeast-trending, 4 miles long, 5 miles westsouthwest of Merced Peak (lat. 37°36' N, long. 119°28'30" W); the ridge is east of Buena Vista Peak. Named on Merced Peak (1953) 15' quadrangle.

Buena Vista Hills [KERN]: *range*, between Buena Vista Valley and Midway Valley, center 2.5 miles north-northeast of Taft (lat. 35° 10'15" N, long. 119°26' W). Named on Fellows (1951), Mouth of Kern (1950), and Taft (1950) 7.5' quadrangles. Arnold and Johnson (p. 19) proposed the name because of the proximity of the range to Buena Vista Lake.

Buena Vista Lake [MADERA]: *lake*, 1500 feet long, less than 0.5 mile north of Buena Vista Peak (lat. 37°36' N, long. 119°31' W; sec. 12, T 4 S, R 22 E). Named on Yosemite (1956) 15' quadrangle.

Buena Vista Lake: see **Buena Vista Lake Bed** [KERN].

Buena Vista Lake Bed [KERN]: *area*, dry bed of Buena Vista Lake 10 miles east-northeast of Taft (lat. 35°11'30" N, long. 119°17'30" W). Named on Mouth of Kern (1950) 7.5' quadrangle The area is called Buena Vista Lake on Millux (1954) 7.5' quadrangle. Buena Vista Lake (1912) 30' quadrangle shows a waterfilled lake 8 miles long. Pedro Fages led a group into San Joaquin Valley in 1772, and gave the name "Buena Vista" to an Indian village by the lake (Boyd, p. 2). Buena Vista Lake was fed by water of Kern River, but diversion of the water in the valley and a levee built in the basin of Buena Vista Lake allowed cultivation of part of the lake bed (Mendenhall, Dole, and Stabler, p. 96).

Buena Vista Peak [MADERA]: *peak*, 17 miles north-northeast of Yosemite Forks (lat. 37°35'40" N, long. 119°31' W; near SW cor. sec. 12, T 4 N, R 22 E). Altitude 9709 feet. Named on Yosemite (1956) 15' quadrangle.

Buena Vista Peak [TULARE]: *peak*, 3.5 miles east-southeast of Wilsonia (lat. 36°42'40" N, long. 118°53'45" W; near SE cor. sec. 14, T 14 S, R 28 E). Altitude 7603 feet. Named on Giant Forest (1956) 15' quadrangle.

Buena Vista Slough [KERN]: *water feature,* extends from near the east end of Elk Hills to Tulare County 50 miles northwest of Bakersfield. Named on Buena Vista Lake (1912) and McKittrick (1912) 30' quadrangles. The feature now is entirely confined by artificial levees, and nearly all of the water is diverted into canals (Davis, Green, Olmsted, and Brown, p. 30).

Buena Vista Valley [KERN]: *valley,* extends northwest from Buena Vista Lake Bed between Elk Hills and Buena Vista Hills. Named on Fellows (1951), Mouth of Kern (1950), Taft (1950), and West Elk Hills (1954) 7.5' quadrangles. Arnold and Johnson (p. 19) proposed the name for the proximity of the valley to Buena Vista Lake.

Buffin Meadow [MADERA]: *area,* 8.5 miles north of Yosemite Forks (lat. 37°29'20" N, long. 119°35'50" W; near N line sec. 19, T 5 S, R 22 E). Named on Bass Lake (1953) 15' quadrangle. The misspelled name is for businessman Edward Wheaton Buffum (Browning, 1986, p. 28).

Buford Mountain [MADERA]: *peak,* 2.5 miles east of Knowles (lat. 37°13'15" N, long. 119°49'50" W; sec. 19, T 8 S, R 20 E). Altitude 2066 feet. Named on Knowles (1962, photorevised 1981) 7.5' quadrangle.

Bug Table [MADERA]: *ridge,* west-northwest-trending, 0.5 mile long, 8 miles south-south-west of the town of North Fork (lat. 37° 07'45" N, long. 119°34'45" W; sec. 21, T 9 S, R 22 E). Named on North Fork (1965) 7.5' quadrangle.

Bullard: see **Figarden** [FRESNO].

Bull Creek [FRESNO]: *stream,* flows 3.5 miles to Deer Creek (3) 6.5 miles north of Balch Camp (lat. 36°59'59" N, long. 119°06' W). Named on Patterson Mountain (1952) 15' quadrangle.

Bull Creek [FRESNO-TULARE]: *stream,* heads in Fresno County and flows 9 miles to Cottonwood Creek 0.5 mile north of Auckland in Tulare County (lat. 36°35'50" N, long. 119°06'25" W; sec. 26, T 15 S, R 26 E). Named on Auckland (1966), Miramonte (1966), and Tucker Mountain (1966) 7.5' quadrangles.

Bullet Lake [FRESNO]: *lake,* 450 feet long, 2.25 miles north-northeast of Blackcap Mountain (lat. 37°06'10" N, long. 118°47' W). Named on Blackcap Mountain (1953) 15' quadrangle.

Bull Flat [KERN]: *area,* 8.5 miles north-north-east of Caliente (lat. 35°24'40" N, long. 118°34'55" W; near NE cor. sec. 18, T 20 S, R 32 E). Named on Breckenridge Mountain (1972) 7.5' quadrangle.

Bullfrog Lake [FRESNO]:
(1) *lake,* 500 feet long, 5.25 miles east-north-east of Dinkey Dome (lat. 37°08'50" N, long. 119°02'25" W; sec. 16, T 9 S, R 27 E). Named on Huntington Lake (1953) 15' quadrangle.
(2) *lake,* 1400 feet long, about 12 miles south of

Mount Pinchot (lat. 36°46'20" N, long. 118°24'10" W). Named on Mount Pinchot (1953) 15' quadrangle. John Muir called the feature Bryanthus Lake (Browning 1986, p. 28).

Bullfrog Lakes [TULARE]: *lakes,* largest 900 feet long, 4.5 miles south-southeast of Mineral King (lat. 36°23'45" N, long. 118°33'15" W). Named on Mineral King (1956) 15' quadrangle.

Bullfrog Meadow [TULARE]: *area,* 11 miles north-northwest of Olancha Peak (lat. 36°24'15" N, long. 118°13' W; on E line sec. 31, T 17 S, R 35 E). Named on Olancha (1956) 15' quadrangle.

Bull Meadow [TULARE]: *area,* 2.25 miles south-southwest of Monache Mountain (lat. 36°10'30" N, long. 118°13' W; near NW cor. sec. 20, T 20 S, R 35 E). Named on Monache Mountain (1956) 15' quadrangle.

Bullpen Canyon [KINGS]: *canyon,* drained by a stream that flows nearly 2 miles to Avenal Canyon 8.5 miles southwest of Avenal (lat. 35°54'55" N, long. 120°14' W; near W line sec. 22, T 23 S, R 16 E). Named on Garza Peak (1953) 7.5' quadrangle.

Bull Run Basin [TULARE]: *relief feature,* 10 miles southeast of California Hot Springs (lat. 35°47'55" N, long. 118°31'15" W; on E line sec. 33, T 24 S, R 32 E); the feature is along Bull Run Creek. Named on California Hot Springs (1958) 15' quadrangle.

Bull Run Creek [KERN-TULARE]: *stream,* heads in Tulare County and flows 11 miles to Kern River 2.25 miles north-northwest of Kernville in Kern County (lat. 35°46'55" N, long. 118°26'40" W; sec. 4, T 25 S, R 33 E); the stream heads near Bull Run Pass. Named on California Hot Springs (1958) and Kernville (1956) 15' quadrangles. On Kernville (1908) 30' quadrangle, the name has the form "Bullrun Creek."

Bull Run Meadow [TULARE]: *area,* 6 miles east-southeast of California Hot Springs (lat. 35°50'25" N, long. 118°34'45" W; sec. 13, T 24 S, R 31 E); the place is west of Bull Run Pass. Named on California Hot Springs (1958) 15' quadrangle.

Bull Run Pass [TULARE]: *pass,* 6 miles east-southeast of California Hot Springs (lat. 35°50'20" N, long. 118°34'35" W; near E line sec. 13, T 24 S, R 31 E). Named on California Hot Springs (1958) 15' quadrangle. Joel Carver used the name "Bull Run Pass" in the early 1880's for a stock trail from Linns Valley to Bull Run Basin (Gudde, 1949, p. 292).

Bull Run Peak [TULARE]: *peak,* 6.25 miles east-southeast of California Hot Springs (lat. 35°50' N, long. 118°34'35" W; near NE cor. sec. 24, T 24 S, R 31 E); the peak is 0.5 mile south of Bull Run Pass. Altitude 8024 feet. Named on California Hot Springs (1958) 15' quadrangle.

Bull Slough [KINGS]: *water feature,* heads at a canal and extends for 2.25 miles to another canal 21 miles east-southeast of Kettleman City (lat. 35°51'45" N, long. 119°37'05" W; at N line sec. 8, T 24 S, R 22 E). Named on Hacienda Ranch (1954) 7.5' quadrangle.

Bull Spring [KERN]:
(1) *spring,* 6 miles west-northwest of Carneros Rocks (lat. 35°28'35" N, long. 119°56'40" W; near E line sec. 20, T 28 S, R 19 E). Named on Las Yeguas Ranch (1959) 7.5' quadrangle.
(2) *spring,* 6.5 miles east-southeast of Caliente (lat. 35°16'05" N, long. 118°30'45" W; near N line sec. 2, T 31 S, R 32 E). Named on Oiler Peak (1972) 7.5' quadrangle.
(3) *spring,* 1.25 miles east of Caliente (lat. 35°17'25" N, long. 118° 36'15" W). Named on Oiler Peak (1972) 7.5' quadrangle.

Bullwheel Ridge [KINGS]: *ridge,* southeast-trending, 2 miles long, nearly 3 miles southwest of Kettleman City (lat. 35°58'25" N, long. 119°59'30" W). Named on Kettleman Plain (1953) and Los Viejos (1954) 7.5' quadrangles. The name refers to a bullwheel used in oil fields that was abandoned on the ridge (United States Board on Geographic Names, 1933b, p. 6).

Bunchgrass Flat [FRESNO]: *area,* 9 miles west of Marion Peak (lat. 36°58'15" N, long. 118°40'40" W). Named on Marion Peak (1953) 15' quadrangle.

Burford [MADERA]: *locality,* 1.5 miles north-west of Yosemite Forks (lat. 37°22'55" N, long. 119°39'10" W; sec. 27, T 6 S, R 21 E). Site named on Bass Lake (1953) 15' quadrangle.

Burham Canyon [KERN]: *canyon,* drained by a stream that flows about 4.5 miles to lowlands 8.5 miles west-northwest of Willow Springs (2) (lat. 34°57' N, long. 118°25' W; near NE cor. sec. 24, T 10 N, R 15 W). Named on Tehachapi South (1966) and Tylerhorse Canyon (1965) 7.5' quadrangles.

Burke Creek: see **Mormon Canyon** [KERN].

Burke Hill [KERN]: *peak,* 6.25 miles north-northwest of Democrat Hot Springs (lat. 35°37' N, long. 118°41'45" W; near SE cor. sec. 36, T 26 S, R 30 E). Named on Democrat Hot Springs (1972) 7.5' quadrangle.

Burkeville: see **Big Blue Mill** [KERN].

Burling [TULARE]: *locality,* 1.5 miles south of downtown Tulare along Southern Pacific Railroad (lat. 36°11'05" N, long. 119°20'35" W; sec. 14, T 20 S, R 24 E). Named on Tulare (1927) 7.5' quadrangle.

Burness [FRESNO]: *locality,* 4.5 miles south-southeast of Clovis along Atchison, Topeka and Santa Fe Railroad (lat. 36°45'55" N, long. 119°39'30" W; on S line sec 26, T 13 S, R 21 E). Named on Clovis (1964) 7.5' quadrangle.

Burning Moscow Spring [KERN]: *spring,* 4.25 miles east-northeast of Claraville (lat. 35°27'40" N, long. 118°15'20" W; sec. 30, T 28 S, R 35 E); the spring is 1.5 miles south-southeast of Burning Moscow mine. Named on Claraville (1972) 7.5' quadrangle.

Burns Flat [FRESNO]: *area,* 5.5 miles east-southeast of Dunlap (lat. 36°41'50" N, long. 119°02'05" W; near NW cor. sec. 22, T 14 S, R 27 E). Named on Miramonte (1966) 7.5' quadrangle.

Burns Meadow [FRESNO]: *area,* 13 miles west-southwest of Marion Peak (lat. 36°51'05" N, long. 118°43'30" W). Named on Marion Peak (1953) 15' quadrangle. The place was the site of Burns sheep camp about 1900 (Forest M. Clingan, personal communication, 1990).

Burns Slough: see **Lonetree Channel** [FRESNO].

Burnt Camp Creek [TULARE]: *stream,* flows 1.5 miles to South Fork Kaweah River 11.5 miles southeast of Kaweah (lat. 36°21'10" N, long. 118°46'30" W; near NE cor. sec. 24, T 18 S, R 29 E). Named on Kaweah (1957) 15' quadrangle.

Burnt Canyon [KERN]: *canyon,* drained by a stream that flows 3.5 miles to Fay Creek nearly 4 miles north-northwest of Weldon (lat. 35°43'05" N, long. 118°18'20" W). Named on Weldon (1972) 7.5' quadrangle.

Burnt Corral Creek [FRESNO]: *stream,* flows 5.5 miles to Post Corral Creek 7.5 miles northwest of Blackcap Mountain (lat. 37° 08' N, long. 118°54'10" W; sec. 22, T 9 S, R 28 E); the stream goes through Burnt Corral Meadow. Named on Blackcap Mountain (1953) 15' quadrangle.

Burnt Corral Meadow [FRESNO]: *area,* 10 miles northwest of Blackcap Mountain (lat. 37°10'15" N, long. 118°55'35" W; near SW cor. sec. 4, T 9 S, R 28 E); the place is along Burnt Corral Creek. Named on Blackcap Mountain (1953) 15' quadrangle. United States Board on Geographic Names (1983d, p. 1) rejected the form "Burnt Corral Meadows" for the name.

Burnt Corral Meadows [TULARE]: *area,* 6.5 miles west of Hockett Peak (lat. 36°13'20" N, long. 118°30' W). Named on Camp Nelson (1956) and Hockett Peak (1956) 15' quadrangles. The name is from a sheep corral that burned at the place (Browning 1986, p. 29).

Burnt House Canyon: see **Cow Canyon** [KERN].

Burnt Mountain [FRESNO]: *peak,* 11.5 miles west of Marion Peak (lat. 36°58'20" N, long. 118°43'30" W). Altitude 10,608 feet. Named on Marion Peak (1953) 15' quadrangle.

Burnt Point [TULARE]: *peak,* 2.5 miles west-northwest of Yucca Mountain (lat. 36°35' N, long. 118°54'40" W; sec. 35, T 15 S, R 28 E). Altitude 3757 feet. Named on Giant Forest (1956) 15' quadrangle.

Burnt Point Creek [TULARE]: *stream,* flows 3 miles to North Fork Kaweah River 1.5 miles west-northwest of Yucca Mountain (lat. 36°34'40" N, long. 118°53'40" W); sec. 36, T 15 S, R 28 E); the mouth of the stream is 1 mile east-southeast of Burnt Point. Named on Giant Forest (1956) 15' quadrangle. United States Board on Geographic Names (1933a,

p. 177) rejected the name "Cow Creek" for the stream.

Burnt Ridge [TULARE]: *ridge,* generally east-trending, 2.5 miles long, 7.5 miles east-north-east of California Hot Springs (lat. 35°54'45" N, long. 118°32'45" W). Named on California Hot Springs (1958) 15' quadrangle.

Burnt Spring [KERN]: *spring,* 5.5 miles southeast of Glennville (lat. 35°39'50" N, long. 118°38'50" W; sec. 16, T 26 S, R 31 E). Named on Glennville (1972) 7.5' quadrangle.

Burr [TULARE]: *locality,* 3 miles north-north-west of Lindsay along Southern Pacific Railroad (lat. 36°14'40" N, long. 119°06'50" W; sec. 25, T 19 S, R 26 E). Named on Lindsay (1951) 7.5' quadrangle.

Burrel [FRESNO]: *village,* nearly 5 miles northwest of Lanare (lat. 36°29'20" N, long. 119°59' W; near S line sec. 35, T 16 S, R 18 E). Named on Burrel (1954) 7.5' quadrangle. Postal authorities established Burrel post office in 1912 (Frickstad, p. 31). The railroad station at the place was named in 1889 for Cuthbert Burrel, or Burrell, a stockman in Fresno County in the 1860's and owner of Elkhorn Ranch (Gudde, 1949, p. 45). Elkhorn Station, located 1.5 miles southeast of present Burrel, was a stop on Butterfield Overland stage line from 1856 until the stage stopped running in 1861 (Hoover, Rensch, and Rensch, p. 92).

Burre Mountain: see **Burrough Mountain** [FRESNO].

Burro Creek [TULARE]: *stream,* flows 3 miles to North Fork of Middle Fork Tule River 6 miles north-northwest of Camp Nelson (lat. 36°13'30" N, long. 118°38'45" W; sec. 32, T 19 S, R 31 E). Named on Camp Nelson (1956) 15' quadrangle.

Burro Flat: see **Bartons Resort** [FRESNO].

Burro Lake [MADERA]: *lake,* 400 feet long, 7 miles south-southeast of Merced Peak (lat. 37°31'55" N, long. 119°21'50" W; sec. 5, T 5 S, R 24 E); the lake is west-northwest of Jackass Lakes. Named on Merced Peak (1953) 15' quadrangle.

Burrough: see **Burrough Valley** [FRESNO].

Burrough Mountain [FRESNO]: *ridge,* northwest-trending, 2.5 miles long, 7.25 miles south-southwest of Shaver Lake Heights (present town of Shaver Lake) (lat. 37°00'30" N, long. 119°21'45" W). Named on Shaver Lake (1953) 15' quadrangle, and on Trimmer (1965) 7.5' quadrangle. Called Burre Mountain on Kaiser (1904) 30' quadrangle.

Burrough Valley [FRESNO]: *valley,* 6.5 miles northwest of Trimmer on upper reaches of Little Dry Creek (2) (lat. 36°58'30" N, long. 119°22' W). Named on Humphreys Station (1965) and Trimmer (1965) 7.5' quadrangles. Mendenhall's (1908) map shows a place called Burrough located at or near present Burrough Valley, and Lippincott's (1902) map shows Burrough P.O. there. California Division of

Highways' (1934) map has the name "Borrough" for a place in present Burrough Valley (near E line sec. 17, T 11 S, R 24 E). Postal authorities established Burrough post office in 1889, moved it 0.5 mile south in 1900, and discontinued it in 1917; the name is for Colonel Henry Burrough, a resident of the neighborhood in 1858 (Salley, p. 30).

Burton Camp [TULARE]: *locality,* 5.5 miles northeast of Fairview (lat. 35°58'40" N, long. 118°25'05" W; sec. 28, T 22 S, R 33 E). Named on Kernville (1956) 15' quadrangle. Called Corral Meadow on Kernville (1908) 30' quadrangle, but United States Board on Geographic Names (1961b, p. 9) rejected this name for the place. The name "Burton" commemorates a rancher who used the site at roundup time (Browning 1986, p. 29).

Burton Meadow [FRESNO]: *area,* 4.25 miles east-southeast of Hume (lat. 36°45'20" N, long. 118°50'40" W). Named on Tehipite Dome (1952) 15' quadrangle. The name commemorates an early-day stockman (Browning, p. 29).

Burton Mill [KERN]: *locality,* 7.5 miles southeast of Bodfish (lat. 35°30'05" N, long. 118°24'20" W; at N line sec. 14, T 28 S, R 33 E). Named on Lake Isabella South (1972) 7.5' quadrangle.

Burton Mountain: see **Burton Pass** [FRESNO].

Burton Pass [FRESNO]: *pass,* 4 miles east-southeast of Hume (lat. 36°45'15" N, long. 118°51' W); the pass is west of Burton Meadow. Named on Tehipite Dome (1952) 15' quadrangle. California Mining Bureau's (1917a) map shows Burton Mountain near present Burton Meadow and Burton Pass.

Burton's Hill: see **Tropico Hill** [KERN].

Burton's Tropico Hill: see **Tropico Hill** [KERN].

Busane Peak [FRESNO]: *peak,* 8.5 miles southsouthwest of Coalinga (lat. 36°01'40" N, long. 120°25'25" W; near E line sec. 11, T 22 S, R 14 E). Altitude 2212 feet. Named on Curry Mountain (1969) 7.5' quadrangle.

Bush Spring [KERN]: *spring,* 2.25 miles southsoutheast of Cummings Mountain (lat. 35°00'25" N, long. 118°33'20" W; near NW cor. sec. 35, T 11 N, R 16 W). Named on Cummings Mountain (1943b) 15' quadrangle.

Butera [TULARE]: *locality,* 5.25 miles south of Earlimart along Southern Pacific Railroad (lat. 35°48'30" N, long. 119°15'25" W; sec. 27, T 24 S, R 25 E). Named on Delano West (1954) 7.5' quadrangle.

Butler [FRESNO]: *locality,* 4 miles northeast of Malaga along Southern Pacific Railroad (lat. 36°43'20" N, long. 119°41' W; near SE cor. sec. 9, T 14 S, R 21 E). Named on Selma (1946) 15' quadrangle.

Butler Spring [KERN]: *spring,* 4.5 miles east-southeast of Woody (lat. 35°41' N, long. 118°45'10" W; sec. 9, T 26 S, R 30 E). Named on Woody (1965) 7.5' quadrangle.

Butterbread Canyon: see **Butterbredt Canyon** [KERN].

Butterbread Peak: see **Butterbredt Peak** [KERN].

Butterbread Spring: see **Butterbredt Spring** [KERN].

Butterbread Well: see **Butterbredt Well** [KERN].

Butterbredt Canyon [KERN]: *canyon,* drained by a stream that flows 8 miles to Alphie Canyon 7 miles northwest of Cinco (lat. 35°21'20" N, long. 118°05' W; sec. 2, T 30 S, R 36 E). Named on Cinco (1972), Dove Spring (1972), and Pinyon Mountain (1972) 7.5' quadrangles. Called Butterbread Canyon on Cross Mountain (1943) 15' quadrangle. United States Board on Geographic Names (1974b, p. 2) gave the name "Butterbread Canyon" as a variant.

Butterbredt Peak [KERN]: *peak,* 5.25 miles south of Pinyon Mountain (lat. 35°23' N, long. 118°09'10" W; sec. 30, T 29 S, R 36 E); the peak is southwest of Butterbredt Canyon. Altitude 5997 feet. Named on Pinyon Mountain (1972) 7.5' quadrangle. Called Butterbread Peak on Cross Mountain (1943) 15' quadrangle. United States Board on Geographic Names (1974b, p. 2) gave the name "Butterbread Peak" as a variant—the name "Butterbredt" is for Frederick Butterbredt, who settled in Kern County in the 1860's.

Butterbredt Spring [KERN]: *spring,* 6 miles south-southeast of Pinyon Mountain (lat. 35°22'55" N, long. 118°06'45" W; near E line sec. 28, T 29 S, R 36 E); the spring is in Butterbredt Canyon. Named on Dove Spring (1972) 7.5' quadrangle. Called Butterbread Spring on Cross Mountain (1943) 15' quadrangle, and United States Board on Geographic Names (1974b, p. 2) gave this name as a variant.

Butterbredt Well [KERN]: *well,* 3.5 miles south-southeast of Pinyon Mountain (lat. 35°24'20" N, long. 118°08'30" W; sec. 17, T 29 S, R 36 E); the well is in Butterbredt Canyon 2.5 miles northwest of Butterbredt Spring. Named on Pinyon Mountain (1972) 7.5' quadrangle. Called Butterbread Well on Cross Mountain (1943) 15' quadrangle, and United States Board on Geographic Names (1974b, p. 2) gave this name as a variant.

Buttonwillow [KERN]: *town,* 26 miles west of Bakersfield (lat. 35° 24' N, long. 119°28'10" W; in and near sec. 14, T 29 S, R 23 E). Named on Buttonwillow (1954) 7.5' quadrangle. Postal authorities established Buttonwillow post office in 1895 (Frickstad, p. 54). The name is from a lone tree that was a landmark in the early days; when the town was laid out in 1895 it was called Buena Vista, but the old name "Buttonwillow" prevailed (Wines, p. 42).

Buttonwillow Peak [TULARE]: *peak,* 2.5 miles east-northeast of Tucker Mountain (lat.

36°38'55" N, long. 119°09'45" W; sec. 5, T 15 S, R 26 E). Altitude 2264 feet. Named on Tucker Mountain (1966) 7.5' quadrangle.

Buttonwillow Ridge [KERN]: *ridge,* northwest-trending, 13 miles long, center 5 miles north-northwest of Buttonwillow (lat. 35°28'15" N, long. 119°29'15" W). Named on Buttonwillow (1954), Lokern (1954), and Semitropic (1954) 7.5' quadrangles.

Buttonwillow Slough [MADERA]: *water feature,* 21 miles west-southwest of Madera, and east of San Joaquin River. Named on Firebaugh (1956) and Poso Farm (1962) 7.5' quadrangles.

Buttresses: see **The Buttresses** [MADERA].

Buzzard Canyon [MADERA]: *canyon,* drained by a stream that flows 2 miles to Fresno River 5 miles south-southeast of Knowles (lat. 37°09' N, long. 119°51'20" W; sec. 13, T 9 S, R 19 E). Named on Knowles (1962) 7.5' quadrangle.

Buzzard Ridge [KERN]: *ridge,* north- to northwest-trending, 1 mile long, 7 miles east-southeast of Caliente (lat. 35°15'45" N, long. 118°30'30" W; sec 2, T 31 S, R 32 E). Named on Oiler Peak (1972) 7.5' quadrangle.

Buzzard Roost [TULARE]: *peak,* 3.5 miles east of Auckland (lat. 36° 34'55" N, long. 119°02'30" W; sec. 33, T 15 S, R 27 E). Altitude 3082 feet. Named on Auckland (1966) 7.5' quadrangle.

Buzzard Roost: see **Ellis Mountain** [TULARE].

Buzzard Spring [KERN]: *spring,* nearly 7 miles east-southeast of Caliente (lat. 35°15'50" N, long. 118°30'40" W; sec. 2, T 31 S, R 32 E); the spring is at the north end of Buzzard Ridge. Named on Oiler Peak (1972) 7.5' quadrangle.

Buzzards' Roost: see **Waukena** [TULARE].

Byles Jamison Camp [FRESNO]: *locality,* 7.25 miles south-southwest of Dinkey Dome in Bear Meadow (3) (lat. 37°01'05" N, long. 119°10'25" W; sec. 31, T 10 S, R 26 E). Named on Huntington Lake (1953) 15' quadrangle.

Byrd Slough [FRESNO]: *water feature,* heads at a canal and extends for 9 miles to Kings River 5.5 miles south of Centerville (lat. 36° 39'05" N, long. 119°28'45" W; sec. 4, T 15 S, R 23 E). Named on Piedra (1965) and Wahtoke (1966) 7.5' quadrangles.

— C —

Cabernet: see **McFarland** [KERN].

Cabin Cove [TULARE]: *locality,* 3.5 miles west-northwest of Mineral King (lat. 36°27'55" N, long. 118°39'15" W). Named on Mineral King (1956) 15' quadrangle.

Cabin Creek [FRESNO]:
(1) *stream,* flows 1.5 miles to Rancheria Creek (3) 12 miles north of Hume (lat. 36°57'25"

N, long. 118°54'15" W). Named on Tehipite Dome (1952) 15' quadrangle.

(2) *stream,* flows 2.5 miles to Kings River 6.25 miles north-northwest of Hume (lat. 36°51'40" N, long. 118°58'15" W). Named on Tehipite Dome (1952) 15' quadrangle.

Cabin Creek [TULARE]: *stream,* flows 2.5 miles to Dorst Creek 4 miles south-southwest of Shell Mountain (lat. 36°38'20" N, long. 118°48'40" W; sec. 10, T 15 S, R 29 E); the stream goes past Cabin Meadow. Named on Giant Forest (1956) 15' quadrangle.

Cabin Lake [MADERA]: *lake,* 900 feet long, 5.5 miles northwest of Devils Postpile (lat. 37°41'05" N, long. 119°09'05" W). Named on Devils Postpile (1953) 15' quadrangle. David Nidever built a log cabin by the lake in the early 1900's (Smith, Genny, p. 61).

Cabin Meadow [FRESNO]:

(1) *area,* 4 miles south-southeast of Dinkey Dome (lat. 37°03'30" N, long. 119°07' W; sec. 14, 15, T 10 S, R 26 E). Named on Huntington Lake (1953) 15' quadrangle.

(2) *area,* 5.5 miles north-northeast of Balch Camp (lat. 36°58'45" N, long. 119°05' W). Named on Patterson Mountain (1952) 15' quadrangle.

Cabin Meadow [TULARE]: *area,* 3 miles south-southwest of Shell Mountain (lat. 36°39'15" N, long. 118°48'35" W; near E line sec. 3, T 15 S, R 29 E). Named on Giant Forest (1956) 15' quadrangle. United States Board on Geographic Names (1933a, p. 180) rejected the name "Guttrie Meadow" for the place. The name "Cabin Meadow" is from a cabin built at the site by an early-day sheepherder (Browning 1986, p. 29).

Cabin Meadow: see **Green Meadow** [TULARE].

Cable [KERN]: *locality,* 3 miles north-northwest of Tehachapi along the railroad (lat. 35°10'05" N, long. 118°28'25" W; at N line sec. 7, T 32 S, R 33 E). Named on Tehachapi North (1966) 7.5' quadrangle. California Mining Bureau's (1917c) map shows a place called Sedwell located about 1 mile west-northwest of Cable along the railroad.

Cache Creek [KERN]: *stream,* flows 19 miles to lowlands 4.5 miles north of Mojave (lat. 35°07' N, long. 118°11'30" W; sec. 26, T 32 S, R 35 E); the stream heads at Cache Peak. Named on California City North (1973), California City South (1973), Mojave (1973), Monolith (1966), Sanborn (1973), and Tehachapi NE (1966) 7.5' quadrangles. Called Tehachapi Creek on Mojave (1947) 7.5' quadrangle.

Cache Peak [KERN]: *peak,* 12.5 miles northnorthwest of Mojave (lat. 35°13'20" N, long. 118°15' W; near W line sec. 20, T 31 S, R 35 E). Altitude 6698 feet. Named on Cache Peak (1973) and Tehachapi NE (1966) 7.5' quadrangles.

Cactus Creek: see **Yucca Creek** [TULARE].

Cactus Mountain: see **Yucca Mountain** [TULARE].

Cactus Point [TULARE]: *peak,* 5 miles southsoutheast of Yucca Mountain (lat. 36°30'40" N, long. 118°49'10" W). Altitude 3738 feet. Named on Giant Forest (1956) 15' quadrangle. National Park Service officials named the peak for the many yuccas growing there (Browning 1986, p. 30).

Cactus Ridge: see **Yucca Ridge** [TULARE].

Cadogan: see **Mendota** [FRESNO].

Caesar: see **Mount Julius Caesar** [FRESNO].

Cahoon Creek [TULARE]: *stream,* flows 3 miles to Horse Creek (1) 6.25 miles westsouthwest of Mineral King (lat. 36°25'05" N, long. 118°42' W); the stream heads at Cahoon Meadow (2). Named on Mineral King (1956) 15' quadrangle. The name commemorates an early settler who had a cabin by the stream (United States Board on Geographic Names, 1933a, p. 183).

Cahoon Gap [TULARE]: *pass,* 12 miles westnorthwest of Triple Divide Peak (lat. 36°38'35" N, long. 118°44'10" W; near SW cor. sec. 4, T 15 S, R 30 E); the pass is about 1 mile north of Cahoon Meadow (1). Named on Triple Divide Peak (1956) 15' quadrangle.

Cahoon Meadow [TULARE]:

(1) *area,* 12 miles west-northwest of Triple Divide Peak (lat. 36°37'50" N, long. 118°44' W; at W line sec. 9, T 15 S, R 30 E); the place is 1 mile south of Cahoon Gap. Named on Triple Divide Peak (1956) 15' quadrangle.

(2) *area,* 7.5 miles southwest of Mineral King (lat. 36°23' N, long. 118°42'10" W); the place is at the head of Cahoon Creek. Named on Mineral King (1956) 15' quadrangle. The name commemorates George Cahoon, an early settler who had a cabin at the place (United States Board on Geographic Names, 1933a, p. 183).

Cahoon Meadow: see **Silliman Meadow** [TULARE].

Cahoon Mountain [TULARE]: *peak,* 8.5 miles southeast of Kaweah (lat. 36°22'20" N, long. 118°49'20" W; sec. 10, T 18 S, R 29 E). Altitude 4229 feet. Named on Kaweah (1957) 15' quadrangle. The name is for George Cahoon of Cahoon Meadow (2) (Hanna, p. 48).

Cahoon Peak: see **Evelyn Lake** [TULARE].

Cahoon Rock: see **Evelyn Lake** [TULARE].

Cain Slough [KINGS]: *stream* and *dry wash,* extends south for 4.5 miles to a point nearly 6 miles west-southwest of Guernsey (lat. 36°11'30" N, long. 119°44'30" W). Named on Guernsey (1929) 7.5' quadrangle. The mostly dry watercourse is called Jacobs Slough on Guernsey (1954) 7.5' quadrangle.

Cain Spring [TULARE]: *spring,* 5 miles northwest of California Hot Springs (lat. 35°55'40" N, long. 118°44'20" W; sec. 16, T 23 S, R 30 E). Named on California Hot Springs (1958) 15' quadrangle.

Cain Spring Gap [TULARE]: *pass,* nearly 5

miles northwest of California Hot Springs (lat. 35°55'10" N, long. 118°44'30" W; near N line sec. 21, T 23 S, R 30 E); the pass is 0.5 mile south-southwest of Cain Spring. Named on California Hot Springs (1958) 15' quadrangle.

Cairns [TULARE]: *locality,* 4.25 miles west-northwest of Woodlake along Atchison, Topeka and Santa Fe Railroad (lat. 36°26' N, long. 119°10' W; at W line sec. 21, T 17 S, R 26 E). Named on Exeter (1952) 15' quadrangle.

Cairns Corner [TULARE]: *locality,* 2.5 miles west of Lindsay (lat. 36°12'40" N, long. 119°08'10" W; at SW cor. sec. 2, T 20 S, R 26 E). Named on Cairns Corner (1950) 7.5' quadrangle.

Calders Corner [KERN]: *locality,* 8 miles south of Shafter (lat. 35° 23' N, long. 119°15'05" W; at SW cor. sec. 24, T 29 S, R 25 E). Named on Rio Bravo (1954) 7.5' quadrangle.

Caldwell [FRESNO]: *locality,* 3 miles southeast of San Joaquin along Southern Pacific Railroad (lat. 36°34'40" N, long. 120°08'45" W). Named on San Joaquin (1925) 7.5' quadrangle.

Caldwell Creek [KERN]: *stream,* flows 7.25 miles to Kern River 3 miles northeast of Wofford Heights (lat. 35°44'25" N, long. 118° 24'55" W; near E line sec. 22, T 25 S, R 33 E). Named on Kernville (1956) 15' quadrangle, and on Lake Isabella North (1972) 7.5' quadrangle. Called Cowell Creek on Kernville (1908) 30' quadrangle, and Cowel Cr. on Olmstead's (1900) map.

Calfax [FRESNO]: *locality,* 20 miles northeast of Coalinga (lat. 36° 20'35" N, long. 120°06'05" W; near NW cor. sec. 26, T 18 S, R 17 E). Named on Calfax (1956) 7.5' quadrangle.

Calf Creek [KERN]: *stream,* flows 2 miles to Cow Creek 10 miles east-northeast of Glennville (lat. 35°46'15" N, long. 118°32' W; at W line sec. 10, T 25 S, R 32 E). Named on California Hot Springs (1958) 15' quadrangle, and on Alta Sierra (1972) 7.5' quadrangle.

Calgro [TULARE]: *locality,* 11 miles north of Visalia along Atchison, Topeka and Santa Fe Railroad (lat. 36°29'20" N, long. 119°17'05" W; near SW cor. sec. 32, T 16 S, R 25 E); the place is 1.5 miles west of Yettem. Named on Monson (1949) 7.5' quadrangle. Called Yettem Sta. on Monson (1927) 7.5' quadrangle. The railroad station was called Yettem from 1910 until 1936; the name "Calgro" is from the term "California Growers Wineries" (Gudde 1949, p. 49, 395). Lippincott's (1902) map shows a place called Lovell near present Calgro. Postal authorities established Lovell post office in 1912 and discontinued it in 1913 (Frickstad, p. 212).

Calico [KERN]: *locality,* 3.5 miles south-southeast of McFarland along Southern Pacific Railroad (lat. 35°38' N, long. 119°12'20" W; near SE cor. sec. 30, T 26 S, R 26 E). Named on McFarland (1954) 7.5' quadrangle.

Caliente [KERN]: *village,* 22 miles east-southeast of Bakersfield (lat. 35°17'25" N, long. 118°37'35" W); the place is along Caliente Creek. Named on Bena (1972) and Oiler Peak (1972) 7.5' quadrangles. Postal authorities established Caliente post office in 1875, discontinued it in 1883, and reestablished it in 1890 (Frickstad, p. 54). The site first was known as Agua Caliente for some nearby hot springs, then as Allen's Camp for Gabriel Allen, and finally as Caliente when Southern Pacific Railroad set up a work camp at the place in 1874 (Bailey, 1967, p. 3).

Caliente Creek [KERN]: *stream,* flows 38 miles to lowlands 5.25 miles southeast of Edison (lat. 35°16'55" N, long. 118°48'40" W; near NE cor. sec. 36, T 30 S, R 29 E). Named on Bena (1972), Edison (1954), Emerald Mountain (1972), Loraine (1972), and Oiler Peak (1972) 7.5' quadrangles. Boyd (p. 170) called the feature Agua Caliente Creek, and noted that the name is from hot springs located near the head of the stream.

Caliente Spring [KERN]: *spring,* 2.25 miles east of Caliente (lat. 35° 17'30" N, long. 118°35'15" W; sec. 30, T 30 S, R 32 E). Named on Oiler Peak (1972) 7.5' quadrangle.

Califa [MADERA]: *locality,* 1 mile northwest of Fairmead along Southern Pacific Railroad (lat. 37°05'05" N, long. 120°12'25" W; near S line sec. 3, T 10 S, R 16 E). Named on Berenda (1918) 7.5' quadrangle. Postal authorities established Califa post office in 1912 and discontinued it in 1915 (Frickstad, p. 85).

California City [KERN]: *town,* desert retirement community 11 miles east-northeast of Mojave (lat. 35°07'30" N, long. 117° 59' W). Named on Boron NW (1973), California City North (1973), California City South (1973), Galileo Hill (1973), Johannesburg (1967), Mohave NE (1973), North Edwards (1973), Saltdale SE (1967), and Sanborn (1973) 7.5' quadrangles. Postal authorities established California City post office in 1960 (Salley, p. 32), and the town incorporated in 1965. California City Development Company started the planned community in 1958; the development covers 158 square miles (Bailey, 1967, p. 3).

California Creek [MADERA]: *stream,* flows 3 miles to Nelder Creek 3.5 miles north-northeast of Yosemite Forks (lat. 37°24'40" N, long. 119°35'45" W; at W line sec. 17, T 6 S, R 22 E). Named on Bass Lake (1953) 15' quadrangle.

California Hot Springs [TULARE]: *locality,* 20 miles east of Ducor (lat. 35°52'45" N, long. 118°40'15" W; sec. 31, T 23 S, R 31 E); the place is along Deer Creek (2). Named on California Hot Springs (1958) 15' quadrangle. Postal authorities established Hot Springs post office in 1900, and changed the name to California Hot Springs in 1926 (Frickstad, p. 211). Four springs with water temperatures of 120°

to 126° Fahrenheit are the basis of a resort; the place first was called Deer Creek Hot Springs (Waring, p. 49).

California Range: see "Regional setting."

Callioud Spring [KERN]: *spring,* 5 miles north of Democrat Hot Springs (lat. 35°36' N, long. 118°39'15" W). Named on Democrat Hot Springs (1972) 7.5' quadrangle.

Caltech Peak [TULARE]: *peak,* 9.5 miles northwest of Mount Whitney (lat. 36°41'15" N, long. 118°23'20" W). Altitude 13,832 feet. Named on Mount Whitney (1956) 15' quadrangle. The name is for <u>Cal</u>ifornia Institute of <u>Tech</u>nology (United States Board on Geographic Names, 1962a, p. 7)

Calwa [FRESNO]: *district,* 4 miles south-southeast of downtown Fresno (lat. 36°42'40" N, long. 119°45'15" W). Named on Fresno South (1963) and Malaga (1964) 7.5' quadrangles. Officials of Atchison, Topeka and Santa Fe Railroad coined the name in 1913 from letters of the term "<u>Cal</u>ifornia <u>W</u>ine <u>A</u>ssociation"—a large winery was near the place (Hanna, p. 52). California Mining Bureau's (1917a) map has the name "Calwa City" along the railroad just southeast of Fresno. Postal authorities established Calwa City post office in 1913 and changed the name to Calwa in 1949 (Salley, p. 33).

Calwa City: see **Calwa** [FRESNO].

Cambio [KERN]: *locality,* nearly 4 miles northeast of Mojave along Southern Pacific Railroad (lat. 35°05'40" N, long. 118°08' W). Named on Mojave (1915) 30' quadrangle.

Camden [FRESNO]: *village,* 3.5 miles east of Riverdale (lat. 36°25'50" N, long. 119°47'50" W; near NW cor. sec. 27, T 17 S, R 20 E). Named on Riverdale (1954) 7.5' quadrangle. Postal authorities established Camden post office in 1903 and discontinued it in 1904 (Frickstad, p. 31).

Cameo [FRESNO]: *locality,* 4 miles south of Clovis along Atchison, Topeka and Santa Fe Railroad (lat. 36°45'50" N, long. 119°42' W; near NE cor. sec. 32, T 13 S, R 21 E). Named on Clovis (1964) 7.5' quadrangle.

Cameron [KERN]: *locality,* 9 miles east-southeast of Tehachapi along the railroad (lat. 35°05'50" N, long. 118°17'45" W; near S line sec. 35, T 32 S, R 34 E); the place is near the mouth of Cameron Canyon. Named on Monolith (1966) 7.5' quadrangle. Postal authorities established Cameron post office in 1899, discontinued it in 1922, reestablished it in 1923, and discontinued it the same year; the name commemorates George W. Cameron, an early settler (Salley, p. 33). Wheeler's (1875-1878) map shows a place called Nadeau located about 5 miles east of Cameron along the railroad.

Cameron Canyon [KERN]: *canyon,* drained by a stream that flows 3.5 miles to the canyon of Cache Creek 8.5 miles east-southeast of Tehachapi (lat. 35°05'35" N, long. 118°18'15"

W; sec. 31, T 12 N, R 13 W). Named on Monolith (1966) 7.5' quadrangle. The stream in the canyon is called Cameron Creek on Tehachapi (1943) 15' quadrangle.

Cameron Creek [TULARE]: *stream,* diverges west from Deep Creek (1) and flows 27 miles to a canal 1.5 miles southwest of Waukena (lat. 36°07'40" N, long. 119°31'45" W; sec. 6, T 21 S, R 23 E). Named on Exeter (1952), Tulare (1942), and Visalia (1949) 15' quadrangles, and on Waukena (1954) 7.5' quadrangle. The name commemorates either Alexander Cameron or Monroe Cameron (Mitchell, A.R., p. 78).

Cameron Creek: see **Cameron Canyon** [KERN].

Cameron Creek Colony [TULARE]: *locality,* 4 miles west-northwest of Exeter (lat. 36°19' N, long. 119°12'15" W; sec. 31, T 18 S, R 25 E); the place is on the south side of Cameron Creek. Named on Exeter (1952) 15' quadrangle.

Cameron Slough [FRESNO]: *water feature,* diverges from Kings River 1.25 miles east-southeast of Centerville and extends for 5.5 miles before rejoining the river 5.5 miles south of Centerville (lat. 36°39'10" N, long. 119°29'45" W; sec. 5, T 15 S, R 23 E). Named on Sanger (1965) and Wahtoke (1966) 7.5' quadrangles.

Cameron Station: see **Tehachapi Valley** [KERN].

Camino Campground [MADERA]: *locality,* 5.5 miles north of Shuteye Peak (lat. 37°25'55" N, long. 119°25'55" W; near SE cor. sec. 3, T 6 S, R 23 E); the place is along Camino Creek. Named on Shuteye Peak (1953) 15' quadrangle.

Camino Creek [MADERA]: *stream,* flows about 3 miles to Beasore Creek 5.25 miles north of Shuteye Peak (lat. 37°25'30" N, long. 119°24'25" W; sec. 12, T 6 S, R 23 E). Named on Shuteye Peak (1953) 15' quadrangle.

Camp Babbitt: see **Visalia** [TULARE].

Camp Badger: see **Badger** [TULARE].

Camp Barbour: see **Old Fort Miller** [FRESNO].

Campbell: see **Big Campbell** [TULARE]; **Campbell Mountain** [FRESNO]; **Little Campbell** [TULARE]; **Mount Ian Campbell**, under **Mount Givens** [FRESNO].

Campbell Creek [TULARE]: *stream,* flows 6.5 miles to Tule River 3.5 miles southwest of Springville (lat. 36°06'05" N, long. 118° 52' W; sec. 17, T 21 S, R 39 E). Named on Springville (1957) 15' quadrangle.

Campbell Mountain [FRESNO]: *mountain,* 5 miles east-southeast of Centerville (lat. 36°41'45" N, long. 119°25'15" W; in and near sec. 24, T 14 S, R 23 E). Altitude 1752 feet. Named on Wahtoke (1966) 7.5' quadrangle. The name is for William Campbell, who had a store at Poole's Ferry on Kings River (Gudde, 1969, p. 51). Eddy's (1854) map shows Campbells Ferry on Kings River, and Bancroft's (1864) map shows Mt. Campbell and a place called Campbell located on the north side of Kings River about where Eddy's (1854) map shows Campbells Ferry.

Campbells Ferry: see **Campbell Mountain** [FRESNO].

Camp Chawanakee [FRESNO]: *locality,* 1.5 miles east-northeast of Shaver Lake Heights (present town of Shaver Lake) on the south side of Shaver Lake (lat. 37°06'45" N, long. 119°17'25" W; sec. 30, T 9 S, R 25 E). Named on Shaver Lake (1953) 15' quadrangle.

Camp Condor [KERN]: *locality,* 6 miles south-west of Eagle Rest Peak (lat. 34°50'55" N, long. 119°12'25" W; on E line sec. 22, T 9 N, R 22 W). Named on Sawmill Mountain (1943) 7.5' quadrangle.

Camp Conifer [TULARE]: *locality,* 5 miles west of Mineral King (lat. 36°27'30" N, long. 118°41'15" W). Named on Mineral King (1956) 15' quadrangle.

Camp Dix [KERN]: *locality,* 18 miles west-northwest of Eagle Rest Peak (lat. 34°57'50" N, long. 119°26'40" W; sec. 9, T 10 N, R 24 W). Named on Ballinger Canyon (1943) 7.5' quadrangle.

Camp Earl-Anna [KERN]: *locality,* 6 miles south-southwest of Tehachapi (lat. 35°03'10" N, long. 118°29'50" W; at S line sec. 8, T 11 N, R 15 W). Named on Tehachapi South (1966) 7.5' quadrangle.

Campfire Lake [FRESNO]: *lake,* 300 feet long, nearly 0.5 mile northeast of Kaiser Peak (lat. 37°17'45" N, long. 119°10'40" W; at N line sec. 30, T 7 S, R 26 E). Named on Kaiser Peak (1953) 15' quadrangle.

Camp Fresno [FRESNO]: *locality,* 3.5 miles south-southwest of Dinkey Dome on the east side of Dinkey Creek (1) (lat. 37°04'10" N, long. 119°09'05" W; near SE cor. sec. 8, T 10 S, R 26 E). Named on Huntington Lake (1953) 15' quadrangle.

Camp Kanawyer: see **Kanawyers** [FRESNO].

Camp Kaweah [KERN]: *locality,* 0.25 mile west-northwest of Alta Sierra (lat. 35°43'50" N, long. 118°33'20" W; near NE cor. sec. 29, T 25 S, R 32 E). Named on Alta Sierra (1972) 7.5' quadrangle.

Camp Kemeric [KERN]: *locality,* 0.5 mile north-northwest of downtown Kernville along Kern River (lat. 35°45'50" N, long. 118°25'50" W; near SW cor. sec. 10, T 25 S, R 33 E). Named on Kernville (1956) 15' quadrangle.

Camp Leonard: see **Weldon** [KERN].

Camp Miller: see **Old Fort Miller** [FRESNO].

Camp Nelson [TULARE]: *town,* 12 miles east of Springville along South Fork of Middle Fork Tule River (lat. 36°08'30" N, long. 118°36'30" W; sec. 33, 34, T 20 S, R 31 E). Named on Camp Nelson (1956) 15' quadrangle. Called Nelson on Kaweah (1909) 30' quadrangle. Postal authorities established

Camp Nelson post office in 1935 (Frickstad, p. 210). The name commemorates John M. Nelson, who homesteaded in the neighborhood in 1884 and opened a summer resort there in 1899 (Hanna, p. 208). The place also was known as Nelson Soda Springs (Waring, p. 243) and Nelson's Soda Springs (Tucker, p. 945).

Camp Nick Williams [KERN]: *locality,* 1.25 miles north-northwest of Claraville (lat. 35°27'35" N, long. 118°20'30" W; sec. 32, T 28 S, R 34 E). Named on Claraville (1972) 7.5' quadrangle.

Camp Oljato [FRESNO]: *locality,* 4 miles east-northeast of the town of Big Creek on the south side of Huntington Lake (lat. 37°14'10" N, long. 119°10'40" W; sec. 18, T 8 S, R 26 E). Named on Huntington Lake (1953) 15' quadrangle.

Camp Owens [KERN]: *locality,* 1 mile north of Kernville along Kern River (lat. 35°46'10" N, long. 118°25'35" W; sec. 10, T 25 S, R 33 E). Named on Kernville (1956) 15' quadrangle.

Camp Santa Teresita [MADERA]: *locality,* 3.5 miles southeast of Yosemite Forks at the northwest end of Bass Lake (1) (lat. 37°19'50" N, long 119°34'55" W; near SW cor. sec. 9, T 7 S, R 22 E). Named on Bass Lake (1953) 15' quadrangle.

Camp Seven [FRESNO]: *locality,* 5 miles east of Hume (lat. 36° 47' N, long. 119°49'40" W). Site named on Tehipite Dome (1952) 15' quadrangle. Hume-Bennett Lumber Company (later called Sanger Lumber Company) built a lumber camp at the spot in 1917 (Browning 1986, p. 30).

Camp 7-C [FRESNO]: *locality,* 4.25 miles north-northwest of Coalinga in Pleasant Valley (lat. 36°12' N, long. 120°22'45" W; sec. 7, T 20 S, R 15 E). Named on Coalinga (1956) 7.5' quadrangle.

Camp Sierra [FRESNO]: *settlement,* 7 miles north-northeast of Shaver Lake Heights (present town of Shaver Lake) (lat. 37°11'30" N, long. 119°15'30" W; sec. 32, T 8 S, R 25 E); the place is in the Sierra Nevada. Named on Shaver Lake (1953) 15' quadrangle. Postal authorities established Sierra Chautauqua post office in 1918, changed the name to Camp Sierra in 1924, and discontinued it in 1935; the name "Chautauqua" is from a place in New York State called Camp Chautauqua (Salley, p. 35, 204).

Camp 61 Campground [FRESNO]: *locality,* 6.5 miles east-northeast of Kaiser Peak (lat. 37°19'10" N, long. 119°04'10" W); the place is along Camp 61 Creek. Named on Kaiser Peak (1953) 15' quadrangle.

Camp 61 Creek [FRESNO]: *stream,* formed by the confluence of East Fork and West Fork, flows 2 miles to South Fork San Joaquin River 8 miles east-northeast of Kaiser Peak (lat. 37°20'30" N, long. 119°03'30" W). Named on Kaiser Peak (1953) 15' quadrangle. East

Fork is 2.5 miles long and West Fork, which heads at Camp 61 Lake, is 1.5 miles long; both forks are named on Kaiser Peak (1953) 15' quadrangle.

Camp 61D Campground [FRESNO]: *locality,* 5 miles east-northeast of Kaiser Peak (lat. 37°19'15" N, long. 119°05'50" W; sec. 14, T 7 S, R 26 E); the place is 1.5 miles west of Camp 61 Campground. Named on Kaiser Peak (1953) 15' quadrangle.

Camp 61 Lake [FRESNO]: *lake,* 450 feet long, 5.25 miles east of Kaiser Peak (lat. 37°18'30" N, long. 119°05'20" W; sec. 24, T 7 S, R 26 E); the lake is at the head of West Fork Camp 61 Creek. Named on Kaiser Peak (1953) 15' quadrangle.

Camp 62 Creek [FRESNO]: *stream,* flows 3.5 miles to South Fork San Joaquin River 9.5 miles east-northeast of Kaiser Peak (lat. 37° 19'35" N, long. 119°01'30" W). Named on Kaiser Peak (1953) 15' quadrangle, which shows the stream diverted into a pipeline.

Camp 35-A [FRESNO]: *locality,* 6.5 miles north-northeast of Coalinga (lat. 36°13'40" N, long. 120°19' W; sec. 35, T 19 S, R 15 E). Named on Coalinga (1956) 7.5' quadrangle.

Camp Three: see **Abbott Mill** [FRESNO].

Camp 25-D [FRESNO]: *locality,* 2.5 miles west-northwest of Coalinga (lat. 36°09'30" N, long. 120°24' W; sec. 25, T 20 S, R 14 E). Named on Coalinga (1956) 15' quadrangle.

Camp Whitsett [TULARE]: *locality,* 10.5 miles south-southeast of Camp Nelson (lat. 36°00'05" N, long. 118°32'10" W; at E line sec. 20, T 22 S, R 32 E). Named on Camp Nelson (1956) 15' quadrangle.

Camp Wishon [TULARE]: *locality,* 4.5 miles northwest of Camp Nelson (lat. 36°11'30" N, long. 118°39'50" W; at N line sec. 18, T 20 S, R 31 E). Named on Camp Nelson (1956) 15' quadrangle. The place is a summer resort named for A.G. Wishon, who was general manager of San Joaquin Power Company, manager of Fresno Water Company, and vice president and manager of Fresno City Railroad (Hanna, p. 357).

Camp Yenis Hante [KERN]: *locality,* 0.5 mile northwest of Alta Sierra (lat. 35°43'55" N, long. 118°33'20" W; at S line sec. 20, T 25 S, R 32 E). Named on Alta Sierra (1972) 7.5' quadrangle.

Canada del Agua Escondida [KERN]: *canyon,* 2.25 miles long, opens into Canyon del Gato-Montes 4.25 miles southwest of Liebre Twins (lat. 34°54'25" N, long. 118°37'10" W). Named on Liebre Twins (1965) 7.5' quadrangle.

Canada de la Oasis: see **Oso Canyon** [KERN].

Cañada de las Uvas: see **Grapevine Creek** [KERN].

Canara Springs: see **Carneros Spring** [KERN].

Canaris Spring: see **Carneros Spring** [KERN].

Canary Spring [KERN]: *spring,* 2.5 miles northwest of Democrat Hot Springs (lat.

35°33'15" N, long. 118°41'40" W; sec. 25, T 27 S, R 30 E). Named on Democrat Hot Springs (1972) 7.5' quadrangle.

Canary Spring: see **Carneros Spring** [KERN].

Cando [FRESNO]: *locality,* 6.5 miles east-northeast of Riverdale along Southern Pacific Railroad (lat. 36°28'50" N, long. 119°45'30" W; sec. 1, T 17 S, R 20 E). Named on Riverdale (1927) 7.5' quadrangle.

Canebrake [KERN]:

(1) *settlement,* 5 miles east-northeast of Onyx (lat. 35°43'40" N, long. 118°08'20" W; sec. 29, T 25 S, R 36 E); the place is along Canebrake Creek. Named on Onyx (1972) 7.5' quadrangle.

(2) *locality,* 5.5 miles north-northwest of Walker Pass (lat. 35°43'45" N, long. 118°04'30" W; near NE cor. sec. 26, T 25 S, R 36 E); the place is along Canebrake Creek. Named on Kernville (1908) 30' quadrangle.

Canebrake Creek [KERN]: *stream,* heads near Walker Pass and flows 15 miles to South Fork Valley 4 miles northeast of Onyx (lat. 35°43'45" N, long. 118°10' W). Named on Lamont Peak (1956) 15' quadrangle, and on Onyx (1972) and Walker Pass (1972) 7.5' quadrangles. Called Chay-o-poo-ya-pah, a version of the Indian name, on Williamson's (1853) map.

Canebrake Flat [KERN]: *area,* 6.5 miles northwest of Walker Pass (lat. 35°44' N, long. 118°06'30" W); the place is along Canebrake Creek. Named on Walker Pass (1972) 7.5' quadrangle.

Cane Canyon [KERN]: *canyon,* drained by a stream that flows 7.5 miles to the canyon of Kelso Creek 6.5 miles west-northwest of Skinner Peak (lat. 35°35'50" N, long. 118°14' W; near E line sec. 8, T 27 S, R 35 E). Named on Cane Canyon (1972) 7.5' quadrangle.

Cane Creek [KERN]: *stream,* flows 3.5 miles to Tillie Creek nearly 2 miles west-northwest of Wofford Heights (lat. 35°42'50" N, long. 118°29' W; at W line sec. 31, T 25 S, R 33 E). Named on Alta Sierra (1972) and Lake Isabella North (1972) 7.5' quadrangles.

Cane Meadow [KERN]: *area,* 7.25 miles east-northeast of Kernville (lat. 35°46'45" N, long. 118°18'05" W; sec. 2, T 25 S, R 34 E). Named on Kernville (1956) 15' quadrangle.

Cane Peak [KERN]: *peak,* 2.25 miles west-northwest of Wofford Heights (lat. 35°43'35" N, long. 118°20'15" W; near E line sec. 25, T 25 S, R 32 E). Altitude 4539 feet. Named on Lake Isabella North (1972) 7.5' quadrangle.

Cane Spring [KERN]:

(1) *spring,* 10.5 miles east of Glennville (lat. 35°45'10" N, long. 118°31' W; at E line sec. 15, T 25 S, R 32 E). Named on California Hot Springs (1958) 15' quadrangle.

(2) *spring,* 4.5 miles east-southeast of Wofford Heights (lat. 35°40'55" N, long. 118°22'50" W; sec. 12, T 26 S, R 33 E). Named on Lake Isabella North (1972) 7.5' quadrangle.

Cane Springs: see **Koehn Spring** [KERN].

Cane Well [KERN]: *well,* 5.5 miles west-north-west of Skinner Peak (lat. 35°35'40" N, long. 118°13' W; near W line sec. 10, T 27 S, R 35 E); the feature is in Cane Canyon. Named on Cane Canyon (1972) 7.5' quadrangle.

Canfield: see **Old River** [KERN].

Cannell Creek [KERN-TULARE]: *stream,* heads in Tulare County and flows 10.5 miles, partly in Kern County, to Kern River 9.5 miles south-southeast of Fairview at Kern-Tulare county line (lat. 35°47'35" N, long. 118°26'50" W; at S line sec. 32, T 24 S, R 33 E); the stream heads near Cannell Peak and goes through Cannell Meadow. Named on Kernville (1956) 15' quadrangle. Called Lit. Brush Cr. on Olmsted's (1900) map.

Cannell Meadow [TULARE]: *area,* 10 miles southeast of Fairview (lat. 35°49'15" N, long. 118°22' W); the place is along Cannell Creek. Named on Kernville (1956) 15' quadrangle.

Cannell Meadow: see **Little Cannell Meadow** [TULARE].

Cannell Peak [TULARE]: *peak,* 8.5 miles east-southeast of Fairview (lat. 35°51'55" N, long. 118°21'35" W; near SW cor. sec. 6, T 24 S, R 34 E). Altitude 9407 feet. Named on Kernville (1956) 15' quadrangle.

Canoas Canyon: see **Canoas Creek** [FRESNO].

Canoas Creek [FRESNO]: *stream,* flows 8 miles to Kettleman Plain 11.5 miles southeast of Coalinga (lat. 36°01'30" N, long. 120°12'05" W; near E line sec. 11, T 22 S, R 16 E). Named on Avenal (1954), Garza Peak (1953), and The Dark Hole (1961) 7.5' quadrangles. Stewart (p. 75) pointed out that *canoa*, which means "canoe" in Spanish, is used in place names in the Mexican sense to mean a trough or ditch for carrying irrigation water, and sometimes is applied to a natural stream. Arnold and Anderson (1908, p. 16) gave the name "Canoas Canyon" to the canyon at the head of Canoas Creek.

Cañon Falls: see **Chagoopa Falls** [TULARE].

Canon Mountain: see **Breckenridge Mountain** [KERN].

Cantil [KERN]: *village,* 6 miles southwest of Saltdale (lat. 35°18'30" N, long. 117°57'05" W; at E line sec. 23, T 30 S, R 37 E). Named on Cantil (1967) 7.5' quadrangle. Postal authorities established Cantil post office in 1916 (Frickstad, p. 54). The place began in 1908 or 1909 as a station on Nevada and California Railroad—*cantil* means "steep rock" in Spanish (Darling, p. 24). Desert Spring, located 1.5 miles northeast of present Cantil, was an important watering place for Indians, early explorers, prospectors, and freighters (Bailey, 1967, p. 6-7).

Can-too-oa Creek: see **Warthan Creek** [FRESNO].

Cantua: see **Cantua Creek** [FRESNO] (2).

Cantua Creek [FRESNO]:
(1) *stream,* heads in San Benito County and flows 19 miles to lowlands 19 miles north of Coalinga (lat. 36°24'40" N, long. 120° 24' W; sec. 36, T 17 S, R 14 E). Named on Ciervo Mountain (1969), Lillis Ranch (1956), and Tres Picos Farms (1956) 7.5' quadrangles. The name commemorates a member of the Cantua family (Gudde, 1949, p. 55).
(2) *settlement,* 11 miles south-southwest of Tranquillity (lat. 36°30'05" N, long. 120°18'50" W; near SW cor. sec. 26, T 16 S, R 15 E). Named on Cantua Creek (1956) 7.5' quadrangle. Postal authorities established and discontinued Cantua post office in 1888, reestablished it in 1890, and discontinued it in 1892; they established Cantua Creek post office in 1941 (Salley, p. 36).

Cantua Creek: see **Warthan Creek** [FRESNO].

Cantua Well [FRESNO]: *well,* 5.25 miles southeast of Ciervo Mountain (lat. 36°24'25" N, long. 120°31'05" W; near E line sec. 35, T 17 S, R 13 E); the well is along a branch of Cantua Creek (1). Named on Ciervo Mountain (1969) 7.5' quadrangle.

Canyon Creek: see **Wilcox Creek** [TULARE].

Canyon de la Lecheria [KERN]: *canyon,* 2.25 miles long, along Pescado Creek above a point 6.5 miles southwest of Liebre Twins (lat. 34°53'20" N, long. 118°39'05" W). Named on Winters Ridge (1966) 7.5' quadrangle.

Canyon del Gato-Montes [KERN]: *canyon,* 3 miles long, opens into lowlands 5 miles south-southwest of Liebre Twins (lat. 34°52'45" N, long. 118°36'15" W). Named on Liebre Twins (1965) and Winters Ridge (1966) 7.5' quadrangles. Called Livsey Canyon on Johnson's (1911) map.

Canyon del Secretario: see **Sacatara Creek** [KERN].

Canyon del Sectario: see **Sacatara Creek** [KERN].

Caparell Creek [KERN]: *stream,* flows 2.5 miles to end in lowlands 10.5 miles south of Arvin (lat. 35°03' N, long. 118°49'05" W; sec. 8, T 11 N, R 18 W). Named on Tejon Hills (1955) 7.5' quadrangle.

Cap Canyon [KERN]: *canyon,* drained by a stream that flows 4.5 miles to South Fork Valley 3 miles east-northeast of Onyx (lat. 35° 42'45" N, long. 118°10'15" W). Named on Onyx (1972) and Walker Pass (1972) 7.5' quadrangles. Called Horse Canyon on Onyx (1943) 15' quadrangle, and United States Board on Geographic Names (1975b, p. 9) gave this name as a variant.

Cape Horn [FRESNO]: *relief feature,* 7.5 miles west-southwest of Blackcap Mountain, where there is a steep drop from the end of a ridge into the canyon of North Fork Kings River (lat. 37°02'45" N, long. 118°55'25" W; sec. 21, T 10 S, R 28 E). Named on Blackcap Mountain (1953) 15' quadrangle.

Capinero Creek [TULARE]: *stream,* flows 6 miles to Deer Creek (2) 0.5 mile east of California Hot Springs (lat. 35°52'50" N, long.

118°39'30" W; sec. 32, T 23 S, R 31 E).
Named on California Hot Springs (1958) 15'
quadrangle.

Capinero Flat: see **Pine Flat** [TULARE] (1).

Capinero Saddle [TULARE]: *pass,* 2.5 miles
southeast of California Hot Springs (lat.
35°51'25" N, long. 118°37'55" W; sec. 9, T
24 S, R 31 E). Named on California Hot
Springs (1958) 15' quadrangle.

Capita Canyon [FRESNO]: *canyon,* drained by
a stream that flows 5 miles to lowlands 17
miles southwest of Firebaugh (lat. 36°41'50"
N, long. 120°41'50" W; sec. 19, T 14 S, R 12
E). Named on Chounet Ranch (1956) and
Mercey Hot Springs (1969) 7.5' quadrangles.

Capital Peak: see **Capitol Rock** [TULARE].

Capitol Rock [TULARE]: *peak,* 11 miles north-
east of California Hot Springs (lat. 35°58'50"
N, long. 118°31'30" W; sec. 28, T 22 S, R 32
E). Altitude 5927 feet. Named on California
Hot Springs (1958) 15' quadrangle. Called
Capital Peak on Olmsted's (1900) map.

Caratan [TULARE]: *locality,* 4.5 miles south
of Earlimart along Southern Pacific Railroad
(lat. 35°49'10" N, long. 119°15'30" W; at S
line sec. 22, T 24 S, R 25 E). Named on
Delano West (1954) 7.5' quadrangle.

Cardinal Lake [FRESNO]: *lake,* 2200 feet long,
4 miles north-northwest of Mount Pinchot (lat.
37°00' N, long. 118°25'40" W); the lake is 1
mile west of Cardinal Mountain. Named on
Big Pine (1950) and Mount Pinchot (1953)
15' quadrangles.

Cardinal Mountain [FRESNO]: *peak,* 3.5 miles
north of Mount Pinchot on Fresno-Inyo
county line (lat. 36°59'55" N, long. 118°
24'45" W). Altitude 13,397 feet. Named on
Mount Pinchot (1953) 15' quadrangle. George
R. Davis of United States Geological Survey
named the peak because the red color at the
summit suggests the cap of a cardinal (Browning 1986, p. 31).

Cargyle Creek [MADERA]: *stream,* flows 4.5
miles to Middle Fork San Joaquin River 8
miles southwest of Devils Postpile (lat. 37°
31'55" N, long. 119°10'50" W; sec. 1, T 5 S,
R 25 E). Named on Devils Postpile (1953)
15' quadrangle. East Fork enters from the
northeast 2 miles upstream from the mouth
of the main creek; it is 3.5 miles long and is
named on Devils Postpile (1953) 15' quadrangle.

Cargyle Meadow [MADERA]: *area,* 5.5 miles
southwest of Devils Postpile (lat. 37°34'25"
N, long. 119°09'30" W); the place is east of
East Fork Cargyle Creek. Named on Devils
Postpile (1953) 15' quadrangle.

Caric [TULARE]: *locality,* 3.5 miles south of
Earlimart along Southern Pacific Railroad
(lat. 35°49'55" N, long. 119°15'40" W; sec.
22, T 24 S, R 25 E). Named on Delano West
(1954) 7.5' quadrangle.

Carillon: see **Mount Carillon** [TULARE].

Carlile: see **Caruthers** [FRESNO].

Carlson Station: see **Balsam Creek** [FRESNO].

Carmelita: see **Reedley** [FRESNO].

Carnaris Spring: see **Carneros Spring**
[KERN].

Carnaros Spring: see **Carneros Spring**
[KERN].

Carneros Canyon [KERN]: *canyon,* 6.5 miles
long, on Kern-San Luis Obispo county line
along Carneros Creek above a point less than
1 mile north of Carneros Rocks (lat. 35°26'45"
N, long. 119° 50'35" W; sec. 32, T 28 S, R 20
E). Named on Carneros Rocks (1959) and Las
Yeguas Ranch (1959) 7.5' quadrangles. United
States Board on Geographic Names (1933a,
p. 196) rejected the name "McLean Canyon"
for the feature.

Carneros Creek [KERN]: *stream,* heads in San
Luis Obispo County and flows 9 miles to
Santos Creek 3.25 miles north-northeast of
Carneros Rocks (lat. 35°28'55" N, long.
119°49'45" W; near NW cor. sec. 21, T 28 S,
R 20 E). Named on Carneros Rocks (1959)
7.5' quadrangle.

Carneros Rocks [KERN]: *relief feature,* 15
miles northwest of McKittrick (lat. 35°26'15"
N, long. 119°50'50" W; sec. 5, T 29 S, R 20
E); the feature is near the mouth of Carneros
Canyon. Named on Carneros Rocks (1959)
7.5' quadrangle.

Carneros Spring [KERN]: *spring,* at Carneros
Rocks (lat. 35°26'20" N, long. 119°50'45" W;
sec. 5, T 29 S, R 20 E). Named on Carneros
Rocks (1959) 7.5' quadrangle. Anderson (p.
169) mentioned Canara Springs. United States
Board on Geographic Names (1933a, p. 196)
rejected the names "Canaris Spring," "Canary
Spring," "Carnaris Spring," and "Carnaros
Spring" for the feature.

Carol Col: see **Humphreys Basin** [FRESNO].

Carter Creek [MADERA]: *stream,* flows 3.25
miles to Fine Gold Creek 4.5 miles northeast
of O'Neals (lat. 37°10'20" N, long. 119° 38' W;
sec. 1, T 9 S, R 21 E). Named on North Fork
(1965) and O'Neals (1965) 7.5' quadrangles.

Carter Creek [MADERA]: *stream,* heads in
Mariposa County and flows 7.5 miles to Miami Creek 4.25 miles west of Yosemite Forks
in Madera County (lat. 37°21'45" N, long.
119°42'20" W; near W line sec. 32, T 6 S, R
21 E). Named on Bass Lake (1953) 15' quadrangle.

Cartridge Creek [FRESNO]: *stream,* flows 6.5
miles to Middle Fork Kings River nearly 4.5
miles northwest of Marion Peak (lat. 36°
59'50" N, long. 118°35'15" W); the stream
heads near Cartridge Pass. Named on Marion
Peak (1953) and Mount Pinchot (1953) 15'
quadrangles. Farquhar (1923, p. 386) connected the name with a story about a man who
had a good shot at a deer near the creek, but
who in his excitement pumped all of the car-
tridges out of the magazine of his rifle—this
act prompted his companions to give the name
"Cartridge" to the creek. South Fork enters

from the south 2 miles upstream from the mouth of the main stream; it is 2.5 miles long and is named on Marion Peak (1953) 15' quadrangle.

Cartridge Pass [FRESNO]: *pass,* 5 miles west-northwest of Mount Pinchot (lat. 36°58'30" N, long. 118°29'10" W); the pass is at the head of Cartridge Creek. Named on Mount Pinchot (1953) 15' quadrangle. The feature first was called Red Pass (Versteeg, p. 423).

Caruthers [FRESNO]: *town,* 15 miles south of downtown Fresno (lat. 36°32'30" N, long. 119°50' W; sec. 18, T 16 S, R 20 E). Named on Caruthers (1963) 7.5' quadrangle. The name commemorates W.A. Caruthers, a local farmer (Gudde, 1949, p. 59). Postal authorities established Caruthers post office in 1891; they established Carlile post office 7 miles northwest of Riverdale in 1894, moved it 1.25 miles east in 1899, and discontinued it in 1905 when they moved the service to Caruthers (Salley, p. 38, 39).

Carver Camp [TULARE]: *locality,* 11 miles south-southeast of Camp Nelson (lat. 36°00'05" N, long. 118°31'25" W; sec. 21, T 22 S, R 32 E). Named on Camp Nelson (1956) 15' quadrangle.

Carver Peak [TULARE]: *peak,* 6 miles south-southwest of California Hot Springs (lat. 35°48'10" N, long. 118°42'20" W; sec. 35, T 24 S, R 30 E). Altitude 4242 feet. Named on California Hot Springs (1958) 15' quadrangle.

Carver Spring [KERN]: *spring,* 3.25 miles west-southwest of Woody (lat. 35°41' N, long. 118°53'20" W; sec. 7, T 26 S, R 29 E). Named on Sand Canyon (1965) 7.5' quadrangle.

Casa Vieja Meadows [TULARE]: *area,* 7 miles east-southeast of Hockett Peak (lat. 36°12' N, long. 118°16'10" W; mainly in sec. 11, T 20 S, R 34 E). Named on Hockett Peak (1956) 15' quadrangle. The name is from an old house or cabin at the place (Browning 1986, p. 33).

Cascada: see **Big Creek** [FRESNO] (3).

Cascada Spring [FRESNO]: *spring,* 18 miles northwest of Coalinga (lat. 36°18' N, long. 120°37'25" W; sec. 1, T 19 S, R 12 E). Named on Santa Rita Peak (1969) 7.5' quadrangle.

Cascade Creek [TULARE]: *stream,* flows 2.25 miles to Yucca Creek 2.5 miles east-northeast of Yucca Mountain (lat. 36°35'20" N, long., 118°49'40" W; near E line sec. 28, T 15 S, R 29 E). Named on Giant Forest (1956) 15' quadrangle.

Cascade Creek: see **Cave Creek** [TULARE].

Cascade Valley [FRESNO]: *canyon,* 3.5 miles long, 5 miles west of Red Slate Mountain along Fish Creek (1) (lat. 37°30'20" N, long. 118°57'30" W). Named on Mount Abbot (1953) and Mount Morrison (1953) 15' quadrangles. J.N. LeConte and J.S. Hutchinson called the place Peninsula Meadow in 1908 for a peninsula that juts into the stream (Farquhar, 1923, p. 386).

Cascadel: see **North Fork** [MADERA].

Cascadel Point [MADERA]: *ridge,* east-trending, 1.5 miles long, 9.5 miles south of Shuteye Peak (lat. 37°13' N, long. 119°26'45" W). Named on Shaver Lake (1953) 15' quadrangle.

Cascajo Hill [KERN]: *peak,* 12 miles north of Blackwells Corner (lat. 35°47' N, long. 119°55' W; near W line sec. 3, T 25 S, R 19 E). Altitude 590 feet. Named on Avenal Gap (1954) 7.5' quadrangle. United States Board on Geographic Names (1933b, p. 6) noted that the name refers to conglomerate that crops out on the peak—*cascajo* means "gravel" in Spanish.

Case Mountain [TULARE]: *peak,* 8 miles east-southeast of Kaweah at the northwest end of Salt Creek Ridge (lat. 36°24'40" N, long. 118°48'10" W). Altitude 5818 feet Named on Kaweah (1957) 15' quadrangle. The name commemorates Bill Case, who hauled shakes from the neighborhood with a team made up of a horse, a mule, a burro, and a steer (Hanna, p. 58).

Cassadys Bar: see **Old Millerton** [FRESNO].

Cassidy Meadows [MADERA]: *areas,* 16 miles northeast of Shuteye Peak (lat. 37°28'45" N, long. 119°11'15" W; sec. 24, T 5 S, R 25 E). Named on Kaiser Peak (1953) 15' quadrangle. Kaiser (1904) 30' quadrangle has the singular form "Cassidy Meadow" for the name, which commemorates James Cassidy, an early sheepman (Browning, 1986, p. 34).

Castac [KERN]: *land grant,* at and southeast of Grapevine. Named on Frazier Mountain (1958), Grapevine (1958), Lebec (1958), and Pastoria Creek (1958) 7.5' quadrangles. Jose Maria Covarrubias received 5 leagues in 1843 and claimed 22,178 acres patented in 1866 (Cowan, p. 25; Cowan gave the form "Castec" as an alternate). The name is of Indian origin (Kroeber, p. 37).

Castac Lake [KERN]: *lake,* 1.25 miles long, 1.25 miles east of Lebec (lat. 34°50'05" N, long. 118°50'35" W); the lake is on Castac grant. Named on Lebec (1958) 7.5' quadrangle. Called Castaic Lake on Lebec (1945) 7.5' quadrangle, but United States Board on Geographic Names (1960b, p. 16) rejected this form of the name. Blake (1857, p. 47) referred to "Salt pond, or Casteca lake (dry)."

Castac Valley [KERN]: *valley,* at and near Lebec on Castac grant; extends into Los Angeles County near the mouth of Cuddy Canyon. Named on Frazier Mountain (1958), Grapevine (1958), and Lebec (1958) 7.5' quadrangles. Called Castaic Valley on Frazier Mountain (1944) and Lebec (1945) 7.5' quadrangles, but United States Board on Geographic Names (1960b, p. 16) rejected this form of the name.

Castaic Lake: see **Castac Lake** [KERN].

Castaic Valley: see **Castac Valley** [KERN].

Castec: see **Castac** [KERN].

Castle Butte [KERN]: *peak,* 17 miles east-northeast of Mojave (lat. 35°06'50" N, long. 117°52'35" W; at SW cor. sec. 26, T 32 S, R 38 E). Altitude 3124 feet. Named on California City South (1973) 7.5' quadrangle. Called Castle Rock on California Mining Bureau's (1917c) map.

Castle Butte Well [KERN]: *well,* 14 miles north-northwest of Boron (lat. 35°11'40" N, long. 117°42'45" W; sec. 32, T 31 S, R 40 E); the well is 11 miles east-northeast of Castle Butte. Named on Boron NW (1973) 7.5' quadrangle.

Castle Creek [TULARE]: *stream,* flows 4 miles to Middle Fork Kaweah River 9.5 miles west-southwest of Triple Divide Peak (lat. 36°32'20" N, long. 118°41'10" W). Named on Mineral King (1956) and Triple Divide Peak (1956) 15' quadrangles. The stream is named from Castle Rocks (Browning 1986, p. 34).

Castle Domes [FRESNO]: *relief feature,* 4.5 miles south-southwest of Mount Pinchot (lat. 36°52'45" N, long. 118°26'45" W). Named on Mount Pinchot (1953) 15' quadrangle.

Castle Lake [MADERA]: *lake,* 600 feet long, nearly 4 miles northwest of Devils Postpile (lat. 37°40'10" N, long. 119°07'10" W). Named on Devils Postpile (1953) 15' quadrangle.

Castle Mountain [FRESNO]: *peak,* 13 miles south of Coalinga on Fresno-Monterey county line (lat. 35°56'20" N, long. 120°20'20" W; sec. 10, T 23 S, R 15 E). Altitude 4343 feet. Named on The Dark Hole (1961) 7.5' quadrangle.

Castle Peak [FRESNO]: *peak,* 14 miles north of Hume (lat. 36°59'15" N, long. 118°51'45" W). Altitude 10,677 feet. Named on Tehipite Dome (1952) 15' quadrangle.

Castle Peak [MADERA]: *peak,* 11.5 miles south of Shuteye Peak (lat. 37°11'05" N, long. 119°26'30" W; near S line sec. 34, T 8 S, R 23 E). Altitude 4082 feet. Named on Shaver Lake (1953) 15' quadrangle. Called Oat Mt. on Kaiser (1904) 30' quadrangle.

Castle Rock [TULARE]:
(1) *peak,* 5 miles southwest of Hockett Peak (lat. 36°10'40" N, long. 118°27'30" W). Altitude 7740 feet. Named on Hockett Peak (1956) 15' quadrangle. The name is for the castlelike appearance of the feature (Browning 1986, p. 34).
(2) *hill,* less than 1 mile northwest of Woodlake (lat. 36°25'25" N, long. 119°05'20" W; sec. 30, T 17 S, R 27 E). Altitude 538 feet. Named on Woodlake (1952) 7.5' quadrangle.

Castle Rock: see **Castle Butte** [KERN].

Castle Rocks [TULARE]: *relief feature,* 12 miles west-southwest of Triple Divide Peak (lat. 36°30' N, long. 118°42'45" W). Named on Mineral King (1956) and Triple Divide Peak (1956) 15' quadrangles. Professor Dean, who had a homestead at the place, named the feature for its resemblance to the medieval castles on the Rhine (Browning 1986, p. 34).

Castro Canyon [FRESNO]: *canyon,* drained by a stream that flows 3 miles to Jacalitos Creek 9 miles southwest of Coalinga (lat. 36°02'20" N, long. 120°27'10" W; sec. 3, T 22 S, R 14 E). Named on Curry Mountain (1969) 7.5' quadrangle.

Castro Spring [FRESNO]: *spring,* 9 miles southwest of Coalinga (lat. 36°02' N, long. 120°27'40" W; sec. 9, T 22 S, R 14 E); the spring is in Castro Canyon. Named on Curry Mountain (1969) 7.5' quadrangle.

Cataract Creek [FRESNO]: *stream,* flows 3 miles to Palisade Creek 12 miles east-south-east of Mount Goddard at Deer Meadow (1) (lat. 37°03'15" N, long. 118°31'10" W). Named on Mount Goddard (1948) 15' quadrangle. J.N. LeConte and his companions named the stream (Browning 1986, p. 34-35).

Cat Canyon [KERN]: *canyon,* 10 miles west of Liebre Twins (lat. 34°59' N, long. 118°44'50" W; on S line sec. 36, T 11 N, R 18 W). Named on Winters Ridge (1966) 7.5' quadrangle.

Cathedral Lake [FRESNO]: *lake,* 1800 feet long, 4.5 miles south-southwest of Mount Goddard (lat. 37°02'25" N, long. 118°44'25" W). Named on Mount Goddard (1948) 15' quadrangle.

Catherine: see **Lake Catherine** [MADERA].

Cats Head Mountain [FRESNO]: *peak,* 4.5 miles north-northeast of Trimmer (lat. 36°57'30" N, long. 119°15'05" W; sec. 21, T 11 S, R 25 E). Altitude 3460 feet. Named on Trimmer (1965) 7.5' quadrangle.

Catskin Canyon [KINGS]: *canyon,* 3 miles long, 13 miles south of Avenal (lat. 35°49'30" N, long. 120°09'30" W). Named on Tent Hills (1942) 7.5' quadrangle.

Cattle Creek: see **Pastoria Creek** [KERN].

Cattle Mountain [MADERA]: *peak,* 11 miles southwest of Devils Postpile (lat. 37°31'05" N, long. 119°13'55" W; on W line sec. 3, T 5 S, R 25 E). Altitude 7946 feet. Named on Devils Postpile (1953) 15' quadrangle.

Caughran Spring [KERN]: *spring,* 2.25 miles northwest of Democrat Hot Springs (lat. 35°33'20" N, long. 118°41'20" W; near NW cor. sec. 30, T 27 S, R 31 E). Named on Democrat Hot Springs (1972) 7.5' quadrangle.

Cave Creek [TULARE]: *stream,* flows nearly 2 miles to Yucca Creek 2.25 miles east-north-east of Yucca Mountain (lat. 36°35'05" N, long. 118°50' W; near N line sec. 33, T 15 S, R 29 E). Named on Giant Forest (1956) 15' quadrangle. United States Board on Geographic Names (1933a, p. 204) rejected the name "Cascade Creek" for the stream.

Cawelo [KERN]: *locality,* 13 miles northwest of Bakersfield along Southern Pacific Railroad (lat. 35°30' N, long. 119°09'55" W). Named on Famoso (1953) and Rosedale (1954) 7.5' quadrangles. The name was coined from letters in names of partners of <u>Ca</u>mp, <u>We</u>st, <u>Lo</u>we, Farm Company (Bailey, 1967, p. 4). In 1909 Harry J. Marten promoted a colony called Martendale that was located a short distance south of Cawelo and made up of 109 Mennonite and Adventist families (Bailey, 1967, p. 16). Postal authorities established Martensdale post office in 1909 and discontinued it in 1910 (Salley, p. 134).

Cecile [FRESNO]: *locality,* 1.5 miles northeast of Malaga along Atchison, Topeka and Santa Fe Railroad (lat. 36°42' N, long. 119° 43' W; near W line sec. 20, T 14 S, R 21 E). Named on Malaga (1964) 7.5' quadrangle.

Cecile Lake [FRESNO]: *lake,* 1300 feet long, 1 mile west of Red Slate Mountain (lat. 37°30'20" N, long. 118°53'20" W). Named on Mount Morrison (1953) 15' quadrangle.

Cecile Lake [MADERA]: *lake,* 1900 feet long, 5.5 miles west-northwest of Devils Postpile at the head of Shadow Creek (lat. 37°39'50" N, long. 119°10' W). Named on Devils Postpile (1953) 15' quadrangle. The feature also is called Upper Iceberg Lake (Smith, p. 62).

Cedarbrook [FRESNO]: *settlement,* 6.5 miles east-southeast of Dunlap (lat. 36°42'30" N, long. 119°00'20" W; sec. 14, T 14 S, R 27 E). Named on Miramonte (1966) 7.5' quadrangle.

Cedar Canyon [FRESNO]: *canyon,* drained by a stream that flows nearly 4 miles to Zapato Chino Creek 10 miles south-southeast of Coalinga (lat. 36°00'45" N, long. 120°17' W; sec. 18, T 22 S, R 16 E). Named on Kreyenhagen Hills (1956) 7.5' quadrangle.

Cedar Canyon [KERN]:

(1) *canyon,* drained by a stream that flows 6.5 miles to Bitterwater Creek (2) 13 miles south-southeast of Orchard Peak (lat. 35°33'35" N, long. 120°02'40" W; sec. 21, T 27 S, R 18 E). Named on Las Yeguas Ranch (1959), Packwood Creek (1961), and Shale Point (1953) 7.5' quadrangles.

(2) *canyon,* drained by a stream that flows 5.5 miles to Tejon Creek nearly 6 miles west of Cummings Mountain (lat. 35°02'45" N, long. 118°40'10" W). Named on Cummings Mountain (1966) and Tejon Ranch (1966) 7.5' quadrangles.

(3) *canyon,* drained by a stream that flows 1.25 miles to El Paso Creek 6.5 miles west-northwest of Liebre Twins (lat. 34°58'45" N, long. 118°40'45" W; sec. 3, T 10 N, R 17 W). Named on Winters Ridge (1966) 7.5' quadrangle.

Cedar Canyon [TULARE]: *canyon,* drained by a stream that flows 3 miles to Durrwood Creek 12 miles south-southwest of Hockett Peak (lat. 36°03'20" N, long. 118°25'55" W). Named on Hockett Peak (1956) 15' quadrangle.

Cedar Creek [KERN]: *stream,* flows 15 miles to Poso Creek 6.25 miles south-southwest of Glennville (lat. 35°38'30" N, long. 118° 44'25" W; near N line sec. 27, T 26 S, R 30 E). Named on California Hot Springs (1958) 15' quadrangle, and on Alta Sierra (1972) and Glennville (1972) 7.5' quadrangles.

Cedar Creek [TULARE]:

(1) *stream,* flows 3.25 miles to Dry Creek (1) 6.25 miles east-southeast of Auckland (lat. 36°32'25" N, long. 119°00'35" W; sec. 14, T 16 S, R 27 E). Named on Giant Forest (1956) 15' quadrangle, and on Auckland (1966) 7.5' quadrangle. Called Elder Creek on Dinuba (1924) 30' quadrangle, but United States Board on Geographic Names (1967c, p. 3) rejected this name for the stream.

(2) *stream,* flows 2.5 miles to Yucca Creek 1.5 miles south-southeast of Yucca Mountain (lat. 36°33'15" N, long. 118°51'20" W). Named on Giant Forest (1956) 15' quadrangle.

(3) *stream,* flows 4 miles to South Fork Tule River 8 miles south-southwest of Camp Nelson (lat. 36°02'20" N, long. 118°40'10" W). Named on Camp Nelson (1956) 15' quadrangle.

(4) *stream,* flows 2 miles to South Fork Kaweah River 10 miles southwest of Mineral King (lat. 36°21'20" N, long. 118°43'55" W). Named on Mineral King (1956) 15' quadrangle. United States Board on Geographic Names (1960b, p. 17) rejected the name "Squaw Creek" for the stream.

Cedar Creek Campground [KERN]: *locality,* 2.25 miles northwest of Alta Sierra (lat. 35°44'55" N, long. 118°34'55" W; sec. 18, T 25 S, R 32 E); the place is along Cedar Creek. Named on Alta Sierra (1972) 7.5' quadrangle.

Cedar Crest [FRESNO]: *town,* 3.5 miles northeast of the town of Big Creek on the north side of Huntington Lake (1) (lat. 37°15' N, long. 119°11'45" W; in and near sec. 11, 12, T 8 S, R 25 E). Named on Huntington Lake (1953) and Kaiser Pass (1953) 15' quadrangles. Postal authorities established Cedar Crest post office in 1923, discontinued it in 1955, and reestablished it in 1962 (Salley, p. 40).

Cedar Grove [FRESNO]: *locality,* 14 miles southwest of Marion Peak in Kings Canyon (lat. 36°47'30" N, long. 118°40'10" W). Named on Marion Peak (1953) 15' quadrangle. Incense-cedar trees are abundant at the place; John Muir called the spot Deer Park (Browning, p. 35).

Cedar Slope [TULARE]: *locality,* 1.5 miles east of Camp Nelson (lat. 36°08'40" N, long. 118°34'40" W; sec. 33, T 20 S, R 31 E). Named on Camp Nelson (1956) 15' quadrangle.

Cedar Spring [TULARE]: *spring,* 1.25 miles south-southwest of California Hot Springs (lat. 35°51'50" N, long. 118°41' W; sec. 1, T 24 S, R 30 E). Named on California Hot Springs (1958) 15' quadrangle.

Cedric Wright: see **Mount Cedric Wright** [FRESNO].

Cella [FRESNO]: *locality,* 3.5 miles southeast of Centerville along Atchison, Topeka and Santa Fe Railroad (lat. 36°41'30" N, long. 119°27'10" W; at S line sec. 22, T 14 S, R 23 E). Named on Wahtoke (1966) 7.5' quadrangle. Called Wahtoke Winery on Wahtoke (1923) 7.5' quadrangle.

Ceneda [KERN]: *locality,* less than 1 mile southwest of Saltdale along Southern Pacific Railroad (lat. 35°21'15" N, long. 117°53'50" W). Named on Cantil (1967) 7.5' quadrangle.

Centennial Peak: see **Colby Pass** [TULARE].

Centennial Ridge [KERN]: *ridge,* west- to westsouthwest-trending, 6 miles long, center 6.25 miles east-northeast of Caliente (lat. 35° 20'10" N, long. 118°32'15" W). Named on Loraine (1972) and Oiler Peak (1972) 7.5' quadrangles.

Center Basin [TULARE]: *relief feature,* 11 miles north-northwest of Mount Whitney (lat. 36°43'30" N, long. 118°21' W); the feature is east of Center Peak. Named on Mount Whitney (1956) 15' quadrangle.

Center Basin Crags [TULARE]: *relief feature,* 11 miles north-northwest of Mount Whitney on Tulare-Inyo county line (lat. 36°44'10" N, long. 118°20'45" W); the feature is northeast of Center Basin. Named on Mount Whitney (1956) 15' quadrangle.

Center Peak [FRESNO]: *peak,* 5.5 miles northwest of Coalinga Mineral Springs (lat. 36°12'10" N, long. 120°37'20" W; sec. 12, T 20 S, R 12 E). Altitude 4536 feet. Named on Sherman Peak (1969) 7.5' quadrangle.

Center Peak [TULARE]: *peak,* 11 miles northnorthwest of Mount Whitney (lat. 36°43'15" N, long. 118°21'40" W). Altitude 12,760 feet. Named on Mount Whitney (1956) 15' quadrangle. Cornelius B. Bradley and his companions named the peak in 1898 for its position in the center of a cirque (Gudde, 1949, p. 62).

Centerville [FRESNO]: *town,* 16 miles east of Fresno on the northwest side of Kings River (lat. 36°44' N, long. 119°29'50" W; sec. 8, T 14 S, R 23 E). Named on Sanger (1923) and Wahtoke (1966) 7.5' quadrangles. A village called Scottsburg started in 1854 on a knoll in the bottom lands of Kings River east of present Sanger, where in the winter of 1861 and 1862 a flood destroyed it; residents rebuilt the place at the foot of a bluff to the northeast, where in 1867 another flood engulfed it; finally the community moved to the top of the bluff and was rechristened Centerville (Hoover, Rensch, and Rensch, p. 92). Postal authorities established Scottsburgh post office in 1856, discontinued it in 1858, reestablished it in 1859, and discontinued it in 1864 (Frickstad, p. 37). Grunsky (p. 40-41) used the name "Centerville Bottoms" for bottom lands that extend for about 9 miles along Kings River near Centerville. California Mining Bureau's (1917a) map has the name "King River" for a locality near present Centerville, and Mendenhall's (1908) map has the name "Kings River" for what appears to be the same place.

Centerville Bottoms: see **Centerville** [FRESNO].

Central Camp [MADERA]: *locality,* 3 miles

west of Shuteye Peak (lat. 37°21' N, long. 119°28'55" W; sec. 5, T 7 S, R 23 E). Named on Shuteye Peak (1953) 15' quadrangle. United States Board on Geographic Names (1994, p. 5) approved the name "Peckinpah Mountain" for a peak bounded by Peckinpah Creek 5.2 miles south-southeast of Central Camp (lat. 37°16'30" N, long. 119°28' W; sec. 33, T 17 S, R 23 E), and rejected the name "Mount Peckinpah" for it.

Central Fork Cottonwood Creek: see **Crystal Creek** [KERN].

Central Fork Rattlesnake Creek: see **Crystal Creek** [KERN].

Central Valley: see "Regional setting."

Cerro Alto [KINGS]: *peak,* 5.25 miles east of Avenal (lat. 35°59'25" N, long. 120°02'05" W; sec. 28, T 22 S, R 18 E). Named on Kettleman Plain (1953) 7.5' quadrangle. United States Board on Geographic Names (1933b, p. 6) noted that the name is descriptive—*cerro alto* means "high hill" in Spanish

Cerro del Sur [KERN]: *hill,* 10 miles north of Blackwells Corner (lat. 35°45'55" N, long. 119°53'20" W; sec. 11, T 25 S, R 19 E). Named on Avenal Gap (1954) 7.5' quadrangle. Altitude 475 feet. United States Board on Geographic Names (1933b, p. 6) pointed out that the feature is the southernmost hill of South Dome, Kettleman Hills.

Cerro Lodoso [KINGS]: *peak,* 2.5 miles northeast of Avenal (lat. 36°02'20" N, long. 120°06'45" W; sec. 3, T 22 S, R 17 E). Altitude 1242 feet. Named on La Cima (1963) 7.5' quadrangle. United States Board on Geographic Names (1933b, p. 6) noted that *cerro lodoso* means "muddy hill" in Spanish.

Cerro Noroeste [KERN]: *peak,* 6.5 miles southwest of Eagle Rest Peak (lat. 34°49'50" N, long. 119°12'10" W; near SW cor. sec. 26, T 9 N, R 22 W). Altitude 8286 feet. Named on Sawmill Mountain (1943) 7.5' quadrangle. United States Board on Geographic Names (1990, p. 9) rejected the names "Abel Mountain" and "Mount Abel" for the feature. The Board (1981c, p. 6) approved the name "Puerta del Suelo" for a pass situated 0.5 mile east-southeast of Cerro Noroeste (lat. 34°49'37" N, long. 119°11'37" W; sec. 35, T 9 N, R 22 W); the name, which has the meaning "passage" in Spanish, is from the legend that Spanish priests used the pass.

Cerro Noroeste Camp [KERN]: *locality,* 6.5 miles southwest of Eagle Rest Peak (lat. 34°49'55" N, long. 119°12'35" W; near SE cor. sec. 27, T 9 N, R 22 W); the place is on the west side of Cerro Noroeste. Named on Sawmill Mountain (1943) 7.5' quadrangle.

Cerro Ultimo [KINGS]: *peak,* 6 miles eastnortheast of Avenal (lat. 35°58'45" N, long. 120°01'20" W; near SE cor. sec. 28, T 22 S, R 18 E). Named on Kettleman Plain (1953) 7.5' quadrangle. The name refers to the feature being the last high peak along the road that

traverses North Dome, Kettleman Hills—
cerro ultimo means "last hill" in Spanish
(United States Board on Geographic Names,
1933b, p. 6).

Chaffee [KERN]: *locality,* 1 mile north of downtown Mojave along Southern Pacific Railroad
(lat. 35°04' N, long. 118°10'15" W; near NE
cor. sec. 8, T 11 N, R 12 W). Named on
Mojave (1973) 7.5' quadrangle. Called Chaffe
on California Mining Bureau's (1917c) map.

Chagoopa Creek [TULARE]: *stream,* flows 7
miles to Kern River 13 miles north-northwest
of Kern Peak (lat. 36°28' N, long. 118° 24'30"
W); Chagoopa Falls is along the stream.
Named on Kern Peak (1956) and Mount
Whitney (1956) 15' quadrangles.

Chagoopa Falls [TULARE]: *waterfall,* 13 miles
north-northwest of Kern Peak (lat. 36°28'10"
N, long. 118°24'45" W); the feature is along
Chagoopa Creek. Named on Kern Peak
(1956) 15' quadrangle. W.B. Wallace, J.W.A.
Wright, and F.H. Wales named the feature
Sha-goo-pah Falls in 1881 to commemorate
an old Piute Indian (Browning 1986, p. 36),
but United States Board on Geographic
Names (1933a, p. 207) rejected the form
"Shagoopah Falls" for the name. The feature
was called Cañon Falls on a Sequoia National
Park map of 1906 (Browning 1986, p. 36).

Chagoopa Plateau [TULARE]: *area,* 15 miles
northwest of Kern Peak (lat. 36°29'15" N, long.
118°26'30" W); Chagoopa Creek crosses the
area. Named on Kern Peak (1956) and Mount
Whitney (1956) 15' quadrangles. William R.
Dudley and his companions named the place
in 1897 (Browning 1986, p. 36).

Chain Lakes [FRESNO]: *lakes,* largest 1100
feet long, 14 miles north of Hume (lat.
36°58'50" N, long. 118°53' W). Named on
Tehipite Dome (1952) 15' quadrangle.

Chain Lakes [MADERA]: *lakes,* largest 1600
feet long, 4.5 miles south of Merced Peak (lat.
37°34'05" N, long. 119°24'15" W). Named
on Merced Peak (1953) 15' quadrangle.

Chalaney Creek [TULARE]: *stream,* flows 6.25
miles to White River (1) nearly 7 miles southeast of Fountain Springs (lat. 35°49'20" N,
long. 118°49'50" W; sec. 22, T 24 S, R 29 E).
Named on White River (1965) 7.5' quadrangle. Called Chanley Creek on White River
(1936) 15' quadrangle, and called Chilean
Creek on White River (1952) 15' quadrangle,
but United States Board on Geographic
Names (1967a, p. 9) rejected both names for
the stream.

Chalk Buttes [KINGS]: *peaks,* on a ridge, nearly
4 miles long, that is 8 miles south-southwest
of Avenal (lat. 35°53'30" N, long. 120°10'45"
W). Named on Garza Peak (1953) 7.5' quadrangle.

Chalk Cliff [KERN]: *relief feature,* 4.25 miles
east-northeast of Knob Hill (lat. 35°35'15" N,
long. 118°52'50" W). Named on Knob Hill
(1965) 7.5' quadrangle.

Chamberlain Lake [FRESNO]: *lake,* 1200 feet
long, 10 miles southwest of Mount Abbot (lat.
37°17'20" N, long. 118°54'35" W). Named on
Mount Abbot (1953) 15' quadrangle. Forest
Service employees Neil Perkins and Harvey
Sauter named the lake for Joel Oliver
Chamberlain of Fresno, who guided a group
to the site in 1947 (Browning 1986, p. 36-37).

Chamberlains Camp [FRESNO]: *locality,* 9
miles west-northwest of Blackcap Mountain
(lat. 37°07' N, long. 118°56'50" W; sec. 29, T
9 S, R 28 E). Named on Blackcap Mountain
(1953) 15' quadrangle. Carl Chamberlain built
a cabin at the place in 1945 when he was running cattle in the neighborhood (Browning
1986, p. 37).

Chamberlin: see **Mount Chamberlin** [TU-
LARE].

Champagne Spring [KERN]: *spring,* 13 miles
north-northwest of Mojave (lat. 35°13'30" N,
long. 118°14'40" W; near N line sec. 20, T 31
S, R 35 E). Named on Cache Peak (1973) 7.5'
quadrangle.

Chanac Canyon: see **Chanac Creek** [KERN].

Chanac Creek [KERN]: *stream,* heads in Cummings Valley and flows 10.5 miles to Tejon
Creek 10 miles west of Cummings Mountain
(lat. 35°04'05" N, long. 118°44'45" W; sec.
1, T 11 N, R 18 E). Named on Cummings
Mountain (1966) and Tejon Ranch (1966) 7.5'
quadrangles. The canyon of the stream was
called Chanac Canyon for François Chanac,
a Frenchman who lived there (Latta, 1976, p.
171).

Chaney Ranch Canyon [FRESNO]: *canyon,*
drained by a stream that flows 1.5 miles to
lowlands 17 miles southwest of Firebaugh (lat.
36°42'30" N, long. 120°42' W; sec. 18, T 14
S, R 12 E). Named on Chounet Ranch (1956)
7.5' quadrangle.

Chaneys: see **Panoche Creek** [FRESNO].

Chanley Creek: see **Chalaney Creek** [TU-
LARE].

Chanz: see **Mojave** [KERN].

Chapel Lake [FRESNO]: *lake,* 800 feet long,
4.5 miles south-southwest of Mount Goddard
(lat. 37°02'45" N, long. 118°44'45" W).
Named on Mount Goddard (1948) 15' quadrangle. William A. Dill of California Department of Fish and Game named the lake in
1948 for its proximity to Cathedral Lake
(Browning 1986, p. 37).

Chapman Creek [MADERA]: *stream,* heads in
Mariposa County and flows 12.5 miles to
Chowchilla River 3 miles northwest of
Raymond in Madera County (lat. 37°15'15"
N, long. 119°56'40" W; sec. 12, T 8 S, R 18
E). Named on Ben Hur (1947) 7.5' quad-
rangle. On Mariposa (1912) 30' quadrangle,
the part of the stream above the mouth of
Becknell Creek is called West Branch.

Charley Mountain [FRESNO]: *peak,* 17 miles
west of Coalinga on Fresno-Monterey county
line (lat. 36°08'25" N, long. 120°39'50" W;

sec. 34, T 20 S, R 12 E). Altitude 3885 feet. Named on Priest Valley (1969) 7.5' quadrangle.

Charlotte Creek [FRESNO]: *stream,* flows 4 miles to Bubbs Creek 13 miles south-southwest of Mount Pinchot (lat. 36°46'20" N, long. 118°29'15" W); the stream heads at Charlotte Lake. Named on Mount Pinchot (1953) 15' quadrangle.

Charlotte Lake [FRESNO]: *lake,* 2100 feet long, 12 miles south of Mount Pinchot (lat. 36°46'35" N, long. 118°25'30" W); the lake is at the head of Charlotte Creek. Named on Mount Pinchot (1953) 15' quadrangle. In the early days the feature was called Rhoda Lake for Mrs. Charles Houle, who camped there frequently in the 1880's (Browning 1986, p. 37).

Charybdis [FRESNO]: *peak,* 3 miles east-southeast of Mount Goddard (lat. 37°05'15" N, long. 118°40' W); the peak is southeast of Ionian Basin and 1.25 miles east-northeast of Scylla. Altitude 13,091 feet. Named on Mount Goddard (1948) 15' quadrangle. Theodore S. Solomons and Ernest C. Bonner named the peak in 1895; the feature also was called Charybdis Peak (Browning 1986, p. 37). United States Board on Geographic Names (1964b, p. 12) rejected the form "Charybois" for the name, and noted that Charybdis is the whirlpool off the Sicilian coast that figures prominently in Greek mythology.

Charybdis Peak: see **Charybdis** [FRESNO].

Charybois: see **Charybdis** [FRESNO].

Chasm Lake [FRESNO]: *lake,* 2300 feet long, 2.5 miles east-southeast of Mount Goddard in Ionian Basin (lat. 37°05'25" N, long. 118°40'40" W). Named on Mount Goddard (1948) 15' quadrangle. Lewis Clark of the Sierra Club proposed the name (Browning 1986, p. 37).

Chawanakee: see **Camp Chawanakee** [FRESNO].

Chawanakee Flat [FRESNO]: *area,* 7.5 miles north of Shaver Lake Heights (present town of Shaver lake) (lat. 37°13' N, long. 119°19'15" W; sec. 23, T 8 S, R 24 E). Named on Shaver Lake (1953) 15' quadrangle.

Chay-o-poo-ya-pah: see **Canebrake Creek** [KERN].

Chepo Saddle [MADERA]: *pass,* 2.5 miles east-southeast of Yosemite Forks (lat. 37°20'55" N, long. 119°35'20" W; sec. 5, T 7 S, R 22 E). Named on Bass Lake (1953) 15' quadrangle.

Cherokee Flat [TULARE]: *area,* 5.5 miles south of Kaweah (lat. 36° 23'35" N, long. 118°54' W; mainly in sec. 1, T 18 S, R 28 E). Named on Kaweah (1957) 15' quadrangle.

Cherokee Strip [KERN]: *locality,* 2.5 miles south-southeast of Shafter (lat. 35°28' N, long. 119°15'35" W; at W line sec. 26, T 28 S, R 25 E). Named on Rio Bravo (1954) 7.5' quadrangle.

Cherry Creek [KERN]: *stream,* flows 2.5 miles to Salt Creek (2) 6.5 miles east-southeast of

Eagle Rest Peak (lat. 34°52'20" N, long. 119°01'55" W; near SE cor. sec. 7, T 9 N, R 20 W). Named on Cuddy Valley (1943) 7.5' quadrangle. United States Board on Geographic Names (1989c, p. 1) rejected the name "Salt Creek" for the stream.

Cherry Creek: see **Salt Creek** [KERN] (2).

Cherry Flat [FRESNO]: *area,* 6 miles north of Trimmer (lat. 36°59'40" N, long. 119°17'40" W; at SE cor. sec. 1, T 11 S, R 24 E). Named on Trimmer (1965) 7.5' quadrangle.

Cherry Flat [TULARE]: *area,* 4.5 miles north-northwest of Yucca Mountain (lat. 36°37'50" N, long. 118°53'50" W; near SE cor. sec. 11, T 15 S, R 28 E). Named on Giant Forest (1956) 15' quadrangle.

Cherry Gap [FRESNO]: *pass,* 2.5 miles west-southwest of Hume (lat. 36°46'35" N, long. 118°57'35" W; sec. 20, T 13 S, R 28 E). Named on Tehipite Dome (1952) 15' quadrangle.

Cherry Gap [KERN]: *pass,* 8 miles northeast of Mount Adelaide (lat. 35°29'55" N, long. 118°37'20" W; near NE cor. sec. 15, T 28 S, R 31 E). Named on Breckenridge Mountain (1972) 7.5' quadrangle.

Cherry Hill [TULARE]: *peak,* 7 miles east of Fairview (lat. 35°55'20" N, long. 118°22'20" W; sec. 13, T 23 S, R 33 E). Altitude 8833 feet. Named on Kernville (1956) 15' quadrangle.

Chetwood Creek [MADERA]: *stream,* flows 2 miles to North Fork San Joaquin River 8.5 miles west-southwest of Devils Postpile (lat. 37°35'50" N, long. 119°14'10" W). Named on Devils Postpile (1953) and Merced Peak (1953) 15' quadrangles. Merced Peak (1953) 15' quadrangle shows Chetwood cabin near the stream.

Chickencoop Canyon [TULARE]: *canyon,* 2.25 miles long, 12.5 miles south of Kaweah (lat. 36°17'30" N, long. 118°55'30" W). Named on Kaweah (1957) 15' quadrangle.

Chicken Spring Lake [TULARE]: *lake,* 1300 feet long, 14 miles north-northwest of Olancha Peak (lat. 36°27'55" N, long. 118°13'35" W; sec. 7, T 17 S, R 35 E). Named on Olancha (1956) 15' quadrangle.

Chicken Spring Pass: see **Cottonwood Pass** [TULARE].

Chico Canyon [KERN-TULARE]: *canyon,* drained by a stream that heads in Kern County and flows 3 miles to Kern River 9 miles southeast of Fairview in Tulare County (lat. 35°48'10" N, long. 118°27'10" W; at E line sec. 31, T 24 S, R 33 E). Named on Kernville (1956) 15' quadrangle.

Chico Martinez Creek [KERN]: *stream,* flows 8 miles to lowlands 3.5 miles east of Carneros Rocks (lat. 35°25'50" N, long. 119°47'10" W; near E line sec. 2, T 29 S, R 20 E). Named on Belridge (1953) and Carneros Rocks (1959) 7.5' quadrangles. The stream, which also is called El Arroyo de Chico Martinez, was named for a Spanish pioneer in the neighborhood (Hoover, Rensch, and Rensch, p. 128).

Chief Lake: see **Big Chief Lake** [FRESNO]; **Warrior Lake** [FRESNO].

Chilean Creek: see **Chalaney Creek** [TULARE].

Chilkoot Campground [MADERA]: *locality*, 5 miles east of Yosemite Forks (lat. 37°21'45" N, long. 119°32'20" W; sec. 35, T 6 S, R 22 E); the place is near the mouth of Chilkoot Creek. Named on Bass Lake (1953) 15' quadrangle.

Chilkoot Creek [MADERA]: *stream*, flows 5.5 miles to North Fork Willow Creek (2) 5 miles east of Yosemite Forks (lat. 37°21'55" N, long. 119°32'20" W; sec. 35, T 6 S, R 22 E); the stream heads at Chilkoot Lake. Named on Bass Lake (1953) and Shuteye Peak (1953) 15' quadrangles. United States Board on Geographic Names (1933a, p. 216) rejected the name "Willow Creek" for the feature.

Chilkoot Lake [MADERA]: *lake*, 1000 feet long, 5 miles northwest of Shuteye Peak (lat. 37°24'40" N, long. 119°28'50" W; sec. 17, T 6 S, R 23 E); the lake is at the head of Chilkoot Creek. Named on Shuteye Peak (1953) 15' quadrangle.

Chilnualna Creek [MADERA]: *stream*, heads along Madera-Mariposa county line and flows 7.5 miles to South Fork Merced River 1.25 miles east-northeast of Wawona (lat. 37°32'45" N, long. 119°38' W; sec. 35, T 4 S, R 21 E). Named on Yosemite (1956) 15' quadrangle. Called Chilnoialny Cr. on Hoffmann and Gardner's (1863-1867) map, but United States Board on Geographic Names (1933a, p. 216) rejected the forms "Chilnoialny Creek," "Chilanoialna Creek," and "Chilnoalna Creek" for the name.

Chilnualna Lakes [MADERA]: *lakes*, 1 mile west of Buena Vista Peak on Madera-Mariposa county line (lat. 37°35'45" N, long. 119°32'15" W); the lakes are on upper reaches of Chilnualna Creek. Named on Yosemite (1956) 15' quadrangle.

Chimney Creek [KERN-TULARE]: *stream*, heads in Tulare County and flows 21 miles to Canebrake Creek 5.5 miles east-northeast of Onyx in Kern County (lat. 35°43'50" N, long. 118°08'15" W; sec. 29, T 25 S, R 36 E); the stream passes east of Chimney Peak. Named on Lamont Peak (1956) 15' quadrangle, and on Onyx (1972) 7.5' quadrangle.

Chimney Lake [FRESNO]: *lake*, 1000 feet long, 6.25 miles west-southwest of Blackcap Mountain (lat. 37°01'40" N, long. 118°53'25" W; sec. 26, T 10 S, R 28 E). Named on Blackcap Mountain (1953) 15' quadrangle.

Chimney Meadow [TULARE]: *area*, 4.5 miles north-northeast of Lamont Peak (lat. 35°51'20" N, long. 118°00'35" W); the place is 2 miles east-southeast of Chimney Peak along Chimney Creek. Named on Lamont Peak (1956) 15' quadrangle. Called Chimney Meadows on Olmsted's (1900) map.

Chimney Peak [TULARE]: *peak*, 5 miles north of Lamont Peak (lat. 35°52' N, long. 118°02'30" W). Altitude 7990 feet. Named on Lamont Peak (1956) 15' quadrangle.

Chimney Rock [TULARE]: *peak*, 5.5 miles north of Yucca Mountain (lat. 36°39'15" N, long. 118°52' W; sec. 6, T 15 S, R 29 E). Altitude 7711 feet. Named on Giant Forest (1956) 15' quadrangle.

Chimney Rock: see **Finger Rock** [FRESNO].

Chimney Spring [FRESNO]: *spring*, 11 miles east-northeast of Clovis (lat. 36°52' N, long. 119°30'55" W; near N line sec. 25, T 12 S, R 22 E). Named on Round Mountain (1964) 7.5' quadrangle, which has a windmill symbol at the place.

Chimney Spring [TULARE]: *spring*, 3.25 miles southeast of Auckland (lat. 36°33'20" N, long. 119°03'55" W; sec. 8, T 16 S, R 27 E). Named on Auckland (1966) 7.5' quadrangle.

Chimo Flat [KERN]: *area*, 6.25 miles north-northwest of Caliente (lat. 35°22'10" N, long. 118°40'55" W). Named on Bena (1972) 7.5' quadrangle.

China Borax Lake: see **China Lake** [KERN] (1).

China Creek [MADERA]: *stream*, flows 5.25 miles to Fresno River 3 miles south-southwest of Yosemite Forks at Oakhurst (lat. 37°19'45" N, long. 119°39'20" W; at N line sec. 15, T 7 S, R 21 E). Named on Bass Lake (1953) 15' quadrangle.

China Garden [KERN]: *area*, 1.5 miles east-northeast of Democrat Hot Springs along Kern River (lat. 35°32'10" N, long. 118°38'35" W). Named on Democrat Hot Springs (1972) 7.5' quadrangle. On Glennville (1956) 15' quadrangle, the name applies to a locality.

China Garden [MADERA]: *area*, 11 miles south of Raymond on the southeast side of Fresno River (lat. 37°03'30" N, long. 119°55' W; mainly in sec. 17, T 10 S, R 19 E). Named on Daulton (1962) 7.5' quadrangle.

China Lake [KERN]:

(1) *dry lake*, mainly in San Bernardino County, but extends west into Kern County 7 miles north-northeast of Ridgecrest (lat. 35° 43' N, long. 117°37'30" W). Named on Ridgecrest North (1973) 7.5' quadrangle. The feature also was called China Borax Lake; this name was from borax operations at the place, presumably carried on by Chinese labor (Gale, p. 269).

(2) *town*, 2.5 miles north-northeast of Ridgecrest on China Lake Naval Weapons Center (lat. 35°39'15" N, long. 117°38'45" W). Named on Ridgecrest North (1973) 7.5' quadrangle. Postal authorities established China Lake post office in 1948 (Frickstad, p. 54). The town took its name from the dry lake (Bailey, 1967, p. 5).

China Lake Naval Weapons Center [KERN]: *military installation*, mainly in Indian Wells

Valley north of Ridgecrest, and at and near China Lake (1). Named on Inyokern (1972), Lone Butte (1973), and Ridgecrest North (1973) 7.5' quadrangles. Construction of the facility began in 1943 (Wines, p. 81).

China Slough [MADERA]: *stream,* flows 3 miles to South Fork Fresno River 13 miles south-southwest of Raymond (lat. 37°01'25" N, long. 119°57'20" W; at N line sec. 36, T 10 S, R 18 E); the stream heads at China Garden. Named on Daulton (1962) 7.5' quadrangle.

China Wells [MADERA]: *locality,* 2 miles north-northwest of Yosemite Forks (lat. 37°23'25" N, long. 119°38'45" W; sec. 23, T 6 S, R 21 E). Site named on Bass Lake (1953) 15' quadrangle.

Chinese Peak [FRESNO]: *peak,* 5 miles east of the town of Big Creek (lat. 37°13'10" N, long. 119°09'15" W; sec. 20, T 8 S, R 26 E). Altitude 8709 feet. Named on Huntington Lake (1953) 15' quadrangle.

Chinowths Corner [TULARE]: *locality,* 2.5 miles west of Visalia (lat. 36°19'35" N, long. 119°20'05" W; at N line sec. 35, T 18 S, R 24 E). Named on Visalia (1949) 7.5' quadrangle.

Chinquapin Creek [FRESNO]: *stream,* flows nearly 3 miles to Camp 62 Creek 9 miles east of Kaiser Peak (lat. 37°18'45" N, long. 119°01'30" W). Named on Kaiser Peak (1953) 15' quadrangle, which shows the water of Camp 62 Creek diverted into a pipeline above the place that Chinquapin Creek reaches the bed of Camp 62 Creek.

Chinquapin Lakes [FRESNO]: *lakes,* largest 400 feet long, 4.5 miles east of Dinkey Dome (lat. 37°06'20" N, long. 119°03'05" W; sec. 32, T 9 S, R 27 E). Named on Huntington Lake (1953) 15' quadrangle.

Chintache Lake: see **Tulare Lake** [KINGS].

Chipmunk Landing: see **Huntington Lake** [FRESNO] (1).

Chipmunk Meadow [MADERA]: *area,* 7 miles east-northeast of Yosemite Forks along Chilkoot Creek (lat. 37°23'45" N, long. 119°30'30" W; near E line sec. 24, T 6 S, R 22 E). Named on Bass Lake (1953) 15' quadrangle.

Chiquita Joaquin River: see **Chiquito Creek** [MADERA].

Chiquita Pass: see **Chiquito Pass** [MADERA].

Chiquito Campground: see **Lower Chiquito Campground** [MADERA]; **Upper Chiquito Campground** [MADERA].

Chiquito Creek [MADERA]: *stream,* flows 20 miles to Mammoth Pool Reservoir on San Joaquin River 5 miles east of Shuteye Peak (lat. 37°20'30" N, long. 119°20' W; sec. 3, T 7 S, R 24 E). Named on Merced Peak (1953) and Shuteye Peak (1953) 15' quadrangles. Called Chiquito Joaquin on Hoffmann and Gardner's (1863-1867) map, and called Chiquita Joaquin River on Lippincott's (1902) map. East Fork enters from the north-northeast 9 miles south of Merced Peak; it is 3.5

miles long and is named on Merced Peak (1953) 15' quadrangle. West Fork enters from the west 2 miles upstream from the mouth of the main creek; it is 11 miles long and is named on Shuteye Peak (1953) 15' quadrangle.

Chiquito Joaquin: see **Chiquito Creek** [MADERA].

Chiquito Lake [MADERA]: *lake,* 1400 feet long, 7 miles south-southwest of Merced Peak (lat. 37°32'10" N, long. 119°26'10" W; on N line sec. 3, T 5 S, R 23 E); the lake is along Chiquito Creek. Named on Merced Peak (1953) 15' quadrangle.

Chiquito Meadows: see **Beasore Meadows** [MADERA].

Chiquito Pass [MADERA]: *pass,* nearly 7 miles south-southwest of Merced Peak (lat. 37°32'30" N, long. 119°26'15" W); the pass is north of Chiquito Lake. Named on Merced Peak (1953) 15' quadrangle. United States Board on Geographic Names (1991, p. 3) rejected the form "Chiquita Pass" for the name.

Chiquito Ridge [MADERA]: *ridge,* generally south-southeast-trending, 6 miles long, Shuteye Peak is near the center of the feature (lat. 37°21' N, long. 119°25'40" W); the ridge is west of Chiquito Creek. Named on Shuteye Peak (1953) 15' quadrangle.

Chittenden Lake [MADERA]: *lake,* 1200 feet long, 5.5 miles south of Merced Peak (lat. 37°33'15" N, long. 119°22'30" W). Named on Merced Peak (1953) 15' quadrangle. Billy Brown, a packer, named the feature in the 1920's for members of the Chittenden family of Fresno (Browning, 1988, p. 24).

Choice Valley [KERN]: *valley,* 8 miles southsouthwest of Orchard Peak on Kern-San Luis Obispo county line (lat. 35°37'40" N, long. 120°11'30" W). Named on Holland Canyon (1961) and Orchard Peak (1961) 7.5' quadrangles.

Choke Creek [FRESNO]: *stream,* flows 2 miles to Grizzly Creek 15 miles southwest of Marion Peak (lat. 36°49'25" N, long. 118°43'45" W). Named on Marion Peak (1953) 15' quadrangle.

Cholla Canyon [KERN]: *canyon,* drained by a stream that flows 3.5 miles to the canyon of Kelso Creek 7 miles west-northwest of Skinner Peak (lat. 35°36'45" N, long. 118°14' W; at W line sec. 4, T 27 S, R 35 E). Named on Cane Canyon (1972) 7.5' quadrangle.

Chollo Well [KERN]: *well,* 6 miles west-northwest of Skinner Peak (lat. 35°36'40" N, long. 118°13'05" W; at W line sec. 3, T 27 S, R 35 E); the well is in Cholla Canyon. Named on Cane Canyon (1972) 7.5' quadrangle.

Cholly Canyon [KERN]: *canyon,* drained by a stream that flows 3 miles to Rancheria Creek (2) 5 miles southwest of Piute Peak (lat. 35°23'45" N, long. 118°26'50" W; sec. 21, T 29 S, R 33 E). Named on Piute Peak (1972) 7.5' quadrangle.

Chowchilla [MADERA]: *town,* 15 miles northwest of Madera (lat. 37°07'10" N, long. 120°15'50" W; in and near sec. 30, T 9 S, R 16 E). Named on Chowchilla (1960) 15' quadrangle. Postal authorities established Chowchilla post office in 1912 (Frickstad, p. 85), and the town incorporated in 1923.

Chowchilla River [MADERA]: *stream,* formed by the confluence of Middle Fork and West Fork in Madera County 9.5 miles northwest of Raymond, flows 80 miles near Madera-Mariposa county line, and then in Merced County, before ending 6 miles northeast of Dos Palos Y (lat. 37°06'30" N, long. 120°32'50" W; sec. 33, T 9 S, R 13 E). Named on Chowchilla (1960), Le Grand (1961), Mariposa (1947), Raymond (1962), and Santa Rita Park (1962) 15' quadrangles. The word "Chowchilla" is a corruption of the name of a warlike Indian tribe that lived along the river; the Indian name is said to have the meaning "murderers" (Hanna, p. 64). Eccleston (p. 31) in 1851 referred to the Indians as the Chou Chili. East Fork heads in Mariposa County and flows 16 miles to Chowchilla River 13 miles southeast of Mariposa in Madera County; it is named on Bass Lake (1953) and Mariposa (1947) 15' quadrangles. Middle Fork is formed in Mariposa County by the confluence of Magoon Creek and Fox Creek; it is 11.5 miles long and is named on Horsecamp Mountain (1947) and Stumpfield Mountain (1947) 7.5' quadrangles. West Fork is formed in Mariposa County by the confluence of Jones Creek and Snow Creek (2); it is 12.5 miles long and is named on Horsecamp Mountain (1947), Mariposa (1947), and Stumpfield Mountain (1947) 7.5' quadrangles. Mendenhall's (1908) map shows a place called Newton Crossing situated along Chowchilla River about 12 miles east-northeast of Chowchilla near the entrance of the river into lowlands (near SW cor. sec. 31, T 8 S, R 18 E). Goddard's (1857) map shows Newtons Crossing.

Chrysoprase Hill [TULARE]: *hill,* 1.25 miles southeast of Lindsay (lat. 36°11'40" N, long. 119°04'05" W; on N line sec. 17, T 20 S, R 27 E). Named on Lindsay (1951) 7.5' quadrangle.

Chuck Pass [FRESNO]: *pass,* 5.5 miles southwest of Blackcap Mountain (lat. 37°00'30" N, long. 118°51'30" W; near NW cor. sec. 6, T 11 S, R 29 E); the pass is near the head of Woodchuck Creek. Named on Blackcap Mountain (1953) 15' quadrangle.

Chuckwalla Mountain [KERN]: *peak,* 3.5 miles west of Cinco (lat. 35°16'20" N, long. 118°05'40" W; near NW cor. sec. 2, T 31 S, R 36 E). Altitude 5029 feet. Named on Cinco (1972) 7.5' quadrangle.

Church Dome [TULARE]: *peak,* 13 miles east-southeast of Fairview (lat. 35°51' N, long. 118°16'15" W; near W line sec. 12, T 24 S, R 34 E). Named on Kernville (1956) 15' quadrangle.

Churchill: see **Yettem** [TULARE].

Church Rock [FRESNO]: *peak,* 9.5 miles southwest of Coalinga (lat. 36°02'05" N, long. 120°28'05" W; sec. 9, T 22 S, R 14 E). Named on Curry Mountain (1969) 7.5' quadrangle.

Chute Spring [TULARE]: *spring,* 3 miles north-northeast of California Hot Springs (lat. 35°55'10" N, long. 119°39' W; sec. 20, T 23 S, R 31 E). Named on California Hot Springs (1958) 15' quadrangle.

Ciatana Creek [MADERA]: *stream,* flows about 3.5 miles to Fish Creek (2) 4.25 miles south-southwest of the town of North Fork (lat. 37°10'05" N, long. 119°31'35" W; sec. 12, T 9 S, R 22 E). Named on North Fork (1965) 7.5' quadrangle.

Cienaga Canyon [KERN]: *canyon,* drained by a stream that flows 9.5 miles to lowlands 3 miles southeast of Maricopa (lat. 35°02'05" N, long. 119°21'55" W; near SW cor. sec. 17, T 11 N, R 23 W). Named on Ballinger Canyon (1943), Pentland (1953), and Santiago Creek (1943) 7.5' quadrangles. United States Board on Geographic Names (1990, p. 6) approved the name "Cienaga Creek" for the stream that flows through Cienega Canyon and ends in the community of Pentland (sec. 8, T 11 N, R 23 W); the Board rejected the form "Cienega Creek" for the name.

Cienaga Creek: see **Cienaga Canyon** [KERN]

Ciervo Hills [FRESNO]: *range,* 28 miles south of Firebaugh on Fresno-San Benito county line between Tumey Gulch and Cantua Creek. Named on Ciervo Mountain (1969), Levis (1956), Lillis Ranch (1956), Monocline Ridge (1955), and Tumey Hills (1956) 7.5' quadrangles.

Ciervo Mountain [FRESNO]: *ridge,* north-trending, 1 mile long, 27 miles south-southwest of Firebaugh (lat. 36°28' N, long. 120°34'40" W; sec. 5, 8, T 17 S, R 13 E); the ridge is in Ciervo Hills. Named on Ciervo Mountain (1969) 7.5' quadrangle.

Ciervo Spring [FRESNO]: *spring,* 1.25 miles northeast of Ciervo Mountain (lat. 36°28'50" N, long. 120°33'25" W; sec. 4, T 17 S, R 13 E); the spring is in Ciervo Hills along Arroyo Ciervo. Named on Ciervo Mountain (1969) 7.5' quadrangle.

Cima Hill [FRESNO]: *peak,* 20 miles southwest of Firebaugh (lat. 36°38'35" N, long. 120°41'40" W; sec. 7, T 15 S, R 12 E). Altitude 1355 feet. Named on Chounet Ranch (1956) 7.5' quadrangle.

Cimarron [KINGS]: *locality,* 1.5 miles west of Lemoore along Southern Pacific Railroad (lat. 36°17'55" N, long. 119°48'45" W; near SW cor. sec. 4, T 19 S, R 20 E). Named on Lemoore (1954) 7.5' quadrangle. Called Heinlen on Lemoore (1927) 7.5' quadrangle.

Cinco [KERN]: *locality,* 6 miles east of Cross Mountain at the edge of Fremont Valley (lat.

35°15'45" N, long. 118°02'10" W; near W line sec. 5, T 31 S, R 37 E). Named on Cinco (1972) 7.5' quadrangle. The place was a construction camp for the aqueduct that takes Owens Valley water from Inyo County to Los Angeles; it was the fifth such camp from Mojave—*cinco* means "fifth" in Spanish (Bailey, 1962, p. 54). California Mining Bureau's (1909a) map shows a place called Pine situated 4.5 miles south of Cinco along the railroad, and a stopping place called 18 Mile House was located just south of present Cinco (Barras, p. 125).

Cincotta [FRESNO]: *locality,* in downtown Fresno along Atchison, Topeka and Santa Fe Railroad (lat. 36°45'40" N, long. 119°45'15" W). Named on Fresno North (1965) 7.5' quadrangle.

Cinnamon Creek [TULARE]: *stream,* flows 3.5 miles to South Fork Kaweah River 7.5 miles south-southeast of Kaweah (lat. 36°22'35" N, long. 118°51'20" W; near E line sec. 8, T 18 S, R 29 E). Named on Kaweah (1957) 15' quadrangle.

Cinnamon Gap [TULARE]: *pass,* 7 miles southeast of Kaweah (lat. 36°24'25" N, long. 118°49'40" W; sec. 33, T 17 S, R 29 E); the pass is near the head of a branch of Cinnamon Creek. Named on Kaweah (1957) 15' quadrangle.

Circle Meadow [TULARE]: *area,* 6.5 miles east of Yucca Mountain (lat. 36°33'55" N, long. 118°45'10" W; on E line sec. 6, T 16 S, R 30 E). Named on Giant Forest (1956) 15' quadrangle.

Cirque Creek [FRESNO]: *stream,* flows 2.5 miles to Bear Creek (2) 8 miles west-southwest of Mount Abbot (lat. 37°21'45" N, long. 118°55'40" W); the stream heads at Cirque Lake. Named on Mount Abbot (1953) 15' quadrangle.

Cirque Crest [FRESNO]: *ridge,* north-northeast- to northeast-trending, 7 miles long, includes Marion Peak (lat. 36°57'25" N, long. 118°31'15" W). Named on Marion Peak (1953) and Mount Pinchot (1953) 15' quadrangles.

Cirque Lake [FRESNO]: *lake,* 2250 feet long, 8 miles west-southwest of Mount Abbot (lat. 37°20' N, long. 118°54'15" W); the lake is at the head of Cirque Creek. Named on Mount Abbot (1953) 15' quadrangle. Scott M. Soule and Jack Criqui of California Department of Fish and Game named the lake in 1948 for its location in a cirque (Browning 1986, p. 39-40).

Cirque Lake: see **Adair Lake** [MADERA].

Cirque Peak [TULARE]: *peak,* 16 miles north-northwest of Olancha Peak on Tulare-Inyo county line (lat. 36°28'40" N, long. 118°14'10" W; on W line sec. 6, T 17 S, R 35 E). Altitude 12,900 feet. Named on Olancha (1956) 15' quadrangle.

Citadel: see **The Citadel** [FRESNO].

Citro [TULARE]: *locality,* 4.25 miles east-southeast of Woodlake along Visalia Electric Railroad (lat. 36°23'35" N, long. 119°01'25" W; sec. 2, T 18 S, R 27 E). Named on Woodlake (1952) 7.5' quadrangle.

Citrus Cove [FRESNO]: *valley,* 5.5 miles northwest of the town of Orange Cove (lat. 36°42'15" N, long. 119°21' W). Named on Orange Cove North (1966) 7.5' quadrangle.

Claire Lake: see **Little Claire Lake** [TULARE].

Clarasillo: see **Claraville** [KERN].

Claraville [KERN]: *locality,* 13 miles north of Emerald Mountain (lat. 35°26'30" N, long. 118°19'45" W; sec. 4, T 29 S, R 34 E). Named on Claraville (1972) 7.5' quadrangle. Postal authorities established Claraville post office in 1940, discontinued it in 1941, reestablished it in 1949, and discontinued it in 1957 (Salley, p. 44). A mining camp called Kelso—later called Claraville for Clara Munckton, the first white girl there—developed in the 1860's, but by 1869 it was deserted; a small community, also called Claraville, grew at the place with a revival of mining in the depression years of the 1930's (Boyd, p. 165; Hensher and Peskin, p. 18). Whipple (p. 149) referred to Clarasillo.

Claraville Flat [KERN]: *area,* at Claraville (lat. 35°26'35" N, long. 118°19'35" W; near E line sec. 4, T 29 S, R 34 E). Named on Claraville (1972) 7.5' quadrangle.

Clarence King: see **Mount Clarence King** [FRESNO].

Clarice Lake [MADERA]: *lake,* 600 feet long, 6.5 miles north-northwest of Devils Postpile (lat. 37°42'20" N, long. 119°08'35" W). Named on Devils Postpile (1953) 15' quadrangle.

Clark Canyon [TULARE]: *canyon,* drained by a stream that flows 1.5 miles to Dry Creek (1) 6.5 miles southeast of Auckland (lat. 36°31'50" N, long. 119°00'35" W; sec. 14, T 16 S, R 27 E). Named on Giant Forest (1956) 15' quadrangle, and on Auckland (1966) 7.5' quadrangle.

Clark Range [MADERA]: *ridge,* northwest- to north-trending, 5 miles long, northwest of Merced Peak (lat. 37°39' N, long. 119°24'30" W). Named on Merced Peak (1953) 15' quadrangle. The feature was known as Obelisk Group and Merced Group at the time of the Whitney survey (Browning, 1986, p. 144).

Clarks Fork: see **Kings River** [KINGS].

Clark Slough [KINGS]: *stream,* flows 6 miles to a ditch 2.5 miles south-southwest of Guernsey (lat. 36°10'35" N, long. 119°39'30" W). Named on Guernsey (1929) 7.5' quadrangle. Called Melga Canal on Guernsey (1954) 7.5' quadrangle.

Clarkson: see **Bakersfield** [KERN].

Clark Valley [FRESNO]: *valley,* 9 miles northwest of Orange Cove along upper reaches of Wahtoke Creek (lat. 36°45' N, long. 119°22' W). Named on Orange Cove North (1966), Piedra (1965), and Pine Flat Dam (1965) 7.5' quadrangles. Called Clarks Valley on Lippincott's (1902) map.

Clavicle: see **Springville** [TULARE].

Claw Lake [FRESNO]: *lake*, 1400 feet long, nearly 5 miles south of Mount Abbot (lat. 37°19'10" N, long. 118°48' W). Named on Mount Abbot (1953) 15' quadrangle.

Clear Creek [KERN]:
(1) *stream*, flows 14 miles to Kern River less than 0.25 mile east-southeast of Miracle Hot Springs (lat. 35°34'30" N, long. 118°31'40" W; near S line sec. 15, T 27 S, R 32 E). Named on Lake Isabella South (1972), Miracle Hot Springs (1972), and Piute Peak (1972) 7.5' quadrangles.
(2) *stream*, flows 6 miles to Tehachapi Creek 0.5 mile southeast of Caliente (lat. 35°17' N, long. 118°38'10" W). Named on Bear Mountain (1966), Keene (1966), and Oiler Peak (1972) 7.5' quadrangles.

Clear Creek Hot Springs: see **Miracle Hot Springs** [KERN].

Clearing: see **The Clearing** [FRESNO].

Clearwater Creek [MADERA]: *stream*, flows 2 miles to Ross Creek 9 miles south-south-east of Shuteye Peak (lat. 37°14'05" N, long. 119°21'10" W; sec. 16, T 8 S, R 24 E). Named on Shaver Lake (1953) 15' quadrangle.

Clicks Creek [TULARE]: *stream*, flows 5.5 miles to Little Kern River 8 miles northeast of Camp Nelson (lat. 36°13'15" N, long. 118°30'10" W; near SE cor. sec. 33, T 19 S, R 32 E). Named on Camp Nelson (1956) 15' quadrangle. The name commemorates Mark, or Martin, Click, a sheepman of 1877 (Browning 1986, p. 41). North Fork enters 2.5 miles upstream from the mouth of the stream; it is 3.25 miles long and is named on Camp Nelson (1956) 15' quadrangle.

Cliff [KERN]: *locality*, 2 miles southeast of Caliente along Southern Pacific Railroad (lat. 35°16'05" N, long. 119°36'25" W). Named on Oiler Peak (1972) 7.5' quadrangle.

Cliff Camp [FRESNO]: *locality*, 14 miles north-northwest of Hume (lat. 36°59'15" N, long. 118°58'25" W). Named on Tehipite Dome (1952) 15' quadrangle.

Cliff Creek [TULARE]: *stream*, flows 8.5 miles to Middle Fork Kaweah River 8 miles west-southwest of Triple Divide Peak (lat. 36°32' N, long. 118°39'20" W). Named on Mineral King (1956) and Triple Divide Peak (1956) 15' quadrangles. The name is from Cliff Pass, an early designation of present Black Rock Pass (Browning 1986, p. 41).

Cliff Lake [FRESNO]: *lake*, 1800 feet long, 5 miles east-northeast of Dinkey Dome (lat. 37°08'30" N, long. 119°02'40" W; near SE cor. sec. 17, T 9 S, R 27 E). Named on Huntington Lake (1953) 15' quadrangle.

Cliff Pass: see **Black Rock Pass** [TULARE].

Cliff Peak [TULARE]: *peak*, 12 miles east of Dinuba (lat. 36°33'25" N, long. 119°10'15" W; near N line sec. 8, T 16 S, R 26 E). Named on Stokes Mountain (1966) 7.5' quadrangle.

Clifton: see **Del Rey** [FRESNO].

Clingans Junction: see **Mill Creek** [FRESNO-TULARE].

Clint [FRESNO]: *locality*, nearly 5 miles east of Riverdale along Atchison, Topeka and Santa Fe Railroad (lat. 36°25'55" N, long. 119°46'20" W; near S line sec. 23, T 17 S, R 20 E). Named on Riverdale (1954) 7.5' quadrangle.

Clotho [FRESNO]: *locality*, 3 miles west-northwest of Sanger along Southern Pacific Railroad (lat. 36°43'15" N, long. 119°36'30" W; near NW cor. sec. 17, T 14 S, R 22 E). Named on Sanger (1965) 7.5' quadrangle. Lippincott's (1902) map has the name "Minneola" at the place, but Grunsky's (1898) map has the name "Minneola" at present Ivesta.

Cloud: see **Lemoore** [KINGS].

Cloudburst Canyon [KERN]: *canyon*, 2.5 miles long, opens into the canyon of San Emigdio Creek 1.25 miles west-southwest of Eagle Rest Peak (lat. 34°53'50" N, long. 119°09'10" W; near E line sec. 6, T 9 N, R 21 W). Named on Eagle Rest Peak (1942) 7.5' quadrangle.

Cloud Canyon [TULARE]: *canyon*, 9 miles long, along Roaring River above a point 8 miles north-northwest of Triple Divide Peak (lat. 36°42'15" N, long. 118°34'30" W). Named on Triple Divide Peak (1956) 15' quadrangle. United States Board on Geographic Names (1933a, p. 225) rejected the names "Cloudy Canyon," "Copper Canyon," and "Deadman Canyon" for the feature. In 1880 Judge W.B. Wallace gave the name "The Cloud mine" to a mining claim near the stream because clouds hung so low overhead, and named the stream at the same time (Farquhar, 1924, p. 47-48).

Cloudy Canyon: see **Cloud Canyon** [TULARE]; **Deadman Canyon** [TULARE] (1).

Clough Cave [TULARE]: *cave*, 12 miles southeast of Kaweah along South Fork Kaweah River (lat. 36°21' N, long. 118°45'40" W). Named on Kaweah (1957) 15' quadrangle. The name is for William O. Clough, who discovered the cave in 1885 (United States Board on Geographic Names, 1933a, p. 225). Goodyear (1888b, p. 647) called the feature Clough's Cave.

Clover Creek [TULARE]:
(1) *stream*, formed by the confluence of East Fork and West Fork, flows 3.5 miles to Marble Fork 12 miles west of Triple Divide Peak (lat. 36°36'10" N, long. 118°44'40" W; sec. 20, T 15 S, R 30 E). Named on Giant Forest (1956) and Triple Divide Peak (1956) 15' quadrangles. East Fork is 2.5 miles long and West Fork is 1.5 miles long; both forks are named on Triple Divide Peak (1956) 15' quadrangle. United States Board on Geographic Names (1933a, p. 225) rejected the name "East Fork" for present Clover Creek, and (1962a, p. 10) rejected the name "Clover Creek" for present East Fork.
(2) *stream*, flows nearly 3 miles to Horse Creek

59

(1) 5.5 miles southwest of Mineral King (lat. 36°24'10" N, long. 118°40'30" W). Named on Mineral King (1956) 15' quadrangle.

Clover Meadow [TULARE]:
(1) *area*, 7.5 miles south-southeast of Monache Mountain along Crag Creek (lat. 36°06'40" N, long. 118°07'30" W). Named on Monache Mountain (1956) 15' quadrangle.
(2) *area*, 6.25 miles northeast of California Hot Springs (lat. 35°56'20" N, long. 118°35'05" W; at N line sec. 13, T 23 S, R 31 E). Named on California Hot Springs (1958) 15' quadrangle.

Clovis [FRESNO]: *city*, 6.5 miles northeast of downtown Fresno (lat. 36°49'25" N, long. 119°42' W; around SE cor. sec. 5, T 13 S, R 21 E). Named on Clovis (1964) 7.5' quadrangle. Officials of Southern Pacific Railroad named the station at the place in 1889 for Clovis Cole, owner of a large wheat ranch that the railroad crossed with a branch line in 1889 (Gudde, 1949, p. 71). Postal authorities established Clovis post office in 1895 (Frickstad, p. 32), and the city incorporated in 1912. They established Garfield post office 12 miles northeast of Fresno in 1891 and discontinued it in 1897 when they moved the service Clovis (Salley, p. 82).

Clyde: see **Norman Clyde Peak**, under **Middle Palisade** [FRESNO].

Coalinga [FRESNO]: *town*, 52 miles southwest of Fresno in Pleasant Valley (lat. 36°08'25" N, long. 120°21'35" W; in and near sec. 32, T 20 S, R 15 E). Named on Coalinga (1956) 7.5' quadrangle. The place was called Coaling Station after officials of Southern Pacific Railroad had a branch line built to the site in 1888 to carry lignitic coal from nearby mines; according to local tradition, the present name was coined when a railroad official added the letter "a" to the word "coaling" (Gudde, 1949, p. 72). Postal authorities established Coalinga post office in 1899 (Frickstad, p. 32), and the town incorporated in 1906. Called Coalingo on California (1891) map, which shows a place called Dathol located along the railroad east of present Coalinga about halfway to Huron. California Division of Highways' (1934) map shows a place called Leroy situated 3.5 miles southwest of Coalinga along Wartham (present Warthan) Creek (near E line sec. 13, T 21 S, R 14 E).

Coalinga Mineral Springs [FRESNO]: *locality*, 11 miles west of Coalinga (lat. 36°08'40" N, long. 120°33'15" W; sec. 34, T 20 S, R 13 E); the place is in Hot Spring Canyon. Named on Sherman Peak (1969) 7.5' quadrangle. Called Fresno Hot Springs on Priest Valley (1915) 30' quadrangle. About 20 springs issue from the canyon wall, and water is piped 0.5 mile from the springs to a resort (Berkstresser, p. A-5). California Mining Bureau's (1909b) map shows a place called Rogers located near present Coalinga Min-

eral Springs. Postal authorities established Rogers post office in 1897 and discontinued it in 1909 (Frickstad, p. 37).

Coalinga Nose [FRESNO]: *ridge*, northeast-trending, 1.5 miles long, 6 miles east-north-east of Coalinga on Anticline Ridge (lat. 36°11'15" N, long. 120°16'15" W; mainly in sec. 18, T 20 S, R 16 E). Named on Coalinga (1956) 7.5' quadrangle.

Coalinga Sulphur Baths [FRESNO]: *locality*, 2.5 miles west-southwest of Coalinga (lat. 36°07'20" N, long. 120°23'50" W; near NW cor. sec. 7, T 21 S, R 15 E). Named on Coalinga (1956) 15' quadrangle. Mineral water comes from a well that was drilled in 1906 for oil, but which tapped an artesian flow of hot sulphur water instead (Laizure, p. 320).

Coalinga Valley: see **Pleasant Valley** [FRESNO].

Coalingo: see **Coalinga** [FRESNO].

Coaling Station: see **Coalinga** [FRESNO].

Coalmine Canyon [FRESNO]: *canyon*, drained by a stream that flows 2.25 miles to Pleasant Valley 3.5 miles west-northwest of Coalinga (lat. 36°09'30" N, long. 120°24'50" W; sec. 26, T 30 S, R 14 E). Named on Alcalde Hills (1969) 7.5' quadrangle.

Coal Oil Canyon [KERN]: *canyon*, drained by a stream that flows 2.5 miles to lowlands 5 miles west-southwest of Mettler (lat. 35°01'45" N, long. 119°02'50" W; near E line sec. 19, T 11 N, R 20 W). Named on Coal Oil Canyon (1955) 7.5' quadrangle. Buena Vista Lake (1912) 30' quadrangle has the form "Coaloil Canyon" for the name.

Coarsegold [MADERA]: *village*, 8 miles south-southwest of Yosemite Forks (lat. 37°15'45" N, long. 119°42' W; sec. 5, T 8 S, R 21 E); the village is along Coarse Gold Creek. Named on Bass Lake (1953) 15' quadrangle. Mariposa (1912) 30' quadrangle has the form "Coarse Gold" for the name. Postal authorities established Coarse Gold Gulch post office in 1878, changed the name to Goldgulch in 1895, and changed it to Coarsegold in 1899 (Frickstad, p. 85). Miners from Texas found gold at the place in 1849 and the community that developed there was known first as Texas Flat (Hoover, Rensch, and Rensch, p. 172). A map of 1874 has the name "Michaels" at the site—Charles Michael had a business there (Clough, p. 78). A Mexican mining camp called Oro Grosso probably was at the place (Gudde, 1975, p. 256). Postal authorities established Rallsville post office 20 miles northeast of Madera in 1881 and discontinued it in 1883, when they moved the service to Coarse Gold Gulch post office; the name "Rallsville" was for George W. Ralls, first postmaster (Salley, p. 180).

Coarse Gold Creek [KERN-TULARE]: *stream*, heads in Kern County and flows 4.5 miles to White River (1) 6.25 miles south-southeast of Fountain Springs in Tulare County (lat.

35°48'25" N, long. 118°52'30" W; near E line sec. 30, T 24 S, R 29 E). Named on Quincy School (1965) and White River (1965) 7.5' quadrangles.

Coarse Gold Creek [MADERA]: *stream*, flows 23 miles to Fresno River 4 miles south-south-east of Knowles (lat. 37°10'05" N, long. 119°50'30" W; sec. 12, T 9 S, R 19 E). Named on Bass Lake (1953), Millerton Lake (1965), and Raymond (1962) 15' quadrangles. The name is from the coarseness of gold found in the stream (Hoover, Rensch, and Rensch, p. 172).

Coarse Gold Gulch: see **Coarsegold** [MADERA].

Cobbs Island [FRESNO]: *island*, 11 miles north of downtown Fresno in San Joaquin River (lat. 36°55' N, long. 119°46' W; sec. 2, 3, T 12 S, R 20 E). Named on Herndon (1965) 15' quadrangle.

Cochran Spring [KERN]: *spring*, nearly 3 miles northwest of Skinner Peak (lat. 35°35'45" N, long. 118°09'40" W). Named on Cane Canyon (1972) 7.5' quadrangle.

Cockscomb: see **Sharktooth Peak** [FRESNO].

Code: see **Terese** [KERN].

Coffee Canyon [KERN]: *canyon*, 5 miles long, along Poso Creek above a point 3.5 miles south-southeast of Knob Hill (lat. 35°31' N, long. 118°55' W; sec. 1, T 28 S, R 28 E). Named on Knob Hill (1965) and Pine Mountain (1965) 7.5' quadrangles.

Coffee Canyon [TULARE]: *canyon*, drained by a stream that flows nearly 3 miles to Middle Fork Tule River 7.5 miles west of Camp Nelson (lat. 36°09'05" N, long. 118°44'15" W). Named on Camp Nelson (1956) 15' quadrangle.

Coffee Creek [KERN]: *stream*, flows 2.5 miles to Little Poso Creek 6 miles north of Democrat Hot Springs (lat. 35°36'55" N, long. 118°40'55" W; near N line sec. 6, T 27 S, R 31 E). Named on Democrat Hot Springs (1972) 7.5' quadrangle.

Coffee Mill Meadow [TULARE]: *area*, 3.5 miles east of Camp Nelson (lat. 36°08'20" N, long. 118°32'50" W; sec. 31, T 20 S, R 32 E). Named on Camp Nelson (1956) 15' quadrangle.

Coffeepot Canyon [TULARE]: *canyon*, drained by a stream that flows 3.25 miles to East Fork Kaweah River 9 miles east-southeast of Kaweah (lat. 36°25'30" N, long. 118°46' W; near NE cor. sec. 25, T 17 S, R 29 E). Named on Kaweah (1957) and Mineral King (1956) 15' quadrangles. The name is said to be from an old coffeepot that hunters found at the place (Browning 1986, p. 43). United States Board on Geographic Names (1933a, p. 227) approved the name "Coffeepot Canyon Creek" for the stream in the canyon.

Coffeepot Canyon Creek: see **Coffeepot Canyon** [TULARE].

Coffin Spring [KERN]: *spring*, 2.5 miles east-

southeast of Caliente (lat. 35°16'55" N, long. 118°35'05" W; at S line sec. 30, T 30 S, R 32 E). Named on Oiler Peak (1972) 7.5' quadrangle.

Coho Creek [TULARE]: *stream*, flows 8.5 miles to White River (1) 6 miles south-southeast of Fountain Springs (lat. 35°48'35" N, long. 118°52'40" W; sec. 30, T 24 S, R 29 E). Named on Gibbon Peak (1965), Quincy School (1965), and White River (1965) 7.5' quadrangles. Called Coko Creek on White River (1936) 15' quadrangle, but United States Board on Geographic Names (1966b, p. 4) rejected this name for the feature.

Coko Creek: see **Coho Creek** [TULARE].

Colby Lake [TULARE]: *lake*, 0.5 mile long, 2.5 miles north-northeast of Triple Divide Peak (lat. 36°37'40" N, long. 118°30'45" W); the lake is 1 mile northwest of Colby Pass. Named on Triple Divide Peak (1956) 15' quadrangle. The name commemorates William E. Colby of the Sierra Club; the club proposed the name in 1927 for what before that time was called Hutchinson Lake (Browning 1986, p. 43).

Colby Meadow [FRESNO]: *area*, 5.25 miles north of Mount Goddard in Evolution Valley (lat. 37°10'45" N, long. 118°43'30" W). Named on Mount Goddard (1948) 15' quadrangle. Forest Service officials named the place in 1915 for William E. Colby of the Sierra Club (Farquhar, 1923, p. 388).

Colby Pass [TULARE]: *pass*, 2.5 miles northeast of Triple Divide Peak on Great Western Divide (lat. 36°37'05" N, long. 118°30' W). Named on Mount Whitney (1956) and Triple Divide Peak (1956) 15' quadrangles. A party from the Sierra Club discovered the route through the pass in 1912 and named the place for the leader of the group, William E. Colby (Farquhar, 1923, p. 388). United States Board on Geographic Names (1990, p. 6) approved the name "Centennial Peak" for a high point located 1 mile northeast of Colby Pass; the name commemorates the one-hundredth anniversary of Sequoia National Park.

Cold Canyon Creek: see **Cold Creek** [FRESNO].

Cold Creek [FRESNO]: *stream*, flows 8.5 miles to Lake Thomas A. Edison 12 miles eastnortheast of Kaiser Peak (lat. 37°22'50" N, long. 119°00'05" W). Named on Kaiser Peak (1953) and Mount Abbot (1953) 15' quadrangles. Called Cold Canyon Creek on Lippincott's (1902) map. United States Board on Geographic Names (1959, p. 2) rejected the name "Cole Creek" for the feature.

Cold Creek [MADERA]: *stream*, flows 1 mile to Middle Fork San Joaquin River 4.5 miles south of Devils Postpile (lat. 37°33'20" N, long. 119°05'30" W). Named on Devils Postpile (1953) 15' quadrangle.

Cold Creek [TULARE]: *stream*, flows 7 miles to Ninemile Creek 2.5 miles east-northeast of Hockett Peak (lat. 36°13'45" N, long. 118°

20'20" W); the stream goes through Cold Meadows. Named on Hockett Peak (1956) and Kern Peak (1956) 15' quadrangles.

Cold Meadows [TULARE]: *area,* nearly 2 miles south-southwest of Kern Peak (lat. 36°17'10" N, long. 118°18' W); the place is along Cold Creek. Named on Kern Peak (1956) 15' quadrangle.

Cold Spring [FRESNO]: *spring,* 3 miles east-northeast of Castle Mountain (lat. 35°57'30" N, long. 120°17'30" W; sec. 6, T 23 S, R 16 E). Named on The Dark Hole (1961) 7.5' quadrangle.

Cold Spring [KERN]:
(1) *spring,* 5 miles north of Democrat Hot Springs (lat. 35°35'55" N, long. 118°38'50" W). Named on Democrat Hot Springs (1972) 7.5' quadrangle.
(2) *spring,* 1 mile north-northwest of Piute Peak (lat. 35°28' N, long. 118°23'45" W; near E line sec. 26, T 28 S, R 33 E). Named on Piute Peak (1972) 7.5' quadrangle.

Cold Spring [TULARE]: *spring,* 7 miles south-east of California Hot Springs (lat. 35°48'30" N, long. 118°34'55" W; sec. 25, T 24 S, R 31 E). Named on California Hot Springs (1958) 15' quadrangle.

Cold Spring: see **North Cold Spring** [TULARE].

Cold Spring Meadow [MADERA]: *area,* 5 miles south-southeast of Shuteye Peak (lat. 37°17' N, long. 119°23'50" W; near NW cor. sec. 31, T 7 S, R 24 E). Named on Shuteye Peak (1953) 15' quadrangle.

Cold Springs Canyon [KERN]: *canyon,* drained by a stream that flows 2 miles to Cuddy Canyon 6 miles west of Lebec (lat. 34°49'15" N, long. 118°58'30" W; at W line sec. 35, T 9 N, R 20 W). Named on Frazier Mountain (1958) 7.5' quadrangle.

Cold Springs Creek [TULARE]: *stream,* flows 4 miles to a presently unnamed stream—called Nigger Rube Creek on Tobias Peak (1936) 30' quadrangle—3.5 miles north-northwest of California Hot Springs (lat. 35°55'20" N, long. 118°42'10" W; sec. 14, T 23 S, R 30 E); the stream heads near Cold Springs Peak. Named on California Hot Springs (1958) 15' quadrangle. Called Cold Spring Cr. on Tobias Peak (1936) 30' quadrangle.

Cold Springs Meadow [MADERA]:
(1) *area,* 9 miles south-southwest of Merced Peak (lat. 37°31'15" N, long. 119°28'45" W; near SW cor. sec. 5, T 5 S, R 23 E). Named on Merced Peak (1953) 15' quadrangle.
(2) *area,* nearly 6 miles northwest of Shuteye Peak (lat. 37°25' N, long. 119°29'30" W; near S line sec. 7, T 6 S, R 23 E). Named on Shuteye Peak (1953) 15' quadrangle.

Cold Springs Peak [TULARE]: *peak,* 3.5 miles north-northeast of California Hot Springs (lat. 35°55'50" N, long. 118°38'50" W; sec. 17, T 23 S, R 31 E); the peak is near the head of Cold Springs Creek. Named on California Hot

Springs (1958) 15' quadrangle. Called Cold Spring Pk. on Tobias Peak (1936) 30' quadrangle.

Cold Springs Saddle [TULARE]: *pass,* 4 miles north-northeast of California Hot Springs (lat. 35°56'05" N, long. 118°38'50" W; sec. 17, T 23 S, R 31 E); the pass is near the head of Cold Springs Creek. Name on California Hot Springs (1958) 15' quadrangle. Called Cold Spring Saddle on Tobias Peak (1936) 30' quadrangle.

Cold Sulfur Spring [TULARE]: *spring,* 5.25 miles east of Auckland along Dry Creek (1) (lat. 36°34'55" N, long. 119°00'35" W; near S line sec. 26, T 15 S, R 27 E). Named on Auckland (1966) 7.5' quadrangle.

Cole Creek: see **Cold Creek** [FRESNO].

Cole Slough [FRESNO-KINGS]: *water feature,* diverges from Kings River 12 miles north-northeast of Hanford in Kings County and extends for 9 miles to rejoin the river 1 mile east-southeast of Laton in Fresno County (lat. 36°25'50" N, long. 119°40'15" W; near SW cor. sec. 23, T 17 S, R 21 E). Named on Burris Park (1954) and Laton (1953) 7.5' quadrangles.

Cole Spring [FRESNO]: *spring,* 5.5 miles north of Trimmer (lat. 36° 59'05" N, long. 119°16'45" W; sec. 7, T 11 S, R 25 E). Named on Trimmer (1965) 7.5' quadrangle. On Watts Valley (1942) 15' quadrangle, the name applies to at a place located 0.5 mile farther east-northeast.

College Lake [FRESNO]: *lake,* 300 feet long, 0.5 mile east-southeast of Kaiser Peak (lat. 37°17'35" N, long. 119°10'35" W; sec. 30, T 7 S, R 26 E); the lake is 1.5 miles north of College Rock. Named on Kaiser Peak (1953) 15' quadrangle.

College Rock [FRESNO]: *relief feature,* 1.5 miles south-southeast of Kaiser Peak (lat. 37°16'20" N, long. 119°10'25" W; sec. 31, T 7 S, R 26 E). Altitude 9076 feet. Named on Kaiser Peak (1953) 15' quadrangle.

Collier Cove [TULARE]: *valley,* 4.5 miles south-southeast of Auckland (lat. 36°31'30" N, long. 119°05' W; in and near sec. 19, T 16 S, R 27 E); the valley is along Collier Creek. Named on Auckland (1966) 7.5' quadrangle.

Collier Creek [TULARE]: *stream,* flows nearly 4 miles to Cottonwood Creek 3.5 miles south of Auckland (lat. 36°32'20" N, long. 119°06'35" W; sec. 14, T 16 S, R 26 E). Named on Auckland (1966) 7.5' quadrangle.

Collins Creek [FRESNO]: *stream,* heads 1.5 miles northeast of Centerville and flows 8 miles to Kings River 2.5 miles southeast of Sanger (lat. 36°31'40" N, long. 119°31'40" W; sec. 36, T 14 S, R 22 E). Named on Sanger (1965) and Wahtoke (1966) 7.5' quadrangles.

Collins Meadow: see **Crown Valley** [FRESNO].

Collins Spring: see **Sulphur Springs** [FRESNO].

Collis: see **Kerman** [FRESNO].

Colony Meadow [TULARE]: *stream,* 3.5 miles south-southeast of Shell Mountain (lat. 36°38'35" N, long. 118°46'40" W; at S line sec. 1, T 15 S, R 29 E). Named on Giant Forest (1956) 15' quadrangle. The name recalls Kaweah Colony (Gudde, 1949, p. 75).

Colony Peak [TULARE]: *peak,* 2.5 miles east-southeast of Yucca Mountain (lat. 36°33'45" N, long. 118°48'15" W). Altitude 6132 feet. Named on Giant Forest (1956) 15' quadrangle. The name commemorates Kaweah Cooperative Commonwealth Colony, organized to cut giant redwoods for lumber in 1886 (United States Board on Geographic Names, 1933a, p. 230).

Colorado Camp [KERN]: *locality,* 3.5 miles northwest of Garlock (lat. 35°26'50" N, long. 117°49'35" W). Named on Garlock (1967) 7.5' quadrangle.

Colored Lady: see **Painted Lady** [FRESNO].

Colorful Creek: see **Salt Creek** [KERN] (2).

Colosseum Mountain [FRESNO]: *peak,* 3.25 miles southeast of Mount Pinchot on Fresno-Inyo county line (lat. 36°54'30" N, long. 118°22'10" W). Altitude 12,473 feet. Named on Mount Pinchot (1953) 15' quadrangle.

Colt Lake [FRESNO]: *lake,* 450 feet long, 1 mile north-northwest of Blackcap Mountain (lat. 37°05'10" N, long. 118°47'50" W). Named on Blackcap Mountain (1953) 15' quadrangle. William A. Dill of California Department of Fish and Game chose the name in 1948 because the outline of the lake on a map has the shape of a colt's head, and because the feature is near Horsehead Lake (Browning 1986, p. 44).

Columbia Well [MADERA]: *well,* 16 miles west of Madera (lat. 36° 56'25" N, long. 120°21'20" W; sec. 29, T 11 S, R 15 E). Named on Kentucky Well (1922) 7.5' quadrangle.

Columbine Lake [TULARE]: *lake,* 0.5 mile long, 2.5 miles east-northeast of Mineral King (lat. 36°27'45" N, long. 118°33' W). Named on Mineral King (1956) 15' quadrangle. Joseph Palmer, a pioneer in the neighborhood, named the lake for the abundance of columbine plants growing around it (Gudde, 1949, p. 75).

Columbine Peak [FRESNO]: *peak,* 10 miles east of Mount Goddard (lat. 37°05'20" N, long. 118°32'25" W). Altitude 12,652 feet. Named on Mount Goddard (1948) 15' quadrangle. The Sierra Club proposed the name before 1939; columbine plants grow nearly to the summit of the peak (Browning 1986, p. 44).

Colvin Mountain [TULARE]: *ridge,* south-southeast-trending, 3.5 miles long, 3.5 miles northwest of Woodlake (lat. 36°26'40" N, long. 119°08'50" W). Named on Exeter (1952) 15' quadrangle.

Colvin Ranch: see **Redbanks** [TULARE].

Comanche Creek [KERN]: *stream,* flows 13 miles to lowlands 5 miles south of Arvin (lat. 35°08'15" N, long. 118°48'45" W). Named on Arvin (1955), Tejon Hills (1955), and Te-

jon Ranch (1966) 7.5' quadrangles. The name commemorates a man who was known as Comanche, and who was believed to be part Comanche Indian—the man lived at a rancheria at Comanche Point (Latta, 1976, p. 199, 201).

Comanche Meadow [TULARE]: *area,* 12 miles northwest of Triple Divide Peak (lat. 36°42'45" N, long. 118°41'05" W; near N line sec. 14, T 14 S, R 30 E). Named on Triple Divide Peak (1956) 15' quadrangle.

Comanche Point [KERN]: *relief feature,* 5 miles south of Arvin at the north end of Tejon Hills (lat. 35°08' N, long. 118°49'15" W); the feature is west of lower reaches of Comanche Creek. Named on Arvin (1955) and Tejon Hills (1955) 7.5' quadrangles.

Comanche Spring [KERN]: *spring,* 5.25 miles south of Arvin (lat. 35°07'55" N, long. 118°48'45" W); the spring is along Comanche Creek. Named on Arvin (1955) 7.5' quadrangle.

Comb Creek [FRESNO]: *stream,* flows 3.5 miles to Lewis Creek (2) 12.5 miles southwest of Marion Peak (lat. 36°49'50" N, long. 118° 40'55" W); the stream heads on Comb Spur. Named on Marion Peak (1953) 15' quadrangle.

Comb Rocks [TULARE]: *relief feature,* 1 mile east-northeast of Kaweah (lat. 36°28'35" N, long. 118°54' W; sec. 1, T 17 S, R 28 E). Named on Kaweah (1957) 15' quadrangle.

Comb Spur [FRESNO]: *ridge,* southeast-trending, 2.5 miles long, 9 miles southwest of Marion Peak (lat. 36°51'15" N, long. 118°37'40" W). Named on Marion Peak (1953) 15' quadrangle.

Compressor Hot Springs: see **Miracle Hot Springs** [KERN].

Condor: see **Camp Condor** [KERN].

Condor Peak [FRESNO]: *peak,* 18 miles northwest of Coalinga (lat. 36°19' N, long. 120°37' W; sec. 36, T 18 S, R 12 E). Altitude 4970 feet. Named on Santa Rita Peak (1969) 7.5' quadrangle.

Conejo [FRESNO]: *settlement,* 7.25 miles west-southwest of Selma (lat. 36°31' N, long. 119°43'10" W; near NE cor. sec. 30, T 16 S, R 21 E). Named on Conejo (1963) 7.5' quadrangle. Postal authorities established Conejo post office in 1898 and discontinued it in 1920 (Frickstad, p. 32).

Cone River: see **Kern-Kaweah River** [TULARE].

Conifer: see **Camp Conifer** [TULARE].

Conifer Ridge [TULARE]: *ridge,* southwest-trending, 3 miles long, nearly 7 miles west of Mineral King (lat. 36°27'45" N, long. 118° 42'50" W). Named on Mineral King (1956) 15' quadrangle. H.Y. Alles suggested the name—conifers grow on the ridge (Browning, p. 44).

Connecting Slough [KERN]: *water feature,* center 2 miles southeast of Millux (lat. 35°10' N, long. 119°10' W); the feature connects Buena Vista Lake Bed to Kern Lake Bed. Named on Conner (1954) and Millux (1954) 7.5' quadrangles.

Conner [KERN]: *locality,* 4.5 miles east of Millux along Sunset Railroad (lat. 35°10'50" N, long. 119°06'55" W; at S line sec. 31, T 31 S, R 27 E). Named on Conner (1954) 7.5' quadrangle. California Mining Bureau's (1917c) map shows a place called Progress located about 2 miles north-northeast of Conner along the railroad. Postal authorities established Progress post office 1913 and discontinued it in 1915 (Frickstad, p. 58).

Connor Station: see **Porterville** [TULARE].

Converse: see **Converse Basin** [FRESNO].

Converse Basin [FRESNO]: *area,* 3 miles west-northwest of Hume (lat. 36°48' N, long. 118°58' W); the place is on upper reaches of Converse Creek southwest of Converse Mountain. Named on Tehipite Dome (1952) 15' quadrangle. The name commemorates Charles F. Converse, who claimed the area in the 1860's (Johnston, p. 58). California Mining Bureau's (1917a) map shows a place called Converse in the area.

Converse Creek [FRESNO]: *stream,* flows 6 miles to Kings River 7 miles northwest of Hume (lat. 36°51'30" N, long. 119°00' W); the stream heads in Converse Basin. Named on Tehipite Dome (1952) 15' quadrangle.

Converse Ferry: see **Friant** [FRESNO].

Converse Mountain [FRESNO]: *peak,* 3 miles northwest of Hume (lat. 36°49'10" N, long. 118°56'45" W); the peak is northeast of Converse Basin. Altitude 7208 feet. Named on Tehipite Dome (1952) 15' quadrangle.

Cony Crags [MADERA]: *ridge,* southwest-trending, 0.5 mile long, 7 miles north-north-east of Merced Peak (lat. 37°44' N, long. 119° 21' W). Named on Merced Peak (1953) 15' quadrangle. The name is for the numerous "conies" that live in talus on the ridge (United States Board on Geographic Names, 1963b, p. 14).

Coon Creek [MADERA]: *stream,* flows nearly 3 miles to Fine Gold Creek 3.5 miles east-northeast of O'Neals (lat. 37°08'45" N, long. 119°38'15" W; sec. 13, T 9 S, R 21 E). Named on North Fork (1965) 7.5' quadrangle.

Cook: see **Alex Cook Spring** [KERN].

Cook Peak [KERN]: *peak,* 3.5 miles northeast of Bodfish (lat. 35°37'20" N, long. 118°26'15" W; sec. 33, T 26 S, R 33 E). Altitude 5405 feet. Named on Lake Isabella South (1972) 7.5' quadrangle. Called Cook's Pt. on Wheeler's (1875-1878) map.

Cooksie Canyon [TULARE]: *canyon,* drained by a stream that flows 0.5 mile to White River (1) nearly 3 miles south of California Hot Springs (lat. 35°50'20" N, long. 118°39'55" W; sec. 18, T 24 S, R 31 E). Named on California Hot Springs (1958) 15' quadrangle.

Cooks Peak [KERN]: *peak,* 1.5 miles south of

Alta Sierra (lat. 35°42'20" N, long. 118°52'50" W; near S line sec. 33, T 25 S, R 32 E). Altitude 6921 feet. Named on Alta Sierra (1972) 7.5' quadrangle.

Cook's Point: see **Cook Peak** [KERN].

Coombs: see **The Loop** [KERN].

Coon Creek [FRESNO]: *stream,* flows about 2.5 miles to Huntington Lake (1) 4.25 miles east-northeast of the town of Big Creek (lat. 37°14'05" N, long. 119°10'25" W; sec. 18, T 8 S, R 26 E). Named on Huntington Lake (1953) 15' quadrangle.

Coon Spring [TULARE]: *spring,* 6 miles southeast of Auckland (lat. 36°31'20" N, long. 119°02'25" W; sec. 21, T 16 S, R 27 E). Named on Auckland (1966) 7.5' quadrangle.

Cooper Canyon [FRESNO]: *canyon,* drained by a stream that flows 7.5 miles to Warthan Creek 3.25 miles southwest of Coalinga (lat. 36°06'20" N, long. 120°24' W; sec. 13, T 21 S, R 14 E). Named on Alcalde Hills (1969) and Curry Mountain (1969) 7.5' quadrangles. Arnold and Anderson (1908, p. 16) called the feature Anticline Canyon because "its course across sections 2, 11, 12 is practically coincident with an anticline."

Copper Canyon: see **Cloud Canyon** [TULARE]: **Deadman Canyon** [TULARE] (1).

Copper Creek [FRESNO]: *stream,* flows 5.25 miles to South Fork Kings River 12 miles south-southwest of Marion Peak in Kings Canyon (lat. 36°47'40" N, long. 118°34'45" W). Named on Marion Peak (1953) 15' quadrangle. Copper deposits were known in the neighborhood as early as the 1860's, and E.C. Winchell called the stream Malachite Creek in 1868—giving it the name of a copper mineral; the name "Copper Creek" was in use in 1890, when two men operated a small mine by the stream (Browning 1986, p. 46).

Copper Mountain: see **Laurel Mountain** [KERN].

Cora Creek [MADERA]: *stream,* flows 3.5 miles to North Fork San Joaquin River 8.5 miles west-southwest of Devils Postpile (lat. 37° 35'25" N, long. 119°13'50" W); the stream heads at Cora Lakes. Named on Devils Postpile (1953) and Merced Peak (1953) 15' quadrangles.

Cora Lakes [MADERA]: *lakes,* largest 1300 feet long, 7.25 miles east-southeast of Merced Peak (lat. 37°35'45" N, long. 119°16'15" W); the lakes are at the head of Cora Creek. Named on Merced Peak (1953) 15' quadrangle. R.B. Marshall of United States Geological Survey named the lakes for Mrs. Cora Cressey Crow (Gudde, 1949, p. 78).

Corbett Lake [FRESNO]: *lake,* 700 feet long, 7.5 miles east of Kaiser Peak (lat. 37°17'25" N, long. 119°03'05" W). Named on Kaiser Peak (1953) 15' quadrangle.

Corcoran [KINGS]: *town,* 17 miles south-southeast of Hanford (lat. 36°05'50" N, long. 119°33'45" W; in and near sec. 14, 23, T 21

S, R 22 E). Named on Corcoran (1954) 7.5' quadrangle. Postal authorities established Corcoran post office in 1901; the name is for a civil engineer of Atchison, Topeka and Santa Fe Railroad (Salley, p. 50). The town incorporated in 1914.

Corcoran: see **South Corcoran** [KINGS].

Corcoran Mountain: see **Mount Corcoran** [TULARE].

Corlew Meadows [FRESNO]: *area,* 6 miles west-southwest of Shaver Lake Heights (present town of Shaver Lake) (lat. 37°04'45" N, long. 119°25'30" W; sec. 11, 12, T 10 S, R 23 E). Named on Shaver Lake (1953) 15' quadrangle. Kaiser (1904) 30' quadrangle shows Corlew Mill in Corlew Meadow.

Corlew Mill: see **Corlew Meadows** [FRESNO].

Corlew Mountain [FRESNO]: *ridge,* west-trending, 2 miles long, 3 miles southwest of Prather (lat. 37°00'10" N, long. 119°33' W; in and near sec. 2, 3, T 11 S, R 22 E). Named on Millerton Lake East (1965) 7.5' quadrangle.

Corn Camp [KERN]: *locality,* 9 miles northeast of McKittrick (lat. 35°24'30" N, long. 119°31'05" W; at E line sec. 17, T 29 S, R 23 E). Named on Lokern (1954) 7.5' quadrangle.

Corn Jack Peak [TULARE]: *peak,* nearly 3 miles east of Tucker Mountain (lat. 36°38'20" N, long. 119°09'30" W; near W line sec. 9, T 15 S, R 26 E). Altitude 2386 feet. Named on Tucker Mountain (1966) 7.5' quadrangle.

Cornwell [KINGS]: *locality,* 7 miles north of Lemoore along Atchison, Topeka and Santa Fe Railroad (lat. 36°23'55" N, long. 119°46'45" W). Named on Riverdale (1927) 7.5' quadrangle. Called Lynn on California Mining Bureau's (1917b) map. California Division of Highways' (1934) map shows Lynn located about 1 mile east of Cornwell along the railroad.

Coronet Lake [FRESNO]: *lake,* 800 feet long, 4 miles south-southwest of Mount Abbot (lat. 37°20' N, long. 118°48'50" W). Named on Mount Abbot (1953) 15' quadrangle.

Corral Canyon [KERN]: *canyon,* drained by a stream that flows 4 miles to Little Creek (1) 5 miles north-northwest of Knob Hill (lat. 35°37'35" N, long. 118°59'15" W; sec. 32, T 26 S, R 28 E). Named on Knob Hill (1965) 7.5' quadrangle.

Corral Creek [TULARE]: *stream,* flows 5.5 miles to Kern River nearly 6 miles south-southeast of Fairview (lat. 35°51' N, long. 118°27'05" W; near NW cor. sec. 17, T 24 S, R 33 E). Named on Kernville (1956) 15' quadrangle.

Corral Creek Campground [TULARE]: *locality,* 5.5 miles south-southeast of Fairview (lat. 35°51'20" N, long. 118°27' W; sec. 8, T 24 S, R 33 E); the place is near the mouth of Corral Creek. Named on Kernville (1956) 15' quadrangle.

Corral Hill [TULARE]: *peak,* 4 miles north-

west of California Hot Springs on Pinnell Camp Ridge (lat. 35°55'20" N, long. 118°43'10" W; near SE cor. sec. 15, T 23 S, R 30 E). Named on California Hot Springs (1958) 15' quadrangle.

Corral Meadow [FRESNO]: *area,* south of Shaver Lake (lat. 37°06'45" N, long. 119°18'15" W; in and near sec. 25, 36, T 9 S, R 24 E). Named on Kaiser (1904) 30' quadrangle. Water of an enlarged Shaver Lake now covers the place.

Corral Meadow [MADERA]: *area,* 6 miles southwest of Devils Postpile (lat. 37°34'25" N, long. 119°10'10" W). Named on Devils Postpile (1953) 15' quadrangle. Mount Lyell (1901) 30' quadrangle shows "77" Corral at about the site of present Corral Meadow—this corral was named for the dry summer of 1877 because it was at one of the few feeding places for stock available that year (Smith, Genny, p. 58).

Corral Meadow [TULARE]: *area,* 12.5 miles south of Hockett Peak (lat. 36°02'15" N, long. 118°22'15" W). Named on Hockett Peak (1956) 15' quadrangle.

Corral Meadow: see **Burton Camp** [TULARE].

Corral Mountain [FRESNO]: *peak,* 7.25 miles west-northwest of Blackcap Mountain (lat. 37°06'15" N, long. 118°55' W; sec. 33, T 9 S, R 28 E). Altitude 9698 feet. Named on Blackcap Mountain (1953) 15' quadrangle.

Corral Spring [KERN]: *spring,* 12 miles north-northwest of Mojave (lat. 35°12'50" N, long. 118°14'35" W; near S line sec. 20, T 31 S, R 35 E). Named on Cache Peak (1973) 7.5' quadrangle.

Corrine Lake [MADERA]: *lake,* 1100 feet long, 13 miles south-southwest of Shuteye Peak (lat. 37°09'35" N, long. 119°29'45" W; on E line sec. 7, T 9 S, R 23 E). Named on Shaver Lake (1953) 15' quadrangle.

Cortez Canyon [KERN]: *canyon,* drained by a stream that flows 6.25 miles to the canyon of Kelso Creek 7 miles west of Skinner Peak (lat. 35°33'15" N, long. 118°14'30" W; sec. 29, T 27 S, R 35 E). Named on Cane Canyon (1972) and Woolstalf Creek (1972) 7.5' quadrangles.

Cortez Spring [KERN]: *spring,* 10 miles south of Weldon (lat. 35° 30'45" N, long. 118°17'55" W; near SW cor. sec. 11, T 28 S, R 34 E); the spring is near the head of Cortez Canyon. Named on Woolstalf Creek (1972) 7.5' quadrangle.

Cottage: see **Visalia** [TULARE].

Cotter: see **Mount Cotter** [FRESNO].

Cotton Center [TULARE]: *locality,* 3.5 miles east-southeast of Woodville (lat. 36°04'05" N, long. 119°08'35" W; near SW cor. sec. 26, T 21 S, R 26 E). Named on Woodville (1950) 7.5' quadrangle.

Cotton Lake [FRESNO]: *lake,* 800 feet long, 9 miles northwest of Mount Abbot (lat. 37°29'05" N, long. 118°53'30" W). Named on Mount Abbot (1953) 15' quadrangle.

Cottonwood Canyon [KERN]: *canyon,* 5.5 miles long, drained by Cottonwood Creek (1) above a point 3.25 miles north-northeast of Orchard Peak (lat. 35°46'55" N, long. 120°06'55" W; near W line sec. 2, T 25 S, T 17 E); the canyon heads at Cottonwood Pass in San Luis Obispo County. Named on Tent Hills (1942) 7.5' quadrangle.

Cottonwood Canyon: see **Los Alamos Creek** [KERN].

Cottonwood Cow Camp [MADERA]: *locality,* 9.5 miles southwest of Madera along Cottonwood Creek (2) (lat. 36°52' N, long. 120° 11'10" W; near S line sec. 23, T 12 S, R 16 E). Named on Madera (1946) 15' quadrangle.

Cottonwood Creek [KERN]:

(1) *stream,* flows 4.5 miles to Kings County 4 miles north-northeast of Orchard Peak (lat. 35°47'20" N, long. 120°06'20" W; at N line sec. 2, T 25 S, R 17 E); the stream drains Cottonwood Canyon. Named on Pyramid Hills (1953) and Tent Hills (1942) 7.5' quadrangles.

(2) *stream,* formed by the confluence of North Fork and South Fork, flows 9 miles to Kern River 4.5 miles west of Mount Adelaide (lat. 35°25'30" N, long. 118°49'30" W; at W line sec. 12, T 29 S, R 29 E). Named on Mount Adelaide (1972) and Rio Bravo Ranch (1954) 7.5' quadrangles. North Fork is 8.5 miles long and is named on Mount Adelaide (1972) 7.5' quadrangle. United States Board on Geographic Names (1975b, p. 9) gave the variant names "Walkers Creek" and "North Fork Cottonwood Creek" for North Fork. South Fork is 12.5 miles long and is named on Breckenridge Mountain (1972) and Mount Adelaide (1972) 7.5' quadrangles.

(3) *stream,* flows 18 miles to Jawbone Canyon 1.5 miles north of Cross Mountain (lat. 35°18' N, long. 118°08'20" W; sec. 29, T 30 S, R 36 E). Named on Claraville (1972), Cross Mountain (1972), and Emerald Mountain (1972) 7.5' quadrangles.

(4) *stream,* flows 11.5 miles to lowlands 10.5 miles west of the village of Willow Springs (lat. 34°54'30" N, long. 118°28'15" W; sec. 33, T 10 N, R 15 W). Named on Fairmont Butte (1965), Liebre Twins (1965), and Tylerhorse Canyon (1965) 7.5' quadrangles.

Cottonwood Creek [MADERA]:

(1) *stream,* flows 11.5 miles to San Joaquin River 9 miles south of O'Neals (lat. 36°59'50" N, long. 119°42'25" W; near W line sec. 5, T 11 S, R 21 E). Named on Little Table Mountain (1962) and Millerton Lake West (1965) 7.5' quadrangles.

(2) *stream,* diverges from Fresno River 10 miles south of Raymond (lat. 37°04'10" N, long. 119°54'35" W; near SW cor. sec. 9, T 10 S, R 19 E) and flows more than 30 miles before ending in lowlands southwest of Madera. Named on Firebaugh (1946), Herndon (1965),

Madera (1946), and Raymond (1962) 15' quadrangles.

Cottonwood Creek [TULARE]: *stream* and *dry wash,* extends for 38 miles to join Elbow Creek and form Cross Creek (1) 9 miles northwest of Visalia (lat. 36°25'55" N, long. 119°23'45" W; sec. 20, T 17 S, R 24 E). Named on Exeter (1952) and Visalia (1949) 15' quadrangles, and on Auckland (1966) and Stokes Mountain (1966) 7.5' quadrangles.

Cottonwood Creek, Central Fork: see **Crystal Creek** [KERN].

Cottonwood Creek: see **Willow Creek** [MADERA] (3).

Cottonwood Pass [TULARE]: *pass,* 14 miles north-northwest of Olancha Peak on Tulare-Inyo county line (lat. 36°27'10" N, long. 118°12'50" W; sec. 17, T 17 S, R 35 E); the pass is at the head of a branch of a Cottonwood Creek that is in Inyo County. Named on Olancha (1956) 15' quadrangle. The feature was known locally as Chicken Spring Pass (Browning 1986, p. 47).

Cottonwood Spring [KERN]: *spring,* 4.25 miles east-northeast of Mount Adelaide (lat. 35°27'10" N, long. 118°40'25" W; near E line sec. 31, T 28 S, R 31 E). Named on Mount Adelaide (1972) 7.5' quadrangle.

Cottonwood Springs Creek [FRESNO]: *stream,* flows 1.25 miles to Kings River 5 miles west-southwest of Balch Camp (lat. 36°52'15" N, long. 119°12'35" W; sec. 23, T 12 S, R 25 E). Named on Patterson Mountain (1952) 15' quadrangle.

Cottonwood Station [KERN]: *locality,* 9 miles south of Bakersfield (lat. 35°14'45" N, long. 118°59' W; at W line sec. 9, T 31 S, R 28 E). Named on Caliente (1914) 30' quadrangle.

Cougar Camp [TULARE]: *locality,* 6.25 miles north of California Hot Springs (lat. 35°58'10" N, long. 118°41' W; sec. 36, T 22 S, R 30 E). Named on California Hot Springs (1958) 15' quadrangle.

Council Lake [FRESNO]: *lake,* 1000 feet long, 7 miles south of Mount Abbot (lat. 37°17'05" N, long. 118°48'20" W). Named on Mount Abbot (1953) 15' quadrangle.

County Line Canyon [KERN]: *canyon,* drained by a stream that flows 1 mile to Indian Wells Valley 11.5 miles north-northwest of Inyokern (lat. 35°47'45" N, long. 117°53'45" W; sec. 4, T 25 S, R 38 E); the feature is on Kern-Inyo county line. Named on Little Lake (1954) 15' quadrangle.

County Well [KERN]: *well,* 2.5 miles east of present Blackwells Corner (lat. 35°36'55" N, long. 119°49'30" W). Named on Lost Hills (1914) 30' quadrangle.

Court House Rock: see **Medlicott Dome** [MADERA].

Courtright Reservoir [FRESNO]: *intermittent lake,* behind a dam on Helms Creek 10 miles west of Blackcap Mountain (lat. 37°04'45" N, long. 118°58'10" W; on E line sec. 12, T 10

S, R 27 E). Named on Blackcap Mountain (1953) 15' quadrangle. The name is for H.H. Courtright, president of San Joaquin Light and Power Corporation and general manager of Pacific Gas and Electric Company (Browning 1986, p. 48).

Cove Canyon [TULARE]: *canyon,* drained by a stream that flows 2.25 miles to White River (1) 3 miles south-southwest of California Hot Springs (lat. 35°50'20" N, long. 118°41'35" W; sec. 13, T 24 S, R 30 E). Named on California Hot Springs (1958) 15' quadrangle.

Covel: see **Easton** [FRESNO].

Covington Mountain: see **Tylerhorse Canyon** [KERN].

Cow Canyon [KERN]: *canyon,* drained by a stream that flows 4.5 miles to Canebrake Creek 6.25 miles north-northwest of Walker Pass (lat. 35°44'35" N, long. 118°04'45" W; sec. 23, T 25 S, R 36 E). Named on Walker Pass (1972) 7.5' quadrangle. Called Burnt House Canyon on Onyx (1943) 15' quadrangle, and United States Board on Geographic Names (1975b, p. 9) gave this name as a variant.

Cow Canyon [TULARE]: *canyon,* drained by a stream that flows 3.5 miles to South Fork Kern River 3.5 miles east-southeast of Monache Mountain (lat. 36°11' N, long. 118°08'20" W; sec. 13, T 20 S, R 35 E). Named on Monache Mountain (1956) 15' quadrangle.

Cow Chip Spring [KERN]: *spring,* 7.25 miles west of Liebre Twins (lat. 34°57'20" N, long. 118°41'50" W; sec. 9, T 10 N, R 17 W). Named on Winters Ridge (1966) 7.5' quadrangle.

Cow Chip Spring: see **Lower Cow Chip Spring** [KERN].

Cow Cove [KERN]: *canyon,* drained by a stream that flows less than 1 mile to Heck Canyon 5.5 miles east-northeast of Caliente (lat. 35°19'25" N, long. 118°32'05" W; at N line sec. 15, T 30 S, R 32 E). Named on Oiler Peak (1972) 7.5' quadrangle.

Cow Cove Spring [KERN]: *spring,* 6 miles east-northeast of Caliente (lat. 35°20' N, long. 118°32'05" W; sec. 10, T 30 S, R 32 E); the spring is near the head of Cow Cove. Named on Oiler Peak (1972) 7.5' quadrangle.

Cow Creek [FRESNO]: *stream,* flows 4 miles to Dinkey Creek (1) 1.25 miles west-southwest of Dinkey Dome (lat. 37°06'30" N, long. 119°09'10" W; sec. 32, T 9 S, R 26 E). Named on Huntington Lake (1953) 15' quadrangle.

Cow Creek [KERN]: *stream,* flows 2.5 miles to Bull Run Creek 10.5 miles east-northeast of Glennville (lat. 35°46'45" N, long. 118°31'40" W; near S line sec. 3, T 25 S, R 32 E). Named on California Hot Springs (1958) 15' quadrangle.

Cow Creek: see **Burnt Point Creek** [TULARE]; **Cow Flat Creek** [KERN]; **Horse Creek** [TULARE] (1).

Cowell Creek: see **Caldwell Creek** [KERN].

Cow Flat [KERN]: *area,* 6 miles northeast of Mount Adelaide (lat. 35°29'50" N, long. 118°40'40" W). Named on Mount Adelaide (1972) 7.5' quadrangle.

Cow Flat Creek [KERN]: *stream,* flows 4 miles to Kern River 2.5 miles southwest of Democrat Hot Springs (lat. 35°30' N, long. 118°41'35" W); the stream goes pass Cow Flat. Named on Democrat Hot Springs (1972) and Mount Adelaide (1972) 7.5' quadrangles. Called Cow Cr. on Caliente (1914) 30' quadrangle.

Cow Heaven Canyon [KERN]: *canyon,* drained by a stream that flows nearly 6 miles to Indian Wells Valley 11 miles west-southwest of Inyokern (lat. 35°34'20" N, long. 117°59'10" W; sec. 22, T 27 S, R 37 E). Named on Freeman Junction (1972), Horse Canyon (1972), and Walker Pass (1972) 7.5' quadrangles.

Cow Heaven Spring [KERN]: *spring,* 6.5 miles east-northeast of Skinner Peak (lat. 35°37'05" N, long. 118°01'30" W); the spring is in Cow Heaven Canyon. Named on Horse Canyon (1972) 7.5' quadrangle.

Cow Meadow [FRESNO]:
(1) *area,* 9 miles north of Kaiser Peak (lat. 37°25'25" N, long. 119°12'25" W; near N line sec. 11, T 6 S, R 25 E). Named on Kaiser Peak (1953) 15' quadrangle.
(2) *area,* 11.5 miles north of Hume (lat. 36°57' N, long. 118°53'05" W). Named on Tehipite Dome (1952) 15' quadrangle.

Cow Mountain [TULARE]: *peak,* 5.25 miles south-southeast of Springville (lat. 36°03'25" N, long. 118°47'05" W). Altitude 3774 feet. Named on Globe (1956) 7.5' quadrangle.

Cow Mountain Creek [TULARE]: *stream,* flows 1.5 miles to the canyon of South Fork Tule River 7 miles south-southeast of Springville (lat. 36°01'50" N, long. 118°47'15" W); the stream heads near Cow Mountain. Named on Globe (1956) 7.5' quadrangle.

Cow Wells: see **Garlock** [KERN].

Coy Creek [TULARE]: *stream,* flows 3 miles to South Fork of Middle Fork Tule River 1 mile southwest of Camp Nelson (lat. 36°07'55" N, long. 118°37'20" W; sec. 3, T 21 S, R 31 E); the stream goes past Coy Flat. Named on Camp Nelson (1956) 15' quadrangle.

Coy Flat [TULARE]: *area,* 1 mile south-southwest of Camp Nelson (lat. 36°07'45" N, long. 118°37'10" W; sec. 3, T 21 S, R 31 E); the place is along Coy Creek. Named on Camp Nelson (1956) 15' quadrangle.

Coyote Canyon [FRESNO]: *canyon,* drained by a stream that flows 5.5 miles to Los Gatos Creek 8 miles northwest of Coalinga (lat. 36°13'05" N, long. 120°27'30" W; sec. 4, T 20 S, R 14 E). Named on Alcalde Hills (1969) and Joaquin Rocks (1969) 7.5' quadrangles.

Coyote Creek [TULARE]: *stream,* flows 6 miles to Kern River 7 miles west-northwest of Kern Peak (lat. 36°20'35" N, long. 118°24'15" W); the stream is north of Coyote Peaks. Named on Kern Peak (1956) 15' quadrangle.

Coyote Flat [TULARE]: *area,* nearly 1 mile south-southeast of Auckland (lat. 36°34'35" N, long. 119°06' W; sec. 36, T 15 S, R 26 E). Named on Auckland (1966) 7.5' quadrangle.

Coyote Gulch [KERN]: *canyon,* drained by a stream that flows 3 miles to Rag Gulch 7.5 miles west-northwest of Woody (lat. 35°44'15" N, long. 118°57'25" W; near E line sec. 21, T 25 S, R 28 E). Named on Quincy School (1965) and Sand Canyon (1965) 7.5' quadrangles.

Coyote Holes: see **Freeman** [KERN].

Coyote Lake [FRESNO]:
(1) *lake,* 1600 feet long, 14 miles east-northeast of Kaiser Peak (lat. 37°27'50" N, long. 119°03'05" W). Named on Kaiser Peak (1953) 15' quadrangle. The lake is one of the group called Margaret Lakes
(2) *lake,* 3000 feet long, 5.5 miles north-northeast of Dinkey Dome (lat. 37°11'10" N, long. 119°05'20" W; near SE cor. sec. 35, T 8 S, R 26 E). Named on Huntington Lake (1953) 15' quadrangle.

Coyote Lakes [TULARE]: *lakes,* two, largest 1100 feet long, 9 miles west of Kern Peak (lat. 36°18'25" N, long. 118°27' W); the lakes are south of Coyote Peaks. Named on Kern Peak (1956) 15' quadrangle.

Coyote Pass [FRESNO]: *pass,* 16 miles north-northeast of Hume on Kettle Ridge (lat. 36°58'50" N, long. 118°45'45" W). Named on Tehipite Dome (1952) 15' quadrangle.

Coyote Pass [TULARE]: *pass,* 11 miles west of Kern Peak on Great Western Divide (lat. 36°20'05" N, long. 118°29' W); the pass is near the head of Coyote Creek. Named on Kern Peak (1956) 15' quadrangle.

Coyote Peaks [TULARE]: *peaks,* 9 miles west of Kern Peak (lat. 36° 18'45" N, long. 118°26'45" W); the peaks are south of Coyote Creek. Altitude of highest is 10,892 feet. Named on Kern Peak (1956) 7.5' quadrangle.

Coyote Ridge [FRESNO]: *ridge,* northwest-trending, 1 mile long, 4.5 miles west of Piedra (lat. 36°48'55" N, long. 119°28' W; sec. 9, 10, T 13 S, R 23 E). Named on Piedra (1965) 7.5' quadrangle.

Coyote Spring [KERN]:
(1) *spring,* 4.25 miles east-northeast of Mount Adelaide (lat. 35°27'10" N, long. 118°40'20" W; sec. 32, T 28 S, R 31 E). Named on Mount Adelaide (1972) 7.5' quadrangle.
(2) *spring,* 6 miles northwest of Woody (lat. 35°45'10" N, long. 118°55'10" W; near W line sec. 13, T 25 S, R 28 E); the spring is in Coyote Gulch. Named on Quincy School (1965) 7.5 quadrangle.
(3) *spring,* nearly 5 miles north-northwest of Walker Pass in Berts Canyon (lat. 35°43'45" N, long. 118°03'20" W). Named on Walker Pass (1972) 7.5' quadrangle.
(4) *spring,* 3.25 miles east of Owens Peak (lat. 35°43'50" N, long. 117°56'15" W; near W line

sec. 30, T 25 S, R 38 E). Named on Owens Peak (1972) 7.5' quadrangle.

Coyote Springs: see **Freeman** [KERN].

Coyote Springs Creek [FRESNO]: *stream,* flows 1 mile to Kings River nearly 7 miles west-southwest of Balch Camp (lat. 36°52'10" N, long. 119°14' W; sec. 22, T 12 S, R 25 E). Named on Patterson Mountain (1952) 15' quadrangle.

Crabtree [FRESNO]: *locality,* nearly 5 miles south-southeast of Balch Camp along Mill Flat Creek (lat. 36°05'40" N, long. 119°05'15" W; sec. 36, T 12 S, R 26 E). Named on Patterson Mountain (1952) 15' quadrangle. The name commemorates John F. Crabtree, who homesteaded in section 36 in 1911 (Browning 1986, p. 48).

Crabtree Creek [TULARE]: *stream,* flows 4 miles to Whitney Creek 4 miles west-southwest of Mount Whitney at Crabtree Meadow (lat. 36°33'30" N, long. 118°21'25" W); the stream goes through Crabtree Lakes. Named on Mount Whitney (1956) 15' quadrangle.

Crabtree Creek: see **Big Arroyo** [TULARE].

Crabtree Lake [FRESNO]: *lake,* 900 feet long, 2.5 miles north of Blackcap Mountain (lat. 37°06'25" N, long. 118°47'45" W). Named on Blackcap Mountain (1953) 15' quadrangle. The name, given in 1945, commemorates Rae Crabtree, a packer (Browning 1986, p. 48).

Crabtree Lakes [TULARE]: *lakes,* largest 0.5 mile long, about 3 miles southwest of Mount Whitney (lat. 36°32'40" N, long. 118° 18' W); the lakes are along Crabtree Creek Named on Mount Whitney (1956) 15' quadrangle.

Crabtree Meadow [TULARE]: *area,* 4 miles west-southwest of Mount Whitney (lat. 36°33'10" N, long. 118°21'20" W); the place is at the mouth of Crabtree Creek. Named on Mount Whitney (1956) 15' quadrangle. The name commemorates W.N. Crabtree, who grazed cattle at the site before 1900 (Browning 1986, p. 48).

Craft: see **Ricardo** [KERN].

Crag Creek [TULARE]: *stream,* flows 3 miles to South Fork Kern River 9 miles south-southeast of Monache Mountain (lat. 36°05'50" N, long. 118°06'50" W); the stream is east of Crag Peak. Named on Monache Mountain (1956) 15' quadrangle.

Crag Peak [TULARE]: *peak,* about 7 miles south-southeast of Monache Mountain (lat. 36°06'45" N, long. 118°09'10" W). Altitude 9455 feet. Named on Monache Mountain (1956) 15' quadrangle.

Cramer: see **Milo** [TULARE].

Crandall Hill: see **Tropico Hill** [KERN].

Crane: see **Joe Crane Lake** [MADERA].

Crane Canyon [KERN]: *canyon,* drained by a stream that heads in Los Angeles County and flows 2 miles to Castac Lake 1.25 miles east-southeast of Lebec (lat. 34°49'35" N, long. 118°50'35" W). Named on Lebec (1958) 7.5' quadrangle.

Crane Meadow [TULARE]: *area,* 9 miles south of Camp Nelson (lat. 36°00'50" N, long. 118°36'30" W; near SE cor. sec. 15, T 22 S, R 31 E). Named on Camp Nelson (1956) 15' quadrangle.

Crane Valley [MADERA]: *valley,* 5 miles southeast of Yosemite Forks along North Fork Willow Creek (2) (lat. 37°19' N, long. 119°33'30" W). Named on Bass Lake (1953) 15' quadrangle. Water of Bass Lake (1) now covers most of the valley.

Crane Valley Creek: see **North Fork**, under **Willow Creek** [MADERA] (2).

Crane Valley Lake: see **Bass Lake** [MADERA] (1).

Crater Creek [FRESNO]: *stream,* flows nearly 3.5 miles to Florence Lake 13 miles southwest of Mount Abbot (lat. 37°16'35" N, long. 118°58'15" W); the stream heads at Crater Lake. Named on Mount Abbot (1953) 15' quadrangle.

Crater Creek [MADERA]: *stream,* flows 6.5 miles to Middle Fork San Joaquin River 4.5 miles south of Devils Postpile (lat. 37°33'30" N, long. 119°05'30" W). Named on Devils Postpile (1953) 15' quadrangle.

Crater Lake [FRESNO]: *lake,* 900 feet long, 10 miles east-southeast of Kaiser Peak (lat. 37°15' N, long. 119°00'25" W). Named on Huntington Lake (1953) and Kaiser Peak (1953) 15' quadrangles.

Crater Lake Meadow [FRESNO]: *area,* in a circular depression 8 miles north-northeast of Kaiser Peak (lat. 37°24'15" N, long. 119° 08'45" W). Named on Kaiser Peak (1953) 15' quadrangle.

Crater Mountain [FRESNO]: *peak,* 2 miles south-southwest of Mount Pinchot (lat. 36°55'20" N, long. 118°25'15" W). Altitude 12,874 feet. Named on Mount Pinchot (1953) 15' quadrangle.

Crawford Camp [TULARE]: *locality,* nearly 5 miles south of Camp Nelson (lat. 36°04'20" N, long. 118°36' W; sec. 26, T 21 S, R 31 E); the place is at the head of Crawford Creek. Named on Camp Nelson (1956) 15' quadrangle.

Crawford Creek [TULARE]: *stream,* flows 1.5 miles to Windy Creek (1) nearly 6 miles south of Camp Nelson (lat. 36°03'30" N, long. 118°37'15" W; sec. 34, T 21 S, R 31 E). Named on Camp Nelson (1956) 15' quadrangle.

Crazy Lake [FRESNO]: *lake,* 750 feet long, 8.5 miles southwest of Mount Abbot (lat. 37°18'05" N, long. 118°53'50" W). Named on Mount Abbot (1953) 15' quadrangle. A group from California Department of Fish and Game gave the name in 1948 because the lake is at such a desolate site that anyone who visits the place must be crazy (Browning 1986, p. 49).

Credow Mountain: see **Quedow Mountain** [TULARE].

Crescent Creek [MADERA]: *stream,* flows 4.5 miles to South Fork Merced River 4.25 miles south-southwest of Buena Vista Peak (lat. 37°32'15" N, long. 119°33' W; at S line sec. 34, T 4 S, R 22 E). Named on Yosemite (1956) 15' quadrangle.

Crescent Creek [TULARE]: *stream,* flows 3.5 miles to Moro Creek nearly 7 miles east-southeast of Yucca Mountain (lat. 36°32'15" N, long. 118°45'25" W). Named on Giant Forest (1956) and Triple Divide Peak (1956) 15' quadrangles.

Crescent Lake [MADERA]: *lake,* 1700 feet long, 2.25 miles south-southwest of Buena Vista Peak (lat. 37°33'55" N, long. 119°32' W; on N line sec. 26, T 4 S, R 22 E); the lake is along Crescent Creek. Named on Yosemite (1956) 15' quadrangle.

Crescent Lake [TULARE]: *lake,* 1300 feet long, 9 miles west-northwest of Triple Divide Peak (lat. 36°38'40" N, long. 118°41' W). Named on Triple Divide Peak (1956) 15' quadrangle.

Crescent Lawn: see **Horse Corral Meadow** [FRESNO].

Crescent Meadow [TULARE]: *area,* 12.5 miles west-southwest of Triple Divide Peak (lat. 36°33'25" N, long. 118°44'45" W; on S line sec. 5, T 16 S, R 30 E). Named on Triple Divide Peak (1956) 15' quadrangle.

Crew Creek [TULARE]: *stream,* flows nearly 4 miles to South Fork Tule River 6.25 miles south-southwest of Springville (lat. 36°02'55" N, long. 118°51'30" W; near E line sec. 5, T 22 S, R 29 E). Named on Globe (1956) 7.5' quadrangle.

Crocker: see **Mount Crocker** [FRESNO].

Crocker Canyon [KERN]: *canyon,* drained by a stream that heads in San Luis Obispo County and flows 5.25 miles in Kern County to Midway Valley 4.25 miles north-northwest of Fellows (lat. 35°13'45" N, long. 119°34'50" W; sec. 14, T 31 S, R 22 E). Named on Fellows (1951) and Panorama Hills (1954) 7.5' quadrangles.

Crocker Flat [KERN]: *area,* 7 miles south-southwest of McKittrick (lat. 35°12'20" N, long. 119°39'40" W; on S line sec. 19, T 31 S, R 22 E); the place is 1.5 miles south of Crocker Canyon. Named on Panorama Hills (1954) 7.5' quadrangle. Arnold and Johnson (p. 20) proposed the name.

Crocker Spring [KERN]: *spring,* 5.5 miles south-southwest of McKittrick (lat. 35°13'35" N, long. 119°40'10" W; at W line sec. 18, T 31 S, R 22 E); the spring is in Crocker Canyon. Named on McKittrick (1912) 30' quadrangle.

Crofton Spring [KERN]: *spring,* 4 miles east-southeast of Caliente (lat. 35°16' N, long. 118°33'50" W; near N line sec. 5, T 31 S, R 32 E). Named on Oiler Peak (1972) 7.5' quadrangle.

Crome [KERN]: *locality,* 12 miles west-northwest of Bakersfield along Atchison, Topeka and Santa Fe Railroad (lat. 35°26'30" N, long.

119°11'50" W; at S line sec. 32, T 28 S, R 26 E). Named on Rosedale (1954) 7.5' quadrangle.

Cromir [FRESNO]: *locality,* 4 miles south-southeast of Firebaugh along Southern Pacific Railroad (lat. 36°48'20" N, long. 120°25'20" W; near NE cor. sec. 15, T 13 S, R 14 E). Named on Firebaugh (1956) 7.5' quadrangle. On Firebaugh (1923) 7.5' quadrangle, the name applies to a place located 1 mile farther west along a former Atchison, Topeka and Santa Fe Railroad line.

Crook Creek [MADERA]: *stream,* flows 4.5 miles to Fresno River 6.5 miles west of Yosemite Forks (lat. 37°21' N, long. 119°44'45" W); the stream is east of Crook Mountain (1). Named on Bass Lake (1953) 15' quadrangle. United States Board on Geographic Names (1984a, p. 3) approved the name "Crooks Creek" for the feature; the name commemorates William H. Crooks, a rancher along the stream from the 1850's until 1912.

Crooked Slough [KINGS]: *stream,* diverges from Kings River and flows 3 miles to South Fork Kings River 4.5 miles north-northwest of Lemoore (lat. 36°21'50" N, long. 119°48'15" W; sec. 16, T 18 S, R 20 E). Named on Lemoore (1954) and Riverdale (1954) 7.5' quadrangles.

Crook Mountain [MADERA]:

(1) *ridge,* north-trending, 3 miles long, 13 miles north-northeast of Raymond (lat. 37°22'30" N, long. 119°46'15" W). Named on Horsecamp Mountain (1947) and Stumpfield Mountain (1947) 7.5' quadrangles. United States Board on Geographic Names (1984a, p. 3) approved the name "Crooks Mountain" for the feature; the name commemorates William H. Crooks, of present Crooks Creek.

(2) *peak,* nearly 6 miles southeast of O'Neals (lat. 37°04'20" N, long. 119°37'05" W; sec. 7, T 10 S, R 22 E). Altitude 2006 feet. Named on Millerton Lake East (1965) 7.5' quadrangle.

Crooks Creek: see **Crook Creek** [MADERA].

Crooks Mountain: see **Crook Mountain** [MADERA] (1).

Cross [TULARE]: *locality,* 2.5 miles south-southeast of Traver along Southern Pacific Railroad (lat. 36°25'20" N, long. 119°28' W; sec. 27, T 17 S, R 23 E); the place is 1.5 miles north-northwest of the railroad crossing of Cross Creek (1). Named on Traver (1949) 7.5' quadrangle.

Cross Creek [FRESNO-TULARE]: *stream,* heads in Tulare County and flows 3 miles to Bubbs Creek 13 miles south-southwest of Mount Pinchot in Fresno County (lat. 36°46'15" N, long. 118°28'50" W). Named on Mount Whitney (1907) 30' quadrangle, and on Mount Pinchot (1953) 15' quadrangle.

Cross Creek [KINGS-TULARE]: *stream,* formed by the confluence of Cottonwood Creek and Elbow Creek in Tulare County, flows 31 miles before it divides to form Middle Branch and West Branch 5.5 miles south of Guernsey in Kings County (lat. 36°07'50" N, long. 119°38' W; sec. 6, T 21 S, R 22 E). Named on Burris Park (1954), Guernsey (1954), Remnoy (1954), Traver (1949), and Waukena (1954) 7.5' quadrangles. Middle Branch is named on Corcoran (1954), El Rico Ranch (1954), and Guernsey (1954) 7.5' quadrangles. West Branch is named on El Rico Ranch (1954) and Guernsey (1954) 7.5' quadrangles. East Branch diverges from Cross Creek 3.5 miles northwest of Corcoran, and flows 7 miles before rejoining Cross Creek 6 miles east of Hanford. East Branch is named on Corcoran (1954), Goshen (1949), Remnoy (1954), Traver (1949), and Waukena (1954) 7.5' quadrangles.

Cross Creek: see **Traver** [TULARE].

Cross Ferry: see **Kern River** [KERN].

Cross Mountain [KERN]: *peak,* 15 miles north of Mojave (lat. 35° 16'45" N, long. 118°08'10" W; sec. 32, T 30 S, R 36 E). Altitude 5203 feet. Named on Cross Mountain (1972) 7.5' quadrangle.

Cross Mountain [TULARE]: *peak,* 10 miles north of Triple Divide Peak (lat. 36°44'10" N, long. 119°30'10" W). Altitude 12,185 feet. Named on Triple Divide Peak (1956) 15' quadrangle.

Cross Mountain: see **Breckenridge Mountain** [KERN].

Crown Basin [FRESNO]: *valley,* 3.25 miles south-southeast of Blackcap Mountain (lat. 37°01'45" N, long. 118°46'15" W); the valley is at the head of Crown Creek. Named on Blackcap Mountain (1953) 15' quadrangle.

Crown Creek [FRESNO]: *stream,* flows 12 miles to Middle Fork Kings River 11 miles northeast of Hume (lat. 36°54'30" N, long. 118°47' W); the stream heads in Crown Basin. Named on Blackcap Mountain (1953) and Tehipite Dome (1952) 15' quadrangles.

Crown Lake [FRESNO]: *lake,* 1800 feet long, 4 miles southwest of Blackcap Mountain (lat. 37°02' N, long. 118°50'50" W). Named on Blackcap Mountain (1953) 15' quadrangle.

Crown Mountain: see **Crown Rock** [FRESNO].

Crown Ridge [FRESNO]: *ridge,* southwest-trending, 2 miles long, 13 miles north of Hume (lat. 36°58' N, long. 118°52'20" W). Named on Tehipite Dome (1952) 15' quadrangle.

Crown Rock [FRESNO]: *relief feature,* 12 miles north-northeast of Hume (lat. 36°57'15" N, long. 118°52' W); the feature is between Crown Valley and Crown Ridge. Altitude 9342 feet. Named on Tehipite Dome (1952) 15' quadrangle. Called Crown Mt. on Tehipite (1903) 30' quadrangle. Frank Dusy gave the name "Crown Mountain" to the feature about 1870 because of its crownlike top (Browning 1986, p. 50).

Crown Valley [FRESNO]: *valley,* 12 miles north-northeast of Hume (lat. 36°57' N, long.

118°50'45" W); the valley is drained by a branch of Crown Creek. Named on Tehipite Dome (1952) 15' quadrangle. Called Collins Meadow on Tehipite (1903) 30' quadrangle.

Crumville: see **Ridgecrest** [KERN].

Crunigen Creek [TULARE]: *stream,* flows 2.5 miles to East Fork Kaweah River 8 miles east-southeast of Kaweah (lat. 36°26'40" N, long. 118°46'30" W; sec. 13, T 17 S, R 29 E). Named on Kaweah (1957) 15' quadrangle. United States Board on Geographic Names (1988b, p. 1) approved the name "Grunigen Creek" for the feature, and noted that the name commemorates John Grunigen, a resident of the neighborhood after 1900.

Crystal Cave [TULARE]: *cave,* 2.5 miles east-northeast of Yucca Mountain (lat. 36°35'20" N, long. 118°49'40" W; near E line sec. 28, T 15 S, R 29 E). Named on Giant Forest (1956) 15' quadrangle. A.L. Medley and C.M. Webster discovered the cave in 1918; Walter Fry named it (Browning 1986, p. 50).

Crystal Creek [FRESNO]: *stream,* flows 2 miles to Middle Fork Kings River 12.5 miles northeast of Hume (lat. 36°55' N, long. 118°45'45" W). Named on Marion Peak (1953) and Tehipite Dome (1952) 15' quadrangles.

Crystal Creek [KERN]: *stream,* flows 2.5 miles to South Fork Cottonwood Creek (2) 6.5 miles east of Mount Adelaide (lat. 35° 24'55" N, long. 118°37'35" W; sec. 11, T 29 S, R 31 E). Named on Breckenridge Mountain (1972) 7.5' quadrangle. Called Central Fork [of Cottonwood Creek (2)] on Breckenridge Mountain (1943) 15' quadrangle. United States Board on Geographic Names (1975b, p. 9) gave the names "Central Fork Cottonwood Creek" and "Central Fork Rattlesnake Creek" as variants.

Crystal Creek [TULARE]: *stream,* flows 1.5 miles to East Fork Kaweah River 1 mile south-southeast of Mineral King (lat. 36°26'10" N, long. 118°35'20" W); the stream heads at Crystal Lake. Named on Mineral King (1956) 15' quadrangle. The stream first was called Silver Creek (Jackson, p. 25).

Crystal Lake [TULARE]: *lake,* 1000 feet long, 2 miles east-southeast of Mineral King (lat. 36°26'30" N, long. 118°33'40" W); the lake is at the head of Crystal Creek. Named on Mineral King (1956) 15' quadrangle. The feature first was called Silver Lake (Jackson, p. 25).

Crystal Springs Campground [FRESNO]: *locality,* 4 miles southwest of Hume (lat. 36°44'40" N, long. 118°57'35" W; sec. 32, T 13 S, R 28 E). Named on Giant Forest (1956) 15' quadrangle.

Cudahy Camp [KERN]: *locality,* 4.25 miles north-northwest of Saltdale in Last Chance Canyon (lat. 35°24'40" N, long. 117°55'30" W). Site named on Saltdale NW (1967) 7.5' quadrangle.

Cuddy Canyon [KERN]: *canyon,* 6.5 miles long, on Kern-Los Angeles county line, opens into Castac Valley 1.5 miles southwest of Lebec (lat. 34°49' N, long. 118°53'15" W; near SW cor. sec. 34, T 9 N, R 19 W). Named on Frazier Mountain (1958) 7.5' quadrangle.

Cuddy Creek [KERN]: *stream,* flows 6 miles to Cuddy Canyon 8 miles west of Lebec (lat. 34°49'05" N, long. 119°00'10" W); the stream goes through Cuddy Valley. Named on Cuddy Valley (1943) 7.5' quadrangle.

Cuddy Valley [KERN]: *valley,* 7 miles southeast of Eagle Rest Peak (lat. 34°50' N, long. 119°03'30" W); the valley is at the head of Cuddy Creek. Named on Cuddy Valley (1943) 7.5' quadrangle. Fairbanks (1894b, p. 494) referred to Cuddy's Valley. The name commemorates John Fletcher Cuddy, a hunter at Fort Tejon who built a log cabin in the valley (Latta, 1976, p. 204).

Cueva Canyon [FRESNO]: *canyon,* drained by a stream that flows 1 mile to Salt Creek (2) 7 miles south-southwest of Coalinga (lat. 36° 03' N, long. 120°24'50" W; sec. 1, T 22 S, R 14 E). Named on Curry Mountain (1969) 7.5' quadrangle.

Cuidado Mountain: see **Quedow Mountain** [TULARE].

Cuidow Mountain: see **Quedow Mountain** [TULARE].

Cummings Creek [KERN]: *stream,* flows 5.5 miles to Cummings Valley 4 miles north-northwest of Cummings Mountain (lat. 35°05'45" N, long. 118°35' W; near S line sec. 31, T 32 S, R 32 E). Named on Cummings Mountain (1966) 7.5' quadrangle.

Cummings Mountain [KERN]: *peak,* 9 miles southwest of Tehachapi (lat. 35°02'30" N, long. 118°34'15" W; sec. 15, T 11 N, R 16 W). Altitude 7725 feet. Named on Cummings Mountain (1966) 7.5' quadrangle. The name is for George Cummings of Cummings Valley (Gudde, 1949, p. 86). This appears to be the feature called Tehachapai Peak on Wheeler's (1875-1878) map.

Cummings Valley [KERN]: *valley,* 5 miles north-northwest of Cummings Mountain (lat. 35°06'30" N, long. 118°36' W). Named on Cummings Mountain (1966), Keene (1966), and Tejon Ranch (1966) 7.5' quadrangles. The name commemorates George Cummings, who bought land in the valley in the late 1850's (Boyd, p. 173).

Cuneo [KINGS]: *locality,* 4 miles north of Stratford along Southern Pacific Railroad (lat. 36°14'50" N, long. 119°50' W). Named on Stratford (1929) 7.5' quadrangle.

Cunningham Creek [TULARE]: *stream,* flows 4 miles to Roaring River 5.5 miles north of Triple Divide Peak (lat. 36°40'20" N, long. 118°32'15" W). Named on Mount Whitney (1956) and Triple Divide Peak (1956) 15' quadrangles.

Cunningham Lake [FRESNO]: *lake,* 600 feet long, 7 miles east of Kaiser Peak (lat. 37°17'10" N, long. 119°03'35" W). Named on Kaiser Peak (1953) 15' quadrangle.

Curry Mountain [FRESNO]: *ridge,* northwest-trending, 2 miles long, 7 miles southwest of Coalinga (lat. 36°05' N, long. 120°27'30" W). Named on Curry Mountain (1969) 7.5' quadrangle.

Curtis Mountain [TULARE]: *ridge,* west-trending, 2.5 miles long, 8 miles east-northeast of Dinuba (lat. 36°35'45" N, long. 119°15'45" W). Named on Orange Cove South (1966) and Stokes Mountain (1966) 7.5' quadrangles.

Cutler [TULARE]: *town,* 5.5 miles east-southeast of Dinuba (lat. 36° 31'30" N, long. 119°17'15" W; sec. 19, 20, T 16 S, R 25 E). Named on Orange Cove South (1966) 7.5' quadrangle. Postal authorities established Cutler post office in 1910 (Frickstad, p. 210). Officials of Atchison, Topeka and Santa Fe Railroad named the place in 1897 for Dr. John Cutler, a pioneer of Tulare County (Mitchell, A.R., p. 67).

Cuts Meadow: see **Cutts Meadow** [FRESNO].

Cuttens: see **Lost Hills** [KERN] (2).

Cutterbank Spring [KERN]: *spring,* 5.25 miles west-northwest of Cinco (lat. 35°17'30" N, long. 118°07'20" W; near SW cor. sec. 28, T 30 S, R 36 E). Named on Cinco (1972) 7.5' quadrangle.

Cutts Meadow [FRESNO]: *area,* 3 miles northwest of Dinkey Dome (lat. 37°08'35" N, long. 119°10'25" W; sec. 18, T 9 S, R 26 E). Named on Huntington Lake (1953) 15' quadrangle. Called Cuts Meadow on Kaiser (1904) 30' quadrangle.

Cyclamen Lake [TULARE]: *lake,* 900 feet long, 2.5 miles east-northeast of Mineral King (lat. 36°28'05" N, long. 118°33'05" W). Named on Mineral King (1956) 15' quadrangle. The name is for cyclamen plants that grow near the lake (United States Board on Geographic Names, 1933a, p. 250).

Cyclone Meadow [TULARE]: *area,* 9.5 miles south-southwest of Mineral King (lat. 36°19'05" N, long. 118°37'50" W; mainly in sec. 32, T 18 S, R 31 E). Named on Mineral King (1956) 15' quadrangle.

Cyrus Canyon [KERN]: *canyon,* drained by a stream that flows 6 miles to Isabella Lake less than 2 miles east of Wofford Heights (lat. 35°42'30" N, long. 118°25'20" W; sec. 34, T 25 S, R 33 E). Named on Lake Isabella North (1972) and Weldon (1972) 7.5' quadrangles.

Cyrus Flat [KERN]: *valley,* 2.5 miles east of Wofford Heights (lat. 35°42'25" N, long. 118°24'20" W); the valley is at the mouth of Cyrus Canyon. Named on Lake Isabella North (1972) 7.5' quadrangle.

– D –

Dabney Canyon [KERN]: *canyon,* drained by a stream that flows 5 miles to Midway Valley nearly 3 miles west-northwest of Fellows (lat. 35°11'45" N, long. 119°35'10" W; near SW

cor. sec. 26, T 31 S, R 22 E). Named on Fellows (1951) and Panorama Hills (1954) 7.5' quadrangles.

Dade: see **Mount Dade** [FRESNO].

Dagany Gap [KERN]: *pass,* 7.5 miles east-northeast of Orchard Peak in Pyramid Hills (lat. 35°46'50" N, long. 120°00'30" W; on E line sec. 3, T 25 S, R 18 E). Named on Pyramid Hills (1953) 7.5' quadrangle. The name commemorates F.P. Daganey, a French stockman who lived at the place (Latta, 1949, p. 335).

Dairyland [MADERA]: *locality,* 7.5 miles south-southwest of Chowchilla (lat. 37°01'05" N, long. 120°18'35" W; on W line sec. 35, T 10 S, R 15 E). Named on Chowchilla (1960) 7.5' quadrangle. Chowchilla (1918) 7.5' quadrangle shows the place 3 miles farther west at the end of Chowchilla Pacific Railroad, and California Division of Highways' (1934) map shows it at the end of a branch of Southern Pacific Railroad (SE quarter sec. 31, T 10 S, R 15 E).

Dale Lake [FRESNO]: *lake,* 900 feet long, 6 miles north-northwest of Blackcap Mountain (lat. 37°09'05" N, long. 118°49'55" W). Named on Blackcap Mountain (1953) 15' quadrangle. Employees of California Department of Fish and Game named the lake for John Dale, a packer, when the lake first was planted with fish in 1936 (Browning 1986, p. 51).

Daley Mill [KERN]: *locality,* 3 miles west-southwest of Saltdale (lat. 35°20'20" N, long. 117°55'55" W). Ruins named on Cantil (1967) 7.5' quadrangle.

Dalton Mountain [FRESNO]: *ridge,* west-northwest-trending, 3.5 miles long, 11 miles southwest of Balch Camp (lat. 36°46'35" N, long. 119°14'30" W). Named on Patterson Mountain (1952) 15' quadrangle, and on Pine Flat Dam (1965) 7.5' quadrangle. The name is from the outlaw Dalton brothers, or from Gratton Dalton, the eldest outlaw brother who hid near the feature after he escaped from jail (Hanna, p. 81).

Damon Mill [FRESNO]: *locality,* 2.25 miles north-northwest of the present town of Shaver Lake (formerly Shaver Lake Heights) (lat. 37°08'20" N, long. 119°19'40" W; near NW cor. sec. 23, T 9 S, R 24 E); the place is near the head of Mill Creek (2). Named on Kaiser (1904) 30' quadrangle. Called Duncan Mill on California Mining Bureau's (1917a) map.

Danner Meadow [TULARE]: *area,* 11.5 miles south of Hockett Peak (lat. 36°03'25" N, long. 118°21'40" W). Named on Hockett Peak (1956) 15' quadrangle.

Darby Pond [FRESNO]: *lake,* 1500 feet long, 3.5 miles west-northwest of Selma (lat. 36°34'55" N, long. 119°40'15" W; sec. 34, T 15 S, R 21 E). Named on Selma (1946) 15' quadrangle. Conejo (1963) 7.5' quadrangle has the name for a dry depression.

Dark Canyon [TULARE]:

(1) *canyon*, drained by a stream that flows 3.25 miles to Trout Creek 14 miles east-northeast of Fairview (lat. 35°58'45" N, long. 118°15'35" W; sec. 25, T 22 S, R 34 E). Named on Hockett Peak (1956) and Kernville (1956) 15' quadrangles.

(2) *canyon*, drained by a stream that flows 1.25 miles to White River (1) 3 miles southeast of California Hot Springs (lat. 35° 50'40" N, long. 118°38'15" W; sec. 16, T 24 S, R 31 E). Named on California Hot Springs (1958) 15' quadrangle.

(3) *canyon*, drained by a stream that flows 2 miles to Chico Canyon 9 miles south-southeast of Fairview (lat. 35°48'10" N, long. 118° 27'30" W; sec. 31, T 24 S, R 33 E). Named on Kernville (1956) 15' quadrangle.

Dark Hole: see **The Dark Hole** [FRESNO-KINGS].

Darwin: see **Mount Darwin** [FRESNO]; **Reedley** [FRESNO].

Darwin Canyon [FRESNO]: *canyon*, 2 miles long, 6 miles north-northeast of Mount Goddard (lat. 37°11'15" N, long. 118°41'W); the feature is 1.5 miles north-northwest of Mount Darwin. Named on Mount Goddard (1948) 15' quadrangle.

Darwin Glacier [FRESNO]: *glacier*, 5.5 miles north-northeast of Mount Goddard (lat. 37°10'20" N, long. 118°40'30" W); the glacier is 0.25 mile north of Mount Darwin. Named on Mount Goddard (1948) 15' quadrangle.

Dathol: see **Coalinga** [FRESNO].

Daulton [MADERA]: *locality*, 8 miles southsouthwest of Raymond (lat. 37°07'10" N, long. 119°58'50" W; sec. 26, T 9 S, R 18 E); the place is along Daulton Creek. Named on Daulton (1962) 7.5' quadrangle. Postal authorities established Daulton post office in 1899 and discontinued it in 1908 (Frickstad, p. 85). Daulton (1921) 7.5' quadrangle shows the place along Southern Pacific Railroad. Officials of the railroad named the station there in the 1860's for Henry C. Daulton, who gave right of way through his property—Mr. Daulton was chairman of the commission that organized Madera County (Gudde, 1949, p. 89).

Daulton Creek [FRESNO]: *stream*, flows 4 miles to Mammoth Pool Reservoir on San Joaquin River 8 miles west-northwest of Kaiser Peak (lat. 37°19'25" N, long. 119°18'50" W; near N line sec. 14, T 7 S, R 24 E). Named on Shuteye Peak (1953) 15' quadrangle. The name commemorates H.C. Daulton, an early stockman in the neighborhood (Browning 1986, p. 52).

Daulton Creek [MADERA]: *stream*, flows 16 miles to Dry Creek 10.5 miles south-southwest of Raymond (lat. 37°04'30" N, long. 119°59'20" W; sec. 10, T 10 S, R 18 E). Named on Daulton (1962) and Raymond (1962) 7.5' quadrangles. The part of the stream

above the mouth of Rawls Gulch is called Gnat Creek on Raymond (1944) 15' quadrangle, but United States Board on Geographic Names (1964a, p. 9) rejected this name for the stream.

Daulton Spring [MADERA]: *spring*, 5.5 miles southeast of Knowles (lat. 37°10'20" N, long. 119°47'30" W; sec. 4, T 9 S, R 20 E). Named on Knowles (1962) 7.5' quadrangle.

Daulton Station [FRESNO]: *locality*, 6 miles west-northwest of Kaiser Peak (lat. 35°20'05" N, long. 119°17'05" W; sec. 7, T 7 S, R 25 E). Named on Shuteye Peak (1953) 15' quadrangle. Kaiser (1904) 30' quadrangle shows Daulton ranger station at the site.

Daunt: see **Springville** [TULARE].

Davis: see **Scarlet and Davis Canyon** [TULARE].

Davis Campground [KERN]: *locality*, 5.25 miles west-northwest of Miracle Hot Springs (lat. 35°36'55" N, long. 118°36'50" W). Named on Miracle Hot Springs (1972) 7.5' quadrangle.

Davis Creek [FRESNO]: *stream*, flows 2.5 miles to Mill Flat Creek nearly 5 miles south-southeast of Balch Camp (lat. 36°50'35" N, long. 119°05'15" W; sec. 36, T 12 S, R 26 E); the stream heads near Davis Flat. Named on Patterson Mountain (1952) 15' quadrangle.

Davis Flat [FRESNO]: *area*, 6 miles southsoutheast of Balch Camp (lat. 36°49'15" N, long. 119°05'15" W; near SW cor. sec. 6, T 13 S, R 27 E). Named on Patterson Mountain (1952) 15' quadrangle.

Davis Lake [FRESNO]:

(1) *lake*, 1600 feet long, nearly 7 miles northnorthwest of Blackcap Mountain (lat. 37°09'55" N, long. 118°04'45" W). Named on Blackcap Mountain (1953) 15' quadrangle.

(2) *lakes*, two joined, 1.5 miles long together, 2 miles north of Mount Goddard (lat. 37°07'45" N, long. 118°43'30" W). Named on Mount Goddard (1948) 15' quadrangle. The name commemorates George R. Davis of United States Geological Survey (United States Board on Geographic Names, 1933a, p. 256).

Davis Mountain [FRESNO]: *ridge*, west-northwest-trending, 1 mile long, nearly 6 miles north of Trimmer (lat. 36°59'15" N, long. 119° 17'50" W; on E line sec. 12, T 11 S, R 24 E). Named on Trimmer (1965) 7.5' quadrangle.

Davis Mountain [TULARE]: *ridge*, west-southwest-trending, about 1.5 miles long, 4.5 miles northeast of Woodlake (lat. 36°28' N, long. 119°02'45" W). Named on Woodlake (1952) 7.5' quadrangle.

Davis Mountain: see **Mount Davis** [MADERA].

Dead Horse Canyon [KERN]: *canyon*, drained by a stream that flows 1.5 miles to Oiler Canyon 3.5 miles northeast of Caliente (lat. 35°19'50" N, long. 118°35'20" W; sec. 7, T 30 S, R 32 E). Named on Oiler Peak (1972) 7.5' quadrangle.

Deadhorse Lake [MADERA]: *lake,* 1000 feet long, 4.5 miles west-northwest of Devils Postpile (lat. 37°39'05" N, long. 119°09'35" W). Named on Devils Postpile (1953) 15' quadrangle.

Dead Horse Meadow [TULARE]: *area,* 4.5 miles east of California Hot Springs (lat. 35°52'25" N, long. 118°35'15" W; sec. 1, T 24 S, R 31 E). Named on California Hot Springs (1958) 15' quadrangle.

Dead Horse Slough [TULARE]: *water feature,* dry watercourse 2 miles long that heads 3.5 miles west-northwest of Porterville (lat. 36°05'40" N, long. 119°04'25" W; near SE cor. sec. 17, T 21 S, R 27 E). Named on Porterville (1929) 7.5' quadrangle.

Dead Horse Spring [KERN]: *spring,* nearly 4 miles north-northeast of Caliente (lat. 35°20'20" N, long. 118°35'40" W; near SW cor. sec. 6, T 30 S, R 32 E); the spring is in Dead Horse Canyon. Named on Oiler Peak (1972) 7.5' quadrangle.

Deadman Canyon [FRESNO]: *canyon,* drained by a stream that flows 3.5 miles to Jacalitos Creek 6.25 miles south of Coalinga (lat. 36°03' N, long. 120°21'55" W; near N line sec. 4, T 22 S, R 15 E). Named on Kreyenhagen Hills (1956) 7.5' quadrangle.

Deadman Canyon [TULARE]:

(1) *canyon,* drained by a stream that flows 8 miles to Roaring River 8.5 miles north-northwest of Triple Divide Peak (lat. 36°42'25" N, long. 118°34'45" W). Named on Triple Divide Peak (1956) 15' quadrangle. The grave of a sheepherder is at the lower end of the canyon (Browning, p. 53). United States Board on Geographic Names (1933a, p. 257) rejected the names "Cloudy Canyon" and "Copper Canyon" for the feature.

(2) *canyon,* drained by a stream that flows 1.5 miles to Kern River 4.5 miles south of Hockett Peak (lat. 36°09'10" N, long. 118°23'55" W). Named on Hockett Peak (1956) 15' quadrangle.

Deadman Canyon: see **Cloud Canyon** [TULARE].

Deadman Creek [KERN]: *stream,* flows 3.25 miles to Tecuya Creek 3.5 miles southwest of Grapevine (lat. 34°53'10" N, long. 118° 58' W; sec, 2, T 9 N, R 20 W). Named on Grapevine (1958) and Frazier Mountain (1958) 7.5' quadrangles. On Frazier Mountain (1944) and Tecuya Creek (1945) 7.5' quadrangles, the name has the form "Dead Man Creek."

Deadman Creek [TULARE]: *stream,* flows 3 miles to South Fork of Middle Fork Tule River 2.5 miles west of Camp Nelson (lat. 36°08'55" N, long. 118°39'10" W). Named on Camp Nelson (1956) 15' quadrangle.

Deadman Gap [KINGS]: *pass,* 12.5 miles south-southeast of Avenal in Pyramid Hills (lat. 35°50'05" N, long. 120°02'45" W; sec. 17, T 24 S, R 18 E). Named on Pyramid Hills (1953) 7.5' quadrangle.

Deadman Pass [MADERA]: *pass,* 4.5 miles north of Devils Postpile on Madera-Mono county line (lat. 37°41'20" N, long. 119°04'10" W); the pass is near the head of Deadman Creek, which is in Mono County. Named on Devils Postpile (1953) 15' quadrangle. Deadman Creek was named for the headless body of a man found along it about 1868 (Browning, 1986, p. 53-54).

Deadmans Corners [FRESNO]: *locality,* 27 miles northeast of Coalinga (lat. 36°29'15" N, long. 120°05'50" W; at SW cor. sec. 35, T 16 S, R 17 E). Named on Five Points (1956) 7.5' quadrangle.

Dead Mule Saddle [TULARE]: *pass,* 2.5 miles north-northeast of California Hot Springs (lat. 35°55' N, long. 118°39'15" W; sec. 20, T 23 S, R 31 E). Named on California Hot Springs (1958) 15' quadrangle.

Dead Ox Creek [KERN]: *stream,* flows 9 miles to Willow Spring Creek (1) 4.5 miles west-southwest of Woody (lat. 35°40'40" N, long. 118°54'35" W; sec. 12, T 26 S, R 28 E). Named on Sand Canyon (1965) and Woody (1965) 7.5' quadrangles. Called Rabbit Creek on Woody (1935) 15' quadrangle, where present Five Dog Creek is called Dead Ox Creek, but United States Board on Geographic Names (1966b, p. 4) rejected the name "Rabbit Creek" for present Dead Ox Creek.

Dead Ox Spring [KERN]: *spring,* 3.5 miles south of Woody (lat. 35° 39'20" N, long. 118°50'25" W; sec. 22, T 26 S, R 29 E); the spring is along Dead Ox Creek. Named on Woody (1965) 7.5' quadrangle.

Dead Pine Ridge [FRESNO]: *ridge,* north-trending, 5 miles long, 7.5 miles west-southwest of Marion Peak (lat. 36°54'30" N, long. 118° 38'45" W). Named on Marion Peak (1953) 15' quadrangle.

Deadwood Gulch [MADERA]: *canyon,* 1.5 miles long, 7.25 miles south-southwest of Yosemite Forks (lat. 37°16'45" N, long. 119° 42' W). Named on Bass Lake (1953) 15' quadrangle.

Deadwood Meadow [TULARE]: *area,* 8 miles east of Fairview (lat. 35°55'35" N, long. 118°21'15" W; sec. 18, T 23 S, R 34 E). Named on Kernville (1956) 15' quadrangle.

Deadwood Peak [MADERA]: *peak,* 4.5 miles southwest of Yosemite Forks on Potter Ridge (lat. 37°18'50" N, long. 119°41'05" W; sec. 21, T 7 S, R 21 E). Altitude 4540 feet. Named on Bass Lake (1953) 15' quadrangle.

Death Canyon [TULARE]: *canyon,* drained by a stream that flows 3 miles to Dry Creek (3) 4 miles north-northwest of Olancha Peak (lat. 36°19'10" N, long. 118°08' W). Named on Olancha (1956) 15' quadrangle.

Deep Canyon [TULARE]:

(1) *canyon,* 1.5 miles long, opens into the canyon of Middle Fork Tule River 2.5 miles east of Springville (lat. 36°07'55" N, long. 118°46'10" W; sec. 5, T 21 S, R 30 E). Named on Springville (1957) 15' quadrangle.

(2) *canyon,* 3.5 miles long, along the lower part of Marble Fork above a point 5.25 miles southeast of Yucca Mountain (lat. 36°31'20" N, long. 118°47'50" W). Named on Giant Forest (1956) 15' quadrangle.

Deep Creek [FRESNO]: *stream,* flows 4.5 miles to Big Creek (2) 7 miles west-northwest of Balch Camp (lat. 36°56' N, long. 119°14'40" W; sec. 33, T 11 S, R 25 E). Named on Patterson Mountain (1952) and Trimmer (1965) 7.5' quadrangles.

Deep Creek [KERN-TULARE]: *stream,* heads in Tulare County and flows 6.5 miles to Cow Creek 10.5 miles east-northeast of Glennville in Kern County (lat. 35°46'35" N, long. 118°31'50" W; at S line sec. 3, T 25 S, R 32 E). Named on California Hot Springs (1958) 15' quadrangle.

Deep Creek [TULARE]:
(1) *stream,* diverges southwest from Kaweah River and flows 11.5 miles to a ditch 5.5 miles south of Visalia (lat. 36°15'05" N, long. 119°16'55" W; sec. 29, T 19 S, R 25 E). Named on Exeter (1952) and Visalia (1949) 15' quadrangles.
(2) *stream,* heads 11 miles southwest of Tulare and flows 5 miles to Tule River 6 miles south of Waukena (lat. 36°03'10" N, long. 119° 30'05" W; sec. 32, T 21 S, R 23 E). Named on Corcoran (1954) and Taylor Weir (1950) 7.5' quadrangles. Lake View School (1927) 7.5' quadrangle shows North Fork, Middle Fork, and South Fork joining to form the stream, but Taylor Weir (1950, photorevised 1969) 7.5' quadrangle fails to name the forks, and has the name "Deep Creek" along the North Fork of the older map.
(3) *stream,* flows 5 miles to Little Kern River 4.5 miles west-southwest of Hockett Peak (lat. 36°12'20" N, long. 118°27'40" W). Named on Hockett Peak (1956) and Kern Peak (1956) 15' quadrangles.

Deep Creek, North Fork: see **Bates Slough** [TULARE].

Deep Creek Cave [TULARE]: *cave,* 8 miles southeast of California Hot Springs (lat. 35°48'40" N, long. 118°33'45" W; sec. 30, T 24 S, R 32 E); the cave is near Deep Creek [KERN-TULARE]. Named on California Hot Springs (1958) 15' quadrangle.

Deep Hollow [MADERA]: *canyon,* drained by a stream that flows nearly 2 miles to Willow Creek (1) 3.5 miles north-northeast of Raymond (lat. 37°15'45" N, long. 119°53'30" W). Named on Ben Hur (1947) and Raymond (1962) 7.5' quadrangles.

Deep Lake: see **Little Deep Lake**, under **Fingerbowl Lake** [FRESNO].

Deep Meadow [TULARE]: *area,* 3.5 miles east-northeast of Camp Nelson along Boulder Creek (2) (lat. 36°09'05" N, long. 118°32'45" W; sec. 30, T 20 S, R 32 E). Named on Camp Nelson (1956) 15' quadrangle.

Deep Well Canyon [FRESNO]: *canyon,* drained by a stream that flows 3.25 miles to Warthan Creek 3.25 miles east-northeast of Smith Mountain (2) (lat. 36°05'15" N, long. 120°32'15" W; sec. 23, T 21 S, R 13 E). Named on Smith Mountain (1969) 7.5' quadrangle.

Deer Canyon [FRESNO]: *canyon,* drained by a stream that flows 5.5 miles to Middle Fork Kings River 4.5 miles north-northeast of Hume (lat. 36°50'25" N, long. 118°52'10" W); the canyon is east of Deer Ridge. Named on Tehipite Dome (1952) 15' quadrangle.

Deer Canyon [KERN]: *canyon,* drained by a stream that flows 1.25 miles to Tehachapi Creek 2.5 miles east-southeast of Caliente (lat. 35°16'10" N, long. 118°35'30" W). Named on Oiler Peak (1972) 7.5' quadrangle.

Deer Cove [FRESNO]: *area,* 14 miles southwest of Marion Peak (lat. 36°49' N, long. 118°43' W). Named on Marion Peak (1953) 15' quadrangle.

Deer Cove Creek [FRESNO]: *stream,* flows 2.5 miles to South Fork Kings River 15 miles southwest of Marion Peak (lat. 36°48'15" N, long. 118°43'15" W); the stream drains Deer Cove. Named on Marion Peak (1953) 15' quadrangle. United States Board on Geographic Names (1989a, p. 3) rejected the name "Deer Creek" for the feature.

Deer Creek [FRESNO]:
(1) *stream,* flows 5.5 miles to Fish Creek (1) 1.5 miles north of Double Peak (lat. 37°32'40" N, long. 119°02'20" W); the stream heads at Deer Lakes. Named on Devils Postpile (1953) and Mount Morrison (1953) 15' quadrangles.
(2) *stream,* flows 2 miles to Huntington Lake (1) 3 miles south of Kaiser Peak (lat. 37°15'05" N, long. 119°10'30" W; sec. 7, T 8 S, R 26 E). Named on Kaiser Peak (1953) 15' quadrangle.
(3) *stream,* flows 10 miles to Dinkey Creek (1) 6 miles south-southeast of the village of Dinkey Creek (lat. 37°00'05" N, long. 119°07'10" W). Named on Huntington Lake (1953) and Patterson Mountain (1952) 15' quadrangles. East Fork enters from the southeast 3.5 miles upstream from the mouth of the main creek; it is 4 miles long and is named on Huntington Lake (1953) and Patterson Mountain (1952) 15' quadrangles.
(4) *stream,* flows 3 miles to Pine Flat Reservoir 5 miles north-northeast of Tivy Mountain (lat. 36°52'05" N, long. 119°20'10" W; sec. 22, T 12 S, R 24 E). Named on Pine Flat Dam (1965) and Trimmer (1965) 7.5' quadrangles.

Deer Creek [TULARE]:
(1) *stream,* flows 2 miles to East Fork Kaweah River 4.25 miles west of Mineral King (lat. 36°27'20" N, long. 118°40'10" W). Named on Mineral King (1956) 15' quadrangle.
(2) *stream,* flows 35 miles to lowlands 6.25 miles north of Ducor (lat. 35°58'55" N, long. 119°02'45" W; sec. 27, T 22 S, R 27 E). Named on California Hot Springs (1958),

Springville (1957), and White River (1952) 15' quadrangles, and on Alpaugh (1953), Ducor (1952), Pixley (1954), and Sausalito School (1954) 7.5' quadrangles. Ducor (1952) and Porterville (1951) 7.5' quadrangles show Old Deer Creek Channel, which diverges northwest from Deer Creek (2) near the entrance of the creek to lowlands.

Deer Creek: see **Deer Cove Creek** [FRESNO]; **Hamilton Creek** [TULARE]; **Little Deer Creek** [TULARE]; **Timber Gap Creek** [TULARE].

Deer Creek Campground [FRESNO]: *locality*, 3 miles south of Kaiser Peak on the north shore of Huntington Lake (1) (lat. 37°15'10" N, long. 119°10'35" W; sec. 7, T 8 S, R 26 E); the place is near the mouth of Deer Creek (2). Named on Kaiser Peak (1953) 15' quadrangle.

Deer Creek Colony [TULARE]: *settlement*, 7.5 miles northwest of Fountain Springs (lat. 35°58'45" N, long. 118°59'55" W; around NW cor. sec. 31, T 22 S, R 28 E); the place is near Deer Creek (2). Named on Ducor (1929) and Fountain Springs (1965) 7.5' quadrangles.

Deer Creek Hot Springs: see **California Hot Springs** [TULARE].

Deer Creek Slough [TULARE]: *water feature*, 5.5 miles long, ends 8 miles north-northwest of Earlimart (lat. 35°59'15" N, long. 19°20'40" W; sec. 26, T 22 S, R 24 E). Named on Pixley (1929) and Tipton (1928) 7.5' quadrangles.

Deer Creek Switch: see **Terra Bella** [TULARE].

Deer Crossing [FRESNO]: *settlement*, 5 miles southeast of Dunlap (lat. 36°41'25" N, long. 119°02'50" W; sec. 21, T 14 S, R 27 E). Named on Miramonte (1966) 7.5' quadrangle.

Deerhorn Mountain [TULARE]: *peak*, 11.5 miles northwest of Mount Whitney (lat. 36°42'45" N, long. 118°24'30" W). Altitude 13,265 feet. Named on Mount Whitney (1956) 15' quadrangle. J.N. LeConte named the peak in 1895 for the resemblance of its double summit to a pair of horns (Browning 1986, p. 54).

Deer Island [TULARE]: *hill*, 2.5 miles east-southeast of Monache Mountain (lat. 36°11'30" N, long. 118°09' W; on N line sec. 14, T 20 S, R 35 E). Named on Monache Mountain (1956) 15' quadrangle.

Deer Lake [FRESNO]: *lake*, 400 feet long, 5 miles east of Kaiser Peak (lat. 37°17'10" N, long. 119°05'35" W; sec. 26, T 7 S, R 26 E). Named on Kaiser Peak (1953) 15' quadrangle.

Deer Lakes [FRESNO]: *lakes*, largest 1000 feet long, 7.5 miles west-northwest of Red Slate Mountain (lat. 33°37'40" N, long. 118°59'15" W); the lakes are at the head of Deer Creek (1). Named on Mount Morrison (1953) 15' quadrangle.

Deer Meadow [FRESNO]:
(1) *area*, 11.5 miles east-southeast of Mount Goddard along Palisade Creek (lat. 37°03'20" N, long. 118°31'20" W). Named on Mount Goddard (1948) 15' quadrangle.

(2) *area*, 8.5 miles east of Hume (lat. 36°46'35" N, long. 118°45'40" W). Named on Tehipite Dome (1952) 15' quadrangle.

(3) *area*, 5.5 miles east-southeast of Dinkey Mountain (lat. 37°00'50" N, long. 119°04' W; sec. 31, T 10 S, R 27 E); the place is along Deer Creek (3). Named on Kaiser (1904) 30' quadrangle.

Deer Mountain [TULARE]: *peak*, 5.5 miles southeast of Monache Mountain (lat. 36°09' N, long. 118°07'20" W; near S line sec. 30, T 20 S, R 36 E). Altitude 9410 feet. Named on Monache Mountain (1956) 15' quadrangle.

Deer Park: see **Cedar Grove** [FRESNO].

Deer Ridge [FRESNO]: *ridge*, south- to southeast-trending, 4.5 miles long, 6 miles north of Hume (lat. 36°52' N, long. 118°53'30" W); the ridge is west of Deer Canyon. Named on Tehipite Dome (1952) 15' quadrangle.

Deer Ridge [TULARE]: *ridge*, southwest-trending, 1.25 miles long, 5 miles east-southeast of Yucca Mountain (lat. 36°32'40" N, long. 118°47'05" W). Named on Giant Forest (1956) 15' quadrangle.

Deer Spring [KERN]: *spring*, 3.25 miles east-southeast of Caliente (lat. 35°16'15" N, long. 118°34'35" W; near SE cor. sec. 31, T 30 S, R 32 E); the spring is in Deer Canyon. Named on Oiler Peak (1972) 7.5' quadrangle.

Deer Spring [TULARE]: *spring*, 12 miles north of Lamont Peak (lat. 35°58' N, long. 118°01'35" W). Named on Lamont Peak (1956) 15' quadrangle.

Delano [KERN]: *town*, 31 miles north-northwest of Bakersfield (lat. 35°46'15" N, long. 119°14'5" W; in and near sec. 11, T 25 S, R 25 E). Named on Delano East (1953) and Delano West (1954) 7.5' quadrangles. Postal authorities established Delano post office in 1874 (Frickstad, p. 55), and the town incorporated in 1915. Officials of Southern Pacific Railroad named their station at the place in 1873 for Secretary of the Interior Columbus Delano, who headed his department from 1870 until 1875 (Bailey, 1967, p. 6). Postal authorities established Shamrock post office 12 miles south of Delano in 1880 and discontinued it in 1881; they established Benita post office 31 miles southwest of Delano in 1888 and discontinued it in 1889; they established Gyle post office 23.5 miles southwest of Delano in 1888 and discontinued it in 1889 (Salley, p. 19, 91, 202).

Delft Colony [TULARE]: *village*, 4 miles west-southwest of Dinuba (lat. 36°30'40" N, long. 119°26'45" W; sec. 26, T 16 S, R 23 E). Named on Reedley (1966) 7.5' quadrangle.

Delkern: see **Greenfield** [KERN].

Delonegha Creek [KERN]: *stream*, flows 3.5 miles to Kern River 4.5 miles west-southwest of Miracle Hot Springs (lat. 35°33'25" N, long. 118°36'25" W). Named on Democrat Hot Springs (1972) and Miracle Hot Springs (1972) 7.5' quadrangles.

Delonegha Hot Springs [KERN]: *springs,* 4.5 miles west-southwest of Miracle Hot Springs along Kern River (lat. 35°33'25" N, long. 118°36'40" W); the springs are near the mouth of Delonegha Creek. Named on Miracle Hot Springs (1972) 7.5' quadrangle. Called Delonegha Springs on Glennville (1956) 15' quadrangle, and United States Board on Geographic Names (1975b, p. 9) gave this name as a variant. The springs supported a small resort in 1908 (Waring, p. 51). The name "Delonegha" is from a gold-mining settlement of the 1830's in Georgia; a mining place of 1866 situated along Kern River near the springs was called Hot Springs Bar (Boyd, p. 57).

Delonegha Springs: see **Delonegha Hot Springs** [KERN].

Delpiedra: see **Piedra** [FRESNO].

Del Rey [FRESNO]: *town,* 3.5 miles southsouthwest of Sanger (lat. 36°39'30" N, long. 119°35'35" W; near E line sec. 5, T 15 S, R 22 E). Named on Sanger (1965) 7.5' quadrangle. The place first was called Clifton, but when the railroad reached the site in 1898 the name was changed to Del Rey because the station was on Rio del Rey ranch (Gudde, 1949, p. 92). Postal authorities established Clifton post office in 1885 and changed the name to Del Rey in 1898; the name "Clifton" was for Clift Wilkinson, founder of the town (Salley, p. 46).

Democrat Hot Springs [KERN]: *locality,* 14 miles south of Glennville along Kern River (lat. 35°31'40" N, long. 118°40' W). Named on Democrat Hot Springs (1972) 7.5' quadrangle. Called Democrat Springs on Glennville (1956) 15' quadrangle, and United States Board on Geographic Names (1975a, p. 4) gave this name as a variant. Dell Hill started a health resort at the site in 1905 (Bailey, 1967, p. 6).

Democrat Spring [KERN]: *spring,* 1.5 miles south-southwest of Democrat Hot Springs (lat. 35°30'25" N, long. 118°40'40" W). Named on Democrat Hot Springs (1972) 7.5' quadrangle.

Democrat Springs: see **Democrat Hot Springs** [KERN].

Den Lake [FRESNO]: *lake,* 1000 feet long, 4.5 miles south of Mount Abbot (lat. 37°19'20" N, long. 118°47'35" W). Named on Mount Abbot (1953) 15' quadrangle. Employees of California Department of Fish and Game named the lake in 1952 (Browning 1986, p. 54).

Dennison Mountain [TULARE]: *peak,* 12.5 miles southwest of Mineral King (lat. 36°19'05" N, long. 118°44'45" W); the peak is at the west end of Dennison Ridge. Altitude 8650 feet. Named on Mineral King (1956) 15' quadrangle.

Dennison Peak [TULARE]: *peak,* 15 miles southeast of Kaweah (lat. 36°17'50" N, long. 118°45'30" W); the peak is 1.5 miles south-

southwest of Dennison Mountain. Altitude 7290 feet. Named on Kaweah (1957) 15' quadrangle.

Dennison Ridge [TULARE]: *ridge,* southwest-to west-trending, 4.5 miles long, 10.5 miles southwest of Mineral King (lat. 36°19'30" N, long. 118°42' W). Named on Mineral King (1956) 15' quadrangle. The name is for a pioneer who built a trail from the foothills to the high part of the Sierra Nevada in the 1860's (Browning 1986, p. 54).

Dent: see **Nellie Dent Creek** [KERN].

Denver Church Campground [MADERA]: *locality,* 4.25 miles southeast of Yosemite Forks on the west side of Bass Lake (1) (lat. 37°19'20" N, long. 119°34'40" W; sec. 16, T 7 S, R 22 E). Named on Bass Lake (1953) 15' quadrangle.

Depot Flat [TULARE]: *area,* 10.5 miles east of Tucker Mountain (lat. 36°38'10" N, long. 119°01'10" W; near W line sec. 11, T 15 S, R 27 E). Named on Miramonte (1966) 7.5' quadrangle.

Depressed Lake [FRESNO]: *lake,* 900 feet long, 8 miles west-southwest of Mount Abbot (lat. 37°19'40" N, long. 118°54'55" W). Named on Mount Abbot (1953) 15' quadrangle. Jack Criqui and Scott M. Soule of California Department of Fish and Game named the lake in 1948 for its position in a depression (Browning 1986, p. 54).

Derby Acres [KERN]: *village,* 5.5 miles north-northwest of Fellows (lat. 35°14'50" N, long. 119°35'40" W; sec. 10, T 31 S, R 22 E). Named on Fellows (1951) and West Elk Hills (1954) 7.5' quadrangles. The community began in the 1930's (Bailey, 1967, p. 6).

Deseret: see **Wildflower** [FRESNO].

Desert Butte [KERN]: *hill,* 4 miles west-southwest of Castle Butte (lat. 35°05'10" N, long. 117°56'20" W; near NE cor. sec. 4, T 11 N, R 10 W). Altitude 2849 feet. Named on California City South (1973) 7.5' quadrangle. The feature is one of Twin Buttes.

Desert Lake [KERN]: *village,* 2.5 miles west of Boron (lat. 35°00'15" N, long. 117°42' W; sec. 35, T 11 N, R 8 W). Named on Boron (1973) 7.5' quadrangle.

Desert Lake: see **Koehn Lake** [KERN].

Desert Spring: see **Cantil** [KERN].

Desert Springs: see **Koehn Spring** [KERN].

Desert Springs Valley: see **Fremont Valley** [KERN].

Desert Wells [KERN]: *wells,* 3.5 miles west-northwest of Castle Butte (lat. 35°08'15" N, long. 117°56' W). Named on Searles Lake (1915) 1° quadrangle.

Desolation Lake [FRESNO]: *lake,* 1 mile long, 2 miles west of Mount Humphreys in Humphreys Basin (lat. 37°16'25" N, long. 118°42'15" W); the lake is 0.5 mile north of Lower Desolation Lake. Named on Mount Tom (1949) 15' quadrangle. J.N. LeConte named the lake in 1898 (Farquhar, 1923, p. 391).

Desolation Lake: see **Lower Desolation Lake** [FRESNO].

De Stazo Hill [KERN]: *hill,* 10.5 miles north-northeast of Rosamond (lat. 34°59'35" N, long. 118°04'30" W; near W line sec. 5, T 10 N, R 11 W). Altitude 2976 feet. Named on Bissell (1973) 7.5' quadrangle. Rosamond (1956) 15' quadrangle shows De Stazo ranch at the place.

Detachment Meadow [MADERA]: *area,* 7.25 miles east-southeast of Merced Peak (lat. 37°36'10" N, long. 119°16'05" W). Named on Merced Peak (1953) 15' quadrangle.

Devel: see **Joe Devel Peak** [TULARE].

Devil Canyon [KERN]: *canyon,* drained by a stream that flows 4.5 miles to Caliente Creek 6 miles east-northeast of Caliente (lat. 35° 18'50" N, long. 118°31'45" W; sec. 15, T 30 S, R 32 E); the canyon is east of Devils Backbone. Named on Oiler Peak (1972) 7.5' quadrangle.

Devils Backbone [KERN]: *ridge,* generally north-trending, 3 miles long, center 5.25 miles east of Caliente (lat. 35°17'15" N, long. 118°32'05" W); the ridge is west of Devil Canyon. Named on Oiler Peak (1972) 7.5' quadrangle.

Devils Bathtub [FRESNO]: *lake,* 3200 feet long, 12 miles west-northwest of Mount Abbot (lat. 37°26' N, long. 118°59'50" W). Named on Mount Abbot (1953) 15' quadrangle. George R. Davis of United States Geological Survey named the lake about 1907 (Farquhar, 1923, p. 391).

Devils Canyon [KERN]: *canyon,* 10 miles west of Liebre Twins (lat. 34°58'45" N, long. 118°44'25" W). Named on Winters Ridge (1966) 7.5' quadrangle.

Devils Canyon [TULARE]: *canyon,* drained by a stream that flows nearly 3 miles to South Fork Kaweah River 10.5 miles southeast of Kaweah (lat. 36°21'10" N, long. 118°47'50" W; near N line sec. 23, T 18 S, R 29 E). Named on Kaweah (1957) 15' quadrangle.

Devils Crags [FRESNO]: *relief feature,* 7.5 miles southeast of Mount Goddard on a north-west-trending ridge 1 mile long (lat. 37°02'10" N, long. 118°36'30" W). Named on Mount Goddard (1948) 15' quadrangle. J.N. LeConte named the feature in 1906 (Farquhar, 1923, p. 391).

Devils Den [KERN]:

(1) *relief feature,* 5 miles east of Orchard Peak (lat. 35°44'15" N, long. 120°02'45" W; at E line sec. 20, T 25 S, R 18 E). Named on Sawtooth Ridge (1961) 7.5' quadrangle. The place was called The Devil's Glen on some old maps (Latta, 1949, p. 296). Arnold and Johnson's (1910) map has the name "Barton Hills" for the range southeast of Devils Den (1), and has the name "Bartons" for a place located 2.5 miles east of Devils Den (1) (near N line sec. 23, T 25 S, R 18 E). According to Arnold and Johnson (p. 19), the name

"Barton's" applied to a group of buildings, including the cabin of Orlando D. Barton, an old settler.

(2) *village,* 12 miles north-northwest of Blackwells Corner (lat. 35°45'55" N, long. 119°58'25" W; at W line sec. 7, T 25 S, R 19 E); the village is 4.5 miles east-northeast of Devils Den (1). Named on Avenal Gap (1954) 7.5' quadrangle. Postal authorities established Devils Den post office in 1946 and discontinued it in 1948 (Frickstad, p. 55). The name applied first to a community located 2 miles south of the present village site (Bailey, 1967, p. 7).

Devils Den [TULARE]: *relief feature,* 6.25 miles north-northwest of California Hot Springs near the head of North Fork Gordon Creek (lat. 35°58' N, long. 118°42'15" W; sec. 35, T 22 S, R 30 E). Named on California Hot Springs (1958) 15' quadrangle.

Devils Den: see **Devils Gate** [FRESNO] (2).

Devils Elbow [KERN]: *bend,* 6 miles east-north-east of Caliente along Caliente Creek (lat. 35°18'50" N, long. 118°31'40" W; sec. 15, T 30 S, R 32 E); the feature is near the mouth of Devil Canyon. Named on Oiler Peak (1972) 7.5' quadrangle.

Devils Gate [FRESNO]:

(1) *narrows,* 4.5 miles northwest of Coalinga Mineral Springs in Hans Grieve Canyon (lat. 36°11' N, long. 120°37'15" W; near N line sec. 24, T 20 S, R 12 E). Named on Sherman Peak (1969) 7.5' quadrangle.

(2) *narrows,* 9 miles south-southwest of Coalinga along Jasper Creek (lat. 36°01'20" N, long. 120°25' W; near N line sec. 13, T 22 S, R 14 E). Named on Curry Mountain (1969) 7.5' quadrangle. Called Devils Den on Coalinga (1956) 15' quadrangle.

Devil's Glen: see **The Devil's Glen**, under **Devils Den** [KERN] (1).

Devils Gulch [KERN]: *canyon,* 4 miles long, opens into lowlands 1 mile south-southwest of Maricopa (lat. 35°03' N, long. 119°24'30" W). Named on Maricopa (1951) 7.5' quadrangle.

Devils Kitchen [KERN]: *canyon,* 2 miles long, along San Emigdio Creek above a point 2.5 miles west-northwest of Eagle Rest Peak (lat. 34°55'15" N, long. 119°10'30" W). Named on Eagle Rest Peak (1942) 7.5' quadrangle.

Devils Kitchen [TULARE]: *area,* nearly 4 miles south-southwest of California Hot Springs in Bear Trap Canyon (lat. 35°49'55" N, long. 118°42'25" W; at N line sec. 23, T 24 S, R 30 E). Named on California Hot Springs (1958) 15' quadrangle.

Devils Postpile [MADERA]: *relief feature,* 17 miles east of Merced Peak along Middle Fork San Joaquin River (lat. 37°37'30" N, long. 119°05' W). Named on Devils Postpile (1953) 15' quadrangle. The feature consists of columns of volcanic rock; it was known locally in 1894 as Devils Woodpile (Hanna, p. 86).

McLaughlin and Bradley (p. 534) used the form "Devil's Post Pile" for the name. United States Board on Geographic Names (1954, p. 3) rejected the names "Devil Postpile" and "Devils Post Pile" for the feature.

Devils Punchbowl [FRESNO]: *lake,* 2000 feet long, 4.25 miles north-northwest of Blackcap Mountain (lat. 37°07'30" N, long. 118°49'50" W). Named on Blackcap Mountain (1953) 15' quadrangle.

Devils Spring [KERN]: *spring,* 6 miles east of Caliente (lat. 35°16'55" N, long. 118°31'15" W; near NW cor. sec. 35, T 30 S, R 32 E); the spring is in Devil Canyon. Named on Oiler Peak (1972) 7.5' quadrangle.

Devils Table [FRESNO]: *ridge,* northwest-trending, 0.25 mile long, 9 miles east-northeast of Kaiser Peak (lat. 37°20'15" N, long. 119°01'40" W). Named on Kaiser Peak (1953) 15' quadrangle.

Devils Thumb [TULARE]: *peak,* 5.25 miles north-northwest of California Hot Springs (lat. 35°56'50" N, long. 118°42'40" W; sec. 11, T 23 S, R 30 E). Named on California Hot Springs (1958) 15' quadrangle.

Devils Top [FRESNO]: *peak,* 1 mile northeast of Double Peak (lat. 37°31'20" N, long. 119°01'45" W). Altitude 9931 feet. Named on Devils Postpile (1953) 15' quadrangle.

Devils Washbowl [FRESNO]: *water feature,* 10 miles southeast of Mount Goddard on Middle Fork Kings River (lat. 37°01' N, long. 118°35' W). Named on Mount Goddard (1948) 15' quadrangle.

Devils Woodpile: see **Devils Postpile** [MADERA].

Devilwater Creek [KERN]: *stream,* flows 4.5 miles to Antelope Plain 6.5 miles south-southwest of Blackwells Corner (lat. 35°31'15" N, long. 119°53'45" W; sec. 2, T 28 S, R 19 E). Named on Las Yeguas Ranch (1959) and Shale Point (1953) 7.5' quadrangles. United States Board on Geographic Names (1933a, p. 264) rejected the form "Devil Water Creek" for the name.

Dewey: see **Wasco** [KERN].

Deweyville: see **Wasco** [KERN].

Dewolf: see **Wolf** [FRESNO].

Diablo Range: see "Regional setting."

Diamond Mesa [TULARE]: *area,* 8 miles north-northwest of Mount Whitney (lat. 36°40'30" N, long. 118°22'10" W). Named on Mount Whitney (1956) 15' quadrangle. Sheepmen named the feature for its shape (Browning 1986, p. 56).

Diamond Peak [FRESNO]: *peak,* 8.5 miles south of Mount Pinchot on Fresno-Inyo county line (lat. 36°49'35" N, long. 118°23'20" W). Altitude 13,126 feet. Named on Mount Pinchot (1953) 15' quadrangle.

Diamond-X Lake [FRESNO]: *lake,* 800 feet long, 6.25 miles north-northwest of Blackcap Mountain (lat. 37°09'40" N, long. 118°49'20" W). Named on Blackcap Mountain (1953) 15'

quadrangle. William A. Dill of California Department of Fish and Game named the lake in 1947 for Diamond-X pack train (Browning 1986, p. 56).

Diaz Canyon [FRESNO]: *canyon,* drained by a stream that flows 8.5 miles to White Creek 6.5 miles north-northeast of Coalinga Mineral Springs (lat. 36°13'40" N, long. 120°30'05" W; sec. 31, T 19 S, R 14 E). Named on Alcalde Hills (1969), Joaquin Rocks (1969), Santa Rita Peak (1969), and Sherman Peak (1969) 7.5' quadrangles.

Dickerson: see **Raco** [FRESNO].

Dicks Creek: see **Avenal Creek** [KINGS].

Dick Wright Spring [FRESNO]: *spring,* 16 miles northwest of Coalinga (lat. 36°19' N, long. 120°32'20" W; sec. 34, T 18 S, R 13 E); the feature is nearly 1 mile south-southwest of Wright Mountain. Named on Santa Rita Peak (1969) 7.5' quadrangle.

Di Giorgio [KERN]: *village,* 6.5 miles south of Edison (lat. 35°15'10" N, long. 118°50'45" W). Named on Arvin (1955) and Edison (1954) 7.5' quadrangles. Postal authorities established Di Giorgio post office in 1944 (Frickstad, p. 55). The name commemorates Joseph Di Giorgio, founder of a huge agricultural enterprise (Hanna, p. 87).

Dillon Canyon [TULARE]: *canyon,* drained by a stream that flows 2 miles to North Fork Tule River 13 miles south-southwest of Mineral King (lat. 36°17'30" N, long. 118°43'15" W; sec. 9, T 19 S, R 30 E); Dillon Mill was situated in the canyon. Named on Mineral King (1956) 15' quadrangle.

Dillon Mill [TULARE]: *locality,* 12 miles south-southwest of Mineral King (lat. 36°18'10" N, long. 118°42'55" W). Named on Kaweah (1909) 30' quadrangle. Nathan P. Dillon started a sawmill at the place in the late 1870's (Browning 1986, p. 56).

Dillons Point: see **Steve Barton Point** [TULARE].

Dinkey Creek [FRESNO]:

(1) *stream,* flows 27 miles to North Fork Kings River at Balch Camp (lat. 36°54'10" N, long. 119°07'15" W; sec. 10, T 12 S, R 26 E); the stream heads at Second Dinkey Lake. Named on Huntington Lake (1953) and Patterson Mountain (1952) 15' quadrangles. Four hunters named the creek in 1863 for their dog, who was injured in a fight with a grizzly bear (Gudde, 1949, p. 95).

(2) *village,* 2.5 miles southwest of Dinkey Dome (lat. 37°05'10" N, long. 119°09'20" W; sec. 5, T 10 S, R 26 E); the village is along Dinkey Creek (1). Named on Huntington Lake (1953) 15' quadrangle. Postal authorities established Dinkey Creek post office in 1925 and discontinued it in 1972 (Salley, p. 59).

Dinkey Dome [FRESNO]: *peak,* 13 miles south-southeast of Kaiser Peak (lat. 37°06'55" N, long. 119°07'50" W; near E line sec. 28, T 9 S, R 26 E); the peak is near Dinkey Creek

(1). Altitude 7697 feet. Named on Huntington Lake (1953) 15' quadrangle.

Dinkey Lake: see **First Dinkey Lake** [FRESNO]; **Second Dinkey Lake** [FRESNO].

Dinkey Meadow [FRESNO]: *area,* 5 miles south-southwest of Dinkey Dome (lat. 37°02'45" N, long. 119°09'45" W; sec. 20, T 10 S, R 26 E). Named on Huntington Lake (1953) 15' quadrangle.

Dinkey Meadow Creek [FRESNO]: *stream,* flows 1 mile to Dinkey Creek (1) nearly 5 miles south-southwest of Dinkey Dome (lat. 37°02'55" N, long. 119°09'25" W; sec. 20, T 10 S, R 26 E); the stream goes through Dinkey Meadow. Named on Huntington Lake (1953) 15' quadrangle.

Dinkey Mountain [FRESNO]: *peak,* 6 miles south-southwest of Dinkey Dome (lat. 37°01'45" N, long. 119°09'45" W; sec. 29, T 10 S, R 26 E); the peak is 1 mile south of Dinkey Meadow. Altitude 6697 feet. Named on Huntington Lake (1953) 15' quadrangle. California Mining Bureau's (1917a) map shows a place called Peterson located a mile northwest of Dinkey Mountain.

Dinuba [TULARE]: *town,* 15 miles north-north-west of Visalia (lat. 36°32'35" N, long. 119°23'10" W; in and near sec. 8, 17, T 16 S, R 24 E). Named on Orange Cove South (1966) and Reedley (1966) 7.5' quadrangles. Postal authorities established Dinuba post office in 1889 (Frickstad, p. 210), and the town incorporated in 1906. The promoters who laid out the townsite in 1888 called the place Sibleyville to honor James Sibley, a landowner there, but officials of Southern Pacific Railroad gave the name "Dinuba" to their station at the site—they coined the name from the first syllables of the names of two teamsters, Dinsmore and Uballis, who hauled grain to the railroad (Hanna, p. 87).

Dinuba: see **North Dinuba** [TULARE].

Dirty Spring [KINGS]: *spring,* 7 miles west-southwest of Avenal (lat. 35°57'50" N, long. 120°14'30" W; near N line sec. 4, T 23 S, R 16 E). Named on Garza Peak (1953) 7.5' quadrangle.

Disappearing Creek [FRESNO]: *stream,* flows 4 miles to Goddard Creek 7 miles south-southeast of Mount Goddard (lat. 37°00'55" N, long. 118°39'35" W). Named on Mount Goddard (1948) 15' quadrangle. Theodore S. Solomons named the stream in 1895 (Farquhar, 1923, p. 392).

Disappointment Lake [FRESNO]: *lake,* 1300 feet long, 5 miles north-northwest of Blackcap Mountain (lat. 37°08'25" N, long. 118°49' W). Named on Blackcap Mountain (1953) 15' quadrangle. Tourists reportedly named the lake after they had poor luck fishing (Browning 1986, p. 57).

Disappointment Peak [FRESNO]: *peak,* 2 miles northwest of Mount Bolton Brown on Fresno-Inyo county line (lat. 37°04'05" N, long. 118°28' W). Altitude 13,917 feet. Named on Big Pine (1950) 15' quadrangle. J. Milton Davis, A.L. Jordan, and H.H. Bliss gave the name "Peak Disappointment" to the feature in 1919, when they made the first ascent and found to their disappointment that it is not the highest point on Middle Palisade (Browning 1986, p. 57).

Discovery Pinnacle [TULARE]: *peak,* 1.5 miles south of Mount Whitney on Tulare-Inyo county line (lat. 36°33'30" N, long. 118°17'25" W). Named on Mount Whitney (1956) 15' quadrangle. Chester Versteeg suggested the name in 1953 (Browning 1986, p. 57).

Discovery Ridge [KINGS]: *ridge,* northeast-trending, 0.5 mile long, 3 miles northeast of Avenal (lat. 36°02'15" N, long. 120°05'35" W). Named on La Cima (1963) 7.5' quadrangle. La Cima (1934) 7.5' quadrangle shows Discovery Well on the ridge—the name of the ridge is from the well (United States Board on Geographic Names, 1933b, p. 8).

Division Lake [FRESNO]: *lake,* 1800 feet long, 2.5 miles east-southeast of Blackcap Mountain (lat. 37°03'40" N, long. 118°45'05" W); the lake is 0.5 mile west-northwest of Battalion Lake. Named on Blackcap Mountain (1953) and Mount Goddard (1948) 15' quadrangles.

Dix: **Camp Dix** [KERN].

Dixie: see **Little Dixie** [KERN].

Dixie Wash: see **Little Dixie Wash** [KERN].

Dobie Spring [KERN]: *spring,* 5.5 miles east of Mount Adelaide (lat. 35°25'35" N, long. 118°38'40" W; near N line sec. 10, T 29 S, R 31 E). Named on Mount Adelaide (1972) 7.5' quadrangle.

Doctor Williams Canyon: see **Williams Canyon** [KERN]

Doc Williams Canyon: see **Williams Canyon** [KERN].

Dodge Hill [FRESNO]: *peak,* 2 miles west-southwest of Coalinga (lat. 36°07'55" N, long. 120°23'40" W; near W line sec. 6, T 21 S, R 15 E). Altitude 1085 feet. Named on Alcalde Hills (1969) 7.5' quadrangle.

Doe Lake [FRESNO]: *lake,* 800 feet long, 13 miles east-southeast of Mount Goddard (lat. 37°02'35" N, long. 118°30'05" W). Named on Mount Goddard (1948) 15' quadrangle.

Doe Meadow [TULARE]: *area,* 2.5 miles south of Hockett Peak (lat. 36°11'10" N, long. 118°23'15" W). Named on Hockett Peak (1956) 15' quadrangle.

Dog Creek [FRESNO]:

(1) *stream,* flows 18 miles to Redbank Slough 4.5 miles southeast of Clovis (lat. 36°46'40" N, long. 119°38'20" W; sec. 25, T 13 S, R 21 E). Named on Academy (1964), Clovis (1964), Humphreys Station (1965), and Round Mountain (1964) 7.5' quadrangles.

(2) *stream,* flows 3.5 miles to Middle Fork Kings River 9.5 miles west of Marion Peak (lat. 36°56'45" N, long. 118°41'20" W). Named on

Marion Peak (1953) 15' quadrangle.

Dogtooth Peak [FRESNO]: *peak,* nearly 6 miles east-northeast of Dinkey Dome (lat. 37°09'15" N, long. 119°02'20" W; near NW cor. sec. 16, T 9 S, R 27 E). Altitude 10,311 feet. Named on Huntington Lake (1953) 15' quadrangle.

Dog Town: see **Mineral King** [TULARE].

Dogtown: see **White River** [TULARE] (2).

Dogwood Canyon [FRESNO]: *canyon,* drained by a stream that flows nearly 3 miles to Warthan Creek 3 miles west-southwest of Coalinga Mineral Springs (lat. 36°07'05" N, long. 120°36'10" W; near W line sec. 5, T 21 S, R 13 E). Named on Sherman Peak (1969) and Smith Mountain (1969) 7.5' quadrangles.

Dollar Lake: see **Big Bird Lake** [TULARE].

Dome: see **Balloon Dome** [MADERA].

Dome Creek [TULARE]:

(1) *stream,* flows 3 miles to Middle Fork Kaweah River 12 miles west-southwest of Triple Divide Peak (lat. 36°31'50" N, long. 118°43'45" W). Named on Triple Divide Peak (1956) 15' quadrangle.

(2) *stream,* flows 2 miles to Dry Meadow Creek 7.25 miles south-southeast of Camp Nelson (lat. 36°03'15" N, long. 118°32'05" W; near NW cor. sec. 4, T 22 S, R 32 E); the stream is west of Dome Rock (1). Named on Camp Nelson (1956) 15' quadrangle.

Dome Land [TULARE]: *area,* 15 miles north-west of Lamont Peak (lat. 35°56' N, long. 118°14'30" W). Named on Kernville (1956) and Lamont Peak (1956) 15' quadrangles.

Domengine Creek [FRESNO]: *stream,* flows 11.5 miles to lowlands 14 miles north-north-east of Coalinga (lat. 36°20'30" N, long. 120°18'45" W; near S line sec. 23, T 18 S, R 15 E). Named on Domengine Ranch (1956) and Joaquin Rocks (1969) 7.5' quadrangles. The name commemorates Adolf Domengine, an early settler in the neighborhood (Anderson and Pack, p. 18).

Domengine Spring [FRESNO]: *spring,* 2.5 miles east-northeast of Joaquin Rocks (lat. 36°19'55" N, long. 120°24'05" W; sec. 25, T 18 S, R 14 E); the spring is along Domengine Creek. Named on Joaquin Rocks (1969) 7.5' quadrangle.

Dome Rock [TULARE]:

(1) *peak,* nearly 7 miles southeast of Camp Nelson (lat. 36°04' N, long. 118°31'45" W; near N line sec. 33, T 21 S, R 32 E). Altitude 7221 feet. Named on Camp Nelson (1956) 15' quadrangle.

(2) *peak,* 8.5 miles northeast of California Hot Springs (lat. 35°58' N, long. 118°33'50" W). Named on Tobias Peak (1936) 30' quadrangle.

Domino: see **Willow Springs** [KERN] (2).

Doney Gulch [KERN]: *canyon,* drained by a stream that flows 3.5 miles to Rag Gulch 1.5 miles north-northeast of Woody (lat. 35°43'25" N, long. 118°49'15" W; sec. 26, T 25 S, R 29 E). Named on Woody (1965) 7.5' quadrangle.

Doney Hill [KERN]: *peak,* 3.25 miles northeast of Woody (lat. 35° 43'40" N, long. 118°47'05" W; sec. 30, T 25 S, R 30 E); the peak is north of Doney Gulch. Altitude 2862 feet. Named on Woody (1965) 7.5' quadrangle.

Donut Rock [FRESNO]: *peak,* 3.5 miles south-southeast of Joaquin Rocks (lat. 36°16'25" N, long. 120°25'20" W; sec. 14, T 19 S, R 14 E). Altitude 3062 feet. Named on Joaquin Rocks (1969) 7.5' quadrangle.

Dora Belle [FRESNO]: *settlement,* at the north edge of Shaver Lake Heights (present town of Shaver Lake) (lat. 37°06'40" N, long. 119°18'50" W; near N line sec. 35, T 9 S, R 24 E). Named on Shaver Lake (1953) 15' quadrangle.

Doris Lake [FRESNO]: *lake,* 1450 feet long, 10 miles east-northeast of Kaiser Peak (lat. 37°20'15" N, long. 119°00'50" W). Named on Kaiser Peak (1953) 15' quadrangle. Ruby Rouch and her daughter Alva planted fish in the lake in 1928 and named the feature for Alva's daughter (Browning 1986, p. 58).

Doris Lake: see **Little Doris Lake** [FRESNO].

Dorst Campground [TULARE]: *locality,* 4.25 miles south-southwest of Shell Mountain (lat. 36°38'10" N, long. 118°48'35" W; near E line sec. 10, T 15 S, R 29 E); the place is near Dorst Creek. Named on Giant Forest (1956) 15' quadrangle. Called Dorst Camp on Tehipite (1903) 30' quadrangle.

Dorst Creek [TULARE]: *stream,* flows 6.5 miles to join Stony Creek and form North Fork Kaweah River 4.5 miles southwest of Shell Mountain (lat. 36°38'35" N, long. 118°50'40" W; near SW cor. sec. 4, T 15 S, R 29 E). Named on Giant Forest (1956) 15' quadrangle. The name commemorates Captain J.H. Dorst, first acting superintendent of Sequoia National Park in 1891 and 1892 (United States Board on Geographic Names, 1933a, p. 270).

Dosados Canyon [FRESNO]: *canyon,* drained by a stream that flows 2.25 miles to lowlands 19 miles southwest of Firebaugh (lat. 36°39'35" N, long. 120°41'35" W; sec. 6, T 15 S, R 12 E). Named on Chounet Ranch (1956) 7.5' quadrangle.

Dos Palos Slough [FRESNO]: *stream,* flows 10 miles to Merced County 6 miles northwest of Oxalis (lat. 36°58' N, long. 120°38'10" W; at NW cor. sec. 23, T 11 S, R 12 E). Named on Panoche (1913) 30' quadrangle.

Double Bunk Creek [TULARE]: *stream,* flows 2.5 miles to join Bear Creek (4) and form South Creek 8 miles northeast of California Hot Springs (lat. 35°57'35" N, long. 118°34'20" W; near E line sec. 1, T 23 S, R 31 E); the stream goes through Double Bunk Meadow. Named on California Hot Springs (1958) 15' quadrangle.

Double Bunk Meadow [TULARE]: *area,* 6.25 miles northeast of California Hot Springs (lat. 35°57'10" N, long. 118°36'05" W; on N line sec. 11, T 23 S, R 31 E); the place is along

Double Bunk Creek. Named on California Hot Springs (1958) 15' quadrangle.

Double Hill [KINGS]: *peaks,* two, 3.25 miles north-northeast of Avenal (lat. 36°02'45" N, long. 120°05'55" W; sec. 2, T 22 S, R 17 E). Named on La Cima (1963) 7.5' quadrangle.

Double Meadow [FRESNO]: *area,* 14 miles north-northwest of Blackcap Mountain (lat. 37°14'55" N, long. 118°54'50" W; sec. 9, 16, T 8 S, R 28 E). Named on Blackcap Mountain (1953) and Mount Abbot (1953) 15' quadrangles.

Double Mountain [KERN]: *peaks,* two, 600 feet apart, 7 miles south-southwest of Tehachapi (lat. 35°02' N, long. 118°29'05" W; on E line sec. 20, T 11 N, R 15 W). Altitude of each peak is 7981 feet. Named on Tehachapi South (1966) 7.5' quadrangle. Called Double Pk. on Wheeler's (1875-1878) map.

Double Peak [FRESNO]: *peaks,* two, 0.25 mile apart, 17 miles north-northeast of Kaiser Peak (lat. 37°30'35" N, long. 119°02'15" W). Altitudes 10,644 and 10,621 feet. Named on Devils Postpile (1953) 15' quadrangle. United States Board on Geographic Names (1971a, p. 2) approved the name "Bench Lakes" for four lakes, largest 650 feet long, situated 1.4 miles east-southeast of Double Peak (lat. 37°30'32" N, long. 119°00'52" W).

Double Peak: see **Double Mountain** [KERN].

Double Spring [KINGS]: *spring,* 10.5 miles southwest of Avenal (lat. 35°52'55" N, long. 120°14'30" W; sec. 33, T 23 S, R 16 E). Named on Garza Peak (1953) 7.5' quadrangle.

Double Trough Spring [FRESNO]: *spring,* 2.25 miles north-northeast of Joaquin Rocks (lat. 36°21'05" N, long. 120°26'05" W; sec. 22, T 18 S, R 14 E). Named on Joaquin Rocks (1969) 7.5' quadrangle.

Double Trough Spring [TULARE]: *spring,* 3.25 miles east-southeast of Auckland (lat. 36°33'50" N, long. 119°03'20" W; sec. 5, T 16 S, R 27 E). Named on Auckland (1966) 7.5' quadrangle.

Dougherty Canyon [KERN]: *canyon,* drained by a stream that flows 1.5 miles to Harper Canyon 6 miles northeast of Caliente (lat. 35° 20'30" N, long. 118°32'25" W; sec. 3, T 30 S, R 32 E). Named on Oiler Peak (1972) 7.5' quadrangle.

Dougherty Creek [FRESNO]: *stream,* formed by the confluence of East Fork and West Fork, flows 3 miles to Middle Fork Kings River 6.5 miles west of Marion Peak (lat. 36°57'45" N, long. 118° 38'30" W). Named on Marion Peak (1953) 15' quadrangle. The name commemorates Bill Dougherty and Bob Dougherty, pioneer sheepmen in the neighborhood (Hanna, p. 89). East Fork heads near Dougherty Peak and is 4.5 miles long. West Fork is 5.25 miles long. Middle Fork is 4 miles long and enters West Fork 0.25 mile upstream from the junction of East Fork and West Fork.

All three forks are named on Marion Peak (1953) 15' quadrangle.

Dougherty Creek [KERN]: *stream,* flows 2.5 miles to Kern River 3.5 miles north-northeast of Mount Adelaide (lat. 35°28'20" N, long. 118°42'45" W). Named on Mount Adelaide (1972) 7.5' quadrangle.

Dougherty Flat [KERN]: *area,* nearly 6 miles northeast of Caliente (lat. 35°21'15" N, long. 118°33'40" W; at NW cor. sec. 4, T 30 S, R 32 E); the place is at the head of Dougherty Canyon. Named on Oiler Peak (1972) 7.5' quadrangle.

Dougherty Meadow [FRESNO]: *area,* 4 miles west-southwest of Marion Peak (lat. 36°55'35" N, long. 118°35'15" W); the place is along East Fork Dougherty Creek. Named on Marion Peak (1953) 15' quadrangle. The name commemorates Bill Dougherty and Bob Dougherty of Dougherty Creek (Hanna, p. 89).

Dougherty Meadow: see **Simpson Meadow** [FRESNO].

Dougherty Peak [FRESNO]: *peak,* 2.5 miles south-southwest of Marion Peak (lat. 36°55'15" N, long. 118°32'45" W). Altitude 12,244 feet. Named on Marion Peak (1953) 15' quadrangle.

Dougherty Spring [KERN]: *spring,* 6 miles northwest of Caliente (lat. 35°21'15" N, long. 118°33'05" W; near N line sec. 4, T 30 S, R 32 E); the spring is in Dougherty Canyon. Named on Oiler Peak (1972) 7.5' quadrangle.

Dover: see **San Joaquin River** [MADERA].

Dove Spring [KERN]: *spring,* 3.25 miles east of Pinyon Mountain (lat. 35°27'10" N, long. 118°05'55" W). Named on Dove Spring (1972) 7.5' quadrangle.

Dove Spring Canyon [KERN]: *canyon,* drained by a stream that flows 7 miles to lowlands 9 miles east-southeast of Pinyon Mountain (lat. 35°26'35" N, long. 118°03'20" W; sec. 6, T 29 S, R 37 E); Dove Spring is in the canyon. Named on Dove Spring (1972) and Pinyon Mountain (1972) 7.5' quadrangles. Called Redrock Canyon on Mojave (1915) 30' quadrangle.

Dove Spring Mill [KERN]: *locality,* 3.25 miles east of Pinyon Mountain (lat. 35°27'10" N, long. 118°05'55" W); the place is at Dove Spring. Named on Cross Mountain (1943) 15' quadrangle.

Dove Well [KERN]: *well,* 2 miles east of Pinyon Mountain (lat. 35° 27'30" N, long. 118°07'15" W); the well is in Dove Spring Canyon 1.25 miles west-northwest of Dove Spring. Named on Dove Spring (1972) 7.5' quadrangle.

Dow: see **Minter Village** [KERN].

Dragon Lake [FRESNO]: *lake,* 1800 feet long, 10 miles south of Mount Pinchot (lat. 36°48'05" N, long. 118°23'05" W); the lake is 1 mile northwest of Dragon Peak. Named on Mount Pinchot (1953) 15' quadrangle.

Dragon Peak [FRESNO]: *peak,* 11 miles south of Mount Pinchot on Fresno-Inyo county line (lat. 36°47'30" N, long. 118°22'30" W). Altitude 12,995 feet. Named on Mount Pinchot (1953) 15' quadrangle. The outline of the peak, as seen from Rae Lakes, resembles a dragon (Browning 1986, p. 59).

Drapersville: see **Kingsburg** [FRESNO].

Drillers Ridge [KINGS]: *ridge,* southeast-trending, 1.25 miles long, 7 miles east-southeast of Avenal (lat. 35°58'25" N, long. 120°00'30" W; in and near sec. 34, T 22 S, R 18 E). Named on Kettleman Plain (1953) 7.5' quadrangle. United States Board on Geographic Names (1933b, p. 8) associated the new name with the oil industry.

Dripping Spring [FRESNO]: *spring,* 8 miles west-southwest of Coalinga (lat. 36°06'55" N, long. 120°29'40" W; sec. 7, T 21 S, R 14 E). Named on Curry Mountain (1969) 7.5' quadrangle.

Dripping Spring [KERN]: *spring,* 2.25 miles south-southeast of Mount Adelaide at the mouth of Barker Creek (lat. 35°24' N, long. 118°43'50" W; at S line sec. 14, T 29 S, R 30 E). Named on Mount Adelaide (1972) 7.5' quadrangle.

Drum Valley [TULARE]: *valley,* 4 miles east of Tucker Mountain, partly along Bull Creek (lat. 36°38'30" N, long. 119°08' W). Named on Miramonte (1966) and Tucker Mountain (1966) 7.5' quadrangles. Called Drums Valley on Mendenhall's (1908) map. Postal authorities established Drum Valley post office in 1877 and discontinued it in 1879 (Frickstad, p. 210).

Dry Canyon [KERN]: *canyon,* drained by a stream that flows 2.5 miles to lowlands 6.25 miles south of Weldon (lat. 35°34'40" N, long. 118°16'20" W). Named on Woolstalf Creek (1972) 7.5' quadrangle.

Dry Creek [FRESNO]: *stream,* flows 22 miles to lowlands 6.5 miles east-northeast of Clovis (lat. 36°52'10" N, long. 119°35'40" W; sec. 20, T 12 S, R 22 E). Named on Shaver Lake (1953) 15' quadrangle, and on Academy (1964), Clovis (1964), Fresno North (1965), Humphreys Station (1965), and Round Mountain (1964) 7.5' quadrangles. Called Big Dry Cr. on Friant (1922) 7.5' quadrangle, and called Tollhouse Cr. on Kaiser (1904) 30' quadrangle—the stream flows through the village of Tollhouse.

Dry Creek [MADERA]: *stream,* flows 20 miles to an artificial watercourse 8.5 miles west of Madera (lat. 36°59' N, long. 120°12'30" W; sec. 10, T 11 S, R 16 E). Named on Le Grand (1961), Madera (1946), and Raymond (1962) 15' quadrangles.

Dry Creek [TULARE]:
(1) *stream,* flows 25 miles to Kaweah River 4.25 miles east of Woodlake and 1 mile west of Limekiln Hill (lat. 36°24'25" N, long. 119°01'20" W; sec. 35, T 17 S, R 27 E). Named on Giant Forest (1956) 15' quadrangle, and on Auckland (1966) and Woodlake (1952,

photorevised 1969) 7.5' quadrangles. Called Limekiln Creek on Lemon Cove (1928) 7.5' quadrangle. East Fork enters 8 miles southeast of Auckland. It is 4 miles long and is named on Giant Forest (1956) 15' quadrangle, and on Auckland (1966) 7.5' quadrangle.
(2) *stream,* flows 7 miles to lowlands 5.25 miles northeast of Exeter (lat. 36°20'25" N, long. 119°03'40" W; near SW cor. sec. 21, T 18 S, R 27 E). Named on Exeter (1952) and Kaweah (1957) 15' quadrangles.
(3) *stream,* flows 4.5 miles to South Fork Kern River 5.25 miles northwest of Olancha Peak (lat. 36°19' N, long. 118°11'05" W; sec. 33, T 18 S, R 35 E). Named on Olancha (1956) 15' quadrangle.

Dry Creek: see **Arroyo Hondo** [FRESNO]; **Big Dry Creek**, under **Academy** [FRESNO]; **Dry Meadow Creek** [TULARE]; **Little Dry Creek** [FRESNO]; **Spring Mountain Gulch** [KERN]; **Willow Spring Creek** [KERN] (1).

Dry Meadow [TULARE]: *area,* 7.5 miles east-southeast of California Hot Springs (lat. 35°50'30" N, long. 118°32'45" W; sec. 17, T 24 S, R 32 E). Named on California Hot Springs (1958) 15' quadrangle.

Dry Meadow: see **Big Dry Meadow** [TULARE]; **Little Dry Meadow** [KERN]; **Little Dry Meadow** [TULARE].

Dry Meadow Creek [KERN]: *stream,* flows 5 miles to Woolstalf Creek 6.5 miles south of Weldon (lat. 35°34'15" N, long. 118° 16' W; near N line sec. 19, T 27 S, R 35 E); the stream heads at Dry Meadows. Named on Woolstalf Creek (1972) 7.5' quadrangle.

Dry Meadow Creek [TULARE]: *stream,* flows 8 miles to Kern River 4.5 miles north of Fairview (lat. 35°59'35" N, long. 118°28'55" W; near SE cor. sec. 23, T 22 S, R 32 E). Named on Camp Nelson (1956) and Kernville (1956) 15' quadrangles. Called Dry Creek on Kaweah (1909) and Kernville (1908) 30' quadrangles.

Dry Meadows [KERN]: *area,* 7.5 miles southsouthwest of Weldon (lat. 35°33'45" N, long. 118°20'10" W). Named on Woolstalf Creek (1972) 7.5' quadrangle.

Dry Meadows [TULARE]: *area,* 7.5 miles east of Hockett Peak along Lost Trout Creek (lat. 36°12'50" N, long. 118°15'10" W; on W line sec. 1, T 20 S, R 34 E). Named on Hockett Peak (1956) 15' quadrangle. United States Board on Geographic Names (1962a, p. 10) rejected the name "Lost Trout Meadow" for the place.

Dry Meadows: see **Big Dry Meadows** [TULARE].

Dry Valley [TULARE]: *valley,* along Dry Creek (1) above a point nearly 6 miles east-northeast of Auckland (lat. 36°36'45" N, long. 119°00'20" W; near SE cor. sec. 14, T 15 S, R 27 E). Named on Giant Forest (1956) 15' quadrangle, and on Auckland (1966) 7.5' quadrangle.

Duck Lake [FRESNO]:

(1) *lake,* 1 mile long, 6 miles west-northwest of Red Slate Mountain (lat. 37°33' N, long. 118°57'40" W). Named on Mount Morrison (1953) 15' quadrangle. One account of the name concerns ducks found frozen in ice on the lake; another account attributes the name to a patch of snow that at certain times resembles the word "DUK" (Smith, Genny, p. 49).

(2) *lake,* 700 feet long, 14 miles north of Hume (lat. 36°59'35" N, long. 118°53'30" W). Named on Tehipite Dome (1952) 15' quadrangle. Rae Crabtree and Bill White named the lake after they saw a duck on it (Browning 1986, p. 59).

Duckworth Canyon [FRESNO]: *canyon,* drained by a stream that flows 3.25 miles to Los Gatos Creek 18 miles west-northwest of Coalinga (lat. 36°16'40" N, long. 120°38'40" W; sec. 14, T 19 S, R 12 E). Named on San Benito Mountain (1969) 7.5' quadrangle.

Ducor [TULARE]: *village,* 12 miles south of Porterville (lat. 35°53'30" N, long. 119°02'50" W; on N line sec. 34, T 23 S, R 27 E). Named on Ducor (1952) 7.5' quadrangle. The place first was called Dutch Corners because four Germans homesteaded there, but when the railroad reached the site in 1889, railroad officials shortened the old name and called their station Ducor (Mitchell, A.R., p. 67). Postal authorities established Ducor post office in 1907 (Frickstad, p. 210).

Dudley [KINGS]: *locality,* 13 miles south-southeast of Avenal in McLure (present Sunflower) Valley (lat. 35°49'40" N, long. 120° 03'25" W; at E line sec. 19, T 24 S, R 18 E). Named on Cholame (1917) 30' quadrangle. Postal authorities established Dudley post office in 1887 and discontinued it in 1918; the name was for Edmund R. Dudley and Benjamin B. Dudley, who developed oil fields in the region (Salley, p. 62). California Mining Bureau's (1909a) map shows a place called Esperanza located 15 miles by stage line north of Dudley. Postal authorities established Esperanza post office in 1889, moved it 5.5 miles northwest in 1893, moved it 1.5 miles northwest in 1896, moved it 4.5 miles southwest in 1900, and discontinued it in 1901 (Salley, p. 70).

Dudley Pond [FRESNO]: *lake,* 1500 feet long, 1.5 miles southwest of Selma (lat. 36°33'25" N, long. 119°37'50" W; sec. 12, T 16 S, R 21 E). Named on Selma (1946) 15' quadrangle. On Conejo (1963) 7.5' quadrangle, the name applies to a dry depression.

Dudley Ridge [KINGS]: *ridge,* west-northwest-trending, 5 miles long, 9 miles southeast of Kettleman City at the south edge of Tulare Lake Bed (lat. 35°55'30" N, long. 119°49'15" W). Named on Dudley Ridge (1954) 7.5' quadrangle.

Dudley Spring [TULARE]: *spring,* 4.5 miles

south of Auckland (lat. 36°31'20" N, long. 119°06'05" W; sec. 24, T 16 S, R 26 E). Named on Auckland (1966) 7.5' quadrangle.

Duff Creek [FRESNO]: *stream,* flows 2.5 miles to Big Creek (2) in Blue Canyon (1) 8.5 miles southwest of Dinkey Dome (lat. 37°01'15" N, long. 119°13'35" W; sec. 34, T 10 S, R 25 E). Named on Huntington Lake (1953) 15' quadrangle.

Dumbell Lakes [FRESNO]: *lakes,* two, each 2400 feet long, located 13 miles east-southeast of Mount Goddard (lat. 37°00'30" N, long. 118°30'40" W). Named on Mount Goddard (1948) 15' quadrangle. The outline of the lakes has a dumbell shape on the map.

Dumtah [TULARE]: *locality,* 6 miles east of Exeter (lat. 36°18'20" N, long. 119°01'50" W; sec. 3, T 19 S, R 27 E). Named on Rocky Hill (1951) 7.5' quadrangle, which has the notation "Indian Camp Ground site" at the place.

Duncan Canyon [FRESNO]: *canyon,* drained by a stream that flows 1 mile to Burrough Valley nearly 7 miles northwest of Trimmer (lat. 36°59'05" N, long. 119°22' W; near E line sec. 8, T 11 S, R 24 E). Named on Trimmer (1965) 7.5' quadrangle.

Duncan Canyon [TULARE]: *canyon,* drained by a stream that flows 1.5 miles to South Fork Tule River 7 miles south-southeast of Springville (lat. 36°02'25" N, long. 118°45'50" W). Named on Globe (1956) 7.5' quadrangle.

Duncan Mill: see **Damon Mill** [FRESNO].

Dunlap [FRESNO]: *settlement,* 13 miles northeast of Orange Cove (lat. 36°44'15" N, long. 119°07'10" W; sec. 2, T 14 S, R 26 E). Named on Miramonte (1966) 7.5' quadrangle. The name commemorates George Dunlap Moss, a school teacher who helped get a post office for the settlement (Hanna, p. 92). Postal authorities established Dunlap post office in 1882, discontinued it for a time in 1885, and moved it 2.5 miles northeast in 1898 (Salley, p. 62).

Dunlap Meadow [TULARE]: *area,* 7 miles east of California Hot Springs (lat. 35°51'45" N, long. 118°32'45" W; sec. 5, 8, T 24 S, R 32 E). Named on California Hot Springs (1958) 15' quadrangle.

Durkas Flat [TULARE]: *area,* 5.5 miles south-southeast of California Hot Springs (lat. 35°48'10" N, long. 118°38'50" W; near NE cor. sec. 32, T 24 S, R 31 E). Named on California Hot Springs (1958) 15' quadrangle.

Durrwood Camp [TULARE]: *locality,* 12 miles south-southwest of Hockett Peak (lat. 36°03'35" N, long. 118°28' W); the place is along Kern River near the mouth of Durrwood Creek. Named on Hockett Peak (1956) 15' quadrangle.

Durrwood Creek [TULARE]: *stream,* flows 6.5 miles to Kern River 12 miles south-southwest of Hockett Peak (lat. 36°03'40" N, long. 118°27'55" W). Named on Hockett Peak

(1956) 15' quadrangle. The name commemorates Billy Durwood (Mitchell, A.R., p. 78; Mitchell gave the name with one "r"). Called Tibbetts Cr. on Olmsted's (1900) map.

Durrwood Meadows [TULARE]: *area,* 8 miles east-northeast of Fairview (lat. 35°59' N, long. 118°22' W; sec. 25, T 22 S, R 33 E). Named on Kernville (1956) 15' quadrangle.

Dustin Acres [KERN]: *settlement,* 6.5 miles north-northeast of Taft (lat. 35°13'10" N, long. 119°23'20" W; sec. 22, T 31 S, R 24 E). Named on Taft (1950) 7.5' quadrangle.

Dusy Basin [KERN]: *area,* 9.5 miles east of Mount Goddard (lat. 37° 05'45" N, long. 118°33' W); the place is at the head of Dusy Branch. Named on Mount Goddard (1948) 15' quadrangle. Lakes in the area are called Dusy Lakes on Mount Goddard (1912) 30' quadrangle.

Dusy Branch [KERN]: *stream,* flows 4 miles to Middle Fork Kings River 7 miles east of Mount Goddard in LeConte Canyon (lat. 37° 05'30" N, long. 118°35'35" W); the stream heads in Dusy Basin. Named on Mount Goddard (1948) 15' quadrangle. L. A. Winchell named the stream in 1879 for Frank Dusy, a stockman in the region as early as 1869 (Farquhar, 1923, p. 392-393).

Dusy Creek [FRESNO]: *stream,* flows 6.5 miles to Helms Creek 10.5 miles west-northwest of Blackcap Mountain in Courtright Reservoir (lat. 37°06'30" N, long. 118°58'20" W; sec. 36, T 9 S, R 27 E). Named on Blackcap Mountain (1953) 15' quadrangle.

Dusy Lakes: see **Dusy Basin** [FRESNO].

Dusy Meadow [FRESNO]: *area,* 10.5 miles west-southwest of Blackcap Mountain along North Fork Kings River (lat. 37°00'45" N, long. 118°58' W; near S line sec. 31, T 10 S, R 28 E). Named on Mount Goddard (1912) 30' quadrangle. Water of Wishon Reservoir now covers the place

Dusy Meadows [FRESNO]: *area,* 11 miles west-northwest of Blackcap Mountain (lat. 37°08'45" N, long. 118°57'40" W; in and near sec. 18, 19, T 9 S, R 28 E); the place is along Dusy Creek. Named on Blackcap Mountain (1953) 15' quadrangle.

Dutch Bar: see **Gordons Ferry** [KERN].

Dutch Corners: see **Ducor** [TULARE].

Dutch Flat [KERN]: *area,* 4.5 miles southwest of Wofford Heights (lat. 35°39'20" N, long. 118°30' W; sec. 24, T 26 S, R 32 E). Named on Alta Sierra (1972) and Lake Isabella North (1972) 7.5' quadrangles.

Dutch John Cut [KINGS]: *water feature,* diverges from Cole Slough and extends for 2.5 miles to Kings River 7 miles north of Hanford (lat. 36°25'50" N, long. 119°38'25" W; near N line sec. 25, T 17 S, R 21 E). Named on Burris Park (1954) and Laton (1953) 7.5' quadrangles.

Dutch John Flat [TULARE]: *area,* 7 miles southeast of Monache Mountain (lat.

36°08'10" N, long. 118°06' W; sec. 32, T 20 S, R 36 E). Named on Monache Mountain (1956) 15' quadrangle.

Dutch Lake [FRESNO]: *lake,* 1000 feet long, 14 miles southwest of Mount Abbot (lat. 37°15'15" N, long. 118°59'15" W). Named on Mount Abbot (1953) 15' quadrangle.

Dutchman Canyon [FRESNO]: *canyon,* drained by a stream that flows 1 mile to Hot Springs Canyon 2.25 miles southeast of Coalinga Mineral Springs (lat. 36°07'30" N, long. 120°31'20" W; near S line sec. 1, T 21 S, R 13 E). Named on Sherman Peak (1969) 7.5' quadrangle.

Dutchman Prospect Spring [KERN]: *spring,* 6.5 miles north of Caliente along Placeritas Creek (lat. 35°23'15" N, long. 118°37'20" W; sec. 23, T 29 S, R 31 E). Named on Breckenridge Mountain (1972) 7.5' quadrangle.

Dutch Oven Meadow [FRESNO]: *area,* 15 miles northwest of Blackcap Mountain (lat. 37°13'30" N, long. 118°59'45" W). Named on Blackcap Mountain (1953) 15' quadrangle.

Dyer Creek [KERN]: *stream,* flows 9.5 miles to lowlands 4.5 miles east-northeast of McFarland (lat. 35°41'40" N, long. 119°09'10" W; near E line sec. 3, T 26 S, R 26 E). Named on Deepwell Ranch (1952) and McFarland (1954) 7.5' quadrangles.

Dyke Ridge: see **Monarch Divide** [FRESNO].

— E —

Eagle Creek [TULARE]:
(1) *stream,* flows nearly 2 miles to East Fork Kaweah River 1 mile south-southeast of Mineral King (lat. 36°26'20" N, long. 118°35'30" W); the stream heads at Eagle Lake. Named on Mineral King (1956) 15' quadrangle. United States Board on Geographic Names (1960b, p. 18) rejected the name "Spring Creek" for the stream.
(2) *stream,* flows 4 miles to Kessing Creek 9.5 miles south-southwest of Camp Nelson (lat. 36°01' N, long. 118°40'50" W). Named on California Hot Springs (1958) and Camp Nelson (1956) 15' quadrangles.

Eagle Hotel [TULARE]: *relief feature,* 2.5 miles northeast of California Hot Springs (lat. 35°54'30" N, long. 118°38'35" W; near W line sec. 21, T 23 S, R 31 E). Named on California Hot Springs (1958) 15' quadrangle.

Eagle Lake [TULARE]: *lake,* 1700 feet long, 2.5 miles south-southwest of Mineral King (lat. 36°24'55" N, long. 118°36'20" W; sec. 28, T 17 S, R 31 E); the lake is at the head of Eagle Creek (1). Named on Mineral King (1956) 15' quadrangle.

Eagle Peak [FRESNO]:
(1) *peak,* 6.5 miles east-southeast of Dinkey Dome (lat. 37°05'20" N, long. 119°01' W; sec. 3, T 10 S, R 27 E). Altitude 10,318 feet.

Named on Huntington Lake (1953) 15' quadrangle.

(2) *peak,* 2.5 miles north-northeast of Trimmer (lat. 36°56'25" N, long. 119°16'35" W; near SW cor. sec. 29, T 11 S, R 25 E). Altitude 3272 feet. Named on Trimmer (1965) 7.5' quadrangle.

Eagle Peak [KERN]: *peak,* 4 miles south-southwest of Loraine (lat. 35°15'10" N, long. 118°28'30" W; near N line sec. 7, T 31 S, R 33 E). Named on Loraine (1972) 7.5' quadrangle.

Eagle Peaks [FRESNO]: *peaks,* 9.5 miles east-northeast of Hume (lat. 36°50'55" N, long. 118°45'40" W); the peaks are at the southeast end of Eagle Spur. Named on Tehipite Dome (1952) 15' quadrangle.

Eagle Rest Peak [KERN]: *peak,* 16 miles west-northwest of Lebec (lat. 34°54'25" N, long. 119°08' W; near SW cor. sec. 33, T 10 N, R 21 W). Altitude 5955 feet. Named on Eagle Rest Peak (1942) 7.5' quadrangle.

Eagle Rock [FRESNO]: *peak,* 10 miles southwest of Coalinga (lat. 36°01'50" N, long. 120°28'10" W; sec. 9, T 22 S, R 14 E). Named on Curry Mountain (1969) 7.5' quadrangle.

Eagle Scout Creek [TULARE]: *stream,* flows 4.25 miles to Middle Fork Kaweah River 7.25 miles west-southwest of Triple Divide Peak (lat. 36°32'20" N, long. 118°38'20" W); the stream heads near Eagle Scout Peak. Named on Triple Divide Peak (1956) 15' quadrangle. United States Board on Geographic Names (1933a, p. 279) rejected the name "North Fork" for the stream.

Eagle Scout Peak [TULARE]: *peak,* 3.5 miles south-southwest of Triple Divide Peak on Great Western Divide (lat. 36°32'45" N, long. 118°33'45" W). Altitude 12,040 feet. Named on Triple Divide Peak (1956) 15' quadrangle. Francis P. Farquhar and three eagle scouts made the first ascent of the peak in 1926 (United States Board on Geographic Names, 1933a, p. 279). United States Board on Geographic Names (1976b, p. 4) approved the name "Lawson Peak" for a feature located 2.8 miles east-northeast of Eagle Scout Peak on Kaweah Peaks Ridge (lat. 36°33'40" N, long. 118°30'50" W); the name commemorates Andrew C. Lawson, professor of geology at University of California.

Eagles Nest [KERN]: *ridge,* northeast-trending, 0.25 mile long, south of Loraine (lat. 35°17'05" N, long. 118°26'25" W; at S line sec. 28, T 30 S, R 33 E). Named on Loraine (1972) 7.5' quadrangle.

Eagle Spring [KERN]: *spring,* 7 miles north-northwest of Mojave (lat. 35°08'45" N, long. 118°13'40" W; sec. 16, T 32 S, R 35 E). Named on Cache Peak (1973) 7.5' quadrangle.

Eagle Spur [FRESNO]: *ridge,* northwest-trending, 3 miles long, 9 miles northeast of Hume (lat. 36°52' N, long. 118°47' W); Eagle Peaks are at the southeast end of the ridge.

Named on Tehipite Dome (1952) 15' quadrangle.

Eaires [KERN]: *locality,* nearly 5 miles north of Rosamond (lat. 34° 55'50" N, long. 118°08'55" W; at E line sec. 28, T 10 N, R 12 W). Named on Soledad Mountain (1947) 7.5' quadrangle.

Earl-Anna: see **Camp Earl-Anna** [KERN].

Earlimart [TULARE]: *town,* 19 miles southwest of Porterville (lat. 35°53' N, long. 119°16'10" W; mainly in sec. 33, T 23 S, R 25 E). Named on Pixley (1954) 7.5' quadrangle. The place first was called Alila, which means "land of flowers," but promoters of the town changed the name to Earlimart to indicate that crops ripen early at the place (Mitchell, A.R., p. 68). Postal authorities established Alila post office in 1885, discontinued it in 1893, reestablished it in 1896, and discontinued it in 1899; they established Earlimart post office in 1907 (Frickstad, p. 209, 210).

Earthquake Spring [KERN]: *spring,* 5.25 miles north-northeast of Caliente (lat. 35°21'50" N, long. 118°36'10" W; sec. 36, T 29 S, R 31 E). Named on Oiler Peak (1972) 7.5' quadrangle.

East Bakersfield: see **Kern**, under **Bakersfield** [KERN].

East Creek [FRESNO-TULARE]: *stream,* heads in Tulare County and flows 12 miles to Bubbs Creek 13 miles south of Mount Pinchot in Fresno County (lat. 36°45'15" N, long. 118°26'25" W); East Lake [TULARE] is along the stream. Named on Mount Whitney (1907) 30' quadrangle, and on Mount Pinchot (1953) 15' quadrangle.

Eastern Brook Lake [FRESNO]: *lake,* 500 feet long, 3.5 miles northeast of Dinkey Dome (lat. 37°09'10" N, long. 199°05'10" W; sec. 13, T 9 S, R 26 E); the lake is 900 feet west of Rainbow Lake (2). Named on Huntington Lake (1953) 15' quadrangle.

East Farmersville [TULARE]: *locality,* 3.25 miles west of Exeter (lat. 36°18'05" N, long. 119°11'40" W; sec. 6, T 19 S, R 26 E); the place is 0.5 mile east of Farmersville. Named on Exeter (1952) 15' quadrangle.

East Fork Spring [TULARE]: *spring,* 2.25 miles southeast of California Hot Springs (lat. 35°51'25" N, long. 118°38'35" W; near W line sec. 9, T 24 S, R 31 E). Named on California Hot Springs (1958) 15' quadrangle.

East Horse Meadow [TULARE]: *area,* 7.5 miles east of California Hot Springs (lat. 35°52'15" N, long. 118°32'25" W; near E line sec. 5, T 24 S, R 32 E). Named on California Hot Springs (1958) 15' quadrangle.

East Kennedy Lake [FRESNO]: *lake,* 900 feet long, 9 miles southwest of Marion Peak (lat. 36°52'35" N, long. 118°39'05" W); the lake is at the head of Kennedy Creek. Named on Marion Peak (1953) 15' quadrangle.

East Lake [FRESNO]: *lake,* 600 feet long, 7.25 miles northeast of Dinkey Dome (lat. 37°10'45" N, long. 119°01'35" W; sec. 4, T 9

S, R 27 E). Named on Huntington Lake (1953) 15' quadrangle.

East Lake [TULARE]: *lake,* 2000 feet long, 13 miles northwest of Mount Whitney (lat. 36°43'30" N, long. 118°26'30" W); the lake is along East Creek. Named on Mount Whitney (1956) 15' quadrangle. State Hydrographic Survey employees named the lake about 1881 for Thomas Benton East, a hunter, trapper, and cattleman of Eshom Valley (Hanna, p. 94). The feature was called Brewer Lake on a map of 1896 (Browning 1986, p. 61).

Eastman Lake [MADERA]: *lake,* on Madera-Mariposa county line behind a dam on Chowchilla River 4.25 miles west of Raymond (lat. 37°13' N, long. 119°59' W; sec. 22, T 8 S, R 18 E). Named on Raymond (1962, photorevised 1981) 7.5' quadrangle, which has the name "Buchanan Dam" for the dam that forms the lake. United States Board on Geographic Names (1975c, p. 5) noted that the name "H.V. Eastman Lake" was mandated by Congressional action and gave the name "Buchanan Reservoir" as a variant. Logan's (1950) map shows a place called Buchanan located about 5 miles west of Raymond near the site of the dam that forms the present lake. Buchanan took its name from Buchanan Hollow, which extends along Chowchilla River for about 2 miles just northeast of the place that Madera County, Mariposa County, and Merced County meet (Clough, p. 78). Postal authorities established Buchanan post office in 1873 and discontinued it in 1904—Buchanan Hollow was named for an early settler (Salley, p. 28).

Easton [FRESNO]: *town,* 7.5 miles south of downtown Fresno (lat. 36°39' N, long. 119°47'20" W; around SW cor. sec. 3, T 15 S, R 30 E). Named on Fresno South (1963) 7.5' quadrangle. Called Covel on Fresno (1923) 7.5' quadrangle. Postal authorities established Easton post office in 1881, moved it 0.5 mile northwest in 1883, discontinued it in 1902, and reestablished it in 1952; the name commemorates O.W. Easton, a land agent (Salley, p. 64).

East Orosi [TULARE]: *village,* 7 miles east of Dinuba (lat. 36°32'55" N, long. 119°15'40" W; sec. 9, T 16 S, R 25 E); the village is 1.5 miles east of Orosi. Named on Orange Cove South (1966) 7.5' quadrangle. Sultana (1923) 7.5' quadrangle shows the place along Atchison, Topeka and Santa Fe Railroad, and the map has the alternate name "Orosi Sta." at the site. Called Arosi on California Mining Bureau's (1917b) map.

East Palo Prieto Creek: see **Bitterwater Creek** [KERN] (2).

East Pinnacles Creek [FRESNO]: *stream,* flows nearly 3 miles to Piute Creek about 9 miles south of Mount Abbot (lat. 37°15'30" N, long. 118°47'45" W); the stream is east of The Pinnacles (1). Named on Mount Abbot (1953) 15' quadrangle.

East Potholes [TULARE]: *area,* 6.5 miles north-northwest of Olancha Peak (lat. 36°21'20" N, long. 118°08'45" W). Named on Olancha (1956) 15' quadrangle. United States Board on Geographic Names (1989a, p. 3) rejected the name "East Potholes Meadow" for the feature.

East Potholes Meadow: see **East Potholes** [TULARE].

East Spur [TULARE]: *ridge,* north-trending, 3 miles long, 12 miles north-northwest of Mount Whitney (lat. 36°43'45" N, long. 118°23'50" W); the ridge is 1 mile east across Vidette Creek from West Spur. Named on Mount Whitney (1956) 15' quadrangle

East Twin Creek: see **Santiago Creek** [KERN].

East Vidette [TULARE]: *peak,* 13 miles north-northwest of Mount Whitney (lat. 36°44'40" N, long. 118°24' W); the peak is 1.25 miles northeast of West Vidette. Altitude 12,350 feet. Named on Mount Whitney (1956) 15' quadrangle.

Echo Canyon [FRESNO]: *canyon,* drained by a stream that flows nearly 3 miles to Warthan Creek 2.5 miles north-northeast of Smith Mountain (2) (lat. 36°07' N, long. 120°34'50" W; sec. 9, T 21 S, R 13 E). Named on Sherman Peak (1969) and Smith Mountain (1969) 7.5' quadrangles.

Eclipse Hill [TULARE]: *peak,* 7.5 miles south-southeast of Fountain Springs near Kern-Tulare county line (lat. 35°47'30" N, long. 118°52'05" W; near S line sec. 32, T 24 S, R 29 E). Altitude 1922 feet. Named on White River (1965) 7.5' quadrangle.

Eden Creek [TULARE]: *stream,* flows 2 miles to East Fork Kaweah River 8 miles west of Mineral King (lat. 36°25'45" N, long. 118°44' W). Named on Mineral King (1956) 15' quadrangle.

Edgemont Acres: see **North Edwards** [KERN].

Edison [KERN]: *town,* 7.5 miles east-southeast of Bakersfield (lat. 35°20'50" N, long. 118°52'10" W; sec. 4, T 30 S, R 29 E). Named on Edison (1954) 7.5' quadrangle. Postal authorities established Edison post office in 1903, discontinued it in 1929, and reestablished it in 1946 (Frickstad, p. 55). Edison Electric Company constructed a substation at the place in 1902; Southern Pacific Railroad built a station called Wade at the site in 1903, but changed the name to Edison the same year (Bailey, 1967, p. 7).

Edison: see **Lake Thomas A. Edison** [FRESNO].

Ediza Lake [MADERA]: *lake,* 1700 feet long, 6.25 miles northwest of Devils Postpile along Shadow Creek (lat. 37°41'05" N, long. 119°09'55" W); the lake is 1.5 miles west-southwest of Shadow Lake. Named on Devils Postpile (1953) 15' quadrangle. The feature also was called Little Shadow Lake (Browning, 1988, p. 37).

Edmiston [FRESNO]: *locality,* 9 miles east-southeast of Clovis (lat. 36°46'40" N, long. 119°32'20" W; near NE cor. sec. 26, T 13 S, R 22 E). Named on Round Mountain (1964) 7.5' quadrangle.

Edmundson Acres [KERN]: *locality,* 1.25 miles north-northeast of Arvin (lat. 35°13'40" N, long. 118°49'20" W; at W line sec. 13, T 31 S, R 29 E). Named on Arvin (1955) 7.5' quadrangle.

Edna Lake [MADERA]: *lake,* 0.5 mile long, nearly 1 mile northeast of Merced Peak (lat. 37°38'35" N, long. 119°22'50" W). Named on Merced Peak (1953) 15' quadrangle. R.B. Marshall of United States Geological Survey named the lake for Edna Bowman of San Jose, who later became Mrs. Charles J. Kuhn (United States Board on Geographic Names, 1934a, p. 7).

Edwards [KERN]: *town,* 16 miles east-southeast of Mojave (lat. 34° 55'30" N, long. 117°56'15" W; around NE cor. sec. 33, T 10 N, R 10 W); the place is on Edwards Air Force Base. Named on Edwards (1973) 7.5' quadrangle. Rogers Lake (1956) 15' quadrangle has the designation "Wherry Housing (Edwards P.O.)" for the place. Postal authorities established Edwards post office in 1951 when they changed the post office name "Muroc" to "Edwards" (Frickstad, p. 55, 57).

Edwards: see **North Edwards** [KERN].

Edwards Air Force Base [KERN]: *military installation,* 11 miles east-southeast of Mojave in Mojave Desert. Named on Los Angeles (1975), San Bernardino (1957), and Trona (1957) 1°x 2° quadrangles. The installation includes more than 301,000 acres (Bailey, 1967, p. 8). The Army Air Corps used Muroc Dry Lake (present Rogers Lake) for bombing practice in 1933; the facility was called Muroc Army Air Field until 1946, when it became Muroc Air Force Base; it was renamed Edwards Air Force Base in 1950 to honor Captain Glen W. Edwards, a test pilot who was fatally injured at the place in 1948 (Wines, p. 145).

Edwards Siding [KERN]: *locality,* 7.5 miles south of Castle Butte along Atchison, Topeka and Santa Fe Railroad (lat. 35°00'20" N, long. 117°53' W; sec. 36, T 11 N, R 10 W). Named on California City South (1973) and North Edwards (1973) 7.5' quadrangles. Called Edwards Station on Castle Butte (1956) 15' quadrangle.

Edwards Station: see **Edwards Siding** [KERN].

Eighteen-mile House: see **Cinco** [KERN]; **Porterville** [TULARE].

Eighteen Mile House [MADERA]: *locality,* 6.25 miles south-southeast of Raymond (lat. 37°07'40" N, long. 119°52'10" W; sec. 23, T 9 S, R 19 E). Named on Daulton (1921) 7.5' quadrangle.

Eisen: see **Mount Eisen** [TULARE].

El Arco [KERN-KINGS]: *ridge,* south-southeast-trending, 2.25 miles long, 12 miles north of Blackwells Corner on Kern-Kings county line (lat. 35°47'20" N, long. 119°55'15" W). Named on Avenal Gap (1954) 7.5' quadrangle. The name is descriptive and means "bow" in Spanish (United States Board on Geographic Names, 1933b, p. 9).

El Arroyo de Chico Martinez: see **Chico Martinez Creek** [KERN].

El Arroyo de Jacalitos: see **Jacalitos Creek** [FRESNO].

Elba [TULARE]: *locality,* 2.5 miles northeast of Tulare (lat. 36°13'55" N, long. 119°18'45" W; at E line sec. 36, T 19 S, R 24 E). Named on Tulare (1927) 7.5' quadrangle.

Elbow: see **Old Millerton** [FRESNO].

Elbow Creek [TULARE]: *stream,* flows 11.5 miles to join Cottonwood Creek and form Cross Creek (1) 9 miles northwest of Visalia (lat. 36°25'55" N, long. 119°23'45" W; sec. 20, T 17 S, R 24 E). Named on Exeter (1952) and Visalia (1949) 15' quadrangles. On Traver (1949, photorevised 1969) 7.5' quadrangle, Elbow Creek ends before it reaches Cottonwood Creek.

El Bulto [KINGS]: *peak,* 5.5 miles south-southwest of Kettleman City (lat. 35°56'05" N, long. 119°59'50" W; near N line sec. 14, T 23 S, R 18 E). Altitude 1005 feet. Named on Los Viejos (1954) 7.5' quadrangle. The name is descriptive and means "the bulk" in Spanish (United States Board on Geographic Names, 1933b, p. 9).

El Caballete [KINGS]: *ridge,* north-northwest-trending, 4 miles long, 8.5 miles south of Kettleman City (lat. 35°53' N, long. 119°58' W). Named on Avenal Gap (1954) and Los Viejos (1954) 7.5' quadrangles. *El Caballete* means "ridge" in Spanish (United States Board on Geographic Names, 1933b, p. 9)

El Campo [KINGS]: *ridge,* north-trending, less than 0.5 mile long, 7 miles east-southeast of Avenal (lat. 35°59'05" N, long. 120°00'25" W; sec. 27, T 22 S, R 18 E). Named on Kettleman Plain (1953) 7.5' quadrangle. *El Campo* means "field" in Spanish (United States Board on Geographic Names, 1933b, p. 9)

El Chichon [KINGS]: *peak,* 2.5 miles east-northeast of Avenal (lat. 36°01'15" N, long. 120°05'15" W; sec. 13, T 22 S, R 17 E). Named on La Cima (1963) 7.5' quadrangle. The name is descriptive; *El Chichon* means "knob" or "lump on the head" in Spanish (United States Board on Geographic Names, 1933b, p. 9).

El Collado [KINGS]: *peak,* 3.5 miles south-southwest of Kettleman City (lat. 35°57'25" N, long. 119°59'50" W; near S line sec. 35, T 22 S, R 18 E). Named on Los Viejos (1954) 7.5' quadrangle. *El Collado* means "small hill" in Spanish (United States Board on Geographic Names, 1933b, p. 9).

Elderberry Springs [KERN]: *springs,* two, 1500 feet apart, 9.5 miles west-southwest of Liebre Twins (lat. 34°55'05" N, long. 118° 44'

W). Named on Winters Ridge (1966) 7.5' quadrangle.

Elder Creek: see **Cedar Creek** [TULARE] (1).

Elderwood [TULARE]: *settlement,* 4 miles north-northwest of Woodlake (lat. 36°28'20" N, long. 119°07'15" W; on S line sec. 2, T 17 S, R 26 E). Named on Woodlake (1952) 7.5' quadrangle.

Elderwood Station [TULARE]: *locality,* 4.5 miles north-northwest of Woodlake at the end of Visalia Electric Railroad (lat. 36°28'45" N, long. 119°06'55" W, at E line sec. 2, T 17 S, R 26 E); the place is 0.5 mile northeast of Elderwood. Named on Woodlake (1952) 7.5' quadrangle. Lemon Cove (1928) 7.5' quadrangle has the name "Elderwood" at the place.

El Dombo [KINGS]: *peak,* 3 miles east of Avenal (lat. 35°59'50" N, long. 120°04'40" W; sec. 24, T 22 S, R 17 E). Altitude 1109 feet. Named on Kettleman Plain (1953) 7.5' quadrangle. The name is descriptive and means "dome" in Spanish (United States Board on Geographic Names, 1933b, p. 9).

El Dorado Camp: see **Sageland** [KERN].

Elephant Back [TULARE]: *ridge,* south-south-east-trending, 2 miles long, 2.5 miles northeast of Lindsay (lat. 36°13'40" N, long. 119°03'10" W). Named on Lindsay (1951) 7.5' quadrangle.

Elephant Butte: see **Standard Hill** [KERN].

Elephant Ear: see **Elephant Knob** [TULARE].

Elephant Hill [FRESNO]: *peak,* 13 miles east-southeast of Coalinga (lat. 36°03'55" N, long. 120°08'25" W; at N line sec. 33, T 21 S, R 17 E). Named on Avenal (1954) 7.5' quadrangle. The name is from discovery of fossil elephant remains on top of the hill (United States Board on Geographic Names, 1933b, p. 9).

Elephant Knob [TULARE]: *peak,* 12 miles northeast of California Hot Springs (lat. 35°59'50" N, long. 118°30'40" W; sec. 22, T 22 S, R 32 E). Altitude 5090 feet. Named on California Hot Springs (1958) 15' quadrangle. Called Elephant Ear on Tobias Peak (1936) 30' quadrangle, but United States Board on Geographic Names (1960a, p. 8) rejected this name for the feature.

Electra Peak [MADERA]: *peak,* 8.5 miles northeast of Merced Peak (lat. 37°42'20" N, long. 119°15'35" W). Altitude 12,442 feet. Named on Merced Peak (1953) 15' quadrangle.

El Hocico [FRESNO]: *relief feature,* 10 miles east-southeast of Coalinga (lat. 36°05'40" N, long. 120°11'25" W). Named on Avenal (1954) 7.5' quadrangle. The name is descriptive; *El Hocico* means "the snout" in Spanish—the feature is the snoutlike protrusion of the northwest end of Kettleman Hills (United States Board on Geographic Names, 1933b, p. 9).

Elizabeth Lake [FRESNO]: *lake,* 300 feet long, 15 miles north-northeast of Hume (lat. 36°59'15" N, long. 118°50'30" W). Named on Tehipite Dome (1952) 15' quadrangle.

Elizabeth Pass [TULARE]: *pass,* 2.5 miles west of Triple Divide Peak (lat. 36°35'55" N, long. 118°34'30" W). Named on Triple Divide Peak (1956) 15' quadrangle. Stewart Edward White named the pass in 1906 for his wife (United States Board on Geographic Names, 1933a, p. 286). The feature also was called Turtle Pass for a large rock that resembles a turtle (Browning 1986, p. 64).

Elk [FRESNO]: *locality,* 7.25 miles southwest of Piedra along Atchison, Topeka and Santa Fe Railroad (lat. 36°45' N, long., 119°29'25" W; near S line sec. 32, T 13 S, R 23 E). Named on Piedra (1965) 7.5' quadrangle. Called Elk Siding on Watts Valley (1942) 15' quadrangle.

Elk Bayou [TULARE]: *stream,* formed by the confluence of Inside Creek and Outside Creek, flows 12 miles to Tule River 8 miles south-southwest of Tulare (lat. 36°05'40" N, long. 119°24'15" W; near N line sec. 20, T 21 S, R 24 E). Named on Taylor Weir (1950, photorevised 1969), Tipton (1950, photorevised 1969), and Tulare (1950, photorevised 1969) 7.5' quadrangles.

Elk Creek [TULARE]: *stream,* flows 2.5 miles to Kaweah River 5.5 miles southeast of Yucca Mountain (lat. 36°30'50" N, long. 118° 48'05" W). Named on Giant Forest (1956) 15' quadrangle.

Elk Hills [KERN]: *range,* center 10 miles north of Taft (lat. 35° 18' N, long. 119°28' W). Named on East Elk Hills (1954), Mouth of Kern (1950), Taft (1950), Tupman (1954), and West Elk Hills (1954) 7.5' quadrangles. Arnold and Johnson (p. 20) proposed the name and noted that "the few remaining elk in this region are said to range in these hills."

Elkhorn Station: see **Burrel** [FRESNO].

Elk Siding: see **Elk** [FRESNO].

El Leon [KINGS]: *peak,* 4.25 miles east of Avenal (lat. 36°00' N, long. 120°03' W; sec. 20, T 22 S, R 18 E). Named on La Cima (1963) 7.5' quadrangle. United States Board on Geographic Names (1933b, p. 9) pointed out that the name means "lion" in Spanish.

Ellings Spring [KERN]: *spring,* 5.25 miles southwest of Orchard Peak (lat. 35°40'35" N, long. 120°11'30" W; near W line sec. 7, T 26 S, T 17 E). Named on Orchard Peak (1961) 7.5' quadrangle.

Elliot Spring [FRESNO]: *spring,* 3.5 miles north-northeast of Coalinga Mineral Springs (lat. 36°11'25" N, long. 120°31'20" W; sec. 13, T 20 S, R 13 E). Named on Sherman Peak (1969) 7.5' quadrangle.

Ellis Meadow [TULARE]: *area,* 10 miles northwest of Triple Divide Peak (lat. 36°42'25" N, long. 118°38'20" W). Named on Triple Divide Peak (1956) 15' quadrangle. The name is for Sam L.N. Ellis, forest ranger and Tulare County supervisor (Gudde, 1949, p. 106).

Ellis Mountain [TULARE]: *peak,* 5.5 miles southeast of Auckland (lat. 36°32'40" N, long.

119°01'15" W; near S line sec. 10, T 16 S, R 27 E). Altitude 2503 feet. Named on Auckland (1966) 7.5' quadrangle. Called Buzzard Roost on Dinuba (1924) 30' quadrangle.

El Lobo [KINGS]: *peak,* 5 miles east of Avenal (lat. 35°59'40" N, long. 120°02'15" W; near SW cor. sec. 21, T 22 S, R 18 E). Altitude 1225 feet. Named on Kettleman Plain (1953) 7.5' quadrangle. United States Board on Geographic Names (1933b, p. 9) pointed out that the name means "wolf" in Spanish.

El Loro [KINGS]: *peak,* nearly 5 miles east of Avenal (lat. 35°59'50" N, long. 120°02'35" W; sec. 20, T 22 S, R 18 E). Named on Kettleman Plain (1953) 7.5' quadrangle. United States Board on Geographic Names (1933b, p. 10) noted that the name means "parrot" in Spanish.

Elmco [TULARE]: *locality,* 7 miles north of Ducor along Southern Pacific Railroad (lat. 35°59'35" N, long. 119°02'30" W; at N line sec. 27, T 22 S, R 27 E). Named on Ducor (1952) 7.5' quadrangle.

Elmer: see **Granite Station** [KERN].

El Mirador [KINGS]: *peak,* 8 miles east-southeast of Avenal (lat. 35°56'40" N, long. 120°00'05" W; sec. 11, T 23 S, R 18 E). Named on Kettleman Plain (1953) 7.5' quadrangle. The name refers to the outstanding location of the feature—it means "watchman" or "balcony" in Spanish (United States Board on Geographic Names, 1933b, p. 10).

El Mirador [TULARE]: *locality,* 4.5 miles east-southeast of Lindsay (lat. 36°10'40" N, long. 119°01'05" W; sec. 23, T 20 S, R 27 E). Named on Lindsay (1951) 7.5' quadrangle. On Lindsay (1928) 7.5' quadrangle, the name applied to a place situated 0.25 mile farther west along Visalia Electric Railroad.

Elmo [KERN]: *locality,* 5.5 miles north of Wasco along Atchison, Topeka and Santa Fe Railroad (lat. 35°40'45" N, long. 119°19'45" W; on W line sec. 7, T 26 S, R 25 E). Named on Pond (1953) 7.5' quadrangle.

El Monte de las Avilas: see **Wheeler Ridge** [KERN] (1).

Elm View [FRESNO]: *village,* 15 miles south of downtown Fresno (lat. 36°32'50" N, long. 119°47'20" W; at NW cor. sec. 15, T 16 S, R 20 E). Named on Caruthers (1963) 7.5' quadrangle.

El Pajaro [KINGS]: *peak,* 2 miles east of Avenal (lat. 36°00'15" N, long. 120°05'40" W; sec. 23, T 22 S, R 18 E). Altitude 1112 feet. Named on La Cima (1963) 7.5' quadrangle. United States Board on Geographic Names (1933b, p. 10) noted that the name means "bird" in Spanish.

El Paso [KINGS]: *pass,* 8 miles east-southeast of Avenal (lat. 35°56'55" N, long. 120°00'10" W; at NW cor. sec. 11, T 23 S, R 18 E). Named on Kettleman Plain (1953) 7.5' quadrangle. United States Board on Geographic Names (1933b, p. 10) pointed out that the feature is

the main pass along the road through Kettleman Hills.

El Paso City: see **Laurel Mountain** [KERN].

El Paso Creek [KERN]: *stream,* flows 18 miles to end 11.5 miles south of Arvin (lat. 35°02'30" N, long. 118°50'55" W; sec. 13, T 11 N, R 19 W). Named on Liebre Twins (1965), Tejon Hills (1955), Tejon Ranch (1966), and Winters Ridge (1966) 7.5' quadrangles.

El Paso Mountains [KERN]: *range,* south of Indian Wells Valley and north of Fremont Valley (center near lat. 35°27' N, long. 117° 50' W). Named on Cantil (1967), El Paso Peaks (1967), Garlock (1967), Inyokern SE (1972), and Saltdale NW (1967) 7.5' quadrangles.

El Paso Peaks [KERN]: *peaks,* 8 miles north-northwest of Randsburg (lat. 35°28'30" N, long. 117°42'30" W; sec. 30, T 28 S, R 40 E); the peaks are at the east end of El Paso Mountains. Altitude of highest peak is 4578 feet. Named on El Paso Peaks (1967) 7.5' quadrangle.

El Perno [KINGS]: *peak,* 4.5 miles east-northeast of Avenal (lat. 36° 01'25" N, long. 120°03'15" W; sec. 8, T 22 S, R 18 E). Named on La Cima (1963) 7.5' quadrangle. The name is descriptive and means "spike" in Spanish (United States Board on Geographic Names, 1933b, p. 10).

El Perro [KINGS]: *peak,* 2.5 miles north of Avenal (lat. 36°02'25" N, long. 120°08'10" W; sec. 4, T 22 S, R 17 E). Named on Avenal (1954) 7.5' quadrangle. United States Board on Geographic Names (1933b, p. 10) noted that the name means "dog" in Spanish.

El Piso [KERN]: *area,* nearly 4 miles east of Avenal (lat. 36°00'10" N, long. 120°03'35" W; sec. 19, T 22 S, R 18 E). Named on La Cima (1963) 7.5' quadrangle. The name refers to slabs of limestone that pave the area—*el piso* means "floor" in Spanish (United States Board on Geographic Names, 1933b, p. 10).

El Piton [FRESNO]: *peak,* 14 miles east-southeast of Coalinga (lat. 36°02'35" N, long. 120°08'40" W; near W line sec. 4, T 22 S, R 17 E). Named on Avenal (1954) 7.5' quadrangle. The name is descriptive and means "protruberance" in Spanish (United States Board on Geographic Names, 1933b, p. 10).

El Portillo [KINGS]: *canyon,* less than 1 mile long, 6.25 miles south-southeast of Kettleman City (lat. 35°55'10" N, long. 119°56'05" W; near NE cor. sec. 20, T 23 S, R 19 E). Named on Los Viejos (1954) 7.5' quadrangle. United States Board on Geographic Names (1933b, p. 10) noted that the name means "gap" or "open pass between hills" in Spanish.

El Prado [FRESNO]:
(1) *locality,* 6 miles north-northwest of Clovis at the junction of Southern Pacific Railroad and San Joaquin and Eastern Railroad (lat. 36°54'20" N, long. 119°43'50" W; near E line

sec. 12, T 12 S, R 20 E). Named on Friant (1922) 7.5' quadrangle. California Mining Bureau's (1917a) map shows a place called Bridge located along San Joaquin River west-southwest of El Prado. Postal authorities established Bridge post office, named for Lanes Bridge, in 1902 and discontinued it in 1907 (Salley, p. 26). Lanes Bridge (1922) 7.5' quadrangle shows Lanes Bridge across San Joaquin River 3.5 miles west-southwest of El Prado (1) (lat. 36°53'35" N, long. 119°47'15" W; near N line sec. 16, T 12 S, R 20 E).

(2) *ridge,* northwest-trending, 1.5 miles long, 12.5 miles east-southeast of Coalinga (lat. 36°03'45" N, long. 120°09'20" W). Named on Avenal (1954) 7.5' quadrangle.

El Pulgar [KINGS]: *peak,* 3 miles east-northeast of Avenal (lat. 36° 01'10" N, long. 120°04'15" W; sec. 18, T 22 S, R 18 E). Named on La Cima (1963) 7.5' quadrangle. The name means "thumb" in Spanish (United States Board on Geographic Names, 1933b, p. 10)

El Rabo [KINGS]: *ridge,* southeast-trending, 1 mile long, 11 miles south of Kettleman City (lat. 35°51' N, long. 119°56'10" W). Named on Avenal Gap (1954) 7.5' quadrangle. The name is for the position of the ridge at the end of the most prominent part of Kettleman Hills—it means "tail" in Spanish (United States Board on Geographic Names, 1933b, p. 10).

El Rascador [KINGS]: *peak,* 5 miles east of Avenal (lat. 36°01'10" N, long. 120°02'30" W; sec. 17, T 22 S, R 18 E). Named on La Cima (1963) 7.5' quadrangle. The name is descriptive and means "scraper" in Spanish (United States Board on Geographic Names, 1933b, p. 10).

El Rico [KINGS]: *locality,* 6 miles south-south-west of Corcoran along Kings Lake Shore Railroad (lat. 36°01'25" N, long. 119° 37' W). Named on Corcoran (1928) 7.5' quadrangle.

El Rincon [KINGS]: *area,* 12.5 miles south of Kettleman City (lat. 35°49'30" N, long. 119°55'30" W; sec. 21, T 24 S, R 19 E). Named on Avenal Gap (1954) 7.5' quadrangle. The name means "corner" in Spanish (United States Board on Geographic Names, 1933b, p. 10).

El Rio de los Santos Reyes: see **Kings River** [FRESNO-KINGS-TULARE].

El Rio de Nuestra Senora de la Merced: see **Merced River** [MADERA].

Emerald Lake [MADERA]: *lake,* 900 feet long, 8 miles north-northwest of Devils Postpile (lat. 37°43'35" N, long. 119°09'50" W); the lake is north of Garnet Lake and Ruby Lake. Named on Devils Postpile (1953) 15' quadrangle.

El Rita: see **Keene** [KERN].

El Serrijon [KINGS]: *ridge,* west-northwest-trending, 0.5 mile long, 3.5 miles east-northeast of Avenal (lat. 36°01'35" N, long. 120°04'15" W; mainly in sec. 7, T 22 S, R 18

E). Named on La Cima (1963) 7.5' quadrangle. United States Board on Geographic Names (1933b, p. 10) pointed out that the name means "small hill" in Spanish.

Elsie: see **Lake Elsie**, under **Fingerbowl Lake** [FRESNO].

El Taco [KINGS]: *peak,* 3.5 miles northeast of Avenal (lat. 36°02'15" N, long. 120°04'55" W; near S line sec. 1, T 22 S, R 17 E). Named on La Cima (1963) 7.5' quadrangle. The name means "stopper" in Spanish (United States Board on Geographic Names, 1933b, p. 10).

El Tejon [KERN]: *land grant,* southeast of Arvin. Named on Arvin (1955), Bear Mountain (1966), Bena (1972), Edison (1954), Pastoria Creek (1958), Tejon Hills (1955), Tejon Ranch (1966), and Winters Ridge (1966) 7.5' quadrangles. Jose Antonio Aguirre and Ignacio del Valle received 22 leagues in 1843 and claimed 97,617 acres patented in 1863 (Cowan, p. 101). The name originated with a dead badger found by early Spanish explorers—it means "badger" in Spanish (Latta, 1976, p. 226).

El Tolete [KINGS]: *peak,* nearly 4 miles east-northeast of Avenal (lat. 36°01'30" N, long. 120°03'50" W; sec. 7, T 22 S, R 18 E). Altitude 1212 feet. Named on La Cima (1963) 7.5' quadrangle. The name is descriptive and means "club" or "cudgel" in Spanish (United States Board on Geographic Names, 1933b, p. 11).

El Vallejo [KERN]: *valley,* 11.5 miles north of Blackwells Corner (lat. 35°46'25" N, long. 119°54'45" W; on N line sec. 10, T 25 S, R 19 E). Named on Avenal Gap (1954) 7.5' quadrangle. The name is descriptive and means "the small valley" in Spanish (United States Board on Geographic Names, 1933b, p. 11).

El Vejon [KERN]: *peak,* 11.5 miles north of Blackwells Corner (lat. 35°46'55" N, long. 119°53'30" W; sec. 2, T 25 S, R 19 E). Altitude 542 feet. Named on Avenal Gap (1954) 7.5 quadrangle. United States Board on Geographic Names (1933b, p. 11) noted that the feature is physiographically old—*vejon* means "very old man" in Spanish.

Ely Creek: see **Ely Meadow** [FRESNO].

Ely Meadow [FRESNO]: *area,* 5 miles north-northeast of Shaver Lake Heights (present town of Shaver Lake) (lat. 37°10'15" N, long. 119°17' W; on S line sec. 6, T 9 S, R 25 E); the place is 1 mile northwest of Ely Mountain. Named on Shaver Lake (1953) 15' quadrangle. United States Board on Geographic Names (1983a, p. 3) approved the name "Ely Creek" for a stream that heads at Ely Meadow and flows 2 miles north to Big Creek (1) 3 miles north of Shaver Lake (lat. 37°11'46" N, long. 119°17'02" W; sec. 31, T 8 S, R 25 E).

Ely Mountain [FRESNO]: *peak,* 4.5 miles northeast of Shaver Lake Heights (present town of Shaver Lake) (lat. 37°09'30" N, long.

119°16'20" W; sec. 8, T 9 S, R 25 E). Altitude 6886 feet. Named on Shaver Lake (1953) 15' quadrangle.

Emerald Lake [TULARE]: *lake,* 800 feet long, 8 miles west of Triple Divide Peak (lat. 36°35'50" N, long. 118°40'30" W; sec. 25, T 15 S, R 30 E). Named on Triple Divide Peak (1956) 15' quadrangle. Superintendent John R. White of Sequoia National Park named the feature in 1925 (Browning 1986, p. 65).

Emerald Mountain [KERN]: *peak,* 12 miles northeast of Tehachapi (lat. 35°15'20" N, long. 118°17' W; near SW cor. sec. 1, T 31 S, R 34 E). Altitude 4990 feet. Named on Emerald Mountain (1972) 7.5' quadrangle.

Emerald Peak [FRESNO]: *peak,* nearly 7 miles north-northeast of Blackcap Mountain (lat. 37°09'55" N, long. 118°45'45" W). Altitude 12,543 feet. Named on Blackcap Mountain (1953) 15' quadrangle. Theodore S. Solomons named the peak in 1895 for its color (Farquhar, 1923, p. 394).

Emigrant Hill [KERN]: *hill,* 10.5 miles northwest of Blackwells Corner (lat. 35°44'20" N, long. 119°58'55" W; sec. 24, T 25 S, R 18 E). Named on Emigrant Hill (1953) 7.5' quadrangle. On Emigrant Hill (1943) 7.5' quadrangle, the name applies to a hill located 0.5 mile farther northeast. The feature is said to have been a landmark for early travelers in the neighborhood (Arnold and Johnson, p. 20).

Emily Lake [MADERA]: *lake,* 800 feet long, 4 miles northwest of Devils Postpile (lat. 37°40'20" N, long. 119°07'15" W). Named on Devils Postpile (1953) 15' quadrangle.

Empire Mountain [TULARE]: *peak,* 1.5 miles northeast of Mineral King (lat. 36°28' N, long. 118°34'30" W). Altitude 11,509 feet. Named on Mineral King (1956) 15' quadrangle.

Enchanted Gorge [FRESNO]: *canyon,* 5.5 miles long, drained by Disappearing Creek, which joins Goddard Creek 7 miles south-southeast of Mount Goddard (lat. 37°00'55" N, long. 118°39'35" W). Named on Mount Goddard (1948) 15' quadrangle. Theodore S. Solomons named the canyon in 1895 (Farquhar, 1923, p. 394).

Engineer Point [KERN]: *peninsula,* 4 miles south of Wofford Heights along Isabella Lake just north of the dam that forms the lake (lat. 35°39'05" N, long. 118°28'05" W; on E line sec. 19, T 26 S, R 33 E). Named on Lake Isabella North (1972) 7.5' quadrangle.

Engle: see **Lake Engle** [KERN].

Enson [TULARE]: *locality,* 1.25 miles northnortheast of Dinuba along Atchison, Topeka and Santa Fe Railroad (lat. 36°33'30" N, long. 119°22'25" W; near NW cor. sec. 9, T 16 S, R 24 E). Named on Orange Cove South (1966) 7.5' quadrangle. Called Giffen on Sultana (1923) 7.5' quadrangle.

Ercil Lake [KERN]: *lake,* 600 feet long, 3.25 miles southwest of Glennville (lat. 35°41'55"

N, long. 118°44'45" W; at E line sec. 4, T 26 S, R 30 E). Named on Glennville (1972) 7.5' quadrangle.

Eric [KERN]: *locality,* 7 miles east of Tehachapi along the railroad (lat. 35°06'35" N, long. 118°19'30" W; at SE cor. sec. 28, T 32 S, R 34 E). Named on Monolith (1966) 7.5' quadrangle.

Eric Spring [FRESNO]: *spring,* 0.5 mile northeast of Smith Mountain (2) (lat. 36°05'05" N, long. 120°35'20" W; sec. 20, T 21 S, R 13 E). Named on Smith Mountain (1969) 7.5' quadrangle.

Ericsson: see **Mount Ericsson** [TULARE].

Ericsson Crags [TULARE]: *relief feature,* 11 miles northwest of Mount Whitney (lat. 36°42'10" N, long. 118°25' W); the feature is north of Mount Ericsson. Named on Mount Whitney (1956) 15' quadrangle.

Erin Lake [TULARE]: *lake,* 1700 feet long, 4.5 miles south of Mount Whitney (lat. 36°30'55" N, long. 118°17'10" W). Named on Mount Whitney (1956) 15' quadrangle. Chester Versteeg suggested the name because the outline of the lake on a map resembles the shape of Ireland on a map (Browning 1986, p. 66).

Ershim Lake [FRESNO]: *lake,* 1500 feet long, 8 miles north-northeast of Dinkey Dome (lat. 37°12'50" N, long. 119°03'20" W). Named on Huntington Lake (1953) 15' quadrangle.

Erskine Creek [KERN]: *stream,* formed by the confluence of East Fork and Middle Fork, flows 8 miles to Kern River 1.5 miles north of Bodfish (lat. 35°36'40" N, long. 118°29'25" W; sec. 1, T 27 S, R 32 E). Named on Lake Isabella South (1972) 7.5' quadrangle. Whipple (p. 149) referred to Erskine's Creek. East Fork is 3 miles long and Middle Fork is 2.25 miles long; both forks are named on Lake Isabella South (1972) and Woolstalf Creek (1972) 7.5' quadrangles. South Fork, which enters from the south just below the confluence of East Fork and Middle Fork, is 6.5 miles long and is named on Lake Isabella South (1972) and Piute Peak (1972) 7.5' quadrangles.

Erskine Creek Cave [KERN]: *cave,* 2 miles east of Bodfish (lat. 35° 35'40" N, long. 118°27'05" W; sec. 8, T 27 S, R 33 E); the cave is above Erskine Creek. Named on Lake Isabella South (1972) 7.5' quadrangle.

Escarpado Canyon [FRESNO]: *canyon,* drained by a stream that flows 2 miles to lowlands 19 miles southwest of Firebaugh (lat. 36°38'30" N, long. 120°40'30" W; near W line sec. 9, T 15 S, R 12 E). Named on Chounet Ranch (1956) 7.5' quadrangle.

Eshel [FRESNO]: *locality,* 3 miles north-northeast of Malaga along Southern Pacific Railroad (lat. 36°43'20" N, long. 119°42'30" W; at S line sec. 8, T 14 S, R 21 E). Named on Malaga (1923) 7.5' quadrangle.

Eshom Creek [TULARE]: *stream,* flows 11 miles to North Fork Kaweah River 3 miles west-northwest of Yucca Mountain (lat. 36° 35'45" N, long. 118°55' W; sec. 27, T 15 S, R 28 E); the stream goes through Eshom Valley. Named on Giant Forest (1956) 15' quadrangle.

Eshom Point [TULARE]: *peak,* 6 miles northwest of Yucca Mountain (lat. 36°38' N, long. 118°56'20" W; sec. 9, T 15 S, R 28 E); the peak is 1.5 miles northeast of Eshom Valley. Named on Giant Forest (1956) 15' quadrangle.

Eshom Valley [TULARE]: *valley,* 6 miles northwest of Yucca Mountain (lat. 36°37'15" N, long. 119°57'45" W); the feature is along Eshom Creek. Named on Giant Forest (1956) 15' quadrangle. John Perry Eshom homesteaded in the valley (Browning 1986, p. 66).

Esperanza: see **Dudley** [KINGS].

Esperanza Canyon [KERN]: *canyon,* drained by a stream that flows 1.25 miles to Kelso Valley 4.5 miles east-southeast of Claraville (lat. 35°25'10" N, long. 118°15'15" W; near E line sec. 18, T 29 S, R 35 E). Named on Claraville (1972) 7.5' quadrangle.

Etheda Springs [FRESNO]: *settlement,* 7 miles east-southeast of Dunlap (lat. 36°41'40" N, long. 119°00'25" W; sec. 23, T 14 S, R 27 E). Named on Miramonte (1966) 7.5' quadrangle.

Eugeneville: see **Garlock** [KERN].

Evans Creek [FRESNO]: *stream,* flows 2.5 miles to Boulder Creek (1) 6.5 miles east of Hume (lat. 36°48'10" N, long. 118°48'05" W). Named on Tehipite Dome (1952) 15' quadrangle. The name commemorates John Evans, who lived near Evans Grove and protected the trees there from fire (Browning 1986, p. 67).

Evans Flat [KERN]: *area,* 6 miles south-southwest of Alta Sierra along Greenhorn Creek (lat. 35°38'45" N, long. 118°35'20" W; near SE cor. sec. 24, T 26 S, R 31 E). Named on Alta Sierra (1972) 7.5' quadrangle.

Evans Flat Campground [KERN]: *locality,* 6.25 miles south-southwest of Alta Sierra (lat. 35°38'30" N, long. 118°35'15" W; near NW cor. sec. 30, T 26 S, R 32 E); the place is near present Evans Flat. Named on Glennville (1956) 15' quadrangle.

Evelyn Lake [TULARE]: *lake,* 750 feet long, 7 miles southwest of Mineral King (lat. 36°23'05" N, long. 118°41' W). Named on Mineral King (1956) 15' quadrangle. The name commemorates Evelyn Clough, sister of William O. Clough of Clough Cave (United States Board on Geographic Names, 1933a, p. 294). United States Board on Geographic Names (1989b, p. 2) approved the name "Cahoon Rock" for a peak located 0.5 mile southwest of Evelyn Lake (lat. 36°22'43" N, long. 118°41'23" W), and rejected the name "Cahoon Peak" for the same feature.

Everts: see **Raco** [FRESNO].

Evolution Basin [FRESNO]: *canyon,* 3.5 miles long, 2 miles northeast of Mount Goddard (lat. 37°08' N, long. 118°41'45" W); the canyon is at the head of Evolution Creek. Named on Mount Goddard (1948) 15' quadrangle.

Evolution Creek [FRESNO]: *stream,* flows 11 miles to South Fork San Joaquin River 9 miles north of Blackcap Mountain (lat. 37°11'45" N, long. 118°47'45" W); the stream heads in Evolution Basin and goes through Evolution Valley. Named on Mount Goddard (1948) 15' quadrangle. Called Middle Branch on Lippincott's (1902) map. In 1895 Theodore S. Solomons named the peaks at the head of the stream (which then was called The Middle Fork of the South Fork of the San Joaquin River) for Darwin, Wallace, Huxley, Haeckel, Spencer, and Fiske—known as the evolution group of philosophers; he gave the name "Evolution Lake" to the lake at the foot of Mount Darwin, and the name was extended to the creek (Farquhar, 1923, p. 395).

Evolution Lake [FRESNO]: *lake,* nearly 1 mile long, 4.5 miles north-northeast of Mount Goddard (lat. 37°10' N, long. 118°41'40" W); the lake is along Evolution Creek 1.25 miles west of Mount Darwin. Named on Mount Goddard (1948) 15' quadrangle. Theodore S. Solomons named the lake in 1895 (Farquhar, 1923, p. 395).

Evolution Meadow [FRESNO]: *area,* 8.5 miles north of Blackcap Mountain (lat. 37°11'45" N, long. 118°46'35" W); the place is near the west end of Evolution Valley. Named on Blackcap Mountain (1953) 15' quadrangle.

Evolution Valley [FRESNO]: *valley,* 6 miles north-northwest of Mount Goddard (lat. 37°11'20" N, long. 118°45' W); Evolution Creek drains the valley. Named on Blackcap Mountain (1953) and Mount Goddard (1948) 15' quadrangles.

Ewe Lake [FRESNO]: *lake,* 500 feet long, 3 miles south-southwest of Mount Goddard (lat. 37°03'50" N, long, 118°44'50" W); the lake is situated next to Ram Lake (2). Named on Mount Goddard (1948) 15' quadrangle. William A. Dill of California Department of Fish and Game named the lake in 1948 for its proximity to Bighorn Lake (2) (Browning 1986, p. 67).

Exchequer Creek [FRESNO]: *stream,* flows 4 miles to Dinkey Creek (1) 4.25 miles southwest of Dinkey Dome (lat. 37°03'30" N, long. 119°09'30" W; sec. 17, T 10 S, R 26 E); the stream goes through Exchequer Meadow. Named on Huntington Lake (1953) 15' quadrangle.

Exchequer Meadow [FRESNO]: *area,* 3 miles south-southeast of Dinkey Dome (lat. 37°04'20" N, long. 119°06'45" W; on W line sec. 11, T 10 S, R 26 E); the place is along Exchequer Creek. Named on Huntington Lake (1953) 15' quadrangle.

Exeter [TULARE]: *town,* 9 miles east-southeast of Visalia (lat. 36° 17'45" N, long. 119°08'15" W; around NE cor. sec. 10, T 19 S, R 26 E). Named on Exeter (1952) 15' quadrangle. D.W. Parkhurst, land agent for Southern Pacific Railroad, named the town in 1888 for his home at Exeter, England; previously the place was called Firebaugh, for John Firebaugh, an owner of the townsite (Mitchell, A.R., p. 68). Postal authorities established Exeter post office in 1889 (Frickstad, p. 210), and the town incorporated in 1911. California Mining Bureau's (1917b) map shows a place called Orangehurst located along the railroad between Exeter and Lindsay. Postal authorities established Orangehurst post office in 1908 and discontinued it in 1916 (Frickstad, p. 212). California Mining Bureau's (1917b) map also shows a place called Kaweah located along the railroad about 4 miles north-northwest of Exeter, and shows a place called Velma situated about 2 miles northwest of Kaweah along the same railroad. Postal authorities established Velma post office 7 miles northwest of Exeter (NW quarter of sec. 21, T 18 S, R 26 E) in 1911 and discontinued in 1913; the name "Velma" was for the postmaster's wife (Salley, p. 230).

— F —

Failing: see **Smith and Failing Meadow** [TULARE].

Faires [KERN]: *locality,* 5 miles north of Rosamond (lat. 34°55'50" N, long. 118°09' W). Named on Rosamond (1943) 15' quadrangle.

Fairmead [MADERA]: *village,* 11 miles northwest of Madera (lat. 37°04'35" N, long. 120°11'35" W; sec. 11, T 10 S, R 16 E). Named on Berenda (1961) 7.5' quadrangle. Postal authorities established Fairmead post office in 1913 and discontinued it in 1940 (Frickstad, p. 85).

Fairview [FRESNO]: *locality,* 9 miles east-southeast of Clovis along Atchison, Topeka and Santa Fe Railroad (lat. 36°45'50" N, long. 119°33'20" W; near NE cor. sec. 34, T 13 S, R 22 E). Named on Round Mountain (1964) 7.5' quadrangle.

Fairview [TULARE]: *locality,* 11 miles east-northeast of California Hot Springs along Kern River (lat. 35°55'30" N, long. 118°29'40" W). Named on Kernville (1956) 15' quadrangle. Called Roads End on Bakersfield (1956) 1°x 2° quadrangle. Postal authorities established Roads End post office in 1936 and discontinued it in 1955; the road north along Kern River formerly ended at the site (Salley, p. 186).

Fairy Gulch [KERN]: *canyon,* 0.25 mile long, 5 miles north of Randsburg near Teagle (lat. 35°26'25" N, long. 117°38'20" W; sec. 1, T 29 S, R 40 E). Named on Randsburg (1911) 15' quadrangle.

Fall Creek [FRESNO]: *stream,* flows 5.5 miles to North Fork Kings River 2.5 miles west of Blackcap Mountain (lat. 37°04'30" N, long. 118°50'30" W). Named on Blackcap Mountain (1953) 15' quadrangle.

Falls: see **The Falls** [MADERA].

Falls Canyon [KINGS]: *canyon,* drained by a stream that flows 1.5 miles to Avenal Canyon 9.5 miles south-southwest of Avenal (lat. 35°52'55" N, long. 120°12'25" W; sec. 35, T 23 S, R 16 E). Named on Garza Peak (1953) 7.5' quadrangle.

Falls Creek [KERN]: *stream,* flows nearly 2 miles to Jawbone Canyon 4 miles west-southwest of Cross Mountain (lat. 35°15'05" N, long. 118°11'50" W; sec. 11, T 31 S, R 35 E). Named on Cache Peak (1973) and Cross Mountain (1972) 7.5' quadrangles.

Famoso [KERN]: *village,* 5.5 miles south-southeast of McFarland along Poso Creek (lat. 35°35'50" N, long. 119°12'20" W; near E line sec. 7, T 27 S, R 26 E). Named on Famoso (1953) 7.5' quadrangle. Wheeler's (1875-1878) map shows a place called Poso at the site. Postal authorities established Spottiswood post office in 1888, changed the name to Famoso in 1895, closed it for a time in 1919, moved it 0.5 mile northwest in 1940, and discontinued it in 1946 (Salley, p. 73, 210). Officials of Southern Pacific Railroad called their station at the site Poso, for Poso Creek, when the rail line reached the place in the 1870's, but postal authorities refused to accept the name (Gudde, 1949, p. 113). California Mining Bureau's (1917c) map shows a place called Page located about 5 miles south of Famoso along the railroad.

Fancher Creek [FRESNO]: *stream,* flows 13 miles to flat lands 9 miles east of Clovis (lat. 36°48' N, long. 119°32'10" W; near W line sec. 13, T 13 S, R 22 E). Named on Humphreys Station (1965), Piedra (1965), and Round Mountain (1964) 7.5' quadrangles. Called Fancy Creek on Round Mountain (1922) 7.5' quadrangle. Grunsky (p. 71) gave the name "Fanshaw Creek" as an alternate.

Fancy Creek: see **Fancher Creek** [FRESNO].

Fane [TULARE]: *locality,* 5.25 miles north of Exeter along Atchison, Topeka and Santa Fe Railroad (lat. 36°22'15" N, long. 119°08' W; near SW cor. sec. 11, T 18 S, R 26 E). Named on Exeter (1952) 15' quadrangle.

Fanshaw Creek: see **Fancher Creek** [FRESNO].

Farewell Canyon [TULARE]: *canyon,* 2 miles long, 3 miles south-southeast of Mineral King at the head of East Fork Kaweah River (lat. 36°24'45" N, long. 118°34'30" W); the canyon heads at Farewell Gap. Named on Mineral King (1956) 15' quadrangle.

Farewell Gap [TULARE]: *pass,* nearly 4 miles south-southeast of Mineral King (lat. 36°24' N, long. 118°34'10" W); the pass is at the head of Farewell Canyon. Named on Mineral King (1956) 15' quadrangle. Miners named the feature about 1872 (Browning 1986, p. 68).

Fargo [FRESNO]: *locality,* 5.25 miles south-southeast of Sanger along Southern Pacific Railroad (lat. 36°38'10" N, long. 119°30'45"

W; sec. 7, T 15 S, R 23 E). Named on Selma (1946) 15' quadrangle. Called Fortuna on Grunsky's (1898) map.

Farmersville [TULARE]: *town,* 4 miles west of Exeter (lat. 36° 18' N, long. 119°12'25" W; around SE cor. sec. 1, T 19 S, R 25 E). Named on Exeter (1952) 15' quadrangle. Postal authorities established Farmersville post office in 1868 and moved it 0.5 mile north in 1900 (Salley, p. 73). The town incorporated in 1960. Settlers named the place about 1860 (Mitchell, A.R., p. 68).

Farmersville: see **East Farmersville** [TULARE].

Farquhar: see **Mount Farquhar**, under **Mount Brewer** [TULARE].

Fat Cow Meadow [TULARE]: *area,* 5.5 miles west-northwest of Olancha Peak (lat. 36°17'45" N, long. 118°12'30" W; sec. 5, 8, T 19 S, R 35 E). Named on Olancha (1956) 15' quadrangle.

Faull Slough [KINGS]: *stream,* flows nearly 2 miles to North Fork Kings River 7.5 miles northwest of Lemoore (lat. 36°22'25" N, long. 119°53'05" W; near SW cor. sec. 11, T 18 S, R 19 E). Named on Burrel (1954), Riverdale (1954), and Vanguard (1956) 7.5' quadrangles. Called N. Fk. Kings River on Riverdale (1927) 7.5' quadrangle, where present North Fork Kings River is called Fresno Slough.

Faust Mill [KERN]: *locality,* 6.5 miles southeast of Bodfish (lat. 35° 30'55" N, long. 118°24'30" W; at S line sec. 2, T 28 S, R 33 E). Ruins of the place are named on Lake Isabella South (1972) 7.5' quadrangle.

Fawn Meadow [FRESNO]: *area,* 10.5 miles north-northeast of Kaiser Peak (lat. 37°26'20" N, long. 119°07'20" W). Named on Kaiser Peak (1953) 15' quadrangle.

Faxon: see **Goshen** [TULARE].

Fay Creek [KERN-TULARE]: *stream,* heads in Tulare County and flows 12.5 miles to South Fork Valley 2 miles north-northwest of Weldon in Kern County (lat. 35°41'35" N, long. 118°18'05" W; sec. 2, T 26 S, R 34 E). Named on Kernville (1956) 15' quadrangle, and on Weldon (1972) 7.5' quadrangle. Called Fay Ranch Cr. on Olmsted's (1900) map.

Fayette [TULARE]: *locality,* 1.5 miles east-southeast of Lindsay along Visalia Electric Railroad (lat. 36°12'05" N, long. 119°03'50" W; sec. 8, T 20 S, R 27 E). Named on Lindsay (1951) 7.5' quadrangle.

Fay Ranch Creek: see **Fay Creek** [KERN-TULARE].

Feather Lake: see **Vermillion Lake** [FRESNO].

Fellows [KERN]: *town,* 5 miles west-northwest of Taft (lat. 35°10'40" N, long. 119°32'25" W; near N line sec. 6, T 32 S, R 23 E). Named on Fellows (1951) 7.5' quadrangle. Postal authorities established Fellows post office in 1910 (Frickstad, p. 55). The name commemorates Charles A. Fellows, a contractor for Sunset Western Railroad (Bailey, 1967, p. 8). California Mining Bureau's (1917c) map shows a place called Vernette located about 1 mile north-northwest of Fellows along the railroad, and a place called Shale situated 1 mile northwest of Vernette along the railroad. Postal authorities established Shale post office in 1912 and discontinued it in 1923 (Frickstad, p. 59). California Mining Bureau's (1909a) map shows a place called Midway located at or near present Fellows.

Femmon: see **Nipinnawasee** [MADERA].

Fence Camp Flat [KERN]: *area,* 5.25 miles north of Caliente along Walker Basin Creek (lat. 35°21'55" N, long. 118°36'55" W; at E line sec. 35, T 29 S, R 31 E); the place is 0.25 mile northwest of Fence Camp Spring. Named on Oiler Peak (1972) 7.5' quadrangle.

Fence Camp Spring [KERN]: *spring,* 5 miles north or Caliente (lat. 35°21'40" N, long. 118°36'40" W; sec. 36, T 29 S, R 31 E). Named on Oiler Peak (1972) 7.5' quadrangle.

Fence Meadow [FRESNO]: *area,* 5.5 miles north-northwest of Balch Camp (lat. 36°58'25" N, long. 119°10'20" W). Named on Patterson Mountain (1952) 15' quadrangle.

Ferguson Creek [TULARE]: *stream,* flows 8.5 miles to Sugarloaf Creek just inside Fresno County 11.5 miles north-northwest of Triple Divide Peak (lat. 36°44'25" N, long. 118°37'35" W). Named on Triple Divide Peak (1956) 15' quadrangle. S.L.N. Ellis named the creek in the early 1920's for Andrew D. Ferguson, who in 1916 was appointed field agent for California Department of Fish and Game; earlier the stream was called Bog Creek (Browning 1986, p. 69). West Fork enters from the south-southwest 2.5 miles upstream from the mouth of the main stream; it is 5.5 miles long and is named on Triple Divide Peak (1956) 15' quadrangle.

Ferguson Meadow [TULARE]: *area,* 6 miles northwest of Triple Divide Peak (lat. 36°39'15" N, long. 118°36'35" W); the place is along Ferguson Creek. Named on Triple Divide Peak (1956) 15' quadrangle. United States Board on Geographic Names (1938, p. 20) rejected the name "Long Meadow" for the feature.

Fernandez Creek [MADERA]: *stream,* flows 1.25 miles to West Fork Granite Creek nearly 4 miles southeast of Merced Peak (lat. 37°35'25" N, long. 119°21'10" W); the stream heads near Fernandez Pass. Named on Merced Peak (1953) 15' quadrangle.

Fernandez Lakes [MADERA]: *lakes,* largest 800 feet long, nearly 4 miles south-southeast of Merced Peak (lat. 37°35' N, long. 119°22'20" W); the lakes are east of Fernandez Pass. Named on Merced Peak (1953) 15' quadrangle.

Fernandez Pass [MADERA]: *pass,* 3.25 miles south of Merced Peak (lat. 37°35'15" N, long. 119°23' W); the pass is near the head of Fernandez Creek. Named on Merced Peak

(1953) 15' quadrangle. Captain H.C. Benson, acting superintendent of Yosemite National Park, named the pass for First Sergeant Joseph Fernandez, who was commended for his assistance in planting fish (United States Board on Geographic Names, 1934a, p. 9).

Fern Lake [FRESNO]: *lake,* 750 feet long, 14 miles northeast of Kaiser Peak (lat. 37°27'25" N, long. 119°02'30" W). Named on Kaiser Peak (1953) 15' quadrangle. The feature is one of the group called Margaret Lakes.

Fern Lake [MADERA]: *lake,* 750 feet long, 3 miles west-southwest of Devils Postpile (lat. 37°36'25" N, long. 119°08' W). Named on Devils Postpile (1953) 15' quadrangle.

Fiddler Gulch [KERN]: *canyon,* drained by a stream that flows 5.5 miles to Fremont Valley 4.5 miles northwest of Randsburg (lat. 35° 24'20" N, long. 117°43' W; near N line sec. 20, T 29 S, R 40 E). Named on El Paso Peaks (1967) and Johannesburg (1967) 7.5' quadrangles. The name is from the fiddlers who made music at the place in the evenings (Wynn, 1963, p. 97).

Figarden [FRESNO]: *village,* 6 miles northwest of downtown Fresno (lat. 36°49'25" N, long. 119°51'35" W; near SW cor. sec. 1, T 13 S, R 19 E). Named on Fresno North (1965) 7.5' quadrangle. Called Bullard on Bullard (1923) 7.5' quadrangle. Postal authorities established Figarden post office in 1925, moved it 0.25 mile east in 1939, discontinued it in 1944, reestablished it in 1947, discontinued it in 1951, and reestablished it in 1952 with the name "Fig Garden Village" (Salley, p. 74). The name "Figarden" was given because of a large fig orchard at the place (Stewart, p. 165). California Mining Bureau's (1917a) map shows a place called Andrews located along the railroad between Fresno and Bullard about 4 miles southeast of Figarden in present Fresno.

Fig Garden Village: see **Figarden** [FRESNO].

Fig Orchard [KERN]: *locality,* nearly 3 miles east-northeast of Caliente along Caliente Creek (lat. 35°18'30" N, long. 118°35' W; near N line sec. 19, T 30 S, R 32 E). Named on Oiler Peak (1972) 7.5' quadrangle.

Fig Spring [FRESNO]: *spring,* 7.25 miles northwest of Coalinga in Post Canyon (lat. 36°11'55" N, long. 120°28' W; sec. 8, T 20 S, R 14 E). Named on Alcalde Hills (1969) 7.5' quadrangle.

Fig Tree Spring [KERN]:

(1) *spring,* nearly 2 miles southwest of Orchard Peak (lat. 34°43'05" N, long. 120°09'20" W; sec. 29, T 25 S, R 17 E). Named on Orchard Peak (1961) 7.5' quadrangle.

(2) *spring,* 6 miles north-northwest of Caliente (lat. 35°22'10" N, long. 118°40'20" W; near N line sec. 32, T 29 S, R 31 E). Named on Bena (1972) 7.5' quadrangle.

Filly Lake [FRESNO]: *lake,* 700 feet long, 1.25 miles north of Blackcap Mountain (lat.

37°05'30" N, long. 118°47'30" W). Named on Blackcap Mountain (1953) 15' quadrangle.

Filo: see **Strathmore** [TULARE].

Finch: see **Rosy Finch Lake** [FRESNO].

Fin Dome [FRESNO]: *peak,* 9 miles south of Mount Pinchot (lat. 36° 48'50" N, long. 118°24'40" W). Altitude 11,693 feet. Named on Mount Pinchot (1953) 15' quadrangle. Bolton C. Brown named the peak in 1899 for the fancied resemblance of the feature to the fin on the back of a sea serpent (Browning 1986, p. 69).

Fine Gold [MADERA]: *locality,* 6.5 miles west-southwest of North Fork (lat. 37°11'30" N, long. 119°37' W; near E line sec. 36, T 8 S, R 21 E); the place is along Fine Gold Creek. Named on Millerton Lake (1945) 15' quadrangle. Postal authorities established Fine Gold post office in 1881 and discontinued it in 1882 (Frickstad, p. 85). When they established a new post office called Gold a little way to the east in 1894, the inhabitants of the community called Fine Gold moved there; postal authorities discontinued Gold post office in 1907 (Clough, p. 79; Frickstad, p. 85). The name "Fine Gold" is the Anglicized form of the Spanish term *Oro Fino* (Gudde, 1975, p. 115).

Fine Gold Creek [MADERA]: *stream,* flows 18 miles to Millerton Lake 5.25 miles southsoutheast of O'Neals (lat. 37°03'30" N, long. 119°38'55" W; sec. 14, T 10 S, R 21 E). Named on Bass Lake (1953) and Millerton Lake (1965) 15' quadrangles. North Fork enters from the northwest 6.5 miles northeast of O'Neals; it is 6.5 miles long and is named on Bass Lake (1953) and Millerton Lake (1965) 15' quadrangles. Clough (p. 79) used the name "Finegold Gulch" for the canyon of Fine Gold Creek.

Fine Gold Creek: see **Little Fine Gold Creek** [MADERA].

Finegold Gulch: see **Fine Gold Creek** [MADERA].

Fine Spring [KERN]: *spring,* nearly 4 miles east of Woody (lat. 35° 42'20" N, long. 118°45'55" W; near SE cor. sec. 32, T 25 S, R 30 E). Named on Woody (1965) 7.5' quadrangle.

Fingerbowl Lake [FRESNO]: *lake,* 400 feet long, 4.25 miles northeast of Dinkey Dome (lat. 37°09' N, long. 119°04'05" W; sec. 18, T 9 S, R 27 E). Named on Huntington Lake (1953) 15' quadrangle. The feature also was called Lake Elsie and Little Deep Lake (Browning 1986, p. 69).

Finger Peak [FRESNO]: *peak,* 5 miles south of Mount Goddard (lat. 37°01'50" N, long. 118°43'45" W). Altitude 12,404 feet. Named on Mount Goddard (1948) 15' quadrangle.

Finger Peak: see **Buck Rock** [TULARE].

Finger Rock [FRESNO]: *relief feature,* 14 miles north of Hume (lat. 36°59'30" N, long. 118°54'35" W). Altitude 9606 feet. Named on Tehipite Dome (1952) 15' quadrangle. The feature originally was called Chimney Rock (Forest Clingan, personal communication, 1989).

Finger Rock [TULARE]: *peak,* 6 miles south-southeast of Monache Mountain (lat. 36°07'15" N, long. 118°10' W; near S line sec. 2, T 21 S, R 35 E). Altitude 9145 feet. Named on Monache Mountain (1956) 15' quadrangle.

Finger Rock: see **Buck Rock** [TULARE].

Fir Camp Saddle [TULARE]: *pass,* nearly 6 miles southeast of California Hot Springs (lat. 35°49'45" N, long. 118°35'20" W; sec. 24, T 24 S, R 31 E). Named on California Hot Springs (1958) 15' quadrangle.

Firebaugh [FRESNO]: *town,* 38 miles west of Fresno on the west side of San Joaquin River (lat. 36°51'30" N, long. 120°27'15" W; in and near sec. 28, 29, T 12 S, R 14 E). Named on Firebaugh (1956) 7.5' quadrangle. A.D. Fierbaugh established a trading post and ferry across San Joaquin River in 1854; the misspelled name "Firebaugh's Ferry" was used as early as 1856 (Gudde, 1949, p. 116). Postal authorities established Firebaugh's Ferry post office in 1860 and discontinued it in 1862; they established Firebaugh post office in 1865 (Frickstad, p. 33). The town incorporated in 1914. The place was a station on Butterfield Overland stage line (Ormsby, p. 120-121).

Firebaugh: see **Exeter** [TULARE].

Firebaugh's Ferry: see **Firebaugh** [FRESNO].

First Dinkey Lake [FRESNO]: *lake,* 1500 feet long, 5 miles northeast of Dinkey Dome (lat. 37°09'50" N, long. 119°04' W; sec. 7, T 9 S, R 27 E); the feature is along upper reaches of Dinkey Creek 1 mile downstream from Second Dinkey Lake. Named on Huntington Lake (1953) 15' quadrangle. Called Dinkey Lake on Kaiser (1904) 30' quadrangle.

First Recess [FRESNO]: *canyon,* drained by a stream that flows 2.5 miles to Mono Creek 5.25 miles west-northwest of Mount Abbot (lat. 37°25'10" N, long. 118°52'10" W); the feature is the first major canyon east of Lake Thomas A. Edison on the south side of Mono Creek. Named on Mount Abbot (1953) 15' quadrangle. Theodore S. Solomons discovered and named the canyon in 1894 (Farquhar, 1925, p. 127).

First Recess Lakes [FRESNO]: *lakes,* two, each about 500 feet long, 4.25 miles west of Mount Abbot (lat. 37°23'40" N, long. 118°51'30" W); the lakes are near the head of First Recess. Named on Mount Abbot (1953) 15' quadrangle.

Fish Camp [FRESNO]: *locality,* nearly 5 miles northwest of Mount Abbot along Mono Creek (lat. 37°25'35" N, long. 118°51'15" W). Named on Mount Abbot (1953) 15' quadrangle.

Fish Canyon: see **Pescado Creek** [KERN].

Fish Creek [FRESNO]:
(1) *stream,* flows 16 miles to Madera County 3.25 miles west-northwest of Double Peak (lat. 37°31'50" N, long. 119°05'25" W). Named on Devils Postpile (1953), Mount Abbot (1953), and Mount Morrison (1953) 15' quadrangles.
(2) *stream,* flows nearly 6 miles to Kings River 2 miles southwest of Piedra (lat. 36°47'35" N, long. 119°24'40" W; near NE cor. sec. 24, T 13 S, R 23 E). Named on Piedra (1965) 7.5' quadrangle.

Fish Creek [MADERA]:
(1) *stream,* flows 5 miles to San Joaquin River 8 miles southeast of Shuteye Peak (lat. 37°15'45" N, long. 119°19'30" W; sec. 2, T 8 S, R 24 E). Named on Shuteye Peak (1953) 15' quadrangle.
(2) *stream,* flows 4.5 miles to Kerckhoff Lake 5.25 miles south of the town of North Fork (lat. 37°09'05" N, long. 119°31'10" W; sec. 13, T 9 S, R 22 E). Named on North Fork (1965) 7.5' quadrangle.
(3) *stream,* heads in Fresno County and flows 2.5 miles in Madera County to Middle Fork San Joaquin River 6 miles south-southwest of Devils Postpile (lat. 37°32'40" N, long. 119°07'55" W). Named on Devils Postpile (1953) 15' quadrangle.

Fish Creek [TULARE]:
(1) *stream,* flows 5.5 miles to Little Kern River 4.25 miles west-southwest of Hockett Peak (lat. 36°12'15" N, long. 118°27'30" W). Named on Camp Nelson (1956) and Hockett Peak (1956) 15' quadrangles.
(2) *stream,* flows 19 miles to South Fork Kern River 13 miles north-northwest of Lamont Peak (lat. 35°57'10" N, long. 118°09'50" W; near W line sec. 1, T 23 S, R 35 E). Named on Hockett Peak (1956), Lamont Peak (1956), and Monache Mountain (1956) 15' quadrangles.

Fish Creek Campground [MADERA]: *locality,* 7.5 miles southeast of Shuteye Peak (lat. 37°15'35" N, long. 119°21'10" W; sec. 4, T 8 S, R 24 E); the place is along Fish Creek (1). Named on Shuteye Peak (1953) 15' quadrangle.

Fish Creek Hot Springs [FRESNO]: *spring,* 1.5 miles north-northeast of Double Peak along Sharktooth Creek (lat. 37°31'55" N, long. 119°01'30" W); the spring is 1 mile upstream from Fish Creek (1). Named on Devils Postpile (1953) 15' quadrangle. United States Board on Geographic Names (1984b, p. 2) approved the name "Iva Bell Hot Springs" for the feature to commemorate a woman who was born at the site.

Fish Creek Meadow [TULARE]: *area,* 11 miles south of Monache Mountain (lat. 36°03' N, long. 118°12' W; sec. 33, T 21 S, R 35 E); the place is along Fish Creek (2). Named on Monache Mountain (1956) 15' quadrangle. United States Board on Geographic Names (1988a, p. 2) approved the name "Rodeo Flat" for the feature.

Fish Creek Mountain [MADERA]: *ridge,* east-trending, 1.5 miles long, 5.5 miles southwest of the town of North Fork (lat. 37°09'50" N, long. 119°34'25" W); the ridge is south of the headwaters of Fish Creek (2). Named on North Fork (1965) 7.5' quadrangle.

Fisher Flat [TULARE]: *area,* 3.5 miles north of Cliff Peak (lat. 36° 36'35" N, long. 119°10'05" W; sec. 20, T 15 S, R 26 E). Named on Stokes Mountain (1966) 7.5' quadrangle.

Fisher Flat: see **Mankins Flat** [TULARE] (1).

Fish Slough [FRESNO]: *water feature,* extends for 2 miles from Fresno Slough to James Bypass 2 miles north of Helm (lat. 36°33'45" N, long. 120°05'30" W). Named on Helm (1963) 7.5' quadrangle.

Fish Valley [FRESNO]: *canyon,* 3 miles long, 2 miles northwest of Double Peak (lat. 37°32' N, long. 119°03'45" W); the canyon is along Fish Creek (1). Named on Devils Postpile (1953) 15' quadrangle.

Fiske: see **Mount Fiske** [FRESNO].

Fiss Hill [KERN]: *hill,* 4 miles northwest of Rosamond (lat. 34° 54' N, long. 118°13' W; near W line sec. 1, T 9 N, R 13 W). Named on Rosamond (1956) 15' quadrangle.

Five Dog Creek [KERN]: *stream,* flows 25 miles to Rag Gulch 12.5 miles east of Delano (lat. 35°45'50" N, long. 119°01'45" W; near SE cor. sec. 11, T 25 S, R 27 E). Named on Deepwell Ranch (1952), Knob Hill (1965), Pine Mountain (1965), Richgrove (1952), Sand Canyon (1965), and Woody (1965) 7.5' quadrangles. Called Dead Ox Creek on Woody (1935) 15' quadrangle, but United States Board on Geographic Names (1966b, p. 4) rejected this name for the stream. Boyd (p. 159) noted that the name "Five Dogs Gulch" is from five dogs at a mining camp of the 1860's.

Five Dogs: see **Granite Station** [KERN].

Five Dogs Gulch: see **Five Dog Creek** [KERN].

Five Fingers [KERN]: *relief features,* 6.25 miles west-northwest of Inyokern (lat. 35°41'15" N, long. 117°54'25" W; sec. 8, T 26 S, R 38 E). Named on Owens Peak (1972) 7.5' quadrangle.

Five Lakes: see **Big Five Lakes** [TULARE]; **Little Five Lakes** [TULARE].

Five Points [FRESNO]: *settlement,* 25 miles northeast of Coalinga (lat. 35°25'45" N, long. 120°06'05" W; near SW cor. sec. 23, T 17 S, R 17 E); five roads meet at the place. Named on Five Points (1956) 7.5' quadrangle. Postal authorities established Five Points post office in 1944 (Frickstad, p 33).

Five Points [KERN]: *locality,* 3.5 miles east of Cummings Mountain (lat. 35°03'05" N, long. 118°30'40" W; at N line sec. 18, T 11 N, R 15 W); five roads meet at the site. Named on Cummings Mountain (1966) 7.5' quadrangle.

Five Springs [FRESNO]: *spring,* 4 miles east-southeast of Tivy Mountain (lat. 36°46'10" N, long. 119°17'35" W; sec. 30, T 13 S, R 25 E).

Named on Pine Flat Dam (1965) 7.5' quadrangle.

Flag Peak [FRESNO]: *peak,* 2.5 miles north-northeast of Coalinga Mineral Springs on Juniper Ridge (lat. 36°10'40" N, long. 120°31'50" W; near W line sec. 24, T 20 S, R 13 E). Altitude 3966 feet. Named on Sherman Peak (1969) 7.5' quadrangle. Called Sherman Peak on Priest Valley (1915) 30' quadrangle.

Flatiron [TULARE]: *relief feature,* 4 miles south-southwest of Hockett Peak between Kern River and Little Kern River (lat. 36° 10' N, long. 118°25' W). Named on Hockett Peak (1956) 15' quadrangle.

Flat Lake [MADERA]: *lake,* 650 feet long, 4.5 miles south-southeast of Merced Peak (lat. 37°34'30" N, long. 119°21'40" W). Named on Merced Peak (1953) 15' quadrangle.

Flat Note Lake [FRESNO]: *lake,* 700 feet long, 7.5 miles south-southwest of Mount Abbot (lat. 37°17'40" N, long. 118°51'10" W); less than 1 mile north of Sharp Note Lake. Named on Mount Abbot (1953) 15' quadrangle.

Flattop [KINGS]: *peak,* 5.5 miles south-southwest of Avenal on Reef Ridge (lat. 35°55'40" N, long. 120°09'15" W; sec. 17, T 23 S, R 17 E). Altitude 2205 feet. Named on Garza Peak (1953) 7.5' quadrangle.

Fleming Creek [FRESNO]: *stream,* flows 7.5 miles to North Fork Kings River 4.25 miles west-northwest of Blackcap Mountain (lat. 37°05'10" N, long. 118°52'05" W; sec. 1, T 10 S, R 28 E). Named on Blackcap Mountain (1953) 15' quadrangle.

Fleming Lake [FRESNO]: *lake,* 700 feet long, 6 miles north-northwest of Blackcap Mountain (lat. 37°08'45" N, long. 118°51' W); the lake is along Fleming Creek 1 mile southsoutheast of Fleming Mountain. Named on Blackcap Mountain (1953) 15' quadrangle.

Fleming Mountain [FRESNO]: *peak,* 7 miles north-northwest of Blackcap Mountain (lat. 37°09'30" N, long. 118°51'25" W); the peak is west of Fleming Creek. Altitude 10,796 feet. Named on Blackcap Mountain (1953) 15' quadrangle.

Fleta [KERN]: *locality,* 3.5 miles south-southeast of Mojave along Southern Pacific Railroad (lat. 35°00'15" N, long. 118°09'25" W; sec. 33, T 11 N, R 12 W). Named on Mojave (1973) and Soledad Mountain (1973) 7.5' quadrangles.

Florence: see **Mount Florence** [MADERA].

Florence Creek [MADERA]: *stream,* heads in Madera County and flows 6 miles to Lewis Creek 7 miles south-southeast of Cathedral Peak in Mariposa County (lat. 37°45'20" N, long. 119°21'15" W). Named on Merced Peak (1953) and Tuolumne Meadows (1956) 15' quadrangles. Browning (1986, p. 72) associated the name with Florence Hutchings, for whom Mount Florence was named.

Florence Lake [FRESNO]: *lake,* behind a dam

on South Fork San Joaquin River 13 miles southwest of Mount Abbot (lat. 37°16'20" N, long. 118°58' W). Named on Blackcap Mountain (1953) and Mount Abbot (1953) 15' quadrangles. Mount Goddard (1912) 30' quadrangle has the name "Lake Florence" for a natural lake in the upper part of the basin of present Florence Lake; Walter H. Starr and his companions camped by this lake in 1896 and named it for Walter's sister (Farquhar, 1923, p. 395-396). United States Board on Geographic Names (1965b, p. 13) rejected the name "Lake Florence" for the present lake.

Florence Lake [MADERA]: *lake,* 850 feet long, 8 miles north-northeast of Merced Peak (lat. 37°45' N, long. 119°20'35" W); the lake is along Florence Creek. Named on Merced Peak (1953) and Tuolumne Meadows (1956) 15' quadrangles. Browning (1986, p. 72) associated the name with Florence Hutchings, for whom Mount Florence was named.

Florence Peak [TULARE]: *peak,* 4 miles southeast of Mineral King on Great Western Divide (lat. 36°24'20" N, long. 118°33' W). Altitude 12,432 feet. Named on Mineral King (1956) 15' quadrangle. United States Board on Geographic Names (1933a, p. 305) once approved the name "Mount Florence" for the feature, and rejected the name "Mount Needham."

Floyd [FRESNO]: *locality,* 11 miles west of downtown Fresno along Southern Pacific Railroad (lat. 36°44'05" N, long. 119°59'30" W; at N line sec. 10, T 14 S, R 18 E). Named on Kearney Park (1923) 7.5' quadrangle.

Fluhr [KERN]: *locality,* 2 miles north-northwest of present Edwards along Atchison, Topeka and Santa Fe Railroad (lat. 34°56'45" N, long. 117°57' W; at W line sec. 21, T 10 N, R 10 W). Named on Rogers Lake (1942) 15' quadrangle. The name commemorates C.G. Fluhr, a superintendent of the railroad (Hanna, p. 108).

Flume Peak [FRESNO]: *peak,* 2.5 miles north-northwest of Shaver Lake Heights (present town of Shaver Lake) (lat. 37°08'40" N, long. 119°20' W; near E line sec. 15, T 9 S, R 24 E). Altitude 5979 feet. Named on Shaver Lake (1953) 15' quadrangle. Kaiser (1904) 30' quadrangle shows a flume belonging to Fresno Flume and Irrigation Co. west of the peak.

Fly Creek [TULARE]: *stream,* flows 2 miles to Bear Creek (1) 6 miles southeast of Auckland (lat. 36°31'35" N, long. 119°01'35" W; sec. 22, T 16 S, R 27 E). Named on Auckland (1966) 7.5' quadrangle.

Flying Dutchman Creek [KERN]: *stream,* flows nearly 3 miles to Havilah Canyon 15 miles north-northeast of Caliente (lat. 35°29'10" N, long. 118°31'30" W; at N line sec. 22, T 28 S, R 32 E). Named on Breckenridge Mountain (1972) 7.5' quadrangle.

Flynn Canyon [TULARE]: *canyon,* flows 3 miles to Tobias Creek 10 miles east-northeast of California Hot Springs (lat. 35°55'05" N, long. 118°30' W; near W line sec. 23, T 23 S, R 32 E). Named on California Hot Springs (1958) 15' quadrangle.

Foerster Creek [MADERA]: *stream,* flows 2.5 miles to Triple Peak Fork 4.5 miles northeast of Merced Peak (lat. 37°41' N, long. 119° 20'10" W); the stream heads near Foerster Peak. Named on Merced Peak (1953) 15' quadrangle.

Foerster Peak [MADERA]: *peak,* 7 miles northeast of Merced Peak (lat. 37°41'25" N, long. 119°17'20" W). Altitude 12,058 feet. Named on Merced Peak (1953) 15' quadrangle. Lieutenant N.F. McClure named the peak in 1895 for Sergeant Lewis Foerster (United States Board on Geographic Names, 1934a, p. 9). United States Board on Geographic Names (1985b, p. 1) approved the name "Mount Ansel Adams" for a peak, altitude 11,760 feet, located 0.8 mile northeast of Foerster Peak (lat. 37°41'52" N, long. 119°16'49" W); the name honors Ansel Easton Adams, photographer and conservationist.

Foolish Lake [FRESNO]: *lake,* 400 feet long, 8.5 miles southwest of Mount Abbot (lat. 37°18'15" N, long. 118°54' W). Named on Mount Abbot (1953) 15' quadrangle. Employees of California Department of Fish and Game gave the name to the lake in 1948 because they thought that it would be foolish for anyone to revisit the place (Browning 1986, p. 72).

Footman Canyon [FRESNO]: *canyon,* drained by a stream that flows 1.25 miles to Boulder Creek (1) 6.5 miles east of Hume (lat. 36°46'45" N, long. 118°46'45" W). Named on Tehipite Dome (1952) 15' quadrangle.

Footman Mountain: see **Footman Ridge** [MADERA].

Ford City [KERN]: *town,* 1 mile north of downtown Taft (lat. 35°09'20" N, long. 119°27'30" W; sec. 12, T 32 S, R 23 E). Named on Taft (1950) 7.5' quadrangle. The name is from the abundance of Model-T Ford cars at the place when it was an oil-boom tent city (Hanna, p. 108).

Ford's Camp: see **Mineral King** [TULARE].

Forester Pass [TULARE]: *pass,* 9 miles northnorthwest of Mount Whitney on Kings-Kern Divide (lat. 36°41'40" N, long. 118°22'15" W). Named on Mount Whitney (1956) 15' quadrangle. Frank Cunningham, supervisor of Sequoia National Forest, named the pass in 1929 for the foresters—including himself—who discovered it (Browning 1986, p. 73).

Forgotten Canyon [TULARE]: *canyon,* drained by a stream that flows 2.5 miles to Rock Creek 13 miles north-northwest of Kern Peak (lat. 36°29'30" N, long. 118°20'30" W). Named on Kern Peak (1956) 15' quadrangle.

Forked Meadow [MADERA]: *area,* 5.25 miles

northeast of Shuteye Peak (lat. 37°23'35" N, long. 119°20'45" W; sec. 21, T 6 S, R 24 E). Named on Shuteye Peak (1953) 15' quadrangle.

Forked Meadow Creek [FRESNO]: *stream,* flows 1 mile to Dinkey Creek (1) 4 miles south-southwest of Dinkey Dome (lat. 37°03'30" N, long. 119°09'30" W; sec. 17, T 10 S, R 26 E). Named on Huntington Lake (1953) 15' quadrangle.

Forks: see **The Forks** [MADERA].

Forks Campground [MADERA]: *locality,* 5 miles southeast of Yosemite Forks on the west side of Bass Lake (1) (lat. 37°18'45" N, long. 119°34'10" W; near N line sec. 21, T 7 S, R 22 E); the place is near The Forks. Named on Bass Lake (1953) 15' quadrangle.

Fort Camp: see **Forthcamp** [FRESNO].

Forthcamp [FRESNO]: *locality,* 4.25 miles south-southeast of Clovis along Atchison, Topeka and Santa Fe Railroad (lat. 36°45'50" N, long. 119°40'20" W; at N line sec. 34, T 13 S, R 21 E). Named on Clovis (1946) 15' quadrangle. Called Fort Camp on Clovis (1922) 7.5' quadrangle, which shows the place along Fresno Interurban Railroad.

Fort Hill: see **Keysville** [KERN].

Fort Keysville: see **Keysville** [KERN].

Fort Miller: see **Old Fort Miller** [FRESNO]; **Old Millerton** [FRESNO].

Fort Tejon: see **Old Fort Tejon** [KERN].

Fortuna: see **Fargo** [FRESNO].

Fort Washington: see **Old Fort Miller** [FRESNO].

Foster Ridge [FRESNO]: *ridge,* northeast-trending, 2.5 miles long, 3 miles north-northwest of Dinkey Dome (lat. 37°09'25" N, long. 119°08'30" W). Named on Huntington Lake (1953) 15' quadrangle.

Fountain Spring: see **Fountain Springs** [TULARE].

Fountain Springs [TULARE]: *locality,* 7 miles east of Ducor (lat. 35°53'25" N, long. 118°54'50" W; near N line sec. 35, T 23 S, R 28 E). Named on Fountain Springs (1965) 7.5' quadrangle. Postal authorities established Fountain Springs post office in 1875, discontinued it for a time in 1878, discontinued it in 1879, reestablished it in 1887, and discontinued it in 1888 (Frickstad, p. 210). A spring at the place called Fountain Spring was long known and used (Waring, p. 336). Officials of Butterfield Overland stage line had one of their stations built at the site in 1858 (Hanna, p. 110).

Fountain Springs Gulch [TULARE]: *canyon,* drained by a stream that flows 22 miles to Deer Creek (2) 6 miles north of Ducor (lat. 35°58'55" N, long. 119°02'35" W; sec. 27, T 22 S, R 27 E); the place called Fountain Springs is in the canyon. Named on Fountain Springs (1965), Gibbon Peak (1965), and Quincy School (1965) 7.5' quadrangles.

Four Canyons [TULARE]: *relief feature,* 5.5

miles north-northwest of Olancha Peak (lat. 36°20'30" N, long. 118°09'20" W). Named on Olancha (1956) 15' quadrangle. United States Board on Geographic Names (1989a, p. 4) rejected the name "Four Canyons Meadow" for the feature.

Four Canyons Meadow: see **Four Canyons** [TULARE].

Four Corners [MADERA]: *locality,* 15 miles south-southeast of Raymond (lat. 37°00'35" N, long. 119°47'35" W; at S line sec. 33, T 10 S, R 20 E). Named on Little Table Mountain (1962) 7.5' quadrangle.

Four Creek Country: see **Kaweah River** [TULARE].

Four Forks Creek [FRESNO]: *stream,* flows 5.5 miles to South Fork San Joaquin River 8 miles north-northeast of Mount Tom (lat. 37° 24'15" N, long. 119°07'45" W). Named on Kaiser Peak (1953) 15' quadrangle.

Four Gables [FRESNO]: *peak,* nearly 3 miles north-northwest of Mount Humphreys on Fresno-Inyo county line (lat. 37°18'25" N, long. 118°41'35" W; near SW cor. sec. 28, T 7 S, R 30 E). Named on Mount Tom (1949) 15' quadrangle.

Four Springs Gulch [KERN]: *canyon,* drained by a stream that flows nearly 4 miles to Dead Ox Creek 3.5 miles southwest of Woody (lat. 35°40' N, long. 118°52'45" W; sec. 17, T 26 S, R 29 E). Named on Sand Canyon (1965) and Woody (1965) 7.5' quadrangles.

Fourth Home Extension Colony: see **Wasco** [KERN].

Fourth Recess [FRESNO]: *canyon,* drained by a stream that flows 3.5 miles to Golden Creek 4.25 miles north of Mount Abbot (lat. 37°26'55" N, long. 118°47'25" W); the feature is the fourth large canyon east of Lake Thomas A. Edison on the south side of Mono Creek. Named on Mount Abbot (1953) 15' quadrangle. Theodore S. Solomons discovered and named the feature in 1894 (Farquhar, 1925, p. 127).

Fourth Recess Lake [FRESNO]: *lake,* 3300 feet long, 3.5 miles north of Mount Abbot (lat. 37°26'15" N, long. 118°47'05" W); the lake is in Fourth Recess. Named on Mount Abbot (1953) 15' quadrangle.

Fowler [FRESNO]: *town,* 11 miles southeast of downtown Fresno (lat. 36°37'50" N, long. 119°40'35" W; in and near sec. 15, T 15 S, R 21 E). Named on Conejo (1963) and Malaga (1964) 7.5' quadrangles. Postal authorities established Fowler post office in 1882 (Frickstad, p. 33), and the town incorporated in 1908. The name commemorates Thomas Fowler, cattle rancher and California state senator, who shipped cattle from a corral at the site (Hanna, p. 110).

Fowler Mountain [MADERA]: *ridge,* south-southeast-trending, 1 mile long, 6 miles south of the town of North Fork (lat. 37°08'30" N, long. 119°31'40" W; on S line sec. 13, T 9 S,

R 22 E). Named on North Fork (1965) 7.5' quadrangle.

Fox Canyon [FRESNO]: *canyon,* drained by a stream that flows nearly 2 miles to Kings River 6 miles east-southeast of Balch Camp (lat. 36°51'35" N, long. 119°00'55" W; sec. 27, T 12 S, R 27 E). Named on Patterson Mountain (1952) 15' quadrangle.

Fox Canyon [KERN]: *canyon,* drained by a stream that flows 4 miles to Indian Creek 2 miles west-northwest of Emerald Mountain (lat. 35°15'50" N, long. 118°19' W; sec. 3, T 31 S, R 34 E). Named on Emerald Mountain (1972) and Tehachapi NE (1966) 7.5' quadrangles.

Fox Creek: see **Hotel Creek** [FRESNO]; **Sheep Creek** [FRESNO].

Fox Flat [TULARE]: *area,* 6 miles west-northwest of Yucca Mountain (lat. 36°35'15" N, long. 118°58'15" W; sec. 30, T 15 S, R 28 E). Named on Giant Forest (1956) 15' quadrangle.

Fox Meadow [TULARE]: *area,* 1.5 miles northwest of Shell Mountain (lat. 36°42'30" N, long. 118°49' W; sec. 15, T 14 S, R 29 E). Named on Giant Forest (1956) 15' quadrangle. The name commemorates John Fox, a packer, hunter, and guide in the Kings River neighborhood (Hanna, p. 110).

Fox Spring [FRESNO]: *spring,* 10 miles southsoutheast of Balch Camp (lat. 36°46'15" N, long. 119°04'45" W; at N line sec. 30, T 13 S, R 27 E). Named on Patterson Mountain (1952) 15' quadrangle.

Fram [KERN]: *locality,* 3 miles north-northwest of Mojave along Southern Pacific Railroad (lat. 35°05'50" N, long. 118°11'10" W; near SE cor. sec. 35, T 32 S, R 35 E). Named on Mojave (1915) 30' quadrangle. California Mining Bureau's (1917c) map shows a place called Reservoir located about 1 mile southsoutheast of Fram along the railroad.

Franciscan Creek [KERN]: *stream,* heads in San Luis Obispo County and flows 6 miles to Antelope Valley (1) 6 miles south-southeast of Orchard Peak (lat. 35°39'25" N, long. 120°05'30" W; sec. 24, T 26 S, R 17 E). Named on Holland Canyon (1961), Packwood Creek (1961), and Sawtooth Ridge (1961) 7.5' quadrangles. Arnold and Johnson (p. 20) proposed the name because rocks of the Franciscan Formation crop out along the stream.

Francis Flat [TULARE]: *area,* 3.5 miles southsoutheast of Auckland (lat. 36°32'15" N, long. 119°05'10" W; near W line sec. 18, T 16 S, R 27 E). Named on Auckland (1966) 7.5' quadrangle.

Frank Canyon [FRESNO]: *canyon,* drained by a stream that flows nearly 1 mile to Salt Creek (2) 7 miles south-southwest of Coalinga (lat. 36°03'05" N, long. 120°25' W; near N line sec. 1, T 22 S, R 14 E). Named on Curry Mountain (1969) 7.5' quadrangle.

Franklin Canyon [TULARE]: *canyon,* 2 miles long, 12.5 miles south of Kaweah (lat.

36°17'30" N, long. 118°57'30" W). Named on Kaweah (1957) 15' quadrangle.

Franklin Creek [TULARE]: *stream,* flows 2.25 miles to East Fork Kaweah River 2 miles south-southeast of Mineral King (lat. 36°25'40" N, long. 118°35' W); the stream heads at Franklin Lakes. Named on Mineral King (1956) 15' quadrangle. United States Board on Geographic Names (1968b, p. 7) rejected the name "East Fork Kaweah River" for the stream.

Franklin Lake [FRESNO]: *lake,* 1400 feet long, 3 miles northwest of Red Slate Mountain at the head of Purple Creek (lat. 37°32' N, long. 118°54'45" W). Named on Mount Morrison (1953) 15' quadrangle.

Franklin Lakes [TULARE]: *lakes,* largest 2200 feet long, 3.25 miles southeast of Mineral King (lat. 36°25' N, long. 118°33'25" W); the lakes are at the head of Franklin Creek. Named on Mineral King (1956) 15' quadrangle. The name is from Lady Franklin mine (United States Board on Geographic Names, 1933a, p. 310), which in turn was named for the widow of Sir John Franklin, the lost English Arctic explorer (Adler, p. 24). Tucker (p. 951) noted that Lady Franklin mine is 1.5 miles southeast of Mineral King on the ridge south of Lady Franklin Cañon. Present Franklin Lakes originally were called Silver Lakes (Browning 1986, p. 74).

Franklin Pass [TULARE]: *pass,* 4 miles southeast of Mineral King on Great Western Divide (lat. 36°24'50" N, long. 118°32'35" W); the pass is near the head of Franklin Creek. Named on Mineral King (1956) 15' quadrangle.

Frazer Spring [KERN]: *spring,* 5 miles westnorthwest of McKittrick (lat. 35°20'45" N, long. 119°41'40" W; at W line sec. 2, T 30 S, R 21 E). Named on Reward (1951) 7.5' quadrangle. Called Frazers Spring on Arnold and Johnson's (1910) map.

Frazer Valley [KERN]: *valley,* 5 miles westnorthwest of McKittrick (lat. 35°20'25" N, long. 119°42' W; in and near sec. 3, T 30 S, R 21 E); Frazer Spring is in the valley. Named on Reward (1951) 7.5' quadrangle. Arnold and Johnson (p. 20) proposed the name.

Frazier [TULARE]: *locality,* 7 miles west-southwest of Springville (lat. 36°06'45" N, long. 118°56'45" W; near W line sec. 10, T 21 S, R 28 E); the place is in Frazier Valley. Named on Kaweah (1909) 30' quadrangle. Postal authorities established Frazier post office in 1882 and discontinued it in 1904 (Frickstad, p. 210). They established Rosedale post office 7.5 miles east of Frazier (NE quarter of sec. 15, T 21 S, R 29 E) in 1883 and discontinued it the same year (Salley, p. 189).

Frazier Creek [TULARE]: *stream,* flows 5.5 miles to lowlands 5.25 miles north-northeast of Porterville (lat. 36°08'35" N, long. 118°59'30" W; near E line sec. 36, T 20 S, R 27 E); the stream drains Frazier Valley. Named on Frazier Valley (1957) and Lindsay (1951) 7.5' quadrangles.

Frazier Park [KERN]: *town,* 5 miles west of Lebec in Cuddy Canyon (lat. 34°49'20" N, long. 118°57' W); the town is 3.5 miles north-northeast of Frazier Mountain, which is in Ventura County. Named on Frazier Mountain (1958) 7.5' quadrangle. Postal authorities established Frazier Park post office in 1927 (Frickstad, p. 55). Harry McBain founded the community in 1925 and named it in 1926 for nearby Frazier Mountain (Bailey, 1967, p. 9).

Frazier Valley [TULARE]: *valley,* 5 miles northeast of Porterville (lat. 36°08' N, long. 118°58' W); the valley is along Frazier Creek. Named on Frazier Valley (1957) and Lindsay (1951) 7.5' quadrangles.

Freckles Meadow [TULARE]: *area,* 8 miles north-northwest of Olancha Peak (lat. 36°22' N, long. 118°10'30" W). Named on Olancha (1956) 15' quadrangle.

Freeman [KERN]: *locality,* 7 miles west-southwest of Inyokern (lat. 35°36' N, long. 117°55'30" W); the place is about 1.25 miles west of present Freeman Junction at the mouth of Freeman Canyon. Named on Searles Lake (1915) 1° quadrangle. Postal authorities established Freeman post office in 1889 and discontinued it in 1909 (Frickstad, p. 55). Freeman S. Raymond started a stage station at a site in 1874 (Bailey, 1967, p. 9). The place first was known as Coyote Holes because water was obtained from shallow pits excavated where coyotes had dug a short distance to water (Waring, p. 340). It also was known as Coyote Springs (Latta, 1976, p. 254).

Freeman Canyon [KERN]: *canyon,* drained by a stream that heads at Walker Pass and flows 7.25 miles to Indian Wells Valley 7 miles west-southwest of Inyokern (lat. 35°36' N, long. 117°55'30" W; sec. 7, T 27 S, R 38 E). Named on Freeman Junction (1972), Owens Peak (1972), and Walker Pass (1972) 7.5' quadrangles.

Freeman Creek [KERN]: *stream,* flows 3 miles to Greenhorn Creek 4.25 miles west of Miracle Hot Springs (lat. 35°35'20" N, long. 118°36'25" W). Named on Democrat Hot Springs (1972) and Miracle Hot Springs (1972) 7.5' quadrangles.

Freeman Creek [TULARE]: *stream,* flows 7.25 miles to Kern River 9 miles south-southwest of Hockett Peak (lat. 36°06'30" N, long. 118°27'15" W). Named on Camp Nelson (1956) and Hockett Peak (1956) 15' quadrangles. Tucker (p. 944) used the form "Freeman's Creek" for the name.

Freeman Gulch [KERN]: *gully,* extends for 4.5 miles from the mouth of Freeman Canyon to Little Dixie Wash 7.5 miles south-southwest of Inyokern (lat. 35°33' N, long. 117°52'30" W; at S line sec. 27, T 27 S, R 38 E). Named on Freeman Junction (1972) 7.5' quadrangle.

Freeman Junction [KERN]: *locality,* 6 miles west-southwest of Inyo Kern (lat. 35°36'05" N, long. 117°45'10" W; near E line sec. 8, T 27 S, R 38 E); the place is near the mouth of Freeman Canyon. Named on Freeman Junction (1972) 7.5' quadrangle.

Freeman Wash Well [KERN]: *well,* 8 miles south-southwest of Inyokern (lat. 35°33' N, long. 117°52'55" W; at SW cor. sec. 27, T 27 S, R 38 E); the well is along Freeman Gulch. Named on Freeman Junction (1972) 7.5' quadrangle.

Freeman Well [KERN]: *well,* 1 mile southeast of Walker Pass (lat. 35°39'05" N, long. 118°00'45" W; sec. 21, T 26 S, R 37 E); the well is in Freeman Canyon. Named on Walker Pass (1972) 7.5' quadrangle.

Freezeout Meadow [TULARE]: *area,* 5.5 miles south-southeast of Camp Nelson (lat. 36°04' N, long. 118°34'40" W; sec. 36, T 21 S, R 31 E). Named on Camp Nelson (1956) 15' quadrangle.

Freitas Spring [FRESNO]: *spring,* 3.25 miles northeast of Coalinga Mineral Springs (lat. 36°10'55" N, long. 120°31'10" W; near N line sec. 24, T 20 S, R 13 E). Named on Sherman Peak (1969) 7.5' quadrangle.

Frémont's Pass: see **Oak Creek Pass** [KERN].

Fremont Valley [KERN]: *area,* east of the south end of the Sierra Nevada and southeast of El Paso Mountains. Named on Bakersfield (1962, revised 1971) and Trona (1957) 1°x 2° quadrangles. Fairbanks (1894a, p. 456) called the area Desert Springs Valley.

French Canyon [FRESNO]: *canyon,* drained by a stream that flows 5 miles to Piute Creek 8.5 miles south of Mount Abbot (lat. 37°15'55" N, long. 118°46'40" W); the canyon heads at French Lake. Named on Mount Abbot (1953) and Mount Tom (1949) 15' quadrangles.

French Gulch [KERN]:

(1) *canyon,* drained by a stream that flows 7 miles to Isabella Lake 4 miles south-south-west of Wofford Heights (lat. 35°39'30" N, long. 118°29'05" W; near NW cor. sec. 19, T 26 S, R 33 E). Named on Alta Sierra (1972) and Lake Isabella North (1972) 7.5' quadrangles.

(2) *canyon,* drained by a stream that flows 4.25 miles to Kelso Creek less than 1 mile north-northeast of Claraville (lat. 35°27'05" N, long. 118°19'15" W; at S line sec. 33, T 28 S, R 34 E); French Meadow is in the canyon. Named on Claraville (1972) 7.5' quadrangle. United States Board on Geographic Names (1975b, p. 9) gave the name "French Meadow Gulch" as a variant.

French Gulch: see **French Ranch Gulch** [KERN].

French Gulch [MADERA]: *canyon,* drained by a stream that flows 1.5 miles to Fresno River 7.25 miles west-southwest of Yosemite Forks (lat. 37°19' N, long. 119°44'45" W; near S line sec. 14, T 7 S, R 20 E). Named on Bass Lake (1953) 15' quadrangle.

French Joe Meadow [TULARE]: *area,* 7 miles northeast of California Hot Springs (lat. 35°56'30" N, long. 118°34'30" W; near SE cor. sec. 12, T 23 S, R 31 E). Named on California Hot Springs (1958) 15' quadrangle.

French Lake [FRESNO]: *lake,* 2800 feet long, 4 miles northwest of Mount Humphreys (lat. 37°18'50" N, long. 118°43' W; sec. 30, T 7 S, R 30 E); the lake is at the head of French Canyon. Named on Mount Tom (1949) 15' quadrangle.

French Meadow [KERN]: *area,* 1.5 miles north-northwest of Claraville (lat. 34°27'45" N, long. 118°20'40" W; sec. 32, T 28 S, R 34 E); the place is in French Gulch (2). Named on Claraville (1972) 7.5' quadrangle. Called Weldon Meadow on Emerald Mountain (1943) 15' quadrangle, where present Weldon Meadow is called French Meadow.

French Meadow Gulch: see **French Gulch** [KERN] (2).

French Ranch Gulch [KERN]: *canyon,* drained by a stream that flows 3.5 miles to Little Poso Creek 4.25 miles northwest of Democrat Hot Springs (lat. 35°34'50" N, long. 118°42'30" W; near W line sec. 13, T 27 S, R 30 E). Named on Democrat Hot Springs (1972) 7.5' quadrangle, which shows French ranch in the canyon. Called French Gulch on Glennville (1956) 15' quadrangle, and United States Board on Geographic Names (1975a, p. 4) gave this name as a variant.

Fresno [FRESNO]: *city,* near the east side of San Joaquin Valley between San Joaquin River and Kings River (lat. 36°46' N, long. 119°47' W). Named on Clovis (1964), Fresno North (1965), Fresno South (1963), and Malaga (1964) 7.5' quadrangles. Postal authorities established Fresno City post office in 1872 and changed the name to Fresno in 1889 (Frickstad, p. 33). The city incorporated in 1885. *Fresno* means "ash tree" in Spanish; the name was applied first to a river because of ash trees along it, and later it was transferred to the city (Stewart, p. 173). Postal authorities established Temperance post office, named for the Christian Temperance Union, 6.5 miles northeast of Fresno in 1881 and discontinued it in 1886; they established Kelso post office, named for Napolean B. Kelso, first postmaster, 10 miles northeast of Fresno in 1891 and discontinued it in 1893; they established Fruitvale post office 5 miles northeast of Fresno City post office in 1883, discontinued it for a time in 1888, and discontinued it finally in 1892 (Salley, p. 81, 110, 219).

Fresno: see **Camp Fresno** [FRESNO]; **Pueblo de las Juntas**, under **Mendota** [FRESNO].

Fresno Beach: see **Scout Island** [FRESNO].

Fresno Branch San Joaquin River: see **Fresno Slough** [FRESNO].

Fresno City: see **Fresno** [FRESNO]; **Tranquillity** [FRESNO].

Fresno Crossing [MADERA]: *locality,* 5.5 miles east-northeast of Knowles along Fresno River near the mouth of Spangle Gold Creek (lat. 37°14'15" N, long. 119°46'25" W; sec. 15, T 8 S, R 20 E). Named on Knowles (1962) 7.5' quadrangle. The place was the main crossing of Fresno River in the mining region (Crampton *in* Eccleston, p. 74).

Fresno Dome [MADERA]: *peak,* 8 miles northeast of Yosemite Forks (lat. 37°27'15" N, long. 119°32'10" W; sec. 35, T 5 S, R 22 E). Altitude 7540 feet. Named on Bass Lake (1953) 15' quadrangle. United States Board on Geographic Names (1991, p. 4) rejected the names "Hogans Dome," "Walemo Rock," "Wameloo Rock," and "Wamelo Rock" for the feature.

Fresno Dome Campground [MADERA]: *locality,* 7.5 miles northeast of Yosemite Forks along Big Creek (lat. 37°27'20" N, long. 119°32'50" W; sec. 34, T 5 S, R 22 E); the place is less than 1 mile west of Fresno Dome. Named on Bass Lake (1953) 15' quadrangle.

Fresno Flats [MADERA]: *valley,* 4.5 miles west-southwest of Yosemite Forks along Fresno River (lat. 37°20'15" N, long. 119° 42' W). Named on Bass Lake (1953) 15' quadrangle.

Fresno Flats: see **Oakhurst** [MADERA].

Fresno Hot Springs: see **Coalinga Mineral Springs** [FRESNO].

Fresno River [MADERA]: *stream,* formed by the confluence of Lewis Fork and Nelder Creek in Madera County, flows 80 miles to San Joaquin River 4.25 miles east-northeast of Dos Palos Y in Merced County (lat. 37°04'35" N, long. 120°33'30" W). Named on Bass Lake (1953), Chowchilla (1960), Firebaugh (1946), Le Grand (1961), Madera (1946), Mariposa (1947), Raymond (1962), and Santa Rita Park (1962) 15' quadrangles. South Fork branches southwest from Fresno River 13 miles south of Raymond and flows 5.5 miles before rejoining the main stream 2.5 miles northeast of Madera; it is named on Herndon (1965) and Raymond (1962) 15' quadrangles. United States Board on Geographic Names (1964c, p. 15) rejected the name "North Fork of Fresno River" for present Lewis Fork [MADERA].

Fresno Slough [FRESNO-KINGS]: *stream,* diverges from North Fork Kings River in Kings County and flows 46 miles to San Joaquin River 7 miles southeast of Firebaugh in Fresno County (lat. 36° 47' N, long. 120°22'05" W; near E line sec. 19, T 13 S, R 15 E). Named on Burrel (1954), Five Points (1956), Helm (1963), Jamesan (1963), Mendota Dam (1956), San Joaquin (1963) and Tranquillity (1956) 7.5' quadrangles. Called Tulare Lake Slough on Coalinga (1912) 30' quadrangle, and called Kings River Slough on Jamesan (1924), Mendota (1924), and Tranquillity (1924) 7.5' quadrangles. The stream also is called South Branch or Fresno Branch San

Joaquin River (Hoover, Rensch, and Rensch, p. 92). Present North Fork Kings River is called Fresno Slough on Riverdale (1927) 7.5' quadrangle, where present Faull Slough is called N. Fk. Kings River.

Fresno Slough By-Pass: see **James Bypass** [FRESNO].

Fresno Springs Canyon: see **Hot Springs Canyon** [FRESNO].

Friant [FRESNO]: *village,* 11.5 miles north of Clovis near San Joaquin River (lat. 36°59'15" N, long. 119°42'35" W; sec. 7, T 11 S, R 21 E). Named on Friant (1964) 7.5' quadrangle. The place was known first as Converse Ferry, for Charles Converse, who established a ferry there in 1852, and later it was called Jones Ferry; when Southern Pacific Railroad reached the site in 1891, the station was called Pollasky for Marcus Pollasky, a railroad agent, and in the early 1920's the village was renamed for Thomas Friant of White-Friant Lumber Company (Gudde, 1949, p. 122). The place also was called Hamptonville (Hanna, p. 114). Postal authorities established Hamptonville post office, named for William R. Hampton, first postmaster, in 1881, changed the name to Pollasky in 1891, and moved it and changed the name to Friant in 1910 (Salley, p. 92, 175). J.R. Jones had a store on the south bank of San Joaquin River just below Converse Ferry that was a noted supply point for many years (Wright, p. 45).

Fridley Canyon [TULARE]: *canyon,* drained by a stream that flows 0.5 mile to Dry Creek (1) 6 miles northeast of Woodlake (lat. 36° 28'35" N, long. 119°01'10" W; sec. 2, T 17 S, R 27 E). Named on Exeter (1952) 15' quadrangle.

Frog Creek [KERN]: *stream,* flows 4 miles to Kelso Creek 6 miles southwest of Skinner Peak (lat. 35°30'20" N, long. 118°12'20" W; sec. 10, T 28 S, R 35 E). Named on Cane Canyon (1972) 7.5' quadrangle.

Frog Lake [FRESNO]:
(1) *lake,* 900 feet long, 13 miles north-north-east of Kaiser Peak (lat. 37°27'25" N, long. 119°03'40" W). Named on Kaiser Peak (1953) 15' quadrangle. The feature is one of the group called Margaret Lakes.
(2) *lake,* 700 feet long, 3.5 miles northwest of Mount Abbot (lat. 37°25'25" N, long. 118°49'35" W). Named on Mount Abbot (1953) 15' quadrangle.

Frog Lakes [TULARE]: *lakes,* two, largest 500 feet long, 11.5 miles south of Mineral King (lat. 36°17'15" N, long. 118°37'15" W). Named on Mineral King (1956) 15' quadrangle.

Frog Meadow [TULARE]: *area,* 5.25 miles east of California Hot Springs (lat. 35°52'25" N, long. 118°34'30" W; on E line sec. 1, T 24 S, R 31 E). Named on California Hot Springs (1958) 15' quadrangle.

Frog Spring [KERN]: *spring,* 5.5 miles southwest of Skinner Peak (lat. 35°30'25" N, long. 118°11'35" W; near NE cor. sec. 10, T 28 S,

E 35 E); the spring is along Frog Creek. Named on Cane Canyon (1972) 7.5' quadrangle.

Front: see **Brown** [KERN].

Fruitvale [KERN]: *settlement,* 4.5 miles west of Bakersfield (lat. 35° 23' N, long. 119°05' W; on S line sec. 21, T 29 S, R 27 E). Named on Oildale (1954) 7.5' quadrangle. The community began in 1891 (Bailey, 1967, p. 9).

Fruitvale: see **Fresno** [FRESNO].

Frypan Meadow [FRESNO]: *area,* 12 miles southwest of Marion Peak (lat. 36°51'10" N, long. 118°41'35" W). Named on Marion Peak (1953) 15' quadrangle.

Frying Pan Lake [MADERA]: *lake,* 300 feet long, 2 miles east-southeast of Merced Peak (lat. 37°37'15" N, long. 119°21'50" W). Named on Merced Peak (1953) 15' quadrangle. John Handley of California Department of Fish and Game named the lake in 1940 (Browning, 1986, p. 75).

Frys Point [TULARE]: *peak,* 4.5 miles south-southeast of Yucca Mountain (lat. 36°30'30" N, long. 118°50'30" W). Altitude 4504 feet. Named on Giant Forest (1956) 15' quadrangle. R. B. Marshall of United States Geological Survey named the peak in 1909 for Walter Fry, who was superintendent of Sequoia and General Grant National Parks from 1914 until 1920 (Hanna, p. 114). United States Board on Geographic Names (1933a, p. 313) rejected the form "Fry's Point" for the name, and noted that Walter Fry entered the first protest against cutting down the big redwood trees after he counted 2000 rings on a stump.

Fuller Acres [KERN]: *locality,* 7.25 miles southeast of downtown Bakersfield (lat. 35°17'55" N, long. 118°54'45" W; near SW cor. sec. 19, T 30 S, R 29 E). Named on Lamont (1954, photorevised 1968) 7.5' quadrangle.

Fuller Buttes [MADERA]: *peaks,* two, 9 miles east-northeast of Shuteye Peak (lat. 37°24'55" N, long. 119°17'05" W; near SW cor. sec. 7, T 6 S, R 25 E). Named on Shuteye Peak (1953) 15' quadrangle.

Fuller Meadow [MADERA]: *area,* 6.25 miles east of Shuteye Peak (lat. 37°21'20" N, long. 119°18'55" W; sec. 35, T 6 S, R 24 E). Named on Shuteye Peak (1953) 15' quadrangle. Called Fullers Meadow on Kaiser (1904) 30' quadrangle. Frank F. Fuller homesteaded in section 35 in 1900 (Browning, 1986, p. 75).

Fulton Creek [KERN]: *stream,* formed by the confluence of McFarland Creek and Peyton Creek, flows nearly 3 miles to Cedar Creek 2.5 miles southeast of Glennville (lat. 35°42' N, long. 118°40'15" W; near N line sec. 5, T 26 S, R 31 E). Named on Glennville (1972) 7.5' quadrangle.

Fulton Peak [KERN]: *peak,* 2.5 miles east of Glennville (lat. 35°43'20" N, long. 118°39'40" W; near E line sec. 29, T 25 S, R 31 E). Altitude 4786 feet. Named on Glennville (1972) 7.5' quadrangle.

Funston Camp: see **Funston Meadow** [TU-LARE].

Funston Creek [TULARE]: *stream,* flows nearly 3 miles to Kern River 12.5 miles northwest of Kern Peak (lat. 36°27'20" N, long. 118°24'45" W); the mouth of the stream is at Upper Funston Meadow. Named on Kern Peak (1956) 15' quadrangle. The name is for James Funston, who ran sheep near the stream in 1870 (United States Board on Geographic Names, 1933a, p. 314).

Funston Lake [TULARE]: *lake,* 2100 feet long, 10.5 miles north-northwest of Kern Peak (lat. 36°26'55" N, long. 118°20'50" W). Named on Kern Peak (1956) 15' quadrangle.

Funston Meadow [TULARE]: *area,* 8.5 miles northwest of Kern Peak in Kern Canyon (lat. 36°23' N, long. 118°24'15" W). Named on Kern Peak (1956) 15' quadrangle. Called Lower Funston Meadow on Olancha (1907) 30' quadrangle. California Mining Bureau's (1917b) map shows a place called Funston Camp located at or near present Funston Meadow.

Funston Meadow: see **Upper Funston Meadow** [TULARE]; **Upper Funston Meadow,** under **Sky Parlor Meadow** [TU-LARE].

Funstons: see **Upper Funston Meadow** [TU-LARE].

– G –

Gabb: see **Mount Gabb** [FRESNO].

Gaggs Camp [MADERA]: *locality,* 2.5 miles west-northwest of Shuteye Peak (lat. 37°21'40" N, long. 119°28' W; sec. 33, T 6 S, R 23 E). Named on Shuteye Peak (1953) 15' quadrangle.

Gail Spring [KERN]: *spring,* 6.5 miles northeast of Caliente (lat. 35° 21'30" N, long. 118°32'40" W; at E line sec. 33, T 29 S, R 32 E). Named on Oiler Peak (1972) 7.5' quadrangle.

Gains: see **Visalia** [TULARE].

Gale Lake [MADERA]: *lake,* 300 feet long, 5.25 miles south of Merced Peak (lat. 37°33'40" N, long. 119°22'50" W); the lake is 0.5 mile south-southeast of Gale Peak. Named on Merced Peak (1953) 15' quadrangle. William A. Dill and a group from California Department of Fish and Game named the lake in 1946 for nearby Gale Peak (Browning, 1986, p. 77).

Galena Creek [TULARE]: *stream,* flows 1.5 miles to North Fork of Middle Fork Tule River 7.5 miles north-northwest of Camp Nelson (lat. 36°14'30" N, long. 118°39'15" W). Named on Mineral King (1956) 15' quadrangle.

Gale Peak [MADERA]: *peak,* 4.5 miles south of Merced Peak (lat. 37°34'05" N, long. 119°23'10" W). Altitude 10,693 feet. Named on Merced Peak (1953) 15' quadrangle. Lieutenant N.F. McClure named the peak for Captain G.H.G. Gale, acting superintendent of Yosemite National Park in 1894 (United States Board on Geographic Names, 1934a, p. 10).

Gale Spring [KERN]: *spring,* 6 miles east-southeast of Caliente (lat. 35°15'15" N, long. 118°31'55" W; at S line sec. 3, T 31 S, R 32 E). Named on Oiler Peak (1972) 7.5' quadrangle.

Galileo Hill [KERN]: *hill,* 10 miles northeast of Castle Butte (lat. 35° 12'45" N, long. 117°45'10" W; at NW cor. sec. 25, T 31 S, R 39 E). Altitude 3310 feet. Named on Galileo Hill (1973) 7.5' quadrangle.

Gallats Lake [TULARE]: *lake,* 1000 feet long, 10.5 miles west of Mount Whitney along Kern-Kaweah River (lat. 36°35'45" N, long. 118°28'25" W). Named on Mount Whitney (1956) 15' quadrangle.

Galley Mountain [TULARE]: *peak,* 6 miles east of Fountain Springs (lat. 35°54'20" N, long. ·118°48'35" W; near S line sec. 23, T 23 S, R 39 E). Altitude 2852 feet. Named on Gibbon Peak (1965) 7.5' quadrangle.

Galt Basin [MADERA]: *area,* 7.5 miles southwest of the town of North Fork (lat. 37°08'50" N, long. 119°36'05" W; near W line sec. 17, T 9 S, R 22 E). Named on North Fork (1965) 7.5' quadrangle.

Gamba: see **Mojave** [KERN].

Gamble Spring Canyon [KERN]: *canyon,* drained by a stream that flows 4 miles to lowlands 9 miles west-northwest of the village of Willow Springs (lat. 34°57'15" N, long. 118°25'30" W; near S line sec. 13, T 10 N, R 15 W). Named on Tehachapi South (1966) and Tylerhorse Canyon (1965) 7.5' quadrangles.

Garcia Canyon [FRESNO]:

(1) *canyon,* drained by a stream that flows 2.5 miles to Los Gatos Creek 20 miles west-northwest of Coalinga (lat. 36°17'10" N, long. 120°39'35" W; near S line sec. 10, T 19 S, R 12 E). Named on San Benito Mountain (1969) 7.5' quadrangle.

(2) *canyon,* drained by a stream that flows 4 miles to Zapato Chino Creek 9.5 miles southeast of Coalinga (lat. 36°01'40" N, long. 120° 15'45" W; sec. 8, T 22 S, R 16 E). Named on Kreyenhagen Hills (1956) 7.5' quadrangle.

Garden City Station [KERN]: *locality,* 9 miles north of Randsburg along Trona Railroad (lat. 35°29'40" N, long. 117°38'20" W; at N line sec. 23, T 28 S, R 40 E). Named on El Paso Peaks (1967) 7.5' quadrangle.

Gardiner: see **Mount Gardiner** [FRESNO].

Gardiner Basin [FRESNO]: *valley,* 9.5 miles south-southwest of Mount Pinchot (lat. 36°49' N, long. 118°27'30" W); the valley is at the head of Gardiner Creek. Named on Mount Pinchot (1953) 15' quadrangle.

Gardiner Creek [FRESNO]: *stream,* flows 6.25 miles to South Fork Kings River 10 miles south of Marion Peak (lat. 36°48'45" N, long.

118°32'50" W); the stream heads in Gardiner Basin. Named on Marion Peak (1953) and Mount Pinchot (1953) 15' quadrangles.

Gardiner Lakes [FRESNO]: *lakes,* 9.5 miles south-southwest of Mount Pinchot (lat. 36°49' N, long. 118°27' W); the lakes are in Gardiner Basin. Named on Mount Pinchot (1953) 15' quadrangle.

Gardiner Pass [FRESNO]: *pass,* 11 miles south-southwest of Mount Pinchot (lat. 36°48' N, long. 118°28'45" W). Named on Mount Pinchot (1953) 15' quadrangle.

Gardner Field [KERN]: *military installation,* 6 miles east-northeast of Maricopa (lat. 35°06'15" N, long. 119°18'30" W). Named on Pentland (1945) 7.5' quadrangle.

Garfield: see **Clovis** [FRESNO].

Garfield Creek [TULARE]: *stream,* flows 3 miles to South Fork Kaweah River 11 miles southwest of Mineral King (lat. 36°20'50" N, long. 118°44'10" W). Named on Mineral King (1956) 15' quadrangle. United States Board on Geographic Names (1933a, p. 318) rejected the name "Board Camp Creek" for the feature. The stream is north of Garfield grove of redwood trees, which R.B. Marshall of United States Geological Survey named for President James A. Garfield (Hanna, p. 117).

Garlic Falls [FRESNO]: *waterfall,* 5.5 miles north-northwest of Hume (lat. 36°51'40" N, long. 118°57' W); the feature is along Garlic Meadow Creek. Named on Tehipite Dome (1952) 15' quadrangle.

Garlic Meadow [FRESNO]: *area,* 9 miles north of Hume (lat. 36°55'05" N, long. 118°55'25" W). Named on Tehipite Dome (1952) 15' quadrangle. Called Garlic Meadows on Lippincott's (1902) map.

Garlic Meadow Creek [FRESNO]: *stream,* flows 4.5 miles to Kings River 5.5 miles north-northwest of Hume (lat. 36°51'35" N, long. 118°57'05" W); the stream heads 1.5 miles west of Garlic Meadow. Named on Tehipite Dome (1952) 15' quadrangle.

Garlic Spur [FRESNO]: *ridge,* south-southeast-trending, 3.5 miles long. 7.5 miles north-northwest of Hume (lat. 36°53'15" N, long. 118°57'45" W); the ridge is west of Garlic Meadow Creek. Named on Tehipite Dome (1952) 15' quadrangle.

Garlock [KERN]: *locality,* 6.25 miles east-northeast of Saltdale (lat. 35°24'15" N, long. 117°47'20" W; at NW cor. sec. 22, T 29 S, R 39 E). Named on Garlock (1967) 7.5' quadrangle. Postal authorities established Garlock post office in 1896, discontinued it in 1904, reestablished it in 1923, and discontinued it in 1926 (Frickstad, p. 55). The name commemorates Eugene Garlock, who built a stamp mill at a watering place called Cow Wells; Garlock called the establishment Eugeneville, but later the site took his surname (Barras, p. 39).

Garlock: see **Old Garlock** [KERN].

Garlock Station [KERN]: *locality,* 1 mile south-southwest of Garlock along Southern Pacific Railroad (lat. 35°23'30" N, long. 117° 47'50" W; sec. 21, T 29 S, R 39 E). Named on Saltdale (1943a) 15' quadrangle.

Garnet Lake [MADERA]: *lake,* 1.5 miles long, 7.25 miles northwest of Devils Postpile (lat. 37°42'35" N, long. 119°09'30" W); the feature is south of Emerald Lake and Ruby Lake. Named on Devils Postpile (1953) 15' quadrangle. Called Badger Lake on maps of the 1890's, where the name "Garnet Lake" applies to present Shadow Lake (Browning, 1988, p. 48). United States Board on Geographic Names (1976c, p. 4) approved the name "Red Top Mountain" for a peak, altitude 10,532 feet, situated 5 miles southeast of Garnet Lake (lat. 37°38'12" N, long. 119°08'04" W).

Garrison Canyon [FRESNO]: *canyon,* drained by a stream that flows 2 miles to Los Gatos Creek 18 miles west-northwest of Coalinga (lat. 36°16'35" N, long. 120°39' W; sec. 14, T 19 S, R 12 E). Named on San Benito Mountain (1969) 7.5' quadrangle.

Garza Creek [FRESNO-KINGS]: *stream,* heads in Kings County and flows 7 miles to Kettleman Plain 12.5 miles southeast of Coalinga in Fresno County (lat. 36°00'30" N, long. 120°11'35" W; near N line sec. 24, T 22 S, R 16 E). Named on Avenal (1954) 7.5' quadrangle. United States Board on Geographic Names (1933a, p. 319) rejected the name "Las Garzas Creek" for the feature.

Garza Peak [KINGS]: *peak,* 6.25 miles southwest of Avenal (lat. 35° 56' N, long. 120°11'55" W; near W line sec. 13, T 23 S, R 16 E). Altitude 2698 feet. Named on Garza Peak (1953) 7.5' quadrangle.

Gassenberg Spring [TULARE]: *spring,* 7.5 miles east of Exeter (lat. 36°17'50" N, long. 119°00'15" W; at S line sec. 1, T 19 S, R 27 E). Named on Rocky Hill (1951) 7.5' quadrangle.

Gates Lake [FRESNO]: *intermittent lake,* 1.25 miles long, 4 miles north of Clovis (lat. 36°53' N, long. 119°41'30" W). Named on Friant (1922) 7.5' quadrangle.

Gautche Point [KERN]: *promontory,* 4.5 miles south-southeast of Wofford Heights along Isabella Lake (lat. 35°39'05" N, long. 118° 25' W; sec. 22, T 26 S, R 33 E). Named on Lake Isabella North (1972) 7.5' quadrangle.

Gautche Springs [KERN]: *springs,* 5 miles east of Bodfish (lat. 35° 36'15" N, long. 118°24'05" W; sec. 2, T 27 S, R 33 E). Named on Lake Isabella South (1972) 7.5' quadrangle.

Gavilan Ridge [FRESNO]: *ridge,* northeast-trending, 1 mile long, 10 miles southwest of Coalinga (lat. 36°01'05" N, long. 120°27'45" W; sec. 16, T 22 S, R 14 E). Named on Curry Mountain (1969) 7.5' quadrangle.

Gavilan Rock [FRESNO]: *peak,* 10 miles south-southwest of Coalinga (lat. 36°01'10" N, long. 120°27'45" W; sec. 15, T 22 S, R 14 E); the feature is on Gavilan Ridge. Named on Curry Mountain (1969) 7.5' quadrangle.

Geghus Ridge [KERN]: *ridge,* west-southwest-trending, 1.25 miles long, 10.5 miles west-southwest of Liebre Twins (lat. 34°54'15" N, long. 118°44'30" W). Named on Winters Ridge (1966) 7.5' quadrangle.

Gem Hill [KERN]: *peak,* 5.5 miles northwest of Rosamond (lat. 34° 55'30" N, long. 118°13'15" W). Named on Soledad Mountain (1973) 7.5' quadrangle.

Gemini [FRESNO]: *peak,* 6.5 miles south-south-west of Mount Abbot (lat. 37°17'45" N, long. 118°49' W). Altitude 12,866 feet. Named on Mount Abbot (1953) 15' quadrangle. Chester Versteeg proposed the name for the double peak (Gudde, 1969, p. 118).

General Canyon [TULARE]: *canyon,* drained by a stream that flows 1 mile to Dry Creek (1) 6.5 miles northeast of Woodlake (lat. 36° 29'05" N, long. 119°00'55" W; near N line sec. 2, T 17 S, R 27 E). Named on Woodlake (1952) 7.5' quadrangle.

General Canyon: see **Liveoak Canyon** [TU-LARE].

Geneva: see **Mount Geneva**, under **Mount Genevra** [TULARE].

Genevra: see **Mount Genevra** [TULARE].

George Lake [FRESNO]: *lake,* 900 feet long, nearly 1 mile east-southeast of Kaiser Peak (lat. 37°17'25" N, long. 119°10'15" W; sec. 30, T 7 S, R 26 E). Named on Kaiser Peak (1953) 15' quadrangle.

Gepford [KINGS]: *locality,* 7 miles north-north-west of Lemoore along Atchison, Topeka and Santa Fe Railroad (lat. 36°23'55" N, long. 119°48'35" W; sec. 4, T 18 S, R 20 E). Named on Riverdale (1954) 7.5' quadrangle.

Geraldine Lakes [FRESNO]: *lakes,* largest 900 feet long, 9 miles north-northeast of Hume (lat. 36°54'50" N, long. 118°52'45" W). Named on Tehipite Dome (1952) 15' quad-rangle.

Gerbracht Camp [KERN]: *locality,* 3.5 miles northwest of Garlock (lat. 35°26'15" N, long. 117°50'20" W). Named on Garlock (1967) 7.5' quadrangle.

Gertrude: see **Ahwahnee** [MADERA].

Gertrude Creek [MADERA]: *stream,* flows 3 miles to Whiskey Creek (2) 8 miles south of Shuteye Peak (lat. 37°14'10" N, long. 119°27'15" W; at W line sec. 15, T 8 S, R 23 E). Named on Shaver Lake (1953) and Shuteye Peak (1953) 7.5' quadrangles.

Gertrude Lake [MADERA]: *lake,* 800 feet long, 3.5 miles west of Devils Postpile (lat. 37°37'10" N, long. 119°08'45" W). Named on Devils Postpile (1953) 15' quadrangle.

Giant Forest: see **Kaweah Camp** [TULARE].

Giant Oak [TULARE]: *locality,* 2.5 miles west-northwest of Exeter along Southern Pacific Railroad (lat. 36°18'20" N, long. 119°11'15"

W; near W line sec. 5, T 19 S, R 26 E). Named on Exeter (1926) 7.5' quadrangle.

Gibbon Canyon: see **Gibbon Creek** [TU-LARE].

Gibbon Creek [TULARE]: *stream,* flows 6.25 miles to South Fork Tule River 7.25 miles south of Springville (lat. 36°01'35" N, long. 118°47'35" W); the stream heads near Gib-bon Peak. Named on Globe (1956) 7.5' quad-rangle. Gibbon Peak (1965) 7.5' quadrangle has the name "Gibbon Canyon" for the can-yon of the stream, but fails to name the stream itself.

Gibbon Peak [TULARE]: *peak,* 9.5 miles east-southeast of Fountain Springs (lat. 35°57'20" N, long. 118°45'50" W; sec. 5, T 23 S, R 30 E). Altitude 4512 feet. Named on Gibbon Peak (1965) 7.5' quadrangle.

Gibonney Canyon [KERN]: *canyon,* drained by a stream that flows 2 miles to South Fork Val-ley 2.5 miles north-northeast of Weldon (lat. 35°41'55" N, long. 118°15'55" W; sec. 6, T 26 S, R 35 E). Named on Weldon (1972) 7.5' quadrangle.

Giffen [KERN]: *locality,* 2.5 miles northeast of Arvin along the railroad (lat. 35°14'20" N, long. 118°47'55" W; at S line sec. 7, T 31 S, R 30 E). Named on Arvin (1933) 7.5' quadrangle. California Division of Highways' (1934) map shows a place called Giffen Jct. located 1.5 miles west of Giffen along the railroad.

Giffen: see **Enson** [TULARE].

Giffen Junction: see **Giffen** [KERN].

Gilbert: see **Mount Gilbert** [FRESNO].

Gilbert Campground [KERN]: *locality,* less then 1 mile north of downtown Kernville along Kern River (lat. 35°46' N, long. 118°25'30" W; sec. 10, T 25 S, R 33 E). Named on Kernville (1956) 7.5' quadrangle.

Gillette [TULARE]: *locality,* 3.5 miles south-east of Lindsay along Atchison, Topeka and Santa Fe Railroad (lat. 36°10'25" N, long. 119°02'10" W; sec. 22, T 20 S, R 27 E). Named on Lindsay (1951) 7.5' quadrangle. On Lindsay (1928) 7.5' quadrangle, the name applies to a place located nearly 1 mile far-ther west at the end of a spur line of Visalia Electric Railroad (sec. 21, T 20 S, R 27 E). The name commemorates King C. Gillette of safety-razor fame, who owned a citrus orchard at the place (Gudde, 1949, p. 127).

Girard: see **Keene** [KERN].

Giraud Peak [FRESNO]: *peak,* 9 miles east of Mount Goddard (lat. 37°04'40" N, long. 118°33'50" W). Altitude 12,585 feet. Named on Mount Goddard (1948) 15' quadrangle. Called Giroud Pk. on Mount Goddard (1912) 30' quadrangle. The name commemorates Alfred R. Giroud, a sheepman of Inyo County (Farquhar, 1923, p. 398).

Giroud Peak: see **Giraud Peak** [FRESNO].

Givens: see **Mount Givens** [FRESNO].

Givens Creek [MADERA]: *stream,* flows 4.5 miles to South Fork Merced River 7.5 miles south-southwest of Merced Peak (lat. 37° 32'40" N, long. 119°28'20" W). Named on Merced Peak (1953) 15' quadrangle.

Givens Lake [MADERA]: *lake,* 900 feet long, 5.25 miles southwest of Merced Peak (lat. 37°35' N, long. 119°27'55" W); the lake is at the head of a branch of Givens Creek. Named on Merced Peak (1953) 15' quadrangle.

Givens Meadow [MADERA]: *area,* 6 miles southwest of Merced Peak (lat. 37°34'45" N, long. 119°28'20" W); the place is 0.5 mile southwest of Givens Lake along Givens Creek. Named on Merced Peak (1953) 15' quadrangle.

Glacier Brook: see **Glacier Creek** [FRESNO] (1).

Glacier Creek [FRESNO]:

(1) *stream,* flows 1.5 miles to Palisade Creek 11 miles east-southeast of Mount Goddard (lat. 37°03'15" N, long. 118°31'10" W). Named on Mount Goddard (1948) 15' quadrangle. J.N. LeConte and his companions gave the name "Glacier Brook" to the stream in 1903 (Browning 1986, p. 81).

(2) *stream,* flows 2.25 miles to South Fork Kings River 11 miles south of Marion Peak (lat. 36°48' N, long. 118°32'45" W); the stream heads near Glacier Monument. Named on Marion Peak (1953) 15' quadrangle.

Glacier Creek: see **Boulder Creek** [FRESNO-TULARE].

Glacier Divide [FRESNO]: *ridge,* west-trending, 9 miles long, 11 miles north-northeast of Blackcap Mountain between Muriel Peak and Pavilion Dome (lat. 37°13'30" N, long. 118°45' W). Named on Blackcap Mountain (1953) and Mount Goddard (1948) 15' quadrangles. United States Board on Geographic Names (1972b, p. 3) approved the name "Matthes Glaciers" for features on Glacier Divide 2.2 miles east of Pavilion Dome; the name honors geologist François E. Matthes, who studied glaciers in the Sierra Nevada.

Glacier Lake [TULARE]: *lake,* 850 feet long, 0.25 mile northwest of Triple Divide Peak (lat. 36°35'45" N, long. 118°32' W). Named on Triple Divide Peak (1956) 15' quadrangle.

Glacier Lake: see **Johnson Lake** [MADERA].

Glacier Lakes [FRESNO]: *lakes,* 5 miles southwest of Marion Peak (lat. 36°54' N, long. 18°35' W). Named on Marion Peak (1953) 15' quadrangle.

Glacier Monument [FRESNO]: *peak,* 11 miles south of Marion Peak (lat. 36°47'55" N, long. 118°30'15" W). Altitude 11,165 feet. Named on Marion Peak (1953) 15' quadrangle.

Glacier Pass: see **Sawtooth Pass** [TULARE].

Glacier Ridge [TULARE]: *ridge,* north-trending, 5.5 miles long, 3 miles north-northwest of Triple Divide Peak between Deadman Canyon and Cloud Canyon (lat. 36°38' N, long. 118°33'15" W). Named on Triple Divide Peak (1956) 15' quadrangle.

Glacier Valley [FRESNO]: *canyon,* drained by

a stream that heads at Glacier Lakes and flows 1.5 miles to East Fork Dougherty Creek 4 miles southwest of Marion Peak (lat. 36°55'20" N, long. 118° 35' W). Named on Marion Peak (1953) 15' quadrangle.

Gladys Lake [MADERA]: *lake,* 600 feet long, 4.5 miles north-northwest of Devils Postpile (lat. 37°40'55" N, long. 119°07'05" W). Named on Devils Postpile (1953) 15' quadrangle.

Glasier Lake: see **Johnson Lake** [MADERA].

Glenburn: see **Bakersfield** [KERN].

Glen Lake [FRESNO]: *lake,* 800 feet long, 4 miles west-northwest of Red Slate Mountain on upper reaches of Purple Creek (lat. 37°32'25" N, long. 118°55'45" W). Named on Mount Morrison (1953) 15' quadrangle.

Glen Meadow [FRESNO]: *area,* 4 miles southwest of Dinkey Dome (lat. 37°04'30" N, long. 119°11' W; near W line sec. 7, T 10 S, R 26 E). Named on Huntington Lake (1953) 15' quadrangle.

Glen Meadow Creek [FRESNO]: *stream,* flows 2.5 miles to Dinkey Creek (1) 3.5 miles south-southwest of Dinkey Dome (lat. 37°03'55" N, long. 119°09'20" W; sec. 17, T 10 S, R 26 E); the stream heads near Glen Meadow. Named on Huntington Lake (1953) 15' quadrangle.

Glennette Lake [FRESNO]: *lake,* 700 feet long, 4 miles west-northwest of Red Slate Mountain on upper reaches of Purple Creek (lat. 37°32'10" N, long. 118°55'45" W); the feature is 750 feet south of Glen Lake. Named on Mount Morrison (1953) 15' quadrangle.

Glennville [KERN]: *village,* 30 miles north-northeast of Bakersfield (lat. 35°43'54" N, long. 118°42'10" W; sec. 25, T 25 S, R 30 E). Named on Glennville (1972) 7.5' quadrangle. Called Glenville on Mendenhall's (1909) map. Postal authorities established Linn's Valley post office in 1860, changed the name to Glenville in 1872, discontinued it in 1874, and reestablished it the same year with the name "Glennville" (Salley, p. 86, 123). The name "Glennville" commemorates James M. Glenn, who had his home and a blacksmith shop at the place (Boyd, p. 156). David Lavers settled in 1858 at a spot situated a mile west-northwest of present Glennville near Poso Creek; the community that grew there was called Lavers' Crossing, and was the trading center for Linns Valley for a decade before Glennville assumed that role (Boyd, p. 153, 156; Hoover, Rensch, and Rensch, p. 130).

Glen Pass [FRESNO]: *pass,* 11 miles south of Mount Pinchot (lat. 36°47'25" N, long. 118°24'40" W). Named on Mount Pinchot (1953) 15' quadrangle. The name (misspelled "Glenn" on early maps) commemorates Glen H. Crow, an assistant with United States Geological Survey in 1905, and later a Forest Service ranger; Bolton C. Brown called the feature Blue Flower Pass in 1899 (Browning 1986, p. 82).

Glenville: see **Glennville** [KERN].
Globe [TULARE]: *settlement,* 2.25 miles south-southwest of Springville (lat. 36°06'05" N, long. 118°49'40" W; sec. 15, T 21 S, R 29 E). Named on Globe (1956) 7.5' quadrangle. Postal authorities established Globe post office in 1890 and discontinued it in 1915 (Frickstad, p. 211).
Globe Rock [MADERA]: *peak,* 9.5 miles north of Shuteye Peak (lat. 37°29'10" N, long. 119°24'45" W; sec. 23, T 5 S, R 23 E). Altitude 7152 feet. Named on Shuteye Peak (1953) 15' quadrangle.
Gloria Meadow [FRESNO]: *area,* 2 miles west-northwest of Kaiser Peak (lat. 37°18'30" N, long. 119°13' W; near NW cor. sec. 23, T 7 S, R 25 E). Named on Kaiser Peak (1953) 15' quadrangle.
Glorietta [FRESNO]: *locality,* 1 mile north-northwest of Clovis along Southern Pacific Railroad (lat. 36°50'20" N, long 119°42'30" W; near SW cor. sec. 32, T 12 S, R 21 E). Named on Clovis (1964) 7.5' quadrangle.
Gloster: see **Actis** [KERN].
Gnat Creek: see **Daulton Creek** [MADERA].
Gnat Meadow [FRESNO]: *area,* 10.5 miles north-northeast of Hume (lat. 36°54'45" N, long. 118°48'40" W). Named on Tehipite Dome (1952) 15' quadrangle. United States Board on Geographic Names (1988a, p. 2) approved the name "Hay Meadow" for the feature, and gave the name "Gnat Meadow" to a nearby area (lat. 36°54'30" N, long. 118°49'17" W).
Goat Crest [FRESNO]: *ridge,* northwest-trending, 1.5 miles long, 6 miles southwest of Marion Peak (lat. 36°53'10" N, long. 118° 35' W). Named on Marion Peak (1953) 15' quadrangle.
Goat Hill [TULARE]: *peak,* 3.5 miles northeast of Auckland (lat. 36° 37'05" N, long. 119°03'15" W; near SE cor. sec. 17, T 15 S, R 27 E). Altitude 2439 feet. Named on Auckland (1966) 7.5' quadrangle.
Goat Mountain [FRESNO]:
(1) *peak,* nearly 7 miles south-southwest of Marion Peak (lat. 36°52'10" N, long. 118°34'25" W); the peak is near the southeast end of Goat Crest. Altitude 12,207 feet. Named on Marion Peak (1953) 15' quadrangle. United States Board on Geographic Names (1978a, p. 4) approved the name "Munger Peak" for a peak located 0.5 mile northwest of Goat Mountain (1) (lat. 36°52'27" N, long. 118°34'45" W); the name honors Maynard Munger, who was instrumental in preserving Kings Canyon, Sequoia, and Yosemite National Parks.
(2) *peak,* 5.25 miles northwest of Coalinga Mineral Springs (lat. 36° 12'30" N, long. 120°36'30" W; sec. 7, T 20 S, R 13 E). Altitude 3721 feet. Named on Sherman Peak (1969) 7.5' quadrangle.
Goat Mountain [MADERA]: *ridge,* south- to

southeast-trending, 3 miles long, 7 miles southeast of Yosemite Forks (lat. 37°17' N, long. 119°33'35" W). Named on Bass Lake (1953) 15' quadrangle.
Goat Peak [KERN]: *peak,* nearly 6 miles south-southeast of Glennville (lat. 35°39'10" N, long. 118°39'40" W; sec. 20, T 26 S, R 31 E). Altitude 5286 feet. Named on Glennville (1972) 7.5' quadrangle.
Goat Ranch Canyon [KERN]: *canyon,* drained by a stream that flows 2.5 miles to lowlands 5.5 miles southwest of Weldon (lat. 35°37'15" N, long. 118°22'15" W; sec. 31, T 26 S, R 34 E). Named on Woolstalf Creek (1972) 7.5' quadrangle.
Goat Spring [FRESNO]: *spring,* 4 miles north of Coalinga Mineral Springs (lat. 36°12'15" N, long. 120°33'10" W; sec. 10, T 20 S, R 13 E). Named on Sherman Peak (1969) 7.5' quadrangle.
Goddard: see **Mount Goddard** [FRESNO].
Goddard Canyon [FRESNO]: *canyon,* 10 miles long, along South Fork San Joaquin River above the confluence of Piute Creek with South Fork 11 miles north-northwest of Blackcap Mountain (lat. 37°13'25" N, long. 118°50' W); the canyon is northwest of Mount Goddard. Named on Blackcap Mountain (1953) 15' quadrangle.
Goddard Creek [FRESNO]: *stream,* flows 10.5 miles to Middle Fork Kings River 6 miles west-northwest of Marion Peak (lat. 36° 58'50" N, long. 118°37'30" W); the stream heads near Mount Goddard. Named on Marion Peak (1953) and Mount Goddard (1948) 15' quadrangles.
Goddard Creek: see **North Goddard Creek** [FRESNO].
Goddard Divide [FRESNO]: *ridge,* extends 5.5 miles east and northeast from Mount Goddard (lat. 37°06'45" N, long. 118°40'15" W). Named on Mount Goddard (1948) 15' quadrangle.
Goethe: see **Mount Goethe** [FRESNO].
Goethe Cirque: see **Goethe Glacier** [FRESNO].
Goethe Glacier [FRESNO]: *glacier,* 7.25 miles north of Mount Goddard on Glacier Divide (lat. 37°12'35" N, long. 118°42'30" W); the feature is west-northwest of Mount Goethe. Named on Mount Goddard (1948) 15' quadrangle. United States Board on Geographic Names (1949b, p. 4) approved the name "Goethe Cirque" for the cirque on the north side of Mount Goethe that encompasses Goethe Glacier and Goethe Lake.
Goethe Lake [FRESNO]: *lake,* 0.5 mile long, 8 miles north of Mount Goddard (lat. 37°13'15" N, long. 118°42'10" W); the lake is 1 mile north of Mount Goethe. Named on Mount Goddard (1948) 15' quadrangle.
Gold: see **Fine Gold** [MADERA].
Gold Canyon [KERN]: *canyon,* drained by a stream that flows 2 miles to Indian Wells Canyon 6 miles west-northwest of Inyokern (lat.

35°40'50" N, long. 117°54'55" W; near SW cor. sec. 8, T 26 S, R 38 E). Named on Owens Peak (1972) 7.5' quadrangle.

Gold Canyon: see **Alphie Canyon** [KERN].

Golden Bear Lake [TULARE]: *lake,* 1700 feet long, 11 miles north-northwest of Mount Whitney in Center Basin (lat. 36°43'35" N, long. 118°21'15" W). Named on Mount Whitney (1956) 15' quadrangle.

Golden Creek [FRESNO]: *stream,* flows 3 miles to Mono Creek 4.25 miles north of Mount Abbot (lat. 37°26'50" N, long. 118°47'35" W). Named on Mount Abbot (1953) 15' quadrangle.

Golden Lake [FRESNO]: *lake,* 1700 feet long, 4.5 miles north-northeast of Mount Abbot (lat. 37°27' N, long. 118°45'55" W); the lake is along Golden Creek. Named on Mount Abbot (1953) 15' quadrangle.

Golden Oaks Spring [KERN]: *spring,* 12.5 miles north-northwest of Mojave (lat. 35°13'30" N, long. 118°14' W; near NW cor. sec. 21, T 31 S, R 35 E). Named on Cache Peak (1973) 7.5' quadrangle.

Golden Trout Creek [TULARE]: *stream,* flows 16 miles to Kern River 7.25 miles west-north-west of Kern Peak (lat. 36°21' N, long. 118°24'15" W). Named on Kern Peak (1956) 15' quadrangle. United States Board on Geographic Names (1933a, p. 328) rejected the names "Volcano Creek" and "Whitney Creek" for the stream.

Golden Trout Creek: see **Stokes Stringer** [TULARE].

Golden Trout Lake [FRESNO]: *lake,* 1800 feet long, about 9.5 miles north of Mount Goddard along Piute Creek (lat. 37°14'25" N, long. 118°43'10" W). Named on Mount Goddard (1948) 15' quadrangle.

Golden Trout Meadows: see **Big Whitney Meadow** [TULARE].

Goldgulch: see **Coarsegold** [MADERA].

Goldleaf [FRESNO]: *locality,* 3 miles north-northeast of Malaga along Southern Pacific Railroad (lat. 36°43'20" N, long. 119°43'05" W; near SE cor. sec. 7, T 14 S, R 21 E). Named on Malaga (1964) 7.5' quadrangle.

Gold Ledge Campground [TULARE]: *locality,* 4 miles south-southeast of Fairview along Kern River (lat. 35°52'40" N, long. 118°27'20" W; sec. 6, T 24 S, R 33 E); the place is near the mouth of Gold Ledge Creek. Named on Kernville (1956) 15' quadrangle.

Gold Ledge Creek [TULARE]: *stream,* flows 3.5 miles to Kern River 4 miles south-south-east of Fairview (lat. 35°52'40" N, long. 118°27'20" W; sec. 6, T 24 S, R 33 E). Named on Kernville (1956) 15' quadrangle. The canyon of the stream is called Brinn Canyon on Olmsted's (1900) map.

Goldpan Canyon [KERN]: *canyon,* drained by a stream that flows 2.5 miles to Caliente Creek 7.25 miles east-southeast of Caliente (lat. 35°18'50" N, long. 118°30'10" W; near SW cor. sec. 13, T 30 S, R 32 E). Named on

Loraine (1972) and Oiler Peak (1972) 7.5' quadrangles.

Gold Peak [KERN]: *peak,* 1 mile south-south-east of Pinyon Mountain (lat. 35°26'40" N, long. 118°09'05" W; sec. 6, T 29 S, R 36 E). Altitude 5963 feet. Named on Pinyon Mountain (1972) 7.5' quadrangle.

Gold Peak Well [KERN]: *well,* 5.5 miles east of Pinyon Mountain in Dove Spring Canyon (lat. 35°26'40" N, long. 118°03'30" W; near NE cor. sec. 1, T 29 S, R 36 E). Named on Dove Spring (1972) 7.5' quadrangle.

Goldstein Peak [TULARE]: *peak,* 3 miles east-southeast of Tucker Mountain (lat. 36°37'45" N, long. 119°09'30" W; near NW cor. sec. 16, T 15 S, R 26 E). Altitude 2821 feet. Named on Tucker Mountain (1966) 7.5' quadrangle. The name commemorates Ike Goldstein of Visalia, who ran hogs near the peak (Gudde, 1949, p. 130).

Gold Town [KERN]: *locality,* 9.5 miles north of Rosamond (lat. 34° 59'55" N, long. 118°10'30" W). Named on Mojave (1943) and Rosamond (1943) 15' quadrangles.

Goler [KERN]: *locality,* 7 miles west-northwest of Randsburg along Southern Pacific Railroad (lat. 35°24'40" N, long. 117°45'30" W); the place is southwest of the mouth of present Goler Gulch. Named on Searles Lake (1915) 1° quadrangle.

Goler Gulch [KERN]: *canyon,* 3.25 miles long, opens into Fremont Valley 6.5 miles north-west of Randsburg (lat. 35°25'45" N, long. 117°44'50" W; sec. 12, T 29 S, R 39 E). Named on El Paso Peaks (1967) and Garlock (1967) 7.5' quadrangles. The name commemorates John Goler (or Goller, or Galler), a forty-niner who reported making a rich gold discovery on his trip out of Death Valley (Gudde, 1969, p. 123-124).

Goler Heights [KERN]: *locality,* 6.5 miles northwest of Randsburg (lat. 35°25'35" N, long. 117°44'40" W; sec. 12, T 29 S, R 39 E); the place is near the mouth of Goler Canyon. Named on El Paso Peaks (1967) 7.5' quadrangle.

Golf Meadow [KERN]:

(1) *area,* 8 miles east-northeast of Mount Adelaide (lat. 35°29'15" N, long. 118°37'20" W; at SW cor. sec. 15, T 28 S, R 31 E). Named on Breckenridge Mountain (1972) 7.5' quadrangle.

(2) *area,* nearly 3 miles south of Hobo (present Miracle) Hot Springs (lat. 35°32' N, long. 118°31'55" W; sec. 34, T 27 S, R 32 E). Named on Glennville (1956) 15' quadrangle. Miracle Hot Springs (1972) 7.5' quadrangle shows Goff ranch at the place.

Gomez Meadow [TULARE]: *area,* 2.5 miles north of Olancha Peak on Tulare-Inyo county line (lat. 36°18'10" N, long. 118°07'10" W). Named on Olancha (1956) 15' quadrangle.

Goodale [TULARE]: *locality,* 4 miles southeast of Woodlake along Visalia Electric Railroad (lat. 36°22'40" N, long. 119°02'35" W; at W line sec. 10, T 18 S, R 28 E). Named on Woodlake (1952) 7.5' quadrangle.

Goodale Pass: see **Silver Pass** [FRESNO].

Goode: see **Mount Goode** [FRESNO]; **Mount Goode**, under **Black Giant** [FRESNO].

Goodmill [FRESNO]: *locality*, 10 miles southsoutheast of Balch Camp along Mill Flat Creek (lat. 36°46'50" N, long. 119°01'20" W; sec. 22, T 13 S, R 27 E). Site named on Patterson Mountain (1952) 15' quadrangle.

Goodwater Spring [KERN]: *spring,* 12.5 miles east-northeast of Tehachapi (lat. 35°12'35" N, long. 118°15'05" W; near NW cor. sec. 29, T 31 S, R 35 E). Named on Tehachapi NE (1966) 7.5' quadrangle.

Gooseberry Campground [TULARE]: *locality,* 6.5 miles southeast of California Hot Springs (lat. 35°49'10" N, long. 118°34'55" W; near S line sec. 24, T 24 S, R 31 E). Named on California Hot Springs (1958) 15' quadrangle.

Gooseberry Flat [MADERA]: *area, 3.25* miles northeast of Yosemite Forks along Nelder Creek (lat. 37°24'20" N, long. 119°35'35" W; near SW cor. sec. 17, T 6 S, R 22 E). Named on Bass Lake (1953) 15' quadrangle.

Goose Lake Bed [KERN]: *area,* 9 miles eastsoutheast of the village of Lost Hills between Semitropic Ridge and Buttonwillow Ridge (lat. 35°33'45" N, long. 119°32'30" W). Named on Semitropic (1954) 7.5' quadrangle. Watts' (1894) map shows Goose Lake at the place.

Goose Lake Slough [KERN]: *stream,* branches west from Kern River 7.25 miles west of Bakersfield (lat. 35°21'15" N, long. 119°07'35" W; near SE cor. sec. 36, T 29 S, R 26 E). Named on Stevens (1954) and Tupman (1954) 7.5' quadrangles. On Buttonwillow (1942) 15' quadrangle, the name applies to present Jerry Slough.

Goose Slough: see **Jerry Slough** [KERN].

Gordon [FRESNO]: *locality,* 5.25 miles northnorthwest of Clovis along Southern Pacific Railroad (lat. 36°53'45" N, long. 119°43'45" W; near NW cor. sec. 18, T 12 S, R 21 E). Named on Friant (1964) 7.5' quadrangle. Called Gordon Siding on Friant (1922) 7.5' quadrangle.

Gordon Creek [MADERA]: *stream,* flows 1.5 miles to Rock Creek 2.5 miles south-southeast of Shuteye Peak (lat. 37°19'05" N, long. 119°24'20" W; sec. 13, T 7 S, R 23 E); the stream heads at Gordon Meadow. Named on Shuteye Peak (1953) 15' quadrangle.

Gordon Creek [TULARE]: *stream,* formed by the confluence of North Fork and South Fork, flows 2.5 miles to Deer Creek (2) 8.5 miles east of Fountain Springs (lat. 35°54'35" N, long. 118°45'55" W; sec. 20, T 23 S, R 30 E). Named on California Hot Springs (1958) and White River (1952) 15' quadrangles. North Fork is 3 miles long and South Fork is 3.5

miles long; both forks are named on California Hot Springs (1958) 15' quadrangle.

Gordon Gulch [KERN]: *canyon,* drained by a stream that flows 8.5 miles to Rag Gulch 5.25 miles west of Woody (lat. 35°43'10" N, long. 118°55'35" W; near S line sec. 26, T 25 S, R 28 E). Named on Sand Canyon (1965), White River (1965), and Woody (1965) 7.5' quadrangles. The name is for John Gordon, a miner and businessman (Boyd, p. 159).

Gordon Hills [TULARE]: *ridge,* west-trending, 1.25 miles long, 7 miles north-northwest of California Hot Springs (lat. 35°58'10" N, long. 118°43'25" W; mainly in sec. 34, T 22 S, R 30 E). Named on California Hot Springs (1958) 15' quadrangle.

Gordon Lake [FRESNO]: *lake,* 900 feet long. 9 miles southwest of Mount Abbot (lat. 37°18'25" N, long. 118°55' W). Named on Mount Abbot (1953) 15' quadrangle. The name is for Gordon Bartholomew, who was damkeeper at Florence Lake (Browning 1986, p. 84).

Gordon Meadow [MADERA]: *area,* 2.5 miles south of Shuteye Peak (lat. 37°18'45" N, long. 119°25'45" W; on S line sec. 14, T 7 S, R 23 E); the place is at the head of Gordon Creek. Named on Shuteye Peak (1953) 15' quadrangle.

Gordons Ferry [KERN]: *locality,* 4 miles northnortheast of downtown Bakersfield along Kern River (lat. 35°25'30" N, long. 118° 58' W; near NE cor. sec. 9, T 29 S, R 28 E). Site named on Oil Center (1954) 7.5' quadrangle. Aneas B. Gordon operated a ferry at the place from 1853 until 1859 (Bailey, 1967, p. 10), and Butterfield Overland stage line had a station there (Ormsby, p. 118). Goddard's (1857) map shows a place called Dutch Bar situated on the south side of Kern River about 12 miles east of Gordons Ferry.

Gordon Siding: see **Gordon** [FRESNO].

Gorge: see **The Gorge** [FRESNO].

Gorge of Despair [FRESNO]: *canyon,* 3 miles long, opens into Tehipite Valley 11.5 miles northeast of Hume (lat. 36°54'30" N, long. 118°46'30" W). Named on Marion Peak (1953) and Tehipite Dome (1952) 15' quadrangles. L.A. Winchell named the canyon in 1879 (Browning 1986, p. 84).

Gosford [KERN]: *locality,* 7 miles southwest of Bakersfield along Southern Pacific Railroad (lat. 35°18'40" N, long. 119°05'45" W; at S line sec. 17, T 30 S, R 27 E). Named on Gosford (1954) 7.5' quadrangle. Southern Pacific Railroad officials started a community at the place in 1893 and named it for the Earl of Gosford, who once owned the property (Bailey, 1967, p. 10).

Goshen [TULARE]: *town,* 7.5 miles west of Visalia (lat. 36°20'55" N, long. 119°25'15" W; on W line sec. 19, T 18 S, R 24 E). Named on Goshen (1949) 7.5' quadrangle. Officials of Southern Pacific Railroad named the place in 1872; the site also was called Goshen Junction (Mitchell, A.R., p. 68). California Mining Bureau's (1917b) map shows a place called Faxon situated along a rail line between Goshen and Visalia.

Goshen Junction: see **Goshen** [TULARE].

Gould: see **Mount Gould** [FRESNO].

Gould Hill [KERN]: *peak,* nearly 5 miles east-southeast of Carneros Rocks (lat. 35°24'50" N, long. 119°45'55" W; near SW cor. sec. 12, T 29 S, R 21 E). Altitude 1402 feet. Named on Carneros Rocks (1959) 7.5' quadrangle.

Government Peak [KERN]: *peak,* 1.5 miles southwest of Randsburg (lat. 35°21'05" N, long. 117°40'20" W; sec. 3, T 30 S, R 40 E). Altitude 4741 feet. Named on Johannesburg (1967) 7.5' quadrangle.

Grabast Canyon [FRESNO]: *canyon,* drained by a stream that flows 2 miles to Hot Springs Canyon 1.5 miles north-northwest of Coalinga Mineral Springs (lat. 36°10' N, long. 120°33'45" W; sec. 27, T 20 S, R 13 E). Named on Sherman Peak (1969) 7.5' quadrangle.

Grabners: see **Marshall Station** [FRESNO].

Graham Creek [TULARE]: *stream,* flows 5.5 miles to Tule River 2.5 miles south-southwest of Springville (lat. 36°05'45" N, long. 118°49'55" W; sec. 15, T 21 S, R 29 E). Named on Globe (1956) 7.5' quadrangle.

Graham Meadow [MADERA]: *area,* 7.5 miles east-southeast of Yosemite Forks (lat. 37°18'45" N, long. 119°30'45" W; on N line sec. 24, T 7 S, R 22 E). Named on Bass Lake (1953) 15' quadrangle.

Graham Mountain [MADERA]: *ridge,* northwest-trending, 1 mile long, 6.25 miles east of Yosemite Forks (lat. 37°21'30" N, long. 119°30'55" W; on S line sec. 36, T 6 S, R 22 E). Named on Bass Lake (1953) 15' quadrangle.

Grahamton: see **San Joaquin** [FRESNO].

Grand Bluff [FRESNO]: *escarpment,* northwest-trending, 0.5 mile long, 6.25 miles west-southwest of Dinkey Dome (lat. 37°04' N, long. 119°13'30" W; near NE cor. sec. 15, T 10 S, R 25 E). Named on Huntington Lake (1953) 15' quadrangle.

Grand Dike [FRESNO]: *ridge,* southeast-trending, 2 miles long, 15 miles west-southwest of Marion Peak (lat. 36°50'15" N, long. 118°44'50" W). Named on Marion Peak (1953) and Tehipite Dome (1952) 15' quadrangles.

Grand Sentinel [FRESNO]: *peak,* 12.5 miles south-southwest of Marion Peak (lat. 36°47' N, long. 118°35' W). Altitude 8504 feet. Named on Marion Peak (1953) 15' quadrangle.

Grandview: see **Traver** [TULARE].

Grangeville [KINGS]: *village,* 3.5 miles west-northwest of Hanford (lat. 36°20'40" N, long. 119°42'35" W; on E line sec. 20, T 18 S, R 21 E). Named on Hanford (1954) 7.5' quadrangle. Postal authorities established Grangeville post office in 1874 and discontinued it in 1920 (Frickstad, p. 61).

Granite: see **Granite Station** [KERN].

Granite Canyon [KERN]: *canyon,* drained by a stream that flows 6.5 miles to Poso Creek 2.5 miles south-southwest of Knob Hill (lat. 35°31'50" N, long. 118°57'50" W; at S line sec. 33, T 27 S, R 28 E). Named on Knob Hill (1965) 7.5' quadrangle.

Granite Creek [FRESNO]: *stream,* flows 6.5 miles to South Fork Kings River 12.5 miles south-southwest of Marion Peak in Kings Canyon (lat. 36°47'30" N, long. 118°36'05" W); the feature heads near Granite Pass. Named on Marion Peak (1953) 15' quadrangle. J.N. LeConte called the stream Kellogg Creek (Browning 1986, p. 85).

Granite Creek [MADERA]: *stream,* formed by the confluence of East Fork and West Fork, flows 6.5 miles to San Joaquin River 13 miles northeast of Shuteye Peak (lat. 37°28'35" N, long. 119° 14' W; near E line sec. 21, T 5 S, R 25 E). Named on Devils Postpile (1953), Kaiser Peak (1953), and Merced Peak (1953) 15' quadrangles. East Fork is 10 miles long and West Fork is 9.5 miles long; both forks are named on Merced Peak (1953) 15' quadrangle.

Granite Creek [TULARE]: *stream,* flows 4.5 miles to Eagle Scout Creek 7 miles west-southwest of Triple Divide Peak (lat. 36°32'25" N, long. 118°38' W). Named on Triple Divide Peak (1956) 15' quadrangle.

Granite Creek Campground [MADERA]: *locality,* 9.5 miles southeast of Merced Peak near the confluence of East Fork Granite Creek and West Fork Granite Creek (lat. 37°32'30" N, long. 119° 16' W). Named on Merced Peak (1953) 15' quadrangle.

Granite Gorge [FRESNO]: *canyon,* 1.5 miles long, 14 miles north-northwest of Hume along North Fork Kings River (lat. 36°58'45" N, long. 118°59' W). Named on Tehipite Dome (1952) 15' quadrangle.

Granite Hill [FRESNO]: *ridge,* northwest- to north-trending, 1.5 miles long, 5.25 miles north-northwest of Orange Cove (lat. 36°41'20" N, long. 119°21'45" W). Named on Orange Cove North (1966) 7.5' quadrangle.

Granite Knob [TULARE]: *peak,* 4 miles south-southwest of Monache Mountain (lat. 36°09'10" N, long. 118°13'25" W; sec. 30, T 20 S, R 35 E). Altitude 9050 feet. Named on Monache Mountain (1956) 15' quadrangle.

Granite Lake [FRESNO]: *lake,* 2400 feet long, 8.5 miles southwest of Marion Peak (lat. 36°51'50" N, long. 118°37'05" W); the lake is near the head of Granite Creek. Named on Marion Peak (1953) 15' quadrangle.

Granite Pass [FRESNO]: *pass,* 7.5 miles southwest of Marion Peak on Monarch Divide (lat. 36°52'40" N, long. 118°36'35" W). Named on Marion Peak (1953) 15' quadrangle.

Granite Ridge [FRESNO]: *ridge,* northwest-trending, 1.5 miles long, about 4 miles west-southwest of Trimmer (lat. 36°52'50" N, long. 119°21'35" W). Named on Pine Flat Dam (1965) and Trimmer (1965) 7.5' quadrangles.

Granite Stairway [MADERA]: *relief feature*, 3 miles southwest of Devils Postpile (lat. 37°35'40" N, long. 119°07'30" W). Named on Devils Postpile (1953) 15' quadrangle.

Grapevine Canyon [MADERA]: *canyon*, drained by a stream that flows 1.5 miles to San Joaquin River 6.5 miles south-southwest of the town of North Fork (lat. 37°08'30" N, long. 119°33'40" W; at S line sec. 15, T 9 S, R 22 E). Named on North Fork (1965) 7.5' quadrangle.

Granite Station [KERN]: *locality*, 6.25 miles west-northwest of Pine Mountain along Five Dog Creek (lat. 35°36'50" N, long. 118°51'30" W; near N line sec. 4, T 27 S, R 29 E). Named on Pine Mountain (1965) 7.5' quadrangle. Postal authorities established Granite post office at the site in 1875 and discontinued it in 1876; they established Elmer post office, named for Elmer Bohana, there in 1890, discontinued it in 1892, reestablished it in 1900, and discontinued it in 1914—the place also was called Five Dogs (Salley, p. 68, 88).

Grant Wells [KERN]: *wells*, 9.5 miles south-southeast of Orchard Peak (lat. 35°37'55" N, long. 120°02'40" W; near W line sec. 33, T 26 S, R 18 E). Named on Packwood Creek (1961) 7.5' quadrangle.

Granz: see **Sunnyside** [FRESNO].

Grapes Spring: see **Lower Grapes Spring** [KERN]; **Upper Grapes Spring** [KERN].

Grapevine [KERN]: *village*, 7 miles north-northwest of Lebec (lat. 34°55'40" N, long. 118°56' W); the village is located near the entrance of Grapevine Creek to lowlands. Named on Grapevine (1958) 7.5' quadrangle. Postal authorities established Grapevine post office in 1923 and discontinued it in 1960 (Salley, p. 88). United States Board on Geographic Names (1982a, p. 3) approved the name "Metralla Canyon" for a feature, 1.2 miles long, that opens into lowlands 1 mile west of Grapevine (lat. 34°55'50" N, long. 118°56'43" W).

Grapevine Canyon [KERN]: *canyon*, drained by a stream that flows 7 miles to lowlands 7.5 miles northwest of Inyokern (lat. 35°44' N, long. 117°53'30" W; sec. 28, T 25 S, R 38 E). Named on Little Lake (1954) 15' quadrangle, and on Owens Peak (1972) 7.5' quadrangle.

Grapevine Canyon: see **Grapevine Creek** [KERN].

Grapevine Creek [KERN]: *stream*, flows 8 miles to lowlands at Grapevine (lat. 34°55'45" N, long. 118°55'35" W). Named on Frazier Mountain (1958), Grapevine (1958), Lebec (1958), and Mettler (1955) 7.5' quadrangles. Called Arroyo de las Uvas on Williamson's (1853) map. The canyon of the stream is called Canada de las Uvas on Parke's (1854-1855) map. Cullimore (p. 12) called the feature

Grapevine Canyon, and noted that when Pedro Fages traversed it in 1771 he called it Pass of Cortes. Francisco Ruiz went through the defile in 1806 and named it *Cañada de las Uvas*, which means "Canyon of the Grapes" in Spanish (Hanna, p. 125).

Grapevine Creek [TULARE]:
(1) *stream*, flows 3 miles to Cottonwood Creek 3 miles southeast of Cliff Peak (lat. 36°31'45" N, long. 119°07'35" W; at S line sec. 15, T 16 S, R 26 E); the stream heads near Grapevine Peak. Named on Auckland (1966) and Stokes Mountain (1966) 7.5' quadrangles.
(2) *stream*, flows 2 miles to Morgan Canyon 2 miles southeast of Auckland (lat. 36°34' N, long. 119°05'10" W; sec. 6, T 16 S, R 27 E). Named on Auckland (1966) 7.5' quadrangle.

Grapevine Peak [KERN]: *peak*, 2 miles southeast of Grapevine (lat. 34°54'10" N, long. 118°54'10" W). Named on Grapevine (1958) 7.5' quadrangle.

Grapevine Peak [TULARE]: *peak*, 2 miles south-southwest of Auckland (lat. 36°33'50" N, long. 119°07'15" W; sec. 2, T 16 S, R 26 E); the peak is near the head of Grapevine Creek (1). Altitude 1935 feet. Named on Auckland (1966) 7.5' quadrangle.

Grasshopper Creek [TULARE]: *stream*, flows 3.5 miles to Kern River 7 miles west-south-west of Kern Peak (lat. 36°16'35" N, long. 118°24'20" W); the mouth of the stream is at Grasshopper Flat. Named on Kern Peak (1956) 15' quadrangle.

Grasshopper Flat [TULARE]: *area*, 7 miles west-southwest of Kern Peak along Kern River (lat. 36°17' N, long. 118°24'20" W); the placed is at the mouth of Grasshopper Creek. Named on Kern Peak (1956) 15' quadrangle.

Grassy Canyon [TULARE]: *canyon*, drained by a stream that flows 2 miles to White River (1) 4.25 miles southwest of California Hot Springs (lat. 35°50'15" N, long. 118°43'30" W; sec. 15, T 24 S, R 30 E). Named on California Hot Springs (1958) 15' quadrangle.

Grassy Lake [FRESNO]: *lake*, 950 feet long, 12 miles northwest of Mount Abbot (lat. 37°28'55" N, long. 118°57'40" W). Named on Mount Abbot (1953) 15' quadrangle.

Gravelly Flat [FRESNO]: *area*, 3 miles northwest of Coalinga Mineral Springs (lat. 36°10'25" N, long. 120°35'35" W; sec. 20, T 20 S, R 13 E). Named on Sherman Peak (1969) 7.5' quadrangle.

Gravelly Fork [MADERA]: *locality*, nearly 7 miles south-southwest of Merced Peak along South Fork Merced River (lat. 37°32'50" N, long. 119°27'10" W). Named on Merced Peak (1953) 15' quadrangle.

Gravesboro [FRESNO]: *settlement*, 3 miles southwest of Piedra on the southeast side of Kings River (lat. 36°46'20" N, long. 119°24'45" W; sec. 25, T 13 S, R 23 E). Named on Piedra (1965) 7.5' quadrangle. Orangedale School (1923) 7.5' quadrangle shows the place along the Atchison, Topeka and Santa Fe Railroad branch line to Piedra.

Graveyard Lakes [FRESNO]: *lakes,* largest 1400 feet long, 11.5 miles west-northwest of Mount Abbot (lat. 37°27' N, long. 118°58'20" W); the lakes are nearly 1 mile east of Graveyard Peak. Named on Mount Abbot (1953) 15' quadrangle.

Graveyard Meadow [MADERA]: *area,* 11 miles northeast of Shuteye Peak (lat. 37°27'50" N, long. 119°17'40" W; sec. 25, T 5 S, R 24 E). Named on Shuteye Peak (1953) 15' quadrangle.

Graveyard Meadow: see **Upper Graveyard Meadow** [FRESNO].

Graveyard Meadows [FRESNO]: *area,* 10 miles west of Mount Abbot along Cold Creek (lat. 37°24'50" N, long. 118°57'35" W). Named on Mount Abbot (1953) 15' quadrangle. Sheepmen named the place for graves there of two murdered men (Farquhar, 1923, p. 400).

Graveyard Peak [FRESNO]: *peak,* 12 miles west-northwest of Mount Abbot (lat. 37°27' N, long. 118°59'15" W); the peak is 3 miles north-northwest of Graveyard Meadows. Altitude 11,494 feet. Named on Mount Abbot (1953) 15' quadrangle.

Gray: see **Jim Gray Creek** [TULARE].

Grayling Lake [MADERA]: *lake,* 750 feet long, 3.5 miles west-northwest of Merced Peak (lat. 37°39'40" N, long. 119°26'50" W). Named on Merced Peak (1953) 15' quadrangle. The name was given in 1930 when grayling first were planted in the lake (Browning, 1986, p. 87).

Gray Peak [MADERA]: *peak,* 3 miles north-northwest of Merced Peak (lat. 37°40'25" N, long. 119°25'05" W). Altitude 11,574 feet. Named on Merced Peak (1953) 15' quadrangle. Members of the Whitney survey named the peak for the color of its upper part (Browning, 1988, p. 53). United States Board on Geographic Names (1933a, p. 336) rejected the name "Hayes Peak" for the feature.

Gray Peak Fork [MADERA]: *stream,* heads in Madera County and flows 7.5 miles to Merced River 8.5 miles south of Cathedral Peak in Mariposa County (lat. 37°43'45" N, long. 119° 23'25" W); the stream heads near Gray Peak [MADERA]. Named on Mount Lyell (1901) 30' quadrangle.

Greasy Creek [TULARE]: *stream,* flows 3.5 miles to Lake Kaweah 5 miles southwest of Kaweah (lat. 36°25'35" N, long. 118°59'30" W; near SW cor. sec. 19, T 17 S, R 28 E). Named on Kaweah (1957) 15' quadrangle.

Great Cliffs [FRESNO]: *relief feature,* 9 miles southeast of Mount Goddard (lat. 37°01' N, long. 118°35'45" W). Named on Mount Goddard (1948) 15' quadrangle.

Great Dome: see **Balloon Dome** [MADERA].

Great Valley: see "Regional setting."

Great Western Divide [TULARE]: *ridge,* 38 miles long, separates the drainage basin of Kern River from the drainage basins of Tulare River and Kings River. Named on Kern Peak (1956), Mineral King (1956), Mount Whitney (1956), and Triple Divide Peak (1956) 15' quadrangles.

Greenacres [KERN]: *town,* 6.25 miles west of Bakersfield (lat. 35° 22'55" N, long. 119°06'45" W; mainly in sec. 30, T 29 S, R 27 E). Named on Oildale (1954) 7.5' quadrangle. Called Green Acres on Bakersfield West (1942) 15' quadrangle. The town began in 1930 (Bailey, 1967, p. 11).

Greenfield [KERN]: *town,* 7 miles south of Bakersfield (lat. 35°16'15" N, long. 119°00'10" W). Named on Gosford (1954) 7.5' quadrangle. Postal authorities established Delkern post office at the place in 1949; the name was coined from letters in the term "Kern Delta," an early designation of the neighborhood (Salley, p. 57).

Greenhorn: see **Petersburg** [KERN].

Greenhorn Cave [KERN]: *cave,* 3.25 miles west of Miracle Hot Springs (lat. 35°34'15" N, long. 118°35'25" W); the cave is along Greenhorn Creek. Named on Miracle Hot Springs (1972) 7.5' quadrangle.

Greenhorn Creek [KERN]: *stream,* flows 8 miles to Kern River 3 miles west-southwest of Miracle Hot Springs (lat. 35°34' N, long. 118°35' W); the stream is in Greenhorn Mountains. Named on Alta Sierra (1972) and Miracle Hot Springs (1972) 7.5' quadrangles.

Greenhorn Mountains [KERN-TULARE]: *range,* north and west of Kern River on Kern-Tulare county line, mainly in Kern County. Named on Bakersfield (1962, revised 1971) 1°x 2° quadrangle. Whipple (p. 149) used the form "Green Horn Mountains" for the name. According to local legend, the name commemorates two novice gold miners—called greenhorns—who were sent into the range to seek gold where gold was thought not to occur, but they found it there anyway (Hanna, p. 126).

Greenhorn Summit [KERN]: *pass,* less than 1 mile north-northwest of Alta Sierra (lat. 35°44'15" N, long. 118°33'20" W; sec. 20, T 25 S, R 32 E); the pass is in Greenhorn Mountains. Named on Alta Sierra (1972) 7.5' quadrangle. Tobias Peak (1943) 30' quadrangle shows Summit store at the place.

Greenleaf: see **Gregg** [MADERA].

Green Meadow [TULARE]: *area,* 7.5 miles south of Mineral King at the head of South Fork Kaweah River (lat. 36°20'25" N, long. 118° 36' W). Named on Mineral King (1956) 15' quadrangle. United States Board on Geographic Names (1938, p. 23) rejected the name "Cabin Meadow" for the feature.

Green Mountain [FRESNO]: *peak,* 2.25 miles east-northeast of Humphreys Station (lat. 36°58'15" N, long. 119°24'25" W; sec. 13, T 11 S, R 23 E). Altitude 3110 feet. Named on Humphreys Station (1965) 7.5' quadrangle.

Green Mountain [MADERA]: *ridge,* east- to southeast-trending, 1.5 miles long, 10 miles west-southwest of Devils Postpile (lat. 37°34'20" N, long. 119°15' W). Named on Devils Postpile (1953) and Merced Peak (1953) 15' quadrangles.

Green Slough [KINGS]: *stream,* flows 5 miles to South Fork Kings River 3.5 miles north-northwest of Lemoore (lat. 36°20'50" N. long. 119°49'05" W; sec. 20, T 18 S, R 20 E). Named on Lemoore (1954) 7.5' quadrangle.

Green Spring [KERN]: *spring,* 5.5 miles southwest of Pinyon Mountain in Kelso Valley (lat. 35°23'50" N, long. 118°13'15" W; sec. 21, T 29 S, R 35 E). Named on Pinyon Mountain (1972) 7.5' quadrangle.

Green Spring [TULARE]: *spring,* 3 miles south of Auckland (lat. 36° 32'35" N, long. 119°06'20" W; at NW cor. sec. 13, T 16 S, R 26 E). Named on Auckland (1966) 7.5' quadrangle.

Green Water Spring [FRESNO]: *spring,* 17 miles north-northwest of Coalinga (lat. 36°22'45" N, long. 120°28'40" W; sec. 8, T 18 S, R 14 E). Named on Lillis Ranch (1956) 7.5' quadrangle.

Greenwich: see **Tehachapi** [KERN].

Gregg [MADERA]: *locality,* 2.5 miles southsoutheast of Trigo along Atchison, Topeka and Santa Fe Railroad (lat. 36°52'55" N, long. 119°56'10" W; near S line sec. 18, T 12 S, R 19 E). Named on Gregg (1965) 7.5' quadrangle. Called Greenleaf on Mendenhall's (1908) map. Postal authorities established Greenleaf post office in 1904 and discontinued it in 1905; they established Gregg post office in 1917, discontinued it for a time in 1928, and discontinued it finally in 1931 (Frickstad, p. 85).

Gregorys Monument [TULARE]: *peak,* 10 miles northwest of Mount Whitney (lat. 36°42'05" N, long. 118°23'40" W). Named on Mount Whitney (1956) 15' quadrangle. Bolton C. Brown named the feature in 1896 (Browning 1986, p. 88).

Gres Canyon [FRESNO]: *canyon,* drained by a stream that flows 1 mile to lowlands 17 miles west-southwest of Firebaugh (lat. 36°43'50" N, long. 120°42'50" W; sec. 12, T 14 S, R 11 E). Named on Chounet Ranch (1956) 7.5' quadrangle.

Grey Meadow [TULARE]: *area,* 7.5 miles northeast of Camp Nelson (lat. 36°12'35" N, long. 118°30'10" W; at E line sec. 4, T 20 S, R 32 E). Named on Camp Nelson (1956) 15' quadrangle.

Grey Rocks [TULARE]: *locality,* 2.5 miles southeast of Exeter along Visalia Electric Railroad (lat. 36°16'05" N, long. 119°06'15" W; at S line sec. 13, T 19 S, R 26 E). Named on Rocky Hill (1927) 7.5' quadrangle.

Grieve: see **Hans Grieve Canyon** [FRESNO].

Grimaud Creek [KERN]: *stream,* flows 7.25 miles to Monotti Creek 5.5 miles west-north-

west of Pine Mountain (lat. 35°35' N, long. 118°52' W; sec. 16, T 27 S, R 29 E). Named on Pine Mountain (1965) 7.5' quadrangle. Called Grimoud Creek on Woody (1935) 15' quadrangle.

Grinnell Lake [FRESNO]: *lake,* 1 mile long, 6.5 miles north-northwest of Mount Abbot (lat. 37°28' N, long. 118°50'55" W). Named on Mount Abbot (1953) 15' quadrangle. Leon A. Talbot of California Department of Fish and Game named the lake in 1946 in memory of Joseph Grinnell, professor of zoology and director of Museum of Vertebrate Zoology at University of California (Gudde, 1949, p. 136; Gudde used the form "Lake Joseph Grinnell" for the name).

Grinnell Lake: see **Little Grinnell Lake** [FRESNO].

Grist Mill Peak [TULARE]: *peak,* 5.5 miles south-southwest of California Hot Springs (lat. 35°48'05" N, long. 118°41'25" W; sec. 36, T 24 S, R 30 E). Named on California Hot Springs (1958) 15' quadrangle.

Grizzly Creek [FRESNO]: *stream,* flows 5 miles to South Fork Kings River 16 miles southwest of Marion Peak (lat. 36°48'15" N, long. 118°44'35" W); the stream heads at Grizzly Lakes. Named on Marion Peak (1953) 15' quadrangle. East Fork enters from the northeast 2 miles upstream from the mouth of the main stream; it is 4 miles long and is named on Marion Peak (1953) 15' quadrangle. Tehipite (1903) 30' quadrangle shows the main stream following present East Fork, and has the name "West Fork" on the present main stream above its confluence with present East Fork.

Grizzly Creek [MADERA]: *stream,* flows 5 miles to South Fork Merced River 8 miles southwest of Merced Peak (lat. 37°32'30" N, long. 119°29' W); the stream heads at Grizzly Lake. Named on Merced Peak (1953) and Shuteye Peak (1953) 15' quadrangles. Called Quartz Cr. on Mount Lyell (1901) 30' quadrangle, but United States Board on Geographic Names (1969a, p. 3) rejected this name for the stream, which is west of Quartz Mountain (1).

Grizzly Gulch [KERN-TULARE]: *canyon,* drained by a stream that heads in Kern County and flows 9.5 miles to White River (1) 7 miles south of Fountain Springs in Tulare County (lat. 35°48'03" N, long. 118°54'20" W; sec. 36, T 24 S, R 28 E). Named on Quincy School (1965) and White River (1965) 7.5' quadrangles.

Grizzly Lake [MADERA]: *lake,* 600 feet long, 10 miles north-northwest of Shuteye Peak (lat. 37°29'10" N, long. 119°29' W; near W line sec. 20, T 5 S, R 23 E); the lake is at the head of Grizzly Creek. Named on Shuteye Peak (1953) 15' quadrangle.

Grizzly Lakes [FRESNO]: *lakes,* largest 300 feet long. 13 miles west-southwest of Marion

Peak (lat. 36°51'50" N, long. 118°43'10" W); the lakes are at the head of Grizzly Creek. Named on Marion Peak (1953) 15' quadrangle.

Grizzly Meadow [MADERA]: *area,* 4 miles north of Shuteye Peak (lat. 37°24'15" N, long. 119°24'45" W; sec. 13, T 6 S, R 23 E). Named on Shuteye Peak (1953) 15' quadrangle.

Groundhog Meadow [TULARE]: *area,* 4.25 miles north-northwest of Kern Peak near Golden Trout Creek (lat. 36°22' N, long. 118°18'25" W; around NW cor. sec. 16, T 18 S, R 34 E). Named on Kern Peak (1956) 15' quadrangle. United States Board on Geographic Names (1933a, p. 342) rejected the name "Volcano Meadow" for the feature. Miners named the place for marmots found there, which the miners misidentified as groundhogs (Adler, p. 22).

Grouse Canyon [TULARE]: *canyon,* drained by a stream that flows 2 miles to Kern River 2.25 miles south-southeast of Hockett Peak (lat. 36°11'30" N, long. 118°22' W). Named on Hockett Peak (1956) 15' quadrangle.

Grouse Creek [FRESNO]: *stream,* flows 1.5 miles to Big Creek (1) 2 miles east-northeast of the town of Big Creek (lat. 37°13'10" N, long. 119°12'50" W; sec. 23, T 8 S, R 25 E). Named on Huntington Lake (1953) 15' quadrangle.

Grouse Creek [TULARE]: *stream,* flows 6.5 miles to South Fork Kaweah River 8 miles south-southeast of Kaweah (lat. 36°22'10" N, long. 118°51'10" W; near NW cor. sec. 16, T 18 S, R 29 E); the stream heads at Upper Grouse Valley and goes through Grouse Valley. Named on Kaweah (1957) 15' quadrangle.

Grouse Lake [FRESNO]:
(1) *lake,* 700 feet long, 3.5 miles east of Dinkey Dome (lat. 37°07'10" N, long. 119°04'15" W; sec. 30, T 9 S, R 27 E). Named on Huntington Lake (1953) 15' quadrangle.
(2) *lake,* 1400 feet long, 8 miles south-southwest of Marion Peak (lat. 36°51'30" N, long. 118°35'15" W). Named on Marion Peak (1953) 15' quadrangle.

Grouse Lake [MADERA]: *lake,* 500 feet long, 2.25 miles southwest of Buena Vista Peak (lat. 37°34'20" N, long. 119°32'45" W; sec. 22, T 4 S, R 22 E). Named on Yosemite (1956) 15' quadrangle.

Grouse Meadow [KERN]: *area,* 2.25 miles south of Claraville (lat. 35°24'35" N, long. 118°20'05" W). Named on Claraville (1972) 7.5' quadrangle.

Grouse Meadow [MADERA]: *area,* 6.25 miles north-northeast of Yosemite Forks (lat. 37°26'55" N, long. 119°34'40" W; at SW cor. sec. 33, T 5 S, R 22 E). Named on Bass Lake (1953) 15' quadrangle.

Grouse Meadow [TULARE]:
(1) *area,* 2 miles south of Wilsonia along Dry Creek (1) (lat. 36°42'15" N, long. 118°57'20" W; sec. 17, T 14 S, R 28 E). Named on Giant

Forest (1956) 15' quadrangle. According to United States Board on Geographic Names (1987b, p. 1), Grouse Meadow is 2.7 miles south-southwest of Wilsonia (lat. 36°41'50" N, long. 118°58'10" W; sec. 19, T 14 S, R 28 E).
(2) *area,* 5 miles north-northwest of Olancha Peak (lat. 36°20'10" N, long. 118°08'40" W). Named on Olancha (1956) 15' quadrangle.

Grouse Meadows [FRESNO]: *area,* 8 miles east-southeast of Mount Goddard along Middle Fork Kings River (lat. 37°03'35" N, long. 118°35'05" W). Named on Mount Goddard (1948) 15' quadrangle. L.A. Winchell named the feature in 1879; the name now has the singular form "Grouse Meadow" (Browning 1986, p. 88).

Grouse Peak [TULARE]: *peak,* 11 miles south-southeast of Kaweah (lat. 36°20' N, long. 118°49'05" W; sec. 27, T 18 S, R 29 E); the peak is northeast of Grouse Valley. Altitude 5317 feet. Named on Kaweah (1957) 15' quadrangle.

Grouse Valley [TULARE]: *valley,* 11.5 miles south-southeast of Kaweah (lat. 36°19' N, long. 118°50' W); the valley is on upper reaches of Grouse Creek. Named on Kaweah (1957) 15' quadrangle.

Grouse Valley: see **Upper Grouse Valley** [TULARE].

Grub Gulch [MADERA]:
(1) *canyon,* 10.5 miles northeast of Raymond (lat. 37°19'25" N, long. 119°46'10" W; sec. 15, T 7 S, R 20 E). Named on Horsecamp Mountain (1947) 7.5' quadrangle. The name is from the local tradition that miners, unsuccessful elsewhere, could always "grub out" enough gold in the canyon to make a living (Hanna, p. 128).
(2) *locality,* 10.5 miles northeast of Raymond (lat. 37°19'30" N, long. 119°46'15" W; sec. 15, T 7 S, R 20 E); the place is in Grub Gulch (1). Named on Mariposa (1912) 30' quadrangle. Postal authorities established Grubgulch post office in 1883 and discontinued it in 1918 (Salley, p 90). They established Miami post office 8 miles southwest of Grub Gulch (2) in 1884 and discontinued it in 1887; the name was from the Miami River region of Ohio (Salley, p. 139).

Grubtree Creek: see **Whitney Creek** [TULARE].

Gruff Lake [FRESNO]: *lake,* 300 feet long, 5 miles south of Mount Abbot (lat. 37°18'59" N, long. 118°47'45" W). Named on Mount Abbot (1953) 15' quadrangle. Employees of California Department of Fish and Game named the lake in 1952 (Browning 1986, p. 89).

Grunigen Creek: see **Crunigen Creek** [TULARE].

Guernsey [KINGS]: *locality,* 9 miles north-northwest of Corcoran along Atchison, Topeka and Santa Fe Railroad (lat. 36°12'45" N, long. 119°38'25" W; sec. 1, T 20 S, R 21

E). Named on Guernsey (1954) 7.5' quadrangle. Postal authorities established Guernsey post office in 1898 and discontinued it in 1918 (Frickstad, p. 61). The name is for James Guernsey, who owned land at the place (Gudde, 1949, p. 138).

Guernsey Mill [TULARE]: *locality*, 4.5 miles southeast of California Hot Springs (lat. 35°50' N, long. 118°36'50" W; near S line sec. 15, T 24 S, R 31 E). Named on California Hot Springs (1958) 15' quadrangle.

Guernsey Slough [KINGS]: *stream*, flows 12 miles to a point nearly 3 miles south of Guernsey (lat. 36°10'20" N, long. 119°38'20" W). Named on Guernsey (1929), Remnoy (1927), and Waukena (1928) 7.5' quadrangles. Remnoy (1954) and Waukena (1954) 7.5' quadrangles have the name on a watercourse that is mainly dry.

Guest Lake [FRESNO]: *lake*, 1300 feet long, nearly 0.5 mile north-northwest of Blackcap Mountain (lat. 37°04'40" N, long. 118°47'50" W). Named on Blackcap Mountain (1953) 15' quadrangle.

Guijarral Hills [FRESNO]: *range*, 8 miles east of Coalinga (lat. 36° 09' N, long. 120°13'30" W). Named on Guijarral Hills (1956) 7.5' quadrangle. Arnold and Anderson (1908, p. 15) named the range, described it as "a small low group of gravelly hills," and noted that *guijarral* means "a heap of pebbles" or "a place abounding in pebbles" in Spanish.

Gulf [KERN]: *locality*, 2 miles east of Millux along Sunset Railroad (lat. 35°10'50" N, long. 119°09'35" W). Named on Millux (1954) 7.5' quadrangle.

Guttrie Meadow: see **Cabin Meadow** [TULARE].

Guyot: see **Mount Guyot** [TULARE].

Guyot Creek [TULARE]: *stream*, flows 32 miles to Rock Creek 13 miles north-northwest of Kern Peak (lat. 36°29'30" N, long. 118° 21' W); the stream is east of Mount Guyot. Named on Kern Peak (1956) and Mount Whitney (1956) 15' quadrangles.

Guyot Flat [TULARE]: *area*, 5.25 miles southwest of Mount Whitney (lat. 36°31'25" N, long. 118°21' W). Named on Mount Whitney (1956) 15' quadrangle. The place also was called Sand Flat (Browning 1986, p. 89).

Gyle: see **Delano** [KERN].

Gypsite [KERN]: *locality*, 3 miles southwest of Saltdale (lat. 35°19'50" N, long. 117°55'50" W). Named on Cantil (1967) 7.5' quadrangle. Postal authorities established Gypsite post office in 1911 and discontinued it in 1912; the name was from a gypsum mine (Salley, p. 91).

– H –

Hacker Mountain [FRESNO]: *peak*, 0.5 mile north-northeast of Trimmer (lat. 36°54'55" N, long. 119°17'35" W; near W line sec. 6, T 12

S, R 25 E). Altitude 2331 feet. Named on Trimmer (1965) 7.5' quadrangle.

Haeckel: see **Mount Haeckel** [FRESNO].

Haggin Well [KERN]: *well*, 9.5 miles north-northwest of Randsburg (lat. 35°29'55" N, long. 117°42'25" W; sec. 18, T 28 S, R 40 E). Named on El Paso Peaks (1967) 7.5' quadrangle. Called Higgins Well on Searles Lake (1915) 1° quadrangle.

Haight Canyon [KERN]: *canyon*, drained by a stream that flows 6.25 miles to Havilah Canyon 4.25 miles south-southwest of Miracle Hot Springs (lat. 35°30'50" N, long. 118°31' W; near NW cor. sec. 11, T 28 S, R 32 E). Named on Breckenridge Mountain (1972), Miracle Hot Springs (1972), and Piute Peak (1972) 7.5' quadrangles.

Haiwee Pass [TULARE]: *pass*, 8.5 miles southeast of Monache Mountain on Tulare-Inyo county line (lat. 36°08'05" N, long. 118° 04'15" W); the pass is near the head of Haiwee Creek, which is in Inyo County. Named on Monache Mountain (1956) 15' quadrangle.

Hale: see **Mount Hale** [TULARE].

Hale McLeod Canyon [KERN]: *canyon*, drained by a stream that heads in San Luis Obispo County and flows 4.5 miles to Midway Valley 1 mile south-southeast of Fellows (lat. 35°09'50" N, long. 119°31'50" W; near N line sec. 8, T 32 S, R 23 E). Named on Fellows (1951) 7.5' quadrangle. The name recalls Hale-McLeod Oil Company, which operated in the neighborhood (Rintoul, p. 92).

Half Corral Meadow [FRESNO]: *area*, 5.25 miles north-northeast of Kaiser Peak (lat. 37°22'05" N, long. 119°09'25" W). Named on Kaiser Peak (1953) 15' quadrangle.

Halfmoon Lake [FRESNO]: *lake*, 2300 feet long, 3.5 miles west-southwest of Blackcap Mountain (lat. 37°03' N, long. 118°50'50" W). Named on Blackcap Mountain (1953) 15' quadrangle.

Halfway House [KERN]: *locality*, nearly 2 miles north-northwest of Knob Hill (lat. 35°35'20" N, long. 118°57'35" W; near SE cor. sec. 9, T 27 S, R 28 E). Named on Knob Hill (1965) 7.5' quadrangle.

Hall Meadow [FRESNO]: *area*, 9 miles southeast of Dinkey Dome (lat. 37°01' N, long. 119°01'15" W; sec. 34, T 10 S, R 27 E); the place is 1.5 miles south of Hall Mountain. Named on Huntington Lake (1953) 15' quadrangle. Called House Meadow on Kaiser (1904) 30' quadrangle. The name "Hall" is for a sheepman and cattle rancher who settled at the place about 1870 (Browning 1986, p. 91).

Hall Mountain [FRESNO]: *ridge*, northwest-trending, 2 miles long 8.5 miles southeast of Dinkey Dome (lat. 37°02'15" N, long. 119° 01' W; in and near sec. 22, 27, T 10 S, R 27 E). Named on Huntington Lake (1953) 15' quadrangle.

Halls Corner [KINGS]: *locality*, about 3 miles north-northwest of Lemoore (lat. 36°20'35"

N, long. 119°48'25" W; at N line sec. 28, T 18 S, R 20 E). Named on Lemoore (1954) 7.5' quadrangle.

Halstead Creek [TULARE]: *stream,* flows 3.5 miles to Marble Fork 5 miles east of Yucca Mountain (lat. 36°34'55" N, long. 118° 47' W; sec. 36, T 15 S, R 29 E); the stream goes through Halstead Meadow. Named on Giant Forest (1956) 15' quadrangle. United States Board on Geographic Names (1933a, p. 349) rejected the name "Suwanee River" for the stream.

Halstead Meadow [TULARE]: *area,* nearly 5.5 miles northeast of Yucca Mountain (lat. 36°37' N, long. 118°47' W; sec. 13, T 15 S, R 29 E); the place is along Halstead Creek. Named on Giant Forest (1956) 15' quadrangle. The name commemorates Sam Halstead, who pastured horses in the neighborhood (United States Board on Geographic Names, 1933a, p. 349).

Hamblin [KINGS]: *settlement,* 2 miles east of Hanford (lat. 36°19'45" N, long. 119°36'30" W; near S line sec. 29, T 18 S, R 22 E). Named on Remnoy (1954) 7.5' quadrangle.

Hambright Canyon [TULARE]: *canyon,* drained by a stream that flows about 0.5 mile to Dry Creek (1) 7 miles northeast of Woodlake (lat. 36°29'30" N, long. 119°01' W; sec. 35, T 16 S, R 27 E). Named on Woodlake (1952) 7.5' quadrangle.

Hamilton Creek [TULARE]: *stream,* flows 3.5 miles to join Lone Pine Creek and form Middle Fork Kaweah River 4.5 miles west-southwest of Triple Divide Peak (lat. 36°33'50" N, long. 118°36'05" W); Hamilton Lakes are along the creek. Named on Triple Divide Peak (1956) 15' quadrangle. United States Board on Geographic Names (1968b, p. 7) rejected the name "Deer Creek" for the stream.

Hamilton Hill: see **Tropico Hill** [KERN].

Hamilton Lake: see **Precipice Lake** [TULARE].

Hamilton Lakes [TULARE]: *lakes,* two, largest 2400 feet long, 3.25 miles southwest of Triple Divide Peak (lat. 36°33'45" N, long. 118°34'30" W); the lakes are along Hamilton Creek. Named on Triple Divide Peak (1956) 15' quadrangle. The name is for James Hamilton, who stocked the lakes with fish that he packed on his back from Big Arroyo (Browning 1986, p. 91).

Hammond [FRESNO]: *locality,* in Fresno where a rail line branches east from the main line of Atchison, Topeka and Santa Fe Railroad (lat. 36°45'35" N, long. 119°47'10" W). Named on Fresno North (1965) 7.5' quadrangle.

Hammond [TULARE]: *locality,* 3.25 miles east of Kaweah along Kaweah River (lat. 36°27'55" N, long. 118°51'40" W; sec. 8, T 17 S, R 29 E). Named on Kaweah (1957) 15' quadrangle. Postal authorities established Hammond post office in 1905 and discontinued it in 1928 (Frickstad, p. 211).

Hamptonville: see **Friant** [FRESNO].

Hamp Williams Pass [KERN]: *pass,* 5.5 miles

north of Emerald Mountain (lat. 35°20'10" N, long. 118°17'10" W). Named on Emerald Mountain (1972) 7.5' quadrangle.

Hanford [KINGS]: *town,* in the north part of Kings County (lat. 36° 20' N, long. 119°38'45" W; in and near sec. 25, T 18 S, R 21 E). Named on Hanford (1954) 7.5' quadrangle. Postal authorities established Hanford post office in 1877 (Frickstad, p. 61), and the town incorporated in 1891. Officials of Central Pacific Railroad named the place for James Hanford, treasurer of the railroad (Hart, J.D., p. 176).

Hanning Flat [KERN]: *valley,* 4.5 miles west-northwest of Weldon (lat. 35°41'15" N, long. 118°21'50" W). Named on Weldon (1972) 7.5' quadrangle.

Hans Grieve Canyon [FRESNO]: *canyon,* drained by a stream that flows 5.25 miles to Warthan Creek 3 miles west-southwest of Coalinga Mineral Springs (lat. 36°07'50" N, long. 120°36'15" W; near E line sec. 6, T 21 S, R 13 E). Named on Priest Valley (1969) and Sherman Peak (1969) 7.5' quadrangles.

Hante: see **Camp Yenis Hante** [KERN].

Happy Gap [FRESNO]:

(1) *pass,* 10 miles east-northeast of Hume (lat. 36°51' N, long. 118° 45'05" W). Named on Tehipite Dome (1952) 15' quadrangle. According to Browning (1986, p. 91), the name describes the feelings of anyone who manages to get a pack train to the place.

(2) *pass,* 6.25 miles southwest of Hume (lat. 36°43'25" N, long. 118°59'30" W; sec. 12, T 14 S, R 27 E). Named on Giant Forest (1956) 15' quadrangle. Early teamsters named the feature (Forest M. Clingan, personal communication, 1990).

Happy Hollow [MADERA]: *canyon,* drained by a stream that flows 3.5 miles to Coarse Gold Creek 6 miles southeast of Knowles (lat. 37°09'35" N, long. 119°47'45" W; sec. 9, T 9 S, R 20 E). Named on Knowles (1962) and Little Table Mountain (1962) 7.5' quadrangles.

Hardcash Gulch [KERN]: *canyon,* less than 1 mile long, 5 miles north of Randsburg (lat. 35°26'35" N, long. 117°38'55" W; on W line sec. 1, T 29 S, R 40 E). Named on El Paso Peaks (1967) 7.5' quadrangle.

Hardwick [KINGS]: *village,* 6.5 miles northwest of Hanford (lat. 36°24'10" N, long. 119°43'10" W; near S line sec. 32, T 17 S, R 21 E). Named on Laton (1953) 7.5' quadrangle. Postal authorities established Hardwick post office in 1895, discontinued it in 1904, reestablished it in 1909, and discontinued it in 1942; the name commemorates an official of Southern Pacific Railroad (Salley, p. 93). A place called Kingston was founded in 1856 on the south bank of Kings River at Whitmore's Ferry, 8.5 miles northwest of present Hanford; L.A. Whitmore started the ferry there in 1854 (Hoover, Rensch, and Rensch, p. 136). Laton (1953) 7.5' quadrangle shows Kingston historical marker 2 miles northeast of Hardwick on the south side of Kings River. Postal authorities established Joneso post office 11 miles southeast of Kingston (NW quarter sec. 14, T 18 S, R 22 E) in 1874 and discontinued it in 1879 (Salley, p. 108).

Harlow: see **Shirley** [KINGS].

Harmon Peak [FRESNO]: *peak,* 2 miles east-southeast of Tivy Mountain (lat. 36°47'05" N, long. 119°19'25" W; sec. 23, T 13 S, R 24 E). Altitude 2190 feet. Named on Pine Flat Dam (1965) 7.5' quadrangle.

Harney: see **Mike Harney Canyon** [KERN].

Harper Canyon [KERN]: *canyon,* drained by a stream that flows 9 miles to Caliente Creek 3.25 miles east-northeast of Caliente (lat. 35°18'30" N, long. 118°34'35" W; near NE cor. sec. 19, T 30 S, R 32 E). Named on Loraine (1972) and Oiler Peak (1972) 7.5' quadrangles.

Harper Peak [KERN]: *peak,* 5.5 miles northwest of Loraine (lat. 35° 22'15" N, long. 118°29'35" W; near SE cor. sec. 25, T 29 S, R 32 E). Altitude 5804 feet. Named on Loraine (1972) 7.5' quadrangle.

Harpertown [KERN]: *locality,* 7 miles southeast of downtown Bakersfield along the railroad (lat. 35°17'40" N, long. 118°55'20" W; at N line sec. 25, T 30 S, R 28 E). Named on Lamont (1954) 7.5' quadrangle.

Harriet Lake [MADERA]: *lake,* 2000 feet long, 5.5 miles east-northeast of Merced Peak (lat. 37°40'25" N, long. 119°18'25" W). Named on Merced Peak (1953) 15' quadrangle.

Harrington: see **Mount Harrington** [FRESNO].

Harris Creek: see **Rattlesnake Creek** [TULARE] (3).

Harris Grade Spring [KERN]: *spring,* 3.5 miles east-northeast of Claraville (lat. 35°27'35" N, long. 118°16'15" W; sec. 36, T 28 S, R 34 E). Named on Claraville (1972) 7.5' quadrangle.

Harrison Pass [TULARE]: *pass,* 10.5 miles northwest of Mount Whitney (lat. 36°41'55" N, long. 118°24' W). Named on Mount Whitney (1956) 15' quadrangle. Called Harrisons Pass on Olmsted's (1900) map. The name commemorates Ben Harrison, a sheepherder who built a monument at the pass in the 1880's (Hanna, p. 134).

Harris Spring [FRESNO]: *spring,* 7 miles south-southeast of Ciervo Mountain (lat. 36°22'50" N, long. 120°31'15" W; sec. 11, T 18 S, R 13 E). Named on Ciervo Mountain (1969) 7.5' quadrangle.

Harry Payne Spring [KERN]: *spring,* 6.5 miles east-southeast of Caliente (lat. 35°15'35" N, long. 118°31' W; sec. 2, T 31 S, R 32 E). Named on Oiler Peak (1972) 7.5' quadrangle.

Harry's Bend: see **Mineral King** [TULARE].

Hart: see **Jack Hart Spring** [FRESNO].

Hart Canyon [KERN]: *canyon,* drained by a stream that flows 2.5 miles to Weaver Creek 7.5 miles north-northwest of Emerald Mountain (lat. 35°21' N, long. 118°21' W; near S line sec. 5, T 30 S, R 34 E); the canyon splits at the head to form Big Hart Canyon and Little Hart Canyon. Named on Emerald Mountain (1972) 7.5' quadrangle.

Hartland [TULARE]: *locality,* 5.5 miles south of Wilsonia (lat. 36° 39'10" N, long. 118°57'25" W; sec. 5, T 15 S, R 28 E). Named on Giant Forest (1956) 15' quadrangle. The name commemorates William Hart, who operated a sawmill near Badger (Browning 1986, p. 93).

Hart Meadow [TULARE]: *area,* 3.5 miles east-southeast of Wilsonia (lat. 36°42'25" N, long. 118°54'05" W; sec. 14, T 14 S, R 28 E). Named on Giant Forest (1956) 15' quadrangle. Mitchel Hart patented land in section 14 in 1890 (Browning 1986, p. 93).

Harts Place [KERN]: *locality,* 13 miles southwest of Inyokern (lat. 35°30'05" N, long. 117°56'50" W; sec. 13, T 28 S, R 37 E). Named on Freeman Junction (1972) 7.5' quadrangle.

Hart Station: see **Old Hart Station** [KERN].

Harvester [KINGS]: *locality,* 18 miles east of Kettleman City along Kings Lake Shore Railroad (lat. 35°58'50" N, long. 119°38'30" W). Named on Harvester (1935) 7.5' quadrangle.

Harvey Lake [FRESNO]: *lake,* 800 feet long, 9 miles southwest of Mount Abbot (lat. 37°18'20" N, long. 118°54'45" W). Named on Mount Abbot (1953) 15' quadrangle. Employees of California Department of Fish and Game named the lake in 1947 for Harvey Sauter of High Sierra Pack Station (Browning 1986, p. 93).

Haskell Meadow [MADERA]: *area,* nearly 2 miles south of Shuteye Peak (lat. 37°19'25" N, long. 119°25'55" W; on W line sec. 14, T 7 S, R 23 E). Named on Shuteye Peak (1953) 15' quadrangle. The name is for Bill Haskell and John Haskell, early sheepmen in the neighborhood (Browning, 1986, p. 93).

Haslett Basin [FRESNO]: *area,* 7 miles northwest of Balch Camp (lat. 36°58' N, long. 119°12'40" W; near SE cor. sec. 14, T 11 S, R 25 E). Named on Patterson Mountain (1952) 15' quadrangle.

Hatchet Peak [TULARE]:
(1) *peak,* 1.5 miles north-northwest of Springville (lat. 36°09' N, long. 118°49'45" W; near SW cor. sec. 27, T 20 S, R 29 E). Altitude 3286 feet. Named on Springville (1957) 7.5' quadrangle.
(2) *peak,* 4.25 miles north-northeast of California Hot Springs (lat. 35°56'30" N, long. 118°39'20" W; sec. 8, T 23 S, R 31 E). Altitude 6385 feet. Named on California Hot Springs (1958) 15' quadrangle.

Hatch Lake [FRESNO]: *lake,* 1100 feet long, 4 miles east-southeast of Dinkey Dome (lat. 37°05'30" N, long. 119°03'45" W; sec. 6, T 10 S, R 27 E). Named on Huntington Lake (1953) 15' quadrangle.

Havala Spring [KERN]: *spring,* 5.25 miles

west-southwest of Cummings Mountain (lat. 35°00'40" N, long. 118°39'15" W; near NE cor. sec. 26, T 11 N, R 17 W). Named on Tejon Ranch (1966) 7.5' quadrangle.

Havilah [KERN]: *village,* 4 miles south-southeast of Miracle Hot Springs (lat. 35°31' N, long. 118°31' W). Named on Miracle Hot Springs (1972) 7.5' quadrangle. Postal authorities established Havilah post office in 1866 and discontinued it in 1918 (Frickstad, p. 56). The community was the first county seat of Kern County. Asbury Harpending (p. 102-103) claimed that he named the place for a biblical country rich in gold.

Havilah Canyon [KERN]: *canyon,* drained by a stream that flows 5.5 miles to Clear Creek (1) 3 miles south-southeast of Miracle Hot Springs (lat. 35°32'05" N, long. 118°30'45" W; sec. 35, T 27 S, R 32 E); Havilah is in the canyon. Named on Breckenridge Mountain (1972) and Miracle Hot Springs (1972) 7.5' quadrangles. On Glennville (1956) 15' quadrangle, the stream in the canyon is called Havilah Creek.

Havilah Creek: see **Havilah Canyon** [KERN].

Hawkins [TULARE]: *locality,* 1.5 miles northeast of Lindsay along Visalia Electric Railroad (lat. 36°13'15" N, long. 119°04'05" W; sec. 5, T 20 S, R 27 E). Named on Lindsay (1928) 7.5' quadrangle.

Hawthorne's Station: see **San Joaquin** [FRESNO].

Hay Corral Ridge [KERN]: *ridge,* generally west-southwest-trending, 2.5 miles long, the center is 2.5 miles east of Caliente (lat. 35°17'25" N, long. 118°34'45" W). Named on Oiler Peak (1972) 7.5' quadrangle.

Hayes: see **Mendota** [FRESNO].

Hayes Canyon [KERN]: *canyon,* drained by a stream that flows 2.5 miles to Winters Canyon 9 miles west-northwest of Liebre Twins (lat. 34°59'25" N, long. 118°43'05" W; sec. 32, T 11 N, R 17 W). Named on Winters Ridge (1966) 7.5' quadrangle.

Hayes Peak: see **Gray Peak** [MADERA].

Hay Flat [KINGS]: *valley,* 8.5 miles south of Avenal (lat. 35°52'50" N, long. 120°08'45" W). Named on Garza Peak (1953) and Tent Hills (1942) 7.5' quadrangles.

Hay Meadow: see **Gnat Meadow** [FRESNO].

Haypress Canyon [KERN]: *canyon,* drained by a stream that flows 2 miles to the canyon of Caliente Creek nearly 4 miles west-northwest of Caliente (lat. 35°18'25" N, long. 118°41'30" W). Named on Bena (1972) 7.5' quadrangle. The name recalls an unsuccessful attempt to haul a hay press through the canyon (Bailey, 1962, p. 43).

Haypress Spring [KERN]: *spring,* 4 miles west of Caliente (lat. 35° 17'40" N, long. 118°41'40" W); the spring is in Haypress Canyon. Named on Bena (1972) 7.5' quadrangle.

Hazelton [KERN]: *locality,* 1.5 miles southeast of Maricopa along Sunset Railroad (lat.

35°02'35" N, long. 119°33' W; on W line sec. 18, T 11 N, R 23 W). Named on Maricopa (1951) 7.5' quadrangle. The place first was called Sunset or Sunset Camp before the railroad reached the site; a locality 2.5 miles farther east (sec. 21, T 11 N, R 23 W) that originally was called Sunset became known as Old Sunset (Latta, 1949, p. 78, 102). Judge Lovejoy gave the name "Sunset" to Old Sunset because of the beautiful sunsets seen there; the name "Hazelton" is for Hazelton Blodget, son of Hugh A. Blodget, a pioneer oilman (Latta, 1949, p. 84, 91).

Hazen: see **Mount Hazen,** under **Table Mountain** [TULARE] (2).

Heald Peak [KERN]: *peak,* 5.25 miles south-southwest of Weldon (lat. 35°35'30" N, long. 118°18'30" W). Altitude 6901 feet. Named on Woolstalf Creek (1972) 7.5' quadrangle. The name commemorates Weldon F. Heald, writer, consultant to Secretary of the Interior, and leader in conservation projects in California (United States Board on Geographic Names, 1974a, p. 3).

Heart Lake [FRESNO]: *lake,* 950 feet long, 9 miles southwest of Mount Abbot (lat. 37°16'55" N, long. 118°52'30" W); the lake has a somewhat heart-shaped outline on a map. Named on Mount Abbot (1953) 15' quadrangle.

Heart Meadow [TULARE]: *area,* 2.5 miles north-northwest of Shell Mountain (lat. 36°43'40" N, long. 118°48'45" W; near N line sec. 10, T 14 S, R 29 E). Named on Giant Forest (1956) 15' quadrangle.

Heather Lake [TULARE]: *lake,* 700 feet long, 9 miles west of Triple Divide Peak (lat. 36°36'05" N, long. 118°41'10" W; near S line sec. 23, T 15 S, R 30 E). Named on Triple Divide Peak (1956) 15' quadrangle. Superintendent White of Sequoia National Park named the feature in 1925 (United States Board on Geographic Names, 1933a, p. 359).

Heather Meadow: see **Lone Pine Meadow** [TULARE].

Heck Canyon [KERN]: *canyon,* drained by a stream that flows 2 miles to Caliente Creek 5.25 miles east-northeast of Caliente (lat. 35°19' N, long. 118°32'10" W; sec. 15, T 30 S, R 32 E). Named on Oiler Peak (1972) 7.5' quadrangle.

Hedrick Meadow [FRESNO]: *area,* 11.5 miles northeast of Kaiser Peak (lat. 37°25'55" N, long. 119°04'05" W). Named on Kaiser Peak (1953) 15' quadrangle.

Heid: see **Redbanks** [TULARE].

Heinlen: see **Cimarron** [KINGS].

Helen Lake [FRESNO]:

(1) *lake,* 600 feet long, 10 miles northwest of Mount Abbot (lat. 37° 28'40" N, long. 118°55'20" W). Named on Mount Abbot (1953) 15' quadrangle. United States Board on Geographic Names (1969a, p. 5) approved the name "Squaw Lake" for the feature.

(2) *lake,* 3000 feet long, 3.25 miles east-north-east of Mount Goddard (lat. 37°07'10" N, long. 118°39'50" W); the lake is northeast of Muir Pass. Named on Mount Goddard (1948) 15' quadrangle. Helen Lake and Wanda Lake, on opposite sides of Muir Pass, were named for daughters of John Muir—this one for Mrs. Helen Muir Funk (Farquhar, 1923, p. 402).

Hell For Sure [TULARE]: *area,* 6.25 miles west-southwest of Kern Peak on the east side of Kern River (lat. 36°16'40" N, long. 118°23'30" W). Named on Kern Peak (1956) 15' quadrangle.

Hell for Sure Lake [FRESNO]: *lake,* 0.5 mile long, 4.5 miles north of Blackcap Mountain (lat. 37°08'20" N, long. 118°48' W); the lake is 0.25 mile southwest of Hell for Sure Pass. Named on Blackcap Mountain (1953) 15' quadrangle.

Hell for Sure Pass [FRESNO]: *pass,* 5 miles north of Blackcap Mountain (lat. 37°08'45" N, long. 118°47'45" W). Named on Blackcap Mountain (1953) 15' quadrangle. J.N. LeConte named the pass in 1904 (Farquhar, 1923, p. 403).

Hell Hole Meadow [FRESNO]: *area,* 12 miles west-southwest of Mount Abbot (lat. 37°18'30" N, long. 118°58'30" W). Named on Mount Abbot (1953) 15' quadrangle.

Hells Half Acre [MADERA]: *area,* 9 miles east-northeast of Shuteye Peak near San Joaquin River (lat. 37°24'15" N, long. 119°16'25" W). Named on Shuteye Peak (1953) 15' quadrangle.

Hells Hole [TULARE]: *area,* 6.25 miles southwest of Kern Peak (lat. 36°15' N, long. 118°22' W). Named on Hockett Peak (1956) and Kern Peak (1956) 15' quadrangles.

Helm [FRESNO]: *village,* 13 miles south of Kerman (lat. 36°31'55" N, long. 120°05'45" W; near SW cor. sec. 14, T 16 S, R 17 E). Named on Helm (1963) 7.5' quadrangle. Postal authorities established Helm post office in 1913 (Frickstad, p. 33). The name commemorates William Helm, a sheepman who came to California in 1859 (Gudde, 1949, p. 146).

Helm Corner [KINGS]: *locality,* 4.5 miles west of Corcoran (lat. 36° 05'50" N, long. 119°38'35" W; at W line sec. 18, T 21 S, R 22 E). Named on El Rico Ranch (1954) 7.5' quadrangle.

Helmke Pond [FRESNO]: *intermittent lake,* 1150 feet long, 5 miles west of Selma (lat. 36°34'15" N, long. 119°41'50" W; sec. 4, T 16 S, R 21 E). Named on Conejo (1963) 7.5' quadrangle. Called Ralmke Pond on Selma (1946) 15' quadrangle, which shows a lake 3000 feet long.

Helms Creek [FRESNO]: *stream,* flows 12 miles to North Fork Kings River about 8.5 miles west of Blackcap Mountain (lat. 37° 03' N, long. 118°56'35" W; sec. 20, T 10 S, R 28 E). Named on Blackcap Mountain (1953) and

Huntington Lake (1953) 15' quadrangles. This apparently is the stream called West Branch on Lippincott's (1902) map.

Helms Creek [MADERA]: *stream,* flows 2.25 miles to Fine Gold Creek 5 miles west-southwest of the town of North Fork (lat. 37° 12'15" N, long. 119°35'45" W; sec. 29, T 8 S, R 22 E). Named on North Fork (1965) 7.5' quadrangle.

Helms Meadow [FRESNO]: *area,* 12.5 miles west-northwest of Blackcap Mountain (lat. 37°08'40" N, long. 119°00' W; mainly in sec. 14, 15, T 9 S, R 27 E); the place is along Helms Creek. Named on Blackcap Mountain (1953) and Huntington Lake (1953) 15' quadrangles. The name commemorates William Helm, an early sheepman (Farquhar, 1923, p. 403).

Hemlock Crossing [MADERA]: *locality,* 8 miles west of Devils Postpile along North Fork San Joaquin River (lat. 37°38'20" N, long. 119°13'25" W). Named on Devils Postpile (1953) 15' quadrangle.

Hengst Peak: see **Mineral King** [TULARE].

Henry: see **Mount Henry** [FRESNO].

Hensley Lake [MADERA]: *lake,* behind a dam on Fresno River 7.5 miles south of Raymond (lat. 37°06'40" N, long. 119°53' W; near N line sec. 34, T 9 S, R 19 E). Named on Daulton (1962, photorevised 1981), Knowles (1962, photorevised 1981), Little Table Mountain (1962, photorevised 1981), and Raymond (1962, photorevised 1981) 7.5' quadrangles.

Herbert: see **Raymond** [MADERA].

Hermit: see **The Hermit** [FRESNO].

Herndon [FRESNO]: *town,* 9 miles northwest of downtown Fresno (lat. 36°50'15" N, long. 119°55' W; on S line sec. 32, T 12 S, R 19 E). Named on Herndon (1964) 7.5' quadrangle. Postal authorities established Herndon post office in 1887, discontinued it in 1893, and reestablished it in 1907 (Frickstad, p. 33). The place was called Sycamore in 1872, when the railroad crossing of San Joaquin River was there; later it was renamed Herndon for a relative of an irrigation promoter (Gudde, 1949, p. 147).

Herrick's Cross: see **Tulare** [TULARE].

Hessian Meadow [TULARE]: *area,* 2.5 miles northeast of Monache Mountain (lat. 36°14'10" N, long. 118°09'55" W; sec. 27, 34, T 19 S, R 35 E). Named on Monache Mountain (1956) 15' quadrangle. Olancha (1907) 30' quadrangle has the form "Hessian Meadows" for the name.

Hester Lake: see **Langille Peak** [FRESNO].

Hewey Valley [TULARE]: *valley,* 2 miles north-northeast of Fountain Springs (lat. 35°55' N, long. 118°54'10" W). Named on Fountain Springs (1965) 7.5' quadrangle. Called Huey Valley on White River (1936) 15' quadrangle, but United States Board on Geographic Names (1967a, p. 9) rejected this form of the name.

Hewitt Valley [MADERA]: *valley,* 7 miles east-southeast of O'Neals (lat. 37°05'05" N, long.

119°34'55" W). Named on Millerton Lake East (1965) 7.5' quadrangle.

Hickman Creek [TULARE]: *stream,* flows 2.5 miles to North Fork Tule River 3.5 miles north-northeast of Springville (lat. 36°10'50" N, long. 118°47'50" W; near SE cor. sec. 14, T 20 S, R 29 E). Named on Springville (1957) 7.5' quadrangle.

Hicko: see **Hiko**, under **Visalia** [TULARE].

Hicks: see **Hiko**, under **Visalia** [TULARE].

Hico: see **Hiko**, under **Visalia** [TULARE].

Hidden Lake [FRESNO]:
(1) *lake,* 850 feet long, 2.5 miles west of Kaiser Peak (lat. 37°18' N, long. 119°14' W; sec. 22, T 7 S, R 25 E). Named on Kaiser Peak (1953) 15' quadrangle.
(2) *lake,* 800 feet long, 16 miles northwest of Blackcap Mountain (lat. 37°15' N, long. 118°59' W). Named on Blackcap Mountain (1953) and Mount Abbot (1953) 15' quadrangles.

Hidden Lake: see **Ruth Lake** [MADERA].

Hidden Lake [TULARE]: *lake,* 300 feet long, 9.5 miles south of Mineral King (lat. 36°18'45" N, long. 118°36'15" W). Named on Mineral King (1956) 15' quadrangle.

Hidden Spring [TULARE]: *spring,* 2.25 miles north-northeast of Yucca Mountain (lat. 36°36'15" N, long. 118°51'30" W; near W line sec. 20, T 15 S, R 29 E). Named on Giant Forest (1956) 15' quadrangle.

Hidden Valley [KERN]: *valley,* 3 miles northnorthwest of Rosamond (lat. 34°54'10" N, long. 118°11'30" W; sec. 6, T 9 N, R 12 W). Named on Soledad Mountain (1973) 7.5' quadrangle.

Hidden Valley: see **Blaney Meadows** [FRESNO].

Hidden Valley Meadows: see **Blaney Meadows** [FRESNO].

Hideaway Lake: see **Ruth Lake** [MADERA].

Higby [TULARE]: *locality,* 3 miles south of Visalia along Atchison, Topeka and Santa Fe Railroad (lat. 36°17'05" N, long. 119°17'10" W; at N line sec. 17, T 19 S, R 25 E). Named on Visalia (1949) 7.5' quadrangle.

Higgins Well: see **Haggin Well** [KERN].

Highberg: see **Actis** [KERN].

High Mountain: see **Pine Top Mountain** [TULARE].

Hights Corner [KERN]: *locality,* 12.5 miles west-northwest of Bakersfield (lat. 35°26'35" N, long. 119°12'10" W; at S line sec. 32, T 28 S, R 26 E). Named on Rosedale (1954) 7.5' quadrangle.

High Sierra: see "Regional setting."

Highway City [FRESNO]: *town,* 2.5 miles southeast of Herndon (lat. 36°48'40" N, long. 119°53'05" W; near SE cor. sec. 10, T 13 S, R 19 E). Named on Herndon (1965) 15' quadrangle. Postal authorities established Highway City post office in 1951 (Salley, p. 97).

Hiko: see **Visalia** [TULARE].

Hildreth [MADERA]: *locality,* 3.5 miles east-

southeast of O'Neals (lat. 37°06'35" N, long. 119°37'55" W; sec. 36, T 9 N, R 21 E). Named on Millerton Lake West (1965) 7.5' quadrangle. Postal authorities established Hildreth post office in 1886 and discontinued it in 1896 (Frickstad, p. 86). The place began in the late 1870's when Tom Hildreth opened a store there (Clough, p. 85). Logan's (1950) map shows a place called Birch located about 3 miles west-northwest of Hildreth.

Hildreth Creek [MADERA]: *stream,* flows 14 miles to Cottonwood Creek (2) 5.5 miles north-northeast of Trigo (lat. 36°59'20" N, long. 119°56' W; sec. 7, T 11 S, R 19 E). Named on Herndon (1965) and Raymond (1962) 15' quadrangles.

Hildreth Mountain [MADERA]: *peak,* 3 miles east of O'Neals (lat. 37°07'15" N, long. 119°38'15" W; near W line sec. 25, T 9 S, R 21 E); the peak is less than 1 mile north-north-west of Hildreth. Altitude 2058 feet. Named on Millerton Lake West (1965) 7.5' quadrangle.

Hilgard: see **Mount Hilgard** [FRESNO].

Hilgard Branch: see **Bear Creek** [FRESNO] (2).

Hilgard Lake [FRESNO]: *lake,* 1100 feet long, 3.25 miles west-southwest of Mount Abbot (lat. 37°22' N, long. 118°50'20" W); the lake is 1 mile northwest of Mount Hilgard at the head of a fork of Hilgard Branch Bear Creek (2). Named on Mount Abbot (1953) 15' quadrangle.

Hill Canyon [KERN]: *canyon,* drained by a stream that flows 1 mile to Oiler Canyon 3 miles northeast of Caliente (lat. 35°19'20" N, long. 118°35'25" W; near NW cor. sec. 18, T 30 S, R 32 E). Named on Oiler Peak (1972) 7.5' quadrangle.

Hillcrest Point [KERN]: *peak,* 6.5 miles east of McKitrrick in Elk Hills (lat. 35°17'15" N, long 119°30'35" W; sec. 28, T 30 S, R 23 E). Altitude 1551 feet. Named on West Elk Hills (1954) 7.5' quadrangle.

Hillmaid [TULARE]: *locality,* 2 miles west of Woodlake along Atchison, Topeka and Santa Fe Railroad and Visalia Electric Railroad (lat. 36°24'50" N, long. 119°08' W; at SW cor. sec. 26, T 17 S, R 26 E). Named on Exeter (1952) 15' quadrangle. Ivanhoe (1926) 7.5' quadrangle has the name "Redbanks" as an alternate.

Hillside: see **Knowles** [MADERA].

Hills Valley [FRESNO]: *valley,* 5 miles north of Orange Cove (lat. 36°41'45" N, long. 119°18'15" W). Named on Orange Cove North (1966) 7.5' quadrangle.

Hillvale Canyon [KERN]: *canyon,* drained by a stream that flows 4.25 miles to Poso Creek 4.25 miles southeast of Knob Hill (lat. 35°30'55" N, long. 118°54'15" W; near SW cor. sec. 6, T 28 S, R 29 E). Named on Knob Hill (1965) and Pine Mountain (1965) 7.5' quadrangles.

Hitchcock: see **Mount Hitchcock** [TULARE].

Hitchcock Lakes [TULARE]: *lakes,* two, largest 3000 feet long, 1.5 miles southwest of Mount Whitney (lat. 36°33'35" N, long. 118°18'30" W); the lakes are northeast of Mount Hitchcock. Named on Mount Whitney (1956) 15' quadrangle. Called Twin Lakes on Mount Whitney (1907) 30' quadrangle, but United States Board on Geographic Names (1933a, p. 367) rejected this name for the pair.

Hitchcock Meadow [TULARE]: *area*, 1.25 miles southwest of Wilsonia (lat. 36°43'25" N, long. 118°58'30" W; sec. 7, T 14 S, R 28 E). Named on Giant Forest (1956) 15' quadrangle.

Hobler Lake [FRESNO]: *lake*, 900 feet long, 9 miles west-northwest of Mount Shinn (lat. 37°08' N, long. 118°56'10" W; sec. 20, T 9 S, R 28 E). Named on Blackcap Mountain (1953) 15' quadrangle. The name reportedly commemorates Sig Hobler, a cattleman (Browning 1986 , p. 97).

Hobo Campground [KERN]: *locality*, less than 0.5 mile east of Miracle (formerly Hobo) Hot Springs along Kern River (lat. 35°34'30" N, long. 118°31'30" W; near S line sec. 15, T 27 S, R 32 E). Named on Miracle Hot Springs (1972) 7.5' quadrangle.

Hobo Hot Springs: see **Miracle Hot Springs** [KERN].

Hobo Ridge [KERN]: *ridge*, north-trending, 3 miles long, center 3.5 miles south-southwest of Miracle Hot Springs (formerly Hobo Hot Springs) (lat. 35°32' N, long. 118°33'30" W). Named on Miracle Hot Springs (1972) 7.5' quadrangle.

Hockett Lakes [TULARE]: *lakes*, largest 1200 feet long, 7.5 miles south-southwest of Mineral King (lat. 36°21'25" N, long. 118° 40' W). Named on Mineral King (1956) 15' quadrangle. The name commemorates John B. Hockett, a pioneer of 1849 and a trail builder (United States Board on Geographic Names, 1933a, p. 368).

Hockett Meadows [TULARE]:
(1) *area*, 6.25 miles south-southwest of Mineral King (lat. 36°22'30" N, long. 118°39'15" W). Named on Mineral King (1956) 15' quadrangle.
(2) *area*, less than 1 mile west-northwest of Hockett Peak (lat. 36° 13'30" N, long. 118°23'50" W). Named on Hockett Peak (1956) 15' quadrangle.

Hockett Peak [TULARE]: *peak*, 15 miles west of Olancha Peak (lat. 36°13'15" N, long. 118°23'05" W). Altitude 8551 feet. Named on Hockett Peak (1956) 15' quadrangle.

Hockett Peak Creek [TULARE]: *stream*, flows 2 miles to Kern River 2.25 miles south-south-east of Hockett Peak (lat. 36°11'30" N, long. 118°22'05" W); the stream heads near Hockett Peak. Named on Hockett Peak (1956) 15' quadrangle.

Hockett Well [KERN]: *well*, 6.5 miles northwest of Woody (lat. 35° 46' N, long. 118°55'20" W; near E line sec. 11, T 25 S, R 28 E). Named

on Quincy School (1965) 7.5' quadrangle.

Hodges Canyon [KERN]: *canyon*, drained by a stream that flows 2.25 miles to Barrel Valley 5 miles south of Orchard Peak (lat. 35° 40'05" N, long. 120°08'40" W; sec. 16, T 26 S, R 17 E). Named on Orchard Peak (1961) 7.5' quadrangle.

Hoffman Canyon [KERN]: *canyon*, drained by a stream that flows 6 miles to Jawbone Canyon 5 miles northwest of Cinco (lat. 35°18'35" N, long. 118°06'10" W; sec. 22, T 30 S, R 36 E). Named on Cinco (1972) and Cross Mountain (1972) 7.5' quadrangles.

Hoffman Creek [FRESNO]: *stream*, flows 3.5 miles to South Fork San Joaquin River 10 miles north of Kaiser Peak (lat. 37°16' N, long. 119°10'15" W); the stream goes through Hoffman Meadow. Named on Kaiser Peak (1953) 15' quadrangle.

Hoffman Meadow [FRESNO]: *area*, 7.5 miles north of Kaiser Peak (lat. 37°24' N, long. 119°11'20" W; sec. 13, T 6 S, R 25 E); the place is on upper reaches of Hoffman Creek. Named on Kaiser Peak (1953) 15' quadrangle.

Hoffman Mountain [FRESNO]: *ridge*, west-southwest-trending, 1.5 miles long, 14 miles north of Hume (lat. 36°59'30" N, long. 118° 55'10" W). Named on Tehipite Dome (1952) 15' quadrangle.

Hoffman Point [FRESNO]: *peak*, 5.5 miles southwest of Dunlap (lat. 36°41'30" N, long. 119°11'45" W; near E line sec. 24, T 14 S, R 25 E). Altitude 1525 feet. Named on Tucker Mountain (1966) 7.5' quadrangle.

Hoffman Summit [KERN]: *pass*, 6.5 miles north-northwest of Cross Mountain (lat. 35°22'20" N, long. 118°09'45" W; on E line sec. 36, T 29 S, R 35 E); the pass is near the head of Hoffman Canyon. Named on Cross Mountain (1972) 7.5' quadrangle.

Hoffman Well [KERN]: *well*, 8 miles north-northwest of Cinco (lat. 35°21'35" N, long. 118°06'35" W; near NE cor. sec. 4, T 30 S, R 36 E). Named on Cinco (1972) 7.5' quadrangle.

Hogans Dome: see **Fresno Dome** [MADERA].

Hogback Peak [FRESNO]: *peak*, 12 miles west-southwest of Marion Peak on Monarch Divide (lat. 36°52'35" N, long. 118°42'35" W). Altitude 11,077 feet. Named on Marion Peak (1953) 15' quadrangle.

Hog Camp [KERN]: *locality*, nearly 2 miles north-northwest of Caliente (lat. 35°18'50" N, long. 118°38'20" W). Named on Bena (1972) 7.5' quadrangle.

Hog Camp Spring [KERN]: *spring*, 2 miles north-northwest of Caliente (lat. 35°19'05" N, long. 118°38'15" W); the spring is 0.25 mile north-northeast of Hog Camp. Named on Bena (1972) 7.5' quadrangle.

Hog Camp Spring: see **Lower Hog Camp Spring** [KERN].

Hog Canyon [FRESNO]: *canyon*, drained by a stream that flows 2 miles to Warthan Creek 3 miles north of Smith Mountain (2) (lat. 36°07'25" N, long. 120°35'45" W; sec. 8, T 21 S, R 13 E). Named on Sherman Peak (1969) 7.5' quadrangle.

Hog Canyon [KERN]: *canyon,* drained by a stream that flows 5.5 miles to Indian Creek 1 mile southeast of Loraine (lat. 35°17'35" N, long. 118°25'15" W; sec. 27, T 30 S, R 33 E). Named on Loraine (1972) and Tehachapi North (1966) 7.5' quadrangles. The stream in the canyon is called Hog Creek on Mojave (1915) 30' quadrangle.

Hog Creek [FRESNO]: *stream,* flows 5.5 miles to Fancher Creek 9.5 miles east of Clovis (lat. 36°49'20" N, long. 119°31'45" W; near N line sec. 12, T 13 S, R 22 E). Named on Piedra (1965) and Round Mountain (1964) 7.5' quadrangles.

Hog Creek: see **Hog Canyon** [KERN].

Hogeye: see **Keyesville** [KERN].

Hogeye Gulch [KERN]: *canyon,* drained by a stream that flows 3.25 miles to Kern River 5.5 miles south-southwest of Wofford Heights (lat. 35°37'55" N, long. 118°29'25" W; near S line sec. 25, T 26 S, R 32 E). Named on Alta Sierra (1972) and Lake Isabella North (1972) 7.5' quadrangles.

Hoggem Lake [MADERA]: *lake,* 600 feet long, 10 miles north-northeast of Yosemite Forks (lat. 37°29'35" N, long. 119°31'45" W; sec. 14, T 5 S, R 22 E). Named on Bass Lake (1953) 15' quadrangle.

Hog Island: see **Alpaugh** [TULARE].

Hog Mountain [FRESNO]: *ridge,* west- to northwest-trending, 1 mile long, nearly 2 miles southwest of Trimmer (lat. 36°53'15" N, long. 119°19' W). Named on Trimmer (1965) 7.5' quadrangle.

Hog Spring [KERN]:
(1) *spring,* 5.5 miles north-northeast of Caliente (lat. 35°21'45" N, long. 118°35'10" W; sec. 31, T 29 S, R 32 E). Named on Oiler Peak (1972) 7.5' quadrangle.
(2) *spring,* 9 miles west of Liebre Twins (lat. 34°57'05" N, long. 118°43'55" W). Named on Winters Ridge (1966) 7.5' quadrangle.

Hog Spring Canyon [TULARE]: *canyon,* drained by a stream that flows 0.5 mile to Dry Creek (1) 7 miles northeast of Woodlake (lat. 36°29'35" N, long. 119°01' W; sec. 35, T 16 S, R 27 E). Named on Woodlake (1952) 7.5' quadrangle. Lemon Cove (1928) 7.5' quadrangle shows Hog Spring Creek in the canyon.

Hog Spring Creek: see **Hog Spring Canyon** [TULARE].

Hoist Ridge [FRESNO]: *ridge,* north-northwest-to northwest-trending, 5 miles long, 4 miles west of Hume (lat. 36°48' N, long. 118° 59'30" W). Named on Patterson Mountain (1952) and Tehipite Dome (1952) 15' quadrangles. Donkey steam engines hoisted logs to the ridge crest, from which place the logs were lowered to a rail line (Browning 1986, p. 99).

Holby Meadow [TULARE]: *area,* 5 miles south-

east of Camp Nelson (lat. 36°06'10" N, long. 118°32'10" W; near E line sec. 17, T 21 S, R 32 E). Named on Camp Nelson (1956) 15' quadrangle.

Holcomb Lake [MADERA]: *lake,* 1400 feet long, 4 miles west of Devils Postpile (lat. 37°37'45" N, long. 119°09'15" W). Named on Devils Postpile (1953) 15' quadrangle.

Hole-in-the-Ground [TULARE]: *area,* 7.5 miles west-southwest of Kern Peak along Kern River (lat. 36°15' N, long. 118°24' W). Named on Hockett Peak (1956) and Kern Peak (1956) 15' quadrangles.

Hole in the Mountain [KERN]: *relief feature,* 8.5 miles east of Mount Adelaide (lat. 35°26'05" N, long. 118°35'45" W; at W line sec. 6, T 29 S, R 32 E). Named on Breckenridge Mountain (1972) 7.5' quadrangle.

Holey Meadow [TULARE]: *area,* 6 miles north-northeast of California Hot Springs (lat. 35°57'15" N, long. 118°36'55" W; at S line sec. 3, T 23 S, R 31 E). Named on California Hot Springs (1958) 15' quadrangle.

Holland Camp [KERN]: *locality,* 4 miles north of Garlock (lat. 35° 27'45" N, long. 117°47'40" W). Named on Garlock (1967) 7.5' quadrangle.

Holland Creek [FRESNO]: *stream,* flows 9 miles to Kings River 3.5 miles southwest of Piedra (lat. 36°46'30" N, long. 119°25'45" W; sec. 26, T 13 S, R 23 E). Named on Piedra (1965) 7.5' quadrangle.

Hollis [KERN]: *locality,* 2.25 miles east-southeast of McFarland along Southern Pacific Railroad (lat. 35°40' N, long. 119°11'25" W; sec. 17, T 26 S, R 26 E). Named on McFarland (1954) 7.5' quadrangle.

Holloway Camp [KERN]: *locality,* 3.5 miles northwest of Saltdale in Last Chance Canyon (lat. 35°24'10" N, long. 117°55'20" W; near N line sec. 20, T 29 S, R 38 E). Named on Saltdale (1943a) 15' quadrangle.

Holly Camp [KERN]: *locality,* 6 miles north of Saltdale (lat. 35°26'50" N, long. 117°53'45" W; at SW cor. sec. 33, T 28 S, R 38 E). Named on Saltdale (1943a) 15' quadrangle. A quarry at the place provided material for Holly-brand cleanser (Schumacher, p. 18).

Hollyhock Spring [FRESNO]: *spring,* 4.5 miles north of Coalinga Mineral Springs (lat. 36°12'40" N, long. 120°33'50" W; near NW cor. sec. 10, T 20 S, R 13 E). Named on Sherman Peak (1969) 7.5' quadrangle.

Holman Mill [FRESNO]: *locality,* 16 miles northwest of Coalinga along White Creek (lat. 36°17'55" N, long. 120°34'45" W; sec. 4, T 19 S, R 13 E). Site named on Santa Rita Peak (1969) 7.5' quadrangle.

Holster Lake [FRESNO]: *lake,* 800 feet long, 2.5 miles north-northeast of Blackcap Mountain (lat. 37°06'25" N, long. 118°47' W). Named on Blackcap Mountain (1953) 15' quadrangle.

Home Camp Creek [FRESNO]: *stream,* flows 4 miles to the west end of Huntington Lake (1) at the village of Huntington Lake (lat. 37°14'10" N, long. 119°14'10" W; near E line sec. 16, T 8 S, R 25 E). Named on Huntington Lake (1953), Kaiser Peak (1953), and Shaver Lake (1953) 15' quadrangles.

Homer Cove [TULARE]: *relief feature,* 7.5 miles northeast of Woodlake (lat. 36°27'40" N, long. 119°00'30" W; sec. 35, T 16 S, R 27 E). Named on Woodlake (1952) 7.5' quadrangle. On Lemon Cove (1928) 7.5' quadrangle, the name "Homer Cove" applies to the lower part of present Indian Canyon.

Homers Nose [TULARE]: *peak,* 9 miles west-southwest of Mineral King (lat. 36°23'05" N, long. 118°44'15" W). Named on Mineral King (1956) 15' quadrangle. The name, given in 1872, commemorates John Homer, a pioneer of 1853 (United States Board on Geographic Names, 1933a, p. 370).

Home Spring [FRESNO]: *spring,* 11 miles east-northeast of Clovis (lat. 36°52'25" N, long. 119°30'35" W; sec. 19, T 12 S, R 23 E). Named on Round Mountain (1964) 7.5' quadrangle.

Home Spring [KERN]: *spring,* 8 miles north-northeast of Caliente (lat. 35°24'15" N, long. 118°34'30" W; sec. 17, T 29 S, R 32 E). Named on Breckenridge Mountain (1972) 7.5' quadrangle.

Homestead: see **Indian Wells** [KERN].

Homestead Spring [FRESNO]: *spring,* 4.25 miles east-northeast of Joaquin Rocks (lat. 36°20'50" N, long. 120°22'45" W; sec. 19, T 18 S, R 15 E). Named on Joaquin Rocks (1969) 7.5' quadrangle.

Honeybee Creek [TULARE]: *stream,* flows 3 miles to South Fork Kern River 7.5 miles southeast of Monache Mountain (lat. 36°08'40" N, long. 118°05'15" W). Named on Monache Mountain (1956) 15' quadrangle.

Honeymoon Lake: see **Lower Honeymoon Lake** [FRESNO]; **Upper Honeymoon Lake** [FRESNO].

Hooker Meadow [TULARE]: *area,* about 7 miles south of Monache Mountain (lat. 36°06'20" N, long. 118°11'45" W; near SE cor. sec. 9, T 21 S, R 35 E). Named on Monache Mountain (1956) 15' quadrangle.

Hookers Cove [MADERA]: *valley,* 11 miles south-southeast of Shuteye Peak (lat. 37°11'50" N, long. 119°22' W; sec. 29, T 8 S, R 24 E); the valley is along Hookers Creek. Named on Shaver Lake (1953) 15' quadrangle.

Hookers Creek [MADERA]: *stream,* flows 3 miles to San Joaquin River 12 miles south-southeast of Shuteye Peak (lat. 37°11'10" N, long. 119°21'05" W; sec. 33, T 8 S, R 24 E); the stream goes through Hookers Cove. Named on Shaver Lake (1953) 15' quadrangle.

Hoopah Lake [FRESNO]: *lake,* 450 feet long, 8 miles south-southwest of Mount Abbot (lat.

37°16'20" N, long. 119°49'10" W). Named on Mount Abbot (1953) 15' quadrangle. Elden H. Vestal of California Department of Fish and Game named the lake in 1951 using a word that he believed was the Indian name for a type of woven carrier for water (Browning 1986, p. 99).

Hooper: see **Mount Hooper** [FRESNO].

Hooper Creek [FRESNO]: *stream,* flows 3.5 miles to the canyon of South Fork San Joaquin River 11 miles west-southwest of Mount Abbot, where it is diverted into a pipeline (lat. 37°18'20" N, long. 118°57' W); the stream heads northwest of Mount Hooper. Named on Mount Abbot (1953) 15' quadrangle.

Hooper Creek: see **South Fork,** under **San Joaquin River** [MADERA].

Hooper Hill [KERN]: *peak,* 1.25 miles east-southeast of Miracle Hot Springs (lat. 35°34' N, long. 118°30'45" W; sec. 23, T 17 S, R 32 E). Altitude 4462 feet. Named on Miracle Hot Springs (1972) 7.5' quadrangle.

Hooper Lake [FRESNO]: *lake,* 750 feet long, 9 miles southwest of Mount Abbot (lat. 37°18' N, long. 118°54'30" W); the lake is 1 mile northwest of Mount Hooper at the head of a branch of Hooper Creek. Named on Mount Abbot (1953) 15' quadrangle.

Hoosier Flat [KERN]: *area,* 4.5 miles east of Mount Adelaide (lat. 35°26'40" N, long. 118°40'05" W; sec. 32, T 28 S, R 31 E). Named on Mount Adelaide (1972) 7.5' quadrangle.

Hoover Creek [MADERA]: *stream,* heads in Madera County and flows 3.5 miles to Buena Vista Creek 8.5 miles southeast of Yosemite Village in Mariposa County (lat. 37°38'55" N, long. 119°30'05" W); the stream heads at Hoover Lakes. Named on Merced Peak (1953) 15' quadrangle. Forest S. Townsley, chief ranger of Yosemite National Park, named Hoover Creek and Hoover Lakes for his friend Herbert C. Hoover (Browning, 1986, p. 99).

Hoover Lakes [MADERA]: *lakes,* three, largest 950 feet long, 4.5 miles west-southwest of Merced Peak (lat. 37°36'35" N, long. 119°28'20" W); the lakes are at the head of Hoover Creek. Named on Merced Peak (1953) 15' quadrangle.

Hopkins: see **Mount Hopkins** [FRESNO].

Hopkins Creek [FRESNO]: *stream,* flows 3 miles to Mono Creek 4.25 miles north-north-west of Mount Abbot (lat. 37°26'25" N, long. 118°49'25" W); the stream heads at Upper Hopkins Lakes near Hopkins Pass. Named on Mount Abbot (1953) 15' quadrangle.

Hopkins Lake: see **Lower Hopkins Lake** [FRESNO]; **Upper Hopkins Lakes** [FRESNO].

Hopkins Pass [FRESNO]: *pass,* 7.25 miles north-northwest of Mount Abbot on Fresno-Mono county line (lat. 37°28'50" N, long. 118° 50'30" W); the pass is near the head of Hopkins Creek. Named on Mount Abbot (1953) 15' quadrangle.

Horned Toad Hills [KERN]: *area,* 3.5 miles northwest of Mojave (lat. 35°05'45" N, long. 118°12'30" W). Named on Mojave (1973) 7.5' quadrangle.

Horn Mountain [TULARE]: *peak,* 6.5 miles southeast of Kaweah (lat. 36°24' N, long. 118°50'30" W). Altitude 4450 feet. Named on Kaweah (1957) 15' quadrangle.

Horsecamp Mountain [MADERA]: *ridge,* north-northwest- to northwest-trending, 1.25 miles long, 8 miles north-east of Raymond (lat. 37°19'50" N, long. 119°50'45" W). Named on Horsecamp Mountain (1947) 7.5' quadrangle.

Horse Canyon [KERN]:
(1) *canyon,* drained by a stream that flows 3 miles to Willow Spring Creek (1) 5 miles west-southwest of Woody (lat. 35°40'30" N, long. 118°54'40" W; at N line sec. 13, T 26 S, R 28 E). Named on Sand Canyon (1965) 7.5' quadrangle.
(2) *canyon,* drained by a stream that flows 4 miles to Cache Creek 9.5 miles east-north-east of Tehachapi (lat. 39°10'50" N, long. 118° 17'30" W; near NE cor. sec. 2, T 32 S, R 34 E). Named on Tehachapi NE (1966) 7.5' quadrangle. The name is from fossil bones of horses found in the neighborhood in the early 1900's (Barras, p. 46).
(3) *canyon,* drained by a stream that flows 6.5 miles to lowlands 5.5 miles east-southeast of Skinner Peak (lat. 35°32'50" N, long. 118° 01'35" W). Named on Horse Canyon (1972) 7.5' quadrangle.

Horse Canyon [KINGS]: *canyon,* drained by a stream that flows less than 1 mile to Kettleman Plain at Avenal (lat. 36°00'40" N, long. 120°07'25" W; sec. 15, T 22 S, R 17 E). Named on La Cima (1963) 7.5' quadrangle.

Horse Canyon [TULARE]: *canyon,* 2 miles long, 6.5 miles south-southeast of Camp Nelson on upper reaches of Dry Meadow Creek (lat. 36°03'30" N, long. 118°33'15" W). Named on Camp Nelson (1956) 15' quadrangle.

Horse Canyon: see **Cap Canyon** [KERN].

Horse Canyon Spring [KERN]: *spring,* 2.5 miles east-northeast of Skinner Peak (lat. 35°34'35" N, long. 118°05' W); the spring is in a branch of Horse Canyon (3). Named on Horse Canyon (1972) 7.5' quadrangle.

Horse Canyon Well [KERN]: *well,* 5.25 miles east of Skinner Peak (lat. 35°33'25" N, long. 118°02' W); the well is in Horse Canyon (3). Named on Horse Canyon (1972) 7.5' quadrangle.

Horse Corral Creek [FRESNO]: *stream,* flows 3.5 miles to Boulder Creek (1) 8 miles east-southeast of Hume (lat. 36°44'25" N, long. 118°47' W); the stream passes through Horse Corral Meadow. Named on Giant Forest (1956) 15' quadrangle.

Horse Corral Meadow [FRESNO]: *area,* 8.5 miles east-southeast of Hume (lat. 36°44'50"

N, long. 118°45'05" W). Named on Giant Forest (1956) and Triple Divide Peak (1956) 15' quadrangles. The name is from a corral that Jasper H. Harrell built for horses at the site in 1877 (Browning 1986, p. 100). Winchell (p. 241) called the place Crescent Lawn in 1868.

Horse Creek [TULARE]:
(1) *stream,* flows 8.5 miles to East Fork Kaweah River 7.5 miles west of Mineral King (lat. 36°25'50" N, long. 118°43'30" W). Named on Mineral King (1956) 15' quadrangle. United States Board on Geographic Names (1933a, p. 373) rejected the name "Cow Creek" for the stream.
(2) *stream,* flows 4.5 miles to Lake Kaweah 6 miles south-southwest of Kaweah (lat. 36°23'05" N, long. 118°56'30" W; sec. 4, T 18 S, R 28 E). Named on Kaweah (1957) 15' quadrangle.

Horsehead Lake [FRESNO]: *lake,* 1800 feet long, 1.25 miles north-northwest of Blackcap Mountain (lat. 37°05'25" N, long. 118°47'55" W); the outline of the lake on a map suggests the head and body of a horse. Named on Blackcap Mountain (1953) 15' quadrangle. William A. Dill and Jack Criqui of California Department of Fish and Game named the lake in 1948 (Browning 1986, p. 100).

Horse Heaven [FRESNO]: *area,* 10.5 miles north-west of Mount Abbot along Fish Creek (1) (lat. 37°29'45" N, long. 118°54'45" W). Named on Mount Abbot (1953) 15' quadrangle.

Horse Meadow [FRESNO]: *area,* 9 miles south-southeast of Dinkey Dome along East Fork Deer Creek (3) (lat. 37°00'05" N, long. 119°02'45" W; sec. 5, T 11 S, R 27 E). Named on Huntington Lake (1953) 15' quadrangle.

Horse Meadow [TULARE]:
(1) *area,* 7 miles north-northeast of California Hot Springs (lat. 35° 58'15" N, long. 118°37'15" W; near SW cor. sec. 34, T 22 S, R 31 E). Named on California Hot Springs (1958) 15' quadrangle.
(2) *area,* 7 miles east-southeast of Fairview along Salmon Creek (lat. 35°54'10" N, long. 118°22'35" W; sec. 25, T 23 S, R 33 E). Named on Kernville (1956) 15' quadrangle.

Horse Meadow: see **East Horse Meadow** [TULARE].

Horse Meadow Creek [TULARE]: *stream,* flows 2 miles to Parker Meadow Creek 6.5 miles north-northeast of California Hot Springs (lat. 35°57'50" N, long. 118°37'05" W; sec. 3, T 23 S, R 31 E); the stream goes through Horse Meadow (1). Named on California Hot Springs (1958) 15' quadrangle.

Horse Meadows: see **Little Horse Meadows** [TULARE].

Horseshoe: see **The Horseshoe** [KERN].

Horseshoe Bend [FRESNO]:
(1) *bend,* 9 miles west of Shaver Lake Heights (present town of Shaver Lake) along San Joaquin River on Fresno-Madera county line (lat.

37°06'40" N, long. 119°28'15" W). Named on Shaver Lake (1953) 15' quadrangle.

(2) *bend,* 5.5 miles east-northeast of Hume along South Fork Kings River (lat. 36°49'15" N, long. 118°49'45" W). Named on Tehipite Dome (1952) 15' quadrangle.

Horseshoe Bend [MADERA]: *bend,* 16 miles south of Shuteye Peak along San Joaquin River on Madera-Fresno county line (lat. 37°06'40" N, long. 119°28'15" W). Named on Shaver Lake (1953) 15' quadrangle.

Horseshoe Creek [FRESNO]: *stream,* flows 4.5 miles to Middle Fork Kings River 6.5 miles west of Marion Peak (lat. 36°58'10" N, long. 118°38'05" W); the stream heads at Horseshoe Lakes. Named on Marion Peak (1953) 15' quadrangle.

Horseshoe Lake [FRESNO]: *lake,* 1600 feet long, 4.25 miles north of Blackcap Mountain (lat. 37°08' N, long. 118°48'15" W); the outline of the lake on a map has the crude shape of a horseshoe. Named on Blackcap Mountain (1953) 15' quadrangle.

Horseshoe Lakes [FRESNO]: *lakes,* largest 1250 feet long, 3 miles west-southwest of Marion Peak (lat. 36°56'45" N, long. 118°34'15" W); the lakes are near the head of Horseshoe Creek. Named on Marion Peak (1953) 15' quadrangle.

Horseshoe Meadows [FRESNO]: *area,* 3.5 miles west of Marion Peak (lat. 36°57' N, long. 118°34'50" W); the place is near Horseshoe Lakes. Named on Marion Peak (1953) 15' quadrangle.

Horsethief Canyon [FRESNO]: *canyon,* drained by a stream that flows 1 mile to Salt Creek (1) 4.25 miles north-northwest of Joaquin Rocks (lat. 36°22'20" N, long. 120°29' W; near SE cor. sec. 7, T 18 S, R 14 E). Named on Joaquin Rocks (1969) 7.5' quadrangle.

Horsethief Canyon [KERN]: *canyon,* drained by a stream that flows 2.5 miles to Oak Creek 8 miles south of Tehachapi (lat. 35°00'50" N, long. 118°26'20" W; sec. 26, T 11 N, R 15 W). Named on Tehachapi South (1966) 7.5' quadrangle.

Horsethief Flat [KERN]: *area,* 9.5 miles northwest of Cummings Mountain (lat. 35°07'25" N, long. 118°42'10" W; on S line sec. 24, T 32 S, R 30 E). Named on Bear Mountain (1966) and Tejon Ranch (1966) 7.5' quadrangles.

Horsethief Lake: see **Lower Horsethief Lake** [FRESNO]; **Upper Horsethief Lake** [FRESNO].

Horsethief Mountain [KERN]: *peak,* 10 miles west-northwest of Cummings Mountain (lat. 35°06'45" N, long. 118°43'20" W; sec. 26, T 32 S, R 30 E). Altitude 3170 feet. Named on Tejon Ranch (1966) 7.5' quadrangle.

Hortense Lake [FRESNO]: *lake,* 1200 feet long, 10 miles northwest of Mount Abbot (lat. 37°29'30" N, long. 118°54'55" W). Named on Mount Abbot (1953) 15' quadrangle.

Hossack Creek [TULARE]: *stream,* flows 2 miles to North Fork of Middle Fork Tule River 4.5 miles northwest of Camp Nelson (lat. 36°11'20" N, long. 118°39'45" W; near N line sec. 18, T 20 S, R 30 E); the stream heads at Hossack Meadow. Named on Camp Nelson (1956) 15' quadrangle.

Hossack Meadow [TULARE]: *area,* 2.5 miles north-northwest of Camp Nelson (lat. 36°10'35" N, long. 118°37'45" W; near NW cor. sec. 21, T 20 S, R 31 E). The place is at the head of Hossack Creek. Named on Camp Nelson (1956) 15' quadrangle. The name commemorates John Hossack, a pioneer stockman (Browning 1986, p. 101).

Hotel Creek [FRESNO]: *stream,* flows 4 miles to South Fork Kings River 14 miles southwest of Marion Peak in Kings Canyon (lat. 36°47'30" N, long. 118°40'10" W). Named on Marion Peak (1953) 15' quadrangle. The name recalls a log hotel that Hugh Robinson built at Cedar Grove in 1897; J.N. LeConte called the stream Fox Creek in 1890 (Browning, p. 101).

Hot Springs [KERN]: *springs,* 3 miles east-northeast of Wofford Heights (lat. 35°43'45" N, long. 118°24'30" W; sec. 26, T 25 S, R 33 E). Named on Lake Isabella North (1972) 7.5' quadrangle. Wheeler's (1875-1878) map shows Hot Sprs. Stage Sta. at or near the place.

Hot Springs: see **California Hot Springs** [TULARE].

Hot Springs Bar: see **Delonegha Hot Springs** [KERN].

Hot Springs Canyon [FRESNO]: *canyon,* drained by a stream that flows 10.5 miles to Warthan Creek nearly 4 miles east of Smith Mountain (1) (lat. 36°05'05" N, long. 120°31'35" W; sec. 24, T 21 S, R 13 E); Coalinga Mineral Springs is in the canyon. Named on Sherman Peak (1969) and Smith Mountain (1969) 7.5' quadrangles. Called Fresno Springs Canyon on Priest Valley (1915) 30' quadrangle, which has the name "Fresno Hot Springs" for present Coalinga Mineral Springs.

Hot Springs Pass [FRESNO]: *pass,* 14 miles northwest of Blackcap Mountain (lat. 37°11'55" N, long. 118°59'40" W). Named on Blackcap Mountain (1953) 15' quadrangle.

Hot Springs Stage Station: see **Hot Springs** [KERN].

Hot Spring Valley [KERN]: *valley,* along Kern River at the town of Lake Isabella (lat. 35°37'30" N, long. 118°28'30" W). Named on Lake Isabella North (1972) and Lake Isabella South (1972) 7.5' quadrangles. The name is from springs of hot water in the valley (Boyd, p. 162).

House Meadow: see **Hall Meadow** [FRESNO].

Houser Camp [KINGS]: *locality,* 12 miles east-southeast of Kettleman City (lat. 35°56' N, long. 119°45'10" W; at NE cor. sec. 13, T 23 S, R 20 E). Named on Dudley Ridge (1954) 7.5' quadrangle.

House Spring [KERN]: *spring,* 1.5 miles north-northeast of Caliente (lat. 35°18'45" N, long. 118°36'50" W). Named on Oiler Peak (1972) 7.5' quadrangle.

House Spring [TULARE]: *spring,* 4.25 miles south-southeast of Auckland (lat. 36°31'35" N, long. 119°07'20" W; sec. 23, T 16 S, R 26 E). Named on Auckland (1966) 7.5' quadrangle.

Howling Gulch [KERN]: *canyon,* drained by a stream that flows 5 miles to Spring Mountain Gulch 0.25 mile west of Woody (lat. 35°42'10" N, long. 118°50'20" W; at N line sec. 3, T 26 S, R 29 E). Named on Woody (1965) 7.5' quadrangle. United States Board on Geographic Names (1966b, p. 5) rejected the name "Wildcat Creek" for the feature.

Howton: see **Success** [TULARE].

Hub [FRESNO-KINGS]: *locality,* 7.25 miles north-northwest of Lemoore on Fresno-Kings county line (lat. 36°24'05" N, long. 119°48'30" W; on N line sec. 4, T 18 S, R 20 E). Named on Riverdale (1954) 7.5' quadrangle. Riverdale (1927) 7.5' quadrangle shows Hub located along Southern Pacific Railroad, which on the map appears to be just inside Kings County.

Huckleberry Creek: see **Huntington Lake** [FRESNO] (1).

Huckleberry Meadow [FRESNO]: *area,* 2 miles southwest of Hume (lat. 36°46' N, long. 118°56'20" W; sec. 28, T 13 S, R 28 E). Named on Tehipite Dome (1952) 15' quadrangle. Called Huckleberry Valley on Tehipite (1903) 30' quadrangle.

Huckleberry Meadow [TULARE]: *area,* 6.5 miles east of Yucca Mountain (lat. 36°33'20" N, long. 118°45'15" W; near SE cor. sec. 6, T 16 S, R 30 E). Named on Giant Forest (1956) 15' quadrangle.

Huckleberry Valley: see **Huckleberry Meadow** [FRESNO].

Hudson Station: see **Rose Station** [KERN].

Huey Valley: see **Hewey Valley** [TULARE].

Hughes Creek [FRESNO]: *stream,* formed by the confluence of North Fork and West Fork, flows 5 miles to Kings River 0.5 mile north-northeast of Piedra (lat. 36°49'10" N, long. 119°22'45" W; sec. 8, T 13 S, R 24 E). Named on Piedra (1965) and Pine Flat Dam (1965) 7.5' quadrangles. North Fork is 2.5 miles long and is named on Humphreys Station (1965) and Trimmer (1965) 7.5' quadrangles. West Fork also is 2.5 miles long and is named on Humphreys Station (1965) and Piedra (1965) 7.5' quadrangles.

Hughes Mountain [FRESNO]: *ridge,* north-west-trending, 1.5 miles long, 3.25 miles north-northeast of Tivy Mountain (lat. 36°50'40" N, long. 119°20'25" W; in and near sec. 34, T 12 S, R 24 E). Named on Pine Flat Dam (1965) 7.5' quadrangle. The name commemorates John R. Hughes, an early settler (Gudde, 1949, p. 156).

Hugh Mann Canyon [KERN]: *canyon,* drained

by a stream that flows 4.25 miles to Weaver Creek 7 miles northwest of Emerald Mountain (lat. 35°20'15" N, long. 118°21'25" W; near W line sec. 8, T 30 S, R 34 E). Named on Emerald Mountain (1972) 7.5' quadrangle.

Hulbert Mountain [MADERA]: *peak,* 5 miles south-southeast of O'Neals (lat. 37°03'20" N, long. 119°40'15" W; near S line sec. 15, T 10 S, R 21 E). Altitude 1847 feet. Named on Millerton Lake West (1965) 7.5' quadrangle.

Hume [FRESNO]: *settlement,* 50 miles east of Fresno (lat. 36°47'10" N, long. 118°54'45" W; in and near sec. 14, 15, T 13 S, R 28 E); the place is near Hume Lake. Named on Tehipite Dome (1952) 15' quadrangle. Postal authorities established Hume post office in 1908, discontinued it in 1924, and reestablished it in 1938 (Frickstad, p. 34).

Hume Lake [FRESNO]: *lake,* 1 mile long, behind a dam on Tenmile Creek 1 mile northeast of Hume (lat. 36°47'40" N, long. 118°54'05" W; sec. 14, T 13 S, R 28 E). Named on Tehipite Dome (1952) 15' quadrangle. The name commemorates Thomas A. Hume, who started a sawmill at the place in 1908 and built the dam that formed the lake in 1909 (Hanna, p. 144).

Hum-pah-ya-mup: see **Kelso Creek** [KERN].

Hum-pah-ya-mup Pass: see **Walker Pass** [KERN].

Humphreys: see **Humphreys Station** [FRESNO]; **Mount Humphreys** [FRESNO].

Humphreys Basin [FRESNO]: *area,* 10 miles north of Mount Goddard (lat. 37°15' N, long. 118°42'30" W); the place is west-southwest of Mount Humphreys. Named on Mount Goddard (1948) and Mount Tom (1949) 15' quadrangles. United States Board on Geographic Names (1978a, p. 3) approved the name "Carol Col" for a pass on the northwest rim of Humphreys Basin 2.9 miles west-north-west of Mount Humphreys (lat. 37°16'42" N, long. 118°43'19" W); the name honors Carol Kassler Ransford, hiker and climber, who spent many summers with youth groups in the neighborhood, and who led a group over the pass in 1973.

Humphreys Lakes [FRESNO]: *lakes,* largest 1400 feet long, 1 mile west-southwest of Mount Humphreys (lat. 37°16' N, long. 118°41'15" W); the lakes are in Humphreys Basin. Named on Mount Tom (1949) 15' quadrangle.

Humphreys Station [FRESNO]: *locality,* 23 miles northwest of Fresno (lat. 36°57'40" N, long. 119°26'40" W; sec. 22, T 11 S, R 23 E). Named on Humphreys Station (1965) 7.5' quadrangle. Called Humphreys on Dinuba (1924) 30' quadrangle. The name commemorates John W. Humphreys, pioneer lumberman and stockman (Gudde, 1969, p. 148).

Hungry Gulch Campground [KERN]: *locality,* 2.5 miles south-southwest of Wofford Heights (lat. 35°40'20" N, long. 118°28'20"

W; near NE cor. sec. 18, T 26 S, R 33 E). Named on Lake Isabella North (1972) 7.5' quadrangle.

Hungry Hollow [TULARE]: *valley,* 6 miles north of Fountain Springs (lat. 35°58'30" N, long. 118°55'45" W). Named on Fountain Springs (1965) 7.5' quadrangle.

Hungry Spring [KERN]: *spring,* 11 miles north-northwest of Mojave (lat. 35°12'15" N, long. 118°13'25" W; sec. 28, T 31 S, R 35 E). Named on Cache Peak (1973) 7.5' quadrangle.

Hunsaker: see **Tulare** [TULARE].

Hunt: see **McFarland** [KERN].

Hunter Creek [TULARE]: *stream,* flows 4.25 miles to South Fork Kaweah River 8 miles south-southwest of Mineral King (lat. 36° 20'25" N, long. 118°38' W; sec. 20, T 18 S, R 31 E). Named on Mineral King (1956) 15' quadrangle. United States Board on Geographic Names (1968b, p. 7) rejected the name "South Fork Kaweah River" for the stream.

Huntington: see **Mount Huntington** [FRESNO].

Huntington Lake [FRESNO]:

(1) *lake,* 4.5 miles long, behind a dam on Big Creek (1) 2.5 miles northeast of the town of Big Creek (lat. 37°14' N, long. 119°12'45" W; sec. 14, T 8 S, R 25 E). Named on Huntington Lake (1953) and Kaiser Peak (1953) 15' quadrangles. Pacific Light and Power Company created the reservoir in 1912 and named it for the company president, Henry E. Huntington (Hart, J.D., p. 199). The place that now holds the lake had the name "The Basin" before the lake formed; a landing place on the lake shore was known as Chipmunk Landing for the abundance of chipmunks there (Redinger, p. 19, 99). United States Board on Geographic Names (1987a, p. 1) approved the name "Huckleberry Creek" for a stream that flows 1.5 miles to Huntington Lake (1) 3.3 miles northeast of the town of Big Creek (lat. 37°14'24" N, long. 119°12'25" W; sec. 14, T 8 S, R 25 E); huckleberry bushes grow along the creek.

(2) *village,* 2 miles north of the town of Big Creek (lat. 37°13'50" N, long. 119°14'10" W; in and near sec. 16, T 8 S, R 25 E); the village is at the west end of Huntington Lake (1). Named on Huntington Lake (1953) 15' quadrangle. Postal authorities established Basin post office in 1913 and changed the name to Huntington Lake in 1916 (Frickstad, p. 31).

Huron [FRESNO]: *town,* 15 miles east-northeast of Coalinga (lat. 36°12'15" N, long. 120°05'55" W; sec. 10, 11, T 20 S, R 17 E). Named on Huron (1956) 7.5' quadrangle. Postal authorities established Huron post office in 1877, discontinued it in 1883, and reestablished it in 1886 (Frickstad, p. 34). The town incorporated in 1951. Postal authorities established Last post office 14 miles southwest of Huron in 1890 and discontinued it in 1895 (Salley, p. 119).

Hutching Creek [MADERA]: *stream,* flows 3.5 miles to Lyell Fork nearly 7 miles northeast of Merced Peak (lat. 37°42'35" N, long. 119°18'40" W). Named on Merced Peak (1953) 15' quadrangle. United States Board on Geographic Names (1978d, p. 2-3) approved the form "Hutchings Creek" for the name, and rejected the names "Hutching Creek" and "North Fork Merced River" for it; the name is for James M. Hutchings, who wrote of Yosemite Valley.

Hutchings Creek: see **Hutching Creek** [MADERA].

Hutchings: see **Mount Hutchings** [FRESNO].

Hutchins [FRESNO]: *locality,* 19 miles southwest of Kaiser Peak along San Joaquin and Eastern Railroad (lat. 37°06'30" N, long. 119°27' W; near N line sec. 34, T 9 S, R 23 E). Named on Kaiser (1904) 30' quadrangle.

Hutchinson Lake: see **Colby Lake** [TULARE].

Hutchinson Meadow [FRESNO]: *area,* 8 miles south of Mount Abbot in Piute Canyon (lat. 37°16'05" N, long. 118°46'50" W). Named on Mount Abbot (1953) 15' quadrangle. The name commemorates James S. Hutchinson, who climbed and explored in the Sierra Nevada for many years (Gudde, 1949, p. 158).

Hutton: see **Mount Hutton**, under **Red Mountain** [FRESNO] (2).

Huxley: see **Mount Huxley** [FRESNO].

H.V. Eastman Lake: see **Eastman Lake** [MADERA].

Hydril [KINGS]: *locality,* less than 2 miles eastnortheast of Avenal (lat. 36°00'50" N, long. 120°06'50" W; sec. 14, T 22 S, R 17 E). Named on La Cima (1963) 7.5' quadrangle.

Hydril Hill [KINGS]: *peak,* 1.5 miles east-northeast of Avenal (lat. 36°00'40" N, long. 120°06'05" W; sec. 14, T 22 S, R 17 E); the peak is 0.25 mile west-southwest of Hydril. Named on La Cima (1963) 7.5' quadrangle. According to United States Board on Geographic Names (1933b, p. 14), the name is in common use locally and was derived from the term "high drill."

— I —

Ian Campbell: see **Mount Ian Campbell**, under **Mount Givens** [FRESNO].

Iceberg Lake [MADERA]: *lake,* about 2000 feet long, 5.5 miles west-northwest of Devils Postpile along Shadow Creek (lat. 37°40'15" N, long. 119°10'05" W). Named on Devils Postpile (1953) 15' quadrangle. The name is for the ice that sometimes floats in the lake until the late summer months (Smith, Genny, p. 62).

Iceberg Lake: see **Upper Iceberg Lake**, under **Cecile Lake** [MADERA].

Ice Creek [TULARE]: *stream,* flows 1 mile to Alder Creek (1) 8.5 miles south-southeast of Camp Nelson (lat. 36°01'50" N, long. 118°32'40" W; sec. 8, T 22 S, R 32 E). Named on Camp Nelson (1956) 15' quadrangle.

Ice House: see **Ice House Creek** [KERN].

Ice House Creek [KERN]: *stream,* flows nearly 2 miles to Shirley Creek 1.25 miles east-southeast of Alta Sierra (lat. 35°43'15" N, long. 118°31'45" W; sec. 27, T 25 S, R 32 E). Named on Alta Sierra (1972) 7.5' quadrangle. California Division of Highways' (1934) map shows a place called Ice House located near present Ice House Creek (sec. 21, T 25 S, R 32 E).

Ickes: see **Mount Ickes** [FRESNO].

Idaho Lake [FRESNO]: *lake,* 650 feet long, 3 miles east of Kaiser Peak (lat. 37°17'35" N, long. 119°07'45" W; sec. 28, T 7 S, R 26 E). Named on Kaiser Peak (1953) 15' quadrangle.

Ida Lake [TULARE]: *lake,* 1000 feet long, behind a dam on Nobe Young Creek 11.5 miles northeast of California Hot Springs (lat. 35°59'55" N, long. 118°31'50" W). Named on California Hot Springs (1958) 15' quadrangle.

Idlewild [TULARE]: *settlement,* 4.5 miles south of California Hot Springs (lat. 35°48'45" N, long. 118°40'10" W; sec. 30, T 24 S, R 31 E). Named on California Hot Springs (1958) 15' quadrangle.

Illilouette Creek [MADERA]: *stream,* heads in Madera County and flows 14 miles to Merced River 2.25 miles southeast of Yosemite Village in Mariposa County (lat. 37°43'30" N, long. 119°33'25" W). Named on Merced Peak (1953) and Yosemite (1956) 15' quadrangles. Called Illilouette Fork on Hoffmann and Gardner's (1863-1867) map. King and Gardner's (1865) map has the designation "Illilouette or South Fork" for the stream. Whitney (1870, p. 65) called it "the South Fork, or the Illilouette." He added: "This is the South Fork of the Middle Fork [Merced River] and not the main South Fork," and, "To avoid confusion, it will be well to call it by the Indian name, Illilouette, one not yet much in use in the Valley." United States Board on Geographic Names (1933a, p. 385) rejected the names "South Canyon Creek" and "Tulu-la-wi-ak" for the stream.

Illinois Mills: see **Visalia** [TULARE].

Ilmon [KERN]: *locality,* 5 miles west-northwest of Caliente along Southern Pacific Railroad (lat. 35°18'45" N, long. 118°41'35" W). Named on Bena (1972) 7.5' quadrangle.

Imhoff [TULARE]: *locality,* 1 mile east-northeast of downtown Tulare along Atchison, Topeka and Santa Fe Railroad (lat. 36°12'55" N, long. 119°19'50" W; at W line sec. 1, T 20 S, R 24 E). Named on Tulare (1927) 7.5' quadrangle.

Indian Basin [FRESNO]: *area,* 2 miles westnorthwest of Hume (lat. 36°48' N, long. 118°56'30" W; on S line sec. 9, T 13 S, R 28 E); Indian Creek drains the place. Named on Tehipite Dome (1952) 15' quadrangle.

Indian Canyon [TULARE]: *canyon,* drained by

a stream that flows 1.5 miles to Dry Creek (1) 6.5 miles northeast of Woodlake (lat. 36°28'50" N, long. 119°01'05" W; sec. 2, T 17 S, R 27 E). Named on Exeter (1952) and Kaweah (1957) 15' quadrangles. The lower part of Indian Canyon is called Homer Cove on Lemon Cove (1928) 7.5' quadrangle, which has the name "Indian Canyon" for a presently unnamed canyon 2 miles farther south.

Indian Creek [FRESNO]: *stream,* flows 5.25 miles to Tenmile Creek 2.5 miles northeast of Hume (lat. 36°49' N, long. 118°53'15" W); the stream goes through Indian Basin. Named on Tehipite Dome (1952) 15' quadrangle.

Indian Creek [FRESNO-TULARE]: *stream,* heads in Fresno County and flows 6.5 miles to Murry Creek (1) 3 miles northeast of Auckland in Tulare County (lat. 36°37'15" N, long. 119°03'55" W; sec. 17, T 15 S, R 27 E). Named on Auckland (1966) and Miramonte (1966) 7.5' quadrangles.

Indian Creek [KERN]: *stream,* flows 14 miles to Caliente Creek at Loraine (lat. 35°18'20" N, long. 118°26'15" W; sec. 21, T 30 S, R 33 E). Named on Emerald Mountain (1972), Loraine (1972), and Tehachapi NE (1966) 7.5' quadrangles.

Indian Head [TULARE]: *relief feature,* nearly 3 miles south of Kern Peak (lat. 36°16'10" N, long. 118°17' W). Named on Kern Peak (1956) 15' quadrangle.

Indian Hill [MADERA]: *peak,* 11 miles northeast of Raymond (lat. 37°19'40" N, long. 119°45'45" W; sec. 15, T 7 S, R 20 E). Named on Horsecamp Mountain (1947) 7.5' quadrangle.

Indian Hill [TULARE]: *peak,* 8 miles east of Tucker Mountain (lat. 36°38'05" N, long. 119°03'30" W; sec. 8, T 15 S, R 27 E); the peak is east of Indian Creek. Altitude 2740 feet. Named on Miramonte (1966) 7.5' quadrangle.

Indian John Spring [KERN]: *spring,* 4.5 miles south-southwest of Tehachapi (lat. 35°04'10" N, long. 118°28'30" W; near S line sec. 4, T 11 N, R 15 E). Named on Tehachapi South (1966) 7.5' quadrangle.

Indian Lake: see **Lower Indian Lake** [FRESNO]; **Upper Indian Lake** [FRESNO].

Indian Meadow [MADERA]: *area,* 10 miles southwest of Devils Postpile (lat. 37°32'35" N, long. 119°14'05" W). Named on Devils Postpile (1953) 15' quadrangle.

Indian Painting Spring [TULARE]: *spring,* 6 miles south-southeast of Auckland (lat. 36°30'20" N, long. 119°03'50" W; sec. 29, T 16 S, R 27 E). Named on Auckland (1966) 7.5' quadrangle.

Indian Rock [FRESNO]: *peak,* 2.5 miles northnortheast of Balch Camp (lat. 36°56'10" N, long. 119°06'15" W). Named on Patterson Mountain (1952) 15' quadrangle.

Indian Rocks [KERN]: *relief feature,* 2.5 miles east-northeast of Orchard Peak (lat. 35°45'10"

N, long. 120°05'20" W; sec. 13, T 25 S, R 17 E). Named on Pyramid Hills (1953) 7.5' quadrangle.

Indian Spring [KERN]: *spring,* nearly 4 miles south-southwest of Orchard Peak (lat. 35°41'05" N, long. 120°09'15" W; near NE cor. sec. 8, T 26 S, R 17 E). Named on Orchard Peak (1961) 7.5' quadrangle.

Indian Spring [TULARE]: *spring,* 5.25 miles south-southeast of Auckland (lat. 36°30'55" N, long. 119°04'30" W; sec. 19, T 16 S, R 27 E). Named on Auckland (1966) 7.5' quadrangle.

Indian Springs [FRESNO]:
(1) *spring,* 7 miles southwest of Blackcap Mountain (lat. 37°00'15" N, long. 118°53' W; sec. 2, T 11 S, R 28 E). Named on Blackcap Mountain (1953) 15' quadrangle.
(2) *spring,* 8 miles northwest of Coalinga (lat. 36°13'10" N, long. 120°27'30" W; sec. 4, T 20 S, R 14 E). Named on Alcalde Hills (1969) 7.5' quadrangle. Called Nunez Spr. on Coalinga (1944) 15' quadrangle.

Indian Springs [MADERA]: *locality,* 5.5 miles south-southwest of O'Neals along Cottonwood Creek (1) (lat. 37°03'05" N, long. 119°43'55" W; sec. 24, T 10 S, R 20 E). Named on Millerton Lake West (1965) 7.5' quadrangle.

Indian Springs: see **Rosamond** [KERN].

Indian Valley [FRESNO]: *valley,* 6.5 miles southeast of Mercey Hot Springs on Fresno-San Benito county line (lat. 36°37'55" N, long. 120°47' W; around SE cor. sec. 8, T 15 S, R 11 E). Named on Mercey Hot Springs (1969) 7.5' quadrangle.

Indian Wells [KERN]: *locality,* 3.5 miles west-northwest of Inyokern (lat. 35°40'05" N, long. 117°52'20" W; near S line sec. 15, T 26 S, R 38 E); the place is at the west edge of Indian Wells Valley. Named on Inyokern (1972) 7.5' quadrangle. Called Homestead on Inyokern (1943) 15' quadrangle. Searles Lake (1915) 1° quadrangle shows a watering place called Indian Wells at the site.

Indian Wells Canyon [KERN]: *canyon,* drained by a stream that flows 8.5 miles to Indian Wells Valley 3.5 miles west-northwest of Inyokern near Indian Wells (lat. 35°40'20" N, long. 117°52'05" W; sec. 15, T 26 S, R 38 E). Named on Owens Peak (1972) 7.5' quadrangle.

Indian Wells Canyon: see **Berts Canyon** [KERN].

Indian Wells Valley [KERN]: *valley,* east of the Sierra Nevada and north of El Paso Mountains at the northeast corner of Kern County; extends into Inyo County and San Bernardino County. Named on Trona (1957) 1°x 2° quadrangle. Called Salt Wells Valley on Wheeler's (1871-1878) map. The feature also was called Inyo-kern Valley and Brown Valley (Thompson, D.G., 1929, p. 144). United States Board on Geographic Names (1933a, p. 388) rejected the names "Salt Wells Valley," "Inyokern Valley," "Inyo-Kern Valley," and "Brown Valley" for the place.

Infant Buttes [FRESNO]: *relief features,* 9.5 miles west-southwest of Mount Abbot (lat. 37°19'30" N, long. 118°56'25" W). Named on Mount Abbot (1953) 15' quadrangle. Theodore S. Solomons gave the name (Farquhar, 1923, p. 406).

Ingle [FRESNO]: *locality,* 7.25 miles east-southeast of Mendota along Southern Pacific Railroad (lat. 36°43'15" N, long. 120°15'25" W; near SW cor. sec. 8, T 14 S, R 16 E). Named on Tranquillity (1956) 7.5' quadrangle.

Ingram Canyon [FRESNO]: *canyon,* drained by a stream that flows 2 miles to Lavrock Canyon 7 miles south of Orchard Peak (lat. 35°38'20" N, long. 120°08'45" W; sec. 28, T 26 S, R 17 E). Named on Orchard Peak (1961) 7.5' quadrangle.

Injun Flats: see **Jackass Meadow** [FRESNO].

Inside Creek [TULARE]: *stream,* diverges from Outside Creek and flows 4 miles to rejoin Outside Creek and form Elk Bayou 5 miles east-southeast of Tulare (lat. 36°11'30" N, long. 119°15'20" W; sec. 15, T 20 S, R 25 E). Named on Cairns Corner (1950, photorevised 1969) and Tulare (1950) 7.5' quadrangles.

Inspiration Point [KERN]: *peak,* 11.5 miles south-southwest of Weldon (lat. 35°30'45" N, long. 118°21'25" W; near SE cor. sec. 7, T 28 S, R 34 E). Altitude 7835 feet. Named on Woolstalf Creek (1972) 7.5' quadrangle.

Inyokern [KERN]: *village,* 8 miles west of Ridgecrest (lat. 35°38'50" N, long. 117°48'45" W; on E line sec. 30, T 26 S, R 39 E). Named on Inyokern (1972) 7.5' quadrangle. Postal authorities established Inyokern post office in 1910 (Frickstad, p. 56). The place started during construction of the aqueduct that takes Owens Valley water from Inyo County to Los Angeles; it was called Siding 16 and Magnolia before 1913, when Robert Thompson, Sr., a resident, suggested the name "Inyokern" for the location near Kern-Inyo county line (Bailey, 1967, p. 11).

Inyo-Kern Valley: see **Indian Wells Valley** [KERN].

Inyo Well [KERN]: *well,* 3.5 miles south of Inyokern along Little Dixie Wash (lat. 35°35'45" N, long. 117°48'55" W; near SE cor. sec. 7, T 27 S, R 30 E). Named on Inyokern SE (1972) 7.5' quadrangle.

Ionian Basin [FRESNO]: *area,* 2.25 miles east-southeast of Mount Goddard (lat. 37°05'40" N, long. 118°40'45" W); the place is near Scylla and Charybdis. Named on Mount Goddard (1948) 15' quadrangle. Lewis Clark of the Sierra Club proposed the name to carry out the Greek theme begun with the names "Scylla" and "Charybdis" (Browning 1986, p. 107).

Iridescent Lake [TULARE]: *lake,* 1500 feet long, 3.5 miles south-southeast of Mount Whitney (lat. 36°32'05" N, long. 118°15'30" W). Named on Mount Whitney (1956) 15' quadrangle.

Iron Canyon [KERN]: *canyon,* drained by a

stream that flows 1.5 miles to Fremont Valley 2 miles northeast of Garlock (lat. 35°25'15" N, long. 117°45'50" W). Named on Garlock (1967) 7.5' quadrangle.

Iron Creek [MADERA]:
(1) *stream,* flows 3.5 miles to South Fork Merced River 4 miles south of Buena Vista Peak (lat. 37°32' N, long. 119°31'30" W; sec. 2, T 5 S, R 22 E); the stream heads at Iron Lakes. Named on Bass Lake (1953) and Yosemite (1956) 15' quadrangles.
(2) *stream,* flows 3 miles to Middle Fork San Joaquin River 7.5 miles west of Devils Postpile (lat. 37°37'10" N, long. 119°13'15" W); the stream heads at Iron Lake on the west side of Iron Mountain (2). Named on Devils Postpile (1953) 15' quadrangle.

Iron Lake [MADERA]: *lake,* 950 feet long, nearly 5 miles west of Devils Postpile (lat. 37°36'45" N, long. 119°10'05" W); the lake is 0.25 mile west of Iron Mountain (2). Named on Devils Postpile (1953) 15' quadrangle.

Iron Lakes [MADERA]: *lakes,* largest 1400 feet long, 10.5 miles north-northwest of Shuteye Peak (lat. 37°29'30" N, long. 119°29'45" W; sec. 18, T 5 S, R 23 E). Named on Shuteye Peak (1953) 15' quadrangle.

Iron Mountain [KERN]: *peak,* 1.5 miles south-southwest of Woody (lat. 35°41'15" N, long. 118°50'55" W; near NW cor. sec. 10, T 26 S, R 29 E). Altitude 2486 feet. Named on Woody (1965) 7.5' quadrangle.

Iron Mountain [MADERA]:
(1) *peak,* 10 miles north-northwest of Shuteye Peak (lat. 37°28'55" N, long. 119°29'15" W; sec. 19, T 5 S, R 23 E). Altitude 9165 feet. Named on Shuteye Peak (1953) 15' quadrangle.
(2) *peak,* 4.5 miles west-southwest of Devils Postpile (lat. 37°36'45" N, long. 119°09'50" W). Altitude 11,149 feet. Named on Devils Postpile (1953) 15' quadrangle.
(3) *peak,* 3.5 miles southwest of Raymond (lat. 37°11'10" N, long. 119°57'35" W; at SW cor. sec. 36, T 8 S, R 18 E). Altitude 984 feet. Named on Raymond (1962) 7.5' quadrangle.

Iron Spring [FRESNO]:
(1) *spring,* 6.25 miles southeast of Smith Mountain (2) (lat. 36°01'35" N, long. 120°30'10" W; sec. 7, T 22 S, R 14 E). Named on Smith Mountain (1969) 7.5' quadrangle.
(2) *spring,* 11 miles southwest of Coalinga (lat. 36°00'35" N, long. 120°28'25" W; near SW cor. sec. 16, T 22 S, R 14 E). Named on Curry Mountain (1969) 7.5' quadrangle.

Iron Spring [TULARE]: *spring,* 5 miles west of Olancha Peak (lat. 36°16'25" N, long. 118°12'20" W; sec. 17, T 19 S, R 35 E). Named on Olancha (1956) 15' quadrangle.

Ironton Flats [MADERA]: *area,* 6.5 miles southwest of the town of North Fork (lat. 37°09'35" N, long. 119°35'45" W; sec. 8, T 9 S, R 22 E). Named on North Fork (1965) 7.5' quadrangle.

Irrigosa [MADERA]: *locality,* 2 miles southwest of Trigo along Southern Pacific Railroad (lat. 36°53'30" N, long. 119°59'10" W; sec. 15, T 12 S, R 18 E). Named on Gregg (1965) 7.5' quadrangle. California Division of Highways' (1934) map shows a place called Tharsa located along the railroad 3.25 miles southeast of Irrigosa (near SW cor. sec. 30, T 12 S, R 19 E).

Isabella [KERN]: *locality,* 4.5 miles north-northeast of Bodfish along Kern River at the mouth of South Fork (lat. 35°39'25" N, long. 118°27'35" W). Named on Isabella (1943) 15' quadrangle. Postal authorities established Isabella post office in 1896, moved it 1.5 miles south in 1953, and changed the name to Lake Isabella in 1957 (Salley, p. 115). Steven Barton founded the town and named it for Queen Isabella of Spain in 1893, the year of the Columbian Exposition celebrating the quadricentennial of the discovery of America (Gudde, 1949, p. 162). Water of Isabella Lake now covers the site.

Isabella: see **Lake Isabella** [KERN].

Isabella Lake [KERN]: *lake,* behind a dam on Kern River 4.5 miles south-southwest of Wofford Heights (lat. 35°38'45" N, long. 118°28'50" W; near SW cor. sec. 19, T 26 S, R 33 E); water of the lake covers the site of the former town of Isabella. Named on Lake Isabella North (1972) and Weldon (1972) 7.5' quadrangles. Called Isabella Reservoir on Isabella (1943) 15' quadrangle. United States Board on Geographic Names (1972a, p. 4) gave the names "Lake Isabella" and "Isabella Reservoir" as variants. The dam that forms the lake was completed in 1953 (Wines, p. 131).

Isabella Reservoir: see **Isabella Lake** [KERN].

Isberg Lakes [MADERA]: *lakes,* two, each about 700 feet long, 4.5 miles east of Merced Peak (lat. 37°38'50" N, long. 119°18'50" W); the lakes are less than 1 mile east of Isberg Pass. Named on Merced Peak (1953) 15' quadrangle.

Isberg Pass [MADERA]: *pass,* nearly 4 miles east of Merced Peak (lat. 37°38'40" N, long. 119°19'30" W). Named on Merced Peak (1953) 15' quadrangle. Lieutenant N.F. McClure named the pass for the soldier who found it in 1895 (United States Board on Geographic Names, 1934a, p. 12).

Isberg Peak [MADERA]: *peak,* 4.25 miles east-northeast of Merced Peak (lat. 37°39'15" N, long. 119°19'15" W); the peak is less than 1 mile north-northeast of Isberg Pass. Altitude 10,996 feet. Named on Merced Peak (1953) 15' quadrangle.

Isham Hill [KERN]: *peak,* 4 miles north-northwest of Woody (lat. 35°45'45" N, long. 118°51' W; near SE cor. sec. 9, T 25 S, R 29 E). Altitude 2196 feet. Named on White River (1965) 7.5' quadrangle.

Island Crossing [FRESNO]: *locality,* 2.25 miles northwest of Double Peak along Fish Creek

(1) (lat. 37°32'05" N, long. 119°04' W). Named on Devils Postpile (1953) 15' quadrangle.

Island Lake [FRESNO]: *lake,* 1100 feet long, 4.5 miles east-northeast of Dinkey Dome (lat. 37°09'05" N, long. 119°03'40" W; sec. 18, T 9 S, R 27 E); the lake contains five islands. Named on Huntington Lake (1953) 15' quadrangle.

Island Number 1 [FRESNO]: *island,* 11 miles north of downtown Fresno in San Joaquin River (lat. 36°55'10" N, long. 119°45'25" W; sec. 2, T 12 S, R 20 E). Named on Herndon (1965) 15' quadrangle.

Island Pass [MADERA]: *pass,* 10 miles northwest of Devils Postpile on Madera-Mono county line (lat. 37°44'10" N, long. 119°11'35" W); the pass is north of Thousand Island Lake. Named on Devils Postpile (1953) 15' quadrangle

Isosceles Peak [FRESNO]: *peak,* 10 miles east of Mount Goddard (lat. 37°05'40" N, long. 118°32'15" W). Named on Mount Goddard (1948) 15' quadrangle. Lewis Clark and Nathan Clark named the peak about 1939 for its appearance from Dusy Basin (Browning, p. 108).

Italian Bar [FRESNO]: *locality,* 9 miles northwest of Shaver Lake Heights (present town of Shaver Lake) along San Joaquin River on Fresno-Madera county line (lat. 37°09'25" N, long. 119°24'15" W; near SW cor. sec. 7, T 9 S, R 24 E). Named on Shaver Lake (1953) 15' quadrangle.

Italian Bar [MADERA]: *locality,* 13 miles south of Shuteye Peak along San Joaquin River on Madera-Fresno county line (lat. 37°09'25" N, long. 119°24'15" W; near SW cor. sec. 7, T 9 S, R 24 E). Named on Shaver Lake (1953) 15' quadrangle.

Italian Creek [FRESNO]: *stream,* flows nearly 3 miles to San Joaquin River 5.5 miles west-northwest of Shaver Lake Heights (present town of Shaver Lake) (lat. 37°08'55" N, long. 119°23'55" W; sec. 18, T 9 S, R 24 E); the stream enters San Joaquin River near Italian Bar. Named on Shaver Lake (1953) 15' quadrangle.

Italy: see **Lake Italy** [FRESNO].

Italy Pass [FRESNO]: *pass,* 2.5 miles south of Mount Abbot on Fresno-Inyo county line (lat. 37°21'05" N, long. 118°47' W); the pass is 1 mile east-southeast of Lake Italy. Named on Mount Abbot (1953) 15' quadrangle.

Iva Bell Hot Springs: see **Fish Creek Hot Springs** [FRESNO].

Ivanhoe [TULARE]: *town,* 7 miles west-southwest of Woodlake (lat. 36°23'15" N, long. 119°13' W; mainly in sec. 1, T 18 S, R 25 E). Named on Exeter (1952) 15' quadrangle. The place was called Klink, for George T. Klink, a railroad auditor, before Mrs. Ellen Boas, a schoolboard member, suggested the name "Ivanhoe" from Ivanhoe school district (Mitchell, A.R., p. 68). Postal authorities established Ivanhoe post office first in 1895 and discontinued it in 1896; they established Klink post office in 1910 and changed the name to Ivanhoe in 1924 (Salley, p. 105, 113). They established Orange Heights post office 12 miles northeast of Visalia in 1910 and discontinued it in 1912, when they moved the service to Klink (Salley, p. 162).

Ive: see **Ivesta** [FRESNO].

Ivesta [FRESNO]: *locality,* 6 miles east-northeast of Malaga along Southern Pacific Railroad (lat. 36°43'20" N, long. 119°38'10" W; on S line sec. 12, T 14 S, R 21 E). Named on Malaga (1964) 7.5' quadrangle. Called Ive on Malaga (1923) 7.5' quadrangle, and called Minneola on Grunsky's (1898) map.

Ivory [TULARE]: *locality,* nearly 3 miles northwest of Dinuba along Southern Pacific Railroad (lat. 36°34'05" N, long. 119°25'25" W; sec. 1, T 16 S, R 23 E). Named on Reedley (1966) 7.5' quadrangle.

Ivy [KERN]: *locality,* 3 miles south of Wasco along Atchison, Topeka and Santa Fe Railroad (lat. 35°33' N, long. 119°19'30" W; sec. 30, T 27 S, R 25 E). Named on Wasco (1953) 7.5' quadrangle.

Izaak Walton: see **Mount Izaak Walton** [FRESNO].

Izaak Walton Lake [FRESNO]: *lake,* 1100 feet long, 9.5 miles southwest of Mount Abbot (lat. 37°29'05" N, long. 118°54' W); the lake is 1 mile north-northwest of Mount Izaak Walton. Named on Mount Abbot (1953) 15' quadrangle.

— J —

Jacalitos Creek [FRESNO]: *stream,* flows 27 miles to Los Gatos Creek 5.5 miles east of Coalinga (lat. 36°08'50" N, long. 120°15'45" W; near W line sec. 32, T 20 S, R 16 E). Named on Coalinga (1956), Curry Mountain (1969), Kreyenhagen Hills (1956), and Smith Mountain (1969) 7.5' quadrangles. Spaniards called the stream El Arroyo de Jacalitos for the many Indian dwellings found near it (Hoover, Rensch, and Rensch, p. 89). *Jacalitos* means "little huts" in Mexican Spanish, with special reference to Indian dwellings (Stewart, p. 225).

Jacalitos Hills [FRESNO]: *range,* 4 miles south of Coalinga between Jacalitos Creek and Warthan Creek (lat. 36°05' N, long. 120°22'30" W). Named on Curry Mountain (1969) and Kreyenhagen Hills (1956) 7.5' quadrangles.

Jackass Butte [MADERA]: *peak,* 11 miles north-northeast of Shuteye Peak (lat. 37°29' N, long. 119°18'30" W; sec. 23, T 5 S, R 24 E); the peak is near Jackass Creek. Altitude 7238 feet. Named on Shuteye Peak (1953) 15' quadrangle.

Jackass Campground: see **Little Jackass Campground** [MADERA].

Jackass Creek [MADERA]: *stream,* flows 15 miles to Mammoth Pool Reservoir 7 miles east-northeast of Shuteye Peak (lat. 37°22'20" N, long. 119°18'15" W; sec. 25, T 6 S, R 24 E); the stream heads at Jackass Lakes and goes past Jackass Butte and Jackass Rock. Named on Merced Peak (1953) and Shuteye Peak (1953) 15' quadrangles. West Fork enters from the northwest 0.5 mile upstream from the mouth of the main stream; it is 6.5 miles long and is named on Shuteye Peak (1953) 15' quadrangle.

Jackass Creek [TULARE]: *stream,* flows 4.5 miles to Fish Creek (2) 10 miles south of Monache Mountain (lat. 36°03'50" N, long. 118° 13'05" W; sec. 29, T 21 S, R 35 E); the stream heads near Jackass Peak and goes through Jackass Meadows. Named on Monache Mountain (1956) 15' quadrangle.

Jackass Dike [FRESNO]: *ridge,* north-north-west-trending, 1.25 miles long, 11.5 miles west-southwest of Mount Abbot (lat. 37°18' N, long. 118°57'40" W); the ridge is 1 mile north of Jackass Meadow. Named on Mount Abbot (1953) 15' quadrangle.

Jackass Flat: see **Jackass Meadow** [FRESNO].

Jackass Lakes [MADERA]: *lakes,* largest 1500 feet long, 7.5 miles south-southeast of Merced Peak (lat. 37°31'40" N, long. 119°21'10" W; sec. 4, 5, T 5 S, R 24 E); the lakes are at the head of Jackass Creek. Named on Merced Peak (1953) 15' quadrangle.

Jackass Meadow [MADERA]: *area,* 11.5 miles north-northeast of Shuteye Peak (lat. 37°30' N, long. 119°20' W); the place is along Jackass Creek. Named on Merced Peak (1953) and Shuteye Peak (1953) 15' quadrangles.

Jackass Meadow: see **Little Jackass Meadow**, under **Soldier Meadow** [MADERA].

Jackass Meadow [FRESNO]: *area,* 12.5 miles southwest of Mount Abbot along South Fork San Joaquin River (lat. 37°16'55" N, long. 118°57'45" W); the place is 1 mile south of Jackass Dike. Named on Mount Abbot (1953) 15' quadrangle. Called Jackass Flat on Lippincott's (1902) map. The place first was called Injun Flats (Browning 1986, p. 109).

Jackass Meadows [TULARE]: *area,* 8 miles southwest of Monache Mountain (lat. 36°05'40" N, long. 118°13'35" W; sec. 17, T 21 S, R 35 E): the place is along Jackass Creek. Named on Monache Mountain (1956) 15' quadrangle.

Jackass Peak [TULARE]: *peak,* nearly 5 miles south of Monache Mountain (lat. 36°08'15" N, long. 118°12'20" W; sec. 32, T 20 S, R 35 E). Altitude 9245 feet. Named on Monache Mountain (1956) 15' quadrangle.

Jackass Rock [MADERA]: *peak,* 9 miles northeast of Shuteye Peak (lat. 37°26' N, long. 119°18' W; sec. 1, T 6 S, R 24 E). Altitude 7112 feet. Named on Shuteye Peak (1953) 15' quadrangle.

Jack Canyon [KERN]: *canyon,* 2 miles long, 4 miles southwest of Orchard Peak on Kern-San Luis Obispo county line (lat. 35°42'30" N, long. 120°11'45" W). Named on Orchard Peak (1961) 7.5' quadrangle.

Jack Hart Spring [FRESNO]: *spring,* 3.5 miles northeast of Coalinga Mineral Springs (lat. 36°10'45" N, long. 120°30'45" W; near NW cor. sec. 19, T 20 S, R 14 E). Named on Sherman Peak (1969) 7.5' quadrangle.

Jackrabbit Hill [KERN]: *hill,* 11.5 miles south-southwest of Boron (lat. 34°50'20" N, long. 117°42'10" W; near SE cor. sec. 27, T 9 N, R 8 W). Altitude 2881 feet. Named on Jackrabbit Hill (1973) 7.5' quadrangle.

Jacks Camp [KERN]: *locality,* 7.5 miles northwest of Cummings Mountain (lat. 35°06'40" N, long. 118°40'20" W; near S line sec. 29, T 32 S, R 31 E). Named on Tejon Ranch (1966) 7.5' quadrangle.

Jacks Creek [KERN]: *stream,* flows 5 miles to Canebrake Creek 2 miles northwest of Walker Pass (lat. 35°41'05" N, long. 118°03'05" W; sec. 7, T 26 S, R 37 E). Named on Walker Pass (1972) 7.5' quadrangle.

Jackson Meadow [FRESNO]: *area,* 13 miles northwest of Mount Abbot (lat. 37°29'45" N, long. 118°58'10" W). Named on Mount Abbot (1953) 15' quadrangle.

Jacksons Hole [KERN]: *relief feature,* 2.5 miles west-southwest of Claraville (lat. 35°25'50" N, long. 118°22'30" W). Named on Claraville (1972) and Piute Peak (1972) 7.5' quadrangles.

Jack Spring [FRESNO]: *spring,* 3.5 miles south-southwest of Coalinga (lat. 36°05'40" N, long. 120°23'05" W; sec. 18, T 21 S, R 15 E). Named on Curry Mountain (1969) 7.5' quadrangle. Called Jack Springs on Coalinga (1956) 15' quadrangle.

Jack Spring [KERN]: *spring,* 4 miles southwest of Orchard Peak (lat. 35°42'05" N, long. 120°11'20" W; near NW cor. sec. 6, T 26 S, R 17 E); the spring is in Jack Canyon. Named on Orchard Peak (1961) 7.5' quadrangle.

Jacks Station [KERN]: *locality,* 2 miles northwest of Walkers Pass (lat. 35°41' N, long. 118°03' W; sec. 7, T 26 S, R 37 E). Named on Kernville (1908) 30' quadrangle.

Jacobsen Meadow [TULARE]: *area,* 6 miles north of Camp Nelson (lat. 36°13'45" N, long. 118°36'10" W; sec. 34, T 19 S, R 31 E); the place is near the head of Jacobson Creek. Named on Camp Nelson (1956) 15' quadrangle.

Jacobson Creek [TULARE]: *stream,* flows nearly 2 miles to South Mountaineer Creek 6.5 miles north-northeast of Camp Nelson (lat. 36°13'50" N, long. 118°34'05" W; sec. 36, T 19 S, R 31 E). Named on Camp Nelson (1956) 15' quadrangle.

Jacobs Slough: see **Cain Slough** [KINGS].

Jamesan [FRESNO]: *locality,* 8 miles west of Kerman along Southern Pacific Railroad (lat. 36°43'10" N, long. 120°12'35" W; at S line sec. 10, T 14 S, R 16 E). Named on Jamesan

(1963) 7.5' quadrangle. Called Jamison on Mendenhall's (1908) map. Postal authorities established Jamison post office in 1893, changed the name to Jameson in 1911, and discontinued it in 1912—the name was for J.G. James, first postmaster (Salley, p. 106).

James Bypass [FRESNO]: *water feature,* artificial watercourse that extends for 14 miles from Fish Slough to Fresno Slough 8 miles southeast of Mendota (lat. 36°40'35" N, long. 120°16' W; sec. 30, T 14 S, R 16 E). Named on Helm (1963), Jamesan (1963), San Joaquin (1963), and Tranquillity (1956) 7.5' quadrangles. Called Main Bypass on San Joaquin (1925) 7.5' quadrangle, and called Fresno Slough By-Pass on Tranquillity (1946) 15' quadrangle.

Jameson: see **Jamesan** [FRESNO].

Jamison: see **Byles Jamison Camp** [FRESNO]; **Jamesan** [FRESNO].

Jasmin [KERN]: *locality,* 6.5 miles northeast of McFarland along Southern Pacific Railroad (lat. 35°44'35" N, long. 119°08'40" W; sec. 23, T 25 S, R 26 E). Named on McFarland (1954) 7.5' quadrangle. Postal authorities established Jasmine (with the final "e") post office at Jasmin in 1913 and discontinued it in 1923 (Salley, p. 106).

Jasmine: see **Jasmin** [KERN].

Jasper Canyon: see **Jasper Creek** [FRESNO].

Jasper Creek [FRESNO]: *stream,* flows nearly 6 miles to Jacalitos Creek 7.5 miles southsouthwest of Coalinga (lat. 36°02'10" N, long. 120°24'05" W; near NW cor. sec. 7, T 22 S, R 15 E). Named on Curry Mountain (1969) and Parkfield (1961) 7.5' quadrangles. The canyon of the stream is called Jasper Canyon on Coalinga (1912) 30' quadrangle. Arnold and Anderson (1908, p. 16) named the stream "from the picturesque and brilliant colored buttes of jasper that surround its upper portion," and applied the name "Jasper Canyon" to the gorge that the stream cut across the northwest end of Reef Ridge.

Jastro [KERN]: *locality,* 4 miles west of Bakersfield along Atchison, Topeka and Santa Fe Railroad (lat. 35°22'35" N, long. 119°04'15" W; near W line sec. 27, T 29 S, R 7 E). Named on Oildale (1954) 7.5' quadrangle.

Jawbone Canyon [KERN]: *canyon,* 16 miles long, opens into Fremont Valley 3 miles northeast of Cinco (lat. 35°18' N, long. 118° 00'20" W; near N line sec. 28, T 30 S, R 37 E). Named on Cache Peak (1973), Cinco (1972), and Cross Mountain (1972) 7.5' quadrangles. The name reportedly is from the discovery of the jawbone of a fossil mammal (Bailey, 1963, p. 13).

Jawbone Canyon: see **Little Jawbone Canyon** [KERN].

Jawbone Lake [FRESNO]: *lake,* 1100 feet long, 7 miles south of Mount Abbot (lat. 37°17'15" N, long. 118°48' W). Named on Mount Abbot (1953) 15' quadrangle.

Jawbone Well [KERN]: *well,* 5.25 miles west-northwest of Cinco (lat. 35°18'05" N, long. 118°07' W; sec. 28, T 30 S, R 36 E); the well is in Jawbone Canyon. Named on Cinco (1972) 7.5' quadrangle.

Jenkins: see **Mount Jenkins**, under **Morris Peak** [KERN].

Jennie Lake [TULARE]: *lake,* 1500 feet long, 2 miles east-southeast of Shell Mountain (lat. 36°40'50" N, long. 118°45'50" W; sec. 30, T 14 S, R 30 E). Named on Giant Forest (1956) 15' quadrangle. S.L.N. Ellis named the lake in 1897 for his wife (Browning 1986, p. 110).

Jenny Creek [TULARE]: *stream,* flows 2.5 miles to North Fork Tule River 14 miles southsouthwest of Mineral King (lat. 36°16'45" N, long. 118°44'10" W). Named on Mineral King (1956) 15' quadrangle.

Jenny Lind Cañon: see **Big Arroyo** [TULARE].

Jenny Lind Canyon [KERN]: *canyon,* drained by a stream that flows 2 miles to Clear Creek (1) 4.5 miles south of Miracle Hot Springs (lat. 35°30'50"N, long. 118°31'05" W; near E line sec. 10, T 28 S, R 32 E). Named on Miracle Hot Springs (1972) 7.5' quadrangle.

Jepson: see **Mount Jepson**, under **Mount Sill** [FRESNO].

Jerkey Meadows [TULARE]: *area,* 6.25 miles west-southwest of Hockett Peak (lat. 36°11'05" N, long. 118°29'15" W). Named on Hockett Peak (1956) 15' quadrangle. United States Board on Geographic Names (1988b, p. 2), approved the singular form "Jerkey Meadow" for the name, and rejected the forms "Jerkey Meadows" and "Jerky Meadow."

Jerry Slough [KERN]: *stream,* flows 7.25 miles to Goose Lake Bed 10.5 miles east-southeast of the village of Lost Hills (lat. 35°33' N, long. 119°31'15" W). Named on Buttonwillow (1954), Semitropic (1954), and Wasco SW (1953) 7.5' quadrangles. Called Goose Slough on Watts' (1894) map. On Buttonwillow (1942) 15' quadrangle, Jerry Slough extends to present Goose Lake Slough; the map has the name "Jerry Slough" for both features.

Jesbel [MADERA]: *locality,* 5.25 miles southsouthwest of Raymond along Southern Pacific Railroad (lat. 37°09' N, long. 119°57'15" W; sec. 13, T 9 S, R 18 E). Named on Raymond (1944) 15' quadrangle.

Jesse Morrow Mountain [FRESNO]: *ridge,* southwest-trending, 3 miles long, 5 miles east of Centerville (lat. 36°44'10" N, long. 119° 24'30" W). Named on Wahtoke (1966) 7.5' quadrangle.

Jewel Lake [FRESNO]: *lake,* 300 feet long, 1200 feet east of Kaiser Peak (lat. 37°17'40" N, long. 119°10'45" W; on W line sec. 30, T 7 S, R 26 E). Named on Kaiser Peak (1953) 15' quadrangle.

Jewetta: see **Saco** [KERN].

Jim Gray Creek [TULARE]: *stream,* flows

about 4 miles to Horse Creek (2) 9 miles south-southwest of Kaweah (lat. 36°20'35" N, long. 118°57' W; sec. 21, T 18 S, R 28 E). Named on Kaweah (1957) 15' quadrangle.

Joaquin Flat [KERN]: *area,* 7 miles west of Cummings Mountain (lat. 35°01'40" N, long. 118°41'30" W; near SE cor. sec. 16, T 11 N, R 17 W). Named on Tejon Ranch (1966) 7.5' quadrangle.

Joaquin Flat [TULARE]: *area,* 5.5 miles south-southeast of Springville (lat. 36°03'15" N, long. 118°47'30" W; sec. 36, T 21 S, R 29 E). Named on Springville (1957) 15' quadrangle.

Joaquin Mill [FRESNO]: *locality,* 16 miles northwest of Coalinga along White Creek (lat. 36°16'20" N, long. 120°35'30" W; sec. 17, T 19 S, R 13 E). Site named on Santa Rita Peak (1969) 7.5' quadrangle.

Joaquin Ridge [FRESNO]: *ridge,* west-trending, 10 miles long, 14 miles north-northwest of Coalinga (lat. 36°19'30" N, long. 120°29'30" W). Named on Joaquin Rocks (1969) and Santa Rita Peak (1969) 7.5' quadrangles. Arnold and Anderson (1908, p. 13) named the ridge and pointed out that the feature called Joaquin Rocks is on it.

Joaquin River: see **San Joaquin River** [FRESNO].

Joaquin Rocks [FRESNO]: *relief feature,* 13 miles north-northwest of Coalinga (lat. 36°19'10" N, long. 120°26'50" W; near E line sec. 33, T 18 S, R 14 E). Named on Joaquin Rocks (1969) 7.5' quadrangle. United States Board on Geographic Names (1933a, p. 399) rejected the name "Tres Piedras" for the feature—Joaquin Rocks has three prominent outcrops.

Joaquin Spring [FRESNO]: *spring,* 0.25 mile southwest of Joaquin Rocks (lat. 36°18'55" N, long. 120°27'10" W; sec. 33, T 18 S, R 14 E). Named on Joaquin Rocks (1969) 7.5' quadrangle.

Joe Bowen Canyon [TULARE]: *canyon,* nearly 3 miles long, 6.5 miles south-southwest of California Hot Springs (lat. 35°48'10" N, long. 118°44'15" W). Named on California Hot Springs (1958) 15' and White River (1965) 7.5' quadrangles.

Joe Crane Lake [MADERA]: *lake,* 1000 feet long, 4.5 miles east of Merced Peak (lat. 37°37'30" N, long. 119°18'50" W). Named on Merced Peak (1953) 15' quadrangle.

Joe Devel Peak [TULARE]: *peak,* 4.25 miles south of Mount Whitney (lat. 36°31' N, long. 118°17'45" W). Altitude 13,325 feet. Named on Mount Whitney (1956) 15' quadrangle. Owen L. Williams of the Sierra Club named the peak in 1937 for Joseph Devel, a member of the Wheeler survey (Browning 1986, p. 111).

Joe Walker Town: see **Walker Basin** [KERN].

Johannesburg [KERN]: *village,* 1 mile east-northeast of Randsburg (lat. 35°22'20" N, long. 117°38' W; sec. 36, T 29 S, R 40 E).

Named on Johannesburg (1967) 7.5' quadrangle. Postal authorities established Johannesburg post office in 1897 (Frickstad, p. 56). The name is from the mining center of Johannesburg in South Africa (Wines, p. 40).

Johnnycakes Lake [KERN]: *lake,* 250 feet long, 3 miles southwest of Glennville (lat. 35°41'45" N, long. 118°44'25" W; sec. 3, T 26 S, R 30 E). Named on Glennville (1972) 7.5' quadrangle.

Johnson: see **Mount Johnson** [FRESNO].

Johnson Canyon [KERN]:

(1) *canyon,* drained by a stream that flows 2.5 miles to Walker Basin 11 miles north-northeast of Caliente (lat. 35°26' N, long. 118°32'10" W; sec. 3, T 29 S, R 32 E). Named on Breckenridge Mountain (1972) 7.5' quadrangle.

(2) *canyon,* drained by a stream that flows 2.5 miles to Castac Valley 3.5 miles south-southeast of Grapevine (lat. 34°52'45" N, long. 118°54'05" W). Named on Frazier Mountain (1958) and Grapevine (1958) 7.5' quadrangles.

Johnson Creek [MADERA]:

(1) *stream,* flows 3.5 miles to South Fork Merced River 4 miles south of Buena Vista Peak (lat. 37°32'15" N, long. 119°31'20" W; near SE cor. sec. 35, T 4 S, R 22 E). Named on Yosemite (1956) 15' quadrangle.

(2) *stream,* flows 4.5 miles to Chiquito Creek 5.5 miles north-northeast of Shuteye Peak (lat. 37°25' N, long. 119°23'05" W; sec. 7, T 6 S, R 24 E). Named on Shuteye Peak (1953) 15' quadrangle.

Johnson Creek [TULARE]: *stream,* flows 6 miles to Golden Trout Creek 5.5 miles northwest of Kern Peak in Little Whitney Meadow (lat. 36°22'30" N, long. 118°20'40" W); the stream heads at Johnson Lake. Named on Kern Peak (1956) 15' quadrangle.

Johnsondale [TULARE]: *village,* 10 miles northeast of California Hot Springs (lat. 35°58'25" N, long. 118°32'20" W; sec. 32, T 22 S, R 32 E). Named on California Hot Springs (1958) 15' quadrangle. Postal authorities established Johnsondale post office in 1939 (Frickstad, p. 211). The name, given in 1938 by Mount Whitney Lumber Company, commemorates Walter Johnson, an officer of the company (Mitchell, A.R., p. 68).

Johnson Flat [FRESNO]: *area,* 4 miles east-southeast of Dunlap (lat. 36°43' N, long. 119°03'20" W). Named on Miramonte (1966) 7.5' quadrangle.

Johnson Lake [MADERA]: *lake,* 900 feet long, 1.5 miles south of Buena Vista Peak (lat. 37°34'05" N, long. 119°31' W; near SW cor. sec. 24, T 4 S, R 22 E); the lake is along Johnson Creek (1). Named on Yosemite (1956) 15' quadrangle. United States Board on Geographic Names (1933a, p. 400) rejected the names "Glacier Lake" and "Glasier Lake" for the feature.

Johnson Lake: see **Johnston Lake** [MADERA].

Johnson Lake [TULARE]: *lake,* 1200 feet long, 9 miles north-northwest of Kern Peak (lat. 36°26' N, long. 118°20'10" W); the lake is less than 1 mile north of Johnson Peak at the head of Johnson Creek. Named on Kern Peak (1956) 15' quadrangle.

Johnson Meadow: see **Johnston Meadow** [MADERA].

Johnson Meadows [MADERA]: *area,* 6 miles north-northeast of Shuteye Peak (lat. 37°25'50" N, long. 119°23'30" W; sec. 6, T 6 S, R 24 E). Named on Shuteye Peak (1953) 15' quadrangle.

Johnson Peak [KINGS]: *peak,* 14 miles south of Avenal (lat. 38° 48' N, long. 120°09'10" W; sec. 32, T 24 S, R 17 E). Named on Tent Hills (1942) 7.5' quadrangle.

Johnson Peak [TULARE]: *peak,* 8 miles north-northwest of Kern Peak (lat. 36°25'10" N, long. 118°20' W; sec. 30, T 17 S, R 34 E). Altitude 11,371 feet. Named on Kern Peak (1956) 15' quadrangle.

Johnson Point [FRESNO]: *peak,* 4 miles southeast of Dunlap (lat. 36°42' N, long. 119°04' W; near NW cor. sec. 20, T 14 S, R 27 E); the feature is 1.5 miles south-southwest of present Johnson Flat. Named on Dinuba (1924) 30' quadrangle.

Johnson Slough [TULARE]: *water feature,* 3 miles north-northwest of Exeter (lat. 36°20' N, long. 119°09'30" W). Named on Exeter (1952) 15' quadrangle. The feature is part of the Kaweah River distributary system.

Johnson Spring [KERN]: *spring,* 12.5 miles north-northeast of Caliente (lat. 35°27'35" N, long. 118°32'40" W; sec. 28, T 28 S, R 32 E); the spring is in Johnson Canyon (1). Named on Breckenridge Mountain (1972) 7.5' quadrangle.

Johns Peak [KERN]: *peak,* 5 miles west-south-west of Piute Peak (lat. 35°24'55" N, long. 118°28' W; near S line sec. 8, T 29 S, R 33 E). Altitude 4917 feet. Named on Piute Peak (1972) 7.5' quadrangle.

Johnston Lake [MADERA]: *lake,* 600 feet long, nearly 2 miles northwest of Devils Postpile (lat. 37°38'45" N, long. 119°06' W); the lake is in Johnston Meadow. Named on Devils Postpile (1953) 15' quadrangle. It first was called Minaret Lake, but Stephen T. Mather suggested the name "Johnston Lake" to honor Taylor Johnston, as well as Mr. Johnston's father and brother—the three men began mining in the neighborhood in 1919 (Browning, 1988, p. 69). United States Board on Geographic Names (1962b, p. 20) rejected the names "Minaret Lake" and "Johnson Lake" for the feature.

Johnston Meadow [MADERA]: *area,* 2 miles northwest of Devils Postpile along Minaret Creek (lat. 37°38'45" N, long. 119°06' W). Named on Devils Postpile (1953) 15' quad-

rangle. Stephen T. Mather suggested the name "Johnston Meadow" for what had been called Minaret Meadow; the new name honors the Johnstons for whom Johnston Lake was named (Browning, 1988, p. 69). United States Board on Geographic Names (1962b, p. 20) rejected the names "Johnson Meadow" and "Minaret Meadow" for the place.

Jo Lake: see **Little Jo Lake** [FRESNO].

Jones Corner [TULARE]: *locality,* 5 miles west of Porterville (lat. 36°03'25" N, long. 119°06'25" W; at SW cor. sec. 30, T 21 S, R 27 E). Named on Porterville (1951) 7.5' quadrangle.

Jones Ferry: see **Friant** [FRESNO].

Joneso: see **Hardwick** [KINGS].

Jon Hill [TULARE]: *ridge,* south-southwest-trending, 1 mile long, 4.5 miles west-north-west of California Hot Springs (lat. 35°54'45" N, long. 118°44'40" W; mainly in sec. 21, T 23 S, R 30 E). Named on California Hot Springs (1958) 15' quadrangle.

J.O. Pass [TULARE]: *pass,* 13 miles west-north-west of Triple Divide Peak (lat. 36°40'30" N, long. 118°44'35" W; sec. 29, T 14 S, R 30 E). Named on Triple Divide Peak (1956) 15' quadrangle. The name is from the initials "J.O." carved on a tree in the early days (United States Board on Geographic Names, 1933a, p. 399).

Jordan: see **Mount Jordan** [TULARE]; **Mount Jordan**, under **North Palisade** [FRESNO]; **Springville** [TULARE].

Jordan Flat [TULARE]: *area,* 9 miles south-southwest of Kaweah (lat. 36°21' N, long. 118°58'30" W; on E line sec. 19, T 18 S, R 28 E). Named on Kaweah (1957) 15' quadrangle.

Jordan Hot Springs [TULARE]: *springs,* 4.5 miles east of Hockett Peak along Ninemile Creek (lat. 36°13'45" N, long. 118°18'05" W). Named on Hockett Peak (1956) 15' quadrangle. According to Waring (p. 53), about 14 springs issue in a little flat along Ninemile Creek and are named for Mr. Jordan, who first blazed a trail through the neighborhood.

Jordan Peak [TULARE]: *peak,* nearly 3 miles north-northeast of Camp Nelson (lat. 36°10'50" N, long. 118°35'50" W; near SE cor. sec. 15, T 20 S, R 31 E). Altitude 9115 feet. Named on Camp Nelson (1956) 15' quadrangle. Browning (1986, p. 112-113) associated the name with John J. Jordan, who built a trail across the Sierra Nevada from Yokohl Valley in 1861.

Jose Basin [FRESNO]: *area,* 3.5 miles west of Shaver Lake Heights (present town of Shaver Lake) (lat. 37°06' N, long. 119°23' W); Jose Creek drains the feature. Named on Shaver Lake (1953) 15' quadrangle.

Jose Creek [FRESNO]: *stream,* flows 7 miles to San Joaquin River nearly 5 miles north-west of Shaver Lake Heights (present town of Shaver Lake) (lat. 37°08'55" N, long. 119°23'15" W; sec. 18, T 9 S, R 24 E). Named on Shaver Lake (1953) 15' quadrangle.

Joseph Grinnell: see **Lake Joseph Grinnell**, under **Grinnell Lake** [FRESNO].

Josephine Lake [TULARE]: *lake,* 1800 feet long, nearly 5 miles north-northwest of Triple Divide Peak (lat. 36°39'45" N, long. 118° 33' W). Named on Triple Divide Peak (1956) 15' quadrangle. S.L.N. Ellis named the lake for Josephine Perkins (Browning 1986, p. 113).

Joughin Cove [KERN]: *embayment,* 5.5 miles southeast of Wofford Heights along Isabella Lake (lat. 35°38'45" N, long. 118°23'35" W; near NW cor. sec. 25, T 26 S, R 33 E). Named on Lake Isabella North (1972) 7.5' quadrangle.

Jovista [TULARE]: *locality,* 10 miles southwest of Ducor along Southern Pacific Railroad (lat. 35°47'50" N, long. 119°10'50" W; sec. 32, T 24 S, R 26 E). Named on Delano East (1953) 7.5' quadrangle, which shows Sierra Vista ranch at the place. Railroad officials coined the name about 1920 by combining the first two letters of Joseph Di Giorgio's given name with the word "vista" (Gudde, 1949, p. 168).

Joyful: see **Bakersfield** [KERN].

Juan Yaqui Spring [KERN]: *spring,* 6.25 miles west-southwest of Liebre Twins (lat. 34°55'45" N, long. 118°40'20" W). Named on Winters Ridge (1966) 7.5' quadrangle.

Jug Spring [TULARE]: *spring,* 5 miles west-southwest of Hockett Peak (lat. 36°11'45" N, long. 118°28' W). Named on Hockett Peak (1956) 15' quadrangle.

Julia Lake [KERN]: *lake,* 450 feet long, 8 miles north-northeast of Caliente along Walker Basin Creek (lat. 35°23'10" N, long. 118° 33'10" W; near S line sec. 21, T 29 S, R 32 E). Named on Breckenridge Mountain (1972) 7.5' quadrangle.

Julius Caesar: see **Mount Julius Caesar** [FRESNO].

Jumble Lake [FRESNO]: *lake,* 1800 feet long, 2.5 miles south-southwest of Mount Abbot (lat. 37°21' N, long. 118°47'45" W). Named on Mount Abbot (1953) 15' quadrangle. Employees of California Department of Fish and Game named the lake in 1952; it first was called Jumble Moraine Lake for the jumble of boulders in a nearby moraine (Browning, p. 113).

Jumble Moraine Lake: see **Jumble Lake** [FRESNO].

Junction Bluffs [MADERA]: *relief feature,* 7 miles south-southwest of Devils Postpile (lat. 37°31'30" N, long. 119°08' W); the feature is on the south side of Middle Fork San Joaquin River east of the junction with North Fork. Named on Devils Postpile (1953) 15' quadrangle.

Junction Butte [MADERA]: *ridge,* north-trending, 2 miles long, 9 miles southwest of Devils Postpile (lat. 37°31'40" N, long. 119°11'45" W; near E line sec. 2, T 5 S, R 25 E); the ridge is southwest of the junction of West Fork San

Joaquin River and Middle Fork San Joaquin River. Named on Devils Postpile (1953) 15' quadrangle.

Junction Lake [MADERA]: *lake,* about 600 feet long, 10.5 miles north-northwest of Shuteye Peak (lat. 37°29'45" N, long. 119°29'45" W; sec. 18, T 5 S, R 23 E). Named on Shuteye Peak (1953) 15' quadrangle.

Junction Meadow [FRESNO]: *area,* 13 miles south of Mount Pinchot along Bubbs Creek (lat. 36°45'15" N, long. 118°26'30" W). Named on Mount Pinchot (1953) 15' quadrangle.

Junction Meadow [TULARE]:
(1) *area,* 7 miles west of Mount Whitney (lat. 36°34'50" N, long. 118°25' W); the place is at the confluence of Kern River and Kern-Kaweah River. Named on Mount Whitney (1956) 15' quadrangle.
(2) *area,* 4.5 miles northeast of Camp Nelson (lat. 36°10'45" N, long. 118°32'40" W; sec. 18, T 20 S, R 32 E). Named on Camp Nelson (1956) 15' quadrangle.

Junction Meadow: see **Log Cabin Meadow** [TULARE].

Junction Pass [TULARE]: *pass,* 9 miles north-northwest of Mount Whitney on Tulare-Inyo county line (lat. 36°41'45" N, long. 118° 21'20" W); the pass is 0.5 mile east-northeast of Junction Peak, for which it is named (United States Board on Geographic Names, 1933a, p. 403). Named on Mount Whitney (1956) 15' quadrangle.

Junction Peak [TULARE]: *peak,* 9 miles north-northwest of Mount Whitney on Tulare-Inyo county line (lat. 36°41'30" N, long. 118° 21'55" W). Altitude 13,888 feet. Named on Mount Whitney (1956) 15' quadrangle. J.N. LeConte named the peak in 1896; the feature is at the junction of Kings-Kern Divide with the crest of the Sierra Nevada (Farquhar, 1923, p. 407).

Junction Ridge [FRESNO]: *ridge,* west-trending, 6 miles long, 7 miles east-northeast of Hume (lat. 36°50'05" N, long. 118°48'15" W); the ridge is the part of Monarch Divide east of the junction of South Fork Kings River and Middle Fork Kings River. Named on Tehipite Dome (1952) 15' quadrangle.

Juniper Ridge [FRESNO]: *ridge,* northwest-trending, 14 miles long, 2.5 miles northeast of Coalinga Mineral Springs (lat. 36°10' N, long. 120°31' W). Named on Alcalde Hills (1969), Curry Mountain (1969), and Sherman Peak (1969) 7.5' quadrangles. Arnold and Anderson (1908, p. 14) named the ridge for its characteristic vegetation.

– K –

Kaiser Campground: see **West Kaiser Campground** [FRESNO].

Kaiser Creek [FRESNO]: *stream,* flows 13 miles to Mammoth Pool Reservoir 7.5 miles

west-northwest of Kaiser Peak (lat. 37°21'20"
N, long. 119°17'30" W; near SE cor. sec. 36,
T 6 S, R 24 E); the stream heads near Kaiser
Pass. Named on Kaiser Peak (1953) and
Shuteye Peak (1953) 15' quadrangles. The
name commemorates Fred Kaiser, who started
to mine along San Joaquin River in 1852
(Gudde, 1975, p. 181).

Kaiser Creek: see **West Kaiser Creek**
[FRESNO].

Kaiser Creek Diggings [FRESNO]: *locality,* 5.5
miles northwest of Kaiser Peak (lat. 37°21'30"
N, long. 119°14'40" W; near N line sec. 4, T
7 S, R 25 E); the place is along Kaiser Creek.
Named on Kaiser (1904) 30' quadrangle.

Kaiser Creek Ford [MADERA]: *locality,* 7
miles east of Shuteye Peak along San Joaquin
River (lat. 37°22' N, long. 119°18' W; sec. 36,
T 6 S, R 24 E); the place is above the mouth
of Kaiser Creek, which is in Fresno County.
Named on Kaiser (1904) 30' quadrangle.

Kaiser Crest: see **Kaiser Ridge** [FRESNO].

Kaiser Pass [FRESNO]: *pass,* 4.5 miles east of
Kaiser Peak (lat. 37° 17'25" N, long.
119°06'05" W; sec. 26, T 7 S, R 26 E); the
pass is on Kaiser Ridge near the head of Kaiser Creek. Named on Kaiser Peak (1953) 15'
quadrangle. Farquhar (1924, p. 49) noted that
the forms "Kaiser Pass" and "Keyser Pass"
both are used locally for the name.

Kaiser Pass Meadow [FRESNO]: *area,* 4.5
miles east of Kaiser Peak (lat. 37°17'40" N,
long. 119°06'10" W; on N line sec. 26, T 7 S,
R 26 E); the place is 0.25 mile north of Kaiser Pass. Named on Kaiser Peak (1953) 15'
quadrangle.

Kaiser Peak [FRESNO]: *peak,* 3 miles north-
northwest of the east end of Huntington Lake
(1) (lat. 37°17'40" N, long. 119°11'05" W;
near NE cor. sec. 25, T 7 S, R 25 E); the peak
is on Kaiser Ridge. Altitude 10,320 feet.
Named on Kaiser Peak (1953) 15' quadrangle.
Farquhar (1924, p. 49) noted that the forms
"Kaiser Peak" and "Keyser Peak" both are
used locally for the name.

Kaiser Peak Meadows [FRESNO]: *area,* nearly
4 miles east-northeast of Kaiser Peak (lat.
37°18'35" N, long. 119°07'10" W; on N line
sec. 22, T 7 S, R 26 E). Named on Kaiser Peak
(1953) 15' quadrangle.

Kaiser Ridge [FRESNO]: *ridge,* mainly west-
trending, 15 miles long, center 2 miles north
of the east end of Huntington Lake (1) (lat.
37°17'15" N, long. 119°09' W). Named on
Kaiser Peak (1953) and Shuteye Peak (1953)
15' quadrangles. United States Board on Geographic Names (1981a, p. 2) rejected the designation "Kaiser Crest" for the ridge.

Kaktus Korner [FRESNO]: *locality,* 6.5 miles
north-northwest of Orange Cove (lat.
36°42'55" N, long. 119°20'50" W; sec. 15, T
14 S, R 24 E). Named on Orange Cove North
(1966) 7.5' quadrangle.

Kanawyers [FRESNO]: *locality,* 12 miles south-

southwest of Marion Peak in Kings Canyon
(lat. 36°47'45" N, long. 118°34'45" W).
Named on Marion Peak (1953) 15' quadrangle. Called Kanawyer on California Mining Bureau's (1917a) map. Postal authorities
established Kanawyer post office in 1908 and
discontinued it in 1914 (Salley, p. 109). According to Forest M. Clingan (personal communication, 1987), Peter Apoleon ("Pole")
Kanawyer started Camp Kanawyer in 1908;
a son, Ione Napoleon ("Poley") Kanawyer,
helped his mother run the place after the death
of the elder Kanawyer, and another son, Thomas Izy Kanawyer, was the first postmaster
of Kanawyer post office.

Kane: see **Koehn Spring** [KERN].

Kane Dry Lake: see **Koehn Lake** [KERN].

Kane Lake: see **Koehn Lake** [KERN].

Kane Springs: see **Koehn Spring** [KERN].

Kates Cow Camp [MADERA]: *locality,* 8 miles
north of Shuteye Peak (lat. 37°27'55" N, long.
119°24'15" W; sec. 25, T 5 S, R 23 E). Named
on Shuteye Peak (1953) 15' quadrangle.

Kaweah [TULARE]: *settlement,* 24 miles north-
northwest of Springville along North Fork
Kaweah River (lat. 36°28'15" N, long. 118°
55' W; near N line sec. 11, T 17 S, R 28 E).
Named on Kaweah (1957) 15' quadrangle.
The place was a townsite of Kaweah Cooperative Colony, founded in 1886 (Kaiser, p.
67). Postal authorities changed the name of
Advance post office to Kaweah in 1890 and
moved it to present Kaweah in 1910 (Mitchell, A.R., p. 64). They discontinued the post
office in 1925 and reestablished it in 1926
(Frickstad, p. 211). Kaiser (fig. 1) showed a
place called Avalon, a townsite of Kaweah
Cooperative Colony, located southeast of
Kaweah on the north side of Kaweah River a
mile or less upstream from the mouth of North
Fork, and a place called Barton Ranch, another townsite of the colony, located on the
west side of Kaweah River about halfway from
Kaweah to Three Rivers.

Kaweah: see **Black Kaweah** [TULARE]; **Camp
Kaweah** [KERN]; **Exeter** [TULARE]; **Lake
Kaweah** [TULARE]; **Mount Kaweah** [TU-
LARE].

Kaweah Basin [TULARE]: *relief feature,* 11
miles west-southwest of Mount Whitney (lat.
36°32'30" N, long. 118°29' W); the feature is
north of Mount Kaweah. Named on Mount
Whitney (1956) 15' quadrangle.

Kaweah Camp [TULARE]: *locality,* 5.25 miles
east of Yucca Mountain (lat. 36°33'55" N,
long. 118°46'25" W). Named on Giant Forest
(1956) 15' quadrangle, which also has the
designation "Sequoia National Park (P.O.)" at
the site. California Mining Bureau's (1909a)
map shows a place called Ranger located 27
miles by stage line northeast of Kaweah.
Postal authorities established Ranger post office at Sequoia National Park ranger headquarters in 1907, changed the name to Giant

Forest in 1915, and moved it when they changed the name to Sequoia National Park in 1918 (Salley, p. 84, 181). The name "Giant Forest" is from huge redwood trees at the place; Hale Tharp discovered the trees in 1858, and John Muir gave them the name "Giant Forest" in 1875 (Hanna, p. 120).

Kaweah Gap [TULARE]: *pass,* 2.5 miles south-southwest of Triple Divide Peak (lat. 36°33'25" N, long. 118°33' W). Named on Triple Divide Peak (1956) 15' quadrangle.

Kaweah Hills: see **Venice Hills** [TULARE].

Kaweah Peaks: see **Kaweah Peaks Ridge** [TULARE].

Kaweah Peaks Ridge [TULARE]: *ridge,* south-southeast-trending, 7 miles long, center 3 miles south-southeast of Triple Divide Peak (lat. 36°33'15" N, long. 118°30'45" W); Black Kaweah, Red Kaweah, and Mount Kaweah are on the ridge. Named on Mount Whitney (1956) and Triple Divide Peak (1956) 15' quadrangles. Mount Whitney (1907) 30' quadrangle has the name "Kaweah Peaks" at the ridge.

Kaweah Queen: see **Black Kaweah** [TULARE].

Kaweah River [TULARE]: *stream,* formed by the confluence of Marble Fork and Middle Fork, flows 32 miles to where it divides 5.5 miles west-northwest of Exeter to form Mill Creek (2) and Packwood Creek (lat. 36°20'10" N, long. 119°13'20" W; sec. 25, T 18 S, R 25 E). Named on Exeter (1952), Giant Forest (1956), and Kaweah (1957) 15' quadrangles. Gabriel Moraga discovered the river in 1806 and called it San Gabriel (Brooks *in* Smith, J.S., p. 142). Derby's (1850) map has the designation "River Francis or San Gabriel" for the stream. Williamson (p. 13) referred to "the Pi-pi-yu-na, or Kah-wée-ya, and very commonly known as Four Creeks," and Blake (1856, p. 367) mentioned "Caweea or Four creeks." The name "Kaweah" is from a tribe of Indians that lived near the spot that the river emerges from the foothills (Kroeber, p. 44). In the early days the river debouched from highlands into a swamp, where it divided into four streams—St. Johns River, Mill Creek (1), Packwood Creek, and Outside Creek; except at times of great freshets, water in the streams sank into the ground before reaching the middle of San Joaquin Valley (Angel, 1890b, p. 728). According to Grunsky (p. 11), four overflow streams gave the name "Four Creek Country" to the neighborhood of Visalia. East Fork enters from the southeast 4.5 miles east of Kaweah; it is 21 miles long and is named on Kaweah (1957) and Mineral King (1956) 15' quadrangles. United States Board on Geographic Names (1968b, p. 7) rejected the name "East Fork of Kaweah River" for East Fork. Marble Fork is 16 miles long and is named on Giant Forest (1956) and Triple Divide Peak (1956) 15' quadrangles. United

States Board on Geographic Names (1962a, p. 13) rejected the names "Marble Fork Creek" and "Marble Fork of Kaweah River" for Marble Fork. Middle Fork is formed by the confluence of Hamilton Creek and Lone Pine Creek; it is 14 miles long and is named on Giant Forest (1956) and Triple Divide Peak (1956) 15' quadrangles. United States Board on Geographic Names (1968b, p. 8) rejected the names "Kaweah River," and "Middle Fork of Kaweah River" for Middle Fork, and rejected the name "Middle Fork Kaweah River" for present Lone Pine Creek [TULARE]. North Fork, formed by the confluence of Stony Creek and Durst Creek, flows 20 miles to join the main stream from the north 2 miles south-southeast of Kaweah; it is named on Giant Forest (1956) and Kaweah (1957) 15' quadrangles. United States Board on Geographic Names (1968b, p. 8) rejected the name "North Fork of Kaweah River" for North Fork. South Fork enters from the southeast 3.25 miles south of Kaweah; it is 23 miles long and is named on Kaweah (1957) and Mineral King (1956) 15' quadrangles. United States Board on Geographic Names (1968b, p. 9) rejected the name "South Fork of Kaweah River" for South Fork.

Kayandee [KERN]: *locality,* 2 miles south of downtown Bakersfield along Southern Pacific Railroad (lat. 35°20'50" N, long. 118°59'40" W; sec. 5, T 30 S, R 28 E). Named on Lamont (1954) 7.5' quadrangle.

Kearney [FRESNO]: *locality,* 7.5 miles west of downtown Fresno along Southern Pacific Railroad (lat. 36°44'45" N, long. 119°55'20" W; sec. 5, T 14 S, R 19 E); a rail line to Kearney Park branched south at the spot. Named on Kearney Park (1923) 7.5' quadrangle. The name "Kearney" for the county park commemorates Martin Theodore Kearney, a rich landholder who came to Fresno County about 1877 (Hanna, p. 159). Postal authorities established Kearney Park post office in 1901 and discontinued it in 1935 (Frickstad, p. 34).

Kearney Park: see **Kearney** [FRESNO].

Kearsarge Lakes [FRESNO]: *lakes,* largest 1600 feet long, 13 miles south of Mount Pinchot (lat. 36°45'45" N, long. 118°23'15" W). Named on Mount Pinchot (1953) 15' quadrangle.

Kearsarge Pass [FRESNO]: *pass,* 12 miles south of Mount Pinchot on Fresno-Inyo county line (lat. 36°46'25" N, long. 118°22'35" W). Named on Mount Pinchot (1953) 15' quadrangle. The name is from Kearsarge mine, which is situated east of the pass in Inyo County (Farquhar, 1924, p. 49).

Kearsarge Pinnacles [FRESNO]: *relief features,* 13 miles south of Mount Pinchot along a northwest-trending ridge 2 miles long (lat. 36°45'35" N, long. 118°23'05" W); the features are southwest of Kearsarge Lakes.

Named on Mount Pinchot (1953) 15' quadrangle.

Kecks Corner [KERN]: *locality,* about 5.5 miles south-southeast of Orchard Peak in Antelope Valley (1) (lat. 35°40'15" N, long. 120° 04'50" W; near NE cor. sec. 13, T 26 S, R 17 E). Named on Sawtooth Ridge (1961) 7.5' quadrangle. Called Kecks Corners on Sawtooth Ridge (1943) 7.5' quadrangle, and called Keck's Corner on California Division of Highways' (1934) map.

Keehn Well: see **Koehn Spring** [KERN].

Keeler Needle [TULARE]: *relief feature,* 1000 feet south of Mount Whitney on Tulare-Inyo county line (lat. 36°34'30" N, long. 118° 17'30" W). Named on Mount Whitney (1956) 7.5' quadrangle. The name commemorates James Edward Keeler, who accompanied S.P. Langley on an expedition to Mount Whitney in 1881, and who later was director of Lick Observatory (Farquhar, 1924, p. 50).

Keene [KERN]: *village,* 8.5 miles northwest of Tehachapi (lat. 35°13'25" N, long. 118°33'50" W; near N line sec. 20, T 31 S, R 32 E). Named on Keene (1966) 7.5' quadrangle, which shows Keene P.O. located 0.5 mile farther southeast at or near Woodford. Postal authorities established Keene post office in 1879, discontinued it in 1881, and reestablished it in 1885 (Frickstad, p. 56). The community began in 1876 as a railroad camp; the station at the place first was called Wells, for Madison P. Wells, a local cattleman, but later was renamed for James R. Keene, a San Francisco financier; the station and village also were called Woodford for a time (Barras, p. 132). Cummings Mountain (1943a) 15' quadrangle shows a place called El Rita situated near present Keene post office, and California (1891) map shows a place called Girard located along the railroad about halfway between Keene and Tehachapi.

Keeneysburg: see **White River** [TULARE] (2).

Keith: see **Mount Keith** [TULARE].

Keller Valley [KERN]: *valley,* 3.5 miles south of Keene (lat. 35°10'25" N, long. 118°33'15" W; on E line sec. 5, T 32 S, R 32 E). Named on Keene (1966) 7.5' quadrangle.

Kelley Canyon: see **Kelly Canyon** [KERN].

Kellogg Creek: see **Granite Creek** [FRESNO].

Kelly Canyon [KERN]: *canyon,* drained by a stream that flows 1.5 miles to Poso Creek 3.25 miles south-southeast of Knob Hill (lat. 35°31'10" N, long. 118°55'40" W; sec. 2, T 28 S, R 28 E). Named on Knob Hill (1965) 7.5' quadrangle. Called Kelley Canyon on Woody (1952) 15' quadrangle.

Kelso: see **Claraville** [KERN]; **Fresno** [FRESNO].

Kelshaw Corners [MADERA]: *locality,* 2.5 miles northwest of O'Neals (lat. 37°09'05" N, long. 119°44' W; sec. 13, T 9 S, R 20 E). Named on O'Neals (1965) 7.5' quadrangle.

Kelso Creek [KERN]: *stream,* flows 27 miles

to South Fork Valley 2.25 miles southeast of Weldon (lat. 35°38'45" N, long. 118°15'15" W; near SE cor. sec. 19, T 26 S, R 35 E). Named on Cane Canyon (1972), Claraville (1972), Onyx (1972), Pinyon Mountain (1972), Weldon (1972), and Woolstalf Creek (1972) 7.5' quadrangles. Called Hum-pah-ya-mup on Williamson's (1853) map.

Kelso Peak [KERN]: *peak,* 6.5 miles west-south-west of Skinner Peak (lat. 35°31' N, long. 118°13'25" W; sec. 4, T 28 S, R 35 E); the peak is west of Kelso Creek. Named on Cane Canyon (1972) 7.5' quadrangle.

Kelso Valley [KERN]: *valley,* about 5.5 miles southwest of Pinyon Mountain (lat. 35°24' N, long. 118°13'30" W). Named on Cross Mountain (1972) and Pinyon Mountain (1972) 7.5' quadrangles. The name commemorates John W. Kelso, a freighter and trader (Boyd, p. 166).

Kelty Meadow [MADERA]: *area,* 7 miles northeast of Yosemite Forks (lat. 37°26'30" N, long. 119°32'35" W; near E line sec. 3, T 6 S, R 22 E). Named on Bass Lake (1953) 15' quadrangle. The misspelled name is for Frank Keltie, who homesteaded in sections 2 and 3 in 1886 (Browning, 1986, p. 116).

Kelty Meadow Campground [MADERA]: *locality,* 7 miles northeast of Yosemite Forks (lat. 37°26'25" N, long. 119°32'35" W; sec. 3, T 6 S, R 22 E); the place is at Kelty Meadow. Named on Bass Lake (1953) 15' quadrangle.

Kemeric: see **Camp Kemeric** [KERN].

Kennedy Canyon [FRESNO]: *canyon,* drained by Kennedy Creek, which flows 4.5 miles to Slide Creek 8.5 miles west of Marion Peak (lat. 36°56'10" N, long. 118°40'10" W). Named on Marion Peak (1953) 15' quadrangle.

Kennedy Creek [FRESNO]: *stream,* flows 4.5 miles to Slide Creek 8.5 miles west of Marion Peak (lat. 36°56'10" N, long. 118°40'10" W); the stream heads at East Kennedy Lake near Kennedy Pass. Named on Marion Peak (1953) 15' quadrangle. West Fork enters from the southwest 3.25 miles upstream from the mouth of the main stream; it is 1 mile long, goes through West Kennedy Lake, and is named on Marion Peak (1953) 15' quadrangle.

Kennedy Lake: see **East Kennedy Lake** [FRESNO]; **West Kennedy Lake** [FRESNO].

Kennedy Meadow [FRESNO]: *area,* 4.5 miles east-southeast of Hume (lat. 36°46'15" N, long. 118°50' W). Named on Tehipite Dome (1952) 15' quadrangle.

Kennedy Meadows [TULARE]: *area,* 15 miles north-northwest of Lamont Peak along South Fork Kern River (lat. 36°00' N, long. 118°07' W); the place is north of Kennedy Peak. Named on Lamont Peak (1956) and Monache Mountain (1956) 15' quadrangles.

Kennedy Meadows Camp [TULARE]: *locality,* 11 miles south-southeast of Monache Mountain along South Fork Kern River (lat. 36°03'10" N, long. 118°07'50" W); the place is at the north end of Kennedy Meadows.

Named on Monache Mountain (1956) 15' quadrangle.

Kennedy Mountain [FRESNO]: *peak,* 10 miles southwest of Marion Peak (lat. 36°52'45" N, long. 118°40'W). Altitude 11,433 feet. Named on Marion Peak (1953) 15' quadrangle.

Kennedy Pass [FRESNO]: *pass,* 9.5 miles southwest of Marion Peak on Monarch Divide (lat. 36°52'30" N, long. 118°39'35" W); the pass is near the head of Kennedy Creek. Named on Marion Peak (1953) 15' quadrangle.

Kennedy Peak [TULARE]: *peak,* 14 miles north-northwest of Lamont Peak (lat. 36°59'05" N, long. 118°07' W; near N line sec. 29, T 22 S, R 36 E). Named on Lamont Peak (1956) 15' quadrangle.

Kennedy Pond [FRESNO]: *intermittent lake,* 450 feet long, 6 miles west-northwest of Selma (lat. 36°35'25" N, long. 119°43'W; near NW cor. sec. 32, T 15 S, R 21 E). Named on Conejo (1963) 7.5' quadrangle. Selma (1946) 15' quadrangle shows a permanent lake 1600 feet long.

Kennedy Spring [KERN]: *spring,* 5 miles south of Piute Peak (lat. 35°22'50" N, long. 118°22'40" W). Named on Piute Peak (1972) 7.5' quadrangle.

Kenyon: see **Pine Ridge** [FRESNO] (3).

Kennedy Table [MADERA]: *ridge,* south-southeast-trending, 4.5 miles long, 6 miles east-southeast of O'Neals (lat. 37°06'30" N, long. 119°35'45" W). Named on Millerton Lake East (1965) and North Fork (1965) 7.5' quadrangles.

Kentucky Well [MADERA]: *well,* 15 miles west of Madera (lat. 36°59'50" N, long. 120°20'20" W; near S line sec. 4, T 11 S, R 15 E). Named on Kentucky Well (1922) 7.5' quadrangle.

Kerckhoff Dome [FRESNO]: *peak,* 0.5 mile east-northeast of the town of Big Creek (lat. 37°12'40" N, long. 119°13'55" W; sec. 27, T 8 S., R 25 E). Named on Huntington Lake (1953) 15' quadrangle. John S. Eastwood, an engineer who made early surveys for power development on San Joaquin River, named the feature to honor William G. Kerckhoff of Kerckhoff Lake (Redinger, p. 8). United States Board on Geographic Names (1983a, p. 4) rejected the form "Kerkhoff Dome" for the name.

Kerckhoff Lake [FRESNO]: *lake,* behind a dam on San Joaquin River 6.25 miles north of Prather on Fresno-Madera county line (lat. 37°07'40" N, long. 119°31'30" W; near S line sec. 24, T 9 S, R 22 E). Named on North Fork (1965) 7.5' quadrangle. The name is from Kerckhoff electric power plant, put into operation in 1920 and named for William G. Kerckhoff, one of the organizers of the company that operated the plant (Gudde, 1949, p. 173).

Kerckhoff Lake [MADERA]: *lake,* 2.25 miles long, behind a dam on San Joaquin River 7 miles south of the town of North Fork on

Madera-Fresno county line (lat. 37°07'40" N, long. 119°31'30" W; near S line sec. 24, T 9 S, R 22 E). Named on North Fork (1965) 7.5' quadrangle. The name is from Kerckhoff power plant, which San Joaquin Power Company put into operation in 1920; the name of the plant commemorates William G. Kerckhoff, one of the organizers of the power company (Gudde, 1949, p. 173).

Kerkhoff Dome: see **Kerckhoff Dome** [FRESNO].

Kerman [FRESNO]: *town,* 15 miles west of Fresno (lat. 36°43'30" N, long. 120°03'30" W). Named on Kerman (1963) 7.5' quadrangle. Postal authorities established Collis post office at the place in 1894, discontinued it in 1899, reestablished it in 1904, and changed the name to Kerman in 1906 (Frickstad, p. 32). The town incorporated in 1946. The Southern Pacific Railroad station built at the site in 1895 was called Collis, for Collis P. Huntington; W.G. Kerckhoff and Jacob Mansar promoted a colony of Germans and Scandinavians from the Middle West at the place in 1906, and called the settlement and station Kerman, a name coined from the first three letters of each promoter's surname (Gudde, 1949, p. 173).

Kern: see **Bakersfield** [KERN].

Kern Canyon [TULARE]: *canyon,* 30 miles long, along Kern River above a point about 7.5 miles west-southwest of Kern Peak (lat. 36°15' N, long. 118°24' W). Named on Kern Peak (1956) and Mount Whitney (1956) 15' quadrangles.

Kern City [KERN]: *locality,* 4 miles west-southwest of downtown Bakersfield (lat. 35°21' N, long. 119°04'15" W). Named on Bakersfield (1962, revised 1971) 1°x 2° quadrangle. Postal authorities established Kern City post office in 1962 and discontinued it in 1976 (Salley, p. 111). The place is a planned retirement community begun in 1961 on 349 acres (Bailey, 1967, p. 13).

Kern City: see **Bakersfield** [KERN].

Kernell [KERN]: *locality,* 5.5 miles west of Delano along Atchison, Topeka and Santa Fe Railroad (lat. 35°45'30" N, long. 119°20'35" W; sec. 13, T 25 S, R 24 E). Named on Delano West (1954) and Pond (1953) 7.5' quadrangles.

Kern Flat [TULARE]: *area,* 3 miles south-southeast of Hockett Peak (lat. 36°10'45" N, long. 118°22'15" W); the place is along Kern River. Named on Hockett Peak (1956) 15' quadrangle.

Kern Hot Spring [TULARE]: *spring,* 13 miles north-northwest of Kern Peak (lat. 36°28'40" N, long. 118°24'15" W); the spring is along Kern River. Named on Kern Peak (1956) 15' quadrangle.

Kern Island: see **Bakersfield** [KERN]; **Kern Lake Bed** [KERN].

Kern-Kaweah River [TULARE]: *stream,* flows

8 miles to Kern River 7.25 miles west of Mount Whitney (lat. 36°34'50" N, long. 118°25'10" W). Named on Mount Whitney (1956) and Triple Divide Peak (1956) 15' quadrangles. Called Kern Kaweah (without the hyphen) River on Mount Whitney (1907) and Tehipite (1903) 30' quadrangles. United States Board on Geographic Names (1933a, p. 424) rejected the name "Cone River" for the stream.

Kern Lake [KERN]: *locality,* 7.5 miles east-southeast of Millux (lat. 35°08'25" N, long. 119°04'30" W; near SE cor. sec. 16, T 32 S, R 27 E); the place is in Kern Lake Bed. Named on Conner (1954) 7.5' quadrangle.

Kern Lake [TULARE]: *lake,* 2400 feet long, 6.5 miles west of Kern Peak along Kern River (lat. 36°19' N, long. 118°24'15" W). Named on Kern Peak (1956) 15' quadrangle. United States Board on Geographic Names (1938, p. 28) rejected the name "Soda Spring Lake" for the feature. Little Yosemite Soda Spring is situated about 2.25 miles north of the lake near Kern River; according to Waring (p. 244), the name probably is from the resemblance of the canyon near the spring to Yosemite Valley.

Kern Lake: see **Kern Lake Bed** [KERN]; **Little Kern Lake** [TULARE].

Kern Lake Bed [KERN]: *area,* 16 miles south-southwest of Bakersfield (lat. 35°08'30" N, long. 119°04' W). Named on Coal Oil Canyon (1955), Conner (1954), and Weed Patch (1955) 7.5' quadrangles. Called Kern Island on Coal Oil Canyon (1934) and Conner (1933) 7.5' quadrangles, but United States Board on Geographic Names (1937, p. 16) rejected this name for the feature. Blake (1857, p. 44) used the name "Posuncula" for the lake, as well as for Kern River (p. 35). Wheeler's (1875-1878) map shows Kern Lake. Buena Vista Lake (1912) 30' quadrangle shows a small Kern Lake near the east end of present Kern Lake Bed.

Kern Lake Creek: see **Little Kern Lake Creek** [TULARE].

Kern Mesa [KERN]: *area,* 16 miles east-southeast of Bakersfield (lat. 35°15' N; long. 118°45' W). Named on Breckenridge Mountain (1943) and Cummings Mountain (1943b) 15' quadrangles.

Kern Peak [TULARE]: *peak,* 18 miles south of Mount Whitney (lat. 36°18'30" N, long. 118°17'10" W; at S line sec. 34, T 18 S, R 34 E). Altitude 11,510 feet. Named on Kern Peak (1956) 15' quadrangle.

Kern Peak Stringer [TULARE]: *stream,* flows 2.5 miles to South Fork Kern River 3.5 miles north-northeast of Kern Peak in Ramshaw Meadows (lat. 36°21'20" N, long. 118°16'05" W; sec. 14, T 18 S, R 34 E); the stream heads near Kern Peak. Named on Kern Peak (1956) 15' quadrangle.

Kern Point [TULARE]: *peak,* 8.5 miles west of Mount Whitney (lat. 36°35'50" N, long.

118°26'35" W); the peak is at the southeast end of Kern Ridge. Altitude 12,789 feet. Named on Mount Whitney (1956) 15' quadrangle.

Kern Ridge [TULARE]: *ridge,* southeast-trending, 4 miles long, 10 miles west-northwest of Mount Whitney (lat. 36°36'45" N, long. 118°27'45" W). Named on Mount Whitney (1956) 15' quadrangle.

Kern River [KERN-TULARE]: *stream,* heads in Tulare County and flows 137 miles to lowlands 2.5 miles north of downtown Bakersfield in Kern County (lat. 35°24'45" N, long. 119°00' W). Named on Bakersfield (1962, revised 1971) and Fresno (1962) 1°x 2° quadrangles. Williamson's (1853) map has the name "Po-sun-co-la or Kern River" for the stream, and Goddard's (1857) map has the designation "Kern or Porsiuncula R." Garces called the stream Rio de San Felipe in 1776, and Padre Zalvidea named it La Porciuncula in 1804; John C. Fremont gave it the name "Kern" to honor his topographer, Edward M. Kern, but the Mexicans called it Rio Bravo (Wines, p. 86). After reaching lowlands, the river forms distributaries; the principal distributary extends for 21 miles to a canal (formerly Buena Vista Slough) near Elk Hills. Wood and Dale (fig. 4) included a sketch map showing Kern River distributaries during pioneer stages of irrigation development, and (p. 21, 23) described Kern River distributaries as follows:

> Near Bakersfield, the river leaves the hills and flows southwestward for 20 mile in a shallow bed ranging in width from 200 to 800 feet to a point near the east tip of Elk Hills, where it branches into two main distributaries, the lesser of which, called Buena Vista Slough, flows northward toward Tulare Lake bed and the other southward into Buena Vista Lake bed. Before irrigation projects changed the natural drainage, the river changed its course many times, after leaving the hills. New channels were formed during floods, because old channels and distributaries had become choked with alluvial debris during low stages. The principal known channels were: Old South Fork, which flowed southward from its head, 2 miles northeast of Bakersfield, to its outfall into Kern Lake; Old River, which flowed southwestward from its head, 1.5 miles west of Bakersfield, toward a point between Kern and Buena Vista Lakes; and Buena Vista Canal Slough, which left the present channel of Kern River 2 miles below the head of Old River and flowed southwestward toward Buena Vista Lake. Of these channels

Old South Fork was the main waterway until the flood of 1862. Old River then became the main channel and remained so until the present Kern River channel was formed by the floods of 1867-68. Since that time, the river has been controlled in one main channel, and many of the distributaries have been modified for use as irrigation canals.

South Fork Kern River heads in Tulare County and flows 90 miles to join the main stream 3.5 miles south of Wofford Heights at Isabella Lake in Kern County (lat. 35°39'35" N, long. 118°27'50" W). South Fork is named on Bakersfield (1962, revised 1971) and Fresno (1962) 1°x 2° quadrangles. Olmstead's (1900) map has the name "North Fork" for present Kern River above the junction with South Fork. A community called Solitaire was located along Kern River in the mid-1850's just above the junction with South Fork (Boyd, p. 51); Cross Ferry, built by James Cross in 1868, was situated along Kern River just below the junction with South Fork (Bailey, 1967, p. 5).

Kern River: see **Little Kern River** [TULARE].

Kern River, East Fork: see **Wallace Creek** [TULARE]; **Wright Creek** [TULARE].

Kern River Channel [KERN-KINGS]: *stream,* flows from Kern River Flood Canal in Kern County north into Kings County 12.5 miles north-northwest of the village of Lost Hills (lat. 35°47'25" N, long. 119°43' W; at N line sec. 4, T 25 S, R 21 E). Named on Lone Tree Well (1954), Lost Hills (1953), and Lost Hills NW (1954) 7.5' quadrangles.

Kern River Slough: see **Lamont** [KERN].

Kernvale: see **Lake Isabella** [KERN].

Kernville [KERN]: *town,* 42 miles northeast of Bakersfield (lat. 35° 45'20" N, long. 118°25'30" W; in and near sec. 15, T 25 S, R 33 E); the town is along Kern River. Named on Kernville (1956) 15' quadrangle. Kernville (1908) 30' quadrangle shows the place along the river 3 miles farther south (lat. 35°42'40" N, long. 118° 26'15" W; sec. 33, T 25 S, R 33 E); the formation of Isabella Lake in 1951 forced removal of the town from its original site to the present place (Bailey, 1967, p. 13). Postal authorities established Kernville post office in 1868 (Frickstad, p. 56). A mining camp called Williamsburg started at the original site of Kernville in 1863; the place also was known as Whiskey Flat for Adam Hamilton's saloon, but in 1864 it became Kernville (Bailey, 1967, p. 13). Kernville Hot Springs were located 2 miles northeast of the first site of Kernville (sec. 34, T 25 S, R 33 E) (Brown, p. 521)—Lake Isabella North (1972) 7.5' quadrangle shows numerous hot springs in that neighborhood.

Kernville Hot Springs: see **Kernville** [KERN].

Kerto [KERN]: *locality,* 1.5 miles northeast of Maricopa along Sunset Railroad (lat.

35°04'45" N, long. 119°22'45" W; near SW cor. sec. 31, T 12 N, R 23 W). Named on Maricopa (1951) 7.5' quadrangle. Postal authorities established Kerto post office in 1912 and discontinued it in 1923; the name was coined from the term "<u>Ker</u>n <u>T</u>rading and <u>O</u>il Company" (Salley, p. 111). California Mining Bureau's (1917c) map shows a place called Signa located about 3 miles northwest of Kerto along the railroad.

Kessing Creek [TULARE]: *stream,* flows 5.5 miles to South Fork Tule River 9 miles south-southwest of Camp Nelson (lat. 36°01'30" N, long. 118°41'25" W). Named on Camp Nelson (1956) 15' quadrangle.

Kettle Dome [FRESNO]: *peak,* 13 miles north-northeast of Hume (lat. 36°56'50" N, long. 118°47' W); the peak is at the southwest end of Kettle Ridge. Altitude 9446 feet. Named on Tehipite Dome (1952) 15' quadrangle.

Kettle Lake: see **Seville Lake** [TULARE].

Kettleman City [KINGS]: *town,* 28 miles southwest of Hanford (lat. 36°00'30" N, long. 119°57'45" W; near S line sec. 18, T 22 S, R 19 E); the place is near the northeast base of Kettleman Hills. Named on Kettleman City (1963) 7.5' quadrangle. A. Mansford Brown laid out the town in 1929 to serve the nearby oil field (Gudde, 1949, p. 174), and postal authorities established Kettleman City post office the same year (Frickstad, p. 61).

Kettleman Hills [FRESNO-KERN-KINGS]: *range,* extends along the southwest side of San Joaquin Valley from Fresno County through Kings County into Kern County. Named on Avenal (1954), Avenal Gap (1954), Emigrant Hill (1953), Kettleman City (1963), Kettleman Plain (1953), La Cima (1963), and Los Viejos (1954) 7.5' quadrangles. The name commemorates David Kettleman, who came to California in 1849 and later pastured cattle in the range (Gudde, 1949, p. 174). United States Board on Geographic Names (1933a, p. 425) rejected the form "Kittleman Hills" for the name. The range has three geographic divisions: North Dome at the north end on Kings-Fresno county line, Middle Dome in the central part, and South Dome at the south end on Kings-Kern county line; the divisions are based on geologic structure, but are applied to geographic units (Woodring, Stewart, and Richards, p. 9). North Dome is named on Avenal (1954), Kettleman Plain (1953), La Cima (1963), and Los Viejos (1954) 7.5' quadrangles. Middle Dome is named on Avenal Gap (1954) and Los Viejos (1954) 7.5' quadrangles. South Dome is named on Avenal Gap (1954) 7.5' quadrangle.

Kettleman Plain [FRESNO-KINGS]: *valley,* between Kettleman Hills and Diablo Range on Fresno-Kings county line, mainly in Kings County. Named on Avenal (1954), Avenal Gap (1954), Garza Peak (1953), Kettleman Plain (1953), La Cima (1963), and Pyramid Hills

(1953) 7.5' quadrangles. United States Board on Geographic Names (1933a, p. 425) rejected the form "Kittleman Plain" for the name.

Kettleman Station [FRESNO]: *locality,* 11 miles southeast of Coalinga (lat. 36°02'55" N, long. 120°11'50" W; near NW cor. sec. 1, T 22 S, R 16 E); the place is in Kettleman Plain. Named on Avenal (1954) 7.5' quadrangle.

Kettleman Station [KINGS]: *locality,* 0.5 mile south of Kettleman City (lat. 35°59'55" N, long. 119°57'45" W; sec. 19, T 22 S, R 19 E); the place is at the east base of Kettleman Hills. Named on Los Viejos (1954) 7.5' quadrangle.

Kettle Peak [TULARE]: *peak,* 12.5 miles westnorthwest of Triple Divide Peak (lat. 36°40'25" N, long. 118°43'55" W; near S line sec. 28, T 14 S, R 30 E). Altitude 10,041 feet. Named on Triple Divide Peak (1956) 15' quadrangle.

Kettle Ridge [FRESNO]: *ridge,* southwest-trending, 7 miles long, 17 miles north-northeast of Hume (lat. 37°00' N, long. 118°45'30" W); Kettle Dome is at the southwest end of the ridge. Named on Blackcap Mountain (1953), Mount Goddard (1948), and Tehipite Dome (1952) 15' quadrangles.

Keyes: see **Sally Keyes Lakes** [FRESNO].

Keyes Gulch: see **Keyesville** [KERN].

Keyesville [KERN]: *locality,* 7.25 miles southeast of Alta Sierra (lat. 35°37'35" N, long. 118°30'40" W; sec. 35, T 26 S, R 32 E); the place is in Hogeye Gulch. Named on Alta Sierra (1972) 7.5' quadrangle. Called Keysville on Glennville (1956) 15' quadrangle, and United States Board on Geographic Names (1975b, p. 10) gave this name as a variant. Richard Keyes discovered a rich quartz vein in what became known as Keyes Gulch; the town that grew there first was called Hogeye, and later Keyesville (Wines, p. 23). Miners built an earthen fort on a hill outside the community in 1855 or 1856 in anticipation of trouble with Indians; the place was called Fort Hill and Fort Keysville (Whiting and Whiting, p. 32).

Keyhole: see **The Keyhole** [FRESNO].

Keyser Pass: see **Kaiser Pass** [FRESNO].

Keyser Peak: see **Kaiser Peak** [FRESNO].

Keys Mountain [FRESNO]: *ridge,* north- to east-trending, 1.25 miles long, 2 miles west-southwest of Humphreys Station (lat. 36°57'10" N, long. 119°28'55" W). Named on Humphreys Station (1965) 7.5' quadrangle.

Keysville: see **Keyesville** [KERN].

Kiavah Mountains: see **Scodie Mountains** [KERN].

Kid Creek [FRESNO]: *stream,* flows 3 miles to South Fork Kings River 4.5 miles south of Marion Peak (lat. 36°53'40" N, long. 118°31'55" W); the stream heads at Kid Lakes. Named on Marion Peak (1953) 15' quadrangle. North Fork enters 0.5 mile upstream from the mouth of the main stream; it is 2.25

miles long and is named on Marion Peak (1953) 15' quadrangle.

Kid Lakes [FRESNO]: *lakes,* 6 miles southsouthwest of Marion Peak (lat. 36°52'45" N, long. 118°33'30" W); the lakes are on upper reaches of Kid Creek. Named on Marion Peak (1953) 15' quadrangle.

Kid Peak [FRESNO]: *peak,* 5.5 miles southsouthwest of Marion Peak (lat. 36°52'40" N, long. 118°33' W). Altitude 11,458 feet. Named on Marion Peak (1953) 15' quadrangle.

Kilmer Spring [KERN]: *spring,* 3.25 miles east of Orchard Peak (lat. 35°44'50" N, long. 120°04'40" W; near SW cor. sec. 18, T 25 S, R 18 E). Named on Sawtooth Ridge (1961) 7.5' quadrangle.

Kilowatt [KERN]: *locality,* 1 mile east of Buttonwillow along Southern Pacific Railroad (lat. 35°23'55" N, long. 119°27' W; near SE cor. sec. 13, T 29 S, R 13 E). Named on Buttonwillow (1954) 7.5' quadrangle.

Kimberlina [KERN]: *locality,* 10.5 miles south of McFarland (lat. 35°31'50" N, long. 119°11'50" W; at S line sec. 32, T 27 S, R 26 E). Named on Famoso (1930) 7.5' quadrangle. The name commemorates J.M. Kimberlin and O.B. Kimberlin, who had a way station at the place in the 1890's (Bailey, 1962, p. 73).

Kimble [KINGS]: *locality,* nearly 5 miles northwest of Hanford along Southern Pacific Railroad (lat. 36°22'05" N, long. 119°43' W; sec. 17, T 18 S, R 21 E). Named on Hanford (1926) 7.5' quadrangle.

King: see **Mount Clarence King** [FRESNO].

King Canyon [KERN]: *canyon,* drained by a stream that flows 2.5 miles to Antelope Valley (1) 3.25 miles south of Orchard Peak (lat. 35°41'25" N, long. 120°08'30" W; near S line sec. 4, T 26 S, R 17 E). Named on Orchard Peak (1961) 7.5' quadrangle.

King Creek [MADERA]: *stream,* flows 6 miles to Middle Fork San Joaquin River 2 miles south-southwest of Devils Postpile (lat. 37°35'50" N, long. 119°05'30" W). Named on Devils Postpile (1953) 15' quadrangle.

Kingfisher Ridge [TULARE]: *ridge,* southtrending, 5 miles long, 2.5 miles northwest of Monache Mountain (lat. 36°13'45" N, long. 118°14' W). Named on Monache Mountain (1956) and Olancha (1956) 15' quadrangles.

Kingfisher Stringer [TULARE]: *stream,* flows 2 miles to Soda Creek (2) 1.5 miles northwest of Monache Mountain (lat. 36°13'10" N, long. 118°12'50" W; near N line sec. 5, T 20 S, R 35 E); the stream is east of Kingfisher Ridge. Named on Monache Mountain (1956) 15' quadrangle.

King George Peak [TULARE]: *peak,* 4 miles west of California Hot Springs (lat. 35°52'15" N, long. 118°44'30" W; sec. 4, T 24 S, R 30 E); the peak is on King George Ridge. Altitude 4377 feet. Named on California Hot Springs (1958) 15' quadrangle.

King George Ridge [TULARE]: *ridge,* west-southwest- to west-trending, 3 miles long, 4.5 miles west of California Hot Springs (lat. 35°52'15" N, long. 118°45' W); King George Peak is on the ridge. Named on California Hot Springs (1958) and White River (1952) 15' quadrangles.

King River: see **Centerville** [FRESNO]; **Kings River** [FRESNO-KINGS-TULARE].

Kingriver: see **Reedley** [FRESNO].

Kingsburg [FRESNO]: *town,* 5 miles southeast of Selma (lat. 36° 31' N, long. 119°33' W); the town is 1.5 miles from Kings River. Named on Selma (1964) 7.5' quadrangle. The place first was called Kings River Switch, then Drapersville, and later Wheatville; Josiah Draper founded the town in the 1870's (Hanna, p. 162). Postal authorities established Wheatville post office in 1874, changed the name to Kingsburgh in 1875, and changed it to Kingsburg in 1876 (Salley, p. 112, 238). The town incorporated in 1908. Postal authorities established Sanders post office 8 miles northeast of Kingsburg in 1879 and discontinued it in 1894; the name was for Charlotte E. Sanders, first postmaster (Salley, p. 193).

Kings Canyon [FRESNO]: *canyon,* 10 miles long, 13 miles south-southwest of Marion Peak (lat. 36°47' N, long. 118°37'30" W); the canyon is along South Fork Kings River. Named on Marion Peak (1953) 15' quadrangle. Called Kings River Canyon on Tehipite (1903) 30' quadrangle.

Kings-Kern Divide [TULARE]: *ridge,* generally west- to southwest-trending, 7 miles long, 11 miles northwest of Mount Whitney (lat. 36°41'30" N, long. 118°25'45" W); the ridge separates Kern River drainage basin from Kings River drainage basin. Named on Mount Whitney (1956) 15' quadrangle.

King Solomons Ridge [KERN]: *ridge,* east- to southeast-trending, nearly 5 miles long, the center is 3.5 miles northwest of Piute Peak (lat. 35°29'30" N, long. 118°25'30" W). Named on Lake Isabella South (1972) and Piute Peak (1972) 7.5' quadrangles.

King Spur [FRESNO]: *ridge,* north-trending, 5 miles long, 8 miles south-southwest of Mount Pinchot (lat. 36°50'15" N, long. 118°26'45" W); Mount Clarence King is near the center of the ridge. Named on Mount Pinchot (1953) 15' quadrangle.

Kings River [FRESNO-KINGS-TULARE]: *stream,* formed in Fresno County by the confluence of Middle Fork and South Fork, flows 125 miles, partly in Tulare County, to Tulare Lake Bed south of Stratford in Kings County. Named on Fresno (1962) 1°x 2° quadrangle. Early Spanish explorers gave the name "El Rio de los Santos Reyes" to present Kings River to honor the Three Wise Men— *El Rio de los Santos Reyes* means "The River of the Holy Kings" in Spanish (Hoover,

Rensch, and Rensch, p. 89). Called Lake Fork on Fremont's (1848) map. The stream also was known as the Wilmilche in the early days of American occupation (Preston, p. 14). The name has the form "King River" on Hamlin's (1904) map, and Williamson (p. 13) used the form "King's river," but United States Board on Geographic Names (1933a, p. 428) rejected both forms. Middle Fork is 35 miles long and is named on Marion Peak (1953), Mount Goddard (1948), and Tehipite Dome (1952) 15' quadrangles. South Fork is 42 miles long and is named on Big Pine (1950), Marion Peak (1953), Mount Pinchot (1953), and Tehipite Dome (1952) 15' quadrangles. North Fork enters from the north 51 miles upstream from the entrance of the main stream into Tulare County; it is 35 miles long and is named on Blackcap Mountain (1953), Patterson Mountain (1952), and Tehipite Dome (1952) 15' quadrangles. Stratford (1942) 15' quadrangle shows Kings River reaching an artificially confined Tulare Lake 10 miles south of Stratford through an artificial watercourse, and Stratford SE (1954) 7.5' quadrangle shows Kings River in an artificial watercourse in Tulare Lake Bed. Kings River splits 6 miles north of Lemoore into a second set of North and South Forks; these forks then join to reform Kings River nearly 5 miles west of Lemoore. The second North Fork is 11 miles long and is named on Burrel (1954), Lemoore (1954), Riverdale (1954), and Vanguard (1956) 7.5' quadrangles; it is called Fresno Slough on Riverdale (1927) 7.5' quadrangle. The second South Fork is 9.5 miles long and is named on Lemoore (1954) and Riverdale (1954) 7.5' quadrangles. Clarks Fork diverges from the second South Fork and flows 5.5 miles to rejoin second North Fork 6 miles west-northwest of Lemoore; it is named on Lemoore (1954) and Vanguard (1956) 7.5' quadrangles.

King's River: see **Kings River** [FRESNO-KINGS-TULARE]; **Reedley** [FRESNO].

Kings River: see **Centerville** [FRESNO].

Kings River Canyon: see **Kings Canyon** [FRESNO].

Kings River Slough: see **Fresno Slough** [FRESNO-KINGS].

Kings River Switch: see **Kingsburg** [FRESNO].

Kingston: see **Hardwick** [KINGS]; **Laton** [FRESNO].

Kinsman Flat [MADERA]: *area,* 11 miles south-southeast of Shuteye Peak (lat. 37°12'15" N, long. 119°21'15" W; sec. 28, T 8 S, R 24 E). Named on Shaver Lake (1953) 15' quadrangle.

Kip Camp [FRESNO]: *locality,* 6.25 miles west-southwest of Mount Abbot along Bear Creek (2) (lat. 37°22'05" N, long. 118°53'35" W). Named on Mount Abbot (1953) 15' quadrangle.

Kip Slough: see **Lonetree Channel** [FRESNO].
Kirch Flat [FRESNO]: *area,* 2.25 miles west-southwest of Balch Camp along Kings River (lat. 36°53'15" N, long. 119°09'15" W; near E line sec. 17, T 12 S, R 26 E). Named on Patterson Mountain (1952) 15' quadrangle.
Kirkman Hill [FRESNO]: *ridge,* west-south-west-trending, 1 mile long, 7.5 miles west-southwest of Piedra (lat. 36°45'50" N, long. 119°30'10" W). Named on Piedra (1965) and Round Mountain (1964) 7.5' quadrangles.
Kismet [MADERA]: *locality,* 6 miles east-southeast of Fairmead along Atchison, Topeka and Santa Fe Railroad (lat. 37°02'50" N, long. 120°05'35" W; near E line sec. 22, T 10 S, R 17 E). Named on Kismet (1961) 7.5' quadrangle. Called Miller on California Mining Bureau's (1917d) map.
Kissack Bay [KERN]: *embayment,* 5 miles southeast of Wofford Heights along Isabella Lake (lat. 35°39' N, long. 118°24'15" W). Named on Lake Isabella North (1972) 7.5' quadrangle.
Kissack Cove [KERN]: *embayment,* 4.5 miles south-southeast of Wofford Heights along Isabella Lake (lat. 35°38'55" N, long. 118° 24'55" W; near SE cor. sec. 22, T 26 S, R 33 E); the feature is at the west end of Kissack Bay. Named on Lake Isabella North (1972) 7.5' quadrangle.
Kittleman Hills: see **Kettleman Hills** [FRESNO-KERN-KINGS-].
Kittleman Plain: see **Kettleman Plain** [FRESNO-KINGS].
Klink: see **Ivanhoe** [TULARE].
Knapsack Pass [FRESNO]: *pass,* 10 miles east of Mount Goddard (lat. 37°05' N, long. 118°32'30" W). Named on Mount Goddard (1948) 15' quadrangle. A.L. Jordan discovered the pass in 1917, and Chester Versteeg suggested the name in 1935 (Browning 1986, p. 121).
Knecht: see **Twin Lakes** [KERN] (1).
Knight Camp: see **Qualls Camp** [FRESNO].
Knob Hill [KERN]: *peak,* 12.5 miles south-southwest of Woody (lat. 35°33'50" N, long. 118°56'55" W; sec. 22, T 27 S, R 28 E). Altitude 1161 feet. Named on Knob Hill (1965) 7.5' quadrangle.
Knob Lake [FRESNO]: *lake,* 950 feet long, 4.25 miles west of Mount Humphreys in Humphreys Basin (lat. 37°16' N, long. 118°44'50" W). Named on Mount Tom (1949) 15' quadrangle. The name is from a knoblike rock tower on the shore of the lake (Browning 1986, p. 121).
Knowles [MADERA]: *settlement,* less than 2 miles east of Raymond (lat. 37°13'10" N, long. 119°52'20" W; sec. 22, T 8 S, R 19 E). Named on Knowles (1962) and Raymond (1962) 7.5' quadrangles. Postal authorities established Knowles post office in 1902 and discontinued it in 1955; the name is for F.E. Knowles, who operated a granite quarry at the place

(Salley, p. 113). California Division of Highways' (1934) map shows a place called Hillside located just southwest of Knowles along Southern Pacific Railroad (near N line sec. 27, T 8 S, R 19 E).
Knowles Junction [MADERA]: *locality,* 1 mile south of Raymond (lat. 37°12'10" N, long. 119°54'30" W; sec. 29, T 8 S, R 19 E); the place is 2.25 miles west-southwest of Knowles. Named on Raymond (1962) 7.5' quadrangle.
Koehn: see **Koehn Spring** [KERN].
Koehn Dry Lake: see **Koehn Lake** [KERN].
Koehn Lake [KERN]: *dry lake,* south of Saltdale in Fremont Valley (lat. 35°19'55" N, long. 117°52'55" W). Named on Cantil (1967) and Saltdale SE (1967) 7.5' quadrangles. Called Koehn Dry Lake on Saltdale (1943a) 15' quadrangle, and Kane Lake on Baker's (1911) map. The feature also was called Kane Dry Lake, Desert Lake, and Salt Lake (Wynn, 1963, p. 29, 32).
Koehn Spring [KERN]: *locality,* 3.25 miles northeast of Cantil (lat. 35°20'30" N, long. 117°55' W); the place is near present Koehn Lake. Named on Searles Lake (1915) 1° quadrangle. Called Kane on Baker's (1911) map. Postal authorities established Koehn post office in 1893 and discontinued it in 1898; the name was for Charles A. Koehn, first postmaster (Salley, p. 113), who homesteaded at the place and operated a store as well as the post office (Wynn, 1963, p. 60). Koehn Spring was known also as Cane Springs, Kane Springs, Mesquite Springs, Desert Springs (Brown, p. 477), and Keehn Well (Mendenhall, 1909, p. 50).
Kolingo Creek [FRESNO]: *stream,* flows 2.25 miles to Cooper Canyon 3.25 miles west-southwest of Coalinga (lat. 36°07' N, long. 120°24'40" W; sec. 12, T 21 S, R 14 E). Named on Alcalde Hills (1969) and Curry Mountain (1969) 7.5' quadrangles.
Kramer Creek [TULARE]: *stream,* flows 5 miles to Backbone Creek 16 miles south-southeast of Kaweah (lat. 36°15'35" N, long. 118° 47'05" W; sec. 24, T 19 S, R 29 E). Named on Kaweah (1957) 15' quadrangle.
Kramer Meadow [MADERA]: *area,* 7 miles north-northeast of Yosemite Forks (lat. 37°27'10" N, long. 119°33'35" W; at E line sec. 33, T 5 S, R 22 E). Named on Bass Lake (1953) 15' quadrangle.
Kramer Meadow [TULARE]: *area,* 5.5 miles east-southeast of Camp Nelson (lat. 36°06'10" N, long. 118°31'15" W; sec. 16, T 21 S, R 32 E). Named on Camp Nelson (1956) 15' quadrangle.
Kreyenhagen Hills [FRESNO-KINGS]: *range,* southwest of Kettleman Plain on Fresno-Kings county line. Named on Avenal (1954), Curry Mountain (1969), Garza Peak (1953), Kettleman Plain (1953), Kreyenhagen Hills (1956), and The Dark Hole (1961) 7.5' quad-

rangles. Arnold and Anderson (1908, p. 14) named the range for three families named Kreyenhagen who owned large tracts of land there, and stated that "they [the Kreyenhagens] are early settlers and practically the only inhabitants, and the region is generally known as the Kreyenhagen country or Kreyenhagen's."

Kreyenhagen Peak [FRESNO]: *peak,* 1 mile north-northeast of Coalinga Mineral Springs (lat. 36°09'30" N, long. 120°32'50" W; near W line sec. 26, T 20 S, R 13 E). Altitude 3561 feet. Named on Sherman Peak (1969) 7.5' quadrangle.

Kurth: see **Porterville** [TULARE].

Kyan [KERN]: *locality,* 11.5 miles east of Taft along Sunset Railroad (lat. 35°07'30" N, long. 119°15'40" W; sec. 23, T 32 S, R 25 E). Named on Mouth of Kern (1932) 7.5' quadrangle.

– L –

La Aleta [KINGS]: *ridge,* east-southeast-trending, 0.5 mile long. 4.5 miles east of Avenal (lat. 36°00'30" N, long. 120°02'40" W; near S line sec. 17, T 22 S, R 18 E). Named on La Cima (1963) 7.5' quadrangle. The descriptive name refers to the curved shape of the feature—*aleta* means "wing" in Spanish (United States Board on Geographic Names, 1933b, p. 15).

La Arena [KERN]: *area,* 11 miles north of Blackwells Corner (lat. 35°46'25" N, long. 119°54'05" W; around NW cor. sec. 11, T 25 S, R 19 E). Named on Avanal Gap (1954) 7.5' quadrangle.

La Bajada [KINGS]: *area,* 5.5 miles south of Kettleman City (lat. 35°55'30" N, long. 119°58'30" W; in and near sec. 13, T 23 S, R 18 E). Named on Los Viejos (1954) 7.5' quadrangle. United States Board on Geographic Names (1933b, p. 15-16) pointed out that *bajada* means "slope" or "descent" in Spanish.

La Brecha [KINGS]: *pass,* 8 miles south of Kettleman City (lat. 35° 53'40" N, long. 119°58'35" W; sec. 25, T 23 S, R 18 E). Named on Los Viejos (1954) 7.5' quadrangle. *Brecha* means "breach" in Spanish (United States Board on Geographic Names, 1933b, p. 16).

La Caldera [KINGS]: *canyon,* 0.5 mile long, 7.5 miles east-southeast of Avenal (lat. 35°57'30" N, long. 120°00'20" W; on E line sec. 3, T 23 S, R 18 E). Named on Kettleman Plain (1953) 7.5' quadrangle. The name is descriptive—*caldera* means "caldron" in Spanish (United States Board on Geographic Names, 1933b, p. 16).

La Cañada Simada [FRESNO]: *canyon,* drained by a stream that flows 1.5 miles to Kettleman Plain 12.5 miles east-southeast of Coalinga (lat. 36°02'25" N, long. 120°09'50" W; near W line sec. 5, T 22 S, R 17 E). Named

on Avenal (1954) 7.5' quadrangle. The name is descriptive and means "deep ravine" in Spanish (United States Board on Geographic Names, 1933b, p. 16).

La Ceja [FRESNO-KINGS]: *ridge,* west-northwest-trending, 3.5 miles long, 4.5 miles north-northeast of Avenal on Kings-Fresno county line (lat. 36°04' N, long. 120°06'15" W). Named on La Cima (1963) 7.5' quadrangle. The name is descriptive and means "summit" in Spanish (United States Board on Geographic Names, 1933b, p. 16).

La Cima [KINGS]: *peak,* 4 miles east of Avenal (lat. 36°00'15" N, long. 120°03'20" W; near W line sec. 20, T 22 S, R 18 E). Altitude 1365 feet. Named on La Cima (1963) 7.5' quadrangle. The name is descriptive and means "summit" in Spanish (United States Board on Geographic Names, 1933b, p. 16).

Lacjac [FRESNO]: *locality,* 2 miles west-northwest of Reedley along Atchison, Topeka and Santa Fe Railroad (lat. 36°36'40" N, long. 119°28'55" W; near W line sec. 21, T 15 S, R 23 E). Named on Reedley (1966) 7.5' quadrangle. Daniel J. Ellis, who built a winery and distillery at the place for the firm of Lachman & Jacobi, coined the name in 1899 from the title of the firm (Gudde, 1949, p. 178).

La Clavija [KINGS]: *peak,* 3.25 miles northeast of Avenal (lat. 36° 02'05" N, long. 120°05' W; sec. 12, T 22 S, R 17 E). Named on La Cima (1963) 7.5' quadrangle. The name is descriptive and means "pin" or "peg" in Spanish (United States Board on Geographic Names, 1933b, p. 16).

La Cuba [KINGS]: *peak,* 4 miles south-southwest of Kettleman City (lat. 35°57'05" N, long. 119°59'05" W; sec. 1, T 23 S, R 18 E). Named on Los Viejos (1954) 7.5' quadrangle. The name is descriptive and means "cask" in Spanish (United States Board on Geographic Names, 1933b, p. 16).

La Cuesta [KINGS]: *peak,* nearly 4 miles east-northeast of Avenal (lat. 36°01'35" N, long. 120°04' W; sec. 7, T 22 S, R 18 E). Named on La Cima (1963) 7.5' quadrangle. United States Board on Geographic Names (1933b, p. 16) pointed out that the name means "hill" or "slope" in Spanish.

La Cumbre [KINGS]: *peak,* 2.5 miles north of Avenal (lat. 36°02'25" N, long. 120°07'15" W; sec. 3, T 22 S, R 17 E). Named on La Cima (1963) 7.5' quadrangle. The name was given because the peak is one of the highest points in Kettleman Hills—*cumbre* means "crest" in Spanish (United States Board on Geographic Names, 1933b, p. 16).

La Cuna [KINGS]: *area,* 4 miles east-northeast of Avenal (lat. 36° 01'10" N, long. 120°03'40" W; sec. 18, T 22 S, R 18 E). Named on La Cima (1963) 7.5' quadrangle. The name is descriptive—*cuna* means "cradle" in Spanish (United States Board on Geographic Names, 1933b, p. 16).

Ladd Creek [MADERA]: *stream,* flows 4.25 miles to Fine Gold Creek 4 miles northeast of O'Neals (lat. 37°09'50" N, long. 119°38'20" W; sec. 12, T 9 S, R 21 E). Named on O'Neals (1965) 7.5' quadrangle. Millerton Lake (1945) 15' quadrangle shows Ladd ranch near the mouth of the stream.

Ladder Lake [FRESNO]: *lake,* 2300 feet long, 6 miles east-southeast of Mount Goddard (lat. 37°04'10" N, long. 118°37'10" W). Named on Mount Goddard (1948) 15' quadrangle.

Lady Franklin Cañon: see **Franklin Lakes** [TULARE].

Lady Lake [MADERA]: *lake,* 1100 feet long, 6.5 miles south-southeast of Merced Peak (lat. 37°32'35" N, long. 119°21'40" W); the lake is one of the group called Madera Lakes. Named on Merced Peak (1953) 15' quadrangle.

La Escudilla [KINGS]: *area,* 7 miles south of Kettleman City (lat. 35°54'25" N, long. 119°57'20" W; near S line sec. 19, T 23 S, R 19 E). Named on Los Viejos (1954) 7.5' quadrangle. United States Board on Geographic Names (1933b, p. 16) pointed out that *escudilla* means "bowl" or "soup plate" in Spanish.

Lagoon Lake [FRESNO]: *lake,* 450 feet long, 12.5 miles northwest of Mount Abbot (lat. 37°29'40" N, long. 118°57'55" W). Named on Mount Abbot (1953) 15' quadrangle.

Laguna de los Tulares: see "Regional setting."

Laguna de Tache [FRESNO-KINGS]: *land grant,* north of Hanford on Fresno-Kings county line, mainly in Kings County. Named on Burrel (1954), Burris Park (1954), Laton (1953), Lemoore (1954), Riverdale (1954), and Vanguard (1956) 7.5' quadrangles. Manuel de Jesus Castro received the land in 1846 and claimed 48,801 acres patented in 1866 (Cowan, p. 101). The name "Tache" is from the Tachi Indians, who lived in the region (Kroeber, p. 60).

Lairds Corner [TULARE]: *locality,* 3.5 miles south-southwest of Woodville (lat. 36°03'05" N, long. 119°13'55" W; at NE cor. sec. 2, T 22 S, R 25 E). Named on Woodville (1950) 7.5' quadrangle.

La Jolla Creek [FRESNO]: *stream,* flows 1.25 miles to Beltran Creek nearly 4 miles northeast of Castle Mountain (lat. 35°58'35" N, long. 120°17'25" W; sec. 31, T 22 S, R 16 E). Named on The Dark Hole (1961) 7.5' quadrangle.

Lake Basin [FRESNO]: *valley,* 2 miles north-northeast of Marion Peak along Cartridge Creek (lat. 36°59' N, long. 118°30' W). Named on Marion Peak (1953) and Mount Pinchot (1953) 15' quadrangles. J.N. LeConte used the name descriptively in 1902 (Browning 1986, p. 122).

Lakecamp Lake [FRESNO]: *lake,* 700 feet long, 8 miles east-southeast of Kaiser Peak (lat. 37°15'25" N, long. 119°03'10" W). Named on Kaiser Peak (1953) 15' quadrangle.

Lake Catherine [MADERA]: *lake,* 1800 feet long, 8 miles northwest of Devils Postpile (lat. 37°41'55" N, long. 119°11'25" W). Named on Devils Postpile (1953) 15' quadrangle.

Lake Elsie: see **Fingerbowl Lake** [FRESNO].

Lake Engle [KERN]: *lake,* 450 feet long, 7.25 miles south-southeast of Glennville along Little Poso Creek (lat. 35°38' N, long. 118°38'45" W; near S line sec. 28, T 26 S, R 31 E). Named on Glennville (1972) 7.5' quadrangle.

Lake Florence: see **Florence Lake** [FRESNO].

Lake Fork: see **Kings River** [FRESNO-KINGS-TULARE].

Lake Isabella [KERN]: *town,* 35 miles east-northeast of Bakersfield along Kern River in Hot Spring Valley (lat. 35°37'30" N, long. 118°28'30" W); the town is below Isabella Lake. Named on Lake Isabella North (1972) and Lake Isabella South (1972) 7.5' quadrangles. Called Isabella on Bakersfield (1962, revised 1971) 1°x 2° quadrangle, which shows a place called Kernvale situated 1.25 miles farther south-southwest. Formation of Isabella Lake forced removal of the original community of Isabella to a site 1.5 miles farther south below the dam that forms the lake. Isabella post office operated at the new site from 1953 until its name was changed to Lake Isabella in 1957 (Salley, p. 115). United States Board on Geographic Names (1975b, p. 10) gave the variant names "Isabella" and "Kernvale" for the town.

Lake Isabella: see **Isabella Lake** [KERN].

Lake Italy [FRESNO]: *lake,* 1.5 miles long, 2.25 miles south-southwest of Mount Abbot (lat. 37°21'30" N, long. 118°48'15" W). Named on Mount Abbot (1953) 15' quadrangle. Members of United States Geological Survey named the feature about 1907 for the resemblance of the outline of the lake on a map to the bootlike shape of Italy on a map (Farquhar, 1923, p. 407).

Lake Joseph Grinnell: see **Grinnell Lake** [FRESNO].

Lake Kaweah [TULARE]: *lake,* behind a dam on Kaweah River 5.25 miles east of Woodlake (lat. 36°25' N, long. 119°00'10" W; sec. 25, T 17 S, R 27 E). Named on Kaweah (1957) 15' quadrangle, and on Woodlake (1952, photorevised 1969) 7.5' quadrangle.

Lake Los Nietos [FRESNO]: *lake,* with three parts, the largest part 250 feet long, located 7 miles northeast of Coalinga (lat. 36°12'40" N, long. 120°16' W; sec. 6, T 20 S, R 16 E). Named on Coalinga (1956) 7.5' quadrangle.

Lake Marion [KERN]: *lake,* 500 feet long, 7 miles south-southeast of Glennville along Little Poso Creek (lat. 35°37'55" N, long. 118°39'55" W; near S line sec. 29, T 26 S, R 31 E). Named on Glennville (1972) 7.5' quadrangle.

Lake Marjorie [FRESNO]: *lake,* 1800 feet long, 1.5 miles west of Mount Pinchot (lat. 36°56'40" N, long. 118°25'45" W). Named on Mount Pinchot (1953) 15' quadrangle. Browning (1986, p. 137) associated the name with Marjorie Mott, daughter of Ernest J. Mott of Mott Lake.

Lake McDermand: see **Mount Goddard** [FRESNO].

Lake Ming [KERN]: *lake,* nearly 1 mile long, 9 miles east-northeast of Bakersfield along Kern River (lat. 35°26'20" N, long. 118°51'50" W). Named on Bakersfield (1962, revised 1971) 1°x 2° quadrangle. The artificial lake was dedicated in 1959 and named for Floyd Ming, a former district supervisor of Kern County (Bailey, 1967, p. 14).

Lake Moic [MADERA]: *lake,* 600 feet long, 7.5 miles south-southeast of Yosemite Forks along Little Fine Gold Creek (lat. 37°16' N, long. 119°34'20" W; sec. 4, T 8 S, R 22 E). Named on Bass Lake (1953) 15' quadrangle.

Lake of the Fallen Moon [FRESNO]: *lake,* 900 feet long, nearly 6 miles west-southwest of Marion Peak (lat. 36°54'50" N, long. 118° 36'50" W). Named on Marion Peak (1953) 15' quadrangle. The author of a poem with the title "Lake of the Fallen Moon" named the feature (Stewart, p. 162).

Lake of the Lone Indian [FRESNO]: *lake,* 1300 feet long, 10.5 miles northwest of Mount Abbot (lat. 37°28'35" N, long. 118°56'10" W). Named on Mount Abbot (1953) 15' quadrangle. The distinct profile of an Indian face and feathered headdress on the slope above the lake suggested the name (Farquhar, 1924, p. 55).

Lake of the Woods [KERN]: *lake,* 550 feet long, 7.5 miles west of Lebec near the head of Cuddy Canyon (lat. 34°49'05" N, long. 118°59'55" W; sec. 33, T 9 N, R 20 W). Named on Frazier Mountain (1958) 7.5' quadrangle.

Lake Paulina [KERN]: *intermittent lake,* 700 feet long, 4.5 miles south-southwest of Weed Patch (lat. 35°10'45" N, long. 118°57'05" W; near NE cor. sec. 3, T 32 S, R 28 E). Named on Weed Patch (1955) 7.5' quadrangle.

Lake Reflection [TULARE]: *lake,* 3500 feet long, 12 miles northwest of Mount Whitney along East Creek (lat. 36°42' N, long. 118°26'40" W). Named on Mount Whitney (1956) 15' quadrangle. Howard Longley and his companions named the lake in 1894 (Browning 1986, p. 181).

Lakeshore [FRESNO]: *village,* nearly 3 miles south-southeast of Kaiser Peak (lat. 37°15'10" N, long. 119°10'25" W; sec. 6, 7, T 8 S, R 26 E); the village is on the north shore of Huntington Lake (1). Named on Kaiser Peak (1953) 15' quadrangle. Postal authorities established Lakeshore post office in 1924 (Frickstad, p. 34).

Lakeside Campground [MADERA]: *locality,* nearly 6 miles southeast of Yosemite Forks on the southwest side of Bass Lake (1) (lat. 37°18'35" N, long. 119°32'45" W; near E line

sec. 22, T 7 S, R 22 E). Named on Bass Lake (1953) 15' quadrangle.

Lake South America [TULARE]: *lake,* 2000 feet long, 9 miles northwest of Mount Whitney (lat. 36°40'45" N, long. 118°24' W). Named on Mount Whitney (1956) 15' quadrangle. Called South American Lake on Mount Whitney (1907) 30' quadrangle, but United States Board on Geographic Names (1933a, p. 707) rejected this form of the name, and noted that Professor Bolton C. Brown of Stanford University named the feature in 1896 for the resemblance of its outline on a map to the outline of South America on a map.

Lake Stockton [KERN]: *lake,* 300 feet long, 7.25 miles south-southeast of Glennville along Little Poso Creek (lat. 35°37'55" N, long. 118°39'05" W; near S line sec. 28, T 26 S, R 31 E). Named on Glennville (1972) 7.5' quadrangle.

Lake Success [TULARE]: *lake,* behind a dam on Tule River 5.5 miles east of Porterville (lat. 36°03'35" N, long. 118°55'05" W; sec. 35, T 21 S, R 28 E); the lake is near the site of the village of Success. Named on Success Dam (1956) 7.5' quadrangle. United States Board on Geographic Names (1962a, p. 17) rejected the name "Success Reservoir" for the lake.

Lake Thomas A. Edison [FRESNO]: *lake,* behind a dam on Mono Creek 11.5 miles west of Mount Abbot (lat. 37°22'10" N, long. 118°59'15" W). Named on Kaiser Peak (1953) and Mount Abbot (1953) 15' quadrangles. The name was given in the early 1950's (Browning 1986, p. 62) to the lake that occupies Vermilion Valley.

Lake Tulare: see **Tulare Lake** [KINGS].

Lakeview [KERN]: *locality;* 8.5 miles west-northwest of Mettler (lat. 35°05'40" N, long. 119°06'30" W; at SW cor. sec. 32, T 32 S, R 27 E); the place is southwest of Kern Lake Bed. Named on Coal Oil Canyon (1955) 7.5' quadrangle.

Lake Virginia [FRESNO]: *lake,* 3700 feet long, 3.5 miles west of Red Slate Mountain (lat. 37°30'40" N, long. 118°56' W). Named on Mount Morrison (1953) 15' quadrangle.

Lake Woollomes [KERN]: *lake,* 2 miles long, 5 miles north-northeast of McFarland (lat. 35°44'20" N, long. 119°10'40" W). Named on McFarland (1954, photorevised 1969) 7.5' quadrangle. The name, given in 1959, is for W.R. Woollomes, a former district supervisor of Kern County (Bailey, 1967, p. 15).

La Liebra [KERN]: *land grant,* on the southeast side of Tehachapi Mountains; extends south into Los Angeles County. Named on La Liebra Ranch (1965), Lebec (1958), Liebre Twins (1965), Neenach School (1965), Tylerhorse Canyon (1965), and Winters Ridge (1966) 7.5' quadrangles. Jose M. Flores received 11 leagues in 1846 and claimed 48,800 acres patented in 1875 (Cowan, p. 45).

La Llanura [KINGS]: *valley,* 5.5 miles south

of Kettleman City (lat. 35°55'30" N, long. 119°57'10" W; in and near sec. 18, T 23 S, R 19 E). Named on Los Viejos (1954) 7.5' quadrangle. The name is descriptive and means "flatness" or "plain" in Spanish (United States Board on Geographic Names, 1933b, p. 16).

La Loba [KINGS]: *ridge,* northwest-trending, 0.25 mile long, 3 miles east-northeast of Avenal (lat. 36°01'35" N, long. 120°04'45" W; sec. 12, T 22 S, R 17 E). Named on La Cima (1963) 7.5' quadrangle. United States Board on Geographic Names (1933b, p. 16) noted that *loba* means "ridge" in Spanish.

La Lomera [FRESNO]: *ridge,* north-trending, nearly 1 mile long, 13 miles east-southeast of Coalinga (lat. 36°03'25" N, long. 120°08'20" W; sec. 33, T 21 S, R 17 E). Named on Avenal (1954) 7.5' quadrangle. The United States Board on Geographic Names (1933b, p. 17) noted that *la lomera* means "the ridge of a house" in Spanish

La Lomica [KINGS]: *peak,* 4 miles south of Kettleman City (lat. 35° 56'55" N, long. 119°57'30" W; on S line sec. 6, T 23 S, R 19 E). Altitude 580 feet. Named on Los Viejos (1954) 7.5' quadrangle. United States Board on Geographic Names (1933b, p. 17) pointed out that *lomica* means "very little hill" in Spanish.

La Luneta [FRESNO]: *peak,* 10.5 miles east-southeast of Coalinga (lat. 36°04'35" N, long. 120°11'10" W; sec. 25, T 21 S, R 16 E). Altitude 999 feet. Named on Avenal (1954) 7.5' quadrangle. The descriptive name refers to the semicircular erosion of the west slope—it means "half moon" in Spanish (United States Board on Geographic Names, 1933b, p. 17).

Lamarck: see **Mount Lamarck** [FRESNO].

Lamarck Col [FRESNO]: *pass,* 6.5 miles north-northeast of Mount Goddard on Fresno-Inyo county line (lat. 37°11'25" N, long. 118° 40' W); the pass is 0.25 mile south-east of Mount Lamarck. Named on Mount Goddard (1948) 15' quadrangle. Art Schober built a trail to the place, which he and his brother John named Schober's Pass in 1939; David Brower suggested the present name, which was in use as early as 1942 (Browning 1986, p. 122).

La Marmita [KINGS]: *relief feature,* closed depression 6.5 miles east of Avenal (lat. 36°00'55" N, long. 120°00'35" W; sec. 15, T 22 S, R 18 E). Named on La Cima (1963) 7.5' quadrangle. La Cima (1934) 7.5' quadrangle shows an intermittent Lake, 350 feet long, in the depression. United States Board on Geographic Names (1933b, p. 17) pointed out that *marmita* means "pot" or "kettle" in Spanish

La Meseta [KINGS]: *peak,* 4.25 miles east of Avenal (lat. 36°00'05" N, long. 120°03' W; sec. 20, T 22 S, R 18 E). Named on La Cima (1963) 7.5' quadrangle. The name refers to the position of the peak about halfway up the north slope of El Leon—*meseta* means "landing

place of a staircase" in Spanish (United States Board on Geographic Names, 1933b, p. 17).

Lamont [KERN]: *town,* 9 miles south-southeast of downtown Bakersfield (lat. 35°15'35" N, long. 118°54'45" W; on W line sec. 6, T 31 S, R 29 E). Named on Lamont (1954) and Weed Patch (1955) 7.5' quadrangles. Postal authorities established Lamont post office in 1947 (Frickstad, p. 56). Promoters started the town in 1923, and Arthur S. McFadden named it for the Scottish clan of his family (Bailey, 1967, p. 15). A station on Butterfield Overland stage line of 1858 to 1861 was located 3 miles west of present Lamont; the station had the name "Kern River Slough" (Bailey, 1967, p. 13).

Lamont Meadow [TULARE]: *area,* about 2 miles north of Lamont Peak along Chimney Creek (lat. 35°49'15" N, long. 118°02'45" W). Named on Lamont Peak (1956) 15' quadrangle. Called La Motte Meadows on Olmsted's (1900) map.

Lamont Peak [TULARE]: *peak,* 37 miles east of California Hot Springs (lat. 35°47'35" N, long. 118°02'35" W). Altitude 7430 feet. Named on Lamont Peak (1956) 15' quadrangle.

La Morra [KINGS]: *peak,* 6.25 miles south-southwest of Kettleman City (lat. 35°55'05" N, long. 119°59'35" W; sec. 23, T 23 S, R 18 E). Altitude 941 feet. Named on Los Viejos (1954) 7.5' quadrangle. The name is descriptive—*morra* means "head" or "top" in Spanish (United States Board on Geographic Names, 1933b, p. 19).

La Motte Meadows: see **Lamont Meadow** [TULARE].

La Muralla [KINGS]: *ridge,* west- to north-northwest-trending, 1 mile long, 5.5 miles east of Avenal (lat. 36°00' N, long. 120°01'35" W). Named on Kettleman Plain (1953) and La Cima (1963) 7.5' quadrangles. The name is descriptive—*muralla* means "wall" or "rampart" in Spanish (United States Board on Geographic Names, 1933b, p. 17).

Lanare [FRESNO]: *village,* 24 miles south-southwest of Fresno (lat. 36°25'55" N, long. 119°55'50" W; near S line sec. 20, T 17 S, R 19 E). Named on Burrel (1954) 7.5' quadrangle. Postal authorities established Lanare post office in 1912 and discontinued it in 1925 (Frickstad, p. 34). The name is from the initials and surname of Llewellyn A. Nares, who with Charles A. Laton purchased a large part of Laguna de Tache grant in 1896 (Hanna, p. 166-167); the name was applied when Laton and Western Railway was built in 1911 (Gudde, 1949, p. 181).

Landco [KERN]: *locality,* 3.5 miles west of Bakersfield along Atchison, Topeka and Santa Fe Railroad (lat. 35°22'50" N, long. 119°03'40" W; sec. 27, T 29 S, R 27 E). Named on Oildale (1954) 7.5' quadrangle.

Land Company Spring [KERN]: *spring,* 5.5 mile east-southeast of Caliente (lat. 35°15'40"

N, long. 118°32' W; sec. 3, T 31 S, R 32 E). Named on Oiler Peak (1972) 7.5' quadrangle.

Landers Creek [KERN]: *stream,* flows 2.25 miles to Kelso Creek less than 1 mile east of Claraville (lat. 35°26'40" N, long. 118°18'55" W; sec. 3, T 29 S, R 34 E). Named on Claraville (1972) 7.5' quadrangle.

Landers Meadow [KERN]: *area,* 2 miles east of Claraville along Kelso Creek (lat. 35°26'50" N, long. 118°17'45" W); the place is above the mouth of Landers Creek. Named on Claraville (1972) 7.5' quadrangle.

Landslide Creek [FRESNO]: *stream,* flows 2.5 miles to Tenmile Creek 1.5 miles southeast of Hume (lat. 36°46'15" N, long. 118°53'35" W; near SE cor. sec. 23, T 13 S, R 28 E). Named on Tehipite Dome (1952) 15' quadrangle.

Lane Slough [TULARE]: *stream,* diverges southwest from St. Johns River and flows 2.5 miles to Kaweah River 4.25 miles north of Exeter (lat. 36°21'30" N, long. 119°08'15" W; sec. 15, T 18 S, R 26 E). Named on Exeter (1952) 15' quadrangle.

Lane Spring [FRESNO]: *spring,* 10.5 miles northwest of Coalinga (lat. 36°14'25" N, long. 120°29'45" W; sec. 30, T 19 S, R 14 E). Named on Alcalde Hills (1969) 7.5' quadrangle.

Langdon: see **Bakersfield** [KERN].

Langille Peak [FRESNO]: *peak,* 6 miles east of Mount Goddard (lat. 37°06' N, long. 118°36'35" W). Altitude 11,991 feet. Named on Mount Goddard (1948) 15' quadrangle. Charles H. Shinn suggested the name to honor Harold Douglas Langille, who visited the region in 1904 as forest inspector of General Land Office (Hanna, p. 167). United States Board on Geographic Names (1961a, p. 18) approved the name "Hester Lake" for a feature, about 1300 feet long, situated 0.8 mile southwest of Langille Peak (lat. 37°05'35" N, long. 118°37'25" W); the name honors both Robert M. Hester, co-pilot of a B-24 bomber that crashed at the lake in 1943 and was found in 1960, and the co-pilot's father, Clinton Hester, who searched for his son's body for more than 14 years.

Langley: see **Mount Langley** [TULARE]; **Mount Langley**, under **Mount Corcoran** [TULARE].

Lang Pond [FRESNO]: *intermittent lake,* 750 feet long, 2.5 miles southwest of Selma (lat. 36°32'35" N, long. 119°38'15" W; sec. 13, T 16 S, R 21 E). Named on Conejo (1963) 7.5' quadrangle. Selma (1946) 15' quadrangle shows a permanent lake 2100 feet long.

Lankershim: see **Trigo** [MADERA].

La Oveja [KINGS]: *peak,* 4 miles east-southeast of Avenal (lat. 35° 59'05" N, long. 120°03'45" W; sec. 30, T 22 S, R 18 E). Altitude 1063 feet. Named on Kettleman Plain (1953) 7.5' quadrangle. The name refers to the raising of sheep in Kettleman Hills—*oveja*

means "sheep" in Spanish (United States Board on Geographic Names, 1933b, p. 17).

La Palomera [KINGS]: *peak,* nearly 6 miles east of Avenal (lat. 36° 00'25" N, long. 120°01'35" W; near N line sec. 21, T 22 S, R 18 E). Altitude 1069 feet. Named on La Cima (1963) 7.5' quadrangle. The name is descriptive—*palomera* means "dove cot" in Spanish (United States Board on Geographic Names, 1933b, p. 17).

La Porciuncula: see **Kern River** [KERN-TULARE].

La Porteria [KINGS]: *pass,* 8 miles south-southeast of Kettleman City (lat. 35°53'55" N, long. 119°55'05" W; sec. 28, T 23 S, R 19 E). Named on Los Viejos (1954) 7.5' quadrangle. The pass is the principal entrance to the interior of Middle Dome Kettleman Hills—*porteria* means "principal opening of a large building" in Spanish (United States Board on Geographic Names, 1933b, p. 17).

La Rambla [KINGS]: *area,* 5 miles southeast of Kettleman City (lat. 35°57'05" N, long. 119°54'35" W). Named on Los Viejos (1954) 7.5' quadrangle. The place is a former beach of Tulare Lake—*rambla* means "sandy place" in Spanish (United States Board on Geographic Names, 1933b, p. 17).

Large Meadow [FRESNO]: *area,* 15 miles north-northeast of Hume (lat. 37°00' N, long. 118°51' W). Named on Blackcap Mountain (1953) and Tehipite Dome (1952) 15' quadrangles.

Larione's Ferry: see **Old Fort Miller** [FRESNO].

La Rose [KERN]: *locality,* nearly 3 miles northwest of Mojave along Southern Pacific Railroad (lat. 35°06'30" N, long. 118°14'45" W; near N line sec. 32, T 32 S, R 35 E). Named on Mojave (1915) 30' quadrangle.

La Rose Creek [KERN]: *stream,* flows 4.5 miles to Cache Creek 10.5 miles east of Tehachapi (lat. 35°06'15" N, long. 118°16'15" W; near W line sec. 31, T 32 S, R 35 E). Named on Monolith (1966) and Tehachapi NE (1966) 7.5' quadrangles.

La Salida [KINGS]: *pass,* 5.5 miles south-southeast of Kettleman City (lat. 35°55'50" N, long. 119°56'15" W; sec. 17, T 23 S, R 19 E). Named on Los Viejos (1954) 7.5' quadrangle. United States Board on Geographic Names (1933b, p. 17) pointed out that *salida* means "exit" or "outlet" in Spanish.

Las Alturas [KINGS]: *ridge,* north-northwest-trending, 9 miles long, 7 miles south of Kettleman City (lat. 35°54' N, long. 119°59' W). Named on Avenal Gap (1954), Kettleman Plain (1953), and Los Viejos (1954) 7.5' quadrangles. The name is descriptive—*las alturas* means "the heights" or "summits" in Spanish (United States Board on Geographic Names, 1933b, p. 18).

Las Colinas [KINGS]: *ridge,* north-trending, 3.5 miles long, 13 miles south of Kettleman City (lat. 35°48'45" N, long. 119°56'30" W). Named on Avenal Gap (1954) 7.5' quadrangle. *Colinas* means "hills" in Spanish (United States Board on Geographic Names, 1933b, p. 18).

Las Garzas Creek: see **Garza Creek** [FRESNO-KINGS].

Las Gatas Creek: see **Los Gatos Creek** [FRESNO].

Las Juntas: see **Pueblo de las Juntas**, under **Mendota** [FRESNO].

Las Lomas [KINGS]: *peaks,* 15 miles south of Kettleman City (lat. 35°48' N, long. 119°54'40" W; in and near sec. 34, T 24 S, R 19 E). Named on Avenal Gap (1954) 7.5' quadrangle. United States Board on Geographic Names (1933b, p. 18) pointed out that *las lomas* means "the little hills" in Spanish.

Las Palmas [FRESNO]: *locality,* 4.5 miles south of Clovis along Southern Pacific Railroad (lat. 36°45'30" N, long. 119°42' W; at W line sec. 33, T 13 S, R 21 E). Named on Clovis (1964) 7.5' quadrangle. Called Los Palmas on California Mining Bureau's (1917a) map. Postal authorities established Womack post office in 1909, changed the name to Las Palmas in 1910, and discontinued it in 1913; the name "Womack" was for D. Donald Womack, first postmaster (Salley, p. 118, 242).

Las Paredes [KINGS]: *ridge,* northwest-trending, 0.5 mile long, 4.5 miles east-northeast of Avenal (lat. 36°01'10" N, long. 120°03'05" W; on N line sec. 17, T 22 S, R 18 E). Named on La Cima (1963) 7.5' quadrangle. The name refers to the precipitous southwest side of the feature—*las paredes* means "the walls" in Spanish (United States Board on Geographic Names, 1933b, p. 18).

Las Perillas [KINGS]: *ridge,* north-northeast-trending, 1 mile long. 12 miles south-southeast of Kettleman City (lat. 35°50'05" N, long. 119°54'30" W; sec. 15, 22, T 24 S, R 29 E). Named on Avenal Gap (1954) 7.5' quadrangle. The name is descriptive; *las perillas* means "knob" or "small pear" in Spanish (United States Board on Geographic Names, 1933b, p. 18).

Last: see **Huron** [FRESNO].

Last Chance Canyon [KERN]: *canyon,* drained by a stream that flows 11.5 miles to Fremont Valley 1.5 miles west-southwest of Saltdale (lat. 35°22'15" N, long. 117°54'25" W). Named on Garlock (1967) and Saltdale NW (1967) 7.5' quadrangles.

Last Chance Canyon: see **Big Last Chance Canyon** [KERN]; **Little Last Chance Canyon** [KERN].

Last Chance Meadow [MADERA]: *area,* 6.5 miles south-southwest of Buena Vista Peak (lat. 37°30'10" N, long. 119°33' W; near N line sec. 15, T 5 S, R 22 E). Named on Yosemite (1956) 15' quadrangle.

Last Chance Meadow [TULARE]: *area,* 10 miles south-southeast of Camp Nelson (lat.

36°00'15" N, long. 118°34' W; sec. 19, T 22 S, R 32 E). Named on Camp Nelson (1956) 15' quadrangle.

Las Tiendas: see **Tent Hills** [KINGS].

Las Tinajas de los Indios: see **Point of Rocks** [KERN].

Latache: see **Lemoore** [KINGS].

Laton [FRESNO]: *town,* 23 miles south-southeast of Fresno (lat. 36° 26'05" N, long. 119°41'05" W; sec. 21, 22, T 17 S, R 21 E). Named on Laton (1953) 7.5' quadrangle. The name commemorates Charles A Laton, who with L.A. Nares acquired part of Laguna de Tache grant in the 1890's (Gudde, 1949, p. 184). Postal authorities established Kingston post office in 1859, discontinued it in 1862, reestablished it in 1866, and moved it 1.5 miles in 1890 when they changed the name to Sans Tache; they changed the name to Lillis in 1891, and moved the post office 1 mile east in 1900 when they and changed the name to Laton (Salley, p. 112, 119, 122, 197). The name "Lillis" was for Simon C. Lillis, superintendent of Laguna de Tache cattle ranch before 1917 (Gudde, 1949, p. 188). California Mining Bureau's (1917a) map has the name "Lillis" for a place located along the railroad about 2 miles west of Laton.

La Tusa [KINGS]: *ridge,* northwest-trending, 0.5 mile long, 3 miles east-northeast of Avenal (lat. 36°01'25" N, long. 120°04'55" W; near S line sec. 12, T 22 S, R 17 E). Named on La Cima (1963) 7.5' quadrangle. The name is descriptive and means "corncob" in Spanish (United States Board on Geographic Names, 1933b, p. 17).

Lauhman Ridge: see **Leuhman Ridge** [KERN].

Laura Lake [MADERA]: *lake,* 700 feet long, 6.25 miles north-northwest of Devils Postpile (lat. 37°42'20" N, long. 119°08'15" W). Named on Devils Postpile (1953) 15' quadrangle.

Laura Peak [KERN]: *peak,* 6 miles east-southeast of Bodfish (lat. 35°34' N, long. 118°23' W; sec. 24, T 27 S, R 33 E). Altitude 5254 feet. Named on Lake Isabella South (1972) 7.5' quadrangle.

Laurel Creek [FRESNO]:

(1) *stream,* flows 2.5 miles to Mono Creek nearly 5 miles northwest of Mount Abbot (lat. 37°25'45" N, long. 118°51' W). Named on Mount Abbot (1953) 15' quadrangle.

(2) *stream,* flows 4 miles to Bear Creek (3) 5 miles south of Dinkey Dome (lat. 37°02'30" N, long. 119°07'45" W; sec. 22, T 10 S, R 26 E). Named on Huntington Lake (1953) 15' quadrangle

Laurel Creek [TULARE]: *stream,* flows 5.5 miles to Kern River 8.5 miles northwest of Kern Peak (lat. 36°23' N, long. 118°23' W). Named on Kern Peak (1956) 15' quadrangle.

Laurel Lake [FRESNO]: *lake,* 700 feet long, 6.5 miles northwest of Mouth Abbot (lat. 37°27'40" N, long. 118°51'30" W); the lake is at the head of a branch of Laurel Creek (1).

Named on Mount Abbot (1953) 15' quadrangle.

Laurel Mountain [KERN]: *peak,* 8 miles north of Randsburg (lat. 35°28'45" N, long. 117°41' W; at NE cor. sec. 29, T 28 S, R 40 E). Named on El Paso Peaks (1967) 7.5' quadrangle. The feature also was known as Copper Mountain (Hess, p. 25). A mining camp called El Paso City was located near Laurel Mountain in the 1860's (Bailey, 1967, p. 8).

Lava Butte [FRESNO]: *peak,* 2.5 miles southeast of Hume (lat. 36° 45'35" N, long. 118°53'15" W; sec. 25, T 13 S, R 28 E). Altitude 6122 feet. Named on Tehipite Dome (1952) 15' quadrangle.

Lava Rock Canyon: see **Lavrock Canyon** [KERN].

La Vega [KINGS]: *area,* 4 miles northeast of Avenal (lat. 37°03'15" N, long. 120°05'10" W; sec. 36, T 21 S, R 17 E). Named on La Cima (1963) 7.5' quadrangle. United States Board on Geographic Names (1933b, p. 17) noted that *la vega* means "the meadow" in Spanish.

Lavers' Crossing: see **Glennville** [KERN].

La Vina [MADERA]: *village,* 6.5 miles south-southwest of Madera (lat. 36°52'50" N long. 120°06'45" W; on S line sec. 16, T 12 S, R 17 E). Named on Madera (1963) 7.5' quadrangle. Postal authorities established La Vina post office in 1891 and discontinued it in 1895 (Frickstad, p. 86). The place began as part of an unsuccessful land-development scheme (Clough, p. 86).

Lavrock Canyon [KERN]: *canyon,* drained by a stream that flows 2 miles to Still Canyon 7 miles south of Orchard Peak (lat. 35°38'15" N, long. 120°08'35" W; sec. 28, T 26 S, R 17 E). Named on Orchard Peak (1961) 7.5' quadrangle. Called Lava Rock Canyon on Annette (1943) 7.5' quadrangle.

Lawson Peak: see **Eagle Scout Peak** [TULARE].

La Zanja [KINGS]: *relief feature,* a line of topographic depressions 9 miles south of Kettleman City (lat. 35°52'30" N, long. 119°57'45" W). Named on Avenal Gap (1954) and Los Viejos (1954) 7.5' quadrangles. The name is descriptive; *la zanja* means "trench" or "furrow" in Spanish (United States Board on Geographic Names, 1933b, p. 17).

Leavis Flat Campground [TULARE]: *locality,* at California Hot Springs (lat. 35°52'45" N, long. 118°40'30" W; sec. 31, T 23 S, R 31 E). Named on California Hot Springs (1958) 15' quadrangle.

Lebec [KERN]: *village,* 38 miles south of Bakersfield (lat. 34°50'05" N, long. 118°51'50" W; sec. 26, T 9 N, R 19 W). Named on Lebec (1958) 7.5' quadrangle. Postal authorities established Tejon post office in 1895; they moved it 3 miles south and changed the name to Lebec the same year (Salley, p. 219). The name "Lebec" commemorates Peter Lebeck, or Lebecque, who

probably was a trapper; according to an epitaph carved on an oak tree at Old Fort Tejon, Lebeck was killed by a bear in 1837 (Cullimore, p. 15-16).

Lecheria Creek: see **Pescado Creek** [KERN].

LeConte: see **Mount LeConte** [TULARE].

LeConte Canyon [FRESNO]: *canyon,* 6 miles long, 7 miles east-southeast of Mount Goddard along Middle Fork Kings River above Palisade Creek (lat. 37°05' N, long. 118°35'40" W). Named on Mount Goddard (1948) 15' quadrangle. The name honors Joseph N. LeConte, professor of engineering mechanics at University of California and president of the Sierra Club (Farquhar, 1924, p. 54). United States Board on Geographic Names (1933a, p. 453) rejected the form "Leconte Canyon" for the name.

LeConte Divide [FRESNO]: *ridge,* 12 miles long, mainly between Mount Henry and Mount Reinstein; center 5 miles north of Blackcap Mountain (lat. 37°09' N, long. 118°48' W). Named on Blackcap Mountain (1953) and Mount Goddard (1948) 15' quadrangles. The name is for Joseph N. LeConte of LeConte Canyon (Farquhar, 1924, p. 53). United States Board on Geographic Names (1933a, p. 453) rejected the form "Leconte Divide" for the name.

Ledger Island [MADERA]: *area,* 18 miles east of Madera on the west side of San Joaquin River (lat. 36°56'55" N, long. 119°44'20" W; sec. 25, T 11 S, R 20 E). Named on Friant (1964) 7.5' quadrangle.

Lee Lake [FRESNO]: *lake,* 1800 feet long, 1 mile west-southwest of Red Slate Mountain (lat. 37°30'05" N, long. 118°53'15" W). Named on Mount Abbot (1953) and Mount Morrison (1953) 15' quadrangles.

Lefever Creek [FRESNO]: *stream,* flows 5.25 miles to Pine Flat Reservoir 7 miles northeast of Tivy Mountain (lat. 36°51'30" N, long. 119°15'15" W; sec. 28, T 12 S, R 25 E). Named on Patterson Mountain (1952) 15' quadrangle, and on Pine Flat Dam (1965) 7.5' quadrangle.

Left Stringer [TULARE]: *stream,* flows 3.5 miles to Right Stringer 4 miles north-north-west of Kern Peak (lat. 36°21'25" N, long. 118° 19'35" W). Named on Kern Peak (1956) 15' quadrangle.

Leggett Creek [TULARE]: *stream,* flows 2.5 miles to Kern River 7 miles west-southwest of Kern Peak (lat. 36°16'30" N, long. 118°24'20" W). Named on Kern Peak (1956) 15' quadrangle.

Leland Gulch [MADERA]: *canyon,* drained by a stream that flows 1.5 miles to Chowchilla River 8 miles northeast of Raymond (lat. 37°18'30" N, long. 119°49'05" W; sec. 19, T 7 S, R 20 E). Named on Horsecamp Mountain (1947) 7.5' quadrangle.

Leliter [KERN]: *locality,* 4.5 miles north-north-west of Inyokern along Southern Pacific Railroad (lat. 35°42'35" N, long. 117°49'45" W;

at NW cor. sec. 6, T 26 S, R 39 E). Named on Inyokern (1943) 15' quadrangle. Searles Lake (1915) 1° quadrangle has the names "Muerto" and "Leliter P.O." at the place. Postal authorities established Leliter post office in 1910 and discontinued it in 1927 (Frickstad, p. 57).

Lemon: see **Lemoncove** [TULARE].

Lemoncove [TULARE]: *village,* 4.5 miles east-southeast of Woodlake (lat. 36°23' N, long. 119°01'30" W; around SW cor. sec. 2, T 18 S, R 27 E); the village is 2 miles south-southwest of Limekiln Hill. Named on Woodlake (1952) 7.5' quadrangle. Called Lemon Cove on Lemon Cove (1928) 7.5' quadrangle, and called Lemon on Mendenhall's (1908) map. J.W.C. Pogue founded the village on his ranch and named it in 1870 (Mitchell, A.R., p. 68). California Mining Bureau's (1909a) map shows a place called Lime Kiln located 2 miles east of Lemoncove along a rail line. Postal authorities established Lime Kiln post office in 1879, moved it 1.25 miles southwest in 1890, and changed the name to Lemoncove in 1898; the name "Lime Kiln" was for a kiln used to produce lime from limestone at the place (Salley, p. 122).

Lemoore [KINGS]: *town,* 7.5 miles west-southwest of Hanford (lat. 36°18'05" N, long. 119°47' W; in and near sec. 3, T 19 S, R 20 E). Named on Lemoore (1954) 7.5' quadrangle. Postal authorities established Lemoore post office in 1875 (Frickstad, p. 61), and the town incorporated in 1900. John Kurtz settled at the place in 1859; Dr. Lovern Lee Moore arrived in 1871 and called the community there Latache, but when Dr. Moore requested a post office, the post office name was coined from his name (Gudde, 1969, p. 176). Postal authorities established Watertown post office 10 miles west of Lemoore in 1896 and discontinued it in 1900; they established Cloud post office 35 miles southwest of Lemoore (SE quarter sec. 26, T 23 S, R 19 E) in 1913 and discontinued it in 1921 (Salley, p. 46, 235).

Lempon [TULARE]: *locality,* 8.5 miles north-northwest of Fountain Springs along Atchison, Topeka and Santa Fe Railroad (lat. 35°59'55" N, long. 118°59'35" W; sec. 19, T 22 S, R 28 E). Named on White River (1936) 15' quadrangle. The name was coined in 1917 from letters in the words "lemon" and "pomegranate" (Gudde, 1949, p. 186; Gudde used the form "Lempom" for the name).

Leonard: see **Camp Leonard**, under **Weldon** [KERN].

Leonards [KERN]: *locality,* 5 miles southwest of Wasco (lat. 35°33'05" N, long. 119°24'10" W; at E line sec. 29, T 27 S, R 24 E). Named on Leonards (1930) 7.5' quadrangle.

Leppy Spring [KERN]: *spring,* 5 miles east of Caliente (lat. 35°16'35" N, long. 118°32'25" W; sec. 33, T 30 S, R 32 E). Named on Oiler Peak (1972) 7.5' quadrangle.

Lerdo [KERN]: *locality,* 12 miles northwest of Bakersfield along Southern Pacific Railroad (lat. 35°29'25" N, long. 119°09'05" W; at W line sec. 14, T 28 S, R 26 E). Named on Rosedale (1954) 7.5' quadrangle. Postal authorities established Lerdo post office in 1890 and discontinued it in 1894 (Frickstad, p. 57).

Lerona [FRESNO]: *locality,* 6.5 miles west-northwest of Shaver Lake Heights (present town of Shaver Lake) (lat. 37°07'45" N, long. 119°25'50" W; sec. 23, T 9 S, R 23 E). Named on Shaver Lake (1953) 15' quadrangle.

Leroy: see **Coalinga** [FRESNO].

Letcher [FRESNO]: *locality,* 12 miles east-northeast of Clovis (lat. 36°54'30" N, long. 119°31' W; sec. 12, T 12 S, R 22 E). Named on Clovis (1946) 15' quadrangle. Postal authorities established Letcher post office in 1886 and discontinued it in 1915; the name commemorates F.F. Letcher, who was a county supervisor (Salley, p. 121).

Lethent [KINGS]: *locality,* 6 miles west of Lemoore along Southern Pacific Railroad (lat. 36°17'10" N, long. 119°53' W; near SW cor. sec. 11, T 19 S, R 19 E). Named on Lethent (1926) 7.5' quadrangle.

Leuhman Ridge [KERN]: *ridge,* northeast-trending, 3 miles long, 4.5 miles south-southwest of Boron (lat. 34°56'30" N, long. 117°41'20" W). Named on Leuhman Ridge (1973) 7.5' quadrangle. Called Lauhman Ridge on Kramer (1956) 15' quadrangle.

Levee: see **Levee Spur** [KERN].

Levee Spur [KERN]: *locality,* nearly 3 miles southwest of Millux along Sunset Railroad (lat. 35°09'15" N, long. 119°14'05" W; near SE cor. sec. 12, T 32 S, R 25 E). Named on Millux (1954) 7.5' quadrangle. Millux (1933) 7.5' quadrangle shows a place called Levee located 1.5 miles farther north along the railroad.

Levis [KERN]: *locality,* 9 miles west-southwest of Tranquillity (lat. 36°37'25" N, long. 120°24'20" W; near E line sec. 14, T 15 S, R 14 E). Named on Levis (1956) 7.5' quadrangle.

Lewis: see **Sam Lewis Camp** [TULARE].

Lewis Creek [FRESNO]:

(1) *stream,* flows 2.5 miles to Holland Creek 3 miles west-southwest of Piedra (lat. 36°48' N, long. 119°26'05" W; sec. 14, T 13 S, R 23 E). Named on Piedra (1965) 7.5' quadrangle.

(2) *stream,* flows 6.5 miles to South Fork Kings River 14 miles southwest of Marion Peak (lat. 36°48'05" N, long. 118°41'45" W); the stream heads at Lewis Lake. Named on Marion Peak (1953) 15' quadrangle. The name commemorates brothers Frank M Lewis and Jeff Lewis, pioneer prospectors and stockmen of the region (Hanna, p. 171). East Fork enters from the northeast 3.5 miles upstream from the mouth of the main stream; it is 3 miles long and is named on Marion Peak (1953) 15' quadrangle.

Lewis Creek [MADERA]: *stream,* heads just

inside Madera County and flows 7.5 miles to Merced River 7.5 miles south of Cathedral Peak (lat. 37°44'15" N, long. 119°24' W). Named on Merced Peak (1953) and Tuolumne Meadows (1956) 15' quadrangles. United States Board on Geographic Names (1934a, p. 14) rejected the name "Maclure Fork" for the stream, and pointed out that the name "Lewis" is for W.B. Lewis, a superintendent of Yosemite National Park.

Lewis Creek: see **Lewis Fork** [MADERA].

Lewis Creek [TULARE]: *stream,* flows 9.5 miles to lowlands 8 miles north of Porterville (lat. 36°11'05" N, long. 119°00' W; sec. 13, T 20 S, R 27 E). Named on Cairns Corner (1927), Frazier Valley (1957), Lindsay (1951), and Springville (1957) 7.5' quadrangles. The name commemorates either Frank Lewis or Jeff Lewis (Mitchell, A.R., p. 78).

Lewis Fork [MADERA]: *stream,* heads just inside Mariposa County and flows 8.5 miles to join Nelder Creek and form Fresno River less than 0.5 mile south-southwest of Yosemite Forks in Madera County (lat. 37°21'40" N, long. 119°37'55" W; near SW cor. sec. 36, T 6 S, R 21 E). Named on Bass Lake (1953) 15' quadrangle. Browning (1986, p. 127) associated the name with Jonathan Lewis, who homesteaded in the neighborhood in 1886. United States Board on Geographic Names (1964c, p. 15) rejected the names "Lewis Creek" and "North Fork of Fresno River" for the stream.

Lewis Hill [TULARE]: *peak,* 2.5 miles north of Porterville (lat. 36° 06'20" N, long. 119°00'40" W). Altitude 1028 feet. Named on Porterville (1951) 7.5' quadrangle.

Lewis Lake [FRESNO]: *lake,* 600 feet long, 10 miles west-southwest of Marion Peak (lat. 36°52'50" N, long. 118°40'35" W); the lake is at the head of Lewis Creek (2). Named on Marion Peak (1953) 15' quadrangle.

Lewis Stringer [TULARE]: *stream,* flows 3.25 miles to South Fork Kern River 8 miles northwest of Olancha Peak in Templeton Meadows (lat. 36°20'05" N, long. 118°13'55" W; sec. 30, T 18 S, R 35 E). Named on Kern Peak (1956) and Olancha (1956) 15' quadrangles.

Liberty [TULARE]: *settlement,* 4.25 miles south-southwest of Visalia (lat. 36°16'15" N, long. 119°18'50" W; near SE cor. sec. 13, T 19 S, R 24 E). Named on Visalia (1949) 15' quadrangle.

Liberty: see **Tonyville** [TULARE].

Liberty Settlement: see **Riverdale** [FRESNO].

Liebel Peak [KERN]: *peak,* 7.5 miles southeast of Bodfish (lat. 35° 30'25" N, long. 118°23'50" W; near E line sec. 11, T 28 S, R 33 E). Altitude 3085 feet. Named on Lake Isabella South (1972) 7.5' quadrangle. The name, given in the 1930's, commemorates Michael Otto Liebel, who came to the region in 1876 and settled near the peak (Gudde, 1949, p. 187).

Liebre Twins [KERN]: *peak,* 24 miles west-northwest of Rosamond (lat. 34°57'20" N, long. 118°34'20" W; near SW cor. sec. 15, T 10 N, R 16 W). Altitude 6413 feet. Named on Liebre Twins (1965) 7.5' quadrangle.

Lieva Springs [KERN]: *springs,* 9.5 miles east of Tehachapi (lat. 35°07'20" N, long. 118°16'55" W; near N line sec. 25, T 32 S, R 34 E). Named on Monolith (1966) 7.5' quadrangle.

Lightner Peak [KERN]: *peak,* 3.5 miles south-southwest of Miracle Hot Springs (lat. 35°31'45" N, long. 118°33'45" W); the peak is 2 miles north of Lightners Flat. Altitude 6430 feet. Named on Miracle Hot Springs (1972) 7.5' quadrangle.

Lightners Flat [KERN]: *area,* 5.25 miles south-southwest of Miracle Hot Springs (lat. 35°30'05" N, long. 118°33'35" W; at S line sec 8, T 28 S, R 32 E); the place is 2 miles south of Lightner Peak. Named on Miracle Hot Springs (1972) 7.5' quadrangle.

Lightning Creek [FRESNO]: *stream,* flows 4 miles to South Fork Kings River 16 miles southwest of Marion Peak (lat. 36°48'10" N, long. 118°44' W). Named on Marion Peak (1953) 15' quadrangle.

Light Well: see **Alamo Solo Spring** [KERN].

Likely Mill: see **Old Likely Mill** [KERN].

Lillian Lake [MADERA]: *lake,* 1550 feet long, 5.25 miles south-southeast of Merced Peak (lat. 37°33'45" N, long. 119°21'50" W). Named on Merced Peak (1953) 15' quadrangle.

Lillis: see **Laton** [FRESNO].

Lilly Canyon [KERN]: *canyon,* drained by a stream that flows nearly 3 miles to Kern River 1.25 miles west of Miracle Hot Springs (lat. 35°34'40" N, long. 118°33'25" W). Named on Miracle Hot Springs (1972) 7.5' quadrangle.

Lilly Mountain [MADERA]: *peak,* 5 miles east-southeast of Knowles (lat. 37°10'55" N, long. 119°47'40" W; sec. 4, T 9 S, R 20 E). Named on Knowles (1962) 7.5' quadrangle.

Lily Lake [MADERA]: *lake,* 500 feet long, 8.5 miles west of Devils Postpile (lat. 37°36'15" N, long. 119°13'50" W). Named on Devils Postpile (1953) 15' quadrangle.

Lime Dyke [KERN]: *relief feature,* 4.25 miles east-southeast of Wofford Heights along Isabella Lake (lat. 35°40'15" N, long. 118° 23'30" W; sec. 13, T 26 S, R 33 E). Named on Lake Isabella North (1972) 7.5' quadrangle.

Lime Kiln: see **Lemoncove** [TULARE].

Limekiln Creek: see **Dry Creek** [TULARE] (1)

Limekiln Hill [TULARE]: *hill,* 5.25 miles east of Woodlake (lat. 36° 24'50" N, long. 119°00'15" W; mainly in sec. 36, T 17 S, R 27 E). Altitude 986 feet. Named on Woodlake (1952) 7.5' quadrangle.

Lime Point [KERN]: *promontory,* 5 miles southeast of Wofford Heights (lat. 35°39'15" N, long. 118°23'30" W; sec. 24, T 26 S, R 33 E).

Named on Lake Isabella North (1972) 7.5' quadrangle.

Limestone Cliff Campground [TULARE]: *locality,* 2.5 miles north-northeast of Fairview along Kern River (lat. 35°57'45" N, long. 118°28'45" W). Named on Kernville (1956) 15' quadrangle.

Lincoln [MADERA]: *locality,* 8 miles south-southwest of Chowchilla along Chowchilla Pacific Railroad (lat. 37°01'10" N, long. 120°20'40" W; near W line sec. 33, T 10 S, R 15 E). Named on Chowchilla (1918) 7.5' quadrangle.

Lind: see **Jenny Lind Cañon**, under **Big Arroyo** [TULARE]; **Jenny Lind Canyon** [KERN].

Lindcove [TULARE]: *village,* 6 miles northeast of Exeter (lat. 36°21'30" N, long. 119°03'45" W; near E line sec. 17, T 18 S, R 27 E). Named on Rocky Hill (1951) 7.5' quadrangle. Rocky Hill (1927) 7.5' quadrangle shows a place called Lind Cove located along Visalia Electric Railroad 0.5 mile south of present Lindcove.

Lindsay [TULARE]: *town,* 10.5 miles north-northwest of Porterville (lat. 36°12'20" N, long. 119°05'20" W; in and near sec 7, T 20 S, R 27 E). Named on Lindsay (1951) 7.5' quadrangle. Postal authorities established Lindsay post office in 1889 (Frickstad, p. 212), and the town incorporated in 1910. Arthur J. Hutchinson, an owner of Lindsay Land Company, gave his wife's maiden name to the town in 1888 (Mitchell, A.R., p. 68).

Lindsay Peak [TULARE]: *peak,* 3 miles north-northeast of Lindsay (lat. 36°14'40" N, long. 119°03'35" W; sec. 28, T 19 S, R 27 E). Altitude 1434 feet. Named on Lindsay (1951) 7.5' quadrangle.

Line Creek [FRESNO]: *stream,* flows 4.25 miles to Huntington Lake (1) nearly 4 miles south of Kaiser Peak (lat. 37°14'25" N, long. 119°12'30" W; sec. 14, T 8 S, R 25 E). Named on Huntington Lake (1953) and Kaiser Peak (1953) 15' quadrangles.

Line Creek Lake [FRESNO]: *lake,* 400 feet long, 0.5 mile west-southwest of Kaiser Peak (lat. 37°17'35" N, long. 119°11'30" W; sec. 25, T 7 S, R 25 E); the lake is near the head of Line Creek. Named on Kaiser Peak (1953) 15' quadrangle.

Linnell Post Office [TULARE]: *locality,* 5 miles west-northwest of Exeter (lat. 36°18'40" N, long. 119°13'25" W; near NW cor. sec. 1, T 19 S, R 25 E). Named on Exeter (1952) 15' quadrangle. Postal authorities established Linnell post office in 1942 (Frickstad, p. 212).

Linn's Valley: see **Glennville** [KERN]; **Linns Valley** [KERN-TULARE].

Linns Valley [KERN-TULARE]: *valley,* on Kern-Tulare county line, mainly in Kern County, 6 miles long, along Poso Creek above a point 1.5 miles south-southwest of Glennville (lat. 35°42'30" N, long. 118°43'

W). Named on California Hot Springs (1958) 15' and Glennville (1972) 7.5' quadrangles. Called Lynn Valley on Tobias Peak (1943) 30' quadrangle, but United States Board on Geographic Names (1960a, p. 8) rejected the names "Lynn Valley" and "Lynns Valley" for the feature. Whitney (1865, p. 221) mentioned Linn's Valley. The name commemorates W.P. Linn, who settled at the place in the 1850's (Barker, p. 2-3).

Lion Canyon [TULARE]: *canyon,* drained by a stream that flows 1 mile to Cedar Creek (1) 6.25 miles east-southeast of Auckland (lat. 36°32'30" N, long. 119°00'25" W; sec. 14, T 16 S, R 27 E). Named on Giant Forest (1956) 15' quadrangle, and on Auckland (1966) 7.5' quadrangle.

Lion Creek [TULARE]:
(1) *stream,* flows 4 miles to Little Kern River 14 miles south-southeast of Mineral King (lat. 36°15'30" N, long. 118°30'55" W; sec. 21, T 19 S, R 32 E); the stream goes through Lion Meadows (1). Named on Kern Peak (1956) and Mineral King (1956) 15' quadrangles.
(2) *stream,* flows 2 miles to Beach Creek 9 miles south-southeast of Hockett Peak (lat. 36°06' N, long. 118°20' W; sec. 17, T 21 S, R 34 E). Named on Hockett Peak (1956) 15' quadrangle.

Lion Flat [KERN]: *area,* 5.25 miles east-southeast of Caliente (lat. 35°15'40" N, long. 118°32'25" W; sec. 4, T 31 S, R 32 E). Named on Oiler Peak (1972) 7.5' quadrangle.

Lion Lake [TULARE]: *lake,* 2400 feet long, 0.5 mile west-southwest of Triple Divide Peak (lat. 36°35'20" N, long. 118°32'20" W); the lake is less than 0.5 mile north-northeast of Lion Rock. Named on Triple Divide Peak (1956) 15' quadrangle.

Lion Meadows [TULARE]:
(1) *area,* 12.5 miles west-southwest of Kern Peak (lat. 36°16' N, long. 118°30' W); the place is along Lion Creek (1). Named on Kern Peak (1956) and Mineral King (1956) 15' quadrangles.
(2) *area,* 7 miles south-southeast of Hockett Peak (lat. 36°07'40" N, long. 118°20'05" W; near W line sec. 5, T 21 S, R 34 E). Named on Hockett Peak (1956) 15' quadrangle.

Lion Point [MADERA]:
(1) *peak,* 11 miles south of Shuteye Peak (lat. 37°11'40" N, long. 119°23'35" W; sec. 31, T 8 S, R 24 E). Altitude 4970 feet. Named on Shaver Lake (1953) 15' quadrangle.
(2) *peak,* nearly 5 miles south-southwest of Devils Postpile (lat. 37° 33'50" N, long. 119°07'30" W). Altitude 8866 feet. Named on Devils Postpile (1953) 15' quadrangle.

Lion Ridge [TULARE]: *ridge,* southwest- to west-trending, 4 miles long, 4 miles east-northeast of California Hot Springs (lat. 35° 54' N, long. 118°36' W). Named on California Hot Springs (1958) 15' quadrangle.

Lion Rock [TULARE]: *peak,* 1 mile southwest

of Triple Divide Peak (lat. 36°35' N, long. 118°32'30" W). Named on Triple Divide Peak (1956) 15' quadrangle. The name, given in 1896, is for the fancied resemblance of the feature to the front of a couchant lion (Browning, 1986, p. 127).

Lion Spring [KERN]: *spring,* 5 miles east-southeast of Caliente (lat. 35°16' N, long. 118°32'30" W; near N line sec 4, T 31 S, R 32 E); the spring is less than 0.5 mile north of Lion Flat. Named on Oiler Peak (1972) 7.5' quadrangle.

Lippincott Mountain [TULARE]: *peak,* 5.25 miles south-southwest of Triple Divide Peak on Great Western Divide (lat. 36°31'15" N, long. 118°33'45" W). Altitude 12,260 feet. Named on Triple Divide Peak (1956) 15' quadrangle. The name is for Joseph Barlow Lippincott, hydrographer for United States Geological Survey and the Reclamation Service (Hanna, p. 172), who allegedly was involved in the acquisition of Owens Valley water by the City of Los Angeles (Kahrl, p. 124-127).

Lisko [TULARE]: *locality,* 2 miles north-northwest of Porterville along Southern Pacific Railroad (lat. 36°05'50" N, long. 119°02'10" W; sec. 15, T 21 S, R 27 E). Named on Porterville (1951) 7.5' quadrangle.

List [TULARE]: *locality,* 1.5 miles south-southeast of Exeter along Atchison, Topeka and Santa Fe Railroad (lat. 36°16'35" N, long. 119°07'35" W; sec. 14, T 19 S, R 26 E). Named on Exeter (1952) 15' quadrangle.

Lithmore: see **Zante** [TULARE].

Little Ash Creek [MADERA]: *stream,* diverges west from Ash Creek (present Ash Slough) 8.5 miles west-southwest of Chowchilla (lat. 37°04'05" N, long. 120°23'50" W; near NW cor. sec. 13, T 10 S, R 14 E), and flows for 5 miles in a westerly direction. Named on Bliss Ranch (1918) 7.5' quadrangle.

Little Avenal Creek [FRESNO-KINGS]: *stream,* heads in Fresno County and flows 15 miles to Avenal Creek 10 miles south of Avenal in Kings County (lat. 35°51'35" N, long. 120°08'45" W; near NW cor. sec. 9, T 24 S, R 17 E). Named on Tent Hills (1942) 7.5' quadrangle.

Little Avenal Creek: see **Avenal Creek** [KINGS]; **Lovel Canyon** [KINGS].

Little Baldy [TULARE]: *peak,* 4.5 miles northeast of Yucca Mountain (lat. 36°36'50" N, long. 118°48'15" W; near S line sec. 14, T 15 S, R 29 E); the peak is 6 miles southeast of Big Baldy. Altitude 8044 feet. Named on Giant Forest (1956) 15' quadrangle.

Little Baldy Saddle [TULARE]: *pass,* 4.5 miles northeast of Yucca Mountain (lat. 36°37'10" N, long. 118°48'30" W; at W line sec. 14, T 15 S, R 29 E); the pass is less than 0.5 mile northwest of Little Baldy. Named on Giant Forest (1956) 15' quadrangle.

Little Bear Canyon [FRESNO]: *canyon,*

drained by a stream that flows nearly 3 miles to Bear Canyon 7.25 miles north-northeast of Charley Mountain (lat. 36°14'30" N, long. 120°37'45" W; sec. 36, T 19 S, R 12 E). Named on Priest Valley (1969) 7.5' quadrangle.

Little Bear Lake [FRESNO]: *lake,* 1400 feet long, 4 miles south-southwest of Mount Abbot (lat. 37°19'50" N, long. 118°48'30" W); the lake is 600 feet downstream from Big Bear Lake. Named on Mount Abbot (1953) 15' quadrangle.

Little Bearpaw Meadow [TULARE]: *area,* 6.25 miles west-southwest of Triple Divide Peak (lat. 36°33'15" N, long. 118°37'50" W); the place is 1 mile south-southwest of Bearpaw Meadow. Named on Triple Divide Peak (1956) 15' quadrangle. United States Board on Geographic Names (1938, p. 31) rejected the name "Wet Meadow" for the feature.

Little Blue Dome [TULARE]: *peak,* 7.5 miles west-southwest of Triple Divide Peak (lat. 36°33'50" N, long. 118°39'25" W). Altitude 7315 feet. Named on Triple Divide Peak (1956) 15' quadrangle.

Little Boulder Creek [FRESNO]: *stream,* flows 3.25 miles to Boulder Creek (1) 6.5 miles east-southeast of Hume (lat. 36°45'55" N, long. 118°47'55" W). Named on Tehipite Dome (1952) 15' quadrangle.

Little Brush Creek: see **Cannell Creek** [KERN-TULARE].

Little Campbell [TULARE]: *hill,* 8 miles east-northeast of Porterville (lat. 36°06'05" N, long. 118°52'35" W; sec. 18, T 21 S, R 29 E); the feature is northwest across Tule River from Big Campbell. Named on Success Dam (1956) 7.5' quadrangle.

Little Cannell Meadow [TULARE]: *area,* 13 miles southeast of Fairview (lat. 35°47'30" N, long. 118°19'50" W; sec. 32, T 24 S, R 34 E); the place is 3 miles southeast of Cannell Meadow. Named on Kernville (1956) 15' quadrangle.

Little Claire Lake [TULARE]: *lake,* 1100 feet long, 4.5 miles east-southeast of Mineral King (lat. 36°25'20" N, long. 118°31'15" W). Named on Mineral King (1956) 15' quadrangle. Ralph Hopping and his companions named the lake in 1900 for Hopping's little daughter (United States Board on Geographic Names, 1933a, p. 464).

Little Creek [KERN]:
(1) *stream,* flows 12 miles to the canyon of Poso Creek 6.5 miles east-southeast of Famoso (lat. 35°33'20" N, long. 119°06'25" W; sec. 30, T 27 S, R 27 E). Named on Knob Hill (1965), North of Oildale (1954), and Sand Canyon (1965) 7.5' quadrangles.
(2) *stream,* flows 1.5 miles to Kern River nearly 3 miles west of Miracle Hot Springs (lat. 35°34'05" N, long. 118°34'55" W). Named on Miracle Hot Springs (1972) 7.5' quadrangle.

Little Deep Lake: see **Fingerbowl Lake** [FRESNO].

Little Deer Creek [TULARE]: *stream,* flows 2 miles to Marble Fork 4.5 miles east of Yucca Mountain (lat. 36°34'30" N, long. 118°47'05" W; sec. 36, T 15 S, R 29 E). Named on Giant Forest (1956) 15' quadrangle. United States Board on Geographic Names (1938, p. 31) rejected the name "Deer Creek" for the feature.

Little Dixie [KERN]: *locality,* 17 miles north-northeast of Cross Mountain (lat. 35°29'50" N, long. 118°00'05" W; sec. 16, T 28 S, R 37 E); the place is along Little Dixie Wash. Named on Mojave (1915) 30' quadrangle.

Little Dixie Wash [KERN]: *stream,* flows for 27 miles from the mouth of Bird Spring Canyon before ending 5.5 miles north-northeast of Inyokern (lat. 35°43' N, long. 117°45'30" W; near W line sec. 35, T 25 S, R 39 E). Named on Dove Spring (1972), Freeman Junction (1972), Inyokern (1972), Inyokern SE (1972), and Saltdale NW (1967) 7.5' quadrangles. On Mojave (1915) 30' quadrangle, the name "Little Dixie Wash" extends up present Bird Spring Canyon.

Little Doris Lake [FRESNO]: *lake,* 400 feet long, nearly 4 miles east-northeast of Dinkey Dome (lat. 37°07'40" N, long. 119°03'50" W; sec. 19, T 9 S, R 27 E). Named on Huntington Lake (1953) 15' quadrangle.

Little Dry Creek [FRESNO]:
(1) *stream,* flows 19 miles to flatlands along San Joaquin River 8 miles north-northwest of Clovis (lat. 36°56'05" N, long. 119°44'45" W; near W line sec. 31, T 11 S, R 21 E). Named on Shaver Lake (1953) 15' quadrangle, and on Academy (1964), Friant (1964), and Humphreys Station (1965) 7.5' quadrangles. Called Dry Creek on Kaiser (1904) 30' quadrangle. North Fork enters from the north 9 miles upstream from the place that the creek reaches flatlands along San Joaquin River; it is 7.5 miles long and is named on Academy (1964) and Millerton Lake East (1965) 7.5' quadrangles.
(2) *stream,* flows 6 miles to Watts Creek nearly 2 miles northwest of Trimmer (lat. 36°55'25" N, long. 119°19'10" W; near S line sec. 35, T 11 S, R 24 E). Named on Trimmer (1965) 7.5' quadrangle.

Little Dry Creek [MADERA]: *stream,* flows 16 miles to Cottonwood Creek (2) 3 miles northwest of Trigo (lat. 36°57' N, long. 119°59'15" W; sec. 27, T 11 S, R 18 E). Named on Herndon (1965) and Raymond (1962) 15' quadrangles.

Little Dry Meadow [KERN]: *area,* 7 miles southwest of Weldon (lat. 35°35' N, long. 118°21'45" W); the place is 2 miles northwest of Dry Meadows. Named on Woolstalf Creek (1972) 7.5' quadrangle.

Little Dry Meadow [TULARE]: *area,* 2.25 miles west-southwest of Monache Mountain

(lat. 36°11'40" N, long. 118°14'05" W; near SW cor. sec. 7, T 20 S, R 35 E); the place is 1.25 miles south-southeast of Big Dry Meadows. Named on Monache Mountain (1956) 15' quadrangle.

Littlefield Mill [FRESNO]: *locality,* 17 miles south-southeast of Kaiser Peak (lat. 37°04'50" N, long. 119°20' W; near NE cor. sec. 10, T 10 S, R 24 E). Named on Kaiser (1904) 30' quadrangle.

Little Fine Gold Creek [MADERA]: *stream,* flows 12 miles to Fine Gold Creek 6.25 miles west-southwest of North Fork (lat. 37°11'45" N, long. 119°37' W; near W line sec. 31, T 8 S, R 22 E). Named on Bass Lake (1953) and Millerton Lake (1965) 15' quadrangles.

Little Five Lakes [TULARE]: *lakes,* 6.5 miles south of Triple Divide Peak (lat. 36°30' N, long. 118°32'45" W); the lakes are northwest of Big Five Lakes. Named on Mineral King (1956) and Triple Divide Peak (1956) 15' quadrangles.

Little Grinnell Lake [FRESNO]: *lake,* 700 feet long, 7.5 miles northwest of Mount Abbot (lat. 37°28'30" N, long. 118°51'40" W); the lake is 1300 feet west-northwest of Grinnell Lake. Named on Mount Abbot (1953) 15' quadrangle.

Little Hart Canyon [KERN]: *canyon,* drained by a stream that flows 1.5 miles to Hart Canyon 8 miles north of Emerald Mountain (lat. 35°22'10" N, long. 118°18'50" W). Named on Claraville (1972) and Emerald Mountain (1972) 7.5' quadrangles.

Little Horse Meadows [TULARE]: *area,* 7 miles southeast of Hockett Peak (lat. 36°08'45" N, long. 118°18'15" W; sec. 33, T 20 S, R 34 E). Named on Hockett Peak (1956) 15' quadrangle.

Little Jackass Campground [MADERA]: *locality,* 6 miles northeast of Shuteye Peak (lat. 37°24' N, long. 119°20'10" W; near S line sec. 15, T 6 S, R 24 E); the place is along West Fork Jackass Creek. Named on Shuteye Peak (1953) 15' quadrangle.

Little Jackass Meadow: see **Soldier Meadow** [MADERA].

Little Jawbone Canyon [KERN]: *canyon,* drained by a stream that flows 4.5 miles to Jawbone Canyon nearly 1.5 miles northwest of Cross Mountain (lat. 35°17'35" N, long. 118°09'10" W; sec. 30, T 30 S, R 36 E). Named on Cross Mountain (1972) 7.5' quadrangle.

Little Jo Lake [FRESNO]: *lake,* 1150 feet long, 1.25 miles north-northeast of Blackcap Mountain (lat. 37°05'15" N, long. 118° 47' W). Named on Blackcap Mountain (1953) 15' quadrangle.

Little Kern: see **Little Kern River** [TULARE].

Little Kern Lake [TULARE]: *lake,* 1100 feet long, 6.5 miles west of Kern Peak (lat. 36°18'25" N, long. 118°24'15" W); the lake is less than 0.5 mile south of Kern Lake.

Named on Kern Peak (1956) 15' quadrangle. Called Little Lake on Olancha (1907) 30' quadrangle, but United States Board on Geographic Names (1938, p. 31) rejected this name for the feature. Called Royal Allen L. on Olmsted's (1900) map.

Little Kern Lake Creek [TULARE]: *stream,* flows 3 miles to Kern River 6.5 miles west of Kern Peak near Little Kern Lake (lat. 36° 18'10" N, long. 118°24'15" W). Named on Kern Peak (1956) 15' quadrangle.

Little Kern River [TULARE]: *stream,* flows 23 miles to Kern River 7 miles south-southwest of Hockett Peak (lat. 36°08' N, long. 118° 26'10" W). Named on Camp Nelson (1956), Hockett Peak (1956), and Mineral King (1956) 15' quadrangles. Called Little Kern on Olmsted's (1900) map.

Little Lake [FRESNO]: *lake,* 1000 feet long, 5.5 miles east-northeast of Dinkey Dome (lat. 37°09'30" N, long. 119°02'35" W; sec. 8, T 9 S, R 27 E). Named on Huntington Lake (1953) 15' quadrangle.

Little Lake: see **Little Kern Lake** [TULARE]; **Little Lakes** [TULARE].

Little Lakes [TULARE]: *lakes,* two, largest 550 feet long, 10.5 miles west-northwest of Triple Divide Peak (lat. 36°38'50" N, long, 118° 42'15" W). Named on Triple Divide Peak (1956) 15' quadrangle. Called Little Lake on Tehipite (1903) 30' quadrangle, but United States Board on Geographic Names (1989b, p. 2) rejected this form of the name.

Little Last Chance Canyon [KERN]: *canyon,* drained by a stream that flows less than 1 mile to Caliente Creek nearly 3 miles west of Loraine (lat. 35°18'20" N, long. 118°29'05" W; near W line sec. 19, T 30 S, R 33 E); the canyon is less than 1 mile west of Big Last Chance Canyon. Named on Loraine (1972) 7.5' quadrangle.

Little Matterhorn: see **Mineral Peak** [TULARE].

Little Moccasin Lake [FRESNO]: *lake,* 400 feet long, 8 miles south of Mount Abbot (lat. 37°16'25" N, long. 118°48'05" W); the lake is 400 feet southwest of Big Moccasin Lake. Named on Mount Abbot (1953) 15' quadrangle.

Little Oak Canyon [KERN]: *canyon,* drained by a stream that flows 2.5 miles to lowlands 2.25 miles east-southeast of Liebre Twins (lat. 34°56'20" N, long. 118°32'15" W). Named on Liebre Twins (1965) 7.5' quadrangle. Johnson's (1911) map has the name "Little Oak Creek" for the stream in the canyon.

Little Oak Creek: see **Little Oak Canyon** [KERN].

Little Oak Flat [FRESNO]: *area,* nearly 2 miles northeast of Coalinga Mineral Springs (lat. 36°09'55" N, long. 120°32'10" W; sec. 23, 26, T 20 S, R 13 E). Named on Sherman Peak (1969) 7.5' quadrangle. Called Oak Flat on Priest Valley (1944) 15' quadrangle.

Little Oak Flat [KERN]: *area,* 3.5 miles north-east of Caliente (lat. 35°19'50" N, long. 118°35'05" W; sec. 7, T 30 S, R 32 E). Named on Oiler Peak (1972) 7.5' quadrangle.

Little Oak Flat [TULARE]: *area,* 7 miles south of Kaweah (lat. 36° 22'10" N, long. 118°55'40" W; on N line sec. 15, T 18 S, R 28 E); the place is north of Oak Flat (1). Named on Kaweah (1957) 15' quadrangle.

Little Oak Spring [FRESNO]: *spring,* 3.5 miles east-northeast of Joaquin Rocks in Ragged Valley (lat. 36°20'05" N, long. 120°23'15" W; sec. 30, T 18 S, R 15 E). Named on Joaquin Rocks (1969) 7.5' quadrangle.

Little Panoche Creek [FRESNO]: *stream,* heads in San Benito County and flows 13 miles to lowlands 18 miles west-southwest of Firebaugh (lat. 36°47'30" N, long. 120°45'40" W; sec. 22, T 13 S, R 11 E). Named on Hammond Ranch (1956), Laguna Seca Ranch (1956), and Mercey Hot Springs (1969) 7.5' quadrangles. United States Board on Geographic Names (1933a, p. 466) rejected the name "Panochita Creek" for the feature. South Fork enters from the south 11 miles above the place that the main stream reaches lowlands; it heads in San Benito County, is 5 miles long, and is named on Mercey Hot Springs (1969) 7.5' quadrangle.

Little Panoche Valley [FRESNO]: *valley,* along Little Panoche Creek and South Fork Little Panoche Creek; partly in Merced and San Benito Counties (lat. 36°43'30" N, long. 120°52' W). Named on Cerro Colorado (1969), Laguna Seca Ranch (1956), Mercey Hot Springs (1969), and Ortigalita Peak (1969) 7.5' quadrangles. United States Board on Geographic Names (1933a, p. 466) rejected the name "Panochita Valley" for the feature.

Little Pete Meadow [FRESNO]: *area,* 6.5 miles east of Mount Goddard along Middle Fork Kings River (lat. 37°06'10" N, long. 118° 35'50" W); the place is 0.5 mile downstream from Big Pete Meadow. Named on Mount Goddard (1948) 15' quadrangle. According to Hanna (p. 120-121), the name probably commemorates Pierre "Little Pete" Giraud.

Little Posé Flat: see **Poso Flat** [KERN].

Little Poso Creek [KERN]: *stream,* flows 12 miles to Poso Creek 4.5 miles northwest of Democrat Hot Springs (lat. 35°34'20" N, long. 118°43'45" W; near SW cor. sec. 14, T 27 S, R 30 E). Named on Alta Sierra (1972), Democrat Hot Springs (1972), and Glennville (1972) 7.5' quadrangles.

Little Rancheria Creek [FRESNO]: *stream,* flows 5 miles to Rancheria Creek (3) 12 miles north-northwest of Hume (lat. 36°57'20" N, long. 118°57'30" W). Named on Tehipite Dome (1952) 15' quadrangle. Called North Fork on Tehipite (1903) 30' quadrangle.

Little Sand Meadow [TULARE]: *area,* 9.5 miles southwest of Triple Divide Peak (lat. 36°30'15" N, long. 118°39'25" W). Named on Triple Divide Peak (1956) 15' quadrangle. United States Board on Geographic Names (1938, p. 32) rejected the name "Sand Meadow" for the place.

Little Sandy Campground [MADERA]: *locality*, 7 miles north-northeast of Yosemite Forks (lat. 37°27'30" N, long. 119°34' W; sec. 33, T 5 S, R 22 E); the place is along Big Creek 1 mile upstream from Big Sandy Campground. Named on Bass Lake (1953) 15' quadrangle.

Little Sandy Creek [FRESNO]: *stream*, flows 4.5 miles to Big Sandy Creek nearly 1 mile east-northeast of Prather (lat. 37°02'30" N, long. 119°30'05" W; sec. 19, T 10 S, R 23 E). Named on Millerton Lake East (1965) 7.5' quadrangle.

Little Santa Maria Valley [KERN]: *valley*, center 5 miles west of McKittrick (lat. 35°18'35" N, long. 119°42'45" W). Named on Reward (1951) 7.5' quadrangle. Called Santa Maria Valley on McKittrick Summit (1959) and Olig (1943) 7.5' quadrangles. United States Board on Geographic Names (1970b, p. 2) listed the variant names "Santa Maria Valley" and "Santa Marie Valley" for the feature.

Little Shadow Lake: see **Ediza Lake** [MADERA].

Little Shuteye Pass [MADERA]: *pass*, 2 miles north-northwest of Shuteye Peak (lat. 37°22'45" N, long. 119°26'10" W; sec. 27, T 6 S, R 23 E); the pass is 2 miles east-southeast of Little Shuteye Peak. Named on Shuteye Peak (1953) 15' quadrangle.

Little Shuteye Peak [MADERA]: *peak*, 4 miles northwest of Shuteye Peak (lat. 37°23'40" N, long. 119°28'10" W; near E line sec. 20, T 6 S, R 23 E). Altitude 8362 feet. Named on Shuteye Peak (1953) 15' quadrangle.

Little Signal Hills [KERN]: *area*, 3 miles northwest of Maricopa (lat. 35°05'35" N, long. 119°26'35" W). Named on Maricopa (1951) 7.5' quadrangle.

Little Spanish Lake [FRESNO]: *lake*, 600 feet long, 10 miles north of Hume (lat. 36°55'40" N, long. 118°54'25" W); the lake is 1750 feet west of Spanish Lake (1). Named on Tehipite Dome (1952) 15' quadrangle.

Little Sycamore Canyon [KERN]:
(1) *canyon*, drained by a stream that flows 6.25 miles to lowlands 3.5 miles southeast of Arvin (lat. 35°10' N, long. 118°47'20" W; near SE cor. sec. 6, T 32 S, R 30 E); the canyon opens into lowlands 3 miles southwest of the mouth of Sycamore Canyon (1). Named on Arvin (1955) and Bear Mountain (1966) 7.5' quadrangles.
(2) *canyon*, drained by a stream that flows 4 miles to lowlands 11 miles southwest of Liebre Twins (lat. 34°50'10" N, long. 118°41'50" W; near E line sec. 29, T 9 N, R 17 W); the canyon opens into lowlands nearly 1 mile west-southwest of the mouth of Big Sycamore Canyon. Named on La Liebre Ranch (1965) 7.5' quadrangle.

Little Table Mountain [MADERA]: *ridge*, south- to south-southeast-trending, 3 miles long, 12 miles east-northeast of Trigo (lat. 36°59' N, long. 119°46' W). Named on Herndon (1965) and Raymond (1962) 15' quadrangles.

Little Tar Canyon [KINGS]: *canyon*, drained by a stream that flows 0.5 mile to Sunflower Valley 7.5 miles south of Avenal (lat. 35°53'35" N, long. 120°07'05" W; sec. 27, T 23 S, R 17 E). Named on Kettleman Plain (1953) 7.5' quadrangle.

Little Tar Canyon: see **Sulphur Spring Canyon** [KINGS] (2).

Little Tehipite Valley [FRESNO]: *valley*, 10 miles northeast of Hume along Middle Fork Kings River (lat. 36°53'15" N, long. 118°47'45" W); the place is 1.5 miles south-southwest of Tehipite Valley. Named on Tehipite Dome (1952) 15' quadrangle.

Little Tenant Spring [KERN]: *spring*, 2 miles north of Democrat Hot Springs (lat. 35°33'20" N, long. 118°40'05" W; near N line sec. 29, T 27 S, R 31 E); the spring is 0.5 mile southwest of Big Tenant Spring in a branch of Tenant Creek. Named on Democrat Hot Springs (1972) 7.5' quadrangle.

Little Trout Creek [TULARE]: *stream*, flows 4.5 miles to Trout Creek 12.5 miles east-northeast of Fairview (lat. 35°58'40" N, long. 118°17' W; near W line sec. 26, T 22 S, R 34 E). Named on Kernville (1956) 15' quadrangle.

Little Troy Meadow [TULARE]: *area*, 10.5 miles south-southwest of Monache Mountain along Mahogany Creek (lat. 36°03'35" N, long. 118°14'10" W; sec. 31, T 21 S, R 35 E); the place is 1 mile south of Troy Meadows. Named on Monache Mountain (1956) 15' quadrangle.

Little White Deer Creek: see **Mill Creek** [FRESNO-TULARE].

Little White Deer Valley: see **Mill Creek** [FRESNO-TULARE].

Little Whitney Meadow [TULARE]: *area*, 5.5 miles northwest of Kern Peak along Golden Trout Creek (lat. 36°22'20" N, long. 118°20'45" W; on W line sec. 7, T 18 S, R 34 E); the place is 6 miles southwest of Big Whitney Meadow. Named on Kern Peak (1956) 15' quadrangle. Called Long Mcadow on Olancha (1907) 30' quadrangle, but United States Board on Geographic Names (1938, p. 32) rejected this name for the feature.

Little Yosemite Soda Spring: see **Kern Lake** [TULARE].

Live Oak Campground [KERN]: *locality*, 0.5 mile southwest of the center of Wofford Heights (lat. 35°42'10" N, long. 118°27'35" W; near N line sec. 5, T 26 S, R 33 E). Named on Lake Isabella North (1972) 7.5' quadrangle.

Live Oak Canyon [KERN]: *canyon*, drained by a stream that flows 2 miles to Cummings Valley 4 miles northwest of Cummings Mountain (lat. 35°04'50" N, long. 118°37'15" W; near N line sec. 6, T 11 N, R 16 W). Named on Cummings Mountain (1966) 7.5' quadrangle.

Liveoak Canyon [KERN]: *canyon,* drained by a stream that flows 6 miles to lowlands 2.5 miles east of Grapevine (lat. 34°56' N, long. 118°52'50" W). Named on Grapevine (1958), Lebec (1958), and Pastoria Creek (1958) 7.5' quadrangles. The stream in the canyon was called Arroyo de las Encinas in the early days (Latta, 1976, p. 205).

Liveoak Canyon [TULARE]: *canyon,* drained by a stream that flows 1.5 miles to Dry Creek (1) 5.5 miles northeast of Woodlake (lat. 36°27'55" N, long. 119°01'30" W; near W line sec. 11, T 17 S, R 27 E). Named on Woodlake (1952) 7.5' quadrangle. Called General Canyon on Lemon Cove (1928) 7.5' quadrangle.

Liveoak Canyon: see **Ragle Canyon** [TULARE].

Live Oak Gulch [TULARE]: *canyon,* drained by a stream that flows 2.5 miles to North Fork Kaweah River 3 miles west-northwest of Yucca Mountain (lat. 36°35'35" N, long. 118°54'45" W; near W line sec. 26, T 15 S, R 28 E). Named on Giant Forest (1956) 15' quadrangle.

Live Oak Pass [TULARE]: *pass,* 4.5 miles west of Yucca Mountain (lat. 36°34'15" N, long. 118°57'05" W; at S line sec. 32, T 15 S, R 28 E); the pass is near the head of Live Oak Gulch. Named on Giant Forest (1956) 15' quadrangle.

Live Oak Spring [FRESNO]: *spring,* 4.5 miles northwest of Coalinga Mineral Springs (lat. 36°11'40" N, long. 120°36'40" W; sec. 18, T 20 S, R 13 E). Named on Sherman Peak (1969) 7.5' quadrangle.

Livermore Mountain: see **Bear Mountain** [KERN].

Livsey Canyon: see **Canyon del Gato-Montes** [KERN].

L Lake [FRESNO]: *lake,* 2400 feet long, 3.25 miles west-northwest of Mount Humphreys (lat. 37°17'45" N, long. 118°43'15" W; sec. 31, T 7 S, R 30 E). Named on Mount Tom (1949) 15' quadrangle, where the outline of the lake on the map resembles a backward letter "L."

Lloyd: see **Lloyd Meadows** [TULARE].

Lloyd Meadows [TULARE]: *area,* 7.5 miles southwest of Hockett Peak (lat. 36°08'40" N, long. 118°28'40" W). Named on Hockett Peak (1956) 15' quadrangle. Olancha (1907) 30' quadrangle has the name "Lloyd" at or near the place. According to Gudde (1949, p. 196), the name is for John W. Loyd, who ran sheep at the place in the 1870's. Tucker (p. 944) used the name "Lloyd Meadows Springs" for springs in the area.

Lloyd Meadows Creek [TULARE]: *stream,* flows 3.5 miles to Freeman Creek 8 miles southwest of Hockett Peak (lat. 36°08'15" N,

long. 118°28'35" W); the stream goes through Lloyd Meadows. Named on Hockett Peak (1956) 15' quadrangle.

Lloyd Meadows Springs: see **Lloyd Meadows** [TULARE].

Lobe Lakes [FRESNO]: *lakes,* largest 1200 feet long, 12 miles north of Blackcap Mountain (lat. 37°14'35" N, long. 118°45'20" W). Named on Blackcap Mountain (1953) 15' quadrangle.

Locans [FRESNO]: *locality,* nearly 5 miles northeast of Malaga along Southern Pacific Railroad (lat. 36°43'20" N, long. 119°39'45" W; near SW cor. sec. 11, T 14 S, R 21 E). Named on Malaga (1964) 7.5' quadrangle. Called Logan on Malaga (1923) 7.5' quadrangle.

Locked Gate Gulch [KERN]: *canyon,* drained by a stream that flows 5.5 miles to Rag Gulch 13 miles east of Delano (lat. 35°45'40" N, long. 119°00'50" W; near N line sec. 13, T 25 S, R 27 E). Named on Sand Canyon (1965) 7.5' quadrangle.

Lockwood Creek [FRESNO]: *stream,* flows 3 miles to South Fork Kings River 4.25 miles northeast of Hume (lat. 36°50'10" N, long. 118°52'10" W). Named on Tehipite Dome (1952) 15' quadrangle.

Loco Bill Canyon [KERN]: *canyon,* 4.5 miles long, along Rancheria Creek (2) above a point 4.5 miles south of Piute Peak (lat. 35°23'10" N, long. 118°23'15" W; sec. 24, T 29 S, R 33 E). Named on Claraville (1972) and Piute Peak (1972) 7.5' quadrangles.

Lodge [FRESNO]: *locality,* 24 miles southwest of Kaiser Peak along Big Creek (2) (lat. 37°02'35" N, long. 119°29'45" W; sec. 19, T 10 S, R 23 E). Named on Kaiser (1904) 30' quadrangle. Postal authorities established Lodge post office in 1888, discontinued it in 1899, reestablished it in 1902, moved it 3 miles north in 1903, and discontinued it in 1904 (Salley, p. 124).

Lodgepole [TULARE]: *locality,* 11 miles west of Triple Divide Peak along Marble Fork (lat. 36°36'15" N, long. 118°43'20" W; sec. 21, T 15 S, R 30 E). Named on Triple Divide Peak (1956) 15' quadrangle.

Logan: see **Locans** [FRESNO].

Logan Meadow [MADERA]: *area,* 5 miles east of Shuteye Peak (lat. 37°21' N, long. 118°20'10" W; in and near sec. 3, T 7 S, R 24 E). Named on Kaiser (1904) 30' quadrangle.

Logan Meadow Campground [MADERA]: *locality,* 5 miles east of Shuteye Peak along Chiquito Creek (lat. 37°21'05" N, long. 119°20'10" W; near N line sec. 3, T 7 S, R 24 E); the place is at Logan Meadow. Named on Shuteye Peak (1953) 15' quadrangle.

Log Bridge Campground [TULARE]: *locality,* 11 miles west of Triple Divide Peak along Marble Fork (lat. 36°36'20" N, long. 118°43'15" W; sec. 21, T 15 S, R 30 E). Named on Triple Divide Peak (1956) 15' quadrangle.

Log Cabin Meadow [TULARE]: *area,* 3.5 miles northeast of Camp Nelson (lat. 36°10'20" N, long. 118°33'40" W; sec. 24, T 20 S, R 31 E). Named on Camp Nelson (1956) 15' quadrangle. United States Board on Geographic Names (1967a, p. 9) rejected the name "Junction Meadow" for the place.

Log Corral Meadow [TULARE]: *area,* 1.25 miles east-southeast of Wilsonia (lat. 36°43'45" N, long. 118°56' W; near S line sec. 4, T 14 S, R 28 E). Named on Giant Forest (1956) 15' quadrangle.

Logger Point [FRESNO]: *ridge,* west-trending, 0.5 mile long, 7 miles east-southeast of Dunlap (lat. 36°42' N, long. 119°00' W). Named on Giant Forest (1956) 15' quadrangle, and on Miramonte (1966) 7.5' quadrangle.

Loggy Meadows [TULARE]: *area,* 5 miles northeast of Camp Nelson along Fish Creek (1) (lat. 36°11'10" N, long. 118°32'10" W; sec. 17, T 20 S, R 32 E). Named on Camp Nelson (1956) 15' quadrangle. United States Board on Geographic Names (1967a, p. 9) rejected the singular form "Loggy Meadow" for the name.

Log Meadow [TULARE]: *area,* 12 miles west-southwest of Triple Divide Peak (lat. 36°33'30" N, long. 118°44'30" W; sec. 5, T 16 S, R 30 E). Named on Triple Divide Peak (1956) 15' quadrangle. Tharps Log, a log made into a dwelling, is in the meadow. United States Board on Geographic Names (1933a, p. 469) rejected the names "Tharpe Meadow," "Tharpe's Log Meadow," and "Wolverton Meadow" for the place. The name "Wolverton" is from James Wolverton, the hunter who named General Sherman tree (Hanna, p. 357).

Lois [TULARE]: *locality,* 3.5 miles south of Porterville along Southern Pacific Railroad (lat. 36°01'05" N, long. 119°01'35" W; sec. 14, T 22 S, R 27 E). Named on Porterville (1951) 7.5' quadrangle.

Lois Lake [MADERA]: *lake,* 650 feet long, 4.25 miles northwest of Devils Postpile (lat. 37°40'30" N, long. 119°07'40" W). Named on Devils Postpile (1953) 15' quadrangle.

Lokern [KERN]: *locality,* 8 miles north-northeast of McKittrick along Southern Pacific Railroad (lat. 35°24' N, long. 119°32'30" W; near S line sec. 18, T 29 S, R 23 E). Named on Lokern (1954) 7.5' quadrangle.

Loma [TULARE]: *locality,* 5 miles south of Visalia along Atchison, Topeka and Santa Fe Railroad (lat. 36°15'25" N, long. 119°17'10" W; at S line sec. 20, T 19 S, R 25 E). Named on Visalia (1949) 7.5' quadrangle.

Loma Atravesada [FRESNO]: *ridge,* west- to northwest-trending, 2 miles long, 18 miles north-northwest of Coalinga (lat. 36°21'20" N, long. 120°31'45" W). Named on Santa Rita Peak (1969) 7.5' quadrangle. The peak called Three Sisters (2) is on the ridge, but United States Board on Geographic Names (1933a,

p. 470) rejected the name "Three Sisters" for the ridge itself.

Lomar Meadow [KERN]: *area,* near Claraville (lat. 35°26'40" N, long. 118°19'35" W; near E line sec. 4, T 29 S, R 34 E). Named on Claraville (1972) 7.5' quadrangle.

London [TULARE]: *town,* 2.5 miles east-northeast of Traver (lat. 36°28'30" N, long. 119°26'30" W; sec. 2, T 17 S, R 23 E). Named on Traver (1949, photorevised 1969) 7.5' quadrangle. Called New London on Visalia (1949) 15' quadrangle.

Lone Doe Lake [FRESNO]: *lake,* 550 feet long, 2 miles north-northwest of Blackcap Mountain (lat. 37°06' N, long. 118°48' W). Named on Blackcap Mountain (1953) 15' quadrangle.

Lone Oak Mountain [TULARE]: *peak,* 3 miles north of Woodlake (lat. 36°27'25" N, long. 119°06'05" W; near N line sec. 13, T 17 S, R 26 E). Altitude 1107 feet. Named on Woodlake (1952) 7.5' quadrangle.

Lone Oak Slough [KINGS]: *stream,* heads near Hanford and flows south 7.5 miles to a point 3 miles west of Guernsey (lat. 36°12'55" N, long. 119°41'45" W). Named on Guernsey (1929) and Hanford (1926) 7.5' quadrangles. Guernsey (1954) and Hanford (1954) 7.5' quadrangles have the name on a dry watercourse.

Lone Pine: see **McFarland** [KERN].

Lone Pine Canyon [FRESNO]: *canyon,* 1 mile long, drained by a stream that joins Kings River 5.5 miles west-southwest of Balch Camp (lat. 36°52'15" N, long. 119°12'40" W; sec. 23, T 12 S, R 25 E). Named on Patterson Mountain (1952) 15' quadrangle.

Lone Pine Canyon [TULARE]: *canyon,* drained by a stream that flows 1 mile to White River (1) 3 miles south-southwest of California Hot Springs (lat. 35°50'20" N, long. 118°41'45" W; sec. 13, T 24 S, R 30 E). Named on California Hot Springs (1958) 15' quadrangle.

Lone Pine Creek [TULARE]: *stream,* flows 4.5 miles to join Hamilton Creek and form Middle Fork Kaweah River 4.5 miles west-southwest of Triple Divide Peak (lat. 36°33'50" N, long. 118°36'05" W); the stream goes through Lone Pine Meadow. Named on Triple Divide Peak (1956) 15' quadrangle. United States Board on Geographic Names (1968b, p. 8) rejected the name "Middle Fork Kaweah River" for the stream.

Lone Pine Meadow [TULARE]: *area,* 2.5 miles west-southwest of Triple Divide Peak (lat. 36°35' N, long. 118°34'15" W); the place is along Lone Pine Creek. Named on Triple Divide Peak (1956) 15' quadrangle. William R. Dudley called the feature Heather Meadow in 1896; the name "Lone Pine" also has the form "Lonepine" (Browning 1986, p. 130).

Lone Pine Mountain [TULARE]: *peak,* 7.25 miles north-northwest of California Hot Springs (lat. 35°58'10" N, long. 118°44'10" W; near E line sec. 33, T 22 S, R 30 E). Altitude 5072 feet. Named on California Hot Springs (1958) 15' quadrangle.

Lone Star [FRESNO]: *locality,* 3.25 miles east-northeast of Malaga along Atchison, Topeka and Santa Fe Railroad (lat. 36°42' N, long. 119°40'45" W; near W line sec. 22, T 14 S, R 21 E). Named on Malaga (1964) 7.5' quadrangle. Called Lonestar on California Mining Bureau's (1909b) map. Postal authorities established Lonestar post office in 1891, discontinued it in 1895, reestablished it in 1900, and discontinued it in 1910; settlers at the place came from the Lone Star State of Texas (Salley, p. 125).

Lone Tree Canyon: see **Pine Tree Canyon** [KERN].

Lonetree Channel [FRESNO]: *water feature,* diverges from Fowler Switch Canal and extends for 7 miles to a ditch 1.5 miles south of Sanger (lat. 36°40'40" N, long. 119°33'35" W). Named on Sanger (1965) 7.5' quadrangle. Grunsky (p. 71) called the feature Lone Tree Slough, and gave the name "Kip Slough" as an alternate; he noted that it was a natural watercourse that became an important distributary of water from a canal system. The name is from a foothill white oak that grew on the west bank of the feature northeast of present Sanger (about on N line sec. 14, T 14 S, R 22 E) (Teilman and Shafer, p. 36). Grunsky (p. 71) mentioned a natural watercourse called Burns Slough that was a tributary of Kip Slough (present Lonetree Channel).

Lone Tree Slough: see **Lonetree Channel** [FRESNO].

Lone Tree Well [KERN]: *well,* 9.5 miles north of the village of Lost Hills (lat. 35°45'10" N, long. 119°39'20" W; sec. 13, T 25 S, R 21 E). Named on Lone Tree Well (1954) 7.5' quadrangle.

Lone Willow Slough [MADERA]: *stream,* diverges northwest from San Joaquin River 18 miles southwest of Madera (lat. 36°46'25" N, long. 120°17'10" W; sec. 25, T 13 S, R 15 E) and flows 23 miles to an artificial watercourse. Named on Firebaugh (1956), Mendota Dam (1956), and Poso Farm (1962) 7.5' quadrangles.

Long Branch [TULARE]: *stream,* flows 5 miles to South Fork Tule River 7.25 miles southsouthwest of Springville (lat. 36°01'40" N, long. 118°50'50" W; sec. 9, T 22 S, R 29 E). Named on Globe (1956) 7.5' quadrangle.

Long Canyon [FRESNO]: *canyon,* 3 miles long, opens into an unnamed valley 6.5 miles west of Red Slate Mountain (lat. 37°30'20" N, long. 118°59'05" W). Named on Kaiser Peak (1953), Mount Abbot (1953), and Mount Morrison (1953) 15' quadrangles.

Long Canyon [KERN]: *canyon,* drained by a stream that flows 3.25 miles to lowlands 4 miles southwest of Weldon (lat. 35°37'15" N, long. 118°20'20" W). Named on Woolstalf Creek (1972) 7.5' quadrangle.

Long Canyon [TULARE]:

(1) *canyon,* 2 miles long, along Long Canyon Creek above a point 3.25 miles northwest of Monache Mountain (lat. 36°14' N, long. 118°14'30" W; sec. 36, T 19 S, R 34 E). Named on Monache Mountain (1956) and Olancha (1956) 15' quadrangles.

(2) *canyon,* drained by a stream that flows nearly 5 miles to Middle Fork Tule River 3.25 miles east-northeast of Springville (lat. 36°08'35" N, long. 118°45'30" W; sec. 32, T 20 S, R 30 E). Named on Camp Nelson (1956) and Springville (1957) 15' quadrangles.

(3) *canyon,* drained by a stream that flows 7 miles to Sacatar Meadow 14 miles north of Lamont Peak (lat. 35°59'40" N, long. 118°04'45" W). Named on Monache Mountain (1956) 15' quadrangle.

Long Canyon: see **Long Hollow** [FRESNO].

Long Canyon Creek [TULARE]: *stream,* flows 5 miles to Ninemile Creek 6 miles east of Hockett Peak (lat. 36°13'15" N, long. 118°16'50" W; at N line sec. 3, T 20 S, R 34 E); the stream drains Long Canyon (1). Named on Hockett Peak (1956) 15' quadrangle.

Long Creek [MADERA]: *stream,* flows 5 miles to North Fork San Joaquin River 8 miles west of Devils Postpile (lat. 37°38'35" N, long. 119°13'40" W); the stream heads near Long Mountain. Named on Devils Postpile (1953) and Merced Peak (1953) 15' quadrangles.

Long Creek [TULARE]: *stream,* flows 7.25 miles to lowlands 2 miles west of Cliff Peak (lat. 36°33'35" N, long. 119°12'35" W; sec. 1, T 16 S, R 25 E); the stream is in Long Valley (1). Named on Stokes Mountain (1966) and Tucker Mountain (1966) 7.5' quadrangles.

Long Hollow [FRESNO]: *canyon,* drained by a stream that flows 6.5 miles to Warthan Creek 7.5 miles west-southwest of Coalinga (lat. 36°05'05" N, long. 120°28'40" W; sec. 20, T 21 S, R 14 E). Named on Alcalde Hills (1969), Curry Mountain (1969), and Sherman Peak (1969) 7.5' quadrangles. Called Long Canyon on Coalinga (1912) 30' quadrangle.

Long Hollow [MADERA]: *canyon,* nearly 3 miles long, opens into the canyon of Coarse Gold Creek 7 miles east-southeast of Knowles (lat. 37°09'40" N, long. 119°46'25" W; sec. 10, T 9 S, R 20 E). Named on Knowles (1962) 7.5' quadrangle.

Long Lake [FRESNO]: *lake,* 1400 feet long, 1 mile north-northeast of Kaiser Peak (lat. 37°18'30" N, long. 119°10'40" W; sec. 19, T 7 S, R 26 E). Named on Kaiser Peak (1953) 15' quadrangle.

Longley Pass [TULARE]: *pass,* 13 miles northwest of Mount Whitney on Great Western Divide (lat. 36°41'20" N, long. 118°28'45" W). Named on Mount Whitney (1956) 15' quadrangle. The name, given in 1895, commemorates Howard Longley, leader of the group that discovered the pass (United States Board on Geographic Names, 1933a, p. 472).

Long Meadow [MADERA]:
(1) *area,* 8.5 miles north-northeast of Yosemite Forks (lat. 37°29'10" N, long. 119°34'45" W; near E line sec. 20, T 5 S, R 22 E). Named on Bass Lake (1953) 15' quadrangle.
(2) *area,* 9 miles north of Shuteye Peak (lat. 37°29' N, long. 119° 25' W; sec. 23, T 5 S, R 23 E). Named on Shuteye Peak (1953) 15' quadrangle.
(3) *area,* 4.5 miles north-northeast of Shuteye Peak (lat. 37°24'30" N, long. 119°23'45" W; near W line sec. 18, T 6 S, R 24 E). Named on Shuteye Peak (1953) 15' quadrangle.

Long Meadow [FRESNO]:
(1) *area,* 8 miles northeast of Dinkey Dome (lat. 37°12' N, long. 119°02' W). Named on Huntington Lake (1953) 15' quadrangle.
(2) *area,* 9 miles west-northwest of Blackcap Mountain (lat. 37°07'45" N, long. 118°55'10" W; sec. 21, T 9 S, R 28 E). Named on Blackcap Mountain (1953) 15' quadrangle. On Mount Goddard (1912) 30' quadrangle, the name has the plural form "Long Meadows."
(3) *area,* at and southwest of Hume (lat. 36°46'45" N, long. 118°55'25" W; in and near sec. 22, T 13 S, R 28 E). Named on Tehipite Dome (1952) 15' quadrangle.

Long Meadow [TULARE]:
(1) *area,* 13 miles south-southwest of Mineral King along North Fork of Middle Fork Tule River (lat. 36°16'30" N, long. 118° 40' W). Named on Mineral King (1956) 15' quadrangle.
(2) *area,* 11 miles west of Triple Divide Peak (lat. 36°35'30" N, long. 118°44'10" W; on·E line sec. 29, T 15 S, R 30 E). Named on Triple Divide Peak (1956) 15' quadrangle.
(3) *area,* 8.5 miles northeast of California Hot Springs (lat. 35° 58'45" N, long. 118°34'55" W; mainly in sec. 36, T 22 S, R 31 E). Named on California Hot Springs (1958) 15' quadrangle.
(4) *area,* 11 miles southeast of Fairview along Fay Creek (lat. 35° 49'30" N, long. 118°20'20" W; sec. 20, T 24 S, R 34 E). Named on Kernville (1956) 15' quadrangle.

Long Meadow: see **Ferguson Meadow** [TULARE]; **Little Whitney Meadow** [TULARE]; **Long Meadow Creek** [FRESNO]; **Rock Meadow** [FRESNO].

Long Meadow Creek [FRESNO]: *stream,* flows 2.5 miles to North Fork Kings River 14 miles north-northwest of Hume (lat. 36°58'10" N, long. 118°59'30" W). Named on Patterson Mountain (1952) and Tehipite Dome (1952) 15' quadrangles. Dinuba (1924) 30' quadrangle shows the stream in a valley called Long Meadow. West Fork enters from the west nearly 1 mile upstream from the mouth of the main stream; it is 1.5 miles long and is named on Patterson Mountain (1952) 15' quadrangle.

Long Meadow Creek [MADERA]: *stream,* flows 2.5 miles to Rainier Creek 8 miles north-northeast of Yosemite Forks (lat. 37° 28'55"

N, long. 119°35'55" W; sec. 19, T 5 S, R 22 E); the stream goes through Long Meadow (1). Named on Bass Lake (1953) 15' quadrangle.

Long Meadow Creek [TULARE]: *stream,* flows 2.5 miles to Bone Creek 11 miles northeast of California Hot Springs (lat. 35°59'55" N, long. 118°32'30" W; sec. 20, T 22 S, R 32 E); the stream heads at Long Meadow (3). Named on California Hot Springs (1958) 15' quadrangle.

Long Mountain [MADERA]: *peak,* 6 miles east-northeast of Merced Peak (lat. 37°40'05" N, long. 119°17'40" W). Altitude 11,502 feet. Named on Merced Peak (1953) 15' quadrangle.

Long Mountain [TULARE]: *ridge,* south-trending, 6 miles long, 6 miles south-southeast of Auckland (lat. 36°30' N, long. 119°02'50" W). Named on Auckland (1966) and Woodlake (1952) 7.5' quadrangles.

Long Ridge [MADERA]: *ridge,* south-trending, 2.5 miles long, 15 miles south of Shuteye Peak (lat. 37°08'15" N, long. 119°28'30" W). Named on Shaver Lake (1953) 15' quadrangle.

Long Stringer [TULARE]:
(1) *stream,* flows 1.5 miles to an unnamed stream 2.5 miles north-northwest of Olancha Peak (lat. 36°18'10" N, long. 118°07'55" W; sec. 1, T 19 S, R 35 E). Named on Olancha (1956) 15' quadrangle.
(2) *stream,* flows 3 miles to Long Canyon Creek 6.5 miles east of Hockett Peak (lat. 36°13'55" N, long. 118°16'20" W). Named on Hockett Peak (1956) and Kern Peak (1956) 15' quadrangles.

Long Tom: see **Long Tom Gulch** [KERN].

Long Tom Gulch [KERN]: *canyon,* drained by a stream that flows 6.5 miles to Poso Creek nearly 5 miles west-southwest of Pine Mountain (lat. 35°31'40" N, long. 118°50'30" W; near N line sec. 3, T 28 S, R 29 E). Named on Pine Mountain (1965) 7.5' quadrangle. The stream in the canyon is called Pine Mountain Creek on Woody (1952) 15' quadrangle, which has the name "Long Tom Gulch" for a branch of present Long Tom Gulch (in sec. 26, T 27 S, R 29 E). United States Board on Geographic Names (1966b, p. 5) rejected the names "Pine Mountain Creek" and "Mountain Creek" for present Long Tom Gulch. A mining camp called Long Tom was situated along Pine Mountain Creek about 1.5 miles north of Poso Creek (Boyd, p. 159).

Long Top [FRESNO]: *ridge,* north-northeast-trending, 2 miles long, 8.5 miles west-north-west of Blackcap Mountain (lat. 37°06' N, long. 118°56'15" W). Named on Blackcap Mountain (1953) 15' quadrangle.

Long Valley [TULARE]:
(1) *valley,* along Long Creek above a point 3.25 miles north-northeast of Cliff Peak (lat. 36°36' N, long. 119°11'20" W; at S line sec. 19, T 15 S, R 26 E). Named on Stokes Mountain (1966) and Tucker Mountain (1966) 7.5' quadrangles.

(2) *valley,* 4 miles long, 7 miles northwest of Lamont Peak (lat. 35° 51'30" N, long. 118°08' W). Named on Lamont Peak (1956) 15' quadrangle.

Lonsmith [KERN]: *locality,* 5 miles east-south-east of downtown Bakersfield along the railroad (lat. 35°20'25" N, long. 118°55'20" W; at S line sec. 1, T 30 S, R 28 E). Named on Lamont (1954) 7.5' quadrangle.

Lookout Hill [KERN]: *hill,* 9 miles north-north-east of Rosamond (lat. 34°59' N, long. 118°05'45" W; at SE cor. sec. 1, T 10 N, R 12 W). Altitude 2744 feet. Named on Bissell (1973) 7.5' quadrangle.

Lookout Mountain [TULARE]: *peak,* 11.5 miles south of Hockett Peak (lat. 36°03'30" N, long. 118°22'30" W). Altitude 9722 feet. Named on Hockett Peak (1956) 15' quadrangle.

Lookout Peak [FRESNO]: *peak,* 17 miles southwest of Marion Peak (lat. 36°46'25" N, long. 118°42'55" W). Altitude 8531 feet. Named on Marion Peak (1953) 15' quadrangle. E.C. Winchell called the feature Winchell's Peak in 1868 for his cousin, Alexander Winchell, State Geologist of Michigan; later L.A. Winchell gave the name "Mount Winchell" to another feature, and the name "Winchell" was lost to present Lookout Peak (Browning 1986, p. 131).

Loop: see **The Loop** [KERN].

Loper Peak [FRESNO]: *peak,* nearly 7 miles west-southwest of Blackcap Mountain (lat. 37°02'20" N, long. 118°54'20" W; on S line sec. 22, T 10 S, R 28 E). Altitude 10,059 feet. Named on Blackcap Mountain (1953) 15' quadrangle. The name commemorates John W. Loper, a cattleman who came to Fresno County in 1883 (Browning 1986, p. 131).

Lopez Flats [KERN]: *area,* 3.5 miles west-southwest of Liebre Twins (lat. 34°56'20" N, long. 118°37'50" W; on S line sec. 19, T 10 N, R 16 E). Named on Winters Ridge (1966) 7.5' quadrangle.

Loraine [KERN]: *village,* 12 miles north of Tehachapi (lat. 35°18'15" N, long. 118°26'05" W; sec. 21, T 30 S, R 33 E). Named on Loraine (1972) 7.5' quadrangle. Emerald Mountain (1943) 15' quadrangle shows the place situated nearly 1 mile west of the present site (sec. 20, T 30 S, R 33 E). Postal authorities established Paris post office in 1903, changed the name to Loraine in 1912, discontinued it in 1918, reestablished it in 1922, and discontinued it in 1926 (Frickstad, p. 57, 58). United States Board on Geographic Names (1975b, p. 10) listed the names "Paris" and "Paris-Loraine" as variants. French and Alsatian miners gave the names "Paris" and "Loraine" to the place (Bailey, 1962, p. 50). California Mining Bureau's (1917c) map shows a place called Amalie located 2.5 miles southwest of Loraine. Postal authorities established Amalie post office in 1894, moved it 2 miles south in

1902, moved it 1.25 miles southeast in 1906, and discontinued it in 1908; the name was from Amalie mine (Salley, p. 6), which Loraine (1972) 7.5' quadrangle shows situated less than 1 mile northeast of Loraine.

Lort [TULARE]: *locality,* 3.5 miles north-north-west of Exeter along Southern Pacific Railroad (lat. 36°20'30" N, long. 119°09'10" W; near SE cor. sec. 21, T 18 S, R 26 E). Named on Exeter (1952) 15' quadrangle.

Los Alamitos: see **Sinks of the Tejon**, under **Tejon Creek** [KERN].

Los Alamos Creek [KERN]: *stream,* flows 3.5 miles to lowlands 11.5 miles southwest of Liebre Twins (lat. 34°50' N, long. 118°42'40" W; near SW cor. sec. 29, T 9 N, R 17 W). Named on La Liebre Ranch (1965) 7.5' quadrangle. The canyon of the stream is called Cottonwood Canyon on Neenach (1943) 15' quadrangle.

Los Alamos y Agua Caliente [KERN]: *land grant,* in southwest part of Tehachapi Mountains. Named on Lebec (1958), Pastoria Creek (1958), and Winters Ridge (1966) 7.5' quadrangles. Francisco Lopez and others received 6 leagues in 1846; Agustin Olivera and others claimed 26,626 acres patented in 1866 (Cowan, p. 14).

Los Gatos Creek [FRESNO]: *stream,* flows 26 miles to Pleasant Valley 5.5 miles northwest of Coalinga (lat. 36°11'45" N, long. 120°25'45" W; sec. 10, T 20 S, R 14 E). Named on Alcalde Hills (1969), Coalinga (1956), Guijarral Hills (1956), San Benito Mountain (1969), Santa Rita Peak (1969), and Sherman Peak (1969) 7.5' quadrangles. Called Las Gatas Creek on Parke's (1854-1855) map, and called Arrojo los Gates on Goddard's (1857) map. The coarse of the stream in San Joaquin Valley is called Arroyo Passajero on Guijarral Hills (1936) 7.5' quadrangle. United States Board on Geographic Names (1933a, p. 475) rejected the names "Arroyo las Gatos," "Las Gatas Creek," and "Polvodero Creek" for the stream, and later (1964c, p. 15) rejected the names "Arroyo Passajero" and "Arroyo Poso de Chane" as well.

Los Jinetes [KINGS]: *peaks,* 3 miles east-north-east of Avenal (lat. 36°01' N, long. 120°04'45" W; sec. 13, T 22 S, R 17 E). Named on La Cima (1963) 7.5' quadrangle.

Los Lobos Creek [KERN]: *stream,* flows 8 miles to lowlands 7.5 miles northwest of Eagle Rest Peak (lat. 34°59'05" N, long. 119° 13'35" W; sec. 4, T 10 N, R 22 W). Named on Conner SW (1955) and Eagle Rest Peak (1942) 7.5' quadrangles.

Los Medanos [KINGS]: *ridge,* southeast-trending, 0.5 mile long, 2 miles south of Kettleman City (lat. 35°58'50" N, long. 119°57'55" W). Named on Los Viejos (1954) 7.5' quadrangle. Sand dunes that cover the side of the ridge account for the name (United States Board on Geographic Names, 1933b, p. 18)—

medanos means "sand banks" or "dunes" in Spanish.

Los Morones [KERN]: *ridge,* southeast-trending, less than 1 mile long, 11 miles north-northwest of Blackwells Corner (lat. 35°45'55" N, long. 119°54'40" W; sec. 10, T 25 S, R 19 E). Named on Avenal Gap (1954) 7.5' quadrangle. United States Board on Geographic Names (1933b, p. 18-19) noted that *los morones* means "little hills" in Spanish.

Los Nietos: see **Lake Los Nietos** [FRESNO].

Los Palmas: see **Las Palmas** [FRESNO].

Los Piramidos: see **Pyramid Hills** [KERN-KINGS].

Lost Canyon [FRESNO]:
(1) *canyon,* 2.5 miles long, 10 miles west of Blackcap Mountain (lat. 37°03'15" N, long. 118°58'20" W); the canyon is 1 mile west of Lost Peak. Named on Blackcap Mountain (1953) 15' quadrangle.
(2) *canyon,* 1.5 miles long, drained by a stream that joins Middle Fork Kings River 11 miles west of Marion Peak (lat. 36°56'25" N, long. 118°43'05" W). Named on Marion Peak (1953) 15' quadrangle.

Lost Canyon [KERN]: *canyon,* drained by a stream that flows 4.5 miles to Pleito Creek 3 miles east-northeast of Eagle Rest Peak (lat. 34°56' N, long. 119°05'20" W; near N line sec. 26, T 10 N, R 21 W). Named on Pleito Hills (1958) 7.5' quadrangle.

Lost Canyon [TULARE]: *canyon,* drained by a stream that flows 4.5 miles to Big Arroyo 14 miles northwest of Kern Peak (lat. 36°27'35" N, long. 118°28'10" W). Named on Kern Peak (1956) and Mineral King (1956) 15' quadrangles. A sheepherder and his sheep were lost in the canyon for six days (Browning 1986, p. 132).

Lost Creek [FRESNO]: *stream,* flows 3.5 miles to Big Creek (2) 9 miles south-southwest of Dinkey Dome (lat. 37°00'20" N, long. 119°13'10" W; sec. 2, T 11 S, R 25 E); the stream heads in Lost Meadow (1). Named on Huntington Lake (1953) 15' quadrangle.

Lost Creek [TULARE]: *stream,* flows 8.5 miles to South Fork Kern River 10.5 miles south-southeast of Monache Mountain (lat. 36°03'40" N, long. 118°07'50" W). Named on Monache Mountain (1956) 15' quadrangle.

Lost Dog Lake [MADERA]: *lake,* 300 feet long, 2.25 miles west-northwest of Devils Postpile (lat. 37°38'20" N, long. 119°07' W). Named on Devils Postpile (1953) 15' quadrangle.

Lost Hills [KERN]:
(1) *ridge,* southeast-trending, 12 miles long, center 7.5 miles west-northwest of the village of Lost Hills (lat. 35°40' N, long. 119°46'15" W). Named on Antelope Plain (1954), Lost Hills (1953), and Lost Hills NW (1954) 7.5' quadrangles. According to one account, the name is from the apparent disappearance of the ridge as it is approached (Hanna, p. 176).
(2) *village,* 42 miles west-northwest of Bakers-field (lat. 35°36'55" N, long. 119°41'20" W; at NE cor. sec. 3, T 27 S, R 21 E); the village is east of the ridge of the same name. Named on Lost Hills (1953) 7.5' quadrangle. Postal authorities established Lost Hills post office in 1911, discontinued it in 1912, reestablished it in 1913, and moved it 0.5 mile mile west in 1937 (Salley, p. 128). They established Cuttens post office, named for Charles R. Cuttens, first postmaster, in 1911 and discontinued it in 1913, when they moved it 10 miles east and reestablished it as Lost Hills post office (Salley, p. 54).

Lost Keys Lakes [FRESNO]: *lakes,* three, each about 750 feet long, 2 miles east of Double Peak (lat. 37°30'50" N, long. 119°00'20" W). Named on Devils Postpile (1953) 15' quadrangle. The group comprises Lower Lost Keyes Lake, Middle Lost Keyes Lake, and Upper Lost Keys Lake (United States Board on Geographic Names, 1971a, p. 2).

Lost Lake [FRESNO]:
(1) *lake,* 850 feet long, 12.5 miles northwest of Blackcap Mountain (lat. 37°12'10" N, long. 118°56'45" W; sec. 31, T 8 S, R 28 E). Named on Blackcap Mountain (1953) 15' quadrangle.
(2) *lake,* nearly 0.5 mile long, 7 miles north-northwest of Clovis near San Joaquin River (lat. 36°58' N, long. 119°44'10" W). Named on Friant (1964) 7.5' quadrangle.

Lost Lake [MADERA]:
(1) *lake,* 750 feet long, 10 miles north of Shuteye Peak (lat. 37°29'45" N, long. 119°27'40" W; sec. 16, T 5 S, R 23 E). Named on Shuteye Peak (1953) 15' quadrangle.
(2) *lake,* 500 feet long, nearly 9 miles west of Devils Postpile (lat. 37°38'10" N, long. 119°14'30" W). Named on Devils Postpile (1953) 15' quadrangle.

Lost Lake [TULARE]: *lake,* 1000 feet long, 11.5 miles west-northwest of Triple Divide Peak (lat. 36°40'25" N, long. 118°42'15" W). Named on Triple Divide Peak (1956) 15' quadrangle.

Lost Lake Creek [MADERA]: *stream,* flows 1 mile to Mugler Creek nearly 10 miles north of Shuteye Peak (lat. 37°29'25" N, long. 119°26'40" W; near SW cor. sec. 15, T 5 S, R 23 E); the stream heads at Lost Lake (1). Named on Shuteye Peak (1953) 15' quadrangle.

Lost Lakes [FRESNO]: *lakes,* largest 1000 feet long, 8.5 miles north-northeast of Mount Goddard (lat. 37°13'25" N, long. 118°41'15" W). Named on Mount Goddard (1948) 15' quadrangle. Art Schober chose the name because the lakes are so well hidden (Browning 1986, p. 132).

Lost Meadow [FRESNO]:
(1) *area,* 6.5 miles south-southwest of Dinkey Dome (lat. 37°02' N, long. 119°11'05" W; on W line sec. 30, T 10 S, R 26 E); the place is near the head of Lost Creek. Named on Huntington Lake (1953) 15' quadrangle.
(2) *area,* 11 miles north of Hume (lat. 36°56'35"

N, long. 118°56'10" W). Named on Tehipite Dome (1952) 15' quadrangle.

(3) *area,* 8 miles east-southeast of Hume (lat. 36°45'10" N, long. 118°46'50" W). Named on Tehipite Dome (1952) 15' quadrangle.

Lost Meadows [TULARE]: *area,* about 4.5 miles south-southeast of Monache Mountain (lat. 36°08'30" N, long. 118°10'15" W; mainly in sec. 34, T 20 S, R 35 E). Named on Monache Mountain (1956) 15' quadrangle.

Lost Peak [FRESNO]: *peak,* 9.5 miles west of Blackcap Mountain (lat. 37°02'50" N, long. 118°57'40" W; sec. 19, T 10 S, R 28 E); the peak is nearly 1 mile east of Lost Canyon (1). Altitude 8476 feet. Named on Blackcap Mountain (1953) 15' quadrangle.

Lost Trout Creek [TULARE]: *stream,* flows 1.5 miles to Long Canyon Creek 7 miles east of Hockett Peak (lat. 36°13'35" N, long. 118°15'35" W). Named on Hockett Peak (1956) 15' quadrangle.

Lost Trout Meadow: see **Dry Meadows** [TULARE].

Los Tulares: see "Regional setting"; **Tulare Lake** [KINGS].

Lost Valley: see **Blaney Meadows** [FRESNO].

Los Viejos [KINGS]: *ridge,* south-southeast-trending, 4 miles long, 5 miles south of Kettleman City (lat. 35°56' N, long. 119°56'45" W). Named on Los Viejos (1954) 7.5' quadrangle. The name refers to the ridge being physiographically older than nearby hills—*los viejos* means "the old men" in Spanish (United States Board on Geographic Names, 1933b, p. 19).

Los Yeguas Creek: see **Yeguas Creek** [KERN].

Lou Beverly Lake [FRESNO]: *lake,* 900 feet long. 6.5 miles southwest of Mount Abbot along South Fork Bear Creek (2) (lat. 37° 19' N, long. 118°51'35" W). Named on Mount Abbot (1953) 15' quadrangle.

Lousy Spring [FRESNO]: *spring,* 4 miles east of Balch Camp (lat. 36°53'45" N, long. 119°02'40" W; near SE cor. sec. 8, T 12 S, R 27 E). Named on Patterson Mountain (1952) 15' quadrangle.

Lovejoy Lake: see **Packsaddle Lake** [FRESNO].

Lovel Canyon [KINGS]: *canyon,* drained by a stream that flows 5 miles to Avenal Canyon 10 miles south-southwest of Avenal (lat. 35°51'40" N, long. 120°11' W; near NE cor. sec. 12, T 24 S, R 16 E). Named on Tent Hills (1942) 7.5' quadrangle. On Cholame (1917) 30' quadrangle, the stream in the canyon is called Little Avenal Creek.

Lovell: see **Calgro** [TULARE].

Lower Araujo Spring [KERN]: *spring,* nearly 6 miles west-southwest of Liebre Twins (lat. 34°55'55" N, long. 118°40'10" W); the spring is 1550 feet west-southwest of Upper Araujo Spring. Named on Winters Ridge (1966) 7.5' quadrangle.

Lower Beck Spring [KERN]: *spring,* 4.5 miles

northeast of Caliente (lat. 35°20'15" N, long. 118°34' W; near N line sec. 8, T 30 S, R 32 E); the spring is in Beck Canyon 0.5 mile south of Upper Beck Spring. Named on Oiler Peak (1972) 7.5' quadrangle.

Lower Boiler Spring [KERN]: *spring,* nearly 7 miles east of Caliente (lat. 35°16'40" N, long. 118°30'45" W; sec. 35, T 30 S, R 32 E); the spring is 0.5 mile north-northwest of Boiler Spring. Named on Oiler Peak (1972) 7.5' quadrangle.

Lower Chiquito Campground [MADERA]: *locality,* 5 miles north-northeast of Shuteye Peak (lat. 37°24'50" N, long. 119°23' W; near N line sec. 18, T 6 S, R 24 E); the place is along Chiquito Creek 7 miles downstream from Upper Chiquito Campground. Named on Shuteye Peak (1953) 15' quadrangle.

Lower Cow Chip Spring [KERN]: *spring,* 7.25 miles west of Liebre Twins (lat. 34°57'10" N, long. 118°41'45" W; at S line sec. 9, T 10 N, R 17 W); the spring is 1150 feet south-southeast of Cow Chip Spring. Named on Winters Ridge (1966) 7.5' quadrangle.

Lower Desolation Lake [FRESNO]: *lake,* 1750 feet long, 2 miles west-southwest of Mount Humphreys in Humphreys Basin (lat. 37° 15'35" N, long. 118°42'25" W); the lake is 0.5 mile south of Desolation Lake. Named on Mount Tom (1949) 15' quadrangle.

Lower Falls [MADERA]: *waterfall,* 2 miles south of Devils Postpile on Middle Fork San Joaquin River (lat. 37°35'40" N, long. 119°05'15" W). Named on Devils Postpile (1953) 15' quadrangle.

Lower Funston Meadow: see **Funston Meadow** [TULARE].

Lower Grapes Spring [KERN]: *spring,* 7 miles east of Caliente (lat. 35°17' N, long. 118°30'05" W; near NW cor. sec. 36, T 30 S, R 32 E); the spring is 0.25 mile east-southeast of Upper Grapes Spring. Named on Oiler Peak (1972) 7.5' quadrangle.

Lower Hog Camp Spring [KERN]: *spring,* nearly 2 miles north-northwest of Caliente (lat. 35°18'45" N, long. 118°38'35" W); the spring is 0.5 mile south-southwest of Hog Camp Spring. Named on Bena (1972) 7.5' quadrangle.

Lower Honeymoon Lake [FRESNO]: *lake,* 1150 feet long, 9.5 miles south of Mount Abbot (lat. 37°15'05" N, long. 118°45'55" W); the lake is 0.25 mile north of Upper Honeymoon Lake. Named on Mount Abbot (1953) 15' quadrangle.

Lower Hopkins Lake [FRESNO]: *lake,* 900 feet long, 5.25 miles north-northwest of Mount Abbot (lat. 35°27'20" N, long. 118°49'40" W); the lake is 1.5 miles south-southeast of Upper Hopkins Lakes at the head of a fork of Hopkins Creek. Named on Mount Abbot (1953) 15' quadrangle.

Lower Horsethief Lake [FRESNO]: *lake,* 450 feet long, 4.5 miles west of Kaiser Peak (lat.

37°17'15" N, long. 119°16'15" W; sec. 29, T 7 S, R 25 E); the lake is 0.25 mile northwest of Upper Horsethief Lake. Named on Shuteye Peak (1953) 15' quadrangle.

Lower Hot Springs: see **Mono Hot Springs** [FRESNO].

Lower Indian Lake [FRESNO]: *lake,* 1700 feet long, nearly 7 miles north-northwest of Blackcap Mountain (lat. 37°09'45" N, long. 118°50'40" W); the lake is 1.5 miles south-southeast of Upper Indian Lake. Named on Blackcap Mountain (1953) 15' quadrangle.

Lower Lost Keys Lake: see **Lost Keys Lakes** [FRESNO].

Lower Merced Pass Lake [MADERA]: *lake,* 1000 feet long, 3 miles west of Merced Peak (lat. 37°37'35" N, long. 119°26'50" W); the lake is less than 0.5 mile west-northwest of Upper Merced Pass Lake. Named on Merced Peak (1953) 15' quadrangle.

Lower Mills Creek Lake [FRESNO]: *lake,* 1300 feet long, 1.5 miles west-northwest of Mount Abbot (lat. 37°23'55" N, long. 118°48'35" W); the lake is along Mills Creek 0.5 mile downstream from Upper Mills Creek Lake. Named on Mount Abbot (1953) 15' quadrangle.

Lower Mineral Hot Springs: see **Mono Hot Springs** [FRESNO].

Lower Mineral Public Camp: see **Mono Hot Springs** [FRESNO].

Lower Ottoway Lake [MADERA]: *lake,* 1900 feet long, 1.5 miles west-northwest of Merced Peak (lat. 37°38'35" N, long. 119°25'05" W); the lake is along Ottoway Creek 1.5 miles west of Ottoway Peak. Named on Merced Peak (1953) 15' quadrangle.

Lower Rancheria Creek [FRESNO]: *stream,* flows 5 miles to Kings River 3.25 miles west-southwest of Balch Camp (lat. 36°52'55" N, long. 119°10'25" W; near SE cor. sec. 18, T 12 S, R 26 E). Named on Patterson Mountain (1952) 15' quadrangle.

Lower Springhill Campground [TULARE]: *locality,* 5.25 miles south-southeast of Fairview along Kern River (lat. 35°51'40" N, long. 118°26'50" W; sec. 8, T 24 S, R 33 E); the place is 0.25 mile south of Upper Springhill Campground. Named on Kernville (1956) 15' quadrangle.

Lower Tent Meadow [FRESNO]: *area,* 9.5 miles south-southwest of Marion Peak (lat. 36°49'30" N, long. 118°34'30" W); the place is nearly 1 mile south-southeast of Upper Tent Meadow. Named on Marion Peak (1953) 15' quadrangle. A large block of granite in the meadow resembles a white tent from a distance (Browning 1986, p. 214).

Lower Tobias Meadow [TULARE]: *area,* 7 miles east of California Hot Springs (lat. 35°52'45" N, long. 118°32'45" W; sec. 32, T 23 S, R 32 E); the place is along Tobias Creek 1.5 miles northeast of Tobias Meadow. Named on California Hot Springs (1958) 15' quadrangle.

Lower Turret Lake [FRESNO]: *lake,* 1700 feet long, 9.5 miles south-southwest of Mount Abbot (lat. 37°15'20" N, long. 118° 50' W); the lake is 0.5 mile south of Middle Turret Lakes along Turret Creek. Named on Mount Abbot (1953) 15' quadrangle.

Lower Twin Lake [FRESNO]: *lake,* 1000 feet long, nearly 2 miles east of Kaiser Peak (lat. 37°17'40" N, long. 119°09'10" W; sec. 29, T 7 S, R 26 E); the lake is 1100 feet east-southeast of Upper Twin Lake. Named on Kaiser Peak (1953) 15' quadrangle. On Kaiser (1904) 30' quadrangle, present Lower Twin Lake and present Upper Twin Lake together are called Twin Lakes.

Lowes Corner [TULARE]: *locality,* 1.5 miles west of Woodville (lat. 36°05'40" N, long. 119°13'55" W; at SW cor. sec. 13, T 21 S, R 25 E). Named on Woodville (1950) 7.5' quadrangle.

Lucas Creek [KERN]: *stream,* flows 7.25 miles to Kern River 4 miles north-northeast of Mount Adelaide (lat. 35°29' N, long. 118° 42'35" W). Named on Breckenridge Mountain (1972) and Mount Adelaide (1972) 7.5' quadrangles.

Lucca [TULARE]: *locality,* 2.5 miles north of Lindsay along Atchison, Topeka and Santa Fe Railroad (lat. 36°14'45" N, long. 119°05'25" W; sec. 30, T 19 S, R 27 E). Named on Lindsay (1951) 7.5' quadrangle.

Lucerne [KINGS]: *locality,* 3.5 miles north of Hanford along Atchison, Topeka and Santa Fe Railroad (lat. 36°22'50" N, long. 119° 39'45" W; sec. 11, T 18 S, R 21 E). Named on Laton (1953) 7.5' quadrangle. The place is in a neighborhood named for Mussel Slough, but in 1887 it received the name "Lucerne Valley" from Lucerne in Europe (Gudde, 1949, p. 197).

Lucerne Valley: see **Mussel Slough** [KINGS].

Luckett Mountain [FRESNO]: *peak,* 8 miles south-southwest of Balch Camp (lat. 36°48'35" N, long. 119°11'30" W; sec. 7, T 13 S, R 26 E). Altitude 3181 feet. Named on Patterson Mountain (1952) 15' quadrangle.

Luck Point [FRESNO]: *peak,* 5 miles east of Kaiser Peak (lat. 37° 18' N, long. 119°05'50" W; sec. 23, T 7 S, R 26 E). Named on Kaiser Peak (1953) 15' quadrangle.

Lucky Canyon [TULARE]: *canyon,* drained by a stream that flows 1.25 miles to Dry Creek (1) 6.5 miles southeast of Auckland (lat. 36°32'05" N, long. 119°00'35" W; sec. 14, T 16 S, R 27 E). Named on Giant Forest (1956) 15' quadrangle, and on Auckland (1966) 7.5' quadrangle.

Lucy Runyon Canyon [TULARE]: *canyon,* drained by a stream that flows 1.5 miles to Dry Creek (1) 5 miles east-southeast of Auckland (lat. 36°34'15" N, long. 119°01'15" W; near N line sec. 3, T 16 S, R 27 E). Named on Auckland (1966) 7.5' quadrangle.

Lucys Foot Pass [TULARE]: *pass,* 11 miles northwest of Mount Whitney on Kings-Kern

Divide (lat. 36°41'45" N, long. 118°25'15" W). Named on Mount Whitney (1956) 15' quadrangle. Browning 1986 (p. 133) associated the name with Lucy Fletcher Brown (Mrs. Bolton C. Brown), who crossed the pass in 1896.

Lumer [TULARE]: *locality,* 2.5 miles south-southeast of Porterville along Atchison, Topeka and Santa Fe Railroad (lat. 36°02'15" N, long. 118°59'25" W; at S line sec. 6, T 22 S, R 28 E). Named on Success Dam (1956) 7.5' quadrangle.

Lumreau Creek [KERN]: *stream,* flows 6.5 miles to Cedar Creek 3 miles south-southeast of Glennville (lat. 35°41'20" N, long. 118°41'15" W; near S line sec. 6, T 26 S, R 31 E). Named on Alta Sierra (1972) and Glennville (1972) 7.5' quadrangles.

Lumreau Mountain [TULARE]: *peak,* 3 miles northeast of Springville (lat. 36°09'55" N, long. 118°46'55" W; near SE cor. sec. 24, T 20 S, R 29 E). Altitude 3085 feet. Named on Springville (1957) 7.5' quadrangle.

Luna [TULARE]: *locality,* 1.5 miles west-northwest of Exeter along Southern Pacific Railroad (lat. 36°18'20" N, long. 119°10'15" W; at W line sec. 4, T 19 S, R 26 E). Named on Exeter (1926) 7.5' quadrangle.

Lunch Meadow [TULARE]: *area,* 17 miles northwest of Lamont Peak (lat. 35°59'20" N, long. 118°13' W; sec. 20, T 22 S, R 35 E). Named on Lamont Peak (1956) 15' quadrangle.

Lupine Campground [MADERA]: *locality,* 6.25 miles southeast of Yosemite Forks on the southwest side of Bass Lake (1) (lat. 37°18'30" N, long. 119°32'35" W; near W line sec. 23, T 7 S, R 22 E). Named on Bass Lake (1953) 15' quadrangle.

Lyell: see **Mount Lyell** [MADERA-TUOLUMNE].

Lurline Wells [KERN]: *wells,* 11 miles northwest of Wasco (lat. 35° 42'45" N, long. 119°27'45" W; sec. 35, T 25 S, R 23 E). Named on Wasco NW (1953) 7.5' quadrangle.

Lyell Fork [MADERA]: *stream,* flows 6 miles to join Merced Peak Fork and form Merced River 5.25 miles north-northeast of Merced Peak (lat. 37°42'05" N, long. 119°20'50" W). Named on Merced Peak (1953) 15' quadrangle. United States Board on Geographic Names (1978d, p. 3) rejected the names "Merced River" and "North Fork" for the stream.

Lynch Canyon [KERN]: *canyon,* drained by a stream that flows 2 miles to lowlands 5 miles east-northeast of Bodfish (lat. 35°36'45" N, long. 118°24'30" W; sec. 2, T 27 S, R 33 E). Named on Lake Isabella South (1972) 7.5' quadrangle.

Lynn: see **Cornwell** [KINGS].

Lynns Valley: see **Linns Valley** [KERN-TULARE].

– M –

Mace Lake [FRESNO]: *lake,* 600 feet long, 10 miles northwest of Mount Abbot (lat. 37°29'05" N, long. 118°54'30" W). Named on Mount Abbot (1953) 15' quadrangle.

Mace Meadow [KERN]: *area,* about 2.5 miles south-southeast of Claraville along Cottonwood Creek (3) (lat. 35°24'20" N, long. 118°18'50" W). Named on Claraville (1972) 7.5' quadrangle.

Machine Creek [TULARE]: *stream,* flows 2.5 miles to Little Trout Creek 12 miles east-northeast of Fairview (lat. 35°58'05" N, long. 118°17'35" W; sec. 34, T 22 S, R 34 E). Named on Kernville (1956) 15' quadrangle.

Mack Meadow [KERN]: *area,* 11 miles south-southwest of Weldon (lat. 35°30'20" N, long. 118°20'45" W; sec. 17, T 28 S, R 34 E). Named on Woolstalf Creek (1972) 7.5' quadrangle.

Maclure: see **Mount Maclure** [MADERA-TUOLUMNE].

Maclure Fork: see **Lewis Creek** [MADERA].

Madera [MADERA]: *town,* in the southwest-central part of Madera County along Fresno River (lat. 36°57'45" N, long. 120°03'30" W). Named on Madera (1963) 7.5' quadrangle. Postal authorities established Madera post office in 1877 (Frickstad, p. 86), and the town incorporated in 1907. Officials of California Lumber Company had the town laid out in 1876 at the end of a flume that brought lumber 63 miles from the mountains to the railroad—madera means "wood" or "timber" in Spanish (Hoover, Rensch, and Rensch, p. 173).

Madera Creek [MADERA]: *stream,* flows 4 miles to West Fork Granite Creek 6.5 miles southeast of Merced Peak (lat. 37°33'45" N, long. 119°18'50" W); the stream heads near Madera Peak. Named on Merced Peak (1953) 15' quadrangle. United States Board on Geographic Names (1933b, p. 19) rejected the name "Black Peak Fork" for the stream.

Madera Equalization Reservoir [MADERA]: *lake,* 1 mile long, 10 miles south of Raymond (lat. 37°04' N, long. 119°56'15" W; on N line sec. 18, T 10 S, R 19 E). Named on Daulton (1962) 7.5' quadrangle.

Madera Lake [MADERA]: *lake,* 1.5 miles long, 14 miles south-southwest of Raymond near Fresno River (lat. 37°01'20" N, long. 119°59'15" W). Named on Daulton (1962) 7.5' quadrangle.

Madera Lakes [MADERA]: *lakes,* three, largest 1100 feet long, 6.5 miles south-southeast of Merced Peak along Madera Creek (lat. 37°32'40" N, long. 119°21'25" W); the group includes Lady Lake and Vandeburg Lake. Named on Merced Peak (1953) 15' quadrangle.

Madera Peak [MADERA]: *peak,* 6.5 miles south of Merced Peak (lat. 37°32'15" N, long.

119°22'30" W). Altitude 10,509 feet. Named on Merced Peak (1953) 15' quadrangle. Called Black Mt. on Hoffmann and Gardner's (1863-1867) map. Members of the Wheeler survey called the feature Black Peak (Browning, 1986, p. 134), but United States Board on Geographic Names (1933a, p. 487) rejected this name.

Madera Station: see **Storey** [MADERA].

Maddox: see **Mount Maddox** [TULARE].

Maddox Canyon [KERN]: *canyon,* nearly 2 miles long, 5.5 miles west-southwest of McKittrick (lat. 35°16'40" N, long. 119°43'50" W). Named on Olig (1943) 7.5' quadrangle.

Maggie Lakes [TULARE]: *lakes,* largest 800 feet long, 12 miles south of Mineral King (lat. 36°16'35" N, long. 118°37'15" W); the lakes are 1 mile north of Maggie Mountain. Named on Mineral King (1956) 15' quadrangle.

Maggie Mountain [TULARE]: *peak,* 13 miles south of Mineral King (lat. 36°15'50" N, long. 118°37'05" W). Altitude 10,042 feet. Named on Mineral King (1956) 15' quadrangle. Frank Knowles named the peak in the 1870's to commemorate Maggie Kincaid, a school teacher in Tulare County (Gudde, 1949, p. 201; Gudde used the name "Mount Maggie.")

Magnesite: see **Success** [TULARE].

Magnesite Junction: see **Success** [TULARE].

Magnet: see **O'Neals** [MADERA].

Magnolia [TULARE]: *locality,* 3.5 miles south-southeast of Porterville along Atchison, Topeka and Santa Fe Railroad (lat. 36°01'20" N, long. 118°59'35" W; at S line sec. 7, T 22 S, R 28 E). Named on Success Dam (1956) 7.5' quadrangle.

Magnolia: see **Inyokern** [KERN].

Magunden [KERN]: *locality,* 4 miles east of downtown Bakersfield (lat. 35°21'45" N, long. 118°55'50" W; at E line sec. 35, T 29 S, R 28 E). Named on Lamont (1954) 7.5' quadrangle.

Mahogany Creek [TULARE]: *stream,* flows 4 miles to Fish Creek (2) 10.5 miles south of Monache Mountain (lat. 36°03'15" N, long. 118°12'30" W; sec. 36, T 21 S, R 35 E). Named on Hockett Peak (1956) and Monache Mountain (1956) 15' quadrangles.

Mahogany Flat [TULARE]: *area,* 3 miles west-northwest of Camp Nelson along South Fork of Middle Fork Tule River (lat. 36°09'05" N, long. 118°39'20" W). Named on Camp Nelson (1956) 15' quadrangle.

Main Bypass: see **James Bypass** [FRESNO].

Major General: see **The Major General** [TULARE].

Malachite Creek: see **Copper Creek** [FRESNO].

Malaga [FRESNO]: *town,* 6 miles south-southeast of downtown Fresno (lat. 36°41' N, long. 119°44' W; mainly in sec. 30, T 14 S, R 21 E). Named on Malaga (1964) 7.5' quadrangle. Postal authorities established Tokay post office in 1886, changed the name to Malaga

later the same year, discontinued it in 1964, and reestablished it in 1965 (Salley, p. 131, 222) The place, named for the popular malaga grape, was the site of a development called The Malaga Colony (Hanna, p. 183).

Malaga Colony: see **The Malaga Colony**, under **Malaga** [FRESNO].

Mallard Lake [FRESNO]: *lake,* 600 feet long, 8 miles east-southeast of Kaiser Peak (lat. 37°15'20" N, long. 119°02'35" W). Named on Kaiser Peak (1953) 15' quadrangle.

Mallory: see **Mount Mallory** [TULARE].

Malpais [TULARE]: *area,* 5 miles northwest of Kern Peak near Golden Trout Creek (lat. 36°22' N, long. 118°20'24" W). Named on Kern Peak (1956) 15' quadrangle.

Malta: see **Maltha** [KERN].

Maltermoro: see **Sunnyside** [FRESNO].

Maltha [KERN]: *locality,* 3.25 miles north of downtown Bakersfield along Southern Pacific Railroad in Kern River oil field (lat. 35°25'20" N, long. 118°59'45" W; sec. 8, T 29 S, R 28 E). Named on Oil Center (1954) 7.5' quadrangle. Called Malta on Oil Center (1940) 7.5' quadrangle. Maltha is a soft form of native asphalt.

Malum Ridge [MADERA]: *ridge,* south-southeast-trending, 5 miles long, 10.5 miles southeast of Yosemite Forks (lat. 37°15' N, long. 119°30'30" W). Named on Bass Lake (1953), Millerton Lake (1965), and Shaver Lake (1953) 15' quadrangles.

Mama Pottinger Canyon [KERN]: *canyon,* 2.25 miles long, opens into Santa Maria Valley (present Little Santa Maria Valley) 5.5 miles west of McKittrick (lat. 35°18' N, long. 119°43'10" W); the canyon is 1 mile east of present Pottinger Canyon. Named on Olig (1943) 7.5' quadrangle.

Mammoth Crest [FRESNO]: *ridge,* 7 miles long, at and southeast of the place that Fresno County, Madera County, and Mono County meet (lat. 37°34'15" N, long. 119°00' W). Named on Devils Postpile (1953) and Mount Morrison (1953) 15' quadrangles.

Mammoth Crest [MADERA]: *ridge,* extends for 7 miles south-southeast and east from Mammoth Pass on Madera-Mono county line and on Fresno-Mono county line (center near lat. 37°34'15" N, long. 119°00' W). Named on Devils Postpile (1953) 15' quadrangle.

Mammoth Mountain [MADERA]: *peak,* nearly 3 miles east of Devils Postpile on Madera-Mono county line (lat. 37°37'50" N, long. 119°01'55" W); the peak is northwest of Mammoth Lakes, which are in Mono County. Altitude 11,053 feet. Named on Devils Postpile (1953) 15' quadrangle. Called Mammoth Pk. on California Mining Bureau's (1917d) map.

Mammoth Mountain: see **Banner Peak** [MADERA].

Mammoth Pass [MADERA]: *pass,* 3 miles east-southeast of Devils Postpile on Madera-Mono county line (lat. 37°36'35" N, long. 119°01'45" W); the pass is west of Mammoth Lakes, which are in Mono County. Named on Devils Postpile (1953) 15' quadrangle. The pass also is called Pumice Gap (Smith *in* Wright, p. 92).

Mammoth Peak: see **Mammoth Mountain** [MADERA].

Mammoth Pool Reservoir [FRESNO]: *lake,* behind a dam on San Joaquin River 8 miles west-northwest of Kaiser Peak on Fresno-Madera county line (lat. 37°19'25" N, long. 119°18'55" W; near N line sec. 14, T 7 S, R 24 E). Named on Shuteye Peak (1953) 15' quadrangle.

Mammoth Pool Reservoir [MADERA]: *lake,* 7.5 miles long, behind a dam on San Joaquin River 6.5 miles east-southeast of Shuteye Peak on Madera-Fresno county line (lat. 37°19'25" N, long. 119° 18'55" W; near N line sec. 14, T 7 S, R 24 E. Named on Shuteye Peak (1953) 15' quadrangle.

Mankins Creek [TULARE]: *stream,* flows 4 miles to North Fork Kaweah River 0.5 mile southeast of Kaweah (lat. 36°27'50" N, long. 118°54'40" W; sec. 11, T 17 S, R 28 E); the stream heads at Mankins Flat (2). Named on Kaweah (1957) 15' quadrangle. Called Mankin Cr. on Kaweah (1909) 30' quadrangle, but United States Board on Geographic Names (1968b, p. 8) rejected the form "Mankin" for the name. According to A.R. Mitchell (p. 78), the name is misspelled and commemorates James Manikin.

Mankins Flat [TULARE]:
(1) *area,* 3.25 miles north of Cliff Peak along Moore Creek (lat. 36° 36'10" N, long. 119°09'50" W; at S line sec. 20, T 15 S, R 26 E). Named on Stokes Mountain (1966) 7.5' quadrangle. Called Fisher Flat on Dunlap (1944) 15' quadrangle, but United States Board on Geographic Names (1967d, p. 5) rejected the names "Fisher Flat" and "Mankin Flat" for the name.
(2) *area,* 3 miles west-northwest of Kaweah (lat. 36°29'30" N, long. 118°57'45" W); the place is near the head of Mankins Creek. Named on Kaweah (1957) 15' quadrangle. Called Mankin Flat on Kaweah (1909) 30' quadrangle, but United States Board on Geographic Names (1968b, p. 8) rejected this form of the name.

Mankins Spring [TULARE]: *spring,* 3 miles north of Cliff Peak along Moore Creek (lat. 36°36' N, long. 119°09'50" W; near N line sec. 29, T 15 S, R 26 E); the spring is at the south end of Mankins Flat (1). Named on Stokes Mountain (1966) 7.5' quadrangle. United States Board on Geographic Names (1968b, p. 8) rejected the form "Mankin Springs" for the name.

Mann: see **Hugh Mann Canyon** [KERN].

Mannot Creek: see **Monotti Creek** [KERN].

Manse Meadow [FRESNO]: *area,* 11 miles east-

southeast of Kaiser Peak (lat. 37°15'35" N, long. 118°55'55" W). Named on Kaiser Peak (1953) and Mount Abbot (1953) 15' quadrangles.

Manter Creek [TULARE]: *stream,* flows 8 miles to South Fork Kern River 10.5 miles west-northwest of Lamont Peak (lat. 35°50'45" N, long. 118°12'50" W); the stream goes through Manter Meadow. Named on Kernville (1956) and Lamont Peak (1956) 15' quadrangles. Called Manter Meadow Cr. on Olmsted's (1900) map. The name is for John Manter and Hiram Manter (Mitchell, A.R., p. 78).

Manter Meadow [TULARE]: *area,* 12.5 miles east-southeast of Fairview (lat. 35°53' N, long. 118°17' W; mainly in sec. 35, T 23 S, R 34 E); the place is along Manter Creek. Named on Kernville (1956) 15' quadrangle.

Manter Meadow Creek: see **Manter Creek** [TULARE].

Mantes Canyon [FRESNO]: *canyon,* drained by a stream that flows 2.5 miles to the canyon of Zapato Chino Creek 9.5 miles southeast of Coalinga (lat. 36°02'15" N, long. 120°15'05" W; near SW cor. sec. 4, T 22 S, R 16 E). Named on Kreyenhagen Hills (1956) 7.5' quadrangle.

Manuel Canyon [KERN]: *canyon,* less than 1 mile long, 10 miles west-northwest of Inyokern (lat. 35°42'05" N, long. 117°58'20" W; on N line sec. 2, T 26 S, R 37 E). Named on Owens Peak (1972) 7.5' quadrangle.

Manzanita: see **Milo** [TULARE].

Manzanita Canyon [TULARE]: *canyon,* drained by a stream that flows 2.5 miles to Kern River 2 miles east-southeast of Hockett Peak (lat. 36°12'40" N, long. 118°21'15" W); the canyon heads near Manzanita Knob. Named on Hockett Peak (1956) 15' quadrangle.

Manzanita Knob [TULARE]: *peak,* 4.5 miles east-southeast of Hockett Peak (lat. 36°12'30" N, long. 118°18'30" W; near SW cor. sec. 4, T 20 S, R 34 E). Altitude 9121 feet. Named on Hockett Peak (1956) 15' quadrangle.

Manzanita Lake [MADERA]: *lake,* behind a dam on North Fork Willow Creek (2) 1.25 miles north-northwest of North Fork (lat. 37°14'40" N, long. 119°30'55" W; sec. 12, T 8 S, R 22 E). Named on Bass Lake (1953) and Millerton Lake (1965) 15' quadrangles.

Manzanita Park: see **Big Creek** [FRESNO] (3).

Manzanita Ridge [KERN]: *ridge,* generally west-trending, 1.5 miles long, center nearly 3 miles east-northeast of Caliente (lat. 35°16'45" N, long. 118°34'45" W). Named on Oiler Peak (1972) 7.5' quadrangle.

Maple Creek [TULARE]: *stream,* flows 1.5 miles to Yucca Creek 1.5 miles south-southeast of Yucca Mountain (lat. 36°33' N, long. 118°51'45" W). Named on Giant Forest (1956) 15' quadrangle.

Marble Canyon [TULARE]: *canyon,* drained by a stream that flows 0.5 mile to Dry Creek (1) 6 miles east-southeast of Auckland (lat.

36°32'50" N, long. 119°00'35" W; sec. 11, T 16 S, R 27 E). Named on Auckland (1966) 7.5' quadrangle.

Marble Cave [TULARE]: *cave,* 4.5 miles east of Yucca Mountain (lat. 36°33'30" N, long. 118°47'30" W); the cave is along Marble Fork near Marble Falls. Named on Tehipite (1903) 30' quadrangle.

Marble Falls [TULARE]: *waterfall,* 4.5 miles east-southeast of Yucca Mountain along Marble Fork (lat. 36°33'20" N, long. 118°47'30" W). Named on Giant Forest (1956) 15' quadrangle.

Marble Fork: see **Kaweah River** [TULARE].

Marble Fork Creek: see **Marble Fork**, under **Kaweah River** [TULARE].

Marble Point [FRESNO]: *peak,* 1.5 miles east-southeast of Dinkey Dome (lat. 37°06'35" N, long. 119°06'20" W; sec. 35, T 9 S, R 26 E). Altitude 8858 feet. Named on Huntington Lake (1953) 15' quadrangle.

Marble Spring Canyon [KERN]: *canyon,* less than 1 mile long, 7.25 miles west-southwest of Liebre Twins (lat. 34°54'30" N, long. 118°41' W). Named on Winters Ridge (1966) 7.5' quadrangle.

Marca Canyon [FRESNO]: *canyon,* drained by a stream that flows 3.5 miles to lowlands 17 miles southwest of Firebaugh (lat. 36° 43' N, long. 120°42'15" W; sec. 18, T 14 S, R 12 E). Named on Chounet Ranch (1956) 7.5' quadrangle.

Marcel [KERN]: *locality,* 3.5 miles southeast of Keene along the railroad (lat. 35°11'25" N, long. 118°31' W; sec. 35, T 31 S, R 32 E). Named on Keene (1966) 7.5' quadrangle.

Marcelin Spring [FRESNO]: *spring,* 11 miles southwest of Coalinga (lat. 36°01'05" N, long. 120°28'50" W; sec. 17, T 22 S, R 14 E). Named on Curry Mountain (1969) 7.5' quadrangle.

Marcella Lake [FRESNO]: *lake,* 650 feet long, 7.5 miles west-southwest of Mount Abbot (lat. 37°20'50" N, long. 118°54'50" W). Named on Mount Abbot (1953) 15' quadrangle.

Mare Spring [FRESNO]: *spring,* 3 miles north-northeast of Joaquin Rocks (lat. 36°21'35" N, long. 120°25'25" W; sec. 14, T 18 S, R 14 E). Named on Joaquin Rocks (1969) 7.5' quadrangle.

Margaret Lake: see **Big Margaret Lake** [FRESNO].

Margaret Lakes [FRESNO]: *lakes,* 14 miles north-northeast of Kaiser Peak (lat. 37°27'45" N, long. 119°02'45" W); Big Margaret Lake is the largest of the group. Named on Kaiser Peak (1953) 15' quadrangle.

Maricopa [KERN]: *town,* 6.5 miles south-southeast of Taft (lat. 35° 03'45" N, long. 119°24' W; around NW cor. sec. 12, T 11 N, R 24 W). Named on Maricopa (1951) 7.5' quadrangle. Postal authorities established Maricopa post office in 1901 (Frickstad, p. 57), and the town incorporated in 1911.

Maricopa Flat [KERN]: *area,* center 5 miles east-northeast of Maricopa (lat. 35°04'30" N, long. 119°18'15" W). Named on Pentland (1953) 7.5' quadrangle.

Maricopa Valley: see **Sunset Valley** [KERN].

Marie Lake [FRESNO]: *lake,* 1 mile long, 7.5 miles southeast of Mount Abbot (lat. 37°18' N, long. 118°52' W). Named on Mount Abbot (1953) 15' quadrangle. R.B. Marshall of United States Geological Survey named the lake for Mary Hooper, daughter of Major William B. Hooper (Gudde, 1949, p. 204); the name of nearby Mount Hooper commemorates the major.

Marilyn Lake: see **Peter Pande Lake** [FRESNO].

Marino Canyon [KERN]: *canyon,* drained by a stream that flows 2.5 miles to lowlands 4.25 miles east of Claraville (lat. 35°26' N, long. 118°15'05" W; near W line sec. 8, T 29 S, R 35 E). Named on Claraville (1972) 7.5' quadrangle.

Marion: see **Lake Marion** [KERN].

Marion Lake [FRESNO]: *lake,* 1300 feet long, 1.25 miles north-northeast of Marion Peak (lat. 36°58'25" N, long. 118°31' W). Named on Marion Peak (1953) 15' quadrangle. J.N. LeConte named the lake in 1902 for his wife, Helen Marion Gompertz LeConte (Hanna, p. 185).

Marion Peak [FRESNO]: *peak,* 24 miles east-northeast of Hume on Cirque Crest (lat. 36°57'25" N, long. 118°31'15" W). Altitude 12,719 feet. Named on Marion Peak (1953) 15' quadrangle. The name commemorates Mrs. J.N. LeConte (Hanna, p. 185).

Marjorie: see **Lake Marjorie** [FRESNO].

Markland Canyon [FRESNO]: *canyon,* drained by a stream that flows 2.5 miles to Hot Springs Canyon nearly 2 miles east-southeast of Coalinga Mineral Springs (lat. 36°07'55" N, long. 120° 32' W; sec. 1, T 21 S, R 13 E). Named on Sherman Peak (1969) 7.5' quadrangle.

Markwood Creek [FRESNO]: *stream,* flows 2.5 miles to Stevenson Creek 6.5 miles west of Dinkey Dome (lat. 37°06'20" N, long. 119°15' W; sec. 33, T 9 S, R 25 E); the stream goes through Markwood Meadow. Named on Huntington Lake (1953) 15' quadrangle.

Markwood Meadow [FRESNO]: *area,* nearly 6 miles west-southwest of Dinkey Dome (lat. 37°05'30" N, long. 119°13'55" W; sec. 3, T 10 S, R 25 E); the place is along Markwood Creek. Named on Huntington Lake (1953) 15' quadrangle. The name commemorates William Markwood, a sheepman of the 1870's (Gudde, 1949, p. 206).

Marmot Lake [FRESNO]: *lake,* 1200 feet long, 1 mile southwest of Mount Humphreys in Humphreys Basin (lat. 37°15'35" N, long. 118°40'55" W). Named on Mount Tom (1949) 15' quadrangle.

Marsala [KINGS]: *locality,* 2.25 miles north-northwest of Stratford along Southern Pacific

Railroad (lat. 37°13'15" N, long. 119° 50' W). Named on Stratford (1929) 7.5' quadrangle.

Marshall Hill [FRESNO]: *hill,* 3.5 miles west-southwest of Prather (lat. 37°01'10" N, long. 119°34'25" W; sec. 33, T 10 S, R 22 E); the feature is 0.5 mile northwest of Marshall Station. Named on Millerton Lake East (1965) 7.5' quadrangle.

Marshall Lake [FRESNO]: *lake,* 1000 feet long, 8 miles southwest of Mount Abbot (lat. 37°18'05" N, long. 118°52'30" W). Named on Mount Abbot (1953) 15' quadrangle. Elden H. Vestal named the lake in 1942 (Browning 1986, p. 138).

Marshall Meadow [TULARE]: *area,* 6.5 miles southeast of California Hot Springs (lat. 35°48'10" N, long. 118°36'10" W; near W line sec. 35, T 24 S, R 31 E). Named on California Hot Springs (1958) 15' quadrangle.

Marshall Station [FRESNO]: *locality,* 3.5 miles west-southwest of Prather near the south end of Auberry Valley (lat. 37°00'50" N, long. 119°34'05" W; sec. 33, T 10 S, R 22 E). Named on Millerton Lake East (1965) 7.5' quadrangle. Called Grabners on Millerton Lake (1945) 15' quadrangle, but United States Board on Geographic Names (1967a, p. 9) rejected this name. Postal authorities established Grabners post office in 1914, discontinued it in 1933, reestablished it in 1939, and discontinued it in 1951; the name was for a landowner at the place (Salley, p. 87).

Marsh Lake [FRESNO]:
(1) *lake,* 900 feet long, 6 miles west of Red Slate Mountain (lat. 37° 30'25" N, long. 118°58'45" W). Named on Mount Morrison (1953) 15' quadrangle.
(2) *lake,* 700 feet long, 6 miles west-southwest of Blackcap Mountain (lat. 37°01'55" N, long. 118°53'25" W; sec. 26, T 10 S, R 28 E). Named on Blackcap Mountain (1953) 15' quadrangle.

Martensdale: see **Cawelo** [KERN].

Martha Lake [FRESNO]: *lake,* 3600 feet long, 1 mile west-southwest of Mount Goddard (lat. 37°05'40" N, long. 118°44'15" W). Named on Mount Goddard (1948) 15' quadrangle. George R. Davis of United States Geological Survey named the lake in 1907 for his mother (Farquhar, 1924, p. 57).

Martina Spring [KERN]: *spring,* 6.25 miles southeast of Arvin (lat. 35°07'55" N, long. 118°46'05" W; near W line sec. 21, T 32 S, R 30 E). Named on Arvin (1955) 7.5' quadrangle.

Martinez: see **Chico Martinez Creek** [KERN].

Martinez Creek [FRESNO]: *stream,* flows 8 miles to lowlands 15 miles north of Coalinga (lat. 36°21'45" N, long. 120°21'15" W; near W line sec. 16, T 18 S, R 15 E). Named on Domengine Ranch (1956) and Joaquin Rocks (1969) 7.5' quadrangles.

Martinez Spring [FRESNO]: *spring,* 2.25 miles northeast of Joaquin Rocks (lat. 36°20'25" N, long. 120°24'55" W; sec. 26, T 18 S, R 14 E); the feature is along a branch of Martinez Creek. Named on Joaquin Rocks (1969) 7.5' quadrangle.

Martin Hill [TULARE]: *hill,* 2 miles south-southeast of Porterville (lat. 36°02'45" N, long. 118°59'45" W; sec. 6, T 22 S, R 28 E). Named on Success Dam (1956) 7.5' quadrangle.

Martin Pond [FRESNO]: *intermittent lake,* 800 feet long, 5.25 miles west of Selma (lat. 36°33'55" N, long. 119°42'10" W; sec. 5, T 16 S, R 21 E). Named on Conejo (1963) 7.5' quadrangle. Selma (1946) 15' quadrangle shows a permanent lake 1900 feet long.

Marvin Pass [TULARE]: *pass,* 15 miles northwest of Triple Divide Peak (lat. 36°43'50" N, long. 118°44'05" W; near SW cor. sec. 4, T 14 S, R 30 E). Named on Triple Divide Peak (1956) 7.5' quadrangle.

Marys Meadow [FRESNO]: *area,* 3 miles southwest of Kaiser Peak (lat. 37°15'40" N, long. 119°13'20" W; sec. 3, T 8 S, R 25 E). Named on Kaiser Peak (1953) 15' quadrangle.

Matchin [TULARE]: *locality,* 2.25 miles northeast of Exeter along Atchison, Topeka and Santa Fe Railroad (lat. 36°19'30" N, long. 119°07'45" W; near N line sec. 35, T 18 S, R 26 E). Named on Exeter (1952) 15' quadrangle.

Mather Pass [FRESNO]: *pass,* 1.5 miles southwest of Mount Bolton Brown (lat. 37°01'50" N, long. 118°27'35" W). Named on Big Pine (1950) 15' quadrangle. Mr. and Mrs. Chauncey J. Hamlin and their companions named the pass in 1921 for Stephen T. Mather, National Park Service director (Farquhar, 1924, p. 57).

Mathews Mill [FRESNO]: *locality,* 3 miles west-northwest of Shaver Lake Heights (present town of Shaver Lake) (lat. 37°07'25" N, long. 119°22'15" W; sec. 29, T 9 S, R 24 E). Named on Shaver Lake (1953) 15' quadrangle.

Mattei [FRESNO]: *locality,* 2.5 miles east-north-east of Malaga along Atchison, Topeka and Santa Fe Railroad (lat. 36°42' N, long. 119° 41'30" W; sec. 21, T 14 S, R 21 E). Named on Malaga (1964) 7.5' quadrangle.

Matterhorn: see **Little Matterhorn**, under **Mineral Peak** [TULARE].

Matthes Glaciers: see **Glacier Divide** [FRESNO].

Maxson Dome [FRESNO]: *peak,* 9.5 miles west-northwest of Blackcap Mountain (lat. 37°07'20" N, long. 118°57'15" W; sec. 30, T 9 S, R 28 E). Altitude 9547 feet. Named on Blackcap Mountain (1953) 15' quadrangles.

Maxson Lake [FRESNO]: *lake,* 450 feet long, 3 miles south-southwest of Blackcap Mountain (lat. 37°01'50" N, long. 118°48'45" W). Named on Blackcap Mountain (1953) 15' quadrangle.

Maxson Meadow: see **Big Maxson Meadow** [FRESNO].

Maxson Meadows [FRESNO]: *area,* 9.5 miles west-northwest of Blackcap Mountain (lat. 37°06'10" N, long. 118°57'20" W; sec. 31, T 9 S, R 28 E); the place is 1.5 miles south of Maxson Dome. Named on Blackcap Mountain (1953) 15' quadrangle. The name commemorates an early stockman (Browning 1986, p. 140).

May: see **Wilbur May Lake** [FRESNO].

Mayan Peak [KERN]: *peak,* 2 miles west of Pinyon Mountain (lat. 35°27'50" N, long. 118°11'40" W; near NE cor. sec. 27, T 28 S, R 35 E). Altitude 6108 feet. Named on Pinyon Mountain (1972) 7.5' quadrangle.

Mayfair [KERN]: *locality,* 5.5 miles east-southeast of downtown Bakersfield (lat. 35°20'10" N, long. 118°54'50" W; sec. 12, T 30 S, R 28 E). Named on Lamont (1954, photorevised 1968) 7.5' quadrangle.

Mayville: see **Visalia** [TULARE].

McAdie: see **Mount McAdie** [TULARE].

McCleod Flat [MADERA]: *area,* 4 miles east of Yosemite Forks along North Fork Willow Creek (2) (lat. 37°21'20" N, long. 119° 33'25" W; near NW cor. sec. 3, T 7 S, R 22 E). Named on Bass Lake (1953) 15' quadrangle. United States Board on Geographic Names (1990, p. 9) approved the name "McLeod Flat" for the feature, and noted that the name is for Malcolm McLeod, district ranger for Fresno Flats in 1911.

McClure Flat [TULARE]: *area,* 5.5 miles southeast of Auckland (lat. 36°31'25" N, long. 119°02'45" W; sec. 21, T 16 S, R 27 E). Named on Auckland (1966) 7.5' quadrangle.

McClure Lake [MADERA]: *lake,* 1100 feet long, 4.5 miles east of Merced Peak (lat. 37°38'30" N, long. 119°18'50" W). Named on Merced Peak (1953) 15' quadrangle. The name commemorates Lieutenant N.F. McClure, who was stationed in Yosemite National Park in 1894 and 1895 (Farquhar, 1924, p. 57).

McClure Meadow [FRESNO]: *area,* 6 miles north-northwest of Mount Goddard in Evolution Valley (lat. 37°11'15" N, long. 118° 44'45" W). Named on Mount Goddard (1948) 15' quadrangle. The name honors Wilbur F. McClure, state engineer of California, for his assistance in building John Muir Trail (Farquhar, 1924, p. 57).

McClure Spring [TULARE]: *spring,* 5.5 miles southeast of Auckland (lat. 36°31'25" N, long. 119°02'40" W; sec. 21, T 16 S, R 27 E); the spring is at McClure Flat. Named on Auckland (1966) 7.5' quadrangle.

McClures Valley: see **Sunflower Valley** [KERN-KINGS].

McConnel Meadow [TULARE]: *area,* 10.5 miles northwest of Olancha Peak (lat. 36°23' N, long. 118°14'25" W; near SE cor. sec. 1, T 18 S, R 34 E). Named on Olancha (1956) 15' quadrangle.

McCreary Meadow [MADERA]: *area,* 13

miles northeast of Shuteye Peak (lat. 37°29'25" N, long. 119°16'20" W; sec. 18, T 5 S, R 25 E). Named on Shuteye Peak (1953) 15' quadrangle.

McDermand: see **Lake McDermand**, under **Mount Goddard** [FRESNO].

McDermott Camp [TULARE]: *locality,* 7.5 miles north-northwest of California Hot Springs (lat. 35°58'55" N, long. 118°42'40" W). Named on California Hot Springs (1958) 15' quadrangle.

McDoogle: see **Mount McDoogle**, under **Mount Cedric Wright** [FRESNO].

McDuffie: see **Mount McDuffie** [FRESNO].

McFarland [KERN]: *town,* 6.5 miles south of Delano (lat. 35°40'40" N, long. 119°13'40" W; in and near sec. 12, T 26 S, R 25 E). Named on McFarland (1954) 7.5' quadrangle. Postal authorities established McFarland post office in 1908 (Frickstad, p. 57), and the town incorporated in 1957. The name is for J.B. McFarland, a founder of the community (Gudde, 1949, p. 199). The place first was known as Hunt, and later as Lone Pine (Wines, p. 86). Darling (p. 19) listed a place called Cabernet located along Southern Pacific Railroad 3 miles south of McFarland.

McFarland Creek [KERN]: *stream,* flows nearly 5 miles to join Peyton Creek and form Fulton Creek 2 miles east-northeast of Glennville (lat. 35°44'05" N, long. 118°40' W; sec. 20, T 25 S, R 31 E). Named on California Hot Springs (1958) 15' quadrangle, and on Alta Sierra (1972) and Glennville (1972) 7.5' quadrangles.

McGee: see **Mount McGee** [FRESNO].

McGee Canyon [FRESNO]: *canyon,* 1.5 miles long, drained by a stream that heads at McGee Lakes and flows to Evolution Creek 5 miles north of Mount Goddard (lat. 37°10'40" N, long. 118°43'15" W). Named on Mount Goddard (1948) 15' quadrangle.

McGee Lake [MADERA]: *lake,* 550 feet long, 5.5 miles east-northeast of Merced Peak (lat. 37°39'15" N, long. 119°18' W). Named on Merced Peak (1953) 15' quadrangle.

McGee Lakes [FRESNO]: *lakes,* largest 2500 feet long, 3 miles north of Mount Goddard (lat. 37°08'55" N, long. 118°43'10" W); the lakes are 1.25 miles northeast of Mount McGee on upper reaches of McGee Creek. Named on Mount Goddard (1948) 15' quadrangle.

McGee Pass [FRESNO]: *pass,* 3500 feet southeast of Red Slate Mountain on Fresno-Mono county line (lat. 37°30'05" N, long. 118°51'35" W); the pass is near the head of McGee Creek, which is in Mono County. Named on Mount Morrison (1953) 15' quadrangle.

McGovern Gap [KERN]: *narrows,* 3.25 miles south of Orchard Peak (lat. 35°41'20" N, long. 120°08'30" W; near S line sec. 4, T 26 S, R 17 E) Named on Orchard Peak (1961) 7.5' quadrangle. A settler named McGovern lived near the place (Arnold and Johnson, p. 21).

McGuire Lake [FRESNO]: *lake,* 900 feet long, nearly 1 mile west-northwest of Blackcap Mountain (lat. 37°04'40" N, long. 118°48'20" W). Named on Blackcap Mountain (1953) 15' quadrangle. United States Board on Geographic Names (1983a, p. 4) approved the name "McGuire Lakes" for this and a nearby lake together.

McIntyre Creek [TULARE]: *stream,* flows 2.5 miles to South Fork of Middle Fork Tule River 1.25 miles east of Camp Nelson (lat. 36°08'20" N, long. 118°35'15" W; sec. 33, T 20 S, R 31 E). Named on Camp Nelson (1956) 15' quadrangle. The name commemorates Thomas McIntyre, who ran sheep in the neighborhood in the 1880's (Gudde, 1949, p. 199).

McIvers Spring [KERN]: *spring,* 5 miles northeast of Skinner Peak (lat. 35°37'15" N, long. 118°04'20" W). Named on Horse Canyon (1972) 7.5' quadrangle, which shows McIvers cabin at the place. Called Melvers Spring on Onyx (1943) 15' quadrangle. United States Board on Geographic Names (1975b, p. 10) gave the name "Melvers Spring" as a variant.

McKays Point [TULARE]: *relief feature,* 3.25 miles east-southeast of Woodlake where Saint Johns River diverges from Kaweah River (lat. 36°23'20" N, long. 119°02'45" W; near E line sec. 4, T 18 S, R 27 E). Named on Woodlake (1952) 7.5' quadrangle.

McKee Canyon [TULARE]: *canyon,* drained by a stream that flows less than 1 mile to Dry Creek (1) 4.25 miles east-northeast of Woodlake (lat. 36°26'25" N, long. 119°01'20" W; near E line sec. 22, T 17 S, R 27 E). Named on Woodlake (1952, photorevised 1969) 7.5' quadrangle.

McKenzie Fire Camp [FRESNO]: *locality,* 12 miles north-northeast of Clovis (lat. 36°58'55" N, long. 119°36'40" W; near S line sec. 7, T 11 S, R 22 E). Named on Clovis (1946) 15' quadrangle.

McKenzie Ridge [FRESNO]: *ridge,* northwest-trending, 7.5 miles long, 11 miles south-southeast of Balch Camp (lat. 36°45'45" N, long. 119°02'30" W). Named on Giant Forest (1956) and Patterson Mountain (1952) 15' quadrangles, and on Miramonte (1966) 7.5' quadrangle.

McKittrick [KERN]: *village,* 14 miles northwest of Taft (lat. 35°18'20" N, long. 119°37'20" W; on W line sec. 21, T 30 S, R 22 E). Named on Reward (1951) and West Elk Hills (1954) 7.5' quadrangles. Postal authorities established McKittrick post office in 1900 (Salley, p. 136). The name commemorates Captain William McKittrick, a local landowner and cattleman; the community incorporated in 1911 (Bailey, 1967, p. 17). California Mining Bureau's (1917c) map shows a place called Asphalto located about 3 miles northeast of McKittrick along a rail

line. Postal authorities established Asphalto post office in 1893, discontinued it in 1894, reestablished it in 1898, and moved it 2 miles southwest in 1900 when they renamed it McKittrick (Salley, p. 11). At least three different places had the name "Asphalto" (Wines, p. 47), which was from deposits of asphaltum nearby (Bailey, 1967, p. 17).

McKittrick Summit [KERN]: *peak,* 8 miles west of McKittrick (lat. 35°17'25" N, long. 119°45'45" W; near N line sec. 30, T 30 S, R 21 E). Altitude 4332 feet. Named on McKittrick Summit (1959) 7.5' quadrangle. Arnold and Johnson (p. 21) proposed the name.

McKittrick Valley [KERN]: *valley,* northwest of and east-southeast of McKittrick (center near lat. 35°17'45" N, long. 119°35'45" W). Named on Reward (1951) and West Elk Hills (1954) 7.5' quadrangles. Arnold and Johnson (p. 21) proposed the name.

McLean Canyon: see **Carneros Canyon** [KERN].

McLeod: see **Hale McLeod Canyon** [KERN].

McLeod Flat: see **McCleod Flat** [MADERA].

McLure Valley: see **Sunflower Valley** [KERNKINGS].

McMillin [FRESNO]: *locality,* 12.5 miles southwest of downtown Fresno along Southern Pacific Railroad (lat. 36°39'20" N, long. 119°58' W; sec. 1, T 15 S, R 18 E). Named on Kearney Park (1923) 7.5' quadrangle.

Meadow Brook [FRESNO]: *stream,* flows 3 miles to North Fork Kings River 3.25 miles west of Blackcap Mountain (lat. 37°04'50" N, long. 118°51'10" W). Named on Blackcap Mountain (1953) 15' quadrangle.

Meadow Creek [TULARE]: *stream,* flows 1.5 miles to North Fork of Middle Fork Tule River 4.5 miles northwest of Camp Nelson (lat. 36°11'15" N, long. 118°40'10" W). Named on Camp Nelson (1956) 15' quadrangle.

Meadow Flat [TULARE]: *area,* 3.5 miles south of Wilsonia along Eshom Creek (lat. 36°41'10" N, long. 118°57' W; at SE cor. sec. 20, T 14 S, R 28 E). Named on Giant Forest (1956) 15' quadrangle.

Meadow Lakes [FRESNO]: *village,* 6.5 miles west-southwest of Shaver Lake Heights (present town of Shaver Lake) in Corlew Meadows (lat. 37°04'50" N, long. 119°25'45" W; sec. 11, T 10 S, R 23 E). Named on Shaver Lake (1953) 15' quadrangle. Postal authorities established Meadow Lakes post office in 1930, discontinued it for a time in 1932, and discontinued it finally in 1933 (Frickstad, p. 35).

Meadows Ridge [TULARE]: *ridge,* south-trending, 1 mile long, 9.5 miles east of Tucker Mountain (lat. 36°39' N, long. 119°02'10" W; on W line sec. 3, T 15 S, R 27 E). Named on Miramonte (1966) 7.5' quadrangle.

Measels Spring [KERN]: *spring,* 6.5 miles southwest of Pinyon Mountain (lat. 35°24' N, long. 118°14'55" W; sec. 20, T 29 S, R 35 E).

Named on Pinyon Mountain (1972) 7.5' quadrangle.

Medano [MADERA]: *locality,* 4.5 miles north-northeast of Fairmead (lat. 37°07'50" N, long. 120°09'10" W; sec. 19, T 9 S, R 17 E). Named on Le Grand (1918) 7.5' quadrangle.

Media: see **Bates Station** [MADERA].

Media Agua Creek [KERN]: *stream,* flows 8.5 miles to Antelope Plain 7 miles south of Blackwells Corner (lat. 35°30'55" N, long. 119°53'20" W; sec. 2, T 28 S, R 19 E). Named on Las Yeguas Ranch (1959) and Shale Point (1953) 7.5' quadrangles. The name is from the location of the stream halfway between Carneros Spring and a well at Point of Rocks—*media agua* means "middle water" in Spanish (Arnold and Johnson, p. 21).

Medley Lake [FRESNO]: *lake,* 1250 feet long, 7 miles south-southwest of Mount Abbot along South Fork Bear Creek (2) (lat. 37°18'10" N, long. 118°51'05" W). Named on Mount Abbot (1953) 15' quadrangle. William A. Dill of California Department of Fish and Game named the lake in 1942 (Browning 1986, p. 143).

Megs Mud Spring [KERN]: *spring,* 11.5 miles north-northwest of Mojave (lat. 35°12'45" N, long. 118°13'25" W; near S line sec. 21, T 31 S, R 35 E). Named on Cache Peak (1973) 7.5' quadrangle.

Mehrten Creek [TULARE]: *stream,* flows 3.5 miles to Middle Fork Kaweah River 10 miles west-southwest of Triple Divide Peak (lat. 36°32'15" N, long. 118°41'30" W). Named on Triple Divide Peak (1956) 15' quadrangle. The name "Mehrten" commemorates James Mehrten, a pioneer cattleman of Three Rivers (Browning 1986, p. 143). United States Board on Geographic Names (1938, p. 34) rejected the form "Merten Creek" for the name.

Mehrten Meadow [TULARE]: *area,* 8.5 miles west of Triple Divide Peak (lat. 36°35' N, long. 118°41' W; at E line sec. 35, T 15 S, R 30 E); the place is near the head of Mehrten Creek. Named on Triple Divide Peak (1956) 15' quadrangle. United States Board on Geographic Names (1938, p. 35) rejected the form "Merten Meadow" for the name.

Melvers Spring: see **McIvers Spring** [KERN].

Melvin [FRESNO]: *locality,* 1 mile south of the center of Clovis along Southern Pacific Railroad (lat. 36°48'25" N, long. 119°41'55" W; near NW cor. sec. 16, T 13 S, R 21 E). Named on Clovis (1964) 7.5' quadrangle.

Menagerie Canyon [KERN]: *canyon,* drained by a stream that flows 4 miles to Caliente Creek 3.25 miles west of Loraine (lat. 35°18'25" N, long. 118°29'35" W; sec. 24, T 30 S, R 32 E). Named on Loraine (1972) 7.5' quadrangle.

Mendel: see **Mount Mendel** [FRESNO].

Mendiburu Canyon [KERN]: *canyon,* drained by a stream that flows 4.25 miles to Tehachapi Valley 3.5 miles southeast of Tehachapi (lat.

35°05'40" N, long. 118°24'10" W; at N line sec. 31, T 12 N, R 14 W). Named on Tehachapi South (1966) 7.5' quadrangle.

Mendota [FRESNO]: *town,* 8.5 miles south-southeast of Firebaugh (lat. 36°45'15" N, long. 120°22'45" W; in and near sec. 31, T 13 S, R 15 E). Named on Coit Ranch (1956), Firebaugh (1956), Mendota Dam (1956), and Tranquillity (1956) 7.5' quadrangles. Postal authorities established Mendota post office in 1892; officials of Southern Pacific Railroad named the place for Mendota, Illinois (Salley, p. 138). The town incorporated in 1942. Postal authorities established Hayes post office, named for William J. Hayes, first postmaster, 18 miles southwest of Mendota in 1893 and discontinued it in 1902; they established Cadogan post office, named for James J. Cadogan, first postmaster, 20 miles south of Mendota in 1894 and discontinued it in 1895 (Salley, p. 31, 95). A place called Pueblo de las Juntas, located at the confluence of San Joaquin River and Fresno Slough (about 2 miles north of present Mendota), was one of the first places in San Joaquin Valley settled by Spaniards—*las juntas,* which means "junction" or "meeting place" in Spanish, may have referred to the location of the site at the confluence of waterways, or to the place being a rendezvous for refugees; the locality also was called Fresno for two large ash trees that grew there on the bank of the river (Hoover, Rensch, and Rensch, p. 91) Derby's (1850) map shows a place called Warsaw situated at about this same site. A place called Rancho de los Californios was located farther east on high ground near the south bank of San Joaquin River (Charles W. Clough, personal communication, 1985); notorious horse thieves hid from Spanish authorities at the locality, which continued as a den of outlaws well into the American period (Hoover, Rensch, and Rensch, p. 91).

Mendota Pool [FRESNO]: *water feature,* behind a dam on San Joaquin River 7 miles southeast of Firebaugh on Fresno-Madera county line (lat. 36°47'15" N, long. 120°22'15" W; sec. 19, T 13 S, R 15 E); the feature is 2.25 miles north of Mendota at the confluence of San Joaquin River and Fresno Slough. Named on Mendota Dam (1956) 7.5' quadrangle.

Mendota Pool [MADERA]: *water feature,* behind a dam on San Joaquin River 21 miles south west of Madera on Madera-Fresno county line (lat. 36°47'15" N, long. 120°22'15" W; sec. 19, T 13 S, R 15 E). Named on Mendota Dam (1956) 7.5' quadrangle.

Mendota Station: see **Tranquillity** [FRESNO].

Mercedes River: see **Merced River** [MADERA].

Merced Group: see **Clark Range** [MADERA].

Merced Pass [MADERA]: *pass,* 3 miles west-southwest of Merced Peak (lat. 37°37' N, long.

119°26'30" W). Named on Merced Peak (1953) 15' quadrangle.

Merced Pass Lake: see **Lower Merced Pass Lake** [MADERA]; **Upper Merced Pass Lake** [MADERA].

Merced Peak [MADERA]: *peak,* 22 miles north-northeast of Yosemite Forks (lat. 37°38'05" N, long. 119°23'35" W); the peak is near the headwaters of Merced River. Altitude 11,726 feet. Named on Merced Peak (1953) 15' quadrangle. United States Board on Geographic Names (1976b, p. 1-2) approved the name "Mount Bruce" for a peak (altitude 9728 feet) located 6 miles southwest of Merced Peak (lat. 37°35'48" N, long. 119°29'32" W); the name commemorates the Bruce family, pioneers in the region in the 1850's.

Merced Peak Fork [MADERA]: *stream,* flows 6 miles to join Lyell Fork and form Merced River 5.25 miles north-northeast of Merced Peak (lat. 37°42'05" N, long. 119°20'50" W); the stream heads north of Merced Peak. Named on Merced Peak (1953) 15' quadrangle.

Merced River [MADERA]: *stream,* formed in Madera County by the confluence of Lyell Fork and Merced Peak Fork, flows 140 miles, partly in Mariposa County, to San Joaquin River 27 miles west of Merced in Merced County (lat. 37°20'55" N, long. 120°58'30" W; near W line sec. 3, T 7 S, R 9 E). Named on Atwater (1961), Coulterville (1947), El Portal (1947), Merced (1962), Merced Falls (1962), Merced Peak (1953), Turlock (1962), and Yosemite (1956) 15' quadrangles. Called Rio de los Merced on Ord's (1848) map, R. de la Merced on Wyld's (1849) map, and Mercedes River on Ellis' (1850) map. United States, Board on Geographic Names (1978d, p. 3) rejected the names "Aux-um-ne," "Aux-um-nes," "Rio de la Merced," "Wa-kal-la," and "El Rio de Nuestra Senora de la Merced" for the stream, and pointed out that Spanish explorers under Sergeant Gabriel Moraga named the river on September 29, 1806, five days after the feast day of Our Lady of Mercy—*merced* means "mercy" in Spanish. North Fork enters the main stream from the north 4.5 miles northeast of the village of Bear Valley in Mariposa County; it is 18 miles long and is named on Coulterville (1947), Lake Eleanor (1956), and Tuolumne (1948) 15' quadrangles. South Fork heads in Madera County and enters the main stream from the southeast 6 miles west-southwest of El Portal in Mariposa County; it is 43 miles long and is named on El Portal (1947), Merced Peak (1953), and Yosemite (1956) 15' quadrangles. United States Board on Geographic Names (1978d, p. 3) rejected the name "North Fork Merced River" for Lyell Fork. Gardiner (p. 139) noted a place called New York Camp that was started in Mariposa County near the mouth of Merced River in 1850.

Merced River: see **Lyell Fork** [MADERA].

Mercer Mountain [MADERA]: *peak,* 1 mile east of O'Neals (lat. 37° 07'40" N, long. 119°40'40" W; near SE cor. sec. 21, T 9 S, R 21 E). Altitude 1921 feet. Named on O'Neals (1965) 7.5' quadrangle.

Mercey Creek [FRESNO]: *stream,* heads just inside Merced County and flows 8 miles, partly in San Benito County, to Little Panoche Creek 2 miles north-northwest of Mercey Hot Springs in Fresno County (lat. 36°44' N, long. 120°52'10" W; sec. 3, T 14 S, R 10 E). Named on Cerro Colorado (1969) and Mercey Hot Springs (1969) 7.5' quadrangles. Called Mercy Creek on Panoche Valley (1944) 15' quadrangle.

Mercey Hot Springs [FRESNO]: *locality,* 25 miles west-southwest of Firebaugh in Little Panoche Valley (lat. 36°42'15" N, long. 120° 51'30" W; near SE cor. sec. 15, T 14 S, R 10 E). Named on Mercey Hot Springs (1969) 7.5' quadrangle. Called Mercy Hot Sprs. on Panoche Valley (1944) 15' quadrangle. The name commemorates J.N. Mercy, an early stockman in the neighborhood (Stewart, p. 291). The springs were known as early as 1848, and were utilized for a health resort after about 1900 (Laizure, p. 322).

Mercy Creek: see **Mercey Creek** [FRESNO].

Mercy Hot Springs: see **Mercey Hot Springs** [FRESNO].

Meridian [KERN]: *locality,* 4.5 miles northeast of Mettler (lat. 35°06'25" N, long. 118°54'50" W; at SE cor. sec. 25, T 32 S, R 28 E). Named on Mettler (1955) 7.5' quadrangle.

Merriam Lake [FRESNO]: *lake,* 1600 feet long, 6.5 miles south of Mount Abbot (lat. 37°17'40" N, long. 118°47'30" W); the lake is 1.5 miles southwest of Merriam Peak. Named on Mount Abbot (1953) 15' quadrangle.

Merriam Peak [FRESNO]: *peak,* 5.5 miles south of Mount Abbot (lat. 37°18'35" N, long. 118°45'55" W). Altitude 13,077 feet. Named on Mount Abbot (1953) 15' quadrangle. California State Geographic Board proposed the name to honor C. Hart Merriam, chief of United States Biological Survey from 1885 until 1910, and chairman of United States Geographic Board from 1914 until 1925 (United States Board on Geographic Names, 1933a, p. 514). United States Board on Geographic Names (1983a, p. 4) rejected the name "Mount Merriam" for the feature.

Merrill: see **Pete Merrill Canyon** [FRESNO].

Merrill Pools [FRESNO]: *water feature,* 10.5 miles south-southwest of Coalinga on upper reaches of Taylor Creek (2) (lat. 36°00'25" N, long. 120°27'15" W; sec. 22, T 22 S, R 14 E). Named on Curry Mountain (1969) 7.5' quadrangle.

Merry Camp [TULARE]: *locality,* 2.5 miles north of California Hot Springs (lat. 35°55' N, long. 118°40'05" W; sec. 19, T 23 S, R 31

E); the place is along Merry Creek. Named on California Hot Springs (1958) 15' quadrangle.

Merry Creek [TULARE]: *stream,* flows 2.5 miles to Tyler Creek 1.25 miles north-northwest of California Hot Springs (lat. 35°53'50" N, long. 118°40'40" W; sec. 30, T 23 S, R 31 E). Named on California Hot Springs (1958) 15' quadrangle.

Merryman [TULARE]: *locality,* 3 miles northeast of Exeter along Visalia Electric Railroad (lat. 36°19'30" N, long. 119°06'20" W; at W line sec. 36, T 18 S, R 26 E). Named on Rocky Hill (1951) 7.5' quadrangle.

Merten Creek: see **Mehrten Creek** [TULARE].

Merten Meadow: see **Mehrten Meadow** [TULARE].

Mesa Lake [FRESNO]: *lake,* 1500 feet long, 2.5 miles west of Mount Humphreys in Humphreys Basin (lat. 37°16'05" N, long. 118°43'10" W). Named on Mount Tom (1949) 15' quadrangle.

Mesa Roida [KINGS]: *area,* 6 miles east of Avenal (lat. 35°59'25" N, long. 120°01'20" W; near NE cor. sec. 28, T 22 S, R 18 E). Named on Kettleman Plain (1953) 7.5' quadrangle. The name is descriptive—*roida* means "eroded" in Spanish (United States Board on Geographic Names, 1933b, p. 20).

Mesa Spring [KERN]: *spring,* 5.25 miles west-northwest of Garlock (lat. 35°26'35" N, long. 117°52'10" W). Named on Garlock (1967) 7.5' quadrangle.

Mesquite Canyon [KERN]: *canyon,* drained by a stream that flows nearly 4 miles to Fremont Valley 1.5 miles west-southwest of Garlock (lat. 35°23'35" N, long. 117°48'55" W). Named on Garlock (1967) 7.5' quadrangle.

Mesquite Springs [KERN]: *springs,* 1.5 miles southwest of Garlock (lat. 35°23'25" N, long. 117°48'45" W; at N line sec. 29, T 29 S, R 39 E); the springs are near the mouth of Mesquite Canyon. Named on Garlock (1967) 7.5' quadrangle.

Mesquite Springs: see **Koehn Spring** [KERN].

Metcalf Gap [MADERA]: *pass,* 15 miles north-northeast of Raymond (lat. 37°24'15" N, long. 119°45'55" W; sec. 15, T 6 S, R 20 E). Named on Stumpfield Mountain (1947) 7.5' quadrangle.

Metralla Canyon: see **Grapevine** [KERN].

Mettler [KERN]: *village,* 21 miles south of Bakersfield (lat. 35°03'50" N, long. 118°58'10" W; on S line sec. 1, T 11 N, R 20 W). Named on Mettler (1955) 7.5' quadrangle. The village was started in 1941 and named for W. H. Mettler, a local agriculturalist (Bailey, 1967, p. 17).

Mexican Colony [KERN]: *locality,* 2 miles south of Shafter (lat. 35° 28'05" N, long. 119°16'05" W; near N line sec. 27, T 28 S, R 25 E). Named on Rio Bravo (1954) 7.5' quadrangle.

Meyer: see **Oscar Meyer Spring** [KERN].

Miami: see **Grub Gulch** [MADERA] (2).

Miami Creek [MADERA]: *stream,* heads in Mariposa County and flows 17 miles to Fresno River 5.5 miles west-southwest of Yosemite Forks in Mariposa County (lat. 37°20'30" N, long. 119°43'40" W; near NE cor. sec. 12, T 7 S, R 20 E). Named on Bass Lake (1953) 15' quadrangle. Called North Fork on Mariposa (1912) 30' quadrangle, but United States Board on Geographic Names (1964b, p. 13) rejected the name "North Fork Fresno River" for the stream.

Michaels: see **Coarsegold** [MADERA].

Middle Creek [TULARE]: *stream,* flows less than 1 mile to Alder Creek (1) 8.5 miles south-southeast of Camp Nelson (lat. 36°01'50" N, long. 118°32'50" W; sec. 8, T 22 S, R 32 E). Named on Camp Nelson (1956) 15' quadrangle.

Middle Dome: see **Kettleman Hills** [FRESNO-KERN-KINGS].

Middle Fork Spring [TULARE]: *spring,* 2.25 miles southeast of California Hot Springs (lat. 35°51'20" N, long. 118°38'45" W; near E line sec. 8, T 24 S, R 31 E). Named on California Hot Springs (1958) 15' quadrangle.

Middle Knob [KERN]: *ridge,* east-northeast-trending, 1 mile long, 8 miles north-northwest of Mojave (lat. 35°09'40" N, long. 118°13'15" W). Named on Cache Peak (1973) 7.5' quadrangle.

Middle Lost Keys Lake: see **Lost Keys Lakes** [FRESNO].

Middle Palisade [FRESNO]: *peak,* 2.5 miles northwest of Mount Bolton Brown on Fresno-Inyo county line (lat. 37°04'15" N, long. 118°28'05" W). Altitude 14,040 feet. Named on Big Pine (1950) 15' quadrangle. A peak 0.5 mile northwest of Middle Palisade is called Norman Clyde Peak for Norman A. Clyde, a mountaineer who made the first ascent of the feature in 1930 (United States Board on Geographic Names, 1974b, p. 3).

Middle Ridge [KERN]: *ridge,* west-northwest-trending, 3 miles long, 5 miles west-north-west of Liebre Twins (lat. 34°58'15" N, long. 118°39'15" W). Named on Winters Ridge (1966) 7.5' quadrangle.

Middle Spring [FRESNO]: *spring,* 4.25 miles north of Coalinga Mineral Springs (lat. 36°12'25" N, long. 120°33'30" W; sec. 10, T 20 S, R 13 E). Named on Sherman Peak (1969) 7.5' quadrangle.

Middle Turret Lakes [FRESNO]: *lakes,* two, largest 700 feet long, 8.5 miles south-south-west of Mount Abbot (lat. 37°16'05" N, long. 118°49'55" W); the lakes are between Lower Turret Lake and Upper Turret Lakes at the head of Turret Creek. Named on Mount Abbot (1953) 15' quadrangle.

Midge Creek [FRESNO]: *stream,* flows nearly 2 miles to Rancheria Creek (1) 3.5 miles southeast of Kaiser Peak (lat. 37°15'25" N, long. 119°08'30" W; sec. 4, T 8 S, R 26 E).

Named on Kaiser Peak (1953) 15' quadrangle.

Midge Lake [FRESNO]: *lake,* 600 feet long, 16 miles northeast of Kaiser Peak (lat. 37°29' N, long. 119°00'40" W). Named on Kaiser Peak (1953) 15' quadrangle.

Midland: see **Midoil** [KERN].

Midoil [KERN]: *locality,* nearly 2 miles southeast of Fellows (lat. 35°09'30" N, long. 119°31'20" W; sec. 8, R 32 S, E 23 E). Named on Fellows (1951) 7.5' quadrangle. McKittrick (1912) 30' quadrangle shows Midland P.O. at the place. Postal authorities established Midland post office in 1908 and discontinued it in 1914 (Frickstad, p. 57).

Mid Ridge [KINGS]: *ridge,* east-southeast-trending, 0.5 mile long, 3.25 miles southwest of Kettleman City (lat. 35°58'10" N, long. 119°59'45" W; sec. 35, T 22 S, R 18 E). Named on Los Viejos (1954) 7.5' quadrangle.

Mid Valley [TULARE]: *locality,* 4 miles south-southeast of Goshen along Southern Pacific Railroad (lat. 36°17'50" N, long. 119°23'05" W; at NE cor. sec. 8, T 19 S, R 24 E). Named on Goshen (1949) 7.5' quadrangle.

Midway: see **Fellows** [KERN].

Midway Lake [FRESNO]: *lake,* 1200 feet long, 3.25 miles southeast of Blackcap Mountain (lat. 37°02'30" N, long. 118°45' W). Named on Blackcap Mountain (1953) 15' quadrangle.

Midway Mountain [TULARE]: *peak,* 12 miles west-northwest of Mount Whitney on Great Western Divide (lat. 36°38'35" N, long. 118°28'55" W). Altitude 13,666 feet. Named on Mount Whitney (1956) 15' quadrangle.

Midway Valley [KERN]: *valley,* southwest of Buena Vista Hills; center near Taft (lat. 35°09' N, long. 119°26' W). Named on Fellows (1951), Taft (1950), and West Elk Hills (1954) 7.5' quadrangles. The name is for the proximity of the place to Midway oil field (Arnold and Johnson, p. 21).

Mike Harney Canyon [KERN]: *canyon,* drained by a stream that flows 1.25 miles to French Ranch Gulch 3.5 miles north of Democrat Hot Springs (lat. 35°34'45" N, long. 118°40'15" W; sec. 17, T 27 S, R 31 E). Named on Democrat Hot Springs (1972) 7.5' quadrangle.

Mike Walker Canyon [MADERA]: *canyon,* drained by a stream that flows 1.5 miles to San Joaquin River 6.25 miles south-southwest of the town of North Fork (lat. 37°08'40" N, long. 119°33'15" W; sec. 15, T 9 S, R 22 E). Named on North Fork (1965) 7.5' quadrangle.

Mile High Curve [MADERA]: *locality,* 5.25 miles east-southeast of Shuteye Peak (lat. 37°18'40" N, long. 119°20'50" W); the feature is along a road 2500 feet above San Joaquin River. Named on Shuteye Peak (1953) 15' quadrangle.

Milestone Bow: see **Milestone Bowl** [TULARE].

Milestone Bowl [TULARE]: *relief feature,* 11.5 miles west-northwest of Mount Whitney (lat. 36°37'30" N, long. 118°29' W); the feature is

south of Milestone Mountain. Named on Mount Whitney (1956) 15' quadrangle. Called Milestone Bow on Mount Whitney (1907) 30' quadrangle, but United States Board on Geographic Names (1933a, p. 519) rejected this name.

Milestone Creek [TULARE]: *stream,* flows 3.5 miles to Kern River 9 miles west-northwest of Mount Whitney (lat. 36°38'25" N, long. 118°25'30" W); the stream heads near Milestone Mountain. Named on Mount Whitney (1956) 15' quadrangle.

Milestone Mountain [TULARE]: *peak,* 11.5 miles west-northwest of Mount Whitney on Great Western Divide (lat. 36°38'05" N, long. 118°29' W). Altitude 13,641 feet. Named on Mount Whitney (1956) 15' quadrangle.

Miley [FRESNO]: *locality,* 5 miles northeast of Selma along Atchison, Topeka and Santa Fe Railroad (lat. 36°37'20" N, long. 119°32'45" W; sec. 14, T 15 S, R 22 E). Named on Selma (1964) 7.5' quadrangle. Postal authorities established Miley post office in 1899 and discontinued it in 1902; the name commemorates Julian J. Miley, first postmaster (Salley, p. 140).

Milham City [KINGS]: *locality,* 3 miles northwest of Kettleman City (lat. 36°02'15" N, long. 120°00' W; near SW cor. sec. 2, T 22 S, R 18 E). Named on Kettleman City (1937) and La Cima (1934) 7.5' quadrangles.

Milk Canyon [TULARE]: *canyon,* drained by a stream that flows 1.5 miles to North Fork of Middle Fork Tule River 5.5 miles west-northwest of Camp Nelson (lat. 36°10'05" N, long. 118°42'10" W). Named on Camp Nelson (1956) 15' quadrangle.

Milk Ranch Canyon [FRESNO]: *canyon,* drained by a stream that flows 6 miles to Mill Creek (3) 2 miles southeast of Dunlap (lat. 36°43'05" N, long. 119°05'35" W; sec. 12, T 14 S, R 26 E). Named on Miramonte (1966) 7.5' quadrangle.

Milk Ranch Peak [TULARE]: *peak,* 8 miles east of Kaweah (lat. 36° 29' N, long. 118°46'50" W; sec. 1, T 17 S, R 29 E); the peak is west of Paradise Ridge. Altitude 6250 feet. Named on Kaweah (1957) 15' quadrangle. United States Board on Geographic Names (1946, p. 2) rejected the name "Paradise Peak" for the feature.

Milk Ranch Peak: see **Paradise Peak** [TULARE].

Mill Creek [FRESNO]:

(1) *stream,* flows 5 miles to Mammoth Pool Reservoir 7.5 miles northwest of Kaiser Peak (lat. 37°21'45" N, long. 119°17'35" W; near E line sec. 36, T 6 S, R 24 E). Named on Kaiser Peak (1953) and Shuteye Peak (1953) 15' quadrangles.

(2) *stream,* flows 2.5 miles to Jose Creek 4 miles northwest of Shaver Lake Heights (present town of Shaver Lake) (lat. 37°08'20" N, long. 119°22'35" W; near N line sec. 20, T 9 S, R 24 E). Named on Shaver Lake (1953) 15'

quadrangle. Kaiser (1904) 30' quadrangle shows Damon Mill situated near the headwaters of the stream.

Mill Creek [FRESNO-TULARE]: *stream,* heads in Tulare County and flows 30 miles to Kings River 1.5 miles north-northeast of Tivy Mountain in Fresno County (lat. 36°49'10" N, long. 119°21' W; near N line sec. 10, T 13 S, R 24 E). Named on Giant Forest (1956) and Patterson Mountain (1952) 15' quadrangles, and on Miramonte (1966), Pine Flat Dam (1965), and Tucker Mountain (1966) 7.5' quadrangles. United States Board on Geographic Names (1981b, p. 4) approved the name "Little White Deer Creek" for a stream that flows 4 miles to Mill Creek 2.5 miles west of Dunlap (lat. 36°44'32" N, long. 119°09'45" W; sec. 5, T 14 S, R 26 E). The Board at the same time approved the name "Little White Deer Valley" for a valley, 2.5 miles long, that is drained by Little White Deer Creek, and (p. 3) approved the name "Clingans Junction" for a locality situated in Little White Deer Valley 3 miles northwest of Dunlap (lat. 36°45'16" N, long. 119°10'10" W; sec. 32, T 13 S, R 25 E)—this name is for William Melrose Clingan, who established the first business at the place in 1946.

Mill Creek [KERN]:

(1) *stream,* flows 2.25 miles to Lumreau Creek 4.25 miles southeast of Glennville (lat. 35°40'45" N, long. 118°39'25" W; sec. 9, T 26 S, R 31 E). Named on Glennville (1972) 7.5' quadrangle.

(2) *stream,* flows 8 miles to Kern River 5.25 miles west-southwest of Miracle Hot Springs (lat. 35°32'35" N, long. 118°37'05" W). Named on Breckenridge Mountain (1972) and Miracle Hot Springs (1972) 7.5' quadrangles.

Mill Creek [KINGS]: *stream,* flows 4 miles to Cross Creek 6.5 miles southeast of Hanford (lat. 36°15'50" N, long. 119°33'35" W; sec. 23, T 19 S, R 22 E). Named on Remnoy (1927) 7.5' quadrangle. On Remnoy (1954) 7.5' quadrangle, the stream is mainly in an artificial watercourse. On Goshen (1926) 7.5' quadrangle, the name applies to a nearby stream that heads in Tulare County.

Mill Creek [TULARE]:

(1) *stream,* heads at Kaweah River and flows 16 miles to Kings County 10.5 miles westsouthwest of Visalia (lat. 36°17'15" N, long. 119°28'25" W; at W line sec. 10, T 19 S, R 23 E). Named on Exeter (1952) and Visalia (1949) 15' quadrangles. Grunsky (p. 11) referred to "Visalia or Mill Creek" as a major high-water channel of Kaweah River. East Fork enters from the east 4.5 miles southsouthwest of Goshen; it is 4.25 miles long and is named on Goshen (1926) 7.5' quadrangle.

(2) *stream,* flows 2 miles to South Creek 9.5 miles northeast of California Hot Springs near Johnsondale (lat. 35°58'05" N, long. 118°32'25" W; sec. 32, T 22 S, R 32 E).

Named on California Hot Springs (1958) 15' quadrangle.

Mill Creek: see **Peel Mill Creek** [TULARE].

Miller: see **Camp Miller** and **Fort Miller**, under **Old Fort Miller** [FRESNO].

Miller: see **Kismet** [MADERA].

Miller Creek [MADERA]: *stream,* flows 4.5 miles to Granite Creek 14 miles northeast of Shuteye Peak (lat. 37°29'35" N, long. 119°14'40" W; sec. 16, T 5 S, R 25 E). Named on Kaiser Peak (1953), Merced Peak (1953), and Shuteye Peak (1953) 15' quadrangles.

Miller Crossing [MADERA]: *locality,* 10 miles southwest of Devils Postpile along San Joaquin River (lat. 37°30'35" N, long. 119° 12' W; sec. 11, T 5 S, R 25 E). Named on Devils Postpile (1953) 15' quadrangle. The name is for William C. Miller, an early-day sheepman (Browning, 1986, p. 147).

Miller Meadow [MADERA]: *area,* 12.5 miles northeast of Shuteye Peak (lat. 37°29'50" N, long. 119°17'30" W; sec. 13, T 5 S, R 24 E). Named on Shuteye Peak (1953) 15' quadrangle.

Miller Meadow Campground [MADERA]: *locality,* 10.5 miles south-southeast of Merced Peak (lat. 37°30'15" N, long. 119°17'20" W; near S line sec. 12, T 5 S, R 24 E). Named on Merced Peak (1953) 15' quadrangle.

Millers Corner: see **Twentytwo Mile House** [MADERA].

Miller Spring [KERN]: *spring,* 5.5 miles north of Caliente (lat. 35° 22'20" N, long. 118°39' W; near E line sec. 28, T 29 S, R 31 E). Named on Bena (1972) 7.5' quadrangle.

Miller Springs [KERN]: *springs,* 3.5 miles north of Emerald Mountain (lat. 35°18'20" N, long. 118°16'50" W). Named on Emerald Mountain (1972) 7.5' quadrangle.

Millersville [KERN]: *locality,* 1.25 miles west of Loraine along Caliente Creek (lat. 35°18'10" N, long. 118°27'20" W; sec. 20, T 30 S, R 33 E). Named on Loraine (1972) 7.5' quadrangle. The place was a mining camp that Bailey (1962, p. 50) called Millerville.

Millerton: see **Old Millerton** [FRESNO].

Millerton Lake [FRESNO]: *lake,* behind a dam on San Joaquin River 11 miles west-southwest of Prather on Fresno-Madera county line (lat. 37°00' N, long. 119°42'15" W; sec. 5, T 11 S, R 21 E). Named on Friant (1964), Millerton Lake East (1965), and Millerton Lake West (1965) 7.5' quadrangles.

Millerton Lake [MADERA]: *lake,* behind a dam on San Joaquin River 9 miles south of O'Neals on Madera-Fresno county line (lat. 37°00' N, long. 119°42'15" W; sec. 5, T 11 S, R 21 E). Named on Friant (1964), Millerton Lake East (1965), and Millerton Lake West (1965) 7.5' quadrangles. Water of the lake covers the site of Old Millerton in Fresno County.

Millerton Ridge [MADERA]: *ridge,* southwest-trending, 1.5 miles long, 5.5 miles south of O'Neals (lat. 37°02'45" N, long. 119° 41' W);

DURHAM'S PLACE-NAMES

the ridge is north of Millerton Lake. Named on Millerton Lake West (1965) 7.5' quadrangle.

Millerton Spring: see **Sulphur Springs** [FRESNO].

Millertown: see **Old Millerton** [FRESNO].

Millerville: see **Millersville** [KERN].

Mill Flat [FRESNO]: *area,* 3.5 miles south-southeast of Balch Camp along Kings River (lat. 36°51'25" N, long. 119°05'30" W; sec. 25, T 12 S, R 26 E). Named on Patterson Mountain (1952) 15' quadrangle.

Mill Flat Creek [FRESNO]: *stream,* flows 12.5 miles to Kings River 3.5 miles south-southeast of Balch Camp at Mill Flat (lat. 36°51'25" N, long. 119°05'40" W; sec. 25, T 12 S, R 26 E). Named on Giant Forest (1956) and Patterson Mountain (1952) 15' quadrangles, and on Miramonte (1966) 7.5' quadrangle.

Mill Potrero [KERN]: *marsh,* 4 miles south-southwest of Eagle Rest Peak (lat. 34°51'10" N, long. 119°10' W; sec. 19, T 9 N, R 21 W). Named on Sawmill Mountain (1943) 7.5' quadrangle. The first steam sawmill in the neighborhood was at the site (Hoover, Rensch, and Rensch, p. 127).

Mills: see **Mount Anna Mills**, under **Mount Guyot** [TULARE]; **Mount Mills** [FRESNO].

Mills Creek [FRESNO]: *stream,* flows 2.25 miles to Second Recess 3.25 miles west-northwest of Mount Abbot (lat. 37°24'15" N, long. 118°50' W); the stream heads at Upper Mills Creek Lake nearly 1 mile west-southwest of Mount Mills. Named on Mount Abbot (1953) 15' quadrangle.

Mills Creek Lake: see **Lower Mills Creek Lake** [FRESNO]; **Upper Mills Creek Lake** [FRESNO].

Mills Spring [FRESNO]: *spring,* 8 miles west of Coalinga (lat. 36°09'25" N, long. 120°29'50" W; sec. 30, T 20 S, R 14 E). Named on Alcalde Hills (1969) 7.5' quadrangle.

Milltown: see **Big Blue Mill** [KERN].

Millux [KERN]: *locality,* 15 miles east-northeast of Taft along Sunset Railroad (lat. 35°10'50" N, long. 119°11'45" W). Named on Millux (1954) 7.5' quadrangle. The name was coined in 1901 from the name of the stock-raising firm of Miller and Lux (Gudde, 1949, p. 216).

Millville: see **Big Blue Mill** [KERN].

Millwood [FRESNO]: *locality,* 6.5 miles east of Dunlap along Mill Flat Creek (lat. 36°44'40" N, long. 119°00'10" W; sec. 35, T 13 S, R 27 E). Site named on Miramonte (1966) 7.5' quadrangle. Postal authorities established Millwood post office in 1894 and discontinued it in 1909 (Frickstad, p. 35). The place was called Sequoia Mills before the post office was established (Forest M. Clingan, personal communication, 1990). Johnston (p. 54) noted a place called Andy Berry's Landing that was located between Millwood and Hoist

Ridge—the Berry brothers had a log landing at the site.

Millys Foot Pass [TULARE]: *pass,* 11 miles northwest of Mount Whitney on Kings-Kern Divide (lat. 36°41'10" N, long. 118°25'45" W). Named on Mount Whitney (1956) 15' quadrangle. The name recalls Mildred Jentsch, who with Sylvia Kershaw made the first crossing of the pass in 1953 (Browning 1986, p. 147).

Milo [TULARE]: *locality,* 6 miles north of Springville (lat. 36°13'10" N, long. 118°48'55" W; near NE cor. sec. 3, T 20 S, R 29 E). Named on Springville (1957) 7.5' quadrangle. Postal authorities established Milo post office in 1888 and discontinued it in 1922 (Salley, p. 141). The name was selected from a list that Henry Murphy submitted; Milo also was known as Mountain View (Mitchell, A.R., p. 68). Postal authorities established Manzanita post office in 1882 and changed the name the same year to Cramer, for Eleanor A. Cramer, first postmaster; they moved Cramer post office 1.5 miles south in 1887, and discontinued it in 1891 when they moved the service to Milo (Salley, p. 52, 132). Thompson's (1892) map shows both Milo P.O. (sec. 2, T 20 S, R 29 E) and Cramer P.O. (sec. 14, T 20 S, R 29 E). Postal authorities established Summerhouse post office in 1890, and discontinued it the same year when they moved the service to Cramer; the post office was at a summer campsite that Andrew J. Doty started in 1885 (Salley, p. 215). California Division of Highways' (1934) map shows a locality called Balch Park situated 8 miles east of Milo (near SE cor. sec. 25, T 19 S, R 30 E).

Minaret Creek [MADERA]: *stream,* flows 5 miles to Middle Fork San Joaquin River less than 1 mile north-northwest of Devils Postpile (lat. 37°38'05" N, long. 119°05'05" W); the stream heads at Minaret Lake. Named on Devils Postpile (1953) 15' quadrangle.

Minaret Falls [MADERA]: *waterfall,* 1.25 miles north-northwest of Devils Postpile (lat. 37°38'25" N, long. 119°05'30" W); the feature is along Minaret Creek. Named on Devils Postpile (1953) 15' quadrangle.

Minaret Falls Campground [MADERA]: *locality,* 1 mile north of Devils Postpile along Middle Fork San Joaquin River (lat. 37°38'20" N, long. 119°05' W); the place is 0.5 mile east-southeast of Minaret Falls. Named on Devils Postpile (1953) 15' quadrangle.

Minaret Lake [MADERA]: *lake,* 2000 feet long, nearly 5 miles west-northwest of Devils Postpile (lat. 37°39'35" N, long. 119°09'25" W); the lake is 1 mile east of Minarets. Named on Devils Postpile (1953) 15' quadrangle.

Minaret Lake: see **Johnston Lake** [MADERA].

Minaret Meadow: see **Johnston Meadow** [MADERA].

Minarets [MADERA]: *relief features,* 6 miles west-northwest of Devils Postpile (lat. 37°39'50" N, long. 119°10'45" W). Named on Devils Postpile (1953) 15' quadrangle. Members of the Whitney survey named the features for their resemblance to mosque spires (Smith, Genny, p. 26).

Minarets: see **North Fork** [MADERA].

Minaret Summit [MADERA]: *pass,* 2.5 miles north-northeast of Devils Postpile on Madera-Mono county line (lat. 37°39'15" N, long. 119°03'25" W). Named on Devils Postpile (1953) 15' quadrangle.

Mine Creek [FRESNO]: *stream,* heads in Merced County and flows 8 miles to Little Panoche Creek nearly 3 miles north of Mercey Hot Springs in Fresno County (lat. 36°44'45" N, long. 120°51'35" W; sec. 3, T 14 S, R 10 E). Named on Cerro Colorado (1969), Mercey Hot Springs (1969), and Ortigalita Peak (1969) 7.5' quadrangles.

Mine Hill [TULARE]: *peak,* 7 miles east of Porterville (lat. 36°03'25" N, long. 118°53'35" W). Altitude 1784 feet. Named on Success Dam (1956) 7.5' quadrangle.

Mine Mountain [FRESNO]: *peak,* 6 miles west-northwest of Castle Mountain on Fresno-Monterey county line (lat. 35°58'10" N, long. 120°26' W; sec. 35, T 22 S, R 14 E). Named on Parkfield (1961) 7.5' quadrangle.

Mineral Creek [TULARE]: *stream,* flows 2 miles to East Fork Kaweah River 1.5 miles west of Mineral King (lat. 36°27'05" N, long. 118°57'10" W; sec. 17, T 17 S, R 31 E); the stream heads at Mineral Lakes. Named on Mineral King (1956) 15' quadrangle. Elden H. Vestal of California Department of Fish and Game named the stream in 1956 (Browning 1986, p. 148).

Mineral Hot Springs: see **Lower Mineral Hot Springs**, under **Mono Hot Springs** [FRESNO].

Mineral King [TULARE]: *locality,* 25 miles north-northeast of Springville along East Fork Kaweah River (lat. 36°27' N, long. 118°35'40" W). Named on Mineral King (1956) 15' quadrangle. In 1874 Harry Parole discovered the valley that contains present Mineral King and set up a camp at a bend in the river there; the place became known as Harry's Bend, and later as Sunny Slope before the dogs attracted to a butcher shop at the site gave it the name "Dog Town" (Jackson, p. 1, 48). The mining district organized in the valley in 1873 took the name "Mineral King," and the settlement there first had the biblical name "Beulah," for the land of promise (Jackson, p. 18). In 1879 the mining district contained separate settlements called Barton's, Ford's Camp, Beulah Camp, and Dog Town, but the whole place was called Mineral King (Jackson, p. 42). Postal authorities established Mineralking post office in 1877, discontinued it in 1882, reestablished it in 1897, and discontinued in it 1969 (Salley, p. 141). They established Redfield post office 6 miles west of Mineral King in 1880 and discontinued it in 1881; the

name was for B. Redfield, first postmaster (Salley, p. 182). United States Board on Geographic Names (1980, p. 4) approved the name "Hengst Peak" for a feature, altitude 11,127 feet, situated 3 miles south-southwest of Mineral King (lat. 36°24'38" N, long. 118°37'15" W; sec. 32, T 17 S, R 31 E)—the name commemorates Albert Alfred Hengst of Three Rivers, who built trails and transplanted golden trout in the Sierra Nevada.

Mineral Lakes [TULARE]: *lakes,* largest 450 feet long, 2.25 miles southwest of Mineral King (lat. 36°25'40" N, long. 118°37'25" W; sec. 20, 29, T 17 S, R 31 E); the lakes are at the head of Mineral Creek. Named on Mineral King (1956) 15' quadrangle. Elden H. Vestal of California Department of Fish and Game named the lakes in 1956 (Browning 1986, p. 148).

Mineral Peak [TULARE]: *peak,* nearly 2 miles east-southeast of Mineral King (lat. 36°26'45" N, long. 118°33'50" W). Altitude 11,550 feet. Named on Mineral King (1956) 15' quadrangle. The feature first was called Little Matterhorn for its resemblance to the peak in Switzerland called The Matterhorn (Jackson, p. 24).

Mineral Public Camp: see **Lower Mineral Public Camp**, under **Mono Hot Springs** [FRESNO].

Miner Creek [TULARE]: *stream,* flows 2.5 miles to South Fork Tule River 5 miles south-southwest of Camp Nelson (lat. 36°04'30" N, long. 118°38'30" W). Named on Camp Nelson (1956) 15' quadrangle. Browning 1986 (p. 148) associated the name with James L. Miner, who patented land in the neighborhood in 1888.

Miner's Peak: see **Sawtooth Peak** [TULARE] (1).

Ming: see **Lake Ming** [KERN].

Miningtown Meadow [FRESNO]: *area,* 3 miles northeast of Dinkey Dome (lat. 37°08'30" N, long. 119°04'45" W; near SE cor. sec. 13, T 9 S, R 26 E). Named on Huntington Lake (1953) 15' quadrangle. The name is from a proposed silver-mining town that Thomas Edward Bacon laid out in 1879, but that failed to develop (Browning 1986, p. 148).

Minkler [FRESNO]: *village,* 2.25 miles east-southeast of Centerville (lat. 36°43'25" N, long. 119°27'20" W; sec. 10, T 14 S, R 23 E). Named on Wahtoke (1966) 7.5' quadrangle. According to Gudde (1949, p. 216), the name probably commemorates Charles O. Minkler, a farmer at nearby Sanger, or a member of his family.

Minnehaha Creek [TULARE]: *stream,* flows 2.5 miles to Cottonwood Creek 5 miles north-northwest of Woodlake (lat. 36°29'05" N, long. 119°07'10" W; near S line sec. 35, T 16 S, R 26 E). Named on Auckland (1966) and Woodlake (1952) 7.5' quadrangles.

Minneola: see **Clotho** [FRESNO]; **Ivesta** [FRESNO].

Minnie Lake [FRESNO]: *lake,* 700 feet long,

12.5 miles west-northwest of Mount Abbot (lat. 37°28' N, long. 118°59'15" W). Named on Mount Abbot (1953) 15' quadrangle. William A. Dill of California Department of Fish and Game named the lake in 1943; the name "Minnie" for the small lake is the diminutive of the word "minnow" (Browning 1986, p. 148).

Minnow Creek [FRESNO]: *stream,* flows 4.5 miles to Fish Creek (1) 6 miles west of Red Slate Mountain in Cascade Valley (lat. 37°30'40" N, long. 118°58'15" W). Named on Mount Abbot (1953) and Mount Morrison (1953) 15' quadrangles.

Minnow Lake [MADERA]: *lake,* 600 feet long, 1 mile south of Buena Vista Peak (lat. 37°34'45" N, long. 119°30'50" W; sec. 24, T 4 S, R 22 E). Named on Yosemite (1956) 7.5' quadrangle.

Minster: see **The Minster** [TULARE].

Minter Field: see **Minter Village** [KERN].

Minter Village [KERN]: *locality,* 13 miles northwest of Bakersfield (lat. 35°30'15" N, long. 119°10'30" W). Named on Famoso (1953) 7.5' quadrangle. The name is from Minter Field, an Army Air Corps facility at the place during World War II; Minter Village was started at the site following the war (Bailey, 1967, p. 17). Postal authorities established Minter Field post office in 1942 and discontinued it in 1949; they established Minter Village post office in 1948 and discontinued it in 1961— the name "Minter Field" honored Lieutenant Hugh C. Minter, who was killed in an air crash in 1932 (Salley p. 142). Famoso (1930) 7.5' quadrangle shows a place called Dow located at the site of present Minter Village.

Minturn [MADERA]: *locality,* 1.5 miles north-northwest of Chowchilla along Southern Pacific Railroad (lat. 37°08'25" N, long. 120° 16'25" W; on W line sec. 19, T 9 S, R 16 E). Named on Chowchilla (1960) 15' quadrangle. Postal authorities established Minturn post office in 1884 and discontinued it in 1922 (Frickstad, p. 86). The name commemorates Jonas Minturn and Thomas Minturn, who raised wheat and arranged for a freight siding when the railroad reached the place in 1872 (Clough, p. 80).

Miracle Hot Springs [KERN]: *village,* 14 miles southeast of Glennville along Kern River (lat. 35°34'35" N, long. 118°32' W; near SW cor. sec. 15, T 27 S, R 32 E); the village is less than 0.25 mile west-northwest of the mouth of Clear Creek (1). Named on Miracle Hot Springs (1972) 7.5' quadrangle. Called Hobo Hot Springs on Glennville (1956) 15' quadrangle. Postal authorities established Hobo Hot Springs post office in 1932 and changed the name to Miracle Hot Springs in 1947 (Frickstad, p. 56). The name "Hobo" recalls workmen on a compressor at the place—local ranchers called them hobos because they stole sheep and cattle (Bailey, 1967, p. 17-

18). The place also was called Clear Creek Hot Springs (Waring, p. 51), Air Compressor Springs (Brown, p. 520), and Compressor Hot Springs (Bailey, 1967, p. 17).

Mirador [TULARE]: *locality,* 4 miles southeast of Lindsay along Atchison, Topeka and Santa Fe Railroad (lat. 36°10' N, long. 119° 02'05" W; near N line sec. 27, T 20 S, R 27 E). Named on Lindsay (1951) 7.5' quadrangle. The place was named in 1923 (Gudde, 1949, p. 217). California Division of Highways' (1934) map shows a locality called Strathmore Jct. along the railroad 1 mile south of Mirador (near N line sec. 34, T 20 S, R 27 E); the site is 1.25 miles east-northeast of Strathmore.

Miramonte [FRESNO]: *settlement,* 5 miles southeast of Dunlap along Mill Creek (3) (lat. 36°41'35" N, long. 119°03' W; sec. 21, T 14 S, R 27 E). Named on Miramonte (1966) 7.5' quadrangle. Postal authorities established Miramonte post office in 1909, discontinued it in 1912 and reestablished it in 1923 (Frickstad, p. 35).

Miramonte: see **Semitropic** [KERN].

Mirror Lake [FRESNO]: *lake,* 800 feet long, 6.5 miles east of the town of Big Creek (lat. 37°12'55" N, long. 119°07'25" W; at SW cor. sec. 22, T 8 S, R 26 E). Named on Huntington Lake (1953) 15' quadrangle.

Mirror Lake [KERN]: *dry lake,* 2 miles northeast of downtown Ridgecrest on Kern-San Bernardino county line (lat. 35°38'45" N, long. 117°38'15" W; on E line sec. 26, T 26 S, R 40 E). Named on Ridgecrest North (1973) 7.5' quadrangle.

Missouri Triangle [KERN]: *locality,* 10 miles north of McKittrick (lat. 35°26'15" N, long. 119°41'20" W; sec. 2, T 29 S, R 21 E). Named on Belridge (1953) 7.5' quadrangle.

Mist Falls [FRESNO]: *waterfall,* 10 miles south of Marion Peak along South Fork Kings River (lat. 36°48'45" N, long. 118°32'55" W). Named on Marion Peak (1953) 15' quadrangle.

Mist Lake [FRESNO]: *lake,* 950 feet long, 3 miles west of Mount Abbot (lat. 37°22'55" N, long. 118°50'05" W). Named on Mount Abbot (1953) 15' quadrangle. Bob Ehlers of California Department of Fish and Game named the lake in 1952 (Browning 1986, p. 149).

Mitchell Canyon [TULARE]: *canyon,* drained by a stream that flows less than 1 mile to Dry Creek (1) 7 miles southeast of Auckland (lat. 36°31'20" N, long. 119°00'40" W; sec. 23, T 16 S, R 27 E). Named on Auckland (1966) 7.5' quadrangle.

Mitchell Corner [TULARE]: *locality,* 4.25 miles west-northwest of Exeter (lat. 36°19'35" N, long. 119°12'20" W; at SW cor. sec. 30, T 18 S, R 26 E). Named on Exeter (1952) 15' quadrangle.

Mitchell Meadow [TULARE]: *area,* 7 miles south-southwest of Mineral King (lat. 36°21'20" N; long. 118°38'25" W; sec. 17, T

18 S, R 31 E). Named on Mineral King (1956) 15' quadrangle. The name commemorates Hyman Mitchell of White River (2) (Gudde, 1949, p. 218).

Mitchell Peak [FRESNO]: *peak,* 4.5 miles south-southeast of Dunlap (lat. 36°40'55" N, long. 119°04'25" W; sec. 30, T 14 S, R 27 E). Altitude 3574 feet. Named on Miramonte (1966) 7.5' quadrangle.

Mitchell Peak [TULARE]: *peak,* 14 miles northwest of Triple Divide Peak (lat. 36°43'55" N, long. 118°42'50" W; near W line sec. 3, T 14 S, R 30 E). Altitude 10,365 feet. Named on Triple Divide Peak (1956) 15' quadrangle. The name commemorates Susman Mitchell, banker, merchant, postmaster of Visalia (Hanna, p. 196), and son of Hyman Mitchell of Mitchell Meadow (Gudde, 1949, p. 218).

Mitchells Corner [KERN]: *locality,* 1.25 miles north-northwest of Arvin (lat. 35°13'25" N, long. 118°50'30" W; at SE cor. sec. 15, T 31 S, R 29 E). Named on Arvin (1955) 7.5' quadrangle.

Mitchell Slough [TULARE]: *stream,* flows 4.25 miles before ending 1.25 miles north-northeast of Tipton (lat. 36°04'40" N, long. 119°18'10" W; at E line sec. 29, T 21 S, R 25 E). Named on Tipton (1950) and Woodville (1950, photorevised 1969) 7.5' quadrangles.

Miter: see **The Miter** [TULARE].

Moccasin Lake: see **Big Moccasin Lake** [FRESNO]; **Little Moccasin Lake** [FRESNO].

Mohave: see **Mojave** [KERN].

Mohave Desert: see "Regional setting."

Mojave [KERN]: *town,* 50 miles east-southeast of Bakersfield (lat. 35°03'10" N, long. 118°10'20" W; in and near sec. 8, 17, T 11 N, R 12 W); the town is in Mojave Desert. Named on Mojave (1973) 7.5' quadrangle. Called Mohave on Mendenhall's (1909) map, but United States Board on Geographic Names (1934b, p. 11) rejected this form of the name. Postal authorities established Mojave post office in 1876 (Frickstad, p. 57). California Mining Bureau's (1909a) map shows a place called Chanz located 37 miles by stage line north of Mojave. Postal authorities established Chanz post office, named for George A. Chanz, first postmaster, in 1906 and discontinued it in 1909 (Salley, p. 42). Mendenhall's (1909) map shows a place called Water Station located 7.5 miles northeast of Mohave (present Mojave); it was a well-known road ranch and stage station (Mendenhall, 1909, p. 57). Thompson's (1921) map shows a place called Gamba located 4.5 miles southeast of Mojave along Atchison, Topeka and Santa Fe Railroad.

Mojave Desert: see "Regional setting."

Monache Creek [TULARE]: *stream,* flows 4.25 miles to South Fork Kern River 1.5 miles northeast of Monache Mountain in Monache Meadows (lat. 36°13'10" N, long. 118°10'15" W; sec. 3, T 20 S, R 35 E). Named on

Monache Mountain (1956) and Olancha (1956) 15' quadrangles. Members of United States Geological Survey gave the name to the stream in 1905 (Gudde, 1949, p. 221).

Monache Meadows [TULARE]: *area,* east of Monache Mountain along South Fork Kern River (lat. 36°12'30" N, long. 118°10' W). Named on Monache Mountain (1956) 15' quadrangle.

Monache Mountain [TULARE]: *peak,* 6 miles southwest of Olancha Peak (lat. 36°12'20" N, long. 118°11'40" W; near N line sec. 9, T 20 S, R 35 E). Altitude 9410 feet. Named on Monache Mountain (1956) 15' quadrangle. Members of United States Geological Survey named the peak in 1905 for Monachi Indians, usually called Mono Indians (Gudde, 1949, p. 221).

Monarch [KERN]: *locality,* nearly 1 mile north of downtown Maricopa at the end of a spur of Sunset Railroad (lat. 35°04'35" N, long. 119°24'20" W; at N line sec. 2, T 11 N, R 24 W). Named on Buena Vista Lake (1912) 30' quadrangle.

Monarch Creek [TULARE]: *stream,* flows 2 miles to East Fork Kaweah River at Mineral King (lat. 36°27'10" N, long. 118°35'50" W); the stream heads at Monarch Lakes. Named on Mineral King (1956) 15' quadrangle.

Monarch Divide [FRESNO]: *ridge,* west-trending, 17 miles long, between South Fork Kings River and Middle Fork Kings River. Named on Marion Peak (1953) and Tehipite Dome (1952) 15' quadrangles. Members of the Whitney survey called the feature Dyke Ridge (Browning 1986, p. 151).

Monarch Lakes [TULARE]: *lakes,* two, largest 2000 feet long, nearly 2 miles east of Mineral King (lat. 36°27'05" N, long. 118°33'45" W); the lakes are at the head of Monarch Creek. Named on Mineral King (1956) 15' quadrangle.

Mon Bluff [KERN]: *relief feature,* nearly 3 miles south of Knob Hill on the south side of Poso Creek (lat. 35°31'30" N, long. 118°57'25" W; at W line sec. 3, T 28 S, R 28 E); the feature is 1 mile east of the mouth of Mon Canyon. Named on Knob Hill (1965) 7.5' quadrangle.

Mon Canyon [KERN]: *canyon,* drained by a stream that flows 2.5 miles to Poso Creek nearly 3 miles south-southwest of Knob Hill (lat. 35°31'45" N, long. 118°58'25" W; near NW cor. sec. 4, T 28 S, R 28 E). Named on Knob Hill (1965) 7.5' quadrangle.

Monmouth [FRESNO]: *village,* 7.25 miles west of Selma (lat. 36°33'55" N, long. 119°44'20" W; sec. 1, T 16 S, R 20 E). Named on Conejo (1963) 7.5' quadrangle. Officials of Atchison, Topeka and Santa Fe Railroad named the place in the 1890's for Monmouth, Illinois, former home of a settler in the village (Gudde, 1949, p. 221). Postal authorities established Monmouth post office in 1908 and discontinued it in 1919 (Frickstad, p. 35).

Monnotti Creek: see **Monotti Creek** [KERN].

Monocline Ridge [FRESNO]: *ridge,* northwest-trending, 12 miles long, 23 miles south-southwest of Firebaugh (lat. 36°32'30" N, long. 120°34' W). Named on Ciervo Mountain (1969), Lillis Ranch (1956), and Moncline Ridge (1955) 7.5' quadrangles. Anderson and Pack (p. 19) proposed the name because of the monoclinal structure of strata at the ridge.

Mono Creek [FRESNO]: *stream,* flows 20 miles to South Fork San Joaquin River 7.5 miles northeast of Kaiser Peak (lat. 37°21'20" N, long. 119°04'15" W). Named on Kaiser Peak (1953) and Mount Abbot (1953) 15' quadrangles.

Mono Creek Campground [FRESNO]: *locality,* 12 miles west of Mount Abbot along Mono Creek below Lake Thomas A. Edison (lat. 37°21'30" N, long. 118°59'50" W). Named on Mount Abbot (1953) 15' quadrangle.

Mono Crossing [FRESNO]: *locality,* 8 miles east-northeast of Kaiser Peak along South Fork San Joaquin River (lat. 37°20'30" N, long. 119°03'25" W); the place is 1.5 miles upstream from the mouth of Mono Creek. Named on Kaiser Peak (1953) 15' quadrangle.

Mono Divide [FRESNO]: *ridge,* extends for 7.5 miles southwest and then northwest from Mount Abbot (center near lat. 37°22'30" N, long. 118°50'30" W); the feature separates the drainage basin of Mono Creek from the drainage basin of Bear Creek (2). Named on Mount Abbot (1953) 15' quadrangle.

Mono Hot Springs [FRESNO]: *locality,* 9.5 miles east-northeast of Kaiser Peak (lat. 37°19'35" N, long. 119°01' W). Named on Kaiser Peak (1953) 15' quadrangle. Called Lower Hot Springs on Kaiser (1904) 30' quadrangle. Postal authorities established Mono Hot Springs post office in 1945 (Frickstad, p. 35). Laizure (p. 322) gave the alternate name "Lower Mineral Hot Springs" for the place, and mentioned that Lower Mineral Public Camp was at the site. Bradley (p. 457) noted that six springs occur at the place, the hottest with water temperature of 112° Fahrenheit.

Monolith [KERN]: *village,* 4.5 miles east of Tehachapi (lat. 35°07'15" N, long. 118°22'20" W; sec. 30, T 32 S, R 34 E). Named on Monolith (1966) 7.5' quadrangle. Postal authorities established Aqueduct post office in 1908 and changed the name to Monolith in 1910 (Salley, p. 9). The place began as a camp for workmen at a plant that supplied cement for construction of the aqueduct that takes Owens Valley water from Inyo County to Los Angeles; William Mulholland, who directed construction of the aqueduct, gave the name "Monolith" (Bailey, 1967, p. 18), which comes from the monolithic body of limestone that provided material for the cement plant (Barras, p. 59). California Mining Bureau's (1917c) map shows a place called Proctor located about 1 mile east of Monolith along the railroad near present Proctor Lake.

Mono Meadow [FRESNO]: *area,* 10 miles east-northeast of Kaiser Peak (lat. 37°20'45" N, long. 119°00'45" W); the place is along Mono Creek. Named on Kaiser Peak (1953) 15' quadrangle.

Mono Pass [FRESNO]: *pass,* 2.5 miles northnortheast of Mount Abbot on Fresno-Inyo county line (lat. 37°25'30" N, long. 118°46'20" W); the pass is at the head of the drainage basin of Mono Creek. Named on Mount Abbot (1953) 15' quadrangle.

Mono Rock [FRESNO]: *peak,* 3.5 miles north of Mount Abbot (lat. 37°26'20" N, long. 118°47'40" W); the feature is near Mono Creek. Altitude 11,555 feet. Named on Mount Abbot (1953) 15' quadrangle.

Monotti Creek [KERN]: *stream,* flows 3 miles to Adobe Canyon 4 miles east of Knob Hill (lat. 35°34'30" N, long. 118°52'40" W; near S line sec. 17, T 27 S, R 29 E). Named on Knob Hill (1965) and Pine Mountain (1965) 7.5' quadrangles. Called Mannot Creek on Woody (1935) 15' quadrangle, but United States Board on Geographic Names (1966a, p. 6) rejected the forms "Mannot Creek" and "Monnotti Creek" for the name.

Monson [TULARE]: *village,* 11.5 miles northnorthwest of Visalia (lat. 36°29'35" N, long. 119°20'10" W; sec. 35, T 16 S, R 24 E). Named on Monson (1949) 7.5' quadrangle. Postal authorities established Monson post office in 1889 and discontinued it in 1920 (Frickstad, p. 212).

Monte Diablo Range: see "Regional setting."

Monterio: see **Rosamond** [KERN].

Montgomery Canyon [KERN]: *canyon,* drained by a stream that flows 4.5 miles to Caliente Creek 4.25 miles east-northeast of Caliente (lat. 35°18'45" N, long. 118°33'25" W; near SW cor. sec. 16, T 30 S, R 32 E). Named on Oiler Peak (1972) 7.5' quadrangle.

Montgomery Spring [KERN]: *spring,* 4.5 miles east of Caliente (lat. 35°17'05" N, long. 118°32'55" W; sec. 28, T 30 S, R 32 E); the spring is east of Montgomery Canyon. Named on Oiler Peak (1972) 7.5' quadrangle.

Monument Hill [TULARE]: *ridge,* southeast-to southwest-trending, 2 miles long, 6.5 miles east of Exeter (lat. 36°17'15" N, long. 119° 01'25" W). Named on Rocky Hill (1951) 7.5' quadrangle.

Monument Lake [MADERA]: *lake,* 450 feet long, 4.25 miles south-southeast of Merced Peak (lat. 37°34'45" N, long. 119°21'40" W). Named on Merced Peak (1953) 15' quadrangle.

Moon Lake [FRESNO]: *lake,* 1400 feet long, 3.5 miles west-northwest of Mount Humphreys (lat. 37°17'35" N, long. 118°43'45" W; sec. 31, T 7 S, R 30 E). Named on Mount Tom (1949) 15' quadrangle.

Moonshine Spring [FRESNO]: *spring,* 3.5 miles northeast of Coalinga Mineral Springs (lat. 36°11'15" N, long. 120°31'05" W; sec.

13, T 20 S, R 13 E). Named on Sherman Peak (1969) 7.5' quadrangle.

Moore: see **Bill Moore Canyon** [TULARE]; **Bill Moore Ridge** [TULARE].

Moore Canyon: see **Sycamore Canyon** [KERN] (2).

Moore Creek [TULARE]: *stream,* flows 3.5 miles to Wilcox Creek 1 mile northeast of Cliff Peak (lat. 36°34'05" N, long. 119°09'15" W; sec. 4, T 16 S, R 26 E). Named on Stokes Mountain (1966) 7.5' quadrangle. Called Wilcox Cr. on Dinuba (1924) 30' quadrangle. Blake (1857, p. 28) referred to Moore's Creek.

Moorehouse Creek [TULARE]: *stream,* flows 2 miles to South Fork of Middle Fork Tule River 3 miles west-northwest of Camp Nelson (lat. 36°09'05" N, long. 118°39'10" W). Named on Camp Nelson (1956) 15' quadrangle. The name commemorates Gus Moorehouse, an early prospector (Gudde, 1949, p. 224).

Moore Mill [FRESNO]: *locality,* 6 miles southsouthwest of Shaver Lake (lat. 37°03'05" N, long. 119°20' W; near N line sec. 22, T 10 S, R 24 E). Named on Kaiser (1904) 30' quadrangle.

Moose Lake [TULARE]: *lake,* 3300 feet long, 6 miles west of Triple Divide Peak (lat. 36°36' N, long. 118°38'15" W). Named on Triple Divide Peak (1956) 15' quadrangle. Hale Tharp named the lake (Browning, p. 153).

Moraine: see **Mount Moraine**, under **Barton Peak** [TULARE].

Moraine Creek [TULARE]: *stream,* flows 5.5 miles to Roaring River 10.5 miles north-northwest of Triple Divide Peak (lat. 36°43'50" N, long. 118°35'25" W); the stream goes through Moraine Meadows. Named on Triple Divide Peak (1956) 15' quadrangle.

Moraine Lake [TULARE]: *lake,* 1900 feet long, 14 miles northeast of Kern Peak (lat. 36°27'45" N, long. 118°27'20" W). Named on Kern Peak (1956) 15' quadrangle.

Moraine Meadow [MADERA]: *area,* 3 miles south-southwest of Merced Peak along South Fork Merced River (lat. 37°35'45" N, long. 119°25'30" W); the place is 1.5 miles eastnortheast of Moraine Mountain. Named on Merced Peak (1953) 15' quadrangle. Mount Lyell (1901) 30' quadrangle has the form "Moraine Meadows" for the name.

Moraine Meadows [TULARE]: *area,* 9 miles north-northwest of Triple Divide Peak (lat. 36°43'10" N, long. 118°34'20" W); the place is northeast of Moraine Ridge along Moraine Creek. Named on Triple Divide Peak (1956) 15' quadrangle. Called Moraine Meadow on Tehipite (1903) 30' quadrangle.

Moraine Mountain [MADERA]: *peak,* 4.5 miles southwest of Merced Peak (lat. 37°35'30" N, long. 119°27'10" W). Altitude 9754 feet. Named on Merced Peak (1953) 15' quadrangle.

Moraine Ridge [TULARE]: *ridge,* northwesttrending, 3 miles long, 9 miles north-north-

west of Triple Divide Peak (lat. 36°42'45" N, long. 118°34'30" W). Named on Triple Divide Peak (1956) 15' quadrangle.

Moreno Gulch [FRESNO]: *canyon,* drained by a stream that flows 4.25 miles to lowlands 17 miles west-southwest of Firebaugh (lat. 36°44'30" N, long. 120°43'30" W; sec. 1, T 14 S, R 11 E). Named on Chounet Ranch (1956) 7.5' quadrangle. Anderson and Pack (p. 19) remarked that the name is appropriate because some of the rocks in the canyon are brown—*moreno* means "brown" in Spanish.

Morgan Canyon [TULARE]: *canyon,* drained by a stream that flows 2.5 miles to Cottonwood Creek 2 miles south of Auckland (lat. 36° 33'35" N, long. 119°06'35" W; sec. 2, T 16 S, R 26 E). Named on Auckland (1966) 7.5' quadrangle.

Morgan Meadow [MADERA]: *area,* 1.5 miles northwest of Shuteye Peak (lat. 37°21'40" N, long. 119°26'15" W; sec. 34, T 6 S, R 23 E). Named on Shuteye Peak (1953) 15' quadrangle.

Morlar Flat [FRESNO]: *area,* 2.5 miles southeast of Dunlap (lat. 36°42'10" N, long. 119°06'05" W; near SW cor. sec. 13, T 14 S, R 26 E). Named on Miramonte (1966) 7.5' quadrangle.

Mormon Canyon [KERN]: *canyon,* drained by a stream that flows 3 miles to Poso Flat 7 miles north-northwest of Democrat Hot Springs, and 1.5 miles west of Burke Hill (lat. 35°37'05" N, long. 118°43'35" W; near SW cor. sec. 35, T 26 S, R 30 E). Named on Democrat Hot Springs (1972) and Glennville (1972) 7.5' quadrangles. The stream in the canyon, and in a branch of the canyon, is called Burke Creek on Glennville (1956) 15' quadrangle. United States Board on Geographic Names (1975a, p. 4) approved the name "Mormon Canyon" for the feature, and gave the name "Burke Creek" as a variant.

Mormon Flat [KERN]: *area,* 3.5 miles north of Garlock (lat. 35°27'15" N, long. 117°47' W); the place is at the head of Mormon Gulch. Named on Garlock (1967) 7.5' quadrangle.

Mormon Gulch [KERN]: *canyon,* 1.5 miles long, opens into Goler Gulch 3.5 miles northnortheast of Garlock (lat. 35°27'05" N, long. 117°45'45" W). Named on Garlock (1967) 7.5' quadrangle.

Mormon Hill [MADERA]: *peak,* 8 miles south of Shuteye Peak (lat. 37°14' N, long. 119°25'35" W; sec. 14, T 8 S, R 23 E). Named on Shaver Lake (1953) 15' quadrangle.

Moro: see **Taft** [KERN].

Moro Creek [TULARE]: *stream,* flows 1.5 miles to Middle Fork Kaweah River 7.5 miles east-southeast of Yucca Mountain (lat. 36° 31'35" N, long. 118°45' W); the stream heads near Moro Rock. Named on Giant Forest (1956) 15' quadrangle.

Moron: see **Taft** [KERN].

Moro Rock [TULARE]: *peak,* 6 miles eastsoutheast of Yucca Mountain (lat. 36°32'40"

N, long. 118°45'50" W). Altitude 6725 feet. Named on Giant Forest (1956) 15' quadrangle. The name is from a blue-roan mustang that ranged near the feature in the 1860's—*moro* is the Mexican term for the color of the animal (Browning 1986, p. 154).

Morris Canyon [KERN]: *canyon,* drained by a stream that flows 2 miles to Indian Wells Canyon 9 miles west-northwest of Inyokern (lat. 35°42'30" N, long. 117°57'05" W). Named on Owens Peak (1972) 7.5' quadrangle.

Morris Peak [KERN]: *peak,* 10 miles west-northwest of Inyokern (lat. 35°41'25" N, long. 117°59'10" W; near SE cor. sec. 3, T 26 S, R 37 E). Altitude 7215 feet. Named on Owens Peak (1972) 7.5' quadrangle. United States Board on Geographic Names (1984c, p. 2) approved the name "Mount Jenkins" for a peak, altitude 7921 feet, situated 1.3 miles north of Morris Peak (lat. 35°42'33" N, long. 117°59'30" W); the name commemorates James Charles Jenkins, authority on the flora, fauna, and history of the southern Sierra Nevada.

Morrow: see **Jesse Morrow Mountain** [FRESNO].

Morton Flat [TULARE]: *area,* 8 miles east of Fountain Springs (lat. 35°54'15" N, long. 118°46'15" W; near NE cor. sec. 30, T 23 S, R 30 E). Named on Gibbon Peak (1965) 7.5' quadrangle.

Moseman Stage Station: see **Walker Basin** [KERN].

Moses Mountain [TULARE]: *peak,* 13 miles south-southwest of Mineral King (lat. 36°16'45" N, long. 118°40'45" W). Altitude 9331 feet. Named on Mineral King (1956) 15' quadrangle. Frank Knowles named the peak in the 1870's for an elderly fisherman who had the nickname "Moses" (Gudde, 1949, p. 226; Gudde used the form "Mount Moses" for the name).

Mosquito Creek [KINGS]: *stream,* flows 4 miles to Cross Creek 6 miles east-southeast of Hanford (lat. 36°17'35" N, long. 119°32'50" W; sec. 11, T 19 S, R 22 E). Named on Goshen (1949) and Remnoy (1954) 7.5' quadrangles.

Mosquito Creek [TULARE]: *stream,* flows 1.5 miles to East Fork Kaweah River 1.25 miles west of Mineral King (lat. 36°27'05" N, long. 118°37' W; near W line sec. 16, T 17 S, R 31 E); the stream heads below Mosquito Lakes. Named on Mineral King (1956) 15' quadrangle.

Mosquito Lakes [TULARE]: *lakes,* largest 1200 feet long, 2.25 miles south-southwest of Mineral King (lat. 36°25'20" N, long. 118°36'45" W); the lakes are above the head of Mosquito Creek. Named on Mineral King (1956) 15' quadrangle.

Mosquito Meadow [TULARE]: *area,* 8 miles east-northeast of Fairview (lat. 35°57'10" N, long. 118°21'15" W; sec. 6, T 23 S, R 34 E). Named on Kernville (1956) 15' quadrangle.

Mosquito Pass [FRESNO]: *pass,* 8.5 miles north-northwest of Blackcap Mountain (lat. 37°11'15" N, long. 118°51'10" W). Named on Blackcap Mountain (1953) 15' quadrangle.

Motte Canyon [FRESNO]: *canyon,* drained by a stream that flows 2.5 miles to Jasper Creek 9 miles south-southwest of Coalinga (lat. 36°01'15" N, long. 120°25' W; sec. 13, T 22 S, R 14 E). Named on Curry Mountain (1969) 7.5' quadrangle.

Mott Lake [FRESNO]: *lake,* 1300 feet long, 7 miles northwest of Mount Abbot (lat. 37°27'15" N, long. 118°52'55" W). Named on Mount Abbot (1953) 15' quadrangle. The name is for Ernest Julian Mott, a mountain explorer (United States Board on Geographic Names, 1933a, p. 533).

Mound [KERN]: *hill,* 3 miles south-southwest of Boron (lat. 34°57'55" N, long. 117°40'40" W; sec. 13, T 10 N, R 8 W). Altitude 2955 feet. Named on Leuhman Ridge (1973) 7.5' quadrangle.

Mount Abbot [FRESNO]: *peak,* 20 miles north of Mount Goddard on Fresno-Inyo county line (lat. 37°23'15" N, long. 118°47'05" W). Altitude 13,715 feet. Named on Mount Abbot (1953) 15' quadrangle. Members of the Whitney survey named the peak in 1864 for Henry Larcom Abbot, a captain of army engineers at the time (Farquhar, 1923, p. 381). United States Board on Geographic Names (1933a, p. 78) rejected the form "Mount Abbott" for the name.

Mount Abel: see **Cerro Noroeste** [KERN].

Mount Adelaide [KERN]: *peak,* 14 miles east-northeast of Bakersfield (lat. 35°25'50" N, long. 118°44'35" W; sec. 3, T 29 S, R 30 E). Altitude 3430 feet. Named on Mount Adelaide (1972) 7.5' quadrangle.

Mount Agassiz [FRESNO]: *peak,* 10.5 miles east of Mount Goddard on Fresno-Inyo county line (lat. 37°06'45" N, long. 118°31'50" W). Altitude 13,891 feet. Named on Mount Goddard (1948) 15' quadrangle. Called Agassiz Needle on Mount Goddard (1912) 30' quadrangle, a name that L.A. Winchell gave in 1879 to honor professor Louis Agassiz of Harvard University (Farquhar, 1923, p. 382).

Mountain Creek: see **Long Tom Gulch** [KERN].

Mountaineer Creek [TULARE]: *stream,* flows 5 miles to Alpine Creek 8 miles northeast of Camp Nelson (lat. 36°14'05" N, long. 118°30'10" W; at NW cor. sec. 33, T 19 S, R 32 E). Named on Camp Nelson (1956) 15' quadrangle.

Mountaineer Creek: see **South Mountaineer Creek** [TULARE].

Mountain Home [TULARE]: *locality,* 8 miles northwest of Camp Nelson (lat. 36°14' N, long. 118°41'35" W; sec. 35, T 19 S, R 30 E). Named on Camp Nelson (1956) 15' quadrangle.

Mountain House Station: see **Willow Springs**

Station, under **Willow Spring** [KERN] (2).

Mountain Meadow [FRESNO]: *area,* 16 miles north-northeast of Hume (lat. 36°59'15" N, long. 118°46'45" W). Named on Tehipite Dome (1952) 15' quadrangle.

Mountain Mesa [KERN]: *locality,* 5.5 miles south-southeast of Wofford Heights near Isabella Lake (lat. 35°38'15" N, long. 118° 24'15" W; sec. 26, T 26 S, R 33 E). Named on Lake Isabella North (1972) 7.5' quadrangle.

Mountain Oak Spring [KERN]: *spring,* 5.25 miles east-southeast of Caliente (lat. 35°16'05" N, long. 118°32'25" W; near NE cor. sec. 4, T 31 S, R 32 E). Named on Oiler Peak (1972) 7.5' quadrangle.

Mountain Rest: see **Tollhouse** [FRESNO].

Mountain View: see **Milo** [TULARE].

Mountain View Peak [MADERA]: *ridge,* east-trending, 1 mile long, 6.5 miles southwest of North Fork (lat. 37°10'35" N, long. 119°36'30" W). Named on North Fork (1965) 7.5' quadrangle.

Mount Anna Mills: see **Mount Guyot** [TULARE].

Mount Ansel Adams: see **Foerster Peak** [MADERA].

Mount Bago [FRESNO]: *peak,* 12.5 miles south of Mount Pinchot (lat. 36°46'15" N, long. 118°26'15" W). Altitude 11,868 feet. Named on Mount Pinchot (1953) 15' quadrangle.

Mount Barnard [TULARE]: *peak,* nearly 4 miles north-northwest of Mount Whitney on Tulare-Inyo county line (lat. 36°37'40" N, long. 118°19'15" W). Altitude 13,990 feet. Named on Mount Whitney (1956) 15' quadrangle. The name commemorates astronomer Edward E. Barnard (United States Board on Geographic Names, 1933a, p. 124).

Mount Baxter [FRESNO]: *peak,* 6.25 miles south-southeast of Mount Pinchot on Fresno-Inyo county line (lat. 36°51'45" N, long. 118°21'50" W). Altitude 13,125 feet. Named on Mount Pinchot (1953) 15' quadrangle. George R. Davis of United States Geological Survey made the first ascent of the peak and named it in 1905 for John Baxter, a rancher of Owens Valley in Inyo County (Browning 1986, p. 12). United States Board on Geographic Names (1969d, p. 8) approved the name "Acrodectes Peak" for a feature situated about 0.5 mile west of Mount Baxter (lat. 36°51'40" N, long. 118°22'26" W).

Mount Bolton Brown [FRESNO]: *peak,* 20 miles east of Blackcap Mountain on Fresno-Inyo county line (lat. 37°02'45" N, long. 118°26'20" W). Altitude 13,538 feet. Named on Big Pine (1950) 15' quadrangle. Chester Versteeg and his companions climbed the peak in 1922 and named it to honor Bolton C. Brown of the Sierra Club (Versteeg, p. 426).

Mount Bradley [TULARE]: *peak,* 10.5 miles north-northwest of Mount Whitney on Tulare-Inyo county line (lat. 36°43'45" N, long.

118°20'15" W). Altitude 13,289 feet. Named on Mount Whitney (1956) 15' quadrangle. The name, given in 1898, commemorates Cornelius Beach Bradley, professor of rhetoric at University of California, and a charter member of the Sierra Club (Browning 1986, p. 24).

Mount Breckenridge: see **Breckenridge Mountain** [KERN].

Mount Brewer [TULARE]: *peak,* 14 miles northwest of Mount Whitney on Great Western Divide (lat. 36°42'30" N, long. 118° 29' W). Altitude 13,570 feet. Named on Mount Whitney (1956) 15' quadrangle. The name commemorates William H. Brewer of the Whitney survey (Hanna, p. 40), who climbed the peak with Hoffmann and Gardner on July 4, 1864 (Whitney 1865, p. 383). United States Board on Geographic Names (1989a, p. 4) approved the name "Mount Farquhar" for a peak, elevation 12,893 feet, located 1.6 miles northwest of Mount Brewer (lat. 36°43'43" N, long. 118° 29'53" W); the name commemorates Francis P. Farquhar, conservationist and writer, who was instrumental in creation of Kings Canyon National Park.

Mount Bruce: see **Merced Peak** [MADERA].

Mount Campbell: see **Campbell Mountain** [FRESNO].

Mount Carillon [TULARE]: *peak,* 1.25 miles northeast of Mount Whitney on Tulare-Inyo county line (lat. 36°35'30" N, long. 118° 16'40" W). Altitude 13,552 feet. Named on Mount Whitney (1956) 15' quadrangle. Chester Versteeg proposed the name for the resemblance of the feature to a bell tower (Browning 1986, p. 31).

Mount Cedric Wright [FRESNO]: *peak,* 3.25 miles south-southeast of Mount Pinchot (lat. 36°54'15" N, long. 118°23'15" W). Altitude 12,372 feet. Named on Mount Pinchot (1953) 15' quadrangle. United States Board on Geographic Names (1962a, p. 9) rejected the name "Mount McDoogle" for the peak, and noted that the name "Cedric Wright" honors photographer George Cedric Wright.

Mount Chamberlin [TULARE]: *peak,* 3.25 miles south-southwest of Mount Whitney (lat. 36°32' N, long. 118°18'35" W). Altitude 13,169 feet. Named on Mount Whitney (1956) 15' quadrangle. Members of the Sierra Club proposed the name to honor geologist Thomas Crowder Chamberlin (Browning 1986, p. 37).

Mount Clarence King [FRESNO]: *peak,* 8 miles south-southwest of Mount Pinchot (lat. 36°50' N, long. 118°26'45" W). Altitude 12,905 feet. Named on Mount Pinchot (1953) 15' quadrangle. Called Mt. King on Mount Whitney (1907) 30' quadrangle. Members of the Whitney survey named the peak in 1864 for Clarence King of the survey (Hanna, p. 65).

Mount Corcoran [TULARE]: *peak,* 4 miles southeast of Mount Whitney on Tulare-Inyo county line (lat. 36°32'10" N, long. 118° 14'50" W). Named on Lone Pine (1958) 15' quadrangle. The name, given about 1868, commemorates philanthropist William Wilson Corcoran (United States Board on Geographic Names, 1968b, p. 6). United States Board on Geographic Names (1933a, p. 236) rejected the names "Mount Langley," "Mount Whitney No. 1," "Old Mount Whitney," and "Sheep Rock" for the peak, and later (1968b, p. 6) rejected the name "Corcoran Mountain" as well. The name "Sheep Rock" was from the large number of mountain sheep found near the peak (Whitney 1865, p. 390).

Mount Cotter [FRESNO]: *peak*, 9 miles south-southwest of Mount Pinchot (lat. 36°49'05" N, long. 118°26'20" W). Altitude 12,721 feet. Named on Mount Pinchot (1953) 15' quadrangle. The name commemorates Richard Cotter, a member of the Whitney survey (United States Board on Geographic Names, 1938, p. 15).

Mount Crocker [FRESNO]: *peak*, 7 miles north-northwest of Mount Abbot on Fresno-Mono county line (lat. 37°29' N, long. 118°49'30" W). Altitude 12,457 feet. Named on Mount Abbot (1953) 15' quadrangle. R.B. Marshall of United States Geological Survey named the peak in memory of Charles Crocker, one of the "Big Four" of Central Pacific Railroad (Gudde, 1949, p. 84); nearby Mount Hopkins, Mount Huntington, and Mount Stanford commemorate the other three railroad magnates. The four peaks surround Pioneer Basin and are called Pioneer Peaks (Gudde, 1949, p. 264; Hanna, p. 237).

Mount Dade [FRESNO]: *peak*, 0.5 mile southeast of Mount Abbot on Fresno-Inyo county line (lat. 37°22'55" N, long. 118°46'45" W). Named on Mount Abbot (1953) 15' quadrangle.

Mount Darwin [FRESNO]: *peak*, 5 miles north-northeast of Mount Goddard on Fresno-Inyo county line (lat. 37°10' N, long. 118°40'15" W); the peak is east of Evolution Lake and Evolution Valley. Altitude 13,830 feet. Named on Mount Goddard (1948) 15' quadrangle. Theodore S. Solomons named the peak in 1895 to honor Charles Darwin (Farquhar, 1923, p. 390).

Mount Davis [MADERA]: *peak*, 9.5 miles northwest of Devils Postpile on Madera-Mono county line (lat. 37°42'55" N, long. 119°13'05" W). Altitude 12,311 feet. Named on Devils Postpile (1953) 15' quadrangle. The name commemorates Milton F. Davis, who climbed the peak in 1891 when he was a Lieutenant under Captain A.E. Wood, first acting superintendent of Yosemite National Park (Farquhar, 1926, p. 305). The feature also was called Davis Mountain (Browning, 1988, p. 31).

Mount Diablo Range: see "Regional setting."

Mount Eisen [TULARE]: *peak*, nearly 7 miles south-southwest of Triple Divide Peak on Great Western Divide (lat. 36°29'55" N, long. 118°34' W). Altitude 12,160 feet. Named on Mineral King (1956) and Triple Divide Peak (1956) 15' quadrangles. The name, given in 1941, commemorates Gustavus A. Eisen, a Swedish scientist who came to the United States in 1872 and was one of the first advocates of a park to protect groves of redwood trees (Hanna, p. 95).

Mount Ericsson [TULARE]: *peak*, 11 miles northwest of Mount Whitney on Kings-Kern Divide (lat. 36°41'50" N, long. 118°24'45" W). Altitude 13,608 feet. Named on Mount Whitney (1956) 15' quadrangle. Bolton C. Brown and his wife named the peak in 1896 for John Ericsson, inventor of the Union ironclad ship *Monitor* (Farquhar, 1923, p. 394).

Mount Farquhar: see **Mount Brewer** [TULARE].

Mount Fiske [FRESNO]: *peak*, 3.5 miles northeast of Mount Goddard on Goddard Divide (lat. 37°08'15" N, long. 118°40' W). Altitude 13,524 feet. Named on Mount Goddard (1948) 15' quadrangle. Theodore S. Solomons named the peak in 1895 for John Fiske, historian and philosopher (Farquhar, 1923, p. 395).

Mount Florence [MADERA]: *peak*, 8 miles north-northeast of Merced Peak (lat. 37°44'25" N, long. 119°19' W); the peak is south of Florence Creek. Altitude 12,561 feet. Named on Merced Peak (1953) 15' quadrangle. The name commemorates Florence Hutchings, daughter of James M. Hutchings and the first white child born in Yosemite Valley (United States Board on Geographic Names, 1934a, p. 9).

Mount Florence: see **Florence Peak** [TULARE].

Mount Gabb [FRESNO]: *peak*, 1.25 miles southwest of Mount Abbot (lat. 37°22'40" N, long. 118°48'10" W). Altitude 13,711 feet. Named on Mount Abbot (1953) 15' quadrangle. Members of the Whitney survey named the peak—or a nearby one—to honor William More Gabb, paleontologist of the survey (Farquhar, 1923, p. 396-397).

Mount Gardiner [FRESNO]: *peak*, 10 miles south-southwest of Mount Pinchot (lat. 36°48'20" N, long. 118°27'30" W). Altitude 12,907 feet. Named on Mount Pinchot (1953) 15' quadrangle. Members of the Whitney survey named the peak in 1865 for James Terry Gardiner (or Gardner), who served with the survey from 1864 until 1867 (Hanna, p. 117).

Mount Geneva: see **Mount Genevra** [TULARE].

Mount Genevra [TULARE]: *peak*, 11 miles northwest of Mount Whitney on Kings-Kern Divide (lat. 36°41' N, long. 118°26' W). Altitude 13,055 feet. Named on Mount Whitney (1956) 15' quadrangle. Helen M. Gompertz and J N. LeConte named the peak in 1899 for

Genevra Magee after they had climbed to the top of Mount Brewer with Mrs. Magee (Hanna, p. 119). Called Mt. Geneva on Olmsted's (1900) map.

Mount Gilbert [FRESNO]: *peak,* 7 miles east-northeast of Mount Goddard on Fresno-Inyo county line (lat. 37°08'15" N, long. 118° 35'45" W; sec. 28, T 9 S, R 31 E). Altitude 13,103 feet. Named on Mount Goddard (1948) 15' quadrangle. The name commemorates geologist Grove Karl Gilbert (Farquhar, 1923, p. 398).

Mount Givens [FRESNO]: *peak,* 7.5 miles east of Kaiser Peak on Kaiser Ridge (lat. 37°16'45" N, long. 119°03'15" W). Altitude 10,648 feet. Named on Kaiser Peak (1953) 15' quadrangle. United States Board on Geographic Names (1982b, p. 3) approved the name "Mount Ian Campbell" for a peak situated 2.3 miles southeast of Mount Givens at the east end of Kaiser Ridge (lat. 37°15'43" N, long. 119°01'11" W); the name commemorates Ian Campbell, who was chief of California Division of Mines and Geology, and first chairman of California Advisory Committee on Geographic Names—Dr. Campbell did geologic work near the peak.

Mount Goddard [FRESNO]: *peak,* 33 miles east of Shaver Lake Heights (present town of Shaver Lake) (lat. 37°06'15" N, long. 118°43'05" W); the peak is at the head of Goddard Creek on Goddard Divide. Altitude 13,568 feet. Named on Mount Goddard (1948) 15' quadrangle. Members of the Whitney survey named the peak for George Henry Goddard, civil engineer and California map maker (Whitney 1865, p. 382). United States Board on Geographic Names (1968c, p. 6) approved the name "Mount Solomons" for a peak situated 2.5 miles east of Mount Goddard; the name commemorates Theodore S. Solomons, who explored and mapped in the Sierra Nevada. The Board (1968a, p. 5) also approved the name "Lake McDermand" for a lake, 0.3 miles long, located 2.5 miles northeast of Mount Goddard; the name is for Charles K. McDermand, outdoorsman, writer, and authority on fishing for golden trout in the High Sierra.

Mount Goethe [FRESNO]: *peak,* 7.25 miles north of Mount Goddard on Glacier Divide (lat. 37°12'25" N, long. 118°42'15" W). Named on Mount Goddard (1948) 15' quadrangle. The name is for Johann Wolfgang Goethe and was given in commemoration of the bicentennial of Goethe's birth (United States Board on Geographic Names, 1949a, p. 3).

Mount Goode [FRESNO]: *peak,* 8.5 miles east of Mount Goddard on Fresno-Inyo county line (lat. 37°07'25" N, long. 118°34'05" W; on W line sec. 35, T 9 S, R 31 E). Altitude 13,092 feet. Named on Mount Goddard (1948) 15' quadrangle. The name commemorates topographer Richard Urquhart Goode of United

States Geological Survey (Farquhar, 1923, p. 399).

Mount Goode: see **Black Giant** [FRESNO].

Mount Gould [FRESNO]: *peak,* 12 miles south of Mount Pinchot on Fresno-Inyo county line (lat. 36°46'50" N, long. 118°22'35" W). Altitude 13,005 feet. Named on Mount Pinchot (1953) 15' quadrangle. The name is for Wilson S. Gould of Oakland, who climbed the peak with J.N. LeConte in 1896; LeConte and some companions had called the feature University Peak in 1890, but that name was transferred to another place (Farquhar, 1923, p. 399).

Mount Guyot [TULARE]: *peak,* 6.25 miles southwest of Mount Whitney (lat. 36°30'30" N, long. 118°21'45" W). Altitude 12,300 feet. Named on Mount Whitney (1956) 15' quadrangle. The name commemorates Arnold H. Guyot, Swiss geologist and geographer (United States Board on Geographic Names, 1933a, p. 345). United States Board on Geographic Names (1985b, p. 1) approved the name "Mount Anna Mills" for a peak located 2.5 miles south of Mount Guyot (lat. 36°28'30" N, long. 118°20'55" W); the name commemorates Anna Mills Johnston, one of the first women to climb Mount Whitney.

Mount Haeckel [FRESNO]: *peak,* 4.5 miles northeast of Mount Goddard on Fresno-Inyo county line (lat. 37°09' N, long. 118°39'35" W). Altitude 13,435 feet. Named on Mount Goddard (1948) 15' quadrangle. Theodore S. Solomons named the peak in 1895 for Ernest Heinrich Haeckel, professor of zoology at University of Jena (Farquhar, 1923, p. 401).

Mount Hale [TULARE]: *peak,* 1.5 miles west-northwest of Mount Whitney (lat. 36°35'15" N, long. 118°18'50" W). Named on Mount Whitney (1956) 15' quadrangle. Sierra Club officials suggested the name to commemorate astronomer George Ellery Hale (Browning 1986, p. 90).

Mount Harrington [FRESNO]: *peak,* 13 miles west-southwest of Marion Peak (lat. 36°52'10" N, long. 118°43'55" W). Altitude 11,005 feet. Named on Marion Peak (1953) 15' quadrangle.

Mount Hazen: see **Table Mountain** [TULARE] (2).

Mount Henry [FRESNO]: *peak,* 8 miles north-northwest of Blackcap Mountain on LeConte Divide (lat. 37°11' N, long. 118°49'35" W). Altitude 12,196 feet. Named on Blackcap Mountain (1953) 15' quadrangle. J.N. LeConte named the peak for physicist Joseph Henry of Smithsonian Institution and National Academy of Sciences (Farquhar, 1923, p. 403).

Mount Hilgard [FRESNO]: *peak,* 3 miles southwest of Mount Abbot (lat. 37°21'40" N, long. 118°49'35" W). Altitude 13,361 feet. Named on Mount Abbot (1953) 15' quadrangle. Ernest C. Bonner suggested the name to honor

E.W. Hilgard of University of California; apparently Bonner meant the name for present Recess Peak (Farquhar, 1923, p. 404).

Mount Hitchcock [TULARE]: *peak,* 2 miles southwest of Mount Whitney (lat. 36°33'15" N, long. 118°18'40" W). Altitude 13,184 feet. Named on Mount Whitney (1956) 15' quadrangle. The Reverend F.H. Wales of Tulare named the peak in 1881 to honor Charles Henry Hitchcock, professor of geology at Dartmouth College (Hanna, p. 139).

Mount Hooper [FRESNO]: *peak,* 9 miles southwest of Mount Abbot (lat. 37°17'30" N, long. 118°53'40" W). Altitude 12,349 feet. Named on Mount Abbot (1953) 15' quadrangle. R.B. Marshall of United States Geological Survey named the peak in memory of Major William B. Hooper (Gudde, 1949, p. 153).

Mount Hopkins [FRESNO]: *peak,* 5.5 miles north-northwest of Mount Abbot (lat. 37°27'50" N, long. 118°48'45" W); the peak is 2 miles southeast of Hopkins Pass. Altitude 12,302 feet. Named on Mount Abbot (1953) 15' quadrangle. R.B. Marshall of United States Geological Survey named the peak to commemorate Mark Hopkins, one of the "Big Four" of Central Pacific Railroad (Hanna, p. 141-142); nearby Mount Crocker, Mount Huntington, and Mount Stanford commemorate the other three railroad magnates. The four peaks surround Pioneer Basin and are called Pioneer Peaks (Gudde, 1949, p. 264; Hanna, p. 237).

Mount Humphreys [FRESNO]: *peak,* 12 miles north of Mount Goddard on Fresno-Inyo county line (lat. 37°16'15" N, long. 118°40'15" W). Altitude 13,986 feet. Named on Mount Tom (1949) 15' quadrangle. Members of the Whitney survey named the peak in 1864 to honor General Andrew Atkinson Humphreys (Farquhar, 1923, p. 405-406).

Mount Huntington [FRESNO]: *peak,* nearly 6 miles north of Mount Abbot on Fresno-Mono county line (lat. 37°28'10" N, long. 118°46'35" W). Altitude 12,405 feet. Named on Mount Abbot (1953) 15' quadrangle. R.B. Marshall of United States Geological Survey named the peak to honor Collis P. Huntington, one of the "Big Four" of Central Pacific Railroad (Hanna, p. 145); nearby Mount Crocker, Mount Hopkins, and Mount Stanford commemorate the other three railroad magnates. The four peaks surround Pioneer Basin and are called Pioneer Peaks (Gudde, 1949, p. 264; Hanna, p. 237).

Mount Hutchings [FRESNO]: *peak,* 9.5 miles south-southwest of Marion Peak (lat. 36°50' N, long. 118°36' W). Altitude 10,785 feet. Named on Marion Peak (1953) 15' quadrangle. The name commemorates J.M. Hutchings, pioneer of the Yosemite region and publisher of *Hutchings' California Magazine* (Farquhar, 1923, p. 406).

Mount Hutton: see **Red Mountain** [FRESNO]

(2).

Mount Huxley [FRESNO]: *peak,* 3 miles northeast of Mount Goddard (lat. 37°08'15" N, long. 118°40'55" W). Altitude 13,117 feet. Named on Mount Goddard (1948) 15' quadrangle. Theodore S. Solomons named the peak in 1895 for Thomas Henry Huxley (Farquhar, 1923, p. 406). United States Board on Geographic Names (1969c, p. 4) approved the name "Mount Warlow" for a peak located 0.7 mile southeast of Mount Huxley; the name commemorates Chester H. Warlow, who helped in the creation of Kings Canyon National Park.

Mount Ian Campbell: see **Mount Givens** [FRESNO].

Mount Ickes [FRESNO]: *peak,* 2 miles west-southwest of Mount Pinchot (lat. 36°56' N, long. 118°26'20" W). Altitude 12,968 feet. Named on Mount Pinchot (1953) 15' quadrangle. 'The name commemorates Harold L. Ickes, Secretary of the Interior from 1933 until 1946 (United States Board on Geographic Names, 1964b, p. 13).

Mount Izaak Walton [FRESNO]: *peak,* 8 miles northwest of Mount Abbot (lat. 37°28'15" N, long. 118°53'20" W). Altitude 12,099 feet. Named on Mount Abbot (1953) 15' quadrangle. Francis P. Farquhar proposed the name in 1919 to honor the author of *The Compleat Angler* (Gudde, 1949, p. 163).

Mount Jenkins: see **Morris Peak** [KERN].

Mount Jepson: see **Mount Sill** [FRESNO].

Mount Johnson [FRESNO]: *peak,* 7.5 miles east-northeast of Mount Goddard on Fresno-Inyo county line (lat. 37°07'45" N, long. 118°35'05" W; on E line sec. 33, T 9 S, R 31 E). Altitude 12,868 feet. Named on Mount Goddard (1948) 15' quadrangle. The name honors Willard D. Johnson of United States Geological Survey (United States Board on Geographic Names, 1933a, p. 401).

Mount Jordan [TULARE]: *peak,* 11.5 miles northwest of Mount Whitney on Kings-Kern Divide (lat. 36°41' N, long. 118°26'50" W). Altitude 13,344 feet. Named on Mount Whitney (1956) 15' quadrangle. The name commemorates David Starr Jordan, who was president of Stanford University (United States Board on Geographic Names, 1933a, p. 401).

Mount Jordan: see **North Palisade** [FRESNO].

Mount Julius Caesar [FRESNO]: *peak,* 2 miles south of Mount Abbot on Fresno-Inyo county line (lat. 37°21'20" N, long. 118°46'50" W); the peak is 1 mile east of Lake Italy. Altitude 13,196 feet. Named on Mount Abbot (1953) 15' quadrangle. Alfred H. Prater and Myrtle Prater made the first ascent of the peak in 1928; they named it for Julius Caesar because of its proximity to Lake Italy (Browning, p. 113). United States Board on Geographic Names (1978b, p. 4) rejected the form "Mount Julius Cesar" for the name.

Mount Kaweah [TULARE]: *peak,* 11 miles

west-southwest of Mount Whitney (lat. 36°31'35" N, long. 118°28'40" W); the peak is at the southeast end of Kaweah Peaks Ridge. Altitude 13,802 feet. Named on Mount Whitney (1956) 15' quadrangle.

Mount Keith [TULARE]: *peak,* 9 miles north-northwest of Mount Whitney on Tulare-Inyo county line (lat. 36°42' N, long. 118°20'30" W). Altitude 13,977 feet. Named on Mount Whitney (1956) 15' quadrangle. Helen M. Gompertz named the peak in 1896 to honor landscape-painter William Keith (Hanna, p. 159).

Mount King: see **Mount Clarence King** [FRESNO].

Mount Lamarck [FRESNO]: *peak,* 7 miles north-northeast of Mount Goddard on Fresno-Inyo county line (lat. 37°11'40" N, long. 118° 40'10" W). Altitude 13,417 feet. Named on Mount Goddard (1948) 15' quadrangle. The name commemorates the French evolutionist Jean Baptiste Pierre Antoine de Monet de Lamarck (Browning 1986, p. 122).

Mount Langley [TULARE]: *peak,* nearly 5 miles southeast of Mount Whitney on Tulare-Inyo county line (lat. 36°31'25" N, long. 118° 14'20" W). Altitude 14,042 feet. Named on Lone Pine (1958) 15' quadrangle. The name commemorates Samuel Pierpont Langley, secretary of Smithsonian Institution from 1877 until 1906, who led an expedition to Mount Whitney in 1881 to study solar heat (Farquhar, 1924, p. 52).

Mount Langley: see **Mount Cocoran** [TULARE].

Mount LeConte [TULARE]: *peak,* 3.5 miles southeast of Mount Whitney on Tulare-Inyo county line (lat. 36°32'30" N, long. 118° 15'05" W). Altitude 13,960 feet. Named on Mount Whitney (1956) 15' quadrangle. The name commemorates Joseph LeConte, professor of geology and natural history at University of California (Farquhar, 1924, p. 53).

Mount Lyell [MADERA-TUOLUMNE]: *peak,* 12 miles south of Tioga Pass on Madera-Tuolumne county line (lat. 37°44'25" N, long. 119°16'15" W); the peak is near the head of Lyell Fork [TUOLUMNE]. Altitude 13,114 feet. Named on Merced Peak (1953) 15' quadrangle. Members of the Whitney survey named the peak for Sir Charles Lyell, distinguished English geologist (United States Board on Geographic Names, 1934a, p. 15).

Mount Maddox [TULARE]: *peak,* 15.miles northwest of Triple Divide Peak (lat. 36°43'40" N, long. 118°44'45" W; sec. 8, T 14 S, R 30 E). Named on Triple Divide Peak (1956) 15' quadrangle.

Mount Maggie: see **Maggie Mountain** [TULARE].

Mount Mallory [TULARE]: *peak,* 2.5 miles southeast of Mount Whitney on Tulare-Inyo county line (lat. 36°33' N, long. 118°15'45" W). Altitude 13,850 feet. Named on Mount Whitney (1956) 15' quadrangle. Norman Clyde, who climbed the peak in 1925, proposed the name to honor the climber who died on Mount Everest in 1924 (Farquhar, 1926, p. 306).

Mount McAdie [TULARE]: *peak,* 2.25 miles south-southeast of Mount Whitney on Tulare-Inyo county line (lat. 36°33' N, long. 118°16'30" W). Named on Mount Whitney (1956) 15' quadrangle. The name is for meteorologist Alexander G. McAdie (Browning 1986, p. 140-141).

Mount Maclure [MADERA-TUOLUMNE]: *peak,* 11.5 miles south of Tioga Pass on Madera-Tuolumne county line (lat. 37°44'40" N, long. 119°16'45" W). Named on Merced Peak (1953) 15' quadrangle. Members of the Whitney survey named the peak for William Maclure, pioneer American geologist (Whitney, 1870, p. 101). United States Board on Geographic Names (1933a, p. 486) rejected the form "Mount McClure" for the name.

Mount McClure: see **Mount Maclure** [MADERA-TUOLUMNE].

Mount McDoogle: see **Mount Cedric Wright** [FRESNO].

Mount McDuffie [FRESNO]: *peak,* 4.5 miles east-southeast of Mount Goddard on Black Divide (lat. 37°04'25" N, long. 118° 38'35" W). Altitude 13,271 feet. Named on Mount Goddard (1948) 15' quadrangle. The name honors Duncan McDuffie for his interest in national parks and work as a conservationist (United States Board on Geographic Names, 1954, p. 3).

Mount McGee [FRESNO]: *peak,* 2.5 miles north-northwest of Mount Goddard (lat. 37°08'20" N, long. 118°44'15" W). Altitude 12,969 feet. Named on Mount Goddard (1948) 15' quadrangle. The name commemorates William John McGee, who was with United States Geological Survey and Bureau of American Ethnology (Browning 1986, p. 142).

Mount Mendel [FRESNO]: *peak,* 5.25 miles north-northeast of Mount Goddard (lat. 37°10'30" N, long. 118°40'50" W). Altitude 13,691 feet. Named on Mount Goddard (1948) 15' quadrangle. Sierra Club officials proposed the name before 1942 to honor Johann Gregor Mendel, Austrian geneticist; the peak was called Mt. Wallace on some maps (Browning 1986, p. 143-144).

Mount Merriam: see **Merriam Peak** [FRESNO].

Mount Mills [FRESNO]: *peak,* 0.5 mile north-northwest of Mount Abbot on Fresno-Inyo county line (lat. 37°23'40" N, long. 118°47'20" W); the peak is near the head of Mills Creek. Altitude 13,468 feet. Named on Mount Abbot (1953) 15' quadrangle. The name commemorates Darius Ogden Mills, California banker, railroad man, and mountaineer (Hanna, p. 193)

Mount Moraine: see **Barton Peak** [TULARE].

Mount Moses: see **Moses Mountain** [TULARE].

Mount Muir [TULARE]: *peak,* 1 mile south of Mount Whitney on Tulare-Inyo county line (lat. 36°33'50" N, long. 118°17'25" W). Altitude 14,015 feet. Named on Mount Whitney (1956) 15' quadrangle. Professor Alexander G. McAdie named the peak for naturalist John Muir (Farquhar, 1924, p. 60).

Mount Needham: see **Florence Peak** [TULARE].

Mount Newcomb [TULARE]: *peak,* 2.5 miles south of Mount Whitney (lat. 36°32'25" N, long. 118°17'35" W). Altitude 13,410 feet. Named on Mount Whitney (1956) 15' quadrangle. Sierra Club officials proposed the name to honor astronomer and political economist Simon Newcomb (Browning 1986, p. 158).

Mount Olive [FRESNO]: *hill,* 3 miles west of Orange Cove (lat. 36° 37'40" N, long. 119°22' W; sec. 16, T 15 S, R 24 E). Named on Orange Cove North (1966) 7.5' quadrangle.

Mount Owen: see **Brown** [KERN].

Mount Peckinpah: see **Peckinpah Mountain**, under **Central Camp** [MADERA].

Mount Perkins [FRESNO]: *peak,* 2 miles southeast of Mount Pinchot on Fresno-Inyo county line (lat. 36°55'40" N, long. 118°22'50" W). Altitude 12,591 feet. Named on Mount Pinchot (1953) 15' quadrangle. Robert D. Pike named the peak in 1906 for George Perkins, governor of California from 1880 until 1883, and senator from 1893 until 1915 (Hanna, p. 233).

Mount Pheasant [KERN]: *peak,* 5.25 miles south-southeast of Woody (lat. 35°38'25" N, long. 118°47'05" W; near NE cor. sec. 30, T 26 S, R 30 E). Altitude 3629 feet. Named on Woody (1965) 7.5' quadrangle.

Mount Pickering [TULARE]: *peak,* 3.5 miles south of Mount Whitney (lat. 36°31'40" N, long. 118°17'30" W). Altitude 13,485 feet. Named on Mount Whitney (1956) 15' quadrangle. Sierra Club officials proposed the name to honor astronomer Edward Charles Pickering (Browning 1986, p. 169).

Mount Pinchot [FRESNO]: *peak,* 6.5 miles east of Marion Peak (lat. 36°56'45" N, long. 118°24'15" W). Altitude 13,495 feet. Named on Mount Pinchot (1953) 15' quadrangle. J.N. LeConte named the peak in 1896 for conservationist Gifford Pinchot, Forest Service chief from 1898 until 1910 (Hanna, p. 236).

Mount Poso [KERN]: *peak,* 14 miles east-south-east of McFarland (lat. 35°35'35" N, long. 119°00'10" W; sec. 7, T 27 S, R 28 E); the peak is north of Poso Creek. Altitude 1215 feet. Named on North of Oildale (1954) 7.5' quadrangle.

Mount Powell [KERN]: *peak,* 5.5 miles east-northeast of Mount Goddard on Fresno-Inyo county line (lat. 37°08'15" N, long. 118°37'40" W; sec. 30, T 9 S, R 31 E). Named on Mount Goddard (1948) 15' quadrangle. According to Farquhar (1924, p. 64), the name presumably commemorates John Wesley Powell.

Mount Prater [FRESNO]: *peak,* 3500 feet south-southeast of Mount Bolton Brown on Fresno-Inyo county line (lat. 37°02'15" N, long. 118°26' W). Altitude 13,329 feet. Named on Big Pine (1950) 15' quadrangle. The name commemorates Alfred Prater, who with his wife ascended the peak in 1928 (United States Board on Geographic Names, 1933a, p. 618).

Mount Raymond Camp [MADERA]: *locality,* 7 miles south-southwest of Buena Vista Peak (lat. 37°30' N, long. 119°29'20" W; sec. 16, T 5 S, R 22 E); the place is 1.5 miles west-south-west of Raymond Mountain. Named on Yosemite (1956) 15' quadrangle.

Mount Reinstein [FRESNO]: *peak,* 2 miles southwest of Mount Goddard (lat. 37°04'45" N, long. 118°44'15" W). Altitude 12,604 feet. Named on Mount Goddard (1948) 15' quadrangle. R.B. Marshall of United States Geological Survey named the peak for Jacob B. Reinstein, a regent of University of California from 1897 until 1912 (Farquhar, 1925, p. 128).

Mount Ritter [MADERA]: *peak,* 8 miles north-west of Devils Postpile (lat. 37°41'20" N, long. 119°11'55" W); the peak is on Ritter Ridge. Altitude 13,157 feet. Named on Devils Postpile (1953) 15' quadrangle. Members of the Whitney survey named the peak for German geographer Karl Ritter (Whitney, 1870, p. 101).

Mount Rixford [FRESNO]: *peak,* 11 miles south of Mount Pinchot (lat. 36°47'05" N, long. 118°23'55" W). Altitude 12,890 feet. Named on Mount Pinchot (1953) 15' quadrangle. Vernon L. Kellogg named the peak in 1899 for Dr. Emmet Rixford, who was the first to climb the feature (Hanna, p. 257).

Mount Royce: see **Royce Peak** [FRESNO].

Mount Ruskin [FRESNO]: *peak,* 4.25 miles west-northwest of Mount Pinchot (lat. 36°58'45" N, long. 118°28'20" W). Altitude 12,920 feet. Named on Mount Pinchot (1953) 15' quadrangle. Bolton C. Brown named the peak in 1895 for English writer John Ruskin (Hanna, p. 261).

Mount Russell [TULARE]: *peak,* less than 1 mile north-northeast of Mount Whitney on Tulare-Inyo county line (lat. 36°35'25" N, long. 118°17'15" W). Altitude 14,086 feet. Named on Mount Whitney (1956) 15' quadrangle. The name commemorates geologist Israel C. Russell (Hanna, p. 261).

Mount Senger [FRESNO]: *peak,* 8.5 miles south-southwest of Mount Abbot (lat. 37°16'40" N, long. 118°51'25" W). Altitude 12,271 feet. Named on Mount Abbot (1953)

15' quadrangle. Theodore S. Solomons named the peak in 1894 for J. Henry Senger, professor of German at University of California and a founder of the Sierra Club (Farquhar, 1925, p. 132).

Mount Shakspere [FRESNO]: *peak,* 11.5 miles east-southeast of Mount Goddard (lat. 37°02'10" N, long. 118°31'55" W). Altitude 12,151 feet. Named on Mount Goddard (1948) 15' quadrangle.

Mount Shinn [FRESNO]: *peak,* 12 miles northwest of Blackcap Mountain (lat. 37°12'45" N, long. 118°55'05" W; sec. 28, T 8 S, R 28 E). Altitude 11,020 feet. Named on Blackcap Mountain (1953) 15' quadrangle. The name is for Charles Howard Shinn, who was supervisor of Sierra National Forest (United States Board on Geographic Names, 1933a, p. 689).

Mount Shinn Lake [FRESNO]: *lake,* 500 feet long, 12 miles northwest of Blackcap Mountain (lat. 37°12'25" N, long. 118°55'25" W; sec. 29, T 8 S, R 28 E); the lake is 0.5 mile southwest of Mount Shinn. Named on Blackcap Mountain (1953) 15' quadrangle.

Mount Sill [FRESNO]: *peak,* 12 miles east of Mount Goddard on Fresno-Inyo county line (lat. 37°05'45" N, long. 118°30'10" W). Altitude 14,162 feet. Named on Mount Goddard (1948) 15' quadrangle. J.N. LeConte named the peak in 1896 for Edward Rowland Sill, professor of literature at University of California from 1874 until 1882 (Farquhar, 1925, p. 133). United States Board on Geographic Names (1971b, p. 2) approved the name "Mount Jepson" for a peak situated 0.7 mile southeast of Mount Sill; the name honors Willis Linn Jepson, professor of botany at University of California from 1899 until 1937. The Board at the same time noted the variant name "Pine Martin Peak" for present Mount Jepson.

Mount Silliman [TULARE]: *peak,* 10 miles west-northwest of Triple Divide Peak (lat. 36°38'40" N, long. 118°41'50" W). Altitude 11,188 feet. Named on Triple Divide Peak (1956) 15' quadrangle. William H. Brewer and other members of the Whitney survey named the peak in 1864 for Professor Benjamin Silliman, Jr., of Yale University (Brewer, p. 523).

Mount Solomons: see **Mount Goddard** [FRESNO].

Mount Spencer [FRESNO]: *peak,* 4 miles north-northeast of Mount Goddard (lat. 37°09'20" N, long. 118°40'50" W). Named on Mount Goddard (1948) 15' quadrangle. Theodore S. Solomons named the peak in 1895 for Herbert Spencer, author of *Principles of Philosophy* (Farquhar, 1925, p. 134).

Mount Stanford [FRESNO]: *peak,* 7 miles north of Mount Abbot on Fresno-Inyo county line (lat. 37°29'25" N, long. 118°47'45" W). Altitude 12,851 feet. Named on Mount Abbot (1953) 15' quadrangle. R.B. Marshall of

United States Geological Survey named the peak for Leland Stanford (Farquhar, 1925, p. 135), one of the "Big Four" of Central Pacific Railroad; nearby Mount Crocker, Mount Hopkins, and Mount Huntington commemorate the other three railroad magnates. The four peaks surround Pioneer Basin and are called Pioneer Peaks (Gudde, 1949, p. 264; Hanna, p. 237). United States Board on Geographic Names (1983a, p. 5) rejected the name "Stanford Peak" for Mount Stanford.

Mount Stanford [TULARE]: *peak,* 10.5 miles north-northwest of Mount Whitney (lat. 36°42'10" N, long. 118°23'40" W). Altitude 13,963 feet. Named on Mount Whitney (1956) 15' quadrangle. Bolton C. Brown named the peak in 1896 for Stanford University (Farquhar, 1925, p. 135).

Mount Starr [FRESNO]: *peak,* 3 miles north-northeast of Mount Abbot on Fresno-Inyo county line (lat. 37°25'40" N, long, 118°45'55" W). Altitude 12,870 feet. Named on Mount Abbot (1953) 15' quadrangle. Sierra Club officials named the peak to honor Walter A. Starr, Jr., mountain climber and author of *Guide to the John Muir Trail and the High Sierra Region* (United States Board on Geographic Names, 1939, p. 33).

Mount Stevenson [FRESNO]: *ridge,* north-northeast-trending, 3 miles long, 1.25 miles north-northwest of Shaver Lake Heights (present town of Shaver Lake) (lat. 37°07'20" N, long. 119°19'40" W); the ridge is south of Stevenson Creek. Named on Shaver Lake (1953) 15' quadrangle.

Mount Stewart [TULARE]: *peak,* 2 miles southwest of Triple Divide Peak on Great Western Divide (lat. 36°34'10" N, long. 118°33'15" W). Altitude 12,205 feet. Named on Triple Divide Peak (1956) 15' quadrangle. United States Board on Geographic Names (1938, p. 52) rejected the form "Stewart Mountain" for the name, and noted that California State Geographical Board named the feature in 1929 to honor Colonel George W. Stewart of Visalia, who was instrumental in creation of Sequoia National Park.

Mount Thompson [FRESNO]: *peak,* 6.5 miles east-northeast of Mount Goddard on Fresno-Inyo county line (lat. 37°08'35" N, long. 118°36'45" W; sec. 29, T 9 S, R 31 E); the peak is 1 mile east-northeast of Mount Powell. Named on Mount Goddard (1948) 15' quadrangle. R.B. Marshall of United States Geological Survey named the peak for Almon Harris Thompson, geographer with the Survey from 1882 until 1906 (Farquhar, 1925, p. 138).

Mount Tom [FRESNO]: *peak,* 5.5 miles north of Kaiser Peak (lat. 37°22'35" N, long. 119°10'40" W). Altitude 9018 feet. Named on Kaiser Peak (1953) 15' quadrangle.

Mount Tyndall [TULARE]: *peak,* 6 miles north-northwest of Mount Whitney on Tulare-Inyo county line (lat. 36°39'20" N, long. 18° 20'10" W). Altitude 14,018 feet. Named on Mount Whitney (1956) 15' quadrangle. Clarence King and Richard Cotter climbed the peak in 1864; King named the feature for John Tyndall, professor of natural philosophy at Royal Institution, London (Farquhar, 1925, p. 140).

Mount Vernon [KERN]: *hill,* 7.5 miles northwest of Blackwells Corner (lat. 35°41'50" N, long. 119°57'55" W; sec. 6, T 26 S, R 19 E). Named on Emigrant Hill (1953) 7.5' quadrangle. Called Wagon Wheel Mt. on Emigrant Hill (1943) 7.5' quadrangle.

Mount Versteeg [TULARE]: *peak,* 5 miles north-northwest of Mount Whitney on Tulare-Inyo county line (lat. 36°38'50" N, long. 118° 19'25" W). Altitude 13,470 feet. Named on Mount Whitney (1956) 15' quadrangle. The name honors Chester Versteeg, who did much to further interest in the Sierra Nevada (United States Board on Geographic Names, 1965a, p. 10-11).

Mount Wallace [FRESNO]: *peak,* 1.5 miles northeast of Mount Goddard on Fresno-Inyo county line (lat. 37°08'45" N, long. 118° 39'20" W). Altitude 13,377 feet. Named on Mount Goddard (1948) 15' quadrangle. Theodore S. Solomons named the peak in 1895 for Alfred Russell Wallace, English scientist and friend of Charles Darwin (Farquhar, 1925, p. 142).

Mount Wallace: see **Mount Mendel** [FRESNO].

Mount Warlow: see **Mount Huxley** [FRESNO].

Mount Whitney [TULARE]: *peak,* 58 miles east-northeast of Visalia on Tulare-Inyo county line (lat. 36°34'45" N, long. 118°17'30" W). Altitude 14,494 feet. Named on Mount Whitney (1956) 15' quadrangle. A field party of the Whitney survey saw the peak in 1864 and named it for their chief, Josiah Dwight Whitney (Whitney 1865, p. 382).

Mount Whitney: see **Old Mount Whitney**, under **Mount Corcoran** [TULARE].

Mount Whitney Number 1: see **Mount Corcoran** [TULARE].

Mount Winchell [FRESNO]: *peak,* 11 miles east of Mount Goddard on Fresno-Inyo county line (lat. 37°06'15" N, long. 118°31'30" W). Altitude 13,768 feet. Named on Mount Goddard (1948) 15' quadrangle. The name honors Alexander Winchell, professor of physics, and later professor of geology at University of Michigan (Farquhar, 1925, p. 144-145).

Mount Woodworth [FRESNO]: *peak,* 6.5 miles east-southeast of Mount Goddard (lat. 37°01'35" N, long. 118°36'55" W). Altitude 12,219 feet. Named on Mount Goddard (1948) 15' quadrangle. The name commemorates Benjamin P. Woodworth, who camped in Simpson Meadow about 1888 (Farquhar, 1925, p. 145).

Mount Wynne [FRESNO]: *peak,* 0.5 mile southsoutheast of Mount Pinchot (lat. 36°56'20" N,

long. 118°24'10" W). Altitude 13,179 feet. Named on Mount Pinchot (1953) 15' quadrangle. The name honors Sedman W. Wynne, who lost his life while working as supervisor of Sequoia National Forest (United States Board on Geographic Names, 1933a, p. 826).

Mount Young [TULARE]: *peak,* 2 miles west of Mount Whitney (lat. 36°45'50" N, long. 118°19'35" W). Altitude 13,177 feet. Named on Mount Whitney (1956) 15' quadrangle. F.H. Wales made the first ascent of the peak in 1881 and named it for Charles Augustus Young of Western Reserve, Dartmouth, and Princeton Universities (Hanna, p. 362).

Movie Stringer [TULARE]: *stream,* flows 2.5 miles to South Fork Kern River 7.5 miles northwest of Olancha Peak in Templeton Meadows (lat. 36°19'50" N, long. 118°13'30" W; sec. 30, T 18 S, R 35 E). Named on Olancha (1956) 15' quadrangle.

Mowery Meadow [TULARE]: *area,* 7 miles north of Camp Nelson (lat. 36°14'30" N, long. 118°55'45" W; sec. 27, T 19 S, R 31 E). Named on Camp Nelson (1956) 15' quadrangle.

Mowry Lake [FRESNO]: *intermittent lake,* 2200 feet long, 4 miles east-northeast of Mendota (lat. 36°46'25" N, long. 120°18'55" W; on E line sec. 27, T 13 S, R 15 E). Named on Firebaugh (1946) 15' quadrangle.

Mud Creek [FRESNO]: *stream,* flows 5.5 miles to a canal 11 miles east-southeast of Clovis (lat. 36°46'05" N, long. 119°31'20" W; sec. 25, T 13 S, R 22 E). Named on Round Mountain (1964) 7.5' quadrangle.

Muddy Creek [KERN]: *stream,* flows 4 miles to lowlands 8 miles northwest of Eagle Rest Peak (lat. 34°59' N, long. 119°15' W; sec. 5, T 10 N, R 22 W). Named on Conner SW (1955), Eagle Rest Peak (1942), and Santiago Creek (1943) 7.5' quadrangles.

Mud Hen Creek [KERN]: *stream,* flows 1.5 miles to French Gulch (1) 4.25 miles south of Alta Sierra (lat. 35°40' N, long. 118°33' W; near W line sec. 16, T 26 S, R 32 E). Named on Alta Sierra (1972) 7.5' quadrangle.

Mud Lakes [FRESNO]: *lakes,* two, each 650 feet long, 3.25 miles east of Dinkey Dome (lat. 37°06'15" N, long. 119°04'25" W; near S line sec. 30, T 9 S, R 27 E). Named on Huntington Lake (1953) 15' quadrangle.

Mud Run [FRESNO]: *stream,* flows nearly 4 miles to Los Gatos Creek 6 miles north-northeast of Coalinga Mineral Springs (lat. 36° 13'35" N, long. 120°31'05" W; near NE cor. sec. 1, T 20 S, R 13 E). Named on Sherman Peak (1969) 7.5' quadrangle.

Mud Spring [KERN]: *spring,* 7.25 miles east-northeast of Caliente (lat. 35°20'40" N, long. 118°31'05" W; sec. 2, T 30 S, R 32 E). Named on Oiler Peak (1972) 7.5' quadrangle.

Mud Spring [TULARE]: *spring,* 3.5 miles north-northeast of California Hot Springs (lat. 35°55'45" N, long. 118°38'30" W; at W line sec. 16, T 23 S, R 31 E). Named on California Hot Springs (1958) 15' quadrangle.

Mud Spring Creek [MADERA]: *stream,* flows 8 miles to Fresno River 9.5 miles south of Raymond (lat. 37°04'40" N, long. 119°53'55" W; sec. 9, T 10 S, R 19 E). Named on Daulton (1962), Knowles (1962), and Little Table Mountain (1962) 7.5' quadrangles.

Mud Spring Gap [TULARE]: *pass,* 5 miles north-northwest of Woodlake (lat. 36°28'20" N, long. 119°08'40" W; at N line sec. 10, T 17 S, R 26 E). Named on Exeter (1952) 15' quadrangle.

Mud Springs [KERN]: *springs,* 8.5 miles northwest of Emerald Mountain (lat. 35°21'30" N, long. 118°22'15" W; sec. 6, T 30 S, R 34 E). Named on Emerald Mountain (1972) 7.5' quadrangle.

Muerto: see **Leiter** [KERN].

Mugler Creek [MADERA]: *stream,* flows 6 miles to Chiquito Creek 6.5 miles north-north-east of Shuteye Peak (lat. 37°26'15" N, long. 119°23' W; sec. 6, T 6 S, R 24 E); the stream goes through Muglers Meadow. Named on Shuteye Peak (1953) 15' quadrangle.

Muglers Meadow [MADERA]: *area,* 9 miles north of Shuteye Peak (lat. 37°28'45" N, long. 119°26' W; sec. 22, T 5 S, R 23 E); the place is along Mugler Creek. Named on Shuteye Peak (1953) 15' quadrangle. Christopher Mugler, a sheepman who was in the neighborhood as early as 1852, had his base camp at the place (Browning, 1986, p. 155).

Muir: see **Mount Muir** [TULARE].

Muir Pass [FRESNO]: *pass,* 2.5 miles east-northeast of Mount Goddard on Goddard Divide (lat. 37°06'45" N, long. 118°40'15" W); the pass is along John Muir Trail. Named on Mount Goddard (1948) 15' quadrangle. William E. Colby named the pass for John Muir (Farquhar, 1924, p. 61).

Mulch Canyon [FRESNO]: *canyon,* drained by a stream that flows 2.5 miles to Warthan Creek 2 miles east-northeast of Charley Mountain (lat. 36°09'20" N, long. 120°38'10" W; near SE cor. sec. 26, T 20 S, R 12 E). Named on Priest Valley (1969) 7.5' quadrangle.

Mule Creek [FRESNO]: *stream,* flows 2 miles to North Fork Kings River nearly 7 miles east-northeast of Balch Camp (lat. 36°55'50" N, long. 119°00'20" W; at E line sec. 34, T 11 S, R 27 E). Named on Patterson Mountain (1952) and Tehipite Dome (1952) 15' quadrangles.

Mule Meadow [TULARE]: *area,* 8.5 miles south of Camp Nelson (lat. 36°01'15" N, long. 118°35'35" W; sec. 14, T 22 S, R 31 E); the place is 1.25 miles east-northeast of Mule Peak. Named on Camp Nelson (1956) 15' quadrangle.

Mule Peak [TULARE]: *peak,* 8.5 miles south of Camp Nelson (lat. 36°01' N, long. 118°36'50" W; sec. 15, T 22 S, R 31 E); the peak is 1.25 miles west-southwest of Mule Meadow. Altitude 8142 feet. Named on Camp

Nelson (1956) 15' quadrangle.

Muley Hole [FRESNO]: *locality,* 7 miles south of Dinkey Dome along Dinkey Creek (1) (lat. 37°00'50" N, long. 119°07'10" W; sec. 34, T 10 S, R 26 E). Named on Huntington Lake (1953) 15' quadrangle. Horses and mules feed at the place (Browning 1986, p. 155).

Mulkey Creek [TULARE]: *stream,* flows 10.5 miles to South Fork Kern River 6.5 miles northwest of Olancha Peak (lat. 36°20'10" N, long. 118°11'50" W; sec. 28, T 18 S, R 35 E); the stream heads near Mulkey Pass. Named on Olancha (1956) 15' quadrangle.

Mulkey Meadows [TULARE]: *area,* 10.5 miles north-northwest of Olancha Peak (lat. 36°24'15" N, long. 118°12'15" W); the place is along Mulkey Creek. Named on Olancha (1956) 15' quadrangle. The name is for Cyrus Mulkey, Inyo County sheriff in the 1870's (Hanna, p. 204).

Mulkey Pass [TULARE]: *pass,* 12 miles north-northwest of Olancha Peak on Tulare-Inyo county line (lat. 36°25'45" N, long. 118°09'55" W; near E line sec. 22, T 17 S, R 35 E); the pass is near the head of Mulkey Creek. Named on Olancha (1956) 15' quadrangle. The feature also is called "old" Mulkey Pass—Trail Pass is called "new" Mulkey Pass (Schumacher, p. 80).

Mullen Ridge [MADERA]: *ridge,* south-trending, 2 miles long, 6.5 miles north of Raymond on Madera-Mariposa county line (lat. 37°18'40" N, long. 119°53'35" W). Named on Ben Hur (1947) 7.5' quadrangle.

Mundgi Flat [KERN]: *area,* 5 miles north of Caliente along Walker Basin Creek (lat. 35°21'35" N, long. 118°38'15" W; sec. 34, T 29 S, R 31 E). Named on Bena (1972) 7.5' quadrangle.

Munger Peak: see **Goat Mountain** [FRESNO] (1).

Munn Camp [KERN]: *locality,* 5.25 miles east-northeast of Glennville (lat. 35°45'40" N, long. 118°37'15" W; near SW cor. sec. 11, T 25 S, R 31 E). Named on California Hot Springs (1958) 15' quadrangle.

Munzer Meadow [KERN]: *area,* 8 miles east-northeast of Mount Adelaide (lat. 35°27'40" N, long. 118°36'50" W; sec. 26, T 28 S, R 31 E). Named on Breckenridge Mountain (1972) 7.5' quadrangle.

Muriel Lake [FRESNO]: *lake,* 3200 feet long, 9 miles north of Mount Goddard (lat. 37°14' N, long. 118°41'45" W); the lake is 1 mile north of Muriel Peak. Named on Mount Goddard (1948) 15' quadrangle.

Muriel Peak [FRESNO]: *peak,* 6 miles north-northeast of Mount Goddard (lat. 37°13'05" N, long. 118°41'30" W). Altitude 12,942 feet. Named on Mount Goddard (1948) 15' quadrangle.

Muro Blanco [FRESNO]: *relief feature,* 2.5 miles south-southeast of Marion Peak on the southeast side of South Fork Kings River (lat.

36°55' N, long. 118°30'30" W). Named on Marion Peak (1953) and Mount Pinchot (1953) 15' quadrangles. The side of the canyon there resembles a solid white wall—*muro blanco* means "white wall" in Spanish (Gudde, 1969, p. 215).

Muroc [KERN]: *locality,* 3 miles east of present Edwards at the edge of Rogers Lake (lat. 34°55'30" N, long. 117°52'20" W; at N line sec. 31, T 10 N, R 9 W); the site now is on Edwards Air Force Base. Named on Rogers Lake (1942) 7.5' quadrangle. Postal authorities established Muroc post office in 1910 and discontinued it in 1951, when they changed the name to Edwards (Frickstad, p. 57). Called Yucca on Campbell's (1902) map, and called Rodriguez on Johnson's (1911) map. The place also had the names "Rogers" and "Rod" (Wines, p. 86). The name "Muroc" is the surname "Corum" spelled backward; Ralph Corum and Clifford Corum were early settlers at the place (Hoover, Rensch, and Rensch, p. 134). California Mining Bureau's (1917c) map shows a place called Neil located less than 1 mile north-northwest of Muroc at the edge of present Rogers Lake.

Muroc: see **North Muroc** [KERN]; **North Muroc**, under **North Edwards** [KERN].

Muroc Air Force Base: see **Edwards Air Force Base** [KERN].

Muroc Army Air Field: see **Edwards Air Force Base** [KERN].

Muroc Dry Lake: see **Rogers Lake** [KERN].

Muroc Junction [KERN]: *locality,* 7.25 miles south of Castle Butte (lat. 35°00'35" N, long. 117°52'45" W; at E line sec. 36, T 11 N, R 10 W). Named on Castle Butte (1956) 15' quadrangle.

Murphy Slough [FRESNO]: *water feature,* diverges from Cole Slough near Laton and extends for 22 miles to Fresno Slough 4.5 miles northwest of Lanare (lat. 36°28'10" N, long. 119°59'50" W; sec. 10, T 17 S, R 18 E). Named on Burrel (1954), Laton (1953), and Riverdale (1954) 7.5' quadrangles.

Murphy Spring [KERN]: *spring,* 12 miles east-northeast of Mount Adelaide (lat. 35°28'50" N, long. 118°32'30" W; sec. 21, T 28 S, R 32 E). Named on Breckenridge Mountain (1972) 7.5' quadrangle.

Murray [KINGS]: *locality,* 9 miles northeast of Avenal (lat. 36°05'35" N, long. 120°00'10" W; near NW cor. sec. 23, T 21 S, R 18 E). Named on La Cima (1963) 7.5' quadrangle. Postal authorities established Murray post office in 1920, discontinued it in 1929, reestablished it in 1936, and discontinued it in 1944 (Frickstad, p. 61). The name commemorates David Murray, a leader in the introduction of olive culture to the neighborhood (Gudde, 1949, p. 229).

Murry Creek [TULARE]:
(1) *stream,* flows 6.5 miles to Cottonwood Creek 1.5 miles north-northeast of Auckland

(lat. 36°36'40" N, long. 119°05'45" W; sec. 24, T 15 S, R 26 E). Named on Auckland (1966) and Miramonte (1966) 7.5' quadrangles.
(2) *stream,* flows 1.5 miles to Bear Creek (1) 5.25 miles southeast of Auckland at Murry Flat (lat. 36°32'20" N, long. 119°02' W; near W line sec. 15, T 16 S, R 27 E). Named on Auckland (1966) 7.5' quadrangle.

Murry Creek: see **Bear Creek** [TULARE] (1).

Murry Flat [TULARE]: *area,* 5.25 miles southeast of Auckland (lat. 36°32'20" N, long. 119°01'55" W; in and near sec. 15, T 16 S, R 27 E). Named on Auckland (1966) 7.5' quadrangle. Called Shadley Flat on Dinuba (1924) 30' quadrangle.

Murry Gulch [TULARE]: *canyon,* drained by a stream that flows less than 1 mile to Murry Creek (1) 4.5 miles northeast of Auckland (lat. 36°37'20" N, long. 119°02'05" W; sec. 15, T 15 S, R 27 E). Named on Auckland (1966) 7.5' quadrangle.

Murry Hill [TULARE]: *hill,* less than 1 mile southeast of Porterville (lat. 36°03'50" N, long. 119°00'15" W; near W line sec. 36, T 21 S, R 27 E. Named on Porterville (1951) 7.5' quadrangle.

Muscatel [FRESNO]: *locality,* 4.5 miles west-northwest of downtown Fresno along Southern Pacific Railroad (lat. 36°47'35" N, long. 119°51'30" W; near NW cor. sec. 24, T 13 S, R 19 E). Named on Fresno North (1965) 7.5' quadrangle.

Mushroom Rock [FRESNO]: *relief feature,* 9 miles north-northeast of Shaver Lake Heights (present town of Shaver Lake) (lat. 37°13'55" N, long. 119°17' W; sec. 18, T 8 S, R 25 E). Named on Shaver Lake (1953) 15' quadrangle.

Musick Creek [FRESNO]: *stream,* flows 4.5 miles to Jose Creek 3.5 miles west-southwest of Shaver Lake Heights (present town of Shaver Lake) (lat. 37°05'30" N, long. 119°22'50" W; sec. 5, T 10 S, R 24 E). Named on Shaver Lake (1953) 15' quadrangle.

Musick Mountain [FRESNO]: *peak,* 4.5 miles north of Shaver Lake Heights (present town of Shaver Lake) (lat. 37°10'10" N, long. 119°18'30" W; sec. 1, 12, T 9 S, R 24 E). Altitude 6807 feet. Named on Shaver Lake (1953) 15' quadrangle. Called Music Pk. on Kaiser (1904) 30' quadrangle. The name "Musick" commemorates either Charles Musick or Henry Musick, both of whom were connected with a sawmill at Shaver Lake (Redinger, p. 79).

Music Peak: see **Musick Mountain** [FRESNO].

Musk [TULARE]: *locality,* 2.5 miles north-northwest of Exeter along Southern Pacific Railroad (lat. 36°19'40" N, long. 119°09' W; near SW cor. sec. 27, T 18 S, R 26 E). Named on Exeter (1926) 7.5' quadrangle.

Mussel Slough [KINGS]: *stream,* flows 20 miles to a ditch 2.5 miles east-northeast of Stratford (lat. 36°12'30" N, long. 19°46'15" W). Named on Burris Park (1926), Guernsey (1929), Hanford (1926), and Stratford (1929) 7.5' quadrangles. On Guernsey (1954) and Stratford (1954) 7.5' quadrangles, the name applies to a watercourse that is mainly dry. Grunsky (p. 87) noted in 1898 that "All of the Kings River delta south of the main channel of the river and west of Cross Creek is commonly known as the Mussel Slough country," and "Many water courses, locally called sloughs, former channels of Kings River, course through this region from the north to south." The name "Mussel Slough" is associated with the bloody conflict in 1880 between hirelings of Southern Pacific Railroad and settlers; after this tragedy, the neighborhood was renamed Lucerne Valley (Hart, J.D., p. 292).

Mustang Hill [KINGS]: *peak,* 2.25 miles southwest of Kettleman City (lat. 35°58'55" N, long. 119°59'05" W; at W line sec. 25, T 22 S, R 18 E). Altitude 738 feet. Named on Los Viejos (1954) 7.5' quadrangle.

Mustang Peak [FRESNO]: *peak,* 5 miles westnorthwest of Castle Mountain on Fresno-Monterey county line (lat. 35°58'30" N, long. 120°24'45" W; sec. 36, T 22 S, R 14 E). Named on Parkfield (1961) 7.5' quadrangle.

Mustang Spring [FRESNO]: *spring,* 7.25 miles west-northwest of Coalinga (lat. 36°10'25" N, long. 120°28'35" W; sec. 20, T 20 S, R 14 E). Named on Alcalde Hills (1969) 7.5' quadrangle.

Mustang Spring [KERN]: *spring,* 4 miles southwest of Skinner Peak (lat. 35°31'25" N, long. 118°10'35" W; sec. 2, T 28 S, R 35 E). Named on Cane Canyon (1972) 7.5' quadrangle.

Myers Canyon [KERN]: *canyon,* drained by a stream that flows 4 miles to Bodfish Creek less than 1 mile east of Bodfish (lat. 35° 35'15" N, long. 118°28'20" W; at S line sec. 7, T 27 S, R 33 E). Named on Lake Isabella South (1972) 7.5' quadrangle.

Myricks Corner [KERN]: *locality,* 1.25 miles northwest of Shafter (lat. 35°30'55" N, long. 119°17'20" W; at S line sec. 4, T 28 S, R 25 E). Named on Wasco (1953) 7.5' quadrangle.

Mystery Lake [FRESNO]: *lake,* 1400 feet long, nearly 4 miles northeast of Dinkey Dome (lat. 37°09'35" N, long. 119°05'15" W; sec. 12, T 9 S, R 26 E). Named on Huntington Lake (1953) 15' quadrangle.

— N —

Nadeau: see **Cameron** [KERN].

Nagel Canyon [KERN]: *canyon,* drained by a stream that flows 1.5 miles to Weaver Creek 8 miles north-northwest of Emerald Mountain (lat. 35°21'20" N, long. 118°21' W; sec. 5, T 30 S, R 34 E). Named on Emerald Mountain (1972) 7.5' quadrangle.

Nanceville [TULARE]: *locality,* 3 miles west of Porterville (lat. 36° 04'10" N, long.

119°04'20" W; sec. 29, T 21 S, R 27 E). Named on Porterville (1951) 7.5' quadrangle.

Napoleon Spring [KERN]: *spring,* 10 miles southwest of Blackwells Corner (lat. 35°30'15" N, long. 119°58'40" W; near W line sec. 7, T 28 S, R 19 E). Named on Shale Point (1953) 7.5' quadrangle.

Naranjo [TULARE]: *locality,* 2 miles eastsoutheast of Woodlake along Visalia Electric Railroad (lat. 36°24'15" N, long. 119°23'40" W; near W line sec. 33, T 17 S, R 27 E). Named on Woodlake (1952) 7.5' quadrangle. Harry Brown and Senator Harding, landowners there, named the place in 1898 (Mitchell, A.R., p. 69). The locality is in a citrus-growing neighborhood—*naranjo* means "orange tree" in Spanish (Gudde, 1949, p. 231). Postal authorities established Naranjo post office in 1901, discontinued it in 1913, reestablished it in 1914, and discontinued it in 1918 (Frickstad, p. 212).

Narbo: see **Quartz Mountain** [MADERA] (2).

Narboe Lake: see **Proctor Lake** [KERN].

Nares [FRESNO]: *locality,* 0.5 mile northwest of Helm along Southern Pacific Railroad (lat. 36°32'15" N, long. 120°06' W). Named on Helm (1925) 7.5' quadrangle.

Narrows: see **The Narrows** [KERN].

Navelencia [FRESNO]: *village,* 7 miles eastsoutheast of Centerville (lat. 36°41' N, long. 119°23' W; sec. 29, T 14 S, R 24 E). Named on Wahtoke (1966) 7.5' quadrangle. Postal authorities established Navelencia post office in 1915 and discontinued it in 1931 (Frickstad, p. 36). The place is in a citrus-growing neighborhood, and the name was coined from the words "navel" and "valencia," two kinds of oranges (Gudde, 1949, p. 232).

Neasons Flat [KERN]: *area,* 3 miles east of Eagle Rest Peak along Pleito Creek (lat. 34°54'45" N, long. 119°04'45" W; near W line sec. 36, T 10 N, R 21 W). Named on Pleito Hills (1958) 7.5' quadrangle.

Needham: see **Mount Needham**, under **Florence Peak** [TULARE].

Needham Mountain [TULARE]: *peak,* 3.25 miles east of Mineral King (lat. 36°27'15" N, long. 118°32'10" W). Altitude 12,467 feet. Named on Mineral King (1956) 15' quadrangle. W.F. Dean named the peak for James Carson Needham, a congressman (Hanna, p. 208).

Needle Camp [TULARE]: *locality,* 10 miles south-southwest of Hockett Peak (lat. 36°05'25" N, long. 118°27'50" W); the place is near the mouth of Needlerock Creek. Named on Hockett Peak (1956) 15' quadrangle.

Needlerock Creek [TULARE]: *stream,* flows 3.5 miles to Kern River 10 miles south-southwest of Hockett Peak (lat. 36°05'20" N, long. 118°27'55" W); the stream is south of The Needles. Named on Camp Nelson (1956) and Hockett Peak (1956) 15' quadrangles.

Needles: see **The Needles** [TULARE].

Neelle Lake [FRESNO]: *lake,* 500 feet long, 3.5 miles north of Mount Abbot (lat. 37°26'10" N, long. 118°46'25" W). Named on Mount Abbot (1953) 15' quadrangle.

Neff Mills: see **Pinehurst** [FRESNO].

Neffs Camp [FRESNO]: *settlement,* nearly 7 miles east-southeast of Dunlap (lat. 36°42'15" N, long. 119°00'10" W; sec. 14, T 14 S, R 27 E). Named on Miramonte (1966) 7.5' quadrangle. Dinuba (1924) 30' quadrangle shows a place called Neff Mills located about 1 mile southwest of present Neffs Camp (near W line sec. 23, T 14 S, R 27 E).

Negit Lake [FRESNO]: *lake,* 1200 feet long, 7.5 miles south of Mount Abbot (lat. 37°16'55" N, long. 118°48'15" W). Named on Mount Abbot (1953) 15' quadrangle. Elden H. Vestal of California Department of Fish and Game named the lake in 1951 using a word that he thought has the meaning "night" or "darkness" in the Piute Indian language (Browning 1986, p. 157).

Negro Creek [TULARE]: *stream,* flows 3.25 miles to lowlands 3.5 miles west-northwest of Cliff Peak (lat. 36°35' N, long. 119°13'40" W; sec. 35, T 15 S, R 25 E). Named on Stokes Mountain (1966) 7.5' quadrangle. Called Niggerhead Cr. on Dinuba (1924) 30' quadrangle.

Negro Rube Creek: see **Nigger Rube Creek** [TULARE].

Ne Hi Canyon [FRESNO]: *canyon,* drained by a stream that flows 3 miles to Diaz Canyon nearly 3 miles southwest of Joaquin Rocks (lat. 36°17'25" N, long. 120°28'55" W; sec. 7, T 19 S, R 14 E). Named on Joaquin Rocks (1969) 7.5' quadrangle.

Nehouse Creek [MADERA]: *stream,* flows 3 miles to West Fork Jackass Creek 6.5 miles east-northeast of Shuteye Peak (lat. 37°23'30" N, long. 119°19'20" W; sec. 23, T 6 S, R 24 E). Named on Shuteye Peak (1953) 15' quadrangle.

Nelder Creek [MADERA]: *stream,* flows 7.5 miles to join Lewis Fork and form Fresno River less than 0.5 mile south-southwest of Yosemite Forks (lat. 37°21'40" N, long. 119°37'55" W; near SW cor. sec. 36, T 6 S, R 21 E). Named on Bass Lake (1953) 15' quadrangle.

Neil: see **Muroc** [KERN].

Neil Lake [FRESNO]: *lake,* 800 feet long, 9 miles southwest of Mount Abbot (lat. 37°17'55" N, long. 118°54'25" W). Named on Mount Abbot (1953) 15' quadrangle. Scott M. Soule and Jack Criqui of California Department of Fish and Game named the lake in 1948 for Neil Perkins, a Forest Service ranger (Browning 1986, p. 157).

Neill's Hot Springs: see **Scovern Hot Springs** [KERN].

Nelder Grove Campground [MADERA]: *locality,* 5 miles north-northeast of Yosemite Forks (lat. 37°15'20" N, long. 119°35' W; sec.

8, T 6 S, R 22 E). Named on Bass Lake (1953) 15' quadrangle. Nelder Grove is a group of redwood trees—John Muir found John A. Nelder living in a cabin at the place in 1875 (Browning, 1986, p. 157).

Nellie Dent Creek [KERN]: *stream,* flows nearly 4 miles to Isabella Lake at Wofford Heights (lat. 35°42'20" N, long. 118°26'50" W; near SW cor. sec. 33, T 25 S, R 33 E). Named on Lake Isabella North (1972) 7.5' quadrangle.

Nellie Lake [FRESNO]: *lake,* 1200 feet long, 3.5 miles west-southwest of Kaiser Peak (lat. 37°16'50" N, long. 119°14'45" W; on S line sec. 28, T 7 S, R 25 E). Named on Kaiser Peak (1953) 15' quadrangle.

Nellies Nipple [KERN]: *peak,* 4 miles southeast of Loraine (lat. 35° 15'25" N, long. 118°23'30" W; near SW cor. sec. 1, T 31 S, R 33 E). Named on Loraine (1972) 7.5' quadrangle.

Nelson: see **Camp Nelson** [TULARE].

Nelson Creek [TULARE]: *stream,* flows 2 miles to South Fork of Middle Fork Tule River at Camp Nelson (lat. 36°08'10" N, long. 118°36'35" W; near S line sec. 33, T 20 S, R 31 E). Named on Camp Nelson (1956) 15' quadrangle. The name commemorates John M. Nelson of Camp Nelson (Browning 1986, p. 157).

Nelson Lakes [FRESNO]: *lakes,* largest 1300 feet long, 5 miles east of Dinkey Dome (lat. 37°06'30" N, long. 119°02'20" W; in and near sec. 28, 33, T 9 S, R 27 E). Named on Huntington Lake (1953) 15' quadrangle.

Nelson Mountain [FRESNO]: *peak,* 5 miles east-southeast of Dinkey Dome (lat. 37°05'25" N, long. 119°02'55" W; sec. 5, T 10 S, R 27 E). Altitude 10,218 feet. Named on Huntington Lake (1953) 15' quadrangle. The name commemorates Thomas P. Nelson, a sheepman in the early days (Browning 1986, p. 158).

Nelson's Hot Springs: see **Scovern Hot Springs** [KERN].

Nelson Soda Springs: see **Camp Nelson** [TULARE].

Neufeld [KERN]: *locality,* nearly 2 miles north of Wasco along Atchison, Topeka and Santa Fe Railroad (lat. 35°37'10" N, long. 119°19'50" W; on E line sec. 36, T 26 S, R 24 E). Named on Wasco (1953) 7.5' quadrangle.

Neuralia [KERN]: *locality,* 12 miles northeast of Mojave along Southern Pacific Railroad (lat. 35°11'50" N, long. 118°02'45" W; near N line sec. 31, T 31 S, R 37 E). Named on Mojave (1956) 15' quadrangle. Postal authorities established Neuralia post office in 1914 and discontinued it in 1916; the name is from the term "new railroad" (Salley, p. 153).

Nevills [FRESNO]: *locality,* 6.5 miles west of downtown Fresno along Southern Pacific Railroad (lat. 36°44'45" N, long. 119°54'10" W; sec. 4, T 14 S, R 19 E). Named on Kearney Park (1923) 7.5' quadrangle.

New Army Pass [TULARE]: *pass,* 17 miles north-northwest of Olancha Peak on Tulare-

Inyo county line (lat. 36°29'25" N, long. 118°14'25" W); the feature is 0.5 mile south of Army Pass. Named on Olancha (1956) 15' quadrangle. The pass is along a trail built in 1955 to bypass the route through Army Pass (Browning 1986, p. 158).

New Auberry [FRESNO]: *village,* 10 miles west of Shaver Lake Heights (present town of Shaver Lake) (lat. 37°05'40" N, long. 119°29'45" W; near NE cor. sec. 6, T 10 S, R 23 E). Named on Shaver Lake (1953) 15' quadrangle. Called Auberry on Kaiser (1904) 30' quadrangle.

Newcomb: see **Mount Newcomb** [TULARE].

New London: see **London** [TULARE].

Newton Crossing: see **Chowchilla River** [MADERA].

New York Camp: see **Merced River** [MADERA].

Nichols Canyon [FRESNO]: *canyon,* drained by a stream that flows 2 miles to North Fork Kings River nearly 4 miles west of Blackcap Mountain (lat. 37°04'20" N, long. 118°51'35" W). Named on Blackcap Mountain (1953) 15' quadrangle.

Nichols Peak: see **Nicolls Peak** [KERN].

Nick Williams: see **Camp Nick Williams** [KERN].

Nicolls Peak [KERN]: *peak,* 3 miles south of Weldon (lat. 35°37'10" N, long. 118°17'50" W; sec. 35, T 26 S, R 34 E). Named on Woolstalf Creek (1972) 7.5' quadrangle. Called Nichols Peak on Isabella (1943) 15' quadrangle. United States Board on Geographic Names (1974b, p. 3) gave the form "Nichols Peak" as a variant; the name "Nicolls Peak" commemorates John Nicoll, who homesteaded near the peak in 1856.

Nicoll Spring [KERN]: *spring,* 2.25 miles southeast of Weldon (lat. 35°38' N, long. 118°16'45" W; sec. 25, T 26 S, R 34 E). Named on Weldon (1972) 7.5' quadrangle.

Niggerhead Creek: see **Negro Creek** [TULARE].

Nigger Rube Creek [TULARE]: *stream,* flows 7.5 miles to Deer Creek (2) 4 miles west-northwest of California Hot Springs (lat. 35°53'50" N, long. 118°30'10" W; near E line sec. 28, T 23 S, R 30 E). Named on Tobias Peak (1936) 30' quadrangle. United States Board on Geographic Names (1988a, p. 3) approved the name "Rube Creek" for the stream, and rejected the names "Nigger Rube Creek" and "Negro Rube Creek" for it.

Nigger Slough [TULARE]: *stream,* flows 6.5 miles to Inside Creek 8.5 miles west of Lindsay (lat. 36°12'10" N, long. 119°14'35" W; near E line sec. 10, T 20 S, R 25 E). Named on Cairns Corner (1927) and Exeter (1926) 7.5' quadrangles.

Nightingale Gulch [KERN]: *canyon,* drained by a stream that flows 7 miles to Five Dog Creek 6 miles southwest of Woody (lat. 35°38'05" N, long. 118°53'40" W; sec. 30, T 26 S, R 29

E). Named on Sand Canyon (1965) and Woody (1965) 7.5' quadrangles.

Nine Lake Basin [TULARE]: *area,* 2 miles south-southwest of Triple Divide Peak at the head of Big Arroyo (lat. 36°33'45" N, long. 118°32'15" W). Named on Triple Divide Peak (1956) 15' quadrangle.

Ninemile Creek [TULARE]: *stream,* flows 8.5 miles to Kern River 2 miles east of Hockett Peak (lat. 36°13'15" N, long. 118°21'05" W). Named on Hockett Peak (1956) 15' quadrangle.

Nipinnawasee [MADERA]: *settlement,* 6.25 miles west-northwest of Yosemite Forks (lat. 37°24'15" N, long. 119°43'55" W; on S line sec. 13, T 6 S, R 20 E). Called Nipinnawassee on Bass Lake (1953) 15' quadrangle, but United States Board on Geographic Names (1981a, p. 2) rejected the forms "Nipinnawassee" and "Nippinawasee" for the name. Postal authorities established Femmon post office 3 miles north of Ahwahnee in 1912, and then moved it and changed the name to Nipinnawasee the same year; the name "Femmon" honored Frank Femmon, who developed a prize-winning apple (Salley, p. 73-74). They discontinued Nipinnawasee post office in 1961; the name is of Indian origin and was transferred from Michigan (Salley, p. 154).

Nobe Young Creek [TULARE]: *stream,* flows 7.5 miles to Dry Meadow Creek 11 miles south-southeast of Camp Nelson (lat. 36° 00'15" N, long. 118°30'05" W; sec. 22, T 22 S, R 32 E); the stream goes through Nobe Young Meadow. Named on California Hot Springs (1958) and Camp Nelson (1956) 15' quadrangles.

Nobe Young Meadow [TULARE]: *area,* 8 miles south-southeast of Camp Nelson (lat. 36°01'40" N, long. 118°34'30" W; sec. 12, T 22 S, R 31 E); the place is along Nobe Young Creek. Named on Camp Nelson (1956) 15' quadrangle.

Noble: see **Stony Flat** [FRESNO].

Nome: see **Bakersfield** [KERN].

Nonada Hill [FRESNO]: *peak,* 18 miles southwest of Firebaugh (lat. 36°42' N, long. 120°43' W; sec. 24, T 14 S, R 11 E). Altitude 1288 feet. Named on Chounet Ranch (1956) 7.5' quadrangle.

No Name Creek: see **Sheep Creek** [TULARE] (1).

Noname Lake [MADERA]: *lake,* 500 feet long, 3.5 miles west of Devils Postpile (lat. 37°37'40" N, long. 119°08'50" W). Named on Devils Postpile (1953) 15' quadrangle.

Noradell: see **Tipton** [TULARE].

Norman Clyde Peak: see **Middle Palisade** [FRESNO].

Norris Creek [MADERA]: *stream,* flows 4.5 miles to Jackass Creek 11.5 miles north-north-east of Shuteye Peak (lat. 37°29'45" N, long. 119°19'15" W); the stream heads near Norris

Lake. Named on Merced Peak (1953) 15' quadrangle.

Norris Lake [MADERA]: *lake,* 400 feet long, 8 miles south-southeast of Merced Peak (lat. 37°31'35" N, long. 119°20'15" W; near W line sec. 3, T 5 S, R 24 E). Named on Merced Peak (1953) 15' quadrangle.

North Alder Creek [TULARE]: *stream,* flows 3 miles to South Alder Creek 4.5 miles north-northwest of Camp Nelson (lat. 36°12'05" N, long. 118°38'45" W; sec. 8, T 20 S, R 31 E). Named on Camp Nelson (1956) 15' quadrangle.

North Cold Spring [TULARE]: *spring,* nearly 7 miles north of California Hot Springs at the head of Bond Creek (lat. 35°58'30" N, long. 118°41'40" W). Named on California Hot Springs (1958) 15' quadrangle.

North Cold Spring Peak [TULARE]: *peak,* 6.5 miles north of California Hot Springs (lat. 35°58'25" N, long. 118°41'15" W); the peak is 0.25 mile east-southeast of North Cold Spring. Altitude 6730 feet. Named on California Hot Springs (1958) 15' quadrangle.

North Dinuba [TULARE]: *locality,* less than 2 miles north-northwest of Dinuba along Atchison, Topeka and Santa Fe Railroad (lat. 36° 34' N, long. 119°23'30" W; at W line sec. 5, T 16 S, R 24 E). Named on Reedley (1966) 7.5' quadrangle.

North Dome [FRESNO]: *peak,* 11 miles south-southwest of Marion Peak (lat. 36°48'25" N, long. 118°35'45" W). Altitude 8717 feet. Named on Marion Peak (1953) 15' quadrangle. John Muir named the peak in 1875 (Browning 1986, p. 159).

North Dome: see **Kettleman Hills** [FRESNO-KERN-KINGS].

North Edwards [KERN]: *town,* 7.25 miles south-southeast of Castle Butte (lat. 35°01' N, long. 117°49'45" W; sec. 27, 28, T 11 N, R 9 W); the town is north of Edwards Air Force Base. Named on North Edwards (1973) 7.5' quadrangle. Called Edgemont Acres on Castle Butte (1956) 15' quadrangle. United States Board on Geographic Names (1975d, p. 4) gave the names "Edgemont Acres" and "North Muroc" as variants.

North Fork [MADERA]: *town,* 22 miles east of Raymond (lat. 37°13'40" N, long. 119°30'30" W; around SE cor. sec. 13, T 8 S, R 22 E); the town is along North Fork Willow Creek (2). Named on North Fork (1965) 7.5' quadrangle. Called Northfork on California Mining Bureau's (1909b) map. Postal authorities established North Fork post office in 1888 (Frickstad, p. 86). Milton Brown was the first settler at the site, and the community that grew there was called Brown's; the place took the name "North Fork" after postal authorities started North Fork post office in the store building of North Fork Lumber Company (Clough, p. 80-81). Postal authorities established Cascadel post office 4 miles east of

North Fork in 1892 and discontinued it in 1896; the name was from Cascadel ranch, which in turn was named for Cascadel Point (Salley, p. 39). Shaver Lake (1953) 15' quadrangle shows Cascadel ranch situated along Whiskey Creek (2) (sec. 16, T 8 S, R 23 E). Postal authorities established a post office called Minarets about 5 miles southeast of North Fork in 1925 and discontinued it in 1933; the place was the terminus of Minarets and Western Railroad (Salley, p. 141). The name "Minarets" was used much earlier, however, when Madera County separated from Fresno County and residents of the mountainous part of Madera County planned to build a town called Minarets 15 miles east of Madera and have the county seat there (Clough, p. 15-16). Postal authorities established Bethel post office 4 miles west of North Fork in 1881 and discontinued it in 1885; James W. Bethel owned the store that housed the post office (Salley, p. 20).

North Goddard Creek [FRESNO]: *stream,* flows 5 miles to South Fork San Joaquin River 4.5 miles north-northeast of Blackcap Mountain in Goddard Canyon (lat. 37°08'05" N, long. 118°45'55" W); the stream heads north of Mount Goddard. Named on Blackcap Mountain (1953) and Mount Goddard (1948) 15' quadrangles.

North Guard [TULARE]: *peak,* 14 miles northwest of Mount Whitney on Great Western Divide (lat. 36°43' N, long. 118°29'15" W); the peak is 1.5 miles north of South Guard. Altitude 13,327 feet. Named on Mount Whitney (1956) 15' quadrangle. Lieutenant Milton F. Davis named the peak on a map in 1896 (Browning 1986, p. 160).

North Guard Creek [FRESNO-TULARE]: *stream,* heads in Tulare County and flows 5.5 miles to Bubbs Creek 13 miles south-southwest of Mount Pinchot in Fresno County (lat. 36°46'05" N, long. 118°28'15" W). Named on Mount Whitney (1907) 30' quadrangle, and on Mount Pinchot (1953) 15' quadrangle.

North Guard Lake [TULARE]: *lake,* 1900 feet long, 15 miles northwest of North Guard (lat. 36°44'35" N, long. 118°28'30" W); the lake is 2 miles north-northeast of North Guard along North Guard Creek. Named on Mount Whitney (1956) 15' quadrangle. J. Hoganson of United States Geological Survey named the lake in 1956 (Browning 1986, p. 160).

North Meadow [TULARE]: *area,* 14 miles south of Hockett Peak (lat. 36°01' N, long. 118°24'15" W). Named on Hockett Peak (1956) 15' quadrangle.

North Meadow Creek [TULARE]: *stream,* flows 4 miles to Brush Creek 4.5 miles northeast of Fairview (lat. 35°58'15" N, long. 118° 26'10" W; sec. 32, T 22 S, R 33 E); the stream heads at North Meadow. Named on Hockett Peak (1956) and Kernville (1956) 15' quadrangles.

North Mountain [FRESNO]: *peak,* 12 miles south-southwest of Marion Peak (lat. 36°48'20" N, long. 118°37'50" W). Altitude 8632 feet. Named on Marion Peak (1953) 15' quadrangle.

North Muroc [KERN]: *locality,* 8 miles southeast of Castle Butte (lat. 35°00'20" N, long. 117°49' W; sec. 34, T 11 N, R 9 W). Named on Castle Butte (1956) 7.5' quadrangle.

North Muroc: see **North Edwards** [KERN].

North Palisade [FRESNO]: *peak,* 11.5 miles east of Mount Goddard on Fresno-Inyo county line (lat. 37°05'40" N, long. 118°30'50" W). Altitude 14,242 feet. Named on Mount Goddard (1948) 15' quadrangle. Called Mt. Jordan on Lippincott's (1902) map. The name "North Palisade" is from the Whitney survey (Farquhar, 1924, p. 62). Members of the Wheeler survey called the feature Northwest Palisade (Browning, p. 164). United States Board on Geographic Names (1985a, p. 3) approved the name "Polemonium Peak" for a feature 0.2 mile southeast of North Palisade on Fresno-Inyo county line (lat. 37°05'37" N, long. 118°30'40" W).

North Shafter [KERN]: *locality,* 1 mile northwest of Shafter (lat. 35° 30'40" N, long. 119°17'05" W; sec. 9, T 28 S, R 25 E). Named on Wasco (1953) 7.5' quadrangle.

North Side: see **Oildale** [KERN].

North Tule: see **Porterville** [TULARE].

Northwest Palisade: see **North Palisade** [FRESNO].

Notarb [MADERA]: *locality,* 6 miles southeast of Fairmead along Southern Pacific Railroad (lat. 37°00'40" N, long. 120°07'05" W; near N line sec. 4, T 11 S, R 17 E). Named on Kismet (1961) 7.5' quadrangle.

Noyer Canyon [KERN]: *canyon,* drained by a stream that flows nearly 2 miles to Kern River 3.5 miles north-northeast of Wofford Heights (lat. 35°45'05" N, long. 118°25'20" W; sec. 15, T 25 S, R 33 E). Named on Lake Isabella North (1972) 7.5' quadrangle.

Number 7 Spring [FRESNO]: *spring,* 4 miles east of Castle Mountain near the head of Canoas Creek (lat. 35°56'50" N, long. 120°16'20" W; near NE cor. sec. 7, T 23 S, R 16 E). Named on The Dark Hole (1961) 7.5' quadrangle.

Nunez Canyon [FRESNO]: *canyon,* drained by a stream that flows 5 miles to Coyote Canyon 8 miles northwest of Coalinga (lat. 36°13'15" N, long. 120°27'30" W; sec. 4, T 20 S, R 14 E). Named on Alcalde Hills (1969) and Joaquin Rocks (1969) 7.5' quadrangles.

Nunez Spring: see **Indian Springs** [FRESNO] (2).

Nutcracker Lake: see **Ruth Lake** [MADERA].

Nutmeg Creek [FRESNO]: *stream,* flows 5.5 miles to Big Creek (2) 7 miles west-north-west of Balch Camp (lat. 36°57'30" N, long. 119°13'40" W; sec. 22, T 11 S, R 25 E); the stream heads at Nutmeg Glen. Named on Huntington Lake (1953) and Patterson Mountain (1952) 15' quadrangles.

Nutmeg Glen [FRESNO]: *locality,* 8 miles south-southwest of Dinkey Dome (lat. 37°00'30" N, long. 119°11'15" W; near SW cor. sec. 31, T 10 S, R 26 E). The place is at the head of Nutmeg Creek. Named on Huntington Lake (1953) 15' quadrangle.

Nydiver Lakes [MADERA]: *lakes,* largest 1000 feet long, 7 miles northwest of Devils Postpile (lat. 37°41'35" N, long. 119°10'15" W). Named on Devils Postpile (1953) 15' quadrangle. Browning (1986, p. 160) associated the name with David Nidever, a prospector of the early 1900's.

– O –

Oak: see **Borden** [MADERA].

Oak Canyon: see **Little Oak Canyon** [KERN].

Oak Creek [KERN]: *stream,* flows 10 miles to lowlands 10 miles southeast of Tehachapi (lat. 35°02'25" N, long. 118°18'30" W; near SW cor. sec. 18, T 11 N, R 13 W). Named on Monolith (1966), Tehachapi South (1966), and Willow Springs (1965) 7.5' quadrangles.

Oak Creek: see **Little Oak Creek**, under **Little Oak Canyon** [KERN].

Oak Creek Canyon [KERN]: *canyon,* 8 miles long, along Oak Creek above a point 10 miles southeast of Tehachapi (lat. 35°02'25" N, long. 118°18'30" W; near SW cor. sec. 18, T 11 N, R 13 W). Named on Monolith (1966) and Tehachapi South (1966) 7.5' quadrangles.

Oak Creek Pass [KERN]: *pass,* 6 miles southeast of Tehachapi (lat. 35°03'40" N, long. 118°23'15" W; sec. 8, T 11 N, R 14 W). Named on Tehachapi South (1966) 7.5' quadrangle. The feature was called Tehachapi Pass before the coming of the railroad in 1876, when the name "Tehachapi" was transferred to present Tehachapi Pass (Hoover, Rensch, and Rensch, p. 127). Whitney 1865 (p. 216) used the name "Frémont's Pass" for present Oak Creek Pass, and noted that John C. Frémont traversed the feature in 1844.

Oak Flat [FRESNO]:
(1) *area,* 5.25 miles north-northwest of Balch Camp (lat. 36°58'45" N, long. 119°08'50" W). Named on Patterson Mountain (1952) 15' quadrangle.
(2) *area,* 7.25 miles west of Coalinga (lat. 36°09'20" N, long. 120° 29'05" W; sec. 30, T 20 S, R 14 E). Named on Alcalde Hills (1969) 7.5' quadrangle.
(3) *valley,* 5 miles east-northeast of Castle Mountain (lat. 35°58'45" N, long. 120°15'45" W). Named on The Dark Hole (1961) 7.5' quadrangle.

Oak Flat [KERN]:
(1) *area,* nearly 4.5 miles northeast of Caliente (lat. 35°20'20" N, long. 118°34'40" W; at SW

cor. sec. 5, T 30 S, R 32 E). Named on Oiler Peak (1972) 7.5' quadrangle.

(2) *area,* 3 miles west of Democrat Hot Springs (lat. 35°31'55" N, long. 118°43' W; sec. 35, T 27 S, R 30 E). Named on Democrat Hot Springs (1972) 7.5' quadrangle.

(3) *area,* 7.25 miles northwest of Cummings Mountain (lat. 35°07'30" N, long. 118°38'50" W). Named on Bear Mountain (1966) and Tejon Ranch (1966) 7.5' quadrangles.

Oak Flat [TULARE]:

(1) *area,* 9 miles south of Kaweah (lat. 36°20'30" N, long. 118°55'30" W). Named on Kaweah (1957) 15' quadrangle.

(2) *area,* 5.5 miles southwest of California Hot Springs (lat. 35° 49' N, long. 118°43'50" W; sec. 27, T 24 S, R 30 E). Named on California Hot Springs (1958) 7.5' quadrangle.

(3) *area,* 8 miles south-southeast of Springville (lat. 36°01'10" N, long. 118°46'10" W). Named on Globe (1956) 7.5' quadrangle.

Oak Flat: see **Little Oak Flat** [FRESNO]; **Little Oak Flat** [KERN]; **Little Oak Flat** [TULARE].

Oak Flat Canyon [FRESNO]: *canyon,* drained by a stream that flows 8.5 miles to Warthan Creek 5 miles southwest of Coalinga (lat. 36° 05'40" N, long. 120°25'45" W; sec. 23, T 21 S, R 14 E); Oak Flat (2) is in the canyon. Named on Alcalde Hills (1969), Curry Mountain (1969), and Sherman Peak (1969) 7.5' quadrangles.

Oak Flat Peak [TULARE]: *peak,* 8 miles south-southeast of Springville (lat. 36°01'10" N, long. 118°46'35" W); the peak is west of Oak Flat (3). Altitude 2734 feet. Named on Globe (1956) 7.5' quadrangle.

Oak Grove [TULARE]: *locality,* 7.25 miles east of Kaweah along East Fork Kaweah River (lat. 36°27'05" N, long. 118°47'25" W; near E line sec. 15, T 17 S, R 29 E). Named on Kaweah (1957) 15' quadrangle. Called Oakgrove on Kaweah (1909) 30' quadrangle.

Oakhurst [FRESNO]: *locality,* 5.25 miles southwest of Piedra along Atchison, Topeka and Santa Fe Railroad (lat. 36°45' N, long. 119° 26'25" W; near S line sec. 35, T 13 S, R 23 E). Named on Watts Valley (1942) 15' quadrangle.

Oakhurst [MADERA]: *settlement,* 3 miles south-southwest of Yosemite Forks along Fresno River (lat. 37°19'45" N, long. 119° 39' W; near NW cor. sec. 14, T 7 S, R 21 E); the place is at the east end of Fresno Flats. Named on Bass Lake (1953) 15' quadrangle. The settlement is called Fresno Flats on Mariposa (1912) 30' quadrangle. Postal authorities established Fresno Flats post office in 1873, and moved it and changed the name to Oakhurst in 1912 (Salley, p. 81, 158). They established Starville post office 23 miles northeast of Fresno Flats post office in 1889 and discontinued it in 1891; the name was from Star mine (Salley, p. 212).

Oak Ridge [KERN]: *ridge,* south-southwest-trending, 1.5 miles long, 4 miles south-south-west of Alta Sierra (lat. 35°40'35" N, long. 118°35'10" W). Named on Alta Sierra (1972) 7.5' quadrangle.

Oak Spring: see **Little Oak Spring** [FRESNO].

Oat Canyon [TULARE]: *canyon,* drained by a stream that flows 4.25 miles to Lewis Creek 8 miles north-northeast of Porterville (lat. 36°11' N, long. 118°58'20" W; near SW cor. sec. 17, T 20 S, R 28 E). Named on Frazier Valley (1957) 7.5' quadrangle.

Oat Knob [TULARE]: *peak,* 6 miles northeast of Woodlake (lat. 36° 29'05" N, long. 119°01'45" W; near NE cor. sec. 3, T 17 S, R 27 E). Named on Woodlake (1952) 7.5' quadrangle.

Oat Knob Canyon [TULARE]: *canyon,* drained by a stream that flows less than 1 mile to Dry Creek (1) 6.5 miles northeast of Woodlake (lat. 36°29' N, long. 119°01' W; sec. 2, T 17 S, R 27 E); the canyon heads near Oat Knob. Named on Woodlake (1952) 7.5' quadrangle.

Oat Mountain [FRESNO]: *ridge,* generally west-trending, 7 miles long, 7 miles southwest of Balch Camp (lat. 36°51' N, long. 119° 12' W). Named on Patterson Mountain (1952) and Watts Valley (1942) 15' quadrangles.

Oat Mountain: see **Castle Peak** [MADERA].

Oat Mountain [TULARE]: *peak,* 9 miles south of Springville (lat. 36°00' N, long. 118°47'55" W). Altitude 3519 feet. Named on Springville (1957) and White River (1952) 15' quadrangles.

Obelisk [FRESNO]: *relief feature,* 9 miles north-northeast of Hume (lat. 36°54'30" N, long. 118°51'10" W). Altitude 9700 feet. Named on Tehipite Dome (1952) 15' quadrangle. Members of United States Geological Survey applied the name in 1903 for the shape of the feature (Gudde, 1949, p. 240).

Obelisk Group: see **Clark Range** [MADERA].

Obelisk Lake: see **Adair Lake** [MADERA].

O'Brien Hill [KERN]: *peak,* 3.5 miles south of Miracle Hot Springs (lat. 35°31'25" N, long. 118°31'55" W; sec. 3, T 28 S, R 32 E); the peak is 1 mile east-northeast of O'Brien Spring. Named on Miracle Hot Springs (1972) 7.5' quadrangle.

O'Brien Spring [KERN]: *spring,* 4 miles south-southwest of Miracle Hot Springs (lat. 35°31'10" N, long. 118°32'55" W; sec. 4, T 28 S, R 32 E); the spring is 1 mile west-south-west of O'Brien Hill. Named on Miracle Hot Springs (1972) 7.5' quadrangle.

Observation Peak [FRESNO]: *peak,* 12 miles east-southeast of Mount Goddard (lat. 37°01'25" N, long. 118°31'20" W). Altitude 12,322 feet. Named on Mount Goddard (1948) 15' quadrangle. J.N. LeConte, who named the peak in 1902, also called it Panorama Point (Browning 1986, p. 160).

Occoya Creek: see **Poso Creek** [KERN-TULARE].

Ockenden [FRESNO]: *locality,* 1.25 miles south of Shaver Lake Heights (present town of Shaver Lake) (lat. 37°05'20" N, long. 119°18'55" W; sec. 2, T 10 S, R 24 E). Named on Shaver Lake (1953) 15' quadrangle. Postal authorities established Ockenden post office in 1893 and discontinued it in 1918; the name is for Thomas J. Ockenden, first postmaster (Salley, p. 159).

O-co-ya Creek: see **Poso Creek** [KERN-TU-LARE].

Octol [TULARE]: *locality,* 4.5 miles north-northwest of Tipton along Southern Pacific Railroad (lat. 36°07'25" N, long. 119°19'40" W; at N line sec. 12, T 21 S, R 24 E). Named on Tipton (1950) 7.5' quadrangle.

Odessa [KINGS]: *locality,* 4 miles south of Hanford along Atchison, Topeka and Santa Fe Railroad (lat. 36°16'15" N, long. 119°38'40" W; near S line sec. 13, T 19 S, R 21 E). Named on Hanford (1926) 7.5' quadrangle.

Oil Canyon [FRESNO]: *canyon,* drained by Oil Creek, which flows 6 miles to Pleasant Valley 6 miles north of Coalinga (lat. 36°13'25" N, long. 120°21'15" W; near NE cor. sec. 5, T 20 S, R 15 E). Named on Domengine Ranch (1956) and Joaquin Rocks (1969) 7.5' quadrangles. Arnold and Anderson (1908, p. 16) named the canyon, which the road to Oil City follows.

Oil Canyon [KERN]: *canyon,* drained by a stream that flows 3.25 miles to Cache Creek 8 miles east of Tehachapi (lat. 35°09'05" N, long. 118°18'25" W; near NE cor. sec. 15, T 32 S, R 34 E). Named on Tehachapi NE (1966) 7.5' quadrangle. The name is from wells that were drilled for oil in the neighborhood in the early 1900's (Barras, p. 42).

Oil Center [KERN]: *locality,* 4.5 miles north of downtown Bakersfield (lat. 35°26'20" N, long. 118°59'15" W; near NE cor. sec. 5, T 29 S, R 28 E); the place is in Kern River oil field. Named on Oil Center (1954) 7.5' quadrangle. Postal authorities established Oilcenter post office in 1901 and discontinued it in 1937 (Frickstad, p. 58).

Oil City [FRESNO]: *locality,* 9 miles north of Coalinga (lat. 36° 16' N, long. 120°21'50" W; sec. 20, T 19 S, R 15 E); the place is in Oil Canyon. Named on Coalinga (1912) 30' quadrangle. William Youle, a pioneer oil man, named the place for Oil City, Pennsylvania (Latta, 1949, p. 139).

Oil City [KERN]: *locality,* 4.25 miles north-northeast of downtown Bakersfield along Kern River (lat. 35°25'35" N, long. 118°57'30" W; at N line sec. 10, T 29 S, R 28 E). Named on Oil Center (1954) 7.5' quadrangle.

Oil Creek [FRESNO]: *stream,* flows nearly 6 miles through Oil Canyon to Pleasant Valley 6 miles north of Coalinga (lat. 36°13'25" N, long. 120°21'15" W; near NE cor. sec. 5, T 20 S, R 15 E). Named on Coalinga (1956) 7.5'

quadrangle.

Oildale [KERN]: *town,* 3.5 miles north-north-west of downtown Bakersfield on the north side of Kern River (lat. 35°25'10" N, long. 119°01'45" W; sec. 12, T 29 S, R 27 E). Named on Oildale (1954) 7.5' quadrangle. Postal authorities established Oildale post office in 1916; the name is from oil tanks at the site (Salley, p. 160). The place first was called North Side (Wines, p. 86). Samuel Dickinson subdivided 10 acres in 1909 to start the town (Bailey, 1967, p. 20).

Oiler Canyon [KERN]: *canyon,* drained by a stream that flows 3.25 miles to the canyon of Caliente Creek 2.5 miles east-northeast of Caliente (lat. 35°18'30" N, long. 118°35' W; near N line sec. 19, T 30 S, R 32 E); the canyon heads near Oiler Peak. Named on Oiler Peak (1972) 7.5' quadrangle.

Oiler Peak [KERN]: *peak,* nearly 5 miles north-northeast of Caliente (lat. 35°21'10" N, long. 118°35'10" W; near N line sec. 6, T 30 S, R 32 E). Altitude 4323 feet. Named on Oiler Peak (1972) 7.5' quadrangle.

Oilfields [FRESNO]: *settlement,* 7.5 miles north-northeast of Coalinga (lat. 36°14'45" N, long. 120°18'50" W; sec. 26, T 19 S, R 15 E). Named on Coalinga (1956) 7.5' quadrangle. Postal authorities established Oilfields post office in 1908 and discontinued it in 1951 (Frickstad, p. 36). The place originally was called Balfour from the firm of Balfour, Williamson & Company, of London, England, an investor in oil of the region, and later the name was changed to Oilfields, from California Oilfields, Ltd., also a British Company; by 1908 the "model oil town" was functioning (Franks and Lambert, p. 133).

Oil Junction [KERN]: *locality,* 4.5 miles north-west of downtown Bakersfield along Southern Pacific Railroad (lat. 35°25'10" N, long. 119°03'25" W; near E line sec. 10, T 29 S, R 27 E). Named on Oildale (1954) 7.5' quad-rangle.

Oil Well Canyon [FRESNO]: *canyon,* drained by a stream that flows 1.25 miles to Salt Creek (2) 7 miles south-southwest of Coalinga (lat. 36°03'05" N, long. 120°25'20" W; near NE cor. sec. 2, T 22 S, R 14 E). Named on Curry Mountain (1969) 7.5' quadrangle.

Olaine Lake [MADERA]: *lake,* 1000 feet long, 5 miles north-northwest of Devils Postpile (lat. 37°41'40" N, long. 119°06'45" W). Named on Devils Postpile (1953) 15' quadrangle. Charles Olaine prospected at the lake about 1910 (Browning, 1986, p. 161).

Olancha Pass [TULARE]: *pass,* 5.25 miles east of Monache Mountain on Tulare-Inyo county line (lat. 36°12'45" N, long. 118°06'15" W; sec. 5, T 20 S, R 36 E); the pass is 4 miles south of Olancha Peak. Named on Monache Mountain (1956) 15' quadrangle.

Olancha Peak [TULARE]: *peak,* 24 miles south-southeast of Mount Whitney on Tulare-

Inyo county line (lat. 36°15'55" N, long. 118° 07' W); the peak is above the village of Olancha, which is in Inyo County. Altitude 12,123 feet. Named on Olancha (1956) 15' quadrangle.

Old Bretz Mill [FRESNO]: *settlement,* 2 miles south-southeast of Shaver Lake Heights (present town of Shaver Lake) (lat. 37°04'55" N, long. 119°18' W; near SE cor. sec. 1, T 10 S, R 24 E). Named on Shaver Lake (1953) 15' quadrangle. Kaiser (1904) 30' quadrangle shows a place called Peteras Mill located near the site.

Old Deer Creek Channel: see **Deer Creek** [TULARE] (2).

Old Fort Miller [FRESNO]: *locality,* 8.5 miles west-southwest of Prather on the south side of San Joaquin River (lat. 37°00'35" N, long. 119°39'45" W; near N line sec. 3, T 11 S, R 21 E); water of Millerton Lake now covers the site. Named on Sulphur Springs (1919) 7.5' quadrangle. Members of the Mariposa Battalion built a post along the river in 1851 and called it Camp Barbour for Indian Commissioner George W. Barbour; later the same year the army built a post at or near the site and called it Camp Miller for Major Albert S. Miller; the name was changed to Fort Miller in 1852, and the post was abandoned in 1858, reoccupied in 1863, and abandoned again in 1864 (Frazer, p. 26-27). Crampton (*in* Eccleston, p. 78) noted that Camp Barbour was along San Joaquin River opposite Larione's ferry, and stated that Larione's corral (which presumably was located near the ferry) was on the south side of the river about 1 mile south of old Fort Washington, which in turn was about 10 miles below Fort Miller. The only evidence of Fort Washington on modern maps is Fort Washington school shown located 11 miles north of downtown Fresno on Herndon (1965) 15' quadrangle (lat. 36°53'45" N, long. 119°45'50" W), and nearby Fort Washington country club. Eddy's (1854) map and Baker's (1855) map both show Washington City below Fort Miller along San Joaquin River, and Rogers and Johnston's (1857) map has the name "Washington" in the same neighborhood.

Old Fort Tejon [KERN]: *locality,* 3.25 miles north-northwest of Lebec (lat. 34°52'25" N, long. 118°53'35" W). Named on Frazier Mountain (1958) 7.5' quadrangle. Fort Tejon was started in 1854, and in 1858 it became a station on Butterfield Overland stage line; the post was evacuated in 1861, reoccupied in 1863 by California volunteer troops, and abandoned in 1864 (Frazer, p. 32). Postal authorities established Fort Tejon post office in 1859, discontinued it in 1862, reestablished it in 1892, and discontinued it the same year (Salley, p. 78).

Old Garlock [KERN]: *locality,* 3 miles south-west of Garlock (lat. 35°22'30" N, long.

117°49'30" W). Named on Saltdale (1943b) 15' quadrangle.

Old Hart Station [KERN]: *locality,* 2.5 miles east of the village of Lost Hills (lat. 35°37' N, long. 119°38'45" W). Named on Hart Station (1942) 15' quadrangle.

Old Likely Mill [KERN]: *locality,* nearly 5 miles southwest of Alta Sierra (lat. 35°40'35" N, long. 118°36'25" W; near SE cor. sec. 12, T 26 S, R 31 E). Site named on Alta Sierra (1972) 7.5' quadrangle.

Old Millerton [FRESNO]: *locality,* 9.5 miles west-southwest of Prather on the south side of San Joaquin River (lat. 37°00'35" N, long. 119°40'40" W; near N line sec. 4, T 11 S, R 21 E). Named on Sulphur Springs (1919) 7.5' quadrangle, which shows Old Fort Miller located 1 mile east of Old Millerton. The place began in 1850 as a mining town called Rootville, and became the county seat when Fresno County was organized in 1856 (Hoover, Rensch, and Rensch, p. 92). By 1853 or 1854 the name "Rootville" was changed to Millerton, for nearby Fort Miller; the place also was called Millertown (Gudde, 1975, p. 295). The leading inhabitants of the town moved to Fresno after 1872 (Bancroft, p. 517). Water of Millerton Lake now covers the site of Old Millerton. Postal authorities established Millerton post office in 1853, discontinued it in 1863, reestablished it in 1864, changed the name to Fort Miller in 1874, and discontinued it in 1876 (Frickstad, p. 33, 35). They established Elbow post office 27 miles southeast of Millerton in 1866 and discontinued it in 1868; the name "Elbow" was from a bend in Kings River (Salley, p. 66). Rich placer-gold deposits were reported in 1850 from San Joaquin River above Millerton at a place called Cassadys Bar (Gudde, 1975, p. 63).

Old Mount Whitney: see **Mount Corcoran** [TULARE].

Old Panama: see **Panama** [KERN].

Old Pipe Lake [FRESNO]: *lake,* 700 feet long, 4.25 miles west-southwest of Blackcap Mountain (lat. 37°03'40" N, long. 118° 52' W; sec. 13, T 10 S, R 28 E). Named on Blackcap Mountain (1953) 15' quadrangle.

Old River [KERN]: *village,* 9.5 miles southwest of Bakersfield (lat. 35°16' N, long. 119°06'30" W; at NW cor. sec. 5, T 31 S, R 27 E). Named on Gosford (1954) 7.5' quadrangle. The place began in the 1870's and took its name from an old channel of Kern River (Bailey, 1967, p. 20). Thomas Barnes laid out a small community in 1859 called Barnes Settlement that was situated on his homestead a short distance west of the present Old River; Charles W. Canfield laid out a townsite in 1874 near the same site and called it Canfield (Bailey, 1967, p. 2).

Old River: see **Kern River** [KERN-TULARE].

Old South Fork: see **Kern River** [KERN-TULARE].

Old Squaw Lake [FRESNO]: *lake,* 1000 feet long, 8 miles south-southwest of Mount Abbot (lat. 37°16'25" N, long. 118°49'40" W). Named on Mount Abbot (1953) 15' quadrangle.

Old Sunset: see **Hazelton** [KERN].

Old Town [KERN]: *locality,* 3 miles west-northwest of Tehachapi (lat. 35°08'35" N, long. 118°29'40" W; sec. 13, T 32 S, R 32 E). Named on Tehachapi North (1966) 7.5' quadrangle. Cummings Mountain (1943b) 15' quadrangle shows the place situated 1.25 miles farther southwest (lat. 35°07'40" N, long. 118°30'20" W; sec. 23, T 32 S, R 32 E). The community first was called Williamsburg for James E. Williams, an early businessman there (Boyd, p. 175). Postal authorities established Tehichipa post office near Oak Creek Pass in 1869, moved it in 1877 to present Old Town, and discontinued it in 1885 (Boyd, p. 176; Salley, p. 219). Gray's (1873) map has the name "Tehichipa" along the railroad.

Oleander [FRESNO]:
(1) *locality,* 9 miles south-southeast of downtown Fresno (lat. 36° 38' N, long. 119°45'15" W; at NE cor. sec. 14, T 15 S, R 20 E). Named on Fresno South (1963) 7.5' quadrangle. Postal authorities established Oleander post office in 1881, moved it 1 mile northeast in 1899, and discontinued it in 1935; the post office name was the middle name of the first postmaster, William O. Johnson (Salley, p. 160).
(2) *locality,* 2.5 miles south-southwest of Malaga along Atchison, Topeka and Santa Fe Railroad (lat. 36°38'40" N, long. 119°45' W; sec. 12, T 15 S, R 20 E); the place is 0.25 mile east of Oleander (1). Named on Selma (1946) 15' quadrangle.

Olig [KERN]: *locality,* 2 miles northwest of McKittrick (lat. 35°19'20" N, long. 119°39'15" W; at N line sec. 18, T 30 S, R 22 E). Named on McKittrick (1912) 30' quadrangle.

Olive: see **Mount Olive** [FRESNO].

Olive Lake [FRESNO]: *lake,* 2000 feet long, 13 miles north-northwest of Mount Abbot (lat. 37°28'25" N, long. 118°59'10" W). Named on Mount Abbot (1953) 15' quadrangle.

Oliver Rock [FRESNO]: *peak,* 10 miles south-southwest of Coalinga (lat. 36°00'35" N, long. 120°26'20" W; near SW cor. sec. 14, T 22 S, R 14 E). Named on Curry Mountain (1969) 7.5' quadrangle.

Oljato: see **Camp Oljato** [FRESNO].

O'Neals [MADERA]: *locality,* 13 miles east-southeast of Raymond along Willow Creek (4) (lat. 37°07'40" N, long. 119°41'40" W; near SW cor. sec. 21, T 9 S, R 21 E). Named on O'Neals (1965) 7.5' quadrangle. Postal authorities established O'Neals post office in 1887 (Frickstad, p. 86). Charles O'Neal bought the store at the place in 1887, operated a small hotel, and was named postmaster of the new

post office that took his name (Clough, p. 82). Postal authorities established Magnet post office 4 miles northeast of O'Neals in 1900 and discontinued in 1907; the name was for Magnet mine (Salley, p. 131).

O'Neil Canyon [KERN]: *canyon,* drained by a stream that flows 3.25 miles to Castac Valley 2 miles north-northwest of Lebec (lat. 34° 51'50" N, long. 118°52'50" W). Named on Frazier Mountain (1958) 7.5' quadrangle.

Onion Meadow [TULARE]: *area,* 7.5 miles south of Camp Nelson (lat. 36°02' N, long. 118°36' W; sec. 11, T 22 S, R 31 E). Named on Camp Nelson (1956) 15' quadrangle.

Onion Meadow Peak [TULARE]: *peak,* 8 miles south of Camp Nelson (lat. 36°01'40" N, long. 118°36'05" W; near S line sec. 11, T 22 S, R 31 E); the peak is south-southwest of Onion Meadow. Named on Camp Nelson (1956) 15' quadrangle.

Onion Spring Meadow [FRESNO]: *area,* 10 miles northeast of Kaiser Peak (lat. 37°24' N, long. 119°04'10" W). Named on Kaiser Peak (1953) 15' quadrangle.

Onyx [KERN]: *village,* 3.5 miles east-northeast of Weldon (lat. 35° 41'25" N, long. 118°13'10" W; sec. 4, T 26 S, R 35 E); the place is at the mouth of Scodie Canyon. Named on Onyx (1972) 7.5' quadrangle. Postal authorities established Onyx post office in 1889 (Frickstad, p. 58). The village first was called Scodie, for William Scodie, who opened a store there in 1861 (Bailey, 1967, p. 20).

Onyx Peak [KERN]: *peak,* 2.25 miles south of Onyx (lat. 35°39'25" N, long. 118°13'30" W; near N line sec. 21, T 26 S, R 35 E). Altitude 5244 feet. Named on Onyx (1972) 7.5' quadrangle.

O'Quinn Meadow [TULARE]: *area,* 3.5 miles east-southeast of California Hot Springs (lat. 35°51'10" N, long. 118°37' W; sec. 10, T 24 S, R 31 E). Named on California Hot Springs (1958) 15' quadrangle.

Ora [FRESNO]: *locality,* 2 miles east-northeast of Coalinga along Southern Pacific Railroad (lat. 36°09'05" N, long. 120°19'30" W; near S line sec. 27, T 20 S, R 15 E). Named on Coalinga (1956) 7.5' quadrangle.

Orange Cove [FRESNO]: *town,* 8 miles east-northeast of Reedley (lat. 36°37'30" N, long. 119°18'45" W; sec. 13, T 15 S, R 24 E). Named on Orange Cove North (1966) and Orange Cove South (1966) 7.5' quadrangles. Postal authorities established Orange Cove post office in 1914 (Frickstad, p. 36), and the town incorporated in 1948. Elmer M. Sheridan founded and named the town in 1914 before the neighborhood became a large producer of citrus (Hanna, p. 219).

Orange Heights: see **Ivanhoe** [TULARE].

Orangehurst: see **Exeter** [TULARE].

Orchard Peak [KERN]: *peak,* 34 miles west-northwest of Bakersfield (lat. 35°44'15" N, long. 120°08' W; near W line sec. 22, T 25 S,

R 17 E). Altitude 3125 feet. Named on Orchard Peak (1961) 7.5' quadrangle. Arnold and Johnson (p. 21) proposed the name to commemorate Joseph E. Orchard, an old resident of McLure Valley (present Sunflower Valley).

Orchard Ridge: see **Bluestone Ridge** [KERN].

Orchid Lake [FRESNO]: *lake,* 750 feet long, 7.25 miles southwest of Mount Abbot (lat. 37°19'35" N, long. 118°53'25" W). Named on Mount Abbot (1953) 15' quadrangle.

Ordinance Creek [FRESNO]: *stream,* flows 3.25 miles to Big Creek (1) 6.5 miles north of Shaver Lake Heights (present town of Shaver Lake) (lat. 37°12' N, long. 119°18'10" W; sec. 25, T 8 S, R 24 E). Named on Shaver Lake (1953) 15' quadrangle.

Orejano Canyon [KERN]:
(1) *canyon,* drained by a stream that flows nearly 3 miles to Caliente Creek 5 miles northwest of Emerald Mountain (lat. 35°18'50" N, long. 118°20'05" W). Named on Emerald Mountain (1972) 7.5' quadrangle.
(2) *canyon,* drained by a stream that flows 4 miles to Tehachapi Creek nearly 3 miles southeast of Caliente (lat. 35°15'50" N, long. 118°35'25" W; at W line sec. 6, T 31 S, R 32 E); the canyon is south of Orejano Ridge. Named on Oiler Peak (1972) 7.5' quadrangle.

Orejano Ridge [KERN]: *ridge,* generally west-trending, 5 miles long, center 5 miles east-southeast of Caliente (lat. 35°15'50" N, long. 118°32'50" W); the ridge is north of Orejano Canyon (2). Named on Oiler Peak (1972) 7.5' quadrangle.

Oren [FRESNO]: *village,* 20 miles southwest of Kaiser Peak (lat. 37° 05'15" N, long. 119°25'40" W; sec. 2, T 10 S, R 23 E). Named on Kaiser (1904) 30' quadrangle. Postal authorities established Oren post office in 1899 and discontinued it in 1905 (Frickstad, p. 36). Called Oro on California Mining Bureau's (1917a) map.

Oriole Lake [TULARE]: *lake,* 400 feet long, 8 miles west of Mineral King (lat. 36°27'35" N, long. 118°44'10" W; sec. 8, T 17 S, R 30 E). Named on Mineral King (1956) 15' quadrangle.

Orion [KINGS]: *locality,* 5.25 miles west-southwest of Hanford along Southern Pacific Railroad (lat. 38°18'40" N, long. 119°44'20" W; sec. 6, T 19 S, R 21 E). Named on Hanford (1926) 7.5' quadrangle.

Orlem [TULARE]: *locality,* 2.25 miles east-southeast of Lindsay along Visalia Electric Railroad (lat. 36°11'30" N, long. 119°03' W; sec. 16, T 20 S, R 27 E). Named on Lindsay (1928) 7.5' quadrangle.

Oro: see **Oren** [FRESNO].

Oro Grosso: see **Coarsegold** [MADERA].

Oro Loma [FRESNO]: *locality,* 13 miles west of Firebaugh (lat. 36° 53'25" N, long. 120°41' W; sec. 17, T 12 S, R 12 E). Named on Dos Palos (1956) 7.5' quadrangle. Postal authorities established Oro Loma post office in 1914

and discontinued it in 1929 (Frickstad, p. 36).

Orosi [TULARE]: *town,* 5.5 miles east of Dinuba (lat. 36°32'40" N, long. 118°17'10" W; around SE cor. sec. 7, T 16 S, R 25 E). Named on Orange Cove South (1966) 7.5' quadrangle. Neal McCallum named the place in 1888, supposedly for golden poppies in the neighborhood—*oro* means "gold" in Spanish (Mitchell, A.R., p. 69). Postal authorities established Orosi post office in 1888 (Frickstad, p. 213).

Orosi: see **East Orosi** [TULARE].

Orosi Station: see **East Orosi** [TULARE].

Orris [TULARE]: *locality,* 2.5 miles south-southwest of Ducor along Southern Pacific Railroad (lat. 35°51'15" N, long. 119°03'40" W; sec. 9, T 24 S, R 27 E). Named on Richgrove (1952) 7.5' quadrangle.

Osa Creek [TULARE]: *stream,* flows 4.5 miles to Kern River 4 miles south of Hockett Peak (lat. 36°09'45" N, long. 118°22'40" W); the stream heads at Osa Meadows. Named on Hockett Peak (1956) 15' quadrangle.

Osa Meadows [TULARE]: *area,* 5.25 miles east-southeast of Hockett Peak (lat. 36°10'55" N, long. 118°18'20" W). Named on Hockett Peak (1956) 15' quadrangle.

Oscar Meyer Spring [KERN]: *spring,* 1 mile south-southwest of Democrat Hot Springs (lat. 35°30'55" N, long. 118°40'15" W). Named on Democrat Hot Springs (1972) 7.5' quadrangle.

Oso Canyon [KERN]: *canyon,* drained by a stream that flows 1 mile to Los Angeles County 4.25 miles east-southeast of Lebec (lat. 34° 49'05" N, long. 118°47'40" W). Named on Lebec (1958) 7.5' quadrangle. United States Board on Geographic Names (1967c, p. 4) rejected the name "Canada de la Oasis" for the feature.

Ottoway Creek [MADERA]: *stream,* flows 3 miles to Illilouette Creek 3.25 miles west of Merced Peak (lat. 37°38' N, long. 119°27'10" W); the stream heads near Ottoway Peak. Named on Merced Peak (1953) 15' quadrangle.

Ottoway Lake: see **Lower Ottoway Lake** [MADERA]; **Upper Ottoway Lake** [MADERA].

Ottoway Peak [MADERA]: *peak,* 0.5 mile north of Merced Peak (lat. 37°38'30" N, long. 119°23'30" W). Named on Merced Peak (1953) 15' quadrangle. Lieutenant N.F. McClure named the peak in 1895 for a corporal in his detachment (United States Board on Geographic Names, 1934a, p. 18).

Ousel Creek: see **Ouzel Creek** [TULARE].

Outside Creek [TULARE]: *stream,* diverges southwest from Johnson Slough 3 miles northwest of Exeter and flows for 12 miles to join Inside Creek and form Elk Bayou 5 miles east-southeast of Tulare (lat. 36°11'30" N, long. 119°15'20" W; sec. 15, T 20 S, R 25 E). Named on Exeter (1952) 15' quadrangle, and on Cairns Corner (1950, photorevised 1969) and Tulare (1950) 7.5' quadrangles. The name is from the location of the stream on the outside edge of marsh formed by the fan of Kaweah River and Saint Johns River (Gudde, 1949, p. 247).

Ouzel Creek [TULARE]: *stream,* flows 2.25 miles to East Lake 13 miles northwest of Mount Whitney (lat. 36°43'30" N, long. 118°26'40" W). Named on Mount Whitney (1956) 15' quadrangle. United States Board on Geographic Names (1933a, p. 578) rejected the form "Ousel Creek" for the name. David Starr Jordan gave the name to the stream in 1899 because John Muir had studied the water ouzel along it (Ristow, p. 424).

Ovejo: see **Tillman** [MADERA].

Overholster Meadow [TULARE]: *area,* 9 miles north-northwest of Olancha Peak along Mulkey Creek (lat. 36°22'25" N, long. 118°12'15" W; sec. 8, T 18 S, R 35 E). Named on Olancha (1956) 15' quadrangle.

Owen: see **Mount Owen**, under **Brown** [KERN].

Owens: see **Camp Owens** [KERN].

Owens Camp [KERN]: *locality,* 5.25 miles west-northwest of Garlock (lat. 35°26'35" N, long. 117°52'10" W). Named on Garlock (1967) 7.5' quadrangle.

Owens Mountain [FRESNO]: *ridge,* west-northwest-trending, 2 miles long, 8 miles north-northeast of Clovis (lat. 36°55'50" N, long. 119°38'30" W). Named on Friant (1964) 7.5' quadrangle. According to Gudde (1949, p. 247), the name probably commemorates George W. Owens, who came to California in 1862 and had a stock ranch in the foothills in the 1870's.

Owens Peak [KERN]: *peak,* 12 miles west-northwest of Inyokern (lat. 35°44'15" N, long. 117°59'45" W). Altitude 8453 feet. Named on Owens Peak (1972) 7.5' quadrangle. Birnie (p. 131) referred to Owen's Peak. The name honors Richard Owens, who was with Fremont's exploring expedition in 1845 (Hanna, p. 222, 223).

Owl Creek [MADERA]: *stream,* flows 2 miles to Whiskey Creek (2) 5.5 miles south of Shuteye Peak (lat. 37°16' N, long. 119°26'15" W; sec. 3, T 8 S, R 23 E). Named on Shuteye Peak (1953) 15' quadrangle.

Owl Mountain [FRESNO]: *peak,* 2.5 miles southeast of Trimmer (lat. 36°52'50" N, long. 119°15'35" W; near SE cor. sec. 17, T 12 S., R 25 E). Altitude 2181 feet. Named on Trimmer (1965) 7.5' quadrangle.

Owl Peak [TULARE]: *peak,* 1.25 miles southsoutheast of Auckland (lat. 36°34'20" N, long. 119°05'40" W; near S line sec. 36, T 15 S, R 26 E). Altitude 2417 feet. Named on Auckland (1966) 7.5' quadrangle.

Oxalis [FRESNO]: *locality,* 6.5 miles northwest of Firebaugh along Southern Pacific Railroad (lat. 36°54'45" N, long. 120°32'55" W; sec. 4, T 12 S, R 13 E). Named on Oxalis (1956) 7.5' quadrangle. Railroad officials gave their

station at the place the botanical name for wood sorrel (Gudde, 1949, p. 247).

Oyster Hill [KINGS]: *peak,* 13 miles south of Kettleman City (lat. 35°49'05" N, long. 119°54'50" W; near NE cor. sec. 28, T 24 S, R 19 E). Named on Avenal Gap (1954) 7.5' quadrangle.

– P –

Packsaddle Canyon [TULARE]: *canyon,* drained by a stream that flows 3.5 miles to Kern River 1.5 miles northeast of Fairview (lat. 35°56'40" N, long. 118°28'35" W). Named on Kernville (1956) 15' quadrangle.

Packsaddle Cave [TULARE]: *cave,* 2 miles east-northeast of Fairview (lat. 35°56'15" N, long. 118°27'45" W); the cave is in Packsaddle Canyon. Named on Kernville (1956) 15' quadrangle.

Packsaddle Creek [TULARE]: *stream,* flows 1.5 miles to Bear Creek (4) 6.5 miles northeast of California Hot Springs (lat. 35°56'40" N, long. 118°35' W; sec. 12, T 23 S, R 31 E); the stream heads near Packsaddle Meadow. Named on California Hot Springs (1958) 15' quadrangle.

Packsaddle Lake [FRESNO]: *lake,* 2000 feet long, 9.5 miles north of Mount Goddard in Humphreys Basin (lat. 37°14'10" N, long. 118° 44'20" W). Named on Mount Goddard (1948) 15' quadrangle. Sierra Club officials named the feature; Toby Way, a packer, called it Lovejoy Lake in 1928 or 1929, when he stocked it with fish (Browning 1986, p. 163).

Packsaddle Meadow [TULARE]: *area,* 5 miles northeast of California Hot Springs (lat. 35°55'30" N, long. 118°35'50" W); the place is at the head of Packsaddle Creek. Named on California Hot Springs (1958) 15' quadrangle.

Packwood [KERN]: *locality,* 11 miles southsoutheast of Orchard Peak (lat. 35°35'15" N, long. 120°03'35" W); the place is near the head of Packwood Creek. Named on Packwood (1943) 7.5' quadrangle. Called Packwood's on Arnold and Johnson's (1910) map.

Packwood Creek [KERN]: *stream,* flows 6.25 miles to Antelope Valley (1) 7.5 miles west of Blackwells Corner (lat. 35°37'15" N, long. 119°59'55" W; sec. 35, T 26 S, R 18 E); the stream heads near Packwood. Named on Emigrant Hill (1953), Packwood Creek (1961), Sawtooth Ridge (1961), and Shale Point (1953) 7.5' quadrangles.

Packwood Creek [TULARE]: *stream,* heads at Kaweah River and flows 15 miles to ditches 9 miles west-southwest of Visalia (lat. 36°15'45" N, long. 119°25'55" W; sec. 24, T 19 S, R 23 E). Named on Exeter (1952) and Visalia (1949) 15' quadrangles. The name commemorates Elisha Packwood (Mitchell,

A.R., p. 78).

Packwood Creek: see **Bates Slough** [TU-LARE].

Page: see **Famoso** [KERN].

Pagliarulo [TULARE]: *locality,* 3 miles south of Earlimart along Southern Pacific Railroad (lat. 35°50'20" N, long. 119°15'50" W; sec. 15, T 24 S, R 25 E). Named on Delano West (1954) 7.5' quadrangle. Called Stone on Earlimart (1942) 15' quadrangle.

Pahute Peak: see **Piute Peak** [KERN].

Paige [TULARE]: *locality,* 4.25 miles west-southwest of Tulare along Atchison, Topeka and Santa Fe Railroad (lat. 36°10'55" N, long. 119°25'10" W; near NW cor. sec. 19, T 20 S, R 24 E). Named on Paige (1950) 7.5' quadrangle. The named was given in the 1890's for landowner Timothy Paige (Gudde, 1949, p. 248). Postal authorities established Paige post office in 1908 and discontinued it in 1914 (Frickstad, p. 213).

Paine Lake [FRESNO]: *lake,* 2250 feet long, 9 miles north of Mount Goddard in Humphreys Basin (lat. 37°13'55" N, long. 118°43'45" W). Named on Mount Goddard (1948) 15' quadrangle. United States Board on Geographic Names (1986, p. 4) approved the form "Payne Lake" for the name, which commemorates Edgar Alwin Payne, painter of scenes in the Sierra Nevada, including a view of this lake. John Schober named the feature (Browning 1986, p. 163).

Painted Lady [FRESNO]: *peak,* 10.5 miles south of Mount Pinchot (lat. 36°47'35" N, long. 118°23'55" W). Altitude 12,126 feet. Named on Mount Pinchot (1953) 15' quadrangle. Bolton C. Brown gave the name "The Pyramid" to the feature in 1899; the peak also was known as Colored Lady (Browning 1986, p. 163).

Painted Rock [FRESNO]: *relief feature,* 12 miles northeast of Hume in Tehipite Valley (lat. 36°54'50" N, long. 118°46'30" W). Named on Tehipite Dome (1952) 15' quadrangle.

Paiute Peak: see **Piute Peak** [KERN].

Pajuela Peak [KERN]: *peak,* 8.5 miles east of Tehachapi (lat. 35°07'15" N, long. 118°17'35" W; sec. 26, T 32 S, R 34 E). Altitude 5764 feet. Named on Monolith (1966) 7.5' quadrangle.

Palisade Basin [FRESNO]: *area,* 11 miles east of Mount Goddard (lat. 37°05' N, long. 118°31'30" W); the place is southwest of North Palisade. Named on Mount Goddard (1948) 15' quadrangle.

Palisade Creek [FRESNO]: *stream,* flows 7.5 miles to Middle Fork Kings River 8.5 miles east-southeast of Mount Goddard (lat. 37°03'10" N, long. 118°34'45" W); the stream heads near Middle Palisade and goes through Palisade Lakes. Named on Big Pine (1950) and Mount Goddard (1948) 15' quadrangles. L.A. Winchell named the stream (Browning

1986, p. 164).

Palisade Crest [FRESNO]: *peak,* 3.5 miles northwest of Mount Bolton Brown on Fresno-Inyo county line (lat. 37°04'40" N, long. 118°29'10" W). Named on Big Pine (1950) 15' quadrangle.

Palisade Lakes [FRESNO]: *lakes,* two, largest 2400 feet long, 2 miles west-northwest of Mount Bolton Brown (lat. 37°03'20" N, long. 118°28'45" W); the lakes are along Palisade Creek. Named on Big Pine (1950) 15' quadrangle.

Palma Plain: see **Antelope Valley** [KERN] (2).

Palmer Cave [TULARE]: *cave,* 11 miles southeast of Kaweah (lat. 36°22'30" N, long. 118°45'35" W). Named on Kaweah (1957) 15' quadrangle. Joseph L. Palmer discovered the cave in 1872 and named it for himself (Browning 1986, p. 164-165).

Palmer Mountain [FRESNO]: *peak,* 19 miles east of Hume (lat. 36° 44'50" N, long. 118°34'05" W). Altitude 11,250 feet. Named on Triple Divide Peak (1956) 15' quadrangle. The name commemorates Joe Palmer, an early prospector in the neighborhood (United States Board on Geographic Names, 1933a, p. 583). The name originally was applied to present Avalanche Peak (Hanna, p. 227).

Palmer Spring [KERN]: *spring,* 2 miles northnortheast of Caliente (lat. 35°19'10" N, long. 118°36'45" W). Named on Oiler Peak (1972) 7.5' quadrangle.

Palmo [KERN]: *locality,* 2.5 miles south of Wasco along Atchison, Topeka and Santa Fe Railroad (lat. 35°33'30" N, long. 119°19'45" W; near SW cor. sec. 19, T 27 S, R 25 E). Named on Wasco (1953) 7.5' quadrangle.

Paloma [KERN]: *locality,* 2 miles east-southeast of Millux (lat. 35° 10'20" N, long. 119°09'50" W). Named on Millux (1933) 7.5' quadrangle.

Paloma Meadows [TULARE]: *area,* 14 miles south-southeast of Hockett Peak (lat. 36°01'20" N, long. 118°19'15" W). Named on Hockett Peak (1956) 15' quadrangle.

Palo Prieto: see **Annette** [KERN].

Palo Prieto Canyon: see **Palo Prieto Pass** [KERN].

Palo Prieto Creek: see **East Palo Prieto Creek**, under **Bitterwater Creek** [KERN] (2).

Palo Prieto Pass [KERN]: *valley,* 6 miles long, 8.5 miles south-southeast of Orchard Peak on Kern-San Luis Obispo county line (lat. 35°37'30" N, long. 120°11' W). Named on Holland Canyon (1961) and Orchard Peak (1961) 7.5' quadrangles. United States Board on Geographic Names (1968a, p. 6) rejected the names "Palo Prieto Canon" and "Palo Prieto Canyon" for the feature.

Palo Prieto Valley: see **Bitterwater Valley** [KERN].

Pampa: see **Bena** [KERN].

Pampa Peak [KERN]: *peak,* 7 miles northwest of Caliente (lat. 35° 21'55" N, long.

118°42'40" W; sec. 36, T 29 S, R 30 E); the peak is 3 miles north-northeast of Bena, which formerly was called Pampa. Altitude 3176 feet. Named on Bena (1972) 7.5' quadrangle.

Panama [KERN]: *village,* 8 miles south-southwest of Bakersfield (lat. 35°16' N, long. 119°03'20" W; at SE cor. sec. 34, T 30 S, R 27 E). Named on Gosford (1954) 7.5' quadrangle. Postal authorities established Panama post office in 1874 and discontinued it in 1876 (Frickstad, p. 58). A Mexican settlement called Rio Bravo, from an early name for Kern River, was started in 1849 about 2 miles north of present Panama; later the settlement of Rio Bravo was called Panama, and later still the name "Panama" was transferred to present Panama, while the site first called Rio Bravo became known as Old Panama (Bailey, 1967, p. 21). The name "Panama" was from a comparison of the place to the low-lying, swampy, mosquito-infested lands of the Isthmus of Panama (Boyd, p. 98).

Panama Slough [KERN]: *water feature,* 2 miles southwest of Panama (lat. 35°15' N, long. 119°04'55" W). Named on Conner (1954) and Gosford (1954) 7.5' quadrangles. Gosford (1932) 7.5' quadrangle shows Panama Slough diverging from Kern River 2.5 miles west of downtown Bakersfield, and Buena Vista Lake (1912) 30' quadrangle shows it extending to Kern Lake Bed 1.25 miles east of Conner.

Pande: see **Peter Pande Lake** [FRESNO].

Panoche Creek [FRESNO]: *stream,* heads in San Benito County and flows 30 miles to lowlands 19 miles southwest of Firebaugh (lat. 36°38' N, long. 120°39'10" W; near N line sec. 15, T 15 S, R 12 E). Named on Chaney Ranch (1955), Chounet Ranch (1956), and Tumey Hills (1956) 7.5' quadrangles. Whitney (p. 55) referred to Big Panoche Creek. Anderson and Pack (p. 19) noted that the lower 3-mile reach of the stream sometimes incorrectly is termed Silver Creek, and United States Board on Geographic Names (1933a, p. 586) rejected the name "Silver Creek" for present Panoche Creek. Mendenhall's (1908) map shows a place called Schunemanns situated on the southeast side of Panoche Creek about 1 mile southwest of the entrance of the stream into lowlands (sec. 16, T 15 S, R 12 E). California Mining Bureau's (1917a) map shows a place called Chaneys located south of Panoche Creek and about 3 miles east of the entrance of Panoche Creek into lowlands—Chaney Ranch (1955) 7.5' quadrangle shows Chaney ranch at about the same site.

Panoche Creek: see **Little Panoche Creek** [FRESNO]; **Silver Creek** [FRESNO] (2).

Panoche Hills [FRESNO]: *range,* 20 miles west-southwest of Firebaugh between Panoche Creek and Little Panoche Creek (lat. 36° 42' N, long. 120°45' W). Named on Chounet Ranch (1956), Hammond Ranch (1956), Laguna Seca Ranch (1956), Mercey Hot Springs

(1969), Panoche (1969), and Tumey Hills (1956) 7.5' quadrangles.

Panoche Junction [FRESNO]: *locality,* 15 miles west-southwest of Tranquillity (lat. 36°32'45" N, long. 120°29'15" W; at N line sec. 18, T 16 S, R 14 E). Named on Levis (1956) 7.5' quadrangle.

Panoche Mountain [FRESNO]: *peak,* 5.5 miles east-northeast of Mercey Hot Springs (lat. 36°43'30" N, long. 120°45'50" W; on E line sec. 9, T 14 S, R 11 E). Altitude 2091 feet. Named on Mercey Hot Springs (1969) 7.5' quadrangle.

Panoche Valley: see **Little Panoche Valley** [FRESNO].

Panochita Creek: see **Little Panoche Creek** [FRESNO].

Panochita Valley: see **Little Panoche Valley** [FRESNO].

Panorama Campground [TULARE]: *locality,* 7.5 miles southeast of California Hot Springs (lat. 35°48'35" N, long. 118°34'15" W; sec. 30, T 24 S, R 32 E). Named on California Hot Springs (1958) 15' quadrangle. Called Panorama Camp on Tobias Peak (1936) 30' quadrangle.

Panorama Heights [TULARE]: *settlement,* 5.5 miles south-southeast of California Hot Springs (lat. 35°48'20" N, long. 118°37'45" W; near SE cor. sec. 28, T 24 S, R 31 E). Named on California Hot Springs (1958) 15' quadrangle.

Panorama Point [TULARE]: *peak,* 4 miles southeast of Yucca Mountain (lat. 36°32'15" N, long. 118°48'40" W). Named on Giant Forest (1956) 15' quadrangle.

Panorama Point: see **Observation Peak** [FRESNO].

Panther Creek [TULARE]: *stream,* flows 3.25 miles to Middle Fork Kaweah River 11 miles west-southwest of Triple Divide Peak (lat. 36°32'20" N, long. 118°43'05" W); the stream heads near Panther Peak. Named on Triple Divide Peak (1956) 15' quadrangle. The name is from a mountain lion that Hale Tharp killed near the feature (Browning 1986, p. 165).

Panther Gap [TULARE]: *pass,* 10 miles west of Triple Divide Peak (lat. 36°35' N, long. 118°42'15" W; near N line sec. 34, T 15 S, R 30 E); the pass is 0.5 mile east of Panther Peak. Named on Triple Divide Peak (1956) 15' quadrangle.

Panther Meadow [TULARE]: *area,* 10.5 miles west of Triple Divide Peak (lat. 36°35'10" N, long. 118°42'50" W; near SW cor. sec. 27, T 15 S, R 30 E); the place is north of Panther Peak. Named on Triple Divide Peak (1956) 15' quadrangle.

Panther Peak [TULARE]: *peak,* 10.5 miles west of Triple Divide Peak (lat. 36°35' N, long. 118°42'50" W; near NW cor. sec. 34, T 15 S, R 30 E). Altitude 9046 feet. Named on Triple Divide Peak (1956) 15' quadrangle.

Paoha Lake [FRESNO]: *lake,* 200 feet long, 7.5

miles south of Mount Abbot (lat. 37°16'55" N, long. 118°48'30" W). Named on Mount Abbot (1953) 15' quadrangle. Elden H. Vestal of California Department of Fish and Game named the lake in 1951; Vestal believed that the word "paoha" has the meaning "white" or "daylight" in the Piute Indian language, and therefore has a meaning opposite to that of the name of nearby Negit Lake (Browning 1986, p. 165).

Papoose Lake [FRESNO]: *lake,* 550 feet long, 10 miles northwest of Mount Abbot (lat. 37°28'15" N, long. 118°55'55" W); the lake is between Warrior Lake and Lake of the Lone Indian. Named on Mount Abbot (1953) 15' quadrangle.

Paradise Canyon [TULARE]: *canyon,* 1.5 miles long, 9 miles south of Kaweah along the lower part of Jim Grey Creek (lat. 36°20'10" N, long. 118°56'15" W). Named on Kaweah (1957) 15' quadrangle.

Paradise Cave [TULARE]: *cave,* 9 miles east of Kaweah (lat. 36°28'45" N, long. 118°45'40" W; sec. 6, T 17 S, R 30 E); the cave is on the south side of Paradise Ridge. Named on Kaweah (1957) 15' quadrangle. H.R. Harmon discovered the cave in 1901; Charles W. Blossom and Walter Fry, rangers of Sequoia National Park, named it in 1906 (Browning 1986, p. 166).

Paradise Cove [KERN]: *embayment,* 4.25 miles south-southeast of Wofford Heights along Isabella Lake (lat. 35°39'10" N, long. 118° 25'30" W; sec. 22, T 26 S, R 33 E). Named on Lake Isabella North (1972) 7.5' quadrangle.

Paradise Cove Campground [KERN]: *locality,* 4.5 miles south-southeast of Wofford Heights (lat. 35°38'55" N, long. 118°25'30" W; sec. 22, T 26 S, R 33 E); the place is at Paradise Cove. Named on Lake Isabella North (1972) 7.5' quadrangle.

Paradise Creek [TULARE]: *stream,* flows 4.5 miles to Middle Fork Kaweah River 7 miles east-southeast of Yucca Mountain (lat. 36° 31'15" N, long. 118°45'45" W). Named on Giant Forest (1956) and Mineral King (1956) 15' quadrangles.

Paradise Peak [TULARE]: *peak,* 6 miles west-northwest of Mineral King (lat. 36°28'35" N, long. 118°41'50" W); the peak is at the east end of Paradise Ridge. Altitude 9362 feet. Named on Mineral King (1956) 15' quadrangle. United States Board on Geographic Names (1933a, p. 588) rejected the name "Milk Ranch Peak" for the feature, and later (1938, p. 40) rejected the name "Paradise Peak Lookout."

Paradise Peak: see **Milk Ranch Peak** [TULARE].

Paradise Peak Lookout: see **Paradise Peak** [TULARE].

Paradise Ridge [TULARE]: *ridge,* west-trending, 4 miles long, 8 miles west-northwest of Mineral King (lat. 36°28'30" N, long. 118°

44' W); the ridge extends west from Paradise Peak. Named on Kaweah (1957) and Mineral King (1956) 15' quadrangles.

Paradise Valley [FRESNO]: *valley,* 7.5 miles south of Marion Peak along South Fork Kings River (lat. 36°51' N, long. 118°32' W). Named on Marion Peak (1953) 15' quadrangle.

Paradise Valley [KERN]: *valley,* 6 miles south-southwest of Tehachapi along Brite Creek (lat. 35°03'15" N, long. 118°30' W). Named on Cummings Mountain (1966) and Tehachapi South (1966) 7.5' quadrangles.

Parejo Hill [KINGS]: *peak,* 7.5 miles south of Kettleman City (lat. 35°54'05" N, long. 119°56'20" W; sec. 29, T 23 S, R 19 E). Altitude 553 feet. Named on Los Viejos (1954) 7.5' quadrangle. The name is descriptive—*parejo* means "even" in Spanish (United States Board on Geographic Names, 1933b, p. 22).

Paris: see **Loraine** [KERN].

Paris-Loraine: see **Loraine** [KERN].

Park: see **The Park**, under **Walker Basin** [KERN].

Parker Bluffs [TULARE]: *relief feature,* 9.5 miles northeast of California Hot Springs (lat. 35°59' N, long. 118°33'30" W); the feature is north of Parker Meadow Creek. Named on California Hot Springs (1958) 15' quadrangle.

Parker Creek: see **Barker Creek** [KERN]; **Parker Meadow Creek** [TULARE].

Parker Meadow [TULARE]: *area,* 6 miles north-northeast of California Hot Springs (lat. 35°57'40" N, long. 118°37'45" W; sec. 4, T 23 S, R 31 E). Named on California Hot Springs (1958) 15' quadrangle.

Parker Meadow: see **Upper Parker Meadow** [TULARE].

Parker Meadow Creek [TULARE]: *stream,* flows 7.25 miles to South Creek 9.5 miles northeast of California Hot Springs near Johnsondale (lat. 35°58'10" N, long. 118°32'15" W; sec. 32, T 22 S, R 32 E); the stream goes through Parker Meadow. Named on California Hot Springs (1958) 15' quadrangle. United States Board on Geographic Names (1960a, p. 9) rejected the name "Parker Creek" for the stream.

Parker Pass [TULARE]: *pass,* nearly 6 miles north-northeast of California Hot Springs (lat. 35°57'10" N, long. 118°37'25" W; near SW cor. sec. 3, T 23 S, R 31 E); the pass is 0.5 mile southeast of Parker Meadow. Named on California Hot Springs (1958) 15' quadrangle.

Parker Peak [TULARE]: *peak,* 6.5 miles north-northeast of California Hot Springs (lat. 35°58'20" N, long. 118°38'45" W; sec. 32, T 22 S, R 31 E). Altitude 7578 feet. Named on California Hot Springs (1958) 15' quadrangle.

Parkfield Junction [FRESNO]: *locality,* 8 miles west-southwest of Coalinga (lat. 36°04'55" N, long. 120°28'45" W; at S line sec. 20, T 21 S, R 14 E). Named on Curry Mountain (1969) 7.5' quadrangle.

Park Ridge [FRESNO-TULARE]: *ridge*, north-to northeast-trending, 7 miles long, 1.5 miles west of Hume on Fresno-Tulare county line, mainly in Fresno County (lat. 36°47' N, long. 118°56'45" W). Named on Giant Forest (1956) and Tehipite Dome (1952) 15' quadrangles.

Park Road Ridge: see **Ash Peaks Ridge** [TULARE].

Parlier [FRESNO]: *town*, 5.5 miles east-northeast of Selma (lat. 36° 36'35" N, long. 119°31'30" W; mainly in sec. 24, T 15 S, R 22 E). Named on Selma (1964) 7.5' quadrangle. Postal authorities established Parlier post office in 1898 and named it for I. N. Parlier, first postmaster (Salley, p. 167), who came to the neighborhood in the 1870's (Hanna, p. 230). The town incorporated in 1921.

Parsons: see **Wible Orchard** [KERN].

Parsons Canyon [FRESNO]: *canyon*, drained by a stream that flows 3.25 miles to Oak Flat Canyon 5.5 miles west of Coalinga (lat. 36° 07'35" N, long. 120°27'20" W; sec. 4, T 21 S, R 14 E). Named on Alcalde Hills (1969) 7.5' quadrangle.

Parsons Peak [MADERA-TUOLUMNE]: *peak*, 9.5 miles south-southwest of Tioga Pass on Madera-Tuolumne county line (lat. 37°46'30" N, long. 119°18'25" W). Named on Tuolumne Meadows (1956) 15' quadrangle. R.B. Marshall of United States Geological Survey named the peak for Edward Taylor Parsons, who for many years was a director of the Sierra Club (United States Board on Geographic Names, 1934a, p. 19).

Paso Slough: see **Poso Slough** [FRESNO].

Pass Creek: see **Tehachapi Creek** [KERN].

Pastoria Creek [KERN]: *stream*, flows 13 miles to lowlands 7 miles north of Lebec (lat. 34°56'20" N long. 118°50'30" W). Named on Pastoria Creek (1958), Tejon Hills (1955), and Winters Ridge (1966) 7.5' quadrangles. Whitney (p. 191) mentioned Arroyo Pastoria. The name was given because the stream passes through land used in the 1850's as pasture for the Indian reservation on El Tejon grant (Gudde, 1949, p. 255)—*pastoria* means "pastoral life" in Spanish. United States Board on Geographic Names (1982b, p. 2) approved the name "Cattle Creek" for a stream that flows 4.3 miles to Pastoria Creek 1.5 miles north-northwest of the entrance of Pastoria Creek into lowlands (lat. 34°57'38" N, long. 118°51'05" W).

Patch [KERN]: *locality*, 10 miles southeast of Bakersfield along the railroad (lat. 35°15'10" N, long. 118°53'40" W; at SW cor. sec. 5, T 31 S, R 29 E). Named on Lamont (1954) 7.5' quadrangle. The site first was known as Weedpatch from the abundance of weeds there, but railroad officials abbreviated the name for their siding (Gudde, 1949, p. 255).

Pattee Rocks [TULARE]: *peak*, 4.5 miles west of Yucca Mountain (lat. 36°33'45" N, long. 118°56'50" W). Altitude 4284 feet. Named on

Giant Forest (1956) 15' quadrangle.

Patterson: see **Trigo** [MADERA].

Patterson Bend [FRESNO]: *bend*, 7.5 miles north-northwest of Prather along San Joaquin River on Fresno-Madera county line (lat. 37°08'40" N, long. 119°33'15" W). Named on North Fork (1965) 7.5' quadrangle.

Patterson Bend [MADERA]: *bend*, 6 miles south-southwest of the town of North Fork along San Joaquin River on Madera-Fresno county line (lat. 37°08'40" N, long. 119°33'15" W). Named on North Fork (1965) 7.5' quadrangle.

Patterson Bluffs [FRESNO]: *escarpment*, west-northwest-trending, 3 miles long, 2.5 miles east-northeast of Balch Camp (lat. 36°55'15" N, long. 119°04'45" W). Named on Patterson Mountain (1952) 15' quadrangle.

Patterson Creek [FRESNO]: *stream*, flows 2.5 miles to North Fork Kings River 2.25 miles east of Balch Camp (lat. 36°54'30" N, long. 119°05' W; near NE cor. sec. 12, T 12 S, R 26 E). Named on Patterson Mountain (1952) 15' quadrangle.

Patterson Mountain [FRESNO]: *ridge*, north-northwest-trending, 4.5 miles long, 6 miles northeast of Balch Camp (lat. 36°58' N, long. 119°03' W). Named on Patterson Mountain (1952) 15' quadrangle. The name commemorates John A. Patterson and Elisha Patterson, who pastured sheep at the place (Browning 1986, p. 167).

Pattiway [KERN]: *locality*, 15 miles west of Eagle Rest Peak (lat. 34°55'40" N, long. 119°23'55" W; at S line sec. 24, T 10 N, R 24 W). Named on Mount Pinos (1903) 30' quadrangle. Postal authorities established Pattiway post office in 1891, moved it 1 mile east in 1903, and discontinued it in 1936; the name is from the Patti family, pioneers at the place (Salley, p. 168).

Paulina: see **Lake Paulina** [KERN].

Pavilion Dome [FRESNO]: *peak*, 11 miles north of Blackcap Mountain at the west end of Glacier Divide (lat. 37°13'50" N, long. 118° 48'30" W). Altitude 11,846 feet. Named on Blackcap Mountain (1953) 15' quadrangle. L.A. Winchell named the peak in 1879 (Browning 1986, p. 167).

Payne: see **Harry Payne Spring** [KERN].

Payne Lake: see **Paine Lake** [FRESNO].

Peak Disappointment: see **Disappointment Peak** [FRESNO].

Pear Lake [TULARE]: *lake*, 1600 feet long, 7.5 miles west of Triple Divide Peak (lat. 36°36'05" N, long. 118°40' W; on S line sec. 24, T 15 S, R 30 E). Named on Triple Divide Peak (1956) 15' quadrangle. Colonel White named the lake in the early 1920's for its pearlike shape (Browning 1986, p. 167).

Pearl Lake [FRESNO]: *lakes*, two connected, largest 2300 feet long, nearly 4 miles south-southwest of Mount Goddard (lat. 37°03'10" N, long. 118°44'55" W). Named on Blackcap

Mountain (1953) and Mount Goddard (1948) 15' quadrangles.

Pecan Spring [MADERA]: *spring,* 5 miles southeast of Knowles (lat. 37°09'35" N, long. 119°49'05" W; sec. 8, T 9 S, R 20 E). Named on Knowles (1962) 7.5' quadrangle.

Pechacho Creek [KERN]: *stream,* flows 2.5 miles to Kern River nearly 3 miles north of Mount Adelaide (lat. 35°28'15" N, long. 118°45' W). Named on Mount Adelaide (1972) 7.5' quadrangle.

Peckinpah Creek [MADERA]: *stream,* flows 4 miles to South Fork Willow Creek (2) 9 miles south-southwest of Shuteye Peak (lat. 37°14'10" N, long. 119°29'45" W; sec. 18, T 8 S, R 23 E); the stream goes through Peckinpah Meadow. Named on Shaver Lake (1953) and Shuteye Peak (1953) 15' quadrangles.

Peckinpah Meadow [MADERA]: *area,* 6 miles south-southwest of Shuteye Peak (lat. 37°15'55" N, long. 119°27'45" W; sec. 4, T 8 S, R 23 E); the place is along Peckinpah Creek. Named on Shuteye Peak (1953) 15' quadrangle.

Peckinpah Mill [MADERA]: *locality,* 6.25 miles south-southwest of Shuteye Peak (lat. 37°15'50" N, long. 119°27'45" W; sec. 4, T 8 S, R 23 E); the place is along Peckinpah Creek. Named on Kaiser (1904) 30' quadrangle. Charlie Peckinpah and his brothers started a sawmill at the spot in 1884 (Browning, 1986, p. 167).

Peckinpah Mountain: see **Central Camp** [MADERA].

Pecks Canyon [TULARE]: *canyon,* drained by a stream that flows 5 miles to Alpine Creek 13 miles south of Mineral King (lat. 36°15'50" N, long. 118°33'10" W). Named on Mineral King (1956) 15' quadrangle. The name commemorates a man who ran sheep in the neighborhood about 1870 (Gudde, 1949, p. 256).

Peel Creek: see **Peel Mill Creek** [TULARE].

Peel Mill Creek [TULARE]: *stream,* flows 4.5 miles to Poso Creek 5.25 miles south of California Hot Springs (lat. 35°48'15" N, long. 118°39'50" W; near SE cor. sec. 30, T 24 S, R 31 E); the stream heads near Peel Peak. Named on California Hot Springs (1958) 15' quadrangle. United States Board on Geographic Names (1960a, p. 10) rejected the names "Mill Creek," "Peel Creek," and "Pell Mell Creek" for the stream.

Peel Peak [TULARE]: *peak,* 6.5 miles southeast of California Hot Springs (lat. 35°48'20" N, long. 118°36'10" W; sec. 26, T 24 S, R 31 E); the peak is on Peel Ridge. Altitude 6788 feet. Named on California Hot Springs (1958) 15' quadrangle.

Peel Ridge [TULARE]: *ridge,* west-southwest-trending, 2.5 miles long, 6.5 miles south-southeast of California Hot Springs (lat. 35° 47'45" N, long. 118°37'10" W); Peel Peak is near the northeast end of the ridge. Named

on California Hot Springs (1958) 15' quadrangle.

Peeping Tom Spring [KERN]: *spring,* 13 miles north of Mojave (lat. 35°14'55" N, long. 118°10' W; near E line sec. 12, T 31 S, R 35 E). Named on Cache Peak (1973) 7.5' quadrangle.

Peerless Valley [KERN]: *valley,* center 4.5 miles east of Castle Butte (lat. 35°06' N, long. 117°48' W). Named on Galileo Hill (1973) and North Edwards (1973) 7.5' quadrangles.

Pelican Island [KERN]: *hill,* 12 miles east-northeast of Taft in Buena Vista Lake Bed (lat. 35°12'40" N, long. 119°16' W). Named on Mouth of Kern (1950) 7.5' quadrangle.

Pelican Island [KINGS]: *area,* 14 miles east-southeast of Kettleman City in Tulare Lake Bed (lat. 35°57' N, long. 119°43'15" W; sec. 4, 5, 8, 9, T 23 S, R 21 E). Named on Hacienda Ranch NW (1954) 7.5' quadrangle.

Pell Mell Creek: see **Peel Mill Creek** [TULARE].

Pemmican Lake [FRESNO]: *lake,* 500 feet long, 9 miles south-southwest of Mount Abbot (lat. 37°15'35" N, long. 118°48'50" W). Named on Mount Abbot (1953) 15' quadrangle.

Penasco Rock [FRESNO]: *peak,* 9.5 miles south-southwest of Coalinga (lat. 36°00'30" N, long. 120°24'50" W; near N line sec. 24, T 22 S, R 14 E); the peak is 800 feet south of Penasco Spring. Named on Curry Mountain (1969) 7.5' quadrangle.

Penasco Spring [FRESNO]: *spring,* 9.5 miles south-southwest of Coalinga (lat. 36°00'35" N, long. 120°24'50" W; sec. 13, T 22 S, R 14 E); the spring is 800 feet north of Penasco Rock. Named on Curry Mountain (1969) 7.5' quadrangle.

Pendant Lake [FRESNO]: *lake,* 1700 feet long, 9 miles south-southwest of Mount Abbot (lat. 37°15'35" N, long. 118°49'15" W). Named on Mount Abbot (1953) 15' quadrangle. Elden H. Vestal of California Department of Fish and Game named the lake in 1951 for its pendantlike shape (Browning 1986, p. 168).

Peninsula Meadow: see **Cascade Valley** [FRESNO].

Pentland [KERN]: *locality,* 2.5 miles east of Maricopa along Sunset Railroad (lat. 35°03'30" N, long. 119°21'15" W; near N line sec. 8, T 11 N, R 23 W). Named on Pentland (1953) 7.5' quadrangle. Called Pentland Junction on Buena Vista Lake (1912) 30' quadrangle.

Pentland Junction: see **Pentland** [KERN].

Peppergrass Flat [FRESNO]: *area,* 1.5 miles east of Ciervo Mountain (lat. 36°27'55" N, long. 120°33' W; sec. 9, 10, T 17 S, R 13 E). Named on Ciervo Mountain (1969) 7.5' quadrangle.

Pepper Grass Valley [KINGS]: *valley,* 9.5 miles south of Kettleman City (lat. 35°52' N, long. 119°56'45" W). Named on Avenal Gap (1954) and Los Viejos (1954) 7.5' quadrangles.

Peppermint Creek [TULARE]: *stream,* flows 7.5 miles to Kern River 13 miles south-south-west of Hockett Peak (lat. 36°02'50" N, long. 118°28' W). Named on Camp Nelson (1956) and Hockett Peak (1956) 15' quadrangles.

Peppermint Meadows [TULARE]: *area,* 12.5 miles south-southwest of Hockett Peak (lat. 36°04' N, long. 118°30' W); the place is along a branch of Peppermint Creek. Named on Camp Nelson (1956) and Hockett Peak (1956) 15' quadrangles.

Peral [TULARE]: *locality,* 6.5 miles north of Visalia along Atchison, Topeka and Santa Fe Railroad (lat. 36°25'35" N, long. 119°17'10" W; sec. 29, T 17 S, R 25 E). Named on Monson (1949) 7.5' quadrangle. Railroad officials gave the name about 1895—*peral* means "pear tree" in Spanish (Gudde, 1949, p. 258).

Perkins: see **Mount Perkins** [FRESNO].

Pernu: see **Porterville** [TULARE].

Pernu Junction: see **Porterville** [TULARE].

Perrin Creek [TULARE]: *stream,* flows 3 miles to Rock Creek 13 miles north of Kern Peak (lat. 36°29'50" N, long. 118°19'45" W). Named on Kern Peak (1956) and Mount Whitney (1956) 15' quadrangles. G.H. Perrin, who surveyed for General Land Office in 1884, named the stream for himself (Browning 1986, p. 168).

Persian Creek [FRESNO-TULARE]: *stream,* heads in Fresno County and flows 5 miles to Murry Creek (1) nearly 3 miles northeast of Auckland in Tulare County (lat. 36°37'15" N, long. 119°04'30" W; sec. 18, T 15 S, R 27 E). Named on Auckland (1966) and Miramonte (1966) 7.5' quadrangles.

Pescado Creek [KERN]: *stream,* flows nearly 5 miles to lowlands 9 miles southwest of Liebre Twins (lat. 34°51'30" N, long. 118°40'15" W; sec. 22, T 9 N, R 17 W). Named on La Liebre Ranch (1965) and Winters Ridge (1966) 7.5' quadrangles. United States Board on Geographic Names (1967c, p. 4) rejected the name "Lecheria Creek" for the stream. Johnson's (1911) map has the name "Fish Canyon" for the canyon of the creek.

Pete Meadow: see **Big Pete Meadow** [FRESNO]; **Little Pete Meadow** [FRESNO].

Pete Merrill Canyon [FRESNO]: *canyon,* drained by a stream that flows 2.25 miles to Jacalitos Creek 5.5 miles south-southeast of Coalinga (lat. 36°03'45" N, long. 120°20'10" W; sec. 34, T 21 S, R 15 E). Named on Kreyenhagen Hills (1956) 7.5' quadrangle.

Peteras Mill: see **Old Bretz Mill** [FRESNO].

Peter Pande Lake [FRESNO]: *lake,* 3100 feet long, 12 miles west-northwest of Mount Abbot (lat. 37°28'05" N, long. 118°58'50" W). Named on Mount Abbot (1953) 15' quadrangle. United States Board on Geographic Names (1961b, p. 11) rejected the name "Marilyn Lake" for the feature.

Peter Peak [FRESNO]: *peak,* 3.25 miles north-northwest of Mount Goddard (lat. 37°08'45"

N, long. 118°44'45" W). Altitude 12,543 feet. Named on Mount Goddard (1948) 15' quadrangle. Officials of Sierra Club named the feature for Peter Grubb, who made the first ascent of the peak in 1936 (Browning 1986, p. 169).

Petersburg [KERN]: *locality,* 4.5 miles west-northwest of Miracle Hot Springs along Greenhorn Creek (lat. 35°36'10" N, long. 118° 36'10" W; near SW cor. sec. 1, T 27 S, R 31 E). Site named on Glennville (1956) 15' quadrangle. Postal authorities established Petersburgh (with a terminal "h") post office in 1858 and discontinued it in 1863 (Salley, p. 170). The name is for Peter Gardett, who opened a store at the place in the early 1850's; the community also was known as Greenhorn (Bailey, 1962, p. 9, 13).

Peterson: see **Dinkey Mountain** [FRESNO].

Peterson Creek [MADERA]: *stream,* heads in Mariposa County and flows 4.5 miles to Carter Creek 4.5 miles west of Yosemite Forks in Madera County (lat. 37°22'10" N, long. 119°42'40" W; sec. 31, T 6 S, R 21 E). Named on Bass Lake (1953) 15' quadrangle.

Peterson Mill [FRESNO]: *locality,* 18 miles south-southwest of Kaiser Peak along Rush Creek (lat. 37°02'30" N, long. 119°17'20" W; sec. 19, T 10 S, R 25 E). Named on Kaiser (1904) 30' quadrangle.

Petro [KERN]: *locality,* 7.25 miles north of Wasco along Atchison, Topeka and Santa Fe Railroad (lat. 35°41'45" N, long. 119°19'50" W). Named on Pond (1930) 7.5' quadrangle.

Peyrone Camp [TULARE]: *locality,* 7.5 miles south of Camp Nelson (lat. 36°02' N, long. 118°36'40" W; sec. 10, T 22 S, R 31 E). Named on Camp Nelson (1956) 15' quadrangle.

Peyton Creek [KERN]: *stream,* flows 2.5 miles to join McFarland Creek and form Fulton Creek 2 miles east-northeast of Glennville (lat. 35°44'05" N, long. 118°40' W; sec. 20, T 25 S, R 31 E). Named on California Hot Springs (1958) 15' quadrangle, and on Glennville (1972) 7.5' quadrangle.

Pheasant: see **Mount Pheasant** [KERN].

Phoenix Gulch [KERN]: *canyon,* 0.5 mile long, 5.25 miles north of Randsburg (lat. 35°26'35" N, long. 117°38'15" W; sec. 1, T 29 S, R 40 E). Named on El Paso Peaks (1967) 7.5' quadrangle.

Picacho Rock [FRESNO]: *relief feature,* 2.5 miles east-northeast of Castle Mountain (lat. 35°57'40" N, long. 120°17'55" W; sec. 1, T 23 S, R 15 E). Named on The Dark Hole (1961) 7.5' quadrangle.

Picayune Creek [MADERA]: *stream,* flows 4.5 miles to Coarse Gold Creek 6.5 miles north of O'Neals (lat. 37°13'10" N, long. 119°42'35" W; sec. 19, T 8 S, R 21 E). Named on O'Neals (1965) 7.5' quadrangle.

Pickering: see **Mount Pickering** [TULARE].

Picket Creek [TULARE]: *stream,* flows nearly 4.5 miles to Kern-Kaweah River 8.5 miles west of Mount Whitney (lat. 36°34'35" N, long. 118°26'30" W). Named on Mount Whitney (1956) 15' quadrangle.

Picket Guard Peak [TULARE]: *peak,* 10 miles west of Mount Whitney (lat. 36°34'35" N, long. 118°28'15" W); the peak is north of Picket Creek. Altitude 12,302 feet. Named on Mount Whitney (1956) 15' quadrangle.

Piedra [FRESNO]: *locality,* 23 miles east of Fresno on the south side of Kings River (lat. 36°48'35" N, long. 119°22'55" W; sec. 8, T 13 S, R 24 E). Named on Piedra (1965) 7.5' quadrangle. Watts Valley (1942) 15' quadrangle has both the names "Piedra" and "Delpiedra P.O." at the place, and Pine Flat Dam (1965) 7.5' quadrangle has the name "Piedra P.O." at a site located about 1.25 miles east-northeast of Piedra (lat. 36°49'20" N, long. 119°21'50" W; near S line sec. 4, T 13 S, R 24 E). When Atchison, Topeka and Santa Fe Railroad built a branch line in 1911 to handle rock from a quarry, the siding near the quarry was called Piedra—*piedra* means "rock" or "stone" in Spanish (Gudde, 1949, p. 261). Postal authorities established Delpiedra post office at the place in 1920 and discontinued it in 1943; they established Piedra post office in 1949 (Frickstad, p. 32, 36).

Pierce Creek [TULARE]: *stream,* flows 6 miles to North Fork Kaweah River 3.5 miles northwest of Yucca Mountain (lat. 36°36'10" N, long. 118°55' W; sec. 22, T 15 S, R 28 E); the stream goes through Pierce Valley. Named on Giant Forest (1956) 15' quadrangle.

Pierce Valley [TULARE]: *area,* 7.25 miles northwest of Yucca Mountain (lat. 36°39'30" N, long. 118°56'40" W; on N line sec. 4, T 15 S, R 28 E); the place is along Pierce Creek. Named on Giant Forest (1956) 15' quadrangle.

Pieto Creek: see **Pleito Creek** [KERN].

Pigeon Creek [TULARE]:

(1) *stream,* flows 1 mile to South Fork Kaweah River 12.5 miles southeast of Kaweah (lat. 36°20'50" N, long. 118°45'15" W). Named on Kaweah (1957) 15' quadrangle.

(2) *stream,* flows 4.25 miles to South Fork Tule River 10 miles southwest of Camp Nelson (lat. 36°02'35" N, long. 118°44'30" W). Named on Camp Nelson (1956) 15' quadrangle.

Pigeon Creek: see **Squaw Creek** [TULARE].

Pigpen Spring [KERN]: *spring,* nearly 7 miles northeast of Mount Adelaide along Flat Creek (lat. 35°29'50" N, long. 118°39'50" W; sec. 16, T 28 S, R 31 E). Named on Mount Adelaide (1972) 7.5' quadrangle.

Pika Lake [FRESNO]: *lake,* 1600 feet long, 5.5 miles west-northwest of Red Slate Mountain (lat. 37°33'05" N, long. 118°57'05" W). Named on Mount Morrison (1953) 15' quadrangle. The name is for the rabbitlike animals called pikas that live near the lake (Smith, Genny, p. 49).

Pilot Knob [FRESNO]: *peak,* 8 miles south of Mount Abbot (lat. 37° 16'25" N, long.

118°45'25" W). Altitude 12,245 feet. Named on Mount Abbot (1953) 15' quadrangle.

Pilot Knob [KERN]: *peak,* 2.5 miles north of Onyx (lat. 35°43'45" N, long. 118°12'40" W). Named on Onyx (1972) 7.5' quadrangle.

Pinchot: see **Mount Pinchot** [FRESNO].

Pinchot Pass [FRESNO]: *pass,* nearly 1 mile south-southwest of Mount Pinchot (lat. 36°56'10" N, long. 118°24'45" W). Named on Mount Pinchot (1953) 15' quadrangle.

Pincushion Mountain [FRESNO]: *peak,* 7.25 miles west of Prather on a peninsula in Millerton Lake (lat. 37°01'55" N, long. 119°38'35" W; sec. 26, T 10 S, R 21 E). Altitude 1582 feet. Named on Millerton Lake West (1965) 7.5' quadrangle.

Pincushion Peak [FRESNO]: *peak,* 13 miles north-northeast of Kaiser Peak (lat. 37°28'20" N, long. 119°06'30" W). Altitude 9819 feet. Named on Kaiser Peak (1953) 15' quadrangle. The name is for the fancied resemblance of the feature to a pincushion (Gudde, 1949, p. 262).

Pine: see **Cinco** [KERN].

Pine Canyon [FRESNO]: *canyon,* drained by a stream that flows 6.5 miles to White Creek 7 miles north-northeast of Coalinga Mineral Springs (lat. 36°14'20" N, long. 120°30'35" W; near S line sec. 30, T 19 S, R 14 E). Named on Santa Rita Peak (1969) and Sherman Peak (1969) 7.5' quadrangles.

Pine Cove [KERN]: *relief feature,* less than 1 mile east-northeast of Claraville (lat. 35°26'45" N, long. 118°19' W; sec. 3, T 29 S, R 34 E). Named on Claraville (1972) 7.5' quadrangle.

Pine Creek [TULARE]: *stream,* flows 4.5 miles to North Fork Tule River 16.miles south-southeast of Kaweah (lat. 36°16'10" N, long. 118°45'40" W; near E line sec. 18, T 19 S, R 30 E). Named on Kaweah (1957) and Mineral King (1956) 15' quadrangles.

Pine Creek Pass [FRESNO]: *pass,* 5 miles northwest of Mount Humphreys on Fresno-Inyo county line (lat. 37°19'05" N, long. 118°44'05" W; near N line sec. 30, T 7 S, R 30 E); the pass is at the head of Pine Creek, which is in Inyo County. Named on Mount Tom (1949) 15' quadrangle.

Pinedale [FRESNO]:

(1) *town,* 5.5 miles north of downtown Fresno (lat. 36°50'30" N, long. 119°47'45" W; in and near sec. 33, T 12 S, R 20 E). Named on Fresno North (1965) 7.5' quadrangle. Postal authorities established Pinedale post office in 1923 (Frickstad, p. 36).

(2) *locality,* 3.5 miles north-northwest of Clovis along Southern Pacific Railroad (lat. 36°52' N, long. 119°43'45" W; near NE cor. sec. 25, T 12 S, R 20 E). Named on Clovis (1946) 15' quadrangle. Called Setch on Clovis (1922) 7.5' quadrangle, and called Pinedale Siding on Clovis (1964) 7.5' quadrangle.

Pinedale Siding: see **Pinedale** [FRESNO] (2).

Pine Flat [FRESNO]: *area,* 5 miles northeast of Piedra along Kings River (lat. 36°51'20" N, long. 119°18'40" W; sec. 25, 26, 35, 36, T 12 S, R 24 E). Named on Watts Valley (1942) 15' quadrangle. Water of Pine Flat Lake now covers the place.

Pine Flat [KERN]: *area,* 6.25 miles east-north-east of Mount Adelaide (lat. 35°28'35" N, long. 118°38'50" W; sec. 21, T 28 S, R 31 E). Named on Mount Adelaide (1972) 7.5' quadrangle.

Pine Flat [MADERA]: *area,* 9.5 miles southwest of Devils Postpile along San Joaquin River (lat. 37°30'50" N, long. 119°11'25" W; near NW cor. sec. 12, T 5 S, R 25 E). Named on Devils Postpile (1953) 15' quadrangle.

Pine Flat [TULARE]:
(1) *area,* 12 miles southeast of Fairview (lat. 35°47'45" N, long. 118°21'15" W; sec. 31, T 24 S, R 34 E). Named on Kernville (1956) 15' quadrangle. The place also is called Capinero Flat (Wells, p. 21).
(2) *settlement,* 1.25 miles east-southeast of California Hot Springs (lat. 35°52'30" N, long. 118°39' W; in and near sec. 5, T 24 S, R 31 E). Named on California Hot Springs (1958) 15' quadrangle.

Pine Flat Lake: see **Pine Flat Reservoir** [FRESNO].

Pine Flat Reservoir [FRESNO]: *lake,* behind a dam on Kings River 3 miles northeast of Tivy Mountain (lat. 36°49'55" N, long. 119°19'30" W; sec. 2, T 13 S, R 24 E). Named on Patterson Mountain (1952) 15' quadrangle, and on Pine Flat Dam (1965) and Trimmer (1965) 7.5' quadrangles. United States Board on Geographic Names (1972a, p. 4) approved the name "Pine Flat Lake," for the feature, and gave the names "Boone Lake" and "Pine Flat Reservoir" as variants.

Pinehurst [FRESNO]: *settlement,* 6.5 miles east-southeast of Dunlap (lat. 36°41'40" N, long. 119°00'55" W; sec. 23, T 14 S, R 27 E). Named on Miramonte (1966) 7.5' quadrangle. Dinuba (1924) 30' quadrangle shows a place called Neff Mills located at or near the site.

Pine Logging Camp [FRESNO]: *settlement,* 4 miles south-southwest of Dinkey Dome (lat. 37°03'50" N, long. 119°09'40" W; sec. 17, T 10 S, R 26 E). Named on Huntington Lake (1953) 15' quadrangle.

Pine Martin Peak: see **Mount Jepson,** under **Mount Sill** [FRESNO].

Pine Meadow: see **Big Pine Meadow** [TULARE].

Pine Mountain [KERN]: *peak,* 10.5 miles southsoutheast of Woody (lat. 35°33'45" N, long. 118°46'05" W; sec. 20, T 27 S, R 30 E). Named on Pine Mountain (1965) 7.5' quadrangle.

Pine Mountain [TULARE]:
(1) *peak,* 13 miles south of Monache Mountain (lat. 36°01'15" N, long. 118°11'10" W). Named on Monache Mountain (1956) 15'

quadrangle.
(2) *peak,* 2 miles southeast of California Hot Springs (lat. 35°51'25" N, long. 118°39'10" W; sec. 8, T 24 S, R 31 E). Altitude 5214 feet. Named on California Hot Springs (1958) 15' quadrangle.

Pine Mountain Creek: see **Long Tom Gulch** [KERN].

Pine Point [KERN]: *promontory,* 3.5 miles south of Wofford Heights along Isabella Lake (lat. 35°39'25" N, long. 118°26'55" W; at W line sec. 21, T 26 S, R 33 E). Named on Lake Isabella North (1972) 7.5' quadrangle.

Pine Point Campground [MADERA]: *locality,* 6.5 miles southeast of Yosemite Forks on the southwest side of Bass Lake (1) (lat. 37°18'20" N, long. 119°32'25" W; sec. 23, T 7 S, R 22 E). Named on Bass Lake (1953) 15' quadrangle.

Pine Ridge [FRESNO]:
(1) *ridge,* east-northeast- to east-trending, 8 miles long, 3 miles southeast of Shaver Lake Heights (present town of Shaver Lake) (lat. 37°05' N, long. 119°17'30" W). Named on Huntington Lake (1953) and Shaver Lake (1953) 15' quadrangles.
(2) *ridge,* north-northwest-trending, 7 miles long, 8 miles south of Balch Camp (lat. 36°47'30" N, long. 119°07' W). Named on Patterson Mountain (1952) 15' quadrangle.
(3) *village,* 4 miles southwest of Shaver Lake Heights (present town of Shaver Lake) (lat. 37°03'45" N, long. 119°21'30" W; sec. 16, T 10 S, R 24 E); the village is at the west end of Pine Ridge (1). Named on Shaver Lake (1953) 15' quadrangle. California Mining Bureau's (1909b) map has the form "Pineridge" for the name. Postal authorities established Kenyon post office in 1890, changed the name to Pine Ridge in 1892, changed it to Pineridge in 1895, and discontinued it in 1944; the name "Kenyon" was for Silas W. Kenyon, first postmaster (Salley, p. 111, 172).

Pine Ridge [TULARE]: *ridge,* generally west- and west-southwest-trending, 6 miles long, 3 miles north-northeast of Yucca Mountain (lat. 36°36'45" N, long. 118°50'30" W). Named on Giant Forest (1956) 15' quadrangle.

Pines: see **The Pines** [MADERA].

Pines Creek [MADERA]: *stream,* flows nearly 2 miles to Bass Lake (1) 5.5 miles southeast of Yosemite Forks (lat. 37°19'20" N, long. 119°32'45" W; near E line sec. 15, T 7 S, R 22 E). Named on Bass Lake (1953) 15' quadrangle.

Pine Slope Campground [MADERA]: *locality,* nearly 5 miles southeast of Yosemite Forks on the west side of Bass Lake (1) (lat. 37°18'55" N, long. 119°34'20" W; near S line sec. 16, T 7 S, R 22 E). Named on Bass Lake (1953) 15' quadrangle.

Pine Spring [KERN]:
(1) *spring,* nearly 4 miles southeast of Caliente (lat. 35°15'25" N, long. 118°34'25" W; near SE cor. sec. 6, T 31 S, R 32 E). Named on

Oiler Peak (1972) 7.5' quadrangle.

(2) *spring,* 1.5 miles northeast of Emerald Mountain (lat. 35°16'05" N, long. 118°15'40" W; sec. 6, T 31 S, R 35 E). Named on Emerald Mountain (1972) 7.5' quadrangle.

Pine Top Mountain [TULARE]: *peak,* 7 miles west of Mineral King (lat. 36°28'05" N, long 118°43'05" W). Altitude 7915 feet. Named on Mineral King (1956) 15' quadrangle. United States Board on Geographic Names (1933a, p. 605) rejected the name "High Mountain" for the peak.

Pine Tree Canyon [KERN]: *canyon,* 13 miles long, opens into Fremont Valley 14 miles north-northeast of Mojave (lat. 35°13'50" N, long. 118°03'45" W; sec. 13, T 31 S, R 36 E). Named on Cache Peak (1973) and Mojave NE (1973) 7.5' quadrangles. Called Lone Tree Canyon on Mojave (1956) 15' quadrangle, and United States Board on Geographic Names (1975d, p. 4) gave this name as a variant. North Fork branches northwest 7.5 miles above the mouth of the main canyon; it is 4 miles long and is named on Cache Peak (1973) 7.5' quadrangle.

Pinewood Camp [TULARE]: *locality,* nearly 6 miles east of Yucca Mountain (lat. 36°34'25" N, long. 118°45'55" W; sec. 31, T 15 S, R 30 E). Named on Giant Forest (1956) 15' quadrangle.

Pinnacles: see **The Pinnacles** [FRESNO].

Pinnacles Creek: see **East Pinnacles Creek** [FRESNO]; **West Pinnacles Creek** [FRESNO].

Pinnell Camp Ridge [TULARE]: *ridge,* generally west-trending, 1 mile long, 4.25 miles northwest of California Hot Springs (lat. 35° 55'20" N, long. 118°43'30" W). Named on California Hot Springs (1958) 15' quadrangle.

Pintojo Ridge [KINGS]: *ridge,* southeast-trending, 1 mile long. 9.5 miles south of Kettleman City (lat. 35°52'10" N, long. 119°56' W). Named on Avenal Gap (1954) 7.5' quadrangle. The name refers to the appearance of strata that crop out on the ridge—*pintojo* means "spotted" in Spanish (United States Board on Geographic Names, 1933b, p. 23).

Pinto Lake [TULARE]: *lake,* 300 feet long, 2.5 miles north-northeast of Mineral King (lat. 36°29'10" N, long. 118°34'45" W). Named on Mineral King (1956) 15' quadrangle.

Pinyon Creek [KERN]: *stream,* flows 5 miles to Kelso Creek 5 miles west-southwest of Skinner Peak (lat. 35°32'50" N, long. 118°12'35" W; sec. 27, T 27 S, R 35 E). Named on Cane Canyon (1972) 7.5' quadrangle.

Pinyon Mountain [KERN]: *peak,* 28 miles north-northeast of Tehachapi (lat. 35°27'30" N, long. 118°09'25" W; at E line sec. 25, T 28 S, R 35 E). Altitude 6182 feet. Named on Pinyon Mountain (1972) 7.5' quadrangle.

Pinyon Peak [KERN]: *peak,* nearly 4 miles west-northwest of Walker Pass (lat. 35°40'55" N,

long. 118°05'20" W). Altitude 6805 feet. Named on Walker Pass (1972) 7.5' quadrangle.

Pinyon Well [KERN]: *well,* 3.25 miles west of Skinner Peak (lat. 35° 33'30" N, long. 118°10'55" W; near SW cor. sec. 24, T 27 S, R 35 E); the well is along Pinyon Creek. Named on Cane Canyon (1972) 7.5' quadrangle.

Piojo Spring [KERN]: *spring,* 6.5 miles east of Mount Adelaide (lat. 35°26'55" N, long. 118°28'40" W; sec. 34, T 28 S, R 31 E). Named on Mount Adelaide (1972) 7.5' quadrangle.

Pioneer [KERN]: *locality,* 2 miles south-southeast of Maricopa (lat. 35°02'20" N, long. 119°23'05" W; near E line sec. 13, T 11 N, R 24 W). Named on Buena Vista Lake (1912) 30' quadrangle. Postal authorities established Pioneer post office in 1901 and discontinued it in 1909; the first settlers, who considered themselves pioneers, named their community (Salley, p. 172).

Pioneer Basin [KERN]: *valley,* 6 miles north of Mount Abbot (lat. 37°28'45" N, long. 118°48' W). Named on Mount Abbot (1953) 15' quadrangle. Mount Crocker, Mount Hopkins, Mount Huntington, and Mount Stanford, which are called Pioneer Peaks, surround the valley (Hanna, p. 237)—R.B. Marshall of United States Geological Survey named the four peaks for pioneer railroad builders, and also named the valley (Gudde, 1949, p. 264).

Pioneer Basin Lakes [FRESNO]: *lakes,* largest 3200 feet long, 6 miles north of Mount Abbot (lat. 37°28'45" N, long. 118°48' W); the lakes are in Pioneer Basin. Named on Mount Abbot (1953) 15' quadrangle.

Pioneer Peaks: see **Pioneer Basin** [FRESNO].

Pioneer Point [KERN]: *promontory,* 4.25 miles south-southwest of Wofford Heights along Isabella Lake (lat. 35°39'05" N, long. 118° 29' W; near W line sec. 19, T 26 S, R 33 E). Named on Lake Isabella North (1972) 7.5' quadrangle.

Pioneer Point Campground [KERN]: *locality,* 4.25 miles south-southwest of Wofford Heights along Isabella Lake (lat. 35°39'05" N, long. 118°29'10" W; on E line sec. 24, T 26 S, R 32 E); the place is just west of Pioneer Point. Named on Lake Isabella North (1972) 7.5' quadrangle.

Pipe Hill [KINGS]: *peak,* 3.5 miles south-southwest of Kettleman City (lat. 35°57'50" N, long. 119°59'30" W; at N line sec. 2, T 23 S, R 18 E). Named on Los Viejos (1954) 7.5' quadrangle. The name refers to a pipeline across the feature (United States Board on Geographic Names, 1933b, p. 23).

Pipe Lake: see **Old Pipe Lake** [FRESNO].

Pipeline Canyon [TULARE]: *canyon,* drained by a stream that flows 1.25 miles to Capinero Creek 2 miles east-southeast of California Hot Springs (lat. 35°52'15" N, long. 118°38'20"

W; sec. 4, T 24 S, R 31 E). Named on California Hot Springs (1958) 15' quadrangle.

Pippin Flat [TULARE]: *area,* 4 miles east-northeast of Auckland (lat. 36°36'30" N, long. 119°02'05" W; near W line sec. 22, T 15 S, R 27 E). Named on Auckland (1966) 7.5' quadrangle.

Pistol Creek [TULARE]: *stream,* flows 1.5 miles to Shotgun Creek 8 miles south-south-east of Mineral King (lat. 36°20'45" N, long. 118°32' W). Named on Mineral King (1956) 15' quadrangle.

Pitco [KINGS]: *locality,* 2 miles north-northwest of Hanford along Atchison, Topeka and Santa Fe Railroad (lat. 36°21'25" N, long. 119°39'45" W; near N line sec. 23, T 18 S, R 21 E). Named on Hanford (1954) 7.5' quadrangle.

Pitman Creek [FRESNO]: *stream,* formed by the confluence of Tamarack Creek and South Fork Tamarack Creek, flows 2.25 miles to Big Creek (1) east of the town of Big Creek (lat. 37°12'15" N, long. 119°14'15" W; sec. 28, T 8 S, R 25 E). Named on Huntington Lake (1953) 15' quadrangle. Called Pittman Cr. on Lippincott's (1902) map. The name commemorates Elias Pitman, who had a hunting cabin by the stream (Gudde, 1949, p. 264).

Pitney Canyon [KERN]: *canyon,* drained by a stream that flows 1 mile to Oak Creek 7.5 miles south-southeast of Tehachapi (lat. 35°01'20" N, long. 118°24'50" W; near NW cor. sec. 30, T 11 N, R 14 W). Named on Tehachapi South (1966) 7.5' quadrangle.

Piute [KERN]: *locality,* 5.25 miles north-north-east of Paris (present Loraine) (lat. 35°21'55" N, long. 118°22'50" W); the place is 6 miles south of present Piute Peak. Named on Mohave (1915) 30' quadrangle. Postal authorities established Piute post office in 1875, discontinued it in 1876, reestablished it in 1894, and discontinued it in 1918 (Frickstad, p. 58).

Piute Branch: see **Piute Creek** [KERN].

Piute Canyon [KERN]: *canyon,* 7.5 miles long, drained by lower Piute Creek, which joins South Fork San Joaquin River 11 miles north-northwest of Blackcap Mountain (lat. 37°13'25" N, long. 118°50' W). Named on Blackcap Mountain (1953) and Mount Abbot (1953) 15' quadrangles.

Piute Creek [KERN]: *stream,* flows 11.5 miles to South Fork San Joaquin River 11 miles north-northwest of Blackcap Mountain (lat. 37°13'25" N, long. 118°50' W); the stream heads near Piute Pass. Named on Mount Abbot (1953), Mount Goddard (1948), and Mount Tom (1949) 15' quadrangles. Called North Branch on Lippincott's (1902) map. J.N. LeConte called the stream Piute Branch in 1904 to avoid the name "North Branch of South Fork San Joaquin River"—the name "Piute" is from Piute Pass (Browning 1986, p. 171; Farquhar, 1924, p. 64).

Piute Mountains [KERN]: *range,* 32 miles north-northeast of Tehachapi (lat. 35°35' N,

long. 118°18' W). Named on Emerald Mountain (1972), Weldon (1972), and Woolstalf Creek (1972) 7.5' quadrangles.

Piute Pass [FRESNO]: *pass,* 9.5 miles north-northeast of Mount Goddard on Fresno-Inyo county line (lat. 37°14'20" N, long. 118° 41' W); the pass is at the head of Piute Creek. Named on Mount Goddard (1948) 15' quadrangle. J.N. LeConte named the pass for Indians, commonly called Piutes, that used it (Gudde, 1949, p. 266).

Piute Peak [KERN]: *peak,* 22 miles north of Tehachapi (lat. 35°27'05" N, long. 118°23'25" W; sec. 36, T 28 S, R 33 E). Altitude 8417 feet. Named on Piute Peak (1972) 7.5' quadrangle. Called Pahute Pk. on Wheeler's (1875-1878) map, but United States Board on Geographic Names (1933a, p. 607) rejected the forms "Pahute Peak," "Pah-ute Peak," and "Paiute Peak" for the name.

Piute Spring [KERN]: *spring,* 0.25 mile south-southeast of Piute Peak (lat. 35°26'50" N, long. 118°23'20" W; sec. 36, T 28 S, R 33 E). Named on Piute Peak (1972) 7.5' quadrangle. United States Board on Geographic Names (1975b, p. 11) gave the name "Piute Springs" as a variant.

Pixley [TULARE]: *town,* 6 miles north-north-west of Earlimart (lat. 35°58'05" N, long. 119°17'25" W; mainly in sec. 32, T 22 S, R 25 E). Named on Pixley (1954) 7.5' quadrangle. Postal authorities established Pixley post office in 1887 (Frickstad, p. 213). The name is for Frank Pixley, a writer and member of the company that owned the townsite (Mitchell, A.R., p. 69).

Placeritas Creek [KERN]: *stream,* flows 4.25 miles to Walker Basin Creek 4.25 miles north-northeast of Caliente (lat. 35°21'15" N, long. 118°39'20" W). Named on Bena (1972), Breckenridge Mountain (1972), and Mount Adelaide (1972) 7.5' quadrangles.

Placeritas Spring [KERN]: *spring,* 5.25 miles north-northwest of Caliente (lat. 35°21'50" N, long. 118°39'20" W; sec. 33, T 29 S, R 31 E); the spring is along Placeritas Creek. Named on Bena (1972) 7.5' quadrangle.

Plains: see **Tillman** [MADERA].

Plainview [TULARE]: *village,* 5 miles south-southwest of Lindsay (lat. 36°08'40" N, long. 119°07'55" W; on W line sec. 35, T 20 S, R 26 E). Named on Cairns Corner (1950) 7.5' quadrangle.

Plano [TULARE]: *locality,* 2 miles south-south-east of Porterville (lat. 36°02'40" N, long. 119°00'25" W; sec. 1, T 22 S, R 27 E). Named on Porterville (1951) 7.5' quadrangle. Postal authorities established Plano post office in 1871 and discontinued it in 1915 (Frickstad, p. 213). A.J. Adams, the postmaster, selected the name (Mitchell, A.R., p. 69).

Plano: see **Sanborn** [KERN].

Plata Creek: see **Pleito Creek** [KERN].

Plato Creek: see **Pleito Creek** [KERN].

Plaza [TULARE]: *locality,* 2 miles southeast of Goshen (lat. 36°19'35" N, long. 119°24' W; near SW cor. sec. 29, T 18 S, R 24 E). Named on Goshen (1949) 7.5' quadrangle.

Pleasant Valley [FRESNO]: *valley,* around and east of Coalinga (lat. 36°08' N, long. 120°17' W). Named on Alcalde Hills (1969), Avenal (1954), Coalinga (1956), Guijarral Hills (1956), and Kreyenhagen Hills (1956) 7.5' quadrangles. Called Coalinga Valley on Mendenhall's (1908) map. Arnold and Anderson (1908, p. 15) noted that at least part of the valley at the mouth of Los Gatos Creek was known as Pleasant Valley, and suggested that the name be applied to the entire lowland around Coalinga.

Pleasant Valley [TULARE]: *valley,* 3 miles west-southwest of Springville (lat. 36°06'30" N, long. 118°51'30" W). Named on Springville (1957) 15' quadrangle.

Pleasant View [TULARE]: *locality,* 5.5 miles south-southeast of California Hot Springs along Von Hellum Creek (lat. 35°48'15" N, long. 118°38'20" W; near S line sec. 28, T 24 S, R 31 E). Named on California Hot Springs (1958) 15' quadrangle.

Pleitito Creek [KERN]: *stream,* flows 7 miles to lowlands 9 miles west-southwest of Mettler (lat. 35°00'30" N, long. 119°07'40" W; sec. 28, T 11 N, R 21 W). Named on Coal Oil Canyon (1955), Conner SW (1955), Eagle Rest Peak (1942), and Pleito Hills (1958) 7.5' quadrangles. The name is from nearby Pleito Creek (Latta, 1976, p. 215).

Pleito Creek [KERN]: *stream,* flows 13 miles to lowlands 9.5 miles west-southwest of Mettler (lat. 35°00'30" N, long. 119°06'45" W; sec. 27, T 11 N, R 21 W). Named on Coal Oil Canyon (1955), Cuddy Valley (1943), and Pleito Hills (1958) 7.5' quadrangles. The name has been attributed to arguments that Indians of the neighborhood had with the Spanish priests who wanted to take the Indians to Santa Barbara mission—*pleito* means "argument" or "debate" in Spanish (Latta, 1976, p. 215). Joy (p. 51) called the stream Plato Creek, but United States Board on Geographic Names (1933a, p. 609) rejected the forms "Plato Creek," "Plata Creek," and "Pieto Creek" for the name.

Pleito Hills [KERN]: *range,* 5 miles east-northeast of Eagle Rest Peak (lat. 34°56'15" N, long. 119°03' W); the range is east of Pleito Creek. Named on Pleito Hills (1958) 7.5' quadrangle.

Pocket Lake [FRESNO]: *lake,* 550 feet long, 16 miles northeast of Kaiser Peak (lat. 37°28'55" N, long. 119°01' W). Named on Kaiser Peak (1953) 15 quadrangle.

Pocket Meadow [FRESNO]: *area,* 7.5 miles west-northwest of Mount Abbot along North Fork Mono Creek (lat. 37°26'05" N, long. 118°54'30" W). Named on Mount Abbot (1953) 15' quadrangle.

Pogue Canyon [TULARE]: *canyon,* drained by a stream that flows 1.25 miles to Dry Creek (1) 4.25 miles east of Woodlake (lat. 36° 25'35" N, long. 119°01'20" W; sec. 26, T 17 S, R 27 E). Named on Woodlake (1952) 7.5' quadrangle.

Point of Rocks [KERN]: *ridge,* southeast-trending, 1 mile long, 8 miles east-southeast of Orchard Peak (lat. 35°41'35" N, long. 120° 00'15" W). Named on Emigrant Hill (1953) and Sawtooth Ridge (1961) 7.5' quadrangles. Spaniards called the ridge Las Tinajas de los Indios; it has natural holes that hold water from winter rains, and apparently it was an important Indian camp—*tinajas* means "tanks" in Spanish (Hoover, Rensch, and Rensch, p. 128).

Poison Meadow [FRESNO]: *area,* 11 miles west-southwest of Mount Abbot along South Fork San Joaquin River (lat. 37°19' N, long. 118°58'35" W). Named on Mount Abbot (1953) 15' quadrangle.

Poison Meadow [MADERA]: *area,* 6.25 miles east-northeast of Yosemite Forks (lat. 37°23'50" N, long. 119°31'15" W; sec. 24, T 6 S, R 22 E). Named on Bass Lake (1953) 15' quadrangle.

Poison Meadow [TULARE]:
(1) *area,* on the northwest side of Shell Mountain (lat. 36°41'50" N, long. 118°47'50" W; mainly in sec. 23, T 14 S, R 29 E). Named on Giant Forest (1956) 15' quadrangle. According to United States Board on Geographic Names (1987b, p. 2), Poison Meadow is at the west base of Shell Mountain (lat. 36°41'50" N, long. 118°48'30" W; sec. 22, T 14 S, R 29 E).
(2) *area,* 6.25 miles east of Fairview (lat. 35°55'30" N, long. 118° 23'10" W; sec. 14, T 23 S, R 33 E). Named on Kernville (1956) 15' quadrangle.
(3) *area,* 6 miles east-southeast of California Hot Springs (lat. 35° 50'50" N, long. 118°34'30" W; near NE cor. sec. 13, T 24 S, R 31 E). Named on California Hot Springs (1958) 15' quadrangle.

Poison Meadow Creek [TULARE]: *stream,* flows 4 miles to Brush Creek 5 miles northeast of Fairview (lat. 35°57'55" N, long. 118° 25'15" W; sec. 33, T 22 S, R 33 E); the stream heads at Poison Meadow (2). Named on Kernville (1956) 15' quadrangle.

Poison Oak Canyon [KINGS]: *canyon,* drained by a stream that flows 1 mile to Falls Canyon 9.5 miles south-southwest of Avenal (lat. 35°52'50" N, long. 120°12'30" W; sec. 35, T 23 S, R 16 E). Named on Garza Peak (1953) and Tent Hills (1942) 7.5' quadrangles.

Poison Oak Spring [KERN]:
(1) *spring,* 2.25 miles north-northeast of Caliente (lat. 35°19'15" N, long. 118°37' W). Named on Oiler Peak (1972) 7.5' quadrangle.
(2) *spring,* nearly 4 miles east-southeast of Caliente (lat. 35°16'15" N, long. 118°33'55"

W; sec. 32, T 30 S, R 32 E). Named on Oiler Peak (1972) 7.5' quadrangle.

Poison Oak Spring [TULARE]: *spring,* 3.5 miles northwest of California Hot Springs (lat. 35°54'40" N, long. 118°43'20" W; sec. 22, T 23 S, R 30 E). Named on California Hot Springs (1958) 15' quadrangle.

Poison Ridge [FRESNO]: *ridge,* west-north-west-trending, 2 miles long, 3.25 miles north-northeast of Balch Camp (lat. 36°57' N, long. 119°06' W). Named on Patterson Mountain (1952) 15' quadrangle.

Poison Spring [KERN]: *spring,* 3 miles west-southwest of Garlock (lat. 35°23'40" N, long. 117°50'15" W). Named on Garlock (1967) 7.5' quadrangle.

Poison Switch: see **Wassamma** [MADERA].

Poleline Canyon [KERN]: *canyon,* drained by a stream that flows 2.5 miles to Jawbone Canyon 3.5 miles north of Cinco (lat. 35°18'45" N, long. 118°01'45" W; sec. 20, T 30 S, R 37 E). Named on Cinco (1972) 7.5' quadrangle.

Polemonium Peak: see **North Palisade** [FRESNO].

Pollasky: see **Friant** [FRESNO].

Polonia Valley: see **Polonio Pass** [KERN].

Polonio Pass [KERN]: *valley,* 3.5 miles west-southwest of Orchard Peak on Kern-San Luis Obispo county line (lat. 35°43'30" N, long. 120°11'35" W). Named on Orchard Peak (1961) 7.5' quadrangle. Angel (1890a, p. 569) mentioned Polonia Valley.

Polvadero Gap [FRESNO]: *pass,* 9 miles east of Coalinga between Guijarral Hills and Kettleman Hills (lat. 36°07'15" N, long. 120°11'45" W). Named on Avenal (1954) and Guijarral Hills (1956) 7.5' quadrangles. Arnold and Anderson (1908, p. 15) attributed the name to dust storms common at the place, and noted the incorrect form "Pulvero" for the name. *Polvadera* and *polvadero* are dialectal variations of *polvareda,* which means "dust storm" or "cloud of dust" in Spanish (Stewart, p. 380). Postal authorities established Pulvadera post office 8 miles southwest of Huron in 1880 and discontinued it in 1882 (Salley, p. 178).

Polvodero Creek: see **Los Gatos Creek** [FRESNO].

Ponca [TULARE]: *locality,* 2 miles south of Porterville along Southern Pacific Railroad (lat. 36°02'30" N, long. 119°01' W; at W line sec. 1, T 22 S, R 27 E). Named on Porterville (1951) 7.5' quadrangle.

Pond [KERN]: *village,* 8.5 miles north of Wasco (lat. 35°43'05" N, long. 119°19'40" W; at NW cor. sec. 31, T 25 S, R 25 E). Named on Pond (1953) 7.5' quadrangle, which shows Pondham school located 1 mile to the east. The community began about 1889 (Bailey, 1967, p. 21). Postal authorities established Pond post office in 1912; the name is from the word "Pondham" (Salley, p. 176). California Mining Bureau's (1917c) map shows a place called

Smyrna located 8 miles west of Pond. Postal authorities established Smyrna post office in 1888 and discontinued it in 1889; the name was for Smyrna, Turkey, the source of imported fig trees planted at the place (Salley, p. 207).

Pond Meadow [TULARE]: *area,* 13 miles northwest of Triple Divide Peak (lat. 36°43' N, long. 118°43' W; near SE cor. sec. 9, T 14 S, R 30 E). Named on Triple Divide Peak (1956) 15' quadrangle. United States Board on Geographic Names (1933a, p. 613) rejected the name "Tamarack Meadow" for the feature.

Pond Lily Lake [MADERA]: *lake,* nearly 6 miles south of Devils Postpile (lat. 37°32'30" N, long. 119°06'05" W). Named on Devils Postpile (1953) 15' quadrangle.

Pond Lily Lake: see **Sotcher Lake** [MADERA].

Pool's Ferry: see **Reedley** [FRESNO].

Pool's Fort: see **Reedley** [FRESNO].

Poop Out Pass [TULARE]: *pass,* 1 mile east-southeast of Shell Mountain (lat. 36°41'15" N, long. 118°46'50" W; sec. 24, T 14 S, R 29 E). Named on Giant Forest (1956) 15' quadrangle.

Popes Valley: see **Watts Valley** [FRESNO].

Poplar [TULARE]: *town,* 4 miles southeast of Woodville (lat. 36°03'20" N, long. 119°08'35" W; on E line sec. 34, T 21 S, R 26 E). Named on Woodville (1950) 7.5' quadrangle. Postal authorities established Poplar post office in 1880 and discontinued it in 1907 (Frickstad, p. 213). Arthur Carpenter named the place in 1879 for poplar trees around his home (Mitchell, A.R., p. 69). Postal authorities established Belleville post office 10 miles southwest of Poplar in 1882, moved it 4.5 miles northeast in 1889, and discontinued it in 1892 (Salley, p. 17).

Porphyry Lake [MADERA]: *lake,* 500 feet long, 3.25 miles east of Merced Peak (lat. 37°37'45" N, long. 119°20' W). Named on Merced Peak (1953) 15' quadrangle.

Porque: see **Treadwell** [KERN].

Porsiuncula River: see **Kern River** [KERN-TULARE].

Portal: see **Big Creek** [FRESNO] (3).

Portal Lake [FRESNO]: *lake,* 500 feet long, nearly 3 miles southeast of Blackcap Mountain (lat. 37°02'35" N, long. 118°45'25" W). Named on Blackcap Mountain (1953) 15' quadrangle.

Porter Slough [TULARE]: *water feature,* heads at Tule River 4 miles east-southeast of downtown Porterville, and extends through Porterville into lowlands. Named on Porterville (1951, photorevised 1969), Success Dam (1956), and Woodville (1950) 7.5' quadrangles, which show a partly dry watercourse. Called Porters Slough on Cairns Corner (1927) 7.5' quadrangle.

Porters Trading Post: see **Porterville** [TULARE].

Porterville [TULARE]: *city,* 24 miles southeast of Visalia where Tule River enters lowlands (lat. 36°04'15" N, long. 119°01' W). Named on Porterville (1951) and Success Dam (1956) 7.5' quadrangles. Tule River station of Butterfield Overland stage line was at the site, and after Royal Porter Putnam started a hotel and trading post there, the place was known as Porters Trading Post, Porterville, and Putnamville (Hanna, p. 241). Postal authorities established Tule post office in 1859, changed the name to Portersville in 1871, and to Porterville in 1915 (Frickstad, p. 213, 214). The city incorporated in 1902. Postal authorities established North Tule post office 23 miles northeast of Porterville (SE quarter sec. 14, T 20 S, R 29 E) in 1874 and discontinued it the same year (Salley, p. 157). Goodyear (1888b, p. 649) noted that a place called Connor Station, or Eighteen-mile House, was located about 17 miles from Visalia on the road to Porterville, and a place called Vandalia was located on the left bank of Tule River at a ford about a mile beyond Porterville and 10.5 miles from Connor Station. California Mining Bureau's (1917b) map shows a place called Kurth located along the railroad just north of Porterville. California Division of Highways' (1934) map shows a place called Pernu located at the end of a rail line 3 miles east of Porterville (near S line sec. 28, T 21 S, R 28 E), a place called Pernu Jct. situated along Southern Pacific Railroad 1 mile farther south (near S line sec. 33, T 21 S, R 28 E), and a place called Tandy located along the railroad 3.5 miles east of Porterville between Pernu Junction and Pernu (sec. 33, T 21 S, R 28 E).

Portex [TULARE]: *locality,* 5.5 miles southeast of Lindsay along Visalia Electric Railroad (lat. 36°08'45" N, long. 119°01'30" W; near W line sec. 35, T 20 S, R 27 E). Named on Lindsay (1928) 7.5' quadrangle.

Portuguese Canyon [FRESNO]: *canyon,* drained by a stream that flows 1.25 miles to enter an unnamed canyon 2 miles west-south-west of Joaquin Rocks (lat. 36°18'35" N, long. 120°29' W; sec. 6, T 19 S, R 14 E). Named on Joaquin Rocks (1969) 7.5' quadrangle.

Portuguese Creek [MADERA]: *stream,* flows 3.5 miles to Chiquito Creek 8.5 miles northnortheast of Shuteye Peak (lat. 37°28'10" N, long. 119°22'45" W; sec. 30, T 5 S, R 24 E). Named on Merced Peak (1953) and Shuteye Peak (1953) 15' quadrangles.

Portuguese Meadow [TULARE]: *area,* 8 miles southeast of California Hot Springs (lat. 35°48' N, long. 118°34'30" W; near E line sec. 36, T 24 S, R 31 E). Named on California Hot Springs (1958) 15' quadrangle.

Portuguese Pass [TULARE]: *pass,* 7.5 miles southeast of California Hot Springs (lat. 35°48' N, long. 118°34'50" W; sec. 36, T 24

S, R 31 E); the pass is less than 1 mile northeast of Portuguese Peak. Named on California Hot Springs (1958) 15' quadrangle.

Portuguese Peak [TULARE]: *peak,* 8 miles southeast of California Hot Springs (lat. 35°47'30" N, long. 118°35'05" W; near S line sec. 36, T 24 S, R 31 E). Altitude 7914 feet. Named on California Hot Springs (1958) 15' quadrangle.

Posa Creek: see Poso Creek [KERN-TULARE].

Pose Creek: see Poso Creek [KERN-TULARE].

Posé Flat: see Poso Flat [KERN].

Posey [TULARE]: *village,* 5.25 miles south of California Hot Springs (lat. 35°48'20" N, long. 118°40'50" W; around SE cor. sec. 25, T 24 S, R 30 E). Named on California Hot Springs (1958) 15' quadrangle. Postal authorities established Posey post office in 1915 (Frickstad, p. 213).

Posey Creek: see Poso Creek [KERN-TULARE].

Posey Flats: see Poso Flat [KERN].

Posey Station: see Poso Creek [KERN-TULARE].

Poso: see Famoso [KERN]; Mount Poso [KERN].

Poso Camp: see Poso Park [TULARE].

Poso Creek [KERN-TULARE]: *stream,* formed by the confluence of Van Hellum Creek and Spear Creek in Tulare County, flows 60 miles to lowlands 1.5 miles east-southeast of Famoso in Kern County (lat. 35°35' N, long. 119°10'55" W; near NW cor. sec. 16, T 27 S, R 26 E). Named on California Hot Springs (1958) 15' quadrangle, and on Allensworth (1954), Democrat Hot Springs (1972), Famoso (1953), Glennville (1972), Knob Hill (1965), McFarland (1954), North of Oildale (1954), Pine Mountain (1965), and Pond (1953) 7.5' quadrangles. Called Pose Cr. on Blake's (1857) map. Goddard's (1857) map has the designation "Occoya or Posa C." for the stream, and Williamson (p. 14) used the form "O-co-ya Creek" for the name. The stream also was called Posey Creek (Wines, p. 86). The name "Poso" is descriptive of pools found along the stream during the dry season—*posa* means "pool" and *poso* means "well" in Spanish (Boyd, p. 153). Posey Station was a stop at Poso Creek for Butterfield Overland stage line from 1858 to 1861 (Bailey, 1967, p. 21).

Poso Creek: see Little Poso Creek [KERN].

Poso Drain 1 [FRESNO]: *water feature,* extends for 3.5 miles to Poso Slough 6.5 miles north-northwest of Firebaugh (lat. 36°57'05" N, long. 120°29'40" W; sec. 25, T 11 S, R 13 E). Named on Poso Farm (1962) 7.5' quadrangle. The feature now is considered to carry the lower reach of Poso Slough (United States Board on Geographic Names, 1964a, p. 13).

Poso Drain 2 [FRESNO]: *water feature,* extends for 2.5 miles to Poso Drain 1 about 6 miles north-northwest of Firebaugh (lat. 36° 56'20" N, long. 120°29'15" W; sec. 30, T 11 S, R 14 E). Named on Poso Farm (1962) 7.5' quadrangle.

Poso Flat [KERN]: *valley,* along Poso Creek above a point 5 miles northwest of Democrat Hot Springs (lat. 35°34'45" N, long. 118° 43'35" W). Named on Democrat Hot Springs (1972), Glennville (1972), Pine Mountain (1965), and Woody (1965) 7.5' quadrangles. Whitney (1865, p. 221) mentioned Posé Flat and Little Posé Flat. The feature also was called Posey Flats (Wines, p. 86). Postal authorities established Pozo Flat post office 9 miles east of Elmer post office at or near present Poso Flat in 1891 and discontinued it the same year (Salley, p. 177).

Poso Park [TULARE]: *settlement,* 5.25 miles south-southeast of California Hot Springs along Spear Creek (lat. 35°48'40" N, long. 118°38'05" W; sec. 28, T 24 S, R 31 E). Named on California Hot Springs (1958) 15' quadrangle. Called Poso Camp on Tobias Peak (1943) 30' quadrangle.

Poso Slough [TULARE]: *water feature,* extends for 8 miles from near San Joaquin River to Merced County 6.5 miles north-northwest of Oxalis (lat. 37°00'20" N, long. 120°35'20" W; sec. 6, T 11 S, R 13 E). Named on Santa Rita Park (1962) 15' quadrangle, and on Oxalis (1956) and Poso Farm (1962) 7.5' quadrangles. United States Board on Geographic Names (1964a, p. 13) rejected the names "Paso Slough" and "Poso Drain 1" for the feature; by this decision the former Poso Drain 1 is considered to be part of Poso Slough.

Post Canyon [FRESNO]: *canyon,* drained by a stream that flows 4.5 miles to Los Gatos Creek 6.5 miles northwest of Coalinga (lat. 36° 12'15" N, long. 120°26'20" W; sec. 10, T 20 S, R 14 E). Named on Alcalde Hills (1969) and Sherman Peak (1969) 7.5' quadrangles.

Post Corral Creek [FRESNO]: *stream,* flows 9 miles to North Fork Kings River 6.25 miles west of Blackcap Mountain (lat. 37°05'05" N, long. 118°54'15" W; sec. 3, T 10 S, R 28 E); the stream goes through Post Corral Meadows. Named on Blackcap Mountain (1953) 15' quadrangle.

Post Corral Meadows [FRESNO]: *area,* 7.5 miles northwest of Blackcap Mountain (lat. 37°08' N, long. 118°54' W; sec. 22, T 9 S, R 28 E). Named on Blackcap Mountain (1953) 15' quadrangle.

Post Creek [MADERA]: *stream,* flows 3.25 miles to West Fork Granite Creek 5.25 miles southeast of Merced Peak (lat. 37°34'50" N, long. 119°19'40" W); the stream heads near Post Peak. Named on Merced Peak (1953) 15' quadrangle.

Post Lakes [MADERA]: *lakes,* two, each about 700 feet long, nearly 3 miles east-southeast of Merced Peak (lat. 37°37'35" N, long. 119°20'40" W); the lakes are 1 mile west of

Post Peak. Named on Merced Peak (1953) 15' quadrangle.

Post Peak [MADERA]: *peak,* 3.5 miles east of Merced Peak (lat. 37° 37'45" N, long. 119°19'40" W). Altitude 11,009 feet. Named on Merced Peak (1953) 15' quadrangle. R.B. Marshall of United States Geological Survey named the peak for William S. Post, an employee of the Survey (United States Board on Geographic Names, 1934a, p. 19).

Post Peak Pass [MADERA]: *pass,* 3.5 miles east of Merced Peak (lat. 37°37'50" N, long. 119°19'40" W); the pass is north of Post Peak. Named on Merced Peak (1953) 15' quadrangle.

Po-sun-co-la River: see **Kern River** [KERN-TULARE].

Posuncula Lake: see **Kern Lake Bed** [KERN].

Potato Butte: see **Black Peak** [FRESNO].

Potato Hill [TULARE]: *peak,* 10.5 miles south of Kaweah (lat. 36° 19'10" N, long. 118°56'35" W; sec. 33, T 18 S, R 28 E). Altitude 2878 feet. Named on Kaweah (1957) 15' quadrangle.

Potato Mountain: see **Black Peak** [FRESNO].

Potato Patch [KERN]:
(1) *area,* nearly 5 miles east of Kernville along Caldwell Creek (lat. 35°45'40" N, long. 118°20'30" W; near NE cor. sec. 17, T 25 S, R 34 E). Named on Kernville (1956) 15' quadrangle.
(2) *area,* 3 miles south of Alta Sierra (lat. 35°41'05" N, long. 118° 33'20" W; sec. 8, T 26 S, R 32 E). Named on Alta Sierra (1972) 7.5' quadrangle.

Pothole: see **The Pothole** [TULARE].

Pothole Creek [TULARE]: *stream,* flows 3 miles to Deer Creek (2) 6.5 miles northeast of Fountain Springs (lat. 35°57'15" N, long. 118°49'35" W; sec. 3, T 23 S, R 29 E); the stream heads at The Pothole. Named on Gibbon Peak (1965) 7.5' quadrangle.

Potholes: see **East Potholes** [TULARE].

Potholes Meadow: see **East Potholes Meadow**, under **East Potholes** [TULARE].

Potter Creek [FRESNO]: *stream,* flows 2.5 miles to Rancheria Creek (1) 3 miles south-southeast of Kaiser Peak (lat. 37°15'20" N, long. 119°09'35" W; sec. 5, T 8 S, R 26 E). Named on Kaiser Peak (1953) 15' quadrangle.

Potter Pass [FRESNO]: *pass,* 2.5 miles east of Kaiser Peak (lat. 37° 14'15" N, long. 119°08'25" W; sec. 28, T 7 S, R 26 E); the pass is near the head of Potter Creek. Named on Kaiser Peak (1953) 15' quadrangle.

Pottinger: see **Mama Pottinger Canyon** [KERN].

Pottinger Canyon [KERN]: *canyon,* 2.5 miles long, opens into Little Santa Maria Valley 6.5 miles west of McKittrick (lat. 35°18'30" N, long. 119°44'10" W; near S line sec. 17, T 30 S, R 21 E). Named on McKittrick Summit (1959) and Reward (1951) 7.5' quadrangles.

Potwisha [TULARE]: *locality,* 5.5 miles southeast of Yucca Mountain near the confluence of Middle Fork Kaweah River and Marble Fork Kaweah River (lat. 36°30'05" N, long. 118°48' W). Named on Giant Forest (1956) 15' quadrangle. Tehipite (1903) 30' quadrangle shows Potwisha Camp at the place. The name commemorates an Indian tribe that lived in the neighborhood (United States Board on Geographic Names, 1933a, p. 617).

Potwisha Camp: see **Potwisha** [TULARE].

Powder Horn Meadow [TULARE]: *area,* 5.5 miles northeast of California Hot Springs (lat. 35°56'25" N, long. 118°36'15" W; near SW cor. sec. 11, T 23 S, R 31 E). Named on California Hot Springs (1958) 15' quadrangle.

Powell: see **Mount Powell** [FRESNO].

Powell Meadow [TULARE]: *area,* 4.5 miles southwest of Monache Mountain (lat. 36°09'15" N, long. 118°14'50" W; sec. 25, T 20 S, R 34 E). Named on Monache Mountain (1956) 15' quadrangle. Called Powell Meadows on Olancha (1907) 30' quadrangle, but United States Board on Geographic Names (1988b, p. 2) rejected the names "Powell Meadows" and "Powers Meadow" for the place.

Powers Meadow: see **Powell Meadow** [TULARE].

Powers Well [KERN]: *well,* 6 miles west-northwest of Inyokern in Indian Wells Canyon (lat. 35°40'40" N, long. 117°54'45" W; sec. 17, T 26 S, R 38 E). Named on Owens Peak (1972) 7.5' quadrangle.

Pozo Flat: see **Poso Flat** [KERN].

Prater: see **Mount Prater** [FRESNO].

Prather [FRESNO]: *settlement,* 25 miles northwest of Fresno (lat. 37°02'15" N, long. 119°30'45" W; near NE cor. sec. 25, T 10 S, R 22 E). Named on Millerton Lake East (1965) 7.5' quadrangle. Postal authorities established Prather post office in 1914, discontinued it in 1935, reestablished it in 1936, and moved it 1.25 miles southwest in 1939 (Salley, p. 177). The name is for Joseph L. Prather, who came to California in 1872 and eventually settled on a ranch at the site where the later settlement is located (Hanna, p. 243-244).

Prather Pond [FRESNO]: *intermittent lake,* 1000 feet long, 8 miles west of Selma (lat. 36°33'05" N, long. 119°45' W; sec. 12, T 16 S, R 20 E). Named on Caruthers (1963) and Conejo (1963) 7.5' quadrangles. Selma (1946) 15' quadrangle shows a permanent lake.

Pratton [FRESNO]: *locality,* 6 miles west of downtown Fresno along Southern Pacific Railroad (lat. 36°44'45" N, long. 119°53'30" W; sec. 3, T 14 S, R 19 E). Named on Kearney Park (1963) 7.5' quadrangle.

Precipice Lake [TULARE]: *lake,* 1000 feet long, 3.25 miles south-southwest of Triple Divide Peak along Hamilton Creek (lat. 36°33'05" N, long. 118°33'35" W). Named on Triple Divide Peak (1956) 15' quadrangle. United States Board on Geographic Names (1968b, p. 9) rejected the name "Hamilton

Lake" for the feature.

Prefedio Creek [KERN]: *stream,* flows 2.5 miles to Kern River near Democrat Hot Springs (lat. 35°31'50" N, long. 118°39'55" W; at S line sec. 32, T 27 S, R 31 E). Named on Democrat Hot Springs (1972) 7.5' quadrangle.

Prefedio Spring [KERN]: *spring,* 1.5 miles north-northwest of Democrat Hot Springs (lat. 35°32'45" N, long. 118°40'50" W; near SE cor. sec. 30, T 27 S, R 31 E); the spring is along Prefedio Creek. Named on Democrat Hot Springs (1972) 7.5' quadrangle. Glennville (1956) 15' quadrangle has the plural form "Prefedio Springs" for the name.

Prewett Station: see **Bates Station** [MADERA].

Prewit [TULARE]: *locality,* 5 miles southeast of Lindsay along Visalia Electric Railroad (lat. 36°09'30" N, long. 119°01'20" W; sec. 26, T 20 S, R 27 E). Named on Lindsay (1928) 7.5' quadrangle.

Prices Camp [FRESNO]: *locality,* 16 miles northeast of Piedra along Dinkey Creek (lat. 36°57'20" N, long. 19°08'35" W). Named on Dinuba (1924) 30' quadrangle.

Primero [TULARE]: *locality,* 7 miles northeast of Dinuba along Atchison, Topeka and Santa Fe Railroad (lat. 36°36' N, long. 119° 17'05" W; near NW cor. sec. 29, T 15 S, R 25 E). Named on Sultana (1923) 7.5' quadrangle. The place is the first station north of Orosi on the railroad branch line to Porterville—*primero* means "first" in Spanish (Gudde, 1949, p. 273).

Primrose Lake [TULARE]: *lake,* 1200 feet long, 4 miles south-southeast of Mount Whitney (lat. 36°31'15" N, long. 118°16'30" W). Named on Mount Whitney (1956) 15' quadrangle. Chester Versteeg proposed the name (Browning 1986, p. 175), which is for the abundance of wild primroses on the shore of the lake (United States Board on Geographic Names, 1938, p. 43).

Proctor: see **Monolith** [KERN].

Proctor Lake [KERN]: *lake,* 6900 feet long, 6 miles east of Tehachapi (lat. 35°07' N, long. 118°20'45" W; sec. 27, 29, T 32 S, R 34 E). Named on Tehachapi (1943) 15' quadrangle. On Monolith (1966) 7.5' quadrangle, the name applies to a dry lake. John Narbo collected salt in the 1860's at the shallow lake, which he called Narboe Lake (Barras, p. 10-11); the feature also was called Salt Lake (Barras, p. 52) and Tehachapi Lake (Bailey, 1962, p. 43).

Profile View [TULARE]: *relief feature,* 14 miles west-northwest of Triple Divide Peak (lat. 36°42' N, long. 118°44'30" W; near N line sec. 20, T 14 S, R 30 E). Named on Triple Divide Peak (1956) 15' quadrangle.

Progress: see **Conner** [KERN].

Prospero [KERN]: *locality,* 10 miles northwest of Bakersfield along Southern Pacific Railroad (lat. 35°28'15" N, long. 119°07'30" W; at S line sec. 24, T 28 S, R 26 E). Named on Oildale (1954) and Rosedale (1954) 7.5' quadrangles.

Providence Creek [FRESNO]: *stream,* flows about 2.5 miles to Big Creek (2) 8 miles southwest of Dinkey Dome (lat. 37°02'15" N, long. 119°14'35" W; near NE cor. sec. 28, T 10 S, R 25 E). Named on Huntington Lake (1953) 15' quadrangle. Kaiser (1904) 30' quadrangle shows Providence mine near the head of the stream.

Pueblo de las Juntas: see **Mendota** [FRESNO].

Puerta del Suelo: see **Cerro Noroeste** [KERN].

Pulvadera: see **Polvadero Gap** [FRESNO].

Pumice Butte [FRESNO]: *peak,* 3 miles northnorthwest of Double Peak (lat. 37°33'10" N, long. 119°03'35" W). Altitude 9533 feet. Named on Devils Postpile (1953) 15' quadrangle.

Pumice Flat [MADERA]: *area,* 1.5 miles north of Devils Postpile along Middle Fork San Joaquin River (lat. 37°39' N, long. 119°04'30" W). Named on Devils Postpile (1953) 15' quadrangle. Waring (p. 239) noted that a meadow located 2 miles south of Pumice Flat is known as Soda Spring Flat for a small spring of carbonated water there that is well known to campers.

Pumice Gap: see **Mammoth Pass** [MADERA].

Pumpkin Canyon [TULARE]: *canyon,* drained by a stream that flows 2 miles to White River (1) 4.25 miles southwest of California Hot Springs (lat. 35°50'15" N, long. 118°43'25" W; sec. 15, T 24 S, R 30 E). Named on California Hot Springs (1958) 15' quadrangle.

Pumpkin Center [KERN]: *town,* 7.5 miles south-southwest of Bakersfield (lat. 35°16' N, long. 119°02' W; on S line sec. 36, T 30 S, R 27 E). Named on Gosford (1954) 7.5' quadrangle. Postal authorities established Pumpkin Center post office in 1945 (Salley, p. 178). The name originated with a crop of pumpkins grown near the place in 1932 (Bailey, 1967, p. 22).

Pup Meadow [TULARE]: *area,* 5.25 miles eastnortheast of California Hot Springs (lat. 35°53'45" N, long. 118°34'45" W; sec. 25, T 23 S, R 31 E). Named on California Hot Springs (1958) 15' quadrangle.

Puppet Lake [FRESNO]: *lake,* 3300 feet long, 3.5 miles west-northwest of Mount Humphreys (lat. 37°17'10" N, long. 118°44' W). Named on Mount Tom (1949) 15' quadrangle.

Purdie Canyon Spring [KERN]: *spring,* 6 miles west-southwest of Liebre Twins (lat. 34°56'10" N, long. 118°40'20" W); the spring is near the west end of Purdie Ridge. Named on Winters Ridge (1966) 7.5' quadrangle.

Purdie Ridge [KERN]: *ridge,* west-southwest of Liebre Twins (lat. 34°56'10" N, long. 118°39'45" W; at N line sec. 23, T 10 N, R 17 W). Named on Winters Ridge (1966) 7.5' quadrangle.

Purdie Spring [KERN]: *spring,* 5 miles westsouthwest of Liebre Twins (lat. 34°56'10" N, long. 118°39'30" W; near N line sec. 23, T 10 N, R 17 W). Named on Winters Ridge (1966)

7.5' quadrangle.

Purple Creek [FRESNO]: *stream,* flows 5.5 miles to Fish Creek (1) 5.5 miles west of Red Slate Mountain in Cascade Valley (lat. 37° 30'40" N, long. 118°58'15" W); Purple Lake is along the stream. Named on Mount Morrison (1953) 15' quadrangle.

Purple Lake [FRESNO]: *lake,* 0.5 mile long, 4.5 miles west-northwest of Red Slate Mountain (lat. 37°31'45" N, long. 118°56'45" W). Named on Mount Morrison (1953) 15' quadrangle. The name is for the purple tint of water in the lake at certain times (Smith, Genny, p. 49).

Putman Canyon: see **Snowslide Canyon** [TULARE].

Putnam Canyon [TULARE]: *canyon,* drained by a stream that flows 1.5 miles to South Fork Kaweah River 11.5 miles southwest of Mineral King (lat. 36°20'50" N, long. 118°45'05" W). Named on Mineral King (1956) 15' quadrangle. Called Snowslide Canyon on Kaweah (1909) 30' quadrangle, where present Snowslide Canyon is called Putman Canyon. United States Board on Geographic Names (1960b, p. 20) rejected the name "Snowslide Canyon" for present Putnam Canyon, and listed the name "Putnam Creek" for the stream in the canyon.

Putnam Creek: see **Putnam Canyon** [TULARE].

Putnamville: see **Porterville** [TULARE].

Pylema: see **Bakersfield** [KERN].

Pyles Camp [TULARE]: *locality,* 8 miles southwest of Hockett Peak along Freeman Creek (lat. 36°08'20" N, long. 118°28'35" W). Named on Hockett Peak (1956) 15' quadrangle.

Pyramid: see **The Pyramid**, under **Painted Lady** [FRESNO].

Pyramid Hill [KERN]: *ridge,* east-southeasttrending, 1.5 miles long, 6.5 miles northwest of Mount Adelaide (lat. 35°29'30" N, long. 118°49'45" W). Named on Rio Bravo Ranch (1954) 7.5' quadrangle.

Pyramid Hills [KERN-KINGS]: *ridge,* northnorthwest- to northwest-trending, 6.5 miles long, 14 miles south-southeast of Avenal on Kern-Kings county line, mainly in Kings County (lat. 35°50' N, long. 120°02'30" W). Named on Pyramid Hills (1953) 7.5' quadrangle. Arnold and Anderson (1908, p. 14) named the feature because it is "capped by a succession of conical hills, which when viewed from the east appear like isolated pyramids." United States Board on Geographic Names (1933a, p. 627) rejected the names "Los Piramidos" and "The Pyramids" for the ridge.

Pyramid Peak [FRESNO]: *peak,* 4.25 miles southwest of Mount Pinchot (lat. 36°54'20" N, long. 118°27'40" W). Altitude 12,777 feet. Named on Mount Pinchot (1953) 15' quadrangle.

Pyramids: see **The Pyramids**, under **Pyramid Hills** [KERN-KINGS].

— Q —

Quail [TULARE]: *locality,* 3.5 miles south of Tipton along Southern Pacific Railroad (lat. 36°00'35" N, long. 119°18'10" W; near SW cor. sec. 17, T 22 S, R 25 E). Named on Tipton (1950) 7.5' quadrangle. Postal authorities established Quail post office in 1912 and discontinued it in 1914 (Frickstad, p. 213).

Quail Canyon [KERN]: *canyon,* drained by a stream that flows 1.25 miles to Oak Creek Canyon 7.5 miles south of Tehachapi (lat. 35°01'25" N, long. 118°25'20" W; near S line sec. 24, T 11 N, R 15 W). Named on Tehachapi South (1966) 7.5' quadrangle.

Quail Flat [TULARE]:
(1) *area,* 3 miles east-southeast of Wilsonia (lat. 36°43'20" N, long. 118°54'25" W; sec. 11, T 14 S, R 28 E). Named on Giant Forest (1956) 15' quadrangle.
(2) *valley,* 5.5 miles south-southeast of Auckland (lat. 36°30'55" N, long. 119°03'45" W; sec. 20, 29, T 16 S, R 27 E). Named on Auckland (1966) 7.5' quadrangle. Called Quail Valley on Dunlap (1944) 15' quadrangle.

Quail Meadows [FRESNO]: *areas,* two, 8 miles west-northwest of Mount Abbot along Mono Creek (lat. 37°24'45" N, long. 118°55'45" W). Named on Mount Abbot (1953) 15' quadrangle.

Quail Spring [KERN]:
(1) *spring,* 6.5 miles southwest of Pinyon Mountain (lat. 35°23'15" N, long. 118°14'10" W; near E line sec. 29, T 29 S, R 35 E). Named on Pinyon Mountain (1972) 7.5' quadrangle.
(2) *spring,* 12 miles north of Mojave (lat. 35°13'30" N, long. 118° 10'45" W; near N line sec. 24, T 31 S, R 35 E). Named on Cache Peak (1973) 7.5' quadrangle.

Quail Trap Canyon [TULARE]: *canyon,* 1 mile long, 5.5 miles south-southwest of California Hot Springs (lat. 35°48'20" N, long. 118°42'30" W; sec. 26, 35, T 24 S, R 30 E). Named on California Hot Springs (1958) 15' quadrangle.

Quail Valley: see **Quail Flat** [TULARE] (2).

Quaker Meadow [TULARE]: *locality,* nearly 4 miles southeast of Camp Nelson (lat. 36°06'35" N, long. 118°33'10" W; near NE cor. sec. 18, T 21 S, R 32 E). Named on Camp Nelson (1956) 15' quadrangle.

Quaking Aspen Camp: see **Quaking Aspen Meadow** [TULARE].

Quaking Aspen Meadow [TULARE]: *area,* 4 miles east-southeast of Camp Nelson (lat. 36°07'10" N, long. 118°32'40" W; sec. 8, T 21 S, R 32 E). Named on Camp Nelson (1956) 15' quadrangle. California Division of Highways' (1934) map shows a place called Quak-ing Aspen Camp situated at or near the site (near E line sec. 5, T 21 S, R 32 E).

Quality [KERN]: *locality,* 7.5 miles east of Delano along Southern Pacific Railroad (lat. 35°47' N, long. 119°07'10" W; sec. 1, T 25 S, R 26 E). Named on Richgrove (1952) 7.5' quadrangle.

Qualls Camp [FRESNO]: *locality,* 7.25 miles northeast of Dinkey Dome (lat. 37°11'15" N, long. 119°02'20" W). Named on Huntington Lake (1953) 15' quadrangle. United States Board on Geographic Names (1983c, p. 6) rejected the name "Knight Camp" for the place. Wesley Qualls had a cow camp there in the 1920's, and Walter Knight used it later (Browning 1986, p. 176).

Quartzburg: see **Big Blue Mill** [KERN].

Quartz Creek: see **Grizzly Creek** [MADERA].

Quartz Mountain [KERN]: *peak,* 3.5 miles west-northwest of Miracle Hot Springs (lat. 35°35'45" N, long. 118°35'30" W). Altitude 5223 feet. Named on Miracle Hot Springs (1972) 7.5' quadrangle.

Quartz Mountain [MADERA]:
(1) *ridge,* northwest-trending, 1 mile long, 8.5 miles south-southwest of Merced Peak (lat. 37°31'10" N, long. 119°26'45" W). Named on Merced Peak (1953) 15' quadrangle.
(2) *peak,* 4.25 miles north of O'Neals (lat. 37°11'30" N, long. 119° 41'05" W; sec. 33, T 8 S, R 21 E). Altitude 2752 feet. Named on O'Neals (1965) 7.5' quadrangle. Quartz Mountain Mill Company, financed in France, started a mining community called Narbo on land that the company had near the peak (Clough, p. 89-90). Postal authorities established Narbo post office in 1884 (SW quarter sec. 33, T 8 S, R 21 E), moved it in 1887 (SW quarter sec. 20, T 8 S, R 21 E), and discontinued it the same year. The name "Narbo" was from the word "Narbonne," which was the name of one of the promoters of the French company (Salley, p. 150).

Quatro Osos Canyon: see **Williams Canyon** [KERN].

Quedow Mountain [TULARE]: *ridge,* northwest-trending, 1.25 miles long, 4 miles northnortheast of Fountain Springs (lat. 35°56'30" N, long. 118°53' W). Named on Fountain Springs (1965) 7.5' quadrangle. Called Credow Mountain on White River (1936) 15' quadrangle, and called Cuidado Mtn. on White River (1952) 15' quadrangle, but United States Board on Geographic Names (1967a, p. 10) rejected the names "Credow Mountain," "Cuidado Mountain," and "Cuidow Mountain" for the feature.

Quinn Peak [TULARE]: *peak,* about 8 miles south of Mineral King (lat. 36°20'05" N, long. 118°35'15" W). Altitude 10,168 feet. Named on Mineral King (1956) 15' quadrangle. The name commemorates Harry Quinn, who settled in California in 1868 (United States Board on Geographic Names, 1933a, p. 629).

– R –

Rabbit Creek: see **Dead Ox Creek** [KERN].
Rabbit Gulch [KERN]: *canyon,* drained by a stream that flows 1.5 miles to Dead Ox Creek 3.5 miles south-southeast of Woody (lat. 35°39'30" N, long. 118°48'15" W; near N line sec. 24, T 26 S, R 29 E). Named on Woody (1965) 7.5' quadrangle.
Rabbit Hill [MADERA]: *peak,* 5.5 miles south-southwest of Raymond (lat. 37°08'10" N, long. 119°55'50" W; near E line sec. 19, T 9 S, R 10 E). Altitude 886 feet. Named on Raymond (1962) 7.5' quadrangle.
Rabbit Island [KERN]: *island,* 450 feet long, 4.5 miles west of Weldon in Isabella Lake (lat. 35°40'20" N, long. 118°22'20" W; near N line sec. 18, T 26 S, R 34 E). Named on Weldon (1972) 7.5' quadrangle.
Rabbit Meadow [TULARE]: *area,* 4.5 miles east-southeast of Wilsonia (lat. 36°42'45" N, long. 118°52'35" W; near NW cor. sec. 18, T 14 S, R 29 E). Named on Giant Forest (1956) 15' quadrangle.
Raco [FRESNO]: *locality,* 4.25 miles southwest of Herndon along Southern Pacific Railroad (lat. 36°48' N, long. 119°58'40" W; sec. 14, T 13 S, R 18 E). Named on Herndon (1964) 7.5' quadrangle. Called Dickerson on Herndon (1923) 7.5' quadrangle. California Mining Bureau's (1917a) map shows a place called Everts located at or just east of present Raco.
Rademacher: see **Rademacher Siding** [KERN].
Rademacher Siding [KERN]: *locality,* 11.5 miles north of Randsburg along Southern Pacific Railroad (lat. 35°32' N, long. 117° 41' W). Named on Searles Lake (1915) 1° quadrangle. Called Rademacher on California Division of Highways' (1934) map.
Radnor [TULARE]: *locality,* nearly 4 miles south of Earlimart along Southern Pacific Railroad (lat. 35°49'50" N, long. 119°15'40" W; sec. 22, T 24 S, R 25 E). Named on Delano West (1954) 7.5' quadrangle.
Rae Lake [FRESNO]: *lake,* 1000 feet long, 6.5 miles north-northwest of Blackcap Mountain (lat. 37°09'05" N, long. 118°50'55" W). Named on Blackcap Mountain (1953) 15' quadrangle. The name commemorates Rae Crabtree, a packer (Browning 1986, p. 177).
Rae Lakes [FRESNO]: *lakes,* largest 3000 feet long, 9.5 miles south of Mount Pinchot at the head of South Fork Woods Creek (lat. 36° 48'30" N, long. 118°24' W). Named on Mount Pnchot (1953) 15' quadrangle. R.B. Marshall of United States Geological Survey named one of the lakes in 1906 for Rachel Colby, wife of William E. Colby (Browning 1986, p. 177).
Ragged Spur [FRESNO]: *ridge,* south-south-east-trending, 4.5 miles long, 4 miles southeast of Mount Goddard (lat. 37°03' N, long.

118°40'30" W). Named on Mount Goddard (1948) 15' quadrangle.
Ragged Top [KINGS]: *peak,* 6 miles south of Avenal on Reef Ridge (lat. 35°54'55" N, long. 120°08'10" W; sec. 21, T 23 S, R 17 E). Altitude 2025 feet. Named on Garza Peak (1953) 7.5' quadrangle.
Ragged Valley [FRESNO]: *valley,* 3 miles east-northeast of Joaquin Rocks (lat. 36°20'15" N, long. 120°23'45" W). Named on Domengine Ranch (1956) and Joaquin Rocks (1969) 7.5' quadrangles.
Rag Gulch [KERN]: *canyon,* drained by a stream that flows 28 miles to a ditch on Kern-Tulare county line 7.5 miles east of Delano (lat. 35°47'25" N, long. 119°06'40" W; at N line sec. 6, T 25 S, R 27 E). Named on Delano East (1953), Quincy School (1965), Richgrove (1952), Sand Canyon (1965), White River (1965), and Woody (1965) 7.5' quadrangles. According to legend, the name is from stew, or ragout, made by French miners (Boyd, p. 159).
Ragle Canyon [TULARE]: *canyon,* drained by a stream that flows 1.5 miles to Dry Creek (1) 4.25 miles east-northeast of Woodlake (lat. 36°26'05" N, long. 119°01'30" W; near W line sec. 23, T 17 S, R 27 E). Named on Woodlake (1952) 7.5' quadrangle. Called Liveoak Canyon on Lemon Cove (1928) 7.5' quadrangle.
Rail Flat [TULARE]: *area,* 5.25 miles southwest of California Hot Springs (lat. 35°49'35" N, long. 118°44'15" W; sec. 21, T 24 S, R 30 E). Named on California Hot Springs (1958) 7.5' quadrangle.
Rail Flat Ridge [TULARE]: *ridge,* generally west-trending, 1.5 miles long, 6 miles southwest of California Hot Springs (lat. 35°49'20" N, long. 118°44'45" W); the ridge is south of Rail Flat. Named on California Hot Springs (1958) 15' quadrangle, and on White River (1965) 7.5' quadrangle.
Railroad Canyon [TULARE]: *canyon,* drained by a stream that flows 1.25 miles to White River (1) 5 miles southwest of California Hot Springs (lat. 35°50'10" N, long. 118°44'30" W; sec. 16, T 24 S, R 30 E). Named on California Hot Springs (1958) 15' quadrangle.
Railroad Spring [KERN]:
(1) *spring,* 0.5 mile southwest of Orchard Peak (lat. 35°44' N, long. 120°08'25" W; sec. 21, T 25 S, R 17 E). Named on Orchard Peak (1961) 7.5' quadrangle.
(2) *spring,* 3 miles northwest of Caliente (lat. 35°19' N, long. 118° 40' W). Named on Bena (1972) 7.5' quadrangle.
Rainbow Falls [MADERA]: *waterfall,* 1.5 miles south of Devils Postpile on Middle Fork San Joaquin River (lat. 37°36'05" N, long. 119°05' W). Named on Devils Postpile (1953) 15' quadrangle.
Rainbow Lake [FRESNO]:
(1) *lake,* 0.5 mile long, 15 miles north-north-

east of Kaiser Peak (lat. 37°28'35" N, long. 119° 02' W); the lake is one of the group called Margaret Lakes. Named on Kaiser Peak (1953) 15' quadrangle.
(2) *lake,* 500 feet long, 3.5 miles northeast of Dinkey Dome (lat. 37° 09'10" N, long. 119°05' W; sec. 13, T 9 S, R 26 E); the lake is 900 feet east of Eastern Brook Lake. Named on Huntington Lake (1953) 15' quadrangle.
(3) *lake,* 1150 feet long, nearly 2 miles east-northeast of Blackcap Mountain (lat. 37°05'05" N, long. 118°45'50" W). Named on Blackcap Mountain (1953) 15' quadrangle.

Rainbow Lake [MADERA]: *lake,* 950 feet long, 4 miles south-southeast of Merced Peak (lat. 37°34'40" N, long. 119°22' W). Named on Merced Peak (1953) 15' quadrangle.

Rainbow Lakes [FRESNO]: *lakes,* largest 1400 feet long, 8.5 miles east of Mount Goddard (lat. 37°05'15" N, long. 118°34' W). Named on Mount Goddard (1948) 15' quadrangle. Mr. Halladay, an early-day packer, named the lakes (Browning 1986, p. 178).

Rainbow Mountain [TULARE]: *peak,* 3.25 miles southeast of Mineral King on Great Western Divide (lat. 36°25'25" N, long. 118°33' W). Named on Mineral King (1956) 15' quadrangle. The name is from the colored rocks at the peak and the shape of the crest (Browning 1986, p. 178).

Rainier Creek [MADERA]: *stream,* flows 5 miles to Big Creek 7.5 miles north of Yosemite Forks (lat. 37°28'40" N, long. 119°36'50" W; near SW cor. sec. 19, T 5 S, R 22 E). Named on Bass Lake (1953) and Yosemite (1956) 15' quadrangles.

Raisin: see **Raisin City** [FRESNO].

Raisin City [FRESNO]: *village,* 13 miles southsouthwest of downtown Fresno (lat. 36°36'05" N, long. 119°54'10" W; sec. 28, T 15 S, R 19 E). Named on Raisin (1963) 7.5' quadrangle, which also shows Raisin P.O. at the place. The village is called Raisin on Raisin (1925) 7.5' quadrangle. Postal authorities established Raisin post office in 1907 (Frickstad, p. 37).

Raljon Lake [KERN]: *lake,* 800 feet long, 2.5 miles southwest of Glennville (lat. 35°42'25" N, long. 118°44'10" W; sec. 34, T 25 S, R 30 E). Named on Glennville (1972) 7.5' quadrangle, which shows Raljon ranch at the lake.

Rallsville: see **Coarsegold** [MADERA].

Ralmke Pond: see **Helmke Pond** [FRESNO].

Rambaud Creek [FRESNO]: *stream,* flows 2 miles to Middle Fork Kings River 9 miles eastsoutheast of Mount Goddard (lat. 37°02'50" N, long. 118°34'50" W). Named on Mount Goddard (1948) 15' quadrangle.

Rambaud Peak [FRESNO]: *peak,* 8 miles eastsoutheast of Mount Goddard (lat. 37°02'20" N, long. 118°35'50" W); the peak is south of Rambaud Creek. Named on Mount Goddard (1948) 15' quadrangle. The name commemorates Pete Rambaud, a Basque sheepman who brought the first sheep into the neighborhood

from Inyo County in 1877 (Farquhar, 1925, p. 127).

Ram Lake [FRESNO]:
(1) *lake,* 1100 feet long, 4 miles northwest of Red Slate Mountain on upper reaches of Purple Creek (lat. 37°32'35" N, long. 118°55'35" W). Named on Mount Morrison (1953) 15' quadrangle.
(2) *lake,* 750 feet long, 2.5 miles east-southeast of Blackcap Mountain (lat. 37°03'50" N, long. 118°45' W); the feature is next to Ewe Lake. Named on Blackcap Mountain (1953) 15' quadrangle. William A. Dill of California Department of Fish and Game named the lake in 1948 because of its proximity to Bighorn Lake (Browning 1986, p. 178).

Ramona Lake [FRESNO]: *lake,* 0.5 mile long, 12.5 miles north of Blackcap Mountain (lat. 37°15' N, long. 118°47' W). Named on Blackcap Mountain (1953) and Mount Abbot (1953) 15' quadrangles.

Rampart Pass: see **Siberian Pass** [TULARE].

Ramshaw Meadows [TULARE]: *area,* 3.5 miles northeast of Kern Peak along South Fork Kern River (lat. 36°21' N, long. 118° 15' W). Named on Kern Peak (1956) and Olancha (1956) 15' quadrangles. The name commemorates Peter Ramshaw, a stockman in the neighborhood from 1861 until 1880 (Gudde, 1949, p. 279).

Rancheria [FRESNO]: *locality,* 6 miles southeast of Balch Camp (lat. 36°50'05" N, long. 119°03'30" W; sec. 5, T 13 S, R 27 E). Site named on Patterson Mountain (1952) 15' quadrangle.

Rancheria Campground [FRESNO]: *locality,* 3 miles south-southeast of Kaiser Peak on the north side of Huntington Lake (1) (lat. 37°15'10" N, long. 119°10' W; near NE cor. sec. 7, T 8 S, R 26 E); the place is near the mouth of Rancheria Creek (1). Named on Kaiser Peak (1953) 15' quadrangle.

Rancheria Canyon [KERN]: *canyon,* drained by a stream that flows 2.5 miles to Rattlesnake Creek (3) nearly 4 miles south of Pine Mountain (lat. 35°30'25" N, long. 118°45'45" W; near W line sec. 9, T 28 S, R 30 E). Named on Democrat Hot Springs (1972) 7.5' quadrangle.

Rancheria Canyon [TULARE]: *canyon,* drained by a stream that flows 1.25 miles to Dry Creek (1) nearly 5 miles east-southeast of Auckland at Rancheria Flat (lat. 36°33'45" N, long. 119°01'25" W; sec. 3, T 16 S, R 27 E). Named on Auckland (1966) 7.5' quadrangle.

Rancheria Creek [FRESNO]:
(1) *stream,* flows 6 miles to Huntington Lake (1) 3 miles south-southeast of Kaiser Peak (lat. 37°15'20" N, long. 119°09'40" W; sec. 5, T 8 S, R 26 E). Named on Kaiser Peak (1953) 15' quadrangle. Called North Fork [of Big Creek (1)] on Kaiser (1904) 30' quadrangle.
(2) *stream,* flows 2.5 miles to White Deer Creek

9 miles southwest of Balch Camp (lat. 36°47'55" N, long. 119°12'30" W; sec. 13, T 13 S, R 25 E). Named on Patterson Mountain (1952) 15' quadrangle.

(3) *stream,* flows 8 miles to North Fork Kings River 7.25 miles east-northeast of Balch Camp (lat. 36°56'45" N, long. 119°00'05" W; sec. 26, T 11 S, R 27 E). Named on Tehipite Dome (1952) 15' quadrangle. On Tehipite (1903) 30' quadrangle, present Little Rancheria Creek is called North Fork [Rancheria Creek (3)].

Rancheria Creek [KERN]:

(1) *stream,* flows 5.25 miles to Rattlesnake Creek (3) 5.25 miles southwest of Pine Mountain (lat. 35°30'50" N, long. 118°50'15" W; near NE cor. sec. 10, T 28 S, R 29 E). Named on Pine Mountain (1965) and Rio Bravo Ranch (1954) 7.5' quadrangles.

(2) *stream,* flows 12.5 miles to Walker Basin Creek 10.5 miles northeast of Caliente in Walker Basin (lat. 35°24'25" N, long. 118° 30'35" W; near E line sec. 14, T 29 S, R 32 E). Named on Breckenridge Mountain (1972), Claraville (1972), and Piute Peak (1972) 7.5' quadrangles. Called Williams Cr. on Wheeler's (1875-1878) map.

Rancheria Creek [MADERA]: *stream,* flows 1.5 miles to China Creek 4.25 miles south of Yosemite Forks (lat. 37°18'15" N, long. 119°37'20" W; sec. 24, T 7 S, R 21 E). Named on Bass Lake (1953) 15' quadrangle.

Rancheria Creek [TULARE]: *stream,* flows 5.5 miles to Bear Creek (2) nearly 6 miles north-northeast of Springville (lat. 36°12'05" N, long. 118°45'40" W; near E line sec. 7, T 20 S, R 30 E). Named on Camp Nelson (1956) and Springville (1957) 15' quadrangles.

Rancheria Creek: see Little Rancheria Creek [FRESNO]; Lower Rancheria Creek [FRESNO].

Rancheria Flat [TULARE]: *area,* nearly 5 miles east-southeast of Auckland along Dry Creek (1) (lat. 36°33'50" N, long. 119°01'25" W; sec. 3, T 16 S, R 27 E); the place is at the mouth of Rancheria Canyon. Named on Auckland (1966) 7.5' quadrangle.

Rancho de los Californios: see Mendota [FRESNO].

Rancho Seco [KERN]: *locality,* 2 miles south-southwest of Cantil (lat. 35°17' N, long. 117°59'20" W). Named on Cantil (1967) 7.5' quadrangle.

Rand [KERN]: *locality,* 4.25 miles north-north-west of Randsburg along Southern Pacific Railroad (lat. 35°25'20" N, long. 117°41'30" W). Named on El Paso Peaks (1967) 7.5' quadrangle.

Rand Camp: see Randsburg [KERN].

Rand Mountains [KERN]: *range,* extends southwest from Randsburg (center near lat. 35°20' N, long. 117°43' W). Named on California City North (1973), Cantil (1967), Johannesburg (1967), and Saltdale SE (1967) 7.5' quadrangles.

Randsburg [KERN]: *village,* 17 miles south of Ridgecrest (lat. 35° 22'05" N, long. 117°39'10" W; sec. 35, T 29 S, R 40 E). Named on Johannesburg (1967) 7.5' quadrangle. Postal authorities established Randsburg post office in 1896 (Frickstad, p. 58). Prospectors found gold in 1895 at Rand mine, named for the gold-producing Rand district of South Africa; the camp that grew there first was called Rand Camp, and later Randsburg (Neal, p. 14-15).

Ranger: see Kaweah Camp [TULARE].

Ranger Lakes [TULARE]: *lakes,* two, largest 900 feet long, 10.5 miles west-northwest of Triple Divide Peak (lat. 36°40' N, long. 118°41'30" W). Named on Triple Divide Peak (1956) 15' quadrangle. United States Board on Geographic Names (1989b, p. 2) approved the name "Ranger Lake" for one of the lakes (lat. 36°39'57" N, long. 118°41'42" W).

Ranger Meadow [TULARE]: *area,* about 5 miles northwest of Triple Divide Peak in Deadman Canyon (1) (lat. 36°38'55" N, long. 118°35' W). Named on Triple Divide Peak (1956) 15' quadrangle.

Rankin Peak [KERN]: *peak,* 3 miles south of Miracle Hot Springs (lat. 35°32' N, long. 118°31'25" W; sec. 34, T 27 S, R 32 E). Altitude 4278 feet. Named on Miracle Hot Springs (1972) 7.5' quadrangle.

Rattlesnake Creek [FRESNO]:

(1) *stream,* flows 2.5 miles to South Fork San Joaquin River 7 miles northeast of Kaiser Peak (lat. 37°21'45" N, long. 119°05'50" W). Named on Kaiser Peak (1953) 15' quadrangle.

(2) *stream,* flows 2 miles to Boulder Creek (1) 6.5 miles east of Hume (lat. 36°47'05" N, long. 118°47'50" W). Named on Tehipite Dome (1952) 15' quadrangle.

(3) *stream,* flows 3.25 miles to Middle Fork Kings River 10.5 miles west of Marion Peak (lat. 36°56'25" N, long. 118°42'40" W). Named on Marion Peak (1953) 15' quadrangle.

Rattlesnake Creek [KERN]:

(1) *stream,* flows 4.5 miles to Isabella Lake 0.5 mile south-southwest of Wofford Heights (lat. 35°41'55" N, long. 118°27'25" W; sec. 5, T 26 S, R 33 E). Named on Alta Sierra (1972) and Lake Isabella North (1972) 7.5' quadrangles.

(2) *stream,* flows 5 miles to South Fork Cottonwood Creek (2) 4 miles east-southeast of Mount Adelaide (lat. 35°24'10" N, long. 118°40'45" W; sec. 17, T 29 S, R 31 E). Named on Mount Adelaide (1972) 7.5' quadrangle.

(3) *stream,* flows 10 miles to Poso Creek 6 miles west-southwest of Pine Mountain (lat. 35°31'05" N, lonyg. 118°51'20" W; near E line sec. 4, T 28 S, R 29 E). Named on Democrat Hot Springs (1972) and Pine Mountain (1965) 7.5' quadrangles.

Rattlesnake Creek [TULARE]:

(1) *stream,* flows 3.5 miles to Cottonwood

Creek 1 mile west of Auckland (lat. 36°35'10" N, long. 119°07'15" W; near NW cor. sec. 35, T 15 S, R 26 E). Named on Auckland (1966) and Stokes Mountain (1966) 7.5' quadrangles.
(2) *stream*, flows 8.5 miles to Kern River 10 miles northwest of Kern Peak (lat. 36°25' N, long. 118°24'45" W). Named on Kern Peak (1956) and Mineral King (1956) 15' quadrangles.
(3) *stream*, flows 13 miles to Kern River 5.5 miles south of Hockett Peak (lat. 36°08'30" N, long. 118°24'05" W). Named on Hockett Peak (1956) 15' quadrangle. This appears to be the stream called Harris Creek on Olmsted's (1900) map.

Rattlesnake Creek, Central Fork: see **Crystal Creek** [KERN].

Rattlesnake Lake [MADERA]: *lake*, 850 feet long, 15 miles northeast of Shuteye Peak (lat. 37°28'40" N, long. 119°11'20" W; sec. 24, T 5 S, R 25 E). Named on Kaiser Peak (1953) 15' quadrangle.

Rattlesnake Meadow [TULARE]: *area*, 15 miles east-southeast of Fairview (lat. 35°48'40" N, long. 118°16'15" W; near W line sec. 25, T 24 S, R 34 E). Named on Kernville (1956) 15' quadrangle.

Rattlesnake Ridge [TULARE]: *ridge*, southwest-trending, 1.5 miles long, 7 miles northwest of California Hot Springs (lat. 35°57'35" N, long. 118°44'35" W; on N line sec. 4, T 23 S, R 30 E). Named on California Hot Springs (1958) 15' quadrangle.

Rattlesnake Spring [FRESNO]: *spring*, 4 miles north-northwest of Joaquin Rocks (lat. 36°22'25" N, long. 120°28'30" W; sec. 8, T 18 S, R 14 E). Named on Joaquin Rocks (1969) 7.5' quadrangle.

Rattlesnake Spring [KERN]:
(1) *spring*, 4.25 miles east-southeast of Mount Adelaide (lat. 35°24'45" N, long. 118°40'20" W; near N line sec. 17, T 29 S, R 31 E); the feature is along Rattlesnake Creek (2). Named on Mount Adelaide (1972) 7.5' quadrangle.
(2) *spring*, 4.5 miles northwest of Caliente (lat. 35°20'15" N, long. 118°40'55" W). Named on Bena (1972) 7.5' quadrangle.

Rattlesnake Spring [TULARE]:
(1) *spring*, 4 miles north of Cliff Peak (lat. 36°37' N, long. 119°09'55" W; near S line sec. 17, T 15 S, R 26 E); the spring is above the head of Rattlesnake Creek (1). Named on Stokes Mountain (1966) 7.5' quadrangle.
(2) *spring*, 6.25 miles south-southeast of Auckland (lat. 36°30'30" N, long. 119°03'05" W; sec. 28, T 16 S, R 27 E). Named on Auckland (1966) 7.5' quadrangle.

Rattlesnake Well [MADERA]: *well*, 12.5 miles west of Madera (lat. 36°57'10" N, long. 120°16'45" W; near N line sec. 25, T 11 S, R 15 E). Named on Kentucky Well (1922) 7.5' quadrangle.

Raven Pass [KERN]: *pass*, 8 miles south-southeast of Orchard Peak (lat. 35°38' N, long.

120°04'15" W; sec. 30, T 26 S, R 18 E). Named on Sawtooth Ridge (1961) 7.5' quadrangle.

Rawls Gulch [MADERA]: *canyon*, drained by a stream that flows 2.5 miles to Daulton Creek 4 miles south-southwest of Raymond (lat. 37°09'50" N, long. 119°56' W; sec. 7, T 9 S, R 19 E). Named on Raymond (1962) 7.5' quadrangle.

Raymond [MADERA]: *village*, 20 miles north-northeast of Madera (lat. 37°13'10" N, long. 119°54'20" W; mainly in sec. 20, 21, T 8 S, R 19 E). Named on Raymond (1962) 7.5' quadrangle. Postal authorities established Raymond post office in 1886 (Frickstad, p. 86). The place first was called Wildcat Station, but when Southern Pacific Railroad reached the site in 1886, the rail stop there was called Raymond for Mr. T. Raymond of Raymond-Whitcomb Travel Association (Clough, p. 90). California Division of Highways' (1934) map shows a place called Herbert located along the railroad 2.25 miles south of Raymond.

Raymond: see **Mount Raymond Camp** [MADERA].

Raymond Mountain [MADERA]: *peak*, 6 miles south-southwest of Buena Vista Peak (lat. 37°30'30" N, long. 119°32'50" W; sec. 10, T 5 S, R 22 E). Altitude 8712 feet. Named on Yosemite (1956) 15' quadrangle. Members of the Whitney survey named the peak for Israel Ward Raymond, who played an active part in persuading the federal government to give Yosemite Valley to the State of California for a park, and who served on the supervisory commission for the park from 1864 until 1866 (Hanna, p. 251).

Raynor Creek [MADERA]: *stream*, heads in Mariposa County and flows 10 miles to Chowchilla River 13 miles northeast of Fairmead in Madera County (lat. 37°12'05" N, long. 120°00'25" W; sec. 28, T 8 S, R 18 E). Named on Ben Hur (1947), Illinois Hill (1962), and Raynor Creek (1961) 7.5' quadrangles.

Rayo [TULARE]: *locality*, 5.5 miles west-north-west of Woodlake along Atchison, Topeka and Santa Fe Railroad (lat. 36°26'50" N, long. 119°11'05" W; near W line sec. 17, T 17 S, R 26 E). Named on Exeter (1952) 15' quadrangle.

Reader Flat [KERN]: *area*, 4 miles northwest of Caliente (lat. 35° 20'20" N, long. 118°40'05" W). Named on Bena (1972) 7.5' quadrangle.

Recess Peak [FRESNO]: *peak*, 4 miles west of Mount Abbot on Mono Divide (lat. 37°23' N, long. 118°51'15" W); the peak is near the head of First Recess. Altitude 12,836 feet. Named on Mount Abbot (1953) 15' quadrangle. Theodore S. Solomons named the peak for its proximity to First Recess (Browning 1986, p. 179).

Rector [TULARE]: *locality*, 6 miles west of Exeter along Southern Pacific Railroad (lat. 36°18'20" N, long. 119°14'30" W; on W line sec. 2, T 19 S, R 25 E). Named on Exeter (1952) 15' quadrangle.

Red and White Lake [FRESNO]: *lake,* 1800 feet long, 8 miles northwest of Mount Abbot (lat. 37°29'05" N, long. 118°52'05" W); the lake is 0.5 mile west-northwest of Red and White Mountain. Named on Mount Abbot (1953) 15' quadrangle.

Red and White Mountain [FRESNO]: *peak,* 7.5 miles north-northwest of Mount Abbot on Fresno-Mono county line (lat. 37°28'50" N, long. 118°51'25" W). Altitude 12,850 feet. Named on Mount Abbot (1953) 15' quadrangle. Theodore S. Solomons named the peak in 1894 for red and white rocks exposed on it (Farquhar, 1925, p. 127).

Red Bank Creek: see **Redbank Slough** [FRESNO].

Redbanks [TULARE]: *locality,* 2.5 miles west-northwest of Woodlake along Atchison, Topeka and Santa Fe Railroad, and along Visalia Electric Railroad (lat. 36°25'20" N, long. 119°08'35" W; sec. 27, T 17 S, R 26 E). Named on Exeter (1952) 15' quadrangle. Called Colvin Ranch on Ivanhoe (1926) 7.5' quadrangle, which has the name "Redbanks" as an alternate designation for present Hillmaid. Railroad officials named the place in 1914 for Redbanks Orchard Company, which itself had been named for the red soil in the neighborhood (Gudde, 1949, p. 282). California Mining Bureau's (1917b) map shows a place called Heid located along the railroad between Redbanks and Seville.

Redbank Slough [FRESNO]: *water feature,* extends for 13 miles to an artificial watercourse 4.5 miles southeast of Clovis (lat. 36°46'15" N, long. 119°39'05" W; sec. 26, T 13 S, R 21 E). Named on Clovis (1964) and Round Mountain (1964) 7.5' quadrangles. Grunsky (p. 71) used the name "Red Bank Creek" for the feature.

Red Buttes [KERN]: *ridge,* south-trending, 2.25 miles long, 4.5 miles north-northwest of Saltdale (lat. 35°25'15" N, long. 118°54'45" W). Named on Saltdale NW (1967) 7.5' quadrangle. On Saltdale (1943a) 15' quadrangle, the name applies to a ridge located 2 miles farther west across Last Chance Canyon.

Red Cones [MADERA]: *peaks,* two, 2.5 miles south-southeast of Devils Postpile (lat. 37°35'30" N, long. 119°03'25" W). Altitudes 8985 and 9015 feet. Named on Devils Postpile (1953) 15' quadrangle.

Red Creek [MADERA]: *stream,* heads near Red Peak in Madera County and flows 4.5 miles to Clark Fork 12.5 miles south-southwest of Cathedral Peak in Mariposa County (lat. 37°40'55" N, long. 119°29'15" W). Named on Merced Peak (1953) 15' quadrangle.

Red Devil Lake [MADERA]: *lake,* 1500 feet long, 2 miles north of Merced Peak (lat. 37°39'55" N, long. 119°23'10" W). Named on Merced Peak (1953) 15' quadrangle.

Redfield: see **Mineral King** [TULARE].

Red Fir Meadow [TULARE]: *area,* 11 miles west of Triple Divide Peak (lat. 36°35'10" N, long. 118°43'20" W; near S line sec. 28, T 15 S, R 30 E). Named on Triple Divide Peak (1956) 15' quadrangle.

Red Hill [KERN]:
(1) *ridge,* west-southwest-trending, 2 miles long, 2.5 miles north-northeast of Glennville (lat. 35°45'35" N, long. 118°41'25" W). Named on California Hot Springs (1958) 15' quadrangle.
(2) *peak,* 4 miles northeast of Knob Hill (lat. 35°35'40" N, long. 118°53'05" W; near W line sec. 8, T 27 S, R 29 E). Altitude 1789 feet. Named on Knob Hill (1965) 7.5' quadrangle.
(3) *peak,* 2.5 miles east of Rosamond (lat. 34°52'10" N, long. 118° 07' W; near SE cor. sec. 14, T 9 N, R 12 W). Altitude 2743 feet. Named on Rosamond Lake (1973) 7.5' quadrangle.

Red Hill [TULARE]:
(1) *peak,* 4.25 miles east of Kaweah (lat. 36°28'20" N, long. 118°50'20" W; at S line sec. 4, T 17 S, R 29 E). Named on Kaweah (1957) 15' quadrangle.
(2) *peak,* 5.25 miles south of Camp Nelson (lat. 36°04' N, long. 118°37'30" W). Altitude 6292 feet. Named on Camp Nelson (1956) 15' quadrangle.

Red Hill: see **Tropico Hill** [KERN].

Red Kaweah [TULARE]: *peak,* nearly 4 miles south-southeast of Triple Divide Peak (lat. 36°32'25" N, long., 118°30'15" W); the peak is on Kaweah Peaks Ridge. Named on Triple Divide Peak (1956) 15' quadrangle.

Red Lake [FRESNO]: *lake,* 1600 feet long, 5.5 miles north of Dinkey Dome (lat. 37°11'30" N, long. 119°06'35" W; sec. 34, T 8 S, R 26 E); the lake is 0.5 mile south-southeast of the top of Red Mountain (1). Named on Huntington Lake (1953) 15' quadrangle.

Red Mountain [FRESNO]:
(1) *peak,* nearly 6 miles north of Dinkey Dome (lat. 37°11'50" N, long. 119°06'50" W; sec. 34, T 8 S, R 26 E). Altitude 9874 feet. Named on Huntington Lake (1953) 15' quadrangle.
(2) *peak,* nearly 5.5 miles north of Blackcap Mountain on LeConte Divide (lat. 37°09' N, long. 118°48' W). Altitude 11,951 feet. Named on Blackcap Mountain (1953) 15' quadrangle. United States Board on Geographic Names (1973a, p. 3) approved the name "Mount Hutton" for a peak located less than 2 miles south of Red Mountain (2) (lat. 37°07'34" N, long. 118°47'52" W); the name honors Scottish geologist James Hutton.
(3) *peak,* nearly 2 miles east of Humphreys Station (lat. 36°57'40" N, long. 119°24'50" W; sec. 24, T 11 S, R 23 E). Altitude 2804 feet. Named on Humphreys Station (1965) 7.5' quadrangle.
(4) *ridge,* north-northwest-trending, 2.5 miles long, 3 miles north-northwest of Piedra (lat.

36°51'30" N, long. 119°23'40" W). Named on Piedra (1965) 7.5' quadrangle.

Red Mountain [KERN]:
(1) *ridge,* generally west- to southwest-trending, 4.5 miles long, center 6 miles west of Piute Peak (lat. 35°28'05" N, long. 118°29'35" W). Named on Breckenridge Mountain (1972) and Piute Peak (1972) 7.5' quadrangles.
(2) *peak,* 4 miles west-southwest of Alta Sierra (lat. 35°41'55" N, long. 118°36'45" W; sec. 2, T 26 S, R 31 E). Altitude 5828 feet. Named on Alta Sierra (1972) 7.5' quadrangle.
(3) *peak,* 10 miles east of Tehachapi (lat. 35°08'55" N, long. 118° 16'20" W; at W line sec. 18, T 32 S, R 35 E). Altitude 5729 feet. Named on Tehachapi NE (1966) 7.5' quadrangle.

Red Mountain [TULARE]: *peak,* 5.25 miles south of Auckland (lat. 36°30'45" N, long. 119°05'55" W; near N line sec. 25, T 16 S, R 26 E). Altitude 2326 feet. Named on Auckland (1966) 7.5' quadrangle.

Red Mountain Basin [FRESNO]: *relief feature,* 4.5 miles north-northwest of Blackcap Mountain (lat. 37°08'10" N, long. 118° 49' W); the feature is 1.25 miles southwest of Red Mountain (2). Named on Blackcap Mountain (1953) 15' quadrangle.

Redoak Creek [FRESNO]: *stream,* flows 2.5 miles to Kings River 3.5 miles west-south-west of Balch Camp (lat. 36°52'45" N, long. 119°10'45" W; sec. 19, T 12 S, R 26 E). Named on Patterson Mountain (1952) 15' quadrangle.

Red Pass: see **Cartridge Pass** [FRESNO].

Red Peak [MADERA]: *peak,* 1.5 miles north-northwest of Merced Peak (lat. 37°39'15" N, long. 119°24'30" W). Altitude 11,699 feet. Named on Merced Peak (1953) 15' quadrangle. Members of the Whitney survey gave the name "Red Mountain" to the feature for the dominant color of its upper part (Browning, 1988, p. 116).

Red Peak Fork [MADERA]: *stream,* flows 4 miles to Merced River 5.25 miles north-north-east of Merced Peak (lat. 37°42'20" N, long. 119°21'40" W); the stream heads near Red Peak. Named on Merced Peak (1953) 15' quadrangle.

Red Point [FRESNO]: *peak,* 4600 feet north-northwest of Marion Peak (lat. 36°58'10" N, long. 118°31'35" W). Named on Marion Peak (1953) 15' quadrangle.

Redrock [KERN]:
(1) *locality,* 2.5 miles north of Cantil near the mouth of Redrock (present Red Rock) Canyon (lat. 35°20'40" N, long. 117°58'10" W; near N line sec. 11, T 30 S, R 37 E). Named on Saltdale (1943a) 15' quadrangle.
(2) *locality,* at Cantil along Southern Pacific Railroad (lat. 35°18'30" N, long. 117°58'30" W; at E line sec. 23, T 30 S, R 37 E). Named on Saltdale (1943a) 15' quadrangle.

Red Rock Canyon [KERN]: *canyon,* 4 miles long, opens into Fremont Valley 2.5 miles north of Cantil (lat. 35°20'45" N, long. 117° 58'10" W; near N line sec. 11, T 30 S, R 37 E). Named on Cantil (1967) and Saltdale NW (1967) 7.5' quadrangles. Saltdale (1943a) 15' quadrangle has the form "Redrock Canyon" for the name.

Redrock Canyon: see **Dove Spring Canyon** [KERN].

Redrock Creek [TULARE]: *stream,* flows 5.5 miles to Ninemile Creek 4.5 miles east of Hockett Peak (lat. 36°13'45" N, long. 118° 18'15" W); the stream drains Redrock Meadows. Named on Hockett Peak (1956) and Kern Peak (1956) 15' quadrangles.

Redrock Meadows [TULARE]: *area,* 3 miles south-southeast of Kern Peak (lat. 36°16'10" N, long. 118°16'15" W); the place is along upper reaches of Redrock Creek. Named on Kern Peak (1956) 15' quadrangle.

Reds Creek [MADERA]: *stream,* flows 1.5 miles to Middle Fork San Joaquin River 1.25 miles north of Devils Postpile (lat. 37°38'35" N, long. 119°04'40" W); the stream heads near Reds Lake. Named on Devils Postpile (1953) 15' quadrangle.

Reds Creek: see **Reds Meadow Hot Springs** [MADERA].

Reds Lake [MADERA]: *lake,* 500 feet long, 1.5 miles northeast of Devils Postpile (lat. 37°38'20" N, long. 119°03'20" W); the lake is near the head of Reds Creek. Named on Devils Postpile (1953) 15' quadrangle.

Red Slate Mountain [FRESNO]: *peak,* 23 miles northeast of Kaiser Peak on Fresno-Mono county line (lat. 37°30'30" N, long. 118°52'10" W). Altitude 13,163 feet. Named on Mount Morrison (1953) 15' quadrangle. Members of the Whitney survey named the peak in 1864 (Browning 1986, p. 180).

Reds Meadow Hot Springs [MADERA]: *springs,* 0.5 mile southeast of Devils Postpile (lat. 37°37'05" N, long. 119°04'25" W); the springs are at Reds Meadows. Named on Devils Postpile (1953) 15' quadrangle. Waring (p. 55) reported that water in a bathing pool at the largest of several small thermal springs at the east side of Reds Meadows has a temperature of 120° Fahrenheit. United States Board on Geographic Names (1984b, p. 2) approved the name "Reds Creek" for a stream that flows 3.5 miles to San Joaquin River 0.5 mile west-southwest of Reds Meadow Hot Springs (lat. 37°36'58" N, long. 119°04'57" W)—the hot springs are along this stream.

Reds Meadows [MADERA]: *area,* 0.5 mile southeast of Devils Postpile (lat. 37°37' N, long. 119°04'30" W). Named on Mount Lyell (1901) 30' quadrangle. The name commemorates Red Sotcher, or Satcher, who came to the place in 1879 to herd sheep (Smith, Genny, p. 14).

Red Spring [KERN]: *spring,* 6 miles east-southeast of Caliente (lat. 35°16'10" N, long.

118°31'20" W; near SE cor. sec. 34, T 30 S, R 32 E). Named on Oiler Peak (1972) 7.5' quadrangle.

Red Spur [TULARE]: *ridge,* generally southeast-trending, 2 miles long, 8.5 miles west-southwest of Mount Whitney (lat. 36°32' N, long. 118°26' W). Named on Mount Whitney (1956) 15' quadrangle.

Red Spur Creek [TULARE]: *stream,* flows 3.5 miles to Kern River 15 miles north-northwest of Kern Peak (lat. 36°29'50" N, long. 118°24'15" W); the stream heads near Red Spur. Named on Kern Peak (1956) and Mount Whitney (1956) 15' quadrangles.

Red Top [MADERA]:
(1) *locality,* 12 miles west-southwest of Chowchilla (lat. 37°05' N, long. 120°29'30" W; near SW cor. sec. 6, T 10 S, R 14 E). Named on Bliss Ranch (1960) 7.5' quadrangle. Postal authorities established Red Top post office in 1952 (Salley, p. 183).
(2) *peak,* 6 miles south of Merced Peak (lat. 37°32'45" N, long. 119°24'10" W). Altitude 9977 feet. Named on Merced Peak (1953) 15' quadrangle. The name also had the form "Redtop" (Browning, 1986, p. 180).

Red Top Mountain: see **Garnet Lake** [MADERA].

Redwood Creek [MADERA]: *stream,* flows 1.5 miles to Nelder Creek 1 mile east of Yosemite Forks (lat. 37°22' N, long. 119°36'35" W; sec. 13, T 6 S, R 22 E). Named on Bass Lake (1953) 15' quadrangle.

Redwood Camp [TULARE]: *locality,* 4.5 miles west-southwest of Camp Nelson (lat. 36°06'50" N, long. 118°41'10" W; sec. 12, T 21 S, R 30 E). Named on Camp Nelson (1956) 15' quadrangle.

Redwood Canyon [TULARE]: *canyon,* drained by Redwood Creek (1), which flows 7.5 miles to North Fork Kaweah River 3.5 miles north-northwest of Yucca Mountain (lat. 36°37'20" N, long. 118° 53'35" W; sec. 13, T 15 S, R 28 E). Named on Giant Forest (1956) 15' quadrangle.

Redwood Corral [TULARE]: *locality,* 7 miles north of California Hot Springs (lat. 35°58'55" N, long. 118°39'40" W); the place is near the head of Redwood Creek (2). Named on California Hot Springs (1958) 15' quadrangle.

Redwood Creek [FRESNO]: *stream,* flows 2.5 miles to South Fork Kings River 5 miles east-northeast of Hume (lat. 36°49' N, long. 118°50'05" W). Named on Tehipite Dome (1952) 15' quadrangle.

Redwood Creek [TULARE]:
(1) *stream,* flows 7.5 miles to North Fork Kaweah River 3.5 miles north-northwest of Yucca Mountain (lat. 36°37'20" N, long. 118° 53'35" W; sec. 13, T 15 S, R 28 E); the stream is east of Redwood Mountain. Named on Giant Forest (1956) 15' quadrangle. East Fork enters from the east 5.5 miles upstream from the mouth of the main stream; it is 1.5 miles

long and is named on Giant Forest (1956) 15' quadrangle.
(2) *stream,* flows 1.5 miles to Eagle Creek (2) 8 miles north of California Hot Springs (lat. 35°59'55" N, long. 118°39'55" W). Named on California Hot Springs (1958) 15' quadrangle.
(3) *stream,* flows 2 miles to East Fork Kaweah River 6 miles west of Mineral King (lat. 36°26'15" N, long. 118°41'50" W). Named on Mineral King (1956) 15' quadrangle.

Redwood Meadow [TULARE]:
(1) *area,* 7.25 miles southwest of Triple Divide Peak (lat. 36°30'50" N, long. 118°38'05" W). Named on Triple Divide Peak (1956) 15' quadrangle. William B. Wallace and his companions named the place in 1887 (United States Board on Geographic Names, 1933a, p. 638).
(2) *area,* 8 miles north-northeast of California Hot Springs (lat. 35° 58'30" N, long. 118°35'40" W; sec. 35, T 22 S, R 31 E). Named on California Hot Springs (1958) 15' quadrangle.

Redwood Mountain [TULARE]: *ridge,* south-trending, 5 miles long, 5.25 miles south-southeast of Wilsonia (lat. 36°40' N, long. 118° 55' W); the ridge is west of Redwood Canyon and Redwood Creek (1). Named on Giant Forest (1956) 15' quadrangle.

Redwood Saddle [TULARE]: *pass,* 2.5 miles southeast of Wilsonia (lat. 36°42'25" N, long. 118°55'15" W; sec. 15, T 14 S, R 28 E). Named on Giant Forest (1956) 15' quadrangle.

Reed Canyon [KERN]: *canyon,* drained by a stream that flows 3.5 miles to Sacramento Canyon 5 miles north-northeast of downtown Bakersfield (lat. 35°26'35" N, long. 118°58'45" W; near S line sec. 32, T 28 S, R 28 E). Named on Oil Center (1954) 7.5' quadrangle.

Reed Canyon: see **Tecuya Creek** [KERN].

Reedley [FRESNO]: *town,* 22 miles east-southeast of Fresno (lat. 36° 35'45" N, long. 119°27' W). Named on Reedley (1966) 7.5' quadrangle. Postal authorities established Reedley post office in 1888 and named to honor Thomas L. Reed, landowner at the place; the suffix was added because Reed objected to use of his name (Salley, p. 183). The town incorporated in 1913. California Mining Bureau's (1917a) map shows a place called Darwin located along the railroad north of Reedley and south of the rail crossing of Wahtoke Creek. The same map shows a locality called Vino situated north of Reedley just north of the rail crossing of Wahtoke Creek. A place called Pool's Ferry was settled as early as 1850 or 1851 along Kings River 2.25 miles northwest of present Reedley (Hoover, Rensch, and Rensch, p. 91). A map of 1863 shows Pool's Fort near the confluence of Kings River and Wahtoke Creek, at or near the site of Pool's Ferry (Whiting and Whiting, p. 63). Smith's Ferry superseded Pool's Ferry; James Smith started it in 1855 near the southwest edge of present Reedley, and it lasted until 1874 (Hoover, Rensch, and Rensch, p. 91-92). Postal authorities established Smith's Ferry post office 7 miles northeast of Sanger in 1865, changed the name to King's River in 1866, changed it to Kingriver in 1895, and discontinued it in 1905; they had established an earlier King's River post office 7 miles northeast of Sanger in 1856 and discontinued it in 1859 (Salley, p. 112, 206). Postal authorities established Carmelita post office 8.5 miles north of Reedley in 1899 and discontinued it in 1900 (Salley, p. 38).

Reedwater Canyon [FRESNO]: *canyon,* drained by a stream that flows 3 miles to Zapato Chino Canyon 4.25 miles north-northwest of Castle Mountain (lat. 35°59'55" N, long. 120°21'45" W; sec. 21, T 22 S, R 15 E). Named on The Dark Hole (1961) 7.5' quadrangle.

Reefer City [KERN]: *locality,* 3.25 miles south-southwest of Mojave (lat. 35°00'25" N, long. 118°11' W; near NW cor. sec. 32, T 11 N, R 12 W). Named on Mohave (1947) 7.5' quadrangle.

Reef Lake [FRESNO]: *lake,* 600 feet long, 16 miles northeast of Kaiser Peak (lat. 37°29' N, long. 119°01'10" W). Named on Kaiser Peak (1953) 15' quadrangle.

Reef Ridge [FRESNO-KINGS]: *ridge,* generally northwest-trending, 18 miles long, on Fresno-Kings county line northwest of Sulphur Spring Canyon [KINGS] (2). Named on Garza Peak (1953), Kettleman Plain (1953), Pyramid Hills (1953), and The Dark Hole (1961) 7.5' quadrangles. Arnold and Anderson (1908, p. 14) noted that the ridge "is formed by the prominent lower Miocene fossiliferous strata termed 'Reef beds,' which dip at a high angle and, owing to their resistance to erosion, rise high above the softer sand hills on the northeast."

Reef Station [KINGS]: *locality,* 8 miles south-southeast of Avenal in Kettleman Plain (lat. 35°54'05" N, long. 120°03'15" W; sec. 29, T 23 S, R 18 E); the place is 2.5 miles east-northeast of Reef Ridge. Named on Kettleman Plain (1953) 7.5' quadrangle.

Reese Canyon [FRESNO]: *canyon,* drained by a stream that flows 1.5 miles to Oak Flat nearly 5 miles northeast of Castle Mountain (lat. 35°58'50" N, long. 120°16'20" W; near SE cor. sec. 30, T 22 S, R 16 E). Named on The Dark Hole (1961) 7.5' quadrangle.

Reese Creek [FRESNO]: *stream,* flows 2 miles to Dinkey Creek (1) 2.5 miles south-southwest of Dinkey Dome (lat. 37°05'05" N, long. 119°09'15" W; sec. 5, T 10 S, R 26 E). Named on Huntington Lake (1953) 15' quadrangle.

Reflection: see **Lake Reflection** [TULARE].

Reinstein: see **Mount Reinstein** [FRESNO].

Reka [FRESNO]: *locality,* 1 mile south-southeast of Sanger along Southern Pacific Railroad (lat. 36°41'20" N, long. 119°33'05" W;

sec. 26, T 14 S, R 22 E). Named on Sanger (1923) 7.5' quadrangle.

Remnoy [KINGS]: *locality,* 5 miles east of Hanford along Southern Pacific Railroad (lat. 36°20'20" N, long. 119°33'15" W; sec. 26, T 18 S, R 22 E). Named on Remnoy (1954) 7.5' quadrangle.

Reservoir: see **Fram** [KERN].

Revis Mountain [MADERA]: *peak,* 5.5 miles north-northwest of O'Neals (lat. 37°11'40" N, long. 119°44'45" W; near E line sec. 35, T 8 S, R 20 E). Named on Knowles (1962) and O'Neals (1965) 7.5' quadrangles.

Reward [KERN]: *locality,* 3.5 miles west-north-west of McKittrick (lat. 35°19'15" N, long. 119°40'30" W; near NW cor. sec. 13, T 30 S, R 21 E). Named on Reward (1951) 7.5' quadrangle. Postal authorities established Reward post office in 1909 and discontinued it in 1937 (Frickstad, p. 58). The small oil-field community began in 1907 (Bailey, 1967, p. 22).

Reynolds [TULARE]: *locality,* nearly 2 miles north-northeast of Lindsay along Visalia Electric Railroad (lat. 36°13'40" N, long. 119°04'20" W; sec. 32, T 19 S, R 27 E). Named on Lindsay (1928) 7.5' quadrangle.

Rhoda Lake: see **Charlotte Lake** [FRESNO].

Rhymes Campground [KERN]: *locality,* 3 miles south-southwest of Alta Sierra (lat. 35°41'10" N, long. 118°34'25" W; sec. 7, T 26 S, R 32 E). Named on Alta Sierra (1972) 7.5' quadrangle.

Rhymes Flat [KERN]: *area,* 6 miles northnortheast of Caliente (lat. 35°21'45" N, long. 118°33'50" W; near E line sec. 32, T 29 S, R 32 E). Named on Oiler Peak (1972) 7.5' quadrangle.

Rhymes Spring [KERN]: *spring,* 6 miles northnortheast of Caliente (lat. 35°21'45" N, long. 118°34' W; sec. 32, T 29 S, R 32 E); the spring is at Rhymes Flat. Named on Oiler Peak (1972) 7.5' quadrangle.

Ribier [KERN]: *locality,* 11 miles southeast of Bakersfield along the railroad (lat. 35°15'10" N, long. 118°52'45" W; at SE cor. sec. 5, T 31 S, R 29 E). Named on Lamont (1954) 7.5' quadrangle.

Ricardo [KERN]: *locality,* nearly 5 miles north-northwest of Cantil in Red Rock Canyon (lat. 35°22'30" N, long. 117°59'20" W; near N line sec. 34, T 29 S, R 37 E). Site named on Cantil (1967) 7.5' quadrangle. Postal authorities established Ricardo post office in 1898, discontinued it in 1907, reestablished it in 1908, discontinued it in 1912, reestablished it in 1913, and discontinued it in 1917 (Frickstad, p. 58). Rudolf Hagen operated a station that he named Ricardo for his son, Richard; the station occupied two sites (Bailey, 1967, p. 23). Postal authorities established Craft post office 7 miles south of Ricardo in 1909 and discontinued it in 1911 (Salley, p. 52).

Rich [KERN]: *locality,* nearly 5 miles west-southwest of Boron along the railroad (lat.

34°58'35" N, long. 117°43'35" W; sec. 9, T 10 N, R 8 W). Named on Leuhman Ridge (1973) 7.5' quadrangle.

Richgrove [TULARE]: *town,* 7.5 miles south-southwest of Ducor (lat. 35°47'50" N, long. 119°06'25" W; on E line sec. 36, T 24 S, R 26 E). Named on Richgrove (1952) 7.5' quadrangle. Officers of Richgrove Land and Development Company named the town in 1909; the place also was known as Wildflower, for Wildflower school district (Mitchell, A.R., p. 69). Postal authorities established Richgrove post office in 1911 (Frickstad, p. 213). California Mining Bureau's (1917b) map has the form "Rich Grove" for the name.

Ridenhour Creek [TULARE]: *stream,* flows about 3 miles to Dry Creek (1) 5.5 miles northeast of Woodlake (lat. 36°28' N, long. 119°01'30" W; sec. 11, R 17 S, E 27 E). Named on Auckland (1966) and Woodlake (1952) 7.5' quadrangles.

Ridgecrest [KERN]: *town,* 48 miles north-northeast of Mojave at the edge of China Lake Naval Weapons Center (lat. 35°37'25" N, long. 117°40'15" W). Named on Ridgecrest North (1973) and Ridgecrest South (1973) 7.5' quadrangles. Postal authorities established Ridgecrest post office in 1941 (Frickstad, p. 58), and the town incorporated in 1963. The community began in 1912, when it was called Crumville for Robert Crum and James Crum, who ran a dairy (Bailey, 1967, p. 23).

Rifle Creek [TULARE]: *stream,* flows 3 miles to Little Kern River 10 miles south-southeast of Mineral King (lat. 36°19'20" N, long. 118°31'40" W); the stream is near Pistol Creek and Shotgun Creek. Named on Mineral King (1956) 15' quadrangle.

Right Angle Canyon [FRESNO]: *canyon,* drained by a stream that flows 4 miles to Panoche Creek 21 miles southwest of Firebaugh (lat. 36°36'35" N, long. 120°40'55" W; sec. 20, T 15 S, R 12 E). Named on Chounet Ranch (1956) 7.5' quadrangle.

Right Stringer [TULARE]: *stream,* flows 2.5 miles to Left Stringer 4 miles north-northwest of Kern Peak (lat. 36°21'25" N, long. 118° 19'35" W). Named on Kern Peak (1956) 15' quadrangle.

Rinaldis Well [KERN]: *well,* 9 miles north-northwest of Randsburg (lat. 35°29'30" N, long. 117°42'20" W; sec. 19, T 28 S, R 40 E). Named on El Paso Peaks (1967) 7.5' quadrangle.

Rincon [TULARE]: *area,* east of Kern River between Fairview and The Needles (center near lat. 36°02'30" N, long. 118°27' W). Named on Hockett Peak (1956) and Kernville (1956) 15' quadrangles.

Rio Bravo [KERN]: *locality,* 7.25 miles south of Shafter along Southern Pacific Railroad (lat. 35°23'50" N, long. 119°17'25" W; near NE cor. sec. 21, T 29 S, R 25 E). Named on Rio Bravo (1954) 7.5' quadrangle. Postal authorities es-

tablished Rio Bravo post office in 1912 and discontinued it in 1919 (Frickstad, p. 58).

Rio Bravo: see **Kern River** [KERN-TULARE]; **Panama** [KERN].

Rio de la Merced: see **Merced River** [MADERA].

Rio de los Merced: see **Merced River** [MADERA].

Rio de San Felipe: see **Kern River** [KERN-TULARE].

Rio San Joaquin: see **San Joaquin River** [MADERA].

Rio Tulare: see **San Joaquin River** [MADERA].

Ripperdan [MADERA]: *village,* 7.5 miles south of Madera (lat. 36° 51'05" N, long. 120°03'20" W; at NE cor. sec. 36, T 12 S, R 17 E). Named on Biola (1963) 7.5' quadrangle.

Ritter: see **Mount Ritter** [MADERA].

Ritter Range [MADERA]: *ridge,* north-northwest-trending, 8 miles long, 8 miles northwest of Devils Postpile (lat. 37°41'30" N, long. 119°12' W); Mount Ritter is near the middle of the ridge. Named on Devils Postpile (1953) 15' quadrangle.

Riverbend [FRESNO]: *locality,* 11.5 miles east-southeast of Clovis along Atchison, Topeka and Santa Fe Railroad (lat. 36°45'25" N, long. 119°30'40" W; sec. 31, T 13 S, R 23 E). Named on Round Mountain (1964) 7.5' quadrangle.

Riverdale [FRESNO]: *town,* 23 miles south of Fresno (lat. 36°25'55" N, long. 119°51'30" W; sec. 24, 25, T 17 S, R 19 E). Named on Riverdale (1954) 7.5' quadrangle. Postal authorities established Riverdale post office in 1875 (Frickstad, p. 37). The place first was called Liberty Settlement; the newer name is for the proximity of Kings River to the town (Gudde, 1949, p. 287).

River Hill [TULARE]: *peak,* 5.5 miles east of Kaweah (lat. 36°27'45" N, long. 118°49'10" W; sec. 10, T 17 S, R 29 E). Altitude 2767 feet. Named on Kaweah (1957) 15' quadrangle.

River Spring [TULARE]: *spring,* 4 miles south of Kern Peak (lat. 36°15'15" N, long. 118°16'40" W). Named on Kern Peak (1956) 15' quadrangle.

River Valley [TULARE]: *canyon,* 2.5 miles long, 5.5 miles west-southwest of Triple Divide Peak along Middle Fork Kaweah River (lat. 36°33'30" N, long. 118°37' W). Named on Triple Divide Peak (1956) 15' quadrangle.

Riverview: see **Bakersfield** [KERN].

Rixford: see **Mount Rixford** [FRESNO].

Roach Canyon [FRESNO]: *canyon,* drained by a stream that flows 3.5 miles to Los Gatos Creek 16 miles west-northwest of Coalinga (lat. 36°15'15" N, long. 120°36'55" W; near NW cor. sec. 30, T 19 S, R 13 E). Named on San Benito Mountain (1969) and Santa Rita Peak (1969) 7.5' quadrangles.

Roads End: see **Fairview** [TULARE].

Road Well [KERN]: *well,* 5.25 miles south-southwest of Pinyon Mountain in Kelso Valley (lat. 35°23'30" N, long. 118°11'50" W; near NW cor. sec. 26, T 29 S, R 35 E). Named on Pinyon Mountain (1972) 7.5' quadrangle.

Roaring River [FRESNO-TULARE]: *stream,* heads in Tulare County and flows 16 miles to South Fork Kings River 13 miles south-south-west of Marion Peak in Fresno County (lat. 36°47'05" N, long. 118°37'30" W). Named on Marion Peak (1953) and Triple Divide Peak (1956) 15' quadrangles. Frank M. Lewis named the stream in the 1870's (Browning 1986, p. 184).

Roaring River Falls [FRESNO]: *waterfall,* 13 miles south-southwest of Marion Peak (lat. 36°46'50" N, long. 118°37'15" W); the feature is along Roaring River. Named on Marion Peak (1953) 15' quadrangle.

Robbers Canyon [FRESNO]: *canyon,* drained by a stream that flows nearly 2 miles to Bear Canyon 6.5 miles north-northwest of Coalinga Mineral Springs (lat. 36°13'25" N, long. 120°36'50" W; sec. 6, T 20 S, R 13 E). Named on Sherman Peak (1969) 7.5' quadrangle.

Robbers Roost [KERN]: *relief feature,* 8.5 miles west-southwest of Inyokern (lat. 35°35'30" N, long. 117°56'55" W; near N line sec. 13, T 27 S, R 37 E). Named on Freeman Junction (1972) 7.5' quadrangle. Outlaws hid at the place, which also was called Bandit Rocks (Wines, p. 36).

Roberts: see **Bob Rabbit Place,** under **Bob Rabbit Canyon** [KERN].

Robinson [KINGS]: *locality,* 8 miles north-northwest of Lemoore along Southern Pacific Railroad (lat. 36°24'05" N, long. 119°50'35" W). Named on Riverdale (1927) 7.5' quadrangle. California Division of Highways' (1934) map shows a lake called Summit Lake located 5.25 miles west-southwest of Robinson (NW quarter sec. 17, T 18 S, R 19 E).

Robinson Bay [KERN]: *embayment,* 4 miles east-southeast of Wofford Heights along Isabella Lake (lat. 35°40'25" N, long. 118°23'35" W; near NW cor. sec. 13, T 26 S, R 33 E); the embayment is east of Robinson Point. Named on Lake Isabella North (1972) 7.5' quadrangle.

Robinson Point [KERN]: *promontory,* nearly 4 miles southeast of Wofford Heights along Isabella Lake (lat. 35°40'25" N, long. 118° 24' W; on S line sec. 11, T 26 S, R 33 E). Named on Lake Isabella North (1972) 7.5' quadrangle.

Robla: see **Tulare** [TULARE].

Rockbound Lake [MADERA]: *lake,* 6.5 miles east-northeast of Merced Peak (lat. 37°40'10" N, long. 119°16'50" W). Named on Merced Peak (1953) 15' quadrangle.

Rock Corral Spring [KERN]: *spring,* 2.5 miles south-southeast of Glennville (lat. 35°41'50" N, long. 118°40'45" W; sec. 6, T 26 S, R 31 E). Named on Glennville (1972) 7.5' quadrangle.

Rock Creek [FRESNO]:
(1) *stream,* flows 5.5 miles to Four Forks Creek 8 miles north-northeast of Kaiser Peak (lat. 37°24'10" N, long. 119°07'20" W). Named on Kaiser Peak (1953) 15' quadrangle.
(2) *stream,* flows 5 miles to Dinkey Creek (1) 2.25 miles southwest of Dinkey Dome at the village of Dinkey Creek (lat. 37°05'15" N, long. 119°09'20" W; sec. 5, T 10 S, R 26 E). Named on Huntington Lake (1953) 15' quadrangle.

Rock Creek [MADERA]: *stream,* flows 7 miles to San Joaquin River 7.5 miles southeast of Shuteye Peak (lat. 37°16'30" N, long. 119° 19'55" W; sec. 34, T 7 S, R 24 E). Named on Shuteye Peak (1953) 15' quadrangle.

Rock Creek [TULARE]: *stream,* flows 12 miles to Kern River 13 miles north-northwest of Kern Peak (lat. 36°28'45" N, long. 118° 24'20" W). Named on Kern Peak (1956) and Mount Whitney (1956) 15' quadrangles. Present Siberian Pass Creek was called South Fork Rock Creek (Browning 1986, p. 198).

Rock Creek Lake [FRESNO]: *lake,* 800 feet long, 13 miles north-northeast of Kaiser Peak (lat. 37°28'10" N, long. 119°04'50" W); the lake is near the head of Rock Creek (1). Named on Kaiser Peak (1953) 15' quadrangle.

Rock Haven [FRESNO]: *settlement,* 1.5 miles north of Shaver Lake Heights (present town of Shaver Lake) (lat. 37°07'40" N, long. 119°19' W; sec. 23, 26, T 9 S, R 24 E). Named on Shaver Lake (1953) 15' quadrangle.

Rockhouse Basin [TULARE]: *valley,* 12.5 miles northwest of Lamont Peak along South Fork Kern River (lat. 35°56'30" N, long. 118°09'45" W). Named on Lamont Peak (1956) 15' quadrangle.

Rockhouse Meadow [TULARE]: *area,* 11 miles northwest of Lamont Peak along South Fork Kern River (lat. 35°53'30" N, long. 118°11'15" W; on S line sec. 27, T 23 S, R 35 E). Named on Lamont Peak (1956) 15' quadrangle. Olmsted's (1900) map has the form "Rock House Meadows" for the name.

Rock Lake [FRESNO]: *lake,* 900 feet long, 5 miles east-northeast of Dinkey Dome (lat. 37°09'10" N, long. 119°03'05" W; sec. 17, T 9 S, R 27 E). Named on Huntington Lake (1953) 15' quadrangle.

Rock Meadow [FRESNO]: *area,* 7 miles northeast of Dinkey Dome (lat. 37°11'45" N, long. 119°03'35" W). Named on Huntington Lake (1953) 15' quadrangle. Called Long Meadow on Kaiser (1904) 30' quadrangle, which has the name "Rock Meadow" for a place situated 2 miles farther east.

Rock Mountain [FRESNO]: *peak,* 4.5 miles north of Prather (lat. 37° 06'15" N, long. 119°31'05" W; sec. 36, T 9 S, R 22 E). Altitude 2869 feet. Named on Millerton Lake East (1965) 7.5' quadrangle.

Rock Pile [KERN]: *hill,* 8.5 miles southeast of Edison (lat. 35°15'40" N, long. 118°45'25" W; sec. 4, T 31 S, R 30 E). Named on Edison

(1931) 7.5' quadrangle.

Rockslide Lake [TULARE]: *lake,* 900 feet long, 8.5 miles west of Mount Whitney along Kern-Kaweah River (lat. 36°34'35" N, long. 118°26'30" W). Named on Mount Whitney (1956) 15' quadrangle.

Rock Spring [FRESNO]: *spring,* 8.5 miles east-northeast of Clovis (lat. 36°51' N, long. 119°33' W; near NE cor. sec. 34, T 12 S, R 22 E). Named on Round Mountain (1964) 7.5' quadrangle.

Rock Spring [KERN]:
(1) *spring,* 5 miles north-northeast of Glennville (lat. 35°47'10" N, long. 118°39'15" W; sec. 4, T 25 S, R 31 E). Named on California Hot Springs (1958) 15' quadrangle.
(2) *spring,* 0.5 mile south-southeast of Mount Adelaide (lat. 35° 25'20" N, long. 118°44'25" W; sec. 10, T 29 S, R 30 E). Named on Mount Adelaide (1972) 7.5' quadrangle. Caliente (1914) 30' quadrangle shows a locality called Rock Springs at the site.
(3) *spring,* 3 miles south-southwest of Loraine (lat. 35°15'45" N, long. 118°27'15" W; sec. 5, T 31 S, R 33 E). Named on Loraine (1972) 7.5' quadrangle.

Rock Spring [TULARE]: *spring,* 3.5 miles southeast of Auckland (lat. 36°33' N, long. 119°03'55" W; sec. 8, T 16 S, R 17 E). Named on Auckland (1966) 7.5' quadrangle.

Rock Springs: see **Rock Spring** [KERN] (2).

Rockwell Pond [FRESNO]: *lake,* 1.25 miles long, 2.25 miles west-northwest of Selma (lat. 36°34'50" N, long. 119°38'45" W; sec. 35, 36, T 15 S, R 21 E). Named on Selma (1946) 15' quadrangle. On Conejo (1963) 7.5' quadrangle, the name applies to a dry depression.

Rocky Basin Lakes [TULARE]: *lakes,* largest 1900 feet long, 10 miles north of Kern Peak (lat. 36°26'45" N, long. 118°19'15" W). Named on Kern Peak (1956) 15' quadrangle.

Rocky Creek [TULARE]: *stream,* flows 6.5 miles to South Fork Tule River 7.25 miles south-southeast of Springville (lat. 36°02'15" N, long. 118°45'20" W). Named on Camp Nelson (1956) and Springville (1957) 15' quadrangles.

Rocky Gulch [KERN]: *canyon,* drained by a stream that flows 2.5 miles to French Gulch (1) 5 miles southeast of Alta Sierra (lat. 35° 40'15" N, long. 118°30' W; near NW cor. sec. 13, T 26 S, R 32 E). Named on Alta Sierra (1972) 7.5' quadrangle.

Rocky Hill [TULARE]:
(1) *ridge,* west-trending, 2 miles long, 3 miles east-northeast of Porterville (lat. 36°05'10" N, long. 118°57'30" W). Named on Success Dam (1956) 7.5' quadrangle.
(2) *peak,* 3 miles east of Exeter (lat. 36°17'15" N, long. 119°05'05" W; sec. 7, T 19 S, R 27 E). Altitude 1580 feet. Named on Rocky Hill (1951) 7.5' quadrangle.
(3) *locality,* 1.25 miles east-northeast of Exeter along Visalia Electric Railroad (lat. 36°18'05"

N, long. 119°07'05" W; near E line sec. 2, T 19 S, R 26 E); the place is 2 miles west-north-west of Rocky Hill (2). Named on Rocky Hill (1951) 7.5' quadrangle.

Rocky Hills [TULARE]: *range,* 10 miles north of Porterville (lat. 36° 12'30" N, long. 119°00' W). Named on Lindsay (1951) and Frazier Valley (1957) 7.5' quadrangles.

Rocky Point [KERN]:
(1) *promontory,* 2.5 miles south-southeast of Wofford Heights along Isabella Lake (lat. 35°40'25" N, long. 118°26'35" W; on S line sec. 9, T 26 S, R 33 E). Named on Lake Isabella North (1972) 7.5' quadrangle.
(2) *relief feature,* 4.5 miles southeast of Bodfish (lat. 35°32'05" N, long. 118°26'30" W; sec. 33, T 27 S, R 33 E). Named on Lake Isabella South (1972) 7.5' quadrangle.
(3) *peak,* 6.25 miles west of Skinner Peak (lat. 35°34'30" N, long. 118°14'20" W; at SE cor. sec. 17, T 27 S, R 35 E). Named on Cane Canyon (1972) 7.5' quadrangle.

Rocky Point Bay [KERN]: *embayment,* 2.5 miles southeast of Wofford Heights on the north side of Isabella Lake (lat. 35°40'45" N, long. 118°25'40" W; sec. 9, 10, T 26 S, R 33 E); the embayment is east of Rocky Point (1). Named on Lake Isabella North (1972) 7.5' quadrangle.

Rocky Point Campground [MADERA]: *locality,* 6.5 miles southeast of Yosemite Forks on the southwest side of Bass Lake (1) (lat. 37° 18'10" N, long. 119°32'20" W; sec. 23, T 7 S, R 22 E). Named on Bass Lake (1953) 15' quadrangle.

Rod: see **Muroc** [KERN].

Rodecker Flat [KERN]: *area,* 1.5 miles northwest of Inyokern in South Fork Sand Canyon (2) (lat. 35°46'05" N, long. 117°57'30" W). Named on Little Lake (1954) 15' quadrangle.

Rodeo Canyon [KERN]: *canyon,* drained by a stream that flows 2.5 miles to Caliente Creek 2.5 miles west of Caliente (lat. 35°17'45" N, long. 118°40'10" W). Named on Bena (1972) 7.5' quadrangle.

Rodeo Flat: see **Fish Creek Meadow** [TULARE].

Rodeo Ridge [KERN]: *ridge,* south-trending, 1.5 miles long, 3.25 miles northwest of Loraine (lat. 35°20' N, long. 118°29' W). Named on Loraine (1972) 7.5' quadrangle.

Rodeo Spring [KERN]: *spring,* 3 miles west of Caliente (lat. 35°17'10" N, long. 118°40'40" W); the spring is in Rodeo Canyon. Named on Bena (1972) 7.5' quadrangle.

Rodger Peak [MADERA]: *peak,* 9.5 miles northeast of Merced Peak on Madera-Mono county line (lat. 37°43'30" N, long. 119°15'25" W). Altitude 12,978 feet. Named on Merced Peak (1953) 15' quadrangle. Called Rodgers Peak on Mount Lyell (1901) 30' quadrangle. United States Board on Geographic Names (1934a, p. 21) approved the form "Rodgers Peak" for the name, which

Lieutenant N.F. McClure gave in 1895 to honor Captain Alexander Rodgers.

Rodgers Creek [FRESNO]: see **Rogers Creek** [FRESNO].

Rodgers Crossing [FRESNO]: *locality,* 3 miles south of Balch Camp along Kings River (lat. 36°51'45" N, long. 119°07'20" W; sec. 27, T 12 S, R 26 E); the place is near the east end of Rodgers Ridge. Named on Patterson Mountain (1952) 15' quadrangle.

Rodgers Peak: see **Rodger Peak** [MADERA].

Rodgers Ridge [FRESNO]: *ridge,* west-trending, 14 miles long, 7 miles east of Balch Camp (lat. 36°54' N, long. 119°00' W). Named on Patterson Mountain (1952) and Tehipite Dome (1952) 15' quadrangles.

Rodrigues Lake: see **Rogers Lake** [KERN].

Rodriguez: see **Muroc** [KERN].

Rogers: see **Coalinga Mineral Springs** [FRESNO]; **Muroc** [KERN].

Rogers Camp [TULARE]: *locality,* 2.5 miles southwest of Camp Nelson (lat. 36°06'30" N, long. 118°38'10" W; near N line sec. 9, T 21 S, R 31 E). Named on Camp Nelson (1956) 15' quadrangle.

Rogers Creek [FRESNO]: *stream,* flows 5.5 miles to Crown Creek 12 miles north-north-east of Hume (lat. 36°55'50" N, long. 118°48'30" W); the stream heads near the east end of Rodgers Ridge. Named on Tehipite Dome (1952) 15' quadrangle. United States Board on Geographic Names (1987b, p. 2) approved the name "Rodgers Creek" for the stream, and noted that the name commemorates John Rodgers, an early stockman in the neighborhood.

Rogers Lake [KERN]: *dry lake,* 21 miles east-southeast of Mojave (lat. 34°54'30" N, long. 117°49'30" W). Named on Edwards (1973), Redman (1973), Rogers Lake North (1973), and Rogers Lake South (1973) 7.5' quadrangles. The feature also was known as Muroc Dry Lake and as Rodrigues Lake (Hoover, Rensch, and Rensch, p. 134).

Rogers Spring [MADERA]: *spring,* 2.5 miles east of Knowles (lat. 37°13'30" N, long. 119°49'40" W; sec. 19, T 8 S, R 20 E). Named on Knowles (1962) 7.5' quadrangle. Called Rogers Sprs. on Raymond (1944) 15' quadrangle, but United States Board on Geographic Names (1965d, p. 11) rejected this form of the name.

Rogersville: see **Big Blue Mill** [KERN].

Rolinda [FRESNO]: *settlement,* 10 miles west of downtown Fresno (lat. 36°44'05" N, long. 119°57'40" W; at S line sec. 1, T 14 S, R 18 E). Named on Kearney Park (1963) 7.5' quadrangle. On Kearney Park (1923) 7.5' quadrangle, the name applies to a place situated 0.5 mile farther north along Southern Pacific Railroad. Postal authorities established Rolinda post office in 1895 and discontinued it in 1902 (Frickstad, p. 37).

Roman Four Lake [FRESNO]: *lake,* 450 feet long, 1.5 miles north of Blackcap Mountain (lat. 37°05'40" N, long. 118°47'45" W). Named on Blackcap Mountain (1953) 15' quadrangle. William A. Dill of California Department of Fish and Game named the lake in 1948 because he thought that its outline on a map resembles the Roman numeral "IV" (Browning 1986, p. 187).

Roof Spring [KINGS]: *spring,* 6.5 miles south of Avenal (lat. 35°54'45" N, long. 120°08'40" W; sec. 21, T 23 S, R 17 E). Named on Garza Peak (1953) 7.5' quadrangle.

Root Creek [MADERA]: *stream,* flows 11.5 miles before ending in lowlands 2 miles east-southeast of Trigo (lat. 36°53'50" N, long. 119°55'45" W; sec. 8, T 12 S, R 19 E). Named on Herndon (1965) 15' quadrangle.

Root Island: see **Alpaugh** [TULARE].

Rootville: see **Old Millerton** [FRESNO].

Rosalie Lake [MADERA]: *lake,* 1100 feet long, nearly 5 miles north-northwest of Devils Postpile (lat. 37°41'15" N, long. 119°07'20" W). Named on Devils Postpile (1953) 15' quadrangle.

Rosamond [KERN]: *town,* 13 miles south of Mohave (lat. 34°51'40" N, long. 118°09'45" W; in and near sec. 21, T 9 N, R 12 W). Named on Rosamond (1973) 7.5' quadrangle. Postal authorities established Rosamond post office in 1885, discontinued it in 1887, and reestablished it in 1888 (Frickstad, p. 58). Officials of Southern Pacific Railroad founded the town in 1876 and named it for the daughter of a railroad official (Wines, p. 80). Baker's (1911) map shows a place called Monterio located about 20 miles west-northwest of Rosamond. Postal authorities established Monterio post office in 1895 and discontinued it in 1899 (Salley, p. 145). Johnson's (1911) map shows some springs, called Indian Springs, situat ed 2.5 miles east of Rosamond (at SE cor. sec. 14, T 9 N, R 12 W).

Rosamond Dry Lake: see **Rosamond Lake** [KERN].

Rosamond Hills [KERN]: *range,* center 5 miles northeast of Rosamond (lat. 34°55' N, long. 118°06'30" W). Named on Bissell (1973), Edwards (1973), and Soledad Mountain (1973) 7.5' quadrangles.

Rosamond Lake [KERN]: *dry lake,* 6 miles east-southeast of Rosamond on Kern-Los Angeles county line (lat. 34°50' N, long. 118° 04' W). Named on Rosamond Lake (1973) 7.5' quadrangle. Called Rosamond Dry Lake on Rosamond (1943) 15' quadrangle.

Rosebud Lake [FRESNO]: *lake,* 700 feet long, 8 miles southwest of Mount Abbot (lat. 37°18'35" N, long. 118°53'30" W). Named on Mount Abbot (1953) 15' quadrangle.

Rose Crossing [FRESNO]: *locality,* 6 miles north of Balch Camp along Dinkey Creek (1) (lat. 36°59'15" N, long. 119°07'30" W). Named on Patterson Mountain (1952) 15' quadrangle.

238

Rosedale [KERN]: *town,* 8 miles west of Bakers-field (lat. 35°23' N, long. 119°08'30" W; on S line sec. 24, T 29 S, R 26 E). Named on Rosedale (1954) 7.5' quadrangle. Rosedale post office was established in 1891 and discontinued in 1913 (Frickstad, p. 58). The place preserves the name of a failed colony of English farmers started in 1891 (Bailey, 1967, p. 23-24).

Rosedale [MADERA]: *locality,* 4.5 miles north-northwest of O'Neals (lat. 37°11'25" N, long. 119°43'40" W; near W line sec. 31, T 8 S, R 21 E). Named on Mariposa (1912) 30' quadrangle.

Rosedale: see **Frazier** [TULARE].

Rosedale Station [KERN]: *locality,* 9 miles west-northwest of Bakersfield along Atchison, Topeka and Santa Fe Railroad 1.5 miles north-northwest of Rosedale (lat. 35°24'10" N, long. 119°09'05" W; sec. 14, T 29 S, R 26 E). Named on Rosedale (1954) 7.5' quadrangle.

Rose Lake [FRESNO]: *lake,* 3000 feet long, 8 miles southwest of Mount Abbot (lat. 37°18'30" N, long. 118°53' W). Named on Mount Abbot (1953) 15' quadrangle. R.B. Marshall of United States Geological Survey named the lake for Rosa Hooper, sister of Selden S. Hooper, a Survey assistant (Farquhar, 1925, p. 130).

Rosemarie Meadow [FRESNO]: *area,* 7 miles southwest of Mount Abbot (lat. 37°19'05" N, long. 118°52'20" W); the place is near Rose Lake and Marie Lake. Named on Mount Abbot (1953) 15' quadrangle.

Rosemarr Spring [KERN]: *spring,* 4.25 miles southwest of Cummings Mountain (lat. 35°00'05" N, long. 118°37'35" W; sec. 31, T 11 N, R 16 W). Named on Tejon Ranch (1966) 7.5' quadrangle.

Rose's Station: see **Rose Station** [KERN].

Rose Station [KERN]: *locality,* 2.5 miles north of Grapevine along Grapevine Creek (lat. 34°57'50" N, long. 118°55' W). Site named on Grapevine (1958) 7.5' quadrangle. Called Rose's Store on Wheeler's (1875-1878) map, and called Roses Station on Mendenhall's (1908) map. Postal authorities established Tejon post office in 1875, moved it 6 miles north and changed the name to Rose's Station in 1877, and discontinued it in 1883 (Salley, p. 189, 219). William W. Hudson and James V. Rosemyre had a sheep ranch at the site in the 1870's and opened a stopping place there called Hudson Station; the place was renamed Rose Station after William B. Rose acquired it (Boyd, p. 42).

Ross Creek [FRESNO]:
(1) *stream,* flows 4.5 miles to Dinkey Creek (1) 4 miles north of Balch Camp (lat. 36°57'50" N, long. 119°07'20" W). Named on Patterson Mountain (1952) 15' quadrangle.
(2) *stream,* flows 2 miles to Big Creek (2) 7 miles west-northwest of Balch Camp (lat. 36°55'30" N, long. 119°14'35" W; near E line

sec. 33, T 11 S, R 25 E). Named on Patterson Mountain (1952) 15' quadrangle.

Ross Creek [MADERA]: *stream,* flows 5 miles to San Joaquin River 10 miles southeast of Shuteye Peak (lat. 37°13'35" N, long. 119° 20' W; near N line sec. 22, T 8 S, R 24 E). Named on Shaver Lake (1953) and Shuteye Peak (1953) 15' quadrangles.

Rossi [KERN]: *locality,* nearly 3 miles west of Lemoore along Southern Pacific Railroad (lat. 36°17'45" N, long. 119°49'55" W; near W line sec. 8, T 19 S, R 20 E). Named on Lemoore (1954) 7.5' quadrangle.

Ross Meadow [FRESNO]: *area,* 4.5 miles northeast of Balch Camp (lat. 36°57'10" N, long. 119°04' W; near S line sec. 19, T 11 S, R 27 E); the place is near the head of Ross Creek (1). Named on Patterson Mountain (1952) 15' quadrangle.

Rosy Finch Lake [FRESNO]: *lake,* 1850 feet long, 7.25 miles northwest of Mount Abbot (lat. 37°27'55" N, long. 118°52'15" W). Named on Mount Abbot (1953) 15' quadrangle. William A. Dill of California Department of Fish and Game named the lake in 1943 (Browning 1986, p. 187).

Roth: see **Strathmore** [TULARE].

Roth Spur: see **Strathmore** [TULARE].

Rough and Ready Mountain [KERN]: *peak,* 5.25 miles west-northwest of Miracle Hot Springs (lat. 35°36'40" N, long. 118°36'55" W). Named on Miracle Hot Springs (1972) 7.5' quadrangle.

Rough Creek [FRESNO]: *stream,* flows 4.5 miles to Kings River 5.25 miles north-northwest of Hume (lat. 36°51'30" N, long. 118° 56'40" W); the stream is east of Rough Spur. Named on Tehipite Dome (1952) 15' quadrangle.

Rough Spur [FRESNO]: *ridge,* south-south-west- to south-trending, 4 miles long, 7.5 miles north-northwest of Hume (lat. 36°53'45" N, long. 118°56'15" W). Named on Tehipite Dome (1952) 15' quadrangle.

Round Corral Meadow [FRESNO]: *area,* 8 miles southwest of Blackcap Mountain (lat. 37°00' N, long. 118°54'45" W; sec. 3, T 11 S, R 28 E). Named on Blackcap Mountain (1953) and Tehipite Dome (1952) 15' quadrangles.

Round Meadow [FRESNO]:
(1) *area,* 2 miles east of Kaiser Peak (lat. 37°17'45" N, long. 119° 08'55" W; on S line sec. 20, T 7 S, R 26 E). Named on Kaiser Peak (1953) 15' quadrangle.
(2) *area,* 3.5 miles south-southwest of Kaiser Peak on the north side of Huntington Lake (1) (lat. 37°14'45" N, long. 119°12'30" W; near N line sec. 14, T 8 S, R 25 E). Named on Kaiser (1904) 30' quadrangle.

Round Meadow [TULARE]:
(1) *area,* 6.5 miles south of Camp Nelson (lat. 36°02'40" N, long. 118°35'45" W; sec. 2, T 22 S, R 31 E). Named on Camp Nelson (1956)

15' quadrangle.

(2) *area,* 8 miles east-northeast of Fairview (lat. 35°57'55" N, long. 118°21'30" W; sec. 36, T 22 S, R 33 E). Named on Kernville (1956) 15' quadrangle.

(3) *area,* 5.25 miles west of Hockett Peak (lat. 36°13'10" N, long. 118°28'35" W). Named on Hockett Peak (1956) 15' quadrangle.

(4) *area,* 5.5 miles east of Yucca Mountain (lat. 36°34'05" N, long. 118°46' W; sec. 6, T 16 S, R 30 E). Named on Giant Forest (1956) 15' quadrangle.

Round Mountain [FRESNO]:

(1) *hill,* 11 miles east of Clovis (lat. 36°49'10" N, long. 119°30'35" W; sec. 7, T 13 S, R 23 E). Altitude 869 feet. Named on Round Mountain (1964) 7.5' quadrangle.

(2) *peak,* 6.5 miles north of Charley Mountain on Fresno-Monterey county line (lat. 36°14'10" N, long. 120°39'55" W; sec. 34, T 19 S, R 12 E). Named on Priest Valley (1969) 7.5' quadrangle.

Round Mountain [KERN]:

(1) *peak,* 5 miles south-southeast of Woody (lat. 35°37'55" N, long. 118°48'40" W; near S line sec. 25, T 26 S, R 29 E). Altitude 2961 feet. Named on Woody (1965) 7.5' quadrangle.

(2) *peak,* 10 miles northeast of Bakersfield (lat. 35°29'10" N, long. 118°53'20" W; near SE cor. sec. 18, T 28 S, R 29 E). Named on Oil Center (1954) 7.5' quadrangle. A ridge known as Sharktooth Hill is located 2.5 miles southwest of the peak; rocks exposed there contain fossils of Miocene marine vertebrates, including the teeth of sharks (Mitchell, Edward, p. III, 11).

Round Mountain [TULARE]: *peak,* 7 miles east of Monache Mountain on Tulare-Inyo county line (lat. 36°11'25" N, long. 118°04'25" W). Altitude 9884 feet. Named on Monache Mountain (1956) 15' quadrangle.

Round Mountain Stringer [TULARE]: *stream,* flows 2.5 miles to South Fork Kern River 1.25 miles east-southeast of Monache Mountain (lat. 36°12'05" N, long. 118°10'25" W; sec. 10, T 20 S, R 35 E). Named on Monache Mountain (1956) 15' quadrangle.

Roundtop [KINGS]: *peak,* nearly 6 miles southwest of Avenal on Reef Ridge (lat. 35°56'20" N, long. 120°11'35" W; sec. 12, T 23 S, R 16 E). Named on Garza Peak (1953) 7.5' quadrangle.

Round Valley [TULARE]: *valley,* 3.5 miles east-northeast of Lindsay (lat. 36°13'05" N, long. 119°01'20" W). Named on Lindsay (1951) 7.5' quadrangle.

Roush Creek [MADERA]: *stream,* flows nearly 2 miles to Whiskey Creek (2) 5.5 miles south of Shuteye Peak (lat. 37°15'50" N, long. 119°26'15" W; sec. 3, T 8 S, R 23 E). Named on Shuteye Peak (1953) 15' quadrangle. Charley Roush had a sawmill in section 3 in the 1920's (Browning, 1986, p. 188).

Rowell Meadow [TULARE]: *area,* 14 miles northwest of Triple Divide Peak (lat. 36°43'

N, long. 118°44'15" W; near SE cor. sec. 8, T 14 S, R 30 E). Named on Triple Divide Peak (1956) 15' quadrangle. The name commemorates Chester Rowell and George Rowell, who ran sheep in the area (Gudde, 1949, p. 291).

Rowen [KERN]: *locality,* 1.5 miles northwest of Keene along the railroad (lat. 35°14'25" N, long. 118°34'35" W; near S line sec. 7, T 31 S, R 32 E). Named on Keene (1966) 7.5' quadrangle. Postal authorities established Rowen post office in 1906 and discontinued it in 1908 (Frickstad, p. 59).

Roy [KINGS]: *locality,* 8 miles north-northwest of Lemoore along Atchison, Topeka and Santa Fe Railroad (lat. 36°23'50" N, long. 119°51' W; at E line sec. 1, T 18 S, R 19 E). Named on Riverdale (1954) 7.5' quadrangle.

Royal Allen Lake: see **Little Kern Lake** [TULARE].

Royal Arch Lake [MADERA]: *lake,* 900 feet long, 1.25 miles southeast of Buena Vista Peak (lat. 37°34'40" N, long. 119°30'10" W; near E line sec. 24, T 4 S, R 22 E). Named on Yosemite (1956) 15' quadrangle.

Royce Lakes [FRESNO]: *lakes,* largest 2400 feet long, 4.5 miles south-southeast of Mount Abbot (lat. 37°19'15" N, long. 118°45'45" W); the lakes are north and east of Royce Peak. Named on Mount Abbot (1953) 15' quadrangle.

Royce Peak [FRESNO]: *peak,* 4.5 miles south of Mount Abbot (lat. 37°19'10" N, long. 118°46'10" W). Altitude 13,253 feet. Named on Mount Abbot (1953) 15' quadrangle. United States Board on Geographic Names (1983a, p. 4) rejected the name "Mount Royce" for the feature, and noted that California State Geographic Board proposed the name in 1929 to honor Josiah Royce.

Rube Creek [FRESNO]: *stream,* flows 5.5 miles to South Fork San Joaquin River 11 miles north of Kaiser Peak (lat. 37°27'10" N, long. 119°10'30" W); the stream heads near Rube Meadow. Named on Kaiser Peak (1953) 15' quadrangle.

Rube Creek: see **Nigger Rube Creek** [TULARE].

Rube Meadow [FRESNO]: *area,* 14 miles north-northeast of Kaiser Peak (lat. 37°29'20" N, long. 119°07'20" W). Named on Kaiser Peak (1953) 15' quadrangle.

Ruby Creek [FRESNO]: *stream,* flows 2.5 miles to Bear Creek (3) 4 miles southeast of Dinkey Dome in Bear Meadow (2) (lat. 37°04'15" N, long. 119°05'10" W; sec. 12, T 10 S, R 26 E). Named on Huntington Lake (1953) 15' quadrangle.

Ruby Lake [MADERA]: *lake,* 1000 feet long, 8 miles north-northwest of Devils Postpile (lat. 37°43'20" N, long. 119°09'35" W); the feature is between Emerald Lake and Garnet Lake. Named on Devils Postpile (1953) 15' quadrangle.

Rucker Spring [FRESNO]: *spring,* 16 miles northwest of Coalinga (lat. 36°18'45" N, long.

120°32'30" W; near S line sec. 34, T 18 S, R 13 E). Named on Santa Rita Peak (1969) 7.5' quadrangle.

Rugg [FRESNO]: *locality*, 3 miles east-northeast of Kerman along Southern Pacific Railroad (lat. 36°43'55" N, long. 120°00'10" W; near W line sec. 10, T 14 S, R 18 E). Named on Kerman (1922) 7.5' quadrangle.

Ruiz Canyon [FRESNO]: *canyon*, drained by a stream that flows nearly 2 miles to Pete Merrill Canyon 6 miles south-southeast of Coalinga (lat. 36°03'25" N, long. 120°19'55" W; sec. 34, T 21 S, R 15 E). Named on Kreyenhagen Hills (1956) 7.5' quadrangle.

Runnington: see **Actis** [KERN].

Runyon: see **Lucy Runyon Creek** [TULARE].

Runyon Spring [KERN]: *spring*, 2 miles northeast of Glennville (lat. 35°45'05" N, long. 118°40'50" W; sec. 18, T 25 S, R 31 E). Named on California Hot Springs (1958) 15' quadrangle.

Rusconi [FRESNO]: *locality*, 2 miles south of Sanger along Southern Pacific Railroad (lat. 36°40'35" N, long. 119°32'55" W; near N line sec. 35, T 14 S, R 22 E). Named on Selma (1946) 15' quadrangle.

Rush Creek [FRESNO]: *stream*, flows 10.5 miles to Big Creek (2) 8 miles northwest of Balch Camp (lat. 36°58'15" N, long. 119°14' W; sec. 15, T 11 S, R 25 E). Named on Patterson Mountain (1952) and Shaver Lake (1953) 15' quadrangles, and on Trimmer (1965) 7.5' quadrangle.

Ruskin: see **Mount Ruskin** [FRESNO].

Russell: see **Mount Russell** [TULARE].

Russells Camp [FRESNO]: *locality*, 17 miles south of Kaiser Peak (lat. 37°02'45" N, long. 119°07'50" W; sec. 22, T 10 S, R 26 E). Named on Kaiser (1904) 30' quadrangle.

Russian Charley Creek [FRESNO]: *stream*, flows nearly 2 miles to Pine Flat Reservoir 5.25 miles northeast of Tivy Mountain (lat. 36° 51'05" N, long. 119°17'15" W; near N line sec. 31, T 12 S, R 25 E). Named on Pine Flat Dam (1965) 7.5' quadrangle.

Rutan Rock [FRESNO]: *peak*, 10 miles southsouthwest of Coalinga (lat. 36°00'40" N, long. 120°25'45" W; sec. 14, T 22 S, R 14 E). Named on Curry Mountain (1969) 7.5' quadrangle.

Ruth Camp Spring [KERN]: *spring*, 11 miles north of Mojave in North Fork Pine Tree Canyon (lat. 35°12'45" N, long. 118°12'25" W; near S line sec. 22, T 31 S, R 35 E). Named on Cache Peak (1973) 7.5' quadrangle.

Rutherford Lake [MADERA]: *lake*, 1900 feet long, nearly 3 miles south-southeast of Merced Peak (lat. 37°35'55" N, long. 119°22'15" W). Named on Merced Peak (1953) 15' quadrangle. The name commemorates Lieutenant Samuel M. Rutherford, who was stationed in Yosemite National Park in 1896 (Farquhar, 1925, p. 130).

Ruth Hill [FRESNO]: *peak*, 4 miles west of Dunlap (lat. 36°43'50" N, long. 119°11'30"

W; near NW cor. sec. 7, T 14 S, R 26 E). Altitude 2731 feet. Named on Tucker Mountain (1966) 7.5' quadrangle.

Ruth Lake [MADERA]: *lake*, 700 feet long, 4.25 miles south-southeast of Merced Peak (lat. 37°34'35" N, long. 119°22'15" W). Named on Merced Peak (1953) 15' quadrangle. A group from California Department of Fish and Game and from the Forest Service named the lake in 1934 to honor Ruth Burghduff, wife of A.E. Burghduff of the Department of Fish and Game; the feature had been called Hidden Lake, Nutcracker Lake, and Hideaway Lake (Browning, 1986. p. 189).

Ryans Lower Cow Camp [MADERA]: *locality*, 4 miles north of Shuteye Peak (lat. 37°24'15" N, long. 119°25' W; near E line sec. 14, T 6 S, R 23 E); the place is 2 miles southsoutheast of Ryans Upper Cow Camp. Named on Shuteye Peak (1953) 15' quadrangle.

Ryans Upper Cow Camp [MADERA]: *locality*, 5.5 miles north of Shuteye Peak (lat. 37°26' N, long. 119°25'55" W; near SW cor. sec. 2, T 6 S, R 23 E); the place is 2 miles northnorthwest of Ryans Lower Cow Camp. Named on Shuteye Peak (1953) 15' quadrangle.

– S –

Sacata Creek [FRESNO]: *stream*, flows nearly 3 miles to Kings River 6.5 miles west-southwest of Balch Camp (lat. 36°53' N, long. 119°13'55" W; sec. 15, T 12 S, R 25 E). Named on Patterson Mountain (1952) 15' quadrangle. United States Board on Geographic Names (1978c, p. 5) approved the name "Sacate Creek" for the feature, and rejected the names "Sacata Creek" and "Secata Creek."

Sacatara Creek [KERN]: *stream*, flows 3.5 miles to lowlands nearly 3 miles south-southeast of Liebre Twins (lat. 34°55' N, long. 118° 33'15" W). Named on Liebre Twins (1965) 7.5' quadrangle. The canyon of the stream is called Tierra Seca on Johnson's (1911) map, and it is called Canyon del Secretario on Neenach (1943) 15' quadrangle. United States Board on Geographic Names (1967c, p. 4) rejected the names "Canyon del Secretario" and "Canyon del Sectario" for the feature.

Sacatar Canyon [TULARE]: *canyon*, 3.5 miles long, 12.5 miles north of Lamont Peak (lat. 35°58'30" N, long. 119°02'30" W). Named on Lamont Peak (1956) 15' quadrangle.

Sacata Ridge [FRESNO]: *ridge*, south-southwest- to southwest-trending, 2.5 miles long, 6 miles west of Balch Camp (lat. 36° 54' N, long. 119°13'30" W). Named on Patterson Mountain (1952) 15' quadrangle. United States Board on Geographic Names (1978c, p. 5) approved the name "Sacate Ridge" for the feature, and rejected the forms "Sacata

Ridge" and "Secata Ridge."

Sacatar Meadow [TULARE]: *area,* 14 miles north of Lamont Peak (lat. 35°59'30" N, long. 118°04'40" W; in and near sec. 22, T 22 S, R 36 E); the place is at the mouth of Sacatar Canyon. Named on Lamont Peak (1956) 15' quadrangle. *Sacatar* is the Spanish word for a place that bunchgrass called sacaton grows (Browning 1986, p. 190).

Sacate Creek: see **Sacata Creek** [FRESNO].

Sacate Ridge: see **Sacata Ridge** [FRESNO]:

Saco [KERN]: *locality,* 7 miles northwest of Bakersfield along Southern Pacific Railroad (lat. 35°26'40" N, long. 119°05'25" W; sec. 32. T 28 S, R 27 E). Named on Oildale (1954) 7.5' quadrangle. Called Jewetta on Oildale (1935) 7.5' quadrangle. Postal authorities established Jewetta post office in 1893, discontinued it in 1896, reestablished it in 1898, and discontinued it in 1903; the name was for Solomon Jewett and Philo D. Jewett, pioneers at the place (Salley, p. 107).

Sacramento Gulch [KERN]: *canyon,* 1 mile long, opens into the canyon of Kern River 4 miles north-northeast of downtown Bakersfield (lat. 35°25'40" N, long. 118°58'25" W; near S line sec. 4, T 29 S, R 28 E). Named on Oil Center (1954) 7.5' quadrangle.

Sacratone Flat [TULARE]: *area,* 5 miles south of Hockett Peak (lat. 36°09' N, long. 118°22'45" W). Named on Hockett Peak (1956) 15' quadrangle.

Saddle [FRESNO]: *village,* 19 miles south-southwest of Kaiser Peak (lat. 37°03'35" N, long. 119°21'55" W; near W line sec. 16, T 10 S, R 24 E). Named on Kaiser (1904) 30' quadrangle.

Saddle Mountain [FRESNO]: *peak,* 13 miles northeast of Kaiser Peak (lat. 37°26'20" N, long. 119°02'40" W). Altitude 11,192 feet. Named on Kaiser Peak (1953) 15' quadrangle.

Saddle Spring [KERN]:
(1) *spring,* 3.5 miles northwest of Emerald Mountain in Orejano Canyon (1) (lat. 35°17'15" N, long. 118°19'50" W). Named on Emerald Mountain (1972) 7.5' quadrangle.
(2) *spring,* 6.5 miles southeast of Bodfish (lat. 35°31'10" N, long. 118°24'40" W; sec. 2, T 28 S, R 33 E). Named on Lake Isabella South (1972) 7.5' quadrangle.

Sadler Lake [MADERA]: *lake,* 1100 feet long, 5 miles east of Merced Peak (lat. 37°38'35" N, long. 119°18'10" W); the lake is 1.5 miles west of Sadler Peak. Named on Merced Peak (1953) 15' quadrangle.

Sadler Peak [MADERA]: *peak,* 6.5 miles east of Merced Peak (lat. 37°38'20" N, long. 119°16'20" W). Altitude 10,567 feet. Named on Merced Peak (1953) 15' quadrangle. Lieutenant N.F. McClure named the peak in 1895 for a corporal in his detachment (Farquhar, 1925, p. 130).

Sage [KERN]: *locality,* 1 mile north-northwest of downtown Mojave along Southern Pacific Railroad (lat. 35°04' N, long. 118°10'40" W; at S line sec. 5, T 11 N, R 12 W). Named on Mojave (1915) 30' quadrangle.

Sagebrush Gulch [TULARE]: *canyon,* drained by a stream that flows 2 miles to Little Kern River 8 miles northeast of Camp Nelson (lat. 36°13'50" N, long. 118°30'45" W; sec. 33, T 19 S, R 32 E). Named on Camp Nelson (1956) and Hockett Peak (1956) 15' quadrangles.

Sage Canyon [KERN]: *canyon,* drained by a stream that flows 7 miles to lowlands 6.25 miles east of Skinner Peak (lat. 35°33'20" N, long. 118°00'55" W; sec. 29, T 27 S, R 37 E). Named on Freeman Junction (1972) and Horse Canyon (1972) 7.5' quadrangles.

Sageland [KERN]: *locality,* 3.5 miles west-north-west of Pinyon Mountain near Kelso Creek (lat. 35°28'45" N, long. 118°12'45" W; at NE cor. sec. 21, T 28 S, R 35 E). Named on Pinyon Mountain (1972) 7.5' quadrangle. A place called El Dorado Camp started at the site in 1866 and it was renamed Sageland the next year (Boyd, p. 166). California Mining Bureau's (1917c) map shows a place called Sorrell's located about 8 miles south of Sageland.

Sage Mill [MADERA]: *locality,* 5.5 miles south of Shuteye Peak (lat. 37°16'15" N, long. 119°25'30" W; near S line sec. 35, T 7 S, R 23 E). Named on Kaiser (1904) 30' quadrangle.

Saginaw Creek [MADERA]: *stream,* flows 4.5 miles to San Joaquin River 13 miles south of Shuteye Peak (lat. 37°09'50" N, long. 119° 25' W; sec. 12, T 9 S, R 23 E). Named on Shaver Lake (1953) 15' quadrangle.

Saint John Ridge [KERN]: *ridge,* generally west-trending, 2.5 miles long, 4.25 miles east of Claraville (lat. 35°27'15" N, long. 118°15'30" W); Saint John mine is near the east end of the ridge. Named on Claraville (1972) and Pinyon Mountain (1972) 7.5' quadrangles. Several structures were moved south from Sageland to Saint John mine in 1872, and the name "St. Johnville" was proposed for the community at the mine (Boyd, p. 166).

Saint Johns [TULARE]: *settlement,* 2 miles south of Woodlake (lat. 36°23'05" N, long. 119°05'55" W; at SE cor. sec. 1, T 18 S, R 26 E). Named on Woodlake (1952) 7.5' quadrangle.

Saint Johns River [TULARE]: *stream,* diverges from Kaweah River 3.5 miles east-southeast of Woodlake and flows 25 miles to Cross Creek (1) 9.5 miles northwest of Visalia (lat. 36°25'20" N, long. 119°24'50" W). Named on Exeter (1952) and Visalia (1949) 15' quadrangles. Monson (1949, photorevised 1969), Traver (1949, photorevised 1969), Visalia (1949, photorevised 1969), and Woodlake (1952, photorevised 1969) 7.5' quadrangles show the stream in an artificial watercourse. The name commemorates Loomis St. Johns, an early settler in the neighborhood (Hoover,

Rensch, and Rensch, p. 561). Freshets of 1861 and 1862 established the stream permanently (Grunsky, p. 12).

Saint Johnville: see **Saint John Ridge** [KERN].

Sales Creek [FRESNO]: *stream,* flows 8.5 miles to Dog Creek 10 miles east-northeast of Clovis (lat. 36°53'25" N, long. 119°32'25" W; sec. 14, T 12 S, R 22 E). Named on Academy (1964) and Humphreys Station (1965) 7.5' quadrangles.

Sallie Keyes Creek: see **Sally Keyes Lakes** [FRESNO]

Sallie Keyes Lakes: see **Sally Keyes Lakes** [FRESNO].

Sally Keyes Creek: see **Sallie Keyes Creek**, under **Sally Keyes Lakes** [FRESNO].

Sally Keyes Lakes [FRESNO]: *lakes,* three, each about 1400 feet long, 9.5 miles south-southwest of Mount Abbot (lat. 37°16'20" N, long. 118°52'30" W). Named on Mount Abbot (1953) 15' quadrangle. United States Board on Geographic Names (1983d, p. 2) approved the name "Sallie Keyes Lakes" for the features, and noted that the name commemorates Sallie Keyes Shipp, whose family members were the principal owners of Blaney Meadows from the 1890's until 1940. The Board at the same time approved the name "Sallie Keyes Creek" for the stream that flows 1.7 miles from Sallie Keyes Lakes to South Fork San Joaquin River at Blaney Meadows (lat. 37°14'26" N, long. 118°53'20" W), and rejected the names "Sally Keyes Creek" and "Senger Creek" for this stream.

Salmon Creek [TULARE]: *stream,* flows 11 miles to Kern River 2.5 miles southeast of Fairview (lat. 35°53'45" N, long. 118°28' W; near N line sec. 31, T 23 S, R 33 E). Named on Kernville (1956) 15' quadrangle.

Salmon Creek Falls [TULARE]: *waterfall,* 3.5 miles east-southeast of Fairview (lat. 35°54'35" N, long. 118°26'05" W); the feature is along Salmon Creek. Named on Kernville (1956) 15' quadrangle. United States Board on Geographic Names (1961b, p. 12) rejected the name "Salmon Falls" for the feature.

Salmon Falls: see **Salmon Creek Falls** [TULARE].

Salt Canyon [FRESNO]:
(1) *canyon,* drained by a stream that heads in Merced County and flows nearly 3 miles in Fresno County to Little Panoche Creek 20 miles west-southwest of Firebaugh (lat. 36°46'50" N, long. 120°48'10" W; near SE cor. sec. 19, T 13 S, R 11 E). Named on Laguna Seca Ranch (1956) 7.5' quadrangle.
(2) *canyon,* drained by a stream that flows 2.5 miles to Los Gatos Creek 6 miles northwest of Coalinga (lat. 36°12' N, long. 120°26'10" W; sec. 10, T 20 S, R 14 E). Named on Alcalde Hills (1969) 7.5' quadrangle.
(3) *canyon,* drained by a stream that flows 2.5 miles to Dogwood Canyon 3.25 miles north-

northwest of Smith Mountain (2) (lat. 36°07'50" N, long. 120°36'45" W; sec. 7, T 21 S, R 13 E). Named on Slack Canyon (1969) and Smith Mountain (1969) 7.5' quadrangles.

Salt Creek [FRESNO]:
(1) *stream,* flows 10.5 miles to lowlands 17 miles north of Coalinga (lat. 36°26'35" N, long. 120°23'30" W; near W line sec. 6, T 18 S, R 15 E). Named on Ciervo Mountain (1969), Joaquin Rocks (1969), Lillis Ranch (1956), Santa Rita Peak (1969), and Tres Picos Farms (1956) 7.5' quadrangles.
(2) *stream,* flows nearly 6 miles to Jacalitos Creek 6 miles south-southwest of Coalinga (lat. 36°02'55" N, long. 120°22'45" W; near E line sec. 31, T 21 S, R 15 E). Named on Curry Mountain (1969) 7.5' quadrangle.

Salt Creek [KERN]:
(1) *stream,* flows 7.25 miles to Temblor Valley 5.5 miles southeast of Carneros Rocks (lat. 35°23'25" N, long. 119°45'55" W; at W line sec. 19, T 29 S, R 21 E). Named on Belridge (1953, photorevised 1973), Carneros Rocks (1959), and McKittrick Summit (1959) 7.5' quadrangles. Called Temblor Creek on Belridge (1953) 7.5' quadrangle, but United States Board on Geographic Names (1968a, p. 7) rejected this name for the stream.
(2) *stream,* flows 10 miles to lowlands 4 miles west-northwest of Grapevine (lat. 34°56'50" N, long. 118°59'20" W; near E line sec. 15, T 10 N, R 20 W). Named on Cuddy Valley (1943), Grapevine (1958), and Pleito Hills (1958) 7.5' quadrangles. United States Board on Geographic Names (1989c, p. 1) rejected the name "Cherry Creek" for the feature. The Board (1982b, p. 2) approved the name "Colorful Creek" for a stream that joins Salt Creek (2) 1 mile south-southwest of the mouth of that creek (lat. 34°56'03" N, long. 118°59'59" W; sec. 22, T 10 N, R 20 W)—the name is from colorful rocks along the stream.

Salt Creek [TULARE]: *stream,* flows 5 miles to Kaweah River 2.5 miles east-southeast of Kaweah (lat. 36°27'35" N, long. 118°52'15" W; near SE cor. sec. 7, T 17 S, R 29 E). Named on Kaweah (1957) 15' quadrangle.

Salt Creek: see **Cherry Creek** [KERN].

Salt Creek Ridge [TULARE]: *ridge,* east-south-east-trending, 4 miles long, 9.5 miles southeast of Kaweah (lat. 36°23'45" N, long. 118°46'45" W). Named on Kaweah (1957) and Mineral King (1956) 15' quadrangle.

Saltdale [KERN]: *village,* 21 miles south-southwest of Ridgecrest near Koehn Lake (lat. 35°21'35" N, long. 117°53'15" W). Named on Cantil (1967) 7.5' quadrangle. Postal authorities established Saltdale post office in 1916 and discontinued it in 1950 (Frickstad, p. 59). The village began when salt production started at Koehn Lake in 1914 (Bailey, 1967, p. 24).

Salt Lake: see **Koehn Lake** [KERN]; **Proctor Lake** [KERN].

Salt Lick Meadow [TULARE]: *area,* 6.5 miles north-northwest of Kern Peak (lat. 36°23'30" N, long. 118°20'05" W; sec. 6, T 18 S, R 34 E). Named on Kern Peak (1956) 15' quadrangle.

Salt Lick Spring [KERN]: *spring,* 4.5 miles east-southeast of Caliente (lat. 35°15'30" N, long. 118°33'25" W; near E line sec. 5, T 31 S, R 32 E). Named on Oiler Peak (1972) 7.5' quadrangle.

Salt Lick Spring: see **Upper Salt Lick Spring** [KERN].

Salt Springs [MADERA]: *locality,* 2 miles south-southwest of present Yosemite Forks along Fresno River (lat. 37°20'30" N, long. 119°38'30" W; sec. 11, T 7 S, R 21 E). Named on Mariposa (1912) 30' quadrangle.

Salt Wells Valley: see **Indian Wells Valley** [KERN].

Sam Lewis Camp [TULARE]: *locality,* 10.5 miles south-southwest of Monache Mountain (lat. 36°03'35" N, long. 118°14'20" W; near N line sec. 31, T 21 S, R 35 E). Named on Monache Mountain (1956) 15' quadrangle.

Sample Meadows [FRESNO]: *area,* 3.25 miles northeast of Kaiser Peak (lat. 37°20' N, long. 119°09' W; sec. 8, 9, T 7 S, R 26 E). Named on Kaiser Peak (1953) 15' quadrangle. Called Sample Meadow on Kaiser (1904) 30' quadrangle. Browning (1986, p. 191) associated the name with D.C. Sample, an early-day sheepman in the neighborhood.

Sampson Creek [FRESNO]: *stream,* flows 4.5 miles to Mill Flat Creek 7.5 miles south-southeast of Balch Camp (lat. 36°48'50" N, long. 119°03'10" W; near NW cor. sec. 9, T 13 S, R 27 E); the stream goes through Sampson Flat. Named on Patterson Mountain (1952) 15' quadrangle. United States Board on Geographic Names (1967a, p. 10) rejected the form "Samson Creek" for the name.

Sampson Flat [FRESNO]: *area,* 8 miles south-southeast of Balch Camp (lat. 36°47'30" N, long. 119°05' W; on W line sec. 18, T 13 S, R 27 E). Named on Patterson Mountain (1952) 15' quadrangle. United States Board on Geographic Names (1967a, p. 10) rejected the form "Samson Flat" for the name. An Indian called Sampson led a party across the Sierra Nevada in 1858, and later his name was given to Sampson's Flats (Chalfant, p. 124).

Samson Creek: see **Sampson Creek** [FRESNO].

Samson Flat: see **Sampson Flat** [FRESNO].

Sam Spring [KERN]: *spring,* 3 miles northeast of Caliente (lat. 35° 19'10" N, long. 118°35'05" W; sec. 18, T 30 S, R 32 E). Named on Oiler Peak (1972) 7.5' quadrangle.

Sam Spring [TULARE]: *spring,* 12 miles south of Hockett Peak along Durrwood Creek (lat. 36°03' N, long. 118°24' W). Named on Hockett Peak (1956) 15' quadrangle.

Sanborn [KERN]: *locality,* 5.5 miles southeast of Mojave along Atchison, Topeka and Santa Fe Railroad (lat. 35°00' N, long. 118° 06'15" W). Named on Bissell (1973) and Sanborn (1973) 7.5' quadrangles. Called Plano on Elizabeth Lake (1917) and Mojave (1915) 30' quadrangles.

Sanborn Hill [KERN]: *hill,* 5.5 miles southeast of Mojave (lat. 35° 00'30" N, long. 118°06' W; sec 36, T 11 N, R 12 W); the feature is 0.5 mile north of Sanborn. Named on Sanborn (1973) 7.5' quadrangle.

Sandberg Lodge [KERN]: *locality,* 3 miles west of Liebre Twins (lat. 34°57' N, long. 118°37'30" W; at N line sec. 19, T 10 N, R 16 W). Named on Neenach (1943) 15' quadrangle.

Sand Canyon [KERN]:

(1) *canyon,* drained by a stream that flows 4.5 miles to Rag Gulch 5.25 miles west of Woody (lat. 35°43'05" N, long. 118°55'35" W; at S line sec. 26, T 25 S, R 28 E). Named on Sand Canyon (1965) 7.5' quadrangle.

(2) *canyon,* drained by a stream that heads in Inyo County and flows 3.5 miles in Kern County to Indian Wells Valley 10 miles north-northwest of Inyokern (lat. 35°46'40" N, long. 117°53'45" W; sec. 9, T 25 S, R 38 E). Named on Little Lake (1954) 15' quadrangle. South Fork branches southwest 3 miles above the mouth of the main canyon; it is 4 miles long and is named on Little Lake (1954) 15' quadrangle.

(3) *canyon,* drained by a stream that flows 6.5 miles to Caliente Creek 1 mile east-northeast of Loraine (lat. 35°18'35" N, long. 118°25' W; sec. 22, T 30 S, R 33 E). Named on Loraine (1972) 7.5' quadrangle. West Fork branches northwest 1.25 miles north of the mouth of the canyon; it is 4.25 miles long and is named on Loraine (1972) 7.5' quadrangle.

(4) *canyon,* 10.5 miles long, along Cache Creek above a point 8.5 miles east-southeast of Tehachapi (lat. 35°05'45" N, long. 118°18'15" W; near SW cor. sec. 35, T 32 S, R 34 E). Named on Monolith (1966) and Tehachapi NE (1966) 7.5' quadrangles. The name "Sand Canyon" also applies to the canyon of Sand Creek above the confluence of Sand Creek and Cache Creek.

(5) *locality,* 0.5 mile northeast of present Loraine along Caliente Creek (lat. 35°18'25" N, long. 118°25'40" W; at W line sec. 22, T 30 S, R 33 E); the place is below the mouth of Sand Canyon (3). Named on Emerald Mountain (1943) 15' quadrangle.

Sand Creek [FRESNO]: *stream,* flows 2.5 miles to Dry Creek 1.25 miles west-northwest of Humphreys Station (lat. 36°58' N, long. 119°27'55" W; near N line sec. 21, T 11 S, R 23 E). Named on Humphreys Station (1965) 7.5' quadrangle.

Sand Creek [FRESNO-TULARE]: *stream,* heads in Fresno County and flows 12.5 miles to lowlands 6.5 miles east-northeast of Dinuba in Tulare County (lat. 36°35'45" N, long.

119°17'10" W; near W line sec. 29, T 15 S, R 25 E). Named on Orange Cove South (1966), Stokes Mountain (1966), and Tucker Mountain (1966) 7.5' quadrangles.

Sand Creek [KERN]: *stream,* flows 6.25 miles to Cache Creek 8 miles east of Tehachapi (lat. 35°08'55" N, long. 118°18'30" W; near E line sec. 15, T 32 S, R 34 E); the stream drains the upper part of Sand Canyon (4). Named on Tehachapi NE (1966) 7.5' quadrangle.

Sand Creek [MADERA]: *stream,* flows 7 miles to join Browns Creek and form South Fork Willow Creek (2) 5 miles southwest of Shuteye Peak (lat. 37°17'55" N, long. 119°29'40" W; near NE cor. sec. 30, T 7 S, R 23 E). Named on Shuteye Peak (1953) 15' quadrangle. North Fork enters from the northnorthwest 2.25 miles upstream from the mouth of the main creek; it is 4.5 miles long and is named on Shuteye Peak (1953) 15' quadrangle. Kaiser (1904) 30' quadrangle shows present North Fork as the main stream.

Sand Cut: see **Bena** [KERN].

Sanders: see **Kingsburg** [FRESNO].

Sand Flat [KERN-TULARE]: *area,* 4.25 miles north of Glennville along Poso Creek on Kern-Tulare county line (lat. 35°47'20" N, long. 118°42'15" W; on N line sec. 1, T 25 S, R 30 E). Named on California Hot Springs (1958) 15' quadrangle.

Sand Flat [TULARE]: *area,* 5.5 miles east of California Hot Springs (lat. 35°53' N, long. 118°34'30" W; near E line sec. 36, T 23 S, 31 E). Named on California Hot Springs (1958) 15' quadrangle.

Sand Flat: see **Guyot Flat** [TULARE].

Sand Gulch [KERN]: *canyon,* less than 1 mile long, opens into Goler Gulch 3 miles northeast of Garlock (lat. 35°26'20" N, long. 117°45'10" W). Named on Garlock (1967) 7.5' quadrangle.

Sand Hill Ridge [TULARE]: *ridge,* west- to northwest-trending, 3 miles long, 14 miles south-southwest of Hockett Peak (lat. 36°02'35" N, long. 118°29'50" W). Named on Camp Nelson (1956) and Hockett Peak (1956) 15' quadrangles.

San Diego Creek [KERN]: *stream,* flows 1 mile to San Luis Obispo County 13 miles westnorthwest of McKittrick (lat. 35°21'05" N, long. 119°50'30" W; at S line sec. 32, T 29 S, R 20 E). Named on McKittrick Summit (1959) 7.5' quadrangle. On McKittrick (1912) 30' quadrangle, the name has the form "Sandiego Creek." United States Board on Geographic Names (1933a, p. 665) once approved this form for the name, but later the Board (1978d, p. 3) reversed this decision.

Sand Lake [FRESNO]: *lake,* 400 feet long, 16 miles northeast of Kaiser Peak (lat. 37°28'50" N, long. 119°01'05" W). Named on Kaiser Peak (1953) 15' quadrangle.

Sand Meadow: see **Little Sand Meadow** [TULARE].

Sand Meadows [FRESNO]: *area,* 10 miles west of Blackcap Mountain (lat. 37°05'55" N, long. 118°58'15" W; near S line sec. 36, T 9 S, R 27 E). Named on Mount Goddard (1912) 30' quadrangle. Water of Courtright Reservoir now covers the place.

Sand Meadows [TULARE]: *area,* 7 miles southsouthwest of Mineral King (lat. 36°21'30" N, long. 118°39'15" W; sec. 18, T 18 S, R 31 E). Named on Mineral King (1956) 15' quadrangle.

Sand Meadows: see **Sandy Meadow** [TULARE].

Sandpiper Lake [FRESNO]: *lake,* 1300 feet long, 6.5 miles southwest of Mount Abbot along South Fork Bear Creek (2) (lat. 37°18'30" N, long. 118°51'05" W). Named on Mount Abbot (1953) 15' quadrangle. Employees of California Department of Fish and Game named the lake in 1942 for sandpipers that nest near South Fork Bear Creek (2) (Browning 1986, p. 191).

Sand Ridge [KINGS]: *ridge,* west-southwest- to west-trending, 12.5 miles long, 20 miles southeast of Kettleman City (lat. 35°50'40" N, long. 119°39' W). Named on Hacienda Ranch (1954), Lone Tree Well (1954), and West Camp (1954) 7.5' quadrangles.

Sand Slough [KINGS]:

(1) *stream,* diverges from North Fork Kings River 7 miles northwest of Lemoore (lat. 36°22'55" N, long. 119°51'45" W; sec. 12, T 18 S, R 19 E) and flows nearly 2 miles to Faull Slough. Named on Burrel (1954) and Riverdale (1954) 7.5' quadrangles.

(2) *stream,* heads near Hanford and flows 9 miles in a ditch 2.25 miles west-southwest of Guernsey (lat. 36°12'10" N, long. 119°40'50" W; sec. 10, T 20 S, R 21 E). Named on Guernsey (1929) and Hanford (1926) 7.5' quadrangles. On Guernsey (1954) and Hanford (1954) 7.5' quadrangles, the name applies to a mainly dry watercourse.

Sandspur [TULARE]: *locality,* nearly 4 miles east-southeast of Woodlake along Visalia Electric Railroad (lat. 36°23'55" N, long. 119°02' W; near N line sec. 3, T 18 S, R 27 E). Named on Lemon Cove (1928) 7.5' quadrangle.

Sandy Bluffs: see **Big Sandy Bluffs** [FRESNO].

Sandy Campground: see **Big Sandy Campground** [MADERA]; **Little Sandy Campground** [MADERA].

Sandy Creek [KERN]:

(1) *stream,* flows 6.25 miles to Poso Creek nearly 3 miles north of Glennville in Linns Valley (lat. 35°46'10" N, long. 118°42'45" W; sec. 11, T 25 S, R 30 E). Named on California Hot Springs (1958) 15' quadrangle.

(2) *stream,* flows 14 miles to end 6.5 miles east of Taft near Buena Vista Lake Bed (lat. 35°08'05" N, long. 119°20'35" W; near NE cor. sec. 24, T 32 S, R 24 E). Named on Mouth of Kern (1950) and Taft (1950) 7.5' quadrangles.

Sandy Creek: see **Big Sandy Creek** [FRESNO]; **Little Sandy Creek** [FRESNO].

Sandy Creek Spring [KERN]: *spring,* 4.25 miles northeast of Glennville (lat. 35°46'25" N, long. 118°39'05" W; at N line sec. 9, T 25 S, R 31 E); the spring is along Sandy Creek (1). Named on California Hot Springs (1958) 15' quadrangle.

Sandy Meadow [TULARE]: *area,* 4.5 miles west of Mount Whitney (lat. 36°34' N, long. 118°22'15" W). Named on Mount Whitney (1956) 15' quadrangle. Called Sand Meadows on Mount Whitney (1907) 30' quadrangle, but United States Board on Geographic Names (1938, p. 47) rejected this name for the feature.

Sandy Plateau: see **Bighorn Plateau** [TULARE].

Sandy Valley: see **Big Sandy Valley** [FRESNO].

San Emedio: see **San Emidio** [KERN] (1).

San Emedio Creek: see **San Emigdio Creek** [KERN].

San Emedio Mountain: see **San Emigdio Mountain** [KERN].

San Emedio Range: see **San Emigdio Mountains** [KERN].

San Emidio [KERN]:

(1) *land grant,* at and south of the mouth of San Emigdio Creek, mainly between San Emigdio Creek and Santiago Creek. Named on Eagle Rest Peak (1942), Pleito Hills (1958), and Santiago Creek (1943) 7.5' quadrangles. United States Board on Geographic Names (1933a, p. 665) approved the form "San Emigdio" for the name, and rejected the forms "San Emidio," "San Emedio," and "San Emidion." Jose Antonio Dominguez received 4 leagues in 1842; Francisco Dominguez and others claimed 17,710 acres patented in 1866 (Cowan, p. 75).

(2) *locality,* 6 miles east-northeast of Maricopa along Sunset Railroad (lat. 34°05'35" N, long. 119°18'15" W; sec. 26, T 12 N, R 23 W). Named on Pentland (1953) 7.5' quadrangle.

San Emidio Creek: see **San Emigdio Creek** [KERN].

San Emidio Mountain: see **San Emigdio Mountain** [KERN].

San Emidio Mountains: see **San Emigdio Mountains** [KERN].

San Emidion: see **San Emidio** [KERN] (1).

San Emidion Creek: see **San Emigdio Creek** [KERN].

San Emidion Mountain: see **San Emigdio Mountain** [KERN].

San Emigdio: see **San Emidio** [KERN] (1); **San Emigdio Creek** [KERN].

San Emigdio Creek [KERN]: *stream,* flows 13 miles to lowlands 6.5 miles north-northwest of Eagle Rest Peak (lat. 34°59'20" N, long. 119°11'05" W; near N line sec. 1, T 10 N, R 22 W). Named on Conner SW (1955), Cuddy Valley (1943), Eagle Rest Peak (1942), and Sawmill Mountain (1943) 7.5' quadrangles.

Called Arroyo San Arminio on Williamson's (1853) map. Joy (p. 51) mentioned San Emigio Cañon, Whitney (1865, p. 186) wrote of San Emidio Cañon, and Fairbanks (1894b, p. 495) described San Emedio Cañon. United States Board on Geographic Names (1933a, p. 665) rejected the forms "San Emedio Creek," "San Emidio Creek," and "San Emidion Creek " for the name. Mendenhall's (1908) map shows a place called San Emigdio situated at the entrance of San Emigdio Creek to the lowlands; Eagle Rest Peak (1942) 7.5' quadrangle shows the headquarters of San Emigdio ranch at the same place. About 3 miles farther north along San Emigdio Creek is the site of a Mexican community that was called San Emigdio (Hoover, Rensch, and Rensch, p. 127). The Mexican place was started before 1824 and was the first white community in Kern County; it was abandoned in the 1890's (Bailey, 1967, p. 24). Postal authorities established San Emigdio post office 25 miles southwest of Bakersfield in 1881 and discontinued it in 1886 (Salley, p. 193).

San Emigdio Mountain [KERN]: *peak,* 3.5 miles southwest of Eagle Rest Peak (lat. 34°52'25" N, long. 119°10'45" W; near S line sec. 12, T 9 N, R 22 W). Altitude 7495 feet. Named on Sawmill Mountain (1943) 7.5' quadrangle. United States Board on Geographic Names (1933a, p. 665) rejected the forms "San Emedio Mountain," "San Emidio Mountain," and "San Emidion Mountain" for the name.

San Emigdio Mountains [KERN]: *range,* south of San Joaquin Valley and west of Grapevine Creek. Named on Los Angeles (1975) 1°x 2° quadrangle. Joy (p. 51) called the range San Emidio Mountains, and Fairbanks (1894b, p. 493) called it San Emedio Range. United States Board on Geographic Names (1973b, p. 3) gave the name "San Emidio Mountains" as a variant.

Sanger [FRESNO]: *town,* 13 miles east-southeast of downtown Fresno (lat. 36°42'15" N, long. 119°33'30" W; around NE cor. sec. 22, T 14 S, R 22 E). Named on Sanger (1965) 7.5' quadrangle. Postal authorities established Sanger post office in 1888 (Frickstad, p. 37), and the town incorporated in 1911. The name honors Joseph Sanger, Jr., who came to San Francisco in 1887 to attend the annual convention of the Railroad Yardmasters Association, of which he was secretary-treasurer (Johnston, p. 27). California Mining Bureau's (1917a) map shows a place called Tarn about 4 miles south-southeast of Sanger along Southern Pacific Railroad.

San Joaquin [FRESNO]: *town,* 11 miles southwest of Kerman (lat. 36°36'30" N, long. 120°11'15" W; mainly in sec. 23, 24, T 15 S, R 16 E). Named on San Joaquin (1963) 7.5' quadrangle. Postal authorities established San Joaquin post office in 1913; at first it was intended to call the post office Grahamton for an early settler (Salley, p. 87, 195). The town incorporated in 1920. A place called Hawthorne's Station was about 1 mile southeast of present San Joaquin along Butterfield Overland stage line from 1858 until 1861 (Hoover, Rensch, and Rensch, p. 92).

San Joaquin Mountain [MADERA]: *peak,* 6.5 miles north of Devils Postpile on Madera-Mono county line (lat. 37°43'10" N, long. 119°06'20" W). Altitude 11,600 feet. Named on Devils Postpile (1953) 15' quadrangle. A pair of peaks, this one and the nearby peak now called Two Teats, together formerly had the name "Two Teats" (Gudde, 1949, p. 373-374).

San Joaquin River [FRESNO-MADERA]: *stream,* formed by the confluence of North Fork and Middle Fork in Madera County 8.5 miles southwest of Devils Postpile, flows 320 miles to Contra Costa and Sacramento Counties 17 miles west of Lodi (lat. 38°05'55" N, long. 121°34'40" W). Named on Fresno (1962, revised 1967), Mariposa (1957, revised 1970), Sacramento (1957, limited revision 1964), San Jose (1962), and Santa Cruz (1958) 1°x 2° quadrangles. Present San Joaquin River is called R. San Joachim on Wilkes' (1841) map, Rio San Joaquin on Fremont's (1848) map, River San Joarquin on Derby's (1850) map, and Rio Tulare or San Joaquin on Sage's (1846) map. Gabriel Moraga named the river about 1805 for Saint Joaquin, father of the Virgin Mary (Hart, p. 379). North Fork is 16 miles long and Middle Fork is 21 miles long; both forks are named on Devils Postpile (1953) 15' quadrangle. South Fork heads in Fresno County and flows 4 miles in Madera County to join San Joaquin River 12 miles east-northeast of Shuteye Peak; it is named on Kaiser Peak (1953) 15' quadrangle. United States Board on Geographic Names (1965c, p. 12) rejected the name "Hooper Creek" for South Fork. A landing place called Dover was situated along San Joaquin River 5 miles above the mouth of Merced River in present Merced County (Hoover, Rensch, and Rensch, p. 206). Postal authorities established Dover post office in 1870 and discontinued it in 1874; wheat was shipped from the place to Dover, England, which suggested the name (Salley, p. 61).

San Joaquin Valley: see "Regional setting."
Sanjon de San Jose: see **Tulare Lake** [KINGS].
San Pedro: see **Tule River** [KINGS-TULARE].
Sans Tache: see **Laton** [FRESNO].
Santa Maria Valley: see **Little Santa Maria Valley** [KERN].
Santa Rita Slough [FRESNO]: *water feature,* diverges from San Joaquin River and extends for 1 mile to Merced County 8 miles north of Oxalis (lat. 37°02' N, long. 120°33'20" W; near W line sec. 27, T 10 S, R 13 E). Named on Santa Rita Bridge (1922) 7.5' quadrangle.

Santa Teresita: see **Camp Santa Teresita** [MADERA].
Santiago Creek [KERN]: *stream,* flows 11 miles to lowlands 9 miles west-northwest of Eagle Rest Peak (lat. 34°58'10" N, long. 119°16'55" W; sec. 12, T 10 N, R 23 W). Named on Apache Canyon (1943), Pentland (1953), Santiago Creek (1943), and Sawmill Mountain (1943) 7.5' quadrangles. United States Board on Geographic Names (1982b, p. 3) approved the name "East Twin Creek" for a stream, 2 miles long, that joins Santiago Creek from the southeast about 2.5 miles upstream from the entrance of Santiago Creek into lowlands (lat. 34°56'02" N, long. 119°18'10" W; sec. 23, T 10 N, R 23 W). The Board at the same time approved the name "West Twin Creek" for a stream, 1.6 miles long, that enters Santiago Creek from the southwest 450 feet upstream from the mouth of East Twin Creek (lat. 34°55'57" N, long. 119°18'12" W; sec. 23, T 10 N, R 23 W).
Santos: see **Strathmore** [TULARE].
Santos Creek [KERN]: *stream,* heads in San Luis Obispo County and flows 4 miles to lowlands 2 miles north-northwest of Carneros Rocks (lat. 35°27'55" N, long. 119°51'25" W; sec. 30, T 28 S, R 20 E). Named on Carneros Rocks (1959) and Las Yeguas Ranch (1959) 7.5' quadrangles. The name commemorates Joe Santos, a settler (Arnold and Johnson, p. 22).
Sapphire Lake [FRESNO]: *lake,* 3000 feet long, 3.5 miles north-northeast of Mount Goddard in Evolution Basin (lat. 37°08'55" N, long. 118°41'40" W). Named on Mount Goddard (1948) 15' quadrangle.
Satcher Lake: see **Sotcher Lake** [MADERA].
Satellite Lake [KERN]: *playa,* 2 miles east of downtown Ridgecrest on Kern-San Bernardino county line (lat. 35°37'40" N, long. 117° 38'05" W; on E line sec. 35, T 26 S, R 40 E). Named on Ridgecrest North (1973) 7.5' quadrangle.
Saturday Peak [KERN]: *peak,* 3.5 miles west-southwest of Democrat Hot Springs (lat. 35°30'25" N, long. 118°43'20" W). Altitude 4143 feet. Named on Democrat Hot Springs (1972) 7.5' quadrangle.
Saturday Spring [KERN]: *spring,* 3 miles west-southwest of Democrat Hot Springs (lat. 35°30'30" N, long. 118°42'45" W); the spring is 0.5 mile east of Saturday Peak. Named on Democrat Hot Springs (1972) 7.5' quadrangle.
Saturday Spring Creek [KERN]: *stream,* flows 2.25 miles to Kern River 1.5 miles southwest of Democrat Hot Springs (lat. 35°30'45" N, long. 118°41'25" W). Named on Democrat Hot Springs (1972) 7.5' quadrangle.
Sawmill Canyon [KERN]: *canyon,* drained by a stream that flows nearly 4 miles to Oak Creek 8 miles south of Tehachapi (lat. 35° 01' N, long. 118°25'50" W; near W line sec. 25, T 11 N, R 15 W). Named on Tehachapi South (1966) 7.5' quadrangle.

Sawmill Flat [FRESNO]: *locality,* 7.5 miles northeast of Balch Camp (lat. 36°58'15" N, long. 119°01' W; sec. 15, T 11 S, R 27 E). Site named on Patterson Mountain (1952) 15' quadrangle.

Sawmill Mountain [KERN]: *peak,* 6.5 miles south-southwest of Eagle Rest Peak on Kern-Ventura county line (lat. 34°48'50" N, long. 119°10' W; on S line sec. 31, T 9 N, R 21 W). Named on Sawmill Mountain (1943) 7.5' quadrangle.

Sawmill Pass [FRESNO]: *pass,* 5 miles south-southeast of Mount Pinchot on Fresno-Inyo county line (lat. 36°53' N, long. 118°21'45" W); the pass is near the head of Sawmill Creek, which is in Inyo County. Named on Mount Pinchot (1953) 15' quadrangle.

Sawtooth Pass [TULARE]: *pass,* 2 miles east-northeast of Mineral King on Great Western Divide (lat. 36°27'10" N, long. 118°33'40" W); the pass is 0.5 mile northwest of Sawtooth Peak. Named on Mineral King (1956) 15' quadrangle. Called Glacier Pass on Kaweah (1909) 30' quadrangle, but United States Board on Geographic Names (1960b, p. 20) rejected this name for the feature.

Sawtooth Peak [TULARE]:
(1) *peak,* 2.25 miles east of Mineral King on Great Western Divide (lat. 36°27'20" N, long. 118°33'15" W). Named on Mineral King (1956) 15' quadrangle. United States Board on Geographic Names (1933a, p. 675) rejected the name "Miner's Peak" for the feature. The name "Sawtooth" is from the shape of the peak (Browning 1986, p. 193).
(2) *peak,* 28 miles south-southeast of Monache Mountain on Tulare-Inyo county line (lat. 35°49'25" N, long. 117°59'50" W). Altitude 7970 feet. Named on Little Lake (1954) 15' quadrangle.

Sawtooth Ridge [KERN]: *ridge,* east-southeast-trending, 1.25 miles long, 3.5 miles southeast of Orchard Peak (lat. 35°41'55" N, long. 120°05'30" W). Named on Sawtooth Ridge (1961) 7.5' quadrangle. Arnold and Johnson (p. 22) gave the name for the jagged appearance of the ridge.

Sawyer: see **Tom Sawyer Lake** [KERN].

Sawyer Peak [TULARE]: *peak,* nearly 3 miles north of Cliff Peak (lat. 36°35'50" N, long. 119°10'10" W; sec. 29, T 15 S, R 26 E). Altitude 2403 feet. Named on Stokes Mountain (1966) 7.5' quadrangle.

Scaffold Meadows [TULARE]: *area,* 9 miles north-northwest of Triple Divide Peak along Roaring River (lat. 36°42'45" N, long. 118°35' W). Named on Triple Divide Peak (1956) 15' quadrangle. Called Scaffold Meadow on Tehipite (1903) 30' quadrangle. Sheepherders built a scaffold at the place to keep food out of the reach of animals (Browning 1986, p. 193).

Scarab Lake [FRESNO]: *lake,* 700 feet long, 16 miles northeast of Kaiser Peak (lat. 37°28'50" N, long. 119°00'50" W). Named on Kaiser Peak (1953) 15' quadrangle.

Scarlet and Davis Canyon [TULARE]: *canyon,* drained by a stream that flows 2 miles to Tobias Creek 7.25 miles east of California Hot Springs (lat. 35°53'15" N, long. 118°32'30" W; sec. 32, T 23 S, R 32 E). Named on California Hot Springs (1958) 15' quadrangle.

Scarlett and Davis Canyon: see **Speas Creek** [TULARE] (1).

Scenic Heights [TULARE]: *ridge,* south-south-east-trending, about 1 mile long, 1.25 miles north-northwest of Porterville (lat. 36°05'20" N, long. 119°01'20" W). Named on Porterville (1951) 7.5' quadrangle.

Scenic Meadow [TULARE]: *area,* 7.25 miles north-northwest of Triple Divide Peak (lat. 36°41' N, long. 118°35'45" W). Named on Triple Divide Peak (1956) 15' quadrangle.

Scepter Creek [FRESNO]: *stream,* flows 7.25 miles to Crown Creek 13 miles north-north-east of Hume (lat. 36°57'05" N, long. 118°48'30" W); the stream heads near Scepter Pass. Named on Blackcap Mountain (1953) and Tehipite Dome (1952) 15' quadrangles.

Scepter Lake [FRESNO]: *lake,* 850 feet long, 3.5 miles southwest of Blackcap Mountain (lat. 37°01'50" N, long. 118°50'05" W); the lake is located along Scepter Creek. Named on Blackcap Mountain (1953) 15' quadrangle.

Scepter Pass [FRESNO]: *pass,* nearly 3 miles southwest of Blackcap Mountain (lat. 37°02'50" N, long. 118°50' W); the pass is at the head of Scepter Creek. Named on Blackcap Mountain (1953) 15' quadrangle.

Schaeffer Meadow [TULARE]:
(1) *area,* 5 miles west-northwest of Olancha Peak (lat. 36°17'15" N, long. 118°12' W; sec. 8, 9, T 19 S, R 35 E). Named on Olancha (1956) 15' quadrangle.
(2) *area,* 11.5 miles south of Hockett Peak (lat. 36°03'20" N, long. 118°24'25" W); the place is 1.5 miles south-southwest of Schaeffer Mountain. Named on Hockett Peak (1956) 15' quadrangle.

Schaeffer Mountain [TULARE]: *peak,* 10 miles south of Hockett Peak (lat. 36°04'30" N, long. 118°23'45" W). Altitude 9292 feet. Named on Hockett Peak (1956) 15' quadrangle.

Schaeffer Stringer [TULARE]: *stream,* flows 2 miles to South Fork Kern River 4.25 miles west of Olancha Peak (lat. 36°16'20" N, long. 118°11'40" W; sec. 16, T 19 S, R 35 E). Named on Olancha (1956) 15' quadrangle.

Schilling [FRESNO]: *locality,* nearly 2 miles south-southeast of Lanare along Atchison, Topeka and Santa Fe Railroad (lat. 36°24'30" N, long. 119°54'45" W; sec. 33, T 17 S, R 19 E). Named on Burrel (1954) 7.5' quadrangle.

Schmidt Camp [KERN]: *locality,* nearly 5 miles west of Garlock (lat. 35°24'40" N, long. 117°52'25" W). Named on Garlock (1967) 7.5' quadrangle.

Schmidt Creek [MADERA]: *stream,* flows 7.5 miles to end 6.5 miles southeast of Fairmead near Notarb (lat. 37°00'15" N, long. 120°07'05" W; sec. 4, T 11 S, R 17 E). Named on Kismet (1961) 7.5' quadrangle.

Schober's Pass: see **Lamarck Col** [FRESNO].

Schoolhouse Spring [TULARE]: *spring,* 4.5 miles south-southeast of Auckland (lat. 36°31'45" N, long. 119°04'15" W; near SE cor. sec. 18, T 16 S, R 27 E). Named on Auckland (1966) 7.5' quadrangle.

Schoolhouse Well [KERN]: *well,* 8 miles northwest of Cross Mountain in Kelso Valley (lat. 35°22'15" N, long. 118°13' W; near E line sec. 33, T 29 S, R 35 E). Named on Cross Mountain (1972) 7.5' quadrangle.

Schoolmarm Lake [FRESNO]: *lake,* 1050 feet long, 2.5 miles north of Blackcap Mountain (lat. 37°06'35" N, long. 118°47'50" W). Named on Blackcap Mountain (1953) 15' quadrangle.

Schultz Creek [TULARE]: *stream,* flows 3 miles to Bull Run Creek 9.5 miles southeast of California Hot Springs (lat. 35°48'05" N, long. 118°32' W; sec. 33, T 24 S, R 32 E). Named on California Hot Springs (1958) 15' quadrangle.

Schunemanns: see **Panoche Creek** [FRESNO].

Scodie: see **Onyx** [KERN].

Scodie Canyon [KERN]: *canyon,* drained by a stream that flows 8.5 miles to South Fork Valley near Onyx (lat. 35°40'55" N, long. 118°12'55" W; sec. 10, T 26 S, R 35 E). Named on Cane Canyon (1972) and Onyx (1972) 7.5' quadrangles.

Scodie Meadow [TULARE]: *area,* 7 miles north-northeast of Lamont Peak along Chimney Creek (lat. 35°53'25" N, long. 118°00'10" W). Named on Lamont Peak (1956) 15' quadrangle.

Scodie Mountains [KERN]: *range,* center 9 miles east of Weldon and west of Walker Pass (lat. 35°38' N, long. 118°08' W). Named on Bakersfield (1962, revised 1971) 1°x 2° quadrangle. Called Kiavah Mountains on Onyx (1943) 15' quadrangle, but United States Board on Geographic Names (1963a, p. 16) rejected the names "Kiavah Mountains" and "Kiavah Mountain" for the feature, and noted that the name "Scodie" commemorates William Scodie, who opened a store at the mouth of Scodie Canyon in the 1860's.

Scodie Spring [KERN]: *spring,* nearly 4 miles south-southeast of Onyx (lat. 35°38'30" N, long. 118°11'10" W; sec. 26, T 26 S, R 35 E); the spring is in Scodie Canyon. Named on Onyx (1972) 7.5' quadrangle.

Scoop Lake [FRESNO]: *lake,* 600 feet long, 7 miles west of Red Slate Mountain (lat. 37°31'05" N, long. 118°59'40" W). Named on Mount Morrison (1953) 15' quadrangle.

Scott Canyon [FRESNO]: *canyon,* drained by a stream that flows 2 miles to Oak Flat Canyon 7.25 miles west of Coalinga (lat. 36°09'20" N,

long. 120°29'10" W; sec. 30, T 20 S, R 14 E). Named on Alcalde Hills (1969) 7.5' quadrangle.

Scottsburg: see **Centerville** [FRESNO].

Scout Island [FRESNO]: *area,* 7.5 miles north-northwest of downtown Fresno on the south side of San Joaquin River (lat. 36°51'30" N, long. 119°50'30" W; sec. 25, T 12 S, R 19 E). Named on Fresno North (1965) 7.5' quadrangle. Bullard (1923) 7.5' quadrangle has the name "Fresno Beach" at the place, which it shows at the end of Fresno Beach Electric Railroad.

Scovern Hot Springs [KERN]: *springs,* 2.25 miles north-northeast of Bodfish (lat. 35°37'15" N, long. 118°28'25" W; sec. 31, T 27 S, R 33 E); the springs are in Hot Spring Valley. Named on Lake Isabella South (1972) 7.5' quadrangle. Spanish settlers called the springs Agua Caliente (Waring, p. 51). Isabella (1943) 15' quadrangle has the name for a resort at the springs; the resort also was called Neill's Hot Springs, Nelson's Hot Springs, and Walser Hot Springs (Bailey, 1962, p. 52; Bailey, 1967, p. 25).

Scraper Canyon [KERN]: *canyon,* drained by a stream that flows 4 miles to Caliente Creek 2.5 miles west-northwest of Caliente (lat. 35°18'10" N, long. 118°40'25" W). Named on Bena (1972) 7.5' quadrangle.

Scraper Spring [KERN]: *spring,* 2.5 miles north-northwest of Caliente (lat. 35°19'20" N, long. 118°38'50" W); the spring is in Scraper Canyon. Named on Bena (1972) 7.5' quadrangle.

Scratch Hill [TULARE]: *peak,* 12 miles southeast of Kaweah (lat. 36°20'45" N, long. 118°46'15" W). Named on Kaweah (1957) 15' quadrangle.

Scylla [FRESNO]: *peak,* 2.25 miles southeast of Mount Goddard (lat. 37°04'50" N, long. 118°41'20" W); the peak is 1.25 miles west-southwest of Charybdis. Altitude 12,939 feet. Named on Mount Goddard (1948) 15' quadrangle. Theodore S. Solomons named the peak in 1895 (Hanna, p. 61). United States Board on Geographic Names (1964b, p. 14) rejected the name "Scylla Peak" for the feature, and noted that the name is from the rock off the Sicilian coast that figures in Greek mythology. At the same time the Board approved the name "The Three Sirens" for three peaks located between Scylla and Charybdis.

Scylla Peak: see **Scylla** [FRESNO].

Searles [KERN]: *locality,* 8 miles north of Randsburg along Southern Pacific Railroad (lat. 35°29' N, long. 117°38'05" W; near W line sec. 23, T 28 S, R 40 E). Named on El Paso Peaks (1967) 7.5' quadrangle. Called Searles Sta. on Searles Lake (1915) 1° quadrangle.

Searles Station: see **Searles** [KERN].

Searles Valley [KERN]: *valley,* mainly in San Bernardino County, but the westernmost end of the feature extends into Kern County 8.5 miles south-southeast of Ridgecrest (lat.

35°30'30" N, long. 117°37'45" W). Named on Ridgecrest South (1973) 7.5' quadrangle. United States Board on Geographic Names (1961b, p. 12) rejected the name "Spangler Valley" for the feature.

Secata Creek: see **Sacata Creek** [FRESNO].

Secata Ridge: see **Sacata Ridge** [FRESNO].

Second Crossing [FRESNO]: *locality,* 2 miles northeast of Double Peak along Fish Creek (1) (lat. 37°32' N, long. 119°00'40" W); the place is 3.5 miles upstream from Island Crossing. Named on Devils Postpile (1953) 15' quadrangle.

Second Dinkey Lake [FRESNO]: *lake,* 600 feet long, 5 miles northeast of Dinkey Dome on upper reaches of Dinkey Creek (lat. 37° 09'20" N, long. 119°03'20" W; on S line sec. 8, T 9 S, R 27 E); the lake is 1 mile upstream from First Dinkey Lake. Named on Huntington Lake (1953) 15' quadrangle.

Second Recess [FRESNO]: *canyon,* drained by a stream that flows 4 miles to Mono Creek 4.5 miles west-northwest of Mount Abbot (lat. 37°25'25" N, long. 118°51'25" W); the feature is the second large canyon east of Lake Thomas A. Edison on the south side of Mono Creek. Named on Mount Abbot (1953) 15' quadrangle. Theodore S. Solomons discovered and named the canyon in 1894 (Farquhar, 1925, p. 127).

Sedge Lake [FRESNO]: *lake,* 500 feet long, 15 miles northeast of Kaiser Peak (lat. 37°28'25" N, long. 119°01'35" W). Named on Kaiser Peak (1953) 15' quadrangle. The lake is one of the group called Margaret Lakes.

Sedwell: see **Cable** [KERN].

Seguro [KERN]: *locality,* 3.25 miles north-northwest of downtown Bakersfield along Southern Pacific Railroad (lat. 35°25'10" N, long. 119°01' W). Named on Oildale (1954) 7.5' quadrangle. Buena Vista Lake (1912) 30' quadrangle has the name "Waits" at or near present Seguro.

Selden Pass [FRESNO]: *pass,* 8.5 miles southwest of Mount Abbot (lat. 37°17'20" N, long. 118°52'20" W). Named on Mount Abbot (1953) 15' quadrangle. R.B. Marshall of United States Geological Survey named the pass for Selden S. Hooper, who was with the Survey from 1891 until 1898 (Farquhar, 1925, p. 131); nearby Mount Hooper was named for Selden's father, and Rose Lake was named for his sister. United States Board on Geographic Names (1933a, p. 680) rejected the form "Seldon Pass" for the name.

Selma [FRESNO]: *town,* 16 miles southeast of Fresno (lat. 36°34'15" N, long. 119°36'30" W). Named on Selma (1964) 7.5' quadrangle. Postal authorities established Selma post office in 1880 and named it for the daughter of Max Gruenberg, an early settler (Salley, p. 201). The town incorporated in 1893.

Semitropic [KERN]: *locality,* 10.5 miles east of the village of Lost Hills (lat. 35°36'05" N,

long. 119°30'25" W; at SW cor. sec. 4, T 27 S, R 23 E). Named on Semitropic (1954) 7.5' quadrangle. California Mining Bureau's (1917c) map has the form "Semi Tropic" for the name. Postal authorities established Semitropic post office in 1893, moved it 2 miles west in 1904, moved it 3.5 miles southeast in 1905, and discontinued it in 1913; the name was for Semitropic Fruit Company (Salley, p. 201). California Mining Bureau's (1917c) map shows a place called Mira Monte located about 5 miles north of Semi Tropic. Postal authorities established Miramonte post office in 1889 and discontinued it in 1902, when they moved the service to Semitropic (Frickstad, p. 57).

Semitropic Ridge [KERN]: *ridge,* southeast-trending, 17 miles long, center 1.5 miles south-southwest of Semitropic (lat. 35°34'45" N, long. 119°31'15" W). Named on Lost Hills NE (1954), Semitropic (1954), and Wasco SW (1953) 7.5' quadrangles.

Seneca Spring [KERN]: *spring,* 3.5 miles west-southwest of Loraine (lat. 35°16'40" N, long. 118°29'35" W; sec. 36, T 30 S, R 32 E). Named on Loraine (1972) 7.5' quadrangle.

Senger: see **Mount Senger** [FRESNO].

Senger Creek [FRESNO]: *stream,* flows 4 miles to an unnamed stream 13 miles north-north-west of Blackcap Mountain (lat. 37°14'30" N, long. 118°53'10" W; at E line sec. 15, T 8 S, R 28 E); the stream heads near Mount Senger. Named on Blackcap Mountain (1953) and Mount Abbot (1953) 15' quadrangles. United States Board on Geographic Names (1983d, p. 2) approved the name "Sallie Keyes Creek" for the previously unnamed stream that Senger Creek joins, and noted (p. 3) that T.S. Solomons named Senger Creek in 1894 to honor professor Joachim H. Senger of University of California, a founder of the Sierra Club.

Senger Creek: see **Sallie Keyes Creek**, under **Sally Keyes Lakes** [FRESNO].

Sentinel [FRESNO]: *locality,* 2.5 miles west of present Humphreys Station (lat. 36°57'50" N, long. 119°29'30" W; near NE cor. sec. 19, T 11 S, R 23 E). Named on Dinuba (1924) 30' quadrangle. Postal authorities established Sentinel post office in 1880, discontinued it in 1883, reestablished it in 1888, discontinued it in 1897, reestablished it in 1905, and discontinued it in 1910; the name is from the way Keys Mountain acts as a sentinel by the place (Salley, p. 201).

Sentinel Butte [TULARE]: *hill,* 2.5 miles north-northwest of Woodlake (lat. 36°26'50" N, long. 119°06'36" W; sec. 13, T 17 S, R 26 E). Altitude 737 feet. Named on Woodlake (1952) 7.5' quadrangle.

Sentinel Dome [FRESNO]: *peak,* 15 miles south-southwest of Marion Peak (lat. 36°45'35" N, long. 118°38'35" W); the peak is on Sentinel Ridge. Altitude 9115 feet. Named on Marion Peak (1953) 15' quadrangle.

Sentinel Peak [TULARE]: *peak,* 10 miles south-southeast of Camp Nelson (lat. 36°01' N, long. 118°31'35" W; sec. 16, T 22 S, R 32 E). Altitude 6159 feet. Named on Camp Nelson (1956) 15' quadrangle.

Sentinel Ridge [FRESNO]: *ridge,* east-north-east-trending, 5 miles long, 16 miles south-southwest of Marion Peak (lat. 36°45'10" N, long. 118°39'45" W). Named on Marion Peak (1953) and Triple Divide Peak (1956) 15' quadrangles.

Sequoia Creek [FRESNO-TULARE]: *stream,* heads in Tulare County and flows 3.5 miles to Sequoia Lake 6 miles southwest of Hume in Fresno County (lat. 36°44'15" N, long. 118°59'15" W; sec. 1, T 14 S, R 27 E). Named on Giant Forest (1956) 15' quadrangle.

Sequoia Lake [FRESNO]: *lake,* 0.5 mile long, 6 miles southwest of Hume (lat. 36°43'55" N, long. 118°59'25" W; sec. 1, T 14 S, R 27 E). Named on Giant Forest (1956) 15' quadrangle.

Sequoia Mills: see **Millwood** [FRESNO].

Sequoia National Park Post Office: see **Kaweah Camp** [TULARE].

Serefin Spring [KERN]: *spring,* 3.5 miles north-northwest of Caliente (lat. 35°19'30" N, long. 118°38'10" W). Named on Bena (1972) 7.5' quadrangle.

Sesame: see **Bellview** [MADERA].

Setch: see **Pinedale** [FRESNO] (2).

Set Creek: see **Setimo Creek** [KERN].

Setimo Creek [KERN]: *stream,* flows about 3.5 miles to Rancheria Creek (2) 4.25 miles south of Piute Peak (lat. 35°23'20" N, long. 118°24'10" W; at E line sec. 23, T 29 S, R 33 E). Named on Piute Peak (1972) 7.5' quadrangle. Called Set Creek on Emerald Mountain (1943) 15' quadrangle. United States Board on Geographic Names (1975b, p. 11) gave the names "Set Creek" and "Setino Creek" as variants.

Seven Gables [FRESNO]: *peak,* 6 miles south-southwest of Mount Abbot (lat. 37°48'45" N, long. 118°50' W). Altitude 13,075 feet. Named on Mount Abbot (1953) 15' quadrangle. Theodore S. Solomons and Leigh Bierce climbed the peak in 1894 and gave it the name suggested by its shape (Farquhar, 1925, p. 132).

Seven Gables Lakes [FRESNO]: *lakes,* largest about 1200 feet long, 5.5 miles south-southwest of Mount Abbot (lat. 37°18'45" N, long. 118°48'45" W); the lakes are 1 mile east of Seven Gables. Named on Mount Abbot (1953) 15' quadrangle.

Sevenmile Hill [TULARE]: *ridge,* south-south-west-trending, 3 miles long, 10 miles west-southwest of Triple Divide Peak (lat. 36°33'45" N, long. 118°42' W). Named on Triple Divide Peak (1956) 15' quadrangle.

Seventeen Canyon [KERN]: *canyon,* drained by a stream that flows 4 miles to Midway Valley 2.25 miles southeast of Fellows (lat. 35°

09'35" N, long. 119°30'30" W; sec. 9, T 32 S, R 23 E); the canyon is partly in section 17. Named on Fellows (1951) 7.5' quadrangle.

"77" Corral: see **Corral Meadow** [MADERA].

Seville [TULARE]: *village,* 8.5 miles northwest of Woodlake (lat. 36° 29' N, long. 119°13'30" W; near NE cor. sec. 2, T 17 S, R 25 E). Named on Exeter (1952) 15' quadrangle. Postal authorities established Seville post office in 1915 and discontinued it in 1931 (Frickstad, p. 213). Officials of Atchison, Topeka and Santa Fe Railroad named the place in 1913 (Mitchell, A.R., p. 70).

Seville Lake [TULARE]: *lake,* 1000 feet long, 12 miles west-northwest of Triple Divide Peak (lat. 36°41' N, long. 118°43' W; on E line sec. 28, T 14 S, R 30 E). Named on Triple Divide Peak (1956) 15' quadrangle. Called Kettle Lake on a map of 1874 (Forest M. Clingan, personal communication, 1990).

Shadequarter Mountain [TULARE]: *ridge,* south-southwest- to west-trending, 2 miles long, 5.5 miles west of Yucca Mountain (lat. 36°33'45" N, long. 118°58' W). Named on Giant Forest (1956) 15' quadrangle.

Shadley Creek [TULARE]: *stream,* flows nearly 2 miles to Warm Sulphur Spring 5 miles east of Auckland (lat. 36°35'20" N, long. 119°00'50" W; sec. 26, T 15 S, R 27 E). Named on Auckland (1966) 7.5' quadrangle. Dinuba (1924) 30' quadrangle shows the stream continuing on to Dry Creek (1).

Shadley Flat: see **Murry Flat** [TULARE].

Shadow Creek [MADERA]: *stream,* flows 4.5 miles to Middle Fork San Joaquin River 5.25 miles north-northwest of Devils Postpile (lat. 37°41'45" N, long. 119°07'05" W); the stream goes through Shadow Lake. Named on Devils Postpile (1953) 15' quadrangle.

Shadow Lake [MADERA]: *lake,* 2400 feet long, 5.5 miles north-northwest of Devils Postpile (lat. 37°41'40" N, long. 119°07'50" W). Named on Devils Postpile (1953) 15' quadrangle. Called Garnet Lake on some early maps (Browning, 1988, p. 128).

Shadow Lake: see **Little Shadow Lake**, under **Ediza Lake** [MADERA].

Shafter [KERN]: *town,* 18 miles west-northwest of Bakersfield (lat. 35°30'05" N, long. 119°16'20" W; in and near sec. 10, T 28 S, R 25 E). Named on Rio Bravo (1954) and Wasco (1953) 7.5' quadrangles. Postal authorities established Shafter post office in 1898, moved it 1.25 miles west in 1902, discontinued it in 1905, and reestablished it in 1914 (Salley, p. 202). The town incorporated in 1938. A railroad loading station was at the site in 1898, and a 7100-acre subdivision was placed on sale there in 1914 (Bailey, 1967, p. 25). The name honors General William Shafter, commander of United States forces in Cuba during the Spanish-American War, who lived on his ranch near Bakersfield after retirement in 1901 (Gudde, 1949, p. 326).

Shafter: see **North Shafter** [KERN].
Shagoopah Falls: see **Chagoopa Falls** [TULARE].
Shakeflat Creek [MADERA]: *stream,* flows 3.25 miles to San Joaquin River 5.5 miles east-southeast of Shuteye Peak (lat. 37°18'50" N, long. 119°20' W). Named on Shuteye Peak (1953) 15' quadrangle.
Shakspere: see **Mount Shakspere** [FRESNO].
Shale: see **Fellows** [KERN].
Shale Hills [KERN]: *range,* 11 miles southeast of Orchard Peak (lat. 35°37' N, long. 112°01' W). Named on Packwood Creek (1961), Sawtooth Ridge (1961), and Shale Point (1953) 7.5' quadrangles. Arnold and Johnson (p. 22) proposed the name.
Shale Point [KERN]: *ridge,* east-southeast-trending, 1 mile long, 5.5 miles west of Blackwells Corner (lat. 35°35'45" N, long. 119°57'45" W); the ridge is at the east end of Shale Hills. Named on Shale Point (1953) 7.5' quadrangle. Arnold and Johnson (p. 22) proposed the name.
Shamrock: see **Delano** [KERN].
Shannon Valley [FRESNO]: *area,* 6 miles west-southwest of Dunlap (lat. 36°42'15" N, long. 119°13' W). Named on Tucker Mountain (1966) 7.5' quadrangle.
Sharknose Ridge [TULARE]: *ridge,* west-northwest-trending, 1.5 miles long, 9.5 miles north-northwest of Olancha Peak (lat. 36°23'35" N, long. 118°10'20" W). Named on Olancha (1956) 15' quadrangle.
Sharktooth Creek [FRESNO]: *stream,* flows nearly 4 miles to Fish Creek (1) 2 miles north of Double Peak in Fish Valley (lat. 37°32'10" N, long. 119°02'35" W); the stream heads near Sharktooth Lake. Named on Devils Postpile (1953) 15' quadrangle.
Sharktooth Hill: see **Round Mountain** [KERN] (2).
Sharktooth Lake [FRESNO]: *lake,* 1100 feet long, 16 miles north-northeast of Kaiser Peak (lat. 37°29'55" N, long. 119°01'50" W); the lake is near the head of Sharktooth Creek. Named on Kaiser Peak (1953) 15' quadrangle.
Sharktooth Peak [FRESNO]: *peak,* 15 miles north-northeast of Kaiser Peak (lat. 37°29' N, long. 119°01'30" W). Altitude 11,630 feet. Named on Kaiser (1904) 30' quadrangle. Theodore S. Solomons named the peak in 1892 (Farquhar, 1925, p. 132). On Kaiser Peak (1953) 15' quadrangle, the name applies to a feature located 1.5 miles farther south-south-west (lat. 37°27'45" N, long. 119°02'35" W), but United States Board on Geographic Names (1969a, p. 4) approved the name "Cockscomb" for this second peak.
Sharon [MADERA]: *locality,* 4 miles east-northeast of Fairmead along Atchison, Topeka and Santa Fe Railroad (lat. 37°06' N, long. 120°07'50" W; near SE cor. sec. 32, T 9 S, R 17 E). Named on Berenda (1961) 7.5' quadrangle. Postal authorities established Sharon

post office in 1898 and discontinued it in 1927 (Frickstad, p. 86). The place began as part of a real estate promotion on land that had been owned by San Francisco financier William Sharon (Clough, p. 91). California Mining Bureau's (1917d) map shows a place called Watt located 2.5 miles north-northwest of Sharon along the railroad.
Sharp Creek: see **Wishon Reservoir** [FRESNO].
Sharp Note Lake [FRESNO]: *lake,* 600 feet long, 8.5 miles south-southwest of Mount Abbot (lat. 37°17'05" N, long. 118°51'20" W); the lake is less than 1 mile south of Flat Note Lake. Named on Mount Abbot (1953) 15' quadrangle.
Sharpville: see **Shipp** [FRESNO].
Shaver [FRESNO]: *village,* 12 miles south-southwest of Kaiser Peak at the north end of Shaver Lake (lat. 37°08'35" N, long. 119°17'50" W; near SE cor. sec. 13, T 9 S, R 24 E). Named on Kaiser (1904) 30' quadrangle. Postal authorities established Shaver post office in 1896 and discontinued it in 1925 (Frickstad, p. 37). Water of an enlarged Shaver Lake now covers the site.
Shaver Crossing [FRESNO]: *locality,* 9 miles south-southwest of Kaiser Peak along San Joaquin and Eastern Railroad (lat. 37°11'10" N, long. 119°16'40" W; near NE cor. sec. 6, T 9 S, R 25 E). Named on Kaiser (1904) 30' quadrangle.
Shaver Lake [FRESNO]: *lake,* behind a dam on Stevenson Creek nearly 3 miles north-north-east of Shaver Lake Heights (present town of Shaver Lake) (lat. 37°08'40" N, long. 119°18'10" W; sec. 13, T 9 S, R 24 E). Named on Shaver Lake (1953) 15' quadrangle. The name commemorates C.B. Shaver, co-founder of Fresno Flume and Irrigation Company; officials of this company had the dam built that forms the lake in what had been known as Stevenson Basin and Stevenson Meadows (Redinger, p. 77).
Shaver Lake: see **Shaver Lake Heights** [FRESNO].
Shaver Lake Heights [FRESNO]: *town,* 14 miles south-southwest of Kaiser Peak (lat. 37°06'25" N, long. 119°19'15" W; in and near sec. 35, T 9 S, R 24 E); the town is at the southwest end of Shaver Lake. Named on Shaver Lake (1953) 15' quadrangle, which also has the name "Shaver Lake P.O." at the place. Postal authorities established Shaver Lake post office in 1928 (Frickstad, p. 37). United States Board on Geographic Names (1983a, p. 4) approved the name "Shaver Lake" for the town.
Shaver Lake Point [FRESNO]: *promontory,* 2.25 miles north-northeast of Shaver Lake Heights (present town of Shaver Lake) (lat. 37°08'15" N, long. 119°18'15" W; sec. 24, T 9 S, R 24 E); the feature is on the west side of Shaver Lake. Named on Shaver Lake (1953)

15' quadrangle.

Sheep Creek [FRESNO]: *stream,* flows 5 miles to South Fork Kings River 14 miles southwest of Marion Peak in Kings Canyon (lat. 36°47'35" N, long. 118°40'25" W). Named on Marion Peak (1953) and Triple Divide Peak (1956) 15' quadrangles. A sheep trail followed the creek in the early days; the stream had the name Fox Creek on a map of 1896 (Forest M. Clingan, personal communication, 1990).

Sheep Creek [TULARE]:
(1) *stream,* flows 2.25 miles to Willow Creek (2) 12 miles west of Kern Peak (lat. 36°17'15" N, long. 118°30' W). Named on Kern Peak (1956) 15' quadrangle. United States Board on Geographic Names (1986, p. 4) approved the designation "No Name Creek" for the stream; at the same time the Board approved the name "Sheep Creek" for a stream that heads 2.2 miles south-southwest of Coyote Peaks and flows for 2.5 miles to Willow Creek (2) 3.5 miles northwest of Angora Mountain (lat. 36°16'47" N, long. 118°30'30" W).
(2) *stream,* flows 4 miles to North Fork Kaweah River 5.25 miles south-southwest of Yucca Mountain (lat. 36°30'10" N, long. 118° 54'40" W); the stream is southwest of Sheep Ridge. Named on Giant Forest (1956) 15' quadrangle.

Sheep Crossing [MADERA]: *locality,* 8 miles west-southwest of Devils Postpile along North Fork San Joaquin River (lat. 37°33'40" N, long. 119°12'30" W). Named on Devils Postpile (1953) 15' quadrangle. A trail used by cattlemen crossed the river at the place on a bridge known as Sheep Crossing (McLaughlin and Bradley, p. 556).

Sheep Mountain [TULARE]: *peak,* 10 miles south of Mineral King (lat. 36°18'30" N, long. 118°37'25" W). Named on Mineral King (1956) 15' quadrangle.

Sheep Mountain: see **Angora Mountain** [TULARE].

Sheep Pass: see **Vacation Pass** [TULARE].

Sheep Ridge [TULARE]: *ridge,* southeast-trending, 3 miles long, 3 miles west-southwest of Yucca Peak (lat. 36°33'10" N, long. 118° 55'15" W); the ridge is northeast of Sheep Creek (2). Named on Giant Forest (1956) 15' quadrangle.

Sheep Rock: see **Mount Corcoran** [TULARE].

Sheep Spring [KERN]: *spring,* 6.5 miles north of Garlock (lat. 35° 29'50" N, long. 117°48'15" W). Named on Garlock (1967) 7.5' quadrangle.

Sheep Springs: see **Willow Springs** [KERN] (1).

Sheep Troughs Spring [KERN]: *spring,* 7.5 miles northeast of Mount Adelaide (lat. 35°29'50" N, long. 118°38'10" W; sec. 15, T 28 S, R 31 E). Named on Mount Adelaide (1972) 7.5' quadrangle.

Shelf Lake [FRESNO]: *lake,* 300 feet long, 10 miles west-northwest of Mount Abbot (lat. 37°25'55" N, long. 118°57'30" W). Named on Mount Abbot (1953) 15' quadrangle.

Charles K. Fisher of California Department of Fish and Game gave the name in 1949 for the position of the lake on a topographic shelf above Cold Creek (Browning 1986, p. 197).

Shell [KINGS]: *locality,* 1 mile east-southeast of Hanford along Southern Pacific Railroad lat. 36°19'40" N, long. 119°37'10" W; at S line sec. 30, T 18 S, R 22 E). Named on Remnoy (1954) 7.5' quadrangle.

Shellenbarger Lake [MADERA]: *lake,* 450 feet long, 6.25 miles west of Devils Postpile (lat. 37°38'35" N, long. 119°11'40" W). Named on Devils Postpile (1953) 15' quadrangle.

Shell Mountain [TULARE]: *peak,* 9.5 miles north-northeast of Yucca Mountain (lat. 36°41'45" N, long. 118°47'45" W; sec. 23, T 14 S, R 29 E). Altitude 9594 feet. Named on Giant Forest (1956) 15' quadrangle.

Shepherd Cove [TULARE]: *relief feature,* wide place in the canyon of Kaweah River 3.5 miles east of Kaweah (lat. 36°28'30" N, long. 118°51'25" W; in and near sec. 5, T 17 S, R 29 E); the feature is 1.5 miles southeast of Shepherd Peak. Named on Kaweah (1957) 15' quadrangle.

Shepherd Pass [TULARE]: *pass,* 7.25 miles north-northwest of Mount Whitney on Tulare-Inyo county line (lat. 36°40'20" N, long. 118°20'35" W). Named on Mount Whitney (1956) 15' quadrangle. The name commemorates the pioneer Shepherd families of Inyo County (United States Board on Geographic Names, 1933a, p. 687).

Shepherd Peak [TULARE]: *peak,* 2.5 miles east-northeast of Kaweah (lat. 36°29'30" N, long. 118°52'35" W). Altitude 3570 feet. Named on Kaweah (1957) 15' quadrangle.

Sherman Creek [TULARE]: *stream,* flows 1.5 miles to Marble Fork 5.5 miles east of Yucca Mountain (lat. 36°34'55" N, long. 118°46'05" W; sec. 31, T 15 S, R 30 E); the stream is near General Sherman redwood tree. Named on Giant Forest (1956) 15' quadrangle.

Sherman Peak [FRESNO]: *peak,* 4 miles north of Coalinga Mineral Springs (lat. 36°12'05" N, long. 120°33'40" W; sec. 10, T 20 S, R 13 E). Altitude 3857 feet. Named on Sherman Peak (1969) 7.5' quadrangle.

Sherman Peak [TULARE]: *peak,* 14 miles south of Hockett Peak (lat. 36°00'40" N, long. 118°23'25" W). Altitude 9909 feet. Named on Hockett Peak (1956) 15' quadrangle.

Sherman Peak: see **Flag Peak** [FRESNO].

Shinn: see **Mount Shinn** [FRESNO].

Shipp [FRESNO]: *locality,* 8.5 miles north of Clovis along San Joaquin and Eastern Railroad (lat. 36°56'40" N, long. 119°40'30" W; near E line sec. 28, T 11 S, R 21 E). Named on Friant (1922) 7.5' quadrangle. California Mining Bureau's (1917a) map shows a place called Sharpville located along the railroad 4 miles east-northeast of Shipp.

Shirley [KINGS]: *locality,* 4.5 miles north of Hanford along Atchison, Topeka and Santa

Fe Railroad (lat. 36°23'55" N, long. 119°39'45" W; sec. 2, T 18 S, R 21 E). Named on Laton (1953) 7.5' quadrangle. Called Harlow on Laton (1927) 7.5' quadrangle.

Shirley Creek [KERN]: *stream,* flows 4 miles to Tillie Creek 2.25 miles west of Wofford Heights (lat. 35°42'55" N, long. 118°29'35" W; sec. 36, T 25 S, R 32 E); the stream heads at Shirley Peak. Named on Alta Sierra (1972) and Lake Isabella North (1972) 7.5' quadrangles.

Shirley Creek [MADERA]: *stream,* flows 1 mile to Madera Creek nearly 6 miles south-south-east of Merced Peak (lat. 37°33'30" N, long. 119°20'50" W). Named on Merced Peak (1953) 15' quadrangle.

Shirley Lake [MADERA]: *lake,* 600 feet long, 5.25 miles south of Merced Peak (lat. 37°33'35" N, long. 119°22'30" W). Named on Merced Peak (1953) 15' quadrangle.

Shirley Meadow Campground [KERN]: *locality,* 1.25 miles south-southwest of Alta Sierra (lat. 35°42'45" N, long. 118°33'35" W; sec. 32, T 25 S, R 32 E); the place is 0.25 mile north of Shirley Peak. Named on Glennville (1956) 15' quadrangle.

Shirley Meadows [KERN]: *locality,* 1.25 miles south-southwest of Alta Sierra (lat. 35°42'35" N, long. 118°33'20" W; sec. 32, T 25 S, R 32 E); the place is 0.25 mile northeast of Shirley Peak along Shirley Creek. Named on Alta Sierra (1972) 7.5' quadrangle.

Shirley Peak [KERN]: *peak,* 1.25 miles south-southwest of Alta Sierra (lat. 35°42'25" N, long. 118°33'35" W; sec. 32, T 25 S, R 32 E); the peak is at the head of Shirley Creek. Altitude 7091 feet. Named on Alta Sierra (1972) 7.5' quadrangle.

Shoemaker Spring [KERN]: *spring,* 5 miles south-southwest of Skinner Peak (lat. 35°30'10" N, long. 118°09'55" W; sec. 12, T 28 S, R 35 E). Named on Cane Canyon (1972) 7.5' quadrangle.

Short Canyon [KERN]:

(1) *valley,* 3.5 miles south of Onyx (lat. 35°38'15" N, long. 118°13'30" W). Named on Onyx (1972) 7.5' quadrangle.

(2) *canyon,* drained by a stream that flows 3 miles to Caldwell Creek nearly 2 miles east of Kernville (lat. 35°45'05" N, long. 118°23'30" W; near W line sec. 13, T 25 S, R 33 E). Named on Lake Isabella North (1972) and Weldon (1972) 7.5' quadrangles.

(3) *canyon,* 2 miles long, opens into lowlands nearly 6 miles northwest of Inyokern (lat. 35°42'25" N, long. 117°53'20" W; sec. 4, T 26 S, R 38 E). Named on Owens Peak (1972) 7.5' quadrangle.

Short Canyon Well [KERN]: *well,* 3.5 miles south-southwest of Onyx (lat. 35°38'20" N, long. 118°14' W; near W line sec. 28, T 26 S, R 35 E); the well is in Short Canyon (1). Named on Onyx (1972) 7.5' quadrangle.

Short Hair Creek [FRESNO]: *stream,* flows 5.5 miles to North Fork Kings River at Wishon

Reservoir 10.5 miles west-southwest of Black-cap Mountain (lat. 37°01'15" N, long. 118°58'10" W; at W line sec. 31, T 10 S, R 28 E); the stream goes through Short Hair Meadow. Named on Blackcap Mountain (1953) and Huntington Lake (1953) 15' quadrangles.

Short Hair Meadow [FRESNO]: *area,* 8 miles east-southeast of Dinkey Dome (lat. 37°03'30" N, long. 119°00'25" W; near E line sec. 15, T 10 S, R 27 E); the place is along Short Hair Creek. Named on Huntington Lake (1953) 15' quadrangle.

Shorty Lake [FRESNO]: *lake,* 500 feet long, 15 miles northeast of Kaiser Peak (lat. 37°28'30" N, long. 119°01'40" W); the feature is one of the group called Margaret Lakes. Named on Kaiser Peak (1953) 15' quadrangle.

Shotgun Creek [TULARE]: *stream,* flows 4.5 miles to Little Kern River about 9 miles south-southeast of Mineral King (lat. 36°20'05" N, long. 118°32' W); the stream heads near Shotgun Pass. Named on Mineral King (1956) 15' quadrangle.

Shotgun Pass [TULARE]: *pass,* 5.5 miles south-east of Mineral King (lat. 36°23'20" N, long. 118°32'10" W); the pass is near the head of Shotgun Creek. Named on Mineral King (1956) 15' quadrangle.

Shuteye Creek [MADERA]: *stream,* flows 2.5 miles to West Fork Chiquito Creek 3 miles northeast of Shuteye Peak (lat. 37°22'50" N, long. 119°23'20" W; sec. 30, T 6 S, R 24 E); the stream heads at Shuteye Peak. Named on Shuteye Peak (1953) 15' quadrangle.

Shuteye Pass [MADERA]: *pass,* 1 mile south-east of Shuteye Peak (lat. 37°20'20" N, long. 119°24'45" W; near NW cor. sec. 12, T 7 S, R 23 E). Named on Shuteye Peak (1953) 15' quadrangle.

Shuteye Pass: see **Little Shuteye Pass** [MADERA].

Shuteye Peak [MADERA]: *peak,* 11 miles east of Yosemite Forks (lat. 37°21' N, long. 119°25'40" W; sec. 2, T 7 S, R 23 E). Altitude 8351 feet. Named on Shuteye Peak (1953) 15' quadrangle. The name commemorates a mountaineer who was called Old Shuteye because he was blind in one eye (Hanna, p. 304).

Shuteye Peak: see **Little Shuteye Peak** [MADERA].

Siberian Outpost [TULARE]: *area,* 11.5 miles north of Kern Peak along Siberian Pass Creek (lat. 36°28'15" N, long. 118°18'15" W). Named on Kern Peak (1956) 15' quadrangle.

Siberian Outpost Creek: see **Siberian Pass Creek** [TULARE].

Siberian Pass [TULARE]: *pass,* 11 miles north of Kern Peak (lat. 36° 28'10" N, long. 118°16'15" W; near NW cor. sec. 11, T 17 S, R 34 E). Named on Kern Peak (1956) 15' quadrangle. United States Board on Geographic Names (1933a, p. 691) rejected the name "Rampart Pass" for the feature.

Siberian Pass Creek [TULARE]: *stream,* flows 5.25 miles to Rock Creek 13 miles north-northwest of Kern Peak (lat. 36°29'40" N, long. 118°20'10" W). Named on Kern Peak (1956) 15' quadrangle. Called Siberian Outpost Cr. on Olmsted's (1900) map. The stream also was called South Fork Rock Creek (Browning, p. 198).

Sibleyville: see **Dinuba** [TULARE].

Sidehill Meadow [TULARE]: *area,* 4 miles southwest of Kern Peak (lat. 36°16'10" N, long. 118°20'10" W). Named on Kern Peak (1956) 15' quadrangle.

Sides [TULARE]: *locality,* 3.5 miles southeast of Exeter along Atchison, Topeka and Santa Fe Railroad (lat. 36°15'10" N, long. 119°05'55" W; near NW cor. sec. 30, T 19 S, R 27 E). Named on Rocky Hill (1927) 7.5' quadrangle.

Siding 18: see **Brown** [KERN].

Siding Number Two: see **Taft** [KERN].

Siding 16: see **Inyokern** [KERN].

Sidney Peak [KERN]: *peak,* 4 miles southwest of Randsburg (lat. 35°19'30" N, long. 117°42' W; near W line sec. 16, T 30 S, R 40 E). Altitude 4372 feet. Named on Johannesburg (1967) 7.5' quadrangle.

Sieretta Peak: see **Sirretta Peak** [TULARE].

Sierra: see **Camp Sierra** [FRESNO]; **High Sierra**, under "Regional setting."

Sierra Chautauqua: see **Camp Sierra** [FRESNO].

Sierra del Monte Diablo: see "Regional setting."

Sierra de San Marcos: see "Regional setting."

Sierra Glen [TULARE]: *locality,* 8.5 miles west-northwest of Yucca Mountain (lat. 36°38'20" N, long. 118°59'55" W; sec. 12, T 15 S, R 27 E). Named on Giant Forest (1956) 15' quadrangle.

Sierra Heights [TULARE]: *locality,* 2 miles southeast of Lindsay along Atchison, Topeka and Santa Fe Railroad (lat. 36°11'10" N, long. 119°03'40" W; near W line sec. 16, T 20 S, R 27 E). Named on Lindsay (1951) 7.5' quadrangle.

Sierra Nevada: see "Regional setting."

Sierra Sky Park [FRESNO]: *locality,* 7 miles northwest of downtown Fresno (lat. 36°50'25" N, long. 119°51'50" W; sec. 35, T 12 S, R 19 E). Named on Fresno North (1965) 7.5' quadrangle.

Sierra Vista [MADERA]: *locality,* 2.5 miles north-northwest of Chowchilla along Southern Pacific Railroad (lat. 37°09' N, long. 120°17'10" W; sec. 13, T 9 S, R 15 E). Named on Plainsburg (1919) 7.5' quadrangle.

Signa: see **Kerto** [KERN].

Signal Hills: see **Little Signal Hills** [KERN].

Silaxo Drain [FRESNO]: *water feature,* extends for 10 miles, partly as an artificial watercourse, to Poso Slough nearly 5 miles north of Oxalis (lat. 36°58'55" N, long. 120°33'25" W; at N line sec. 16, T 11 S, R 13 E). Named on Oxalis (1956) and Poso Farm (1962) 7.5' quadrangles. Oxalis (1956) 7.5' quadrangle shows a place called Silaxo Oil Pumping Sta. located 1.5 miles east-southeast of Oxalis along Southern Pacific Railroad. The name "Silaxo" is the word "oxalis" spelled backwards (Gudde, 1949, p. 247).

Silaxo Drain 1 [FRESNO]: *water feature,* extends for 3.5 miles to Silaxo Drain about 2.5 miles east-southeast of Oxalis (lat. 36°54'15" N, long. 120°30'15" W; sec. 12, T 12 S, R 13 E. Named on Poso Farm (1962) 7.5' quadrangle.

Sill: see **Mount Sill** [FRESNO].

Silliman: see **Mount Silliman** [TULARE].

Silliman Creek [TULARE]: *stream,* flows 4 miles to Marble Fork 12 miles west of Triple Divide Peak (lat. 36°36'10" N, long. 118°44'15" W; sec. 20, T 15 S, R 30 E); the stream heads near Mount Silliman. Named on Triple Divide Peak (1956) 15' quadrangle.

Silliman Crest [TULARE]: *ridge,* generally north-northwest-trending, 2.5 miles long, 11 miles west-northwest of Triple Divide Peak (lat. 36°39'30" N, long. 118°42'20" W); Mount Silliman is at the south end of the ridge. Named on Triple Divide Peak (1956) 15' quadrangle.

Silliman Lake [TULARE]: *lake,* 700 feet long, 10 miles west-northwest of Triple Divide Peak (lat. 36°38'10" N, long. 118°42' W); the lake is 0.5 mile south-southwest of Mount Silliman at the head of a branch of Silliman Creek. Named on Triple Divide Peak (1956) 15' quadrangle.

Silliman Meadow [TULARE]: *area,* 11 miles west-northwest of Triple Divide Peak (lat. 36°37'50" N, long. 118°43'15" W; sec. 9, T 15 S, R 30 E); the place is along Silliman Creek. Named on Triple Divide Peak (1956) 15' quadrangle. United States Board on Geographic Names (1938, p. 49) rejected the name "Cahoon Meadow" for the feature.

Silliman Pass [TULARE]: *pass,* 11 miles west-northwest of Triple Divide Peak (lat. 36°39'45" N, long. 118°42'20" W); the pass is 1.5 miles north-northwest of Mount Silliman on Silliman Crest. Named on Triple Divide Peak (1956) 15' quadrangle.

Silver City [TULARE]: *locality,* 3 miles west-northwest of Mineral King (lat. 36°28' N, long. 118°38'45" W). Named on Mineral King (1956) 15' quadrangle. Miners on the way to Mineral King started a camp at the site in 1874 (Browning 1986, p. 199).

Silver Creek [FRESNO]:
(1) *stream,* flows 6.5 miles to Fish Creek (1) 3.25 miles west-northwest of Double Peak (lat. 37°31'50" N, long. 119°05'25" W); the stream heads on Silver Divide. Named on Devils Postpile (1953) and Kaiser Peak (1953) 15' quadrangles. Theodore S. Solomons named the creek in 1892 for its silvery appearance (Farquhar, 1925, p. 133-134).

(2) *stream,* heads in San Benito County and flows 13 miles to Panoche Creek 23 miles southwest of Firebaugh (lat. 36°36'30" N, long. 120°41'10" W; sec. 20, T 15 S, R 12 E). Named on Tumey Hills (1956) 7.5' quadrangle. United States Board on Geographic Names (1933a, p. 693) rejected the name "Panoche Creek" for the stream.

(3) *stream,* flows 4 miles to Middle Fork Kings River 9.5 miles northeast of Hume (lat. 36°53'05" N, long. 118°47'40" W); the stream is south of Silver Spur. Named on Tehipite Dome (1952) 15' quadrangle.

Silver Creek [KERN]: *stream,* flows 1.5 miles to Indian Creek 5 miles west-northwest of Emerald Mountain (lat. 35°16'20" N, long. 118°22'15" W; near N line sec. 6, T 31 S, R 34 E). Named on Emerald Mountain (1972) 7.5' quadrangle.

Silver Creek [TULARE]: *stream,* flows 2.5 miles to North Fork of Middle Fork Tule River 7 miles north-northwest of Camp Nelson (lat. 36°14'10" N, long. 118°39'05" W; near SE cor. sec. 30, T 19 S, R 31 E). Named on Camp Nelson (1956) and Mineral King (1956) 15' quadrangles.

Silver Creek: see **Crystal Creek** [TULARE]; **Panoche Creek** [FRESNO].

Silver Divide [FRESNO]: *ridge,* generally west- and northwest-trending, 13 miles long, between the drainage areas of South Fork San Joaquin River and Middle Fork San Joaquin River. Named on Devils Postpile (1953), Kaiser Peak (1953), and Mount Abbot (1953) 15' quadrangles.

Silver Lake [TULARE]: *lake,* 700 feet long, nearly 6 miles southeast of Mineral King along Shotgun Creek (lat. 36°22'55" N, long. 118° 31'55" W). Named on Mineral King (1956) 15' quadrangle.

Silver Lake: see **Crystal Lake** [TULARE].

Silver Lakes: see **Franklin Lakes** [TULARE].

Silver Pass [FRESNO]: *pass,* 9.5 miles northwest of Mount Abbot (lat. 37°28'05" N, long. 118°55'20" W); the pass is on Silver Divide. Named on Mount Abbot (1953) 15' quadrangle. United States Board on Geographic Names (1982b, p. 3) approved the name "Goodale Pass" for a place located west of Silver Pass (lat. 37°27'50" N, long. 118°56'18" W).

Silver Pass Creek [FRESNO]: *stream,* flows 2 miles to North Fork Mono Creek 8 miles west-northwest of Mount Abbot (lat. 37°26'15" N, long. 118°54'30" W); the stream heads at Silver Pass Lake. Named on Mount Abbot (1953) 15' quadrangle.

Silver Pass Lake [FRESNO]: *lake,* 2200 feet long, 9 miles west-northwest of Mount Abbot (lat. 37°27'35" N, long. 118°55'20" W); the lake is 0.5 mile south of Silver Pass. Named on Mount Abbot (1953) 15' quadrangle.

Silver Peak [FRESNO]: *peak,* 15 miles northeast of Kaiser Peak (lat. 37°28'15" N, long.

119°01'15" W); the peak is on Silver Divide. Altitude 11,878 feet. Named on Kaiser Peak (1953) 15' quadrangle. Theodore S. Solomons named the peak in 1892 for nearby Silver Creek (1) (Farquhar, 1925, p. 134).

Silver Spray Falls [FRESNO]: *waterfall,* 11.5 miles northeast of Hume along Crown Creek (lat. 36°54'50" N, long. 118°47'15" W). Named on Tehipite Dome (1952) 15' quadrangle.

Silver Spur [FRESNO]: *ridge,* west-trending, 3 miles long, 11 miles northeast of Hume (lat. 36°53' N, long. 118°46' W). Named on Marion Peak (1953) and Tehipite Dome (1952) 15' quadrangles.

Simmons Peak [MADERA-TUOLUMNE]: *peak,* 10.5 miles south of Tioga Pass on Madera-Tuolumne county line (lat. 37°45'40" N, long. 119°17'35" W). Altitude 12,503 feet. Named on Tuolumne Meadows (1956) 15' quadrangle. R.B. Marshall of United States Geological Survey named the peak in 1909 for Dr. Samuel E. Simmons of Sacramento (United States Board on Geographic Names, 1934a, p. 22).

Simmons Post Camp [TULARE]: *locality,* 3.5 miles southwest of Camp Nelson (lat. 36°06'40" N, long. 118°39'45" W; sec. 7, T 21 S, R 31 E). Named on Camp Nelson (1956) 15' quadrangle.

Simpson Meadow [FRESNO]: *area,* 6.5 miles west of Marion Peak along Middle Fork Kings River (lat. 36°58' N, long. 118°38'10" W). Named on Marion Peak (1953) 15' quadrangle. Called Simpson Meadows on Lippincott's (1902) map. The Simpson family ran sheep at the place in the 1880's and patented the land in 1900; the area first was called Dougherty Meadow for Bill Dougherty and Bob Dougherty, who pastured horses there (Browning 1986, p. 201).

Sing Peak [MADERA]: *peak,* 5.5 miles south of Merced Peak (lat. 37°33'15" N, long. 119°23'15" W). Altitude 10,552 feet. Named on Merced Peak (1953) 15' quadrangle. R.B. Marshall of United States Geological Survey named the peak in 1899 for Tie Sing, cook for the Survey from 1888 until he died in an accident in 1918 (United States Board on Geographic Names, 1934a, p. 22).

Sink: see **Tejon Creek** [KERN].

Sinks of Tehachapa: see **Tehachapi Valley** [KERN].

Sinks of the Tejon: see **Tejon Creek** [KERN].

Siphon Canyon [TULARE]: *canyon,* drained by a stream that flows 2 miles to Middle Fork Tule River 2.5 miles east of Springville (lat. 36°08'05" N, long. 118°46'10" W; near N line sec. 5, T 21 S, R 30 E). Named on Springville (1957) 7.5' quadrangle, which shows a siphon in the canyon.

Sirretta Meadows [TULARE]: *areas,* 10 miles east of Fairview (lat. 35°56'30" N, long. 118°19'15" W); the meadows are 1.5 miles north-northeast of Sirretta Peak. Named on Kernville (1956) 15' quadrangle.

Sirretta Peak [TULARE]: *peak,* 9 miles east of Fairview (lat. 35°50'30" N, long. 118°20' W; sec. 17, T 23 S, R 34 E). Altitude 9977 feet. Named on Kernville (1956) 15' quadrangle. California Mining Bureau's (1917b) map has the name "Sieretta Pk."

Sivert [KERN]: *locality,* 5 miles east-southeast of Edison along Southern Pacific Railroad (lat. 35°19'40" N, long. 118°47'15" W). Named on Edison (1931) 7.5' quadrangle. Called Treves on Caliente (1914) 30' quadrangle.

Sixmile House [MADERA]: *locality,* 14 miles south-southwest of Raymond (lat. 37°00'45" N, long. 119°57'50" W; near SW cor. sec. 36, T 10 S, R 18 E). Named on Daulton (1921) 7.5' quadrangle.

Six Shooter Lake [FRESNO]: *lake,* 800 feet long, 2.5 miles north of Blackcap Mountain (lat. 37°06'35" N, long. 118°47'10" W). Named on Blackcap Mountain (1953) 15' quadrangle.

Sixty Lake Basin [FRESNO]: *valley,* 9 miles south of Mount Pinchot at the head of a branch of South Fork Woods Creek (lat. 36°49' N, long. 118°25'30" W). Named on Mount Pinchot (1953) 15' quadrangle.

Skeleton Spring [FRESNO]: *spring,* 4.25 miles north-northeast of Coalinga Mineral Springs (lat. 36°12'20" N, long. 120°32'15" W; sec. 11, T 20 S, R 13 E). Named on Sherman Peak (1969) 7.5' quadrangle.

Skinner Flat [KERN]: *area,* 3 miles south-southwest of Piute Peak (lat. 35°24'55" N, long. 118°25' W; near SW cor. sec. 11, T 29 S, R 33 E). Named on Piute Peak (1972) 7.5' quadrangle.

Skinner Peak [KERN]: *peak,* 10 miles south-southeast of Onyx (lat. 35°34' N, long. 118°07'35" W). Altitude 7120 feet. Named on Cane Canyon (1972) and Horse Canyon (1972) 7.5' quadrangles.

Skull Island: see **Alpaugh** [TULARE].

Skull Spring [KERN]: *spring,* nearly 4 miles north of Caliente in Tollhouse Canyon (lat. 35°20'40" N, long. 118°38'25" W). Named on Bena (1972) 7.5' quadrangle.

Skunk Canyon [FRESNO]: *canyon,* drained by a stream that flows 1.5 miles to Salt Canyon (3) 3 miles north-northwest of Smith Mountain (2) (lat. 36°07'10" N, long. 120°37'20" W; sec. 12, T 21 S, R 12 E). Named on Slack Canyon (1969) and Smith Mountain (1969) 7.5' quadrangles.

Skunk Hollow [FRESNO]: *area,* 10.5 miles north-northeast of Coalinga (lat. 36°16'50" N, long. 120°18' W; near NE cor. sec. 14, T 19 S, R 15 E). Named on Domengine Ranch (1956) 7.5' quadrangle.

Skunk Spring [TULARE]: *spring,* 4.25 miles north-northwest of California Hot Springs (lat. 35°56' N, long. 118°42'40" W; near N

line sec. 14, T 23 S, R 30 E). Named on California Hot Springs (1958) 15' quadrangle.

Skunk Spring Saddle [TULARE]: *pass,* 4.5 miles northwest of California Hot Springs (lat. 35°56'05" N, long. 118°43' W; near SW cor. sec. 11, T 23 S, R 30 E); the pass is 0.25 mile west-northwest of Skunk Spring. Named on California Hot Springs (1958) 15' quadrangle.

Sky-Blue Lake [TULARE]: *lake,* 2000 feet long, 3.25 miles south-southeast of Mount Whitney (lat. 36°32' N, long. 118°16'20" W). Named on Mount Whitney (1956) 15' quadrangle.

Sky Parlor Meadow [TULARE]: *area,* 14 miles northwest of Kern Peak along Funston Creek (lat. 36°27'40" N, long. 118°26'30" W). Named on Kern Peak (1956) 15' quadrangle. United States Board on Geographic Names (1933a, p. 699) rejected the name "Upper Funston Meadow" for the feature.

Slab Lakes [MADERA]: *lakes,* largest 800 feet long, 2.5 miles east-southeast of Merced Peak (lat. 37°37'05" N, long. 119°21'25" W). Named on Merced Peak (1953) 15' quadrangle.

Slapjack Creek [TULARE]: *stream,* flows 1 mile to East Fork Kaweah River 6.5 miles west of Mineral King (lat. 36°26' N, long. 118°42'45" W). Named on Mineral King (1956) 15' quadrangle.

Slate Mountain [TULARE]: *ridge,* north-trending, 6 miles long, 4.25 miles south-southeast of Camp Nelson (lat. 36°05' N, long. 118°34'30" W). Named on Camp Nelson (1956) 15' quadrangle.

Slater [KERN]: *locality,* 3 miles south of Famoso along Southern Pacific Railroad (lat. 35°32'55" N, long. 119°11'45" W; sec. 29, T 27 S, R 26 E). Named on Famoso (1953) 7.5' quadrangle.

Slickrock Canyon [TULARE]: *canyon,* 3.25 miles long, along Cottonwood Creek above a point 1.5 miles north-northeast of Auckland (lat. 36°36'40" N, long. 119°05'45" W; sec. 24, T 15 S, R 26 E). Named on Auckland (1966) and Miramonte (1966) 7.5' quadrangles.

Slick Rock Creek [KERN]: *stream,* flows 2.5 miles to Cedar Creek 2.5 miles west of Alta Sierra (lat. 35°43'55" N, long. 118°35'35" W; near SE cor. sec. 24, T 25 S, R 31 E). Named on Alta Sierra (1972) 7.5' quadrangle.

Slide Bluffs [FRESNO]: *relief feature,* 8.5 miles west of Marion Peak on the south side of the canyon of Middle Fork Kings River (lat. 36°56'15" N, long. 118°40'45" W). Named on Marion Peak (1953) 15' quadrangle.

Slide Canyon: see **Snowslide Canyon** [TULARE].

Slide Creek [FRESNO]: *stream,* flows 4.5 miles to Middle Fork Kings River 8.5 miles west of Marion Peak (lat. 36°56'50" N, long. 118°40'15" W); the stream heads at Slide Lakes and joins Middle Fork Kings River at the base of Slide Bluffs. Named on Marion Peak (1953) 15' quadrangle.

Slide Creek [MADERA]:
(1) *stream,* flows 3.5 miles to Bass Lake (1) nearly 4 miles southeast of Yosemite Forks (lat. 37°19'50" N, long. 119°34'40" W; sec. 9, T 7 S, R 22 E). Named on Bass Lake (1953) 15' quadrangle.
(2) *stream,* flows 2.5 miles to Rock Creek 5.5 miles southeast of Shuteye Peak (lat. 37°17'15" N, long. 119°21'25" W; sec. 28, T 7 S, R 24 E). Named on Shuteye Peak (1953) 15' quadrangle.
(3) *stream,* flows 2.5 miles to North Fork San Joaquin River 8 miles west of Devils Postpile (lat. 37°38'20" N, long. 119°13'25" W). Named on Devils Postpile (1953) 15' quadrangle.

Slide Lakes [FRESNO]: *lakes,* largest 600 feet long, 10 miles west-southwest of Marion Peak (lat. 36°53'30" N, long. 118°41' W); the lakes are at the head of Slide Creek. Named on Marion Peak (1953) 15' quadrangle.

Slide Peak [FRESNO]: *peak,* 10 miles west-southwest of Marion Peak (lat. 36°54' N, long. 118°41'25" W). Altitude 10,915 feet. Named on Marion Peak (1953) 15' quadrangle.

Smiley Mountain [MADERA]: *peak,* 3.25 miles west-northwest of the town of North Fork (lat. 37°14'35" N, long. 119°33'55" W; near SE cor. sec. 9, T 8 S, R 22 E). Altitude 3648 feet. Named on North Fork (1965) 7.5' quadrangle.

Smith and Failing Meadow [TULARE]: *area,* 3 miles east-northeast of Camp Nelson (lat. 36°09'25" N, long. 118°33'20" W; at W line sec. 30, T 20 S, R 32 E). Named on Camp Nelson (1956) 15' quadrangle.

Smith Canyon [KERN]:
(1) *canyon,* drained by a stream that flows 8.5 miles to South Fork Valley near Onyx (lat. 35°41'20" N, long. 118°12'55" W; near SW cor. sec. 3, T 26 S, R 35 E). Named on Onyx (1972) and Walker Pass (1972) 7.5' quadrangles.
(2) *canyon,* drained by a stream that flows 2.5 miles to Nagel Canyon 8 miles north-north-west of Emerald Mountain (lat. 35° 22' N, long. 118°19'55" W). Named on Claraville (1972) and Emerald Mountain (1972) 7.5' quadrangles.

Smith Corner [KERN]: *locality,* 1.5 miles south of Shafter (lat. 35° 28'45" N, long. 119°16'40" W; on E line sec. 21, T 28 S, R 25 E). Named on Rio Bravo (1954) 7.5' quadrangle.

Smith Creek: see **Beach Creek** [TULARE].

Smith Meadow [FRESNO]: *area,* 10.5 miles north-northwest of Hume (lat. 36°56' N, long. 118°58' W). Named on Tehipite Dome (1952) 15' quadrangle.

Smith Meadow [TULARE]: *area,* 16 miles northwest of Lamont Peak (lat. 35°57'50" N, long. 118°13'40" W; on W line sec. 32, T 22 S, R 35 E). Named on Lamont Peak (1956) 15' quadrangle.

Smith Meadows [TULARE]: *area,* 5 miles south-southwest of Monache Mountain (lat. 36°08'35" N, long. 118°14'30" W; sec. 36, T 20 S, R 34 E); the place is 1.5 miles north-west of Smith Mountain (2). Named on Monache Mountain (1956) 15' quadrangle.

Smith Mill [TULARE]: *locality,* 4.5 miles south-west of Camp Nelson (lat. 36°05'25" N, long. 118°39'30" W; near NW cor. sec. 20, T 21 S, R 31 E). Named on Camp Nelson (1956) 15' quadrangle.

Smith Mountain [FRESNO]: *peak,* 14 miles west-southwest of Coalinga (lat. 36°04'45" N, long. 120°35'40" W; sec. 29, T 21 S, R 13 E). Altitude 3947 feet. Named on Smith Mountain (1969) 7.5' quadrangle.

Smith Mountain [FRESNO-TULARE]: *ridge,* south-trending, 3 miles long, 3.5 miles north-east of Dinuba on Fresno-Tulare county line (lat. 37°34'55" N, long. 119°20'45" W). Named on Orange Cove South (1966) 7.5' quadrangle.

Smith Mountain [TULARE]: *peak,* 5.5 miles south-southwest of Monache Mountain (lat. 36°07'35" N, long. 118°13'25" W; sec. 5, T 21 S, R 35 E). Altitude 9515 feet. Named on Monache Mountain (1956) 15' quadrangle.

Smith's Ferry: see **Reedley** [FRESNO].

Smyrna [TULARE]: *locality,* 2.25 miles south-southeast of Dinuba along Southern Pacific Railroad (lat. 36°31' N, long. 119°23'50" W; at S line sec. 21, T 16 S, R 24 E). Named on Sultana (1923) 7.5' quadrangle.

Smyrna: see **Pond** [KERN].

Snail Head [TULARE]: *peak,* 0.5 mile south-southeast of Springville (lat. 36°07'15" N, long. 118°48'40" W; near N line sec. 11, T 21 S, R 29 E). Altitude 1901 feet. Named on Globe (1956) 7.5' quadrangle.

Snake Creek [TULARE]: *stream,* flows 6 miles to South Fork Kern River 3 miles southeast of Monache Mountain (lat. 36°10'45" N, long. 118°09'20" W; near S line sec. 14, T 20 S, R 35 E). Named on Monache Mountain (1956) 15' quadrangle.

Snake Meadow [MADERA]: *area,* 7.5 miles southwest of Devils Postpile (lat. 37°33'35" N, long. 119°11'20" W). Named on Devils Postpile (1953) 15' quadrangle.

Snow Bend [FRESNO]: *locality,* nearly 4 miles east-southeast of Kaiser Peak (lat. 37°16'05" N, long. 119°07'25" W; near W line sec. 3, T 8 S, R 26 E). Named on Kaiser Peak (1953) 15' quadrangle.

Snow Canyon [MADERA]: *canyon,* 2.5 miles long, 1.5 miles southwest of Devils Postpile along King Creek (lat. 37°36'35" N, long. 119°06'45" W). Named on Devils Postpile (1953) 15' quadrangle.

Snow Corral Creek [FRESNO]: *stream,* flows 2.25 miles to Deer Creek (3) 8 miles south-southeast of Dinkey Dome (lat. 37°00'40" N, long. 119°03'55" W; sec. 31, T 10 S, R 27 E); the stream heads near Snow Corral Meadow.

Named on Huntington Lake (1953) 15' quadrangle.

Snow Corral Meadow [FRESNO]: *area,* 7 miles south-southeast of Dinkey Dome (lat. 37°01'40" N, long. 119°04'20" W; sec. 30, T 10 S, R 27 E). Named on Huntington Lake (1953) 15' quadrangle.

Snow Creek [TULARE]: *stream,* flows 3 miles to Little Trout Creek 12 miles east-northeast of Fairview (lat. 35°58' N, long. 118°17'35" W; sec. 34, T 22 S, R 34 E). Named on Kernville (1956) 15' quadrangle.

Snow Lakes [FRESNO]: *lakes,* two, each 1400 feet long, 2 miles north of Mount Abbot in Fourth Recess (lat. 37°25' N, long. 118° 47'25" W). Named on Mount Abbot (1953) 15' quadrangle.

Snowslide Canyon [TULARE]: *canyon,* drained by a stream that flows 1.5 miles to Garfield Creek 10.5 miles southwest of Mineral King (lat. 36°20'50" N, long. 118°40'05" W). Named on Mineral King (1956) 15' quadrangle. Called Putman Can. on Kaweah (1909) 30' quadrangle, where present Putnam Canyon is called Snowslide Canyon. United States Board on Geographic Names (1967b, p. 2) rejected the names "Putman Canyon" and "Slide Canyon" for present Snowslide Canyon.

Snowslide Creek [FRESNO]: *stream,* flows 1 mile to Pittman Creek just east of the town of Big Creek (lat. 37°12'10" N, long. 119°14'10" W; sec. 28, T 8 S, R 25 E). Named on Huntington Lake (1953) 15' quadrangle.

Snowy Mountains: see "Regional setting."

Snowy Range: see "Regional setting."

Soaproot Flat [FRESNO]: *area,* 7 miles south-southeast of Shaver Lake Heights (present town of Shaver Lake) (lat. 37°01'10" N, long. 119°15'50" W; sec. 32, T 10 S, R 25 E); the place is west-southwest of Soaproot Saddle. Named on Shaver Lake (1953) 15' quadrangle.

Soaproot Saddle [FRESNO]: *pass,* 7 miles south-southeast of Shaver Lake Heights (present town of Shaver Lake) (lat. 37°01'30" N, long. 119°15'05" W; near S line sec. 28, T 10 S, R 25 E); the pass is east-northeast of Soaproot Flat. Named on Shaver Lake (1953) 15' quadrangle.

Soda Butte [TULARE]: *peak,* 9 miles south of Mineral King (lat. 36° 19'20" N, long. 118°34'15" W); the peak is near the head of Soda Spring Creek. Named on Mineral King (1956) 15' quadrangle.

Soda Creek [TULARE]:
(1) *stream,* flows 1.5 miles to South Fork of Middle Fork Tule River 3.25 miles west-northwest of Camp Nelson (lat. 36°09'15" N, long. 118°39'50" W). Named on Camp Nelson (1956) 15' quadrangle.
(2) *stream,* flows 3 miles to South Fork Kern River 1.25 miles east of Monache Mountain near Soda Springs (1) (lat. 36°12'35" N, long. 118°10'30" W; sec. 3, T 20 S, R 35 E); the stream joins South Fork near Soda Springs

(1). Named on Monache Mountain (1956) 15' quadrangle.
(3) *stream,* flows 6 miles to Big Arroyo 14 miles northwest of Kern Peak (lat. 36°27'30" N, long. 118°28'05" W). Named on Kern Peak (1956) and Mineral King (1956) 15' quadrangles.
(4) *stream,* flows 3.5 miles to Kern River 4.25 miles south of Hockett Peak (lat. 36°09'30" N, long. 118°23' W). Named on Hockett Peak (1956) 15' quadrangle.

Soda Flat [TULARE]: *area,* 2.5 miles east of Hockett Peak along Ninemile Creek (lat. 36°13'40" N, long. 118°20'20" W). Named on Hockett Peak (1956) 15' quadrangle.

Soda Spring [FRESNO]: *spring,* 1.5 miles north of Double Peak along Fish Creek (1) (lat. 37°32'15" N, long. 119°02'50" W). Named on Mount Lyell (1901) 30' quadrangle.

Soda Spring [MADERA]: *spring,* 8 miles southwest of Devils Postpile near Sheep Crossing (lat. 37°33'15" N, long. 119°12'30" W). Named on Mount Lyell (1901) 30' quadrangle.

Soda Spring [TULARE]:
(1) *spring,* 7.25 miles west-northwest of Kern Peak in Kern Canyon (lat. 36°20'45" N, long. 118°24'25" W). Named on Kern Peak (1956) 15' quadrangle. A group of campers named the spring in 1873 (Browning 1986, p. 204).
(2) *spring,* 7.5 miles southwest of Hockett Peak (lat. 36°08'10" N, long. 118°28'30" W). Named on Hockett Peak (1956) 15' quadrangle.
(3) *spring,* on the west side of Tule River at Springville (lat. 36°07'45" N, long. 118°48'55" W; sec. 2, T 21 S, R 29 E). Named on Springville (1957) 7.5' quadrangle.

Soda Spring: see **Upper Funston Meadow** [TULARE].

Soda Spring Creek [TULARE]: *stream,* flows 8 miles to Little Kern River 14 miles southsoutheast of Mineral King (lat. 36°15'15" N, long. 118°31' W; sec. 21, T 19 S, R 32 E); the stream heads near Soda Butte. Named on Mineral King (1956) 15' quadrangle.

Soda Spring Flat: see **Pumice Flat** [MADERA].

Soda Spring Lake: see **Kern Lake** [TULARE].

Soda Springs [KERN]: *spring,* 3 miles westnorthwest of Emerald Mountain along Indian Creek (lat. 35°16'05" N, long. 118°19'55" W; sec. 4, T 31 S, R 34 E). Named on Emerald Mountain (1972) 7.5' quadrangle.

Soda Springs [TULARE]:
(1) *spring,* 1 mile east-northeast of Monache Mountain in Monache Meadows (lat. 36°12'35" N, long. 118°10'30" W; sec. 3, T 20 S, R 35 E). Named on Monache Mountain (1956) 15' quadrangle.
(2) *locality,* 7 miles south-southeast of Springville along South Fork Tule River (lat. 36°02'20" N, long. 118°45'25" W). Named on Globe (1956) 7.5' quadrangle.

Soda Springs Campground [MADERA]: *lo-*

cality, 3 miles northeast of Shuteye Peak (lat. 37°22'50" N, long. 119°23'20" W; sec. 30, T 6 S, R 24 E). Named on Shuteye Peak (1953) 15' quadrangle.

Soldier Meadow [MADERA]: *area,* 10 miles southeast of Merced Peak (lat. 37°32'35" N, long. 119°15' W). Named on Devils Postpile (1953) and Merced Peak (1953) 15' quadrangles. The place first was called Little Jackass Meadow; the present name is from use of the area as a patrol camp when the army administered Yosemite National Park (Browning, 1986, p. 204).

Soldier Meadow [TULARE]: *area,* 7 miles north-northeast of California Hot Springs (lat. 35°58'40" N, long. 118°37'45" W; sec. 33, T 22 S, R 31 E). Named on California Hot Springs (1958) 15' quadrangle.

Soldier Wells [KERN]: *springs,* 7.5 miles west-southwest of Inyokern in Freeman Canyon (lat. 35°36'40" N, long. 117°56'20" W; near SE cor. sec. 1, T 27 S, R 37 E). Named on Freeman Junction (1972) 7.5' quadrangle.

Soledad Mountain [KERN]: *range,* 8.5 miles north of Rosamond (lat. 34°58'55" N, long. 118°11'15" W). Named on Soledad Mountain (1973) 7.5' quadrangle.

Solitaire: see **Kern River** [KERN-TULARE].

Solomons: see **Mount Solomons,** under **Mount Goddard** [FRESNO].

Solon [KERN]: *locality,* 8 miles east-northeast of present Edwards along Atchison, Topeka and Santa Fe Railroad (lat. 34°57'10" N, long. 117°47'50" W; near N line sec. 23, T 10 N, R 9 W). Named on Rogers Lake (1942) 15' quadrangle.

Solo Peak [TULARE]: *peak,* 4.5 miles southwest of Camp Nelson (lat. 36°06'15" N, long. 118°40'15" W; sec. 18, T 21 S, R 31 E). Altitude 7310 feet. Named on Camp Nelson (1956) 15' quadrangle.

Sontag Point [FRESNO]: *peak,* 2.5 miles east-northeast of Dunlap (lat. 36°44'50" N, long. 119°04'30" W; sec. 31, T 13 S, R 27 E). Altitude 4223 feet. Named on Miramonte (1966) 7.5' quadrangle. The name commemorates John Sontag, an outlaw of the 1890's, who with his partner, Chris Evans, had a shootout with a posse at a cabin situated about 0.5 mile north of the place (Forest M. Clingan, personal communication, 1989).

Soquel Campground [MADERA]: *locality,* 4.5 miles northeast of Yosemite Forks along North Fork Willow Creek (2) (lat. 37°24'15" N, long. 119°33'40" W; near SE cor. sec. 16, T 6 S, R 22 E). Named on Bass Lake (1953) 15' quadrangle.

Soquel Meadow [MADERA]: *area,* 6 miles northeast of Yosemite Forks (lat. 37°25'40" N, long. 119°33'15" W; in and near sec. 10, T 6 S, R 22 E). Named on Bass Lake (1953) 15' quadrangle. Smith Comstock moved his sawmill to the place from Soquel in Santa Cruz County in 1881, and applied the name of the

old site to the new one (Browning, 1986, p. 205).

Sorrell Peak [KERN]: *peak,* 3 miles southeast of Claraville (lat. 35° 25'05" N, long. 118°17'20" W). Altitude 7704 feet. Named on Claraville (1972) 7.5' quadrangle. Called Sorell Peak on Emerald Mountain (1943) 15' quadrangle. United States Board on Geographic Names (1975b, p. 11) gave the forms "Sorell Peak" and "Sorrel Peak" as variants, and noted that the name "Sorrell" commemorates Hiram H. Sorrell, a homesteader in Kelso Valley.

Sorrell's: see **Sageland** [KERN].

Sotcher Lake [MADERA]: *lake,* 1600 feet long, 0.5 mile east of Devils Postpile (lat. 37°37'35" N, long. 119°04'25" W). Named on Devils Postpile (1953) 15' quadrangle. Called Satcher Lake on Mount Lyell (1901) 30' quadrangle. The name commemorates "Red" Sotcher (or Satcher), for whom Reds Meadows was named; the feature also is known as Pond Lily Lake for the mass of yellow lilies that cover its surface near the outlet (Smith, Genny, p. 14).

Source Point [MADERA]: *peak,* 9 miles south-southeast of Shuteye Peak (lat. 37°13'30" N, long. 119°23'20" W; near N line sec. 19, T 8 S, R 24 E). Altitude 6182 feet. Named on Shaver Lake (1953) 15' quadrangle.

South Alder Creek [TULARE]: *stream,* flows 3.5 miles to North Fork of Middle Fork Tule River 5 miles north-northwest of Camp Nelson (lat. 36°12'10" N, long. 118°39' W; near W line sec. 8, T 20 S, R 31 E). Named on Camp Nelson (1956) 15' quadrangle.

South American Lake: see **Lake South America** [TULARE].

South Bear Creek [TULARE]: *stream,* flows 2.25 miles to Bear Creek (2) 6 miles northeast of Springville (lat. 36°12'05" N, long. 118°45'25" W). Named on Camp Nelson (1956) and Springville (1957) 15' quadrangles.

South Canyon Creek: see **Illilouette Creek** [MADERA].

South Corcoran [KINGS]: *locality,* 0.5 mile south-southeast of Corcoran along Atchison, Topeka and Santa Fe Railroad (lat. 36°05'30" N, long. 119°33'15" W; on E line sec. 23, T 21 S, R 22 E). Named on Corcoran (1928) 7.5' quadrangle.

South Creek [TULARE]: *stream,* formed by the confluence of Double Bunk Creek and Bear Creek (4), flows 6 miles to Kern River 3 miles north of Fairview (lat. 35°58'05" N, long. 118°29'10" W; sec. 35, T 22 S, R 32 E). Named on California Hot Springs (1958) and Kernville (1956) 15' quadrangles. Called Wade Cr. on Olmsted's (1900) map.

South Creek Falls [TULARE]: *waterfall,* 3.25 miles north of Fairview (lat. 35°58'15" N, long. 118°29'30" W; sec. 35, T 22 S, R 32 E); the waterfall is along South Creek. Named on Kernville (1956) 15' quadrangle.

South Dome: see **Kettleman Hills** [FRESNO-KERN-KINGS].

Southeast Palisade: see **Split Mountain** [FRESNO].

South Fork [MADERA]: *village,* 9 miles south-southeast of Shuteye Peak along South Fork Willow Creek (2) (lat. 37°14' N, long. 119° 29'30" W; sec. 18, T 8 S, R 23 E). Named on Shaver Lake (1953) 15' quadrangle.

South Fork Bluffs [MADERA]: *relief feature,* 6 miles south-southwest of Shuteye Peak on the east side of South Fork Willow Creek (2) (lat. 37°16'30" N, long. 119°29' W). Named on Shuteye Peak (1953) 15' quadrangle.

South Fork Meadows [TULARE]:
(1) *area,* 8 miles south-southwest of Mineral King (lat. 36°20'50" N, long. 118°38'30" W; sec. 20, T 18 S, R 31 E); the place is along South Fork Kaweah River. Named on Mineral King (1956) 15' quadrangle.
(2) *area,* 12.5 miles northwest of Olancha Peak (lat. 36°24'45" N, long. 118°14'35" W; on S line sec. 25, T 17 S, R 34 E); the place is along South Fork Kern River. Named on Olancha (1956) 15' quadrangle.

South Fork Meadows: see **Tunnel Meadow** [TULARE].

Southfork Pass [FRESNO]: *pass,* 1.5 miles north-northwest of Mount Bolton Brown on Fresno-Inyo county line (lat. 37°04'05" N, long. 118°27'05" W); the pass is at the head of a branch of South Fork Big Pine Creek, which is in Inyo County. Named on Big Pine (1950) 15' quadrangle.

South Fork Valley [KERN]: *valley,* extends for 11 miles along South Fork Kern River above Isabella Lake. Named on Onyx (1972) and Weldon (1972) 7.5' quadrangles.

South Guard [TULARE]: *peak,* 13 miles northwest of Mount Whitney on Great Western Divide (lat. 36°41'40" N, long. 118°29' W); the peak is 1.5 miles south of North Guard. Altitude 13,224 feet. Named on Mount Whitney (1956) 15' quadrangle. Lieutenant Milton F. Davis named the feature (Browning 1986, p. 205).

South Guard Lake [TULARE]: *lake,* 2100 feet long, 14 miles northwest of Mount Whitney (lat. 36°41'30" N, long. 118°29'40" W); the lake is 0.5 mile west of South Guard. Named on Mount Whitney (1956) 15' quadrangle.

South Lake [FRESNO]: *lake,* 1200 feet long, 4.5 miles northeast of Dinkey Dome (lat. 37°09'30" N, long. 119°03'35" W; sec. 7, T 9 S, R 27 E). Named on Huntington Lake (1953) 15' quadrangle.

South Lake [KERN]: *settlement,* 4.5 miles west-southwest of Weldon (lat. 35°38'15" N, long. 118°21'45" W; mainly in sec. 30, T 26 S, R 34 E); the place is south of the east end of Isabella Lake. Named on Weldon (1972) 7.5' quadrangle.

South Mountaineer Creek [TULARE]: *stream,* flows 3 miles to Mountaineer Creek nearly 7 miles north-northeast of Camp Nelson (lat. 36°13'55" N, long. 118°33'50" W; sec. 36, T 19 S, R 31 E). Named on Camp Nelson (1956) 15' quadrangle.

South Palisade: see **Split Mountain** [FRESNO].

South Taft [KERN]: *district,* 0.5 mile south of downtown Taft (lat. 35°08' N, long. 119°27'20" W; near N line sec. 24, T 32 S, R 23 E). Named on Taft (1950) 7.5' quadrangle.

Spa [TULARE]: *locality,* 10.5 miles west-north-west of Earlimart along Atchison, Topeka and Santa Fe Railroad (lat. 35°56'35" N, long. 119°26'30" W; sec. 12, T 23 S, R 23 E). Named on Alpaugh (1929) 7.5' quadrangle. Postal authorities established Spa post office in 1911 and discontinued it in 1920 (Frickstad, p. 213).

Spangle Gold Creek [MADERA]: *stream,* flows 3.5 miles to Fresno River 5.5 miles east-north-east of Knowles (lat. 37°14'15" N, long. 119°46'25" W; sec. 15, T 8 S, R 20 E). Named on Horsecamp Mountain (1947) and Knowles (1962) 7.5' quadrangles. Crawford (p. 207) referred to Spangle Gold Gulch.

Spangle Gold Gulch: see **Spangle Gold Creek** [MADERA].

Spangler Valley: see **Searles Valley** [KERN].

Spanish Camp [TULARE]: *locality,* 11.5 miles north-northeast of Porterville (lat. 36°12'35" N, long. 118°54'40" W; near S line sec. 2, T 20 S, R 28 E). Named on Frazier Valley (1957) 7.5' quadrangle.

Spanish Lake [FRESNO]:
(1) *lake,* 1300 feet long, 10 miles north of Hume (lat. 36°55'50" N, long. 118°53'55" W); the lake is 1.5 miles north-northwest of Spanish Mountain. Named on Tehipite Dome (1952) 15' quadrangle.
(2) *lake,* 700 feet long, 18 miles northwest of Coalinga (lat. 36° 19'50" N, long. 120°34'30" W; sec. 29, T 18 S, R 13 E). Named on Santa Rita Peak (1969) 7.5' quadrangle.

Spanish Lake: see **Little Spanish Lake** [FRESNO].

Spanish Meadow [FRESNO]: *area,* 10 miles north of Hume (lat. 36° 55'55" N, long. 118°54'20" W); the place is nearly 2 miles north-northwest of Spanish Mountain. Named on Tehipite Dome (1952) 15' quadrangle.

Spanish Mountain [FRESNO]: *peak,* 9 miles north of Hume (lat. 36° 54'30" N, long. 118°53'25" W). Altitude 10,051 feet. Named on Tehipite Dome (1952) 15' quadrangle.

Spanish Needle Creek [KERN]: *stream,* flows 5.5 miles to Canebreak Creek 3.5 miles north-northwest of Walker Pass (lat. 35°45'05" N, long. 118°40'40" W). Named on Lamont Peak (1956) 7.5' quadrangle.

Spear Creek [TULARE]: *stream,* flows 4.5 miles to join Von Hellum Creek and form Poso Creek 5.25 miles south of California Hot Springs (lat. 35°48'15" N, long. 118°39'10" W; near S line sec. 29, T 24 S, R 31 E). Named on California Hot Springs (1958) 15' quadrangle.

Spear Creek Summer Home Tract [TULARE]: *locality,* 6 miles southeast of California Hot Springs (lat. 35°49'10" N, long. 118° 35'35" W; near SE cor. sec. 23, T 24 S, R 31 E); the place is near Spear Creek. Named on California Hot Springs (1958) 15' quadrangle.

Spearpoint Lake [FRESNO]: *lake,* 2250 feet long, 9 miles south-southwest of Mount Abbot (lat. 37°15'45" N, long. 118°49'05" W). Named on Mount Abbot (1953) 15' quadrangle. Elden H. Vestal of California Department of Fish and Game named the lake in 1951 for its shape (Browning 1986, p. 206).

Speas Creek [TULARE]:
(1) *stream,* flows 3.5 miles to Tobias Creek 9 miles east of California Hot Springs (lat. 35°54'10" N, long. 118°31' W; sec. 27, T 23 S, R 32 E). Named on California Hot Springs (1958) 15' quadrangle. On Tobias Peak (1936) 30' quadrangle, the canyon of the stream is called Scarlett and Davis Can., but United States Board on Geographic Names (1960a, p. 10) rejected this name for the feature.
(2) *stream,* flows 2.5 miles to White River (1) 4.5 miles southwest of California Hot Springs (lat. 35°50'20" N, long. 118°43'45" W; sec. 15, T 24 S, R 30 E). Named on California Hot Springs (1958) 15' quadrangle.

Speas Dirty Camp [TULARE]: *locality,* 6.5 miles east-northeast of California Hot Springs (lat. 35°55'30" N, long. 118°33'55" W; sec. 18, T 23 S, R 32 E); the place is in Speas Meadow. Named on California Hot Springs (1958) 15' quadrangle.

Speas Meadow [TULARE]: *area,* about 7 miles east-northeast of California Hot Springs (lat. 35°55'35" N, long. 118°33'45" W; sec. 18, T 23 S, R 32 E); the place is near the head of Speas Creek (1). Named on California Hot Springs (1958) 15' quadrangle.

Speas Ridge [TULARE]: *ridge,* northeast- to east-trending, 5 miles long, 9 miles east-northeast of California Hot Springs (lat. 35° 57' N, long. 118°32' W). Named on California Hot Springs (1958) 15' quadrangle.

Specimen Springs [MADERA]: *spring,* 6.25 miles north-northeast of Raymond (lat. 37°18'25" N, long. 119°52'05" W; sec. 23, T 7 S, R 19 E). Named on Horsecamp Mountain (1947) 7.5' quadrangle.

Speckerman Mountain [MADERA]: *peak,* 6.5 miles north-northeast of Yosemite Forks (lat. 37°27'15" N, long. 119°34'45" W; near E line sec. 32, T 5 S, R 22 E). Altitude 7137 feet. Named on Bass Lake (1953) 15' quadrangle. The name, given in the 1850's, commemorates a settler who lived near the feature (Gudde, 1949, p. 340).

Speck Spring [FRESNO]: *spring,* 5.25 miles west-southwest of Coalinga in Oak Flat Canyon (lat. 36°07'10" N, long. 120°27' W; near W line sec. 10, T 21 S, R 14 E). Named on Curry Mountain (1969) 7.5' quadrangle.

Spellacy [KERN]: *locality,* 5.25 miles northwest of Maricopa (lat. 35°06'45" N, long. 119°28'15" W; sec. 26, T 32 S, R 23 E). Named on Maricopa (1951) 7.5' quadrangle.

Spellacy Hill [KERN]: *ridge,* northwest-trending, 1 mile long, 1.5 miles west-southwest of Taft (lat. 35°07'45" N, long. 119°29' W; on E line sec. 22, T 32 S, R 23 E). Named on Taft (1950) 7.5' quadrangle. Arnold and Johnson (p. 22) proposed the name to commemorate the Spellacy brothers, early investors in oil development of the neighborhood.

Spencer: see **Mount Spencer** [FRESNO]:

Sphinx: see **The Sphinx** [FRESNO].

Sphinx Creek [FRESNO-TULARE]: *stream,* heads at Sphinx Lakes in Tulare County and flows 8 miles to Bubbs Creek 12 miles south of Marion Peak in Fresno County (lat. 36°46'50" N, long. 118°32'15" W). Named on Marion Peak (1953) and Triple Divide Peak (1956) 15' quadrangles.

Sphinx Crest [TULARE]: *ridge,* northwest-trending, 3 miles long, 9 miles north of Triple Divide Peak (lat. 36°43'40" N, long. 118° 32' W). Named on Triple Divide Peak (1956) 15' quadrangle.

Sphinx Lakes [TULARE]: *lakes,* largest 2000 feet long, 9.5 miles north of Triple Divide Peak (lat. 36°44' N, long. 118°31' W); the lakes are northeast of Sphinx Crest on upper reaches of Sphinx Creek. Named on Triple Divide Peak (1956) 15' quadrangle.

Spicer City [KERN]: *locality,* 9 miles south-southeast of the village of Lost Hills (lat. 35°30'05" N, long. 119°36'10" W). Named on Semitropic (1954) 7.5' quadrangle.

Spinecup Ridge [MADERA]: *ridge,* southwest-trending, 1.5 miles long, 1.5 miles east-northeast of Raymond (lat. 37°13'30" N, long. 119°53' W). Named on Raymond (1962) 7.5' quadrangle.

Spinks Corner [TULARE]: *locality,* 8 miles west of Lindsay (lat. 36° 12'40" N, long. 119°13'55" W; at N line sec. 11, T 20 S, R 25 E). Named on Cairns Corner (1950) 7.5' quadrangle.

Split Mountain [FRESNO]: *peak,* 2 miles south-southeast of Mount Bolton Brown on Fresno-Inyo county line (lat. 37°01'15" N, long. 118°25'15" W). Altitude 14,058 feet. Named on Big Pine (1950) 15' quadrangle. Bolton C. Brown named the peak for its double summit; members of the Wheeler survey called the feature Southeast Palisade in 1876—it also was known as South Palisade (Farquhar, 1925, p. 135).

Split Mountain [KERN]: *ridge,* generally east-trending, 1.25 miles long, 3 miles west of Kernville (lat. 35°45'05" N, long. 118°28'30" W). Named on Kernville (1956) 15' quadrangle, and on Lake Isabella North (1972) 7.5' quadrangle.

Sportsman Lake [FRESNO]: *lake,* 900 feet long, 4.5 miles east-southeast of Dinkey Dome (lat. 37°05'45" N, long. 119°03'20" W;

near N line sec. 5, T 10 S, R 27 E). Named on Huntington Lake (1953) 15' quadrangle.

Spotted Lakes [MADERA]: *lakes,* largest 1400 feet long, nearly 6 miles south of Merced Peak (lat. 37°33'05" N, long. 119°24' W). Named on Merced Peak (1953) 15' quadrangle.

Spottiswood: see **Famoso** [KERN].

Spout Spring [KERN]: *spring,* 8 miles east-northeast of Glennville (lat. 35°45'05" N, long. 118°33'30" W; sec. 17, T 25 S, R 32 E). Named on California Hot Springs (1958) 15' quadrangle.

Spring Canyon [KERN]: *canyon,* drained by a stream that flows 1.5 miles to Canebreak Flat 6 miles northwest of Walker Pass (lat. 35° 43'15" N, long. 118°06'25" W; near SW cor. sec. 27, T 25 S, R 36 E). Named on Walker Pass (1972) 7.5' quadrangle.

Spring Cove Campground [MADERA]: *local-ity,* 6.5 miles southeast of Yosemite Forks on the southwest side of Bass Lake (1) (lat. 37° 18' N, long. 119°32'30" W; near S line sec. 23, T 7 S, R 22 E). Named on Bass Lake (1953) 15' quadrangle.

Spring Creek [FRESNO]:
(1) *stream,* flows 1 mile to Huntington Lake 3 miles south of Kaiser Peak (lat. 37°15'05" N, long. 119°10'45" W; sec. 7, T 8 S, R 26 E). Named on Kaiser Peak (1953) 15' quadrangle.
(2) *stream,* flows 3.5 miles to Kings River 6.5 miles northwest of Hume (lat. 36°51'45" N, long. 118°58'55" W). Named on Tehipite Dome (1952) 15' quadrangle.

Spring Creek: see **Eagle Creek** [TULARE] (1).

Springfield Spring [KERN]: *spring,* 11 miles north-north-west of Mojave (lat. 35°12'25" N, long. 119°12'40" W; sec. 27, T 31 S, R 35 E). Named on Cache Peak (1973) 7.5' quadrangle.

Spring Gulch [KERN]: *canyon,* 1 mile long, opens into the canyon of Erskine Creek 4.25 miles east of Bodfish (lat. 35°34'30" N, long. 118°24'45" W; near SW cor. sec. 14, T 27 S, R 33 E). Named on Lake Isabella South (1972) 7.5' quadrangle.

Springhill Campground: see **Lower Springhill Campground** [TULARE]; **Upper Springhill Campground** [TULARE].

Spring Lake [TULARE]: *lake,* 1400 feet long, 2.5 miles east-northeast of Mineral King (lat. 36°28'15" N, long. 118°33'25" W). Named on Mineral King (1956) 15' quadrangle.

Spring Mountain Creek: see **Spring Mountain Gulch** [KERN].

Spring Mountain Gulch [KERN]: *canyon,* drained by a stream that flows 3.5 miles to Rag Gulch 0.5 mile west of Woody (lat. 35° 42'10" N, long. 118°50'45" W; near S line sec. 34, T 25 S, R 29 E). Named on Woody (1965) 7.5' quadrangle. United States Board on Geographic Names (1966b, p. 6) rejected the names "Dry Creek" and "Spring Mountain Creek" for the feature.

Springville [TULARE]: *town,* 12 miles east-northeast of Porterville along Tule River (lat.

36°07'55" N, long. 118°49' W; in and near sec. 2, T 21 S, R 29 E). Named on Globe (1956) and Springville (1957) 7.5' quad-rangles. A.M. Coburn, a lumberman who had mills at the place, founded the town in 1889; it first was called Daunt, for William G. Daunt, a settler of the 1860's, and later was named for Soda Spring (3) (Hanna, p. 314). Postal authorities established Daunt post office in 1886 and changed the name to Springville in 1911 (Frickstad, p. 210). California Division of Highways' (1934) map shows a place called Clavicle located 2 miles south of Springville along Southern Pacific Railroad (near E line sec. 15, T 21 S, R 29 E). Postal authorities established Jordan post office 11 miles northeast of Springville in 1951 and discontinued it in 1952 (Salley, p. 108).

Square Lake [FRESNO]: *lake,* 650 feet long, 3 miles west of Mount Humphreys in Humphreys Basin (lat. 37°16' N, long. 118°43'35" W). Named on Mount Tom (1949) 15' quadrangle.

Squaw Creek [TULARE]: *stream,* flows 2.5 miles to South Fork Kaweah River 12.5 miles southeast of Kaweah (lat. 36°20'50" N, long. 118°45'05" W). Named on Kaweah (1957) and Mineral King (1956) 15' quadrangles. United States Board on Geographic Names (1960b, p. 21) rejected the name "Pigeon Creek" for the stream. The name "Squaw Creek" was given about sixty years after a Mexican murdered his wife near the stream (Browning 1986, p. 207).

Squaw Creek: see **Cedar Creek** [TULARE] (4).

Squaw Dome [MADERA]: *peak,* about 13 miles northeast of Shuteye Peak (lat. 37°28'55" N, long. 119°15'50" W; sec. 20, T 5 S, R 25 E). Altitude 7818 feet. Named on Shuteye Peak (1953) 15' quadrangle. Called Squaw Nipple Peak on California Mining Bureau's (1917d) map.

Squaw Lake: see **Helen Lake** [FRESNO] (1); **Old Squaw Lake** [FRESNO].

Squaw Leap [FRESNO]: *peak,* nearly 3 miles northwest of Prather (lat. 37°04'10" N, long. 119°32'45" W; near SW cor. sec. 11, T 10 S, R 22 E). Named on Millerton Lake East (1965) 7.5' quadrangle.

Squaw Nipple Peak: see **Squaw Dome** [MA-DERA].

Squaw Valley [FRESNO]:
(1) *valley,* 6.5 miles west of Dunlap (lat. 36°44' N, long. 119° 14' W). Named on Orange Cove North (1966) and Tucker Mountain (1966) 7.5' quadrangles.
(2) *locality,* 7 miles west of Dunlap (lat. 36°44'25" N, long. 119°14'40" W; sec. 3, T 14 S, R 25 E); the place is in Squaw Valley (1). Named on Tucker Mountain (1966) 7.5' quadrangle. Postal authorities established Squaw Valley post office in 1879, changed the name to Squawvalley in 1895, discontin-ued it in 1918, reestablished it in 1923,

changed the name back to Squaw Valley in 1932, discontinued the post office in 1945, and reestablished it in 1960 (Salley, p. 211). United States Board on Geographic Names (1959, p. 2) rejected the form "Squawvalley" for the name.

Squirrel Creek [TULARE]: *stream,* flows 4 miles to East Fork Kaweah River 8.5 miles east-southeast of Kaweah (lat. 36°26'25" N, long. 118°46'15" W; at S line sec. 13, T 17 S, R 29 E). Named on Kaweah (1957) and Mineral King (1956) 15' quadrangles.

Squirrel Meadow [KERN]: *area,* 10 miles east-northeast of Mount Adelaide (lat. 35°28'30" N, long. 118°34'35" W; sec. 19, T 28 S, R 32 E). Named on Breckenridge Mountain (1972) 7.5' quadrangle.

Squirrel Mountain Valley [KERN]: *settlement,* 5 miles northeast of Bodfish (lat. 38°37'30" N, long. 118°24'30" W; sec. 35, T 26 S, R 33 E). Named on Lake Isabella North (1972) and Lake Isabella South (1972) 7.5' quadrangles.

Stable Creek [KERN]: *stream,* flows nearly 3 miles to French Gulch (1) 4.5 miles south-southeast of Alta Sierra (lat. 35°39'55" N, long. 118°31'15" W; sec. 15, T 26 S, R 32 E). Named on Alta Sierra (1972) 7.5' quadrangle.

Stag Canyon [KERN]: *canyon,* drained by a stream that flows 1.25 miles to Montgomery Canyon 4.25 miles east of Caliente (lat. 35° 17'35" N, long. 118°33'10" W; sec. 28, T 30 S, R 32 E). Named on Oiler Peak (1972) 7.5' quadrangle.

Stag Dome [FRESNO]: *peak,* 14 miles southwest of Marion Peak (lat. 36°49'15" N, long. 118°42' W). Altitude 7710 feet. Named on Marion Peak (1953) 15' quadrangle.

Stag Saddle [KERN]: *pass,* 5.25 miles east of Caliente on Devils Backbone (lat. 35°17'15" N, long. 118°32'05" W; sec. 27, T 30 S, R 32 E); the pass is near the head of Stag Canyon. Named on Oiler Peak (1972) 7.5' quadrangle.

Stag Spring [KERN]: *spring,* 4 miles southwest of Cummings Mountain (lat. 35°00'20" N, long. 118°37'20" W; sec. 31, T 11 N, R 16 W). Named on Cummings Mountain (1966) 7.5' quadrangle.

Stag Thicket Spring [KERN]: *spring,* 5.5 miles east of Caliente (lat. 35°17'15" N, long. 118°31'35" W; sec. 27, T 30 S, R 32 E). Named on Oiler Peak (1972) 7.5' quadrangle.

Stairway Creek [MADERA]: *stream,* flows 4.5 miles to Middle Fork San Joaquin River 6.5 miles south-southwest of Devils Postpile (lat. 37°32'25" N, long. 119°08'15" W); the stream heads near Granite Stairway. Named on Devils Postpile (1953) 15' quadrangle.

Stairway Meadow [MADERA]: *area,* 3.25 miles southwest of Devils Postpile (lat. 37°35'50" N, long. 119°07'45" W); the place is northwest of Granite Stairway. Named on Devils Postpile (1953) 15' quadrangle.

Stalf Creek: see **Woolstalf Creek** [KERN].

Standard Hill [KERN]: *hill,* 3 miles south of

Mojave (lat. 35°00'25" N, long. 118°10'25" W; sec. 32, T 11 N, R 12 W). Altitude 3128 feet. Named on Mojave (1973) 7.5' quadrangle. Called Elephant Butte on Mojave (1947) 7.5' quadrangle, and United States Board on Geographic Names (1975c, p. 5) gave this name as a variant.

Standard Mill [MADERA]: *locality,* 4 miles northeast of O'Neals (lat. 37°09'55" N, long. 119°38'20" W; near W line sec. 12, T 9 S, R 21 E). Named on Mariposa (1912) 30' quadrangle.

Stanford: see **Mount Stanford** [FRESNO]; **Mount Stanford** [TULARE].

Stanford Lakes [MADERA]: *lakes,* largest 1100 feet long, nearly 6 miles south-southeast of Merced Peak (lat. 37°33'15" N, long. 119° 21'40" W). Named on Merced Peak (1953) 15' quadrangle. Billy Brown, a local packer, applied the misspelled name about 1920; he intended to honor the Kenneth J. Staniford family of Fresno (Browning, 1986, p. 207).

Stanford Peak: see **Mount Stanford** [FRESNO].

Stanley: see **Turk** [FRESNO].

Stark Creek [KERN]: *stream,* flows 6.5 miles to Kern River 3.25 miles north-northeast of Mount Adelaide (lat. 35°28'35" N, long. 118°43'25" W). Named on Mount Adelaide (1972) 7.5' quadrangle. Called Stork Creek on Breckenridge Mountain (1943) 15' quadrangle, and United States Board on Geographic Names (1975b, p. 12) gave this name as a variant.

Starkweather Lake [MADERA]: *lake,* 600 feet long, 2.5 miles north of Devils Postpile (lat. 37°39'50" N, long. 119°04'25" W). Named on Devils Postpile (1953) 15' quadrangle. The name commemorates a prospector who had claims above the lake in the 1920's (Smith, Genny, p. 13).

Star Lakes [MADERA]: *lakes,* largest 900 feet long, 5.5 miles south-southwest of Buena Vista Peak (lat. 37°30'55" N, long. 119°32'45" W; sec. 10, T 5 S, R 22 E). Named on Yosemite (1956) 15' quadrangle, which shows Star mine southwest of the lakes.

Starr: see **Mount Starr** [FRESNO].

Starvation Creek [TULARE]: *stream,* flows 4 miles to Tyler Creek 2 miles northeast of California Hot Springs (lat. 35°54'10" N, long. 118°38'50" W; sec. 29, T 23 S, T 31 E). Named on California Hot Springs (1958) 15' quadrangle.

Starville: see **Oakhurst** [MADERA].

State Lakes [FRESNO]: *lakes,* 2 miles southwest of Marion Peak (lat. 36°55'50" N, long. 118°33'30" W); the lakes are about 1 mile west of State Peak. Named on Marion Peak (1953) 15' quadrangle.

State Peak [FRESNO]: *peak,* 2 miles southwest of Marion Peak (lat. 36°55'55" N, long. 118°32'40" W). Altitude 12,620 feet. Named on Marion Peak (1953) 15' quadrangle.

Statham Creek: see **Statum Creek** [FRESNO].

Statham Meadow: see **Statum Meadow** [FRESNO].

Statum Creek [FRESNO]: *stream,* flows about 4 miles to Rancheria Creek (3) 12 miles north of Hume (lat. 36°57'15" N, long. 118°56'10" W). Named on Tehipite Dome (1952) 15' quadrangle. United States Board on Geographic Names (1987b, p. 2) approved the name "Statham Creek" for the stream, and pointed out that the name commemorates Albert Statham, an early-day sheepman in the neighborhood.

Statum Meadow [FRESNO]: *area,* 11 miles north of Hume (lat. 36° 56'40" N, long. 118°54'50" W); the place is along Statum (present Statham) Creek. Named on Tehipite Dome (1952) 15' quadrangle. United States Board on Geographic Names (1987b, p. 2) approved the name "Statham Meadow" for the feature.

Steelhead Lake [FRESNO]: *lake,* 2600 feet long, 3 miles northwest of Mount Humphreys (lat. 37°18'05" N, long. 118°42'40" W; near NW cor. sec. 32, T 7 S, R 30 E). Named on Mount Tom (1949) 15' quadrangle.

Stephenson Hill [FRESNO]: *peak,* 6.25 miles northwest of Piedra (lat. 36°52'15" N, long. 119°27'45" W; sec. 21, T 12 S, R 23 E). Altitude 1059 feet. Named on Piedra (1965) 7.5' quadrangle.

Steve Barton Point [TULARE]: *peak,* 4 miles east of Woodlake (lat. 36°24'15" N, long. 119°01'45" W; sec. 34, T 17 S, R 27 E). Altitude 859 feet. Named on Woodlake (1952) 7.5' quadrangle. Grunsky (p. 11) called the feature Dillons Point.

Stevens [KERN]: *locality,* 11.5 miles west-south-west of Bakersfield along Southern Pacific Railroad (lat. 35°18'50" N, long. 119°11'20" W; sec. 16, T 30 S, R 26 E). Named on Stevens (1954) 7.5' quadrangle.

Stevens Creek: see **Stevenson Creek** [FRESNO].

Stevenson: see **Mount Stevenson** [FRESNO].

Stevenson Basin: see **Shaver Lake** [FRESNO].

Stevenson Creek [FRESNO]: *stream,* flows 12 miles, including through Shaver Lake, to San Joaquin River 5 miles north-northwest of Shaver Lake Heights (present town of Shaver Lake) (lat. 37°10'15" N, long. 119°21'35" W; at N line sec. 9, T 9 S, R 24 E). Named on Huntington Lake (1953) and Shaver Lake (1953) 15' quadrangles. United States Board on Geographic Names (1933a, p. 721) rejected the names "Stevens Creek" and "Stevensons Creek" for the stream. North Fork enters Shaver Lake 3.5 miles east-northeast of Shaver Lake Heights (present town of Shaver Lake); it is 3.5 miles long and is named on Huntington Lake (1953) and Shaver Lake (1953) 15' quadrangles.

Stevenson Creek [KERN]: *stream,* flows 4.5 miles to Indian Creek 4 miles east-southeast of Loraine (lat. 35°16'20" N, long. 118°22'30" W; near NW cor. sec. 6, T 31 S, R 34 E); the stream is located 1 mile south-southeast of Stevenson Peak. Named on Emerald Mountain (1972), Loraine (1972), and Tehachapi NE (1966) 7.5' quadrangles.

Stevenson Gulch [TULARE]: *canyon,* drained by a stream that flows 2 miles to South Fork of Middle Fork Tule River 4.5 miles west-northwest of Camp Nelson (lat. 36°09'30" N, long. 118°41'15" W). Named on Camp Nelson (1956) 15' quadrangle.

Stevenson Meadow [MADERA]: *area,* 8.5 miles west-northwest of Devils Postpile (lat. 37°39'35" N, long. 119°13'50" W). Named on Devils Postpile (1953) 15' quadrangle.

Stevenson Meadows: see **Shaver Lake** [FRESNO].

Stevenson Peak [KERN]: *peak,* 3 miles east-southeast of Loraine (lat. 35°17'10" N, long. 118°23' W; sec. 25, T 30 S, R 33 E). Altitude 5026 feet. Named on Loraine (1972) 7.5' quadrangle.

Stevensons Creek: see **Stevenson Creek** [FRESNO].

Steve Spring [KERN]: *spring,* 11 miles south-southwest of Weldon (lat. 35°30'45" N, long. 118°20'05" W; at E line sec. 8, T 28 S, R 34 E). Named on Woolstalf Creek (1972) 7.5' quadrangle.

Stewart Mountain: see **Mount Stewart** [TULARE].

Still Canyon [KERN]: *canyon,* drained by a stream that flows 3.5 miles to Barrel Valley nearly 6 miles south of Orchard Peak (lat. 35°39'10" N, long. 120°07'45" W; sec. 22, T 26 S, R 17 E). Named on Orchard Peak (1961) 7.5' quadrangle.

Still Lake [KERN]: *intermittent lake,* about 600 feet long, 7.5 miles south-southwest of Orchard Peak (lat. 35°38'10" N, long. 120°11'20" W; sec. 30, T 26 S, R 17 E). Named on Orchard Peak (1961) 7.5' quadrangle.

Stine Cove [KERN]: *embayment,* 3.25 miles southeast of Wofford Heights on the north side of Isabella Lake (lat. 35°40'40" N, long. 118°24'30" W; sec. 11, T 26 S, R 33 E). Named on Lake Isabella North (1972) 7.5' quadrangle.

Stine Point [KERN]: *promontory,* 3.25 miles southeast of Wofford Heights along Isabella Lake (lat. 35°40'35" N, long. 118°24'50" W; near SE cor. sec. 10, T 26 S, R 33 E). Named on Lake Isabella North (1972) 7.5' quadrangle.

Stocking Lake [FRESNO]: *lake,* 1800 feet long, 5.5 miles south-southeast of Mount Pinchot (lat. 36°52'15" N, long. 118°22'15" W). Named on Mount Pinchot (1953) 15' quadrangle.

Stockton: see **Lake Stockton** [KERN].

Stoil [TULARE]: *locality,* 9 miles west-north-west of Earlimart along Atchison, Topeka and Santa Fe Railroad (lat. 35°55'05" N, long. 119°25'25" W; sec. 19, T 23 S, R 24 E). Named on Alpaugh (1953) 7.5' quadrangle.

The name is an abbreviated form of the term "Standard Oil"—Standard Oil Company had a pumping station at the place (Gudde, 1949, p. 344).

Stoker Canyon [KERN-KINGS]: *canyon,* drained by a stream that heads in Kings County and flows 3.5 miles to Cottonwood Canyon 3.5 miles northwest of Orchard Peak in Kern County (lat. 35°46'25" N, long. 120°10'25" W; near N line sec. 7, T 25 S, R 17 E). Named on Tent Hills (1942) 7.5' quadrangle.

Stokes Mountain [TULARE]: *ridge,* south-southwest- to west-trending, 5 miles long, 10 miles east of Dinuba (lat. 36°31' N, long. 119° 11'45" W). Named on Stokes Mountain (1966) 7.5' quadrangle.

Stokes Stringer [TULARE]: *stream,* flows 3 miles to Golden Trout Creek 9 miles north of Kern Peak in Big Whitney Meadow (lat. 36°26'05" N, long. 118°15'35" W; sec. 23, T 17 S, R 34 E). Named on Kern Peak (1956) and Olancha (1956) 15' quadrangles. United States Board on Geographic Names (1989a, p. 4) rejected the name "Golden Trout Creek" for the feature.

Stone: see **Pagliarulo** [TULARE].

Stone Corral Canyon [TULARE]: *canyon,* drained by a stream that flows 1 mile to lowlands 3 miles south of Cliff Peak (lat. 36°30'40" N, long. 119°10'45" W; sec. 30, T 16 S, R 26 E). Named on Stokes Mountain (1966) 7.5' quadrangle.

Stoney Point [FRESNO]: *peak,* 4.5 miles west-northwest of Piedra (lat. 36°50'15" N, long. 119°27'10" W; near SW cor. sec. 34, T 12 S, R 23 E). Named on Piedra (1965) 7.5' quadrangle.

Stony Creek [TULARE]: *stream,* flows 4.5 miles to join Dorst Creek and form North Fork Kaweah River 4.5 miles southwest of Shell Mountain (lat. 36°38'35" N, long. 118°50'40" W; near SW cor. sec. 4, T 15 S, R 29 E). Named on Giant Forest (1956) 15' quadrangle.

Stony Creek Campground [TULARE]: *locality,* 3 miles southwest of Shell Mountain (lat. 36°39'50" N, long. 118°50' W; sec. 33, T 14 S, R 28 E); the place is along Stony Creek. Named on Giant Forest (1956) 15' quadrangle. Called Stony Creek Camp on Tehipite (1903) 30' quadrangle.

Stony Flat [FRESNO]: *area,* 5 miles east-southeast of Dunlap (lat. 36°42'55" N, long. 119°01'50" W). Named on Miramonte (1966) 7.5' quadrangle. Postal authorities established Noble post office at the place in 1892 (Forest M. Clingan, personal communication, 1990). They moved it 2 miles north in 1896, moved it 1.5 miles northwest the same year, and discontinued it in 1902 (Salley, p. 154).

Stony Meadow [TULARE]: *area,* 10 miles south of Hockett Peak (lat. 36°04'40" N, long. 118°24' W). Named on Hockett Peak (1956) 15' quadrangle.

Storey [MADERA]: *locality,* 2.5 miles east-northeast of Madera along Atchison, Topeka and Santa Fe Railroad (lat. 37°58'30" N, long. 120°01'05" W; near W line sec. 16, T 11 S, R 18 E). Named on Madera (1963) 7.5' quadrangle. Madera (1946) 15' quadrangle has the designation "Storey (Madera Sta.)" at the place.

Stork Creek: see **Stark Creek** [KERN].

Stormy Canyon [KERN]: *canyon,* drained by a stream that flows 3.5 miles to South Fork Valley less than 1 mile north-northwest of Onyx (lat. 35°42'15" N, long. 118°13'35" W; sec. 4, T 26 S, R 35 E). Named on Onyx (1972) 7.5' quadrangle.

Stormy Canyon [TULARE]: *canyon,* drained by a stream that flows 4 miles to Kern River 8 miles south-southeast of Fairview (lat. 35° 49'05" N, long. 118°27'30" W; sec. 30, T 24 S, R 33 E). Named on California Hot Springs (1958) and Kernville (1956) 15' quadrangles.

Story Creek [TULARE]: *stream,* flows nearly 3 miles to Long Creek 2 miles west of Cliff Peak (lat. 36°33'40" N, long. 119°12'25" W; sec. 1, T 16 S, R 25 E). Named on Stokes Mountain (1966) 7.5' quadrangle.

Stout [TULARE]: *locality,* 1.5 miles south-southeast of Lindsay along Southern Pacific Railroad (lat. 36°10'55" N, long. 119°04'50" W; near SW cor. sec. 17, T 20 S, R 27 E). Named on Lindsay (1951) 7.5' quadrangle.

Stove Canyon [FRESNO]: *canyon,* drained by a stream that flows 1 mile to Hot Springs Canyon 3 miles north-northwest of Coalinga Mineral Springs (lat. 36°11'10" N, long. 120°34'15" W; sec. 16, T 20 S, R 13 E). Named on Sherman Peak (1969) 7.5' quadrangle.

Stove Ridge [FRESNO]: *ridge,* north- to north-northeast-trending, 1 mile long, 4 miles north of Coalinga Mineral Springs (lat. 36° 12' N, long. 120°32'45" W; in and near sec. 11, T 20 S, R 13 E); the ridge is east of Stove Spring. Named on Sherman Peak (1969) 7.5' quadrangle.

Stove Spring [FRESNO]: *spring,* 4.25 miles north of Coalinga Mineral Springs (lat. 36°12'20" N, long. 120°32'45" W; sec. 11, T 20 S, R 13 E). Named on Sherman Peak (1969) 7.5' quadrangle.

Strader: see **Wible Orchard** [KERN].

Strand [KERN]: *locality,* 13 miles west of Bakersfield along Southern Pacific Railroad (lat. 35°20'30" N, long. 119°13'20" W; near S line sec. 6, T 30 S, R 26 E). Named on Stevens (1932) 7.5' quadrangle.

Stratford [KINGS]: *town,* 14 miles southwest of Hanford (lat. 36°11'20" N, long. 119°49'20" W; sec. 17, T 20 S, R 20 E). Named on Stratford (1954) 7.5' quadrangle. Called Stratton on California Mining Bureau's (1909a) map. The place was named Stratton in 1901 for William Stratton of Empire Land and Water Company, which operated in the neighborhood; the name was changed to Stratford in 1906 through the efforts of the local woman's club (Hanna, p. 318). Postal authorities established Stratford post office in 1910 (Frickstad, p. 61).

Strathmore [TULARE]: *town,* 4.25 miles south-southeast of Lindsay (lat. 36°08'50" N, long. 119°03'35" W; sec. 32, 33, T 20 S, R 27 E). Named on Lindsay (1951) 7.5' quadrangle. Mary Burness named the town in 1906 with the word that she said means "beautiful valley" in her native Scotland; the place also was called Balfour, Roth Spur, and Filo—the name "Balfour" was for Balfour-Guthrie Company, owner of land at the site, and the name "Roth" was for the Roth family, pioneer grain farmers (Mitchell, A.R., p. 69). The place also was called Santos (Gudde, 1949, p. 345). Postal authorities established Roth post office in 1896 and discontinued it in 1899; they established Strathmore post office in 1907 (Frickstad, p. 213).

Strathmore Junction: see **Mirador** [TULARE].

Stratton: see **Stratford** [KINGS].

Stratton Canyon [KERN]: *canyon,* drained by a stream that flows about 2.5 miles to Bronco Canyon (2) 4.5 miles west-northwest of Liebre Twins (lat. 34°58'50" N, long. 118°38'45" W; at N line sec. 1, T 10 N, R 17 W). Named on Liebre Twins (1965) and Winters Ridge (1966) 7.5' quadrangles.

Strawberry Creek [TULARE]: *stream,* flows 3.25 miles to South Fork Kern River 4 miles west-northwest of Olancha Peak (lat. 36° 17'50" N, long. 118°10'45" W; sec. 3, T 19 S, R 35 E); the mouth of the stream is in Strawberry Meadows. Named on Olancha (1956) 15' quadrangle.

Strawberry Lake [FRESNO]: *lake,* 600 feet long, 7.25 miles east of the town of Big Creek (lat. 37°12'15" N, long. 119°06'45" W; sec. 27, T 8 S, R 26 E). Named on Huntington Lake (1953) 15' quadrangle.

Strawberry Meadow Creek [FRESNO]: *stream,* flows nearly 1 mile to Dinkey Creek (1) 5 miles south of Dinkey Dome (lat. 37°02'35" N, long. 119°08'50" W; sec. 21, T 10 S, R 26 E). Named on Huntington Lake (1953) 15' quadrangle.

Strawberry Meadows [TULARE]: *area,* 4.5 miles northwest of Olancha Peak (lat. 36°18' N, long. 118°11' W). Named on Olancha (1956) 15' quadrangle. Called Templeton Meadows on Olancha (1907) 30' quadrangle, but United States Board on Geographic Names (1961b, p. 12) rejected the names "Templeton Meadow" and "Templeton Meadows" for the feature.

Street Canyon [TULARE]: *canyon,* drained by a stream that flows 2 miles to Gibbon Creek 9 miles south-southeast of Springville (lat. 36°00'10" N, long. 118°46'35" W). Named on Springville (1957) and White River (1952) 15' quadrangles.

Stringer District [KERN]: *locality,* 2 miles south of Randsburg (lat. 35°20'30" N, long. 117°39'15" W; sec. 11, 12, T 30 S, R 40 E). Named on Randsburg (1911) 15' quadrangle.

String Meadows [FRESNO]: *areas,* two, 3.5 miles west-southwest of Double Peak (lat. 37°30' N, long. 119°06'15" W). Named on Devils Postpile (1953) and Kaiser Peak (1953) 15' quadrangles. United States Board on Geographic Names (1985c, p. 3) rejected the singular form "String Meadow" for the name.

String Town: see **Gertrude**, under **Ahwanee** [MADERA].

Striped Mountain [FRESNO]: *peak,* 1.25 miles north of Mount Pinchot on Fresno-Inyo county line (lat. 36°57'55" N, long. 118°24'10" W). Named on Mount Pinchot (1953) 15' quadrangle. Bolton C. Brown named the feature in 1895 for its appearance (Browning 1986, p. 210).

Striped Rock Creek [MADERA]: *stream,* heads in Mariposa County and flows 11 miles to Chowchilla River 6.25 miles north-northeast of Raymond in Madera County (lat. 37°18'05" N, long. 119°51'45" W); the stream goes past Striped Rock. Named on Ben Hur (1947), Horsecamp Mountain (1947), and Mariposa (1947) 7.5' quadrangles.

Stub Lake [FRESNO]: *lake,* 900 feet long, 5.25 miles south-southwest of Mount Abbot (lat. 37°19' N, long. 118°49'15" W). Named on Mount Abbot (1953) 15' quadrangle.

Studebaker Flat [KERN]: *area,* 4 miles south-southeast of Bodfish (lat. 35°32'10" N, long. 118°27'05" W; near E line sec. 32, T 27 S, R 33 E). Named on Lake Isabella South (1972) 7.5' quadrangle.

Studhorse Canyon [FRESNO]: *canyon,* drained by a stream that flows 3 miles to Los Gatos Creek 5.5 miles north-northeast of Coalinga Mineral Springs (lat. 36°13'25" N, long. 120°31'40" W; sec. 1, T 20 S, R 13 E). Named on Sherman Peak (1969) 7.5' quadrangle.

Studhorse Canyon [KERN]: *canyon,* drained by a stream that flows 4.25 miles to Caliente Creek 1 mile west of Loraine (lat. 35°18'05" N, long. 118°27'20" W; sec. 20, T 30 S, R 33 E). Named on Loraine (1972) 7.5' quadrangle. The stream in the canyon is called Studhorse Creek on Mojave (1915) 30' quadrangle.

Studhorse Creek: see **Studhorse Canyon** [KERN].

Success [TULARE]: *village,* 5 miles southwest of Springville (lat. 36°04'40" N, long. 118°52'45" W; sec. 30, T 21 S, R 29 E). Named on Kaweah (1909) 30' quadrangle. Postal authorities established Success post office in 1903 and discontinued it in 1912 (Frickstad, p. 213). California Division of Highways' (1934) map shows a place called Magnesite located 2 miles east-southeast of Success along Southern Pacific Railroad (near S line sec. 30, T 21 S, R 29 E), a place called Magnesite Jct. situated nearly 1 mile south-southwest of Success along the railroad (sec. 26, T 21 S, R 28 E), and a place called Howton located nearly 3 miles east-southeast of Success at the end of a rail line (sec. 32, T 21 S, R 29 E).

Success: see **Lake Success** [TULARE].

Success Reservoir: see **Lake Success** [TULARE].

Sugarbowl Dome [TULARE]: *peak,* 7.25 miles west-southwest of Triple Divide Peak (lat. 36°33'15" N, long. 118°38'50" W). Named on Triple Divide Peak (1956) 15' quadrangle. The name is descriptive; a depression in the top of the feature holds snow most of the summer and suggests a sugar-filled bowl (Browning 1986, p. 210).

Sugarloaf [KERN]: *peak,* 5.25 miles north of Cinco (lat. 35°20'20" N, long. 118°02'45" W; sec. 7, T 30 S, R 37 E). Altitude 4132 feet. Named on Cinco (1972) 7.5' quadrangle.

Sugarloaf [TULARE]:
(1) *peak,* 12 miles northwest of Triple Divide Peak (lat. 36°43'50" N, long. 118°39'30" W). Altitude 8002 feet. Named on Triple Divide Peak (1956) 15' quadrangle. A field party of the Whitney survey led by William H. Brewer gave the name "Sugar Loaf Rock" to the feature in 1864 (Browning 1986, p. 210).
(2) *peak,* 2.5 miles southeast of Auckland (lat. 36°33'50" N, long. 119°04' W; sec. 5, T 16 S, R 27 E). Altitude 2653 feet. Named on Auckland (1966) 7.5' quadrangle.

Sugarloaf Creek [FRESNO-TULARE]: *stream,* heads in Tulare County and flows 9 miles to Roaring River 15 miles south-southwest of Marion Peak in Fresno County (lat. 36°45'10" N, long. 118°36'50" W); the stream goes past Suglarloaf [TULARE] (1). Named on Triple Divide Peak (1956) 15' quadrangle. South Fork enters from the south 12 miles northwest of Triple Divide Peak and is 5 miles long. East Fork enters 1 mile east-northeast of the mouth of South Fork and is 6.25 miles long. Both forks are named on Triple Divide Peak (1956) 15' quadrangle.

Sugarloaf Hill [FRESNO]: *peak,* 4.25 miles west-northwest of Shaver Lake Heights (present town of Shaver Lake) (lat. 37°07'15" N, long. 119°23'35" W; sec. 30, T 9 S, R 24 E). Altitude 3580 feet. Named on Shaver Lake (1953) 15' quadrangle.

Sugarloaf Meadow [TULARE]: *area,* 12 miles northwest of Triple Divide Peak (lat. 36°43'30" N, long. 118°39'50" W; near E line sec. 12, T 14 S, R 30 E); the place is about 0.5 mile southwest of Sugarloaf (1). Named on Triple Divide Peak (1956) 15' quadrangle.

Sugarloaf Mountain [KERN]: *peak,* 8.5 miles northeast of Tehachapi (lat. 35°13' N, long. 118°20'20" W; at W line sec. 21, T 31 S, R 34 E). Altitude 6244 feet. Named on Tehachapi NE (1966) 7.5' quadrangle.

Sugarloaf Mountain Park [TULARE]: *locality,* 4.5 miles southeast of California Hot Springs (lat. 35°50'15" N, long. 118°36'10" W; sec. 14, T 24 S, R 31 E); the place is 1 mile northeast of Sugarloaf Peak. Named on California Hot Springs (1958) 15' quadrangle.

Sugarloaf Park [KERN]: *area,* 4.5 miles north of Cinco (lat. 35°19'40" N, long. 118°01'55" W; near W line sec. 17, T 30 S, R 37 E); the place is 1 mile southeast of Sugarloaf. Named on Cinco (1972) 7.5' quadrangle.

Sugarloaf Peak [TULARE]: *peak,* 4.5 miles southeast of California Hot Springs (lat. 35°49'40" N, long. 118°37' W; sec. 22, T 24 S, R 31 E). Altitude 6265 feet. Named on California Hot Springs (1958) 15' quadrangle.

Sugar Loaf Rock: see **Sugarloaf** [TULARE] (1).

Sugarloaf Valley [FRESNO-TULARE]: *valley,* 12 miles north-northwest of Triple Divide Peak on Fresno-Tulare county line (lat. 36°44'15" N, long. 118°38' W); the valley is along Sugarloaf Creek [FRESNO-TULARE] east of Sugarloaf [TULARE] (1). Named on Triple Divide Peak (1956) 7.5' quadrangle.

Sugar Pine [MADERA]: *village,* 5 miles north of Yosemite Forks (lat. 37°26'30" N, long. 119°37'45" W; near W line sec. 1, T 6 S, R 21 E). Named on Bass Lake (1953) 15' quadrangle. Postal authorities established Sugar Pine post office in 1907 and discontinued it in 1934 (Frickstad, p. 86). Madera Sugar Pine Company built a town at the site in 1899 and 1900 (Clough, p. 47).

Sugarpine Hill [FRESNO]: *peak,* 12.5 miles north-northwest of Hume (lat. 36°57'15" N, long. 118°58'55" W). Altitude 7027 feet. Named on Tehipite Dome (1952) 15' quadrangle.

Sulfur Spring [KERN]: *spring,* 5 miles south of Orchard Peak (lat. 35°40' N, long. 120°08'55" W; sec. 16, T 26 S, R 17 E). Named on Orchard Peak (1961) 7.5' quadrangle.

Sullivan [KERN]: *locality,* 2.5 miles east of Tehachapi along Southern Pacific Railroad (lat. 35°07'30" N, long. 118°24'05" W). Named on Mojave (1915) 30' quadrangle.

Sulphur Creek [FRESNO]: *stream,* flows 3.5 miles to Warthan Creek 3.25 miles east-northeast of Smith Mountain (2) (lat. 36°05'45" N, long. 120°32'30" W; near N line sec. 23, T 21 S, R 13 E). Named on Smith Mountain (1969) 7.5' quadrangle.

Sulphur Flat [FRESNO]: *area,* 4 miles east of Joaquin Rocks (lat. 36°19'35" N, long. 120°22'35" W; near NE cor. sec. 31, T 18 S, R 15 E). Named on Joaquin Rocks (1969) 7.5' quadrangle.

Sulphur Flat Spring [FRESNO]: *spring,* nearly 4 miles east of Joaquin Rocks (lat. 36°19'20" N, long. 120°22'50" W; sec. 31, T 18 S, R 15 E); the spring is 0.25 mile southwest of Sulphur Flat. Named on Joaquin Rocks (1969) 7.5' quadrangle.

Sulphur Meadow [FRESNO]: *area,* 12 miles south-southwest of Kaiser Peak on the northeast side of Shaver Lake (lat. 37°08'20" N, long. 119°17'30" W). Named on Kaiser (1904) 30' quadrangle. Water of an enlarged Shaver Lake now covers the place.

Sulphur Ridge [TULARE]: *ridge,* west- to southwest-trending, 1.5 miles long, 3.5 miles west of Kaweah (lat. 36°28'35" N, long. 118° 59' W). Named on Kaweah (1957) 15' quadrangle.

Sulphur Spring [FRESNO]:

(1) *spring,* 16 miles north-northwest of Coalinga along Salt Creek (1) (lat. 36°22'30" N, long. 120°25'50" W; sec. 10, T 18 S, R 14 E). Named on Lillis Ranch (1956) 7.5' quadrangle.

(2) *spring,* 9 miles south-southwest of Coalinga (lat. 36°01'45" N, long. 120°26'15" W; sec. 11, T 22 S, R 14 E). Named on Coalinga (1956) 15' quadrangle.

(3) *spring,* 9 miles south of Coalinga (lat. 36°00'55" N, long. 120° 23'20" W; sec. 18, T 22 S, R 15 E). Named on Coalinga (1956) 15' quadrangle.

Sulphur Spring [KERN]:

(1) *spring,* 11 miles south-southeast of Orchard Peak along Packwood Creek (lat. 35°35'15" N, long. 120°03'25" W; sec. 8, T 27 S, R 18 E). Named on Packwood Creek (1961) 7.5' quadrangle.

(2) *spring,* 3.5 miles west of McKittrick (lat. 35°18'35" N, long. 119°41' W; sec. 14, T 30 S, R 21 E). Named on Reward (1951) 7.5' quadrangle.

Sulphur Spring [KINGS]: *spring,* 6.5 miles west-southwest of Avenal (lat. 35°57'25" N, long. 120°13'40" W; sec. 3, T 23 S, R 16 E). Named on Garza Peak (1953) 7.5' quadrangle.

Sulphur Spring Canyon [KINGS]:

(1) *canyon,* drained by a stream that flows 2.25 miles to Willow Spring Canyon 8 miles south-southwest of Avenal (lat. 35°54'20" N, long. 120°12'35" W; near N line sec. 26, T 23 S, R 16 E). Named on Garza Peak (1953) 7.5' quadrangle.

(2) *canyon,* drained by a stream that flows 3.5 miles to lowlands 10 miles south-southeast of Avenal (lat. 35°52'15" N, long. 120°03'50" W; sec. 6, T 24 S, R 18 E). Named on Kettleman Plain (1953) and Pyramid Hills (1953) 7.5' quadrangles. Called Little Tar Canyon on Cholame (1917) 30' quadrangle.

Sulphur Spring Canyon: see **Arroyo Pinoso** [FRESNO].

Sulphur Springs [FRESNO]: *locality,* 10 miles west-southwest of Prather on the south side of San Joaquin River (lat. 37°00'40" N, long. 119°41'15" W; near NW cor. sec. 4, T 11 S, R 21 E). Named on Sulphur Springs (1919) 7.5' quadrangle. Water of Millerton Lake now covers the site. Bradley (p. 457-458) noted that a spring at the place was called Millerton Spring, or locally Collins Spring for an owner; it was known as early as 1856 and the water was used by a resort after 1907.

Sultana [TULARE]: *village,* 2.5 miles east of Dinuba (lat. 36°32'40" N, long. 119°20'20" W; around SW cor. sec. 11, T 16 S, R 24 E). Named on Orange Cove South (1966) 7.5' quadrangle. Postal authorities established Sultana post office in 1900 (Frickstad, p. 214). Officials of Atchison, Topeka and Santa Fe Railroad named the place in 1897 for Sultana grapes grown in the neighborhood; the railroad station also had the name "Alta" (Mitchell, A.R., p. 70).

Summerhouse: see **Milo** [TULARE].

Summers Ridge [TULARE]: *ridge,* east-trending, 1.5 miles long, 1.5 miles south-southeast of Monache Mountain (lat. 36°11'15" N, long. 118°11' W). Named on Monache Mountain (1956) 15' quadrangle.

Summit [KERN]: *locality,* 2 miles east of Tehachapi along the railroad (lat. 35°07'40" N, long. 118°24'50" W; near E line sec. 22, T 32 S, R 33 E). Named on Tehachapi North (1966) 7.5' quadrangle. Called Summit Switch on California Division of Highways' (1934) map.

Summit Creek [FRESNO]: *stream,* flows 4.25 miles to Big Creek (2) 5 miles southeast of Shaver Lake Heights (present town of Shaver Lake) (lat. 37°03'30" N, long. 119°15'15" W; sec. 16, T 10 S, R 25 E); one branch of the stream heads at Summit Meadow (1). Named on Huntington Lake (1953) and Shaver Lake (1953) 15' quadrangles.

Summit Creek [TULARE]: *stream,* flows 5 miles to South Fork Kern River 6 miles east-southeast of Monache Mountain (lat. 36° 10'10" N, long. 118°06'10" W; sec. 20, T 20 S, R 36 E); the stream goes through Summit Meadows. Named on Monache Mountain (1956) 15' quadrangle.

Summit House [MADERA]: *locality,* 6 miles northeast of Raymond (lat. 37°16'50" N, long. 119°49'30" W; sec. 31, T 7 S, R 20 E). Named on Horsecamp Mountain (1947) 7.5' quadrangle.

Summit Lake [MADERA]: *lake,* 600 feet long, 8 miles north-northwest of Devils Postpile (lat. 37°44' N, long. 119°08'35" W; sec. 31, T 2 S, R 26 E). Named on Devils Postpile (1953) 15' quadrangle.

Summit Lake [FRESNO]:

(1) *lake,* 900 feet long, 3.25 miles north-northeast of Mount Abbot (lat. 37°25'55" N, long. 118°46'05" W). Named on Mount Abbot (1953) 15' quadrangle.

(2) *lake,* 1100 feet long, 14 miles northwest of Blackcap Mountain (lat. 37°12'15" N, long. 118°59'25" W). Named on Blackcap Mountain (1953) 15' quadrangle.

(3) *lake,* 700 feet long, 9.5 miles north of Mount Goddard (lat. 37° 14'20" N, long. 118°41'20" W). Named on Mount Goddard (1948) 15' quadrangle.

Summit Lake [TULARE]: *lake,* 700 feet long, 10 miles south-southwest of Mineral King (lat. 36°18'35" N, long. 118°38'10" W; near S line sec. 32, T 18 S, R 31 E). Named on Mineral King (1956) 15' quadrangle.

Summit Lake: see **Robinson** [KINGS].

Summit Meadow [FRESNO]:

(1) *area,* 5 miles west-southwest of Dinkey Dome (lat. 37°04'55" N, long. 119°12'25" W; near NE cor. sec. 11, T 10 S, R 25 E); the place is near the head of Summit Creek. Named on Huntington Lake (1953) 15' quadrangle.

(2) *area,* 17 miles southwest of Marion Peak (lat. 36°46'10" N, long. 118°43'05" W). Named on Marion Peak (1953) 15' quadrangle.

Summit Meadow [MADERA]:

(1) *area,* 5.5 miles east-northeast of Shuteye Peak (lat. 37°22'30" N, long. 119°19'45" W; sec. 27, T 6 S, R 24 E). Named on Shuteye Peak (1953) 15' quadrangle.

(2) *area,* nearly 3 miles southwest of Devils Postpile (lat. 37°36' N, long. 119°07'15" W). Named on Devils Postpile (1953) 15' quadrangle.

Summit Meadow [TULARE]: *area,* 10 miles south-southwest of Mineral King (lat. 36°19'45" N, long. 118°41' W). Named on Mineral King (1956) 15' quadrangle.

Summit Meadows [TULARE]: *area,* 4.5 miles east of Monache Mountain (lat. 36°13' N, long. 118°06'45" W; in and near sec. 5, 6, T 20 S, R 36 E); the place is along Summit Creek. Named on Monache Mountain (1956) 15' quadrangle.

Summit Range [KERN]: *range,* mainly in San Bernardino County, but extends west into Kern County 6 miles north of Randsburg (lat. 35°27' N, long. 117°38' W). Named on El Paso Peaks (1967) 7.5' quadrangle. A branch line of Southern Pacific Railroad reaches its highest point in the range, which accounts for the name (Gudde, 1949, p. 347).

Summit Station: see **Tehachapi** [KERN].

Summit Switch: see **Summit** [KERN].

Sumner: see **Bakersfield** [KERN].

Sumner's [KERN]: *locality,* 15 miles south of Orchard Peak along Bitterwater Creek (2) (lat. 35°31'55" N, long. 120°05'10" W; near W line sec. 31, T 27 S, R 18 E). Named on Cholame (1917) 30' quadrangle.

Sunday Peak [KERN]: *peak,* 8 miles east-northeast of Glennville (lat. 35°46'55" N, long. 118°35' W; sec. 6, T 25 S, R 32 E). Altitude 8295 feet. Named on California Hot Springs (1958) 15' quadrangle.

Sunflower Valley [KERN-KINGS]: *valley,* 12 miles south-southeast of Avenal on Kern-Kings county line. Named on Garza Peak (1953), Kettleman Plain (1953), Pyramid Hills (1953), Sawtooth Ridge (1961), and Tent Hills (1942) 7.5' quadrangles. Called McLure Valley on Kettleman Plain (1933), Pyramid Hills (1943), and Reef Ridge (1937) 7.5' quadrangles, but United States Board on Geographic Names (1968b, p. 9) rejected the

names "McLure Valley," "McLures Valley," and "McClures Valley" for the feature. The name "McLure" was for an early settler, and the name "Sunflower" is for the abundant growth of wild sunflowers at the place (Arnold and Anderson, 1908, p. 15).

Sunland [TULARE]: *locality,* 3.5 miles south-southeast of Porterville at the end of a spur of Atchison, Topeka and Santa Fe Railroad (lat. 36°01'25" N, long. 118°58'50" W; at SW cor. sec. 8, T 22 S, R 28 E). Named on Springville (1957) 15' quadrangle.

Sunnyside [FRESNO]: *locality,* 5 miles north-northeast of Malaga along Southern Pacific Railroad (lat. 36°44'55" N, long. 119°41'55" W; near NW cor. sec. 4, T 14 S, R 21 E). Named on Malaga (1964) 7.5' quadrangle. Called Granz on Selma (1946) 15' quadrangle, and called Maltermoro on Mendenhall's (1908) map. Postal authorities established Maltermoro post office in 1894 and discontinued it in 1913; the name was coined using the surname of postmaster George H. Malter (Salley, p. 131). California Mining Bureau's (1917a) map shows a place called Barton located along the railroad between present Sunnyside and Fresno. Postal authorities established Barton post office in 1949 (Salley, p. 15).

Sunny Slope: see **Mineral King** [TULARE].

Sunset: see **Hazelton** [KERN].

Sunset Camp: see **Hazelton** [KERN].

Sunset Campground [TULARE]: *locality,* 0.5 mile west-northwest of Wilsonia (lat. 36°44'15" N, long. 118°57'50" W; near E line sec. 6, T 14 S, R 28 E). Named on Giant Forest (1956) 15' quadrangle.

Sunset Meadow [TULARE]: *area,* 3 miles north-northwest of Shell Mountain (lat. 36°44' N, long. 118°46'15" W; near W line sec. 6, T 14 S, R 30 E). Named on Giant Forest (1956) 15' quadrangle.

Sunset Point [FRESNO]: *peak,* 1 mile north-northeast of the town of Big Creek (lat. 37°13' N, long. 119°14'20" W; sec. 21, T 8 S, R 25 E). Altitude 7264 feet. Named on Huntington Lake (1953) 15' quadrangle.

Sunset Point [KERN]: *peak,* 6 miles southeast of Bodfish (lat. 35°31'35" N, long. 118°24'50" W; near NE cor. sec. 3, T 28 S, R 33 E). Named on Lake Isabella South (1972) 7.5' quadrangle.

Sunset Rock [TULARE]: *relief feature,* 5.25 miles east of Yucca Mountain (lat. 36°34'40" N, long. 118°46'30" W; sec. 36, T 15 S, R 29 E). Named on Giant Forest (1956) 15' quadrangle.

Sunset Valley [KERN]: *valley,* southwest of Maricopa along Bitterwater Creek (1) (center near lat. 35°03' N, long. 119°25'30" W). Named on Maricopa (1943) 7.5' quadrangle. Arnold and Johnson (p. 21) proposed the name "Maricopa Valley" for the feature.

Superior Lake [MADERA]: *lake,* 850 feet long,

3.25 miles west of Devils Postpile (lat. 37°38'05" N, long. 119°08'25" W). Named on Devils Postpile (1953) 15' quadrangle.

Surprise Arroyo [FRESNO]: *stream,* flows 1.5 miles to Arroyo Vadoso 13 miles east-southeast of Coalinga (lat. 36°04'50" N, long. 120°08'25" W; near S line sec. 21, T 21 S, R 17 E). Named on Avenal (1954) 7.5' quadrangle. The name is from the surprising discovery of oil in a well at the place, which is considerably north of other producing oil wells (United States Board on Geographic Names, 1933b, p. 26).

Suwanee Creek [TULARE]: *stream,* flows 2.5 miles to Marble Fork nearly 5 miles east of Yucca Mountain (lat. 36°34'50" N, long. 118°47' W; sec. 36, T 15 S, R 29 E). Named on Giant Forest (1956) 15' quadrangle.

Suwanee River: see **Halstead Creek** [TULARE].

Swale Campground [TULARE]: *locality,* 1 mile west-northwest of Wilsonia (lat. 36°44'25" N, long. 118°58'25" W; near N line sec. 6, T 14 S, R 28 E). Named on Giant Forest (1956) 15' quadrangle.

Swall [TULARE]: *locality,* 4 miles northeast of Tulare along Atchison, Topeka and Santa Fe Railroad (lat. 36°14'25" N, long. 119°17'10" W; at S line sec. 29, T 19 S, R 25 E). Named on Tulare (1950) 7.5' quadrangle.

Swallow Rock [FRESNO]: *relief feature,* 10 miles southwest of Coalinga (lat. 36°01'55" N, long. 120°28'35" W; near E line sec. 8, T 22 S, R 14 E). Named on Curry Mountain (1969) 7.5' quadrangle.

Swamp Creek [FRESNO]: *stream,* flows about 2.5 miles to Dinkey Creek (1) 1.5 miles east-northeast of Dinkey Dome (lat. 37°07'30" N, long. 119°06'15" W; near N line sec. 26, T 9 S, R 26 E); one branch of the stream heads at Swamp Lake and goes through Swamp Meadow. Named on Huntington Lake (1953) 15' quadrangle.

Swamp Lake [FRESNO]: *lake,* 1200 feet long, 3.5 miles east-northeast of Dinkey Dome (lat. 37°07'45" N, long. 119°04'05" W; sec. 19, T 9 S, R 27 E); the lake is at the head of Swamp Creek. Named on Huntington Lake (1953) 15' quadrangle.

Swamp Lake [MADERA]: *lake,* 500 feet long, 7 miles south-southwest of Merced Peak (lat. 37°32'50" N, long. 119°27'15" W). Named on Merced Peak (1953) 15' quadrangle.

Swamp Lakes [FRESNO]: *lakes,* largest 2750 feet long, 11 miles west-southwest of Marion Peak (lat. 36°53'30" N, long. 118°42'30" W). Named on Marion Peak (1953) 15' quadrangle.

Swamp Meadow [FRESNO]: *area,* 3.5 miles east-northeast of Dinkey Dome (lat. 37°08'10" N, long. 119°04'20" W; sec. 19, T 9 S, R 27 E); the place is along Swamp Creek. Named on Huntington Lake (1953) 15' quadrangle.

Swede Lake [FRESNO]: *lake,* 1100 feet long,

4.25 miles northeast of Dinkey Dome (lat. 37°09'25" N, long. 119°04'35" W; sec. 7, T 9 S, R 27 E). Named on Huntington Lake (1953) 15' quadrangle.

Sweet Ridge [KERN]: *ridge,* generally south-trending, 1.5 miles long, 11.5 miles north-northwest of Mojave (lat. 35°12'10" N, long. 118°14'05" W). Named on Cache Peak (1973) 7.5' quadrangle.

Sweet Water Campground [MADERA]: *locality,* 4.5 miles east of Shuteye Peak along Chiquito Creek (lat. 37°21'30" N, long. 119°20'40" W; near E line sec. 33, T 6 S, R 24 E). Named on Shuteye Peak (1953) 15' quadrangle.

Sweetwater Spring [KERN]: *spring,* 9 miles east of Tehachapi (lat. 35°08'45" N, long. 118°17'20" W; on W line sec. 13, T 32 S, R 34 E). Named on Tehachapi NE (1966) 7.5' quadrangle.

Switchback Peak [TULARE]: *peak,* 5 miles east-southeast of Yucca Mountain (lat. 36°32'20" N, long. 118°47'25" W). Altitude 5016 feet. Named on Giant Forest (1956) 15' quadrangle. The name is from a zigzag trail, and later a road, on the east slope of the feature (United States Board on Geographic Names, 1933a, p. 734).

Swortzels Camp [MADERA]: *locality,* 5.5 miles north of Shuteye Peak (lat. 37°26' N, long. 119°24'45" W; near E line sec. 2, T 6 S, R 23 E). Named on Shuteye Peak (1953) 15' quadrangle.

Sycamore: see **Herndon** [FRESNO].

Sycamore Canyon [KERN]:

(1) *canyon,* drained by a stream that flows 10 miles to lowlands 4 miles east of Arvin (lat. 35°12' N, long. 118°45'30" W; sec. 28, T 31 S, R 30 E). Named on Arvin (1955) and Bear Mountain (1966) 7.5' quadrangles. Called Arroyo de los Alizos on Williamson's (1853) map.

(2) *canyon,* drained by a stream that flows 7.25 miles to Poso Creek 5.5 miles southeast of Knob Hill (lat. 35°30'25" N, long. 118° 53' W; sec. 8, T 28 S, R 29 E). Named on Knob Hill (1965) and Pine Mountain (1965) 7.5' quadrangles. Called Moore Canyon on Woody (1952) 15' quadrangle.

(3) *canyon,* drained by a stream that flows 2.5 miles to Tehachapi Creek 2 miles southeast of Caliente (lat. 35°16'25" N, long. 118°35'50" W). Named on Oiler Peak (1972) 7.5' quadrangle.

(4) *canyon,* drained by a stream that flows 2 miles to Caliente Creek 1.5 miles west of Loraine (lat. 35°18'15" N, long. 118°27'35" W; sec. 20, T 30 S, R 33 E). Named on Loraine (1972) 7.5' quadrangle. Emerald Mountain (1943) 15' quadrangle has the name "Sycamore Creek" for the stream in the canyon.

Sycamore Canyon: see **Big Sycamore Canyon** [KERN]; **Little Sycamore Canyon** [KERN].

Sycamore Creek [FRESNO]:

(1) *stream,* flows 14 miles to Pine Flat Reservoir 1.5 miles northeast of Trimmer (lat.

36°55'10" N, long. 119°16'40" W; near E line sec. 6, T 12 S, R 25 E). Named on Shaver Lake (1953) 15' quadrangle, and on Trimmer (1965) 7.5' quadrangle. North Fork enters from the north-northeast 9.5 miles upstream from the mouth of the main stream; it is 2.5 miles long and is named on Shaver Lake (1953) 15' quadrangle.

(2) *stream,* flows 2 miles to Mill Creek (3) 10 miles southwest of Balch Camp (lat. 36°47'30" N, long. 119°14'10" W; sec. 15, T 13 S, R 25 E). Named on Patterson Mountain (1952) 15' quadrangle.

Sycamore Creek [KERN]: *stream,* flows 2.25 miles to Kern River 5 miles west-southwest of Miracle Hot Springs (lat. 35°33'05" N, long. 118°36'50" W). Named on Democrat Hot Springs (1972) and Miracle Hot Springs (1972) 7.5' quadrangles.

Sycamore Creek [TULARE]: *stream,* flows 5 miles to North Fork Tule River 4 miles north-northeast of Springville (lat. 36°11'10" N, long. 118°47'50" W; near E line sec. 14, T 20 S, R 29 E). Named on Springville (1957) 7.5' quadrangle.

Sycamore Creek: see **Sycamore Canyon** [KERN] (4).

Sycamore Flat 1 Campground [FRESNO]: *locality,* 2.25 miles east of Trimmer near Pine Flat Reservoir (lat. 36°54'10" N, long. 119° 15'25" W; sec. 9, T 12 S, R 25 E). Named on Trimmer (1965) 7.5' quadrangle.

Sycamore Flat 2 Campground [FRESNO]: *locality,* 2 miles east of Trimmer near Pine Flat Reservoir (lat. 36°54'05" N, long. 119°15'30" W; sec. 9, T 12 S, R 25 E). Named on Trimmer (1965) 7.5' quadrangle.

Sycamore Gap [TULARE]: *pass,* 3 miles west-northwest of California Hot Springs (lat. 35°53'35" N, long. 118°43'15" W; near SE cor. sec. 27, T 23 S, R 30 E). Named on California Hot Springs (1958) 15' quadrangle.

Sycamore Spring [KERN]: *spring,* 2.5 miles east-southeast of Caliente (lat. 35°17' N, long. 118°34'45" W; at S line sec. 30, T 30 S, R 32 E); the spring is in Sycamore Canyon (3). Named on Oiler Peak (1972) 7.5' quadrangle.

Sycamore Spring [TULARE]: *spring,* 2 miles north-northeast of California Hot Springs (lat. 35°54'20" N, long. 118°39'40" W; near SW cor. sec. 20, T 23 S, R 31 E). Named on California Hot Springs (1958) 15' quadrangle.

Sycamore Springs [FRESNO]: *spring,* 2 miles west-northwest of Balch Camp (lat. 36°55' N, long. 119°09' W; sec. 4, T 12 S, R 26 E). Named on Patterson Mountain (1952) 15' quadrangle.

Sycamore Springs Creek [FRESNO]: *stream,* flows 2.5 miles to Kings River 2.5 miles west-southwest of Balch Camp (lat. 36°53'15" N, long. 119°09'30" W; sec. 17, T 12 S, R 26 E); the stream heads near Sycamore Springs. Named on Patterson Mountain (1952) 15' quadrangle.

– T –

Table Creek [TULARE]: *stream,* flows 3.25 miles to Roaring River 4 miles north of Triple Divide Peak (lat. 36°39'10" N, long. 118° 32' W); the stream heads near Table Mountain (2). Named on Mount Whitney (1956) and Triple Divide Peak (1956) 15' quadrangles.

Tableland [TULARE]: *area,* 5.5 miles west-northwest of Triple Divide Peak (lat. 36°37'30" N, long. 118°37' W). Named on Triple Divide Peak (1956) 15' quadrangle.

Table Meadow Creek [TULARE]: *stream,* flows 3 miles to the Little Kern River nearly 15 miles south of Mineral King (lat. 36°15' N, long. 118°30'55" W; at N line sec. 28, T 19 S, R 32 E). Named on Kern Peak (1956) and Mineral King (1956) 15' quadrangles.

Table Meadows [TULARE]: *area,* 6.25 miles west-northwest of Triple Divide Peak (lat. 36°37' N, long. 118°38' W); the place is west of Tableland. Named on Triple Divide Peak (1956) 15' quadrangle.

Table Mountain [FRESNO]: *ridge,* northeast-to north-trending, 2.5 miles long, 13 miles north-northeast of Clovis (lat. 37°00' N, long. 119°36'15" W). Named on Academy (1964) and Millerton Lake East (1965) 7.5' quadrangles.

Table Mountain [FRESNO-KINGS]: *ridge,* east- to southeast-trending, 10 miles long, 12 miles southwest of Avenal, where Fresno County, Kings County, and Monterey County meet at a point (lat. 35°54'30" N, long. 120°19' W). Named on Garza Peak (1953) and The Dark Hole (1961) 7.5' quadrangles.

Table Mountain: see **Little Table Mountain** [MADERA].

Table Mountain [TULARE]:

(1) *peak,* 8.5 miles north-northeast of California Hot Springs (lat. 35°59'20" N, long. 118°36'10" W; sec. 26, T 22 S, R 31 E). Named on California Hot Springs (1958) 15' quadrangle.

(2) *peak,* 11.5 miles west-northwest of Mount Whitney on Great Western Divide (lat. 36°39'35" N, long. 118°28'20" W). Altitude 13,630 feet. Named on Mount Whitney (1956) 15' quadrangle. Captain Michaelis, who commanded the signal service on a scientific expedition to Mount Whitney, named the peak Mount Hazen in 1881 to honor General Hazon, chief signal officer of the army (Browning 1986, p. 211).

Taboose Pass [FRESNO]: *pass,* 2.5 miles north of Mount Pinchot on Fresno-Inyo county line (lat. 36°59'05" N, long. 118°24'45" W); the pass is at the head of Taboose Creek, which is in Inyo County. Named on Mount Pinchot (1953) 15' quadrangle.

Tache Lake: see **Tulare Lake** [KINGS].

Taft [KERN]: *town,* 30 miles west-southwest of Bakersfield (lat. 35° 08'25" N, long.

119°27'25" W; sec. 13, T 32 S, R 23 E). Named on Taft (1950) 7.5' quadrangle. Buena Vista Lake (1912) 30' quadrangle has both the names "Moron" and "Taft P.O." at the place. Postal authorities established Taft post office in 1909 (Frickstad, p. 59), and the town incorporated in 1910. The place began as Siding Number Two along Sunset Railroad, but the cluster of businesses that sprang up there was called Moro; the name "Moro" was changed to Moron to avoid confusion with the name "Morro," but postal authorities rejected the name "Moron" because a place in Colorado already had that name—the community was renamed Taft for newly elected President William Howard Taft (Wines, p. 54).

Taft: see **South Taft** [KERN].

Taft Heights [KERN]: *town,* 1 mile west-southwest of downtown Taft (lat. 35°08'05" N, long. 119°28'15" W; near N line sec. 23, T 32 S, R 23 E). Named on Taft (1950) 7.5' quadrangle. The place first was called Boust City for E.J. Boust, an oil pioneer who started the community (Bailey, 1967, p. 2).

Tagus [TULARE]: *locality,* 6 miles southwest of Visalia along Southern Pacific Railroad (lat. 36°16'15" N, long. 119°22' W; near SE cor. sec. 16, T 19 S, R 24 E). Named on Visalia (1949) 7.5' quadrangle. Called Tagus Ranch on California Division of Highways' (1934) map. Railroad officials named the place in 1872 (Gudde, 1949, p. 351).

Tagus Ranch: see **Tagus** [TULARE].

Tah-ee-chay-pah Pass: see **Tehachapi Pass** [KERN].

Tailholt: see **White River** [TULARE] (2).

Talbot [MADERA]: *locality,* 9 miles east of Fairmead along Southern Pacific Railroad (lat. 37°04'30" N, long. 120°11'45" W; sec. 8, T 10 S, R 18 E). Named on Kismet (1920) 7.5' quadrangle.

Talus Lake [TULARE]: *lake,* 800 feet long, 4.25 miles north-northeast of Triple Divide Peak (lat. 36°38'55" N, long. 118°30'05" W). Named on Triple Divide Peak (1956) 15' quadrangle.

Tamarack Creek [FRESNO]: *stream,* flows 7 miles to join South Fork Tamarack Creek and form Pitman Creek 2.5 miles east-southeast of the town of Big Creek (lat. 37°11'30" N, long. 119°12'10" W; sec. 35, T 8 S, R 25 E). Named on Huntington Lake (1953) 15' quadrangle. South Fork is 5 miles long and is named on Huntington Lake (1953) 15' quadrangle.

Tamarack Creek [TULARE]: *stream,* flows nearly 4 miles to Little Kern River 11 miles south-southeast of Mineral King (lat. 36°18'05" N, long. 118°31'05" W). Named on Kern Peak (1956) and Mineral King (1956) 15' quadrangles.

Tamarack Lake [TULARE]: *lake,* 1600 feet long, 2 miles west-southwest of Triple Divide Peak along Lone Pine Creek (lat. 36°34'50"

N, long. 118°33'50" W). Named on Triple Divide Peak (1956) 15' quadrangle.

Tamarack Meadow [FRESNO]: *area,* 4 miles northwest of Dinkey Dome (lat. 37°09'15" N, long. 119°11'05" W; near NW cor. sec. 18, T 9 S, R 26 E); the place is 2.5 miles southeast of Tamarack Mountain. Named on Huntington Lake (1953) 15' quadrangle. Called Tamarack Meadows on Kaiser (1904) 30' quadrangle.

Tamarack Meadow: see **Pond Meadow** [TULARE].

Tamarack Mountain [FRESNO]: *ridge,* north-northeast-trending, 1.5 miles long, 2.25 miles southeast of the town of Big Creek (lat. 37°10'40" N, long. 119°13'15" W; in and near sec. 2, 3, T 9 S, R 25 E). Named on Huntington Lake (1953) 15' quadrangle.

Tandy: see **Porterville** [TULARE].

Tarbel Pocket [TULARE]: *relief feature,* 4.5 miles west-northwest of Yucca Mountain along Eshom Creek (lat. 36°36'15" N, long. 118°56'25" W; sec. 21, T 15 S, R 28 E). Named on Giant Forest (1956) 15' quadrangle.

Tar Canyon: see **Arroyo del Camino** [KINGS]; **Big Tar Canyon** [KINGS]; **Little Tar Canyon**, under **Sulphur Spring Canyon** [KINGS] (2).

Tar Creek: see **Big Tar Creek** [KINGS].

Tar Gap [TULARE]: *pass,* 3.5 miles southwest of Mineral King (lat. 36°25'20" N, long. 118°38'35" W; sec. 30, T 17 S, R 31 E). Named on Mineral King (1956) 15' quadrangle.

Tarn: see **Sanger** [FRESNO].

Tar Peak [KINGS]: *peak,* 5.5 miles south-southwest of Avenal on Reef Ridge (lat. 35°56'05" N, long. 120°10'40" W; near N line sec. 18, T 23 S, R 17 E); the peak is west of Big Tar Canyon. Named on Garza Peak (1953) 7.5' quadrangle.

Tarpey [FRESNO]: *locality,* 2.25 miles south of Clovis along Southern Pacific Railroad (lat. 36°47'15" N, long. 119°41'55" W; near W line sec. 21, T 13 S, R 21 E). Named on Clovis (1964) 7.5' quadrangle. Postal authorities established Tarpey post office in 1892, discontinued it in 1914, reestablished it in 1958, and discontinued it in 1961; the named was for Arthur B. Tarpey (Salley, p. 218).

Tarpey Village [FRESNO]: *district,* 2 miles south of Clovis (lat. 36° 47'45" N, long. 119°42' W); the place is at and near Tarpey. Named on Clovis (1964) 7.5' quadrangle.

Taurusa [TULARE]: *locality,* 6.5 miles north-northeast of Visalia along Southern Pacific Railroad (lat. 36°25' N, long. 119°15'05" W; sec. 27, T 17 S, R 25 E). Named on Monson (1949) 7.5' quadrangle. California Mining Bureau's (1917b) map shows a place called Venice Hill located along the railroad between Taurusa and Klink, about 1 mile northwest of Klink.

Tawny Boy: see **Tawny Point** [TULARE].

Tawny Point [TULARE]: *peak,* 6 miles northwest of Mount Whitney (lat. 36°37'40" N, long. 118°22'30" W). Altitude 12,332 feet. Named on Mount Whitney (1956) 15' quadrangle. Chester Versteeg suggested the name "Tawny Boy" for the feature in 1953 (Browning 1986, p. 213).

Taylor Canyon: see **Taylor Creek** [FRESNO] (2).

Taylor Creek [FRESNO]:
(1) *stream,* flows 2 miles to Rush Creek 4 miles south-southeast of Shaver Lake Heights (present town of Shaver Lake) (lat. 37°03'10" N, long. 119°18' W; near N line sec. 24, T 10 S, R 24 E). Named on Shaver Lake (1953) 15' quadrangle.
(2) *stream,* flows 3.25 miles to Jacalitos Creek 9 miles southwest of Coalinga (lat. 36°02'05" N, long. 120°27' W; sec. 10, T 22 S, R 14 E). Named on Curry Mountain (1969) 7.5' quadrangle. Coalinga (1912) 30' quadrangle shows the stream in Taylor Canyon.

Taylor Creek [TULARE]: *stream,* flows 6.5 miles to South Fork Kern River 10 miles west-northwest of Lamont Peak (lat. 35°50'05" N, long. 118°12'55" W). Named on Kernville (1956) and Lamont Peak (1956) 15' quadrangles. The name commemorates Charlie Taylor (Browning 1986, p. 213).

Taylor Meadow [TULARE]: *area,* 13 miles east-southeast of Fairview (lat. 35°59'50" N, long. 118°17'30" W; on E line sec. 22, T 24 S, R 34 E); the place is along Taylor Creek. Named on Kernville (1956) 15' quadrangle.

Taylor Mountain [MADERA]: *ridge,* west-northwest-trending, 1.5 miles long, 2 miles southeast of Yosemite Forks (lat. 37°20'50" N, long. 119°36' W; on E line sec. 6, T 7 S, R 22 E). Named on Bass Lake (1953) 15' quadrangle.

Taylor Spring [KERN]: *spring,* 5.5 miles west-northwest of Carneros Rocks (lat. 35°27'45" N, long. 119°56'20" W; sec. 28, T 28 S, R 19 E). Named on Las Yeguas Ranch (1959) 7.5' quadrangle.

Teaford Saddle [MADERA]: *pass,* 6 miles south-southeast of Yosemite Forks (lat. 37°17'15" N, long. 119°34'55" W; near SW cor. sec. 28, T 7 S, R 22 E). Named on Bass Lake (1953) 15' quadrangle, which shows Teaford ranch located 1 mile south of the pass.

Teagle [KERN]: *locality,* 5 miles north of Randsburg along Southern Pacific Railroad (lat. 35°26'15" N, long. 117°38'20" W; near S line sec. 1, T 29 S, R 40 E). Named on Randsburg (1911) 15' quadrangle. Called Teague on California Mining Bureau's (1917c) map.

Teagle Wash [KERN]: *stream,* flows nearly 2 miles to San Bernardino County 8 miles south-southeast of Ridgecrest in Searles Valley (lat. 35°30'30" N, long. 117°37'45" W; near NE cor. sec. 14, T 28 S, R 40 E). Named on Ridgecrest South (1973) 7.5' quadrangle.

Teague: see **Teagle** [KERN].

Teakettle Creek [FRESNO]: *stream,* flows 3.5 miles to North Fork Kings River 7.25 miles east-northeast of Balch Camp (lat. 36°56'45" N, long. 119°00'10" W; sec. 26, T 11 S, R 27 E). Named on Patterson Mountain (1952) 15' quadrangle.

Tecuya Creek [KERN]: *stream,* flows 7.5 miles to lowlands 2 miles west of Grapevine (lat. 34°55'45" N, long. 118°57'25" W); the stream heads near Tecuya Mountain. Named on Coal Oil Canyon (1955), Frazier Mountain (1958), Grapevine (1958), and Mettler (1955) 7.5' quadrangles. Kroeber (p. 61) stated that the word "Tecuya" is from the name by which Indians of the neighborhood were known to other Indians. Latta (1976, p. 211) used the name "Arroyo de Tecuya," and attributed the word "Tecuya" to the Indian term for a large white rock at the mouth of the canyon of the stream. United States Board on Geographic Names (1982a, p. 3) approved the name "Reed Canyon" for a feature, 2.5 miles long, that opens into lowlands less than 0.25 mile east of the place that Tecuya Creek reaches lowlands (lat. 34°55'40" N, long. 118°57'15" W).

Tecuya Mountain [KERN]: *peak,* 6.5 miles west of Lebec (lat. 34°50'30" N, long. 118°58'50" W; near SE cor. sec. 22, T 9 N, R 20 W); the peak is near the head of Tecuya Creek. Altitude 7155 feet. Named on Frazier Mountain (1958) 7.5' quadrangle. United States Board on Geographic Names (1989c, p. 2) approved the name "Tecuya Ridge" for a feature that extends west for 10.5 miles from O'Neil Canyon to a point 1 mile south of Antimony Peak—Tecuya Mountain is the high point on the ridge. The Board at the same time attributed the name "Tecuya" to Chief Tecuya, the Indian leader whose tribe worked the so-called lost Los Padres mine in the nineteenth century.

Tecuya Ridge: see **Tecuya Mountain** [KERN].

Teddy Bear Lake [FRESNO]: *lake,* 700 feet long, 3 miles south-southwest of Mount Abbot (lat. 37°20'45" N, long. 118°48'50" W). Named on Mount Abbot (1953) 15' quadrangle.

Tehachapai Pass: see **Tehachapi Pass** [KERN].

Tehachapai Peak: see **Cummings Mountain** [KERN].

Tehachapai Station: see **Tehachapi** [KERN].

Tehachapi [KERN]: *town,* 35 miles east-southeast of Bakersfield (lat. 35°07'50" N, long. 118°26'45" W; in and near sec. 20, 21, T 32 S, R 33 E); the town is in Tehachapi Valley. Named on Tehachapi North (1966) and Tehachapi South (1966) 7.5' quadrangles. Called Tehachapai Sta. on Wheeler's (1875-1878) map, but United States Board on Geographic Names (1933a, p. 747) rejected the form "Tehachapai" for the name. Tehachapi incorporated in 1909. Peter D. Greene founded a place in the 1870's called Greenwich that was located about 3 miles east of

Old Town; in 1876 officials of Southern Pacific Railroad laid out another community situated by the railroad about a mile northeast of Greenwich, gave it the name Summit Station, and later called it Tehachapi (Boyd, p. 177). Postal authorities established Greenwich post office in 1875 and discontinued it in 1893, when they moved it to Tehachapi (Salley, p. 90, 219).

Tehachapi Creek [KERN]: *stream,* flows 22 miles to Caliente Creek near Caliente (lat. 35°17'20" N, long. 118°37'40" W); the stream heads at Tehachapi Valley. Named on Keene (1966), Oiler Peak (1972), and Tehachapi North (1966) 7.5' quadrangles. Fremont used the name "Pass Creek" for the stream (Williamson, p. 19).

Tehachapi Creek: see **Cache Creek** [KERN].

Tehachapi Lake: see **Proctor Lake** [KERN].

Tehachapi Mountain [KERN]: *peak,* 6 miles south-southwest of Tehachapi (lat. 35°02'50" N, long. 118°29' W; at W line sec. 16, T 11 N, R 15 W). Named on Tehachapi South (1966) 7.5' quadrangle.

Tehachapi Mountains [KERN]: *range,* between Tehachapi Pass and Grapevine Creek. Named on Bakersfield (1962, revised 1971) and Los Angeles (1975) 1°x 2° quadrangles.

Tehachapi Pass [KERN]: *canyon,* 2.5 miles long, along Cache Creek 9.5 miles east-southeast of Tehachapi (lat. 35°06'05" N, long. 118°17' W). Named on Monolith (1966) 7.5' quadrangle. Called Tah-ee-chay-pah Pass on Williamson's (1853) map. United States Board on Geographic Names (1933a, p. 747) rejected the form "Tehachapai Pass" for the name, which is of Indian origin (Kroeber, p. 61).

Tehachapi Pass: see **Oak Creek Pass** [KERN].

Tehachapi Valley [KERN]: *valley,* at and near Tehachapi (center near lat. 35°07' N, long. 118°25' W). Named on Cummings Mountain (1966), Keene (1966), Monolith (1966), Tehachapi North (1966), and Tehachapi South (1966) 7.5' quadrangles. Alexander M. Cameron and George W. Cameron lived in the east part of the valley in the early days at what was known as Cameron Station (Boyd, p. 173). Cameron Station was called Sinks of Tehachapa in the late 1860's (Barras, p. 125).

Tehichipa: see **Old Town** [KERN].

Tehipite Dome [FRESNO]: *peak,* 12 miles northeast of Hume (lat. 36°55'10" N, long. 118°46'45" W). Altitude 7708 feet. Named on Tehipite Dome (1952) 15' quadrangle.

Tehipite Valley [FRESNO]: *valley,* 11.5 miles northeast of Hume along Middle Fork Kings River (lat. 36°54'30" N, long. 118°46'45" W); the valley is 0.5 mile south of Tehipite Dome. Named on Tehipite Dome (1952) 15' quadrangle. The word "Tehipite" is of Indian origin (Kroeber, p. 62)

Tehipite Valley: see **Little Tehipite Valley** [FRESNO].

Tejon: see **Lebec** [KERN]; **Old Fort Tejon** [KERN]; **Rose Station** [KERN].

Tejon Canyon [KERN]: *canyon,* 11 miles long, along Tejon Creek above a point 4.25 miles west of Cummings Mountain (lat. 35°02'25" N, long. 118°39'15" W). Named on Cummings Mountain (1966), Tehachapi South (1966), and Tejon Ranch (1966) 7.5' quadrangles. Parke's (1854-1855) map has the name "Tejon Pass" for the feature.

Tejon Creek [KERN]: *stream,* flows 23 miles to lowlands 8 miles south of Arvin (lat. 35°05'30" N, long. 118°49' W; sec. 29, T 12 N, R 18 W); the stream drains Tejon Canyon. Named on Arvin (1955), Tejon Hills (1955), Tejon Ranch (1966), and Weed Patch (1955) 7.5' quadrangles. The feature was known to Mexicans by the names "Arroyo del Tejon" and "Arroyo de los Alamos" (Latta, 1976, p. 201). Water of Tejon Creek sinks into sand in lowlands at a place called Sinks of the Tejon; Mexicans called the site Agua de los Alamos, or Los Alamitos, because of a spring there— the place was a gathering spot for Indians before it became an important station on Butterfield Overland stage line from 1858 until 1861 (Hoover, Rensch, and Rensch, p. 129). Postal authorities established Sink post office there in 1859 and discontinued it in 1861 (Salley, p. 205).

Tejon Hills [KERN]: *ridge,* west- to northwest-trending, 9 miles long, between Comanche Creek and Tejon Creek, center 9 miles southeast of Arvin (lat. 35°05'30" N, long. 118°46'45" W). Named on Arvin (1955), Tejon Hills (1955), and Tejon Ranch (1966) 7.5' quadrangles.

Tejon Pass: see **Tejon Canyon** [KERN].

Tejon Reservoir Number 1 [KERN]: *lake,* 600 feet long, 10 miles west of Cummings Mountain (lat. 35°02'05" N, long. 118°44'40" W; sec. 13, T 11 N, R 18 W); the lake is nearly 2 miles west-northwest of Tejon Reservoir Number 2. Named on Tejon Ranch (1966) 7.5' quadrangle.

Tejon Reservoir Number 2 [KERN]: *lake,* 2000 feet long, 8.5 miles west of Cummings Mountain (lat. 35°01'20" N, long. 118°43' W); the lake is nearly 2 miles east-southeast of Tejon Reservoir Number 1. Named on Tejon Ranch (1966) 7.5' quadrangle.

Telegraph Flat [TULARE]: *area,* 5.5 miles south of Fountain Springs (lat. 35°48'40" N, long. 118°55'55" W; sec. 27, T 24 S, R 28 E). Named on Quincy School (1965) 7.5' quadrangle.

Telephone Canyon [KERN]: *canyon,* drained by a stream that flows 2.5 miles to the canyon of Caliente Creek at Caliente (lat. 35°17'30" N, long. 118°37'40" W). Named on Bena (1972) and Oiler Peak (1972) 7.5' quadrangles.

Telephone Canyon Spring [KERN]: *spring,* 2 miles north of Caliente (lat. 35°19'10" N, long.

118°37'30" W); the spring is near the head of Telephone Canyon. Named on Bena (1972) 7.5' quadrangle.

Telephone Hills [KERN]: *range,* 3.5 miles south of McKittrick (lat. 35°15' N, long. 119°38' W). Named on Fellows (1951), Panorama Hills (1954), and Reward (1951) 7.5' quadrangles.

Telephone Ridge [KERN-TULARE]: *ridge,* west-trending, 5 miles long, 5.5 miles northeast of Glennville on Kern-Tulare county line (lat. 35°47'15" N, long. 118°38'15" W). Named on California Hot Springs (1958) 15' quadrangle.

Temblor Creek [KERN]: *stream,* flows 6 miles to Salt Creek (1) 5.5 miles southeast of Carneros Rocks in Temblor Valley (lat. 35°23'25" N, long. 119°45'55" W; near W line sec. 19, T 29 S, R 21 E). Named on Carneros Rocks (1959) and McKittrick Summit (1959) 7.5' quadrangles. Present Salt Creek (1) is called Temblor Creek on Belridge (1953) 7.5' quadrangle, but United States Board on Geographic Names (1968a, p. 7) rejected this name for it.

Temblor Range [KERN]: *range,* southwest of the San Joaquin Valley on Kern-San Luis Obispo county line. Named on Bakersfield (1962, revised 1971) and San Luis Obispo (1956, revised 1969) 1°x 2° quadrangles. Arnold and Anderson (1908, p. 13) applied the name—*temblor* means "earthquake" in Spanish—and stated that it is particularly suited to the range "because the great California fault line [San Andreas fault], along which earthquakes have repeatedly originated, follows the range from one end to the other," and because the well-known old Temblor ranch is on the west flank of the range. United States Board on Geographic Names (1933a, p. 748) rejected the form "Temploa Range" for the name.

Temblor Valley [KERN]: *valley,* 9.5 miles northwest of McKittrick (lat. 35°23' N, long. 119°46' W); the valley is near the northeast base of Temblor Range. Named on Belridge (1953), Carneros Rocks (1959), and Reward (1950, photorevised 1973) 7.5' quadrangles.

Temperance: see **Fresno** [FRESNO].

Temperance Flat [FRESNO]: *area,* 4 miles west-northwest of Prather (lat. 37°03'35" N, long. 119°35' W; sec. 16, 17, T 10 S, R 22 E). Named on Millerton Lake East (1965) 7.5' quadrangle.

Temple Slough [FRESNO]: *water feature,* mainly an artificial watercourse that diverges west-northwest from San Joaquin River 5.5 miles north-northeast of Oxalis (lat. 36°59' N, long. 120°30' W). Named on Oxalis (1922) 7.5' quadrangle. Oxalis (1956) 7.5' quadrangle shows the feature as the route of a canal.

Templeton Meadows [TULARE]: *area,* 7.5 miles northwest of Olancha Peak along South Fork Kern River (lat. 36°20' N, long. 118°13' W); the place is northwest of Templeton Mountain. Named on Olancha (1956) 15'

quadrangle. The name is for Benjamin S. Templeton, a sheepman (Gudde, 1949, p. 358). United States Board on Geographic Names (1961b, p. 12) rejected the singular form "Templeton Meadow" for the name.

Templeton Meadows: see **Strawberry Meadows** [TULARE].

Templeton Mountain [TULARE]: *peak,* 6 miles northwest of Olancha Peak (lat. 36°18'50" N, long. 118°12'20" W); the peak is southeast of Templeton Meadows. Named on Olancha (1956) 15' quadrangle.

Temploa Range: see **Temblor Range** [KERN].

Tenant Creek [KERN]: *stream,* flows 2.5 miles to Kern River 0.5 mile east-northeast of Democrat Hot Springs (lat. 35°31'55" N, long. 118°39'20" W). Named on Democrat Hot Springs (1972) 7.5' quadrangle. Called Tenant Mine Cr. on Glennville (1956) 15' quadrangle, and United States Board on Geographic Names (1975a, p. 4) gave this name as a variant.

Tenant Mine Creek: see **Tenant Creek** [KERN].

Tenant Spring: see **Big Tenant Spring** [KERN]; **Little Tenant Spring** [KERN].

Tenmile Creek [FRESNO-TULARE]: *stream,* heads in Tulare County and flows 11.5 miles to Kings River 4.25 miles north-northeast of Hume in Fresno County (lat. 36°50'20" N, long. 118°52'45" W). Named on Giant Forest (1956) and Tehipite Dome (1952) 15' quadrangles.

Tennessee Knob [TULARE]: *peak,* 6.5 miles north-northwest of Fountain Springs (lat. 35°58'45" N, long. 118°57'15" W; near S line sec. 28, T 22 S, R 28 E); the peak is on Tennessee Ridge. Altitude 1406 feet. Named on Fountain Springs (1965) 7.5' quadrangle.

Tennessee Point [FRESNO]: *peak,* 6 miles east-northeast of Kaiser Peak (lat. 37°19'45" N, long. 119°05'10" W; sec. 12, T 7 S, R 26 E). Named on Kaiser Peak (1953) 15' quadrangle.

Tennessee Ridge [TULARE]: *ridge,* northwest-to north-trending, 4 miles long, 5 miles north-northwest of Fountain Springs (lat. 35° 57'30" N, long. 118°56'40" W); Tennessee Knob is on the ridge. Named on Fountain Springs (1965) 7.5' quadrangle.

Tent Hills [KINGS]: *peaks,* 11 miles south of Avenal along a northwest-trending ridge 3.25 miles long (lat. 35°50'45" N, long. 120° 09' W). Named on Tent Hills (1942) 7.5' quadrangle. Arnold and Anderson (1908, p. 14) named the feature for "the resemblance of the individual hills to tents." United States Board on Geographic Names (1933a, p. 749) rejected the names "Las Tiendas" and "The Tents" for the peaks.

Tent Meadow: see **Lower Tent Meadow** [FRESNO]; **Upper Tent Meadow** [FRESNO].

Tents: see **The Tents**, under **Tent Hills** [KINGS].

Terese [KERN]: *locality,* 6 miles south-southeast of Inyokern along Southern Pacific Railroad (lat. 35°34'10" N, long. 117°46'45" W; sec. 21, T 27 S, R 39 E). Named on Inyokern (1943) 15' quadrangle. Searles Lake (1915) 1° quadrangle shows Terese Siding situated about 2.5 miles south-southeast of present Terese along the railroad, and Lee's (1912) map has the name "Code" for a place located 4 miles south-southeast of Terese along the railroad (sec. 2, T 28 S, R 39 E).

Terese Siding: see **Terese** [KERN].

Terminus [TULARE]: *locality,* 4.5 miles east of Woodlake (lat. 36° 24'45" N, long. 119°00'50" W; near N line sec. 35, T 17 S, R 27 E). Site named on Woodlake (1952) 7.5' quadrangle. Lemon Cove (1928) 7.5' quadrangle shows the place at the end of a spur line of Visalia Electric Railroad.

Terra Bella [TULARE]: *town,* nearly 5 miles north of Ducor (lat. 35° 57'40" N, long. 119°02'30" W; sec. 3, T 23 S, R 27 E). Named on Ducor (1952) 7.5' quadrangle. Postal authorities established Terrabella post office in 1891, discontinued it the same year, and reestablished it with the name "Terra Bella" in 1909 (Salley, p. 220). The place first was called Deer Creek Switch; officials of Edward Silent Real Estate Company gave the new name in 1908 (Mitchell, A.R., p. 70).

Tether Lake [FRESNO]: *lake,* 450 feet long, 8 miles south-southwest of Mount Abbot (lat. 37°16'30" N, long. 118°49'25" W). Named on Mount Abbot (1953) 15' quadrangle. Elden H. Vestal of California Department of Fish and Game chose the name because the lake is tied, or tethered, by water to two adjacent lakes (Browning 1986, p. 214).

Texas Flat [MADERA]: *area,* 7.25 miles north-northwest of Shuteye Peak (lat. 27°26'25" N, long. 119°29'45" W; sec. 6, T 6 S, R 23 E). Named on Shuteye Peak (1953) 15' quadrangle.

Tharpe Meadow: see **Log Meadow** [TULARE].

Tharpe's Log Meadow: see **Log Meadow** [TULARE].

Tharps Peak [TULARE]: *peak,* 5.25 miles south of Kaweah (lat. 36° 23'40" N, long. 118°55'50" W; sec. 3, T 18 S, R 28 E). Altitude 2760 feet. Named on Kaweah (1957) 15' quadrangle. United States Board on Geographic Names (1968b, p. 10) rejected the form "Thorps Peak" for the name.

Tharps Peak: see **Alta Peak** [TULARE].

Tharps Rock [TULARE]: *relief feature,* 8 miles west of Triple Divide Peak (lat. 36°35'05" N, long. 118°40' W; at S line sec. 25, T 15 S, R 30 E). Named on Triple Divide Peak (1956) 15' quadrangle. The name applies to a boulder, about 1100 feet high, named to honor Hale D. Tharp, first explorer in the vicinity (United States Board on Geographic Names, 1933a, p. 751).

Tharsa: see **Irrigosa** [MADERA].

The Basin: see **Huntington Lake** [FRESNO]

(1).

The Big Arroyo: see **Big Arroyo** [TULARE].

The Buttresses [MADERA]: *escarpment,* 1 mile south-southwest of Devils Postpile on the west side of Middle Fork San Joaquin River (lat. 37°36'45" N, long. 119°05'15" W). Named on Devils Postpile (1953) 15' quadrangle.

The Citadel [FRESNO]: *peak,* 6.5 miles east-southeast of Mount Goddard (lat. 37°04' N, long. 118°36'30" W). Altitude 11,744 feet. Named on Mount Goddard (1948) 15' quadrangle. The Sierra Club proposed the name in 1941 (Browning 1986, p. 40).

The Clearing [FRESNO]: *area,* 1.5 miles east of Joaquin Rocks (lat. 36°19' N, long. 120°25'15" W; in and near sec. 35, T 18 S, R 14 E). Named on Joaquin Rocks (1969) 7.5' quadrangle.

The Dark Hole [FRESNO-KINGS]: *canyon,* drained by a stream that heads in Fresno County and flows 3.25 miles to Avenal Canyon 10 miles southwest of Avenal in Kings County (lat. 35°55'30" N, long. 120°16'15" W; at W line sec. 17, T 23 S, R 16 E). Named on The Dark Hole (1961) 7.5' quadrangle.

The Devil's Glen: see **Devils Den** [KERN] (1).

The Falls [MADERA]: *locality,* 4 miles southeast of Yosemite Forks near the northwest end of Bass Lake (1) (lat. 37°19'55" N, long. 119°34'15" W; sec. 9, T 7 S, R 22 E). Named on Bass Lake (1953) 15' quadrangle.

The Five Lakes: see **Big Five Lakes** [TULARE].

The Forks [MADERA]: *locality,* 5 miles southeast of Yosemite Forks on the west side of Bass Lake (1) (lat. 37°18'50" N, long. 119°34'20" W; on N line sec. 21, T 7 S, R 22 E). Named on Bass Lake (1953) 15' quadrangle.

The Gorge [FRESNO]: *canyon,* drained by a stream that flows 1.5 miles to Bear Canyon 5.5 miles north-northwest of Coalinga Mineral Springs (lat. 36°13' N, long. 120°36'05" W; sec. 5, T 20 S, R 13 E). Named on Sherman Peak (1969) 7.5' quadrangle.

The Hermit [FRESNO]: *peak,* 4 miles north of Mount Goddard (lat. 37°09'50" N, long. 118°43' W). Altitude 12,360 feet. Named on Mount Goddard (1948) 15' quadrangle.

The Horseshoe [KERN]: *locality;* bend in the road nearly 4 miles northeast of Caliente (lat. 35°19'55" N, long. 118°34'55" W; sec. 7, T 30 S, R 32 E). Named on Oiler Peak (1972) 7.5' quadrangle.

The Keyhole [FRESNO]: *relief feature,* 8 miles north-northwest of Mount Goddard (lat. 37°12'55" N, long. 118°40'50" W). Named on Mount Goddard (1948) 15' quadrangle. Climbers from the Sierra Club applied the name to a notch in Glacier Divide (Browning 1986, p. 119).

The Loop [KERN]: *locality,* 2 miles southeast of Keene (lat. 35°12'05" N, long. 118°32'10" W; at W line sec. 27, T 31 S, R 32 E). Named on Keene (1966) 7.5' quadrangle. The name applies to the place that the railroad makes a loop to gain elevation and thereby crosses over itself. Wheeler's (1875-1878) map shows a place called Coombs located near the site.

The Major General [TULARE]: *peak,* 5 miles south-southeast of Mount Whitney (lat. 36°30'45" N, long. 118°30' W). Named on Mount Whitney (1956) 15' quadrangle. Chester Versteeg suggested the name in 1939 (Browning 1986, p. 135).

The Malaga Colony: see **Malaga** [FRESNO].

The Minster [TULARE]: *peak,* 12 miles northwest of Mount Whitney (lat. 36°42'55" N, long. 118°25'15" W). Named on Mount Whitney (1956) 15' quadrangle. David Starr Jordan named the peak in 1899 (Browning 1986, p. 148).

The Miter [TULARE]: *peak,* 3.5 miles south-southeast of Mount Whitney (lat. 36°32'05" N, long. 118°15'50" W). Altitude 12,770 feet. Named on Mount Whitney (1956) 15' quadrangle. The name is from the shape of the peak (United States Board on Geographic Names, 1938, p. 36).

The Narrows [KERN]: *narrows,* 3.5 miles north-northeast of Garlock in Goler Gulch (lat. 35°27' N, long. 117°45'45" W). Named on Garlock (1967) 7.5' quadrangle.

The Needles [TULARE]: *relief features,* 9.5 miles southwest of Hockett Peak (lat. 36°06'30" N, long. 118°28'45" W). Named on Hockett Peak (1956) 15' quadrangle.

The Park: see **Walker Basin** [KERN].

The Pines [MADERA]: *settlement,* 5.25 miles southeast of Yosemite Forks on the northeast side of Bass Lake (1) (lat. 37°19'10" N, long. 119°33'15" W; sec. 15, T 7 S, R 22 E). Named on Bass Lake (1953) 15' quadrangle.

The Pinnacles [FRESNO]:
 (1) *relief feature,* 7.5 miles south-southwest of Mount Abbot along a south-trending ridge, 1.5 miles long, situated between the head of East Pinnacles Creek and the head of West Pinnacles Creek (lat. 38°16'40" N, long. 118°48'45" W). Named on Mount Abbot (1953) 15' quadrangle.
 (2) *peak,* 1.5 miles southeast of Smith Mountain (2) on Fresno-Monterey county line (lat. 36°03'40" N, long. 120°34'45" W; sec. 33, T 21 S, R 13 E). Named on Smith Mountain (1969) 7.5' quadrangle.

The Pothole [TULARE]: *relief feature,* 9 miles northeast of Fountain Springs (lat. 35°58'40" N, long. 118°47'45" W); the feature is near the head of Pothole Creek. Named on Gibbon Peak (1965) 7.5' quadrangle.

The Pyramid: see **Painted Lady** [FRESNO].

The Pyramids: see **Pyramid Hills** [KERN-KINGS].

Thermal: see **Auberry** [FRESNO].

The Sphinx [FRESNO]: *peak,* 13 miles south of Marion Peak (lat. 36°45'15" N, long. 118°32'55" W); the peak is west of Sphinx Creek. Altitude 9146 feet. Named on Marion

Peak (1953) 15' quadrangle. John Muir named the peak in 1891; Hutchings called it The Watch Tower in 1875 (Browning 1986, p. 206).

The Tents: see **Tent Hills** [KINGS].

The Three Sirens: see **Scylla** [FRESNO].

The Thumb [FRESNO]: *peak,* 4.5 miles north of Double Peak (lat. 37°34'35" N, long. 119°01'30" W). Altitude 10,285 feet. Named on Devils Postpile (1953) 15' quadrangle.

The Tombstone [FRESNO]: *relief feature,* 11 miles southwest of Mount Abbot (lat. 37°16'10" N, long. 118°54'55" W; sec. 4, T 8 S, R 28 E). Named on Mount Abbot (1953) 15' quadrangle. The shape of the feature suggested the name (Gudde, 1949, p. 365).

The Tunnel [TULARE]: *locality,* 4 miles north of Kern Peak (lat. 36° 22' N, long. 118°17'20" W; near NW cor. sec. 15, T 18 S, R 34 E). Named on Olancha (1907) 30' quadrangle. The name recalls a tunnel dug in the 1880's to divert water from Golden Trout Creek to meadows on South Fork Kern River (Browning 1986, p. 226).

The Turtle Hole [KINGS]: *canyon,* 0.25 mile long, opens into Avenal Canyon from the southwest 8.5 miles southwest of Avenal (lat. 35°54'55" N, long. 120°14'15" W; sec. 21, T 23 S, R 16 E). Named on Garza Peak (1953) 7.5' quadrangle.

The Washboard [FRESNO]: *area,* 12.5 miles east of Coalinga (lat. 36°07' N, long. 120°08' W). Named on Avenal (1954), Guijarral Hills (1956), and La Cima (1963) 7.5' quadrangles. The name describes the series of parallel ridges and depressions in the area (United States Board on Geographic Names, 1933b, p. 28).

The Watch Tower: see **The Sphinx** [FRESNO].

The Wye [TULARE]: *locality;* road junction less than 1 mile south of Wilsonia (lat. 36°43'25" N, long. 118°57'15" W; sec. 8, T 14 S, R 28 E). Named on Giant Forest (1956) 15' quadrangle.

Third Recess [FRESNO]: *canyon,* drained by a stream that flows 2.5 miles to Mono Creek 4 miles north-northwest of Mount Abbot (lat. 37°26'35" N, long. 118°48'20" W); the feature is the third large canyon east of Lake Thomas A. Edison on south side of Mono Creek. Named on Mount Abbot (1953) 15' quadrangle. Theodore S. Solomons discovered and named the feature in 1894 (Farquhar, 1925, p. 127).

Third Recess Lake [FRESNO]: *lake,* 1300 feet long, 2.5 miles north-northwest of Mount Abbot (lat. 37°25'20" N, long. 118°48'10" W); the lake is in Third Recess. Named on Mount Abbot (1953) 15' quadrangle.

Thomas A. Edison: see **Lake Thomas A. Edison** [FRESNO].

Thomas Lane [KERN]: *locality,* 1.25 miles south-southwest of Shafter (lat. 35°29'15" N, long. 119°17' W; near S line sec. 16, T 28 S, R 25 E). Named on Rio Bravo (1954) 7.5'

quadrangle.

Thompson: see **Mount Thompson** [FRESNO].

Thompson Camp [TULARE]: *locality*, 3.5 miles northwest of California Hot Springs (lat. 35°55'15" N, long. 118°42'30" W; at S line sec. 14, T 23 S, R 30 E); the place is near the south end of Thompson Ridge. Named on California Hot Springs (1958) 15' quadrangle.

Thompson Camp Spring [TULARE]: *spring*, 8 miles northeast of California Hot Springs (lat. 35°57'35" N, long. 118°34'15" W; near W line sec. 6, T 23 S, R 32 E). Named on California Hot Springs (1958) 15' quadrangle.

Thompson Creek [KERN]: *stream*, flows 4.5 miles to Walker Basin Creek 3.5 miles west of Piute Peak (lat. 35°26'25" N, long. 118°27'10" W; near NW cor. sec. 4, T 29 S, R 33 E). Named on Piute Peak (1972) 7.5' quadrangle.

Thompson Creek: see **Walker Basin Creek** [KERN].

Thompson Lake: see **Thomson Lake** [FRESNO].

Thompson Peak [TULARE]: *peak*, 4.5 miles north-northwest of California Hot Springs (lat. 35°56'15" N, long. 118°42'25" W; sec. 11, T 23 S, R 30 E); the peak is on Thompson Ridge. Altitude 4322 feet. Named on California Hot Springs (1958) 15' quadrangle.

Thompson Ridge [TULARE]: *ridge*, southwest-to south-trending, 2.5 miles long, 4.5 miles north-northwest of California Hot Springs (lat. 35°56'15" N, long. 118°42'30" W); Thompson Peak is on the ridge. Named on California Hot Springs (1958) 15' quadrangle.

Thompson Spring [KERN]: *spring*, 3 miles west-southwest of Piute Peak (lat. 35°26'05" N, long. 118°26'30" W; sec. 4, T 29 S, R 33 E); the spring is near Thompson Creek. Named on Piute Peak (1972) 7.5' quadrangle.

Thomson Lake [FRESNO]: *lake*, 900 feet long, 13 miles northwest of Blackcap Mountain (lat. 37°12'10" N, long. 118°57'25" W; near NW cor. sec. 31, T 8 S, R 28 E). Named on Blackcap Mountain (1953) 15' quadrangle. United States Board on Geographic Names (1978c, p. 5) approved the name "Thompson Lake" for the feature and rejected the names "Thomson Lake" and "Tompson Lake."

Thornberry Mountain [MADERA]: *ridge*, east- to east-northeast-trending, 4.5 miles long, 6.5 miles south of Yosemite Forks (lat. 37°16'15" N, long. 119°37' W). Named on Bass Lake (1953) 15' quadrangle.

Thornton Meadow [KERN]: *area*, 4.5 miles south-southeast of Claraville in Big Hart Canyon (lat. 35°22'45" N, long. 118°18'35" W). Named on Claraville (1972) 7.5' quadrangle.

Thorps Peak: see **Tharps Peak** [TULARE].

Thousand Island Lake [MADERA]: *lake*, 1.5 miles long, 8.5 miles northwest of Devils Postpile (lat. 37°43'15" N, long. 119°11' W). Named on Devils Postpile (1953) 15' quadrangle.

Three Corners [FRESNO]: *locality*, 2.5 miles north of Coalinga (lat. 36°10'50" N, long. 120°21'15" W; at NW cor. sec. 21, T 20 S, R 15 E); three roads join at the place. Named on Coalinga (1956) 7.5' quadrangle.

Three Island Lake [FRESNO]: *lake*, 4000 feet long, 7.5 miles south-southwest of Mount Abbot (lat. 37°17'25" N, long. 118°50'50" W). Named on Mount Abbot (1953) 15' quadrangle, which shows four islands in the lake. A survey party led by William A. Dill of California Department of Fish and Game named the lake in 1942 (Browning 1986, p. 216).

Three Peaks [KINGS]: *peaks*, 14 miles south of Avenal (lat. 35°48'10" N, long. 120°10' W; near NE cor. sec. 31, T 24 S, R 17 E). Named on Tent Hills (1942) 7.5' quadrangle.

Three Pines Canyon [KERN]: *canyon*, drained by a stream that flows 4.5 miles to Canebrake Creek 3 miles northwest of Walker Pass (lat. 35°41'50" N, long. 118°03'25" W; near W line sec. 6, T 26 S, R 37 E). Named on Owens Peak (1972) and Walker Pass (1972) 7.5' quadrangles.

Three Rivers [TULARE]: *settlement*, 2.25 miles south-southeast of Kaweah along Kaweah River (lat. 36°26'20" N, long. 118°54'15" W; in and near sec. 24, T 17 S, R 28 E). Named on Kaweah (1957) 15' quadrangle. Mrs. Louisa Rockwell named the place in 1879 for the three forks of Kaweah River (Mitchell, A.R., p. 70). Postal authorities established Three Rivers post office in 1879, changed the name to Threerivers in 1895, changed it back to Three Rivers in 1932, and moved the post office 0.5 mile north in 1940 (Salley, p. 221).

Three Sirens: see **The Three Sirens**, under **Scylla** [FRESNO].

Three Sisters [FRESNO]:
(1) *peak*, 4.5 miles east-northeast of Dinkey Dome (lat. 37°08'30" N, long. 119°03'35" W; near SE cor. sec. 18, T 9 S, R 27 E). Altitude 10,619 feet. Named on Huntington Lake (1953) 15' quadrangle.
(2) *peak*, 18 miles north-northwest of Coalinga on Loma Atravesada (lat. 36°21'25" N, long. 120°32'05" W; near SW cor. sec. 14, T 18 S, R 13 E). Altitude 4220 feet. Named on Santa Rita Peak (1969) 7.5' quadrangle.

Three Sisters: see **Loma Atravesada** [FRESNO].

Three Springs [FRESNO]: *springs*, 12 miles north of Hume (lat. 36° 57'35" N, long. 118°56'30" W). Named on Tehipite Dome (1952) 15' quadrangle, which shows two springs. Bradley (p. 459) reported three large perennial springs at the place.

Thumb: see **The Thumb** [FRESNO].

Thunderbolt Peak [FRESNO]: *peak*, 11 miles east of Mount Goddard on Fresno-Inyo county line (lat. 37°05'50" N, long. 118° 31' W). Named on Mount Goddard (1948) 15' quadrangle. Francis P. Farquhar and six companions made the first ascent of the peak in 1931;

they named it after they experienced a violent thunder storm there (Browning 1986, p. 216-217).

Thunder Mountain [TULARE]: *peak,* 12 miles west-northwest of Mount Whitney on Great Western Divide (lat. 36°40'10" N, long. 118°28'30" W). Altitude 13,588 feet. Named on Mount Whitney (1956) 15' quadrangle. George R. Davis of United States Geological Survey named the feature when he made the first ascent in 1905 (Browning 1986, p. 216).

Tibbets Creek [TULARE]: *stream,* flows 5.5 miles to South Fork Kern River 12 miles northwest of Lamont Peak in Rockhouse Basin (lat. 35°55'45" N, long. 118°10' W; near E line sec. 14, T 23 S, R 35 E). Named on Lamont Peak (1956) 15' quadrangle.

Tibbetts Creek: see **Durrwood Creek** [TULARE].

Tick-Tack-Toe Hill [MADERA]: *ridge,* west-southwest-trending, 1 mile long, nearly 7 miles south of O'Neals (lat. 37°01'45" N, long. 119°42'15" W). Named on Millerton Lake West (1965) 7.5' quadrangle. Millerton Lake (1945) 15' quadrangle has the form "Tick-tack-toe Hill" for the name.

Tierra Seca: see **Sacatara Creek** [KERN].

Tiffin [TULARE]: *locality,* 4 miles east-southeast of Lindsay along Visalia Electric Railroad (lat. 36°11' N, long. 119°01'30" W; near SW cor. sec. 14, T 20 S, R 27 E). Named on Lindsay (1928) 7.5' quadrangle.

Tiger Flat: see **Tiger Flat Campground** [KERN].

Tiger Flat Campground [KERN]: *locality,* 8.5 miles east-northeast of Glennville (lat. 35°46'40" N, long. 118°34' W; near SW cor. sec. 5, T 25 S, R 32 E). Named on California Hot Springs (1958) 15' quadrangle. Tobias Peak (1943) 30' quadrangle shows Tiger Flat at or near the site.

Tillie Creek [KERN]: *stream,* flows 5 miles to Isabella Lake 0.5 mile south of the center of Wofford Heights (lat. 35°42'05" N, long. 118°27'15" W; sec. 5, T 26 S, R 33 E). Named on Alta Sierra (1972) and Lake Isabella North (1972) 7.5' quadrangles. Called Tilly Cr. on Olmsted's (1900) map.

Tillie Creek Campground [KERN]: *locality,* 0.5 mile south of the center of Wofford Heights (lat. 35°42'05" N, long. 118°27'20" W; sec. 5, T 26 S, R 33 E); the place is near the mouth of Tillie Creek. Named on Lake Isabella North (1972) 7.5' quadrangle.

Tillman [MADERA]: *locality,* 6.25 miles southwest of Chowchilla along Chowchilla Pacific Railroad (lat. 37°02'30" N, long. 120°19'35" W; near SW cor. sec. 22, T 10 S, R 15 E). Named on Chowchilla (1918) 7.5' quadrangle. California Division of Highways' (1934) map shows a place called Plains located along Southern Pacific Railroad nearly 2 miles southwest of Tillman (near E line sec. 32, T 10 S, R 15 E), a place called Ovejo lo-

cated along the railroad 1.25 miles northeast of Tillman (near N line sec. 22, T 10 S, R 15 E), and a place called Ash located along the railroad 1.5 miles northeast of Ovejo (near S line sec. 11, T 10 S, R 15 E).

Tilly Creek: see **Tillie Creek** [KERN].

Timber Creek [MADERA]:
(1) *stream,* flows 2 miles to West Fork Granite Creek 6 miles southeast of Merced Peak (lat. 37°34'20" N, long. 119°19' W); the stream heads near Timber Knob. Named on Merced Peak (1953) 15' quadrangle.
(2) *stream,* flows 2.5 miles to Sand Creek 3.5 miles west-southwest of Shuteye Peak (lat. 37°19'45" N, long. 119°29'25" W; near SE cor. sec. 7, T 7 S, R 23 E). Named on Shuteye Peak (1953) 15' quadrangle.

Timber Gap [TULARE]: *pass,* 1 mile north of Mineral King (lat. 36° 28'05" N, long. 118°35'50" W). Named on Mineral King (1956) 15' quadrangle.

Timber Gap Creek [TULARE]: *stream,* flows 2 miles to Cliff Creek 3.5 miles north-northwest of Mineral King (lat. 36°29'55" N, long. 118°36'55" W); the stream heads near Timber Gap. Named on Mineral King (1956) 15' quadrangle. United States Board on Geographic Names (1933a, p. 757) rejected the name "Deer Creek" for the stream.

Timber Knob [MADERA]: *peak,* 6 miles east-southeast of Merced Peak (lat. 37°35'20" N, long. 119°18' W); the peak is east of Timber Creek (1). Altitude 9945 feet. Named on Merced Peak (1953) 15' quadrangle.

Tipton [TULARE]: *town,* 10.5 miles south of Tulare (lat. 36°03'35" N, long. 119°18'40" W; sec. 31, T 21 S, R 25 E). Named on Tipton (1950) 7.5' quadrangle. Postal authorities established Tipton post office in 1873 (Frickstad, p. 214). According to A.R. Mitchell (p. 70), the place first was called Tip Town because it was at the tip of the railroad when construction halted there for several months. According to Hanna (p. 330), the name commemorates John Tipton, the first white child born in the neighborhood. Postal authorities established Noradell post office about 9 miles southeast of Tipton in 1879 and discontinued it in 1881; the name "Noradell" was coined from the given names of Mrs. Dellia Carey, first postmaster, and a member of her family called Nora (Salley, p. 155).

Tip Town: see **Tipton** [TULARE].

Titcomb Flat [MADERA]: *area,* 5.25 miles southwest of North Fork (lat. 37°10'35" N, long. 119°34'40" W; sec. 4, T 9 S, R 22 E). Named on North Fork (1965) 7.5' quadrangle.

Titus and Manly Ferry: see **San Joaquin City** [MADERA].

Tivy Mountain [FRESNO]: *peak,* 24 miles east of Fresno (lat. 36° 48' N, long. 119°21'30" W; near E line sec. 16, T 13 S, R 24 E); the peak is 3 miles northeast of Tivy Valley. Altitude 2848 feet. Named on Pine Flat Dam

(1965) 7.5' quadrangle. On Watts Valley (1942) 15' quadrangle, the name applies to the ridge on which the peak is the high point.

Tivy Valley [FRESNO]: *valley,* 3 miles south-southwest of Piedra (lat. 36°46'15" N, long. 119°24'15" W; in and near sec. 30, T 13 S, R 24 E). Named on Piedra (1965) 7.5' quadrangle.

Tobias Creek [TULARE]: *stream,* flows 6.5 miles to Kern River 0.5 mile south-southeast of Fairview (lat. 35°55'05" N, long. 118°29'30" W; sec. 23, T 23 S, R 32 E). Named on California Hot Springs (1958) and Kernville (1956) 15' quadrangles. The name commemorates Tobias Minter (Mitchell, A.R., p. 78).

Tobias Meadow [TULARE]: *area,* 5.5 miles east-southeast of California Hot Springs (lat. 35°51'50" N, long. 118°34'15" W; on S line sec. 6, T 24 S, R 32 E); the place is at the head of Tobias Creek. Named on California Hot Springs (1958) 15' quadrangle.

Tobias Meadow: see **Lower Tobias Meadow** [TULARE].

Tobias Pass [TULARE]: *pass,* 5.5 miles east-southeast of California Hot Springs (lat. 35°51'30" N, long. 118°43'30" W; near E line sec. 12, T 24 S, R 31 E); the pass is 0.5 mile north-northwest of Tobias Peak near the head of Tobias Creek. Named on California Hot Springs (1958) 15' quadrangle.

Tobias Peak [TULARE]: *peak,* 6 miles east-southeast of California Hot Springs (lat. 35°51' N, long. 118°34'20" W; near SW cor. sec. 7, T 24 S, R 32 E); the peak is near the head of Tobias Creek. Altitude 8284 feet. Named on California Hot Springs (1958) 15' quadrangle. John Minter and Tobe Minter named the peak in 1884 in memory of their father, Tobias Minter, who homesteaded near the feature (Gudde, 1949, p. 363).

Toby [KERN]: *locality,* 2.25 miles east-northeast of Saltdale (lat. 35° 22'30" N, long. 117°51' W). Named on Saltdale (1943b) 15' quadrangle.

Tocher Lake [FRESNO]: *lake,* 900 feet long, nearly 4 miles north-northeast of Dinkey Dome (lat. 37°10'10" N, long. 119°06'40" W; near NW cor. sec. 11, T 9 S, R 26 E). Named on Huntington Lake (1953) 15' quadrangle. The name commemorates Dr. Lloyd Tocher of Fresno (Browning 1986, p. 218).

Todds Hill [TULARE]: *ridge,* south-trending, 1 mile long, 1.25 miles north-northeast of Lindsay (lat. 36°13'25" N, long. 119°04'55" W). Named on Lindsay (1951) 7.5' quadrangle. Called Wards Hill on Porterville (1942) 15' quadrangle.

Toe Lake [FRESNO]: *lake,* 1100 feet long, 1.5 miles south-southwest of Mount Abbot (lat. 37°21'45" N, long. 118°47'25" W); the lake is near the northeast or "toe" end of boot-shaped Lake Italy. Named on Mount Abbot (1953) 15' quadrangle.

Tokay [TULARE]: *locality,* nearly 2 miles east-northeast of Dinuba along Atchison, Topeka and Santa Fe Railroad (lat. 36°33'05" N, long. 119°21'20" W; near W line sec. 10, T 16 S, R 24 E). Named on Orange Cove South (1966) 7.5' quadrangle.

Tokay: see **Malaga** [FRESNO].

Tokopah Falls [TULARE]: *waterfall,* 9 miles west of Triple Divide Peak on Marble Fork (lat. 36°36'30" N, long. 118°41'20" W; sec. 23, T 15 S, R 30 E); the feature is above Tokopah Valley. Named on Triple Divide Peak (1956) 15' quadrangle.

Tokopah Valley [TULARE]: *canyon,* 1.5 miles long, 10 miles west of Triple Divide Peak along Marble Fork (lat. 36°36'40" N, long. 118°42'15" W; sec. 22, 23, T 15 S, R 30 E). Named on Triple Divide Peak (1956) 15' quadrangle. The name is from an Indian word that has the meaning "high" (United States Board on Geographic Names, 1933a, p. 760).

Tollgate Canyon [KERN]: *canyon,* drained by a stream that flows 6.25 miles to Indian Creek 2 miles southeast of Loraine (lat. 35°17'05" N, long. 118°24'45" W; near SW cor. sec. 26, T 30 S, R 33 E). Named on Loraine (1972) and Tehachapi North (1966) 7.5' quadrangles.

Tollhouse [FRESNO]: *village,* 7.5 miles southwest of Shaver Lake Heights (present town of Shaver Lake) (lat. 37°01'10" N, long. 119°24' W; sec. 31, T 10 S, R 24 E). Named on Shaver Lake (1953) 15' quadrangle. Lippincott's (1902) map shows Toll House P.O. at the place. Postal authorities established Toll House post office in 1876, discontinued it in 1884, reestablished it in 1885, and changed the name to Tollhouse in 1894 (Salley, p. 222). The village began in 1867 when a building was constructed where toll was levied on vehicles passing up or down a 10-mile road that led to mills near Shaver Lake; toll was collected until 1878 (Hoover, Rensch, and Rensch, p. 94). Postal authorities established Mountain Rest post office 6 miles north of Tollhouse in 1945, discontinued it in 1947, reestablished it in 1948, and discontinued it in 1953 (Salley, p. 147).

Tollhouse Canyon [KERN]: *canyon,* drained by a stream that flows 4 miles to Walker Basin Creek 4.25 miles north-northwest of Caliente (lat. 35°20'55" N, long. 118°39'25" W). Named on Bena (1972) and Oiler Peak (1972) 7.5' quadrangles—the last-named map shows a tollhouse in the canyon.

Tollhouse Creek [FRESNO]: *stream,* flows 1.5 miles to Dry Creek 6.5 miles southwest of Shaver Lake Heights (present town of Shaver Lake) (lat. 37°02'25" N, long. 119°23'50" W; sec. 19, T 10 S, R 24 E); the stream is 1.5 miles north of Tollhouse. Named on Shaver Lake (1953) 15' quadrangle. On Kaiser (1904) 30' quadrangle, Dry Creek and this tributary together are called Tollhouse Cr.

Tollhouse Flat [KERN]: *area,* 3.25 miles north

of Caliente (lat. 35° 20'20" N, long. 118°37'55" W); the place is in Tollhouse Canyon. Named on Bena (1972) 7.5' quadrangle.

Tolly Spring [KERN]: *spring,* 12 miles north of Mojave (lat. 35°13'20" N, long. 118°09'10" W; sec. 19, T 31 S, R 36 E). Named on Cache Peak (1973) 7.5' quadrangle.

Tom: see **Mount Tom** [FRESNO].

Tomahawk Lake [FRESNO]: *lake,* 1900 feet long, 3 miles west-southwest of Mount Humphreys in Humphreys Basin (lat. 37°15'25" N, long. 118°43'35" W). Named on Mount Tom (1949) 15' quadrangle.

Tombstone: see **The Tombstone** [FRESNO].

Tombstone Creek [FRESNO]:

(1) *stream,* flows 2 miles to South Fork San Joaquin River 12 miles southwest of Mount Abbot (lat. 37°16'45" N, long. 118°57'35" W); the stream heads near the feature called The Tombstone. Named on Mount Abbot (1953) 15' quadrangle.

(2) *stream,* flows 4 miles to Middle Fork Kings River 7.5 miles northeast of Hume (lat. 36°52' N, long. 118°49'30" W). Named on Tehipite Dome (1952) 15' quadrangle.

Tombstone Ridge [FRESNO]: *ridge,* southeast-trending, 3 miles long, 9.5 miles north-northeast of Hume (lat. 36°53'45" N, long. 118°49' W). Named on Tehipite Dome (1952) 15' quadrangle.

Tompson Lake: see **Thomson Lake** [FRESNO].

Tom Sawyer Lake [KERN]: *lake,* 1250 feet long, 3 miles west-northwest of Tehachapi along Brite Creek (lat. 35°09'05" N, long. 118°29'30" W; sec. 13, T 32 S, R 32 E). Named on Tehachapi North (1966) 7.5' quadrangle.

Toms Hill [KERN]: *peak,* 4.25 miles north-northwest of Cross Mountain (lat. 35°20'15" N, long. 118°09'40" W; at W line sec. 7, T 30 S, R 36 E). Altitude 5048 feet. Named on Cross Mountain (1972) 7.5' quadrangle. On Cross Mountain (1943) 15' quadrangle, the name applies to a peak located 1 mile farther north (near SW cor. sec. 6, T 30 S, R 36 E).

Ton Tache: see **Tulare Lake** [KINGS].

Tonyville [TULARE]: *locality,* 3 miles north of Lindsay (lat. 36°14'55" N, long. 119°05'25" W; sec. 30, T 19 S, R 27 E). Named on Lindsay (1951) 7.5' quadrangle. Called Liberty on Lindsay (1928) 7.5' quadrangle, which shows the place along Visalia Electric Railroad.

Toolville [TULARE]: *locality,* 1.5 miles east-southeast of Exeter (lat. 36°17'10" N, long. 119°06'55" W; at W line sec. 12, T 19 S, R 26 E). Named on Rocky Hill (1951) 7.5' quadrangle.

Toolwass: see **Bakersfield** [KERN].

Toomey Gulch: see **Tumey Gulch** [FRESNO].

Tooth Lake [FRESNO]: *lake,* 700 feet long, 5 miles south of Mount Abbot (lat. 37°19' N, long. 118°47'55" W). Named on Mount Abbot (1953) 15' quadrangle.

Toowa Range [TULARE]: *ridge,* east-southeast-to southeast-trending, 5.5 miles long; Kern

Peak is near the center (lat. 36°18'30" N, long. 118°17'10" W). Named on Kern Peak (1956) and Olancha (1956) 15' quadrangles. Called Too-wa Range on Olmsted's (1900) map.

Tornado Creek [FRESNO]: *stream,* flows 3.5 miles to Tenmile Creek 1.5 miles northeast of Hume (lat. 36°48' N, long. 118°53'30" W); the stream heads at Tornado Meadow. Named on Tehipite Dome (1952) 15' quadrangle.

Tornado Meadow [FRESNO]: *area,* 3.5 miles east of Hume (lat. 36° 46'45" N, long. 118°50'45" W). Named on Tehipite Dome (1952) 15' quadrangle. The name is from a tangle of trees felled by a windstorm (Forest M. Clingan, personal communication, 1990).

Tower Rock [TULARE]: *peak,* 6.5 miles west-northwest of Kern Peak (lat. 36°20'20" N, long. 118°23'50" W). Altitude 8469 feet. Named on Kern Peak (1956) 15' quadrangle.

Towne: see **Towne Oil Station** [FRESNO].

Town Oil Station [FRESNO]: *locality,* 26 miles north-northeast of Coalinga (lat. 36°28'20" N, long. 120°08'45" W; near N line sec. 8, T 17 S, R 17 E). Abandoned site named on Westside (1956) 7.5' quadrangle. Mendenhall's (1908) map has the name "Towne" at the place.

Townsend: see **Yettem** [TULARE].

Trabuco Mountain [MADERA]: *peak,* 8.5 miles north-northwest of O'Neals (lat. 37°14'50" N, long. 119°44'10" W; sec. 12, T 8 S, R 20 E). Altitude 2647 feet. Named on Bass Lake (1953) and Millerton Lake (1965) 15' quadrangles.

Trail Crest [TULARE]: *locality,* 1.5 miles south of Mount Whitney on Tulare-Inyo county line (lat. 36°33'35" N, long. 118°17'30" W); the trail to Mount Whitney reaches the crest of the Sierra Nevada at the spot. Named on Mount Whitney (1956) 15' quadrangle.

Trail Lakes [FRESNO]: *lakes,* two, largest 700 feet long, 3.5 miles north of Mount Abbot (lat. 37°26'25" N, long. 118°46'30" W). Named on Mount Abbot (1953) 15' quadrangle.

Trail Pass [TULARE]: *pass,* 12 miles north-northwest of Olancha Peak on Tulare-Inyo county line (lat. 36°25'40" N, long. 118°10'30" W; sec. 22, T 17 S, R 35 E). Named on Olancha (1956) 15' quadrangle. Trail Pass has been called "new" Mulkey Pass, and Mulkey Pass has been called "old" Mulkey Pass (Schumacher, p. 80).

Trail Peak [TULARE]: *peak,* 12 miles north-northwest of Olancha Peak on Tulare-Inyo county line (lat. 36°25'40" N, long. 118°11'20" W; sec. 21, T 17 S, R 35 E); the peak is less than 1 mile west of Trail Pass. Altitude 11,623 feet. Named on Olancha (1956) 15' quadrangle.

Trail Spring [KERN]: *spring,* 13 miles north of Mojave (lat. 35°14'20" N, long. 118°11'25" W; near N line sec. 14, T 31 S, R 35 E). Named on Cache Peak (1973) 7.5' quadrangle.

Tranquillity [FRESNO]: *town,* 10 miles southeast of Mendota (lat. 36°38'50" N, long. 120°15' W; sec. 5, 8, T 15 S, R 16 E). Named on Jamesan (1963) and Tranquillity (1956) 7.5' quadrangles. Postal authorities established Tranquillity post office in 1910 (Frickstad, p. 38). A place called Fresno City was begun about 1855 at the head of navigation on Fresno Slough, less than 2 miles north and slightly west of present Tranquillity; Fresno City was practically abandoned by 1865 (Hoover, Rensch, and Rensch, p. 92). Postal authorities established Fresno City post office in 1860 and discontinued it in 1863 (Frickstad, p. 33). Mendenhall's (1908) map shows a place called Mendota Station located 3.5 miles west-southwest of present Tranquillity.

Traver [TULARE]: *village,* 14 miles northwest of Visalia (lat. 36°27'15" N, long. 119°29'05" W; sec. 16, T 17 S, R 23 E). Named on Traver (1949) 7.5' quadrangle. The name, given in 1884, commemorates Charles Traver, a member of 76 Land and Water Company (Mitchell, A.R., p. 70). Postal authorities established Cross Creek post office in 1874, changed the name to Grandview in 1876, and changed it to Traver in 1884 (Frickstad, p. 210, 211).

Travers Creek [FRESNO-TULARE]: *stream,* heads in Fresno County and flows 11 miles to a canal 2.5 miles west of Dinuba in Tulare County (lat. 36°32'45" N, long. 119°25'40" N; near SW cor. sec. 12, T 16 S, R 23 E). Named on Reedley (1966) 7.5' quadrangle.

Treadwell [KERN]: *locality,* 4 miles north-northwest of downtown Bakersfield along Southern Pacific Railroad (lat. 35°25'40" N, long. 118°58'20" W; near S line sec. 4, T 29 S, R 28 E). Named on Oil Center (1954) 7.5' quadrangle. California Mining Bureau's (1917c) map shows a place called Porque located about 3 miles north of Treadwell along a railroad.

Trescope [KERN]: *locality,* 8 miles northeast of Mojave along Southern Pacific Railroad (lat. 35°08'30" N, long. 118°04'30" W; near SW cor. sec. 13, T 32 S, R 36 E). Named on Mojave (1915) 30' quadrangle. Called Trescape on Mojave (1943) 15' quadrangle.

Tres Piedras: see **Joaquin Rocks** [FRESNO].

Tretten Canyon [FRESNO]: *canyon,* drained by a stream that flows 3.5 miles to Mill Creek (3) nearly 4 miles east-southeast of Tivy Mountain (lat. 36°47'15" N, long. 119°17'35" W; sec. 19, T 13 S, R 25 E). Named on Pine Flat Dam (1965) 7.5' quadrangle.

Treves: see **Sivert** [KERN].

Trigo [MADERA]: *village,* 7 miles east-south-east of Madera (lat. 36° 54'35" N, long. 119°57'30" W; sec. 1, T 12 S, R 18 E). Named on Gregg (1965) 7.5' quadrangle. Called Patterson on Mendenhall's (1908) map. Postal authorities established Trigo post office in 1912 and discontinued it in 1942 (Frickstad, p. 86). Logan's (1950) map shows a place called Lankershim located about 3.5 miles

northwest of Trigo along Atchison, Topeka and Santa Fe Railroad.

Trimmer [FRESNO]: *locality,* 8 miles north-northeast of Piedra (lat. 36°54'20" N, long. 119°17'45" W; on E line sec. 12, T 12 S, R 24 E). Named on Trimmer (1965) 7.5' quadrangle. Watts Valley (1942) 15' quadrangle shows Trimmer situated 0.5 mile farther southeast within the limits of present Pine Flat Reservoir (near center of sec. 7, T 12 S, R 25 E). Postal authorities established Trimmer post office in 1889, discontinued it in 1890, reestablished it in 1892, moved it 1 mile south in 1894, moved it 1 mile northwest in 1895, and discontinued it in 1919 (Salley, p. 224). A resort called Trimmer Springs, for owner Morris Trimmer (Hanna, p. 333), operated before 1911 along Kings River (sec. 18, T 12 S, R 25 E) less than 1 mile south of Trimmer post office (Bradley, p. 459)—water of Pine Flat Reservoir now covers the site.

Trimmer Springs: see **Trimmer** [FRESNO].

Trinity Lakes [MADERA]: *lakes,* 3.25 miles north-northwest of Devils Postpile (lat. 37°40' N, long. 119°06' W). Named on Devils Postpile (1953) 15' quadrangle.

Triple Divide Peak [MADERA]: *peak,* 1.5 miles east of Merced Peak (lat. 37°37'55" N, long. 119°22'10" W). Altitude 11,607 feet. Named on Merced Peak (1953) 15' quadrangle. Lieutenant N.F. McClure named the peak in 1895 (Browning, 1988, p. 147).

Triple Divide Peak [TULARE]: *peak,* 13 miles west of Mount Whitney on Great Western Divide (lat. 36°35'35" N, long. 118°31'50" W). Altitude 12,634 feet. Named on Triple Divide Peak (1956) 15' quadrangle.

Triple Falls [FRESNO]: *waterfall,* 2.5 miles northwest of Marion Peak along Cartridge Creek (lat. 36°59'05" N, long. 118°33'15" W). Named on Marion Peak (1953) 15' quadrangle.

Triple Peak Fork [MADERA]: *stream,* flows 5.5 miles to Merced Peak Fork 5 miles north-northeast of Merced Peak (lat. 37°41'45" N, long. 119°20'50" W); the stream heads near Triple Divide Peak. Named on Merced Peak (1953) 15' quadrangle. United States Board on Geographic Names (1978d, p. 4) rejected the form "Tripple Peak Fork" for the name.

Trocha [TULARE]: *locality,* 8.5 miles southwest of Ducor along Southern Pacific Railroad (lat. 35°47'50" N, long. 119°08'45" W; sec. 34, T 24 S, R 26 E). Named on Delano East (1953) 7.5' quadrangle.

Tropico Hill [KERN]: *hill,* 4 miles west-north-west of Rosamond (lat. 34°52'45" N, long. 118°13'55" W). Named on Soledad Mountain (1973) 7.5' quadrangle. The feature also was known as Red Hill, Crandall Hill, Hamilton Hill, Burton's Hill, and Burton's Tropico Hill (Settle, p. 58, 62; Wynn, 1951, p. 16). The name "Hamilton" was for Ezra Hamilton, who recognized gold in rock at the hill; the name

"Burton" was for the Burton brothers, who erected a mill at the place (Wynn, 1951, p. 16).

Trout Creek [TULARE]: *stream,* flows 15 miles to South Fork Kern River 12.5 miles northwest of Lamont Peak (lat. 35°56'35" N, long. 118°10' W; sec. 11, T 23 S, R 35 E). Named on Hockett Peak (1956), Kernville (1956), and Lamont Peak (1956) 15' quadrangles.

Trout Creek: see **Little Trout Creek** [TULARE].

Trout Meadows [TULARE]: *area,* 2 miles west-southwest of Hockett Peak (lat. 36°12'45" N, long. 118°25'10" W). Named on Hockett Peak (1956) 15' quadrangle.

Troy Meadow: see **Little Troy Meadow** [TULARE].

Troy Meadows [TULARE]: *area,* 9.5 miles south-southwest of Monache Mountain along Fish Creek (2) (lat. 36°04'20" N, long. 118°14'15" W; in and near sec. 30, T 21 S, R 35 E). Named on Monache Mountain (1956) 15' quadrangle.

True Meadow [TULARE]: *area,* 14 miles southeast of Fairview (lat. 35°48'10" N, long. 118°18'25" W; near NW cor. sec. 34, T 24 S, R 34 E). Named on Kernville (1956) 15' quadrangle. Browning (1986, p. 221) associated the name with Henry B. True, who patented land in the neighborhood in 1891.

Tucker Creek [KERN]: *stream,* flows 2.5 miles to Kern River 2.25 miles east-northeast of Democrat Hot Springs (lat. 35°32'20" N, long. 118°37'40" W). Named on Democrat Hot Springs (1972) 7.5' quadrangle.

Tucker Mountain [TULARE]: *peak,* 12 miles northeast of Dinuba (lat. 36°38'20" N, long. 119°12'30" W; sec. 12, T 15 S, R 25 E). Altitude 2611 feet. Named on Tucker Mountain (1966) 7.5' quadrangle. The name is for a homesteader east of the peak (Gudde, 1949, p. 370).

Tulainyo Lake [TULARE]: *lake,* 0.5 mile long, 1.5 miles north-northeast of Mount Whitney (lat. 36°35'50" N, long. 118°16'46" W); the lake is near Tulare-Inyo county line. Named on Mount Whitney (1956) 15' quadrangle. R.B. Marshall of United States Geological Survey coined the name in 1917 from the words "Tulare" and "Inyo" (United States Board on Geographic Names, 1933a, p. 771).

Tula Lake: see **Tulare Lake** [KINGS].

Tulare [TULARE]: *city,* 8.5 miles south-southwest of Visalia (lat. 36°12'30" N, long. 119°20'50" W). Named on Tulare (1950) 7.5' quadrangle. Postal authorities established Tulare post office in 1872 (Frickstad, p. 214), and the city incorporated in 1888. Officials of Southern Pacific Railroad named the city in 1872 (Mitchell, A.R., p. 70). California Mining Bureau's (1917b) map shows a place called Robla located along the railroad about halfway between Tulare and Paige. Postal authorities established Hunsaker post office 10.5 miles southeast of Tulare in 1872 and discontinued it in 1884; the name was for Henry Hunsaker, a pioneer settler (Salley, p. 101). They established Herrick's Cross post office 14 miles southeast of Tulare in 1878 and discontinued it in 1882; the place was at a crossroads named for the local landowner (Salley, p. 96).

Tulare Lake [KINGS]: *lake,* south of Lemoore. Named on La Rambla (1942) and Stratford (1942) 15' quadrangles, which show the lake confined within artificial banks. Wilkes' (1841) map has the name "L. Chintache," and Wilkes (p. 47) in his report referred to Tula Lake, "called by the Indians, Chintache Lake." Fremont's (1848) map has the name "L. d. l. Tulares." Derby's (1850) map has the name "Tache Lake" and the designation "Bed of the Ton Tache" for marsh south of the lake. Eddy's (1854) map has the designation "Tulare or Tache Lake," Parke's (1854-1855) map has the name "Tulare Lake," and Rogers and Johnston's (1857) map has the name "L. Tulare." Pedro Fages discovered the lake in 1772 and gave the name "Los Tulares" to marshlands of San Joaquin Valley—*los tulares* means "the place of rushes" in Spanish (Hoover, Rensch, and Rensch, p. 135). *Tule* means "reed" or "bullrush" in American Spanish, and a place where reeds grow should be called *Tular,* but a new American term was derived from the plural form *Tulares,* apparently by simply dropping the final letter (Stewart, p. 497). According to Derby (p. 13), water overflowed north from the lake to San Joaquin River through a slough known as Sanjon de San Jose, but the lake has not overflowed to San Joaquin River since 1878, chiefly because water is diverted from Kings River for irrigation (Davis, Green, Olmsted, and Brown, p. 29). During reclamation of the lake bed for agriculture, dikes and levees restricted the lake to the northwest part of its old bed (Davis, Green, Olmsted, and Brown, p. 29), and the most recent maps show no lake at all. Tulare Lake Bed is named on Corcoran (1954), Dudley Ridge (1954), El Rico Ranch (1954), Hacienda Ranch NE (1954), Hacienda Ranch NW (1954), Kettleman City (1963), Los Viejos (1954), Stratford (1954), Stratford SE (1954), and Westhaven (1956) 7.5' quadrangles.

Tulare Lake Bed: see **Tulare Lake** [KINGS].

Tulare Lake Slough: see **Fresno Slough** [FRESNO].

Tulare Peak [TULARE]: *peak,* 3.25 miles southeast of Mineral King (lat. 36°24'45" N, long. 118°33'45" W). Altitude 11,588 feet. Named on Mineral King (1956) 15' quadrangle.

Tulare Plains: see "Regional setting."

Tulare Valley: see "Regional setting."

Tule: see **North Tule,** under **Porterville** [TULARE]; **Porterville** [TULARE].

Tule Lake [FRESNO]: *lake,* 900 feet long. 9.5 miles east-northeast of Kaiser Peak (lat.

37°20'30" N, long. 119°01'20" W). Named on Kaiser Peak (1953) 15' quadrangle.

Tule Meadow [FRESNO]:
(1) *area,* 8 miles north-northeast of Kaiser Peak (lat. 37°23'30" N, long. 119°07' W). Named on Kaiser Peak (1953) 15' quadrangle.
(2) *area,* 10 miles southeast of Dinkey Dome (lat. 37°00' N, long. 119°01'45" W; sec. 4, T 11 S, R 27 E). Named on Huntington Lake (1953) and Patterson Mountain (1952) 15' quadrangles.

Tule River [KINGS-TULARE]: *stream,* formed by the confluence of North Fork and Middle Fork in Tulare County, flows 38 miles to Kings County 7.25 miles south-southwest of Waukena (lat. 36°02'05" N, long. 119°32'05" W); in Kings County the stream flows through Tulare Lake Bed in an artificial watercourse. Named on Corcoran (1954), El Rico Ranch (1954), Globe (1956), Porterville (1951, photorevised 1969), Springville (1957), Stratford SE (1954), Success Dam (1956), Taylor Weir (1950, photorevised 1969), Tipton (1950, photorevised 1969), and Woodville (1950, photorevised 1969) 7.5' quadrangles. Derby's (1850) map has the designation "Tule River or San Pedro" for the stream. Middle Fork Tule River is formed 5.5 miles west-northwest of Camp Nelson by the confluence of North Fork of Middle Fork and South Fork of Middle Fork; it is 7 miles long and is named on Camp Nelson (1956) and Springville (1957) 15' quadrangles. North Fork of Middle Fork is 14 miles long and is named on Camp Nelson (1956) and Mineral King (1956) 15' quadrangles. South Fork of Middle Fork is 11.5 miles long and is named on Camp Nelson (1956) 15' quadrangle; it also is called East Fork of Middle Fork (Waring, p. 243). North Fork Tule River is 18 miles long and is named on Kaweah (1957), Mineral King (1956), and Springville (1957) 15' quadrangles. South Fork Tule River joins Tule River 6 miles east of Porterville in Lake Success; it is 22 miles long and is named on Camp Nelson (1956) and Springville (1957) 15' quadrangles. Tule River splits 3.25 miles east of Woodville to form North Branch and South Branch. North Branch flows 13 miles before it joins South Branch to reform Tule River 3 miles north-northwest of Tipton; it is named on Cairns Corner (1950, photorevised 1969), Tipton (1950, photorevised 1969), Tulare (1950, photorevised 1969), and Woodville (1950, photorevised 1969) 7.5' quadrangles. South Branch is 11.5 miles long and is named on Tipton (1950, photorevised 1969) and Woodville (1950, photorevised 1969) 7.5' quadrangles. North Branch is unnamed on Tipton (1928) 7.5' quadrangle, which has the name "Tule River" for present South Branch. Middle Branch diverges from South Branch 1 mile north-northeast of Woodville and flows 4.5 miles before it rejoins South Branch; it is

named on Woodville (1950, photorevised 1969) 7.5' quadrangle. Lake View School (1927) 7.5' quadrangle shows Tule River situated 1 to 2 miles farther south in a watercourse called Old Channel Tule River on Taylor Wier (1950, photorevised 1969) 7.5' quadrangle.

Tule River: see **Porterville** [TULARE].

Tule Spring [FRESNO]: *spring,* 4 miles north-northwest of Coalinga Mineral Springs (lat. 36°11'10" N, long. 120°36' W; sec. 17, T 20 S, R 13 E). Named on Sherman Peak (1969) 7.5' quadrangle.

Tule Spring [KERN]: *spring,* 10 miles west of Liebre Twins in Devils Canyon (lat. 34°56'45" N, long. 118°44'25" W; at W line sec. 6, T 10 N, R 17 W). Named on Winters Ridge (1966) 7.5' quadrangle.

Tully Hole [FRESNO]: *relief feature,* 3 miles west of Red Slate Mountain (lat. 37°31'10" N, long. 118°55'15" W). Named on Mount Morrison (1953) 15' quadrangle. The feature contains marsh. Gene Tully, a Forest Service ranger, used the place to rest his stock when he was on patrol in the neighborhood (Browning 1986, p. 222).

Tully Lake [FRESNO]: *lake,* 1350 feet long, 9 miles northwest of Mount Abbot (lat. 37°29'15" N, long. 118°53' W). Named on Mount Abbot (1953) 15' quadrangle.

Tumey Gulch [FRESNO]: *canyon,* drained by a stream that heads in San Benito County and flows 14 miles to lowlands 20 miles south-southwest of Firebaugh (lat. 36°35' N, long. 120°36' W; sec. 31, T 15 S, R 13 E). Named on Monocline Ridge (1955) and Tumey Hills (1956) 7.5' quadrangles. The name also had the form "Toomey Gulch" (Gudde, 1969, p. 347).

Tumey Hills [FRESNO]: *range,* 25 miles south-southwest of Firebaugh on Fresno-San Benito county line (lat. 36°33' N, long. 120° 39' W); the range is west of Tumey Gulch. Named on Monocline Ridge (1955) and Tumey Hills (1956) 7.5' quadrangles.

Tunemah Lake [FRESNO]: *lake,* 2000 feet long, 6 miles south of Mount Goddard (lat. 37°00'55" N, long. 118°42'10" W). Named on Mount Goddard (1948) 15' quadrangle.

Tunemah Pass [FRESNO]: *pass,* 8 miles west of Marion Peak (lat. 36°58'45" N, long. 118°40' W); the pass is 2 miles southeast of Tunemah Peak. Named on Tehipite (1903) 30' quadrangle. The name originated with a curse vented by Chinese cooks who accompanied sheepmen through the pass (Hanna, p. 336).

Tunemah Peak [FRESNO]: *peak,* 10 miles west-northwest of Marion Peak (lat. 36°59'45" N, long. 118°41'51" W). Altitude 11,894 feet. Named on Marion Peak (1953) 15' quadrangle. The name is from Tunemah Pass (Hanna, p. 336).

Tunis Creek [KERN]: *stream,* flows 15 miles to El Paso Creek 12.5 miles south of Arvin (lat. 35°01'40" N, long. 118°49'25" W; sec. 20, T 11 N, R 18 W). Named on Pastoria Creek

(1958), Tejon Hills (1955), and Winters Ridge (1966) 7.5' quadrangles.

Tunnabora Peak [TULARE]: *peak,* 2 miles north-northeast of Mount Whitney on Tulare-Inyo county line (lat. 36°36'15" N, long. 118°16'50" W). Altitude 13,565 feet. Named on Mount Whitney (1956) 15' quadrangle.

Tunnel: see **The Tunnel** [TULARE].

Tunnel Air Camp [TULARE]: *locality,* 5 miles north-northeast of Kern Peak (lat. 36°22'50" N, long. 118°15'50" W; at N line sec. 11, T 18 S, R 34 E); the place is in Tunnel Meadow. Named on Kern Peak (1956) 15' quadrangle.

Tunnel Meadow [TULARE]: *area,* 5 miles north-northeast of Kern Peak along South Fork Kern River (lat. 36°22'40" N, long. 118° 16' W; mainly in sec. 10, 11, T 18 S, R 34 E); the place is northeast of The Tunnel. Named on Kern Peak (1956) 15' quadrangle. Called South Fork Meadows on Olancha (1907) 30' quadrangle, but United States Board on Geographic Names (1938, p. 56) rejected this name for the place.

Tunnel Spring [KERN]:

(1) *spring,* 2.25 miles northeast of Kernville (lat. 35°46'30" N, long. 118°23'40" W; near NW cor. sec. 12, T 25 S, R 33 E). Named on Kernville (1956) 15' quadrangle.

(2) *spring,* 3.5 miles west-northwest of Pinyon Mountain (lat. 35° 28'50" N, long. 118°12'45" W; near SE cor. sec. 16, T 28 S, R 35 E). Named on Pinyon Mountain (1972) 7.5' quadrangle.

(3) *spring,* nearly 3 miles northeast of Mount Adelaide along Stark Creek (lat. 35°27'40" N, long. 118°42'45" W). Named on Mount Adelaide (1972) 7.5' quadrangle.

Tuohy Creek [TULARE]: *stream,* flows 1.5 miles to South Fork Kaweah River 8 miles south-southwest of Mineral King (lat. 36° 20'50" N, long. 118°40'15" W); the stream goes through Tuohy Meadow. Named on Mineral King (1956) 15' quadrangle.

Tuohy Meadow [TULARE]: *area,* 9 miles south-southwest of Mineral King (lat. 36°20'15" N, long. 118°40'10" W). Named on Mineral King (1956) 15' quadrangle.

Tupman [KERN]: *village,* 20 miles west-southwest of Bakersfield (lat. 35°17'50" N, long. 119°21' W; at S line sec. 24, T 30 S, R 24 E). Named on Tupman (1954) 7.5' quadrangle. Postal authorities established Tupman post office in 1921 (Frickstad, p. 59). The name, given at a public meeting in 1920, commemorates H.V. Tupman, from whom Standard Oil Company purchased the land at the place (Gudde, 1949, p. 372).

Turf Lakes [FRESNO]: *lakes,* largest 500 feet long, 7.5 miles north-northwest of Blackcap Mountain (lat. 37°10'30" N, long. 118°49'55" W). Named on Blackcap Mountain (1953) 15' quadrangle.

Turk [FRESNO]: *locality,* 8 miles east-northeast of Coalinga along Southern Pacific Railroad (lat. 36°10'15" N, long. 120°13'15" W;

sec. 22, T 20 S, R 16 E). Named on Guijarral Hills (1956) 7.5' quadrangle. Called Stanley on Arnold and Anderson's (1910) map.

Turman Spring [KERN]: *spring,* 2.5 miles north-northeast of Caliente (lat. 35°19'15" N, long. 118°36'15" W). Named on Oiler Peak (1972) 7.5' quadrangle.

Turnbull [TULARE]: *locality,* 6.25 miles south of Waukena along Atchison, Topeka and Santa Fe Railroad (lat. 36°02'55" N, long. 119°31'10" W; near NE cor. sec. 6, T 22 S, R 23 E). Named on Corcoran (1928) 7.5' quadrangle.

Turner Flat [TULARE]: *area,* 4.5 miles southwest of California Hot Springs (lat. 35°50'30" N, long. 118°44'30" W; sec. 16, T 24 S, R 30 E); the place is 1.25 miles south of Turner Peak. Named on California Hot Springs (1958) 15' quadrangle.

Turner Lake [MADERA]: *lake,* 1200 feet long, 2.5 miles east of Merced Peak (lat. 37°38'30" N, long. 119°20'50" W). Named on Merced Peak (1953) 15' quadrangle. The name is for Henry Ward Turner of United States Geological Survey, who pioneered geologic mapping in and near Yosemite National Park (United States Board on Geographic Names, 1963b, p. 15).

Turner Peak [TULARE]: *peak,* 4.25 miles west-southwest of California Hot Springs (lat. 35°51'30" N, long. 118°44'30" W; sec. 9, T 24 S, R 30 E). Altitude 3731 feet. Named on California Hot Springs (1958) 15' quadrangle.

Turret Creek [FRESNO]: *stream,* flows 2.5 miles to Piute Canyon 12 miles north of Blackcap Mountain (lat. 37°14'20" N, long. 118° 49'30" W); the stream heads near Turret Peak. Named on Blackcap Mountain (1953) 15' quadrangle.

Turret Lake: see **Lower Turret Lake** [FRESNO]; **Middle Turret Lakes** [FRESNO]; **Upper Turret Lakes** [FRESNO].

Turret Peak [FRESNO]: *peak,* 9 miles south-southwest of Mount Abbot (lat. 37°15'50" N, long. 118°50'30" W). Named on Mount Abbot (1953) 15' quadrangle.

Turtle Creek [FRESNO]: *stream,* flows 2.5 miles to Ross Creek (1) 4 miles north of Balch Camp (lat. 36°57'45" N, long. 119°07'15" W). Named on Patterson Mountain (1952) 15' quadrangle.

Turtle Hole: see **The Turtle Hole** [KINGS].

Turtle Pass: see **Elizabeth Pass** [TULARE].

Tweedy Creek [KERN]: *stream,* flows 9 miles to Tehachapi Creek 0.5 mile north-northwest of Keene (lat. 35°13'55" N, long. 118° 34' W; sec. 17, T 31 S, R 32 E). Named on Keene (1966) and Tehachapi North (1966) 7.5' quadrangles.

Twelvemile House [MADERA]: *locality,* 10 miles south of Raymond (lat. 37°04'20" N, long. 119°54'10" W; sec. 9, T 10 S, R 19 E). Named on Daulton (1921) 7.5' quadrangle.

Twentyfive Canyon [FRESNO]: *canyon,* drained by a stream that flows nearly 5 miles to Salt Creek (1) 3.5 miles north of Joaquin

Rocks (lat. 36°22'20"N, long. 120°27'35" W; near S line sec. 9, T 18 S, R 14 E). Named on Joaquin Rocks (1969) 7.5' quadrangle. Joaquin Rocks (1943) 15' quadrangle has the form "Twenty Five Canyon" for the name.

25 Hill [KERN]: *ridge,* southeast- to east-trending, 1 mile long, 5.25 miles northwest of Maricopa (lat. 35°06'50" N, long. 119°28' W; sec. 25, 26, T 32 S, R 23 E). Named on Maricopa (1951) 7.5' quadrangle.

Twentyfive Spring [FRESNO]: *spring,* 2.5 miles west-northwest of Joaquin Rocks (lat. 36°19'40" N, long. 120°29'35" W; near S line sec. 30, T 18 S, R 14 E); the spring is near the head of Twentyfive Canyon. Named on Joaquin Rocks (1969) 7.5' quadrangle. Joaquin Rocks (1943) 15' quadrangle has the form "Twenty Five Spr." for the name.

Twentyone Canyon [KERN]: *canyon,* drained by a stream that flows 4.5 miles to Midway Valley 3.5 miles southeast of Fellows (lat. 35°08'25" N, long. 119°30' W; near E line sec. 9, T 32 S, R 23 E); the canyon is in section 21. Named on Elkhorn Hills (1954) and Fellows (1950, photorevised 1973) 7.5' quadrangles.

Twentysix Camp [FRESNO]: *locality,* 3.5 miles east-northeast of Castle Mountain (lat. 35°57'15" N, long. 120°16'50" W; sec. 6, T 23 S, R 16 E). Named on The Dark Hole (1937) 7.5' quadrangle.

Twentytwo Mile House [MADERA]: *locality,* 14 miles south-southeast of Raymond (lat. 37°02'20" N, long. 119°46'50" W; near S line sec. 22, T 10 S, R 20 E). Named on Little Table Mountain (1962) 7.5' quadrangle. Called Millers Corner on Raymond (1944) 15' quadrangle.

Twin Buck Lakes [FRESNO]: *lakes,* two, largest 900 feet long, 2 miles north of Blackcap Mountain (lat. 37°06'10" N, long. 118° 48' W). Named on Blackcap Mountain (1953) 15' quadrangle.

Twin Buttes [KERN]: *hills,* two, 1 mile apart, 4 miles southwest of Castle Butte (lat. 35°05'10" N, long. 117°56'20" W; and lat. 35°04'20" N, long. 117°55'35" W). Named on California City South (1973) 7.5' quadrangle; the northwesternmost of the two hills is called Desert Butte.

Twin Buttes [TULARE]:
(1) *hills,* two, 5.5 miles west of Woodlake (lat. 36°25'35" N long. 119°11'50" W; sec. 30, T 17 S, R 26 E). Altitudes 584 and 651 feet. Named on Exeter (1952) 15' quadrangle.
(2) *locality,* 7 miles west-northwest of Woodlake along Atchison, Topeka and Santa Fe Railroad (lat. 36°28' N, long. 119°12'15" W; at E line sec. 12, T 17 S, R 25 E); the place is 2.5 miles north of Twin Buttes (1). Named on Exeter (1952) 15' quadrangle.

Twin Creek: see **East Twin Creek** and **West Twin Creek,** under **Santiago Creek** [KERN].

Twinky Spring [KERN]: *spring,* 5.5 miles east-southeast of Caliente (lat. 35°15'15" N, long.

118°32'15" W; at SE cor. sec. 4, T 31 S, R 32 E). Named on Oiler Peak (1972) 7.5' quadrangle.

Twin Island Lakes [MADERA]: *lakes,* two, largest 1800 feet long, 9.5 miles west-northwest of Devils Postpile (lat. 37°41'30" N, long. 119°13'55" W); each lake contains a small island. Named on Devils Postpile (1953) 15' quadrangle.

Twin Lake: see **Lower Twin Lake** [FRESNO]; **Upper Twin Lake** [FRESNO].

Twin Lakes [FRESNO]:
(1) *lakes,* two, largest 450 feet long, 9.5 miles north of Hume (lat. 36°55'15" N, long. 118°53'50" W). Named on Tehipite Dome (1952) 15' quadrangle.
(2) *lakes,* two, largest 1100 feet long, 2.5 miles south-southeast of Mount Pinchot (lat. 36°54'35" N, long. 118°23'30" W). Named on Mount Pinchot (1953) 15' quadrangle.

Twin Lakes [MADERA]: *lakes,* two, largest 400 feet long, 5 miles southeast of Merced Peak (lat. 37°34'30" N, long. 119°20'25" W). Named on Merced Peak (1953) 15' quadrangle.

Twin Lakes [KERN]:
(1) *lakes,* two, largest 1000 feet long, 4.25 miles east-northeast of Liebre Twins (lat. 34°59'10" N, long. 118°30'20" W; at E line sec. 6, T 10 N, R 15 W). Named on Neenach (1943) 15' quadrangle. Johnson's (1911) map shows a place called Knecht located 1.25 miles south of the lakes.
(2) *locality,* 4 miles east-northeast of Liebre Twins (lat. 34°59'15" N, long. 118°30'45" W; sec. 6, T 10 N, R 15 W); the place is at Twin Lakes (1). Named on Liebre Twins (1965) 7.5' quadrangle.

Twin Lakes [TULARE]:
(1) *lakes,* two, largest 1000 feet long, 11 miles west-northwest of Triple Divide Peak (lat. 36°39'30" N, long. 118°42'50" W). Named on Triple Divide Peak (1956) 15' quadrangle.
(2) *lakes,* two, largest 400 feet long, 10.5 miles south of Mineral King (lat. 36°18' N, long. 118°37'10" W). Named on Mineral King (1956) 15' quadrangle.

Twin Lakes: see **Hitchcock Lakes** [TULARE]; **Lower Twin Lake** [FRESNO].

Twin Meadows [FRESNO]: *areas,* two, 13 miles northeast of Kaiser Peak (lat. 37°24'30" N, long. 119°00'20" W). Named on Kaiser Peak (1953) 15' quadrangle.

Twin Oaks [KERN]: *locality,* 1.5 miles east-northeast of Loraine (lat. 35°18'45" N, long. 118°24'30" W; on S line sec. 14, T 30 S, R 33 E). Named on Loraine (1972) 7.5' quadrangle. Postal authorities established Twin Oaks post office in 1926 and discontinued it in 1931 (Salley, p. 226).

Twin Peak [TULARE]: *peak,* 5.5 miles south-southwest of California Hot Springs (lat. 35°48'35" N, long. 118°42'50" W; near W line sec. 26, T 24 S, R 30 E). Altitude 4168 feet. Named on California Hot Springs (1958) 15' quadrangle.

Twin Peaks [FRESNO]: *peaks,* two, 5.5 miles north of Charley Mountain on Fresno-Monterey county line (lat. 36°13'15" N, long. 120°38'40" W; sec. 2, T 20 S, R 12 E). Named on Priest Valley (1969) 7.5' quadrangle.

Twin Peaks [TULARE]: *peaks,* two, 11 miles west-northwest of Triple Divide Peak on Silliman Crest (lat. 36°39'55" N, long. 118° 42'25" W). Altitude of highest is 10,485 feet. Named on Triple Divide Peak (1956) 15' quadrangle.

Twin Sisters [MADERA]: *peaks,* two, 11 miles northeast of Raymond (lat. 37°20'25" N, long. 119°46'15" W; sec. 10, T 7 S, R 20 E). Altitudes 2697 and 2789 feet. Named on Horsecamp Mountain (1947) 7.5' quadrangle.

Twin Springs [TULARE]: *spring,* 3 miles south of California Hot Springs (lat. 35°50'10" N, long. 118°40'15" W; sec. 18, T 24 S, R 31 E). Named on California Hot Springs (1958) 15' quadrangle.

Twisselmann Well [KERN]: *well,* 10 miles south-southeast of Orchard Peak (lat. 35°36'10" N, long. 120°03'25" W; sec. 5, T 27 S, R 18 E). Named on Packwood Creek (1961) 7.5' quadrangle.

Two Springs Campground [MADERA]: *locality,* 5 miles southeast of Yosemite Forks on the south side of Bass Lake (1) (lat. 37°18'50" N, long. 119°33'50" W; near SW cor. sec. 15, T 7 S, R 22 E). Named on Bass Lake (1953) 15' quadrangle.

Two Teats [MADERA]: *peak,* 6 miles north of Devils Postpile on Madera-Mono county line (lat. 37°42'45" N, long. 119°05'55" W). Altitude 11,387 feet. Named on Devils Postpile (1953) 15' quadrangle. This peak and nearby San Joaquin Mountain together also were called Two Teats (Gudde, 1949, p. 373-374).

Tyler [MADERA]: *locality,* 5 miles south-southwest of Chowchilla along Chowchilla Pacific Railroad (lat. 37°03'20" N, long. 120°18'50" W; sec. 15, T 10 S, R 15 E). Named on Chowchilla (1918) 7.5' quadrangle.

Tyler Creek [TULARE]: *stream,* flows 8 miles to Deer Creek (2) 2 miles west of California Hot Springs (lat. 35°53' N, long. 118°42'25" W; sec. 35, T 23 S, R 30 E). Named on California Hot Springs (1958) 15' quadrangle. The name is for J.D. Tyler (Mitchell, A.R., p. 78).

Tyler Gulch [TULARE]: *canyon,* drained by a stream that flows 2 miles to White River (1) 5.25 miles south of Fountain Springs (lat. 35°48'50" N, long. 118°55'35" W; sec. 26, T 24 S, R 28 E). Named on Quincy School (1965) 7.5' quadrangle.

Tylerhorse Canyon [KERN]: *canyon,* drained by a stream that flows 5.5 miles to lowlands 10 miles west-northwest of the village of Willow Springs (lat. 34°57'10" N, long. 118°27' W; near SW cor. sec. 14, T 10 N, R 15 W). Named on Tehachapi South (1966) and Tylerhorse Canyon (1965) 7.5' quadrangles.

United States Board on Geographic Names (1983c, p. 4) approved the name "Covington Mountain" for a peak, altitude 7877 feet, located 8 miles south-southwest of Tehachapi at the head of Tylerhorse Canyon (lat. 35°00'53" N, long. 118°28'25" W; sec. 28, T 11 N, R 15 W); the name is for John D. Covington, an early resident of the neighborhood.

Tyler Meadow [TULARE]: *area,* 7.5 miles east-southeast of California Hot Springs (lat. 35°50' N, long. 118°33'15" W; at NW cor. sec. 20, T 24 S, R 32 E). Named on California Hot Springs (1958) 15' quadrangle.

Tyler Peak [TULARE]: *peak,* 2 miles west-northwest of California Hot Springs (lat. 35°53'45" N, long. 118°42' W; sec. 26, T 23 S, R 30 E); the peak is northwest of Tyler Creek. Altitude 3885 feet. Named on California Hot Springs (1958) 15' quadrangle.

Tyndall: see **Mount Tyndall** [TULARE].

Tyndall Creek [TULARE]: *stream,* flows 7.5 miles to Kern River 7.25 miles west-northwest of Mount Whitney (lat. 36°36'15" N, long. 118°25' W); the stream heads near Mount Tyndall. Named on Mount Whitney (1956) 15' quadrangle.

– U –

Uhl Hill [TULARE]: *peak,* 2.5 miles west-southwest of California Hot Springs (lat. 35°52' N, long. 118°42'45" W; near W line sec. 2, T 24 S, R 30 E). Named on California Hot Springs (1958) 15' quadrangle.

Uhl Pocket [TULARE]: *relief feature,* 1.25 miles south-southwest of California Hot Springs (lat. 35°51'50" N, long. 118°40'45" W; on E line sec. 1, T 24 S, R 30 E). Named on California Hot Springs (1958) 15' quadrangle.

Uhl Station [TULARE]: *locality,* 1.5 miles east-northeast of California Hot Springs (lat. 35°53'10" N, long. 118°38'45" W; near E line sec. 32, T 23 S, R 31 E). Named on California Hot Springs (1958) 15' quadrangle.

Ultra [TULARE]: *locality,* 7 miles northwest of Fountain Springs along Atchison, Topeka and Santa Fe Railroad (lat. 35°57'55" N, long. 118°59'50" W; near SW cor. sec. 31, T 22 S, R 28 E). Named on Fountain Springs (1965) 7.5' quadrangle.

Una [KERN]: *locality,* 10.5 miles west-northwest of Bakersfield along Atchison, Topeka and Santa Fe Railroad (lat. 35°25'25" N, long. 119°10'35" W; sec. 10, T 29 S, R 26 E). Named on Rosedale (1954) 7.5' quadrangle. Rosedale (1933) 7.5' quadrangle shows Una Siding situated 2 miles farther northwest along the railroad (sec. 31, T 28 S, R 26 E).

Unadilla: see **Bakersfield** [KERN].

Una Siding: see **Una** [KERN].

University Peak [FRESNO-TULARE]: *peak,* 12.5 miles north-northwest of Mount Whitney at the spot that Fresno County, Tulare County, and Inyo County meet (lat. 36°44'50" N, long. 118°21'40" W). Altitude 13,632 feet. Named on Mount Whitney (1956) 15' quadrangle. J.N. LeConte and his party made the first ascent of the peak in 1896 and named it for University of California (Browning 1986, p. 226).

University Peak: see **Mount Gould** [FRESNO].

Upper Araujo Spring [KERN]: *spring,* 5.5 miles west-southwest of Liebre Twins (lat. 34°56' N, long. 118°39'50" W; sec. 23, T 10 N, R 17 W); the spring is 1550 feet east-northeast of Lower Araujo Spring. Named on Winters Ridge (1966) 7.5' quadrangle.

Upper Basin [FRESNO]: *area,* 2.5 miles south-southwest of Mount Bolton Brown (lat. 37°01' N, long. 118°27'30" W). Named on Big Pine (1950) and Mount Pinchot (1953) 15' quadrangles.

Upper Beck Spring [KERN]: *spring,* 5 miles northeast of Caliente (lat. 35°20'35" N, long. 118°34'05" W; sec. 5, T 30 S, R 32 E); the feature is in Beck Canyon 0.5 mile north of Lower Beck Spring. Named on Oiler Peak (1972) 7.5' quadrangle.

Upper Chiquito Campground [MADERA]: *locality,* 10 miles north of Shuteye Peak (lat. 37°29'55" N, long. 119°24'30" W; sec. 13, T 5 S, R 23 E); the place is along Chiquito Creek 7 miles upstream from Lower Chiquito Campground. Named on Shuteye Peak (1953) 15' quadrangle.

Upper Funston Meadow [TULARE]: *area,* 12 miles northwest of Kern Peak in Kern Canyon (lat. 36°27' N, long. 118°24'40" W); the place is 4.5 miles north of Funston Meadow at the mouth of Funston Creek. Named on Kern Peak (1956) 15' quadrangle. Olmsted's (1900) map shows a place called Funstons at or near the place. Tucker (p. 946) listed a feature called Soda Spring, located in Upper Funston Meadow between two branches of Kern River.

Upper Funston Meadow: see **Sky Parlor Meadow** [TULARE].

Upper Grapes Spring [KERN]: *spring,* 7 miles east of Caliente (lat. 35°17'05" N, long. 118°30'15" W; near SE cor. sec. 26, T 30 S, R 32 E); the spring is 0.25 mile west-northwest of Lower Grapes Spring. Named on Oiler Peak (1972) 7.5' quadrangle.

Upper Graveyard Meadow [FRESNO]: *area,* 10.5 miles west-northwest of Mount Abbot (lat. 37°26'30" N, long. 118°57'35" W); the place is 1.5 miles upstream along Cold Creek from Graveyard Meadows. Named on Mount Abbot (1953) 15' quadrangle.

Upper Grouse Valley [TULARE]: *valley,* 13 miles south-southeast of Kaweah (lat. 36°18' N, long. 118°48'45" W); the valley is 2 miles southeast of Grouse Valley at the head of Grouse Creek. Named on Kaweah (1957) 15' quadrangle.

Upper Honeymoon Lake [FRESNO]: *lake,* 1200 feet long, 12 miles north of Blackcap Mountain (lat. 37°14'45" N, long. 118°01'05" W); the lake is 0.25 mile south of Lower Honeymoon Lake. Named on Blackcap Mountain (1953) 15' quadrangle.

Upper Hopkins Lakes [FRESNO]: *lakes,* three, largest 950 feet long, 10 miles north-north-west of Mount Abbot (lat. 37°28'30" N, long. 118°50'30" W); the lakes are 1.5 miles north-northwest of Lower Hopkins Lake at the head of Hopkins Creek. Named on Mount Abbot (1953) 15' quadrangle.

Upper Horsethief Lake [FRESNO]: *lake,* 500 feet long, 4.25 miles west of Kaiser Peak (lat. 37°17' N, long. 119°16' W; sec. 29, T 7 S, R 25 E); the lake is 0.25 mile southeast of Lower Horsethief Lake. Named on Shuteye Peak (1953) 15' quadrangle.

Upper Iceberg Lake: see **Cecile Lake** [MADERA].

Upper Indian Lake [FRESNO]: *lake,* 1200 feet long, 8.5 miles north-northwest of Blackcap Mountain (lat. 37°11'05" N, long. 118°51'05" W); the lake is 1.5 miles north-northwest of Lower Indian Lake. Named on Blackcap Mountain (1953) 15' quadrangle.

Upper Lost Keys Lake: see **Lost Keys Lakes** [FRESNO].

Upper Merced Pass Lake [MADERA]: *lake,* 450 feet long, 2.5 miles west-southwest of Merced Peak (lat. 37°37'25" N, long. 119°26'30" W); the lake is 0.5 mile north of Merced Pass. Named on Merced Peak (1953) 15' quadrangle.

Upper Mills Creek Lake [FRESNO]: *lake,* 1300 feet long, 1 mile west-northwest of Mount Abbot (lat. 37°23'25" N, long. 118°48'10" W); the lake is 0.5 mile upstream from Lower Mills Creek Lake at the head of Mills Creek. Named on Mount Abbot (1953) 7.5' quadrangle.

Upper Ottoway Lake [MADERA]: *lake,* 1650 feet long, 0.5 mile west-northwest of Merced Peak (lat. 37°38'25" N, long. 119°24'15" W); the lake is less than 1 mile east of Lower Ottoway Lake. Named on Merced Peak (1953) 15' quadrangle.

Upper Parker Meadow [TULARE]: *area,* 6.25 miles north-northeast of California Hot Springs (lat. 35°58' N, long, 118°38'05" W; on N line sec. 4, T 23 S, R 31 E); the place is 0.5 mile northwest of Parker Meadow along Parker Meadow Creek. Named on California Hot Springs (1958) 15' quadrangle.

Upper Salt Lick Spring [KERN]: *spring,* 4.5 miles east-southeast of Caliente (lat. 35°15'35" N, long. 118°33'25" W; near E line sec. 5, T 31 S, R 32 E); the spring is 250 feet north-northeast of Salt Lick Spring. Named on Oiler Peak (1972) 7.5' quadrangle.

Upper Springhill Campground [TULARE]: *locality,* 5 miles south-southeast of Fairview along Kern River (lat. 35°51'55" N, long. 118°26'50" W; near N line sec. 8, T 24 S, R 33 E); the place is 0.25 mile north of Lower Springhill Campground. Named on Kernville

(1956) 15' quadrangle.

Upper Tent Meadow [FRESNO]: *area,* 9 miles south-southwest of Marion Peak (lat. 36°50'05" N, long. 118°35' W); the place is nearly 1 mile north-northwest of Lower Tent Meadow. Named on Marion Peak (1953) 15' quadrangle. Called Tent Meadow on Tehipite (1903) 30' quadrangle.

Upper Turret Lakes [FRESNO]: *lakes,* largest 500 feet long, 8 miles south-southwest of Mount Abbot (lat. 37°16'30" N, long. 118° 50' W); the lakes are 0.5 mile north of Middle Turret Lakes, and 1 mile north-northeast of Turret Peak. Named on Mount Abbot (1953) 15' quadrangle.

Upper Twin Lake [FRESNO]: *lake,* 1400 feet long, 1.25 miles east of Kaiser Peak (lat. 37°17'45" N, long. 119°09'35" W; on S line sec. 20, T 7 S, R 26 E); the lake is 1100 feet west-northwest of Lower Twin Lake. Named on Kaiser Peak (1953) 15' quadrangle. This lake and Lower Twin Lake together are called Twin Lakes on Kaiser (1904) 30' quadrangle.

Urcado Springs [KERN]: *springs,* two, 1500 feet apart, 9 miles west-southwest of Liebre Twins (lat. 34°55'15" N, long. 118°43'15" W). Named on Winters Ridge (1966) 7.5' quadrangle.

Urruttia Canyon [FRESNO]: *canyon,* drained by a stream that flows nearly 5 miles to Salt Creek (1) 3.5 miles north of Joaquin Rocks (lat. 36°22'10" N, long. 120°26'30" W; near N line sec. 15, T 18 S, R 14 E). Named on Joaquin Rocks (1969) 7.5' quadrangle.

Ursa Lake [FRESNO]: *lake,* 900 feet long, nearly 4 miles south-southwest of Mount Abbot (lat. 37°19'55" N, long. 118°47'50" W); the lake is between Big Bear Lake and Bearpaw Lake. Named on Mount Abbot (1953) 15' quadrangle. Elden H. Vestal of California Department of Fish and Game named the lake in 1952 (Browning 1986, p. 226).

Uva [FRESNO]: *locality,* 2.5 miles northwest of Reedley along Southern Pacific Railroad (lat. 36°37'10" N, long. 119°29'20" W; near S line sec. 17, T 15 S, R 23 E). Named on Reedley (1966) 7.5' quadrangle.

— V —

Vacation Pass [TULARE]: *pass,* 2.5 miles north-northwest of Mount Whitney on Tulare-Inyo county line (lat. 36°36'45" N, long. 118° 18' W). Named on Mount Whitney (1956) 15' quadrangle. Called Sheep Pass on Mount Whitney (1907) 30' quadrangle.

Vaccaro [KERN]: *locality,* 1.25 miles south-southeast of Arvin along the railroad (lat. 35°11'40" N, long. 118°48'50" W; at N line sec. 36, T 31 S, R 29 E). Named on Arvin (1933) 7.5' quadrangle.

Valhalla [TULARE]: *locality,* 3.5 miles west-southwest of Triple Divide Peak (lat.

36°34'05" N, long. 118°35' W). Named on Triple Divide Peak (1956) 15' quadrangle.

Valley Acres [KERN]: *settlement,* 5.25 miles north-northeast of Taft (lat. 35°12'20" N, long. 119°24'20" W; sec. 28, T 31 S, R 24 E). Named on Taft (1950) 7.5' quadrangle. The subdivision community began in 1937 (Bailey, 1967, p. 27).

Valor Lake [FRESNO]: *lake,* 1000 feet long, 2 miles southwest of Mount Goddard (lat. 37°04'55" N, long. 118°44'40" W). Named on Mount Goddard (1948) 15' quadrangle. William A. Dill of California Department of Fish and Game named the lake in 1948 (Browning 1986, p. 226).

Vance [TULARE]: *locality,* 1.5 miles north-northwest of Lindsay along Southern Pacific Railroad (lat. 36°13'25" N, long. 119°06'10" W; near SE cor. sec. 36, T 19 S, R 26 E). Named on Lindsay (1951) 7.5' quadrangle.

Vandalia: see **Porterville** [TULARE].

Vandeburg Lake [MADERA]: *lake,* 900 feet long, 6 miles south-southeast of Merced Peak (lat. 37°32'55" N, long. 119°21'05" W); the lake is one of the group called Madera Lakes. Named on Merced Peak (1953) 15' quadrangle. United States Board on Geographic Names (1991, p. 7) approved the form "Vanderburgh Lake" for the name.

Vanderburgh Lake: see **Vandeburg Lake** [MADERA].

Vandever Mountain [TULARE]: *peak,* 3 miles south-southeast of Mineral King (lat. 36°23'50" N, long. 118°34'50" W). Altitude 11,947 feet. Named on Mineral King (1956) 15' quadrangle. The name commemorates William Vandever, the congressman who introduced the bills that established Yosemite, Sequoia, and General Grant National Parks in 1890; the *Visalia Delta* newspaper proposed the name on September 4, 1890 (Hanna, p. 343).

Van Gordon Creek [TULARE]: *stream,* flows 7.25 miles to Yokohl Creek 14 miles south of Kaweah (lat. 36°16'15" N, long. 118°55'30" W; sec. 15, T 19 S, R 28 E). Named on Kaweah (1957) 15' quadrangle.

Vanguard [KINGS]: *locality,* 10 miles west-southwest of Lemoore (lat. 36°15'20" N, long. 119°57'15" W; sec. 30, T 19 S, R 19 E). Named on Vanguard (1956) 7.5' quadrangle.

Van Ness Slough [FRESNO]: *stream,* flows 2.25 miles to Murphy Slough nearly 2 miles north-west of Riverdale (lat. 36°27'10" N, long. 119°52'30" W; sec. 14, T 17 S, R 19 E). Named on Riverdale (1954) 7.5' quadrangle.

Vanris [FRESNO]: *locality,* 3.25 miles south of Clovis along Southern Pacific Railroad (lat. 36°46'30" N, long. 119°42' W; on W line sec. 28, T 13 S, R 21 E). Named on Clovis (1922) 7.5' quadrangle.

Vaquero Spring [KINGS]: *spring,* 10 miles southwest of Avenal (lat. 35°54'10" N, long. 120°15'25" W; sec. 29, T 23 S, E 16 E).

Named on The Dark Hole (1961) 7.5' quadrangle.

Vasquez Creek [FRESNO]: *stream,* heads in San Benito County and flows 6.5 miles to Mercey Creek 2 miles northwest of Mercey Hot Springs in Fresno County (lat. 36°43'45" N, long. 120°53' W; sec. 9, T 14 S, R 10 E). Named on Cerro Colorado (1969) 7.5' quadrangle.

Vaughn: see **Bodfish** [KERN].

Vee Lake [FRESNO]: *lake,* 3400 feet long, 4.5 miles south-southwest of Mount Abbot (lat. 37°19'20" N, long. 118°48'30" W). Named on Mount Abbot (1953) 15' quadrangle, where the outline of the lake on the map resembles the letter "V."

Velma: see **Exeter** [TULARE].

Venice Cove [TULARE]: *relief feature,* re-entrant into Venice Hills 6 miles west-southwest of Woodlake (lat. 36°22'15" N, long. 119°11'20" W; at SE cor. sec. 7, T 18 S, R 26 E). Named on Exeter (1952) 15' quadrangle.

Venice Hill: see **Taurusa** [TULARE].

Venice Hills [TULARE]: *range,* 5 miles west-southwest of Woodlake (lat. 36°22'45" N, long. 119°10'30" W). Named on Exeter (1952) 15' quadrangle. Early pioneers knew the feature as Kaweah Hills (Hoover, Rensch, and Rensch, p. 561).

Venida [TULARE]: *locality,* 2.5 miles north-northeast of Exeter along Atchison, Topeka and Santa Fe Railroad (lat. 36°19'55" N, long. 119°07'45" W; sec. 26, T 18 S, R 26 E). Named on Exeter (1952) 15' quadrangle. On Exeter (1926) 7.5' quadrangle, the name applies to a place located 0.25 mile farther west at a crossroad.

Venida: see **West Venida** [TULARE].

Vennacher Needle [FRESNO]: *peak,* 5.25 miles northwest of Mount Pinchot (lat. 36°59'55" N, long. 118°28'25" W). Altitude 12,996 feet. Named on Mount Pinchot (1953) 15' quadrangle.

Venola [KERN]: *locality,* 5.25 miles south-southwest of Bakersfield along Southern Pacific Railroad (lat. 35°18'40" N, long. 119°03'15" W; near SW cor. sec. 14, T 30 S, R 27 E). Named on Gosford (1954) 7.5' quadrangle.

Vermilion Cliffs [FRESNO]: *escarpment,* east-northeast-trending, 2 miles long, 8.5 miles west-northwest of Mount Abbot (lat. 37°25'30" N, long. 118°55'30" W); the feature is northeast of the east end of Vermilion Valley. Named on Mount Abbot (1953) 15' quadrangle. United States Board on Geographic Names (1978b, p. 5) ruled against the form "Vermilion Cliffs" for the name. Theodore S. Solomons named the feature in 1894 (Browning 1986, p. 226).

Vermilion Lake [FRESNO]: *lake,* 500 feet long, 8.5 miles west-northwest of Mount Abbot (lat. 37°25'50" N, long. 118°55'35" W); the lake is north of Vermilion Cliffs. Named on Mount Abbot (1953) 15' quadrangle. United States Board on Geographic Names (1965d, p. 8) approved the name "Feather Lake" for a feature situated 3400 feet northwest of Vermilion Lake (lat. 37°26'15" N, long. 118°56'15" W), and rejected the name "Vermilion Lake" for this second feature.

Vermilion Valley [FRESNO]: *valley,* 10 miles west of Mount Abbot along Mono Creek (lat. 37°23' N, long. 118°58' W). Named on Mount Goddard (1912) 30' quadrangle. Water of Lake Thomas A. Edison now covers most of the valley, which Theodore S. Solomons named in 1894 (Farquhar *in* Brewer, p. 548).

Vernette: see **Fellows** [KERN].

Vernon: see **Mount Vernon** [KERN].

Verplank Creek [FRESNO]: *stream,* flows 4.5 miles to Kings River nearly 6 miles east-south-east of Balch Camp (lat. 36°51'35" N, long. 119°02' W; sec. 28, T 12 S, R 27 E); the stream is northeast of Verplank Ridge. Named on Patterson Mountain (1952) 15' quadrangle.

Verplank Ridge [FRESNO]: *ridge,* northwest-trending, 4 miles long, 9 miles southeast of Balch Camp (lat. 36°48'45" N, long. 119° 01' W). Named on Patterson Mountain (1952) and Tehipite Dome (1952) 15' quadrangles.

Verplank Saddle [FRESNO]: *pass,* nearly 7 miles southeast of Balch Camp (lat. 36°50'10" N, long. 119°02'10" W; near NE cor. sec. 4, T 13 S, R 27 E); the pass is at the northwest end of Verplank Ridge. Named on Patterson Mountain (1952) 15' quadrangle.

Versteeg: see **Mount Versteeg** [TULARE].

Vestal [TULARE]: *locality,* 4 miles south-southwest of Ducor (lat. 35°50'25" N, long. 119°05'05" W; sec. 17, T 24 S, R 27 E). Named on Richgrove (1952) 7.5' quadrangle. Officials of California Edison Company named the place in 1919 for the virgin priestesses who tended the sacred fire of Vesta, Roman goddess of the hearth; the company had a substation at the site (Gudde, 1949, p. 379).

Vichy Spring [MADERA]: *spring,* 7.25 miles east-southeast of Raymond (lat. 37°09'35" N, long. 119°47'35" W; sec. 9, T 9 S, R 20 E). Named on Raymond (1944) 15' quadrangle.

Vidette: see **East Vidette** [TULARE]; **West Vidette** [TULARE].

Vidette Creek [FRESNO-TULARE]: *stream,* heads in Tulare County and flows 5.25 miles to Bubbs Creek 13 miles south of Mount Pinchot in Fresno County (lat. 36°45'15" N, long. 118°24'10" W). Named on Mount Whitney (1907) 30' quadrangle, and on Mount Pinchot (1953) 15' quadrangle.

Vidette Lakes [TULARE]: *lakes,* about 1300 feet long, 13 miles north-northwest of Mount Whitney (lat. 36°44'30" N, long. 118°24'30" W); the lakes are along Vidette Creek. Named on Mount Whitney (1956) 15' quadrangle.

Vidette Meadow [FRESNO]: *area,* 13 miles south of Mount Pinchot (lat. 36°45'20" N, long. 118°24'05" W); the place is at the confluence of Vidette Creek and Bubbs Creek. Named on Mount Pinchot (1953) 15' quadrangle.

Vincent Meadow [TULARE]: *area,* nearly 7 miles east of California Hot Springs (lat. 35°52'35" N, long. 118°33' W; near N line sec. 5, T 24 S, R 32 E). Named on California Hot Springs (1958) 15' quadrangle.

Vinland [KERN]: *locality,* 2.5 miles north of McFarland along Southern Pacific Railroad (lat. 35°42'50" N, long. 119°14'05" W; sec. 36, T 25 S, R 25 E). Named on McFarland (1954) 7.5' quadrangle.

Vino: see **Reedley** [FRESNO].

Virginia: see **Lake Virginia** [FRESNO].

Virginia Lake [FRESNO]: *lake,* 1000 feet long, 2.5 miles east-southeast of Dinkey Dome (lat. 37°06'15" N, long. 119°05'15" W; sec. 36, T 9 S, R 26 E). Named on Huntington Lake (1953) 15' quadrangle.

Visalia [TULARE]: *city,* in the northwest part of Tulare County (lat. 36°19'50" N, long. 119°17'30" W). Named on Visalia (1949) 7.5' quadrangle. In 1852 Nathaniel Vise led a group of settlers to the site, which then was known as Buena Vista; the community that grew there was named Visalia, probably by Vise himself (Hoover, Rensch, and Rensch, p. 561-562). According to Barker (p. 1), the name originally had the spelling "Vicealia," and the place is called "Visaija" on Goddard's (1857) map. The area east of Visalia that was subject to overflow by Kaweah River generally was referred to as Visalia Swamp (Grunsky, p. 11). After the county seat moved to Visalia in 1853, the supervisors changed the name of the community to Buena Vista, but changed the name back to Visalia in 1854 (Gudde, 1949, p. 380). Postal authorities established Visalia post office in 1855 (Frickstad, p. 214), and the city incorporated in 1874. In 1862 Lieutenant Colonel George S. Evans selected a site 1 mile north of the center of Visalia for a post called Camp Babbitt, named to honor Lieutenant Colonel E.B. Babbitt, deputy quartermaster general, Department of the Pacific; the camp was set up to help control Southern sympathizers during the Civil War (Hart, H.M., p. 44). When the state legislature created Tulare County in 1852, it placed the seat of justice at a cabin built by John Wood and his companions in late 1849 or early 1850 about 7 miles east of present Visalia on the south side of Kaweah River, and provided that the county seat be called Woodsville (Hoover, Rensch, and Rensch, p. 561). Postal authorities established Woodville post office at the place in 1853 and discontinued it in 1855 (Salley, p. 243). Later they authorized a number of other post offices in the neighborhood of Visalia. They established Illinois Mills post office 8 miles east of Visalia (SW quarter sec. 28, T 18 S, R 26 E) in 1867 and discontinued it in 1868; the operator of a grain mill at the place came from Illinois (Salley, p. 103). They established Wambat post office 35 miles east of Visalia in 1874 and discontinued it in 1876; the name was from badgers that were misidentified as wombats, animals of Australia (Salley, p. 234). They established Mayville post office 12.5 miles northeast of Visalia (NW quarter of sec. 18, T 18 S, R 27 E) in 1878 and discontinued it the same year; the name was from the given name of the postmaster's wife (Salley, p. 135). They established Hiko post office 6 miles east of Visalia in 1880 and discontinued it in 1881; the name was from Hicks Company, a dairy operated by Benjamin Hicks—the place also was known as Hico, Hicko, and Hicks (Salley, p. 97). They established Cottage post office 12 miles east of Visalia in 1885 and discontinued it in 1886; the name was from the location of the post office in a cottage (Salley, p. 51). Thompson's (1892) map shows Gains P.O. located about 15 miles northeast of Visalia (sec. 35, T 16 S, R 26 E). Postal authorities established Gains post office in 1890 and discontinued it in 1891; the name was for Thomas Gains, first postmaster (Salley, p. 82).

Visalia Creek: see **Mill Creek** [TULARE] (1).

Visalia Swamp: see **Visalia** [TULARE].

Volcan [KERN]: *locality,* 3.25 miles north of downtown Bakersfield along Southern Pacific Railroad (lat. 35°25'20" N, long. 118°59'20" W; sec. 8, T 29 S, R 28 E). Named on Oil Center (1954) 7.5' quadrangle.

Volcanic Cone [FRESNO]: *peak,* 14 miles north-northeast of Hume (lat. 36°58'35" N, long. 118°50' W). Altitude 9177 feet. Named on Tehipite Dome (1952) 15' quadrangle.

Volcanic Falls: see **Volcano Falls** [TULARE].

Volcanic Knob [FRESNO]: *peak,* 6 miles west of Mount Abbot (lat. 37°23'50" N, long. 118°53'20" W). Altitude 11,168 feet. Named on Mount Abbot (1953) 15' quadrangle. Theodore S. Solomons named the peak in 1894 (Farquhar, 1925, p. 141).

Volcanic Lakes [FRESNO]: *lakes,* largest 0.5 mile long, 8 miles southwest of Marion Peak (lat. 36°53'15" N, long. 118°37'50" W). Named on Marion Peak (1953) 15' quadrangle.

Volcanic Ridge [MADERA]: *ridge,* west- to southwest-trending, 2.25 miles long, 5.5 miles northwest of Devils Postpile (lat. 37°40'40" N, long. 119°09'15" W). Named on Devils Postpile (1953) 15' quadrangle.

Volcano Creek: see **Golden Trout Creek** [TULARE].

Volcano Falls [TULARE]: *waterfall,* 6.5 miles west-northwest of Kern Peak along Golden Trout Creek (lat. 36°21'10" N, long. 118°23'30" W). Named on Kern Peak (1956) 15' quadrangle. United States Board on Geographic Names (1933a, p. 792) rejected the name "Volanic Falls" for the feature.

Volcano Meadow [TULARE]: *area,* 3.5 miles north-northwest of Kern Peak (lat. 36°21'10" N, long. 118°19'20" W; at SW cor. sec. 17, T 18 S, R 34 E). Named on Kern Peak (1956) 15' quadrangle.

Volcano Meadow: see **Groundhog Meadow** [TULARE].

Von Hellum Creek [TULARE]: *stream,* flows 3 miles to join Spear Creek and form Poso Creek 5.25 miles south of California Hot Springs (lat. 35°48'15" N, long. 118°39'10" W; near S line sec. 29, T 24 S, R 31 E). Named on California Hot Springs (1958) 15' quadrangle.

– W –

Wade: see **Edison** [KERN].

Wade Baxter Spring [KINGS]: *spring,* 4.25 miles southwest of Avenal (lat. 35°57'15" N, long. 120°10'20" W; sec. 6, T 23 S, R 17 E). Named on Garza Peak (1953) 7.5' quadrangle.

Wade Creek: see **South Creek** [TULARE].

Wagonshed Creek [TULARE]: *stream,* flows 1 mile to East Fork Dry Creek (1) 8 miles southeast of Auckland (lat. 36°30'15" N, long. 119°00'40" W; sec. 26, T 16 S, R 27 E). Named on Auckland (1966) 7.5' quadrangle.

Wagon Wheel Mountain [KERN]: *hill,* 9.5 miles northwest of Blackwells Corner (lat. 35°42'35" N, long. 119°59'10" W; sec. 36, T 25 S, R 18 E). Named on Emigrant Hill (1953) 7.5' quadrangle. On Emigrant Hill (1943) 7.5' quadrangle, the name applies to present Mount Vernon. Lost Hills (1914) 30' quadrangle has the form "Wagonwheel Mountain" for the name.

Wagy Flat [KERN]: *area,* 4.5 miles south of Alta Sierra in French Gulch (1) (lat. 35°39'55" N, long. 118°32'05" W; on E line sec. 16, T 26 S, R 32 E). Named on Alta Sierra (1972) 7.5' quadrangle.

Wah Hoo Lake [FRESNO]: *lake,* 350 feet long, 2.5 miles north of Blackcap Mountain (lat. 37°06'30" N, long. 118°47' W). Named on Blackcap Mountain (1953) 15' quadrangle.

Wahoo Lakes [FRESNO]: *lakes,* largest 1100 feet long, 9 miles north of Mount Goddard (lat. 37°13'45" N, long. 118°42'45" W). Named on Mount Goddard (1948) 15' quadrangle. Art Schober named the lakes for exclamations made by a fisherman (Browning 1986, p. 229).

Wahtoka: see **Wahtoke** [FRESNO].

Wahtoke [FRESNO]: *locality,* 4.5 miles south-southeast of Centerville along Atchison, Topeka and Santa Fe Railroad (lat. 36°40'35" N, long. 119°27'20" W; near N line sec. 34, T 14 S, R 23 E). Named on Wahtoke (1966) 7.5' quadrangle. Postal authorities established Wahtoka (with the final "a") post office in 1905 and discontinued it in 1916 (Frickstad, p. 38). Kroeber (p. 66) identified the name as

of Indian origin.

Wahtoke Creek [FRESNO]: *stream,* flows 20 miles to Kings River 1.5 miles north-north-west of Reedley (lat. 36°36'55" N, long. 119°27'55" W; near W line sec. 22, T 15 S, R 23 E). Named on Orange Cove North (1966), Pine Flat Dam (1965), and Wahtoke (1966) 7.5' quadrangles. Mendenhall's (1908) map has the form "Wah to ke" for the name.

Wahtoke Lake [FRESNO]: *lake,* 4000 feet long, behind a dam on Wahtoke Creek 6.5 miles southeast of Centerville (lat. 36°40'45" N, long. 119°24'10" W; sec. 30, T 14 S, R 24 E). Named on Wahtoke (1966) 7.5' quadrangle.

Wahtoke Winery: see **Cella** [FRESNO].

Waits: see **Seguro** [KERN].

Wa-kal-la: see **Merced River** [MADERA].

Walemo Rock: see **Fresno Dome** [MADERA].

Wales Lake [TULARE]: *lake,* 4000 feet long, 2 miles northwest of Mount Whitney (lat. 36°36' N, long. 118°18'50" W). Named on Mount Whitney (1956) 15' quadrangle. The name commemorates the Reverend F.H. Wales, who visited Mount Whitney in 1881 (United States Board on Geographic Names, 1933a, p. 799).

Walker: see **Joe Walker Town**, under **Walker Basin** [KERN].

Walker: see **Mike Walker Canyon** [MADERA].

Walker Basin [KERN]: *valley,* 10 miles northeast of Caliente (lat. 35°24'30" N, long. 118°31' W). Named on Breckenridge Mountain (1972) 7.5' quadrangle, and on Piute Peak (1972) 7.5' quadrangle, which shows Joe Walker mine at the east edge of the valley (lat. 35°25'20" N, long. 118°29'35" W; near E line sec. 12, T 29 S, R 32 E). The valley is called The Park on Williamson's (1853) map. Joe Walker mine was named for the mountain man for whom Walker Pass was named; a settlement at the mine in the 1870's was called Joe Walker Town (Boyd, p. 168, 170). Wheeler's (1875-1878) map shows a place called Moseman Stage Sta. situated along Basin (present Walker Basin) Creek near the place that the stream leaves Walker Basin. Waring (p. 52) referred to a group of small thermal springs at the north edge of Walker Basin as Williams Hot Springs—they were on Williams ranch.

Walker Basin Creek [KERN]: *stream,* flows 25 miles to the canyon of Caliente Creek 6.5 miles west-northwest of Caliente (lat. 35°19'45" N, long. 118°44'15" W); the stream goes through Walker Basin. Named on Bena (1972), Breckenridge Mountain (1972), Oiler Peak (1972), and Piute Peak (1972) 7.5' quadrangles. Called Basin Creek on Emerald Mountain (1943) 15' quadrangle, and United States Board on Geographic Names (1975b, p. 12) gave the names "Basin Creek" and "Thompson Creek" as variants. North Fork enters from the northeast 5 miles west of Piute Peak; it is 5 miles long and is named on Piute Peak (1972) 7.5' quadrangle.

Walker Pass [KERN]: *pass,* 11.5 miles east of Onyx (lat. 35°39'45" N, long. 118°01'35" W; near SE cor. sec. 17, T 26 S, R 37 E). Named on Walker Pass (1972) 7.5' quadrangle. Called Walker's Pass on Williamson's (1853) map, which has the name "Hum-pah-ya-mup Pass" for a feature located about 6 miles farther south, apparently at the head of present Kelso Creek. Fremont (p. 248) named Walker Pass in 1844 for Joseph Walker, the mountain man who discovered it.

Walkers Creek: see **North Fork**, under **Cottonwood Creek** [KERN] (2).

Walker Well [KERN]: *well,* 9 miles west of Inyokern (lat. 35°39'15" N, long. 117°58'20" W; sec. 23, T 26 S, R 37 E). Named on Owens Peak (1972) 7.5' quadrangle.

Wallace: see **Mount Wallace** [FRESNO]; **Mount Wallace**, under **Mount Mendel** [FRESNO].

Wallace Center [KERN]: *locality,* 2 miles north-northwest of Taft (lat. 35°10'05" N, long. 119°27'50" W; on W line sec. 1, T 32 S, R 23 E). Named on Taft (1950) 7.5' quadrangle.

Wallace Creek [TULARE]: *stream,* flows 7 miles to Kern River nearly 7 miles west of Mount Whitney (lat. 36°34'35" N, long. 118°24'45" W). Named on Mount Whitney (1956) 15' quadrangle. Called East Fork [of Kern River] on Mount Whitney (1907) 30' quadrangle, but United States Board on Geographic Names (1933a, p. 799) rejected this name, and noted that the name "Wallace" is for Judge William R. Wallace, a pioneer of the Kaweah neighborhood.

Wallace Lake [TULARE]: *lake,* 3600 feet long, 2.5 miles north-northwest of Mount Whitney (lat. 36°36'40" N, long. 118°18'35" W); the lake is situated along Wallace Creek. Named on Mount Whitney (1956) 15' quadrangle.

Waller: see **Betty Waller Meadow** [TULARE].

Walling Lake [FRESNO]: *lake,* 600 feet long, 1 mile northeast of Kaiser Peak (lat. 37°18'10" N, long. 119°10'20" W; sec. 19, T 7 S, R 26 E). Named on Kaiser Peak (1953) 15' quadrangle.

Walnut Creek [KERN]: *stream,* flows 2.25 miles to San Luis Obispo County 8.5 miles west-northwest of Carneros Rocks (lat. 35°27'55" N, long. 119°59'45" W; at W line sec. 25, T 28 S, R 18 E). Named on Las Yeguas Ranch (1959) 7.5' quadrangle.

Walnut Spring [KERN]: *spring,* 7.5 miles west-northwest of Carneros Rocks (lat. 35°28'35" N, long. 119°58'20" W; sec. 19, T 28 S, R 19 E); the spring is at the head of a branch of Walnut Creek. Named on Las Yeguas Ranch (1959) 7.5' quadrangle.

Walong [KERN]: *locality,* 2.25 miles southeast of Keene along the railroad (lat. 35°11'55" N, long. 118°32'15" W; near SE cor. sec. 28, T 31 S, R 32 E). Named on Keene (1966) 7.5' quadrangle. The designation, a contraction of the name of W.A. Long, a Southern Pacific

Railroad trainmaster, was given in 1876 (Gudde, 1949, p. 383).

Walser Hot Springs: see **Scovern Hot Springs** [KERN].

Walsh Mill [FRESNO]: *locality,* 17 miles south-southwest of Kaiser Peak near Pine Ridge (3) (lat. 37°04'15" N, long. 119°20'30" W; sec. 10, T 10 S, R 24 E). Named on Kaiser (1904) 30' quadrangle.

Waltham Creek: see **Warthan Creek** [FRESNO].

Waltham Valley: see **Warthan Creek** [FRESNO].

Walton: see **Izaak Walton Lake** [FRESNO]; **Mount Izaak Walton** [FRESNO].

Walton Lake [MADERA]: *lake,* 500 feet long, 2 miles east-southeast of Merced Peak (lat. 37°37'20" N, long. 119°21'50" W). Named on Merced Peak (1953) 15' quadrangle. John Handley of California Department of Fish and Game named the lake in 1940 (Browning, 1986, p. 231).

Wambat: see **Visalia** [TULARE].

Wamelo Rock: see **Fresno Dome** [MADERA].

Wampum Lake [FRESNO]: *lake,* 1000 feet long, 8 miles south-southwest of Mount Abbot (lat. 37°16'10" N, long. 118°49'30" W). Named on Mount Abbot (1953) 15' quadrangle. Elden H. Vestal of California Department of Fish and Game named the lake in 1951 (Browning 1986, p. 231).

Wanda Lake [FRESNO]: *lake,* 1 mile long, 2 miles northeast of Mount Goddard in Evolution Basin (lat. 37°07'15" N, long. 118° 41'30" W); the lake is 1 mile west-northwest of Muir Pass. Named on Mount Goddard (1948) 15' quadrangle. R.B. Marshall named the lake for a daughter of John Muir (Browning 1986, p. 231)—Helen Lake (2), on the other side of Muir Pass, is named for another of Muir's daughters.

Ward Canyon [TULARE]: *canyon,* 1.5 miles long, opens into the canyon of Middle Fork Tule River 2.5 miles east of Springville (lat. 36°07'30" N, long. 118°46'15" W; near E line sec. 6, T 21 S, R 30 E). Named on Springville (1957) 15' quadrangle.

Ward Lake [FRESNO]: *lake,* 900 feet long, 13 miles west-southwest of Mount Abbot (lat. 37°18'05" N, long. 118°59'15" W). Named on Mount Abbot (1953) 15' quadrangle. The name commemorates Dr. George C. Ward, of Ward Mountain (Browning 1986, p. 231).

Ward Lakes [MADERA]: *lakes,* two, largest 1200 feet long, 4 miles east of Merced Peak (lat. 37°38'15" N, long. 119°19'10" W). Named on Merced Peak (1953) 15' quadrangle.

Ward Mountain [FRESNO]: *peak,* 12 miles north-northwest of Blackcap Mountain (lat. 37°13'15" N, long. 118°53'40" W; near S line sec. 22, T 8 S, R 28 E). Altitude 10,862 feet. Named on Blackcap Mountain (1953) 15' quadrangle. The name honors Dr. George Clinton Ward, who directed hydroelectric power development in the region (United States Board on Geographic Names, 1936, p. 25).

Ward Mountain [MADERA]: *peak,* nearly 5 miles north-northeast of O'Neals (lat. 37°11'10" N, long. 119°38'50" W; near S line sec. 35, T 8 S, R 21 E). Altitude 2788 feet. Named on O'Neals (1965) 7.5' quadrangle.

Ward Mountain Lake [FRESNO]: *lake,* 1100 feet long, 12 miles north-northwest of Blackcap Mountain (lat. 37°13'25" N, long. 118°54' W; sec. 22, T 8 S, R 28 E); the lake is 0.25 mile west of Ward Mountain. Named on Blackcap Mountain (1953) 15' quadrangle.

Wards Hill: see **Todds Hill** [TULARE].

Ward Spring [TULARE]: *spring,* 2.5 miles east-southeast of Springville (lat. 36°07' N, long. 118°46'30" W; sec. 7, T 21 S, R 30 E); the spring is in Ward Canyon. Named on Globe (1956) 7.5' quadrangle.

Warlow: see **Mount Warlow**, under **Mount Huxley** [FRESNO].

Warm Creek [FRESNO]: *stream,* flows 6 miles to South Fork San Joaquin River 7.5 miles northeast of Kaiser Peak (lat. 37°21'45" N, long 119°04'35" W). Named on Kaiser Peak (1953) 15' quadrangle.

Warm Creek Meadow [FRESNO]: *area,* 11 miles northeast of Kaiser Peak near the west end of Lake Thomas A. Edison (lat. 37° 22'45" N, long. 119°01'30" W); the place is along Warm Creek. Named on Kaiser Peak (1953) 15' quadrangle.

Warm Spring [KERN]: *spring,* 5 miles south-southeast of Arvin (lat. 35°08'50" N, long. 118°47' W; sec. 17, T 32 S, R 30 E). Named on Arvin (1955) 7.5' quadrangle.

Warm Sulfur Spring [TULARE]: *spring,* 5 miles east of Auckland (lat. 36°35'20" N, long. 119°00'50" W; sec. 26, T 15 S, R 27 E). Named on Auckland (1966) 7.5' quadrangle.

Warren [KERN]:
(1) *locality,* 1.25 miles southeast of Fellows along Sunset Railroad (lat. 35°10' N, long. 119°31'25" W; near S line sec. 5, T 32 S, R 23 E). Named on McKittrick (1912) 30' quadrangle.
(2) *locality,* 4 miles north-northwest of Mojave along the railroad (lat. 35°06'50" N, long. 118°12'10" W; sec. 27, T 32 S, R 35 E). Named on Mojave (1956) 15' quadrangle.

Warrior Lake [FRESNO]: *lake,* 1200 feet long, 10 miles northwest of Mount Abbot (lat. 37°28'15" N, long. 118°55'35" W). Named on Mount Abbot (1953) 15' quadrangle. United States Board on Geographic Names (1969a, p. 4) approved the name "Chief Lake" for the feature.

Warrior Lake: see **Bobs Lake** [FRESNO].

Warsaw: see **Pueblo de las Juntas**, under **Mendota** [FRESNO].

Wartham Creek: see **Warthan Creek** [FRESNO].

Warthan: see **Alcalde** [FRESNO].

Warthan Creek [FRESNO]: *stream,* flows 30 miles to Los Gatos Creek nearly 1.25 miles east-northeast of Coalinga (lat. 36°08'40" N, long. 120°20'10" W; near E line sec. 33, T 20 S, R 15 E). Named on Coalinga (1956), Curry Mountain (1969), Kreyenhagen Hills (1956), Priest Valley (1969), Sherman Peak (1969), and Smith Mountain (1969) 7.5' quadrangles. Called Waltham Creek on Coalinga (1912) and Priest Valley (1915) 30' quadrangles. Arnold and Anderson (1908, p. 15) used the form "Waltham Creek" for the name, and noted that the stream was known as Wartham Creek, Warthan Creek, Waltham Creek, and Alcalde Creek; they also pointed out that the stream heads in a valley known as Waltham Valley. United States Board on Geographic Names (1933a, p. 800) rejected the names "Alcalde Creek," "Can-too-oa Creek," "Canuta Creek," and "Wartham Creek" for the stream. The name "Warthan" is from a pioneer rancher (Salley, p. 234).

Wasco [KERN]: *town,* 24 miles northwest of Bakersfield (lat. 35°35'35" N, long. 119°20'05" W; in and near sec. 12, T 27 S, R 24 E). Named on Wasco (1953) 7.5' quadrangle. The place first was called Dewey, and then Deweyville (Bailey, 1967, p. 27). Postal authorities established Deweyville post office, named for Admiral George Dewey of Spanish-American War fame, in 1899 and changed the name to Wasco in 1900 (Salley, p. 58). The town incorporated in 1945. According to Hanna (p. 349), the name "Wasco" was coined from the title "Western American Sugar Company." According to Bailey (1967, p. 27), a former resident of Wasco County, Oregon, named the town. Officials of California Home Extension Association founded Fourth Home Extension Colony at the place in 1907 (Hanna, p. 349).

Washapie Mountain [TULARE]: *peak,* 3 miles east-northeast of Tucker Mountain near Fresno-Tulare county line (lat. 36°39'30" N, long. 119°09'20" W; near N line sec. 4, T 15 S, R 26 E). Named on Tucker Mountain (1966) 7.5' quadrangle. The name is from an Indian village in Drum Valley (Gudde, 1949, p. 383).

Washboard: see **The Washboard** [FRESNO].

Washburn Cove [TULARE]: *relief feature,* wide place in the canyon of Kaweah River 2 miles east-southeast of Kaweah (lat. 36°27'40" N, long. 118°53' W; in and near sec. 7, T 17 S, R 29 E). Named on Kaweah (1957) 15' quadrangle.

Washburn Lake [MADERA]: *lake,* 0.5 mile long, 5.5 miles north-northeast of Merced Peak along Merced River (lat. 37°42'55" N, long. 119°22'15" W). Named on Merced Peak (1953) 15' quadrangle. Lieutenant N.F. McClure named the lake in 1895 for Albert Henry Washburn of Wawona (United States Board on Geographic Names, 1934a, p. 27).

Washington: see **Fort Washington**, under **Old**

Fort Miller [FRESNO].
Washington City: see **Old Fort Miller** [FRESNO].
Wassamma [MADERA]: *locality,* 6 miles west-southwest of present Yosemite Forks (lat. 37°21' N, long. 119°44' W; sec. 1, T 7 S, R 20 E); the place is 1.25 miles west-southwest of present Ahwahnee. Named on Mariposa (1912) 30' quadrangle. The name is from an Indian village located nearby (Kroeber, p. 66). United States Board on Geographic Names (1933a, p. 803) rejected the name "Ahwah-nee" for the place, which was a stage station. McLaughlin and Bradley (p. 532) gave the name "Poison Switch" as an alternate. Clough (p. 80) described Poison Switch as a cross-roads just outside of Gertrude, where team-sters after unloading their cargo of lumber at the head of the flume to Madera would "switch off" to a saloon.
Watch Tower: see **The Watch Tower**, under **The Sphinx** [FRESNO].
Water Canyon [KERN]:
(1) *canyon,* drained by a stream that flows 2 miles to Kelso Valley 5 miles east-southeast of Claraville (lat. 35°24'45" N, long. 118°15'10" W; at E line sec. 18, T 29 S, R 35 E). Named on Claraville (1972) 7.5' quad-rangle.
(2) *canyon,* drained by a stream that flows 4 miles to Jawbone Canyon 3 miles north of Cinco (lat. 35°18'20" N, long. 118°01'25" W; near S line sec. 20, T 30 S, R 37 E). Named on Cinco (1972) 7.5' quadrangle.
(3) *canyon,* drained by a stream that flows nearly 4 miles to Tehachapi Valley 3 miles southwest of Tehachapi (lat. 35°06'25" N, long. 118°29'30" W; near N line sec. 36, T 32 S, R 32 E). Named on Tehachapi South (1966) 7.5' quadrangle.
(4) *canyon,* drained by a stream that flows 1.25 miles to Cummings Creek 2 miles north of Cummings Mountain (lat. 35°04'15" N, long. 118°34' W). Named on Cummings Mountain (1966) 7.5' quadrangle.
Water Canyon Creek [KERN]: *stream,* flows 3.5 miles to Tehachapi Creek 0.5 mile south-east of Keene near Keene post office (lat. 35°13'10" N, long. 118°33'20" W; near E line sec. 20, T 31 S, R 32 E). Named on Keene (1966) 7.5' quadrangle.
Waterfall Canyon [KERN]: *canyon,* drained by La Rose Creek, which flows 4.5 miles to Cache Creek 10 miles east of Tehachapi (lat. 35°06'15" N, long. 118°16'15" W; near W line sec. 31, T 32 S, R 35 E). Named on Monolith (1966) and Tehachapi NE (1966) 7.5' quad-rangles.
Water Gap Spring [KERN]: *spring,* 8 miles northeast of Glennville (lat. 35°47'20" N, long. 118°35'10" W; near NW cor. sec. 6, T 25 S, R 32 E). Named on California Hot Springs (1958) 15' quadrangle.
Water Gulch [MADERA]: *canyon,* drained by

a stream that flows 3.5 miles to Fresno River 5.5 miles east of Knowles (lat. 37°13'20" N, long. 119°46'25" W). Named on Knowles (1962) and O'Neals (1965) 7.5' quadrangles.
Waterhole Mine Spring [KERN]: *spring,* 1 mile east-southeast of Claraville (lat. 35°26'20" N, long. 118°18'40" W; near SE cor. sec. 3, T 29 S, R 34 E). Named on Claraville (1972) 7.5' quadrangle. Emerald Mountain (1943) 15' quadrangle shows Waterhole mine at the place.
Water Station: see **Mojave** [KERN].
Watertown: see **Lemoore** [KINGS].
Watt: see **Sharon** [MADERA].
Watts Creek [FRESNO]: *stream,* flows about 7.5 miles to Sycamore Creek (1) 1.25 miles northwest of Trimmer (lat. 36°55'15" N, long. 119°18'35" W; sec. 1, T 12 S, R 24 E). Named on Humphreys Station (1965) and Trimmer (1965) 7.5' quadrangles.
Watts Valley [FRESNO]: *valley,* 4 miles west-northwest of Trimmer (lat. 36°56' N, long. 119°22' W); Watts Creek drains the valley. Named on Humphreys Station (1965) and Trimmer (1965) 7.5' quadrangles. Postal au-thorities established Watt's Valley post office in 1912 and discontinued it in 1919 (Frickstad, p. 39). The name commemorates C.B. Watts, who settled at what was known as Popes Valley before Watts' arrival (Gudde, 1949, p. 385).
Wauken: see **Waukena** [TULARE].
Waukena [TULARE]: *village,* 10 miles west-southwest of Tulare (lat. 36°08'20" N, long. 119°30'30" W; near SW cor. sec. 32, T 20 S, R 23 E). Named on Waukena (1954) 7.5' quadrangle. Postal authorities established Waukena post office in 1889, discontinued it in 1901, and reestablished it in 1904 (Frickstad, p. 214). The name may be a cor-ruption of the word "Joaquin"—the place also was known as Wauken and Buzzards' Roost (Mitchell, A.R., p. 70).
Weaver Creek [KERN]: *stream,* flows 9.5 miles to Caliente Creek 2.5 miles east of Loraine (lat. 35°18'45" N, long. 118°23'30" W; near SW cor. sec. 13, T 30 S, R 33 E). Named on Claraville (1972), Emerald Mountain (1972), and Loraine (1972) 7.5' quadrangles.
Weaver Creek [TULARE]: *stream,* flows 1 mile to Meadows Creek 2 miles north-northwest of Shell Mountain (lat. 36°43'30" N, long. 118°48'20" W; near W line sec. 11, T 14 S, R 29 E). Named on Giant Forest (1956) 15' quadrangle.
Weaver Lake [TULARE]: *lake,* 1000 feet long, 0.5 mile north-northwest of Shell Mountain (lat. 36°42'10" N, long. 118°47'50" W; sec. 14, T 14 S, R 29 E). Named on Giant Forest (1956) 15' quadrangle.
Webstone: see **Basin** [FRESNO].
Wedge Lake [FRESNO]: *lake,* 800 feet long, 2.25 miles west of Mount Humphreys in Humphreys Basin (lat. 37°16'20" N, long. 118°42'45" W). Named on Mount Tom (1949)

15' quadrangle, which shows that the lake has a wedge-shaped outline.

Weed Patch [KERN]: *town,* 10 miles south-southeast of Bakersfield (lat. 35°14'15" N, long. 118°54'50" W; at SE cor. sec. 12, T 31 S, R 28 E). Named on Weed Patch (1955) 7.5' quadrangle. The town was founded in 1922 (Wines, p. 85). The name was given to the site as early as 1874 because of the abundance of weeds there; the community also was called Alexander's Corner for Cal Alexander, a resident of the place (Bailey, 1967, p. 27).

Weedpatch: see **Algoso** [KERN]; **Patch** [KERN].

Weir Creek [FRESNO]: *stream,* flows 1.5 miles to North Fork Kings River 4 miles east of Balch Camp (lat. 36°54'10" N, long. 119° 03' W; sec. 8, T 12 S, R 27 E). Named on Patterson Mountain (1952) 15' quadrangle.

Weiss Canyon [KERN]: *canyon,* 2.25 miles long, along South Fork Cottonwood Creek (2) above a point 8 miles east of Mount Adelaide (lat. 35°25'10" N, long. 118°36'10" W; sec. 12, T 29 S, R 31 E). Named on Breckenridge Mountain (1972) 7.5' quadrangle.

Welcome Valley [KERN]: *valley,* 8 miles northwest of Blackwells Corner (lat. 35°41'15" N, long. 119°58'45" W). Named on Emigrant Hill (1953) 7.5' quadrangle.

Weldon [KERN]: *village,* 9 miles east-southeast of Wofford Heights in South Fork Valley (lat. 35°40' N, long. 118°17'20" W; on W line sec. 13, T 26 S, R 34 E). Named on Weldon (1972) 7.5' quadrangle. Postal authorities established Weldon post office in 1871 and moved it 0.5 mile east in 1938 (Salley, p. 236); the name commemorates William B. Weldon, a pioneer cattleman in the neighborhood (Bailey, 1962, p. 78). A temporary army post called Camp Leonard was set up near present Weldon in 1863 (Bailey, 1967, p. 3).

Weldon Meadow [KERN]: *area,* 3 miles north of Claraville (lat. 35° 29' N, long. 118°20'15" W; near SE cor. sec. 20, T 28 S, R 34 E). Named on Claraville (1972) 7.5' quadrangle. Called French Meadow on Emerald Mountain (1943) 15' quadrangle, where present French Meadow is called Weldon Meadow. United States Board on Geographic Names (1975b, p. 12) gave the name "French Meadow" as a variant.

Weldon Peak [KERN]: *peak,* 7 miles north of Emerald Mountain (lat. 35°21'25" N, long. 118°17'20" W). Named on Emerald Mountain (1972) 7.5' quadrangle.

Weldon Pond [KERN]: *lake,* 100 feet long. 12.5 miles northwest of Mojave (lat. 35°13'25" N, long. 118°13'45" W; near N line sec. 21, T 31 S, R 35 E). Named on Cache Peak (1973) 7.5' quadrangle.

Wells: see **Keene** [KERN].

Wells Creek [TULARE]: *stream,* flows 2.5 miles to Jim Gray Creek 9 miles south of Kaweah in Oak Flat (1) (lat. 36°20'30" N, long.

118°55'40" W; at N line sec. 27, T 18 S, R 28 E). Named on Kaweah (1957) 15' quadrangle.

Welport [KERN]: *locality,* 6 miles north-north-west of McKittrick (lat. 35°22'35" N, long. 119°40'45" W). Named on Belridge (1943) 7.5' quadrangle.

Weringdale: see **Woody** [KERN].

West Alpaugh [TULARE]: *locality,* 13 miles west of Earlimart (lat. 35°53'20" N, long. 119°30'30" W; sec. 32, T 23 S, R 23 E); the place is 1 mile west of Alpaugh. Named on West Alpaugh (1929) 7.5' quadrangle.

West Baker [KERN]: *locality,* nearly 4 miles northwest of Boron (lat. 35°02'35" N, long. 117°41'25" W; at S line sec. 14, T 11 N, R 8 W); the place is 1.25 miles west of Baker. Named on Boron (1954) 15' quadrangle.

West Camp [KERN]: *locality,* 12 miles north of Blackwells Corner (lat. 35°47'20" N, long. 119°49'20" W; near N line sec. 4, T 25 S, R 20 E). Named on West Camp (1954) 7.5' quadrangle.

Western Creek: see **Woodward Creek** [TULARE].

Westfall Creek [FRESNO]: *stream,* flows 4.5 miles to Kaiser Creek 5.5 miles northwest of Kaiser Peak (lat. 37°20'40" N, long. 119°16'10" W; sec. 5, T 7 S, R 25 E). Named on Kaiser Peak (1953) and Shuteye Peak (1953) 15' quadrangles. The name commemorates Eldridge Westfall, one of the first forest rangers in the region (Browning 1986, p. 234).

Westhaven [FRESNO]: *settlement,* 16 miles south-southwest of Riverdale (lat. 36°13'35" N, long. 119°59'35" W; near SE cor. sec. 35, T 19 S, R 18 E). Named on Westhaven (1956) 7.5' quadrangle. Postal authorities established Westhaven post office in 1918 and discontinued it in 1958 (Salley, p. 237).

Westhaven Siding [FRESNO]: *locality,* 15 miles south-southwest of Riverdale along Southern Pacific Railroad (lat. 36°14'40"N, long. 119°59'35" W; near W line sec. 26, T 19 S, R 18 E); the place is 1.25 miles north of Westhaven. Named on Westhaven (1956) 7.5' quadrangle. Called Westhaven Station on Westhaven (1929) 7.5' quadrangle.

Westhaven Station: see **Westhaven Siding** [FRESNO].

West Kaiser Campground [FRESNO]: *locality,* 4.5 miles northwest of Kaiser Peak (lat. 37°20'40" N, long. 119°14'20" W; sec. 4, T 7 S, R 25 E); the place is along West Kaiser Creek. Named on Kaiser Peak (1953) 15' quadrangle.

West Kaiser Creek [FRESNO]: *stream,* flows 5.5 miles to Kaiser Creek 5.25 miles northwest of Kaiser Peak (lat. 37°20'55" N, long. 119°15' W; sec. 4, T 7 S, R 25 E). Named on Kaiser Peak (1953) 15' quadrangle.

West Kennedy Lake [FRESNO]: *lake,* 2000 feet long, 9 miles west-southwest of Marion Peak (lat. 36°53'20" N, long. 118°39'45" W); the lake is at the head of West Fork Kennedy

Creek. Named on Marion Peak (1953) 15' quadrangle.

West Lake [FRESNO]: *lake,* 800 feet long, 6.25 miles east of the town of Big Creek (lat. 37°12' N, long. 119°07'45" W; near S line sec. 28, T 8 S, R 26 E). Named on Huntington Lake (1953) 15' quadrangle.

West Meadow: see **Big West Meadow**, under **Big Wet Meadow** [TULARE].

Weston Meadow [TULARE]: *area,* 4 miles east-southeast of Wilsonia (lat. 36°43'20" N, long. 118°53'15" W; sec. 12, T 14 S, R 28 E). Named on Giant Forest (1956) 15' quadrangle. The name commemorates Austin Weston of Visalia, who used the place as his headquarters for summer stock grazing (Gudde, 1949, p. 387).

West Park [FRESNO]: *settlement,* 5 miles southwest of downtown Fresno (lat. 36°42'35" N, long. 119°51'10" W; sec. 13, T 14 S, R 19 E). Named on Fresno South (1963) 7.5' quadrangle.

West Pinnacles Creek [FRESNO]: *stream,* flows 3.5 miles to Piute Canyon 12 miles north of Blackcap Mountain (lat. 37°14'40" N, long. 118°49' W); the stream heads west of The Pinnacles (1). Named on Blackcap Mountain (1953) and Mount Abbot (1953) 15' quadrangles.

West Shore Gulch [KERN]: *canyon,* drained by a stream that flows 4.5 miles to the canyon of Kern River 3 miles north of downtown Bakersfield (lat. 35°25'40" N, long. 118°59'15" W; at S line sec. 5, T 29 S, R 28 E). Named on Oil Center (1954) 7.5' quadrangle.

Westside [FRESNO]: *settlement,* 22 miles northeast of Coalinga (lat. 36°24' N, long. 120°08'20" W; near NE cor. sec. 5, T 18 S, R 17 E). Named on Westside (1956) 7.5' quadrangle.

West Spring [FRESNO]: *spring,* 4.5 miles north of Coalinga Mineral Springs (lat. 36°12'35" N, long. 120°33'50" W; sec. 10, T 20 S, R 13 E). Named on Sherman Peak (1969) 7.5' quadrangle.

West Spur [TULARE]: *ridge,* generally north-trending, 3 miles long, 12.5 miles northwest of Mount Whitney (lat. 36°43'30" N, long. 118°25'10" W); the ridge is 1 mile west across Vidett Creek from East Spur. Named on Mount Whitney (1956) 15' quadrangle.

West Stringer [TULARE]: *stream,* flows 3.5 miles to Cold Creek 4.25 miles southwest of Kern Peak (lat. 36°15'40" N, long. 118° 20'10" W). Named on Kern Peak (1956) 15' quadrangle.

West Stringer Saddle [TULARE]: *pass,* 2 miles west of Kern Peak (lat. 36°18'45" N, long. 118°19'20" W; sec. 32, T 18 S, R 34 E); the pass is near the head of West Stringer. Named on Kern Peak (1956) 15' quadrangle.

West Twin Creek: see **Santiago Creek** [KERN].

West Venida [TULARE]: *locality,* 3.25 miles north of Exeter along Atchison, Topeka and

Santa Fe Railroad (lat. 36°20'30" N, long. 119°07'45" W; at S line sec. 23, T 18 S, R 26 E); the place is 0.5 mile north of Venida. Named on Exeter (1952) 15' quadrangle.

West Vidette [TULARE]: *peak,* 13 miles north-northwest of Mount Whitney (lat. 36°44' N, long. 118°25'10" W); the peak is 1.25 miles southwest of East Vidette on West Spur. Named on Mount Whitney (1956) 15' quadrangle.

Wet Meadow [FRESNO]: *area,* 12 miles north of Hume (lat. 36° 57' N, long. 118°52'25" W). Named on Tehipite Dome (1952) 15' quadrangle.

Wet Meadow: see **Big Wet Meadow** [TULARE]; **Little Bearpaw Meadow** [TULARE].

Wet Meadows [TULARE]: *area,* 7 miles south of Mineral King (lat. 36°21'10" N, long. 118°34'50" W). Named on Mineral King (1956) 15' quadrangle.

Whaleback [TULARE]: *ridge,* generally north-trending, 3 miles long, center 2 miles north of Triple Divide Peak (lat. 36°37'20" N, long. 118°31'55" W). Named on Triple Divide Peak (1956) 15' quadrangle.

Wheat Camp [TULARE]: *locality,* 7 miles south of Waukena (lat. 36°02'35" N, long. 119°31'35" W; sec. 6, T 22 S, R 23 E). Named on Corcoran (1954) 7.5' quadrangle.

Wheatville [FRESNO]: *locality,* 29 miles northeast of Coalinga (lat. 36°27'35" N, long. 120°02'05" W; near SW cor. sec. 9, T 17 S, R 18 E). The place is named on Wheatville (1931) 7.5' quadrangle, and the site is named on Five Points (1956) 7.5' quadrangle. Postal authorities established Wheatville post office in 1891 and discontinued it in 1920 (Salley, p. 239).

Wheatville: see **Kingsburg** [FRESNO].

Wheeler Ridge [KERN]:
(1) *ridge,* generally southeast- to east-trending, 5 miles long, 4 miles south-southwest of Mettler (lat. 35°00'40" N, long. 119°00'45" W). Named on Coal Oil Canyon (1955), Mettler (1955), and Pleito Hills (1958) 7.5' quadrangles. The name commemorates the driller of an unsuccessful oil well on the ridge, which earlier was called El Monte de las Avilas for Danurio Avila and his son, Ignacio, who ran horses and cattle there (Latta, 1976, p. 213, 215).
(2) *village,* 4.25 miles south-southeast of Mettler (lat. 35°00'15" N, long. 118°56'55" W; at S line sec. 30, T 11 N, R 19 W); the village is west of Wheeler Ridge (1). Named on Mettler (1955) 7.5' quadrangle. Postal authorities established Wheeler Ridge post office in 1923 and discontinued it in 1972 (Salley, p. 239).

Wheel Mountain [FRESNO]: *peak,* 6.5 miles southeast of Mount Goddard on Black Divide (lat. 37°02'45" N, long. 118°37'45" W). Altitude 12,781 feet. Named on Mount Goddard

(1948) 15' quadrangle. Lewis Clark, Marjory Bridge, John Poindexter, and John Cahill made the first ascent of the peak in 1933 and named it for the configuration of the summit, which reminded them of the spokes of a wheel (Browning 1986, p. 235).

Wherry Housing: see **Edwards** [KERN].

Whiskers Campground [MADERA]: *locality,* nearly 4 miles west-southwest of Shuteye Peak along North Fork Sand Creek (lat. 37° 20'05" N, long. 119°29'35" W; sec. 7, T 7 S, R 23 E). Named on Shuteye Peak (1953) 15' quadrangle.

Whiskey Creek [MADERA]:
(1) *stream,* flows nearly 3 miles to Willow Creek (3) at Knowles (lat. 37°12'55" N, long. 119°52'35" W; sec. 2, T 8 S, R 19 E). Named on Knowles (1962) 7.5' quadrangle.
(2) *stream,* flows 11.5 miles to Willow Creek (2) 13 miles south of Shuteye Peak (lat. 37°09'50" N, long. 119°28'20" W; sec. 9, T 9 S, R 23 E). Named on Shaver Lake (1953) and Shuteye Peak (1953) 15' quadrangles. The stream first was called Alder Creek, but after a store that sold a lot of whiskey opened near the feature at present Cascadel, Indians gave the stream the name "Whiskey Creek" (Clough, p. 80).

Whiskey Falls [MADERA]: *locality,* 4.5 miles south of Shuteye Peak along Whiskey Creek (2) (lat. 37°17'10" N, long. 119°26'25" W; sec. 27, T 7 S, R 23 E). Named on Shuteye Peak (1953) 15' quadrangle.

Whiskey Flat: see **Kernville** [KERN].

Whiskey Ridge [MADERA]: *ridge,* south-trending, 6 miles long, 5.5 miles south of Shuteye Peak (lat. 37°16' N, long. 119°24'45" W); the ridge is east of Whiskey Creek (2). Named on Shaver Lake (1953) and Shuteye Peak (1953) 15' quadrangles.

White Bear Lake [FRESNO]: *lake,* 850 feet long, 3.5 miles south-southwest of Mount Abbot (lat. 37°20'20" N, long. 118°48' W). Named on Mount Abbot (1953) 15' quadrangle.

White Chief Branch [MADERA]: *stream,* flows 2.5 miles to Big Creek 7.5 miles north-northeast of Yosemite Forks (lat. 37°28'20" N, long. 119°35'05" W; sec. 29, T 5 S, R 22 E); the stream heads near White Chief Mountain. Named on Bass Lake (1953) 15' quadrangle.

White Chief Lake [TULARE]: *lake,* 500 feet long, 3 miles south of Mineral King (lat. 36°24'30" N, long. 118°35'55" W); the lake is 0.25 mile north-northwest of White Chief Peak. Named on Mineral King (1956) 15' quadrangle.

White Chief Mountain [MADERA]: *peak,* 10 miles north-northeast of Yosemite Forks (lat. 37°29'20" N, long. 119°32' W; near N line sec. 23, T 5 S, R 22 E). Altitude 8676 feet. Named on Bass Lake (1953) 15' quadrangle.

White Chief Peak [TULARE]: *peak,* 3 miles south of Mineral King (lat. 36°24'20" N, long. 118°35'50" W). Named on Mineral King

(1956) 15' quadrangle.

White City Canyon [KERN]: *canyon,* drained by a stream that flows 4 miles to Sunflower Valley 3.5 miles east of Orchard Peak (lat. 35°44'15" N, long. 120°04'15" W). Named on Sawtooth Ridge (1961) 7.5' quadrangle. The name is for the white tents of a camp known as White City that J.D. Spreckels put up in 1900 when he drilled for oil in the canyon (Marsh, p. 41).

White Cow Canyon [KERN]: *canyon,* drained by a stream that flows 2.25 miles to Tejon Canyon 4 miles west of Cummings Mountain (lat. 35°02'10" N, long. 118°38'15" W). Named on Cummings Mountain (1966) and Tejon Ranch (1966) 7.5' quadrangles.

White Creek [FRESNO]: *stream,* flows 14 miles to Los Gatos Creek 10 miles northwest of Coalinga (lat. 36°13'15" N, long. 120°29'50" W; sec. 6, T 20 S, R 14 E). Named on Alcalde Hills (1969), Santa Rita Peak (1969), and Sherman Peak (1969) 7.5' quadrangles.

White Deer Creek [FRESNO]: *stream,* flows 7.5 miles to Mill Creek (3) 13 miles southwest of Balch Camp (lat. 36°47'25" N, long. 119°13'35" W; near SW cor. sec. 14, T 13 S, R 25 E); the stream goes through White Deer Flat. Named on Patterson Mountain (1952) 15' quadrangle.

White Deer Creek: see **Little White Deer Creek**, under **Mill Creek** [FRESNO-TULARE].

White Deer Flat [FRESNO]: *area,* 6 miles south-southwest of Balch Camp (lat. 36°49'35" N, long. 119°10' W; sec. 4, 5, 6, T 13 S, R 26 E). Named on Patterson Mountain (1952) 15' quadrangle. The name is from an albino deer seen by early settlers (Forest M. Clingan, personal communication, 1990).

White Deer Saddle [FRESNO]: *pass,* 4.5 miles south-southwest of Balch Camp (lat. 36°50'35" N, long. 119°08'50" W; sec. 33, T 12 S, R 26 E); the pass is near the head of White Deer Creek. Named on Patterson Mountain (1952) 15' quadrangle.

White Deer Valley: see **Little White Deer Valley**, under **Mill Creek** [FRESNO-TULARE].

White Divide [FRESNO]: *ridge,* north-northwest-trending, 8.5 miles long, 5 miles south of Mount Goddard (lat. 37°02' N, long. 118°44' W). Named on Marion Peak (1953) and Mount Goddard (1948) 15' quadrangles.

White Dome [TULARE]: *peak,* 11 miles westnorthwest of Lamont Peak (lat. 35°51'50" N, long. 118°12'45" W). Altitude 7555 feet. Named on Lamont Peak (1956) 15' quadrangle.

White Fork: see **Woods Creek** [FRESNO].

White Meadow [TULARE]: *area,* 4.25 miles north-northeast of Camp Nelson (lat. 36°11'40" N, long. 118°34'10" W; near S line sec. 12, T 20 S, R 31 E). Named on Camp Nelson (1956) 15' quadrangle.

White Mountain [KERN]: *peak,* 1 mile northnorthwest of Cross Mountain (lat. 35°17'40"

N, long. 118°08'40" W; on E line sec. 30, T 30 S, R 36 E). Named on Cross Mountain (1972) 7.5' quadrangle.

White Mountain [TULARE]: *peak,* 11 miles west-southwest of Kern Peak (lat. 36°15'30" N, long. 118°28'30" W). Named on Kern Peak (1956) 15' quadrangle.

White Oak Lodge [KERN]: *locality,* 4 miles northwest of Liebre Twins at present Twin Lakes (2) (lat. 34°59'15" N, long. 118°30'45" W; sec. 6, T 10 S, R 15 W). Named on Neenach (1943) 15' quadrangle. Postal authorities established White Oak Lodge post office in 1930 and discontinued it in 1932 (Frickstad, p. 60).

White River [TULARE]:
(1) *stream,* flows 33 miles to lowlands 3 miles southwest of Ducor (lat. 35°51'30" N, long. 119°05'20" W; near W line sec. 8, T 24 S, R 27 E). Named on California Hot Springs (1958) and White River (1952) 15' quadrangles, and on Delano East (1953), Delano West (1954), and Richgrove (1952) 7.5' quadrangles.
(2) *locality,* 7 miles southeast of Fountain Springs (lat. 35°48'40" N, long. 118°50'35" W; sec. 28, T 24 S, R 29 E); the place is along White River (1). Named on White River (1965) 7.5' quadrangle. A mining camp called Dogtown was situated about 2 miles east of present White River (2) in Coarse Gold Gulch; when the first road built into Linns Valley bypassed Dogtown, a new settlement, also called Dogtown, grew at the site of present White River (2) (Hoover, Rensch, and Rensch, p. 563). Later the new settlement was called Tailholt, perhaps either because a miner used a cow's tail as a handle for the door to his cabin (Gudde, 1975, p. 345), or because a lady stagecoach passenger caught her dog by the tail as the dog jumped from a coach at the place (Hoover, Rensch, and Rensch, p. 563). Postal authorities established White River post office in 1862, discontinued it in 1864, reestablished it in 1866, discontinued it in 1868, reestablished it in 1873, and discontinued it in 1933 (Frickstad, p. 214). Levi Mitchell substituted the name "White River" for the name "Tailholt" when the post office was established (Gudde, 1949, p. 388). A place called Keeneysburg was the center of trading in the neighborhood before Tailholt, or White River, replaced it (Hensher and Peskin, p. 9). Postal authorities established Keeneysburgh post office, named for Mr. Keeney, owner of a trading post, in 1859 and discontinued it in 1860; the post-office site now is in Kern County (Salley, p. 110).

White River Camp: see **White River Summer Home Tract** [TULARE].

White River Summer Home Tract [TULARE]: *locality,* 3.25 miles southeast of California Hot Springs (lat. 35°50'55" N, long. 118° 37'30" W; near SW cor. sec. 10, T 24 S, R 31 E); the place is along White River (1). Named on California Hot Springs (1958) 15' quadrangle. Called White River Camp on Tobias Peak (1936) 30' quadrangle.

Whiterock Creek [KERN]: *stream,* flows 5.25 miles to Tehachapi Valley 4 miles east of Tehachapi (lat. 35°08'30" N, long. 118°22'40" W; near SW cor. sec. 18, T 32 S, R 34 E). Named on Tehachapi North (1966) 7.5' quadrangle. Wheeler's (1875-1878) map has the form "White Rock Creek" for the name. Whitney (1865, p. 216) noted the occurrence of beds of white rock along the stream.

Whites Bridge [FRESNO]: *locality,* 2.5 miles east-southeast of Mendota along Fresno Slough (lat. 36°44' N, long. 120°20'30" W; sec. 9, T 14 S, R 15 E). Named on Tranquillity (1956) 7.5' quadrangle. Postal authorities established White's Bridge post office in 1879 and discontinued it in 1893; the name commemorates James R. White, first postmaster, who built the bridge across San Joaquin River at Fresno Slough (Salley, p. 239).

White Tank Spring [FRESNO]: *spring,* 1.5 miles south of Piedra (lat. 36°47'10" N, long. 119°23'10" W; sec. 20, T 13 S, R 24 E). Named on Piedra (1965) 7.5' quadrangle.

White Wolf Spring: see **Bear Mountain** [KERN].

Whitman Creek [TULARE]: *stream,* flows 5.25 miles to Horse Creek (1) 5.5 miles southwest of Mineral King (lat. 36°23'45" N, long. 118°39'55" W). Named on Mineral King (1956) 15' quadrangle. Soldiers named the stream for their commanding officer, Captain William Whitman, acting superintendent of Sequoia National Park in 1912 (Browning 1986, p. 236).

Whitmore's Ferry: see **Kingston**, under **Hardwick** [KINGS].

Whitney: see **Mount Whitney** [TULARE]; **Mount Whitney Number 1** and **Old Mount Whitney**, under **Mount Corcoran** [TULARE].

Whitney Creek [TULARE]: *stream,* flows 7.5 miles to Kern River 6.5 miles west-southwest of Mount Whitney (lat. 36°33'10" N, long. 118°24'10" W); the stream heads near Mount Whitney. Named on Mount Whitney (1956) 15' quadrangle. Called Grubtree Cr. on Olmsted's (1900) map.

Whitney Creek: see **Golden Trout Creek** [TULARE].

Whitney Meadow: see **Big Whitney Meadow** [TULARE]; **Little Whitney Meadow** [TULARE].

Whitney Meadows: see **Big Whitney Meadow** [TULARE].

Whitney Pass [TULARE]: *pass,* less than 2 miles south-southeast of Mount Whitney on Tulare-Inyo county line (lat. 36°33'15" N, long. 118°16'40" W). Named on Mount Whitney (1956) 15' quadrangle.

Whitney Well [KERN]: *well,* 5 miles west-southwest of Pinyon Mountain (lat. 35°25'50" N, long. 118°14'25" W; sec. 8, T 29 S, R 35 E). Named on Pinyon Mountain (1972) 7.5' quadrangle.

Whitsett: see **Camp Whitsett** [TULARE].

Whitton Spring [KERN]: *spring,* 6.25 miles east-southeast of Caliente (lat. 35°15'20" N, long. 118°31'35" W; near S line sec. 3, T 31 S, R 32 E). Named on Oiler Peak (1972) 7.5' quadrangle.

Wible: see **Wible Orchard** [KERN].

Wible Orchard [KERN]: *locality,* 4.25 miles south-southwest of Bakersfield along Southern Pacific Railroad (lat. 35°19' N, long. 119°01'35" W; sec. 13, T 30 S, R 27 E). Named on Gosford (1954) 7.5' quadrangle, and called Wible on Gosford (1932) 7.5' quadrangle. The name commemorates Simon William Wible, who came to Kern County in 1874 (Wines, p. 16). The place is called Wible Orchards on California Division of Highways' (1934) map, which shows a locality called Strader situated 2 miles farther northeast along the railroad (near NE cor. sec. 7, T 30 S, R 28 E). California Mining Bureau's (1917c) map shows a place called Parsons located about 4 miles northeast of Wible along the railroad.

Wiesman Spring [FRESNO]: *spring,* 6 miles east of Balch Camp (lat. 36°53'45" N, long. 119°00'50" W; near S line sec. 10, T 12 S, R 27 E). Named on Patterson Mountain (1952) 15' quadrangle.

Wiggletail [TULARE]: *stream,* flows 1.5 miles to the canyon of Deer Creek (2) 7 miles north-northeast of Fountain Springs (lat. 35°59'10" N, long. 118°53'15" W; sec. 30, T 22 S, R 29 E). Named on White River (1952) 15' quadrangle.

Wik Spring [KERN]: *spring,* 4.25 miles northeast of Caliente (lat. 35°20'30" N, long. 118°34'55" W; sec. 6, T 30 S, R 32 E). Named on Oiler Peak (1972) 7.5' quadrangle.

Wilbur May Lake [FRESNO]: *lake,* 1900 feet long, 11 miles west-northwest of Mount Abbot (lat. 37°28' N, long. 118°57'15" W). Named on Mount Abbot (1953) 15' quadrangle.

Wilcox Canyon [TULARE]: *canyon,* drained by a stream that flows less than 1 mile to Wilcox Creek 1 mile east-northeast of Cliff Peak (lat. 36°33'35" N, long. 119°09'25" W; sec. 4, T 16 S, R 26 E). Named on Stokes Mountain (1966) 7.5' quadrangle.

Wilcox Creek [TULARE]: *stream,* flows 5.5 miles to Cottonwood Creek 3.5 miles southeast of Cliff Peak (lat. 36°30'50" N, long. 119°07'55" W; at S line sec. 22, T 16 S, R 26 E). Named on Stokes Mountain (1966) 7.5' quadrangle. Called Canyon Creek on Dinuba (1924) 30' quadrangle.

Wilcox Creek: see **Moore Creek** [TULARE].

Wildcat Canyon [FRESNO]: *canyon,* drained by a stream that heads in Merced County and flows 6 miles to lowlands 18 miles west of Firebaugh (lat. 36°49'45" N, long. 120°46'15"

W; sec. 4, T 13 S, R 11 E). Named on Laguna Seca Ranch (1956) 7.5' quadrangle.

Wildcat Creek [FRESNO]: *stream,* flows 3 miles to Fancher Creek 5.5 miles south of Humphreys Station (lat. 36°52'50" N, long. 119° 27'30" W; near NE cor. sec. 21, T 12 S, R 23 E); the stream heads near Wildcat Mountain. Named on Humphreys Station (1965) and Piedra (1965) 7.5' quadrangles.

Wildcat Creek [KERN]: *stream,* flows 3 miles to Howling Gulch 0.5 mile south-southwest of Woody (lat. 35°41'50" N, long. 118°50'15" W; sec. 3, T 26 S, R 29 E). Named on Woody (1965) 7.5' quadrangle.

Wildcat Creek: see **Howling Gulch** [KERN].

Wildcat Creek [MADERA]: *stream,* flows 7 miles to Chowchilla River 5 miles west of Raymond (lat. 37°12'15" N, long. 119°59'55" W; sec. 28, T 8 S, R 18 E). Named on Raymond (1962) 15' quadrangle.

Wildcat Mountain [FRESNO]: *peak,* 5.5 miles south of Humphreys Station (lat. 36°53' N, long. 119°25'45" W; sec. 14, T 12 S, R 23 E). Altitude 2227 feet. Named on Humphreys Station (1965) 7.5' quadrangle.

Wildcat Rock [FRESNO]: *peak,* 9 miles southwest of Coalinga (lat. 36°02'20" N, long. 120°28'05" W; near S line sec. 4, T 22 S, R 14 E). Named on Curry Mountain (1969) 7.5' quadrangle.

Wildflower [FRESNO]: *locality,* 6 miles southwest of Selma (lat. 36° 30'10" N, long. 119°40'55" W; near NE cor. sec. 33, T 16 S, R 21 E). Named on Conejo (1963) 7.5' quadrangle. Postal authorities established Wild Flower post office in 1878 and discontinued it in 1898; they established Deseret post office 6 miles west of Wild Flower in 1887 and discontinued it in 1890—Deseret was a Mormon farm community (Salley, p. 58, 240).

Wildflower: see **Richgrove** [TULARE].

Wild Hog Canyon [FRESNO-TULARE]: *canyon,* on Fresno-Tulare county line, drained by a stream that flows 2 miles to Wooley Canyon 8.5 miles east of Tucker Mountain [TULARE] (lat. 36°38'40" N, long. 119°03' W; sec. 4, T 15 S, R 27 E). Named on Miramonte (1966) 7.5' quadrangle.

Wild Hog Canyon [MADERA]: *canyon,* drained by a stream that flows 2.5 miles to Fresno River 4.25 miles east of Knowles (lat. 37°12'35" N, long. 119°47'50" W; near W line sec. 28, T 8 S, R 20 E). Named on Knowles (1962) 7.5' quadrangle.

Wildman Meadow [FRESNO]: *area,* 13 miles southwest of Marion Peak (lat. 36°50'45" N, long. 118°42'20" W). Named on Marion Peak (1953) 15' quadrangle. Frank Lewis and Jeff Lewis named the place about 1881 because the noise that an owl made there resembled the cries of a wild man (Browning 1986, p. 238).

Williams: see **Camp Nick Williams** [KERN]; **Hamp Williams Pass** [KERN].

Williamsburg: see **Kernville** [KERN]; **Old Town** [KERN].

Williams Canyon [KERN]: *canyon,* drained by a stream that flows 4.25 miles to San Emigdio Creek 2.5 miles west-northwest of Eagle Rest Peak (lat. 34°55'25" N, long. 119°10'35" W). Named on Eagle Rest Peak (1942) 7.5' quadrangle. United States Board on Geographic Names (1990, p. 7) approved the name "Doc Williams Canyon" for this feature, and rejected the names "Williams Canyon," "Arroyo de los Osos," "Doctor Williams Canyon," and "Quatro Osos Canyon."

Williams Creek [FRESNO]: *stream,* flows 2.5 miles to Black Rock Reservoir nearly 6 miles east-northeast of Balch Camp (lat. 36°55'20" N, long. 119°01'10" W; near N line sec. 3, T 12 S, R 27 E). Named on Patterson Mountain (1952) 15' quadrangle.

Williams Creek: see **Rancheria Creek** [KERN] (2).

Williams Hot Springs: see **Walker Basin** [KERN].

Williams Meadow [TULARE]: *area,* 13 miles northwest of Triple Divide Peak (lat. 36°43'45" N, long. 118°41'10" W; on S line sec. 2, T 14 S, R 30 E). Named on Triple Divide Peak (1956) 15' quadrangle.

Willow Creek [FRESNO]: *stream,* flows 2.5 miles to a ditch 3.5 miles east-northeast of Reedley (lat. 36°36'55" N, long. 119°23'35" W; near W line sec. 20, T 15 S, R 24 E). Named on Orange Cove North (1966), Reedley (1966), and Wahtoke (1966) 7.5' quadrangles. On Reedley (1924) 7.5' quadrangle, the stream extends to Travers Creek.

Willow Creek [MADERA]:

(1) *stream,* flows 6 miles to Chowchilla River nearly 4 miles north-northeast of Raymond (lat. 37°16'20" N, long. 119°53'40" W; near N line sec. 4, T 8 S, R 19 E). Named on Ben Hur (1947), Horsecamp Mountain (1947), and Knowles (1962) 7.5' quadrangles. North Branch enters from the northeast 3 miles northeast of Raymond; it is 4.5 miles long and is named on Horsecamp Mountain (1947) 7.5' quadrangle.

(2) *stream,* formed by the confluence of North Fork and South Fork, flows 6.25 miles to San Joaquin River 14 miles south of Shuteye Peak (lat. 37°08'45" N, long. 119°27'40" W; sec. 16, T 9 S, R 23 E). Named on Shaver Lake (1953) 15' quadrangle. United States Board on Geographic Names (1937, p. 32) rejected the name "North Fork, San Joaquin River" for the stream and (p. 21) for its North Fork. North Fork Willow Creek is 24 miles long and is named on Bass Lake (1953), Millerton Lake (1965), Shaver Lake (1953), and Shuteye Peak (1953) 15' quadrangles. North Fork is called Willow Creek on Mariposa (1912) 30' quadrangle. United States Board on Geographic Names (1933a, p. 216), under the entry "Chilkoot," called present North Fork Willow

Creek by the name "Crane Valley Creek." South Fork is formed by the confluence of Browns Creek and Sand Creek; it is 6.5 miles long and is named on Bass Lake (1953), Shaver Lake (1953), and Shuteye Peak (1953) 15' quadrangles.

(3) *stream,* flows 12 miles to Fresno River 7.5 miles south of Raymond (lat. 37°06'15" N, long. 119°53'15" W; sec. 34, T 9 S, R 19 E). Named on Daulton (1962), Knowles (1962), and Raymond (1962) 7.5' quadrangles. Called Cottonwood Cr. on Mariposa (1912) 30' quadrangle.

(4) *stream,* flows 8 miles to Fine Gold Creek 4.5 miles south-southeast of O'Neals (lat. 37°04'15" N, long. 119°38'55" W; sec. 11, T 10 S, R 21 E). Named on Millerton Lake West (1965) and O'Neals (1965) 7.5' quadrangles.

Willow Creek [TULARE]:

(1) *stream,* flows 2.5 miles to Big Arroyo 13 miles northwest of Kern Peak (lat. 36°26'45" N, long. 118°27' W). Named on Kern Peak (1956) 15' quadrangle.

(2) *stream,* flows 4.5 miles to Little Kern River 13 miles south-southeast of Mineral King (lat. 36°16'30" N, long. 118°31' W; sec. 16, T 19 S, R 32 E). Named on Kern Peak (1956) and Mineral King (1956) 15' quadrangles.

Willow Creek: see **Chilkoot Creek** [MADERA].

Willow Glen [MADERA]: *locality,* 6 miles north of O'Neals (lat. 37° 12'45" N, long. 119°42'30" W; near NW cor. sec. 29, T 8 S, R 21 E). Named on Mariposa (1912) 30' quadrangle.

Willow Flat [KERN]: *area,* 3 miles southwest of Wofford Heights (lat. 35°40'30" N, long. 118°29'30" W; on S line sec. 12, T 26 S, R 32 E). Named on Lake Isabella North (1972) 7.5' quadrangle.

Willow Gulch [KERN]: *canyon,* drained by a stream that flows 3.25 miles to Erskine Creek 5.25 miles east-southeast of Bodfish (lat. 35°34' N, long. 118°23'50" W; sec. 23, T 27 S, R 33 E). Named on Lake Isabella South (1972) and Woolstalf Creek (1972) 7.5' quadrangles.

Willow Lake [FRESNO]: *intermittent lake,* 0.25 mile long, 6.25 miles west of Selma (lat. 36°33'35" N, long. 119°43'20" W; sec. 7, T 16 S, R 21 E). Named on Conejo (1963) 7.5' quadrangle. Selma (1946) 15' quadrangle shows a permanent lake 4000 feet long.

Willow Meadow [FRESNO]: *area,* 2.5 miles north-northeast of Dinkey Dome (lat. 37°09' N, long. 119°06'45" W; on E line sec. 15, T 9 S, R 26 E). Named on Huntington Lake (1953) 15' quadrangle.

Willow Meadow [TULARE]: *area,* 11.5 miles west of Triple Divide Peak along Silliman Creek (lat. 36°36'55" N, long. 118°44'05" W; near SW cor. sec. 16, T 15 S, R 30 E). Named on Triple Divide Peak (1956) 15' quadrangle.

Willow Meadows Campground [TULARE]: *locality,* nearly 2 miles west-northwest of Hockett Peak (lat. 36°13'55" N, long.

118°24'50" W). Named on Hockett Peak (1956) 15' quadrangle.

Willow Spring [FRESNO]:

(1) *spring,* 3.5 miles northwest of Coalinga Mineral Springs (lat. 36°11'10" N, long. 120°35'40" W; sec. 17, T 20 S, R 13 E). Named on Sherman Peak (1969) 7.5' quadrangle.

(2) *spring,* 7 miles west of Coalinga (lat. 36°09'05" N, long. 120°29'55" W; sec. 30, T 20 S, R 14 E); the feature is at the head of Willow Springs Canyon. Named on Alcalde Hills (1969) 7.5' quadrangle.

(3) *spring,* 6.5 miles east-northeast of Castle Mountain (lat. 35°58'40" N, long. 120°14'05" W; near NW cor. sec. 34, T 22 S, R 16 E). Named on Garza Peak (1953) 7.5' quadrangle.

Willow Spring [KERN]:

(1) *spring,* 2.25 miles north-northeast of Caliente (lat. 35°19'15" N, long. 118°36'25" W). Named on Oiler Peak (1972) 7.5' quadrangle.

(2) *spring,* nearly 5 miles west of Woody (lat. 35°41'35" N, long. 119°55' W; near SW cor. sec. 1, T 26 S, R 28 E); the spring is along Willow Spring Creek (1). Named on Sand Canyon (1965) 7.5' quadrangle. On Woody (1952) 15' quadrangle, the name applies to a spring located 2000 feet farther southeast (near N line sec. 12, T 26 S, R 28 E). On Mendenhall's (1908) map, the name applies to a locality. Boyd (p. 158) mentioned Willow Springs Station, apparently located at this place, and noted the alternate name "Mountain House Station" for the place.

(3) *spring,* 2 miles north-northwest of Skinner Peak (lat. 35°35'30" N, long. 118°08'20" W). Named on Cane Canyon (1972) 7.5' quadrangle.

(4) *spring,* 2.5 miles west-southwest of Democrat Hot Springs (lat. 35°31'15" N, long. 118°42'30" W). Named on Democrat Hot Springs (1972) 7.5' quadrangle.

(5) *spring,* 1.5 miles northwest of Pinyon Mountain (lat. 35°28'25" N, long. 118°10'25" W; near W line sec. 24, T 28 S, R 35 E). Named on Pinyon Mountain (1972) 7.5' quadrangle.

(6) *spring,* 2.5 miles east-southeast of Caliente (lat. 35°16'25" N, long. 118°35'15" W; sec. 31, T 30 S, R 32 E). Named on Oiler Peak (1972) 7.5' quadrangle.

Willow Spring [KINGS]: *spring,* 7.5 miles south-southwest of Avenal (lat. 35°54'45" N, long. 120°12'15" W; sec. 23, T 23 S, R 16 E); the spring is in Willow Spring Canyon. Named on Garza Peak (1953) 7.5' quadrangle.

Willow Spring: see **Willow Spring Well** [KERN].

Willow Spring Canyon [KINGS]: *canyon,* drained by a stream that flows 2.5 miles to Avenal Canyon 9 miles south-southwest of Avenal (lat. 35°53'20" N, long. 120°12'45" W; sec. 35, T 23 S, R 16 E); Willow Spring is in the canyon. Named on Garza Peak (1953) 7.5'

quadrangle.

Willow Spring Creek [KERN]:

(1) *stream,* flows 8 miles to Rag Gulch 5.25 miles west of Woody (lat. 35°43'05" N, long. 118°55'30" W; at N line sec. 35, T 25 S, R 28 E); Willow Spring (2) is along the stream. Named on Sand Canyon (1965) and Woody (1965) 7.5' quadrangles. United States Board on Geographic Names (1966b, p. 6) rejected the name "Dry Creek" for the stream.

(2) *stream,* flows nearly 2 miles to Kern River 0.5 mile west-southwest of Democrat Hot Springs (lat. 35°31'35" N, long. 118°40'30" W). Named on Democrat Hot Springs (1972) 7.5' quadrangle.

Willow Springs [KERN]:

(1) *spring,* 7 miles west-northwest of McKittrick (lat. 35°20'45" N, long. 119°44'05" W; sec. 5, T 30 S, R 21 E); the spring is just north of Willow Springs Valley. Named on Reward (1951) 7.5' quadrangle. Called Sheep Springs on McKittrick (1912) 30' quadrangle.

(2) *village,* 7.5 miles west of Rosamond (lat. 34°52'45" N, long. 118°17'40" W; at S line sec. 7, T 9 N, R 13 W). Named on Willow Springs (1965) 7.5' quadrangle. Postal authorities established Willow Springs post office in 1909 and discontinued it in 1918 (Frickstad, p. 60). Springs at the site provided water for Indians and early travelers in the neighborhood; the place was an important stop on stage and freight lines—Ezra Hamilton built most of the stone buildings at the community about 1900 (Bailey, 1967, p. 28). Thompson's (1921) map shows a place called Domino located 8 miles west-southwest of the village of Willow Springs. Postal authorities established Domino post office in 1913 and discontinued it in 1929 (Frickstad, p. 55).

Willow Springs Butte [KERN]: *ridge,* west-trending, 1.5 miles long, east of the village of Willow Springs (lat. 34°53' N, long. 118°16'30" W). Named on Willow Springs (1965) 7.5' quadrangle.

Willow Springs Canyon [FRESNO]: *canyon,* drained by a stream that flows nearly 5 miles to Oak Flat Canyon 5 miles west-southwest of Coalinga (lat. 36°06'35" N, long. 120°26'30" W; near N line sec. 15, T 21 S, R 14 E); the canyon heads at Willow Spring (2). Named on Alcalde Hills (1969) and Curry Mountain (1969) 7.5' quadrangles.

Willow Springs Station: see **Willow Spring** [KERN] (2).

Willow Springs Valley [KERN]: *valley,* 7.25 miles west-northwest of McKittrick (lat. 35°20'30" N, long. 119°44'30" W); Willow Springs (1) is near the valley. Named on McKittrick Summit (1959) and Reward (1951) 7.5' quadrangles.

Willow Spring Well [KERN]: *well,* 8.5 miles north-northwest of Randsburg (lat. 35°28'55" N, long. 117°41'45" W; near S line sec. 20, T

28 S, R 40 E). Named on El Paso Peaks (1967) 7.5' quadrangle. Called Willow Spring on Randsburg (1911) 15' quadrangle.

Wilmilche: see **Kings River** [FRESNO-KINGS-TULARE].

Wilson Creek [TULARE]: *stream,* flows 2.5 miles to South Fork of Middle Fork Tule River nearly 2 miles west of Camp Nelson (lat. 36°08'25" N, long. 118°38'30" W). Named on Camp Nelson (1956) 15' quadrangle.

Wilsonia [TULARE]: *village,* 12.5 miles north-northwest of Yucca Mountain (lat. 36°44'05" N, long. 118°57'20" W; sec. 14 S, R 28 E). Named on Giant Forest (1956) 15' quadrangle.

Wimp [TULARE]: *locality,* 5.5 miles southwest of Cliff Peak along Atchison, Topeka and Santa Fe Railroad (lat. 36°30'05" N, long. 119°14'35" W; at S line sec. 27, T 16 S, R 25 E). Named on Stokes Mountain (1966) 7.5' quadrangle.

Winchell: see **Mount Winchell** [FRESNO].

Winchell Bay [FRESNO]: *embayment,* 8.5 miles west-southwest of Prather on the south side of Millerton Lake (lat. 37°00' N, long. 119°39'30" W); the embayment occupies the lower part of the canyon of Winchell Creek. Named on Friant (1964) and Millerton Lake West (1965) 7.5' quadrangles.

Winchell Creek [FRESNO]: *stream,* flows nearly 3 miles to Millerton Lake 12.5 miles north-northeast of Clovis (lat. 36°59'50" N, long. 119°38'55" W; sec. 2, T 11 S, R 21 E). Named on Friant (1964) and Millerton Lake East (1965) 7.5' quadrangles.

Winchell's Peak: see **Lookout Peak** [FRESNO].

Windmill Tree Peak [KERN]: *peak,* 5.5 miles south of Glennville (lat. 35°39' N, long. 118°41'55" W; sec. 24, T 26 S, R 30 E). Altitude 4587 feet. Named on Glennville (1972) 7.5' quadrangle.

Window Cliffs [TULARE]: *relief feature,* precipice 8 miles northwest of Kern Peak (lat. 36°23'50" N, long. 118°22'20" W). Named on Kern Peak (1956) 15' quadrangle. The name is from a windowlike opening at the place (United States Board on Geographic Names, 1933a, p. 821).

Window Peak [FRESNO]: *peak,* 5 miles southwest of Mount Pinchot (lat. 36°53'25" N, long. 118°27'25" W). Altitude 12,085 feet. Named on Mount Pinchot (1953) 15' quadrangle.

Windy Canyon [FRESNO]: *canyon,* drained by a stream that flows 3 miles to Middle Fork Kings River 5 miles west-northwest of Marion Peak (lat. 36°59'25" N, long. 118°35'55" W); the canyon is east of Windy Peak and west of Windy Ridge. Named on Marion Peak (1953) 15' quadrangle.

Windy Cliff [FRESNO]: *relief feature,* 11 miles southeast of Mount Goddard (lat. 37°00'20" N, long. 118°33'40" W). Named on Mount Goddard (1948) 15' quadrangle.

Windy Cliffs [FRESNO]: *relief feature,* 6 miles east-northeast of Hume on the south side of

South Fork Kings River (lat. 36°48'35" N, long. 118°48'55" W); the feature is east of the mouth of Windy Gulch. Named on Tehipite Dome (1952) 15' quadrangle.

Windy Creek [TULARE]:
(1) *stream,* flows 4 miles to South Fork Tule River 6 miles south-southwest of Camp Nelson (lat. 36°03'40" N, long. 118°38'45" W); the stream heads near Windy Gap (2). Named on Camp Nelson (1956) 15' quadrangle.
(2) *stream,* flows 1.25 miles to Packsaddle Creek 6.25 miles northeast of California Hot Springs (lat. 35°56'20" N, long. 118°35'10" W; near NW cor. sec. 13, T 23 S, R 31 E). Named on California Hot Springs (1958) 15' quadrangle.

Windy Gap [MADERA]: *pass,* 11.5 miles northeast of Raymond (lat. 37°20'55" N, long. 119°46'10" W; sec. 3, T 7 S, R 20 E). Named on Horsecamp Mountain (1947) 7.5' quadrangle.

Windy Gap [TULARE]:
(1) *pass,* 8 miles south of Mineral King (lat. 36°19'50" N, long. 118°36'05" W); the feature is on Windy Ridge. Named on Mineral King (1956) 15' quadrangle.
(2) *pass,* 7 miles south of Camp Nelson (lat. 36°02'40" N, long. 118°35'10" W; near W line sec. 1, T 22 S, R 31 E). Named on Camp Nelson (1956) 15' quadrangle.

Windy Gulch [FRESNO]: *canyon,* drained by a stream that flows 2.5 miles to South Fork Kings River 6 miles east-northeast of Hume (lat. 35°48'45" N, long. 118°48'55" W); the mouth of the canyon is near Windy Cliffs. Named on Tehipite Dome (1952) 15' quadrangle.

Windy Lake [MADERA]: *lake,* 700 feet long, 1.25 miles north-northeast of Buena Vista Peak (lat. 37°36'45" N, long. 119°30'40" W; sec. 1, T 4 S, R 22 E). Named on Yosemite (1956) 15' quadrangle.

Windy Peak [FRESNO]: *peak,* 5 miles west-northwest of Marion Peak (lat. 36°58'20" N, long. 118°36'35" W). Altitude 8867 feet. Named on Marion Peak (1953) 15' quadrangle.

Windy Point [KERN]: *relief feature,* 4 miles northeast of Caliente (lat. 35°20'10" N, long. 118°34'30" W; near NW cor. sec. 8, T 30 S, R 32 E). Named on Oiler Peak (1972) 7.5' quadrangle.

Windy Ridge [FRESNO]: *ridge,* northwest-trending, 4 miles long, 2.5 miles west of Marion Peak (lat. 36°57'30" N, long. 118°33'45" W). Named on Marion Peak (1953) 15' quadrangle.

Windy Ridge [TULARE]: *ridge,* northeast-trending, 4.5 miles long, 8.5 miles south of Mineral King (lat. 36°19'45" N, long. 118°36'15" W). Named on Mineral King (1956) 15' quadrangle.

Windy Springs [TULARE]: *spring,* 13 miles south-southeast of Monache Mountain (lat.

36°01'30" N, long. 118°06'10" W; sec. 9, T 22 S, R 36 E). Named on Monache Mountain (1956) 15' quadrangle.

Wineland [FRESNO]: *locality,* 2.25 miles southeast of Selma along Southern Pacific Railroad (lat. 36°32'35" N, long. 119°35'05" W; sec. 16, T 16 S, R 22 E). Named on Selma (1964) 7.5' quadrangle.

Winter Garden: see **Alameda** [KERN].

Winters Canyon [KERN]: *canyon,* drained by a stream that flows 3.5 miles to El Paso Creek 8.5 miles west-southwest of Cummings Mountain (lat. 35°00'40" N, long. 118°42'40" W). Named on Tejon Ranch (1966) and Winters Ridge (1966) 7.5' quadrangles.

Winters Ridge [KERN]: *ridge,* east- to east-southeast-trending, 3.5 miles long, 7.5 miles west of Liebre Twins (lat. 34°57'30" N, long. 118°42' W). Named on Winters Ridge (1966) 7.5' quadrangle.

Wirts [TULARE]: *locality,* 1 mile east-northeast of Exeter along Visalia Electric Railroad (lat. 36°18'05" N, long. 119°07'25" W; sec. 2, T 19 S, R 26 E). Named on Rocky Hill (1927) 7.5' quadrangle.

Wisdom Well [FRESNO]: *locality,* 9 miles southwest of Firebaugh (lat. 36°45'25" N, long. 120°34'35" W; sec. 33, T 13 S, R 13 E). Named on Wisdom Well (1923) 7.5' quadrangle.

Wishon: see **Camp Wishon** [TULARE].

Wishon: see **Wishon Cove** [MADERA].

Wishon Campground [MADERA]: *locality,* 7 miles southeast of Yosemite Forks on the west side of Bass Lake (1) (lat. 37°17'15" N, long. 119°32' W; sec. 26, T 7 S, R 22 E); the place is near Wishon Cove. Named on Bass Lake (1953) 15' quadrangle.

Wishon Cove [MADERA]: *embayment,* nearly 7 miles southeast of Yosemite Forks on the west side of Bass Lake (1) (lat. 37°18' N, long. 119°32'15" W; on N line sec. 26, T 7 S, R 22 E). Named on Bass Lake (1953) 15' quadrangle. The name "Wishon" commemorates A. Emory Wishon of San Joaquin Light and Power Corporation, later vice-president and general manager of Pacific Gas and Electric Company (Gudde, 1969, p. 366). A place called Wishon is situated along Minaret and Western Railroad on the south shore of Bass Lake (1) near the dam that forms the lake (Clough, p. 95). Postal authorities established Wishon post office in 1923 to serve a vacation community (Salley, p. 242).

Wishon Reservoir [FRESNO]: *intermittent lake,* behind a dam on North Fork Kings River 11 miles west-southwest of Blackcap Mountain (lat. 37°00'15" N, long. 118°58' W; sec. 6, T 11 S, R 28 E). Named on Blackcap Mountain (1953) and Tehipite Dome (1952) 15' quadrangles. Tehipite Dome (1952) 15' quadrangle shows a permanent lake, and Mount Goddard (1912) 30' quadrangle shows Dusy Meadow along the river where the lake is now. United States Board on Geographic Names (1976a, p. 5) approved the name "Sharp Creek" for a stream that flows 0.6 mile to Wishon Reservoir 10.5 miles west-southwest of Blackcap Mountain; the name commemorates Kenneth Sharp, a Pacific Gas and Electric Company civil engineer who died in an accident in 1972.

Witch Creek [KERN]: *stream,* flows 1.25 miles to El Paso Creek 5.25 miles west of Liebre Twins (lat. 34°57'45" N, long. 118°39'50" W; sec. 11, T 10 N, R 17 W). Named on Winters Ridge (1966) 7.5' quadrangle.

W-K Hill [FRESNO]: *ridge,* northwest-trending, 0.5 mile long, 6 miles north-northeast of Coalinga on Anticline Ridge (lat. 36°13'25" N, long. 120°19'30" W; on N line sec. 3, T 20 S, R 15 E). Named on Coalinga (1956) 7.5' quadrangle.

Wofford Heights [KERN]: *town,* 3.5 miles south-southwest of Kernville (lat. 35°42'30" N, long. 118°27'15" W; in and near sec. 32, T 25 S, R 33 E). Named on Lake Isabella North (1972) 7.5' quadrangle. Postal authorities established Wofford Heights post office in 1953 (Frickstad, p. 60). The name is for I.L. Wofford, who started the resort community in 1948 (Bailey, 1967, p. 28).

Wolf [FRESNO]: *locality,* 5.5 miles east of Malaga along Atchison, Topeka and Santa Fe Railroad (lat. 36°41'40" N, long. 119°38'15" W; sec. 24, T 14 S, R 21 E). Named on Malaga (1964) 7.5' quadrangle. Called Dewolf on Lippincott's (1902) map, and called DeWolf on Mendenhall's (1908) map.

Wolverton Creek [TULARE]: *stream,* flows 3.25 miles to Marble Fork 6.5 miles east-northeast of Yucca Mountain (lat. 36°35'50" N, long. 118°45'10" W; near W line sec. 29, T 15 S, R 30 E). Named on Triple Divide Peak (1956) 15' quadrangle. Browning (1986, p. 240) associated the name with James Wolverton, who discovered and named General Sherman tree in 1879.

Wolverton Meadow: see **Log Meadow** [TULARE].

Womack: see **Las Palmas** [FRESNO].

Wood Canyon [KERN]: *canyon,* 2 miles long, opens into Santa Maria Valley (present Little Santa Maria Valley) 7.5 miles west of McKitttrick (lat. 35°18'45" N, long. 119°45'10" W; sec. 18, T 30 S, R 21 E). Named on McKittrick Summit (1959) and Reward (1951) 7.5' quadrangles.

Woodchoppers Canyon [KERN]: *canyon,* 1 mile long, opens into Canada del Agua Escondido 4 miles southwest of Liebre Twins (lat. 34°54'45" N, long. 118°37'10" W; sec. 31, T 10 N, R 16 W). Named on Liebre Twins (1965) and Winters Ridge (1966) 7.5' quadrangles.

Woodchopper Spring [KERN]: *spring,* 7.5 miles northeast of Caliente (lat. 35°22'20" N, long. 118°32'25" W; sec. 27, T 29 S, R 32 E). Named on Oiler Peak (1972) 7.5' quadrangle.

Woodchuck Country [FRESNO]: *area,* 6.5 miles southwest of Blackcap Mountain (lat. 37°01' N, long. 118°53'30" W); the place is drained by Woodchuck Creek. Named on Blackcap Mountain (1953) 15' quadrangle.

Woodchuck Creek [FRESNO]: *stream,* flows nearly 7 miles to North Fork Kings River 10.5 miles west-southwest of Blackcap Mountain in Wishon Reservoir (lat. 37°00'50" N, long. 118°58' W; sec. 31, T 10 S, R 28 E); the stream heads near Chuck Pass and goes through Woodchuck Country. Named on Blackcap Mountain (1953) 15' quadrangle.

Woodchuck Lake [FRESNO]: *lake,* 2200 feet long, 5.25 miles west-southwest of Blackcap Mountain (lat. 37°02'30" N, long. 118°52'50" W; on E line sec. 23, T 10 S, R 28 E). Named on Blackcap Mountain (1953) 15' quadrangle.

Woodcock Meadow [TULARE]: *area,* 4 miles east-southeast of Wilsonia (lat. 36°42'45" N, long. 118°53'20" W; sec. 13, T 14 S, R 28 E). Named on Giant Forest (1956) 15' quadrangle.

Woodford [KERN]: *locality,* nearly 1 mile southeast of Keene along the railroad (lat. 35°12'45" N, long. 118°33'05" W; near W line sec. 21, T 31 S, R 32 E). Named on Keene (1966) 7.5' quadrangle. Cummings Mountain (1943b) 15' quadrangle has the designation "Woodford (Keene P.O.)" at or near the place.

Wood Lake: see **Bravo Lake** [TULARE].

Woodlake [TULARE]: *town,* 12 miles east-northeast of Visalia (lat. 36°24'50" N, long. 119°05'50" W; around SE cor. sec. 25, T 17 S, R 26 E). Named on Woodlake (1952) 7.5' quadrangle. Gilbert F. Stevenson developed the townsite in 1907, and named the town for nearby Wood Lake (present Bravo Lake) (Hanna, p. 358). Postal authorities established Woodlake post office in 1908 (Frickstad, p. 214), and the town incorporated in 1941.

Woodlake Junction [TULARE]: *locality,* 1 mile west of Woodlake along Visalia Electric Railroad (lat. 36°24'50" N, long. 119°06'55" W; at SW cor. sec. 25, T 17 S, R 26 E). Named on Woodlake (1952) 7.5' quadrangle.

Woodlake Mountain: see **Antelope Mountain** [TULARE].

Woodlake Valley [TULARE]: *valley,* 3.5 miles southeast of Cliff Peak along Cottonwood Creek (lat. 36°30'45" N, long. 119°08' W). Named on Dinuba (1924) 30' quadrangle.

Woodpecker Meadow [TULARE]: *area,* 14 miles east-northeast of Fairview (lat. 35°58'45" N, long. 118°15'40" W; sec. 25, T 22 S, R 34 E). Named on Kernville (1956) 15' quadrangle.

Woods Canyon [KERN]: *canyon,* drained by a stream that flows 3.25 miles to Antelope Valley (1) 3.25 miles south of Orchard Peak (lat. 35°41'25" N, long. 120°08'30" W; near S line sec. 4, T 26 S, R 17 E). Named on Orchard Peak (1961) 7.5' quadrangle.

Woods Creek [FRESNO]: *stream,* flows 11 miles to South Fork Kings River 6.25 miles south of

Marion Peak (lat. 36°52' N, long. 118°31'10" W). Named on Marion Peak (1953) and Mount Pinchot (1953) 15' quadrangles. J.N. LeConte named the stream for Robert Martin Woods, a sheepman in the vicinity of Kings River (Browning 1986, p. 241). South Fork enters from the southeast 5 miles upstream from the mouth of the main stream and is 9 miles long. White Fork enters 6 miles upstream from the mouth of the main stream and is 3.25 miles long. Both forks are named on Mount Pinchot (1953) 15' quadrangle.

Woods Lake [FRESNO]: *lake,* 0.5 mile long, 4.25 miles south-southeast of Mount Pinchot (lat. 36°53'05" N, long. 118°22'55" W); the lake is near the head of a branch of Woods Creek. Named on Mount Pinchot (1953) 15' quadrangle. J.N. LeConte named the feature for Robert Martin Woods of Woods Creek (Browning 1986, p. 241)

Woodsville: see **Visalia** [TULARE].

Woodville [TULARE]: *town,* 10 miles west of Porterville (lat. 36°05'35" N, long. 119°12' W; near sec. 19, T 21 S, R 26 E). Named on Woodville (1950) 7.5' quadrangle. Postal authorities established Woodville post office in 1871, discontinued it in 1908, and reestablished it in 1949 (Salley, p. 243).

Woodville: see **Visalia** [TULARE].

Woodward Creek [KERN]: *stream,* flows about 2.5 miles to French Gulch (1) 4.25 miles south of Alta Sierra (lat. 35°39'25" N, long. 118°32'45" W; sec. 16, T 26 S, R 32 E). Named on Alta Sierra (1972) 7.5' quadrangle.

Woodward Creek [TULARE]: *stream,* flows 4 miles to Stony Creek nearly 4 miles southwest of Shell Mountain (lat. 36°39'25" N, long. 118°50'40" W; near NE cor. sec. 5, T 15 S, R 29 E). Named on Giant Forest (1956) 15' quadrangle. The feature also had the names "Western Creek" and "Beartrap Creek" (Forest M. Clingan, personal communication, 1990).

Woodward Peak [KERN]: *peak,* 6 miles south-southwest of Alta Sierra (lat. 35°38'40" N, long. 118°34'50" W; near N line sec. 30, T 26 S, R 32 E). Named on Alta Sierra (1972) 7.5' quadrangle.

Woodworth: see **Mount Woodworth** [FRESNO].

Woody [KERN]: *village,* 25 miles north-northeast of Bakersfield (lat. 35°42'15" N, long. 118°50' W; near SE cor. sec. 34, T 25 S, R 29 E). Named on Woody (1965) 7.5' quadrangle. Postal authorities established Woody post office in 1889 (Frickstad, p. 60). The name commemorates Dr. Sparrell Walter Woody, a pioneer in the neighborhood (Bailey, 1967, p. 28). Joseph Weringer laid out a community at present Woody in 1891 and called the place Weringdale, but that name did not last (Bailey, 1962, p. 41-42).

Woody Flats [KERN]: *area,* 5.25 miles northeast of Woody along Bear Hollow Creek (lat.

35°44'40" N, long. 118°45'20" W; near NW cor. sec. 21, T 25 S, R 30 E). Named on Woody (1952) 15' quadrangle.

Wooley Canyon [FRESNO-TULARE]: *canyon,* drained by a stream that heads in Fresno County and flows about 4.5 miles to Murry Creek (1) 4 miles northeast of Auckland in Tulare County (lat. 36°37'25" N, long. 119°03'05" W; near W line sec. 16, T 15 S, R 27 E). Named on Miramonte (1966) 7.5' quadrangle.

Woollomes: see **Lake Woollomes** [KERN].

Woolstalf Creek [KERN]: *stream, flows* 7.25 miles to Kelso Creek nearly 7 miles south-southeast of Weldon (lat. 35°34'35" N, long. 118°15'05" W; sec. 17, T 27 S, R 35 E); Woolstalf Meadow is along upper reaches of the stream. Named on Woolstalf Creek (1972) 7.5' quadrangle. Called Stalf Creek on Kernville (1908) 30' quadrangle.

Woolstalf Meadow [KERN]: *area,* 10 miles south of Weldon (lat. 35°31'35" N, long. 118°19' W; on E line sec. 4, T 28 S, R 34 E). Named on Woolstalf Creek (1972) 7.5' quadrangle.

Wooten Creek [FRESNO-TULARE]: *stream,* heads in Fresno County and flows 3.5 miles to Tulare County 3 miles northeast of Orange Cove (lat. 36°39'35" N, long. 119°17' W; at S line sec. 32, T 14 S, R 25 E). The stream flows less than 2 miles in Tulare County before it reenters Fresno County near Orange Cove in an artificial watercourse. Named on Orange Cove North (1966) 7.5' quadrangle.

Worth [TULARE]: *locality,* 4.5 miles east-southeast of Porterville near an old railroad grade (lat. 36°03'10" N, long. 118°56'10" W; near S line sec. 34, T 21 S, R 28 E). Named on Success Dam (1956) 7.5' quadrangle.

Worthing [TULARE]: *locality,* 1.25 miles south-southeast of Lindsay along Southern Pacific Railroad (lat. 36°11'10" N, long. 119° 04'55" W; sec. 18, T 20 S, R 27 E). Named on Lindsay (1928) 7.5' quadrangle.

Wren Creek [FRESNO]:
(1) *stream,* flows 2.5 miles to Middle Fork Kings River 8.5 miles northeast of Hume (lat. 36°52'30" N, long. 118°48'20" W); the stream heads near Wren Peak. Named on Tehipite Dome (1952) 15' quadrangle.
(2) *stream,* flows 2.5 miles to Grizzly Creek 15 miles southwest of Marion Peak (lat. 36°49' N, long. 118°44'15" W). Named on Marion Peak (1953) and Tehipite Dome (1952) 15' quadrangles.

Wren Peak [FRESNO]: *peak,* 8 miles east-northeast of Hume (lat. 36°50'20" N, long. 118°47'30" W). Altitude 9450 feet. Named on Tehipite Dome (1952) 15' quadrangle.

Wright: see **Dick Wright Spring** [FRESNO]; **Mount Cedric Wright** [FRESNO].

Wright Creek [TULARE]: *stream,* flows 5.5 miles to Wallace Creek 5.5 miles west of Mount Whitney (lat. 36°35'20" N, long.

118°23'15" W). Named on Mount Whitney (1956) 15' quadrangle. United States Board on Geographic Names (1933a, p. 825) rejected the name "East Fork, Kern River" for the stream, and noted that the name "Wright" commemorates Captain J.W.A. Wright, who in 1881 visited Mount Whitney with Judge William R. Wallace, for whom Wallace Creek is named.

Wright Lakes [TULARE]: *lakes,* 5 miles northwest of Mount Whitney (lat. 36°37'45" N, long. 118°21'30" W); the lakes are at the head of Wright Creek. Named on Mount Whitney (1956) 15' quadrangle. The name commemorates Captain J.W.A. Wright of Wright Creek (United States Board on Geographic Names, 1933a, p. 825).

Wright Mountain [FRESNO]: *peak,* 16 miles northwest of Coalinga (lat. 36°19'40" N, long. 120°32'10" W; near SE cor. sec. 27, T 18 S, R 13 E). Altitude 4566 feet. Named on Santa Rita Peak (1969) 7.5' quadrangle.

Wutchumna Hill [TULARE]: *hill,* 4 miles east-southeast of Woodlake (lat. 36°23'15" N, long. 119°01'55" W; sec. 3, T 18 S, R 27 E). Altitude 928 feet. Named on Woodlake (1952) 7.5' quadrangle.

Wye: see **The Wye** [TULARE].

Wyeth [TULARE]: *locality,* 7 miles east-southeast of Dinuba along Atchison, Topeka and Santa Fe Railroad (lat. 36°31'10" N, long. 119°15'50" W; sec. 21, T 16 S, R 25 E). Named on Orange Cove South (1966) 7.5' quadrangle. The name, applied in 1913 and 1914, is from the term "wye" for a place that railroad tracks join in the configuration of a letter "Y" (Gudde, 1949, p. 394).

Wygal Spring [KERN]: *spring,* 4.5 miles west of Carneros Rocks (lat. 35°27' N, long. 119°55'45" W; sec. 33, T 28 S, R 19 E). Named on Las Yeguas Ranch (1959) 7.5' quadrangle.

Wyleys Knob [KERN]: *peak,* 2.25 miles south-southwest of Skinner Peak (lat. 35°32'10" N, long. 118°08'20" W). Named on Cane Canyon (1972) 7.5' quadrangle.

Wynne: see **Mount Wynne** [FRESNO].

— X-Y —

Yankee Canyon [KERN]: *canyon,* drained by a stream that flows 1.25 miles to Isabella Lake 3.5 miles south of Wofford Heights (lat. 35°39'30" N, long. 118°26'25" W; near N line sec. 21, T 26 S, R 33 E). Named on Lake Isabella North (1972) 7.5' quadrangle.

Yaqui: see **Juan Yaqui Spring** [KERN].

Yates Hot Springs [KERN]: *springs,* 5.25 miles west-southwest of Piute Peak near Walker Basin Creek (lat. 35°25'55" N, long. 118° 28'55" W; sec. 6, T 29 S, R 33 E). Named on Piute Peak (1972) 7.5' quadrangle. Called Yates Hot Spring on Emerald Mountain

(1943) 15' quadrangle. United States Board on Geographic Names (1975b, p. 12) gave the singular form "Yates Hot Spring" as a variant name.

Yeguas Creek [KERN]: *stream*, heads in San Luis Obispo County and flows 4.25 miles in Kern County before reentering San Luis Obispo County 8.5 miles west of Carneros Rocks (lat. 35°27' N, long. 119°59'45" W; at W line sec. 36, T 28 S, R 18 E). Named on Las Yeguas Ranch (1959) 7.5' quadrangle. Arnold and Johnson (p. 21) called the feature Los Yeguas Creek, and noted that many brood mares were pastured about the head of the stream—*yeguas* means "mares" in Spanish.

Yeguas Mountain [KERN]: *ridge*, generally southeast-trending, 4.5 miles long, 17 miles south-southeast of Orchard Peak (lat. 35°30'30" N, long. 120°01'30" W). Named on La Panza NE (1966) and Packwood Creek (1961) 7.5' quadrangles.

Yellow Aster Mill [KERN]: *locality*, 6.25 miles northwest of Randsburg near the mouth of Goler Canyon (lat. 35°25'15" N, long. 117°44'50" W; near S line sec. 12, T 29 S, R 39 E). Ruins named on El Paso Peaks (1967) 7.5' quadrangle.

Yellow Jacket Canyon [TULARE]: *canyon*, drained by a stream that flows 1.25 miles to Bear Trap Canyon nearly 4 miles south-southwest of California Hot Springs (lat. 35°49'55" N, long. 118°42'25" W; at N line sec. 23, T 24 S, R 30 E). Named on California Hot Springs (1958) 15' quadrangle.

Yellow Jacket Spring [KERN]: *spring*, 2 miles north of Skinner Peak (lat. 35°35'40" N, long. 118°07'35" W). Named on Cane Canyon (1972) 7.5' quadrangle.

Yenis Hante: see **Camp Yenis Hante** [KERN].

Yettem [TULARE]: *settlement*, 11 miles north of Visalia (lat. 36°29'10" N, long. 119°15'30" W; on S line sec. 33, T 16 S, R 25 E). Named on Monson (1949) 7.5' quadrangle. The Reverend Jenanyan gave the name in 1902 to an Armenian settlement—*yettem* means "paradise" in Armenian (Gudde, 1949, p. 395). Postal authorities established Yettem post office in 1905 (Frickstad, p. 214). The place is in what has been called the Churchill district (Mitchell, A.R., p. 71). Postal authorities established Churchill post office, named for Enos Churchill, first postmaster, in 1881 and discontinued it in 1887 (Salley, p. 43-44). They established Townsend post office 8 miles southeast of Churchill post office in 1879 and discontinued it in 1887; the name was for Homer C. Townsend, first postmaster (Salley, p. 223-224).

Yettem Station: see **Calgro** [TULARE].

Yokohl [TULARE]: *locality*, 4 miles northeast of Exeter along Visalia Electric Railroad (lat. 36°19'30" N, long. 119°04'50" W; at SE cor. sec. 30, T 18 S, R 27 E); the place is near the rail crossing of Yokohl Creek. Named on

Rocky Hill (1951) 7.5' quadrangle.

Yokohl Creek [TULARE]: *stream*, flows 17 miles to lowlands 4 miles east-northeast of Exeter (lat. 36°19'30" N, long. 119°04'45" W; near NW cor. sec. 32, T 18 S, R 27 E); the stream goes through Yokohl Valley. Named on Exeter (1952), Kaweah (1957), and Springville (1957) 15' quadrangles.

Yokohl Valley [TULARE]: *valley*, 5 miles east of Exeter (lat. 36° 16' N, long. 119°01'30" W); the valley is along lower reaches of Yokohl Creek. Named on Exeter (1952), Kaweah (1957), and Springville (1957) 15' quadrangles. The name is from an Indian tribe of the region (Kroeber, p. 67).

Yosemite Forks [MADERA]: *locality*, 18 miles northeast of Raymond, where the road to Yosemite Valley branches from the road to Bass Lake (1) (lat. 37°22' N, long. 119°37'45" W; sec. 36, T 6 S, R 21 E). Named on Bass Lake (1953) 15' quadrangle.

Yosemite Soda Spring: see **Little Yosemite Soda Spring**, under **Kern Lake** [TULARE].

Young: see **Mount Young** [TULARE]; **Nobe Young Creek** [TULARE]; **Nobe Young Meadow** [TULARE].

Yucca: see **Muroc** [KERN].

Yucca Creek [TULARE]: *stream*, flows 8 miles to North Fork Kaweah River 2.5 miles southwest of Yucca Mountain (lat. 36°32'45" N, long. 118°53'45" W; sec. 12, T 16 S, R 28 E). Named on Giant Forest (1956) 15' quadrangle. United States Board on Geographic Names (1933a, p. 831) rejected the name "Cactus Creek" for the stream.

Yucca Mountain [TULARE]: *peak*, 29 miles northeast of Visalia (lat. 36°34'15" N, long. 118°52'10" W; near S line sec. 31, T 15 S, R 29 E); the peak is at the southwest end of Yucca Ridge. Altitude 4927 feet. Named on Giant Forest (1956) 15' quadrangle. United States Board on Geographic Names (1933a, p. 831) rejected the name "Cactus Mountain" for the feature.

Yucca Point [FRESNO]: *relief feature*, 3.5 miles northeast of Hume (lat. 36°49'30" N, long. 118°52'20" W). Named on Tehipite Dome (1952) 15' quadrangle.

Yucca Ridge [TULARE]: *ridge*, extends 3 miles northeast and north from Yucca Mountain (lat. 36°35' N, long. 118°51'15" W). Named on Giant Forest (1956) 15' quadrangle. United States Board on Geographic Names (1933a, p. 831) rejected the name "Cactus Ridge" for the feature.

– Z –

Zante [TULARE]: *locality*, 3.5 miles north-northwest of Porterville along Southern Pacific Railroad (lat. 36°06'55" N, long. 119°02'40" W; sec. 10, T 21 S, R 27 E). Named on Porterville (1951) 7.5' quadrangle.

California Mining Bureau's (1917b) map shows a place called Lithmore located along the railroad about halfway from Zante to Kurth.

Zapato Canyon: see **Zapato Chino Canyon** [FRESNO].

Zapato Chino Canyon [FRESNO]: *canyon,* 14 miles long, drained by Zapato Chino Creek, which enters lowlands 9 miles east-southeast of Coalinga (lat. 36°04'10" N, long. 120°13'45" W). Named on Kreyenhagen Hills (1956), Parkfield (1961), and The Dark Hole (1961) 7.5' quadrangles. Called Zapato Canyon on Cholame (1917) and Coalinga (1912) 30' quadrangles, but United States Board on Geographic Names (1964c, p. 16) rejected the names "Zapato Canyon" and "Zapatos Canyon" for the feature.

Zapato Chino Creek [FRESNO]: *stream,* flows 14 miles to lowlands 9 miles east-southeast of Coalinga (lat. 36°04'10" N, long. 120°13'45" W; sec. 27, T 21 S, R 16 E). Named on Avenal (1954), Guijarral Hills (1956), Kreyenhagen Hills (1956), and The Dark Hole (1961) 7.5' quadrangles. Called Zapato Creek on Coalinga (1912) 30' quadrangle, but United States Board on Geographic Names (1964c, p. 17) rejected the names "Zapato Creek" and "Zapatos Creek."

Zapato Creek: see **Zapato Chino Creek** [FRESNO].

Zapato Creek, West Fork: see **Arroyo Pinoso** [FRESNO].

Zapatos Canyon: see **Zapato Chino Canyon** [FRESNO].

Zapatos Creek: see **Zapato Chino Creek** [FRESNO]

Zebe Creek [FRESNO]: *stream,* flows 3.5 miles to Pine Flat Reservoir 4.25 miles northeast of Tivy Mountain (lat. 36°50'20" N, long. 119°18'05" W; near S line sec. 36, T 12 S, R 24 E). Named on Pine Flat Dam (1965) 7.5' quadrangle.

Zebra: see **Zebra Station** [MADERA].

Zebra Station [MADERA]: *locality,* 10 miles southeast of Raymond (lat. 37°06'45" N, long. 119°46'40" W; sec. 27, T 9 S, R 20 E). Named on Little Table Mountain (1962) 7.5' quadrangle. Postal authorities established Zebra post office 6 miles northeast of Bates in 1886, discontinued it in 1888, reestablished it in 1890, discontinued it for a time in 1894, moved it 4.5 miles southwest in 1901, and discontinued it in 1904; the name was from Zebra mine, which had light and dark ore veins that suggested the stripes of a zebra (Salley, p. 246).

Zediker [FRESNO]: *locality,* 11 miles east-southeast of Clovis along Atchison, Topeka and Santa Fe Railroad (lat. 36°45'25" N, long. 119°31'15" W; near E line sec. 36, T 13 S, R 22 E). Named on Round Mountain (1964) 7.5' quadrangle.

Zemorra Creek [KERN]: *stream,* flows 2.5 miles to Chico Martinez Creek 2 miles southeast of Carneros Rocks (lat. 35°25'10" N, long. 119°49' W; sec. 10, T 29 S, R 20 E). Named on Carneros Rocks (1959) 7.5' quadrangle.

Zentner [KERN]: *locality,* 3.5 miles east-north-east of McFarland along Southern Pacific Railroad (lat. 35°42'10" N, long. 119°10'05" W; at NE cor. sec. 4, T 26 S, R 26 E). Named on McFarland (1954) 7.5' quadrangle.

Zumwalt Meadows [FRESNO]: *area,* 12 miles south-southwest of Marion Peak in Kings Canyon (lat. 36°47'30" N, long. 118°35'40" W). Named on Marion Peak (1953) 15' quadrangle. The name is for Daniel Kindle Zumwalt, former owner of the place and a conservation leader in the creation of Sequoia and General Grant National Parks (Hanna, p. 364).

Zwang Peak: see **Avenal** [KINGS]

REFERENCES CITED

BOOKS AND ARTICLES

Alder, Pat. 1963. *Mineral King guide.* Glendale, California: La Siesta Press, 36 p.

Anderson, Frank M. 1905. "A stratigraphic study in the Mount Diablo Range of California." *Proceedings of the California Academy of Sciences* (series 3), v. II, no. 2, p. 156-248.

Anderson, Robert, and Pack, Robert W. 1915. *Geology and oil resources of the west border of the San Joaquin Valley north of Coalinga, California.* (United States Geological Survey Bulletin 603.) Washington: Government Printing Office, 220 p.

Angel, Myron. 1890a. "San Luis Obispo County." *Tenth annual report of the State Mineralogist, for the year ending December 1, 1890.* Sacramento: California State Mining Bureau, p. 567-585.

_____1890b. "Tulare County." *Tenth annual report of the State Mineralogist, for the year ending December 1, 1890.* Sacramento: California State Mining Bureau, p. 728-733.

Arnold, Ralph, and Anderson, Robert. 1908. *Preliminary report on the Coalinga oil district, Fresno and Kings Counties, California.* (United States Geological Survey Bulletin 357.) Washington: Government Printing Office, 142 p.

_____1910. *Geology and oil resources of the Coalinga district, California.* (United States Geological Survey Bulletin 398.) Washington: Government Printing Office, 354 p.

Arnold, Ralph, and Johnson, Harry R. 1910. *Preliminary report on the McKittrick-Sunset oil region, Kern and San Luis Obispo Counties, California.* (United States Geological Survey Bulletin 406.) Washington: Government Printing Office, 225 p.

Bailey, Richard C. 1962. *Explorations in Kern.* Bakersfield, California: Kern County Historical Society, 81 p.

_____1963. "To Claraville and the Burning Moscow mine." *Desert Magazine,* v. 26, no. 7, p. 12-15, 137.

_____1967. *Kern County place names.* Bakersfield, California: Kern County Historical Society, 28 p.

Baker, Charles Laurence. 1911. "Notes on the later Cenozoic history of the Mohave Desert region in southeastern California." *University of California Publications, Bulletin of the Department of Geology,* v. 6, no. 15, p. 333-383.

Bancroft, Hubert Howe. 1888. *History of California, Volume VI, 1848-1859.* San Francisco: The History Company, Publishers, 787 p.

Barker, John. 1955. *San Joaquin vignettes, The reminiscences of Captain John Barker.* Bakersfield, California: Kern County Historical Society, 111 p.

Barras, Judy. 1976. *The long road to Tehachapi.* Tehachapi, California: (Author), 231 p.

Berkstresser, C.F., Jr. 1968. *Data for springs in the Southern Coast, Transverse, and Peninsular Ranges of California.* (United States Geological Survey, Water Resources Division, Open-file report.) Menlo Park, California, 21 p. + appendices.

Birnie, R., Jr. 1876. "Executive report of Lieutenant R. Birnie, Jr., Thirteenth United States Infantry, on the operations of party no. 2, California section, field-season of 1875." *Annual report upon the geographical surveys west of the one hundredth meridian, in California, Nevada, Utah, Colorado, Wyoming, New Mexico, Arizona, and Montana.* (Appendix JJ of *The Annual Report of the Chief of Engineers for 1876.*) Washington: Government Printing Office, p. 130-135.

Blake, William P. 1856. "On the rate of evaporation on the Tulare Lakes of California." *American Journal of Science and Arts* (series 2), v. 21, no. 63, p. 365-368.

_____1857. "Geological report." *Reports of explorations and surveys, to ascertain the most practicable and economical route for a railroad from the Mississippi River to the Pacific Ocean.* Volume V, Part II. (33d Cong., 2d Sess., Sen. Ex. Doc. No. 78.) Washington: Beverley Tucker, Printer, 370 p.

Boyd, William Harland. 1972. *A California middle border; The Kern River country, 1772-1880.* Richardson, Texas: The Havilah Press, 226 p.

Bradley, Walter W. 1915. "Fresno County." *Report XIV of the State Mineralogist.* Sacramento: California State Mining Bureau, p. 429-470.

Brewer, William H. 1949. *Up and down California in 1860-1864.* (Edited by Francis P. Farquhar.) Berkeley and Los Angeles: University of California Press, 583 p.

Brown, G. Chester. 1915. "Kern County." *Report XIV of the State Mineralogist.* Sacramento, California: California State Mining Bureau, p. 471-523.

Browning, Peter. 1986. *Place names of the Sierra Nevada.* Berkeley: Wilderness Press, 253 p.

_____. 1988. *Yosemite place names.* Lafayette, California: Great West Books, 241 p.

Buffum, E. Gould. 1850. *Six months in the gold mines; From a journal of three years' residence in Upper and Lower California, 1847-8-9.* Philadelphia: Lea and Blanchard, 172 p.

California Division of Highways. 1934. *California highway transportation survey, 1934.* Sacramento: Department of Public Works, Division of Highways, 130 p. + appendices.

Campbell, Marius R. 1902. *Reconnaissance of the borax deposits of Death Valley and Mohave Desert..* (United States Geological Survey Bulletin 200.) Washington: Government Printing Office, 23 p.

Carson, James H. 1950. *Recollections of the California mines.* Oakland, California: Biobooks, 113 p.

Chalfant, W.A.. 1933. *The story of Inyo.* (Revised edition.) (Author), 430 p.

Clough, Charles W. 1968. *Madera.* Madera, California: Madera County History, 96 p.

Cowan, Robert G. 1956. *Ranchos of California.* Fresno, California: Academy Library Guild, 151 p.

Coy, Owen C. 1923. *California county boundaries.* Berkeley: California Historical Survey Commission, 335 p.

Crawford, J.J. 1896. "Report of the State Mineralogist." *Thirteenth report (Third Biennial) of the State Mineralogist for the two years ending September 15, 1896.* Sacramento: California State Mining Bureau, p. 10-646.

Cullimore, Clarence. 1949. *Old adobes of forgotten Fort Tejon.* (Second printing, revised and enlarged.) Bakersfield, California: Kern County Historical Society, 93 p.

Darling, Curtis. 1988. *Kern County place names.* (No place): Kern County Historical Society, 135 p.

Davidson, J.W. 1976. *The expedition of Capt. J.W. Davidson from Fort Tejon to the Owens Valley in 1859.* (Edited by Philip J. Wilke and Harry W. Lawton.) Socorro, New Mexico: Ballena Press, 55 p.

Davis, G.H., Green, J.H., Olmsted, F.H., and Brown, D.W. 1959. *Ground-water conditions and storage capacity in the San Joaquin Valley, California.* (United States Geological Survey Water-Supply Paper 1469.) Washington: Government Printing Office, 287 p.

Derby, Geo. H. 1852. "A report of the Tulare valley." *Report of the Secretary of War.* (32d Cong., 1st Sess., Sen. Ex. Doc. 110.) 17 p.

Dillon, Richard H. 1960. *La Panza.* San Francisco: Printed for private circulation by the Grabhorn Press, 12 p.

Eccleston, Robert. 1957. *The Mariposa Indian War, 1850-1851.* (Edited by C. Gregory Crampton.) Salt Lake City: University of Utah Press, 168 p.

Fairbanks, Harold W. 1894a. "Red Rock, Goler, and Summit mining districts, in Kern County." *Twelfth report of the State Mineralogist, (Second Biennial,) two years ending September 15, 1894.* Sacramento: California State Mining Bureau, p. 456-458.

_____1894b. "Geology of northern Ventura, Santa Barbara, San Luis Obispo, Monterey, and San Benito Counties." *Twelfth report of the State Mineralogist, (Second Biennial,) two years ending September 15, 1894.* Sacramento: California State Mining Bureau, p. 493-526.

_____1897. "An interesting case of contact metamorphism." *American Journal of Science* (series 4), v. 4, no. 19, p. 36-38.

Farquhar, Francis P. 1923. "Place names of the High Sierra [Part I]." *Sierra Club Bulletin,* v. 11, no. 4, p. 380-407.

_____1924. "Place names of the High Sierra, Part II." *Sierra Club Bulletin,* v. 12, no. 1, p. 47-64.

_____1925. "Place names of the High Sierra, Part III." *Sierra Club Bulletin,* v. 12, no. 2, p. 126-147.

_____1926. "Mountaineering notes." *Sierra Club Bulletin,* v. 12, no. 3, p. 304-307.

Franks, Kenny A., and Lambert, Paul F. 1985. *Early California oil, A photographic history, 1865-1940.* College Station: Texas A&M University Press, 243 p.

Frazer, Robert W. 1965 *Forts of the West.* Norman: University of Oklahoma Press, 246 p.

Fremont, J.C. 1845. *Report of the exploring expedition to the Rocky Mountains in the year 1842, and to Oregon and North California in the years 1843-'44.* Washington: Blair and Rives, Printers, 583 p.

Frickstad, Walter N. 1955. *A century of California post offices, 1848 to 1954.* Oakland, California: Philatelic Research Society, 395 p.

Gale, Hoyt S. 1914. "Salines in the Owens, Searles, and Panamint basins, southeastern California." *Contributions to economic geology, 1913.* (United States Geological Survey Bulletin 580-L.) Washington: Government Printing Office, p. 251-323.

Gardiner, Howard C. 1970. *In pursuit of the golden dream, Reminiscences of San Francisco and the Northern and Southern Mines, 1849-1857.* (Edited by Dale L. Morgan.) Stoughton, Massachusetts: Western Hemisphere, Inc., 390 p.

Gist, Brooks D. 1976. *Empire out of the tules.* Tulare, California: (Author), 234 p.

Goodyear, W.A. 1888a. "Kern County." *Eighth annual report of the State Mineralogist, for the year ending October 1, 1888.* Sacramento: California State Mining Bureau, p. 309-324.

_____1888b. "Tulare County." *Eighth annual report of the State Mineralogist, for the year ending October 1, 1888.* Sacramento: California State Mining Bureau, p. 643-652.

Grunsky, Carl Ewald. 1898. *Irrigation near Fresno, California.* (United States Geological Survey Water-Supply and Irrigation Papers No. 18.) Washington: Government Printing Office, 94 p.

Gudde, Erwin G. 1949. *California place names.*

Berkeley and Los Angeles: University of California Press, 431 p.

——1969. *California place names.* Berkeley and Los Angeles: University of California Press, 416 p.

——1975. *California gold camps.* Berkeley, Los Angeles, London: University of California Press, 467 p.

Hamlin, Homer. 1904. *Water resources of the Salinas Valley, California.* (United States Geological Survey Water-Supply and Irrigation Paper No. 89.) Washington: Government Printing Office, 91 p.

Hanna, Phil Townsend. 1951. *The dictionary of California land names.* Los Angeles: The Automobile Club of Southern California, 392 p.

Harpending, Asbury. 1913. *The great diamond hoax and other stirring incidents in the life of Asbury Harpending.* San Francisco: The James H. Berry Co., 283 p.

Hart, Herbert M. 1965. *Old forts of the Far West.* New York: Bonanza Books, 192 p.

Hart, James D. 1978. *A companion to California.* New York: Oxford University Press, 504 p.

Hensher, Alan, and Peskin, Jack. 1980. *Ghost towns of the Kern and eastern Sierra, A concise guide.* Los Angeles: (Authors), 32 p.

Hess, Frank L. 1910. "Gold mining in the Randsburg quadrangle, California." *Contributions to economic geology, 1911.* (United States Geological Survey Bulletin 430-A.) Washington: Government Printing Office, p. 23-47.

Hoover, Mildred Brooke, Rensch, Hero Eugene, and Rensch, Ethel Grace. 1966. *Historic spots in California.* (Third edition, revised by William N. Abeloe.) Stanford, California: Stanford University Press, 642 p.

Jackson, Louise A. 1988. *Beulah, A biography of the Mineral King Valley of California.* Tucson, Arizona: Westernlore Press, 179 p.

Johnson, Harry R. 1911. *Water resources of Antelope Valley, California.* (United States Geological Survey Water-Supply Paper 278.) Washington: Government Printing Office, 92 p.

Johnston, Hank. 1966. *They felled the redwoods.* Corona del Mar, California: Trans-Anglo Books, 160 p.

Joy, Douglas A. 1876. "San Emidio district, California." *Annual report upon the geographical surveys west of the one hundredth meridian, in California, Nevada, Utah, Colorado, Wyoming, New Mexico, Arizona, and Montana.* (Appendix JJ of *The Annual Report of the Chief of Engineers for 1876.*) Washington: Government Printing Office, p. 51-52.

Kahrl, William L. 1982. *Water and power, The conflict over Los Angeles' water supply in the Owens Valley.* Berkeley, Los Angeles, London: University of California Press, 583 p.

Kaiser, William. 1977. "The Kaweah co-opera-tive colony—A geographical appraisal of nineteenth century socialism in the mountains." *The California Geographer,* v. 17, p. 63-72.

Kip, Leonard. 1946. *California sketches, with recollections of the gold mines.* Los Angeles: N.A. Kovach, 58 p.

Kroeber, A.L. 1916. "California place names of Indian origin." *University of California Publications in American Archæology and Ethnology,* v. 12, no. 2, p. 31-69.

Laizure, C. McK. 1929. "San Francisco field division (Fresno and Lake Counties)." *Mining in California,* v. 25, no. 3, p. 301-365.

Latta, Frank F. 1949. *Black gold in the Joaquin.* Caldwell, Idaho: The Caxton Printers, 344 p.

——1976. *Saga of Rancho El Tejon.* Santa Cruz, California: Bear State Books, 293 p.

Lee, Charles H. 1912. "Ground water resources of Indian Wells Valley, California." *Report of the Conservation Commission of the State of California to the Governor and Legislature of California.* Sacramento, California: Superintendent of State Printing, p. 401-429.

Lippincott, Joseph Barlow. 1902. *Storage of water on Kings River, California.* (United States Geological Survey Water-Supply and Irrigation Paper No. 58.) Washington: Government Printing Office, 101 p.

Logan, C.A. 1950. "Mines and mineral resources of Madera County, California." *California Journal of Mines and Geology,* v. 46, no. 4, p. 445-482.

Lyman, C.S. 1849. "Observations on California." *American Journal of Science and Arts* (series 2), v. 7, no. 20, p. 290-292, 305-309.

Marsh, Owen T. 1960. *Geology of the Orchard Peak area, California.* (California Division of Mines Special Report 62.) San Francisco: California Division of Mines, 42 p.

McLaughlin, R.P., and Bradley, Walter W. 1916. "Madera County." *Report XIV of the State Mineralogist.* Sacramento: California State Mining Bureau, p. 531-568.

Mendenhall, Walter C. 1908. *Preliminary report on the ground waters of San Joaquin Valley, California.* (United States Geological Survey Water-Supply Paper 222.) Washington: Government Printing Office, 52 p.

——1909. *Some desert watering places in southeastern California and southwestern Nevada.* (United States Geological Survey Water-Supply Paper 224.) Washington: Government Printing Office, 98 p.

Mendenhall, W.C., Dole, R.B., and Stabler, Herman. 1916. *Ground water in San Joaquin Valley, California.* (United States Geological Survey Water-Supply Paper 398.) Washington: Government Printing Office, 310 p.

Mitchell, Annie R. 1972. *Land of the tules.* Fresno, California: Valley Publishers, 80 p.

Mitchell, Edward. 1965. *History of research at Sharktooth Hill, Kern County, California.* Bakersfield, California: Kern County Historical Society, 48 p.

Neal, Howard. 1974. "The mines of Rand." *Desert*, v. 37, no. 5, p. 12-15, 34-35.

Olmsted, Frank H. 1901. "Physical characteristics of Kern River, California, with special reference to electric power development." *Reconnaissance of Kern and Yuba Rivers, California.* (United States Geological Survey Water-Supply and Irrigation Paper No. 46.) Washington: Government Printing Office, p. 11-38.

Ormsby, Waterman L. 1968. *The Butterfield Overland Mail.* San Marino, California: The Huntington Library, 179 p.

Preston, William L. 1981. *Vanishing landscapes, Land and life in the Tulare Lake basin.* Berkeley, Los Angeles, London: University of California Press, 278 p.

Redinger, David H. 1949. *The story of Big Creek.* Los Angeles, California: Angelus Press, 182 p.

Rintoul, William. 1978. *Oildorado.* Santa Cruz, California: Valley Publishers, 241 p.

Ristow, Walter N. 1970. "A covey of names." *Surveying and Mapping,* v. 30, no. 3, p. 419-426.

Salley, H.E. 1977. *History of California post offices, 1849-1976.* La Mesa, California: Postal History Associates, Inc., 300 p.

Schumacher, Genny (editor). 1962. *Deepest Valley.* San Francisco: Sierra Club, 206 p.

Settle, Glen A. 1963. *Here roamed the antelope.* Rosamond, California: The Kern-Antelope Historical Society, Inc., 64 p.

Smith, Jedediah S. 1977. *The southwest expedition of Jedediah S. Smith, His personal account of the journey to California, 1826-1827.* (Edited by George R. Brooks.) Glendale, California: The Arthur H. Clark Company, 259 p.

Smith, Genny (editor). 1976. *Mammoth Lakes Sierra.* (Fourth edition.) Palo Alto, California: Genny Smith Books, 147 p.

Stewart, George R. 1970. *American place-names, A concise and selective dictionary for the continental United States of America.* New York: Oxford University Press, 550 p.

Teilman, I., and Shafer, W.H. 1943. *The historical story of irrigation in Fresno and Kings Counties in central California.* Fresno, California: (Authors), 55 p.

Thompson, David G. 1921. *Routes to desert watering places in the Mohave Desert region, California.* (United States Geological Survey Water-Supply Paper 490-B.) Washington: Government Printing Office, p. 87-269.

_____1929. *The Mohave Desert region, California.* (United States Geological Survey Water-Supply Paper 578.) Washington: Government Printing Office, 759 p.

Thompson, Thomas H. 1892. *Official historical atlas of Tulare County:* Tulare, California: Thos. H. Thompson, 147 p. (Reprinted in 1973 by Limited Editions of Visalia, Inc.)

Troxel, B.W., and Morton, P.K. 1962. *Mines and mineral resources of Kern County, California.* (California Division of Mines and Geology County Report l.) San Francisco: California Division of Mines and Geology, 370 p.

Tucker, W. Burling. 1919. "Tulare County." *Report XV of the State Mineralogist.* Sacramento: California State Mining Bureau, p. 900-954.

Uhte, Robert F. 1951. "Yosemite's pioneer cabins." *Sierra Club Bulletin,* v. 36, no. 5, p. 49-71.

United States Board on Geographic Names (under name "United States Geographic Board"). 1933a. *Sixth report of the United States Geographic Board, 1890 to 1932.* Washington: Government Printing Office, 834 p.

_____(under name "United States Geographic Board"). 1933b. *Decisions of the United States Geographic Board, No. 20—Decisions October 5, 1932.* Washington: Government Printing Office, 29 p.

_____(under name "United States Geographic Board"). 1934a. *Decisions of the United States Geographic Board, No. 30—June 30, 1932.* (Yosemite National Park, California.) Washington: Government Printing Office, 29 p.

_____(under name "United States Geographic Board"). 1934b. *Decisions of the United States Geographic Board, No. 34—Decisions June 1933-March 1934.* Washington: Government Printing Office, 20 p.

_____(under name "United States Board on Geographical Names"). 1936. *Decisions of the United States Board on Geographical Names, Decisions rendered between July 1, 1934, and June 30, 1935.* Washington: Government Printing Office, 26 p.

_____(under name "United States Board on Geographical Names"). 1937. *Decisions of the United States Board on Geographical Names, Decisions rendered between July 1, 1936, and June 30, 1937.* Washington: Government Printing Office, 33 p.

_____(under name "United States Board on Geographical Names"). 1938. *Decisions of the United States Board on Geographical Names, Decisions rendered between July 1, 1937, and June 30, 1938.* Washington: Government Printing Office, 62 p.

_____(under name "United States Board on Geographical Names"). 1939. *Decisions of the United States Board on Geographical Names, Decisions rendered between July 1, 1938, and June 30, 1939.* Washington: Government Printing Office, 41 p.

_____1946 (under name "United States Board on Geographical Names"). *Decision lists nos. 4604, 4605, 4606, April, May, June, 1946.* Washington: Department of the Interior, 9 p.

_____1949a. *Decision lists nos. 4905, 4906, May, June, 1949.* Washington: Department of the Interior, 10 p.

_____1949b. *Decision lists nos. 4907, 4908, 4909, July, August, September, 1949.* Washington: Department of the Interior, 24 p.

_____1954. *Decisions on names in the United States, Alaska and Puerto Rico, Decisions rendered from July 1950 to May 1954.* (Decision list no. 5401.) Washington: Department of the Interior, 115 p.

_____1959. *Decisions on names in the United States, Puerto Rico and the Virgin Islands, Decisions rendered from April 1957 through December 1958.* (Decision list no. 5901.) Washington: Department of the Interior, 100p.

_____1960a. *Decisions on names in the United States, Decisions rendered from September 1959 through December 1959.* (Decision list no. 5904.) Washington: Department of the Interior, 68 p.

_____1960b. *Decisions on names in the United States and the Virgin Islands, Decisions rendered from May 1960 through August 1960.* (Decision list no. 6002.) Washington: Department of the Interior, 77 p.

_____1961a. *Decisions on names in the United States, Decisions rendered from September through December 1960.* (Decision list no. 6003.) Washington: Department of the Interior, 73 p.

_____1961b. *Decisions on names in the United States, Decisions rendered from January through April 1961.* (Decision list no. 6101.) Washington: Department of the Interior, 74hp.

_____1962a. *Decisions on names in the United States, Decisions rendered from September through December 1961.* (Decision list no. 6103.) Washington: Department of the Interior, 75 p.

_____1962b. *Decisions on names in the United States, Decisions rendered from May through August 1962.* (Decision list no. 6202.) Washington: Department of the Interior, 81 p.

_____1963a. *Decisions on geographic names in the United States, January through April 1963.* (Decision list no. 6301.) Washington: Department of the Interior, 78 p.

_____1963b. *Decisions on geographic names in the United States, May through August 1963.* (Decision list no. 6302.) Washington: Department of the Interior. 81 p.

_____1964a. *Decisions on geographic names in the United States, September through December 1963.* (Decision list no. 6303.) Washington: Department of the Interior, 66 p.

_____1964b. *Decisions on geographic names in the United States, January through April 1964.* (Decision list no. 6401.) Washington: Department of the Interior, 74 p.

_____1964c. *Decisions on geographic names in the United States, May through August 1964.* (Decision list no. 6402.) Washington: Department of the Interior, 85 p.

_____1965a. *Decisions on geographic names in the United States, September through December 1964.* (Decision list no. 6403.) Washing-

ton: Department of the Interior, 66 p.

_____1965b. *Decisions on geographic names in the United States, January through March 1965.* (Decision list no. 6501.) Washington: Department of the Interior, 85 p.

_____1965c. *Decisions on geographic names in the United States, April through June 1965.* (Decision list no. 6502.) Washington: Department of the Interior, 39 p.

_____1965d. *Decisions on geographic names in the United States, July through September 1965.* (Decision list no. 6503.) Washington: Department of the Interior, 74 p.

_____1966a. *Decisions on geographic names in the United States, January through March 1966.* (Decision list no. 6601.) Washington: Department of the Interior, 44 p.

_____1966b. *Decisions on geographic names in the United States, April through June 1966.* (Decision list no. 6602.) Washington: Department of the Interior, 36 p.

_____1967a. *Decisions on geographic names in the United States, July through September 1966.* (Decision list no. 6603.) Washington: Department of the Interior, 38 p.

_____1967b. *Decisions on geographic names in the United States, January through March 1967.* (Decision list no. 6701.) Washington: Department of the Interior, 20 p.

_____1967c. *Decisions on geographic names in the United States, April through June 1967.* (Decision list no. 6702.) Washington: Department of the Interior, 26 p.

_____1967d. *Decisions on geographic names in the United States, July through September 1967.* (Decision list no. 6703.) Washington: Department of the Interior, 29 p.

_____1968a. *Decisions on geographic names in the United States, October through December 1967.* (Decision list no. 6704.) Washington: Department of the Interior, 46 p.

_____1968b. *Decisions on geographic names in the United States, January through March 1968.* (Decision list no. 6801.) Washington: Department of the Interior, 51 p.

_____1968c. *Decisions on geographic names in the United States, April through June 1968.* (Decision list no. 6802.) Washington: Department of the Interior, 42 p.

_____1969a. *Decisions on geographic names in the United States, October through December 1968.* (Decision list no. 6804.) Washington: Department of the Interior, 33 p.

_____1969b. *Decisions on geographic names in the United States, January through March 1969.* (Decision list no. 6901.) Washington: Department of the Interior, 31 p.

_____1969c. *Decisions on geographic names in the United States, April through June 1969.* (Decision list no. 6902.) Washington: Department of the Interior, 28 p.

_____1969d. *Decisions on geographic names in the United States, July through September 1969.* (Decision list no. 6903.) Washington:

Department of the Interior, 36 p.

_____1970a. *Decisions on geographic names in the United States, April through June 1970.* (Decision list no. 7002.) Washington: Department of the Interior, 20 p.

_____1970b. *Decisions on geographic names in the United States, July through September 1970.* (Decision list no. 7003.) Washington: Department of the Interior, 15 p.

_____1971a. *Decisions on geographic names in the United States, October through December, 1970.* (Decision list no. 7004.) Washington: Department of the Interior, 28 p.

_____1971b. *Decisions on geographic names in the United States, July through September 1971.* (Decision list no. 7103.) Washington: Department of the Interior, 18 p.

_____1972a. *Decisions on geographic names in the United States, January through March 1972.* (Decision list no. 7201.) Washington: Department of the Interior, 32 p.

_____1972b. *Decisions on geographic names in the United States, July through September 1972.* (Decision list no. 7203.) Washington: Department of the Interior, 17 p.

_____1973a. *Decisions on geographic names in the United States, April through June 1973.* (Decision list no. 7302.) Washington: Department of the Interior, 16 p.

_____1973b. *Decisions on geographic names in the United States, July through September 1973.* (Decision list no. 7303.) Washington: Department of the Interior, 14 p.

_____1974a. *Decisions on geographic names in the United States, October through December 1973.* (Decision list no. 7304.) Washington: Department of the Interior, 15 p.

_____1974b. *Decisions on geographic names in the United States, July through September 1974.* (Decision list no. 7403.) Washington: Department of the Interior, 34 p.

_____1975a. *Decisions on geographic names in the United States, October through December 1974.* (Decision list no. 7404.) Washington: Department of the Interior, 32 p.

_____1975b. *Decisions on geographic names in the United States, January through March 1975.* (Decision list no. 7501.) Washington: Department of the Interior, 36 p.

_____1975c. *Decisions on geographic names in the United States, April through June 1975.* (Decision list no. 7502.) Washington: Department of the Interior, 32 p.

_____1975d. *Decisions on geographic names in the United States, July through September 1975.* (Decision list no. 7503.) Washington: Department of the Interior, 33 p.

_____1976a. *Decisions on geographic names in the United States, October through December, 1975.* (Decision list no. 7504.) Washington: Department of the Interior, 45 p.

_____1976b. *Decisions on geographic names in the United States, April through June 1976.* (Decision list no. 7602.) Washington: Depart-

ment of the Interior, 26 p.

_____1976c. *Decisions on geographic names in the United States, July through September 1976.* (Decision list no. 7603.) Washington: Department of the Interior, 25 p.

_____1978a. *Decisions on geographic names in the United States, January through March 1978.* (Decision list no. 7801.) Washington: Department of the Interior, 18 p.

_____1978b. *Decisions on geographic names in the United States, April through June 1978.* (Decision list no. 7802.) Washington: Department of the Interior, 30 p.

_____1978c. *Decisions on geographic names in the United States, July through September 1978.* (Decision list no. 7803.) Washington: Department of the Interior, 32 p.

_____1978d. *Decisions on geographic names in the United States, October through December 1978.* (Decision list no. 7804.) Washington: Department of the Interior, 48 p.

_____1980. *Decisions on geographic names in the United States, April through June 1980.* (Decision list no. 8002.) Washington: Department of the Interior, 33 p.

_____1981a. *Decisions on geographic names in the United States, October through December 1980.* (Decision list no. 8004.) Washington: Department of the Interior, 21 p.

_____1981b. *Decisions on geographic names in the United States, January through March 1981.* (Decision list no. 8101.) Washington: Department of the Interior, 23 p.

_____1981c. *Decisions on geographic names in the United States, July through September 1981.* (Decision list no. 8103.) Washington: Department of the Interior, 20 p.

_____1982a. *Decisions on geographic names in the United States, October through December 1981.* (Decision list no. 8104.) Washington: Department of the Interior, 26 p.

_____1982b. *Decisions on geographic names in the United States, January through March 1982.* (Decision list no. 8201.) Washington: Department of the Interior, 17 p.

_____1983a. *Decisions on geographic names in the United States, July through September 1982.* (Decision list no. 8203.) Washington: Department of the Interior, 25 p.

_____1983b. *Decisions on geographic names in the United States, January through March 1983.* (Decision list no. 8301.) Washington: Department of the Interior, 33 p.

_____1983c. *Decisions on geographic names in the United States, April through June 1983.* (Decision list no. 8302.) Washington: Department of the Interior, 29 p.

_____1983d. *Decisions on geographic names in the United States, October through December 1983.* (Decision list no. 8304.) Washington: Department of the Interior, 20 p.

_____1984a. *Decisions on geographic names in the United States, April through June 1984.* (Decision list no. 8402.) Washington: Department of the Interior, 22 p.

_____1984b. *Decisions on geographic names in the United States, July through September 1984.* (Decision list no. 8403.) Washington: Department of the Interior, 10 p.

_____1984c. *Decisions on geographic names in the United States, October through December 1984.* (Decision list no. 8404.) Washington: Department of the Interior, 18 p.

_____1985a. *Decisions on geographic names in the United States, January through March 1985.* (Decision list no. 8501.) Washington: Department of the Interior, 18 p.

_____1985b. *Decisions on geographic names in the United States, April through June 1985.* (Decision list no. 8502.) Washington: Department of the Interior, 12 p.

_____1985c. *Decisions on geographic names in the United States, October through December 1985.* (Decision list no. 8504.) Washington: Department of the Interior, 12 p.

_____1986. *Decisions on geographic names in the United States, October through December 1986.* (Decision list no. 8604.) Washington: Department of the Interior, 22 p.

_____1987a. *Decisions on geographic names in the United States, April through June 1987.* (Decision list no. 8702.) Washington: Department of the Interior, 17 p.

_____1987b. *Decisions on geographic names in the United States, October through December 1987.* (Decision list no. 8704.) Washington: Department of the Interior, 15 p.

_____1988a. *Decisions on geographic names in the United States, January through March 1988.* (Decision list no. 8801.) Washington: Department of the Interior, 16 p.

_____1988b. *Decisions on geographic names in the United States, April through June 1988.* (Decision list no. 8802.) Washington: Department of the Interior, 19 p.

_____1989a. *Decisions on geographic names in the United States, January through March 1989.* (Decision list no. 8901.) Washington: Department of the Interior, 9 p.

_____1989b. *Decisions on geographic names in the United States, July through September 1989.* (Decision list no. 8903.) Washington: Department of the Interior, 10 p.

_____1989c. *Decisions on geographic names in the United States, October through December 1989.* (Decision list no. 8904.) Washington: Department of the Interior, 9 p.

_____1990. *Decisions on geographic names in the United States.* (Decision list 1990.) Washington: Department of the Interior, 35 p.

_____1991. *Decisions on geographic names in the United States.* (Decision list 1991.) Washington: Department of the Interior, 40 p.

_____1994. Decisions on geographic names in the United States. (Decision list 1994.) Washington: Department of the Interior, 17 p.

Versteeg, Chester. 1923. "The peaks and passes of the Upper Basin, South Fork of the Kings River." *Sierra Club Bulletin,* v. 11, no. 4, p. 421-426.

Waring, Gerald A. 1915. *Springs of California.* (United States Geological Survey Water-Supply Paper 338.) Washington: Government Printing Office, 410 p.

Watts, W.L. 1894 *The gas and petroleum yielding formations of the Central Valley of California.* (California State Mining Bureau Bulletin 3.) Sacramento: California State Mining Bureau, 100 p.

Wells, Harry L. 1938. *California names.* Los Angeles, California: Kellaway-Ide Co., 88 p.

Whipple, C.W. 1876. "Executive report of Lieutenant C.W. Whipple, Ordnance Corps, on the operations of special party, California section, field-season of 1875." *Annual report upon the geographical surveys west of the one hundredth meridian, in California, Nevada, Utah, Colorado, Wyoming, New Mexico, Arizona, and Montana.* (Appendix JJ of *The Annual report of the Chief of Engineers for 1876.*) Washington: Government Printing Office, p. 147-150.

Whiting, J.S., and Whiting, Richard J. 1960. *Forts of the State of California.* (Authors), 90 p.

Whitney, J.D. 1865. *Report of progress and synopsis of the field-work from 1860 to 1864.* (Geological Survey of California, Geology, Volume I.) Published by authority of the Legislature of California, 498 p.

_____1870. *The Yosemite guide-book.* Published by authority of the Legislature [of California], 155 p.

Wilkes, Charles. 1958. *Columbia River to the Sacramento.* Oakland, California: Biobooks, 140 p.

Williamson, R.S. 1855. "Report." *Reports of explorations and surveys, to ascertain the most practicable and economical route for a railroad from the Mississippi River to the Pacific Ocean.* Volume V, part I. (33d Cong., 2d Sess., Sen. Ex. Doc. No. 78.) Washington: Beverley Tucker, Printer, 43 p.

Winchell, E.C. 1926. "Kings River Cañon in 1868." *Sierra Club Bulletin,* v. 12, no. 3, p. 237-251.

Wines, Howie (editor). 1966. *Kern County centennial almanac.* Bakersfield, California: Kern County Centennial Observance Committee, 176 p.

Wood, P.R., and Dale, R.H. 1964. *Geology and ground-water features of the Edison-Maricopa area, Kern County, California.* (United States Geological Survey Water-Supply Paper 1656.) Washington: Government Printing Office, 108 p.

Woodring, W.P., Stewart, Ralph, and Richards, R.W. 1940. *Geology of the Kettleman Hills Oil Field, California.* (United States Geological Survey Professional Paper 195.) Washington: Government Printing Office, 170 p.

Wright, James W.A. 1984. *The Lost Cement mine.* (Edited by Genny Smith.) Mammoth

Lakes, California: Genny Smith Books, 95 p.

Wynn, Marcia Rittenhouse 1951. "When Ezra Hamilton found gold at Willow Springs." *Desert Magazine*, v. 14, no. 13, p. 15-18.

_____1963. *Desert bonanza, The story of early Randsburg, Mojave Desert mining camp.* Glendale, California: The Arthur H. Clark Company, 275 p.

MISCELLANEOUS MAPS

Arnold and Anderson. 1910. "Geologic and structural map of the Coalinga district, California." (Plate I *in* Arnold and Anderson, 1910.)

Arnold and Johnson. 1910. "Preliminary geologic and structural map of the McKittrick-Sunset oil region, California." (Plate I *in* Arnold and Johnson.)

Baker. 1855. "Map of the mining region, of California." Drawn by Geo. A. Baker.

Baker. 1911. (Untitled map. Plate 34 *in* Baker.)

Bancroft. 1864. "Bancroft's map of the Pacific States." Compiled by Wm. H. Knight. Published by H.H. Bancroft & Co., Booksellers and Stationers, San Francisco, Cal.

Blake. 1857. "Geological map of a part of the State of California explored in 1855 by Lieut. R.S. Williamson, U.S. Top. Engr." (*Accompanies* Blake, 1857.)

California. 1891. (Map reproduced in *Early California, Southern Edition.* Corvalis, Oregon: Western Guide Publishers, p. 44-45.)

California Division of Highways. 1934. (Appendix "A" *of* California Division of Highways.)

California Mining Bureau. 1909a. "Kings, Tulare, and Kern Counties." (*In* California Mining Bureau Bulletin 56.)

_____1909b. "Madera and Fresno Counties." (*In* California Mining Bureau Bulletin 56.)

_____1917a. (Untitled map *in* California Mining Bureau Bulletin 74, p. 168.)

_____1917b. (Untitled map *in* California Mining Bureau Bulletin 74, p. 169.)

_____1917c. (Untitled map *in* California Mining Bureau Bulletin 74, p. 171.)

_____1917d. (Untitled map *in* California Mining Bureau Bulletin 74, p. 167.)

Campbell. 1902. "Sketch map of Mohave Desert and Death Valley." (Plate I *in* Campbell.)

Derby. 1850. "Reconnaissance of the Tulares Valley." Lieut. G.H. Derby, Topl. Engrs., April and May, 1850.

Eddy. 1854. "Approved and declared to be the official map of the State of California by an act of the Legislature passed March 25th 1853." Compiled by W.M. Eddy, State Surveyor General. Published for R.A. Eddy, Marysville, California, by J.H. Colton, New York.

Ellis. 1850. "Map of the gold region of California." Taken from a recent survey by Robert H. Ellis.

Fremont. 1848. "Map of Oregon and Upper California from the surveys of John Charles Frémont and other authorities." Drawn by Charles Preuss. Washington City.

Goddard. 1857. "Britton & Rey's map of the State of California." By George H. Goddard.

Gray. 1873. "Gray's Atlas, New rail road and county map of the States of Oregon, California and Nevada." Compiled and drawn by Frank A. Gray. Published by O.W. Gray. Philadelphia.

Grunsky. 1898. "Map of East side of San Joaquin Valley, from Kings River to Fresno River." (Plate IV *in* Grunsky.)

Hamlin. 1904. "Map of the drainage basin of the Salinas River, showing hydrographic features." (Plate I *in* Hamlin.)

Hoffmann and Gardner. 1863-1867. "Map of a portion of the Sierra Nevada adjacent to Yosemite Valley." From surveys made by Chs. F. Hoffmann and J.T. Gardner, 1863-1867. Geological Survey of California.

Jefferson. 1849. "Map of the emigrant road from Independence Mo. to St. Francisco, California." By T.H. Jefferson.

Johnson. 1911. "Reconnaissance hydrographic map of Antelope Valley region, California." (Plate VI *in* Johnson, H.R.)

King and Gardner. 1865. "Map of the Yosemite Valley." From surveys made by order of the Commissioners to Manage the Yosemite Valley and Mariposa Big Tree Grove, by C. King and J.T. Gardner.

Lee. 1912. "Map of Indian Wells Valley, California, showing China Dry Lake, approximate surface contours and location of wells." (Plate II *in* Lee.)

Lippincott. 1902. "Map of drainage basin of Kings River, California, showing route traversed by exploring parties." [Plate I *in* Lippincott.)

Logan. 1950. "Map of Madera County showing location of mines and mineral deposits." (Plate 73 *in* Logan.)

Mendenhall. 1908. "Artesian areas and groundwater levels in the San Joaquin Valley, California." (Plate I *in* Mendenhall, 1908.)

_____1909. "General map showing approximate location of better known springs and wells in the Mohave and adjacent deserts, southeastern California and southwestern Nevada." (Plate I *in* Mendenhall, 1909.)

Olmstead. 1900. "Map of upper Kern River." (Plate III *in* Olmstead.)

Ord. 1848. "Topographical sketch of the gold and quicksilver district of California, July 25th 1848." By E.O.C.O. [E.O.C. Ord]. Lt. U.S.A.

Parke. 1854-1855. "Map No. 1, San Francisco Bay to the plains of Los Angeles." From explorations and surveys made by Lieut. John C. Parke. Constructed and drawn by H. Custer. (In *Reports of explorations and surveys, to ascertain the most practicable and economical route for a railroad from the Mississippi River to the Pacific Ocean.* Volume XI. 1861.)

Rogers and Johnston. 1857. "State of California." By Prof. H.D. Rogers & A. Keith Johnston.

Sage. 1846. "Map of Oregon, California, New Mexico, N.W. Texas, & the proposed Territory of Ne-Bras-ka." By Rufus B. Sage.

Thompson. 1892. "Map of Tulare County, California." (*Accompanies* Thompson, T.H.)

Thompson. 1921. "Relief map of part of Mohave Desert region, California, showing desert watering places." (Plates IX-XIII *in* Thompson, D.G.)

United States Geological Survey. 1906. "Bakersfield Special." Scale 1:62,500.

Watts. 1894. "Map of the Great Central Valley of California." (*Accompanies* Watts.)

Wheeler. 1871-1878. "Part of southern California." (Atlas Sheet No. 73.) Expeditions of 1871, 1875-'76 & 1878 under the command of 1st Lieut. Geo. M. Wheeler.

_____1875-1878. "Part of southern California."

(Atlas Sheet No. 83A.) Expeditions of 1875 & 1878 under the command of 1st Lieut. Geo. M. Wheeler.

Wilkes. 1841. "Map of Upper California." By the U.S. Ex. Ex. and best authorities.

_____1849. "Map of Upper California." By the best authorities.

Williamson. 1853. "Map of passes in the Sierra Nevada from Walker's Pass to the Coast Range." By Lieut. R.S. Williamson, Topl. Engr., assisted by Lieut. J.G. Parke, Topl. Engr., and Mr. Isaac William Smith, Civ. Engr. (In *Reports of explorations and surveys, to ascertain the most practicable and economical route for a railroad from the Mississippi River to the Pacific Ocean,.* Volume XI. 1861.)

Wyld. 1849. "Map of the gold regions of California." Compiled from original surveys by James Wyld, Geographer to the Queen & Prince Albert, Charing Cross East & 2 Royal Exchange, London.

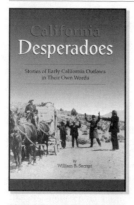
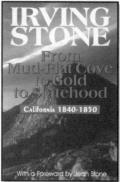

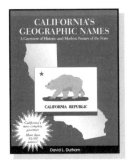

M any years ago in connection with his more than three-decade-long career as a geologist with the United States Geological Survey, David L. Durham often needed to know the whereabouts of some obscure or vanished place in California. He searched for a suitable gazetteer to help him locate these features but found no such volume. To meet his needs he began compiling his own gazetteer for part of the state and, as his interests expanded, so did his gazetteer.

For the first twelve years of his retirement, Mr. Durham compiled information for the gazetteer nearly full-time. Eventually he extended coverage to all of California. The definitive gazetteer of California, *California's Geographic Names: A Gazetteer of Historic and Modern Names of the State* is the result. The Durham's Place-Names of California series, of which this volume is one, contains the same information as *California's Geographic Names* but in thirteen regional divisions.

Mr. Durham was born in California, served as an infantryman in France and Germany during World War II and holds a Bachelor of Science degree from the California Institute of Technology. He and his wife Nancy have two grown children.